Understanding Human Behavior

Understanding Human Behavior

Sixth Edition

James V. McConnell

The University of Michigan

Holt, Rinehart and Winston, Inc.
Fort Worth   Chicago   San Francisco   Philadelphia
Montreal   Toronto   London   Sydney   Tokyo

Publisher Susan Driscoll
Acquisitions Editor Eve Howard
Developmental Editor Jane Knetzger
Senior Project Manager Françoise Bartlett
Art Director Lou Scardino
Production Manager Annette Mayeski
Text design Caliber Design Planning, Inc.
Cover design Lou Scardino

Library of Congress Cataloging-in-Publication Data

McConnell, James V.
   Understanding human behavior.

   Bibliography: p.
   Includes indexes.
   1. Psychology. 2. Human behavior. I. Title.
BF121.M42   1988   150   88-12980

ISBN 0-03-014229-6

Printed in the United States of America

9 0 1 2   061   9 8 7 6 5 4 3 2

Holt, Rinehart and Winston, Inc.
The Dryden Press
Saunders College Publishing

Photo credits are on page 627.

DEDICATION

To everybody who helped, including Lois, Bonnelle, and Beth Ann
But most of all to my students . . .

Preface

By tradition, authors of introductory psychology texts use the preface as a vehicle for describing what their books are like. Let me follow tradition by (1) talking briefly about how the first edition of *Understanding Human Behavior* came into being, and (2) by telling you how the sixth edition differs from previous editions.

Readability and Human Interest

The first edition of *UHB* was published in 1974. Compared to the other introductory texts on the market at that time, *UHB* was fairly revolutionary. First of all, it was *readable*. The average "Reading Ease" score of other introductory texts in 1974—as measured by the Flesch test—was slightly above "Grade 16." That score meant that the students who read the texts needed vocabularies (and the verbal fluency) of a beginning graduate student in order to comprehend the material in the books. The Flesch "Human Interest" scores for those texts were even worse. Put bluntly, in 1974 most introductory psychology texts were both dull and fairly incomprehensible to *the average introductory student*.

The first edition of *UHB* departed from this dreary norm for a very simple reason: While the book was still in manuscript, I asked some 150 students to critique the book. I then revised the manuscript again and again until the majority of those students could understand the material—and said they found it interesting. As a consequence, the Flesch scores for the first edition were twice as high as those for almost any other text on the market.

Because student evaluations of the early editions of *UHB* were so strongly positive, most authors of other introductory psychology texts soon began writing in simpler prose too. And fortunately for the students who are required to read college textbooks, authors in other academic disciplines soon also began to strive to make their books more comprehensible.

Writing texts that *meet student needs* now seems the obvious thing to do. However, as far as I know, *UHB* was the first major text in any field that was created using the sort of student feedback I employed when preparing the first edition of this text. And because I have continued to use student evaluations while preparing each new edition, the Flesch scores for *UHB-6* are still higher than those of almost any other text on the market.

Narration Versus "Lists of Facts"

In 1969, I edited the first edition of the *Psychology Today* text. More than thirty psychologists each contributed a chapter to that text. Most of those chapters consisted of little more than unrelated "lists of facts" about whatever topics the authors had been assigned to cover. My task was to edit the chapters, give the book some coherence, and make the text more appealing to students. To liven the material up, I added several case histories and tried to recast many of the chapters into a sort of "functional narrative" that fleshed out the facts with a kind of story line. It took no great genius on my part to adopt this approach. In his classic work on memory—published a century ago—Hermann Ebbinghaus had noted that material presented in "narrative style" is ten times as easy to learn and remember as are lists of unrelated facts (Ebbinghaus, 1885).

When I asked my students at Michigan to evaluate the *Psychology Today* text, the *only* parts of the book they gave high ratings to were the case histories and the narratives. Thus, when I prepared the first edition of *UHB,* I added "vignettes" at the beginning of each chapter, and tried to give a "narrative flow" to each chapter, as well.

Many other textbook writers have now tried to adopt the "narrative style" that has always been the hallmark of *UHB*. Little wonder they have done so, since recent research has confirmed my original guess that students prefer this approach—and benefit greatly from it (Fernald, 1987).

Running Glossary

Psychologists don't always practice what they preach (McConnell, 1985a). We *know* we ought to listen to our students if we wish to maximize the amount they learn. However, it's often difficult for us to break long-standing habits that prevent us from teaching as effectively as we should.

When I tested *Psychology Today* with my own classes in 1970, I discovered an amazing fact: Although there was a glossary at the end of that book, less than half the students didn't know it existed. And most of those students who did discover the glossary didn't bother to read it. When I asked why they ignored the glossary, they made it clear that it simply was "too much trouble" to interrupt their reading to look up a term whose definition was buried at the end of the text. It didn't take much insight on my part to realize that I could encourage the students to learn more about the complex terms used in psychology if I defined those terms *on the same page* where they were first used. I called this the "running glossary," and it turned out to be a highly effective pedagogical device that many other textbook authors have now adopted. As far as I know, however, *UHB* was the first text to make use of a running glossary.

In 1974, when several hundred students evaluated the first edition of my text, they gave their highest ratings to the vignettes, the simple language, the narrative style, and the running glossary. These features have been retained in all subsequent editions.

What's New

Given the strengths of the previous editions, the question becomes, "What's new about *UHB-6*?" There are, I believe, three major (and noticeable) improvements:

First, the book has a far more contemporary and colorful design. Instructors who were shown sample pages of the new design preferred it, by far, to the format we used in *UHB-5*. I hope you and your students find it more attractive, too.

Second, the 1400 references for this edition are presented in alphabetical order at the end of the text. In previous editions, following the lead of authors of basic science texts, I put "Suggested Readings" at the end of each chapter and banished the references to the *Instructor's Manual*. However, since some instructors encourage their students to make use of the references, they are now presented in the text itself. The citations are noticeably current: Some 34 percent of the reference citations in *UHB-6* are dated 1985 or later, and 64 percent are from the 1980's.

Third, while *UHB-5* had 26 chapters, *UHB-6* has but 22. This reduction was made possible by an almost complete rewrite of much of the material in the text. Let's look at what some of the changes are.

In *UHB-5*, the material on the central nervous system and neural functioning was spread over Chapters 2, 3, and 4. In *UHB-6*, all of these data are presented in Chapter 2.

The material on history and systems, which made up most of Chapter 5 in *UHB-5*, has either been omitted or included within the other chapters.

In *UHB-5*, two chapters were devoted to sensory psychology. In *UHB-6*, both the major and the minor senses are covered in a single chapter.

Also, in *UHB-5*, social psychology took up three chapters. In *UHB-6*, this material has been increased in scope and extensively updated, but is covered in two rather than three chapters.

All told, almost half the material in *UHB-6* is new or different from what was in the previous edition. There is now a complete chapter devoted to cognitive functions (Chapter 12), and the material on memory (Chapter 11) has been extensively revised to take into account the increased focus on cognitive issues in the field itself. There also is more material on cognitive *development* in Chapter 15, including some important new material on cognitive processes in older individuals. The chapter on "person-oriented" personality theories (Chapter 16) is almost entirely new, and includes a much more elaborate description of Freudian theory, of Adler's and Jung's approaches, of the humanistic viewpoint, and of social learning theory. Following Christopher Monte's lead, I have tried to show how early experiences in the theorist's life influenced his or her theorizing (Monte, 1987). And at the suggestion of many instructors, I have now included a section on H. J. Eysenck's approach in Chapter 17, which covers what I call the "trait-oriented" personality theorists. Material on Sternberg's triarchic theory of intelligence has been added to this chapter as well.

In Chapter 18, which covers abnormal psychology, the emphasis now is on the recently revised version of DSM-III (which is called DSM-III-R) rather than on the original version of the manual. I have also added several case histories and increased the coverage of biologically oriented explanations of "mental" disorders to the chapter. In similar fashion, there is now more material on chemotherapy (and on behavior and family therapy) in Chapter 19, which covers various forms of therapy.

Finally, while social psychology now is covered in two chapters rather than three, there is more material on Bandura's theory of "self-efficacy" as well as greater coverage of recent research on body language and the *cognitive* approach to social psychology.

What's Much the Same

Despite all these changes, *UHB-6* is as personal a book as were its predecessors. Research shows that most students are put off by a very formal, academic approach to their first psychology course. They are interested in *people*—themselves and others—and not in esoteric data, statistical equations, and the fine points of experimental design. Many of us who teach the first course forget that 95 percent of our students are *not* psychology majors, and probably 90 percent of them will *never* perform a real psychological experiment. Why then should we require that they memorize "unrelated lists of facts" when ample research shows they will actively forget such lists as soon as they can? Why not try to "turn the students on" instead? *UHB-6* is a practical, people-oriented textbook that deals with real-life issues and gives students material they can put to practical use immediately. Is there any better way to make science understandable to students than by exciting their interest and giving them practical rewards for learning?

J. V. McC.

The Ancillaries

A full set of ancillary materials accompanies the sixth edition of *Understanding Human Behavior*. The package contains a wide range of materials in several different media that serve as enrichments for both the instructor and the student.

Student Manual
Learning Psychology, by Al Siebert of Portland State University and Tim Walter of the University of Michigan, provides a self-paced review of each chapter in *UHB*. Learning objectives, which are repeated in the Instructor's Manual and help to organize the Test Bank, begin each chapter. Concepts are reviewed in a variety of sections: list of key terms and concepts, predicting exam questions, fill-in-the-blank chapter highlights, true/false and multiple-choice questions, action projects, and provocative questions and issues. The Student Manual begins with the popular section "How to Do Well in College and Still Have Time for Your Friends," followed by a general study program for *UHB*. Efforts have been made to ensure an error-free answer key in this edition.

Instructor's Manual
Robert Burke of South Dakota State University has revised the Instructor's Manual with both the novice and experienced instructor in mind. The manual includes general suggestions for developing the course and chapter-by-chapter teaching tips for using *UHB*. Each chapter includes a list of learning objectives; a brief synopsis of the chapter in *UHB;* lecture, discussion, and student project ideas; recommended films and videotapes; and special sections featuring additional cross-cultural and methodological material. The manual ends with a comprehensive list of films and videotapes.

Test Bank
Grace Galliano of Kennesaw College has provided an entirely new Test Bank that features approximately 125 multiple-choice questions per chapter. The questions require either simple recall of material or application of knowledge. This edition of the Test Bank provides far more application questions than the previous edition. The questions are grouped by learning objectives listed in the Instructor's Manual and the Student Manual. In addition, several questions in each chapter are taken from the Student Manual and are so labeled.

Computerized Test Bank
The Test Bank is available for IBM or Apple computers. The program *Testbase* allows the instructor to modify or add questions and to create, scramble, and print tests and answer keys. With *Testbase* the instructor can choose questions either by scrolling through an entire chapter or by having the program isolate questions by the desired learning objective, type of question (recall or application), and/or whether it appears in the Student Manual. A hotline is available for anyone who experiences difficulty with the program or its interface with a particular printer.

Whole Psychology Catalog
This perforated manual contains page after page of innovative student handouts, questionnaires, and lecture outlines.

Psychlearn
This interactive software for students contains five experiments for IBM and Apple computers: Schedules of Reinforcement, Short-term Memory, Reaction Time, Self-consciousness Scale, and Social Dilemma. This full-color program comes with a guide containing instructional

information and discussion questions for each lesson.

Overhead Transparency Acetates
Over one hundred acetates and an accompanying guide are available.

Slides
A set of 300 color slides and an accompanying guide are available.

Video Segments
Please consult your local Holt, Rinehart and Winston sales representative for information on videos and other ancillaries available upon adoption of *UHB*-6.

Acknowledgments

According to the title page, this is "my" book. Nothing could be further from the truth. It takes the combined efforts of hundreds of people to produce a decent introductory psychology text. The author gets most of the credit, but the others do much of the real work. And without their signal contributions, no book would ever see final publication. In this brief note, let me acknowledge my great indebtedness to many individuals.

To begin with, my continuing thanks to Louise Waller, Johnna Barto, Fran Bartlett, and Rosalind Sackoff, who helped the first five editions through their various birth pangs. And my special thanks to Fran for "keeping on" in such fine fashion.

Next, let me thank Nick Suino and Jim Samons, who helped me sustain life while I was in the throes of preparing the sixth edition.

I owe thanks too to Susan Driscoll, who helped steer me in the right direction while preparing the sixth edition. And thanks as well to Chris Olson for getting the project off to a fine start.

A special blessing goes to Elsa Peterson, who did the photo research for the sixth edition. What a pleasure she's been to work with!

Most important, my deep-felt gratitude to Jane Knetzger, who was the developmental editor for this edition. Much of the credit for making this version "the best ever" goes to her.

A strong vote of thanks goes to Eve Howard, Dave Dusthimer, John Howard, Ed Hunter, Ted Buchholz, Geri Badler, and Matt McGuinness for their considerable efforts to make *UHB* so successful.

Then there are the production people who, under Vic Calderon's astute direction, took my scribbles and turned them into the book you're reading. In addition to Fran, my thanks go to Lou Scardino, Annette Mayeski, and Herman Makler.

In the final analysis, a good share of the success of previous editions was due to the enthusiastic reception given *UHB* by many HRW marketing and salespeople. I cannot begin to name them all, but without their help the book never would have been a success.

Many of my professional colleagues gave generously of their time in reading all or parts of the manuscript and offering their thoughtful comments. In particular,

Ira B. Albert, Dundalk Community College

Leon H. Albert, East Los Angeles College

Thomas R. Alley, Clemson University

Stephen R. Baumgardner, University of Wisconsin–Eau Claire

Michael G. Bergmire, Jefferson College

Conrad Brombach, Christian Brothers College

Mark Byrd, University of Kansas

Roland Calhoun, Humboldt State University

William H. Calhoun, University of Tennessee, Knoxville

John J. Colby, Providence College

Margaret E. Condon, Northeastern Illinois University

Eric J. Cooley, Western Oregon State College

Donald R. Cusumano, St. Louis Community College at Forest Park

Ananta Mohan Dasgupta, University of Wisconsin–Eau Claire

Eugene B. Doughtie, University of Houston, University Park

Morton P. Friedman, University of California, Los Angeles

Douglas L. Grimsley, University of North Carolina, Charlotte

George Gerald Gumeson, Cabrillo College

James E. Hart, Edison State Community College

Glenn R. Hawkes, Virginia Commonwealth University

Phyllis A. Hornbuckle, Virginia Commonwealth University

William L. Hoover, Suffold Community College

Patricia Keith-Spiegel, California State University, Northridge

Gary T. King, Rose State College

Stephen B. Klein, Fort Hays State University

Bernard H. Levin, Blue Ridge Community College

Pennie Medina, Bee County College

Terry A. Miller, Iowa Western Community College

Christopher F. Monte, Manhattanville College

Bill Moy, Washtenaw Community College

William W. Nish, Georgia College

Maureen O'Neill, Endicott College

Russell G. Peckens, William Penn College

Kent A. Pierce, Purdue University, Calumet

Darla J. Quesnell, Central Oregon Community College

Richard L. Reiner, Rogue Community College

Stephen Royce, The University of Portland

Ann Rusk, Yuba Community College

Bill Ryan, Polk Community College

S. Therezon Sheerin, Regis College

Al Siebert, Portland State University

Norman Silverman, Loyola University of Chicago

Kenneth Smoot, University of Wisconsin–Eau Claire

Tim Walter, University of Michigan

Carolyn West, Western Piedmont Community College

Several instructors allowed us to test out various text design concepts with their students: Teashia Adkins, University of Houston; Tracy Henley, University of Tennessee; Quentin Pulliam, Nashville State Technical College; Michele Reinhold, Lincolnland Community College; and Rodney G. Triplet, Northern State College.

Then there are my many friends in Ann Arbor and elsewhere, comrades all, who gave me most of my ideas and whose names I have taken in vain in some of the short stories. To my poker-playing cronies—Brian and Grant Healy, Kevin Lynn, Mike Keller, John Holland, Peter Steiner, Chuck Philips, Art Rich, R. M. Doughterty, and Andy Nagy—my thanks for keeping me amused (and broke) during the book's gestation period.

Last, but most assuredly not least, it is my students—past and present—who deserve my thanks. They taught me how to write and shaped me into learning more about psychology and about people than I had any intention of learning. Whatever is best in this book is their doing, not mine.

Bless 'em all.

J. V. McC.

Senior Editorial Consultants

Elliot Aronson, University of California, Santa Cruz

Robert E. Beck, Wake Forest University

Ross Buck, University of Connecticut

Tiffany Field, University of Miami

Kay Deaux, Purdue University

Christopher Hertzog, Georgia Institute of Technology

Daniel P. Kimble, University of Oregon

Michael Kubovy, Rutgers—The State University of New Jersey

John C. Malone, Jr., University of Tennessee

Margaret Matlin, State University of New York, Geneseo

Richard E. Mayer, University of California, Santa Barbara

Stephen Nowicki, Emory University

Alan O. Ross, The State University of New York at Stony Brook

Norman N. Silverman, Loyola University of Chicago

Contents
in Brief

Contents

Contents

Contents

Introduction

"Talk of Mysteries"

> Talk of mysteries! Think of our life in nature—daily to be shown matter, to come in contact with it—rocks, trees, wind on our cheeks! the *solid* earth! the *actual* world! the *common sense!* Contact! Contact! Contact! *Who* are we? *where* are we?
>
> Henry David Thoreau, *The Maine Woods, Ktaadn*

I was sitting at my kitchen table, reading the newspaper, when the phone rang. "Hello," I said.

"Hello, Jim? This is Marcello Truzzi. How would you like to drive down to Toledo to look at a little girl who can read minds?"

Marcello Truzzi is a long-time friend of mine. He is also professor of sociology at Eastern Michigan University, a very good school that is some 5 miles from the kitchen table I was sitting at.

"Why me, Marcello?" I asked. "You're the expert on mind-readers, not me." And indeed he is an expert on such things. For many years, Professor Truzzi has made a study of the **para-normal**, which we can define as "events that seem to be beyond normal explanations." The news media often contain sensational reports of people who (so it is claimed) can read other people's thoughts, or bend spoons through "mental effort," or predict the future. As you might have guessed, most of these reports turn out to be hoaxes or delusions. But since there is *always the chance* that a mind-reader or spoon-bender may actually have genuine paranormal powers, scientists like Dr. Truzzi try to investigate as many of these reports as possible.

"I called you because the little girl is also supposed to be **autistic**," Marcello replied.

"Oh," I said, suddenly realizing why Marcello had called me. For the past several years, my colleagues and I at Michigan have been working with autistic children. *Juvenile autism* is a psychological disorder that affects about one child in 2,000. Most autistic children are quite normal in appearance, and few of them have any measurable brain damage. It is their *behavior* that is unusual or abnormal. These youngsters seldom talk, even though they are physically capable of doing so. For the most part, they are unable (or unwilling) to relate to the people around them, including members of their own families. My colleagues and I at the University of Michigan have been trying to find ways to help autistic children communicate more effectively (Smith *et al.*, 1985).

"Okay, Marcello, tell me about this little girl who can read minds," I said to my friend.

"It's a very interesting story," he said with considerable enthusiasm. "The girl's name is Mary Smith. She's nine years old. She apparently suffers from some kind of brain damage, and limps a bit when she walks. She seldom if ever speaks, which is why she was diagnosed as autistic, I gather."

"Who did the diagnosis?" I asked.

"The school psychologist, I presume," Dr. Truzzi replied. "Mrs. Smith said Mary's teachers believe she's retarded as well as autistic. And Mrs. Smith thinks the teachers are wrong. She says Mary is potentially quite bright, even though the girl doesn't talk. That's why she taught Mary to communicate with her by using a computer."

"A computer?" I said, puzzled. "I thought Mary could read minds."

"Oh, she *supposedly* does," Marcello said. "At least, that's what Mrs. Smith claims. Whether she *really* can read minds remains to be proven scientifically, of course. However, since Mary can't talk, she needs some way of expressing her thoughts. It was only when Mrs. Smith taught Mary how to type on a computer keyboard that the mother learned that her daughter could read minds. Because, up until then, Mary had no way of letting people know what her mental skills were."

"I see," I said, scratching my head. "How long did it take Mary to learn to use the computer?"

"I don't know," Dr. Truzzi said. "But I gather she learned fairly quickly."

"How does she use this computer?"

Marcello paused for just a fraction of a second, as if searching his memory banks. "I think the mother stands behind the girl and asks her questions. Mary then types on the keyboard, and the answers appear on the computer screen."

"Oh?" I said. "Marcello, are you sure this thing is 'for real'?"

Dr. Truzzi laughed. "Of course not. You're never sure about these things until you investigate. But a **psychiatrist** who studied the girl says she really can read minds. And one of the Toledo TV stations broadcast a story about her that apparently impressed a lot of people. So there may be something to it after all. That's why it's important that someone checks this thing out. I don't have time right now, but I thought perhaps you'd be interested in looking into the situation because the girl presumably is autistic."

I stalled for time. "Well, I don't know."

"Oh, come on, Jim. It's a fascinating mystery story, and I know how much you love mysteries."

"Well, all right."

Most texts have word lists or glossaries at the end of the book that give definitions of technical terms. These glossaries are often difficult to find and to use, and few of them tell you how to say the word aloud. In this book, we have reserved the top of the left-hand column of odd-numbered pages for definitions and explanations of the sometimes complicated words or phrases you may encounter in each chapter. We call this the "running glossary." Every time you see a **boldfaced** word on a page, you will know that the word is defined (and often a pronunciation given) in the "running glossary" at the top of the left-hand column of the next odd-numbered page.

If you already understand the boldfaced word, don't bother checking it out immediately. However, if you have any doubts about the meaning of the word—or if you are interested in the Latin or Greek derivation of the term—you may wish to check the item at once, without having to lose your place by turning to the back of the book (where the glossary is located in most other texts).

Also, when you study for an examination, you may find it helpful to check all the terms in the "running glossary" since most of the key words or thoughts will appear there. Many (but not all) of these same important terms will also be **boldfaced** in the summary that appears at the end of most chapters.

If you run across a word you don't understand that does not appear in the "running glossary," please check the index at the end of the book to see if the word is defined elsewhere in the text. There is both an index of people's names and an index of subjects at the end of the book.

The pronunciations given in the definitions are in the Midwestern dialect that is used by many radio and TV announcers and newscasters. Pronunciations of many words vary from one part of the country to another. If you have doubts about how to say a word, please ask your teacher about it.

And finally, one very important point: Any dictionary contains thousands of words that you *already know*, as well as thousands that you *don't* know. I hope you will use the "running glossary" in this text as you would a dictionary. Don't be upset if I define terms you think every student ought to be familiar with. I selected the terms in the glossary by asking several hundred students to circle every word they didn't understand. The items that appear are those that *at least 10 percent* of these students weren't sure of—including some words that have no direct connection with the science of psychology.

This book is for *everybody*—for people with large vocabularies, and for people with limited knowledge but a large desire to learn. If you know most of the words defined in the "running glossary," congratulations! However, you should remember that other students may need all the help any of us can give.

Paranormal (PAIR-ah-NOR-mal). *Para* means "beyond." Therefore, *paranormal* means "events that seem to be beyond normal explanations."

Autistic (aw-TISS-tic). A type of mental disorder characterized by a lack of communication and an avoidance of social contact, as well as by repetitive behaviors and vocalizations.

Psychiatrist (sigh-KIH-ah-trist). A physician (M.D.) who treats mentally disordered individuals. The psychiatrist may or may not have had extensive training in experimental psychology. A clinical psychologist (Ph.D.) also treats mentally disordered individuals, but does not usually have medical training and cannot legally prescribe drugs or perform surgery, as can the psychiatrist. There is an old joke—told chiefly by psychologists—that the major differences between a psychiatrist and a psychologist is about $100,000 a year.

THE MYSTERY OF HUMAN BEHAVIOR

Marcello had me dead to rights. I *do* love mysteries. Like many psychologists, I consider human behavior a fascinating puzzle, begging to be solved. If you enjoy guessing what other people are really like, you probably feel much the same way. So, just for the moment, let's assume that you and I are detectives, trying to figure out whether nine-year-old Mary Smith can really read minds.

Like most sleuths, we'll gather evidence and follow our hunches. But as you will soon learn, modern psychologists have several tools available to them that not even the great Sherlock Holmes possessed.

1. The first tool is that collection of data and theories called *scientific psychology*. Because psychologists have been studying human behavior in the laboratory and in real-life settings for more than a century, we simply know more *facts* about people than most detectives do. And we also have many *theories* about human behavior that have stood the test of time. We frequently draw on these theoretical viewpoints to help us understand human behavior.

2. Our second tool is just as important. It's called the *scientific method*, and it gives us an extremely powerful way of collecting and evaluating the information we need to help us solve human mysteries.

Reading this book can be a useful first step as you try to master the facts and theories that make up modern psychology. And following my train of thought as I puzzle over the matter of Mary Smith may demonstrate rather dramatically why psychologists depend so heavily on the scientific method.

There is another point I should make immediately. I have immense respect for people's privacy. So, I've changed some of the names and descriptions of the people involved in this case history, particularly those involving the "Smith" family. But I also respect accuracy, so I've done my best to report what I actually saw and experienced.

Please keep these points in mind as we return to the mystery of "Mary Smith."

Clues and Data

As I listened to Dr. Truzzi describe Mary Smith, I paid much more attention to some things he said than to others. Several events that Marcello described bothered me. (When you read Chapter 5, you'll learn that the way you perceive the world is strongly influenced by certain *perceptual principles*. One such principle is that you tend to "see what you expect to see." When you perceive something that violates your expectancies, you often tend to focus on it. Small wonder, then, that I focused more on what was unusual in Marcello's description than in what was—to me—rather predictable.)

Let's call the things that bothered me "discrepancies," or *clues*. If we can resolve enough of these discrepancies, perhaps we can decide whether Mary Smith could really read minds, or whether we should explain what she was doing in other ways.

Clue #1. Some children diagnosed as *autistic* do suffer from obvious brain damage. But, as I've already said, most of them appear to have fairly normal nervous systems. So the first thing I asked myself was, "Is Mary Smith really autistic, or is there something else wrong?"

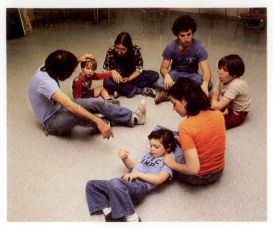

By studying autistic children, psychologists hope to find ways to cure this developmental disorder.

Clue #2 is related to #1. Most autistic children are **mute**. It's very difficult to teach them to speak, or to write, or even to communicate using sign language. While some autistic children do learn to talk eventually, they usually express themselves rather poorly and imprecisely. Thus, it seemed highly unlikely to me that Mary Smith could (a) be autistic, and (b) quickly learn to communicate using the precise language demanded by a computer.

The third discrepancy was more a vague hunch than a clue. For, as Marcello described how Mary "typed out the answers to her mother's questions," I got the uncomfortable feeling that I had heard this story before. I couldn't recall quite where or when I had encountered something similar in the past. But I was pretty sure that if I could just remember, I might come up with a solution to the mystery of Mary Smith. So I asked Dr. Truzzi a few more questions in an attempt to jog my memory.

More about Mary

"Marcello, tell me something. You said she's brain-damaged and limps a bit. So she probably has poor control of her hands as well as of her legs. If that's the case, how does she use the computer?"

"The mother had a special keyboard made with very large letters on it. All Mary has to do, really, is to poke a finger at the letters and she can type out whatever words she supposedly reads in her mother's mind."

I thought for a moment. "Can Mary read anybody else's mind other than her mother's?"

"I haven't seen Mary perform," Marcello said, "so I don't know whether she can read *my* mind or not. But I'm told she can answer almost any question you care to ask her."

"*Any* question?" I asked, my memory stirring a little.

Dr. Truzzi responded almost immediately. "Remember I said a psychiatrist went to see her? Well, she apparently knew things about

him that she couldn't have learned in any ordinary way. Or, at least, that's what Mrs. Smith claims."

My memory nudged me again. "Where does the mother stand when Mary's answering all these questions?"

"Behind the girl. But I think the mother usually touches Mary on the head, supposedly to establish telepathic contact."

Telepathic contact is a fancy way of saying "mind reading," or **mental telepathy**. But to qualify as *mental* telepathy, an event must involve no *physical* contact between the telepath and the mind he or she is "reading." Thus, if Mary Smith was actually a telepath, why would her mother need to touch her on the head in order to establish telepathic contact? Surely this was Clue #4, so I asked another question.

"Couldn't Mrs. Smith be giving her daughter cues as to what to type?"

"That's always possible," Marcello responded in a bemused tone of voice. I sensed that he was almost leading me along, hoping I'd raise the same sort of questions that had already occurred to him. "But the girl apparently types out her answers very quickly. Wouldn't she have to be awfully clever to respond that fast to just a light touch on the head?"

And then the clues all fell into place, and I was sure I had part of the solution to the mystery of Mary Smith. "Clever Hans," I said.

"Clever Hans indeed," Dr. Truzzi replied. "I presumed you'd see the possible similarities."

A Horse Named "Clever Hans"

Some 80 years ago, the newspapers of Berlin, Germany, were filled with exciting stories about a horse named Clever Hans. According

Mr. van Osten shows off Clever Hans and the "answer board" he built for Hans to use.

to these reports, Hans could not only "read minds" but could also solve difficult mathematical problems. People by the thousands flocked to see Hans perform his amazing feats.

Hans was owned by a Mr. van Osten, who was so impressed by the horse's abilities that he built a large "answer board" for Hans to use (see photo). If you gave Mr. van Osten a question for Hans, the man would look directly at the horse and repeat the question in what seemed a normal tone of voice. Hans would then lift his hoof and tap out the answer. If you asked, "What is 2 + 2?" Hans would tap the ground four times. But if your question was "Who is president of the United States?" Hans would point at the letters on the answer board that spelled out the correct response. Frequently, after Hans had done well, Mr. van Osten would pat the animal on its neck or give it a bit of food as a reward.

There were a number of intriguing aspects to Hans's performance. First, if you tried to trick him, he'd almost always catch you at it. For instance, if you said, "2 + 2 is 5, isn't it?" Hans would usually signal "No," using the answer board. Many people believed this response proved Hans was an "independent thinker" and wasn't just responding to subtle cues given him by Mr. van Osten.

Second, if the answer to your question was a long one, Hans would tap much more rapidly than if the answer were short. Many newspaper reporters took this as evidence that Hans was so bright, he knew the length of the answer *before he started responding.* (If the horse merely started and stopped responding when given some cue by Mr. van Osten, the animal obviously wouldn't know in advance which answers were going to be long and which would be short.)

Third, Hans would respond to questions given to him even by strangers. Thus, the horse obviously wasn't just picking up on unintentional cues from his owner.

Given these facts, it's not surprising most people concluded Hans was a genuine telepath. But a few skeptics remained convinced that the animal was merely reacting to cues of some kind from the people who asked Hans questions. The controversy became so heated that, in 1904, several of the best-known scientists in Germany formed a "commission" to study the animal. The commission included a zoologist, a physiologist, a veterinarian, a psychologist, the director of the Berlin Zoo, and

even the manager of a circus that featured animal acts. After months of study, the commission issued its report. These distinguished scientists stated boldly that they could find no evidence Hans was responding to external cues from his questioners. Hence, the commission said, Hans was a "special case," and perhaps really could read minds.

However, like most scientific commissions, this distinguished group recommended that "further research be done." So Professor Carl Stumpf, the psychologist on the commission, told one of his graduate students to look into the matter. This student, a young man named Oskar Pfungst, did just that.

Pfungst to the Rescue

Unlike Professor Stumpf, Oskar Pfungst simply didn't believe that Hans could "read minds." So, for many months, he observed Mr. van Osten very carefully as the owner talked to his horse. Then, in a *controlled and systematic way*, Pfungst began to *change* the conditions under which Hans worked.

For example, Pfungst put blinders on Hans so the animal couldn't watch the people who were asking him questions. The horse's ability to respond correctly decreased significantly. This result strongly suggested that Hans was responding to some unintentional visual cue given him by the person asking the questions. And when Pfungst found ways to keep Hans from hearing the tiny noises that people made when asking him questions, Hans did even worse. Indeed, when Pfungst cut out *both* visual and auditory cues after someone asked the horse a question, Hans either refused to respond or gave the wrong answer.

To test the animal's ability to "think independently," Pfungst did something a little different. First, he asked Hans to add two numbers, such as 23 + 49. Hans immediately responded by tapping out 72. Then Pfungst asked a friend of his to select a number at random and whisper it in the horse's ear. Pfungst then did the same, and asked Hans to add the

Unlike Pfungst, most animal trainers are aware of the cues they give.

two numbers. If *either* Pfungst or his friend knew *both* numbers, Hans invariably got the correct answer. But if neither man was aware of what number the other had chosen, the horse usually failed the test.

These results indicated Clever Hans was indeed a "genius of a horse," but surely wasn't a mind-reader. Rather, the animal was superb at reading "body-language" cues that questioners almost always gave to the animal. But these cues were so slight and so subtle that most people were completely unaware they were giving Hans signals.

For example, the moment most people finished asking Hans a question, they inclined their heads forward a fraction of an inch. This was a signal to Hans to start tapping. When Hans had tapped out the correct response, the people leaned back just slightly. This cue told Hans to stop tapping. (Other people inhaled sharply when they asked a question, and then exhaled when Hans had reached the right number of taps.) Similar cues helped the animal point his hoof to letters on the "answer board" that Mr. van Osten had constructed.

Pfungst also noticed that people tended to lean farther forward when they asked questions requiring long answers than when they asked questions with short answers. This response gave Hans his cue as to how fast to tap. Indeed, the horse was so sensitive to slight head movements that if anyone present raised an eyebrow or twitched a nostril while Hans was responding, he would stop instantly.

A final point: Once Pfungst became aware that Clever Hans was reacting to the body-language cues he was giving the horse, he deliberately tried to stop making these telltale twitches and snorts when he asked Hans questions. But no matter how hard Pfungst struggled to control his body language, Hans could almost always detect some sort of signal that told the animal when and how to respond.

After months of study, Pfungst concluded Hans was a very bright horse indeed, even if the animal couldn't "read minds."

One Reason People Are a Puzzle

The Clever Hans story is important for several reasons. First, it taught psychologists that most of us continuously give cues in our body language that suggest how we feel and what we're thinking about. Usually, we're unaware we're giving off these signals, but they're visible (or audible) to anyone who cares to notice.

Second, the Pfungst research demonstrates just how critical *scientific experiments* are to understanding human behavior. The commission of distinguished scientists that studied Clever Hans observed the horse carefully, asked questions, and gave the matter a lot of thought. Then they concluded that Hans could "read minds." But they didn't do *adequately*

extensive scientific experiments to test out their conclusions. Pfungst observed the animal too, because the scientific method always begins with careful observations. But he alone took the crucial next step. He guessed at the environmental stimuli (or cues) that could be affecting the horse's behavior, and then he altered these stimulus cues in a very systematic way. This creative use of *scientific experiments* led Pfungst to quite a different set of conclusions about Clever Hans than the commission had reached.

Third, when the name "Clever Hans" popped into my memory, I thought I had come up with an answer to the mystery of Mary Smith—even if it was one that Marcello Truzzi had already considered. But, like Pfungst, I couldn't be sure of my conclusions until I too had put the scientific method to good use and done some experiments of my own.

We'll get back to the Mary Smith story in just a moment. First, however, we need to take time out for what we might call an "academic commercial"—that is, a plug for the scientific method.

Science as a "Detective Story"

One of the main purposes of any science is that of solving mysteries. Nature gives us a puzzle, human or otherwise. For some reason, perhaps due to our own peculiar nature as human beings, we are motivated to solve the puzzle. We could just use our "hunches," of course, and make wild guesses about the answer. But scientists prefer to adopt a logical process of some kind when trying to find the solution to the puzzle.

The approach most scientists use is called the *scientific method*, which is based on the belief that most mysteries have *measurable causes*. To use the scientific method properly, you must follow several steps

1. You have to recognize that a mystery of some kind exists which needs solving, and that the mystery probably has a natural cause. We might call this step *perceiving the problem*.
2. You make as many *initial observations* about the mysterious circumstances as you can. And you try to make your observations as exact and complete as possible.
3. You use the results of your initial observations to come up with a *tentative solution* or "first guess" as to what the answer is. Scientists often call this step "making a hypothesis." The solution you pick, however, will be determined by how you view the problem—and the world. If you think events that take place in the world around you are affected primarily by *supernatural powers*, then the scientific method won't help you much. But if you believe that the mysterious event

might have a *natural cause*, then perhaps you can state your "tentative solution" or hypothesis in a way that will help you determine what that cause is.

4. You draw up a plan for *testing objectively* whether or not your first hunch about the solution was correct. This test may merely involve making further observations about the puzzling affair. Or it may involve performing an experiment in which you "do something" to the puzzle in order to get a reaction of some kind.

5. Whether you merely observe things, or whether you undertake an experiment of some kind, you then look over the data you've gathered and try to decide whether your tentative solution to the problem was right or wrong. If your initial hypothesis was wrong, you will revise it and make some more observations. But if your first hunch was correct, you probably will refine your solution to the mystery by *testing it again and again*. And to do so, you will need to make further predictions about future events.

6. If these further predictions turn out to be accurate, then most likely your solution to the puzzle was correct. But if your predictions were incorrect, you should realize that you "goofed" somewhere along the way. And you will have to start the problem-solving process all over again.

The Importance of Objectivity

The key concept in any definition of the scientific method is **objectivity**. And "being objective" means standing back and looking at the puzzle as unemotionally and impersonally as you can. True, your subjective, personal feelings are very useful in *motivating* you to want to solve problems. But your emotions can cloud your judgment if you don't know how to control them when necessary.

For example, Pfungst was *objective* in his study of Clever Hans. His initial hypothesis was that the horse was responding to unconscious cues from Mr. van Osten and other questioners. Pfungst notes, for example, that van Osten never charged anyone for talking to Hans, and made not a penny out of the animal's fame. But Pfungst didn't allow his affection for either the man or the horse to get in the way of his pursuit of objective truth. Mr. van Osten, on the other hand, let his emotions blind him to what was really going on. He loved Hans and was

convinced the horse could "read minds." Shortly after Pfungst proved otherwise, van Osten went into a deep depression. A few months later, he died, a bitter and very disappointed man (Rosenthal, 1965).

Given these facts, perhaps you can understand why I worried a bit about how Mrs. Smith might react if someone proved scientifically that Mary was merely responding to subtle cues from her mother. As you will see, however, those fears were groundless.

A Trip to Toledo

As I mentioned earlier, Marcello was pleased when I said the words "Clever Hans." For, like most behavioral scientists, Dr. Truzzi knew all about Mr. van Osten's horse. Indeed, as I discovered later on, Marcello had published an article on the subject (Truzzi, 1981).

"Oh, yes," Marcello said. "The girl could just be responding to subtle cues from her mother. But what are the cues, and how does the whole thing work? That's what I hope you can find out."

And so we agreed that I would pay a visit to the Smiths. Thus, a week or so later, I drove down to Toledo with a man I'll call Charles Barnwell. Charlie was trained as a social worker, had a long-standing interest in autistic children, and had been to the Smith house previously. He also was convinced that Mary Smith could actually "read minds." After all, Charlie had asked the girl questions himself, and she had gotten the right answers! How could she possibly fake something like that? I told Charlie about Clever Hans, but he really didn't see the connection at first.

At any rate, after an hour's drive, Charlie and I arrived at the Smith house. It was a small but well-kept home on the outskirts of Toledo. Mrs. Smith smiled at us warmly as she opened the door, took our coats, and then invited us back to the kitchen.

My first impression was that I had wandered by mistake into a computer showroom, for the tiny kitchen and dining room were filled with electronic equipment of various kinds. I spotted an Apple computer, a slide projector and a movie screen, a voice synthesizer, and a large keyboard connected to the computer by wires. A sort of highchair, covered with comfortable cushions, sat in front of the computer screen. "This is what Mary uses to communicate with me," Mrs. Smith explained. "The equipment was given to us by one of the service clubs when they learned about Mary's special talents."

I asked about the slide projector. "Mary doesn't see very well," Mrs. Smith said. "She can't always read the tiny letters on the computer screen. I hooked the slide projector up so it can magnify what she types and project it on the movie screen."

Next I asked about Mary herself. "She's adopted, you know," the woman said. "Our first child was born handicapped. Most people are a little put off by handicapped children. But my husband and I think they're the most loving children there are. So we've adopted three of them."

"How old was Mary when you adopted her?" I asked.

"About five," Mrs. Smith replied. "She was like a frightened little animal when we first got her. She hid in the bathroom and wouldn't come out. So I just stayed in the bathroom with her for the first six weeks or so, until she calmed down. Now she's quite comfortable with me. Of course, she still has a few problems, but she's a very special child, as you'll see."

"What kind of problems does she have?"

"Well, her brain didn't develop properly. She's **hydrocephalic**, you know. The doctors have operated on her brain, to relieve the pressure. And it does seem to have helped a little. But she's very bright, despite all her difficulties."

Because Mary Smith's brain had fewer nerve cells than does a normal child's brain, it was understandable that she "had a lot of problems." It also seemed likely she was profoundly handicapped rather than autistic. "Did Mary learn to use the computer rapidly?" I asked.

Mrs. Smith shook her head. "Mary can't control her hands very well, so she can't use the keyboard that came with the computer. So I had that big alphabet board built. Even so, it seemed to take her a long time to learn how to use it. And then one day she just started typing out words and complete sentences."

"Just like that?" I asked.

"Well, more or less. You see, I made the mistake of trying to move her hands for her at first. I'd ask her a question, like, 'How do you spell "cat"?' And then I'd guide her fingers over the board, and show her how to type out the answer. But she just didn't seem to understand what I was trying to get her to do. And then one day I got frustrated and stopped pushing her fingers around."

"How did she respond?"

"I was teaching her how to spell a word—'dog,' I think it was. Well, she got angry with me when I tried to help her type the answer. So I just let go of her hands. She began poking at the keys, slowly. I was screaming DOG, DOG, DOG in my mind, I was so angry. Then I looked over at the screen. She had typed out DOG, DOG, DOG on the keys. 'My Lord,' I said to myself. 'Mary can read my mind.'"

A Mother's Touch

For several seconds, the three of us were completely silent. I glanced at Charlie, who was wide-eyed, as if in amazement. I looked back at Mrs. Smith. Her face wore a quiet smile.

Finally I said, "And ever since that day, Mary has been able to read your thoughts and type them out on the computer?"

Mrs. Smith nodded. "Of course, she got better at it, as time went on."

I cleared my throat. "That first day, when Mary typed out the word 'dog' for you, were you touching her?"

"Oh, yes. I was standing behind her, resting my hands on her head, like I always do when she types. She can't read my mind unless I'm touching her, you know."

"Do you always touch her on the head?"

"No. Her teachers came and saw her perform. They said I must be giving her cues of some kind—turning her head, or something. So now I touch her on the arm instead."

Charlie interrupted. "But it still works, doesn't it?"

Mrs. Smith nodded again.

"Could we see Mary?" Charlie continued. "Could you show us how it works?"

"Of course," the woman said. "I'll get her right away. She's just downstairs, playing."

As soon as Mrs. Smith had left the room, Charlie turned to me. "Amazing, isn't it?"

I sighed. "Yes, it is. Mrs. Smith knows, doesn't she?"

"Knows what?"

"Knows that Mary can't really read minds, Charlie. Knows that she's cueing the girl's responses in some fashion."

Charlie frowned. "Well, I suppose you could be right. But it certainly does seem like the girl can read minds. I mean, I've seen it with my own eyes!"

An Eye-opening Demonstration

Before I could respond, Mrs. Smith returned with her daughter. Charlie and I shook hands with the girl. Then Mrs. Smith put her up on the well-cushioned highchair in front of the computer screen. "Dr. McConnell, if you'd care to write out some questions on a piece of paper, I'll try to have Mary answer them for you."

"What kinds of questions?" I asked.

"Oh, anything at all. Write out some words, for example. Show them to me, but don't say them out loud."

"Okay," I said, and began jotting some words down on a piece of paper. While I was writing, Mrs. Smith got out the alphabet board and put it in Mary's lap. It was a long, thin, flat piece of equipment. The front of the board contained letters and numbers, divided into a sort of grid.

Mrs. Smith showed us that just touching any of the squares on the grid would make the computer display the appropriate letter or number.

Hydrocephalic (HIGH-droh-see-FALL-ic). From the words *hydro* (meaning "water") and *cephalo* (meaning "brain"). Special cells in the brain continuously secrete a watery fluid that surrounds and cushions the brain. In a normal child, this fluid drains off through a sort of tube and becomes the spinal fluid. In the hydrocephalic child, however, the tube is blocked so the fluid can't escape. The pressure inside the skull becomes so great that the child's brain cells can't grow properly. The child is left with a skull full of fluid—and with an underdeveloped brain.

A	B	C	D	E	F	1	2	3
G	H	I	J	K	L	4	5	6
M	N	O	P	Q	R	7	8	9
S	T	U	V	W	X	Y	Z	0

I wrote the words "Rat," "Banana," and "Weather" on the paper and gave it to Mrs. Smith. She glanced at the words, nodded, and then stood behind Mary's chair, draping her arms around the girl's shoulders. Almost at once, the girl lifted her right hand and pointed her right index finger at the letter "A." Without touching any of the squares, her finger swept across the top row of the board. When she reached the end of the first row, her hand jerked back and rapidly swept across the second row. As she neared the "R" in the third row, her hand slowed slightly. Her index finger hovered over the "R" for a fraction of a second. Then she touched it, and the letter "R" appeared on the computer screen.

Instantly, Mary's hand returned to the "A" on the top row. She hesitated momentarily, touched the letter, and then began to sweep out the rest of the top row. This time, her hand didn't slow down until she reached the bottom row. She touched the "T." The word "RAT" now appeared on the computer screen. It had taken Mary less than five seconds to produce the first word I had shown to Mrs. Smith.

"Incredible!" Charlie said, staring at the screen in astonishment.

"Yes, it is," I said, staring at Mrs. Smith's hands as they gently caressed her daughter's arms. "Try the second word, would you please?"

Mrs. Smith nodded. Mary touched the "B" and "A" so quickly that I couldn't follow her movements. But as her finger neared the "N," I was looking intently at the tendons on Mrs. Smith's right hand. The closer the little girl's finger came to the "N," the more visible the tendons on the mother's hand became. And when Mary's finger was right over the letter "N," the mother's tendons popped into full view for a fraction of a second. Mary touched the "N." The tendons in the mother's hand relaxed, and Mary's fingers moved to the top row of the alphabet board once more. Each time the mother's hand tensed, Mary poked the key-

board. Within a few seconds, the word "BANANA" appeared on the computer screen. A few moments later, so did the word "WEATHER."

"Fantastic," Charlie said. "I wouldn't have believed it if I hadn't seen it with my own eyes."

"It is fantastic," I said. I thought for a moment. "Mrs. Smith, I noticed that you were looking at Mary's fingers as she typed. Can she read your mind if you have your eyes closed?"

"No, she can't," the woman replied. "I've tried shutting my eyes, and looking away. Mary just gets confused when I do. That's one of the things that puzzles me."

"What else puzzles you?" I asked.

The woman frowned. "Well, at first I thought she was a mathematical genius. That made me happy, because it would prove to her teachers that she's brighter than they think she is. Anyhow, I'd write out two numbers, add them myself, and then give her the numbers to do on her own. She always got the right answer very quickly. Except one day I added the numbers wrong myself, and Mary typed out the same wrong answer I had, not the correct answer."

"What did you conclude from that?"

"That's when I realized she was reading my mind, not doing the math on her own."

I nodded. "And what did you conclude from the fact that she can't read your mind when you shut your eyes?"

Mrs. Smith gave a deep sigh. She patted Mary lovingly on the head, and then sat down wearily in a kitchen chair. She glanced at the floor for a moment, then looked up at me. "Maybe I am giving her a cue of some kind, maybe not. If I am, I don't know what it is. But that isn't what bothers me."

Mary slid down from her highchair and limped over to her mother. She climbed up in the woman's lap and began pulling at her mother's earring. "Don't do that, dear," Mrs. Smith said gently. She gathered the girl into her arms to keep her quiet.

"What does bother you?" I asked.

The woman sighed again. "The fact that I can't seem to reach *her*. I can hold her in my arms, like this, but I can't reach deep down inside her. Even if she's reading my mind, she's just telling me what *I* think, not what *she* thinks and feels. She may have a damaged brain, but there's a little girl in there somewhere. How do I get to her, Dr. McConnell? *How do I find out who my little girl really is?*"

THREE EXPLANATORY VIEWS OF HUMAN BEHAVIOR

How would you have described Mary to Mrs. Smith had you been in my place? In fact, there are thousands of responses I might have given, all of them accurate in a limited sort of way. For example, I could have replied, "She's a nine-year-old, hydrocephalic human female." Or, "She's your *daughter*, someone you have a warm, loving relationship with." Or even, "She's *herself*, that's who she is."

If you asked a thousand psychologists to define Mary Smith, the answers you'd get would probably include one or more of the descriptive phrases mentioned above. For these responses represent the three major theoretical viewpoints within the behavioral sciences today. Let's look briefly at these three main ways of explaining human behavior.

The Biological Viewpoint

Some psychologists emphasize the importance of biological factors in determining who you are and what you do. These scientists believe that everything you think and feel is controlled by electrical and chemical activity in your brain and the rest of your body. Thus, to these theorists, the body controls the mind, and not the other way around.

From the *biological viewpoint*, Mary Smith would be defined primarily in terms of her damaged nervous system. Her inability to speak, her lack of muscle coordination, her limited comprehension—all these *psychological* or *behavioral* difficulties would be viewed as "natural consequences" of her poorly developed brain. And given this perspective, biological psychologists might well recommend that the best way to help Mary Smith would be through surgery, or the use of drugs.

Mary Smith did have physical handicaps, and there's no way of "defining" her without taking these problems into account. But just as we cannot explain who you are merely by describing the flow of electricity through your nervous system, so we cannot take just a narrow biological view of who Mary Smith really is.

The Intra-Psychic Viewpoint

The majority of behavioral scientists would probably take an *intra-psychic viewpoint* toward Mary Smith. Most psychologists believe that everything that goes wrong (or right) about someone's **psyche** or behavior cannot be explained in simple biological terms. These scientists try to look (as best they can) at what goes on *inside the individual's mind*, rather than just looking at how a person's brain functions.

Intra-psychic psychologists are primarily interested in *mental processes*. Scientists study these inner processes in many ways. First, they observe what people actually do and say in a variety of settings. Second, they give people standardized tests of various kinds, and then compare their responses with those that other individuals make (see Chapter 17). Third, they

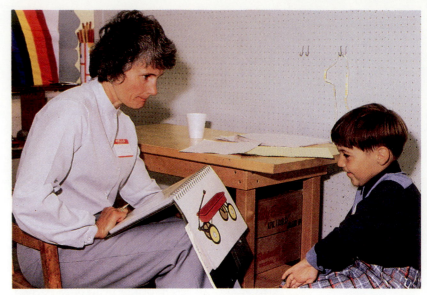

Psychologists use standardized tests to measure and understand an individual's mental processes. This boy is being tested to determine if his language and cognitive skills make him ready for kindergarten.

listen very closely to statements that people make about their inner thoughts and feelings. The intra-psychic psychologists then try to explain the behaviors they've measured *objectively* in terms of *mental processes*—such as perceptions, motives, values, attitudes, memories, and personality traits.

From the biological viewpoint, the body exercises almost complete control over the mind. From the intra-psychic standpoint, however, the mind dominates most bodily activities.

Both viewpoints can be very useful in helping you understand yourself (and others). But both viewpoints are—in and of themselves—incomplete.

The Social/Behavioral Viewpoint

Mary Smith had both a mind and a body. But she was also a *social being*. Mary's thoughts and behaviors were strongly influenced by the people and things around her, and her thoughts and behaviors strongly influenced the people she was around. Even her "mental disabilities" were affected as much by her environment as by her hydrocephalic condition. Children with very similar brain damage often show quite different behavior patterns, depending on what type of home they have grown up in.

Mary had a mother and father, two adopted sisters, and a brother. She had many friends living in her neighborhood, and at school she worked and played with teachers and schoolmates. In the past she had been in a hospital and an adoption agency home. At the moment, she was in contact not only with her mother, but also with a psychologist (me) and with someone trained in social work (Charlie). In her brief life, therefore, Mary Smith had met

1 / Introduction

Psyche (SIGH-key). From the Greek word meaning *mind*. The term *intra-psychic* means "inside the mind." The English word *mind* comes from an Old English term meaning "memory." *Webster's New Collegiate Dictionary* defines *mind* as "that element or complex of elements in an individual that feels, perceives, thinks, wills, and especially reasons." The same book also calls *mind* "The conscious mental events and capabilities in an organism." Mind, then, has to do with your *inner* experiences.

and interacted with hundreds of individuals, all of whom had played their parts in helping make her what she was today. Indeed, from the *social/behavioral viewpoint*, there was little about Mary's actions and emotions that couldn't be explained in terms of what she had learned from her social environment.

Most people ignore the importance of the environment in shaping human thoughts and actions. For example, Mrs. Smith apparently defined her daughter primarily in intra-psychic terms, since she explained the girl's behaviors in terms of "mental telepathy." In fact, mother and daughter had become a smoothly functioning *social team*. Each gave subtle cues to the other, and each responded to subtle cues received from the other. Do we have to know anything at all about brain damage or mental processes in order to explain how both members of this social team responded? Indeed, from the social/behavioral viewpoint, appealing to such concepts as "hydrocephalism" and "mind reading" might well blind us to the social factors that so strongly influenced Mary Smith's responses.

THE HOLISTIC APPROACH

Which of the three viewpoints—the biological, the intra-psychic, or the social/behavioral—gives you the greatest understanding of Mary and her problems?

The holistic point of view takes into account the biological, mental, and social aspects of each person.

The answer is, *all three of them taken together*. Like Mary, you are an incredibly complex living system. There is a biological side to your nature, a mental side, and a social side. You cannot hope to understand yourself—or Mary, or anyone else—unless you are willing to view human beings *holistically*. That is to say, you must learn to perceive people *simultaneously* from the biological, intra-psychic, and social/behavioral perspectives.

Let's keep this *holistic* approach to understanding human behavior in mind as we look more closely at Mary Smith.

Mary and the Three Viewpoints

What had I learned about Mary so far?

From a biological viewpoint, I knew that she had much less brain tissue than a normal child her age would have, and nothing anyone could do would help her recover the lost brain tissue. However, this fact didn't necessarily mean she couldn't recover *psychologically* and *socially* if given the proper training.

From an intra-psychic viewpoint, I knew that Mary suffered from behavioral and mental problems related to her physical difficulties. However, she had strengths and abilities as well as weaknesses and disabilities. Like Hans the horse, Mary was particularly clever at picking up subtle cues from the people around her—cues that most "normal" children probably would have missed. She could communicate her needs and feelings in at least a rudimentary way. And most of all, she could *learn*.

From a social/behavioral viewpoint, it was clear that the girl and her mother made up an incredible team. The woman's love for Mary was obvious. Few of us would have had the stamina, motivation, or guts to stay in a bathroom for weeks just to calm a frightened child's fears. And few of us probably would have worked as hard, or spent as much money, trying to devise ways to help a brain-damaged child learn to communicate with the world around her. Thus, to find out more about who Mary was—and what sort of person she could become—I obviously would need to discover more about how she and her mother interacted.

And I needed to use the scientific method to help me accomplish my task.

THE SCIENTIFIC METHOD

Once Mrs. Smith admitted that she was cueing most of Mary's responses at the computer keyboard, I was reasonably confident the girl wasn't a telepath. Oddly enough, however, Charlie remained unconvinced. So I knew I'd have to do something more to prove my conclusion was right.

I paused for a moment, trying to figure out how to explain to Charlie what I wanted to do, and why. Before I could say anything, however, Mary demanded that her mother take her to the bathroom. While the two were gone, I talked at length with Charlie.

"Look," I said. "You have one explanation for Mary's behavior—you call it 'mind reading.' I have another explanation. Probably we could come up with several more theories if we really tried. The important thing is to find some way to put our notions to a scientific test of some kind, isn't it?"

Charlie nodded in agreement.

"Okay, when Mrs. Smith and Mary come back, suppose we ask Mrs. Smith to help us run an experiment. Okay?"

When Charlie nodded again, I told him what I had in mind.

Independent, Dependent, and Intervening Variables

When psychologists perform experiments to test their hunches, they typically "do something new or unusual" to some organism or group. Then they sit back to see what *changes* occur.

When you "do something new or unusual" to an individual, you decide on the ways you are going to *vary* that person's environment. Since *you* make the choice, this *variable* in the experiment is "independent" of the subject's wishes. Psychologists call "what you do to a subject" the *independent variable* because it is under the experimenter's control.

When you act, people react. The subject's reaction is called the *dependent variable* because the response the subject makes obviously depends on what you've done to the individual.

To summarize, the "independent variable" is what the experimenter does to the subject, while the "dependent variable" is the reaction the subject gives.

But *why* do subjects react as they do? Psychologists aren't always sure. When we find that a certain act of ours almost always evokes the same response in someone else, however, we can often "make guesses." These guesses or hypotheses are our ways of explaining what goes on inside the person that *connects* the act with the reaction. Put another way, we guess at what processes inside the person "intervene" between the independent and dependent variable. And we call these inner processes *intervening variables*. But we can't observe or measure these intervening variables *directly,* for they are just our guesses about why the person acts as he or she does.

Suppose you show Mary Smith a kitten because you want to see how she will react to it. She smiles and pets the animal. "Aha!" you say. "She petted the beast because she loves cats." Showing Mary the kitten is the *independent variable*, because you could have shown her a snake. Smiling and petting are *dependent*

variables, because her response depended on what you showed her. If you'd shown her a snake, she might have run away. "Love" is an *intervening variable*, because it's your explanation of why she responded as she did.

You can *see* kittens and petting behaviors. So independent and dependent variables are things that you can measure objectively. But you *can't see* "love" or "fear" or "mental telepathy." Therefore, intervening variables are usually *internal processes* that you can't measure directly. Indeed, you can't even be sure they actually exist. You merely presume that they do, because intervening variables give you a way of *explaining* the relationship you have observed between the independent and the dependent variables.

Charlie had watched Mary Smith perform at the computer keyboard, and had come up with an explanation for what he saw. The words I had shown to Mrs. Smith were the independent variable in this case, because I could have written three other words. Mary's responses at the keyboard were the dependent variable, because what she wrote obviously depended on the words I had chosen. Charlie then *invented* an intervening variable called "mind reading" to explain the relationship between my independent variable and Mary's dependent response.

I had watched the same performance, but offered a different intervening variable—one called "social cueing." Either hypothesis could be correct. How shall we judge between the two?

How do you decide which of two financial experts is the better? You ask both of them to predict what the stock market will do in the next six months or so, and then you check to see which expert gave the more accurate prediction. Scientists do the same sort of thing when they test two competing hypotheses. They design an experiment and then let each hypothesis predict what will happen. Then they actually run the experiment and compare the results with the predictions. The theory that *predicts and explains* things better usually wins.

With this thought in mind, I said, "Charlie, what would it take to prove to you that Mary is just responding to cues her mother is giving her?"

Charlie thought a moment. "Well, if you can show me what the cues actually are . . ."

"The hands, Charlie. Watch her hands." And then I told Charlie what I had observed and what I wanted to do next.

Using Control Groups in Experiments

Suppose you wanted to prove to Charlie that Mary was just reacting to her mother's body language. What would you do?

To begin with, it might be helpful if you performed some scientific tests. For instance, you might have Mary try "mind reading" again. But sometimes you would let her mother cue her, and sometimes you would remove the cues. If the *only* time Mary responded appropriately was when she got the cues, then you could place some faith in the "cueing" hypothesis.

We'll return to Mary Smith in just a moment. First, however, we need to find out how behavioral scientists actually *design* their experiments. As you will see, sometimes they compare the responses of *different groups of subjects*. We call this the **between-subjects design** because you end up comparing responses *between* different groups. But at other times, the scientists compare responses made by the *same subject* under different conditions. We call this the **within-subjects design** because you end up looking for differences *within each subject's set of responses*. Let's talk about using *different groups* of subjects first.

● ### Between-Subjects Design

When using the "between-subjects" design, psychologists typically expose one group of subjects to what the psychologists believe is the important independent variable. Then, to make sure they can depend on the results they've gotten, the psychologists expose one or more additional groups of subjects to unimportant or trivial independent variables. By *comparing the responses* of these various groups, the scientists can usually decide whether the independent variable they're studying is really important in determining the subjects' responses.

For instance, let's assume you discovered a drug you thought would cure headaches. How would you prove it really worked? You could just give the drug to 100 people with headaches and count how many of your subjects got better. Suppose 65 percent of them got immediate relief. Wouldn't that prove that your drug was effective? Not really. For many scientific studies show that some people get better immediately even if you just give them a sugar pill. And many subjects recover even if you give them nothing at all. So, maybe your new drug is just another sugar pill.

To make sure your drug was really effective, you'd need to test some additional groups. You might give a sugar pill to one such group, and nothing at all to a second bunch of subjects. You could then *compare* the recovery rates shown by these two groups with the recovery rate shown by your original subjects.

In this study, the subjects you gave the "real" pill to would be called the *experimental group*. The two "comparison groups" are referred to as *control groups* because each comparison group you run actually "controls" for another possible explanation of the results shown by the experimental group.

Now, suppose the experimental-group subjects showed a significantly higher recovery rate than did the subjects in the two control groups. The fact that you compared their responses with those of the two control groups *strongly suggests* that your drug was effective in curing headaches.

● ### Within-Subjects Design

In the headache study we've just described, you used the "between-subjects" design because you compared the responses of several groups, and you tested each group under a single experimental condition. However, you could have accomplished much the same thing by using the "within-subjects" design. That is, you could have tested each subject *several times, under different experimental conditions*.

For example, you could find people who get frequent headaches and use them as subjects. The first time they complain of a headache, you give them the sugar pill. The second time, you give them the drug. Then you would compare *each subject's individual responses— once to the sugar pill, once to the drug*.

In fact, you'd want to *randomize your order of presentations*. That is, you'd want to give some people the drug first, then the sugar pill. And you'd want to give other people the sugar pill first, then the drug. And, of course, you should make sure the subjects didn't know which pill they were taking.

Many things can affect the outcome of a scientific study. In the experiment we've just described, for instance, you'd want to make sure that neither the person giving out the pills nor the subjects themselves knew which was the "real" drug and which was the sugar pill. We'll talk more about such matters both in Chapter 13 and in the Statistical Appendix at the end of this book.

Psychologists tend to use the "between-subjects" design when they have a lot of subjects available. The more subjects they test, of course, the more likely it becomes that the results will apply to all people everywhere.

"IT WAS MORE OF A 'TRIPLE-BLIND' TEST. THE PATIENTS DIDN'T KNOW WHICH ONES WERE GETTING THE REAL DRUG, THE DOCTORS DIDN'T KNOW, AND, I'M AFRAID, NOBODY KNEW."

We typically use the "within-subjects" design when we have just a few subjects available—or when we're primarily interested in discovering some of the factors influencing the responses of just one person.

Since I had but one Mary Smith available, I decided to use the "within-subjects" design in trying to discover what variables actually controlled her "mind-reading" responses.

We Use Mary as Her Own Control

Once Mrs. Smith and her daughter returned to the kitchen, I asked Charlie to write out some words and show them to Mrs. Smith. Mary typed them out on the computer just as quickly as she had the words I selected. But this time, of course, Charlie was watching the tendons on Mrs. Smith's hands rather than looking at what Mary was doing. I could tell by the look on his face that he saw what I had seen. (This was the first, or experimental, condition, which involved giving Mary cues from her mother.)

Next, we asked Mrs. Smith to close her eyes and try to communicate with Mary. The girl typed out a couple of random letters and then quit responding. (This was the second, or control, condition because Mrs. Smith couldn't give Mary cues if she couldn't see what Mary was doing. Since we exposed Mary to both conditions, we had employed a "within-subjects design," and had used Mary as her own control.)

"Amazing," Charlie said. "Simply amazing."

"Yes, she is an amazing little girl, isn't she?" I replied. "We can learn a lot from her."

What You Can Learn from Mary Smith— and from This Book

Learning about psychology doesn't consist of finding a set of magic keys that will unlock the "great secrets of your mind." Rather, understanding human behavior is chiefly a matter of discovering thousands of things that you've been thinking and feeling and responding to—but were never really aware of.

Many fields of knowledge can offer you a *subjective* understanding of human behavior. Art, literature, and religion are good examples of subjective approaches that can give you important information about people. But psychology offers you two things that no other field can:

- First, a set of *objective* facts about how you think, feel, and behave.
- Second, theories and insights that attempt to explain in *objective* terms why you think, feel, and act as you do.

But taking an unbiased, objective view of yourself (and others) is a skill that you have to "learn by doing." And not everyone appreciates—or even agrees with—the facts that psychologists have discovered about human nature. Whether it's worth your time to learn how to be objective about people, only you can decide. Perhaps it will help if we discuss what types of psychologists there are, and what these psychologists actually do.

WHAT PSYCHOLOGISTS DO

There are many types of psychologists. Some psychologists *generate* facts and theories; others *apply* this information in real-life settings.

Many psychologists do both.

Experimental and Academic Psychology

Experimental psychologists mostly work in scientific laboratories. These scientists typically perform experiments to help develop a basic understanding of human nature. Some of these individuals study such processes as perception, learning, or motivation in human and animal subjects. Others, called biological psychologists, investigate such things as the effects of drugs and surgery on performance. We will describe biological psychology in Chapters 2 and 3, and other types of experimental psychology in Chapters 4–13. Reading these chapters will give you some idea of what experimental psychologists are like, and the sorts of things they do and are interested in.

Developmental psychologists look at how people grow and mature from conception to old age. They study human behavior in a variety of settings, from hospitals and nurseries to homes for the elderly. We will discuss the sorts

Experimental psychologists study the effects of particular stimuli on particular behaviors, such as how a method of teaching affects learning, or how a drug affects performance in a maze. They often use animal subjects in their experiments.

of experiments that developmental psychologists perform in several chapters, but primarily in Chapters 14 and 15.

Social psychologists study the behavior of people in groups and organizations. Some social psychologists work primarily in laboratories, where they can maintain tight controls over the variables that affect the behaviors of the subjects they study. Other social psychologists work "in the field," which is to say that they perform their research in real-world environments. We will describe both types of studies in Chapters 20–22.

Educational psychologists are primarily interested in how humans learn in schools and other educational settings. The creation of standardized tests and other measures of academic and intellectual performance is one of the chief tasks performed by educational psychologists. We will discuss these sorts of tests in Chapter 17.

In addition to the research they perform, most *experimental psychologists* teach in academic settings such as colleges and universities. Others work in government and industrial laboratories, or at private institutes.

Clinical and Applied Psychology

More than half of the psychologists in the US work in what are called "applied settings." While many of these professionals perform occasional research studies or teach classes, their main focus is generally that of helping people solve real-life problems.

Clinical psychologists, for example, usually deal with individuals who have personal difficulties, or who suffer from mental or behavioral disorders of some kind. Most clinical psychologists work in clinics or hospitals, or treat patients in their own offices. According to a

Clinical psychologists work with people who have various types of problems. This therapy group is for recovering drug addicts, and is led by a clinical psychologist.

"OF COURSE MY ADVICE MAKES SENSE. I'M A GYPSY, BUT I ALSO HAVE A DEGREE IN PSYCHOLOGY."

recent survey, about a third of the clinical psychologists in the US take an **eclectic** approach to therapy; that is, they tend to use therapeutic techniques taken from many different theoretical viewpoints (Watkins *et al.*, 1986). Another third of practicing clinical psychologists are Freudian or psychoanalytic in their outlook. We will have more to say about clinical psychology in Chapters 18 and 19.

Counseling psychologists usually offer expert advice on personal, educational, or career problems. Some counseling psychologists are in private practice; others work in schools or clinics. Generally speaking, counseling psychologists deal with less severe problems than do clinical psychologists. For example, a person wanting help deciding on a career might well go to a counseling psychologist. But someone with a major emotional difficulty might well seek the aid of a clinical psychologist. According to a recent study, however, the differences between the *types* of patients treated by clinical and counseling psychologists has narrowed in recent years. For example, clinical psychologists are now more likely to deal with work-related problems than once they did, and counseling psychologists are now more likely to work with severely disturbed patients than they used to (Watkins *et al.*, 1986). We will describe some of the work done by counseling psychologists in Chapters 9 and 17.

Industrial psychologists tend to be employed by business or government organizations. For the most part, they deal with personnel problems and management decision making. You will find a description of industrial psychology in Chapter 22.

Experimental psychologists may observe behavior either in the laboratory or in real-life settings. They also create tests and take surveys.

Generally speaking, experimental psychologists try to be as objective as possible in their descriptions of people.

Applied psychologists may also develop knowledge in a variety of ways. But chiefly they conduct interviews, give tests, and apply information gathered from experiments, questionnaires, case histories, and surveys. Clinical and counseling psychologists usually deal with one person at a time, although occasionally they work with groups. Industrial psychologists tend to focus on work groups and organizations.

These are very brief descriptions of highly complex and challenging professions. For more information about what it's like to be a psychologist, you might wish to talk to your instructor.

THE AUTHOR'S BIASES

Some psychologists are primarily teachers. Although they may do some research, their main goal is passing information along to the students who take their classes or read their textbooks. As you will see in Chapter 11, I spent many years studying the biochemistry of memory in a scientific laboratory. And in recent years, I've done research on autistic children. However, I've also consulted with various industrial organizations and, during the late 1970's, I helped run a private psychological clinic. So, like most psychologists, I'm something of a hybrid.

And also like most other psychologists, I have my own set of biases or subjective viewpoints about people and psychology. I've mentioned some of these prejudices already. But there are others you should be aware of too.

1. To begin with, I believe the study of human behavior is the most fascinating, awe-inspiring, and important occupation imaginable. I hope that some of my enthusiasm for psychology rubs off on you by the time you finish the book, for it is the greatest gift I can give you.
2. I believe that learning should be both challenging *and* fun. My way of making the study of psychology enjoyable in this book is to focus on the experiences of people such as Mary Smith. For example, I begin and end each chapter with a story or a case history built around the lives of real or imagined human beings. However, you may find that you can *understand* the people in the stories better after you have read the scientific material in the chapter itself.
3. At various points, I have included "thought questions" that often are not answered directly in the text. The purpose of these questions is to push your mind beyond the facts on the printed page. However, if you

find these questions a bore, or if the answers don't come easily, pass the questions by or ask your instructor to help you.
4. I place a great deal more faith in facts than I do in theories and opinions. If you try to understand people before you have enough facts, you run the danger of seeing what you want to see—instead of seeing *objectively* what the people are like. (See Chapter 5.)
5. I am an incurable optimist. I believe that, through the wise and humane application of the *holistic approach*, we can all come closer to achieving our personal goals in life. This moral viewpoint, like most others, rests on faith as well as on science; but it is a faith that is shared by most psychologists or they wouldn't *be* psychologists.
6. Finally, you have theories about human behavior, just as I do. But unless you have studied psychology before, chances are your present theories are based more on your subjective impressions than on objective data. Thus, you may find that many of your feelings or theories about yourself and others are challenged by the facts presented in this textbook. I do not ask that you give up your present views, merely that you try to examine them afresh in the light of what new information this book gives you.

Your author,
James V. McConnell

All of which brings us back again to Mary Smith. For, as it turned out, the results of our little experiment caused both Charlie and Mrs. Smith to re-examine the way in which they perceived the girl.

Psychology's Limits

As you know, we used the "within-subjects" design in testing Mary. And after we were done, Charlie, Mrs. Smith, Mary, and I sat around the kitchen talking.

"What cues am I giving her?" Mrs. Smith asked.

I told her how she tensed her grip on Mary's arm when the girl's finger got close to the correct key.

Mrs. Smith nodded in understanding. "I didn't *feel* myself doing that. But I guess you're right." She thought for a moment, then asked, "How bright do you think Mary is?"

"Bright enough to pick up very subtle cues from you," I replied. "Bright enough to learn how to use a computer keyboard."

"Yes, but is she bright enough to *communicate* with me?"

"She does that all the time. She tells you that she loves you when she seeks you out, and when she cuddles in your arms. By her actions, she tells you when she's happy, when she's angry, when she's excited, and when she's bored. You read her social cues as precisely as she reads yours."

"All mothers do that," the woman said. "That's part of what being a parent is all about—learning to respond to your child's needs, even when the child can't tell you in words. But that's the problem, you see. Do you think Mary is bright enough so that she can learn to talk in words?"

I gave the matter serious consideration. What Mrs. Smith was really asking me was this—what are my child's limits? And whatever these limits are, has my child reached them yet, or can she go farther? But psychology has its limits too, and I wasn't sure I knew enough to help Mrs. Smith find the sort of answer she really wanted to find.

"Look," I said. "I haven't worked with children like Mary before, so I don't know what's possible—or impossible. But I do know that she has two things going for her that might help."

"What two things?" Mrs. Smith asked.

"First, your loving desire to help her. That's a big plus. Second, she's bright enough to pick up on very subtle cues. You taught her how to use a complicated computer keyboard. Perhaps you can use her sensitivity to your cues to teach her to express herself either in speech, or through the computer. Give it a try. But don't expect miracles."

Mrs. Smith frowned, but after a few seconds, she nodded rather reluctantly. She asked what I had in mind, so we talked about the specifics of what she might do. And then, finally, Charlie and I left and drove back to Ann Arbor. The next day, I called Marcello Truzzi and told him he had been right to remind me of the "Clever Hans" story. And I thought the matter would end there.

But a few months later, Mrs. Smith called on the phone. She wanted me to write a letter encouraging her to continue her work with Mary. The girl's teachers remained skeptical that Mary would ever show any progress. Mrs. Smith hoped that a letter from a psychologist might get them to change their minds. I told her I'd be happy to oblige. Then I asked how Mary was doing.

"She's coming along. Slowly, of course, but I do see some change. And working on this brings us closer together. So it's a benefit, no matter how things turn out."

"How far do you think you can go with Mary?"

"I don't know. I'm still convinced she'll learn to express herself some day. But that's my faith talking. The fact is that she still doesn't talk."

"Does that fact bother you still?"

"No, not really. How can you understand people, or hope to help them, if you don't know the objective facts about them?" Mrs. Smith laughed gently. "I remember you told me not to expect miracles. But I'll tell you something. Now that I understand her better, I know I'll love her just as much whether she talks or not. Maybe that's the real miracle."

"Maybe it is," I said.

STUDY QUESTIONS

As you read through the chapter, see if you can find the answers to the following questions:

1. From a psychological point of view, what is the single most important part of your body?
2. What is the *cortex,* and what does it do?
3. Psychologically speaking, what is the primary purpose of your brain?
4. What are the three main parts of the neuron, and what is the major purpose of each?
5. What happens when a neuron "fires"?
6. What is the synapse, and how does it function?
7. What is the difference between pre- and post-synaptic inhibition?
8. What are the major structural and psychological differences between the two cerebral hemispheres?
9. What are the four lobes of the cerebrum, and what functions does each appear to mediate?
10. What do we know about left-handedness?
11. What is the corpus callosum, and what happens when it is cut?
12. What happens in the brain when an epileptic seizure occurs?
13. In split-brain patients, what evidence suggests that the right hemisphere is more aware of what the left is doing than vice versa?
14. What evidence suggests that your "stream of conscious experience" results from the combined activities of several different cognitive and emotional systems?

Structure and Function of the Brain

"On the Other Hand"

· C·H·A·P·T·E·R ·

2

"**Y**oung man, you are an epileptic?"

Patrick looked the woman over carefully. Her closely-cropped white hair was peppered with black, rather like ashes sprinkled on fresh snow. She was wearing a colonel's uniform with a lot of gold braid on it. The other soldiers seemed to be afraid of this woman, so Pat guessed she was a pretty important person. But Pat's friend, Dr. Tavela, had told him not to fear people just because they wore fancy uniforms. So Pat looked straight at the woman and said, "I used to be."

Colonel Garcia picked up a yellow pencil and began tapping it slowly on her desk. She looked squarely at the youth sitting in front of her for a moment, then said, "Before Dr. Tavela operated on you, then, you were subject to epileptic attacks?"

"Yes."

"These attacks occurred frequently?"

Pat shivered a bit, then ran his fingers nervously over the plaster cast on his left hand. It had been six weeks now since he had last felt the "aura," that strange feeling which hit him each time just before he had an epileptic seizure. He had gone six weeks now without the headaches—without once losing consciousness, falling to the floor, and embarrassing himself by "having a fit." Despite the bandages on his head and all the terrible things that had happened since his operation, Pat felt so different now that he tried not to think of what the seizures had been like. But since she asked, Pat answered truthfully. "The attacks came several times a day, sometimes."

Colonel Garcia turned to the officer sitting beside Patrick in front of her desk. "Captain Hartman, this has been confirmed?"

The blond-haired man nodded quickly. "Yes, Colonel. When Patrick was three, a severe fever caused considerable damage to his cortex. We have tested him on the EEG machine. Abnormal, spike-shaped brain waves show up in the motor areas of his right hemisphere. Epileptic seizures are almost always associated with 'spikes' in the motor cortex."

"Yes, of course," the woman responded, gazing back at Patrick. "And after the operation, you have been free of these attacks?"

Pat tried to smile politely. "Yes, ma'am."

"Then how did you hurt your left hand?"

Pat rubbed his right hand over the plaster cast covering his entire left hand and forearm. Only the tips of his fingers were free of the plaster. "After the operation, I couldn't walk very well at first. I fell and broke my hand."

Colonel Garcia looked back at Captain Hartman. "This too is confirmed?"

"Yes, Colonel. The X-rays show a compound fracture of the metacarpal bone. The wound is about three weeks old. Patrick will not be able to use his left hand freely for another month or so—except to scratch his nose."

Patrick gently rubbed a finger along the side of his nose.

"Was Dr. Tavela angry with you for breaking your hand?" the woman asked.

Patrick frowned. "He was angry because he said I might have hurt my head. But then, just before he left, he smiled and said it was a good sign."

"A sign of your recovery?"

Pat thought about it a moment. "He didn't say."

"I wish he had," Colonel Garcia said, then breathed a deep sigh. "Patrick, although Dr. Tavela lived in a foreign country, he was our friend."

Pat interrupted. "You mean he was your spy. Anyhow, that's what the secret police said when they questioned me."

Colonel Garcia glanced uneasily at Captain Hartman, then back at the boy.

"You know Dr. Tavela was a good man, and he would want you to cooperate with us. I know you have told your story many times, Patrick. But I would like to hear it again. Tell me everything that happened, if you don't mind."

The young man shrugged his shoulders. "I don't mind."

"First, why were you sent to see a surgeon in a foreign country? Are there no good physicians here?"

"Because they said that Dr. Tavela was the only doctor in the world who did the sort of operation I needed."

"Dr. Tavela was a brilliant neurosurgeon," Colonel Garcia said quietly. "We will miss him. But tell me what happened to you at his clinic."

"He gave me a lot of tests for a week or so, and then my seizures got real bad. He said it was the stress that made them worse. Then they shaved my head and put me to sleep and he cut out the part of my brain that was making me sick."

"How soon afterward could you get up out of bed?"

"After a few days. Just to go to the bathroom. I guess it was a week or so before I could really walk much."

Colonel Garcia nodded sympathetically. "You said Dr. Tavela gave you some tests before the operation. Did he test you afterward?"

"Yeah. He had this sort of mask that I looked into. It blocked off part of what I could see. Then he showed me things and asked what they were."

The woman smiled with growing excitement. "What sort of things did he show you?"

"Oh, pictures of cows and horses. Circles and squares. Sometimes he showed me printed words and asked me to read them. Sometimes he made me wear earphones and then he asked me to do things or say things."

"What kinds of things?"

"Oh, point at a circle, or say words like 'cat' and 'dog.'"

Colonel Garcia leaned forward eagerly. "And perhaps he talked about a chemical formula, or even showed you a drawing of a particular molecule?"

Pat laughed. "That's what the secret police asked, too. Did I know anything about chemistry? And did Dr. Tavela read me the name of a formula, or show me a picture, or anything like that?"

"And you said . . ."

"I said I that he never read anything to me except the Bible. Mostly *Proverbs*."

"Why *Proverbs*?"

Patrick had never thought to question the actions of the adults around him. "I don't know. He seemed to like them. He said they contained all the wisdom of Solomon."

A startled look appeared on Captain Hartman's face. "Colonel . . ."

The woman interrupted. "Yes, Captain, I know. Tavela's first name was Solomon. You will please get a copy of the Bible from the library."

Captain Hartman rose and left the room.

Putting the pencil carefully down on her desk, Colonel Garcia continued. "Patrick, just before Dr. Tavela was killed by the secret police, a man brought him a very important secret—the outline of the molecular structure of a new chemical compound."

"That would be the funny little man in the dark overcoat, I suppose," Patrick said, trying to be helpful.

"Perhaps so, Patrick. Tell me about him."

Pat picked at one of the bandages on his head with his right hand. "It was that last day, you know, the day the secret police came and . . . and . . ."

"I know. Go on, please."

"Well, I had the earphones on and was looking into the mask. Dr. Tavela was showing me some pictures and asking me questions over the earphones. Sometimes it hurt a little."

"Hurt?"

"Yeah. My ears. Sometimes he would whisper in one ear while he was making a very loud noise in the other. The noise hurt sometimes."

"What did he whisper to you, Patrick?"

Pat sighed. "I couldn't hear most of the time because of the noise. I guess he asked me to point to something, sometimes with my left hand, sometimes with my right."

"But your left hand is in a cast."

"I can point with my fingers," Pat said, poking his left index finger at the pencil on the woman's desk to demonstrate his abilities. "That wasn't the problem."

"What was the problem, Patrick?"

"You're going to think this is pretty funny. I could do what he told me to do over the earphones. I pointed my left fingers at the thing he wanted me to touch. But I never was sure what it was he had asked me to do, even when I did it just like he said to do it." The young man stopped, a puzzled look on his face. "I mean, how can you do something when you don't know what it is you're supposed to be doing?"

Colonel Garcia frowned. Then she said, "Tell me about the man in the overcoat, please."

"Well, Dr. Tavela was testing me when this man came into the lab. He looked nervous and excited, I guess. He pulled on Dr. Tavela's arm, and they went out of the room for a while. Then when Dr. Tavela came back, he was awful excited too. He said that something good had happened, something he had been waiting for a long time." Patrick's left hand reached out and touched the pencil again, almost unconsciously.

"And then . . ."

"And then he said we had work to do. So he whispered at me for a long time, maybe half an hour or so, and had me trace things with my left hand again and again."

Colonel Garcia leaned forward. "What sort of things, Patrick? Numbers and letters?"

"That's what the secret police asked, but I don't know. I really don't!" Patrick's voice cracked with emotion. "I couldn't see the things; I just pointed at them with my left hand. The usual cat and dog pictures, I guess. That's what we usually worked on."

"You told the secret police about this?"

"Of course, but they didn't believe me at first. So they hooked me up to a polly . . . a polly . . ."

"A polygraph, Patrick. That's what you would call a 'lie detector.'"

"Yeah, well, they stuck this wet, metal thing on the palm of my right hand. It was connected with wires to a machine that made squiggles on a sheet of paper. And they asked me questions and looked at the squiggles." Patrick sighed deeply. "They did it for hours and hours and hours. One man kept insisting that I was lying and said they ought to give me a whipping for lying so much."

"Did they punish you?"

Patrick shook his head. "No, the other man kept saying that the squiggles showed I was telling the truth. And I was!"

Colonel Garcia nodded sympathetically. "I believe you, Patrick. You see, the secret police thought that Dr. Tavela had given you the formula or the drawing of the shape of the molecule. We put a lot of pressure on them, but they wouldn't release you until they made sure that you didn't know what it was." The woman picked up the pencil again and tapped it nervously. "He must have known they would arrest him shortly, and I'll bet a million dollars he told you something. He must have hidden some clue deep within your brain, where the secret police couldn't find it, but we could."

"He didn't tell me anything, ma'am." Patrick started to cry a little. "Except, when the police came to the door to get him, he told me to be brave, and tell the truth. He said he was glad I had broken my hand, and that whenever I was troubled, I should read the Bible and seek out a pattern of understanding."

Captain Hartman entered the Colonel's office bearing a tattered book. "You'd be surprised how difficult it was to find a copy of the Bible around this place," he said, handing the book to the woman.

Colonel Garcia gave the man a bemused look, then turned to Patrick. "What part of *Proverbs* did Dr. Tavela read to you the most?"

"The third chapter, I think it was."

The woman leafed through the book, found a place, then began to read. "'Happy is the man that findeth wisdom, and the man that getteth understanding.'" The woman looked at the boy. "Is that the part?"

"Further on, I think."

"'Understanding is more precious than rubies: and all the things thou canst desire are not to be compared unto her. Length of days is in her right hand; and in her left hand riches and honor.'"

Patrick became excited. "Yes, that's it. He read that verse to me several times."

Colonel Garcia put the Bible face down on the desk, and picked up the pencil in her right hand. She tapped it gently on the desk, again and again.

After a moment she stared at Patrick's left hand, encased as it was in the plaster cast. She gazed intently at the bandages on his shaven head. Next she looked at the innocent smile on the young man's face.

Then she laughed warmly, jubilantly. "Of course!" she said loudly.

Captain Hartman was startled. "Have you found the secret, Colonel?"

"Of course I have, Captain. Where the secret police failed, I have succeeded. Thanks to Dr. Tavela's clue from the Bible, and my knowledge of Patrick's problems, I know the truth." She got up and walked around the desk, pulling up a chair to sit by Patrick. She hugged him in her arms momentarily, then gently touched his head.

(Continued on page 45.)

"What an appropriate place to hide a secret," she said.

YOUR BRAIN

Your brain is the master organ of your body. During open heart surgery, a machine can take over many of the functions of your heart and kidneys. But even though a machine is cleaning and pumping your blood, you remain YOU. Which is to say that your thoughts, dreams, hopes, and general behavior patterns aren't much affected by mechanical substitutes for most of your bodily functions.

However, even a small amount of damage to certain *critical parts of your brain* may—under certain circumstances—cause you to lose consciousness for the rest of your life. More extensive damage might even lead to rather dramatic changes in your personality. Why? Because your brain is the seat of your self-awareness, the locus of your intelligence, your compassion, and your creativity. All of your mental activities—your thoughts, emotions, and feelings—and all of your bodily processes are affected by the functioning of your brain.

On the other hand, sometimes people can sustain massive damage to major portions of their brains and, if given proper therapy, still recover all the mental and physical abilities they had before the damage occurred (see Chapter 22). Thus, while your brain is very much the master organ of your body, YOU are a great deal more than the mere sum of all the

A nuclear magnetic resonance photograph of the brain inside the skull.

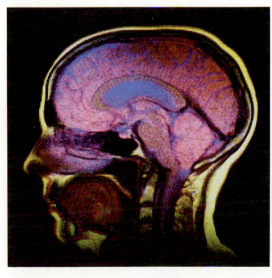

complex physical activities that occur inside your skull.

Still and all, from a psychological point of view, your brain is the *single most important part of your body*. Therefore, if you are to understand why you think and feel and act as you do, you *must* first have some notion of how this master organ operates. With this thought in mind, we will begin our survey of the field of psychology by looking closely at your brain and nervous system.

Inputs, Internal Processes, Outputs

First, let us see what your brain actually looks like. If you enjoy analogies, consider this one for a moment. In a *very limited sense*, your brain is like a wrinkled mushroom packed tightly inside a bony shell we call the skull (see Fig. 2.1). Not counting the skull, your brain weighs about 3 pounds. In their 1980 book, *Behavioral Neuroscience*, Carl Cotman and James McGaugh state the human nervous system contains almost a trillion nerve cells (1,000,000,000,000) (Cotman & McGaugh, 1980). Most of these **neurons**, or nerve cells, are in the brain. The biological activities of these neurons help determine what you think and feel and learn and do.

Psychologists often consider business organizations to be "complex social systems," much as your body is a "complex living system." To make this point clearer, let's compare your body to a corporation. This analogy is pertinent, since the word *corporation* actually comes from the Latin word meaning "body."

All living systems have three main types of functions—*inputs, internal activities*, and *outputs*. A large manufacturing company such as Ford takes in orders from customers and purchases raw materials. These are its *inputs*. The cars that Ford produces are its *outputs*. But producing cars also involves such tasks as "information processing" and "decision making," which are *internal processes*. The management at Ford serves as the "brain" of that corporation and thus "processes the information" and "makes the decisions" that keep the company functioning smoothly.

You too take in information from the world around you and make decisions based on these informational inputs. For example, you must decide what food to eat, what material to study for your next exam, and how you should act in most situations. Food and information are inputs to your body. Decision making and digestion are *internal activities* in your own "corporation." And what you say and do are your outputs. Your brain is your own "top management" that helps run your body in an efficient manner.

● *Corporate Organization*

Ford could not survive unless its management team was organized into various levels of deci-

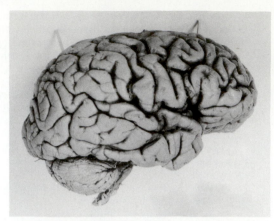

FIG. 2.1 The human brain, viewed from the right. The *cerebellum* (a Latin word meaning "little brain") at the bottom of the photograph is not a part of the cerebrum but is one of the "lower centers." The cerebellum is involved in coordinating such complex movements as walking, playing the piano, driving a car, and so on.

sion making. At the top are the executive officers, who send orders *down* the organizational ladder to "middle-level management." The men and women in middle-level management supervise the various internal functions that keep the organization alive and carry out the orders they receive from top management. Middle-level managers also send messages *up* to the executive officers letting them know how things in the offices and factories are going.

At the bottom of the organizational chart are the front-line supervisors and workers. Some of these lower-level employees receive messages from the outside world, process them, and send them up the chain of command. Other employees produce most of the actual "outputs" of the car company. But what these people do, for the most part, is to follow instructions they receive from higher management.

● *Organization of Your Brain*

Your brain is organized in "levels" much as is Ford. For instance, a large collection of neurons (nerve cells) gathered together at the very top of your brain serves as your own "top management." These neurons make up what is called the **cortex** of your brain.

Cortex is a Latin word meaning the "bark" of a tree or the "skin" of a mushroom. The thin outer skin of a mushroom is often darker and tougher than the tissue inside, and the cortex or thin outer layer of your brain is likewise different from the neurons inside. Your cortex contains millions of very special neurons that seem to be intimately related to your "stream of consciousness," or your moment-to-moment thoughts. It is mostly in your cortex that conscious decisions are made about what your

2 / Structure and Function of the Brain

Neuron (rhymes with "YOUR on"). A single nerve cell.

Cortex (CORE-tex). The thin outer layer of the brain, about 0.6 centimeters (¼ inch) thick. The millions of nerve cells (neurons) in your cortex influence most of what you think, feel, and do.

Sensory pathways. Bundles of nerves rather like telephone cables that feed information about the outside world (inputs) into your brain for processing.

Motor pathways. In biological terms, the word *motor* means "muscular," or "having to do with movement." The motor pathways are bundles of nerves rather like telephone cables that run from your brain out to your muscles (also called "output pathways").

Neural sub-centers. The word *neural* means "having to do with neurons or nerve cells." Certain groups or "centers" of neurons in your brain have highly specific functions, unlike those of any other part of your brain. For instance, one neural sub-center called the thalamus (THALL-ah-muss) acts as a sort of switchboard through which most input messages pass before reaching your cortex. The thalamus is called a sub-center because it is "lower" than your cortex, which is the "highest" part of your brain.

Exercise. In several of these chapters, we will suggest experiments that you can try on yourself—if you like doing such things. You can probably understand the material covered just as well, however, even if you prefer not to take the time to do what's suggested in the exercise.

Cerebrum (sair-REE-brum). The big, thick "cap" on the top of your brain. Humans have bigger cerebrums than any other animal. The word *cerebral* (meaning "mental") comes from "cerebrum." Most of your important mental functions take place in your cerebrum.

own "corporation" or body is going to do. But your cortex must have informational inputs to process if it is to function properly. And your cortex must have ways of sending messages to the muscles and glands in your body if you are to produce the proper outputs.

Sensory and Motor Pathways

Information about the outside world flows into your cortex along a number of routes called **sensory pathways**. Your eyes, ears, nose, tongue, and skin all send messages to your brain about what is happening around you—and inside you. These inputs go first to the lower parts of your brain, and then to your cortex. Your cortex pays attention to this incoming sensory information, checks its memory files, and then "decides" what you should do or think or feel in a given situation. Paying attention, checking memory files, and "deciding how to respond" are some of the ways in which your cortex *processes* (acts on) sensory inputs (see Chapter 12).

Once your cortical "top management" has processed an input and decided on a response, it sends command messages along **motor pathways** to your body's muscles and glands telling them how to react. But before these messages reach your muscles, they must first pass through the lower parts of your brain.

Sub-centers of the Brain

Lying beneath your cortex are a large number of **neural sub-centers,** which are the "middle management" of your brain. These "neural sub-centers" have many functions. They screen out trivial inputs from your body and from the outside world. But they send important inputs on up to your cortex. The lower centers in your brain also execute commands they receive from "upper management" (such as your cortex). However, they make certain types of response outputs on their own (see Chapter 12).

The sub-centers of your brain are important to your very existence, for they control such *automatic* responses as breathing and digestion. They also execute the complex muscle movements involved in walking and running. For example, when you decide to walk to class, the *decision* to do so is made in your cortex. But are you conscious of each tiny movement the muscles in your legs and feet must make to get you there? Surely not, for you would be hard-pressed to keep up with the millions of different neural commands that the lower centers in your brain must issue to your muscles each time you take a simple stroll. Your neural sub-centers handle these movements automatically, without conscious effort on your part. However, in emergency situations, your cortex may assume direct and voluntary control over almost any of your automatic responses.

For the most part, though, your cortical "top management" is free to dream and scheme as it wishes, leaving most of your *physical behavior* to be directly controlled by the lower parts of your brain.

☐ ☐ **QUESTION** ☐ ☐

If you had to consciously think about keeping your heart pumping and your lungs breathing, what would happen when you went to sleep at night?

The Cerebrum

If you would like to get a better feel for the physical structure of your brain, you might try this little **exercise**. Pause for a moment and go look at yourself in a mirror. If by some magic the skin on and skull in your head could be made invisible, you would see the front part of your brain as you stared into the mirror. Viewed this way, your brain would look much like the mountain ranges along the California coast as seen from an airplane (see Fig. 2.2). That is, your brain would appear to be a series of rounded hills with deep valleys in between.

The outer crust of this brainy landscape is, as we said, the *cortex*. It is about ¼ inch thick. This cortical "peel" covers the biggest part of your brain, which is called the **cerebrum** (from the Latin word for "brain").

Your cerebrum sits on top of the rest of your brain much as the huge cap of a mushroom sits on top of its skinny stem. If you could look at your brain from the top, all you would see would be the cortical covering, or the cap of the cerebral mushroom. The lower centers, or sub-units, are all buried deep in your cerebrum or in the stem itself.

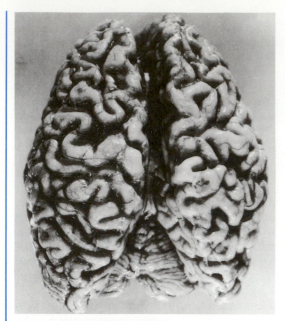

FIG. 2.2 Top view of the brain.

Evolution of the Cerebrum

In evolutionary terms, the cerebrum has been one of the last parts of the brain to develop. If you inspected the brains of lower animals, you would find that a human has a better-developed cerebrum than a monkey, that a monkey has more cerebral tissue than a dog, a dog more than a rat, a rat more than a pigeon, and a pigeon more than a goldfish. Most psychologists believe that, in general terms, the better developed an animal's cerebrum is, the more complex its behavior patterns are likely to be (Kimble, 1987).

Complex intellectual functions—such as writing song lyrics and performing scientific experiments—are controlled by your cerebrum and its cortex. Perhaps this fact explains why biology students are able to study the earthworm, but no one has ever noticed a worm taking notes on human behavior. It takes a very large corporate structure indeed to produce such complex outputs as songs or automobiles.

THE BRAIN AND BEHAVIOR

The *primary purpose* of your brain is to create neural, muscular, and glandular reactions, just as Ford's primary purpose is to produce cars and profits. The "employees" that make up your corporate brain and produce your thoughts, feelings, and behaviors are your individual nerve cells, or neurons. Given the importance of the neurons to your well-being, perhaps we should look at them in detail.

The Neuron

One major purpose of the individual nerve cells in your brain is to *pass information from one part of the body to another*. Although neurons vary considerably among themselves in size and shape, they tend to have three main parts—the **dendrites**, the **soma** (cell body), and the **axon**. As you will see, all three parts of the neuron are involved in transmitting "neural messages" through your body—and hence help produce thoughts and behaviors.

The Dendrites

The front end, or *input* side, of a cortical neuron is a network of tiny fibers called *dendrites*. The dendrites project out from the cell body like the branches of a tree to make contact with surrounding nerve cells. The major activity of the dendrites is to *receive information* from other nerve cells. We will see how the dendrites accomplish this miracle in a moment. Dendrites also generate electrical activity that causes the *brain waves* we will discuss later on.

The Soma

The main part, or body, of the cell is called the *soma*. The soma seems to have two major functions. First, like the dendrites, it can receive inputs from other neurons. But second and just as important, the soma is the neuron's "housekeeper." Most of the complex chemical reactions involved in cellular **metabolism**—

FIG. 2.3 A motor output neuron in the brain. The treelike structures at the top are the dendrites, the pyramid-shaped structure in the middle is the soma, and the thin "wires" at the bottom are part of the axon.

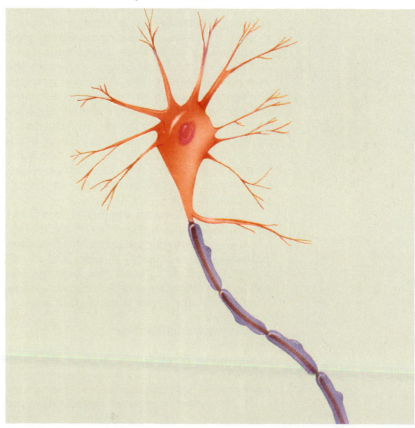

Dendrite (DEN-dright). Tiny fibers at the front or "input" end of a neuron that are chemically excited by neurotransmitters released into the synapse.

Soma (SO-mah). The cell body of a neuron. Contains the cell nucleus (NEW-klee-us). The center or main part of a neuron that "processes" some types of inputs to the cell.

Axon (AX-on). The "tail" or "output" end of a neuron. Axonic end-fibers release neural transmitters into the synaptic cleft which stimulate the next neuron in line.

Metabolism (mett-TAB-boh-lism). From a Greek word meaning "change." The sum total of biological processes inside the cell that (a) build up energy to be released, and (b) repair the cell and keep it functioning in a normal fashion.

Resting potential. The amount of electrical energy stored up by a nerve cell that can be discharged in a short burst. The amount of money you have to spend at any one time is, in a sense, your "financial potential."

Action potentials. Waves of electro-chemical energy that sweep down the axon of a neuron when the nerve cell releases its resting potential and hence "fires."

which keep the cell functioning in a healthy fashion—take place inside the soma.

The Axon

The action end, or *output* system, of the neuron is called the *axon*. The axon stretches back from the soma like a branching telephone cable.

At the end of each axonic branch or cable are tiny fibers which make contact with the dendrites and cell bodies of nearby neurons, or with the muscles and glands in the rest of the body. The axon is the *output area* of the neuron because the axonic fibers actually pass messages along to other nerve cells, and to the muscles and glands.

Many axons are covered with an insulating sheath that serves to speed up neural transmission (see Chapter 13) and prevent "message mixing." This sheath is actually a special type of "support cell," separate from the neuron. The support cell wraps itself around the axon early in life, when the brain is first developing.

As we will see in a moment, the axonic fibers come close to, but *do not touch,* the dendrites and cell bodies of the neurons and muscles they make contact with.

Types of Neurons

There are many different types of neurons in your nervous system. Some nerve cells have complex axons, but no dendrites at all. Just the opposite is shown in Fig. 2.3—a nerve cell with a highly complex dendritic structure but a relatively simple axon. Generally speaking, however, when we speak of "the" neuron, we have something in mind like the nerve cells shown in Fig. 2.4, which have dendrites, a soma, and a single axon with many branches.

Action Potentials

One of the major functions of the neuron is to send information from one part of your body to another. Each nerve cell contains a certain amount of stored-up electrical energy—the **resting potential**—that it can discharge in short bursts. The battery in your car releases a similar burst of stored-up electrical energy when you turn the ignition key. These bursts of energy are called **action potentials**.

The action potential is one the major parts of the complex electro-chemical process by which your neurons pass messages from one part of your body to another. For example, consider three nerve cells in your brain that are connected together in sequence, in *A-B-C* fashion. As Fig. 2.4 shows, one axonic branch of *A* makes contact with the dendrites and soma of *B*, and one axonic branch of *B* makes contact with the dendrites and soma of *C*.

A, B, and *C* all have a certain (and very similar) resting potential to call upon when necessary. When a message is to be passed from *A* to *C*, a chemical change occurs in the axon of *A*

FIG. 2.4 Three neurons in a row. The axonic fibers of A make synapse with the dendrites and cell body of B, and the axonic fibers of B make synapse with the dendrites and cell body of C.

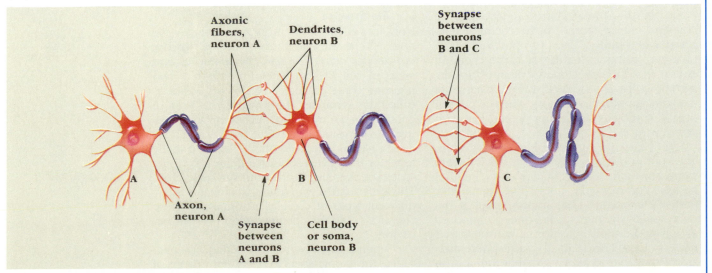

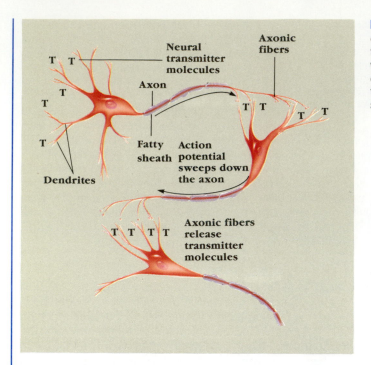

FIG. 2.5 Transmitter molecules (T's) excite the dendrites of a neuron, causing the neuron to fire. During "firing," a wave of electrochemical activity sweeps down the axon, causing the axonic fibers to release more T's (transmitters), which stimulate the next neuron in line.

that affects both the dendrites and the cell body of *B*. Neuron *B* responds by releasing its stored-up electrical energy. That is, when *A* stimulates *B*, an action potential sweeps down the length of *B*'s axonic branches in much the same fashion as fire sweeps down a fuse. When the action potential reaches the tips of *B*'s axonic fibers, it causes a chemical change to occur that sets off a similar burst of electrical energy in neuron *C* (see Fig. 2.5).

Thus, the message passes from *A* to *B* to *C* as each cell produces an action potential which stimulates the next neuron in line.

● *Neural Firing*

Whenever an action potential passes along a neuron's axon, we say that the nerve cell has *fired*, because the action involved is much like the firing of a gun. For example, consider how a gun actually "fires." There is a great deal of *potential* energy stored in the chemical gunpowder in a bullet. When you pull the trigger on a gun, you translate this *potential* chemical energy into the *active* energy of an explosion, and the bullet is propelled down the barrel of the gun. In similar fashion, when a neuron fires, it translates its resting potential into an action potential.

Let's carry the bullet analogy a step further. The neuron behaves in some ways as if it were a machine gun loaded with electro-chemical bullets. For example, a machine gun either fires, or it doesn't. The bullets travel at the same speed whether you fire one or a hundred in a row. In similar fashion, a neuron either fires, or doesn't fire. And all its action potentials are of the *same strength*, whether the neuron

produces one action potential a second, or a hundred.

Also, if you press and release the trigger on a machine gun very quickly, you can fire the shells slowly, one by one. But if you hold the trigger down, you can fire off whole bursts of bullets in a second or two. In like manner, if you tap lightly on your arm, the receptor (input) nerve cells in your skin will fire at a very slow rate—a few times a second. If you press very hard on your arm, however, these same input neurons can fire hundreds or even thousands of times per second.

Every time you move a muscle—or think a thought, or experience an emotion—you do so in part because groups of nerve cells in your brain *fire off* messages to your muscles, glands, or to other groups of neurons.

● *The Synapse*

Now, let's go back to neurons *A*, *B*, and *C*. As we noted, the axonic end-fibers of *A* come close to, *but do not actually touch*, the dendrites and soma of cell *B*. The general area where two neurons come in contact with each other is called the **synapse**. This synapse (or "area of contact") is so tiny you would have trouble seeing it even using a powerful microscope.

As we said, neurons *A* and *B* don't actually touch at their synapse. Instead, there is a tiny space between them called the **synaptic cleft**. This cleft is filled with fluid that contains many different types of chemical substances. These chemicals all have a definite effect on your behavior.

When a neuron fires, the action potential causes the axonic fibers to release tiny drops of chemicals into the synaptic cleft. These chemicals move across the cleft and stimulate the dendrites and soma of the next cell. These stimulating chemicals are called "neural transmitters" or "neurotransmitters." The function of the neurotransmitters is to transmit information from one cell to another. The more neurotransmitters that A's axonic end-fibers release into the synaptic cleft between A and B, the more often cell B will be triggered into firing.

- ### Receptor Sites
The dendrites and cell bodies of neurons have tiny "receptor sites" that are particularly sensitive to neural transmitters. These "receptor sites" are really *complex molecules* which are embedded in the membrane covering the dendrite or cell body (see Fig. 2.6). As we will see shortly, these molecules form "pockets" into which neurotransmitters fit. If a neurotransmitter from A lands on one of the receptor "pockets" on B, the neurotransmitter triggers off a chemical reaction that causes B to fire. An action potential then pulses down B's axon, causing B's axonic end fibers to release neurotransmitters at the synapse between B and C.

If a neurotransmitter molecule from neuron A *doesn't* land on a receptor site—or if the "pockets" are already filled by other molecules—the transmitter will rapidly break down chemically and lose its effectiveness. And even if the

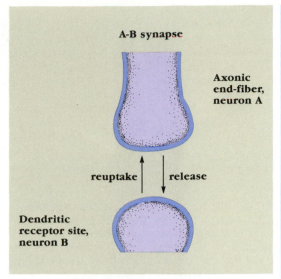

FIG. 2.7 Chemical transmitters released by axonic end-fibers of neuron A find a receptor site on the dendrites (or cell body) of neuron B, causing B to fire. The transmitters then break up, and the pieces are taken up by A and put together again.

transmitter molecule *does* find a receptor site on B, it still will break down quickly—so another transmitter molecule can take its place and cause B to fire once more. The broken pieces of the transmitter will, *in either case*, mostly be taken up by A's axon, put together, and used again (see Fig. 2.7).

Of course, you are not directly aware of all the chemical activity that goes on inside your brain. Yet it is exactly true that you cannot lift a finger, see a sunset, solve a problem, or even remember your own name unless these transmitter substances in your brain function properly.

- ### "Lock and Key Hypothesis"
Our view of what actually happens at the synapse when one neuron causes another to "fire" has changed dramatically in recent years. For example, in 1965, brain researchers knew of only two or three neurotransmitters. Now we realize there are hundreds of different molecules that can act as neurotransmitters. And even 10 years ago, most scientists believed that a given neuron could secrete just one neurotransmitter. However, recent research suggests strongly that *almost all nerve cells produce two or more neurotransmitters* (Kimble, 1987).

Just as there are many different neurotransmitters, there also are many different kinds of receptor sites. We presently believe only one general class of transmitter molecule will "fit into" a given receptor site. When a molecule of the right size and shape from A lands on the proper receptor site on neuron B, the transmitter "unlocks" B and causes B to fire. A molecule of the wrong shape can't "unlock"

FIG. 2.6 When neuron A fires, its axonic fibers release transmitter (T) molecules into the synapse with neuron B. These molecules bind to receptor sites on the dendrites and cell body of B, causing B to fire.

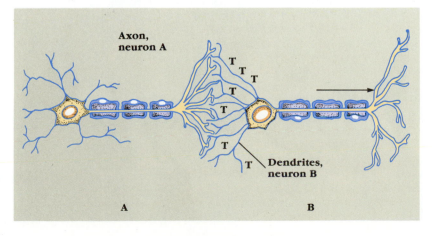

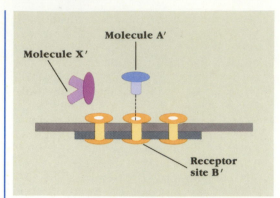

FIG. 2.8 The "lock-key" hypothesis states that a transmitter molecule (the "key") must be the right size and shape to fit into a given receptor site (the "lock") on neuron B. In this drawing, molecule A fits receptor site B and thus can "unlock" neuron B and cause it to fire. Molecule X, however, has the wrong shape and thus cannot "unlock" neuron B.

B—just as a key of the wrong shape can't unlock your front door (see Fig. 2.8).

The belief that *specific transmitters* will only fit into *specific receptor sites* is called the **lock and key hypothesis** of synaptic transmission. As we will see in Chapter 3, this hypothesis helps explain why various drugs can affect highly specific parts of the brain.

Finally, this brief discussion of the "lock and key hypothesis" should illustrate one important fact: We are gathering new information about the nervous system at an explosive rate of speed. Thus, we may well take a *substantially different view* of neural functioning in the 1990's than is presented in these pages. As you read this book, therefore, please remember that everything you learn is "subject to revision" as further data come from the laboratory.

● *Function of the Synapse*

The neurons in your cortex are so incredibly tiny that 20,000 of them could fit on the head of a pin. The synaptic cleft *between* neurons is much smaller yet. Indeed, several transmitter molecules placed one atop the other are enough to bridge the gap between most neurons.

The major purpose of the synapse seems to be this—it helps *control the flow of information through your nervous system*. With certain minor exceptions, neurons "fire" in just one direction—from the dendrite to the axon. Thus, in the illustration we have been using, *A* can cause *B* to fire, and *B* can cause *C* to react. But *C* can't fire *B*, and *B* can't fire *A*.

Information about the world around you enters your body through such sensory receptors as your eyes and ears. Your receptors respond by sending messages to your brain along input pathways in your nervous system up to your brain. But to get from your eye to your

brain, a visual input must pass along several neurons in *A-B-C* fashion, crossing many synapses in the process. When you respond to these inputs, messages from your brain flow down output pathways in *A-B-C* fashion, again crossing several synapses before they reach your muscles.

Input and output pathways are one-way streets that, generally speaking, carry neural messages in just one direction. The synapses act as "traffic cops" that prevent the messages from going the wrong way.

The *amount* of traffic passing along a neural pathway is determined by the number of transmitter molecules each neuron secretes. Anything that causes your neurons to fire faster—and hence release more neurotransmitters—will increase the number of messages the pathways carry. Likewise, anything that decreases the rate of neural firing will also decrease the number of messages flowing through the nervous system. The importance of these statements will become clear as we look closely at **excitation** and **inhibition** in the nervous system.

Excitation and Inhibition

Suppose that, later on today, you are sitting quietly in your chair, reading. Suddenly you get an urge to eat an apple lying on the table beside you. So you decide to reach out and take the apple in your hand. Both the "urge" and the "decision" are communicated from one part of your brain to another by electro-chemical means.

The motor centers in your cortex transmit the order "reach for the apple" by sending an output message to the muscles in your arm tell-

Our sense organs give us information about the world around us and allow us to learn — and teach — specialized skills.

Lock and key hypothesis (high-POTH-ee-sis). The theory that neurons secrete many types of transmitters, each of which can fit into just a limited number of receptor sites. If a transmitter "key" fits into a receptor "lock," it unlocks the neuron and causes it to fire.

Excitation. A neuron is said to be "excited" when it "fires"—that is, when it produces an action potential. The more action potentials it produces, the more "excited" the neuron is.

Inhibition. The opposite of excitation. Anything that prevents neural firing is said to inhibit the neuron.

Tarantula (tah-RAN-chew-lah). A large, hairy, black spider found in Europe and the American Southwest. In fact, while the tarantula is a great jumper and can deliver a mean bite, it is not particularly poisonous to humans.

Pre-synaptic (PREE-sin-NAP-tick). Any process or event that occurs on the "front" side (i.e., the axonic side) of the synapse.

Post-synaptic. Any process or event that occurs on the "back" side (i.e., the dendritic or somatic side) of the synapse.

ing them to get to work. The motor nerves that make synapse with your arm muscles respond by dumping transmitter chemicals into those "neuro-muscular" (nerve-muscle) synapses. These neurotransmitters cause *chemical reactions* in your muscles so they extend and contract in just the right way for your arm to be guided toward the apple.

Now, let's add some complications. Suppose that, just as your hand nears that big red fruit, you notice something that greatly disturbs you. For crouched just behind the apple is a huge, hairy black spider that you recognize as a **tarantula!** Suddenly a great many nerve cells in the emotional sub-centers of your brain will shift into emergency gear. Put more formally, these neurons will begin dumping a great many transmitter chemicals into a great many synapses all over your nervous system!

Your first impulse may be to jerk back your hand as quickly as you can. But any quick movement on your part might disturb the spider and make it jump at you. So what you really should do is to *freeze* for a moment before you slowly retract your hand. (And then perhaps you should exit from the scene as gracefully but as rapidly as possible.)

● Excitatory and Inhibitory Synapses

At the instant you spotted the spider, your hand was in the process of *reaching out* for the apple. How do you go about explaining to your hand that you've changed your mind, and that it should *freeze*? The problem is, you see, that your motor nerves have already dumped a rather large supply of neurotransmitters into their synapses. So how does your brain *recall* those molecules once they've been launched into the synaptic cleft?

Actually, your brain will do three things at once:

1. For each muscle that (when chemically stimulated) will cause your hand to reach

out, there is another muscle that will make your hand pull back. So first, your brain will order the "pull-back" muscles to get *excited* and rescue you. Your neurons will obey this first order by releasing neurotransmitters into the synapses that control the "pull-back" muscles.

2. Next, the motor centers in your cortex will *stop* sending output messages to the "stretch-out" muscles, so that no further neurotransmitters are released into those synaptic canals.

3. Finally, your brain goes one step farther. There are many neurons in your brain that can *inhibit* other nerve cells from firing. Whenever your brain needs to "shut down" neural transmission, it simply orders the inhibitory neurons to do their job.

● Pre- and Post-Synaptic Inhibition

How can the *firing* of one neuron *inhibit* the *firing* of another? We're not entirely sure, but there seem to be two rather distinct types of inhibition. One is called **pre-synaptic** inhibition, because it prevents the axon from *releasing* neurotransmitters into the synapse. The other is called **post-synaptic** inhibition, because it prevents the dendrites and cell bodies from *responding* to neurotransmitters (Kimble, 1987).

Pre-synaptic inhibition is shown in Fig. 2.9. Here, neuron *A* makes synapse with *B*, as usual. As you can see, neurotransmitters released by *A*'s axonic end-fibers cross the *A-B* synapse, find receptor sites on *B*, and cause *B* to fire. However, as Fig. 2.9 shows, if neuron *I* happens to fire, it releases molecules which prevent *A*'s axon from releasing its transmitters. If *A* doesn't release any transmitters, obvi-

FIG. 2.9 Pre-synaptic inhibition. Neuron A's released neurotransmitters find receptor sites on neuron B and cause B to fire. If, however, neuron I happens to fire, it releases molecules that prevent A's axon from releasing its transmitters, and thus B will not fire.

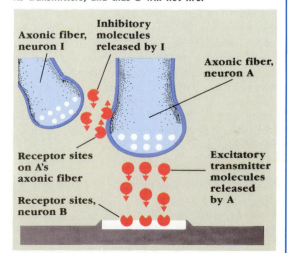

Axonic fiber, neuron I

Inhibitory molecules released by I

Axonic fiber, neuron A

Receptor sites on A's axonic fiber

Excitatory transmitter molecules released by A

Receptor sites, neuron B

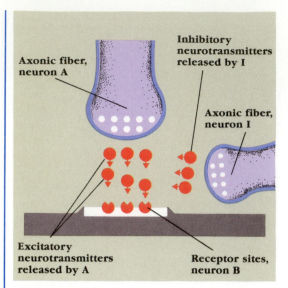

FIG. 2.10 Post-synaptic inhibition. Neurotransmitters released by neuron A's axonic fibers find receptor sites on neuron B and thus "excite" B into firing. But inhibitory neurotransmitters released by neuron I compete for receptor sites on B with those released by A. I's transmitter molecules inhibit B from firing. Whether B fires or not depends on the relative number of excitatory or inhibitory molecules that land on B's receptor sites.

The EEG

If a scientist wanted to get an idea of how your brain was performing, she or he might place one or more small pieces of metal—called **electrodes**—on the outside of your head. These electrodes would be connected by wires to an **electro-encephalo-graph**, or EEG machine (see Fig. 2.12).

This EEG machine translates electrical energy from your brain into *visual patterns on a screen*—much as a television set translates electrical energy into patterns you can see on the face of the picture tube. The dendrites in your brain produce "waves of electrical activity" that are related to (but different from) the "action potentials" already described. An electrode placed on your head can detect these "brain waves," just as a TV antenna can detect the electrical waves in the atmosphere that make up the television signal. The electrode then sends the "brain waves" over a wire to the EEG machine, just as the TV antenna sends the television signal to the TV set. And the EEG machine displays the brain waves on a tube just as the television set displays the TV signal. (Some EEG machines print the waves out on a

ously *B* won't become excited and fire. In this figure, *I-A* is an **inhibitory synapse**, while *A-B* is an **excitatory synapse**.

Post-synaptic inhibition is shown in Fig. 2.10. Here, again, *A* releases its excitatory neurotransmitters into the *A-B* synapse. But now neuron *I* releases its inhibitory molecules directly into the *A-B* synapse too, just as *A* does. The synapse has now become an *A-I-B* synapse. Whether *B* fires at any moment depends on whether *A* or *I* happens to release *the most neurotransmitters*. If more *excitatory* molecules are present in the synaptic cleft, *B* will fire. If more *inhibitory* molecules are present, *B* is inhibited from firing.

In truth, most synapses in the central nervous system are of the *A-I-B* type. That is, any given neuron *B* in your brain is likely to receive simultaneous inputs from dozens of *A*s and dozens of *I*s. Whether *B* fires at any given moment depends on the *balance* of excitatory and inhibitory neurotransmitters it receives at that time. If there are more excitatory molecules than inhibitory molecules present in the synaptic cleft, *B* will fire. If there are more inhibitory than excitatory molecules present, *B* will be inhibited and won't fire (see Fig. 2.11).

□ □ **QUESTION** □ □
How does activity in the synaptic cleft resemble an election in which two candidates, "Fire" and "Don't Fire," are running for office?

FIG. 2.11 A neuron, showing the cell body and dendrites.

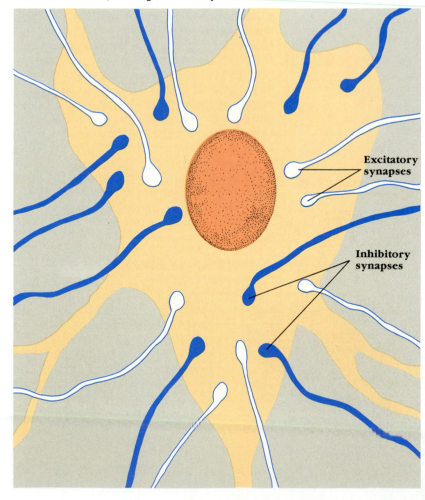

Excitatory synapses

Inhibitory synapses

Inhibitory synapse (inn-HIBB-it-tory), **excitatory synapse** (ex-SIGHT-tah-tory). Neuron *A* causes *B* to fire when *A*'s axonic fibers release transmitters into the *A-B* synapse. This is an excitatory synapse. Neuron *I* can inhibit *A* from releasing transmitters, however, if *I* releases inhibitory molecules onto *A*'s axon. The *I-A* connection is an inhibitory synapse.

Electrode (ee-LEK-trode). A device used to detect electrical activity in the brain. Disk electrodes are coin-shaped pieces of metal that can be placed against the head to read brain waves. Needle electrodes are thin wires inserted through holes in the skull directly into the brain.

Electro-encelphalo-graph (ee-LEK-tro en-SEF-uh-low-graf). An electronic machine that makes a graphic record of brain waves. *Cephalo* is the Greek word for "head."

Beta waves (BAIT-tah). Low-voltage, rapid brain waves with rather a random pattern that typically are a sign that you are concentrating on some cognitive task, or experiencing some emotion.

Alpha waves (AL-fa). When you are resting peacefully with your eyes closed, the visual regions of your brain at the back of your head will show a brain wave that repeats itself about 9–12 times per second. These are alpha waves. If you are listening to music with your eyes closed, the visual regions of your brain will show alpha waves, but the hearing regions will typically show the activity pattern. When you are reading a good book, the situation is often reversed—the visual brain will show the activity pattern and the hearing regions of your brain will show alpha waves.

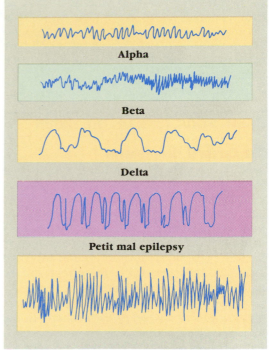

Alpha

Beta

Delta

Petit mal epilepsy

Grand mal epilepsy

|⊢ 1 sec. ⊣|

FIG. 2.13 Alpha waves in the brain made up of electrical waves that have a frequency of 9 to 12 or so cycles per second. The delta waves register on an EEG machine as large, slow waves with a frequency of about 0.1 to 4 cycles per second. The brain waves that occur during epileptic seizures are larger and more synchronous than normal.

piece of paper rather than showing them on a screen.)

The EEG doesn't "read" the activity of one or two *specific* neurons, however. Rather, the EEG gives you the same sort of fuzzy, imprecise picture of what is going on inside the skull that you would get outside a huge football stadium if you tried to guess what was happening inside by listening to the roar of the crowd. Standing outside the stadium, you could tell whether the football game was exciting, and when an important play had been made. But you couldn't always tell which team had the ball, or what the score was—much less what individual members of the crowd were doing or experiencing.

The EEG electrode "listens" outside the skull to the electrical noise made inside by the dendrites of thousands of individual neurons. But all the EEG record can tell you is how active the bulk of the nerve cells are, not the precise behavior patterns of each *single* neuron.

● **Brain Waves**

When you are actively engaged in thought—trying to work through a difficult problem, for example—your EEG record would show a rapid but rather irregular pattern of electrical activity. We call this sort of electrical output **beta waves**, or the *activity pattern* (see Fig. 2.13). The appearance of this irregular brain wave pattern on the EEG usually means your mind is engaged in some kind of "deliberate cognitive processing" or some type of *emotional reaction* (Ray & Cole, 1985).

The visual areas of your cortex are located primarily on the rear surface of your brain, in the occipital lobe. When you relax and close your eyes, these visual parts of your brain will show regular but rather fast waves called **alpha waves**.

FIG. 2.12 A subject hooked up to an EEG machine; a technician reads the tracings as they print out.

When you go to sleep, your brain wave activity generally slows down. The large, slow sleep waves that occur when you are deeply asleep are called "delta waves." (We will have more to say about sleep and delta waves in the next chapter.)

BASIC STRUCTURE OF THE BRAIN

The Cerebral Hemispheres

Now that you've learned a few simple facts about how your neurons work, let's go back to your brain's basic structure. As we noted earlier, your cerebrum has "mountains" and "valleys" in it. The biggest "valley of the brain" is a deep groove that runs down the center from front to back, dividing your brain in two parts called the **left cerebral hemisphere** and the **right cerebral hemisphere**.

For the most part, the two hemispheres are physical *mirror images* of each other—just as the left half of your face is (more or less) a mirror image of your right half, and your left hand is a mirror image of your right hand.

The Lobes of the Brain

There are four main sections, or **lobes**, in *each* cerebral hemisphere:

- The **frontal lobe**, which lies just under the skull in the region of the forehead.

- The **temporal lobe**, which lies under the skull just above each ear, in the general region of your temple.
- The **parietal lobe**, which lies under the top center of your skull.
- The **occipital lobe**, which lies at the back of your head, just above your neck.

As you will see, each of the four lobes of the cerebrum controls or *mediates* a different set of psychological and physiological functions.

Mapping the Cortex Electrically

If someone stuck a pin in your arm, you would experience pain. Surprisingly enough, though, if someone stuck a pin directly into your exposed cortex, you probably wouldn't consciously experience any discomfort at all.

With certain minor exceptions, there simply are no "pain receptors" in the brain. (There are pain receptors in the membrane covering the brain, however.) Because brain tissue is insensitive to pain, patients undergoing brain surgery are often conscious, so they can help the doctor locate whatever damaged section might need to be treated. During such surgery, the doctor may stimulate various parts of the patient's cortex electrically and ask what the patient feels the moment the current is turned on.

What would you experience if you were willing to let a scientist "map" your *entire cor-*

FIG. 2.14 A diagram of the brain.

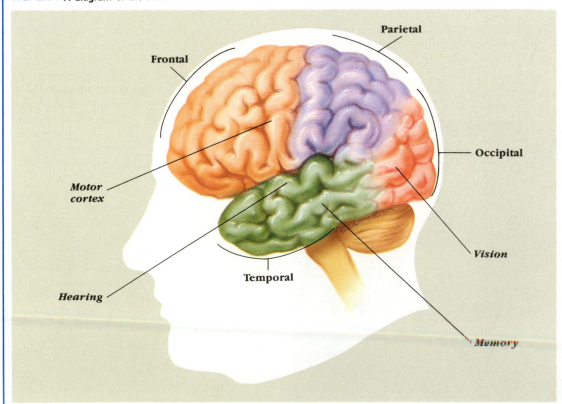

2 / Structure and Function of the Brain

Left cerebral hemisphere, right cerebral hemisphere (ser-REE-bral HEM-ee-sphere). The two halves of the globe-shaped, or spherical, cerebrum.

Lobes. Rounded bumps that typically project out from the organs of the body. Each half of your cerebrum has four main lobes, or projections.

Frontal lobe. The part of your cerebrum which lies just above your eyes at the front of the brain. Experiments suggest this part of your brain may be involved in decision making, among many other things. The *motor cortex* is part of the frontal lobe.

Temporal lobe (TEM-por-al). Part of your cerebrum that lies just above your ears, underneath your temples. It seems to be involved in hearing, in speech production, and in emotional behavior, among many other things.

Parietal lobe (pair-EYE-uh-tal, or puh-RYE-uh-tal). Part of your cerebrum at the very top of your brain. Sensory input from your skin receptors and muscles comes to this part of your cerebrum.

Occipital lobe (ox-SIP-it-tal). The lower, rear part of your cerebrum just above the back of your neck. The visual input area of your brain, among other things.

Association areas. Those parts of your cortex which, when stimulated electrically, do not yield any sensory experiences. Although the full functions of these "silent areas" of your cortex are not fully understood, we assume that they are involved in cortical processing—that is, in evaluating incoming sensory information and in storing memories.

tex with an electrical stimulator? Well, the most dramatic results of all would surely come if the scientist touched the probe to your *motor output area* (motor cortex), which lies at the rear of each frontal lobe (see Fig. 2.14). Stimulation of the nerve cells in the motor cortex in your left hemisphere would cause the muscles on the right side of your body to twitch or jerk—even though you didn't *consciously will* these muscles to move. Stimulation of the motor cortex in your right hemisphere would, of course,

Neurons in the motor areas of the brain make synapse with muscles and glands, allowing us to move about.

make the muscles on the left side of your body move involuntarily.

When the probe was applied to the *occipital lobe* at the back of your head, you would see brief flashes of light or "shooting stars."

If the scientist stimulated parts of your *temporal lobe*, you would hear brief bursts of sounds.

And if the probe were touched to parts of the *parietal lobe* at the top of your head, you might feel odd "prickly" sensations in your skin.

Strangely enough, however, the scientist could apply the probe to large areas of all four lobes without your experiencing *anything at all!*

● Sensory, Motor, and "Silent" Areas

The researchers who first mapped the brain electrically concluded your cerebral cortex has three general types of areas:

1. Sensory input areas, where axons in nerve pathways carrying messages from your sense organs make synapse with dendrites of cortical neurons. We will discuss these areas in detail beginning with Chapter 4.
2. Motor output areas, which contain nerve cells whose axons reach out to make contact with the muscles and glands of your body.
3. "Silent" areas, which have no function that can be determined *directly* from electrical stimulation.

The early brain researchers were surprised to find that most of the surface area of the cortex is "silent" to an electrical probe. At first, these early scientists assumed the silent areas were where memories—or *associations* between sensory inputs and motor outputs—were located. So these silent parts of the cortex were nicknamed the **association areas**. But many lines of evidence now suggest these are the *cortical processing areas*. For it is in these regions that incoming sensory information is processed and evaluated, and where "command decisions" seem to be made.

● Hemispheric Differences

Despite the fact that your two cerebral hemispheres are reversed images of each other, there are important physical and psychological differences between them. The major *physical* difference between the two halves of the brain is that the *left* hemisphere is usually slightly larger in the temporal lobe area just above the left ear (see Fig. 2.15). The major *psychological* difference is the fact that, in most people, the left hemisphere "dominates" in producing language and other coordinated muscular reactions. As you might guess, these physical and psychological differences are closely related.

Damage to the *left* temporal lobe often produces a disorder known as **aphasia**, or the inability to recognize and produce spoken language—at least, it does in *right-handed* individuals. However, damage to the *right* temporal lobe usually has but a minor effect on speech production—at least, it does in *right-handed* individuals. Damage of the same areas in the brains of people who are *left-handed*, however, produces rather a different picture. Furthermore, *aphasia* following temporal lobe damage is far more common in men than in women (Kimura, 1985).

To make these facts a bit more comprehensible, let's continue our study of the nervous system by looking at "handedness" and *hemispheric dominance*.

□□ **QUESTION** □□

If you are right-handed, you probably can't write very well with your left hand. Why is this the case? Do you think the problem lies in your hands (which are almost identical) or in your brain? And why is it that some people seem to be able to write better with their left hands? Furthermore, why is it that men are much more likely to be left-handed than women are?

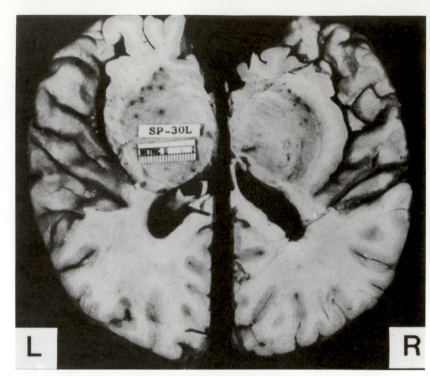

FIG. 2.15 A "slice" through the middle of the human brain at the level of the "speech center" in the temporal lobe. Notice that there is more brain tissue in the area below and to the left of the marker (Sp-30L) in the left hemisphere than in the right hemisphere.

Handedness and Hemispheric Dominance

As confusing as it may seem to you at first, your *right* cerebral hemisphere mainly controls the *left* side of your body, and your *left* cerebral hemisphere mainly controls the *right* side of your body. Thus, the left half of your brain controls your right hand (and foot), and the right half of your brain controls your left hand (and foot).

If you are strongly right-handed, your left hemisphere is your *dominant hemisphere*. A better name for the left half of your brain, however, might be "motor control hemisphere," since this is the side of your brain that coordinates most of your bodily movements.

When you write, your left hemisphere issues the orders that your right hand and fingers follow. And when you speak, it is this same "dominant" left side of your brain that makes your tongue, lips, and vocal cords move. Furthermore, your left hemisphere is better, not merely at *producing* language, but also at *understanding* it than is your right hemisphere. Indeed, your left hemisphere "processes" language *production* even if you are deaf, and use sign language (Damasio, 1986).

Your *right* hemisphere is called by many names—*minor hemisphere*, "perceptual" hemisphere, "emotional" hemisphere, or "monitoring" hemisphere. It understands language, but neither talks nor writes except under rather unusual circumstances. Your right hemisphere does seem to be better at understanding (and producing) art, music, and abstract mathematics than is your left hemisphere. For example, the noted Canadian neuropsychologist Brenda Milner found that right-handed people show a left-ear (right hemisphere) advantage for detecting and identifying musical patterns (cited in Kimura, 1985).

If you are left-handed, it may be that the right half of your cerebrum is the "talking

Aphasia (a-FAZE-ee-ah). The inability to recognize the meaning of words, or to speak or write in meaningful terms. Some experts limit aphasia to an inability to process spoken language, and use the term *agraphia* (a-GRAF-ee-ah) to refer to the inability to process written language. Either disorder is usually a symptom of some kind of brain damage.

Archeological (ark-ee-oh-LODGE-ih-cal). Archeology (ark-ee-OL-oh-gee) is the scientific study of the material remains of past human life. An archeologist typically digs up old bones, pots, etc., in an attempt to find out what human life was like in the past.

Migraine headaches (MY-grain). From the Greek word *hemicrania*, meaning "half-head." A migraine headache usually involves intense pain in just half of the brain, often accompanied by nausea and vomiting.

Autoimmune (AW-toe-im-MUNE). The immune system in your body attacks and destroys intruders such as germs. To function effectively, therefore, it must have some way of "recognizing" your own body parts so it doesn't attack them too. Autoimmune diseases are characterized by a breakdown in the immune system's recognition system, which leads your body to attack itself.

Neurologist (new-ROLL-oh-gist). A scientist who studies nerves or treats nervous disorders.

Testosterone (tess-TOSS-ter-own). A hormone (HORR-moan) or chemical produced chiefly by the male sex organs. See Chapter 7.

such drugs as aspirin and antihistimines than do right-handed people (Irwin, 1985). On the more positive side, however, Jordan Grafman and his associates have found that left-handed people are able to withstand moderate brain damage with relatively few of the motor problems observed in right-handed victims of brain damage (Grafman *et al.*, 1985).

□ □ **QUESTION** □ □

Because our society is built primarily for "right-handed" people, some parents attempt to impose right-handedness on children who are naturally left-handed. What might happen to speech development in a left-handed child who was forced to learn to write and speak with the "wrong" hemisphere of her or his brain? (Hint: A large number of stutterers are left-handed.)

hemisphere" and produces most of your spoken and written language. More usually, however, your left hemisphere will be dominant for language (though not for other motor activities) whether you're right- or left-handed. However, in some left-handers, both hemispheres share the ability to speak and write, and neither of them is really "dominant." We don't really know why the pattern of hemispheric dominance is so confused in left-handed people.

• Left-Handedness

According to most experts, about 90 percent of the world's population is right-handed. Of the remaining 10 percent, about half are "strongly" left-handed. **Archeological** evidence suggests that this strong bias toward right-handedness in humans has existed for at least the last two million years (Toth, 1985).

Left-handedness is associated with many traits—some good, some not so good. Almost twice as many males as females are left-handed. And according to British psychologists Marian Annett and Doris Kilshaw, more than twice as many artists, musicians, mathematicians, and engineers are left-handed as would be expected by chance (Annett & Kilshaw, 1982; Kilshaw & Annett, 1983). For example, two of the greatest artists who ever lived—Michelangelo and Leonardo da Vinci—were left-handed.

However, about 10 percent of left-handers suffer from language disorders and reading disabilities, while only 1 percent of right-handers do. And recent studies suggest that left-handers are three times more likely to suffer severe **migraine headaches** and certain types of **autoimmune** diseases than are right-handed people (Garmon, 1985).

In recent research, Peter Irwin reports that left-handed individuals react more strongly to

• Testosterone and Handedness

According to Harvard **neurologist** Norman Geschwind, the cause for left-handedness may lie in **testosterone**, the male hormone. Geschwind, who died in 1984, began studying the relationship between brain function and behavior in 1961. He is sometimes referred to as "the father of behavioral neurology in this country" (Garmon, 1985). Geschwind believed testosterone *slows the growth of the left hemisphere*, thus favoring greater development of the right. "Consequently, males end up right-handed less often than females," Geschwind said.

Since the *left* hemisphere is specialized for language, males in general might be expected to experience more reading and speech disorders than do females. According to Geschwind, several studies suggest this is the case.

Many highly accomplished individuals throughout history have been left-handed, including Leonardo de Vinci, who drew this portrait of himself in old age.

But the problems are most severe in left-handed males. However, because the right hemisphere is specialized for spatial perception and pattern recognition, left-handers "tend to be more talented in these areas," Geschwind believed.

In an interview he gave just prior to his death, Geschwind suggested that, during the time a child is in the womb, testosterone attacks not only the left hemisphere, but parts of the body's *immune* system as well. Thus, as males grow up, they are much more likely to suffer from such diseases as asthma. However, Geschwind said, being left-handed is neither a curse nor a blessing. He presumed that left-handers who were "at risk" for some diseases probably had a reduced risk of getting cancer and certain other diseases. And as he noted, the population of left-handers is certainly not decreasing and may, in fact, be increasing (Garmon, 1985).

□□ QUESTION □□

Why does it seem logical that right-handers should be better at language, while left-handers are better at painting and abstract mathematics?

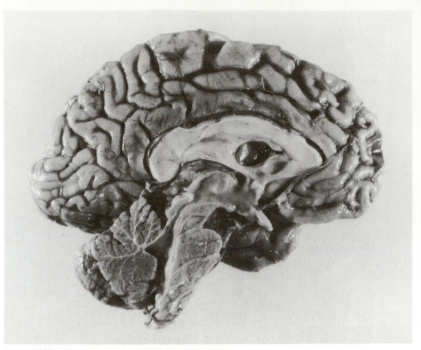

FIG. 2.16 If you cut the human brain in half from front to rear, then looked at the "inside view" of the left hemisphere, this is what you would see. The corpus callosum that connects the two hemispheres is the white tissue in the center of the photograph.

The Corpus Callosum

We will continue our discussion of "handedness" and "hemispheric dominance" in just a moment. First, let's look at how the two halves of your brain manage to cooperate.

The two cerebral hemispheres of your brain are joined together by a bridge of very special tissue—much as the North American hemisphere is joined to the southern by a narrow bridge of land we call Central America. The tissue connecting the two hemispheres of your brain is called the **corpus callosum**, two Latin words meaning "thick or hardened body." The corpus callosum contains a large number of axonic fibers that act like telephone cables running from one side of your brain to the other. Your "talking" hemisphere and your "perceiving" hemisphere keep in touch with each other *primarily* through your corpus callosum (see Fig. 2.16).

Sensory inputs that reach one of your hemispheres are almost automatically flashed to the other. Thus, if one of your hemispheres learns something, it usually shares the information with the other hemisphere almost immediately.

The situation is similar with your behavioral *outputs*. Suppose, for instance, your left hemisphere sends a message to the muscles in your right hand telling them to write the word "dog" with a pencil. Your dominant hemisphere would immediately let your right hemisphere know what it had commanded your hand to do.

• *Handedness and the Corpus Callosum*

Recent research by Sandra Witelson at McMaster University suggests that the corpus callosum is about 11 percent larger in left-handed and **ambidextrous** people than it is in right-handers. Why this difference? According to Witelson, right-handed people tend to use their left hemispheres for speech, but process spatial information more efficiently with the right hemisphere. Left-handers, however, tend to use *both* hemispheres for both types of tasks. For that reason, Witelson says, left-handers may simply require better communication between their hemispheres and thus may have larger corpus callosums than right-handers do (Witelson, 1985).

• *Handedness and Emotionality*

If you are right-handed, your left hemisphere is dominant as far as executing most *sequential muscle movements* is concerned. However, there is conflicting evidence as far as the expression of *emotional reactions* goes.

According to Nathan Fox and Richard Davidson, there is a substantial amount of research suggesting that the right hemisphere mediates negative emotions, while the left hemisphere mediates positive emotions. For example, the right hemisphere seems to be more active in patients suffering from depression, while the left hemisphere is more active in patients suffering from manic attacks. There also is some evidence suggesting that the left side of the face (controlled by the right hemisphere) is involved more frequently than the right in the deliberate production of frowns and the expression of other negative emotions (Fox & Davidson, 1984).

However, as you will shortly learn, patients who have undergone what is called "split-brain surgery" show quite a different pattern. In these patients, *almost all* emotional responses—both positive and negative—are controlled by the right hemisphere.

In addition, hemispheric control of emotionality seems to be *different* in left-handers than in right-handers. University of Wisconsin professor K.U. Smith has studied *facial expressiveness* in hundreds of people using computerized analyses of lip, tongue, and jaw movements. According to Smith, most people are either "left-faced" or "right-faced," which is to say that one side of the face is more *active* and *expressive* than the other. In both right- and left-faced individuals, Smith reports, the dominant side of the face expresses *both* positive and negative emotions more readily than does the non-dominant side (cited in Trotter, 1985).

About 90 percent of the people Smith has examined are "right-faced," and most of them are right-handers. However, Smith states that 98 percent of the opera singers he studied—and almost all of the talented musicians—were left-faced.

□ □ **QUESTION** □ □

If you met an opera star, why might it surprise you to learn she or he was right-handed?

- ### "Male" and "Female" Brains
According to Doreen Kimura, women's brains are organized more "tightly" than men's brains are—at least as far as speech production is concerned (Kimura, 1985). Kimura and her associates at the University of Western Ontario studied the differences between male and female brain-damaged patients. Generally speaking, Kimura's findings tend to confirm the strong influence that sex hormones have on the developing human brain.

To begin with, Kimura notes that there is some evidence that the corpus callosum itself is larger in women than in men. However, while the left temporal lobe is slightly larger than the right in *both* males and females, this difference is less marked in women than in men.

Kimura's research shows that men are likely to lose the ability to *produce speech* if they experience damage to *almost any part of the left hemisphere*. Women, however, develop *severe* speech production problems *only* if the damage occurs to the speech centers in the temporal lobe area. When it comes to damage to the *right* hemisphere, however, the picture is reversed. Women are likely to suffer a *mild* loss in *the ability to define words* whether brain damage occurs to either their left or right hemispheres. Men, however, suffer the same mild loss in word-defining skills *only* if the damage is to the left hemisphere.

According to Kimura, *speech production* is more "tightly organized" in women's brains than in men's. However, she believes that *abstract verbal skills* are more "tightly organized" in men's brains than in women's. Kimura presumes that the differences between male and female brains are due to the influence of sex hormones during development (Kimura, 1985).

Additional data supporting Kimura's views were reported by Henry Nasrallah at the 1986 meeting of the American College of Neuropsychopharmacology. Nasrallah and his associates at Ohio State University studied the *number of nerve fibers* found in various parts of the corpus callosum in right-handed men and women. They found that men had more fibers connecting the two frontal lobes than did women, while women had more fibers connecting the two occipital lobes (at the rear of the cerebrum) than did men. Oddly enough, Nasrallah reports in the December 27, 1986, issue of *Science News*, the reverse is true in schizophrenic males and females.

- ### Hemisphere Development during Childhood
At birth (or shortly thereafter), one hemisphere starts to gain the lead over the other and eventually takes over major control of the whole body. Why the left hemisphere usually "wins out" is a matter for **conjecture** although, as we noted, testosterone and other sex hormones may be influential in determining handedness.

During childhood, too, the left hemisphere tends to develop more quickly—and to a greater extent—than does the right. It may well be, therefore, that the left hemisphere comes to dominate in certain tasks because it is more highly developed during childhood than is the right (Thatcher, Walker, & Giudice, 1987).

In a recent article, Washington University researchers Suzanne Craft, Lee Willerman, and Erin Bigler tested both schizophrenic and normal subjects. They report that, compared with normals, the schizophrenics had difficulty performing tasks that required the subject to compare sensory inputs to the right hemisphere

Early in childhood, the left hemisphere gains dominance over the right, preparing children to learn cognitive skills.

with similar inputs to the left hemisphere. Craft and her colleagues suggest that schizophrenia may be related to a failure of the corpus callosum to develop properly during childhood (Craft, Willerman, & Bigler, 1987).

Once the left hemisphere has become dominant (for such tasks as talking and motor movements), however, how does it *exercise control* over the right hemisphere? R.W. Doty and his colleagues found that the left half of the brain actively *inhibits* the right half when issuing motor output commands. Thus, if you are right-handed, your left hemisphere *suppresses* any attempts the right might make to speak or "take control" of your bodily movements. These "suppression orders," of course, are sent from the left hemisphere to the right across the corpus callosum (Doty *et al.*, 1973).

Now, with all these facts in mind, can you guess what would happen to you if your corpus callosum were cut, and the two hemispheres of your brain were suddenly split apart?

This is precisely the question that psychologists R.W. Sperry and R.E. Myers were trying to answer when, in the 1950's, they performed their first *split-brain operations* on cats. They ended up making one of the most exciting discoveries in modern psychology. Sperry has continued in this field of research for the past 30 years. In 1981 he was awarded the Nobel Prize in medicine and physiology in large part because of his split-brain studies.

Two Minds in the Same Body

The surgical technique used by Sperry and Myers involved opening up the cat's skull, then slicing the animal's corpus callosum. They also split part of the optic nerve that runs from the cat's eyes to its brain.

Normally, sensory input from *each eye* goes to *both* cerebral hemispheres along the **optic nerve**. When Sperry and Myers cut the corpus callosum—and also split part of the optic nerve—they left the cat's *eyes* as isolated from each other as were the *two halves of its cerebrum*. Now, whatever the animal's left eye saw was recorded only in the left hemisphere. And whatever the animal's right eye saw was recorded only in the cat's right hemisphere.

Once a cat had recovered from the surgery, Sperry and Myers gave the animal a variety of behavioral tests. First, they blindfolded its left eye and taught the cat to solve a visual problem using *just* its right eye (and, of course, just the right hemisphere of its brain). The cat learned this lesson very well.

Next, they covered the trained right eye with the blindfold and tested the cat on the same problem with its untrained left eye (and left hemisphere). The question was, would any information about the problem have "leaked" from the right half of the cat's brain to the left?

The answer was a resounding *no*. Using just its untrained left eye/left brain, the cat appeared to be entirely ignorant of what it had learned with its right eye/right brain. When Sperry and Myers subsequently trained *just* the left eye (on a different task), the right eye (and hemisphere) seemed unaware of what the left part of the brain had learned.

Sperry and Myers concluded that the cat now had two "minds," either of which was capable of learning *on its own*—and of responding intelligently to changes in the world around it *on its own* (Myers & Sperry, 1958).

Subsequent experiments with rats and monkeys gave similar results. However, the animals recovered so nicely that, if you hadn't known about their operation, you might not have guessed there were two more-or-less independent "entities" inside each animal's body.

The split-brain surgery was seemingly safe and relatively easy to perform in animals. But what would the operation do to a human, and why would anyone want to find out? To answer that question, we must look more closely at that odd and unfortunate condition known as epilepsy.

Epilepsy

Although four million people in the US suffer from epilepsy, most of us have little understanding of what causes the condition. Nor do most of us appreciate the problems that epileptic individuals must face. And because of our ignorance of (and superstitions about) epilepsy, we often discriminate unjustly against people who suffer seizures.

Just for a moment, then, try to imagine what it might be like if you were unfortunate enough to sustain brain damage and have an epileptic attack.

If the site of the damaged nerve cells were in the *input* or *processing* areas of your brain, you might never recognize that you suffered from epilepsy. For seizures in the input and processing areas of the brain typically lead to little more than momentary lapses in consciousness. This type of epileptic attack is called a **petit mal seizure**. If the injured neurons were in your *output* system, however, you might suffer from a full-blown *motor seizure*—a condition that is very hard to overlook.

If your epilepsy resulted from mild brain damage—or if the attack was caused by an overdose of some drug—your seizures would occur infrequently. But if your brain damage was severe, your attacks might happen several times a day—so frequently that you did not regain consciousness between seizures. This rare condition must be treated promptly, for it can lead to death.

Optic nerve (OP-tick). The visual input pathway that runs from each eye to the brain. Half of the optic nerve from each eye runs to the left brain, half to the right brain. In order to make sure that input from the cat's left eye went only to its left hemisphere, and that input from the right eye went only to the right hemisphere, Sperry and Myers had to cut half of the optic nerve from each eye.

Petit mal seizure (petty mahl). From the French words meaning "small evil," or "little badness." A person suffering a petit mal attack loses consciousness for a few seconds, but no "motor seizure" occurs. Often the person's eyes remain open during this loss of consciousness.

Hypersynchrony (HIGH-purr-SINK-kron-ee). *Hyper* means "high" or "above." *Synchrony* means "coordinated activities." Neurons show hypersynchrony when too many of them fire in unison.

Spikes. Unusual, very large bursts of electrical activity that usually are symptoms of brain damage when they appear on an EEG record.

Grand mal seizure (grahn mahl). Perhaps the most dramatic, terrifying type of motor epilepsy. The French words *grand mal* mean "big sickness" (the final "d" in "grand" is not pronounced).

- ### Hypersynchrony

Generally speaking, the neurons in your brain tend to function in small but relatively independent units. In brain-damaged people, however, *all* the nerve cells in a given part of the brain occasionally begin to fire in unison. We call this type of neural activity **hypersynchrony**, and it typically shows up on an EEG record as **spikes** (see Fig. 2.13).

When hypersynchrony occurs, huge and jagged waves of electrical activity sweep across the surface of the brain like a thunderstorm sweeping across the Atlantic Ocean. And just as you can tell something about the intensity of an Atlantic storm by measuring the size and shape of the ocean waves it stirs up, so you can tell something about that "stormy condition" called epilepsy by reading EEG records taken when a seizure occurs.

- ### Epilepsy and the Corpus Callosum

The brain damage that causes most epileptic seizures usually has a specific *focus* or location on one side of the brain. If you took an EEG record from this damaged area, you would see continual "spike" responses.

But remember that the two hemispheres are more-or-less "mirror images." What would happen if you took an EEG record at the same point in the undamaged hemisphere? In fact, the EEG record from the unscarred hemisphere would usually look pretty normal. However, at the onset of an epileptic attack, you would detect spikes on *both sides of the brain.*

How could there be spike responses coming from apparently healthy tissue? Almost every neuron in your *left* hemisphere has a nerve cell in your *right* hemisphere that is its "identical twin," or mirror image. Many of these nerve cells are tied together by axonic fibers that pass through the corpus callosum. Whenever a neuron in your dominant hemisphere fires, it may send a "command mes-

sage" telling its mirror-image cell in the minor hemisphere to fire too. And whenever the mirror-image neuron fires, it sends a message back to the dominant hemisphere saying that it has fired.

These command messages are the primary way in which your dominant hemisphere coordinates muscular activities on both sides of your body (Kimble, 1987).

Whenever an epileptic seizure begins at a focal point in one hemisphere, the mirror-image neurons in the other hemisphere receive a "seizure message" via the corpus callosum. This "seizure message" causes the mirror-image neurons to fire very, very rapidly themselves. The cells may even start showing spike activity on their own as they "catch fire" from all the stimulation they are receiving from the other hemisphere. So the spike activity begins to build up simultaneously at the *same spot in both hemispheres.*

In addition, the mirror-image neurons may send seizure messages back to the original site of the trouble. This return message from the undamaged hemisphere sets off even more spiking in the damaged area, which then sends even wilder messages back to the mirror-image cells, which causes them to fire even more rapidly.

Each time the seizure message flashes back and forth across the corpus callosum, a few more cells in each hemisphere get caught up in the spiking. Within a few seconds, the whole brain can become involved, and a **grand mal seizure** occurs.

An epileptic seizure, therefore, is a good example of what is called a *positive feedback loop* (see Fig. 2.17).

"Cutting the Feedback Loop"

When medical doctors learned of the Sperry-Myers split-brain operation, they reasoned that if they cut the corpus callosum and separated the two hemispheres of the brain, they could cut the positive feedback loop that typically causes an epileptic attack. And by "cutting the loop," they might prevent full-blown seizures from occurring in patients whose seizures couldn't be controlled by drugs or other medical treatment.

And the doctors were right. They tried the operation on a middle-aged man whom we shall call John Doe. During the Korean War, John Doe had served in the armed forces. After parachuting behind the enemy lines, he had been captured and put in a concentration camp. While in the prison camp, he had been struck on the head several times with a rifle butt.

Shortly thereafter, John Doe's epileptic seizures began. By the time he was released from the concentration camp, his brain was in such

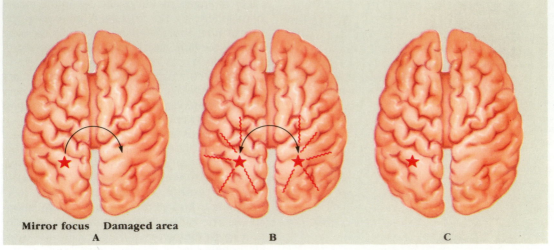

Mirror focus   Damaged area
A   B   C

FIG. 2.17 (A) Damaged cells in the left hemisphere cause abnormal electrical activity in nearby cells and send an "excited" message to their "mirror image" cells in the right hemisphere. (B) The "mirror image" cells are stimulated to fire by this abnormal input and feed an "excited" message back to the right hemisphere. Soon the whole brain is "on fire" with neural excitation, and an epileptic seizure results. (C) Cutting the corpus callosum "cuts the feedback loop" and reduces the likelihood of a seizure.

bad physical shape that drugs couldn't help very much. His seizures increased in frequency and intensity until they were occurring a dozen or more times a day. Without the split-brain operation, John Doe would probably have died—or committed suicide, as had many other epileptic patients with similar problems.

But after the surgeons cut John Doe's corpus callosum, his seizures stopped almost completely—just as the surgeons had expected. Obviously, "cutting the positive feedback loop" had prevented the *grand mal* attacks from occurring.

However, when the doctors split John Doe's brain, they apparently cut his "mind" into two separate but similar personalities as well. Each of these "minds" seemed to exist more-or-less independently of the other, and each of them had its own unique claim on his body (Sperry, 1968).

As far as his mental activities were concerned, John Doe had suddenly become Siamese twins!

John-Doe-Left and John-Doe-Right

Immediately after the operation, John Doe was able to communicate in almost normal fashion. Some of his speech was slurred, as if he didn't have complete control over the muscles in his tongue. But his thinking seemed clear and logical, and he suffered no noticeable loss in intelligence.

But John Doe did have moments of confusion, and he was often unable to coordinate his body movements and his emotional reactions. Every now and then, he reported, the left half of his body "did odd things," *as if it had a will of its own.*

John Doe was right-handed, so his "talking hemisphere" controlled his right hand and leg. Occasionally, when John was dressing, his right hand would zip up his pants (as it normally did) and John would start to go about his business. Moments later, however, his left hand (controlled by the right hemisphere), would casually reach down and unzip his pants. His left hand did other odd things too, mostly in fairly emotional situations. These behaviors almost always embarrassed John Doe's dominant hemisphere, because he could offer no logical (verbal) explanation for why his left hand was behaving so peculiarly.

The doctors soon began to suspect that when John Doe answered their questions and reported his thoughts, it was *only* his left hemisphere that was doing the talking. Indeed, the left side of his brain seemed blissfully unaware of the perceptions and emotions that were occurring in his right hemisphere. And since his left hemisphere controlled speech output, the right hemisphere couldn't communicate by talking. So, it offered its comments behaviorally—by occasionally doing odd things that would *disrupt* the ongoing flow of behavior controlled by John Doe's left hemisphere.

The psychologists working with John Doe soon devised ways of communicating with either side of his brain without the other side's knowing what was going on. John-Doe-Left responded *verbally* to most questions the psychologists asked him, since this hemisphere possessed full language control. John-Doe-Right could not talk, but he could *point* to things (with the left hand) in response to questions that John-Doe-Left couldn't hear (Sperry, 1968).

As soon as John-Doe-Left responded out loud to a question that only it could hear, why would John-Doe-Right usually know what the question had been?

Similar Personalities

According to Roger Sperry, psychological tests showed that both John Does had remarkably similar personalities. Except for language ability, they were about as much alike as identical twins. Their attitudes and opinions seemed to be the same; their perceptions of the world were the same; and they woke up and went to sleep at almost the same times (Sperry, 1968).

There were differences, however. John-Doe-Left could express himself in language and was somewhat more logical and better at orderly planning than was John-Doe-Right. John-Doe-Right tended to be somewhat more aggressive, impulsive, emotional—and frequently expressed frustration with what was going on. Sperry believes this frustration was caused by the fact that John-Doe-Right often knew what he wanted to say or do, but was unable to express himself verbally.

The split-brain operation was so successful in reducing epileptic attacks that it was tried with more than a dozen patients who might otherwise have died from uncontrollable seizures. In some of these patients, one hemisphere (usually the dominant one) was able to gain control of both sides of the body. In most cases, however, the two halves learned to cooperate and share control, but the dominant

"I CLAIMED MY LEFT BRAIN DIDN'T KNOW WHAT MY RIGHT BRAIN WAS DOING, BUT THEY DIDN'T BUY IT."

hemisphere was in the driver's seat most of the time. In one or two patients, though, neither half of the brain ever gained the ability to coordinate all bodily movements (Sperry, 1982).

HOW THE HEMISPHERES DIFFER

The split-brain studies have given us fascinating insights into the ways that the two hemispheres may function in individuals (like yourself) with intact brains. Given their importance, perhaps we should look at these experiments in greater detail.

Visual Perception, "Monitoring," and the Right Hemisphere

Research performed by Roger Sperry (and many others) suggests that the right hemisphere is much better at *perceiving visual patterns* than is the left.

In one experiment, Sperry showed a male patient a complex design and then asked the man to reproduce the pattern by putting colored blocks together. When the patient used his left hand (right hemisphere), he completed the task rapidly. But when the man tried to match the design using his right hand (left hemisphere), he proceeded slowly, clumsily, and made many mistakes. And much to the surprise of both Sperry and the patient, the man's left hand often tried to "correct" the mistakes the right hand made (Sperry, 1982).

Oddly enough, there are no reports of cases in which the left hemisphere tries to correct any responses made by the right half of the brain. Indeed, the left hemisphere usually tends to *deny responsibility* for any of the right hemisphere's actions. And if it cannot deny responsibility, then the left hemisphere will *make up a story* explaining why the left half of the body behaved as it did.

In a recent report, Michael Gazzaniga (one of Sperry's students) reports on his own research with split-brain patients. In one study, Gazzaniga presented a picture of a snow scene to the patient's right hemisphere while showing a different picture (a chicken's claw) to the left hemisphere (see Fig 2.18). Had Gazzaniga asked the patient to report *verbally* what he saw, the patient would have answered, "A chicken's claw." The patient also would have *denied* seeing anything else, for only the left hemisphere controlled speech and all it saw was the chicken's claw.

In fact, however, Gazzaniga showed the patient drawings of various objects and asked him to select which of the objects "went with the scene." The patient's *right* hand pointed to the drawing of the chicken, but the patient's *left* hand pointed to the shovel. As Gazzaniga puts it, "After his response, I asked him why he did that; he looked up and without a moment's hesitation said from his left hemisphere, 'Oh, that's easy. The chicken claw goes with the chicken, and you need a shovel to clean out the chicken shed.'"

Gazzaniga believes that, when asked to explain his left hand's "odd behavior," the patient's left hemisphere simply *made up a logical story* that would excuse the actions (Gazzaniga, 1985).

In a second study, Gazzaniga used a drug that put the left hemisphere to sleep for a few minutes while leaving the right hemisphere awake and alert. While the left hemisphere was asleep, Gazzaniga put a spoon into the patient's left hand and asked the patient to remember what it was. Then, after the patient's left hemisphere had recovered consciousness, Gazzaniga asked the patient what it was that had been placed in his left hand while he was asleep. The patient flatly denied that anything had occurred. However, when shown several objects and asked to guess which it was, the patient immediately said, "Of course, the spoon" (Gazzaniga, 1985).

Gazzaniga's research—and that from other experimenters, as well—suggests that the right hemisphere is better at "monitoring" and remembering the activities of the left than the left hemisphere is at observing and recording the activities of the right.

Emotions and the Right Hemisphere

There is a fair amount of data connecting the right hemisphere with emotionality. For example, in 1979 Elliott Ross and Marek-Marsel Mesulam reported that one of their patients—a 39-year-old woman—had to give up teaching school for a time after suffering a **stroke** in her right hemisphere. She could still speak fluently, but she no longer could "put emotion into her speech and actions." All her words came out in a flat tone of voice, and neither her pupils at school nor her own children could tell when she "meant business" when she talked. To compensate, she learned to say things like "I am angry and mean it" when she wanted to express dissatisfaction.

For a period of time after her stroke, this patient found it impossible to laugh, and she was unable to cry even at her father's funeral. Some six months after the stroke, however, she started to regain the ability to express her feelings. Two months later she was again able to express emotions normally. Apparently, various undamaged parts of her brain had been able to "take over" the right-brain functions lost when the stroke occurred (Ross & Mesulam, 1979).

Similar evidence about the importance of the right hemisphere in processing emotional responses comes from a study on split-brain patients reported by Howard Gardner in 1981. According to Gardner, these patients—using just their left hemispheres—seem incapable of

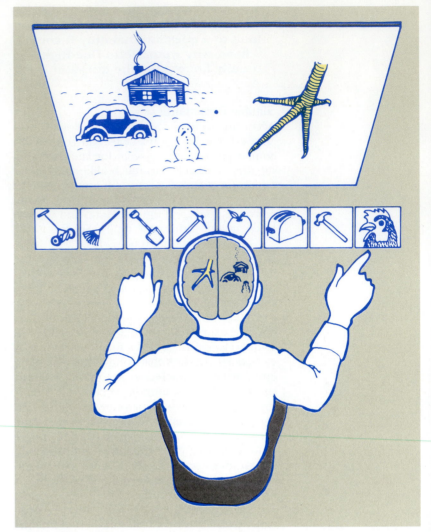

FIG. 2.18 Two problems are presented simultaneously, one to the talking left brain and one to the nontalking right brain. The answers for each problem are available in full view in front of the patient.

"getting a joke." When told the beginning of a funny story, then offered several possible "punch lines," the patients usually do not choose the appropriate endings. Rather, they tend to pick a highly inappropriate ending—and then defend their choice rather vigorously (Gardner, 1981).

Language and the Left Hemisphere

The split-brain research—and many other studies with both normal and brain-damaged individuals—suggests strongly that language is *primarily* processed on the left side of the brain. For instance, in 1978 Ruben Gur and his colleagues at the University of Pennsylvania gave 13 right-handed males various tasks to solve. Half of these tasks involved the use of complex language. The other half of the problems involved the visual perception of incomplete patterns. When the subjects were working on the verbal problems, the blood flow through their *left* hemispheres increased markedly, but the blood flow through their *right*

Stroke. Brain damage usually caused by ruptured blood vessels. When deprived of blood, the neurons in a given area of the brain die. The stroke victim then loses the psychological and biological functions controlled by that part of the brain.

Gestalt (guess-TALT). A mental or perceptual pattern. From the German word meaning "figure," "pattern," or "good form." The ability to see something "as a whole"—rather than just see its parts—is the ability to "form a Gestalt."

hemispheres did not increase at all. And those subjects who did best at solving the visual problems showed an increased blood flow through their right hemispheres, but not through the left half of their brains (Gur *et al.*, 1978).

In a similar set of experiments, David Galin and his associates at the Langley Porter Institute in San Francisco found that normal subjects show increased electrical activity in their left hemispheres when attempting to solve verbal tasks, but increased activity in their right hemispheres when solving tasks requiring spatial ability (Galin *et al.*, 1978).

Galin believes that "each hemisphere is specialized for a different cognitive style—the left for an analytical, logical mode for which words are an excellent tool, and the right for a holistic **Gestalt** mode, which happens to be particularly suitable for spatial relations."

Cooperation across the Corpus Callosum

If it seems highly unlikely to you that you have two minds locked away inside your skull, the reason is not hard to find. Although the split-brain research suggests that each of your hemispheres *specializes* in certain types of tasks, for the most part the two halves of your brain *cooperate* so quickly and efficiently that they operate as a "functional unit" rather than as two separate entities. It is only when the two hemispheres are isolated that their differing abilities can readily be measured. And even these "differences" are not always obvious to the split-brain patient.

Roger Sperry reports that, following their split-brain operations, none of his patients was aware that "anything was missing." Although their left (verbal) hemispheres had lost most of what we call *depth perception*, and could no longer hear music in "full stereophonic sound," the patients did not become aware of this loss until it was demonstrated to them in the laboratory (Sperry, 1982).

More than this, the patients often verbally rejected those few responses that clearly came from their right hemispheres. When Sperry would show a picture of some kind to the right hemisphere, the left hand would identify the picture correctly—but the patient would frequently deny having seen anything at all. And just as often, when the patient's left hand would "correct" the right hand as it tried to reproduce

a pattern, the patient would say something like, "Now, I know it wasn't me who did that!"

• Case of J.W.

Studies in which only part of the corpus callosum is cut tell us even more about how the hemispheres communicate with each other. In 1981 Michael Gazzaniga and his colleagues reported the case history of J.W., a bright young man whose epileptic seizures became so severe he underwent split-brain surgery when he was 26. The operation took place in two stages, however. During the first stage, the surgeon cut *just the rear half* of the callosum. Then, 10 weeks later, the surgeon cut the *front half* as well. Gazzaniga and his co-workers gave J.W. psychological tests several times—before any surgery at all, after the first stage of the operation, and again after the entire corpus callosum had been cut.

Prior to the operation, when the word "knight" was shown just to J.W.'s right hemisphere, he immediately said the word aloud. After the rear half of the callosum was cut, however, J.W. gave the following response when his right hemisphere was again shown the word "knight": "I have a picture in my mind but can't say it. . . . Two fighters in a ring. . . . Ancient . . . wearing uniforms and helmets . . . on horses . . . trying to knock each other off. . . . Knights?"

After his entire corpus callosum was cut, though, J.W. was unable to report *anything at all* about the stimuli presented to his right hemisphere. Indeed, he now denied having "seen" anything, and his guesses at what the right hemisphere had been shown were no better than chance (Gazzaniga & LeDoux, 1978).

Gazzaniga believes that *words* and other types of *specific* sensory information pass back and forth between the two hemispheres in the rear half of the corpus callosum. However, the front half of the callosum apparently is the highway across which the two hemispheres exchange perceptual and emotional information (thoughts, feelings, "pictures," and "meanings") (Gazzaniga, 1985).

□□ **QUESTION** □□
When J.W.'s right hemisphere was shown the word "knight" after the first operation, his left hemisphere responded by talking about "two fighters in a ring wearing ancient armor." But the printed word "knight" sounds just the same as "night" when the two words are spoken aloud. What does the fact that J.W.'s left hemisphere didn't confuse "knight" with "night" tell you about what kind of sensory information the right hemisphere was sending to the left?

The Whole Brain Versus the Split Brain

The chances are very good that no surgeon will ever cut your corpus callosum, and that you will not suffer the type of stroke which destroys your ability to express emotions. What then can all this study of brain-damaged individuals tell you about the normal functioning of the whole, intact brain? Although the split-brain research does give a partial answer to this question, you should realize five things:

1. Almost all of the theories we have today are "subject to recall," which is to say they may be drastically changed as new data come from the laboratory. For example, in 1783 the noted British poet William Cowper wrote, "If man had been intended to fly, God would have provided him with wings." What would Cowper have thought of today's jet airplanes? (And do you really believe that, if your corpus callosum were cut, you would end up with two separate and distinct minds inside your skull?)

2. Because we place a high premium on language production and coordinated activities, we tend to call the left hemisphere the *dominant* half of the brain. The term "dominant" may be a poor choice of words, however. For the right hemisphere surely "dominates" the production of emotional and perceptual responses. And, in normal individuals, both hemispheres are involved in *almost all activities*.

3. Until recently, many experimental psychologists assumed that the "mind" was a highly complex biological machine that "processed information" much as a giant computer might "process data." Other psychologists preferred to view the mind as a mental (or even spiritual) thing. But almost everybody thought of the mind as being a *single system*. However, as Michael Gazzaniga points out, the split-brain research suggests that you have *several different cognitive and emotional systems*, each of which processes sensory inputs (and thoughts and feelings) in different ways. It is the *combined activity* of these various systems that presumably makes up what we might call "the stream of conscious experience" (Gazzaniga, 1985).

4. The split-brain research has taught us a great deal about human individuality, particularly as regards our "mental processes." Roger Sperry puts it this way: "The more we learn, the more we recognize the unique complexity of any one individual intellect and the stronger the conclusion becomes that the individuality inherent in our brain networks makes that of fingerprints or facial features gross and simple by comparison" (Sperry, 1982).

5. As Sigmund Freud put it years ago, studying the abnormal often tells us what the normal is like. Trying to figure out what the right hemisphere's "stream of consciousness" is like has taught us much about what "ordinary consciousness" consists of. But so has research on "altered states of consciousness," such as sleep, dreaming, and drug-induced "highs." Some of the experiences people have when asleep or "on drugs" may well be caused by a disruption of the orderly flow of thoughts and emotions back and forth across the corpus callosum.

To understand better how your *whole brain* works when it is functioning normally, then, we must turn once more to the abnormal—to such "altered states of consciousness" as sleep and drug intoxication.

SUMMARY

1. Your **brain** contains almost a trillion nerve cells, weighs about 3 pounds, and is the master organ of your body that coordinates or controls many of the functions of the other organs.

2. The largest parts of your brain are the two **cerebral hemispheres** that sit atop the stem of your brain like the cap on a mushroom.

3. The thin outer covering of the cerebral hemispheres is called the **cortex**. Many of the functions of the brain that relate to conscious decision making are located in the cortex.

4. The **major function** of your brain is to **process information** in order to produce **thoughts**, **feelings**, and **behaviors**.

5. Most cortical neurons have three main parts—the **dendrites**, the cell body or **soma**, and the **axon**.

6. The main purpose of most neurons is to **pass messages from one part of the body to another**. These messages are really waves of electro-chemical energy called **action potentials**.

7. When the dendrites are stimulated by **neurotransmitters**, the action potential sweeps down the axon like a bullet speeding down the barrel of a gun.

8. When the action potential reaches the end of the axon, it causes the axon to release **neurotransmitters** into the **synaptic cleft**—the fluid-filled space between the axon of one neuron and the dendrites and cell body of a second neuron.

9. Neurotransmitters released into the **synaptic cleft** excite the dendrites of the second neuron. It typically responds by **firing**, or generating an action potential of its own.

10. Neurons have **receptor sites** on their dendrites and cell bodies that are particularly sensitive to **neurotransmitters**.

11. The **lock and key hypothesis** states that if a specific transmitter molecule "fits" a specific receptor site, it "unlocks" the neuron and makes it fire.

12. Your brain contains both **excitatory** and **inhibitory synapses**.

13. **Pre-synaptic inhibition** prevents the axon from releasing neurotransmitters. **Post-synaptic inhibition** prevents the dendrites and cell bodies from responding to neurotransmitters.

14. Electrical activity in the dendrites creates **brain waves** that show up on an **EEG** machine.

15. About 90 percent of the population is **right-handed**. Twice as many men as women are **left-handers**.

16. Left-handers are more likely to suffer **developmental disorders** and **language difficulties**, and are three times more likely to experience **migraine headaches** and **autoimmune disorders** as are right-handers. However, a higher percentage of left-handers are artists, musicians, mathematicians, and engineers.

17. The two hemispheres of your brain are connected by a bridge of tissue called the **corpus callosum**.

18. Damage to various parts of the brain can cause a condition known as **epilepsy**. Epileptic seizures show up on an EEG machine as **spike-shaped brain waves**.

19. If epileptic seizures become too frequent or severe, a surgeon may cut the corpus callosum. This **split-brain operation** may leave the patient with "two minds in the same body."

20. In right-handed people, the left hemisphere is **dominant**, mediates speech, and controls coordinated movements of the body.

21. The minor or **perceptual/emotional hemisphere** can understand most language, but does not usually speak. It seems more specialized to handle perceptual patterns and emotional expression than is the dominant hemisphere.

22. In split-brain patients, the minor hemisphere can **communicate** with the outside world by moving the left hand. However, the dominant (speaking) hemisphere will often **deny** that responses initiated by the minor hemisphere actually occurred, or will **fabricate** excuses to explain the response.

23. In normal individuals, what we call the **stream of conscious awareness** seems to be mediated primarily by the dominant hemisphere, but it is strongly influenced by activities in many other cognitive and emotional systems, particularly those in the minor hemisphere.

(Continued from page 21.)

"What an appropriate place to hide a secret," Colonel Garcia said, caressing Patrick's head again.

"I don't understand," said Captain Hartman. "How can the boy have a secret in his brain that the police over there could not discover?"

Colonel Garcia beamed. "Because Tavela knew more than they did, for one thing. Because they know nothing about the Bible, for another."

"Are you trying to tell me that Tavela hid the secret in Patrick's soul?" Captain Hartman said, a touch of sarcasm in his voice.

"Not quite, Captain, but perhaps you are closer than you know." The woman turned to the young man sitting beside her. "Tell me, Patrick, did you mention the Bible to the secret police when they questioned you?"

"Yes."

"And I'll bet they laughed and spoke of fairy stories, didn't they?"

Patrick nodded his agreement.

"But 'understanding is more precious than rubies,' Patrick. Don't ever forget that. Tavela knew we would understand. And we do."

"I don't understand at all," said Captain Hartman.

Colonel Garcia grew serious. "It is simple, when you know how the brain actually works. Patrick, when Dr. Tavela operated on you, he cut your corpus callosum, didn't he?"

"Yes, I think that was it. He said it would stop the seizures."

Nodding, Colonel Garcia continued. "And then he tested the two hemispheres of your brain to determine what each could see and hear and respond to."

"What has that got to do with the pattern of the secret molecule?" asked the Captain.

"Everything, if you understand the third chapter of *Proverbs*. You see, the 'mask' that Patrick looked into was a device which presented stimuli to just one half of his brain. If Dr. Tavela showed something to the left hemisphere, Patrick would be conscious of it and could answer questions about it verbally." She looked at the young man. "Is that not so? Didn't he ask you what you could see?"

"All the time," replied Patrick. "Sometimes I could tell him, and sometimes I couldn't."

"But even if you couldn't tell him what you saw, you could point to it with your left hand, couldn't you? You could trace patterns with your left hand, couldn't you? Not with your right hand, of course, but with your left hand?"

Patrick considered the matter. "Yeah, you're right."

"Ah," said Captain Hartman. "I think I see what you mean. 'And in her left hand is riches and honor.' When Tavela knew the police were coming for him, he had half an hour to hide the pattern for the new molecule where we could find it later. Not in the cast or in the bandages, because the police would check them."

Patrick nodded excitedly. "Yes, they took off my cast and and changed my bandages. And they took lots of X-rays."

"And they didn't find anything, because they rejected the clue to the Bible," continued the Colonel.

Hartman smiled. "Because Dr. Tavela had hidden the pattern in the right half of Patrick's brain. But how did he do that?"

"He must have shown it to Patrick's right hemisphere, and had Patrick trace it again and again with his left hand," replied Colonel Garcia.

Hartman frowned. "But his left hemisphere doesn't *know* what the formula is at all! The lie detector tests showed that."

"They tested Patrick's *right* hand during the polygraph test, Captain. And the right hand is controlled by the left hemisphere, which was ignorant of what the right hemisphere had learned. They couldn't test Patrick's *left* hand during the tests because he's wearing a cast on his left hand. That's why Dr. Tavela said the broken left hand was a 'good thing.' So his right brain knows, but Patrick doesn't know, eh?" She smiled at the young man. "You really aren't conscious of knowing the pattern for the secret molecule, are you?"

"No," he said, a puzzled look on his face.

"We'll see about that." The woman picked up the pencil from her desk and wrote "Yes" and "No" on a sheet of paper. Then she put the paper close to Patrick's left hand. "Now, Patrick, I'm going to ask you some questions, but I don't want you to answer out loud. Instead, I want you to point to 'Yes' or 'No' on the paper with your *left* hand. All right?"

"All right," he responded, his left hand moving toward the paper.

"Patrick," the Colonel continued, "I want to talk to your right hemisphere. If you hear what I am saying, please point to 'Yes.'"

Patrick's fingers touched "Yes."

"Patrick, did Dr. Tavela show you the drawing of the secret molecule?"

"No," said Patrick out loud. But his left hand pointed to "Yes."

"Weird," Captain Hartman said softly.

Patrick stared at his left hand in amazement. "I don't understand what I'm doing."

Colonel Garcia gave the young man a hug. "In the world of espionage we tell our agents, 'Never let your right hand know what your left is doing.' You are the only person I know of who can actually follow that advice. Because of your special brain, you have helped us, and Dr. Tavela, and even yourself. Be proud of that." Then she sighed and stood up. "Come, Patrick. It is time that your left hand had a long talk with one of our chemists."

Patrick's left hand pointed to "Yes."

Biological Rhythms: Sleep, Drugs, and Consciousness

"Perchance to Dream"

· C·H·A·P·T·E·R ·
3

STUDY QUESTIONS

As you read through the chapter, see if you can find the answers to the following questions:

1. What are "altered states of consciousness"?
2. Psychologically speaking, what are the four most important points about consciousness?
3. What are circadian rhythms?
4. How are biological clocks "reset"?
5. What are the six stages of sleep?
6. During which stage does most dreaming occur, and how do we know that's the case?
7. How do the effects of sleep deprivation differ from those of dream deprivation?
8. What is narcolepsy?
9. What is lucid dreaming?
10. What "natural pain-killers" does the body produce, and how are they implicated in opiate addiction?
11. How many people in the US died from cocaine overdose in 1986?
12. What effects do hallucinogens typically have on information processing in the brain?
13. How do "expectations" affect your response to alcohol?
14. What is the relationship between stress and the release of endorphins in the brain?

The Washington Bureaucrat leaned back in his overstuffed chair, puffed on his pipe, and meditated quietly as he looked at the man and woman sitting in front of his desk. They were nice people, really—bright, eager academics—and he did want to help them. They needed research funds to study some savages living in a jungle in South America. But it was a pity they knew so little about the savages who lived in that "jungle by the Potomac" called Washington, DC.

"Look," the Bureaucrat said, putting down his pipe. "It's a simple trade-off, really. You, Dr. Ogdon, and your husband are both psychologists. You want to go study language development in some very primitive people who live near the Amazon. Right?"

Susan Ogdon looked at her husband and then nodded assent.

"Well," continued the Bureaucrat, "our department wants someone to study marijuana use, and in just the same sort of back-woods people. We don't care what language these people speak or how they learn to speak it. But we do want to find out how pot-smoking affects their lives, their health, and their ability to get along in the world. You make our study for us, and we'll pay for the research." The Bureaucrat picked up his pipe again and leaned back in his chair. "What you choose to do in your spare time is your own affair, naturally. If you want to study language development on the side, we couldn't care less."

The woman cleared her throat. "What do you wish us to prove for you?"

The Bureaucrat sat bolt upright. "Nothing! Nothing at all! We have no preconceived notions of what your findings will be." The man paused, remembering how upset the Deputy Assistant Secretary got at the mere mention of marijuana. "Well, no *official* preconceived notions, you understand. But truthfully, we'll accept and let you publish whatever results you get."

"Why us?" asked Roger Ogdon.

"Because you've been there, and you know the people. Otherwise you wouldn't want to do your own research there." The Bureaucrat's voice softened and he put on his warmest smile. "Speaking personally, I do happen to be quite interested in language development. But the department simply is not able to fund such projects these days. So, when I read the proposal you sent us on language development in primitives, I thought . . ." He let his words drift slowly toward the ceiling like verbal pipe smoke.

The woman's face brightened. "Roger," she said, turning to her husband. "I do believe we ought to consider it. But we'd surely have to think about how to measure the effects of long-term marijuana smoking on anybody, much less on the natives."

"You're right, Sue," Roger Ogdon said. He turned in his chair and looked straight at the Bureaucrat. "Why do you want us to study Amazon primitives? If you want to know the effects of pot-smoking on American citizens—and I suspect you do—why not do your research right here in Washington? Or even at Harvard? Wasn't there a Supreme Court nominee . . ."

"You're thinking of the Previous Administration," said the Bureaucrat quickly. "But really, you know we can't get a really random sample of long-term pot smokers here, or at Harvard, because the people who would volunteer wouldn't be representative. Besides, I suspect those natives have been smoking pot for many generations. You can look for long-term genetic effects as well as measuring the problems it gives them today."

Sue Ogdon frowned. "I thought you said you had no preconceived notions of what we'd find. What if there aren't any long-term genetic effects, or any real problems today?"

Now it was the Bureaucrat's turn to frown. These people were giving him a mild headache. Surely they saw that he was trying to help them. Why didn't they just take the money, and do what they were told? He reached in a desk drawer and took out an aspirin. Taking a sip of water, he swallowed the tablet quickly.

"Look, Dr. Ogdon," he said. "I will be frank with you. It would greatly please certain people upstairs if you found that marijuana had bad effects on the natives. Maybe that's what you'll find, and maybe not. But let's get things straight. I don't care what you find. Just plan the best study possible, use as many controls as you can, and get the facts. We'll pay the bills no matter what."

"Haven't you supported similar studies before?" asked the woman.

The Bureaucrat's face went slightly white. "Er, yes, I believe so. A couple, perhaps. But the more research is repeated, the more firmly we can believe in the data. As my senior professor said in graduate school, 'Replication is good for the soul.'"

Susan Ogdon persisted. "What did the other investigators find?"

"Now, now," said the Bureaucrat in a soothing tone of voice. "I'd rather you approached this problem with fresh minds. Just make sure that you measure the biological, psychological, and social effects of marijuana use, and do so as objectively as you can. That's the important thing."

Roger Ogdon was puzzled. "I don't think I've read the results of those 'couple of studies' you've already funded."

"Well," said the Bureaucrat, reaching for another aspirin. "I don't believe we've published the results yet. Later this year, perhaps . . ." He let his words drift off again.

Susan Ogdon frowned in surprise. "You mean, you didn't publish the results because the data didn't come out the way you expected them to? Then why do you want to pay for still another study whose results you may have to suppress?"

The Bureaucrat put down his pipe in an angry gesture. "Listen to me. You both are psychologists, and you're supposed to be able to understand why people and organizations act like they do. You know perfectly well that it takes a long time for an organization to change its mind on a subject. It takes a lot of data to accomplish that miracle, and a lot of gentle pushing from inside.

You go do the study, and report anything you find. Do your own work on the side, if you wish. And leave it up to me to see that your data have the maximum impact. Okay?"

The man and woman exchanged glances. Then the man said, "Well, I think we understand each other. We'll go plan a study, and submit a proposal to you. If we agree on the details, you'll get us the funding. And, as you said, any other research we do 'on the side' is our business."

The Bureaucrat beamed. "Marvelous! I hoped you'd see it that way. Now, let's go find a drink somewhere and celebrate!"

(Continued on page 73.)

CONSCIOUSNESS

This chapter is about *biological rhythms*—those short- and long-term patterns of physiological activity that affect the behavior patterns of all living organisms. At the human level, the most obvious of these patterns is the daily *sleep/wakefulness cycle.*

As you might guess, there are *psychological* changes associated with many of these *biological* rhythms. Some of these psychological changes involve alterations in your state of **consciousness,** or "mental awareness." So, we will also discuss various *altered states of consciousness* in this chapter.

Some altered states of awareness occur naturally. For instance, that blissful condition called *sleep*, and those sometimes unblissful experiences we call *nightmares*, are examples of "natural" altered states of awareness. But there are "unnatural" states, as well—unnatural in the sense that they are *artificially* brought about. The **intoxication** that you get from drugs such as alcohol is a good example of an artificially-induced altered state of consciousness.

Before we get too far into our investigation of these topics, however, perhaps a brief discussion of *consciousness* is in order.

□ □ **QUESTION** □ □
How would *you* define "consciousness"?

Primitive Terms

Every science has what are called *primitive terms*. That is, every science has ideas or concepts which are so *elemental* that they are exceptionally difficult to define.

For example, "energy" and "matter" are two primitive terms in the field of physics. You must have a rough notion of what these words mean, but you should also realize that great philosophical battles have been fought over their exact definitions.

Psychology has its primitive terms too. One of these is *consciousness*. (Another, in case you're wondering, is *mind*.) The dictionary gives many definitions of "consciousness," most of which have to do with awareness, awakeness, understanding, being alert, or even being alive. Some of the dictionary meanings have to do with *self*-awareness, or the experience of knowing that you are having the expe-

rience of knowing. But no two psychologists will agree completely on the precise meaning of "consciousness" (or of "mind," for that matter).

● *Four Important Points about Consciousness*

We will have more to say about primitive terms (and consciousness and mind) in many other chapters. For the moment, there are four important points we should make about consciousness:

First, consciousness is a *process*, not a thing. Processes are much harder to measure—and to describe scientifically—than are things. You can describe a track shoe rather easily. Describing the *process of running*, however, is a more difficult task.

Second, consciousness is usually marked by a *subjective awareness of the passage of time*. When you are awake, you are aware that "the meter is running." When you are asleep, or when you are intoxicated, your sense of temporal duration is usually badly distorted, if not entirely absent. Thus, one important characteristic of an altered state of consciousness is a change in your *perception* of the passage of time.

The third point has to do with what we might call the "reality" of consciousness. Stevan Harnad notes that "self-awareness" is marked by a kind of *immediate certainty* that "settles all my doubts about whether I really have experiences. . . ." When you are in a state of "ordinary consciousness," Harnad believes, you don't have to ask people around you if you're dreaming; you *know* you're not. But when you've drunk too much booze, or gotten "high" on some drug, you may not always be so sure. Thus, a *change in the subjective experience of reality* is another hallmark of an "altered state of consciousness" (Harnad, 1984).

Fourth, there is an odd and little understood relationship between *language* and *consciousness*. For example, consider the views of Michael Gazzaniga, whose research on split-brain patients we discussed in the previous chapter. Gazzaniga believes that your "stream of consciousness" is a continuous *story* or narrative that your left hemisphere produces in order to *explain* what happens to you—and why you do what you do (Gazzaniga, 1985). Not all psychologists agree with Gazzaniga, but

Normal consciousness includes the awareness of the passage of time.

almost everyone admits there is *some connection* between "being conscious" and the "inner dialogue with yourself" that you engage in while you are awake.

Consciousness is a *subjective state* or "internal process." But it is controlled in large part by physical activities in our brains and bodies. Before we can discuss consciousness further, therefore, we must take a closer look at the biological rhythms that influence our states of awareness.

BIOLOGICAL RHYTHMS

Your body goes through rather regular *biological cycles* every day. Many of these cycles reach a peak at some regular point during the day or night. These cycles are often called **circadian rhythms**, a technical term that means "a repeating pattern of activity that runs about 24 hours in length."

Your temperature, for instance, is usually lowest in the middle of the night. It begins to rise a few hours before you get up in the morning, and reaches the "normal" (98.6° F.) around 6 p.m. Then your temperature begins to drop, moving down toward its nighttime low.

Your blood sugar level, pulse rate, and blood pressure also reach peaks around 5 or 6 p.m. Your sensory abilities—hearing, vision, taste, and smell—also are at their best in the late afternoon. Unlike blood pressure and temperature, however, your sensory acuity reaches a second peak around 3 a.m. (Moore-Ede, Sulzman, & Fuller, 1982).

Other biological cycles reach their high points at different times of day. For example, the amount of male hormone present in the bodies of most men is greatest at about 9 a.m. And the amount of calcium in the blood in both males and females usually peaks at midnight (Moore-Ede, Sulzman, & Fuller, 1982).

The most obvious circadian rhythm is probably the sleep/waking cycle. Most of us are active for some 16 hours each day, but are inactively asleep for the other 8 hours. Before we discuss the sleep/waking cycle, though, there are several general points we should make about biological rhythms.

1. Most **biological clocks** run on a circadian rhythm (under normal conditions). But some cycles are shorter or longer than 24 hours.
2. There is tremendous individual variability among people as far as their biological rhythms are concerned.
3. Most of your biological clocks are controlled by various sub-centers in your brain. The overall pattern of activity in these sub-centers was probably determined by your genes and "set" at birth. However, day-to-day *changes* in your activity cycles are

strongly influenced by inputs from your external environment (Moore-Ede, Sulzman, & Fuller, 1982).

Let's look at all three points in detail.

• Short and Long Cycles

Sleep is a good example of a biological rhythm that runs less than a day in length. As you will soon see, sleep is actually made up of a repeating sequence of events. Each individual sleep cycle runs about 90 minutes (Moore-Ede, Sulzman, & Fuller, 1982).

The female menstrual cycle, which runs about 28 days, is an example of a much longer biological rhythm.

• Individual Variability

Your biological rhythms may peak at quite different times than do those of the people around you. And, as you surely know, your own cycles may be disrupted under many different circumstances, such as sickness or a long trip on a jet airplane (Aschoff, Daan, & Groos, 1982).

Research conducted on Swedish soldiers by T. Akerstedt and J.E. Froberg suggests there may be "morning persons" and "evening persons." Akerstedt and Froberg asked their subjects a series of questions designed to find out whether the men were more active during the day or at night. Some of the men preferred daytime activities and were early risers (the "morning persons" group). Others said they typically did better at night and hence were late risers (the "evening persons" group). The rest of the soldiers (the "intermediate group") had no clear-cut preference (Akerstedt & Froberg, 1976; Torsvall, Akerstedt, & Froberg, 1985).

Next, Akerstedt and Froberg measured the soldiers over a period of several months. The scientists found that, overall, **adrenalin** levels for "morning persons" tended to be higher than for "evening persons." Thus, "morning persons" probably are a bit more active physically than "evening persons" are. However, as you might suspect, adrenalin levels were higher *early in the day* for "morning persons," but higher *at night* for "evening persons." The circadian rhythm for temperature differed significantly for the two groups as well. The results for the "intermediate group" were, as expected, in between these two extremes.

• Genetic Influences on Circadian Rhythms

Recent studies suggest that your genes probably determine whether you become a "morning person" or an "evening person." University of Florida researchers Wilse Webb and Scott Campbell studied the sleep patterns of identical and fraternal twins. Webb and Campbell found that *identical* twins were remarkably similar in terms of their sleep patterns. They took about the same length of time to fall asleep, had about the same number and duration of waking and dream periods during the night, alternated between the various stages of sleep in similar ways, and slept for similar lengths of time. However, *fraternal* twins were alike *only* in terms of the amount of time they slept.

Wilse Webb concludes that "The centers in the brain that control our sleep requirements and patterns appear, in large measure, to be genetically programmed from birth" (Webb, 1983).

Early Influences on Biological Rhythms

According to S.M. Reppert, circadian rhythms begin to show up in rat fetuses several days *before the pups are born*. Once these rhythms appear, they are "set" by chemical signals from the mother's body that apparently pass through the **placenta**. As a consequence, the fetuses'

biological clocks run on the same schedule as does the mother's prior to birth. "The fetus always knows what time of day it is relative to the outside world," Reppert says.

Once the fetuses are born, their rhythms remain **entrained** to the mother's rhythms for at least a week or so, according to Reppert. However, if the newborn pups are nursed by a foster mother with different rhythms, the infant rats' rhythms slowly begin to drift toward the foster mother's cycles. Infant monkeys show a similar *entrainment* to their mother's biological clocks as do infant rats (Reppert, 1985).

□ □ **QUESTION** □ □
Most rat mothers give birth at night. Why might it be important for the mother and her unborn pups to have similar biological rhythms?

Resetting Your Biological Clocks

Biological clocks are typically *set* by external events. If you live on the East Coast of the US, and you are a "morning person," your clocks will normally operate on Eastern Time. If you fly to Los Angeles, you will often experience several days of confusion as your body tries to reset all its clocks so they operate on Pacific Time. When you fly back to the East Coast, you will undergo a similar sort of *jet lag*. In either case, however, once your biological clocks have stabilized, they still will run on a 24-hour cycle.

Scientists have, on occasion, studied the effects of putting people in highly controlled environments that ran on "22-hour days" or "28-hour days." In these laboratory situations, for example, the lights might be on for 11 hours, then off for 11 hours. Generally speaking, the subjects adapted fairly readily to a change in length of day that wasn't more than an hour or two different from the normal 24-hour cycle. They did not adjust well to extremes, however, such as 18-hour or 30-hour days (Moore-Ede, Sulzman, & Fuller, 1982).

Oddly enough, if we remove all environmental cues, you won't set your own "24-hour cycle" and follow it without fail. Rather, if you have no *sensory inputs* to tell you what time of day it really is, your sleep/waking rhythm will soon settle down on a day-length of about 25 hours (Moore-Ede, 1982). Unfortunately, there is not much agreement among the experts as to why your sleep/waking rhythm runs on a 25-hour cycle rather than a 24-hour cycle in the absence of all external cues.

People who travel across many time zones, or who "change shifts" on the job, often must reset their biological clocks radically, and in a brief period of time. Various types of sleeping pills can often speed up the process of putting you on a new sleep cycle, but the drugs also typically cause you to perform poorly on men-

WIZ FIPPLE AND HIS CIRCADIAN RHYTHMS!

tal tasks for several days thereafter (Winfree, 1986). Swedish researcher T. Akerstedt believes that both "jet lag" and "changing shifts" should be considered *types of insomnia*. He recommends that the best way to overcome such problems is to force yourself to follow a new sleep/waking cycle as soon as possible (Akerstedt, 1985). As we will see, that prescription is probably the best advice for handling *any* type of insomnia.

□□ **QUESTION** □□

When President Reagan flew to China, he stopped en route for several days in Hawaii. What have you learned about jet lag that would suggest this was a good idea?

Effects of Melatonin on Biological Clocks

Buried away inside your brain is a tiny subcenter called the **pineal gland**. More than 2,000 years ago, a Greek physician named Herophilus stated that the pineal gland was the "gatekeeper" which regulated the flow of thoughts through the mind. The noted French philosopher René Descartes called the pineal gland "the seat of the soul." In fact, the pineal gland is neither. Rather, as very recent studies show, its main function seems to be that of producing *melatonin,* a hormone that affects both the sleep/waking cycle and the body's responses to the annual cycle of seasons.

• Melatonin and the Sleep Cycle

Under normal circumstances, the level of melatonin builds up in the body during darkness, but decreases during the day. In most "morning persons," the peak amount of melatonin tends to occur at 2 a.m.—just when they report they are most sleepy (Fellman, 1985). And according to MIT scientist Harris Lieberman, volunteers given injections of melatonin at noon got very sleepy and showed a significant slowdown in their reaction times (Lieberman, 1985).

This daily build-up of melatonin occurs in most animals as well as in humans, and seems to be controlled by the onset and offset of *visual stimulation* from the external environment. If you blind an animal—or if you cut the neural pathways running from the optic nerve to the pineal gland—the melatonin cycle no longer matches the environmental light/dark cycle and the animal's sleep/wake cycle changes dramatically (Fellman, 1985).

Daily injections of melatonin in laboratory animals tend to "set" their activity cycles to the time of the injection rather than to normal cues from the external environment. Rats are nocturnal, which is to say they are typically more active at night than during the day. Jenny Redman, Stuart Armstrong, and Kim Ng at La Trobe University in Australia found that injecting mel-

Seasonal behaviors in many species, including the migratory habits of birds, are influenced by melatonin.

atonin into rats caused the animals to *begin* their daily activity cycles at the time of the injection instead of when darkness fell. However, similar injections given to birds (who are active during the day) caused the animals to *end* their activity cycles and go to sleep even when the injections were given early in the day (Redman, Armstrong, & Ng, 1983).

□□ **QUESTION** □□

How might melatonin be used to help fight the effects of "jet lag"?

Melatonin, Mating, and Seasonal Depression

Recent evidence suggests that melatonin influences not only the day/night activity cycle, but also the annual cycle that most animals show to the year-long parade of seasons. Animals whose pineal glands are removed become abnormal in many respects: Deer grow antlers at the wrong time of the year, some birds fail to migrate south for the winter, and many species fail to hibernate at the proper time of the year (Fellman, 1985).

• Melatonin and Mating

University of Texas biologist Russel Reiter and his colleagues have studied the influence of seasonal change on the mating behavior of the Syrian hamster. In the wild, the animal only breeds during the spring and summer and hibernates during the winter. At the start of the autumn season, as the days grow shorter and the nights grow longer, the hamster's reproductive organs shrivel and all but disappear. At the same time, there is a build-up of melatonin in the animal's body. About half way through the winter hibernation, however—just when the days start growing longer again— melatonin levels decrease and the hamster's reproductive organs begin to grow. By the time the animal emerges in the spring, it is ready to mate and reproduce. This same pattern also is found in other hibernating animals (Brainard *et al.*, 1982; Stanton, Craft, & Reiter, 1984).

If the pineal gland is removed, the hamster's sex organs don't regress and the animal continues to mate even during the winter months. According to Reiter, "By mechanisms we still don't understand, the pineal system influences seasonal variation in such things as temperature regulation, deposition of body fat, hibernation, and reproduction" (cited in Fellman, 1985).

In humans there is some evidence—still highly controversial—that a decrease in melatonin levels may "trigger" the hormonal changes that occur at the onset of puberty. For example, MIT biologist Richard Wurtman and his colleagues reported in 1984 that the amount of melatonin children produce declines by 75 percent between early childhood and puberty (Wurtman & Waldhauser, 1984). However, several other scientists have been unable to confirm these results, so the issue still is in doubt. It is true, however, that the *amount of sleep* children need decreases significantly between early childhood and puberty. And since high melatonin levels seem to trigger sleep onset (and duration) in humans, perhaps Wurtman and his colleagues are on the right track.

• Melatonin and SAD

Recent research also suggests that melatonin may be involved in the onset of what is called **seasonal affective disorder**, or SAD.

As the length of day decreases in the fall, some people living far north of the equator begin to overeat, oversleep, and become severely depressed. Come springtime—and the increase in daylight hours—their problems tend to disappear. (The symptoms of SAD also diminish significantly if the person "goes south for the winter"—that is, goes to a part of the world where the days are longer during the winter months.) Some—but not all—of the patients also go through a "manic phase" during the summer months, when the days are particularly long.

Recent research by Alfred J. Lewy and his colleagues in Portland, Oregon, suggests that almost all individuals afflicted with SAD may have abnormal daily melatonin rhythms. In 18 out of 19 patients studied by Lewy and his group, melatonin levels peaked several hours *after* the normal maximum reached at 2 a.m. Such a late melatonin peak, of course, would suggest that SAD patients become sleepiest late in the morning, rather than late in the evening. Lewy reports that exposure to two hours of very bright light as soon as the individuals woke up each morning has led to a marked improvement in almost all SAD patients tested so far (Lewy *et al.*, 1987). Lewy believes that daily treatment with bright light may "reset" the patients' abnormal melatonin cycles.

We might note two things: First, while SAD patients suffer from depression, there is as yet no reliable evidence that *all* depressive patients can be helped with "bright light" treatment. Second, there is no agreement among researchers as to what type of light is needed, how bright the light should be, or at what time of day (or night) the SAD patient should be exposed to the light (Bower, 1986c).

□ □ **QUESTION** □ □
What kind of melatonin cycle would you expect to find in people who suffer from insomnia?

SLEEP

Sleep is obviously an interruption in your normal stream of consciousness—that much is clear. But scientists are still uncertain as to what sleep actually is or what functions it serves. In his book *Sleep: The Gentle Tyrant*, University of Florida psychologist Wilse Webb notes there are two major theoretical explanations for sleep:

- The first is that sleep is an *adaptive response* that increases an organism's chances of surviving.
- The second theory is that sleep is a "restorative process" that allows the body (and perhaps the mind) to repair the day's damages (Webb, 1975).

Let's look briefly at both these theories.

• Sleep as an Adaptive Response

Imagine yourself as a primitive human living on earth thousands of years ago. What sorts of behaviors would increase your chances of surviving? During the day, you'd have to be actively engaged in finding things to eat—and in protecting yourself from those animals that would like to dine on *you*.

But what would you do at night? For, without artificial light, you wouldn't be able to see either food or danger. If you went to sleep at night instead of remaining active, you could conserve your energy and avoid the terrors of the night. As Wilse Webb puts it, "Sleep, then, can be thought of an an instinctive response which is useful in 'keeping us out of harm's way'" (Webb, 1975).

• Sleep as a Restorative Process

If you ask people why they sleep, Wilse Webb says, most of them will respond, "To rest." According to the "restorative theory of sleep," you burn up energy during the day. Thus, you need to remain quiet for long hours each night to "recharge your batteries" (Webb, 1983).

It certainly is true that you often go to bed feeling tired and out of sorts, and wake up the next day feeling much better. It's also the case that, when you're weary, you *feel* the need for sleep—just as you feel the need for food when you're hungry. But does *unconscious* sleep help your body recover more than would "deep rest" in which you stayed peacefully awake? The answer seems to be "no." For scientists have yet to discover any type of restorative process that functions *only* when you are unconscious (Webb, 1982).

• Comparing the Two Theories

Wilse Webb points out there is no way to know which of the two approaches to explaining sleep is correct. Indeed, Webb says, both theories have some validity to them. Because you are relatively immobile when you sleep, you do tend to stay out of harm's way. But it is also more likely you will get your daily "restorative rest" if you feel a need for sleep—and if you are unconscious while resting (Webb, 1975).

□ □ QUESTION □ □
People spend about one-third of their lives in sleep. But less than 2 percent of all psychological research is on sleep and dreaming. How many reasons can you think of to explain why scientists have studied "awakeness" so much more than "sleep"?

SLEEP CYCLES

Sleep is part of your daily activity cycle. But how much you sleep—and when and how deeply you sleep—are determined as much by psychological and social factors as by biological "needs."

Amount of Sleep

Generally speaking, the younger you are, the more you sleep and the deeper your sleep is likely to be. Newborn infants sleep about 16 hours each day/night cycle. This sleep is scattered in six or more bursts of a few hours each, for newborns sleep as much during the day as at night.

During the first year of life, the amount of sleep an infant needs decreases by two hours or more. By six months of age, 80 percent of the infants in one recent study were "sleeping through the night" and taking short naps during the day. By age two, the child sleeps about 12 hours a day, including about 90 minutes of daytime naps (Webb, 1975).

According to Wilse Webb, the major change during the infant's first two years is a decrease in the *amount of daytime sleep*. This change occurs in almost all infants. Therefore, this developmental sequence probably is controlled primarily by genetic factors.

By adolescence and early adulthood, the amount of daily sleep has dropped to about 8 hours. Wilse Webb found that University of Florida students averaged about 7 hours and 40 minutes of sleep at night. In addition, they napped about 25 minutes per day. During the two-week period the students were studied, 84 percent of them took at least one nap and about 42 percent napped daily or almost every day. There was considerable variation, however. Some students averaged but 6 hours per day; others got as much as 10 hours of sleep per 24-hour period. And almost all the students slept more on weekends than during the week (Webb, 1982).

Older people tend to sleep less deeply than do infants or young adults. By 40 or 50 years of age, people wake up more frequently during the night. And by age 60, almost everyone naps on a regular basis. A recent study of 77-year-old men and women suggests these older individuals nap (on the average) twice a day and get about 10 percent of their daily sleep during the day (Moore-Ede, Sulzman, & Fuller, 1982).

These data, however, are for people in the US who live in more-or-less normal circumstances. In other countries, a nap or "siesta" is part of the daily routine for people of all ages. And in the US, people in institutions, individuals who work at night, and persons who are

Wilse Webb

Afternoon naps, or siestas, are as common for adults as for children in many countries.

sick or experiencing other unusual situations will often show quite different sleep patterns no matter what their age.

Sleep Stages

As Wilse Webb puts it, "Sleep is not simply a 'turning off' or 'going flat' or a 'nothingness' in which we lie awash. It is a very busy and active state of affairs" (Webb, 1975). In fact, there are at least six different stages of sleep, each marked by its own pattern of brain waves that can be measured with an EEG machine. If you are an average sleeper, your cycle will go something like this:

- ### Stage 0 Sleep

When you first try to fall asleep, your muscles will relax, and your breathing will slow and become quite regular. Your brain waves slow down a bit too, with alpha waves predominating (see Fig. 3.1). This period is called *Stage 0 sleep*, or "pre-sleep." Stage 0 sleep is little more than a transition from being awake to being asleep. According to Wilse Webb, you spend from 0 to 3 percent of a night's sleep in Stage 0.

- ### Stage 1 Sleep

For the next few minutes, as you relax more deeply, you will be in *Stage 1* of the sleep cycle. Alpha waves disappear and your brain waves show irregular patterns. The disappearance of the alpha rhythm marks the real start of sleep. You spend from 1 to 10 percent of a night's sleep in Stage 1 sleep.

- ### Stage 2 Sleep

It is during this stage that your brain shows **sleep spindles** (see Fig. 3.2), which are bursts of waves that occur about 13–16 times per second. According to Webb, you spend from 40 to 60 percent of a night's sleep in Stage 2.

- ### Stage 3 Sleep

Stage 3 sleep is a brief transition period, during which your brain waves slow down even more and sleep spindles tend to disappear. The slow waves that characterize deep sleep also begin to appear. From 3 to 12 percent of sleep generally occurs at the Stage 3 level.

- ### Stage 4 Sleep

About 40–60 minutes after you lose consciousness, you typically reach the deepest sleep of all. Your brain will show **delta waves**, and it will be very difficult for anyone to awaken you. This is *Stage 4 sleep*, and it is during this stage that sleeptalking, sleepwalking, nightmares, and (in young children) bedwetting occur. Webb states that from 5 to 25 percent of your night's sleep is at Stage 4 (Webb, 1975).

- ### Stage 1-REM Sleep

You may think that you stay at this deep fourth stage all the rest of the night, but that turns out not to be the case. Instead, about 90 minutes after you fall into slumber, your activity cycle will increase slightly. The delta waves will disappear, to be replaced by the *beta waves* that signal an active or "awake" brain. Your eyes will begin to dart around under your closed eyelids as if you were looking at something occurring in front of you. This period of *Rapid Eye Movements* is called **REM** sleep. During the first sleep cycle, REM sleep usually lasts from 8 to 15 minutes. In subsequent cycles, REM sleep may last for 40 minutes or more. Overall, you spend from 15 to 35 percent of the night in REM sleep. (This and subsequent "Stage 1" periods differ from the first Stage 1 episode of the night since they typically involve REM and dreaming, while the first Stage 1 period doesn't.)

- ### Later Cycles

The description we've just given is for the first sleep cycle, which usually lasts about 90 minutes. Occasionally (particularly if you are older) you may wake up briefly during the transition between Stage 4 and Stage 1-REM sleep. But if you don't awaken, your brain waves will slow again. If this is your first cycle of the night, you probably will slip down all the way to Stage 4 sleep once more. Later in the evening, you may go only as deep as Stage 2 or 3. Whatever the case, in the later stages of each subsequent cycle, your brain waves will speed up and you will go through another REM period (Webb, 1982).

According to Wilse Webb, "It is rare, once sleep has begun and is not interrupted, that a stage is 'skipped,' for instance, from 1 to 4 or 4 to 2. REM typically emerges from Stage 2" (Webb, 1975).

If you are like most people, you will experience four to five complete sleep cycles per night, but both the quality and the intensity of the experiences change the longer you stay asleep (see Fig. 3.3). Your first cycle usually yields the longest period of Stage 4 deep sleep, while your first Stage 1-REM period is typically the shortest. However, as Wilse Webb points out, "Although it does appear that there is an approximately 90 minute cycle associated with REM, we must recognize this as a group characteristic which contains a considerable variance

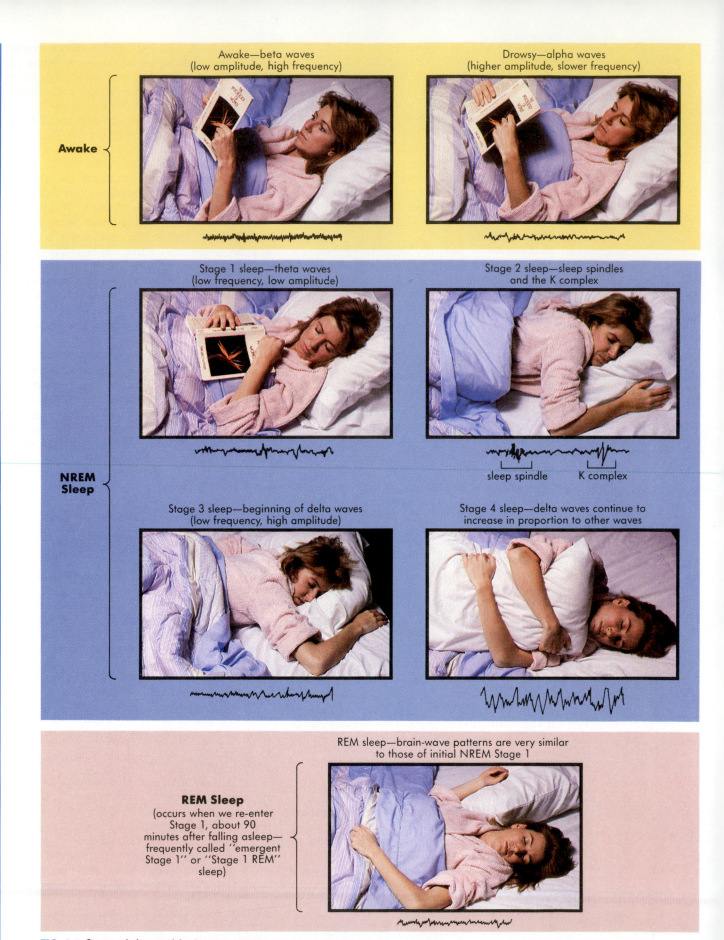

FIG. 3.1 Stages of sleep and brain wave patterns.

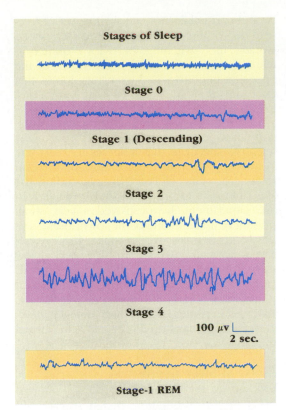

Stages of Sleep

Stage 0

Stage 1 (Descending)

Stage 2

Stage 3

Stage 4

100 μv |
2 sec.

Stage-1 REM

FIG. 3.2 Stages of sleep. The EEG records show the five stages of sleep, including Stage 1-REM. The brain-wave activity during Stage 0 is similar to the "activity rhythm" (beta waves) present when you are awake and conscious.

. . ." (Webb, 1982). Put more bluntly, people have widely different sleep patterns, most of which lie within the "normal range."

REM Sleep

Your eyes do not move constantly during REM sleep. Rather, as Webb notes, eye movements "tend to occur in 'bursts' of different 'densities' (eye movements per minute), with as much as five minutes between such bursts." However, there is much individual variation in such matters. Generally speaking, people who don't recall their dreams very well tend to have fewer eye movements per unit of time than do those who recall their dreams readily (Webb, 1982).

At the onset of Stage 1-REM sleep, males frequently experience an erection of the penis, and females frequently experience vaginal swelling and sometimes a hardening of their nipples. This sexual arousal typically occurs as the sleeper's brain "rises" from Stage 2 sleep and begins a Stage 1-REM sleep period.

Dreams, in one form or another, tend to occur throughout the sleep period. The way we know this is by waking people up at different points in the sleep cycle and asking them if they were dreaming. Generally speaking, most *organized* and *detailed* dreams occur during REM sleep. However, the connection between dreaming and REM sleep depends on how you define dreaming.

FIG. 3.3 The sleep record of one subject tested for three nights by Wilse Webb at the University of Florida. The first night, the subject had some difficulty adjusting to sleeping in the laboratory. Note that the REM periods increase significantly in length in the later sleep cycles of each night. In a good night's sleep, wakefulness gives way to deep sleep, then to the REM stage where most dreams occur. As the night wears on, dreams tend to lengthen.

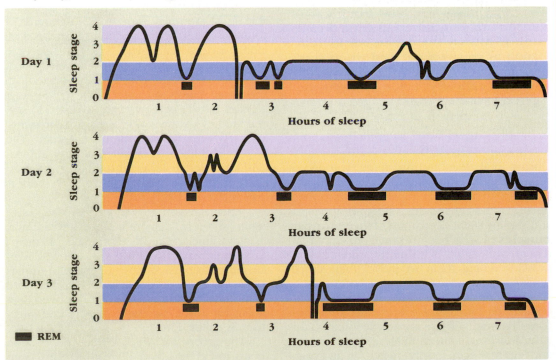

After looking over several experiments in which subjects were awakened at various times, Webb concludes that "If one required the dream to be a clearly present, visual, storylike event, then almost all such 'dreams' occurred with REM awakenings." However, Webb says, "If one accepted the presence of any mental content—'thinking about something' or a brief or vague recall of 'something' . . ." then *dreaming* occurs during all stages of sleep. Webb states that REM dreams produce more of what we tend to think of as dreams—visual, hallucinatory-type events. Non-REM awakenings produce more "thoughtlike" and realistic material (Webb, 1975).

The amount of REM sleep people need tends to decrease from infancy to adulthood. Infants spend about 40 percent of their sleep time in Stage 1-REM. Young adults get more sleep than do very old persons, but the amount of REM sleep is about 20 percent in both groups (Long, 1987).

Dreaming seems to be primarily a function of the right hemisphere. Scientists from several laboratories have found that the right half of the brain is much more active electrically during dreaming than is the left. And Roger Sperry notes that while many of his split-brain patients reported having vivid dreams prior to the surgery, they reported no dreams at all after the operation (Sperry, 1968). However, patients in other laboratories have given different reports, so the question is still in some doubt. It does seem possible, though, that the right hemisphere takes the lead during dreaming.

□ □ **QUESTION** □ □
Why might you have trouble consciously remembering your dreams unless you say the dream out loud as soon as you awaken? And when you first awaken in the morning, why might you have difficulty "talking sensibly and getting your act together" for a short period of time?

• *Dream "Paralysis"*
During REM sleep and dreaming, you are almost incapable of moving. The muscles in your body are relaxed but capable of movement during both light and deep sleep. However, as you slip into REM sleep, most of the **voluntary muscles** in your body become *paralyzed*. Although your brain often sends orders to your muscles telling them to move, they simply don't respond.

In more technical terms, REM sleep is accompanied by extensive *muscular inhibition* (see Chapter 2). There is one exception to this rule, however. During REM sleep your arms and legs may occasionally "twitch" in an irregu-

lar and unusual fashion. According to UCLA researchers Michael Chase and Francisco Morales, this "twitching" behavior is quite normal (in moderation) and is the result of the opposing inhibitory and excitatory forces that exist during REM sleep (Chase & Morales, 1983).

No one knows why this muscular inhibition takes place during REM sleep, but many scientists speculate that it serves to keep you from acting out your dreams. Adrian Morrison at the University of Pennsylvania studied the effect of brain lesions on REM sleep in cats. In one experiment, he destroyed a very small amount of tissue in one of the lower brain centers of his animals. While awake, the cats behaved normally. When an REM period occurred during their sleep, though, the animals raised their heads, moved about, and struck out at imaginary objects. Morrison believes that the lower brain center he destroyed *actively inhibits* the acting out of dream behavior in normal animals (Morrison, 1983).

Effects of Sleep Deprivation

You can go for many days without sleep—if circumstances force you to stay awake. But eventually your body will force you to drift off into slumber. Missing one night's sleep causes little change in your behavior. However, if you stay awake for more than 48 hours, you will probably begin to show an increased irritability and impulsiveness. Your decision-making processes will be affected, and you will react more slowly and make poorer intellectual judgments than you would when rested (Webb, 1982).

If you are deprived of sleep for 100 hours or more, you will very likely show considerable stress. You may experience "moments of confusion," lose your train of thought, become momentarily irritated, feel "spacy," or become quite **apathetic**. You may "misperceive" what is going on around you, become inattentive, and show bursts of anger. A few people—perhaps 5 to 10 percent of those tested in several studies—show panic behaviors or symptoms of some type of mental disorder. The surprising thing is, however, that most individuals can tolerate long periods of total sleep deprivation with so little change in performance (Webb, 1982).

Whenever you are allowed to sleep after being severely deprived, your cycles may change to include much more Stage 4 (deep) sleep than usual—and a good deal less REM sleep than than usual. However, several studies suggest that you are unlikely to sleep for more than 11–16 hours even after you've been kept awake for 10 days straight (Moore-Ede, Sulzman, & Fuller, 1982).

The record for *normal* sleep deprivation seems to be held by a 17-year-old San Diego

Roger Sperry

man. In 1966, he stayed awake for 11 days and nights (264 hours) in an attempt to set a record. When he finally went to bed, he slept but 14 hours, and needed no more than 8 hours a night thereafter (Moore-Ede, 1982).

Until recently, scientists assumed that no one had ever died of lack of sleep. However, in 1986 Italian and American researchers reported the case history of a 53-year-old man who died of exhaustion because he could no longer sleep. During his younger years, the man's sleep patterns had been more-or-less normal. However, at age 52, the man abruptly began to lose the ability to fall asleep. Within a few months, he was getting less than one hour of sleep a night. He sank deeper and deeper into a **stupor**, was unable to perform even the simplest of tasks, did not respond to sleep medication, and soon died. An **autopsy** showed a dramatic loss of nerve cells in the man's **thalamus**—a very important sub-center that channels inputs from the sense organs to the cortex. Further study showed that none of the man's family had normal brain wave activity during sleep, and that one of the man's sisters had also died from lack of sleep (Lugaresi *et al.*, 1986).

● *REM-Sleep Deprivation*

Several researchers have attempted to deprive human subjects of REM sleep by waking the subjects up each time REM sleep occurred. These subjects were allowed all the Stage 2, 3, and 4 sleep they needed. But whenever the subjects cycled up to Stage 1-REM, they were awakened. A few experimenters reported their subjects soon became cross and anxious and showed some signs of mental disturbance. However, most recent studies show little or no evidence of these kinds of symptoms. What is true, though, is that when REM-deprived subjects are allowed to sleep normally, they show what is called a **rebound effect**. That is, they show a great increase in Stage 1-REM sleep, and a marked decrease in Stage 4 deep sleep, for a night or two thereafter (Webb, 1982).

Brain damage may reduce the amount of REM sleep a person gets. Israeli researcher Peretz Lavie recently treated a 33-year-old man whose wife complained that he "shouted in his sleep." When Lavie studied the man's sleep patterns, Lavie discovered that the man showed no REM sleep at all for the first five nights, and only five minutes of REM for each of the next five nights. A brain scan revealed that the man had a piece of shrapnel buried deep in his brain—a "souvenir," Lavie says, of the 1970 war. Other than the occasional shouting while asleep, however, the man seemed to be completely normal (cited in Lawren, 1986).

Animals may be more sensitive to sleep- and dream-deprivation than humans are. University of Chicago scientists Carol Eastman and Allan Rechtschaffen found that rats totally deprived of sleep died after an average of 19 days. Animals deprived of REM sleep—but allowed as much Stage 4 sleep as they needed—died after 37 days (Eastman & Rechtschaffen, 1985).

Wilse Webb calls sleep a "gentle tyrant," and this tyrant struggles to assert its rights. As Webb puts it, "Sleep cannot be ignored or lost without worry or care. Sleep is a fundamental, built-in way of behavior. It is not something we can choose to do or choose not to do . . ." except for short periods of time (Webb, 1975).

SLEEP DISORDERS

There are a number of different types of *sleep disorders*. These include such things as involuntary sleep, the inability to get to sleep in the first place, the inability to stay asleep for very long, disruption of normal breathing during sleep, involuntary leg movements, and walking and talking while asleep. Let's look at these problems in some detail.

Narcolepsy

Suppose you were sitting in a chair after lunch, listening to a friend tell a very funny joke. At the "punch line," of course, you laughed loudly. And just as you did so, you fell asleep involuntarily and stayed asleep for several minutes. How would you explain this odd behavior?

The best explanation would be that you had just experienced an attack of **narcolepsy**, or a "sleep attack." This rare condition seems to affect 2 to 5 people per 1,000 (Herbert, 1983).

Narcolepsy can strike at any time, but according to Swedish psychiatrist Olle Hambert, it usually is associated with *pleasurable events*.

The person with this problem can often "ward off" the attacks in dangerous situations—but not always. The attacks typically occur one or more times per day, and sometimes are so severe that the individual cannot drive and may have problems getting (and keeping) a normal job (Hambert, 1984).

Many scientists believe that narcolepsy is a "hereditary disorder." However, French researchers Jacques Montplaisir and Gaetan Poirier doubt this is the case, since narcolepsy can affect one identical twin, but not the other (Montplaisir & Poirier, 1987).

Narcolepsy is *not* a form of epilepsy, since the EEG record shows the normal Stage 1-REM sleep pattern during an attack. Nor are there any known personality traits that are associated with narcolepsy. However, drugs that tend to suppress REM sleep are sometimes of considerable help to narcoleptic patients (Hambert, 1984).

Insomnia

People who suffer from narcolepsy have trouble staying awake. Individuals who experience **insomnia** have the opposite problem. William Dement, who founded the Sleep Laboratory at Stanford, says that almost everyone occasionally has problems getting to sleep. However, Dement estimates that more than 30 million Americans suffer from a *chronic* inability to initiate or to maintain sleep (cited in Hopson, 1986).

According to Wilse Webb, *insomnia* is "a summary term for all real and imagined failures of the sleep process." The word "imagined" is important for, as Webb notes, some people who claim to be insomniacs in fact show normal sleep when tested in the laboratory (Webb, 1975).

There are four main types of *real* insomnia:

1. *Sleep-onset insomnia*, in which the person cannot get to sleep in the first place.
2. *Sleep-awakening insomnia*, in which the person goes to sleep normally, then wakes up five or more times per night and spends at least 30 minutes awake during the night (while trying to go back to sleep).
3. *Early-termination insomnia*, in which the person wakes up after less than 6 hours of sleep and can't return to sleep at all.
4. *Light-sleep insomnia*, which is characterized by excessive amounts of Stage 1-REM sleep and/or greatly reduced amounts of Stage 4 deep sleep.

As you might suspect, insomnia is more common among older persons than young adults. According to William Dement, the average healthy older person either wakes up or

comes close to doing so about 153 times during a normal seven-hour sleep period. The typical 25-year-old, however, experiences only 10 arousals during the same period of sleep (cited in Fischman, 1986).

There are now numerous sleep clinics around the country that deal with insomnia and related sleep disorders with varying degrees of success. If you suffer from insomnia, the Sleep Disorders Center at Stanford recommends that you set up a *regular schedule* for going to bed and for getting up. The Center also states that sleeping pills are not a long-term solution to "the insomnia problem."

□ □ **QUESTION** □ □
Since sleep is a "gentle tyrant," you eventually get what sleep you really need. Why does this fact suggest that the *psychological discomfort* of insomnia is more important than the *physical effects*?

Sleepwalking

Until the 1960's, sleepwalking was considered to be either a personality disorder of some kind or an "acting out of dreams." Recent research suggests there is little connection between personality problems and sleepwalking. It does seem to "run in families," however, and is associated with other deep sleep disturbances, such as night terrors, sleeptalking, and (to some extent) bedwetting (Chase & Weitzman, 1983).

Sleepwalking almost always occurs during Stage 4 deep sleep, and almost never during Stage 1 REM sleep. Children—particularly those between 9 and 12 years of age—tend to sleepwalk more than do adults. And the problem seems to be more common than originally was thought to be the case. In one recent survey, almost 20 percent of the people questioned could recall one or more sleepwalking episodes (Chase & Weitzman, 1983).

Sleeptalking

Although there are many old beliefs that people who talk in their sleep tend to "tell secrets," the truth is quite different. Some 90 percent of sleeptalk occurs during dream-free sleep and is marked by rather unemotional and "situation-bound" discussions. The 10 percent or so of sleeptalk that occurs during dream sleep is more emotional and usually relates to the "dream in progress" (Kales & Kales, 1984).

Generally speaking, most sleeptalk occurs during Stage 0 or dreamless Stage 1 sleep. Thus the "talker" is really more awake than asleep—which explains why the person can respond to questions. There is no indication that sleeptalking is related to any personality traits or disorders and, at worst, it usually is little more

Insomnia (in-SOM-knee-ah). From Latin and Greek words meaning "sleeplessness." The most common type of sleep disorder.

Enuresis (en-your-REE-sis). From the Greek word *ourein*, meaning "urine." A fancy name for "bedwetting."

Apnea (AP-knee-ah). A brief cessation of breathing.

Nocturnal myoclonus (knock-TURN-al MY-oh-CLONE-us). *Nocturnal* means "night." *Myo* is the Greek word for "muscle," while *clonus* is the Greek word for "an involuntary series of alternating contractions and relaxations." Nocturnal myoclonus, therefore, is an involuntary series of "leg jerks" that occurs during sleep, or while you're trying to go to sleep.

than a minor social problem. However, sleep-talk can be a symptom of other difficulties; thus it usually is included in the list of "sleep disorders."

Bedwetting

Bedwetting, or **enuresis**, is one of the most common types of sleep disorders. In a large sample of children aged 4 to 14, some 29 percent reported recent episodes of bedwetting. The problem is more common in younger children than in older ones. But a recent survey suggests 1 percent of the 14-year-olds still wet the bed with some frequency. Boys are significantly more likely to experience the problem than are girls (Chase & Weitzman, 1983).

Enuresis tends to occur during non-REM sleep, and often happens during Stage 4 deep sleep. Bedwetting may occur for many reasons, including stress, physical problems, and poor training. The behavior therapies (see Chapter 19) are often of some help in solving the problem.

□ □ **QUESTION** □ □

Why can we be reasonably sure that neither sleeptalking nor enuresis would generally occur during REM sleep?

Apnea and Myoclonus

One of the most common sleep disorders—particularly among older people—is sleep **apnea**, or the tendency to stop breathing during sleep. Another, and apparently related sleep disorder, is **nocturnal myoclonus**—uncontrollable leg movements during sleep. A recent study in San Diego of 427 individuals age 65 or older reveals that 48 percent of them suffered from either sleep apnea or myoclonus, while an additional 10 percent suffered from both problems (Fischman, 1986).

The most common type of sleep *apnea* involves a blockage of the throat muscles involved in breathing. It occurs much more frequently in people who snore than those who don't. But apnea may also be caused by activity in the brain itself—perhaps by the same mechanisms that paralyze the voluntary muscles during dreaming. Psychiatrist Anthony Kales be-

lieves that many older persons who die "of natural causes" while asleep may have stopped breathing for too long a period during an attack of sleep apnea (Kales *et al.*, 1982).

People who suffer from *nocturnal myoclonus* usually kick and jerk their legs uncontrollably during sleep. Many of them also suffer from "nervous legs"—tingling feelings in the legs, or a vague uneasiness that can be relieved only by moving them about. myoclonus is usually not "life threatening," but can cause insomnia because the person usually wakes up after each episode—and myoclonus can occur hundreds of times each night.

Scientists are not yet sure what causes nocturnal myoclonus. However, learning to sleep in a different position—and learning to relax prior to going to sleep—are two suggestions most sleep clinics make to people who suffer from apnea and myoclonus (Kales & Kales, 1982).

□ □ **QUESTION** □ □

About half the people who seek treatment for "excessive daytime sleepiness" also suffer from apnea and/or myoclonus. Why isn't this fact particularly surprising?

DREAMS

We've always known that sleeping people dream, but we didn't know much about the frequency of dreaming until the early 1950's. Prior to that time, scientists could do little more than record what people remembered about their dreams. However, some people insisted they never dreamed at all; other individuals were confident that they dreamed the whole night long. Little wonder we learned so little about dreaming until recently.

We now know that everyone dreams *several times a night*, during each sleep cycle. For in 1953 Nathaniel Kleitman and Eugene Aserinsky discovered the connection between REM sleep and dreaming by waking up their subjects at various times during the sleep cycle (Aserinsky & Kleitman, 1953).

If Kleitman and Aserinsky woke up their subjects during deep sleep (Stages 3 and 4), the subjects seldom reported they were dreaming. However, if the subjects were awakened during Stage 1, or particularly during REM sleep, the subjects frequently stated they had been dreaming and could almost always describe what they had just dreamed.

● *Dream Frequency*

According to Kleitman (and most other authorities), you usually have several dreams within each REM period. Each dream probably runs from a few seconds to several minutes in length. And since REM periods at the beginning of your sleep tend to be the shortest, you probably dream less in the early evening than later on (Kleitman, 1987).

Dream Content

If you are like most people, your first dreams of the night will tend to be rather dull and trivial—mostly having to do with things you have done during the day. In later REM periods, however, your dreams will probably become more unusual, vivid, colorful, easier to remember, and sometimes more anxiety-provoking. During any one REM period, you are likely to experience a *sequence of related dreams*, or to run through the *same dream two or three times*. Mostly, though, you will dream about things that are of some interest or importance to you (Corsi-Cabrera *et al.*, 1986; Webb, 1975; see Table 3.1).

There is little or no agreement among the experts as to the *significance* of what people dream. As we will see in a later chapter, Sigmund Freud thought that dreams revealed a person's fears and anxieties. And there is some evidence that people who have dreams that recur almost nightly for long periods of time may suffer from stress and anxiety (Bower, 1986a). Most modern-day sleep experts, however, disagree with Freud. Indeed, at an international conference during the 1970's, nine noted sleep researchers "agreed to disagree" on whether the content of dreams tells us anything important about the dreamer (Cartwright, 1972).

• *Lucid Dreaming*

Most people state they have little conscious control over what happens in their dreams. In recent years, however, psychologists have developed ways of helping people maintain "conscious awareness" that they are dreaming even while the dream is taking place (Galvin, 1982).

The act of maintaining some low level of consciousness during REM periods is often called *lucid dreaming*. According to Stanford psychologist Stephen P. LaBerge, lucid dreaming is most likely to occur during the last dream cycles of the night. LaBerge states that, during a lucid dream, you are aware that your "experiences" were dreams rather than reality, and you can remember the dream quite well after you have wakened.

"Dreaming lucidly of doing something is more like doing it than imagining it," LaBerge reports. During sexual lucid dreams, for example, you undergo physiological changes that are remarkably similar to those that occur during actual sexual activity, LaBerge claims. Sometimes you can even evaluate what is happening during the dream, and take an active role in resolving the conflict that occurs in a lucid dream (Gackenbach *et al.*, 1985; LaBerge, 1985).

TABLE 3.1 Percentage of College Students Who Have Experienced Common Dream Themes

Have you ever dreamed of . . . ?	%
1. being attacked or pursued	82.8
2. falling	77.2
3. trying again and again to do something	71.2
4. school, teachers, studying	71.2
5. being frozen with fright	58.0
6. sexual experiences	66.4
7. eating delicious food	61.6
8. falling with fear	67.6
9. arriving too late, e.g., missing the train	63.6
10. fire	40.8
11. swimming	52.0
12. dead people as though alive	46.0
13. being locked up	56.4
14. loved person as dead	57.2
15. snakes	48.8
16. being on verge of falling	46.8
17. finding money	56.0
18. failing an examination	38.8
19. flying or soaring through air	33.6
20. being smothered, unable to breathe	44.4
21. falling without fear	33.2
22. wild, violent beasts	30.0
23. being inappropriately dressed	46.0
24. seeing self as dead	33.2
25. being nude	42.8
26. killing someone	25.6
27. being tied, unable to move	30.4
28. having superior knowledge or mental ability	25.6
29. lunatics or insane people	25.6
30. your teeth falling out	20.8
31. creatures, part animal, part human	14.8
32. being buried alive	14.8
33. seeing self in mirror	12.4
34. being hanged by the neck	2.8

If you could control the content of your dreams, you'd probably make them pleasant experiences. However, the most vivid (and disturbing) type of dream you are likely to have is one that you seldom have much influence over—the *night terror*. Let us now examine these terrifying dreams in some detail.

□□ **QUESTION** □□

How might the differing abilities of the two hemispheres help explain lucid dreaming—that is, the fact that one part of your mind can be dreaming while another is aware that a dream is taking place?

Night Terrors

Imagine yourself comfortably sleeping in your bed, unaware of everything around you. Then you slowly regain enough consciousness to realize that you are suffocating, that some heavy weight is lying on your chest and crushing your lungs. Realizing that your breathing has almost stopped, and that you are dying for air, you become terrified and scream. At once, you seem to awaken and perceive there is this

3 / Biological Rhythms: Sleep, Drugs, and Consciousness

thing hovering over you, crushing the very life out of your lungs. Despite a strange feeling of paralysis, you start to resist. Your pulse begins to race, your breathing becomes rapid, and you push futilely at the *thing* that is choking you to death. Your legs tremble, then begin to thrash about under the covers. You sweep the bed-clothes aside, stumble to your feet, and mumbling loudly to yourself, you flee into the darkness.

And then, all at once, you find yourself in your living room. The lights come on, the *thing* instantly retreats to the shadows of your mind, and you are awake. You are safe now, but you are intensely wrought up and disturbed. You shake your head, wondering what has happened to you. You can remember that you were fleeing from the *thing* which was crushing you. But you have forgotten your scream and talking in your sleep.

□ □ **QUESTION** □ □
What relationship do you see between this "night terror" dream and the behaviors that occur during sleep apnea and noctural myoclonus?

- **Stage 4 Night Terror**

The *thing* dream is a classic example of a *night terror*. According to Anthony Kales, a scientist at the Penn State Medical School, night terrors occur to but one person in several hundred. However, if someone else in your family has a history of night terrors, you are 10 times more likely to experience night terrors than would ordinarily be the case (Kales & Kales, 1984).

Unlike normal dreams and nightmares, which occur during REM sleep, a night terror typically occurs during Stage 4 sleep.

Unlike most other dreams, the night terror begins during Stage 4 (deep) sleep and not during an REM period. According to Vanderbilt psychologists Charles Carlson and David White, night terrors are a "nighttime disorder of arousal" that are often stress-related. Night terrors can also be triggered by highly-emotional environmental events, and by anti-depressant drugs (Carlson & White, 1982).

Night terrors are more frequent in children than in adults. They are almost always associated with sleepwalking, sleeptalking, and other types of sleep disorders. In a study by Charles Fisher and his colleagues at Mount Sinai Medical Center in New York, some 58 percent of the subjects who suffered from night terrors could remember part of what they experienced during the attack. The dream episodes included such things as being crushed, being enclosed, being abandoned, choking, dying, falling, and aggressive acts by others. Their sleeptalk typically matched the content of the dream. However, the subjects seldom remembered the extensive sleeptalking and screaming that characteristically appeared at the start of the attack (Fisher *et al.*, 1974).

Night terrors can be dangerous. Sleep researcher Ernest Hartmann reports the case history of a man who experienced a night terror while sleeping in his car by the side of a major highway. The man "sleep-drove" his car onto the highway and crashed into another automobile, killing three people. Hartmann admits this is an extreme case, but believes that night terrors are always a *potentially* dangerous experience for those few people who experience them (and for others who are around when the attack occurs) (Hartmann, 1983).

There are several reports in the literature suggesting that psychotherapy, behavior therapy, and use of tranquilizing drugs can be effective in reducing both the number and the severity of *night terror* attacks (Kales & Kales, 1984).

- **Anxiety REM Nightmare**

Much more common than the night terror is the *anxiety nightmare*, which occurs late in the sleep cycle at the end of a very long REM period. If you have an anxiety nightmare, your body will seldom be aroused to a panic state. In fact, there will really be little change in your body's *biological responses* during the nightmare. It is, therefore, the *psychological content* of the dream itself (being chased, falling, witnessing frightening events) that leads to the anxiety attack.

According to Ernest Hartmann, anxiety nightmares are most frequent when your psychological need for REM sleep is greatest. In his book *The Sleeping Pill*, Hartmann notes that various illnesses and high fevers often reduce the amount of REM sleep you experience. So do sleeping pills. Thus, anxiety nightmares often occur when you are recovering from sickness, or just after you have stopped taking sleeping pills. Hartmann warns that taking drugs to help you sleep can be dangerous. For once you stop using the drug, your REM sleep "rebounds" and you may have almost constant anxiety nightmares for several nights in a row. You may then return to the pills—not to put yourself to sleep, but to reduce your REM periods and hence get rid of all those disturbing anxiety nightmares (Hartmann, 1978).

Sleep and dreams are altered states of consciousness that most of us experience every evening. Now that we have talked about them at some length, suppose we look at some other types of altered awareness and then try to determine what *causes* your conscious awareness to shift from one state to another.

□ □ **QUESTION** □ □
A common anxiety nightmare is that of "running through molasses"—trying to escape something terrible, but not being able to move. What happens to your muscles during REM sleep that might help explain the commonness of this type of anxiety nightmare?

ALTERED STATES OF CONSCIOUSNESS

Psychologists generally assume that everything you feel or experience is mirrored in some way by the functioning of your body—particularly by the way in which your nervous system reacts. For example, when some change occurs in the *speed* at which your brain takes in and processes information, there is usually some corresponding change (1) in the way that you think and feel about yourself, and (2) in how pleasant or unpleasant you perceive the world around you to be.

Drugs are a *direct* or chemical method of speeding up or slowing down neural firing—a quick if sometimes deadly way that people have chosen for a great many centuries. When we look at the effects of drugs on human behavior in just a moment, we will find there is a chemical compound that can affect your brain almost any way you wish—but *usually at a cost of some kind*. However, the *environment* in which you take a drug—and your own *past experience* with and *personal expectations* about drugs—can strongly influence the actual effect the drug has on your thoughts, feelings, and behaviors. We'll talk about these environmental effects at the end of the chapter. First, let's look more closely at *drugs*.

DRUGS

A *drug* is usually defined as any substance that can affect the structure or functioning of your body. Actually, that definition doesn't mean very much. Almost any chemical will have some kind of effect on you—if you take a large enough dose, or take it the wrong way. For instance, water is not usually considered a drug, but if you get too much of it in your lungs, you may drown.

A more useful definition is the one we will use in this book: A drug is any chemical which, when taken in relatively small amounts, *significantly increases or decreases cellular activities somewhere in your body*.

Most of the drugs we will discuss in this chapter have their main effects on neural firing, usually by altering the rate or *speed* at which your nerve cells release synaptic transmitters. There are other ways that drugs can affect neural responses, but changing the *rapidity* of neural firing is perhaps the most common. Some drugs—such as caffeine—tend to *increase* the rate at which your neurons fire. Other drugs—such as sleeping pills—have an *inhibitory* effect on neuronal firing (Ray, 1983).

However, the actual effects a particular drug will have on a particular person are often complex and hard to predict. Thus, a drug that affects you one way might affect another person in quite a different manner. And a drug that has a mild effect on you at one time of day may be much more potent at some other point in your daily activity cycle. For example, *stimulants* are much more dangerous if taken at the height of your daily activity cycle than at the low point (Moore-Ede, Sulzman, & Fuller, 1982). We might assume, therefore, that "morning persons" should particularly avoid stimulants early in the day, while "evening persons" should particularly avoid stimulants at night. (And, since stimulants are dangerous drugs, the safest course is not to take them at all.)

Thus, in categorizing drugs, we will find it useful to ask four questions:

- Does the drug have a *specific* or a *general* effect on neural transmission?
- If the effect is general, does the chemical tend to *excite* (increase) or to *inhibit* (decrease) neural firing?
- If the effect is specific, does the drug mostly affect inputs, cortical processes, or outputs? That is, *where in the brain* does the drug produce its effects?
- Are the effects of the drug altered in any way by the *time of day* the drug is taken?

Let us begin by looking at drugs that influence almost every one of your nerve cells.

Drugs Affecting General Activity Levels

One of the most common effects a drug can have is to change your activity level. The more active you are physically, the more rapidly *most* of your neurons must fire. Anything that in-

Caffeine increases the rate at which neurons fire, thus speeding up all types of motor activities.

3 / Biological Rhythms: Sleep, Drugs, and Consciousness

Autonomic nervous system (aw-toh-NOM-ick). That part of the nervous system which controls involuntary activities such as breathing, heart rate, digestion, and so forth. See Chapter 8.

Amphetamines (am-FETT-ah-meens). A class of stimulants or "uppers," any of which may also be called "speed."

Paranoid schizophrenia (PAIR-uh-noid skits-zoh-FREE-knee-uh). The major symptoms of this type of "mental illness" are illogical thought patterns, changeable delusions, and sometimes vivid hallucinations. Delusions of persecution ("They're controlling my mind by radio waves") are most common.

Barbiturates (bar-BITT-your-rates). Neural inhibitors that come from barbituric acid, often used as sleeping pills. Not to be confused with narcotics, most of which come from opium or alcohol. Narcotics are more effective as pain-killers than are barbiturates, but both types of drug are habit-forming.

Analgesic (an-al-GEE-sick). From the Greek words meaning "no pain." Technically speaking, any drug that reduces pain without causing a loss of consciousness.

creases your activity level also causes more transmitters to be dumped into the excitatory synapses in your brain and also in the synapses between your motor nerves and your muscles (see Chapter 2).

- **"Uppers"**

"Uppers," or *psychic energizers*, are drugs that typically facilitate or increase synaptic transmission. "Uppers" therefore usually make you physically and mentally more active. They do this by affecting nerve cells in your **autonomic nervous system**, which controls such involuntary activities as breathing, heart rate, and so forth (Ray, 1983). We will have more to say about your autonomic nervous system in Chapter 8. For the moment, all you need to know is that psychic energizers speed up many of your bodily processes that are controlled by synaptic transmission. "Uppers" are also called

"I'LL HAVE TO GET DR. CURTIS TO REDUCE HIS DOSAGE OF THE MOOD-ELEVATOR."

stimulants, because they chemically stimulate your neurons into firing more often. And, as we noted, "uppers" have a more profound effect when taken at the height of your normal activity cycle (Moore-Ede, Sulzman, & Fuller, 1982).

Caffeine is perhaps the most common "upper" in our society. Less common—and considerably more dangerous—is a class of drugs called by such names as **amphetamines**, or pep pills. Amphetamine itself is often referred to as Benzedrine. Two other similar but more powerful drugs are Dexedrine and Methedrine. Since they all increase neural activity, any or all of these "uppers" can be referred to as *speed*.

Like any other drugs, "uppers" can be dangerous. For example, continued use of amphetamine (or any other type of "speed") can produce symptoms that are much the same as a severe mental disorder called **paranoid schizophrenia** (Ray, 1983).

- **"Downers"**

Drugs that slow down or inhibit neural activity go by the general name of "downers." The strongest "downers" in general use are the **barbiturates**, which are sometimes called "sleeping pills" because they depress neural activity so much they often put a person to sleep.

The *tranquilizers* are both more specific in their effects and usually less powerful than the barbiturates. Tranquilizers affect the nervous system in several different ways. However, many of them act by exciting those neurons which *inhibit* other nerve cells from firing.

"Downers" have physical and psychological side effects that range from mildly unpleasant to downright deadly. Wisely used, these drugs can be of considerable medical help. When abused, these chemicals can lead to depression and other severe types of mental disorders. According to many reports, "downers" are particularly likely to be abused by women (see Chapter 19) (Ray, 1983).

Drugs Affecting Sensory Input

Information about the world around you comes to you through your sensory receptors. As we will see in Chapter 12, if you were totally cut off from the outside world, you would rapidly stop being a normal human being. But not all of the sensory messages that reach your brain bring pleasant news. Some messages involve the experience of *pain*, a highly complex psychological experience we will discuss more fully in Chapter 13.

Aspirin is perhaps the most common **analgesic,** or pain-killing drug, known to humans. Along with caffeine, aspirin is one of the few drugs that almost everyone reading this book will have tried at least once. Aspirin occurs naturally in the bark of the willow tree and was first synthesized in 1860. Some 12 million kilograms (27 million pounds) of aspirin are consumed annually in the United States—enough to treat 17 billion headaches. As potent a painkiller as aspirin is, though, it is also a deadly poison that must be treated with respect. Perhaps 20 percent of the deaths by poisoning that occur in the United States each year are due to an overdose of aspirin. And when taken in large doses by a pregnant woman, aspirin may either kill the unborn child or cause the child to be badly deformed (Ray, 1983).

The Opiates

Aspirin is a mild pain-killer. In case of severe pain, a more potent medicine—such as an **opiate**—is needed. *Opiates* are derived from opium, a drug used for centuries as an analgesic in the Near and Far East. When the seed pods of the opium poppy are slashed, a sticky resin oozes out. This resin is collected by hand, heated and rolled into balls, and then smoked in tiny pipes as opium.

In 1806, **morphine** was first synthesized from opium. Since morphine can be injected directly into the body in controlled amounts, and since it lacks some of the side effects of opium, morphine rapidly gained wide use in medical circles.

No one really knows why the opiates reduce or kill the experience of pain. It seems likely, however, that these drugs stimulate inhibitory neurons which then "turn off" the synapses in your brain which are involved in processing the painful inputs (Ray, 1983).

The Opioid Peptides

Morphine has one terrible side effect: It is very *addictive*. The exact biological mechanism underlying addiction is still not fully understood. However, there is considerable evidence suggesting that *natural pain-killers* produced by the body itself may be involved. These naturally-occurring analgesics have many names, including **enkephalin**, and **endorphin**. However, they all fall into a class of compounds known as the **opioid peptides**. And when you learn how these natural analgesics work, you will understand a bit more about how they may be involved in morphine addiction (Krieger, 1983).

During the 1970's, scientists both in Great Britain and in the United States isolated the first of these natural pain-killers. The name they gave to this opioid peptide was *enkephalin*. We now know there are at least two enkephalins, which differ from each other only slightly. There also are several other similar substances found in the body that are known loosely as the "endorphins." Almost all these opioid peptides have pain-killing properties, and all are *neurotransmitters* (Krieger, 1983).

When an enkephalin—or an endorphin—is injected into the body, it appears to reduce pain at least as much as does morphine. However, the effects the opioid peptides have on both physical and mental processes are complex and—as we will see at the end of this chapter—perhaps a little surprising (Iversen, Iversen, & Snyder, 1983).

Solomon Snyder and his associates at Johns Hopkins University were among the first to identify enkephalin. Snyder believes the natural pain-killers your body normally produces are sufficient to protect you from many of the ordinary aches and pains of life. When you experience severe pain, however, you are likely to turn to stronger medicine, and morphine is one of the strongest yet available (Snyder, 1984a).

Opiate Addiction

If, for medical reasons, you were to take morphine, it would act much as the enkephalins and other opioid peptides do. That is, morphine (1) would block neural transmission in your pain centers, and (2) would stimulate certain nerve centers involved in experiencing pleasure. But according to Solomon Snyder, morphine also *inhibits the production of opioid peptides*. So, when you take morphine for any length of time, your body *stops* manufacturing its natural pain-killers almost entirely (Snyder, 1987).

If you use morphine daily for a month or so, you are likely to become **addicted** to the drug. Then, if you don't get your "daily fix," you feel miserable, you ache all over, you are depressed, and you may even experience convulsions. Why? Because, when you stop taking morphine, your body needs several weeks before it can replenish its supply of natural pain-killers. During this period of time, your body has no defense against pain. Thus, even the slightest cut or bruise will be **excruciatingly** unpleasant. Little wonder, then, that so few morphine addicts voluntarily withdraw from using the drug.

When enkephalin was first discovered, Snyder hoped that it might be useful in treating morphine addiction. After all, if we could find some way to get the body to manufacture large amounts of opioid peptides, we could probably reduce the **withdrawal symptoms** that occur when an addict is cut off from morphine. However, recent research suggests that the enkephalins are as addictive as morphine (Iversen, Iversen, & Snyder, 1983; Wei & Loh, 1976). If this is indeed the case, history will have repeated itself.

Late in the 1800's, scientists hunting for a non-addictive opiate (to replace morphine) stumbled upon **heroin**, which is also made from opium. Heroin is several times more powerful than morphine as a pain-killer. It gets

Opiate (OH-pee-ate or OH-pee-at). Any of the narcotic drugs that come from the opium poppy. Almost all opiates are habit-forming.

Morphine (MORE-feen). A product of opium. Morphine is a dream- or sleep-inducing drug and, like all opiates, is a powerful pain-killer.

Enkephalin (enn-KEFF-uh-linn). A natural pain-killer discovered in the brain by scientists in the US and Great Britain. There are two known types of enkephalins.

Endorphin (en-DORF-in). A type of natural pain-killer found in the body. Both the endorphins and the enkephalins are opioid peptides.

Opioid peptides (OH-pee-oid PEP-tides). Peptides are rather small molecules of a fairly specific type. The endorphins and the enkephalins are all peptides that resemble opiates such as morphine. Thus the endorphins and the enkephalins are included in a class of molecules called opioid peptides.

Addicted. There are at least two types of addiction, biological and psychological. In biological addiction, some "outside" drug (such as morphine) replaces an internal product, such as the endorphins. Thus, the body develops a physical "need" for the replacement chemical. Psychological addiction is a very strong habit not usually marked by a physical need. Most drug addictions have both physical and psychological components.

Excruciatingly (ex-CREW-she-ate-ting-ly). From the Latin word meaning "to nail to a cross." Anything that is excruciating is extremely painful.

Withdrawal symptoms. Those physical and psychological changes that accompany giving up a drug after you have become addicted to it. Vomiting, fever, loss of appetite, compulsive shivering, and hallucinations often accompany withdrawal from narcotics such as heroin.

Heroin (HAIR-oh-in). An opiate derived from morphine. Very addictive, or habit-forming.

Procaine (PRO-cane). Like Novocain (NO-voh-cane), a synthetic form of cocaine.

Euphoria (you-FOR-ee-ah). From the Greek word meaning "good feeling," hence a rush of pleasure.

NIMH. Short for National Institute of Mental Health. A government agency near Washington, DC that (1) performs psychological and psychiatric research "in house" and (2) offers financial support to scientists at various universities.

its name from *hero,* because this drug was supposed to be a "heroic" solution to the "morphine problem." So, in the early 1900's, morphine addicts were given heroin instead. Unfortunately, heroin soon proved to be even more addictive and dangerous than morphine. Because of its addictive qualities, heroin is seldom used as an analgesic in the US today—except by the million or so drug addicts who take it as regularly as their funds allow them to (Platt, 1986).

● **Local Anesthetics**

Laughing gas, or nitrous oxide, is another example of a pain-killer that once enjoyed great medical popularity but which is not used very much today. First discovered in 1799, nitrous oxide was employed by dentists and surgeons as an analgesic because it made their patients so "happy" that tooth-pulling and minor surgery didn't seem to hurt very much.

The effects of laughing gas were often unpredictable, however, and dentists soon began using cocaine instead. However, as Oakley Ray puts it, "The potential for misuse [of cocaine] soon became clear, and a search began for synthetic agents with similar anesthetic characteristics but little or no potential for misuse. This work was rewarded in 1905 with the discovery

of **procaine** (Novocain), which is still widely used" (Ray, 1983, p. 299). Both cocaine and procaine are *local anesthetics* that kill pain by *inhibiting neural transmission* wherever they are injected into the body.

Cocaine is a moderately strong drug made from the leaves of the coca plant. Cocaine, or "coke," is notorious for the rush of pleasure, or **euphoria**, it gives almost immediately after a person takes it (usually by sniffing). Frequent use of cocaine can lead to a variety of problems, however, including severe damage to the nose and throat. And recent research by **NIMH** researcher Robert Post suggests that repeated consumption of cocaine can lead to seizures and death (cited in Bower, 1986b).

Cocaine was first used as a local anesthetic in the late 1800's by a Viennese doctor named Carl Koller. Sigmund Freud, who also lived in Vienna, learned of Koller's work and began experimenting with the drug. Freud found it such a pleasurable medication he recommended it to his patients as a substitute for aspirin. In a letter to his future wife, written in 1884, Freud told her, "I take very small doses of [cocaine] regularly against depression and against indigestion, and with the most brilliant success." When he saw the bad effects cocaine frequently had, though, he changed his mind (Byck, 1974).

Americans were much slower to use cocaine "recreationally" than were Europeans. In a government study taken in 1972, 48 percent of young adults between 18 and 25 had used marijuana, but only 9 percent had tried cocaine. A similar study conducted in 1985 suggests that at least 40 percent of young adults had tried cocaine at least once. The percentage of young adults who admitted they had used cocaine at least once in the past 30 days increased from 1.6 million in 1977 to 5.8 million in 1985. In 1973, a national committee reported that there were "virtually no cocaine-related deaths" reported in the US. In 1985, however,

The thousands of deaths due to drug addiction are not confined to the U.S. These men are processing cocaine in a clandestine factory in Bolivia, a country where cocaine addiction is a serious problem.

some 580 people were reported to have died from an overdose of the drug that year (Kozel & Adams, 1986).

According to Vanderbilt psychologist Oakley Ray, "It has been known for many years that prolonged high doses of either cocaine or amphetamine produce the same toxic syndrome: enhanced sense of physical and mental capacity, loss of appetite, grinding of teeth . . . repetitious behavior, and paranoia" (Ray, 1983). Oakley Ray also points out that alcohol affects the way in which the body reacts both to uppers and downers. Thus, taking these drugs *in combination with alcohol* is particularly dangerous.

For the most part, cocaine users inhale, or "snort," the drug in powder form. However, by 1986 the number of users who "smoke" a processed type of cocaine known as *crack* had increased dramatically. In 1977, less than 1 percent of the people who sought emergency hospital assistance for cocaine abuse had smoked the drug. By 1986, however, this figure had increased to 14 percent (Kozel & Adams, 1986).

Drugs Affecting Central Processing

Analgesics reduce pain in one of two ways: They either prevent painful inputs from occurring, or they keep the inputs from stimulating the "pain centers" in your brain by inhibiting neural transmission (see Chapter 13). Which is to say that analgesics "work" because they prevent you from experiencing the world (and your body) as it really exists.

• Hallucinogens

The **hallucinogens** are a class of drug that work in quite a different way. Rather than affecting inputs, hallucinogenic drugs act on the central processing areas of the brain that try to "make sense" out of these sensory messages. And by speeding up some brain centers and inhibiting others, hallucinogens make you experience or perceive the world as it actually *isn't*.

LSD, **mescaline**, **psilocybin**, and **PCP** are perhaps the best-known hallucinogens in our society, although a wide variety of other drugs also fall into this category (Ray, 1983).

• LSD

According to Oakley Ray, LSD is an artificial or synthetic chemical not found in nature. It was first made in a Swiss laboratory in 1938. However, its rather profound effects on human behavior were not appreciated until five years later. In 1943 Albert Hofmann—the Swiss scientist who had first synthesized LSD—accidentally licked some of the drug off his fingers. About half an hour later, knowing that something unusual was happening to him, Hofmann decided to stop work and bicycle home

from the lab. Wobbling and weaving all the way, he finally made it. But by the time he reached his house, everything he saw looked so terrifying, Hofmann was sure he had gone mad (Ray, 1983).

Because LSD caused people who took it to experience some of the symptoms associated with schizophrenia, Hofmann believed the drug might be useful in brain research. Therefore, he suggested it be given to people with mental disorders. LSD was first tried with patients in a Swiss mental hospital. And, as is often the case when *any* new therapy is first tried, a few of these patients did seem to get better. Whether this improvement was due to the drug or to the special attention the patients got was never proven, however. Oakley Ray notes that "The potential value of the hallucinogens in the treatment of many disorders is still very much discussed and studied, and, as with most issues, a final resolution has not yet been reached" (Ray, 1983). However, a 1975 report from the National Institute of Mental Health states that "Research on the therapeutic use of LSD has shown that it is not a generally useful therapeutic drug."

Oakley Ray

• Mescaline and Psilocybin

Mescaline is a chemical found in buttons on the peyote cactus. It can also be produced in synthetic form in a laboratory. The hallucinogenic effects of mescaline have been known for centuries to Native Americans, who at times have eaten peyote buttons as part of their religious ceremonies.

Less well known is a drug called *psilocybin*, found in a mushroom that grows wild in certain parts of the world. Psilocybin also produces hallucinations and also has been used in religious ceremonies.

• PCP

PCP, or "Angel Dust," has replaced LSD and mescaline as the most abused hallucinogen in the US. Discovered in 1956 by Victor Maddox and Graham Chen in Detroit, PCP was used for a time as an anesthetic for both humans and animals. However, it was banned for human use after tests showed that in large doses it produced convulsions, uncontrollable rage, **coma**, and death.

In his 1981 book on PCP, Edward Domino notes that PCP acts as a **dissociative anesthetic**. That is, the drug doesn't make patients unconscious. Rather, it "disconnects" them from their bodies—and environments. One male subject who took PCP in an experiment reported his legs were "ten miles long." A female subject said, "I feel like the head of a pin in a completely black atmosphere." Domino believes that PCP inhibits neural activity in the *processing areas* of the brain. And by doing so, it induces psychological symptoms similar to

Hallucinogens (hal-LEW-sin-oh-jens). Drugs that affect sensory input neurons, or "processing" neurons, and hence "trick" you into seeing or hearing or feeling things that really aren't there.

LSD. Common name for d-lysergic acid di-ethyl-amide (dee-lie-SIR-gick A-sid di-ETH-ill-A-midd). Also called "acid." Synthetic hallucinogen first synthesized in Switzerland.

Mescaline (MESS-kah-lin). An hallucinogen found in the peyote (pay-YO-tee) cactus.

Psilocybin (SILL-oh-SIGH-bin). An hallucinogenic drug that comes from a wild mushroom.

PCP. Common name for phencyclidine (fenn-SIGH-kli-deen). Also called "Angel Dust."

Coma (KOH-mah). A deep sleep or state of unconsciousness usually brought on by illness or brain damage.

Dissociative anesthetic (diss-SOH-see-ah-tive ann-ness-THET-tick). To dissociate means "to pull apart." A dissociative anesthetic is a drug that kills pain by separating the mind from the body.

Psychosis (sigh-KO-sis). A very severe form of "mental disorder" which often requires hospitalization. Schizophrenia is a type of psychosis.

Cannabis (KAN-ah-biss). The common hemp plant, from which come such drugs as marijuana (also spelled marihuana) and hashish. In the Western world, the most widespread species is cannabis sativa (SAT-ee-vah), which grows wild in most of the continental US.

THC. An abbreviation for tetra-hydro-cannabinol (TET-trah HIGH-dro kan-NAB-ih-nol). Marijuana contains many chemicals, of which THC seems the main one that induces a "high." The "street drugs" sold as THC are usually some other substance, since THC loses its powers when exposed to air.

Chemotherapy (KEY-moh-THER-a-pee). Treatment that involves giving a person drugs or other chemicals to help the person get better.

those reported by people suffering from a variety of mental disorders (Domino, 1981).

One of the greatest dangers of PCP seems to be the *unpredictability* of its effects. Sometimes it causes euphoria, sometimes fear, sometimes rage, sometimes severe depression, and sometimes a complete loss of reality. In 1980, almost 50 percent of the patients admitted to mental hospitals for drug-related problems suffered from PCP **psychosis**. However, as Domino said recently, by 1988 abuse of PCP seemed to be falling off markedly. Oddly enough, Domino says, while street use of PCP has decreased, medical use has increased. For recent studies suggest that, when given to heart attack victims, PCP can protect against brain damage during the recovery period.

Effects of Hallucinogens

No one really knows why the hallucinogens affect people as they do. But according to Edward Domino, hallucinogenic drugs seem to influence neural processing in two important ways. First, they decrease the brain's ability to screen out many types of sensory inputs. And second, the drugs seem to disrupt the brain's attempts to *integrate complex stimuli* (Domino, 1981).

Hallucinogens cause little physical damage to the body. Their danger comes from their effects on mental processes and behavior. One of the most frequent problems associated with use of these drugs is that the user "loses con-

trol" of his or her flow of thoughts and emotions. This sort of experience is often called a "bad trip." In a recent interview, Albert Hofmann notes that almost everyone who takes LSD has a bad trip now and again. And Edward Domino believes that almost anyone who takes a sufficiently large dose of PCP—or who takes small doses regularly—is likely to need medical or psychological help (Domino, 1981).

Marijuana

Marijuana is a product of the hemp or **cannabis** plant, a weed found in abundance in many parts of the world. The "active ingredient" in marijuana is a chemical that goes by the complex name of delta-9-trans-tetrahydrocannabinol—which we can gladly abbreviate as **THC**.

As Solomon Snyder points out in his book *Uses of Marijuana*, cannabis has a long and interesting history. A century ago cannabis was almost as commonly used for medicinal purposes as aspirin is today and could be purchased without a prescription in any drug store (Snyder, 1972). Cannabis became illegal in the US in 1937, but scientific evidence suggests that it still might be useful as a medicine. It seems particularly effective against diseases caused by tension and high blood pressure, menstrual bleeding, and glaucoma (a build-up of pressure within the eyeball). But its most important use may be that of helping relieve the nausea that cancer patients often experience when given **chemotherapy** (Ray, 1983).

Very little is known about how cannabis affects the central nervous sytem, for it is chemically very different from the opiates, from all other known hallucinogens, and from cocaine. In small doses cannabis can produce a pleasant change of mood. In larger amounts it can produce mild hallucinations similar to those brought about by a small dose of LSD or mescaline. In very large doses it can induce vomiting, chills, and fever—as well as the bad-trip "loss of control" caused by hallucinogens (Ray, 1983).

● *Use of Marijuana in the US*

According to Kozel and Adams, use of marijuana in the US peaked about 1979 and has been decreasing ever since. In 1979, 60.4 percent of some 17,000 high school students questioned admitted to having used marijuana at least once, while almost 11 percent said they used the drug on a daily basis. By 1985, only 54.2 percent of the students said they had tried marijuana, and less than 5 percent used it daily (Kozel & Adams, 1986).

Kozel and Adams suggest that this decrease in consumption is due primarily to a change in the *perception* of the dangers of using the drug. In 1978, only 12 percent of the high school students surveyed said they believed there was

Marijuana has been used to treat glaucoma, and to relieve the nausea brought on by chemotherapy for cancer.

"great risk of harm" associated with occasional use of marijuana, and only 35 percent perceived "great risk" with regular use. By 1985, 25 percent of the students said they thought that occasional use could be very harmful, while 70 percent perceived "great risk" was associated with regular use (Kozel & Adams, 1986). Kozel and Adams fail to mention, however, that the *availability* of marijuana decreased significantly while the *price* of the drug increased dramatically during the same time period. However, the availability of cocaine increased while its price actually decreased slightly during the same time span.

● *Is Marijuana Dangerous?*

There is little doubt that marijuana affects performance, particularly on complex tasks. In a recent study, psychiatrist Jerome Yesavage and his associates at Stanford tested the effects of smoking marijuana on the ability to fly and land an airplane. The tests were given (in a flight simulator) to trained pilots at intervals of 1, 4, and 24 hours after the subjects had smoked a marijuana cigarette. All the subjects had smoked marijuana previously. As you might expect, performance one hour after smoking marijuana was affected the most. However, even 24 hours later, the pilots experienced problems handling the airplane—even though they reported no awareness of any after-effects on their mood or alertness. Yesavage and his colleagues conclude that "In actual flight [the errors the subjects made] can easily lead to crashes" (Yesavage *et al.*, 1985).

A number of researchers have found that THC causes at least a temporary reduction in the immune reaction, a fact that leads medical scientists to warn that smoking pot may increase your chances of getting flu, herpes, or even cancer (Dunnett, 1986). To date, however, there is no *clinical* evidence that pot smokers have a higher incidence of these diseases.

In the spring of 1982, the National Academy of Sciences released a study on the dangers of marijuana. According to this report, there is no evidence that cannabis causes permanent, long-term health effects in humans. But the number of short-term reactions to the drug "justifies serious national concern." The scientists conducting the NAS study state there is no conclusive evidence the drug is addictive, that it leads to use of "harder" drugs, affects the structure of the brain, or causes birth defects. But it does affect motor coordination, short-term memory, oral communication, and may disrupt sperm production in males and ovulation in females—at least on a temporary basis (Relman *et al.*, 1982).

University of Michigan psychologist Jerald Bachman has studied marijuana use in high school students for some 15 years. "It is very worthwhile to report on the physical effects of these drugs," Bachman said in a recent interview. But drug education campaigns have to be realistic, Bachman believes. "Telling people about the consequences of drug abuse works. Scare tactics don't work" (cited in Misle, 1988).

Drugs Affecting Motor Output

Almost all of the "uppers" and "downers" affect motor outputs as well as sensory inputs and central processing. However, many drugs have their major influence on muscular reactions.

Perhaps the best known of these drugs is **meprobamate**, also called Miltown or Equanil. When meprobamate was first introduced, it was called a "psychic" tranquilizer. Later research indicated it does not affect central processing all that much, but rather increases the output of inhibitory molecules at the neuro-muscular synapses, thus lowering the level of muscular activity (Ray, 1983).

● *Alcohol*

The social and financial costs of alcohol in the US are, to coin a phrase, fairly sobering. In November 1987, the US Health and Human Services Department held a conference on alcohol. At the conference, Thomas Burke, the agency's chief of staff, reported that alcoholism and alcohol abuse cost $117 billion annually. Direct medical costs account for roughly $15 billion of that total. Burke expects the figure to rise to $136 billion by 1990, and to $150 billion by 1995.

Alcohol is partially or wholly responsible for some 100,000 deaths each year, and it is involved in some half of the automobile accidents on American highways. More than half the people in the US who commit murders each year have measurable amounts of alcohol in their blood at the time of the crime. At least 25 percent of the admissions to US mental hospitals involve alcohol abuse.

An estimated 5 to 10 percent of the work force suffers from alcoholism. Employees with drinking problems are absent 16 times more often than are non-drinkers. They have an accident rate four times greater, use a third more sickness benefits, and have five times more compensation claims than do other employees. Some 40 percent of industrial fatalities and 47 percent of industrial injuries can be traced to alcohol abuse (Ray, 1983).

Alcohol affects the brain in many ways, but two effects seem most important. First, alcohol kills nerve cells—but in a highly selective fashion. In a recent article, Charles Golden and his associates report that alcohol tends to destroy brain tissue *primarily in the dominant hemisphere*. The behavioral changes associated with chronic drunkenness tend to support Golden's findings. For example, the slurred speech, the inability to think logically and to plan effectively, and the emotional outbursts shown by

Meprobamate (mepp-pro-BAMM-ate). A drug that acts to relax the muscles.

many alcoholics all suggest that alcohol disrupts the dominance normally shown by the left hemisphere. Indeed, Golden and his colleagues believe these symptoms result from the right hemisphere's attempts to take over the functions lost through destruction of tissue in the left hemisphere (Golden *et al.*, 1981).

Second, alcohol appears to affect the same inhibitory synapses in the brain that are blocked by cocaine and morphine. Consumed in larger amounts, however, alcohol disrupts motor coordination—presumably by making it difficult for the person to inhibit many types of muscle movements (Snyder, 1987).

In a recent article, G. Alan Marlatt and his associates note that, at low doses, alcohol acts as a stimulant. However, at higher doses, it acts as a depressant. A heavy drinker may consume alcohol for its stimulating effects, but then fall into a depression that triggers further consumption. Little wonder, Marlatt and his colleagues say, that alcohol is such an addictive substance (Mooney *et al.*, 1987).

We will have much more to say about alcoholism (and its treatment) in Chapter 10. At the moment, we will merely note that while use of marijuana and hallucinogens seems to be decreasing, consumption of alcohol remains high. For more than 13 years, University of Michigan psychologists Jerald Bachman, Lloyd Johnston, and Patrick O'Malley have conducted an annual survey of drug habits among American teenagers. Each year, the psychologists give questionnaires to a new sample of 17,000 high school students. The researchers also question

The Behavioral Alcohol Research Laboratory (BARLAB) is a simulated tavern at the University of Washington, equipped with audio-videotaping and one-way-mirror observation facilities, stereo music system, dim lighting, and full wet bar. It is used to study drinking behavior unobtrusively in a naturalistic setting.

2,400 students from previous years. Early in 1988, Bachman, Johnston, and O'Malley released their results for the 1987 survey. They found that almost 6 percent of the teenagers questioned used alcohol daily, almost 70 percent used alcohol at least once a month, and about 40 percent said they had consumed five or more drinks at a time during the two weeks before the survey (Bachman, Johnston, & O'Malley, 1988).

DRUGS AND MENTAL PROCESSES

For the most part, we take drugs because certain chemical compounds make us feel better than we do without the drugs—or because we *believe* the drugs will make us feel better. And beliefs often can have just as strong an influence on the "drug experience" as does the biochemistry of the drug itself.

For example, G.A. Marlatt and D.J. Rohsenow report that most of the "social effects" of alcohol may be due to people's expectations about the drug. In one study by Marlatt and Rohsenow, subjects who drank tonic water but thought it was alcohol showed most of the "classic" symptoms of intoxication, while subjects who drank alcohol but thought it was tonic water failed to get "high." More specifically, men who thought they had consumed alcohol became less anxious in social situations. The men also became more aggressive and sexually aroused. Women who consumed tonic water thinking it was alcohol became more anxious in social situations and less aggressive. The women *reported* they became sexually aroused, but physically they actually became less so (Marlatt & Rohsenow, 1981).

Marlatt and Rohsenow also tested alcoholics by giving them tonic water but telling them it was vodka. The alcoholics experienced the same "craving" for more alcohol after drinking the tonic water as they typically did when consuming alcohol. The alcoholics did *not* report this craving after drinking vodka they thought was just tonic water.

The *social setting* has a strong influence on how you react to all drugs, including alcohol. According to Marlatt and Rohsenow, solitary drinkers describe the effects of drinking primarily in terms of physical symptoms—they feel dizzy or numb. Drinkers in social situations (who have consumed the same amount of alcohol) tend to say they feel more "outgoing" or "friendly."

Marlatt and Rohsenow conclude that the setting in which alcohol is consumed and the drinker's expectations are even more influential in determining the drinker's reactions than are the physical effects of the alcohol itself (Marlatt & Rohsenow, 1981).

Marlatt and Rohsenow's research is still controversial, but recently has been confirmed in part by Harvard psychiatrist Norman Zinberg, who studied the effects of expectations and social settings on drug abuse. Some of Zinberg's subjects were able to control their use of drugs; other subjects could not. Zinberg concludes that the *social setting* and the *social skills* of the user are "a major, if not the primary, element in determining degree of control" (Zinberg, 1984). Put more simply, people who learn to control their use of intoxicants are significantly less likely to have drug-related problems than are people who have never learned self-control. (We will have more to say about this problem in Chapter 10.)

□ □ **QUESTION** □ □

Some people believe alcoholism is a "disease," and that even one drink will set off a strong physical reaction in an alcoholic. Why does the research by Marlatt and Rohsenow—and by Zinberg—cast some doubt on this belief?

Shock, "Getting High," and the Endorphins

Almost all descriptions of that altered state of consciousness we call "getting high" have two important aspects to them: (1) The person feels no pain, and (2) the person feels detached from his or her body and from ordinary reality. Oddly enough, these experiences may well be like those brought about by great shock—and with the release of massive amounts of the endorphins (and other opioid peptides) inside the brain.

William McDermott of the Harvard Medical School speculates that the onset of intense shock may lead the brain to create an abnormal amount of one or more of the endorphins. The sudden release of all these "natural pain-killers" apparently puts the organism in a *trance state* similar to that occasionally achieved by Eastern mystics. This altered state of consciousness is also akin to the euphoria caused by

some drugs, and to the insensitivity to pain associated with hypnosis (McDermott, 1980).

Evidence supporting McDermott's views comes from a study by Bowling Green psychologists Barbara Herman and Jaak Panksepp. They found that *decreasing* the amount of enkephalin in an animal's brain seems to *increase* its sensitivity to pain and to social isolation (Herman & Panksepp, 1981).

There is additional evidence relating the release of endorphins to stress and pain. University of Michigan researchers Huda Akil and Cheryl Cahill reported in 1982 that pregnancy causes women's bodies to make more of one type of endorphin. In a study of 10 women from early pregnancy to labor, Akil and Cahill state, the amount of endorphin in the blood "doubled or tripled in every subject from the first trimester until birth" (Cahill & Akil, 1982).

Given these data, it is tempting to speculate that *almost all altered states of consciousness* are associated with the release of natural pain-killing chemicals within the brain. Sometimes you secrete opioid peptides because of the drugs you have taken. But just as often, you secrete these peptides because of your *expectations* about how the drugs will affect you. Thus, some of the effects of alcohol, the opiates, marijuana, and cocaine are due to biochemical changes these drugs cause at various synapses. But other effects of these drugs are caused by the types of neural transmitters and inhibitors your brain secretes in response to what you *think* the drugs ought to be doing to you.

To restate a point we have already made, your mental processes have as much influence on the behavior of your neurons as the behavior of your neurons has on what you think and feel.

Now that we have briefly surveyed how your nervous system *inputs* sensory data, *processes* it, and then *outputs* behaviors, it's time to look at each of these three elements of information processing in more detail. We'll begin by discussing *sensory inputs* in the next chapter.

SUMMARY

1. **Consciousness** is a **primitive term** that is defined as your ordinary state of mental functioning.
2. Certain experiences—such as falling asleep, dreaming, and taking various drugs—can lead to unusual or **altered states of consciousness**.
3. Your body has certain **biological rhythms**, such as daily fluctuations in temperature, that follow predictable patterns. These **circadian rhythms** suggest there are **biological clocks** in the body that control many

physical processes, including sleep and waking.
4. **Circadian rhythms** are typically determined at (or before) birth, but can be **reset** by inputs from the environment.
5. **Melatonin**, a hormone produced by the **pineal gland**, affects both the sleep/waking cycle and the body's responses to the annual cycle of seasons.
6. Sleep is both an **adaptive response** that helped early humans survive, and an innate **restorative process** that allows the body

72

3 / Biological Rhythms: Sleep, Drugs, and Consciousness

and mind to rejuvenate themselves.

7. **Infants** sleep about 16 hours per 24. **Young adults** sleep about 8 hours, but **older people** sleep slightly less. Both infants and elderly individuals nap more than do young adults.

8. The stages of sleep run from **Stage 0** (pre-sleep) to **Stage 4** (deep sleep). Following Stage 4, you typically go into **Stage 3**, then **Stage 2**, and from there into **Stage 1-REM sleep** during which you will have one or more dreams.

9. Each **sleep cycle** is about 90 minutes long, including an REM period that runs from 8–15 minutes (first cycle of the night) to more than 40 minutes (final sleep cycle of the night). Stage 4 (deep) sleep predominates during the first and second sleep cycles of the night. Stage 2 sleep, Stage 1-REM periods, and **dreaming** increase during later cycles.

10. Stage 1-REM sleep usually develops out of Stage 2 sleep. During REM, most of the **voluntary muscles** in your body are paralyzed—except for those that control eye movements.

11. **Dreaming** seems to be primarily a function of the right hemisphere.

12. If **deprived of sleep** for 100 hours or more, you will typically feel stress and some mental confusion. When you do go to sleep again, you will usually sleep 11–16 hours at most and normal amounts thereafter.

13. People deprived of REM or Stage 4 sleep usually show a **rebound effect** when allowed to sleep normally.

14. Sleep disorders include **narcolepsy** (involuntary "attacks" of sleep), **sleep apnea**, **nocturnal myoclonus** (involuntary leg movements), **insomnia**, **sleepwalking**, **sleeptalking**, and **enuresis**.

15. You **dream** several dreams during each REM period. REM dreams are noted for their completeness and their fantastic quality. Dreams that occur during Stages 2, 3, or 4 are at best **brief** and **fragmentary**, and are "reality-oriented."

16. Some people have **lucid dreams** in which they can control the content and outcome of their dreaming.

17. There are two main types of nightmares: **anxiety nightmares** and **night terrors**. Anxiety nightmares develop out of Stage

1-REM sleep, while night terrors develop out of Stage 4 sleep and occasionally are followed by sleepwalking.

18. **Drugs** can affect many neural processes, but typically cause either an increase or decrease in **neural firing** at specific synapses.

19. The **opiates** inhibit sensory inputs and thus reduce the intensity of painful stimulation. However, the opiates also have a strong effect on **moods**.

20. Your brain produces a variety of natural pain-killers called the **opioid peptides**.

21. **Morphine** inhibits the production of the natural pain-killers. **Withdrawal** from morphine addiction is painful because your body has no **opioid peptides** to inhibit the perception of pain.

22. Use of **cocaine** by young people has increased dramatically in recent years, while use of **marijuana** and **hallucinogens** has decreased. Use of **alcohol** has remained relatively constant.

23. Drugs that affect **cortical processing** can also alter the experience of pain, change moods, and cause you to **hallucinate** or misinterpret your sensory inputs.

24. **PCP** is a **dissociative anesthetic** that disconnects people's minds from their bodies.

25. **Marijuana** affects motor coordination, short-term memory, oral communication, sperm production in males, and ovulation in females. But there is no conclusive evidence that it causes long-term health problems.

26. **Alcohol** is the most widely abused drug in the US and is a major health and social problem.

27. The effects of all drugs are strongly influenced by **psycho-social factors**, including expectations. Experienced drinkers cannot tell the difference between **alcohol** and tonic water.

28. The brain reacts to shock and stress by secreting opioid peptides. In large amounts, these natural pain-killers can bring about a **trance state** or **euphoria**.

29. Your **mental processes** have as much influence on the behavior of your neurons as the behavior of your neurons has on what you think and feel.

(Continued from page 49.)

"Well," said the Bureaucrat, puffing nervously on his pipe. "Back from the Amazon so soon?"

"It's been 18 months," said Dr. Susan Ogdon.

"Ah, yes. Well, time certainly flies, doesn't it?" The Bureaucrat carefully inspected the faces of the two psychologists sitting in his office. They seemed tanned and relaxed. He wished that he could go buzzing off to tropical climes any time he wished. "And how were the pot-smoking natives? Still lost in the 'Stoned Age,' I suppose?" He chuckled over his little joke.

Roger Ogdon smiled wanly. "The natives are decent human beings, just like you and me. Some of them do smoke marijuana, of course, but I doubt theirs is any more of a 'Stoned Age' than ours."

"Um, yes," said the Bureaucrat, quickly swallowing his chuckle. "And what were the results of your study?" In fact, he had a copy of the Ogdons' report lying on his desk in front of him. But he had only found time to skim the first page or so. Besides, he preferred to hear such things first-hand. "I trust you didn't come up with anything too radical?"

Susan Ogdon sighed. "No, our results were about the same as those that Vera Rubin and Lambros Comitas found in their study of marijuana use in Jamaica, and that Paul Doughty and his colleagues at the University of Florida found in their work in Costa Rica."

The Bureaucrat frowned. "Oh, you read those studies, did you?" He wondered why scientists were always checking out the literature when it seemed that tackling a problem with a fresh mind might be so rewarding. He stirred his cup of coffee and took a small sip to perk him up a bit.

"Well," said the woman, "we began by looking at the various ways in which our natives used marijuana. They chew it, smoke it, brew it as tea, and use it in their cooking."

"Oh, my," said the Bureaucrat. "That much, eh?"

"Yes," Roger Ogdon responded. "And they give it to their children as a medicine, so they start using cannabis at a very early age. But, of course, not all of the natives use it."

"Good," the Bureaucrat said. "That means that you could find a control group of non-users, I presume?"

"Yes," said Susan Ogdon. "We found 30 men who were long-time, heavy pot smokers, and 30 who had never used it at all. The users smoked an average of 8 'joints' a day, except that they call them 'spliffs' instead of joints. And, as we note in our report, they refer to pot as 'ganja,' just as the Jamaicans do. It has much more THC in it than does the pot that usually finds its way to the US."

"Excellent!" said the Bureaucrat, reaching for his pipe. "And the non-users were similar to the users in all respects other than the use of this 'ganja'?"

Roger Ogdon nodded. "They were of about the same height, age, occupation, and educational background. And the men in both the experimental and control groups were heavy smokers of tobacco."

The Bureaucrat refilled his pipe and lit it. "Well, if the groups were that similar, then any differences in their mental or physical health most probably was due to the fact that one group smoked marijuana, and the other didn't, right?"

"That's what we presume," said the woman.

"And what was the major difference?" asked the Bureaucrat. "Something startling, I presume?"

Susan Ogdon laughed softly. "Very startling. The ganja smokers weighed, on the average, seven pounds less than did the non-smokers."

The Bureaucrat frowned. "Seven pounds?" he asked. He rubbed his stomach and wondered if he shouldn't lose a little weight. Perhaps those diet pills his wife was taking would help. Then a stray thought popped into his mind. "Wait a minute," he said. "I thought pot smoking gave you 'the blind munchies.' How come the ganja smokers weighed less, not more, than the natives in your control group?"

Roger Ogdon answered. "It's a cultural thing, I suppose. Here the myth is that pot makes you hungry. In the Amazon, they believe it calms your stomach. As I'm sure you know, our expectations about the effects of drugs often reflect our cultural backgrounds and social biases."

"Everyone knows that," responded the Bureaucrat. "But stop teasing me. What else did you find? Surely the ganja smokers had poorer health. I mean, wasn't there a study reported in the *New England Journal of Medicine* in February 1988 showing that pot smokers are at high risk for lung cancer and heart attacks?"

"We read that study," Susan Ogdon said. "It's by UCLA researcher Donald Tashkin. He found that heavy pot smokers have as much bronchitis as do heavy cigarette smokers. But when pressed, Tashkin admits that 'there is no direct evidence that pot smokers actually suffer an unusually high incidence of lung cancer.' Nor could he find any proof that they actually have more heart attacks, or more emphysema. What looks bad in the laboratory doesn't always turn out to be bad in real life."

"And that's what you found in the Amazon?"

"Yes. We took X-rays of the natives' lungs. Both pot smokers and non-smokers showed fairly normal tissue, except that the men who didn't smoke ganja had a bit more scarring of the lungs. But then, as we said, both groups were heavy tobacco smokers as well."

The Bureaucrat put down his pipe. "Well, imagine that. But what about genetic damage?"

Susan Ogdon responded. "The ganja smokers all had parents and grandparents who had been heavy smokers. You'd expect some genetic problems from that, wouldn't you? Yet the ganja smokers actually showed slightly fewer genetic abnormalities than did the men in our control group."

"Oh, my," replied the Bureaucrat as he poked a nasal inhaler up one of his nostrils and inhaled deeply. "I don't think the Deputy Assistant Secretary is going to like your data at all. But that's his problem, now isn't it?" He put the inhaler back in his desk before continuing. "Well,

3 / Biological Rhythms: Sleep, Drugs, and Consciousness

what about personality differences between your experimental and control group subjects?"

"None," said the woman. "We found no significant differences in personality, intelligence, tendency toward mental illness, or brainwave recordings between the two groups."

The Bureaucrat reached in a desk drawer and extracted a small, white capsule. He had spent the morning in a conference with the Deputy Assistant Secretary, and the meeting had not been particularly pleasant. A mild "downer" might help soothe his nerves, he told himself. He swallowed the pill and then picked up the thread of the conversation. "But what effect did the ganja have on the men's intelligence?"

"No effects that we could detect," the woman said. "Which is just what we might expect, given the data reported in a recent article by UCLA psychiatrist Jeffrey Schaeffer and his colleagues."

"They studied savages in the Amazon too?"

"No," Susan Ogdon replied. "They studied 10 Americans living in a Southern state who had been smoking ganja daily for an average of 7.4 years as part of their religious ceremonies. The UCLA psychiatrists found no impairment of cognitive function among their subjects."

"Um," said the Bureaucrat. "But what of the social consequences? What of motivation? Some scientists insist that pot-smoking decreases the desire to work and to get along in society. Did you find that was true in the Amazon?"

"Of course not," Roger Ogdon replied. "The smokers had no more trouble getting or holding a job than did the non-smokers."

"But how long had the pot smokers been puffing on this 'ganja'?" asked the Bureaucrat.

"On the average, about 18 years," said Susan Ogdon.

"And all that ganja didn't even affect their sex lives?" the Bureaucrat said with a gasp.

Roger Ogdon laughed. "Not that we could tell. Or at least not that their wives or girl friends noticed. More objectively, the men in both groups had normal amounts of male hormone."

"Oh, my," said the Bureaucrat. He couldn't imagine how he'd explain this to the Deputy Assistant Secretary. His stomach rumbled. He patted it gently, then helped himself to an antacid tablet he had tucked away in his desk for just such emergencies.

"You must understand," Roger Ogdon said. "It's clear that smoking marijuana can be hazardous to your physical, and perhaps your mental, health. We don't think smoking pot is a particularly smart thing to do. But . . ."

"But?"

"But we don't think the best way to discourage young people from smoking pot is to use scare tactics, or to lie about what the actual dangers are. There's a lot of research showing that telling them the actual facts is far more effective."

"I see," the Bureaucrat said, feeling a tad better.

"You aren't going to object to our publishing the results of our study, are you?" Susan Ogdon asked.

The Bureaucrat smiled. "No, surely not. As you obviously know, your findings really aren't all that surprising, given the results of the Jamaica and Costa Rica studies."

"But what about your Deputy Assistant Secretary?" she questioned.

"Well," responded the Bureaucrat, "I take my cue from Winston Churchill. He once said, 'The truth is incontrovertible. Panic may resent it; ignorance may deride it; malice may distort it; but there it is.'" The man chuckled for a moment. "Leave the Deputy Assistant Secretary to me. Besides, rumor has it that he will be leaving for another position shortly. So let the truth prevail."

"'And the truth will set you free,'" replied Roger Ogdon, smiling.

"Let's hope so," said the Bureaucrat. "But the truth is, I still don't understand why some of the natives smoke ganja, and others don't."

"Individual choice, we presume," Roger Ogdon replied.

The woman nodded. "Yes, and perhaps some difference in their sensitivity to pain."

"Pain?"

"Look," Roger Ogdon continued. "Those men work 10 hours a day or more in the fields, doing very difficult manual labor. They use cannabis as a pain-killer. They probably produce less per hour when they're stoned, but they seem to be able to work longer."

"Then what do they do at night, when they want to relax?" asked the Bureaucrat.

Donald Ogdon laughed. "They drink alcohol."

"No kidding?" responded the Bureaucrat. "Perhaps they're not so different from us after all. But that's what we wanted to find out about, and that's why we supported your research. Please do publish it, wherever you wish. And in conclusion, let me say that it's been a real pleasure to work with you two."

The Bureaucrat shook their hands and walked the two psychologists to the door. Then he returned to his desk, gathered up his papers, and put them in his briefcase. He tossed in a box of aspirin, and then glanced briefly at his watch. It had been a long, hard day, and he hoped his wife would have a martini waiting for him at home.

Then a sad thought crossed his mind. "Pity about those natives having to work so long and hard in the fields," he said aloud. "I suppose they need a little something too, just to get them through the day." He picked up his pipe and tucked it into his briefcase. "Ah, well, different smokes for different folks."

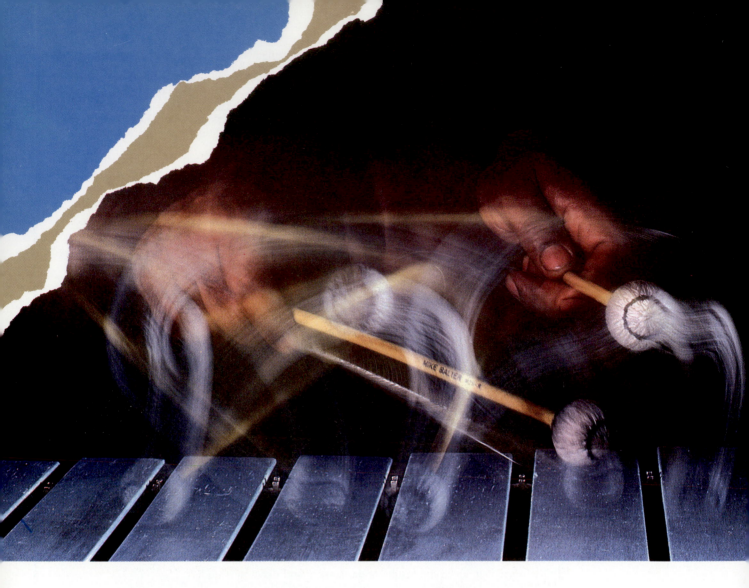

The Senses

"How to Build a Better Robot"

· C · H · A · P · T · E · R ·
4

"Okay, dear, which kid do you want?"

Judy Jones looked around the room. There were children of all ages, all sizes, all colors. Some were playing together; some were fighting; some were sitting quietly in corners minding their own business. Judy glanced quickly at Mrs. Dobson, the woman who had asked the question, and then gazed back at the dozens of children packed into the room.

"How about that little girl over there, in the pink dress?" Judy asked, pointing her finger at a dark-skinned, handsome girl who was playing with several other youngsters. "She looks adorable."

Mrs. Dobson turned to see which child Judy was pointing to. "Oh, Arabella. Sorry, dear, but somebody's already working with her. The pretty ones are always picked first, you know. Pick an ugly one instead, if you want my opinion. They're starved for love, and they need your help just as much as the cute ones do."

Judy was shocked at Mrs. Dobson's bluntness, but guessed the woman might be right. Judy inspected the room carefully, then spotted a little boy with red hair sitting by the window, looking at a magazine. He was by far the most unattractive child in the room. His eyes were watery, his hair uncombed, his skin covered with brown blotches and blemishes. His face was lopsided, and his head seemed too large for his body. Not only that, but he was white. Judy, a black student at a college near the Children's Home, had hoped to work with someone of her own race.

"What about him?" Judy said, pointing again.

"Oh, that's Woodrow Wilson Thomas. Ten years old. Nice little fella, but ugly as home-made sin."

"Home-made sin?" Judy asked.

"Sorry, dear. It's a saying I got from my mother," Mrs. Dobson replied. "Appropriate enough in his case. Woodrow is a bastard, you see."

Judy was shocked. "You mean, he's nasty?"

"No, dear," came the calm response. "I mean bastard in a technical sense. A love child, a natural-born child, the offspring of an unwed mother. I read his record a couple of years back. His mother was 16 when she got pregnant, and she didn't quite remember who the father was. Maybe somebody in the family, for all we know. Anyhow, the mother got rubella—that's the German measles—while she was carrying poor little Woodrow, and he just didn't turn out right. They thought of putting him up for adoption when he was born. But he was so ugly, they figured nobody would take him. So they kept him for a while."

"For a while?" Judy asked, beginning to sympathize with the little boy more and more.

"Yes, 'for a while.' Woodrow not only got off to a bad start in life, he didn't grow up very well either. The record says he crawled and walked at a normal age, but his speech was very retarded. Made animal noises and grunts instead of talking words. Still does, poor little fella. Doesn't understand much when you talk to him, and he won't usually do what you tell him to do. When you try to get through to him, he just stares at you with those watery eyes, and then he looks out the window while you're trying to say something. No wonder his folks put him in the Home here so the state could take care of him. Retarded, that's what Woodrow Wilson Thomas is."

Judy turned the matter over in her mind. "Do you think there's anything I can do for him? I mean, it's part of an assignment for my psych class. We're supposed to show that we can help a retarded or emotionally disturbed child. Can I help Woodrow?"

Mrs. Dobson sighed. "I don't see why not. There must be something you can do. We're so overcrowded here, and we've got such a small staff, I reckon nobody's worked with that child for two or three years. He's no trouble, you see. Doesn't have temper tantrums or act up. Never plays with the other kids, or gets into difficulties. He just sits by the window and looks at his books and magazines all day long."

"Well, if he can read magazines at his age, he can't be all that retarded."

Mrs. Dobson laughed. "Read? Don't be foolish, dear. He just looks at the pretty pictures, and smiles. One day, a year or so ago, I saw him puzzling over a picture like he was trying to figure out what it was. So I asked him what he saw. He just ignored me. Maybe you can get through to him, but I don't promise. But you should learn a lot, and he won't give you any trouble."

Judy accepted the challenge. She went over to the window and tried to talk to Woodrow, but he didn't seem to want to listen. Finally, in desperation, she tugged on his shirt and pulled him over to a nearby table. Woodrow seemed happy to come along with her.

"Now, Woodrow, we're going to draw some pictures. You like pictures, don't you?"

The boy's watery blue eyes drifted toward the window.

Judy pulled on his shirt again until he looked back at her, then she picked up a crayon. She drew a crude picture of a cow while Woodrow watched, seemingly interested. She gave him the crayon and motioned to him that she wanted him to draw. Woodrow took the crayon carefully in his right hand, then looked up at Judy, a puzzled stare on his face.

"Draw a cow, please, Woodrow," Judy said, making scribbling motions with her hand and pointing to the drawing she had just made.

Woodrow smiled serenely as he touched the crayon to the paper. Within three minutes, he handed back to her a crude but recognizable picture of a cow. Judy was so pleased that she wrote the letters C-O-W beneath the drawing. Woodrow took the scratch paper back and copied his own version of the letters underneath those Judy had written.

Judy was thrilled by his response. She got out some of the textbooks she had brought along and hunted through them until she found other pictures for Woodrow to draw. He made a horse, and an auto, and a house. When Judy wrote their names on the scratch paper, Woodrow copied the letters as carefully as he could.

When her time with Woodrow was up, and she had to catch the bus back to the college, Judy kissed Woodrow on the forehead.

"I don't care if you are retarded, young man. You're going to learn to read. I just know you are!" Then she gathered up her textbooks and rushed off.

In her excitement at wanting to tell the other students how well things had gone, Judy failed to notice that she had left her algebra textbook behind. Woodrow picked it up and began to look through it. Although it didn't have any real pictures in it, he found the book utterly fascinating.

The next week, when Judy came back to the State Home for the Retarded to be with Woodrow again, he solemnly presented her with a sheet of scratch paper. On one side were childish drawings of a cow, a tree, a car, and a house, each correctly labeled several times over. On the other side, in very poor but legible script, were written out the first two review problems at the end of the introductory chapter of the algebra textbook.

"My God," said Judy when she saw them. "You've done the algebra correctly!"

(Continued on page 114.)

THE SENSES

According to popular opinion, there are but five senses—vision, hearing, taste, smell, and touch. But there is also "common sense," which is unfortunately rare; "non-sense," which is unfortunately common; and the "sixth sense," which some people claim warns them of impending disaster (and which may be just ordinary "horse sense").

In truth, there are *more* than five senses, no matter how you wish to define the word "senses." For example, in this chapter, you will discover that what most people call "touch" is not one sense, but several: (1) pressure, (2) temperature, (3) feedback from your muscles that lets you know where your arms and legs are, and (4) detection of changes in motion. To make matters even more complex, you will

"WHAT I LIKE ABOUT THIS OFFICE IS I CAN SEE THE CITY, BUT I CAN'T HEAR IT OR SMELL IT."

also find out that taste is both simpler and more complicated than you might have imagined, that smell has a decided effect on your sex life, and that vision and hearing are both "vibratory" senses. And in case you have any doubts, some of these facts are guaranteed to be sensational!

In order to help you "make sense" of your senses, let's begin by taking an imaginary journey into the world of computer technology and "robotics." That is, let's try to figure out what sorts of sensory information a *robot* would need in order to survive in outer space. For if you can understand what inputs a complex machine would need to survive "out there," perhaps you'll understand better what sorts of sensory experiences *you* require in order to survive on the planet Earth.

Project "Robot"

A few years from now, our first real inter-planetary space ships will blast off from earth and take *people* out to one or more of the planets. As you may know, the US space program is directed by the National Aeronautics and Space Administration. Let us suppose that, some time in the future, NASA decides the environments on the eight other planets are so hostile that *robots* should be sent out first to investigate—to make sure *human beings* can survive in space suits if and when we do arrive.

For many reasons, NASA further concludes the robot ought to be human-sized. It should be mobile, and it must carry its own protection against the elements. The robot should also have a means of *sensing and measuring its environment*, and a way of sending messages back to its home base to report the data it gathers.

Let's assume further that you are hired by NASA to help with "Project Robot." Your first assignment is to worry about what kinds of *sensory inputs* the robot should have. You begin by asking yourself, "What kinds of sensory stimulation are humans sensitive to, and what use

This human-sized, mobile robot reacts to sensory inputs much as humans do.

4 / The Senses

Coherent (ko-HERE-ent). Anything that is coherent is logically consistent. When you put all of your sensory inputs together—sight, sound, taste, smell, and "touch"—you are able to perceive the world in a logical manner.

Transduce (trans-DOOSE). To transduce is to change something from one form into another. Your eyes transduce light waves into neural energy which is sent to your brain as a sensory input message.

do we make of the information we get from our bodies and the world around us?"

● **Sensory Coherence**

The robot you will design will have a purpose of some kind. That is, it must execute certain commands, maintain itself in reasonable order, and be able to move about in one fashion or another. All of these actions require that the robot be in touch both with the external world and with its own bodily functions. In this respect, the robot is little different from you. For if *you* are to survive, you too must be able to interact with your environment and know what's going on inside your own body.

The *major purpose* of sensory inputs, then, is to give you a **coherent** picture of both your internal and your external environments so you can achieve your goals in life (including that of surviving). You might be the brightest person ever born, but if you don't get the proper inputs (or don't use them correctly), you won't be around for very long.

Getting the proper inputs is not too difficult for most of us—we have but to open our eyes and ears and "take in the world." But how do you *make sense* out of these inputs? Well, that's one of the chief functions your brain serves—to tie together sight and sound and touch and smell and taste into one *coherent whole* (Uttal, 1978).

To "make sense" of an input may seem easy—after all, your brain performs this task routinely millions of times a day. But think about the *sensory process* for a moment. Suppose you look at a bright red sports car passing by. You "see" the car because of light rays which are reflected to your *eyes* from the automobile. But your *brain* itself is not sensitive to light. So somehow your eyes must *translate* or **transduce** those light rays into a pattern of neural messages. Then your eyes send those input messages to your brain. Your brain momentarily "stores" these neural signals while it checks its memory banks, and "recognizes" the pattern as one it has experienced before. Your brain then combines the *sight* of the car with the deep rumbling *sounds* its engine is making (and perhaps the *smell* of the exhaust) and somehow produces a coherent mental image— that of a noisy, smelly, bright red sports car.

Sensory psychology deals with each of the various types of inputs you can detect—sight, sound, smell, taste, and "touch." *Perception* is

the means by which your brain puts these inputs together to make a coherent experience. *Cognition* is the set of "inner mental processes" describing how you acquire, store, retrieve, and use knowledge about yourself and the world, particularly knowledge that involves either language or "mental images." Thus, cognition includes elements of sensory and perceptual psychology, as well as those processes involved in memory (Matlin, 1983b).

We'll have more to say about perception, cognition, and memory in later chapters. For the moment, let's first try to figure out what your sensory inputs *really are*, and how your brain detects what's going on inside your body and in the outer world.

THE SKIN

Your skin is *one of the most important sensory organs* your body has. It is by far the largest organ in your body: It weighs about 9 pounds, on the average, while your brain is but a third that weight. And your skin not only gives you sensory information; it gives you physical protection from the elements as well. Thus, when your boss at NASA assigns you the task of deciding what kind of "skin" the robot should have, you are rather pleased. Because you have been asked to design one of the most critical parts of the robot's body.

To start matters off, you ask yourself a very important question: "What purpose does the skin serve?" A little thought convinces you that your skin answers many needs. It keeps your vital organs "inside" where they belong, and keeps the outside world "outside" where it belongs. Your skin stretches as you gain weight and shrinks when you shed a few pounds. It also helps regulate your internal temperature, for it has several layers that help insulate you against the cold. And when you get too hot, your skin has sweat glands that release water which cools you by evaporation (Solomon & Davis, 1983).

Most important, however, your skin is filled with *receptors* that let you know what the world around you is like. If you had no skin receptors, you wouldn't know when you had hurt yourself. You also wouldn't know when you were touching something, and whether what you touched was hard or soft, cold or hot. Imagine trying to type a term paper—or play a musical instrument—if your skin didn't give you *feedback* on what your fingers were doing. How long, therefore, do you think you could survive without having *sensory knowledge* from your skin as to what your body was doing?

But would *your* skin serve a robot's specialized needs? After due consideration, you conclude you can't tell what type of covering the robot ought to have until you know more about what this robot is going to have to do. So

The Skin

you begin to think about what types of *sense organs* the robot is going to need in whatever skin it gets.

THE SKIN RECEPTORS

If you like to experiment on yourself, please go find several small objects—things like a pencil, a glass, a rubber band, a ring, a key, a piece of cloth—and put them on a table near you. Now, close your eyes and *feel* each object. Begin by just pressing the palm of your hand down on the objects.

What can you tell about these small objects using what we call *passive touch*—that is, without fingering the objects? That they are hard or soft, large or small, that they have points or sharp edges or rounded **contours**—and that is about all you can tell. A pencil or key is hard; a rubber band or an eraser yields when you press on it and hence feels soft.

But to ask what may at first seem a stupid question, *how do you know what is hard and soft?*

The Pressure Receptors

When you touch an object gently (passively), you depress or deform your skin. Very sensitive nerve cells detect this *deformation of your skin* and fire off a message to your cortex. This input message moves down the axons of the receptor cells until it reaches your spinal cord, then moves up the cord to the stem of your brain. From your brain stem, the message flows through several "lower centers" and finally works its way up to your cortex. Your body may respond automatically and unconsciously to these inputs *before* they reach your cortex. But only when the sensory message arrives at your cortex do you realize *consciously* that your skin has encountered a foreign object of some sort (Barlow & Mollon, 1982).

Now, with the fingers of one hand, gently pinch the palm of your other hand. You will notice that the skin on your palm feels fairly thick. Next, gently pinch the skin on your forearm. The skin is much thinner there. But the major *biological* difference is that the skin on your forearm has hairs on it, while the skin on your palm does not. Some 95 percent of the skin on your body (whether you are male or female) is *hairy* skin. Only the palms of your hands, the soles of your feet, your lips and mouth, your eyeballs, some parts of your sex organs, and a few other scattered areas are made up of *hairless* skin.

- ### Hairless Skin

Hairless skin contains tiny receptor cells that are called **encapsulated nerve endings**. Some of these encapsulated nerve endings look much like small onions and are known as **corpuscles**. The corpuscles are more or less

People who are sightless "see" art through their fingertips. Many museums have "touch collections" especially designed for the visually impaired.

round in shape, much like small onions. And if you were to cut one open, you'd find that these "onion-shaped" corpuscles have many layers to them (see Fig. 4.1) (Solomon & Davis, 1983).

- ### Hairy Skin

Hairy skin has a few encapsulated nerve endings in it. But it also has a unique type of *touch-receptor neuron* buried at the base of each hair. The fibers of these nerve cells are woven around the bottom of each stalk of hair. Whenever the hairstalk is pushed or pulled in any direction, the nerve fibers are squeezed so that they fire off a "pressure" message to your brain. These hairy-skin receptors are called *basket cells* because they look like a wicker basket wrapped around the bottom of the hair stalk (Solomon & Davis, 1983). (It is the basket cell, not the hair itself, that is the "receptor," of course.)

- ### Free Nerve Endings

Both hairy and hairless skin also contain receptor neurons called *free nerve endings*. "Free" in this case means the "input ends" of the receptor are not attached to any particular place (see Fig. 4.1). The free nerve endings are very simple nerve cells whose fibers spread out freely like the branches of a vine just under the outer layers of your skin. Since the free nerve endings are found everywhere on the surface of your body, they are by far the *most common sort* of skin receptor that you have (Solomon & Davis, 1983).

All three types of receptors—the encapsulated nerve endings (including the corpuscles), the basket cells, and the free nerve endings—yield a simple "pressure sensation" when they are stimulated (Hensel, 1982). (As we will see,

Contours (KONN-tours). From the Latin word meaning "to round off," or "to smooth the edges." Contours are the outside edges of a figure.

Encapsulated nerve endings (en-CAP-sue-lated). *Encapsulate* means "to enclose," or "to envelop." When you put on a cap, you encapsulate your head.

Corpuscles (KOR-pus-sulls). The Latin word *corpus* means "body." We get our English words "corpse" (a dead body), "corps" (the Marine Corps), and "corporation" (a body of people) from this same Latin term. A corpuscle is a "little body" or "little cell," particularly one that is isolated from others like it. The red blood cells, for instance, are called the "red corpuscles."

however, some of the free nerve endings and basket cells are also sensitive to temperature.)

Primary Sensory Qualities

Now, go back to the objects you were feeling on the table near you. Close your eyes and have someone place first a *wooden* object and then a *metal* object in your hands. You can tell wood from metal in two ways: (1) The wood is softer than the metal; and (2) the wood will feel warm while the metal feels cold.

Your skin receptors give rise to two qualitatively different sensory experiences—*pres-*

sure and *temperature*. The encapsulated nerve endings in the hairless regions and the basket cells around each hair are primarily *pressure receptors*. The free nerve endings detect both *pressure* and *temperature*.

It may come as a surprise to you that these two sensations (plus pain, which we will discuss later) are the *only primary sensory qualities* your skin can tell you about. However, most psychologists believe that all the information you get from your skin about the world around you is merely a *combination* of pressure sensations and temperature sensations—plus, occasionally, the experience of pain (see Chapter 13) (Hensel, 1981).

• Complex Pressure Sensations

Next, rub the palm of your hand over your clothes, the surface of the table, the cover of this book, the upholstery of a chair, or the top of a rug. Some objects feel smooth to your touch; others feel rough. How does your skin tell you which is which if it can experience just pressure and temperature?

FIG. 4.1 A schematic diagram of the skin. Basket cell receptors are found only in hairy skin. Corpuscles are found primarily in hairless skin. Free nerve endings are found in hairy and hairless regions.

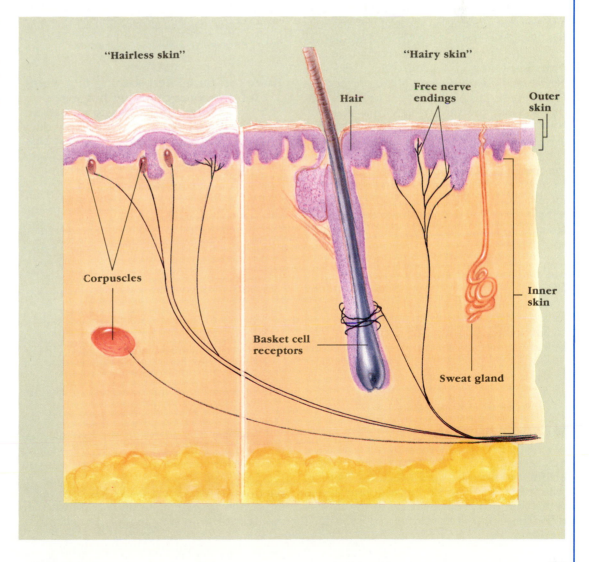

"Hairless skin" "Hairy skin"

Hair Free nerve endings Outer skin

Corpuscles

Basket cell receptors

Sweat gland Inner skin

The answer comes from this fact—when you move your hand across a surface, using what we call *active touch*, you stimulate many receptors at once. Generally speaking, large objects will stimulate a larger and more widely-distributed group of sensory cells than will small objects. Thus, you can gain some notion of the *size* of an object by noting how many receptors—and *which* receptors—fire in response to the stimulation (Geldard & Sherrick, 1986).

If the surface of an object is rough, some parts of your skin "vibrate" vigorously as you rub your palm across the object. Other parts of your skin vibrate little, if at all. Your brain perceives this *pattern of incoming sensory information* as "roughness" or "smoothness" (Smith *et al.*, 1982).

You might think that your robot could recognize most objects *visually*. However, according to University of Rochester researcher C.M. Brown, most modern-day robots can't as yet discriminate small objects (such as a screw) visually (Brown, 1984). Carnegie-Mellon scientists Melvin Siegel and Gregory Toto believe that giving the robots "a sense of touch" may be the simplest way to handle this problem. Siegel and Toto are working on an "artificial skin" that has *pressure-sensitive dots* in it. The dots, of course, are modeled after the receptors in your own skin (cited in Tyndall, 1986). And Gale Nevill and Robert Patterson of the University of Florida have invented a silicon rubber *sensor* that acts like the tiny "ridges" that make up your fingerprint. When the sensor is rubbed across an object, the rubber ridges vibrate. A computer "reads" the pattern of vibration and matches it to those produced by various objects. As of 1986, this sensor could read Braille, identify various grades of sandpaper, and could tell in which direction the slot in the head of a screw is pointing (cited in Tyndall, 1986; Patterson, 1986).

So, let's presume you put pressure receptors similar to those being developed by Nevill and Patterson in your robot's fingers. You (or a computer in the robot's brain) then could tell if an object the robot touched was hard or soft, or rough or smooth, simply by decoding the *pattern of signals* from the robot's pressure receptors. You could also put temperature detectors in the robot's fingers and learn whether the object was hot or cold.

But hot or cold in relation to what?

The Temperature Receptors

When you first crawl into a tub of hot water, it may seem that you are going to be boiled alive before the bath is over. The water feels intensely hot, and your skin turns lobster red as your brain orders an increase in the flow of blood through your skin to help cool you off. If

you manage to stay in the tub for a while, the water feels cooler and cooler even if you keep the temperature of the water constant. When you get out, the air in the bathroom may seem surprisingly cool to your naked skin.

"Hot" and "cold" are *relative* terms that, in your body's case, are always related to whatever your skin temperature is. Anything you touch that is *colder* than your skin will seem *cool* to you. Anything you touch that is *hotter* than your skin will seem *warm*. The warmer or colder the object is in relation to your skin temperature, the more rapidly your temperature receptors will fire (Hensel, 1981).

Many years ago, it was thought there were separate receptors for "warm" and for "cold." However, German psychologist Herbert Hensel notes this simply isn't the case. Areas of hairy skin with no receptors other than the basket cells can detect both warmth and cold. So can areas of the white of the eye, which contains only free nerve endings. Hensel believes that the basket cells and the free nerve endings can signal *either* warm or cold. And they do so primarily by detecting *changes* in the temperature of the skin. Thus, the receptors actually are sensitive to temperature *changes* rather than to "warm" and "cold" in any absolute sense (Hensel, 1982).

□ □ **QUESTION** □ □
After you have been soaking in a warm tub for some time, the hot water typically will seem cooler to you than when you first got in the tub. How does this fact support Hensel's view that the skin is sensitive to temperature changes rather than "hot" or "cold" in any absolute sense?

The Somatic Cortex

The messages that your skin receptors send to your brain tell you four things:

1. The *location* of the experience—that is, what part of your body is detecting the sensations.
2. The *quality* of the experience—that is, pressure or temperature.
3. The *quantity* or strength of the experience—intense pressure or weak, slightly warm or very cold.
4. The *duration* of the stimulation—whether it is brief or continuing.

Let's see why all of this sensory information is important. Suppose you are walking along barefooted and you step on a tack. As you probably well know, you realize almost instantly *what part* of which foot has been punctured, how *intense* the wound is, and whether the tack is *still* in your foot or has fallen out.

To duplicate human abilities, a robot needs to have many more pressure and temperature sensors in its fingers and hands than in most other parts of its body.

How do you become conscious of all this information so quickly?

Well, think for a moment about the NASA robot you are helping design. If you want the robot to *localize* its skin sensations, how would you hook the robot's skin receptors up to its brain? Probably you would want to put in a direct "telephone line" between each receptor and a *specific* part of the "brain." Each receptor would, in effect, have its own "telephone number." The robot could tell where the stimulation was coming from simply by checking to see which telephone line the message was coming over.

Your nervous system is "constructed" in much the same way. Each receptor cell in your skin is connected to a specific region in the *sensory input areas* in your **parietal lobes** (see Fig. 4.2). Thus, your brain can tell the location of any stimulation on your body by noting *where* the input message arrives in the parietal lobe (Solomon & Davis, 1983).

You may recall from Chapter 2 that the parietal lobe in each of your cerebral hemi-spheres is located at the very top center of your brain. The front edge of the parietal lobe is immediately adjacent to the *motor output area* at the rear of the frontal lobe. The cortex at this front edge of the parietal lobe is often called the **somatic cortex**. *Soma* is the Greek word for "body," and it is to this part of your cortex that all of your body or *somatic receptors* send their sensory messages. Receptors in the left side of your body send their inputs primarily to the somatic cortex in the right half of your brain. The receptors in the right side of your body send their messages to your left somatic cortex (Kimble, 1987).

THE DEEP RECEPTORS

If you made the NASA robot much like yourself, it could tell the hardness, smoothness, and temperature of an object it had picked up just by noting what its "skin" receptors were signaling. But what about the object's size, shape, and weight?

Pick up a pencil, close your eyes, and roll the pencil around in your hand. You can tell at once what size, shape, and weight the pencil has. But it is not just your surface or skin receptors that give you this information. For we could anesthetize all the nerves in the skin of your hand, and you would still be able to tell the size, shape, and weight of the pencil.

The muscles, joints, tendons, and bones in your hand (and in much of the rest of your

FIG. 4.2 The four lobes of the brain.

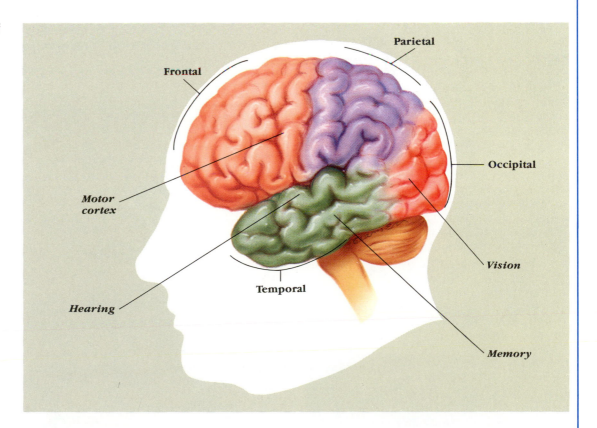

body) all have sensory receptors in them. These are called *deep receptors*, to distinguish them from the *surface receptors* in your skin. Whenever you contract a muscle in your hand, a tiny nerve cell buried in that muscle sends a feedback signal to your somatic cortex saying the muscle is in operation. The heavier an object is, the harder your muscle must work to lift the object and hold it steady. And the harder the muscle pulls or contracts, the more vigorously the tiny receptor neuron buried in the muscle fires—and the more intense feedback you get (Solomon & Davis, 1983).

Distribution of Receptors

If you were building a robot, you would surely want its *fingers* to be more sensitive to pressure and temperature than, say, the middle of its *back*. For robots (like people) would seldom be called upon to make fine discriminations about objects with the "skin" on their backs. So you would probably put *more* sensory receptors in the robot's fingers than on its back.

In zero gravity conditions, your balance detectors can't tell "up" from "down."

Generally speaking, those parts of your body that you use most to make sensory discriminations have the most pressure receptors, while those parts that you use least have fewer receptor neurons. Thus, there are more pressure receptors in your fingertips, your lips, your eyeball, and on the tip of your tongue than elsewhere on your body (Geldard & Herrick, 1986).

Motion-Change Detectors

By using electronic circuits that would operate much the way the neural circuits in your body operate, you could design a robot able to pick things up, measure them with its fingers, and keep track of where its arms and legs were in the process. But what about movement? How could you tell whether your robot was standing still, walking, or twirling around violently in space?

• Two Types of Motion Detectors

Whether you are considering robots or people, there are two basic types of motion that a "body" must be sensitive to: (1) straight-line or linear movements, and (2) rotary or circular movements.

Buried away inside each of your ears are two types of receptor organs that detect *changes* in the motion of your body. The detectors in your ear that sense *changes in linear motion* are two small organs called the **saccule** and the **utricle**. Whenever your body starts or stops moving in a straight-line fashion, *neural receptors* in the saccule and the utricle fire off messages to your brain letting it know that *linear* movement has begun or is slowing down (see Fig. 4.3).

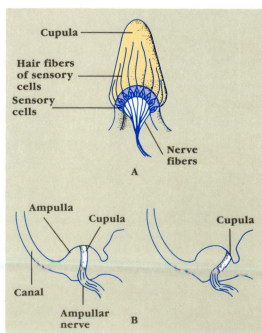

FIG. 4.3 Receptor cells in the cupula of the semicircular canals detect rotary motion.

4 / The Senses

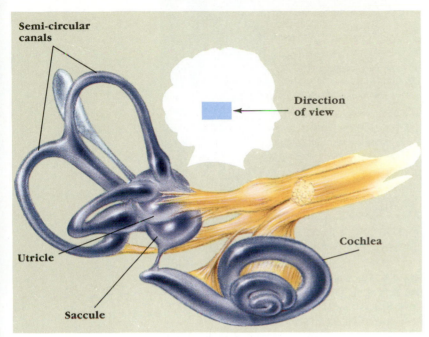

FIG. 4.4 The saccule, utricle, and semi-circular canals are motion detectors in the inner ear.

Any *change in rotary motion* your body makes is detected by the *semi-circular canals* in your ear. These three canals are positioned at right angles to each other inside your ear so they can detect changes in circular motion in any of the three dimensions of space (see Fig. 4.4).

ADAPTATION AND HABITUATION

Your brain is your main organ of survival. And if you are to survive, you must usually pay more attention to *changes* in your environment than to stimuli that *remain constant* for a period of time.

There are at least two ways in which your nervous system adjusts to constant inputs: first, by what we will call *receptor adaptation*; second, by what we will refer to as *central habituation* to a stimulus input. Receptor adaptation occurs in the receptor neurons themselves, while central habituation occurs in your brain.

• *Receptor Adaptation*

As an example of *receptor adaptation*, consider what happens when you first sink into a tub of water that is 20° warmer than your skin. As you know, your temperature receptors will begin to fire vigorously. But as you remain lying in the tub, your skin itself warms up. After a short period of time, your free nerve endings will fire less vigorously because the temperature of your skin is now much closer to that of the water. Because your skin and your free nerve endings have *adapted* to the heat, the water will now seem much less hot to you (Hensel, 1981).

• *Central Habituation*

As an example of *central habituation*, think of what happens when you move into a house beside a busy highway. At first, you notice the sounds of the traffic almost continuously. But after a few days, your brain will stop paying much attention to the continual drone of the passing cars and trucks. Indeed, you may be surprised when a visiting friend asks how you can stand the noise. But in this case, it is your *brain* that has changed its way of responding to a constant input, not the receptors in your *ears*.

In general, we use the term *adaptation* whenever your receptor cells themselves slow down or reduce their firing rates in response to a constant stimulus. We use the term *habituation*, however, to refer to your brain's tendency to ignore sensory inputs that seem of little interest or importance.

□ □ **QUESTION** □ □

When you have been soaking in a hot tub for a while, can you make the water "feel" warmer just by paying attention to it? When you have lived by a noisy highway for a while, can you hear the traffic just by paying attention to it? What do your answers to these two questions tell you about the differences between receptor adaptation and central habituation?

A Window of Skin

Your skin senses are surely as critical to your survival as are vision and hearing. And yet, since you seldom use them *consciously* for communication or artistic expression, you may have overlooked their complexity, their beauty, and their incredible usefulness.

As an example of your skin's importance, consider the story of Helen Keller. She was born a normal child, but an illness when she was 19 months old left her deaf and blind. Although she had learned to say a few words before the illness, she soon stopped speaking. For the next several years, Helen Keller was little more than an animal, trapped in a black and silent cage, completely unable to communicate with those around her.

When Helen Keller was 6, however, her parents appealed to Alexander Graham Bell for help. Bell, the inventor of the telephone, recommended as a teacher a young woman

Helen Keller "saw" many prominent people through her sense of touch, including U.N. representative Eleanor Roosevelt.

FIG. 4.5 Taste buds on the surface of the epiglottis (the back of the throat).

named Anne Sullivan. Within a month Anne Sullivan had taught Helen to make sense of the myriad sensations her skin receptors poured into her brain. Helen learned how to "talk" using her fingers, and how to "listen" when someone "wrote" on the palm of her hand. Later she learned to "read speech" by placing her fingers on the lips of the person who was speaking.

Helen Keller's skin was her only window to the world, but she "saw" through this window with exceptional clarity (Keller, 1970).

TASTE

Your skin is an important "input organ" in part because it protects you from things in the outside world that shouldn't get inside your body. But there are times when you *must* "input" certain items—such as food and water—if you are to survive. And much as it may surprise you, your skin helps you determine what to eat and drink—and what not to. For, as we will soon see, receptor cells in the skin that lines your tongue, mouth, and nose are responsible for mediating those sensory qualities we call "taste" and "smell."

Let's look first at what taste is all about. Pick your favorite food and imagine it in your mind's eye. Let's say you picked a steak—3 inches thick, wrapped in bacon, and cooked just the way you like it. Now, ask yourself what may seem a very stupid question: Why does the *steak* taste good to you?

Whatever reasons you come up with, chances are they're partly wrong. For even the best of steaks has almost no *taste* at all—at least if we restrict "taste" to the sensory qualities that come from the skin receptors in your tongue. Steak *smells* good; it *looks* good; it has a fine *texture* to it as you chew it. And if it comes to your table sizzling hot, steak both *sounds* good and has just the right *temperature*.

But none of these sensory qualities has anything to do with the *taste* of steak. In fact, if we could block out all the other sensory qualities except those that come from your taste receptors, you'd find you could hardly tell the difference between the taste of steak and that of old shoe leather.

The Taste Receptors

Your *taste buds* contain the hair cells which are your taste receptors. The taste buds are your body's "poor relations" (see Fig. 4.5). Impoverished in almost every sense of the word, your taste buds are scattered in nooks and crannies all across the surface and sides of your tongue. Mostly, however, they are found clumped together in bumps on your tongue called **papillae** (from the Latin word meaning "nipples"). If you stick out your tongue and look at it, you will see the papillae very clearly (Solomon & Davis, 1983).

Most of the papillae have grooves around their sides, like the moats or canals that circled old European castles. The taste buds line the sides of the papillae, like windows in the outer wall of a castle (see Fig. 4.6).

There are about 10,000 taste buds in your mouth, each made up of several receptor cells. Most of the buds are on your tongue, but there are also a few scattered elsewhere in your mouth. Each of the receptor cells in the taste bud has a hair at one end which pokes out into

Papillae (pap-PILL-eye, or pap-PILL-ee). The bumps on your tongue that contain the taste buds.

Neonates (KNEE-oh-nates). From the Latin words *neo*, meaning "new," and *nate*, meaning "born." Literally, *neonate* means "newborn."

"MY COMPLIMENTS TO THE FOOD TASTER."

the "moat" around the papilla much as the hairs on the skin of your arm stick out into the air. When you eat or drink something, the liquids in your mouth fill up the moats around the papillae. Various molecules in the food stimulate the hair cells *chemically*. The cells then fire off sensory input messages to your brain, and you experience the sensation of taste (Solomon & Davis, 1983).

Taste Qualities

There are only four basic taste qualities: *sweet, sour, bitter,* and *salty*—a paltry few primary qualities compared to the richness of the sensory experiences you get from vision, hearing, and smell. The noted Cornell psychologist E.B. Titchener once estimated that you can discriminate about 3,000 different tastes. However, all of them appear to be *mixtures* of the four basic taste qualities.

Research suggests there are four different taste receptors—one for each of the four primary taste qualities. However, we still aren't sure just how your nervous system *processes* information from your taste receptors. Thus, as simple a sense as taste is, so far it has defied our attempts to understand it completely (Cotman & McGaugh, 1980).

• *Individual Variability in Taste Sensitivity*

Newborn infants will usually drink milk shortly after birth, but will spit out sour substances. For the first several weeks of life, infants seem to be indifferent both to salty and bitter tastes (Blass & Teicher, 1980). However, by the time they are five months old, most **neonates** begin to show a slight preference for salty-tasting liquids (Beauchamp, 1987). The liking for sweet or slightly salty substances thus seems "built into your genes." But a fondness for beer (and other sour substances), or for "gin and tonic" (and other bitter tastes), and for exceptionally

hot or spicy foods (which trigger off the perception of pain) would seem to be a learned response (Shell, 1986).

However, there is great variability in sensitivity to the taste of various substances, both in infants and adults. Some people are insensitive to the taste of certain foods—you must really saturate their tongues with these foods for these people to detect the substance at all. This *taste blindness* is far from rare, and seems to be caused by some inherited deficiency in the chemical composition of the person's saliva. However, the taste-blind individual can sometimes detect the substance if you first dissolve the food in the saliva of a person with normal taste sensitivity.

The taste receptors in your tongue apparently are "worn down" by the act of chewing and swallowing food—and thus must be replaced every four or five days. Older individuals often cannot regrow lost tissue as readily as younger individuals and therefore may have reduced numbers of receptors in their later years. Perhaps this fact explains why some older people add more seasoning to their food than most younger individuals prefer (Shell, 1986).

Taste is a necessary but not a particularly rich "sense." For the truth is, most of the food qualities that you ascribe to your tongue really should be credited to your nose.

☐☐ **QUESTION** ☐☐
When you catch a cold, and your nose is clogged but your tongue is not affected, why does food suddenly lose its "taste"?

FIG. 4.6 A papilla in the tongue.

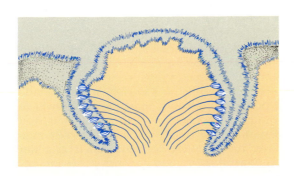

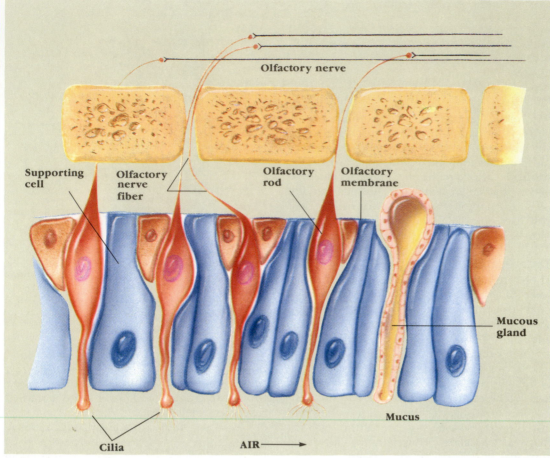

FIG. 4.7 Schematic representation of olfactory membrane, showing the olfactory rods and the cilia in the layer of mucus.

SMELL

Your nose has two cavities or open spaces inside it. The roof of each of these nasal cavities is lined with a thick covering called the **olfactory membrane**, which is really a type of skin. Covering the olfactory membrane is a thin layer of **mucus**. Embedded in the membrane itself are millions of receptor cells called *olfactory rods* (see Fig. 4.7).

At the base end of each of the olfactory rods is an axon that runs directly to your brain. At the front end is a branched set of **cilia**, which act in much the same fashion as dendrites do. These cilia stick out of the olfactory membrane into the layer of mucus (Solomon & Davis, 1983).

The stimuli that excite your olfactory rods are complex chemicals in *gaseous form* that are suspended in the air you breathe. As air passes over the olfactory membrane, some of the complex chemicals in the air are absorbed into the mucus. These gaseous molecules appear to lock onto specific receptor sites on the cilia. This "locking on" causes the olfactory rods to fire off an input message to your brain (Engen, 1982).

• *Smell Qualities*

There have been several attempts to break the experience of smell down into its "primary qualities," such as the "salt, sweet, sour, and bitter" qualities of taste. Perhaps the most successful scheme is that proposed by John Amoore, at the University of California Medical Center in San Francisco. Amoore believes there are seven primary smell qualities:

- camphor (moth balls)
- musky
- floral (roses)
- peppermint
- ethereal (dry-cleaning fluid)
- pungent (vinegar)
- putrid (rotten eggs)

Amoore believes there are several different kinds of *receptor sites* on the olfactory cilia. Stimulus molecules that fit within a *single* receptor site trigger off a *single*, "primary" smell experience. However, most molecules will fit within two or more receptor sites. Thus, you perceive most smells as being complex mixtures of the seven primary smell qualities (Amoore, 1977).

John E. Amoore

Olfactory membrane (oal-FACK-torr-ee). "Olfaction" (oal-FACK-shun) is the process of smelling. The olfactory membrane is a layer of tissue at the top of each nasal cavity that contains the receptors for smell. There are two olfactory membranes in your nose—one inside each nostril.

Mucus (MEW-kuss). The thick, slippery substance that covers (and protects) the olfactory membrane.

Cilia (SILL-ee-ah). From the Latin word meaning "eyelash." A hair-like structure attached to or projecting from many cells.

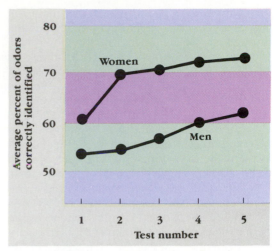

FIG. 4.8 Outcome of an experiment by William Cain, who tested men and women on their ability to learn 80 odors. The ability of both women and men to come up with correct names improves over time. But, on the average, women correctly identified more items on the initial test and maintained this superiority in four later trials.

• Smell—an Ancient Sense

Smell is a unique sense in at least two important ways. First, it is perhaps the most ancient sense of all. Single-celled organisms could detect molecules in the water around them long before they became sensitive to sights or sounds. Second, smell seems more directly related to emotion and motivation than are the other senses. Sensory inputs from your skin, eyes, and ears pass through the thalamus and are relayed directly to your cortex (see Chapter 2). However, the olfactory nerve mostly bypasses the thalamus and runs directly to those sub-centers of the brain that process *emotions*, not *thoughts*.

According to Brown University psychologist Trygg Engen, "*smell may be to emotion what sight or hearing is to cognition. . . . When odor is involved it may well cause a feeling before it elicits a concern with the meaning of the odor*" (Engen, 1982). Engen notes, for instance, that the first thing you typically notice about an odor is whether it's *pleasant* or *unpleasant*. Only after you have reacted to the odor *emotionally* do you usually (1) identify it, and (2) remember its name (Engen, 1987).

□ □ **QUESTION** □ □
Many people report that a home or apartment they have lived in for a long time has a characteristic odor. Usually, these people report they can *recognize* the odor, but have trouble describing it in words. Why do you think they find this task difficult?

Genes, Hormones, and Sensory Acuity

According to psychologists Avery Gilbert and Charles Wysocki, many people lack the ability to smell specific substances. In a recent survey, Gilbert and Wysocki found that 37 percent of American men and 30 percent of American women could not detect the odor associated with "sweaty" armpits. Surprisingly enough, Americans seem worse at detecting this scent than do people almost anywhere else in the world. Gilbert and Wysocki also found that 25 percent of American women and 33 percent of American men couldn't detect the "musky" smell (Gilbert & Wysocki, 1987).

Judging from most recent research, your genes influence your ability to detect various odors. But recent experiments suggest that your olfactory thresholds are also influenced by the amount of sex hormones present in your body.

According to Georgetown University scientist Robert Henkin, a woman's olfactory sensitivity increases "up to 1,000 fold" in the middle of her menstrual cycle (cited in Niemark, 1986). Why this great increase in olfactory sensitivity when ovulation occurs? Hormones seem to be the answer. A woman's estrogen levels are highest during the middle of the cycle, lowest during menstruation. And when menstruation occurs, Trygg Engen says, the mucus layer in the nose is much thicker and odor molecules are less likely to reach the olfactory receptors. During ovulation, there is much less mucus and therefore it is easier for odor molecules to excite the receptors (Engen, 1982).

According to William Cain, women appear to be superior to men at such tasks as identifying and remembering smells. Cain asked 102 men and 103 women subjects to name and identify 80 different odors. Cain exposed the subjects to the smells a total of five times. As Fig. 4.8 shows, the women were superior to the men on each of the tests. Cain believes this superiority is a matter of experience, however, for all the subjects showed improvement over time. And by the fifth test, the men were performing as well as the women had at the start of the experiment. In present-day American society, Cain says, women are more likely to deal with foods, perfumes, and other "smelly" objects than men are (Cain, 1979).

Research by University of Pennsylvania psychologist Richard Doty tends to support

Cain's work. Doty had 33 male and female college students breathe into glass tubes passing through a screen. Judges on the other side tried to guess the sex of the "breather" by smelling the breath. Doty states the majority of judges were accurate most of the time. But several female judges were correct on 95 percent of the tests, and were particularly good at picking out men's breath. Doty concludes that "Though humans don't use their sense of smell in many situations, in some cases people can be as discriminating as animals" (Doty, 1983).

The relationship between smell and memory is exceptionally complex (Engen, 1987). As we will see in Chapter 11, smells tend to evoke rather different types of memories than do inputs from the other senses. However, there seems to be little doubt that you *learn* the qualities associated with most of the odors you encounter in daily life. Indeed, many scientists are now working on systems that will allow computers to recognize scents (Weisburd, 1988).

• "Odor Signatures"
Vanderbilt University researcher Richard Porter believes that each person has a characteristic and unique "odor signature." In one study, Porter and his colleagues found that mothers of newborn infants could correctly identify their child's clothes by smell alone even when the mothers had but two hours' exposure to the just-born infant. Mothers don't lose this ability as their children grow up, either. Porter and his associates report that 17 out of 18 mothers tested could, by smell alone, pick out the T-shirt worn by their three- to eight-year-old child. And 16 out of 18 parents with two children could tell which T-shirt was worn by which child (Porter *et al.*, 1985).

In another study, Porter asked 28 adults to try to match the smell of T-shirts worn by 15 mothers with those worn by their children. The subjects were able to match mother and child at well above chance level. However, when Porter asked his subjects to try to match T-shirts worn by husbands and wives, the subjects had considerable difficulty doing so. Porter believes these results show that genes, not environmental factors, are the primary determinants of "odor signatures" (Porter, 1986).

□□ **QUESTION** □□
William Cain notes that learning to give a "verbal label" to an odor helps considerably in identifying it at a later time. Why might attaching a name to a smell help you remember it?

• Smell and Aging
There is considerable evidence that, in *some* people, the sense of smell diminishes in old age. According to a group of olfactory researchers at the University of Warwick (England), older people often find it more difficult to *detect* odors. More than this, however, the smells older people can still sense often lose their subjective (or emotional) characteristics. The British scientists suggest that this age-related loss may explain why some "senior citizens" don't always eat as balanced a diet as they did when younger. However, older individuals often can *compensate* for this loss in olfactory sensitivity by adding more spices and other flavorings to their food (van Toller, Dodd, & Billing, 1985).

Smells and the Menstrual Cycle
The relationship between smells and sexual behavior is a complex but very interesting one. To begin with, the menstrual cycle itself seems to be controlled in part by olfactory inputs.

There are many "old wives' tales" suggesting that women who live together tend to have menstrual periods that are "in synch" with each other. In 1971, Martha McClintock tested this folk belief by studying the menstrual cycles of 135 women living in a dormitory at Wellesley College. McClintock found that, as the college year progressed, the menstrual cycles of good friends and roommates did in fact become more similar (McClintock, 1971).

An explanation for this "menstrual synchrony" may come from research reported by California psychologist Michael Russell and his colleagues. Russell believes that when we sweat, the **apocrine glands** under our arms release sexual substances. To test this notion, Russell and his group asked a woman with a very regular menstrual cycle to wear cotton pads under her arms daily. The experimenters then rubbed portions of these pads on the upper lips of female volunteers who agreed not to wash their faces for several hours afterwards. A "control" group of volunteers was treated with pads not containing human sweat. The women in the control group maintained their usual menstrual cycle. However, the menstrual cycles of the women who smelled the sweat pads daily became strikingly similar to that of the woman who had donated the sweat (Russell *et al.*, 1977).

The Sweet Smell of Sex
It has long been known that both male and female animals secrete chemicals that attract the opposite sex. These chemicals are called **pheromones**. But what about humans? Do we secrete sex pheromones as do other mammals?

For the past two decades, Naomi Morris and Richard Udry have studied the relationship between smells and sexual intercourse in various groups of married women. Udry and Morris reported that many of the subjects in their first study were more likely to engage in intercourse—and to achieve orgasm—during the

4 / The Senses

middle of their menstrual cycles than at any other time. The woman's hormone production (and hence her sensitivity to smells) is, of course, greatest in mid-cycle. But how could an increase in olfactory acuity account for an increase in sexual behavior (Morris & Udry, 1978)?

● *Copulins*

In the 1960's, Richard Michael and his colleagues at Emory University reported that female monkeys secrete pheromones called **copulins** which are sexually attractive to males. More recently, Michael has discovered that these same copulins are produced by human females. Michael believes that the peak production of copulins occurs in the middle of the menstrual cycle, when ovulation is most likely to take place (Michael *et al.*, 1974).

According to Trygg Engen, the exact effects that odors have on human sexual behavior is still an "open question." However, no one denies the strong influence that smell has on sexuality in the lower animals. To cite just one study, Elliott Blass and Thomas Fillion put lemon scent on the nipples of a group of mother rats who had just given birth. When the infant males who nursed on lemon-smelling mothers were themselves adults, they mated more quickly with females whose genitals were

lemon-scented than they did with normal females. Blass and Fillion believe that, at least in rats, infantile olfactory experiences can influence adult sexual behavior (Fillion & Blass, 1986).

"Local" Versus "Distance" Senses

Smell and taste are often called *chemical senses* because the stimulus that excites the receptors in your tongue and nose are *complex chemical molecules*.

But there is a very important difference between taste and smell—whatever your tongue tastes must ordinarily be brought to your mouth, while your nose can detect stimuli that are some distance away.

The skin senses, including taste, are *local* senses—that is, they give your brain information about the exact point on your body that is being stimulated. Olfaction, hearing, and vision are *distance* senses—that is, they typically tell your brain what is going on some distance away from the surface of your body.

Of the "five" senses, vision and hearing surely predominate—in part because of their sensory richness, but in part because, being "distance senses," vision and hearing are the main channels by which you *communicate with others*.

If you were designing a robot for NASA, you'd surely want it to be able to see and hear. For robots, like people, adapt more easily to the world around them if they have vision and hearing. And they can communicate with others more readily using speech and visual signs than with tastes and smells.

Whether you're designing a NASA robot or trying to learn more about yourself, therefore, it will pay you to find out how your eyes and ears function.

□ □ **QUESTION** □ □
Would you want your NASA robot to be able to detect tastes and smells? Why (or why not)?

HEARING

From a physical point of view, what do your eyes and ears have that your skin, nose, and tongue lack? One answer is—*separation*.

Let's first compare hearing with olfaction. If you block one of your ears with cotton, your ability to localize the *position* of sounds diminishes considerably. But if just one of your nostrils is stopped up when you have a cold, you could locate a rotten egg just about as rapidly as if both your nasal chambers were operating unimpaired.

One important difference between hearing and smell, then, is this: Your ears are some 6 inches apart; your nasal chambers are separated by less than 1/2 inch.

If you would like to demonstrate to your-self the importance of the "space between your ears," you might try a musical experiment. Find a **stereo** hi-fi set with two *movable* speakers. Put the speakers as far apart in the room as you can. Now put on your favorite stereo record and sit between the two speakers with your eyes closed. You will hear music coming at you from all directions. But some sounds will seem to be on your left, while others seem to be on your right.

Now, put the two speakers right next to each other and repeat the experiment. Chances are, the music will seem compressed, pushed together, cut down in size to a *point source*. In short, the stereo music will now sound monaural, or "mono."

Your ears are like the two speakers spread far apart. Your nose and tongue are like the two speakers put close together.

Localizing Sounds

In a sense, your ears are similar to the micro-phones used to record music. To get a stereo effect, the record company must use at least two mikes that are some distance apart. When a band performs, each mike "hears" a slightly different version of the music.

Suppose the lead guitarist in the band is on the left. The mike on the left would then "hear" the guitarist much more loudly than would the mike on the right. If the drummer is on the right, then the right microphone would pick up the sounds of the drum more loudly than would the mike on the left.

Record companies typically make a *completely separate* recording of what the left mike "hears" and what the right mike "hears." These two different records make up the two chan-nels of stereophonic music that are pressed on stereo disks or dubbed on tapes.

By keeping the two channels *separate* dur-ing both recording and playback, you can maintain left-right relationships. That is, when you hear the record, the sounds made by the lead guitarist come primarily from the left speaker. The drummer's beat, however, will come to you mostly from the right speaker.

Your ears are just far enough apart so that you can readily detect left-right differences in sound sources. Sound waves travel at a speed of some 750 miles per hour at sea level. If a cricket 6 feet to the left of your head chirps loudly, the noise will reach your left ear a frac-tion of a second before it reaches your right ear. And since the insect is closer to your left ear than to your right, the noise will be louder when it reaches your left ear than when it fi-nally gets around your head and reaches your right ear (Levine & Shefner, 1981).

Your brain *interprets* the difference in the auditory inputs from your left and right ears to mean that the cricket is to your left. But, as we

Stereo recording duplicates human hearing by using two microphones, placed several inches apart, as "ears" to pick up the sound. Playing it back on stereo speakers, the lis-tener has the impression of "being there."

will soon see, your brain can be fooled in such matters if you know how to go about it.

The farther apart your ears are, the more precisely you can detect the location of a sound—because there is a greater difference in what your two ears would hear. When a re-cording company sets its microphones 10 feet apart, they are effectively increasing the *appar-ent* distance between your ears to 10 feet—particularly if you listen to the music with stereo headphones.

Now go back to your stereo set and put one speaker on the floor and the other as high up in the air as you can directly above the first. Sit with your head upright between the two speakers. When you play music now, it will seem strangely "mono," for each of your ears is the *same distance from both speakers*.

Your ears can detect the location of sounds spread out in the *left-right* dimension rather well. But your ears do very poorly in locating sounds in the *up-down* dimension (Levine & Shefner, 1981).

□ □   **QUESTION**   □ □
Why might it help to "cock your head to one side" when trying to locate the source of a sound over your head?

THE AUDITORY STIMULUS

Hearing is a *vibratory sense*. That is, the **audi-tory** receptors in your ears are sensitive to vi-brations of the molecules in the air around you. These vibrations usually come in waves, which we call "sound waves." Thus, the stimu-lus for hearing (or "audition") is usually a vi-bratory wave of some kind. (Words such as "au-dition," "audio," and "auditorium" all come from the Latin word *audire*, meaning "to hear.")

Imagine yourself seated a couple of feet above a very quiet pool in a forest. You take a stone and toss it in the center of the pond, and what happens? Wave after wave of ripples circle out from the center until they strike the edges of the pool. If you looked closely, you would see that when one of the waves reached the

When a bass fiddle is played, you can often see the string vibrate as it produces sound waves.

Stereo. Short for "stereophonic." From a Greek word meaning "solid," or having to do with three dimensions. Stereo sound has a "three-dimensional" quality to it, quite different from "mono" sound, which seems one-dimensional.

Auditory (AW-ditt-tory). From the Greek word meaning "to hear." Audition is the technical word for "hearing."

Outer ear. The fleshy outer part of the ear. Also called the auricle (AW-rick-cull), the pinna (PIN-nah), or the auditory meatus (me-ATE-us). The outer ear catches sound waves and reflects them into the auditory canal.

Auditory canal (AW-dit-tor-ee). The hollow tube running from the outer to the middle ear.

Middle ear. Contains the hammer, anvil, and stirrup. Lies between the eardrum and the oval window.

Hammer, anvil, and *stirrup* (STIR-up). Three small, connected bones in your middle ear that make sounds louder.

Oval window. The thin membrane lying between your middle and inner ears. The stirrup is connected to one side of the oval window. The basilar membrane (see below) is connected to the other.

Inner ear. A fluid-filled "worm hole" in your skull that contains both the motion detectors (the saccule, utricle, and semi-circular canals) and your receptor neurons for hearing.

Cochlea (COCK-lee-ah). The snail-shaped portion of your inner ear that contains the basilar membrane.

Organ of Corti (KOR-tie). A highly complex structure lying on the basilar membrane that contains the sensory receptor cells for hearing.

Basilar membrane (BASS-ill-ar). A ribbon of tissue that supports the organ of Corti. One end of the basilar membrane connects to the oval window, the other to the round window.

"I HEARD WHAT YOU SAID. I'M PROCESSING IT."

shore, it "bounced back" in a kind of watery echo.

The sound waves that stimulate the *auditory receptors* in your ear are not very different from the ripples that you create by dropping the rock in the pond. Whenever any fairly rigid object is struck forcibly, it tends to *vibrate*. As this object vibrates back and forth, it "makes ripples" in the molecules of air around it. These "ripples" are really *sound waves*. That is, they are waves of energy that pass through the air just as the ripples pass across the surface of the water when you throw a stone in the pond. When these *sound waves* reach your ear, they set part of your eardrum to moving back and forth in rhythm with the vibrating object. Other parts of your ear then translate the vibrations of the eardrum into *patterns of neural energy* that are sent to your brain so that you can "hear" (Levine & Shefner, 1981).

Parts of the Ear

Your ear has three main divisions: (1) the outer ear, (2) the middle ear, and (3) the inner ear (see Fig. 4.9).

1. The **outer ear** is that fleshy flap of skin and other tissue sticking out from either side of your head. Your outer ear tends to "catch" sound waves and direct them into a narrow tunnel called the **auditory canal**. At the inner end of this auditory canal is your *eardrum*, a thin membrane stretched tautly across the auditory canal like the skin on a drum. The eardrum separates your outer ear from your middle ear.

2. The **middle ear** is a hollow cavity in your skull that contains three little bones called the **hammer**, the **anvil**, and the **stirrup**. If you inspected these three little bones under a microscope, they would look much like the real-world objects they are named after. One end of the hammer is connected to the eardrum. When your eardrum moves, it pulls the hammer back and forth rhythmically (Pickles, 1982).

The hammer transmits this "wave" of sound energy to the anvil, making the anvil move back and forth. The anvil pulls the stirrup back and forth in similar fashion.

The stirrup is connected to another membrane called the **oval window**. As the stirrup moves, it forces part of the membrane on your oval window to wiggle back and forth in rhythm too.

The three little bones and the two membranes act as the *amplifiers* in your own biological stereo system. By the time the sound stimulus has reached your oval window, it is many times stronger than it was when it first struck your eardrum.

3. The oval window separates the middle ear from the **inner ear**. Your inner ear is a fluid-filled cavity that runs through your skull bone like a tunnel coiling through a mountain. This inner ear of yours has two main parts: (1) the **cochlea**, and (2) the motion detectors we discussed earlier in this chapter (the saccule, the utricle, and the semi-circular canals).

The cochlea gets its name from the Latin word for "snail shell," which is just what your cochlea looks like. Your auditory receptors are the 24,000 hair cells that are a part of the **organ of Corti** inside your cochlea. The organ of Corti lies on the **basilar membrane**, which runs the length of

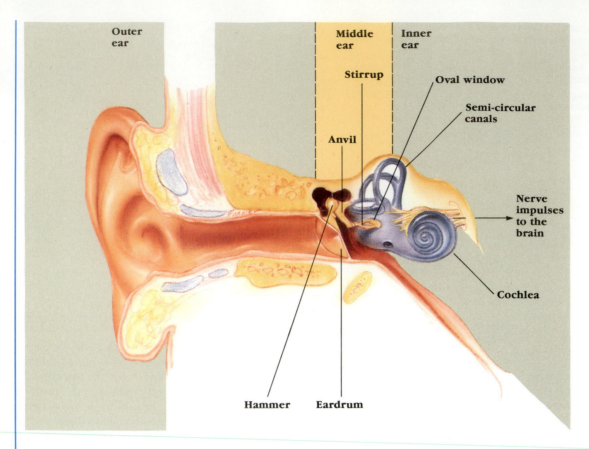

Outer ear

Middle ear   Inner ear

Stirrup

Oval window

Semi-circular canals

Anvil

Nerve impulses to the brain

Cochlea

Hammer   Eardrum

FIG. 4.9 Structure of the human ear.

the cochlea (see Fig. 4.10). Input messages from the hair cells pass along the auditory nerve to the lower centers of the brain, which relay them up to the temporal lobe of your cortex. Generally speaking, you are not *consciously aware* of hearing anything until the auditory message reaches your cortex (Hudspeth, 1983).

Frequency and Amplitude

Sound waves have two important physical aspects: **frequency** and **amplitude**.

The *frequency* of a musical tone is related to how *high* or *low* the tone sounds to your ear. Put more precisely, the psychological *pitch* of a

FIG. 4.10 A cross-section of the tunnel-like tube of the cochlea, with the organ of Corti.

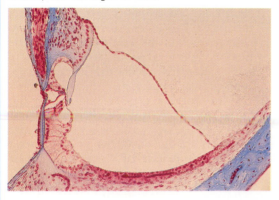

tone is primarily determined by the physical *frequency* of the sound wave.

The *amplitude* of a musical tone is related to how *loud* or *soft* the tone sounds to you. Put more precisely, the subjective *loudness* of a tone is primarily determined by the objective *amplitude* of the sound.

"Pitch" and "loudness" are terms that describe *psychological* attributes of the subjective experience of hearing. "Frequency" and "amplitude" are terms that describe the *physical* characteristics of the auditory stimulus (Moore, 1982).

● *Pitch and Frequency*

If you drop a stone in a deep pond, you set up just one big wave that moves out from the point at which the stone hits the water. But if you drop several pebbles in, one after the other, you set up a *series of waves*. If you dropped in 10 pebbles each second, you would set up 10 waves a second (under perfect conditions). The *frequency* of the waves would then be 10 per second.

When you pluck a string on a guitar, you are doing much the same thing as dropping a rock in a pond. For the string creates sound waves that have *exactly the same frequency as* the number of vibrations that the string makes per second. Your ear detects these sound waves, and your brain turns them into musical tones. The *faster* a particular string vibrates, the

Frequency. In auditory terms, the number of times a sound source vibrates each second. The frequency of a musical tone is measured in Hertz.

Amplitude (AM-plee-tood). From the Latin word meaning "muchness." We get our word "ample" from the same Latin source. Amplitude is the amount of sound present, or the strength of a musical tone. Literally, the "height" of a sound wave.

Hertz (hurts). The frequency of any wave, such as a sound wave. Used to be called "cycles per second," or cps. Named for the German scientist Heinrich Hertz, who made the first definitive studies of energy waves.

more "waves per second" it creates—and the *higher* the pitch of the tone will seem to be when you hear it.

If you plucked the "A" string on a guitar, it would vibrate 440 times per second. This number is called the *frequency* of the musical tone "A." In technical terms, we would say this tone has a frequency of 440 "cycles per second," or 440 **Hertz** (440 Hz). In general, the thinner and shorter a string is, the higher the frequency at which it vibrates—and the higher the pitch of the tone that it makes.

• Amplitude and Loudness

The loudness of a tone is determined primarily by the tone's *amplitude*, not by its frequency. If you happen to pluck the "A" string of the guitar *very gently*, it vibrates 440 times per second.

But if you plucked the string *as hard as you could*, it would still vibrate at about 440 Hz. If it didn't, you wouldn't hear the note as being an "A."

But surely something different happens, for the more energetically you pluck a string, the louder the note sounds. The answer is that the string moves *farther up and down* during each vibration—but it still vibrates at about 440 times per second (see Fig. 4.11A and B). In similar fashion, if you gently drop 10 pebbles per second into a pond, you create 10 very small waves. But if you throw 10 pebbles per second into a pond as hard as you can, you create 10 very tall waves. In either case, however, there are still just *10 waves per second*.

In technical terms, the "taller the wave," the greater its *amplitude*. And the greater the amplitude that a sound wave has, the louder it will sound to you (Moore, 1982).

The Range of Hearing

What kinds of musical tones can your ear hear?

Your range of hearing is, roughly speaking, from *20 Hz to about 20,000 Hz*. But you are not equally sensitive to all frequencies within this range. Your hearing is best from about 400 to 4,000 Hz. Human conversation ranges between 200 and 800 Hz. The lowest tone a bass singer can produce is about 100 Hz, while the

FIG. 4.11A A sound wave "cycle" or "Hertz" is measured from peak to peak.

FIG. 4.11B A vibrating guitar string.

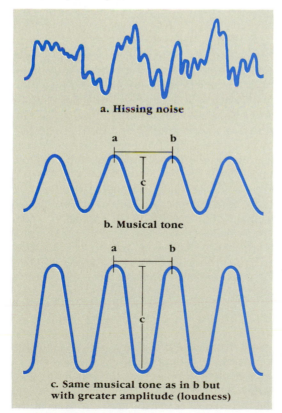

a. Hissing noise

b. Musical tone

c. Same musical tone as in b but with greater amplitude (loudness)

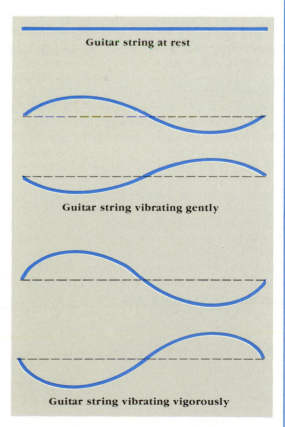

Guitar string at rest

Guitar string vibrating gently

Guitar string vibrating vigorously

highest tone most sopranos can produce is about 1,000 Hz. Thus, your ear is "tuned" to listen to other people speak (and sing) (Moore, 1982).

There seems to be a general rule that holds *across animal species*: The smaller the cochlea, the higher the animal's range of hearing is likely to be. The dog can hear notes at least as high as 25,000 Hz, while the bat is sensitive to tones as high as 100,000 Hz. Elephants, on the other hand, probably have a hearing range that cuts off at about 7,000 Hz (Stebbins, 1983).

▢▢ QUESTION ▢▢

If you wanted to design a whistle that could be used for calling dogs but couldn't be heard by human beings, what frequency range would you want to investigate?

Deafness

What difference would it make to your life if you became deaf?

Hearing is the major channel for *informal* social communication. Our customs, social graces, and moral beliefs are still passed down from one generation to another primarily by word of mouth rather than in writing. And most of us (textbook writers included!) prefer the informal transmission of knowledge that comes from talking to the formalness of the written word.

● *Bone Deafness and Nerve Deafness*

When people grow older, the three small bones in the middle ear often become brittle and thus do not work properly. Since the hammer, anvil, and stirrup serve to *amplify* the sound waves as they come into the ear, you could become deaf (or partially so) when these bones malfunction. This type of *bone deafness* can usually be corrected if you are fitted for a hearing aid, a device that acts like a miniature hi-fi set and "turns up the volume" electronically. Bone deafness can also occur because of disease, birth defects, and exposure to loud sounds. The more severe types of bone deafness sometimes require surgery (Levine & Shefner, 1981).

Many types of infection can attack the hair cells on the organ of Corti. If your receptor cells were permanently damaged for any reason, you would suffer from *nerve deafness*. If only a small section of your basilar membrane were affected, you would lose the ability to hear just high notes, or low notes, or even notes in the middle of the auditory **spectrum** (see Fig. 4.12). If the damage to your nerve cells was widespread, however, you might become totally deaf for *all frequencies*.

In the past, nerve deafness could seldom be corrected either by surgery or by a hearing aid. In the past few years, however, scientists

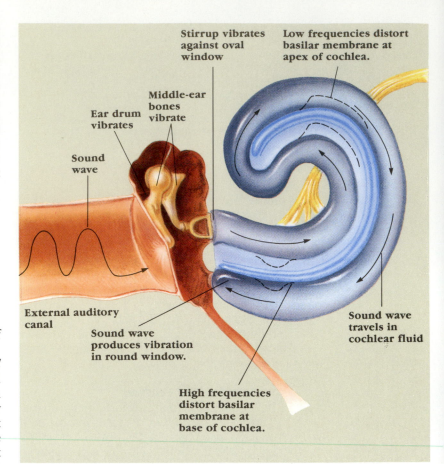

FIG. 4.12 Sound waves arriving through the auditory canal make the eardrum (tympanic membrane) vibrate. The three small bones in the inner ear amplify the sound and cause the oval window to vibrate. Sound waves travel through the cochlear fluid and cause the basilar membrane to distort or vibrate. The hair cells lying on the basilar membrane respond by sending an input message along the auditory nerve (not shown).

have begun implanting tiny electrodes *directly into the ear*. These electrodes deliver short bursts of electricity to the auditory nerve. Normal speech is picked up by a small microphone and "translated" into pulses of electrical current by a pocket-sized computer. These devices by-pass the damaged receptor cells on the basilar membrane by stimulating the auditory nerve itself.

The major causes for nerve deafness are birth defects, disease, and exposure to extremely loud sounds. The jet engines on modern airplanes create ear-splitting sounds, which is why people who work around jets wear protective earphones. The sound levels in many factories can cause damage too if the workers are exposed to the noise for too long a time.

According to Clarkson University psychologists Thomas Ayres and Paul Hughes, loud sounds can also cause a temporary decrease in *visual acuity*. Ayres and Hughes tested the ability of a group of students to discriminate visual stimuli while listening to a recording of a rock group called the Mahavishnu Orchestra. When the recording was playing at a normal level, the

Spectrum (SPECK-trum). From the Latin word meaning "to look," from which we also get the words "specter" (ghost) and "spectacle." The word "spectrum" means a set or array of related objects or events, usually a set of sights or sounds.

Paranoia (pair-ah-NOI-ya). A severe type of mental disorder characterized by delusions of grandeur and suspicions that people are whispering or trying to control your behavior.

students' visual acuity was normal. However, when the recording was playing at about the loudness of a live concert, 80 percent of the students suffered a significant decrease in their visual acuity (cited in Meer, 1985).

☐☐ QUESTION ☐☐
Ayres and Hughes found that many students turn up the volume on their car stereos to "live concert levels" while driving. Why might these students be more likely to have accidents than would students who kept the volume at a lower level?

- ### *Deafness and Paranoia*
According to Stanford psychologist Philip Zimbardo, older individuals who slowly lose their hearing may be reluctant to admit their growing deafness. For to do so, Zimbardo says, would be to admit that they are "growing old." Thus, many older people with hearing losses tend to blame their hearing problems on the behavior of others rather than on their own faulty ears. This "blaming behavior" often takes the form of a mild **paranoia**, in which the

older person grows highly suspicious that other people are whispering about the person behind her or his back (Zimbardo, Andersen, & Kabat, 1981).

In a recent study, Zimbardo and two of his associates report the results of a study they performed on "experimental deafness" at Stanford. The psychologists began by hypnotizing some students in a discussion group and telling them that they would have severe difficulties hearing the other members of the group talk. (As you will see in Chapter 13, this sort of temporary hearing loss under hypnosis is completely reversible.) As predicted, most of the temporarily deaf students became convinced other members of their discussion groups were "talking ill of them," or were trying to do the subjects harm. They also became more hostile, confused, agitated, irritable, and less creative. Zimbardo and his colleagues believe the tendency to blame other people for one's own faults may explain many personality disorders, including some types of paranoia (Zimbardo, Andersen, & Kabat, 1981).

☐☐ QUESTION ☐☐
If you don't "speak up" around a person with hearing problems, how might your own behaviors increase the deaf person's feelings of paranoia?

- ### *Deafness and Television-watching*
In a recent study, Bruce Austin and John Myers of the Rochester Institute of Technology found that hearing-impaired students watch television more hours a week—and like television more—than do students with normal hearing. Furthermore, Austin and Myers report, hearing-impaired students "were more likely than hearing respondents to perceive TV as depicting reality." Austin and Myers believe that people with hearing difficulties may use "television as a social substitute. The hearing-impaired are often cut off from social participation and inclusion in a largely hearing and aurally related world; television makes no social judgments and demands no special social skills" (Austin & Meyers, 1984).

- ### *Language Learning, Deafness, and Feedback*
Learning to sing, dance, play the guitar, or drive a car—all these complex motor tasks require *feedback*. A girl who is born deaf—or partially deaf—has trouble learning to talk because she cannot hear what noises her voice is making. Without the auditory feedback from her vocal cords, the girl can never learn to shape her spoken words properly, because she simply does not know *what her own voice sounds like*.

Until scientists discovered how necessary some kind of feedback is in learning to talk, we often thought that partially-deaf children were

Learning a complex motor task, such as ballet dancing, requires feedback from a skilled instructor as well as from our own senses.

dumb or stupid. Occasionally we mistakenly confined these children to homes for the mentally retarded—although many of them were very intelligent. Fortunately, now that hearing tests for young children are much more common than they used to be, we are less likely to confuse partial deafness with mental retardation (Braginsky & Braginsky, 1971).

□□ **QUESTION** □□
Suppose that a very bright but partially-deaf child is mistakenly put in a home for the mentally retarded. Would anyone be likely to try to train the child to read? Under some circumstances, could the child perhaps learn to read on his or her own?

VISION

Psychologically speaking, hearing is a far more complex sense than is "touch," taste, or smell. But when it comes to "richness" of sensory experience, vision is perhaps more complicated than all the other sensory modalities put together. And because vision dominates so much of our lives, psychologists have studied it in greater detail than the other senses. As a result, we know more about how and why you see than we do about how you experience the rest of your sensory world.

Vision has often been called "the sense of wonder." To appreciate how your ability to see influences your thoughts and behaviors, however, you need to understand at least three things:

- What the visual stimulus (light) is like.
- How your eye converts light into a sensory input to send to your brain.
- How your brain interprets this incoming sensory information.

Once you have learned something about how the eye operates, perhaps you will understand why Robert Boynton recently said, "The seemingly simple act of vision requires the most sophisticated biological instrumentation

FIG. 4.13 The electro-magnetic spectrum.

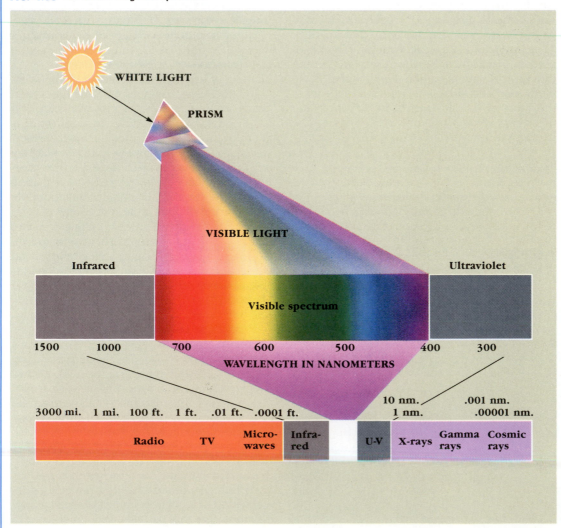

WHITE LIGHT

PRISM

VISIBLE LIGHT

Infrared

Ultraviolet

Visible spectrum

1500   1000   700   600   500   400   300
WAVELENGTH IN NANOMETERS

3000 mi. 1 mi. 100 ft. 1 ft. .01 ft. .0001 ft.   10 nm.   .001 nm.
                                                        1 nm.   .00001 nm.

| Radio | TV | Micro-waves | Infra-red | | U-V | X-rays | Gamma rays | Cosmic rays |

Electro-magnetic spectrum. The entire range of frequencies or wave-lengths of electro-magnetic radiation ranging from gamma rays to the longest radio waves. Includes the visible spectrum.

Photon (FO-tohn). A tiny packet of energy which is the smallest unit of light. Under ideal circumstances, your eye is so incredibly sensitive that it can detect a single photon.

Velocity (vee-LOSS-sit-tee). The speed at which an object or wave moves. From the Latin word meaning "to be quick."

Visible spectrum (SPECK-trum). When you look at a rainbow in the sky, you see the array (spectrum) of visible colors that make up sunlight. For most purposes, "rainbow" and "visible spectrum" can be considered the same things.

Nanometers (NAN-oh-meters). A nanometer is one-billionth of a meter, or about 1/40,000,000,000th of an inch.

Light passing through a prism is broken up into an orderly progression of wave lengths, resulting in a "rainbow" of colors.

of any device in the entire world" (Boynton, 1980).

☐☐ QUESTION ☐☐
If you were designing a robot for NASA, where on the robot's body would you put its hearing and vision receptors? Why?

THE VISUAL STIMULUS

The stimulus for vision is *light*, which is a very small part of the **electro-magnetic spectrum**. The electro-magnetic spectrum also includes X-rays and radio waves (see Fig. 4.13).

The smallest, most elementary unit of light is called the **photon**, which gets its name from the Greek word meaning "light." The flame from one match produces millions of photons. A flashlight produces a great many more photons than does a match. Thus, in general, the *stronger* the light source, the *more* photons it produces in a given unit of time (such as a second).

When you turn on a flashlight, photons stream out from the bulb at an incredible speed, or **velocity**. To give you a better "feel" for this speed, consider the fact that the velocity of sound waves is about 750 miles per *hour*. The speed of light, on the other hand, is about 186,000 miles per *second*.

☐☐ QUESTION ☐☐
Sound travels at slightly more than 2 miles a second. If you saw a lightning bolt hit the ground during a storm, and heard thunder about 4 seconds later, approximately how far away from you did the lightning bolt hit?

Wave-Lengths of Visual Inputs
The bulb of a flashlight produces photons in waves—much as the string on a guitar produces sound waves when the string vibrates, or the wind produces waves on the surface of the ocean. If you want to understand how scientists study light waves, learning something about ocean waves first might be of help.

If you wanted to, you could take a boat out on the sea and actually measure the distance *between* one ocean wave and another. And if you did so, you would find the distance between the crests of the waves was remarkably consistent. On a calm, peaceful day, as the waves moved slowly and majestically, the distance between waves would be rather large. But on windy, choppy days, this wave-length would be rather small. Thus, if you knew the *strength* of the wind, even without going out on the water you would have some notion of what the *length* between the crests of the ocean waves would be.

Much the same sort of consistency holds for the wave-length of light and what color it appears to be. The "rainbow of colors" make up what is technically called the **visible spectrum**. The blue colors have very short wave-lengths. The reds, at the other end of the spectrum, have much longer wave-lengths. The colors between red and blue have wave-lengths that fall between these two extremes.

Thus, if you know what *wave-length* a visual input has, you will know what *color* it ordinarily will appear to be.

However, the distance between the crests of light waves is much, much smaller than the distance between any two ocean waves. The wave-length for red is so short that it takes about 38,000 "red waves" to make an inch. The wave-length for blue is much shorter—it takes about 70,000 "blue waves" to make an inch.

Scientists seldom measure the wave-length of light in fractions of an inch, because the figures are just too clumsy to use. Instead, scientists measure wave-lengths in **nanometers**. The Greek word for "dwarf" is *nanos*. From this fact, you can perhaps guess that the nanometer is a "dwarf" or fraction of a meter (39.37 inches). In fact, there are one billion nanometers in each meter.

Amplitude of Visual Inputs

The physical wave-length of a light stimulus usually determines the color that it will appear to you, such as blue or red. But some blue lights are bright, while others are dim. The physical intensity of a light determines how bright it will seem, and this *physical intensity* can be measured in terms of the height or *amplitude* of the wave.

If you measured the *length* between crests of ocean waves on a calm day, you might find that the wave-length was about 20 feet. The *height* of each wave, however, might be no more than 3 feet. During a storm, the wave-length might still be 20 feet, but the *height* of each ocean wave might now be 10 to 13 feet.

In similar fashion, a dim blue light might have a wave-length of 423 nanometers. If you "turned up the intensity" of this blue light until it was very bright, it would still have a *wave-length* of 423 nanometers—but the *amplitude* (height) of each wave would be many times greater.

When you make a light brighter, you *amplify* the height of each light wave—just as when you turn up the volume on your stereo set you *amplify* the height of each sound wave the machine puts out.

The *psychological color* of a visual input, therefore, is determined primarily by its *physical wave-length*. And the *psychological brightness* of a visual stimulus is determined primarily by the *physical amplitude* of the light wave.

The Visible Spectrum

In a manner of speaking, light waves are much like X-rays and radio waves—except that X-rays have such short wave-lengths that they are invisible to your eye, and radio waves have such a long wave-length that you can't see them. As Fig. 4.13 suggests, the only waves you can *see* lie between 400 and 760 nanometers. We call this range of waves the *visible spectrum*.

Why does a psychologist interested in human behavior bother with such technical measures as wave-length and amplitude? For two reasons, really.

First, because visual inputs *stimulate* people to act and respond. And the more precisely we can specify the stimulus that evokes a certain reaction, the better we can understand the *behavior* itself.

Second, because we are often interested in individual differences. If we show *exactly the same* visual stimulus to two people, and they report *different* psychological experiences, we know these reports are due to differences in the people and not to some variability in the physical stimulus itself. We will have more to say about this point when we discuss color vision disorders (or "color blindness") later in this chapter.

□□ **QUESTION** □□
How many "eyes" should the NASA robot have? Why?

THE EYE

What biological processes occur when you see? These processes are so complex we still don't understand them completely.

If we stretch the facts a bit, we can say that your eye is like a color TV camera. (Your eye is far more complex and compact than a TV camera, but the similarities between the two may help you understand how your eye actually works.) Both your eye and the TV camera are "containers" that have a small hole at one end which admits light. The light then passes through a lens that focuses an image on a **photo-sensitive surface**. In both your eye and in the color TV camera, the "hole" can be opened to let in more light, or closed to keep light out. And in both, the lens can be adjusted to bring near or far objects into focus.

In the case of the color television camera, the light coming through the lens falls on an electronic tube that contains several complex

FIG. 4.14 A diagram of the eye.

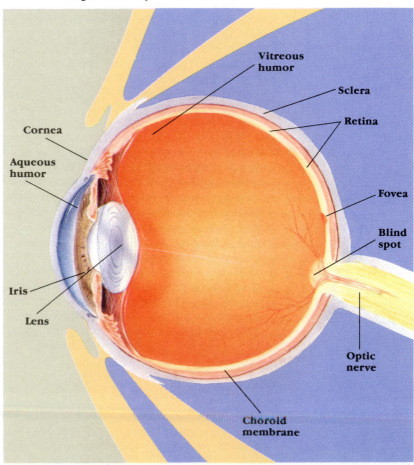

Photo-sensitive surface. Light waves can set off rather dramatic reactions in some chemicals. These light-sensitive chemicals are said to be "photo-sensitive." The film in a camera reacts to light—hence, film is photo-sensitive. The inner surface of your eye contains pigments (colored chemicals) that are also photo-sensitive.

Cornea (CORN-ee-ah). From the Latin word meaning "horn-like." We get our words "horn" and "corn" (the kind of blister you get on your foot) from this same Latin source. The cornea is the tough, transparent tissue in front of the aqueous humor.

Aqueous humor (A-kwi-us). The watery substance between the iris and the cornea that keeps the front of your eyeball "inflated" to its proper size and provides nutrients to the cornea.

Iris (EYE-riss). The colored or pigmented area of the eye. When you say that someone has brown eyes, you really mean the person has brown irises. The Greek word for "rainbow" is iris.

Vitreous humor (VITT-tree-us). From the Latin word meaning "glass." The vitreous humor is a clear, glass-like substance in the center of the eyeball that keeps your eye in its proper rounded shape. Light must pass through the vitreous humor before it strikes your retina.

Retina (RETT-tin-ah). The photo-sensitive inner surface of your eye. Contains the visual receptor organs.

Sclera (SKLAIR-ah). The tough outer layer of the eyeball.

Choroid membrane (KOR-oid). The dark, middle layer of the eyeball that contains blood vessels and pigment cells.

Fovea (FOE-vee-ah). The tiny "pit" or depression right at the center of your retina that contains only cones, and where your vision is at its clearest and sharpest.

Rhodopsin (row-DOP-sin). The visual pigment in the rods that, when bleached by light, causes the rods to send a signal to the brain that a visual input has occurred. The great visual researcher, W.A.H. Rushton, once wrote, "Molecules respond to light as do people to music. Some absorb nothing. Others respond by the degraded vibration of foot or finger. But some there are who rise and dance and change partners." Depending on the situation, when rhodopsin is struck by light rays, it does little or nothing or "rises and dances."

chemicals. These chemicals are photo-sensitive—that is, they react chemically when struck by photons. The camera then produces several different images which, when properly combined on a TV set, reproduce the scene in vivid color.

In the case of your eye, light first passes through the **cornea** and the **aqueous humor** (see Fig. 4.14). Once past the aqueous humor, light enters your inner eye through an opening called the *pupil*. The **iris** is the colored part of your eye which, by expanding and contracting around the pupil, controls the amount of light admitted inside your eye.

Just beyond the pupil is the *lens*. The purpose of the lens in your eye—like the lens in a camera—is to allow you to *focus clearly* whether you are looking at something close or far away. As you change your point of focus from a near object to something several feet away, muscles inside your eye pull on the lens to change its shape and thus refocus the light.

The lens *focuses* the image of what you are looking at. The lens also *projects* this image through the **vitreous humor** onto the inner surface of your eyeball—just as the lens in a camera focuses an image and projects it on the film in the back of the camera.

The inner surface of your eyeball is called the **retina**, from the Latin word meaning "net" or "network." Your retina is a network of millions of cells that—like the picture tube in the TV camera—contains several photo-sensitive chemicals.

The Retina

In a sense, your eyeball is a hollow sphere whose shell has three layers.

- The outer layer—which contains the cornea—is called the **sclera**. The sclera is really the "skin" of your eyeball. Like most other skin tissue, the sclera contains *free nerve endings* that are sensitive to pressure, temperature—and pain (see Fig. 4.14).
- The middle layer of the "shell" of your eye is a dark lining that is called the **choroid membrane**, or coat.
- The third layer is the *retina*, which is really the inner surface of your hollow eyeball.

- #### The Fovea
The inner layer of your retina contains the receptor cells that translate the physical energy of a light wave into the patterns of neural energy that your brain interprets as "seeing" (see Fig. 4.15).

There are two special parts of your retina that you should know about. The first is called the **fovea**. The second is your *blind spot*.

Fovea is the Latin word for "small pit." The fovea in your eye is a tiny pit in the center of your retina where your vision is at its sharpest. Although the fovea is only about the size of a head of a pin, the fovea is crucial for such specialized tasks as reading or inspecting the fine detail of any object.

The *blind spot* is a small area of your retina near the fovea which is, for all practical purposes, totally "sightless." We will discuss the blind spot in greater detail later in this chapter. The reason that this part of your eye is sightless, however, is that it has no *receptor neurons* in it.

- #### The Rods and Cones
The receptor neurons for vision are the *rods* and *cones*. Their names are fairly descriptive of their shapes. In the human eye, the rods are slim, pencil-shaped nerve cells. The cones are thicker and have a cone-shaped tip at their "business" end. An actual photograph of the rods and cones appears in Fig. 4.16.

Both the rods and cones contain chemicals that are very sensitive to light. When a beam of light strikes a rod, it causes the *bleaching* or breakdown of a chemical called **rhodopsin**, or visual purple (the Greek word *rhod* means "rose-colored"). In ways that we still don't entirely understand, this bleaching action causes

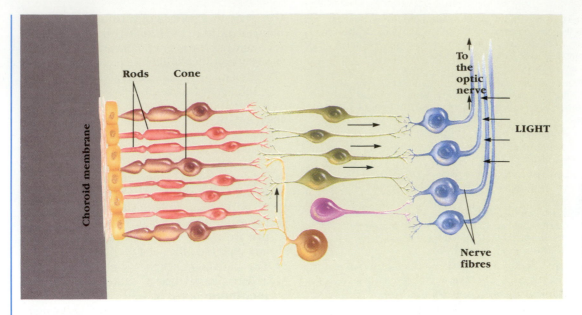

Rods   Cone

Choroid membrane

To
the
optic
nerve

LIGHT

Nerve
fibres

FIG. 4.15 The arrangement of synaptical connections in the primate retina. The right and left sides illustrate areas outside the fovea that contain rods; the center section from the middle of the fovea has no rods.

the rod to respond electrically. This visual input message passes up through the lower centers of your brain and eventually reaches the occipital lobe (see Fig. 4.17). At this point, you become "consciously aware" that you have actually seen something (Stryer, 1987).

● The Rods

Your rods are *color-blind*. They "see" the world in blacks and whites no matter how colorful the world actually is. Your rods respond much like a "fast but grainy" black-and-white film you might use in a camera. That is, the rods need less light to operate than the cones

FIG. 4.16 The rods are the slim, pencil-shaped cells on the left of the photograph; the cones are the two fat cells squeezed in between the rods. Light enters the retina from the right; the back of the eye (choroid coat) is to the left in the photograph.

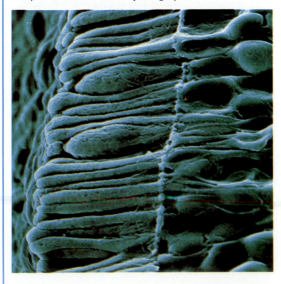

do, but they give a less detailed picture of the world than the colorful view provided by your cones.

For the most part, the rods are concentrated in the outer reaches or **periphery** of the retina. There are almost no rods in the central regions of the retina, and none at all in the fovea. All told, there are about 100 million rods in each of your eyes (Stryer, 1987).

● The Cones

Your cones contain photo-sensitive chemicals which break down when struck by light waves. This chemical reaction triggers off an electrical response in your cones which passes along the optic nerve until it reaches the visual input area in your occipital lobes.

Current research suggests there are three different types of cones. One type of cone is sensitive primarily to *red* light, a second is sensitive to *blue* light, and a third is sensitive to *green*. Each type of cone has its own unique photo-sensitive chemical (Nathans, Thomas, & Hogness, 1986).

There are a few cones in the periphery of the retina, but most of the cones are bunched together in the center of your retina near the fovea. The fovea contains *only cones*. There are some three million cones in each of your eyes (Stryer, 1987).

Since your cones are located *primarily* in the center of your retina, this is the part of your eye that is *most sensitive to color*.

When you look at something straight on, the light waves coming from that object strike your fovea and stimulate the cones, giving you clear color vision. When the same object is at the outer edges (periphery) of your vision, the light waves from the object strike primarily the rods in the periphery of the retina. Since the rods are color-blind, you will see anything that appears at the edges of your visual world as lacking in color. However, you can see some color (very weakly) even in the periphery of your vision because there are a few cones scattered about in the periphery (Barlow & Mollon, 1982).

Structure of the Retina

If you were called upon to design the eyes for a NASA robot, the odds are that you would never think of making the robot's retina like yours.

To begin with, your retina has *ten distinct layers*, with the rods and cones making up the *back layer*. The tips of your rods and cones—which contain the photo-sensitive chemicals

FIG. 4.17 A cross section of the visual system. Any object (such as the gray part of the line) in the left half of your visual field will be focused on the right half of the retinas in both your left and right eyes. Inputs from the right half of both retinas are sent to the visual cortex in your right hemisphere. Inputs from the left half of both retinas go to the left visual cortex. In this drawing, your left brain perceives the red half of the line, while your right brain perceives the gray half of the line.

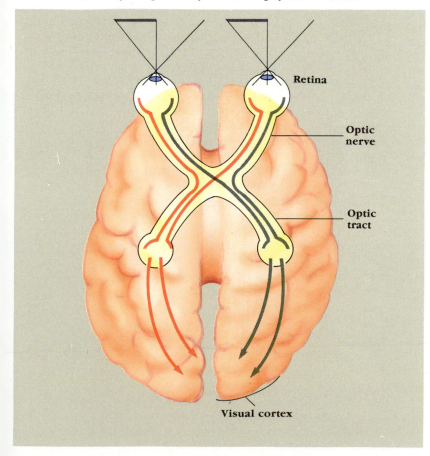

that react to light—are actually pointed away from the outside world. For light to strike your rods and cones, it must first pass through *all nine other layers of your retina* (see Fig. 4.15) (Weale, 1982).

The receptor cells in your skin are a part of your **peripheral nervous system**. That is, they are nerve cells which lie outside your brain and spinal cord. The retina evolved directly from the brain, however, and is considered by most authorities to be a part of the central nervous system (Barlow & Mollon, 1982).

The top layers of your retina contain a great many "large neurons" that are very similar in structure to those found in your cortex. These "large neurons" begin processing visual information right in the retina, before sending messages along to your visual cortex (in the occipital lobes at the back of your brain). Your retina is the *only receptor organ* in your body that processes inputs so extensively before sending them along to the cortex (Boynton, 1980).

The top layers of your retina also contain a few of the tiny blood vessels that serve the retina. Surprisingly enough, light must pass through these "large neurons" and the blood vessels before it can stimulate the rods and cones. Fortunately, these neurons and blood vessels are pushed aside at the point of the fovea. This fact helps explain why the fovea look like a "pit," and why vision is clearest at this point.

The Blind Spot

It is probably hard for you to imagine that each of your eyes has a spot that is, for all practical purposes, *totally blind*. Thus, there actually is a "hole" in your visual field where you see nothing at all.

Why this hole in your visual field? Well, your eyeball is hollow like a balloon, and your retina is *inside* the eyeball. The axons from the "large neurons" must somehow get through the walls of the eyeball if they are to reach their destinations in your brain. These axons meet at a point near the fovea to form the *optic nerve*, which exits from your eye at the *blind spot*. There are no receptors at this point in your retina—only axonic fibers and blood vessels. So, the part of your visual world that falls on the blind spot is not recorded in your brain (Weale, 1982).

You are usually unaware of this "hole in your vision" because what one eye misses, the other usually picks up (see Fig. 4.15). However, it is also true that your brain "cheats" just a bit. That is, your brain fills in the hole by making the empty spot in your visual world look like whatever surrounds it. You can prove this to yourself by following the instructions given in Fig. 4.18A. If you look at the picture from just

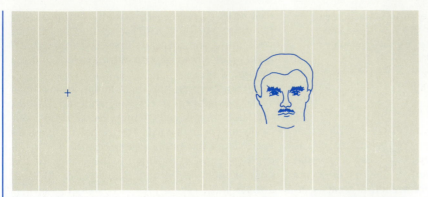

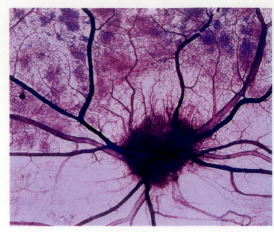

FIG. 4.18A There are no photoreceptors where the optic nerve leaves the eye. This creates a blind spot in our vision. To demonstrate this, close your left eye, fix your right eye on the "+," and move the book slowly toward your face. At a viewing distance of about 14 inches the obnoxious person will disappear but the vertical lines will not.

FIG. 4.18B The "blind spot."

the right position, the man's face disappears. But notice too that the spot where the man's face should be is filled in by your brain with the lines that surround the man's picture.

Optical Defects

Many distortions of your visual world are caused by misinterpretations made by your brain. But quite a few distortions stem from physical problems with the eye itself.

For example, the chances are one in four you either wear glasses or should wear them to help you overcome correctable visual difficulties. Many of these problems come from slight abnormalities in the shape of your eyeball.

● *Near-sightedness and Far-sightedness*

If your eyeball is *too long*, the lens tends to focus the visual image a little *in front* of your retina rather than clearly on it. You then see *near* objects rather clearly, but distant objects would appear fuzzy and blurred to you. We call this condition *near-sightedness* (see Fig. 4.19).

If your eyeball is *too short*, the lens tends to focus the visual image *behind* the retina rather than directly on it. Close objects are therefore indistinct to you, but *far* or distant objects are usually in clear focus. We call this condition *far-sightedness*.

If you watch carefully in the next movie you attend, you may notice something like the following: A woman standing close to the camera is talking with a man some distance away. When the woman is speaking, the camera focuses on her face, which you see clearly—but the image of the distant man is blurred and

"K, C, Ǝ..."

FIG. 4.19 From bottom to top, a far-sighted, a near-sighted, and a normal eye. Notice where the image focuses in each case.

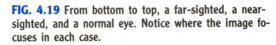

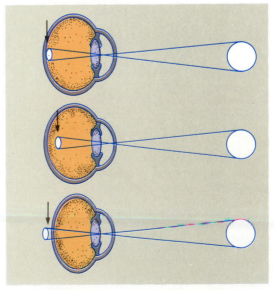

fuzzy. *This is approximately the way the near-sighted person sees the world* (see left photo this page).

Now, as the dialogue in the movie continues and the man begins to speak, the camera changes focus (but not position). Suddenly the woman's face, which is close to the camera, becomes blurred—but the distant image of the man sharpens and becomes distinct. *This is approximately the way the far-sighted person sees things in the world* (see right photo this page).

The lens in your eye operates much the same as does a camera lens, changing the focus from far to near as the occasion demands. As you grow older, however, your lenses become brittle, and you cannot focus back and forth between near and far objects as well as when you were young. This condition is called **old-sightedness**, or *presbyopia*. The typical solution to this problem is *bifocal glasses*. The upper part of the lens gives a clear picture of distant objects, while the lower half of the lens allows the person to see near objects clearly.

If your cornea is irregularly-shaped, you could suffer from a common visual defect called **astigmatism**. Fortunately, you can usually overcome this problem by wearing the proper prescription glasses.

Visual Acuity

When you go to an eye doctor to be tested for glasses, or when you apply for a driver's license, you will be given one of several tests to determine how accurately your eyes *discriminate* small objects. Your ability to discriminate

such things as the small print in a phone book is called your *visual acuity*.

One very common visual test is the **Snellen chart**, which presents letters of different sizes for you to read (see Fig. 4.20). A person with normal vision can barely read the largest letter on this chart at a distance of 200 feet (60 meters), and can just make out the next largest letters standing 100 feet away.

If you took this test yourself, you probably would be asked to stand 20 feet away from the Snellen chart. If you could read the "normal" line of letters at this distance, we would say that you can "see at 20 feet what the normal person can see at 20 feet." Hence, you would have 20/20 vision.

If you stood 20 feet away from the chart and could only read what the normal person can easily see at 100 feet, your vision would be 20/100, which is fairly poor. But if you could make out the very small letters on the bottom line when you were standing 20 feet away, you would be able to read letters that normal people can discriminate only when they are 10 feet away from the chart. In this case, you would have 20/10 or superior visual acuity.

Visual Contrast

Visual acuity alone is not enough for excellent vision. For you also must be able to see *brightness* differences as well. *Visual contrast* is the difference in the levels of brightness between adjoining areas of your visual world. A black dot on a white background has a lot of contrast. A gray cat sitting on a fog-covered rock has little contrast.

According to Robert Sekuler and Patrick Mulvanny, some individuals seem innately to be able to perceive visual contrast better than others. Other people apparently lose the ability to detect subtle contrast effects because of disease or brain damage. At the moment, there is no "optical correction" that will improve your ability to see contrasts. However, it is known that people who can detect contrasts well when wearing ordinary glasses sometimes lose that

A view of a scene as a nearsighted person sees it.

The same scene as viewed by a farsighted person.

The Eye

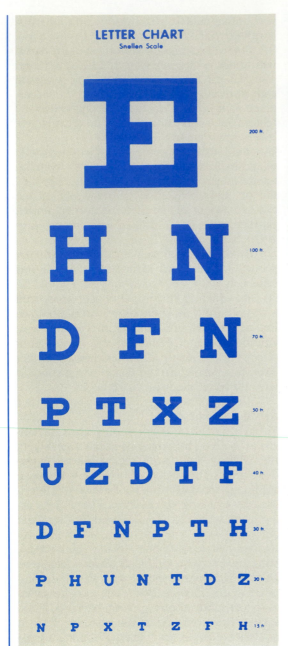

LETTER CHART
Snellen Scale

E — 200 ft.

H N — 100 ft.

D F N — 70 ft.

P T X Z — 50 ft.

U Z D T F — 40 ft.

D F N P T H — 30 ft.

P H U N T D Z — 20 ft.

N P X T Z F H — 15 ft.

FIG. 4.20 The Snellen chart.

Rods, which we rely on for seeing in dim light, are weak at discerning fine detail, such as reading road signs at night.

ability when wearing soft contact lenses. Sekuler and Mulvanny believe that when you apply for a driver's license, you should be tested not merely for visual acuity but for visual contrast as well (Sekuler & Mulvanny, 1982).

Visual Sensitivity

Under normal circumstances—in daylight, for instance—your *visual acuity* depends primarily on your cones. But at night or in any dim illumination—when you are often more interested in *detecting* faint sources of light than in *discriminating* fine details—your rods come into play. Your rods are much more sensitive to light than are your cones. Indeed, under the best of conditions, your rods are capable of detecting *a single photon of light* (Stryer, 1987). Your cones, however, are better than your rods at "seeing things in fine detail."

• *Visual Adaptation*

When light strikes one of your rods or cones, the light causes the photo-sensitive chemicals in your receptors to *bleach*, or break down. Your eye replaces the "broken down" photo-sensitive molecules fairly rapidly. But, as you might guess, your eye can replace these "visual chemicals" more rapidly in the dark than in bright illumination. Thus, after you have "adapted" to the darkness for a while, your ability to detect faint light sources is much better than when you've been sitting in bright sunlight.

As Fig. 4.21 suggests, your *cones* adapt more quickly in darkness than do your *rods*. Your cones become almost as sensitive as they are ever going to get in a matter of 10 minutes or so. Your rods continue to adapt for 30 minutes or more. Because they build up a larger "surplus" of photo-sensitive chemicals, your rods are a thousand times better at *detecting* weak visual inputs when fully dark-adapted than are your cones (Uttal, 1981).

□ □ **QUESTION** □ □
How long do you think an airplane pilot should be required to adapt to the dark before she or he is allowed to fly at night?

• *Night-blindness*

Some people do not see at all well at night. Usually this defect is caused by some disability of the rods. Night-blindness may have many causes, but a lack of Vitamin A is perhaps the

Hue (rhymes with "few"). The colors of the rainbow, or of the visible spectrum. Technically speaking, "color" includes not only the hues of the rainbow, but all the mixtures of hues plus blacks, whites, and grays. Black and white are not considered hues, although technically they are "colors." Pink (red + white) is a color; its hue, however, is red.

Saturation (sat-your-RAY-shun). The intensity or richness of a color. Pink is a weak (desaturated) red. The colors of the rainbow are about as saturated as any colors can be.

most common one. Vitamin A is necessary for the build-up of rhodopsin in the rods.

In daylight, your eyes automatically focus the image of an object on your fovea—where your visual acuity is best in good illumination. But your fovea contains only cones; hence it is "blind" at night. So when you stare directly at an object in dim light, the object may "disappear" because you're trying to see it with your cones.

If you want to see something at night, stare at the object "out of the corner of your eye," so that the object's visual image will fall on the periphery of your retina. That way, you can look at the object with your rods, not your cones. And that way, you can actually see better in dim illumination.

□ □ **QUESTION** □ □
Why do most objects look less colorful at twilight than at bright noon? (Hint: Remember the distribution of cones in the retina.)

COLOR VISION

For the most part, there is a very close connection between the physical attributes of a stimulus and the psychological experiences the stim-

FIG. 4.21 This figure demonstrates that the amount of light necessary for detection is a function of the amount of time a person spends in the dark. The major dark adaptation occurs within the rods, which reach their full sensitivity to minimal light in about 30 minutes. The cones, which adapt less to darkness, reach maximum sensitivity in about 10 minutes.

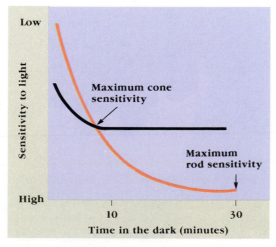

ulus creates inside your head. That's why it is very important that you learn something about the physical aspects of various stimuli. As we will see, however, there are times when your eyes (and brain) respond to inputs in ways that cannot be explained in purely "physical" terms. This point becomes particularly important when we try to describe *color vision*.

Hue

In *physical* terms, when you speak of the color of something, you really are talking about that object's **hue**, or the wave-length of light the object produces or reflects. Each wave-length of light in the rainbow (visible spectrum) produces a unique *hue*. The psychological experience of *color* is closely associated with the physical *hue* or wave-length of the stimulus object.

Most of the familiar colors appear on what psychologists call the *color circle*, which is made by joining the ends of the rainbow (see Fig. 4.22). Arranged around the outer edge of this circle are all of the spectral colors that you can see, and each point on the circle has a unique hue and wave-length.

Saturation

Hue alone is not enough to explain all the colorful visual experiences you have. For example, what is pink? It isn't a mixture of any two colors, but rather is a pale or *diluted* red. The vividness or richness of a color is what we call **saturation**.

Saturated colors are rich-looking and strong. Desaturated colors are weak and diluted. For example, suppose you poured red coloring into a bowl filled with tap water. The water would become deep red—a highly saturated color. Now suppose you pour in a lot more tap water. What happens? The ruby red soon becomes a pale, *desaturated* pink.

The hues around the outer edge of the color circle were carefully picked to be the most saturated possible (see Fig. 4.22). As you move inward toward the center of the circle, the colors become less and less saturated until you reach gray, which has *no hue at all*.

The *color solid* shown in Fig. 4.23 is an "expansion" of the color circle into three-dimensional space. Notice, though, that the color solid is not a perfect globe. The light blue colors simply do not seem as *saturated* to most observers as do the dark blue colors. And the dark yellow colors do not seem as saturated as do the light yellows. There is no general agreement among scientists as to why light blue and dark yellows aren't as fully saturated as are dark blues and light yellows.

• Complementary Colors

Any two colors that are *opposite* one another on the color circle are *complementary*. If you

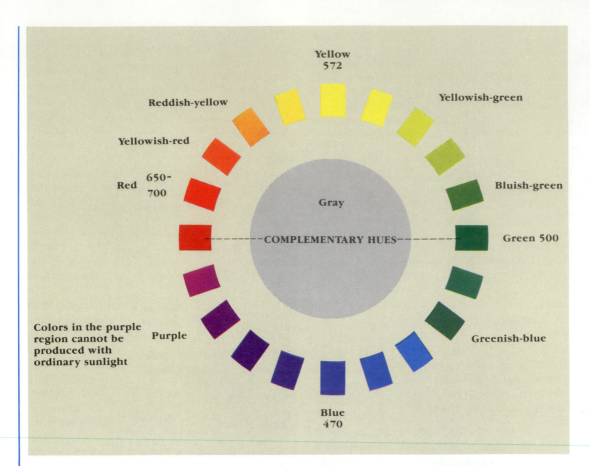

FIG. 4.22 The color circle illustrates the facts of color and color light mixture. The color names and their corresponding wavelengths (in nanometers) are given along the outside of the circle. Complementary colors are those colors opposite each other in the circle (such as reddish-yellow and greenish-blue); they will result in gray when mixed. The mixing of any two other wavelengths gives us an intermediate color. By proper mixing of three wavelengths equidistant in the circle (such as blue, green, and reddish-yellow), we can produce all color sensations.

FIG. 4.23 The purple-blue to yellow color solid on the left is viewed from the green side. The yellow to purple-blue range on the right side is viewed from the red side.

Additively. There are two types of color mixtures, additive and subtractive. If you shine a blue light and a yellow light on the same spot on a movie screen, the screen reflects back almost all of the light and thus "adds" the blue to the yellow light. This is an additive mixture. The pigments in most paints, however, give a subtractive mixture. If you shine a white light on an object painted blue, the pigments in the blue paint will "subtract," or block out, all the spectrum other than the hues in the blue area (that is, all the hues except blue and a little green). Thus, the object appears blue. Yellow paint blocks out ("subtracts") all the hues in white light except those at the yellow end of the spectrum (that is, all but yellow and a little green and a little orange). If you mix blue and yellow paints, the blue pigments subtract out the yellows and the yellow pigments subtract out the blues. But both pigments will leave some of the greens unblocked. Thus, a subtractive mixture of blue and yellow paints often yields a green color.

additively mix two complementary colored lights in more or less equal amounts, you get a completely desaturated gray. Thus, if you add green to a red, the red becomes less and less saturated until it becomes gray. However, the red light *never turns green* until it has passed through gray.

If you (additively) mix two colors that are *close to each other* on the circle, you get a "mixture color," not a gray. Thus, if you add yellow to red, the red turns first orange and then finally becomes a slightly reddish yellow—without first passing through gray.

Lightness

Look again at the color solid shown in Fig. 4.23. As we mentioned, this globe is really a three-dimensional "color circle." The hue changes as you go around the figure, while saturation decreases as you move from the outer edge toward the center of the globe. But there is a third dimension to this figure aside from hue and saturation. This third dimension is called *lightness*. The "north pole" of the solid is pure white. The "south pole" is pure black. Gray lies in the very center of the solid. The "lightness"

of a visual stimulus, then, ranges from white to gray to black.

By definition, black and white are completely desaturated colors. And like gray, black and white are "colors," but not "hues."

□□ **QUESTION** □□
What is the difference between "lightness" and "brightness?" (Hint: Does the saturation of a colored light change when you make it brighter? What about when you make it lighter?)

● *Negative After Images*

For reasons we still don't entirely understand, if you stare at a colored object for a minute or so, then close your eyes or look at a white wall, you will see the image in "reverse color." Technically speaking, this "reverse color" is called a *negative after image*. Negative after images are *always* the "complementary" of the color that you looked at. (See Fig. 4.24.)

COLOR DEFICIENCIES

Suppose you wanted to determine whether other people "saw the world" in the same colorful way that you do. How would you go about finding out?

Well, you might just show a variety of objects—a rose, a lime, a blueberry, and a lemon—to a random sample of subjects and *ask* them what colors the objects were. But even if everyone in your sample announced that "the rose is red-colored," how would you know the subjects actually *saw* the rose as being the same color you did? Red, after all, is a *subjective experience*, not a physical dimension.

One way to bring some objectivity to your experiment might be to show your subjects a rose and then ask them to *mix three colored*

FIG. 4.24 Stare at the center of this flag for about 30 seconds. Then look at a white wall or sheet of paper. You will see a negative after image in the colors complementary to those shown here.

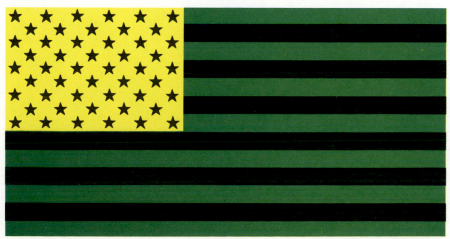

lights until they just matched the redness of the rose. (Technically speaking, this is an *additive* color mixture since it involves lights, not paints or pigments. See Fig. 4.25A and 4.25B.) You could pick almost any three colored lights from the spectrum for your "mix colors," of course. But let's say you picked red, blue, and green because you know you have a specific cone-receptor for each of these colors. You could then use these same three "mix colors" when you asked your subjects to match the greenness of a lime, the redness of a rose, and the blue of a berry (Barlow & Mollon, 1982).

FIG. 4.25A Additive color mixing.   FIG. 4.25B Subtractive color mixing.

● *Color Weakness*

If you tested enough people using an additive color mixture technique, you would soon find that a few of your subjects needed an abnormally large amount of red in order to reproduce the redness of a rose. These people would be *red-weak*. That is, they *see* the color red, but it appears much weaker to them than do green, blue, and yellow. If you asked a red-weak individual to mix red and blue to match the purpleness of a plum, this person would mix in much more red than would a subject with normal "red vision."

A few other subjects might need an unusually large amount of green to match a lime-colored light. These people would be *green-weak*. If you asked a person with normal color vision to mix green and blue to match a turquoise-colored light, the person might mix the two colors in equal proportions. A green-weak individual, however, might well need 80 percent green and 20 percent blue to get a "subjective match" for the turquoise-colored light.

Most *color-weak* individuals have difficulties seeing either red or green—or have problems with both these hues.

● *Color Deficiencies*

About 5 percent of the people in the world are almost totally insensitive to one or more hues on the color circle, although they can see most of the other hues perfectly well. The majority of these **color-deficient** people are *men*, for color deficiency is a sex-linked, inherited problem that seldom affects women.

The color-deficient person can reproduce all of the colors she or he can see by mixing just *two* basic hues. The main types of color deficiency involve a red deficiency or a green deficiency. Blue or yellow color deficiency is very rare.

A person suffering from either red or green deficiency sees the world almost entirely in terms of blues and yellows (plus black and white). Colors at the blue-green end of the spectrum appear blue, while colors at the red-yellow end of the spectrum appear yellow. Thus, to someone with *either* red or green deficiency, a bright red fire engine will look a dull

yellow, and grass would appear to be a desaturated blue (see Fig. 4.26).

The rare individual who is blue-yellow deficient sees the world entirely in reds and greens (plus black and white).

According to W.A.H. Rushton, red-deficient individuals simply don't have any "red cones" in their retinas. Similarly, green-deficient individuals lack the cone that mediates the psychological experience of green (Rushton, 1975).

Very recently, Jeremy Nathans and his colleagues at Stanford have shown that there are unique *genes* on the X-chromosome that "code" for the red, green, and blue cones in your retina. If you lack the "red gene," for example, no red cones appear in your retina and you are completely blind to the color red. Oddly enough, while just one gene determines red and one gene determines blue, some individuals have two (or more genes) that appear to code for green (Nathans *et al.*, 1986a, 1986b). MIT geneticist David Botstein believes

Does everyone see colors the same way? If you think so, try naming the colors of these flowers.

that, as humans evolve over time, these "extra" green genes may allow us to perceive one or more colors we currently are "blind" to (Botstein, 1986).

□ □ **QUESTION** □ □
Suppose your NASA robot could perceive colors that you were blind to. Why would the robot have as much trouble describing these colors to you as you would have trying to describe red, green, and blue to someone who was totally color-blind?

FIG. 4.26 This watercolor is similar to the colorful inkblots used in the Rorschach test. A psychologist can gather data about an individual's personality by asking that person to report what he or she sees in the inkblots.

Total Color-Blindness

Only about one person in 40,000 is totally color-blind. A few of these totally color-blind individuals were born with normal vision, but lost the ability to see hues as a result of disease. Others became totally color-blind because their cones were poisoned by such pollutants as lead or carbon disulfide. Many of these people can recover at least some of their color vision if given proper therapy—including large doses of Vitamin A (Pokorny *et al.*, 1979).

Most totally color-blind people, however, suffer from **albinism**—an inherited condition involving a lack of pigment throughout their bodies. Like albino rabbits and rats, these people have colorless hair, pink-white skin, and pinkish irises. Since the photo-sensitive chemicals in the cones are, in fact, *pigments*, albino people lack functional cones and *cannot see color at all*.

□ □ **QUESTION** □ □
When albino people look directly at an object, it tends to "disappear" from their sight. Why?

Tests for Color Deficiencies

Odd as it may seem, many color-deficient individuals reach maturity without knowing they have a visual defect. For instance, Karl Dallenbach, a psychologist who spent his professional life studying sensory processes, learned of his red deficiency in an introductory psychology class.

Students in this particular class were seated alphabetically to make checking attendance easier for the teacher. Dallenbach was in the front row. During a lecture on vision, the professor wished to demonstrate an old color-deficiency test called the **Holmgren wools**. The test consists of a large number of strands of colored wool that the subject is asked to sort into various piles according to their hues. Dallenbach was tapped for the honor of being a subject simply because he was right under the teacher's nose.

When asked to sort the reds into one pile, Dallenbach included all the wools with a greenish hue as well as those that were clearly red. When asked to sort all the greens, he included the reds.

At first the teacher thought that Dallenbach was playing a joke, but subsequent tests proved he was red-deficient. Like most color-deficient people, Dallenbach had learned to compensate for his handicap while growing up. Since everyone said that grass was green, he saw it as being somehow different from red roses—although, under controlled conditions, Dallenbach could not tell the color of grass from that of most red roses.

Despite this visual problem, however, Dallenbach went on to become a noted psycholo-

FIG. 4.27 A test for color-blindness, which is not very accurate and is no longer used, is to ask a person to separate yarn by color.

FIG. 4.28 These two illustrations are from a series of color-blindness tests. In the left plate, people with normal vision see a number 6, while those with red-green color-blindness do not. Those with normal vision see a number 12 in the right plate; red-green blind people may see one number or none. These reproductions of color-recognition tests cannot be used for actual testing. The examples are only representative of the total of 15 charts necessary for a complete color recognition examination. (American Optical Corporation from their AO Pseudo-Isochromatic Color Tests.)

gist. But perhaps because of his red deficiency, Dallenbach specialized in the study of taste and smell—not of color vision.

The Holmgren wools are but one (and perhaps the least accurate) of many different tests for color deficiencies. Most of the other tests contain hundreds of tiny dots of colors. These dots are so arranged that a person with normal vision sees letters, numbers, or geometric figures in the dots. A person with color deficiency, however, sees only a random jumble of dots or a different number than would the normal person. Examples of these kinds of color deficiency tests are shown in Figs. 4.27 and 4.28.

• *Sensation and Perception*

Sensory inputs are but the first stage of that marvelous process called *perception*. So, even if you could figure out what kinds of sensory receptors your NASA robot ought to have, you still would have to figure out how the robot would *recognize* stimuli and "make sense" out of its sensory inputs.

We will continue our study of *information processing* in the next chapter, when we discuss how your brain "gives meaning" to sensory stimuli.

SUMMARY

1. Your skin is your window to a great part of the outside world. **Receptor cells** in your skin provide sensory inputs to your **somatic cortex (parietal lobe)** telling your cortex what your body is doing, what your skin is touching, and whether the outside world is warm or cold.

2. The **corpuscles** in the hairless regions of your skin detect pressure. The **basket cells** in the hairy regions, and the **free nerve endings** found in all skin, detect both pressure and temperature.

3. Any object warmer than your skin will be sensed as warm. Any object cooler than your skin will be sensed as cold.

4. The **deep receptors** in your muscles, joints, tendons, and bones tell your cortex the position and condition of various parts of your body.

5. Buried away in your inner ear are your motion-change detectors—the **saccule**, the **utricle**, and the **semi-circular canals**. The saccule and utricle sense changes in straight-line or **linear motion**. The semi-circular canals respond to changes in circular or **rotary motion**.

6. Receptor **adaptation** is a slowing down of the firing rate of your sensory receptors which occurs when the receptors are stimulated at a constant rate. Central **habituation** is a process that occurs in your brain when you no longer pay attention to a **constant stimulus input**.

7. Taste and smell are called "chemical senses" because the receptors in the nose and tongue are stimulated primarily by complex chemical molecules.

8. The primary receptors for taste are the receptor cells in the **taste buds**, which are located in mushroom-shaped bumps called **papillae**. Most taste receptors lie on the surface of the tongue, but a few can be found elsewhere in the mouth.

9. The four basic taste qualities are **sweet**, **sour**, **bitter**, and **salty**, but most of the "taste" of food is really the smell of the food rather than its taste.

10. The smell receptors are the **olfactory rods**, which lie on the **olfactory membrane** inside each of the two nostrils.

11. Chemical molecules in the air are absorbed into the **mucus** covering the olfactory

membrane and excite the **cilia** of the olfactory rods. The rods respond by firing off a message to the brain.

12. The primary smell qualities seem to be **camphor**, **musky**, **floral**, **peppermint**, **ethereal**, **pungent**, and **putrid**.

13. Smell is an **ancient sense** more associated with **emotion** and **motivation** than with cognition.

14. Women are more sensitive to all types of sensory inputs in the middle of their **menstrual cycles**—when their **hormone level** is high—than at any other point in the cycle.

15. Women who are housed together tend to experience similar menstrual cycles. This **menstrual synchrony** seems to be caused by chemicals that the women release in their sweat.

16. Women (and many female animals) release chemicals called **copulins** that can be sexually attractive to some males.

17. Smell and taste are both **mono** (one-dimensional) senses in that they seldom help us locate objects in space very well. Hearing is a **stereo** sense. Your brain converts differences in what your two ears hear into an understanding of whether the source of the sound is to the left or right. While your ears discriminate **left-right differences** in sounds very well, they do not discriminate **up-down differences** at all well.

18. The middle ear contains three bones—the **hammer**, **anvil**, and **stirrup**—that amplify sound waves. The **eardrum** separating the outer from the middle ear is connected to the hammer. The stirrup is connected to the **oval window**, which separates the middle from the inner ear.

19. The inner ear is a snail-shaped space called the **cochlea**. The hair cells that are the true **auditory receptors** are part of the **organ of Corti**. The organ of Corti lies on the **basilar membrane**, which runs the length of the cochlea.

20. Sound waves have both **frequency** and **amplitude**. The greater the frequency of a musical tone, the higher it generally sounds. The larger the amplitude of a sound, the louder it will usually seem to be.

21. **Bone deafness** is a hearing loss caused by improper functioning of the bones in your middle ear. **Nerve deafness** results from damage to the hair cell receptors.

22. Children **born deaf** have problems learning to speak because they cannot hear the sound of their own voice.

23. The stimulus input for vision is light, which is made up of waves of energy particles called **photons**.

24. The **frequency** of a light wave helps determine the color the light will appear to be. The **amplitude** (intensity) of the light wave generally determines how bright it will seem.

25. The **wave-lengths** for the visible spectrum run from 400 **nanometers** (blue) through 760 nanometers (red).

26. Light enters your eye through the **cornea** and **aqueous humor**, then passes through the **pupil**, the **lens**, and the **vitreous humor**. The light then strikes your **retina**, which is the **photo-sensitive** inner surface of the hollow eyeball.

27. The retina contains your **visual receptors**—the **rods** and **cones**. There are three types of cones, one sensitive to red, one to blue, and one to green. The rods contain **rhodopsin**, and are sensitive only to blacks, whites, and shades of gray.

28. In the center of your retina is a small pit called the **fovea** that contains only cones. Your vision is at its sharpest when the visual image falls on the fovea.

29. Near the fovea is the **blind spot**, which contains no visual receptors. The optic nerve, which runs from your retina to your brain, exits from the eyeball at the blind spot.

30. **Near-sighted** people typically see close objects more clearly than they do far objects. **Far-sighted** people typically see distant objects more clearly than they do objects that are close to their eyes.

31. A person with normal **visual acuity** (keenness of vision) is said to have **20/20 vision**. This means that the person can see at a distance of 20 feet what the average person can see at a distance of 20 feet. However, the ability to perceive **visual contrast** is also important to good vision.

32. Your rods are more sensitive at night (or in dim illumination) than are your cones. If your rods malfunction, you may suffer from **night-blindness**.

33. Colors have **hue** (red, green, blue, yellow) and **saturation** or richness.

34. Black, white, and gray are completely **desaturated colors**. The black-white axis of the **color solid** runs from white to gray to black, and is called **lightness**.

35. If a person can see a color, but only when it is very intense, the person is said to be **color-weak**. If a person cannot see a particular color no matter how intense it is, that person is said to be **color-deficient**.

36. Men tend to be "color-weak" and "color-deficient" more frequently than women. The most common form of color deficiency is the failure to see reds and/or greens as people with normal color vision do.

37. **Albino** humans and animals lack the pigments necessary for normal color vision. They therefore see only with their rods and are **totally color-blind**. They are also totally blind in their foveas.

Dear Judy Jones:

(Continued from page 78.)

I was going through some of my stuff today, packing it all up, when I found this old sheet of scratch paper. It had a cow on it, and a horse and an automobile. On the back was a couple of algebra problems, written out in long hand. My ticket to the world, I always used to call it. Reminded me that I hadn't written you a letter in some time, so maybe I ought to catch you up with the news.

I'm going to college! Can you believe it! That's what I was packing for, when I found the scratch paper. Bet you never thought, the first time you saw this ugly boy, Woodrow Wilson Thomas, that he'd be going off to college someday. I don't remember that first day you came to the Home too well, maybe because I didn't know the words to remember things with back then. But the algebra book, that is something I sure won't ever forget. I guess I learned how to read with that book. And your help too, and then Mrs. Dobson's. She told me later you had a real argument with her. She thought I was retarded, but you insisted I must just be deaf. Then there was a doctor checking me out, and the hearing aid that the State bought me. Did I ever tell you, the first day I had the hearing aid, I just sat and listened to the birds all day long? Can you imagine not knowing what a bird sounds like until you're 10 years old?

Anyhow, as you know, it took me a couple of years to learn how to talk like normal people do. Still not too good at it, I guess. But I went to school, and I caught up, and now I'm going to college. I still can't believe it. I guess I did pretty good in high school, except maybe in English. But real good in math. Good enough to get a scholarship. How 'bout that? I'm going to study math in college. Hope to be a teacher some day. My complexion has cleared up a lot since you saw me last, and maybe I'm not so ugly any more. Anyhow, I've got me a girl friend. Sort of.

It's been so long, maybe you're married now and have kids of your own. If you do, I bet you'll have their ears checked out early, won't you?

Anyhow, I just wanted to let you know how things are going, and about the college bit. I guess if it hadn't been for you, I'd still be at the Home, sitting in the window, looking at the pretty pictures in the magazines. I guess I really owe the world to you, Judy Jones. So I thought I'd write and say thank you.

Best,
Woody

4 / The Senses

Perception and ESP

"Great Expectations"

· C · H · A · P · T · E · R ·
5

STUDY QUESTIONS

As you read through the chapter, see if you can find the answers to the following questions:

1. What is the "nature-nurture" problem?
2. What are the four main theoretical approaches to the study of perception?
3. According to the Law of Dynamic Direction, what tendencies do all perceptual systems show?
4. According to James Gibson, what is the major determinant of perception?
5. How do the empirical and the information processing approaches differ?
6. What does it mean to say that "perception is a top-down process?"
7. What is the Law of Praegnanz?
8. In Gestalt psychology, what does the phrase "The whole is greater than the sum of its parts" *really* mean?
9. What visual cues allow you to perceive distance as clearly as you do?
10. What effect does expectancy have on perception?
11. What effect does attitude have on pupil size?
12. What do studies on the "visual cliff" tell us about innate fears in infant children and animals?
13. Why don't blind children usually learn the proper use of "I" and "you" until they are five or six years old?
14. Although there is little *scientific* evidence that ESP actually exists, why do so many people continue to believe in it?

The Professor was sitting on a large box, cursing like a trooper and sweating like a stallion. Several other boxes, covered with address labels, were stacked nearby. On the smallest label of all there was just room for

Dr. M.E. Mann
Dept. of Psych.
Univ. of the Mid-West, USA

Moments before, a group of porters had unloaded the boxes from an ancient pickup truck and trundled the cartons inside the airport, dumping them near the Customs office. Professor Mann sat on the cartons, sweating and cursing.

Outside the airport the African sun shone fiercely, roasting any man or beast foolish enough to venture forth unprotected. Even inside the airport building the temperature was nearly 100°, reason enough for the Professor's clothing to be soaked with sweat. The cursing was no doubt due to the fact that Dr. Mann was going home royally frustrated.

A small, dark man walked briskly out of the Customs office and headed toward Mann. Despite the heat, he looked as crisp and elegant as a fashion model in his silk suit.

"Ah, my dear Professor, all is in order, all is in readiness," the man said in a suave tone of voice. "I assure you we will tuck your boxes of scientific equipment on the plane as gently as a mother tucks a child into bed. Let no one say that the Republic of Lafora treats visiting scientists shabbily." The elegantly-dressed man smiled radiantly. "And now, perhaps we might repair to what passes for a cocktail lounge in this ancient airport. I am certain that the limited budget of the Ministry of Science and Technology can be stretched to provide us with a glass or two of cheer while we await the arrival of your jet."

Mann's response was sharp and unprintable.

"Ah," the small man replied. "You are still angry because we cannot approve your venturing into our back country to complete your research. But surely, my dear Professor, you understand my country's position. We are responsible for your safety, and the tribes you wish to study are still little more than savages."

The Professor made a savage remark.

"No, no," the small man continued hastily. "We could not in good conscience let you go among those tribes unprotected, for they would surely murder you. Your research grant is not of sufficient magnitude to allow you to hire bodyguards to protect you. And, as you know, all of our military personnel are required at our borders at this dangerous time in our nation's existence. Now, come and have a drink and soothe yourself while we wait . . ."

Mann interrupted. "Oh, come off it, Freddie. All this formality and politeness is just a cover up for the truth. It's prejudice. Pure and simple prejudice. You're a city-born, Oxford-educated, wealthy, sophisticated man. You hold two cabinet posts in the Laforan government. You've been wined and dined in half the capitals of the world, but I'll bet a year's pay that you've never broken bread with one of your backland natives. If they occasionally wipe out one of your tax collectors or military types, I don't doubt they've been provoked into doing so. But *murderers*? No, that's pure, superstitious prejudice on your part. I've talked to those natives, and many of my anthropologist friends have been out there. You don't understand the backlanders, so you're afraid of them. You shouldn't be. The truth is that they're frightened to death of you city people."

The sharply-dressed Minister of Science and Technology began to sweat a little. "My dear Professor, I took your case to the highest authorities in my government, and the answer was no. Absolutely not. What more could I do?"

"You could have pleaded my case with the President himself, that's what," the irate American continued.

"Our great leader is too busy to concern himself with such trivial matters. As you no doubt are aware, we are threatened by enemies on all sides. Even though you are a noted scientist from a country that has long supported our freedom and independence, I would not dare bother the President with such minor problems at this time."

Mann laughed gruffly. "That's hogwash! You still see the world in terms of absolutes, in blacks and whites. You wouldn't dare turn down my request if your native prejudice wasn't so great that . . ."

The scream of a shrill siren interrupted them. A large black automobile screeched to a halt in front of the airport, and out popped a huge man dressed in the uniform of a Laforan general. The big man came striding into the building at top speed. Then, catching sight of the Minister and Mann, the General rushed up to them.

"Ah, Freddie," said the General, "Thank God I found you. We have a terrible emergency on our hands. Perhaps you can help."

Freddie said, "Of course," and then quickly introduced General Chambro, head of security for the Republic of Lafora, to Professor Mann.

"Charmed, I'm sure," the General said, bowing slightly to acknowledge the American's presence. Then he continued in an excited tone of voice, "Freddie, the Snake is coming!"

Freddie looked puzzled. "The Snake?"

"Yes, on the next airplane. We just got the message from our agents in Paris. They're sure he's coming to kill the President! You must help us figure out what to do!"

5 / Perception and ESP

"Well, why don't you just arrest this 'Snake' as soon as he gets off the airplane?" asked the American in a matter-of-fact tone of voice.

"I'm afraid you don't understand," the General said, giving Dr. Mann a withering look. "The Snake is the most dangerous terrorist in the world, responsible for some of the foulest political assassinations you could imagine. The problem is, we simply don't know what the Snake looks like! Is he young, old, tall, short, fat, skinny? All we know is that he usually kills his victims by injecting snake venom into them with a fang-shaped needle. The victim dies in horrible convulsions. And to arrange to arrive on this plane! No wonder they call him the Snake!"

Freddie paled visibly during the General's speech. Turning to the American, he said quietly, "There is something you don't understand, Dr. Mann. This particular flight brings to Lafora almost a hundred of the biggest munitions dealers in the world. They are wormy characters, all of them. But we need them because, as you know, we refuse to accept military supplies from any of the major powers. So we spread the word that we wished to buy guns, and chartered a special plane to bring in from Europe anyone interested in selling us weapons. That is one of the reasons I am at the airport now, to greet these men and make them welcome. If we treat them badly . . ."

The General interrupted. "And we cannot check out their passports because most of them travel with forged papers."

"What about giving them a lie detector test?" Freddie asked.

"They wouldn't submit to such a test, of course," said the General contemptuously.

"The lie detector measures emotionality, not truthfulness," the American added. "And I'd guess that your 'Snake' isn't exactly the sort who would lose his cool very readily."

"Too true," said the General, and mopped his face again. "But we must find some way of separating the Snake from er, the worms, or we are in grave danger."

Freddie cleared his throat and ventured a question. "Professor Mann, you are an expert in the field of perceptual responses. You told me you wished to give certain tests to our backland natives that would tell you about their minds even if they did not understand the purpose of the tests, and even though you could not speak their language. I don't suppose that now . . ."

Professor Mann was suddenly all business. "Yes, Freddie, it might work. We could set up my equipment right here in the airport and test everyone as they get off the plane. I would have to draw up some new stimulus cards, but that shouldn't take long. Of course, I don't guarantee anything. The error rate is really very high, you know, and I could easily make a dreadful mistake. But if you're really desperate, perhaps it's better than nothing."

The General looked confused. "I don't understand . . ."

Freddie turned to the military man and said, "You aren't expected to understand—this is a matter for scientists such as Dr. Mann and me. We will screen the men on the plane with the Professor's equipment. You have your soldiers standing by, looking as innocent as possible. When we detect the Snake, we will give you a signal and you must move in for the arrest at once. More than that, you need not know."

"But what will we tell the arms dealers?" the General wailed. "They will want an explanation . . ."

"We will say that Paris has reported an outbreak of a highly infectious eye disease, and we must check each person on the flight to make sure they are not carrying the illness," Dr. Mann said brusquely. "I will put on a white uniform and be very efficient about it all."

At this final comment, Freddie smiled broadly. "You are a positive genius, my dear Professor. We will do just what you say!" And then he turned to some porters standing idly by. "Here, you men! Help us open these crates and set up this equipment!"

(Continued on page 145.)

PERCEPTION

Psychology is, in many ways, the scientific study of the obvious. For example, look at Fig. 5.1. Obviously, it's a photograph of a coin. But what *shape* is it, and how do you know it's a "coin"? Well, you say, it's round, and you know it's a coin because you recognize it from past experience. However, let's push matters a bit. How do you *know* the shape of the coin is "round"? Is the concept of "roundness" somehow *hardwired* into your neural circuits? Or did you have to learn what "roundness" is all about?

These are the sorts of "obvious questions" that seldom concern people other than philosophers and behavioral scientists. And, as you have already learned, different theorists are likely to answer such questions in radically different ways. Let's begin this chapter by looking at four major approaches to understanding what perception is all about.

Nature Versus Nurture

One of the great battles in psychology is this: How much of what you experience is learned, and how much is innately determined by your genes? We call this the **nature-nurture problem**, and we will discuss it frequently in future chapters (as well as in this one). In the field of perception, the "nature" position is represented primarily by two theoretical schools— the **Gestalt** psychologists, and the **Gibsonians**. The "nurture" position is best represented by the **empirical** approach, and

FIG. 5.1 What is the shape of this coin?

by what is now called the **information processing** viewpoint. Let's look briefly at all four positions.

The Gestalt Approach

The Gestalt movement began in Germany around 1912. It was started by several psychologists who believed perception was determined by the *interaction* between (1) the physical properties of the external stimulus, and (2) various innately-determined psychological principles or laws. One of these innate principles, called the **Law of Dynamic Direction**, holds that perceptual systems tend to move toward a state of balance, or "equilibrium."

What is the most balanced shape you can think of? Surely, the circle. Indeed, as a general rule, the "simpler the shape, the more in equilibrium it tends to be." Therefore, according to the Law of Dynamic Direction, as you look at objects such as coins, you tend to perceive these objects in the simplest manner possible—in this case, a *round* coin. However, if we showed you a "square" coin, you'd see it as square, not round, because the stimulus factors would be too strong for you to do otherwise. According to the Gestalt position, it is always the *interaction* between "external stimulus" and "internal psychological principles" that determines what you actually perceive (Arnheim, 1986).

☐☐ **QUESTION** ☐☐
If we showed you a picture of an oval, and asked you to draw what you had just been shown, you probably would make the oval rounder than it actually was. Why?

The Gibsonian Approach

The Gestalt view is that your mind *imposes* a kind of psychological order on the inputs you get from the outside world. Cornell psychologist James J. Gibson took the opposite point of view. He held that perception is *direct* and *immediate*. Gibson believed sensory inputs *impose order on your mind* (Gibson, 1950).

According to James Gibson, your brain is "hard-wired" to *see the world as it really is*. The coin *is* round, and the light rays coming from the coin are rich in sensory cues describing its roundness. The pattern of excitation the light rays make on your retina is round. Thus, how could you perceive the coin as anything other than circular in shape (Gibson, 1950)?

Put more precisely, Gibson believed that we can explain almost all perceptual experiences in terms of information to be found in the stimulus itself. Therefore, we should study *stimuli*, not "internal processes." Gibson believed there is a one-to-one correspondence between sensory inputs and perceptual experiences, and that this correspondence is determined by the genes. Put more simply, as far as perception goes, Gibson didn't ask what goes on "inside your head," but rather asked, "what kind of stimulus world is your head inside of?"

Look at Fig. 5.2. Here's the same coin again, but now it's turned away from you in space. Do you still see it as round? Probably so, even though the "image" the coin casts on your retina is actually an **ellipse**. The Gestalt view would be that, since the circle is a "simpler form" than the ellipse, the law of dynamic distribution *forces* you to perceive the coin as round. Gibson, however, would say that sensory cues determine what you perceive, not some "innate tendency toward perceptual equilibrium." For instance, notice that the "detail" on the face of the coin is bold and clear on the left side of the coin. But the features on the right side are "compressed" and less distinct. These *sensory inputs* would force you to perceive the coin as round but turned away from you in space (Bickhard & Richie, 1983).

☐☐ **QUESTION** ☐☐
According to both Gibson and the Gestalt psychologists, how would a newborn infant perceive the coin shown in Fig. 5.2?

The Empirical Approach

Both Gibson and the Gestalt psychologists took the genetic (or "naturist") viewpoint. And, as we will see, both approaches contributed greatly to our understanding of perceptual processes. However, the more traditional viewpoint puts greater emphasis on learning ("nurture") than on nature.

According to the *empirical* position, perception is determined by two independent fac-

FIG. 5.2 What is the shape of this coin?

Nature-nurture problem. One of the major controversies in psychology is over the amount of behavior that is inherited ("nature") and the amount that is learned through experience ("nurture"). For a more complete account of this controversy, see Chapter 14.

Gestalt (guess-SHTALT). A German word that is difficult to translate. Literally, a Gestalt is a "good form" or "good figure." Also means the tendency to see things as "wholes" rather than as jumbled bits and pieces.

Gibsonians. James Gibson was a noted perceptual psychologist who performed most of his research at Cornell. He believed we can account for almost all aspects of visual perception in terms of stimulus inputs, and that the nervous system is "hard-wired" to make use of these inputs to perceive the world "as it really is."

Empirical (em-PEER-ih-cal). To be empirical is to rely on observation and experimental data more than on theory.

Information processing. The scientific study of how informational inputs are received by the nervous system, processed, and stored, and how they lead to various decisions and response outputs.

Law of Dynamic Direction. One of the two principal Gestalt laws of perception. According to Wolfgang Koehler (VULF-gang CURL-er), all systems tend to move toward (in the direction of) a state of equilibrium, where the energy needed to keep the systems going is minimized. Generally speaking, the simpler a visual form is, the less energy it requires to perceive and remember it. Therefore, you tend to perceive ovals as circles because the circle is in better perceptual equilibrium than the oval. The law of dynamic direction is similar to the principle of homeostasis, discussed in Chapter 6, and is opposed by the Law of Praegnanz (PREG-nants), discussed later in this chapter.

Ellipse (el-LIPS). An oval-shaped figure.

tors—*present sensations* and *mental images of past experiences*. Put another way, the empirical view is that "perception = sensory inputs + memories."

The empirical position holds that you were not born with the innate knowledge that the coin is round, nor with the ability to make use of the sensory stimuli coming from the coin. Rather, you *learned* through "empirical observations" that these types of inputs are typically associated with a class of "round objects called coins." From the *empirical viewpoint*, you acquired the ability to see the world the way you see it—including the "roundness" of coins (Sekuler & Blake, 1985).

● The Information Processing Approach

According to the empirical viewpoint, *sensations* are "pure experiences not influenced by learning." Thus, sensory inputs presumably arrive at your cortex "unprocessed" in any significant way by the lower centers in your brain. Once these inputs *register* on your consciousness, your mind checks through its memory files and *interprets* the inputs according to past experience. To the empiricists, perception is the process by which your mind "adds meaning to sensations."

Much of perception does seem to consist of "adding meaning to sensory inputs." But the *manner* in which your mind accomplishes this miracle is far more complex than most early empiricists dreamed. For instance, many neurons in your visual system seem sensitive to

certain *critical features* of visual inputs. Dozens of studies suggest that some cells in your *retina* probably are more responsive to movement than to stationary objects. Other studies show that some neurons in your brain respond to vertical lines, but not to horizontal lines. Yet other nerve cells react to corners and sharp angles, but not to straight or curved lines. Thus, by the time a "circle" has *registered* on your consciousness, this input surely has been "analyzed" or "processed" in a variety of ways (Glass & Holyoak, 1986). (We will have more to say about all this in Chapter 12.)

According to the information processing approach, stimulus inputs flow up to your brain in a series of steps or *stages*. For example, your rods and cones translate light rays coming from the coin into patterns of neural energy. The rods and cones then pass this information along to complex cells in your retina. These complex cells respond to *critical features* of the visual input, and send this "processed information" to the thalamus (and other lower brain centers). Neurons in the thalamus detect certain *patterns of information* coming from the retinal cells, and pass the information "upstream" to your visual cortex.

How do the cells in your brain "process" information? First, by searching for various *specific features* in sensory inputs. For example, when you look at a picture of a coin, the cells might ask the following sorts of questions: Does this input have corners? (No.) Does this input have rounded lines? (Yes.) The cortical neurons then check through your memory banks to see if you have experienced this type of input before. (You've seen a lot of circles.) Your cortex then tries to *match* the present input with an image stored in memory. Since the input matches the image of a coin, you "perceive" a coin!

There are several different types of information-processing theories. However, they all assume that, at each "processing stage," your neurons *extract* some types of information from the input and pass it on. But your neurons also *simplify* the input by failing to pass on "unimportant" information. Indeed, one of the *most important* jobs the lower centers in your brain apparently have is that of *filtering out trivial sensory information*. For example, when you're at a noisy party, or listening to a rock group, you can still talk to a friend because your brain *screens out* the background noise.

Thus, you don't really see (or hear) "what's there." Rather, information processing theories say, you typically perceive only certain *critical features* of the stimulus input. You then *construct* a perception of a stimulus such as a coin from these critical features. But it is your *construction* of the coin—not the coin *itself*—that you perceive.

THE CAT

FIG. 5.3 After you read the words, look at the middle letter in each word.

□ □ **QUESTION** □ □

Without looking at Fig. 5.1 again, can you tell what date was on the coin? If you can't, did you simply "forget," or were you never consciously aware of what the date was?

The Four Viewpoints Compared

The Gestalt and Gibsonian positions emphasize the *innate properties* of perception. The empirical and information processing theories focus on those aspects of perception that are learned.

Gibson made the *stimulus* the most important part of perception. The empirical and the information processing views emphasize "internal processing." The Gestalt theorists talked about the importance of both stimulus and internal processing.

Gibson and the empirical theorists believe that "sensations" arrive at the cortex relatively unprocessed and thus free of cortical influence. The Gestalt position is that cortical processes "shape" perceptions, but the Gestalt psychologists are relatively silent on "processing" in the lower centers of the brain. The information processing viewpoint is that the input is highly processed by these lower centers, and that your cortex can influence what goes on in the "lower centers" in a variety of ways. For example, look at Figure 5.3. Did you read the words as "The cat"? Look again. The "h" and the "a" are identical; thus they must have identical "critical features." But you *perceived* them in different ways because your brain *forced* these letters to fit within the images of well-known words. The other viewpoints have problems explaining this type of perceptual "error."

Gibson saw *sensation* and *perception* as being pretty much the same thing. The Gestalt and empirical theorists believe that sensation and memory are totally independent processes, but that both influence perception. However, the information processing theorists hold that sensation, perception, memory, and **cognition** are all part of the same "global process" by which you *construct* your own representation of external reality. We cannot separate the individual processes because each affects the other (Glass & Holyoak, 1986).

□ □ **QUESTION** □ □

How could you prove to someone else that a coin you held in your hand really existed, independent of your own perception of it?

Perception: A Bottom-up or Top-down Process?

In a sense, the study of perception is the investigation of how you *come to know the world around you*. But there is a knotty problem buried in this seemingly simple definition: Namely, can you *ever* really know what the external world is like? As University of Oregon psychologist David Presti pointed out recently, there are at least two well-known answers to this question (Presti, 1987):

Naive realists believe there is a "real world" that exists independent of your knowledge about it. From this viewpoint, you come to know that world *directly* because of the informational inputs you receive from your sensory receptors. Naive realists believe that perception is primarily a *bottom-up process* which is "driven" by sensory inputs. Gibson and the empirical theorists would probably fit best into this category.

Structural realists hold that you come to know about the external world *indirectly* because your brain *processes* sensory inputs before you are aware of them. As Ulric Neisser puts it, "The world of experience is produced by the man who experiences it. . . . There certainly is a real world of trees and people and cars . . . however, we have no direct, immediate access to the world nor to its properties. Whatever we know of reality has been mediated not only by the organs of sense, but by complex systems which interpret and reinterpret information" (Neisser, 1967).

Therefore, according to Neisser, you can never know what the external world is *really* like, for all you are aware of is your own "construction of reality." However, because you *survive* in this external world using your subjective constructs, it does seem likely that most of your perceptions are reasonably accurate. But you shouldn't be surprised if, from time to time, your perception of things turns out to be radically wrong.

From the structural realism viewpoint, perception is a *top-down process* that is "driven" primarily by your own cognitive constructs. The information processing theorists obviously fit best in this category as, perhaps, do most of the Gestalt theorists (Dodwell & Caelli, 1984).

As David Presti also points out, when we're talking about the perception of physical objects (such as coins and carrots), there's little difference between naive realism and structural realism. When it comes to the perception of *people*, however, the constructionist viewpoint has much to offer. As Presti puts it, "We form hypotheses about the behavior of individuals (ourselves and others) based on very little information and tend to hold our beliefs in the face of massive amounts of disconfirming evidence. . . . We are accountable for the nature of our social experience to an astounding degree" (Presti, 1987). We will have more to say about this point both later in this chapter and in Chapter 20.

Each of the four major theoretical approaches to the study of perception has made its own contributions to our understanding of how you perceive the world. As we discuss perception, we will try to show what the strengths (and problems) associated with each of the theories seem to be.

VISUAL PERCEPTION

Your eyes are more than "the windows to your soul." Unless you are visually handicapped, your eyes are also the main sensory route by which you acquire information about the outside world. Thus, the bulk of perceptual research deals with vision—as does much of the material in this chapter. So let us begin by asking, "How do you perceive the world around you visually?"

Contours

The simplest form of visual information is the difference between light and darkness. A visual **contour** is a place where there is a sharp or sudden change in brightness—from light to dark, or vice versa. Fig. 5.4 has two contours— one at the inner edge of the circle, and one at the outer edge. It is these two contours, actually, that give *shape* to the circle.

The two contours shown in Fig. 5.4 are *objective*. That is, there is a *real* change in brightness between the black of the circle and the beige paper it is printed on. But now look at

FIG. 5.4 The "contour" of this circle is the outer edge.

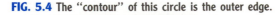

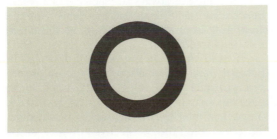

FIG. 5.5 Do you see a solid beige triangle that partially covers up a triangle with black edges? Look again, and see if the solid beige triangle is really there.

Fig. 5.5. Do you see two triangles? Most people see a large beige triangle (pointing up) superimposed on a triangle pointing down. If this is what you see, look at the center of the beige triangle. Doesn't it somehow look *brighter* than the background outside the figure does? And don't you see a sharp contrast between the *imaginary lines* setting off the top triangle and the space outside the triangle? These are *subjective* contours, since they are generated by your brain, not by objective changes in brightness.

What causes subjective contours? One interesting answer was given by Canadian psychologist Stanley Coren and his colleagues. Coren and his associates believe we have an innate tendency to perceive the world in meaningful but simple terms. You could perceive Fig. 5.5 as a collection of (1) three black circles with pie-shaped wedges cut out of them and (2) three V-shaped black lines. However, it is both simpler and more meaningful to see the drawing as a beige triangle lying on top of three black circles and thereby partially covering a second triangle as well (Coren, Porac, & Ward, 1984).

□ □ **QUESTION** □ □
Fig. 5.5 contains an important clue about depth perception. We will discuss it later, but can you guess what it is?

Shape

Look at Fig. 5.6. What do you see? Most people see a solid black circle and a rather formless blob of black ink. Notice that the *contours* give shape to both figures.

Now, close your eyes and try to imagine both black figures. Chances are, you have no

FIG. 5.6 Both the circle and the "blob" have contours.

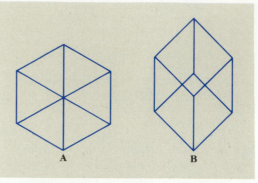

A   B

FIG. 5.7 Most people see the figure on the left as two-dimensional, but see the figure on the right in three dimensions. Why?

problem with the circle. But what about the blob? Why is it so difficult to remember *in detail?*

There are many answers to this question. For one thing, the blob is a much more complex figure than is the circle. For another, you are quite familiar with circles, but you probably never have seen a blob just like this one before. (These facts should tell you something about the importance of memory in shaping your perceptions.)

When the Gestalt psychologists tried to answer this same question, they came up with two opposing principles which, acting jointly, tend to determine all perceptions. The first of these principles is the Law of Dynamic Direction, which we discussed at the beginning of this chapter. According to the Law of Dynamic Direction, you will *remember* the blob as being more circular than it really is because circles are simpler and thus more in perceptual equilibrium than blobs are.

However, a blob is obviously not a circle. Which is to say that blobs have their own unique characteristics that set them apart from circles and squares and other regular shapes. It would help you remember the blob, therefore, if somehow your memory would *sharpen* or *enhance* these unique "blobular" properties. This tendency to perceive objects in their *most clear-cut or unique form* is often called the **Law of Praegnanz** (Arnheim, 1986). And if *only* the Law of Praegnanz affected perception, you would remember the blob as being *even more irregular than it really is.*

However, according to Gestalt psychologist Rudolf Arnheim, the perception of visual shapes is actually determined by the *balance* between two opposing forces—dynamic direction and Praegnanz. The Law of Dynamic Direction pushes your perception of shapes toward simplicity and regularity. The Law of Praegnanz pushes your perception of shapes toward complexity and uniqueness. Arnheim believes that what you actually perceive is the *dynamic balance* your brain achieves between these two forces at any point in time (Arnheim, 1986). And this "balance" is determined *both* by stimulus factors and by your own internal needs.

For example, look at Fig. 5.7. Most people see the drawing on the left as a six-sided figure

with three lines in the middle. But what about the drawing on the right? Do you see it as a two-dimensional figure, or does it somehow project itself into three dimensions? Since the two drawings are really quite similar, why do you perceive Fig. 5.7A as two-dimensional, but Fig. 5.7B in three dimensions?

According to Gestalt theorist Julian Hochberg, Fig. 5.7A is a simple figure when viewed in two dimensions. Therefore, the Law of Dynamic Direction prevails, and you see the figure in two dimensions. However, you *could* project it into three dimensions if you needed to do so. But the *unique properties* of Fig. 5.7B are so strong that (following the Law of Praegnanz) you tend to project the figure into three dimensions to preserve its uniqueness. However, you *could* perceive it as a highly complex two-dimensional form if you needed to do so. Therefore, your perception of either figure is determined not only by the two Gestalt "laws," but also by your own personal situation at the time that you look at the figures (Hochberg, 1984).

☐☐ **QUESTION** ☐☐
From this description, does the Gestalt position on perception seem to be "bottom-up" (determined by stimulus inputs) or "top-down" (determined by cognitive factors)?

Figure-Ground Relationships

According to the Gestalt position, you never perceive an object such as a circle "all by itself." Rather, you always see a circle as a shape *on a background.* The contours that define the circle as a "shape" also differentiate the circle from its surroundings.

In studying visual perception, the Gestalt theorists made many discoveries about *figure-ground relationships.* One such fact is that the figure almost always seems *brighter* and *closer* to you than does the background. Look again at Fig. 5.5. Doesn't the (subjective) beige triangle

FIG. 5.9 Do you see two profile faces? Or a wine glass?

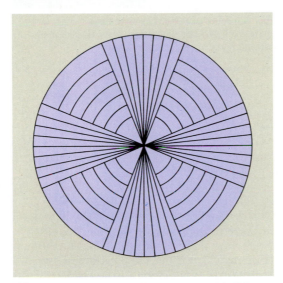

FIG. 5.8 What is figure and what is ground in this drawing? Why?

seem brighter than its surround? And doesn't it seem closer to you than the rest of the figure?

Another aspect of figure-ground relationships is this—the background seems to *continue behind the figure*. Look at Fig. 5.8. Which is figure and which is background? Probably you see a cross on a background of concentric circles. Does the cross seem nearer to you than the circles? Why? If you stare at this figure long enough, you may get a "reversal" and see a cross with radial lines as the "figure." Why is it so hard to see the "radial cross" as *figure*? (Hint: Remember that the background always "continues behind the figure.")

● Ambiguous Figure-Ground Relationships

Now look at Fig. 5.9. What do you see? A blue vase on a green background? Or two green profiles facing each other? Or do these two perspectives alternate?

Fig. 5.9 is a very famous example of what the Gestalt psychologists called **ambiguous** figure-ground relationships. Almost all these ambiguous figures involve *reversible perspectives*. Notice that when the wine glass (or vase) is figure, it seems closer. But when the faces become figure, the glass (or vase) retreats into the background and becomes *less important* psychologically. Generally speaking, you will also perceive the figure as having more *reality*

or "thing-ness" than does the background (Hoffman, 1983).

Now, try to see *both* the vase and the faces as "figure" *at the same time*. Chances are, you'll find it impossible to do. Why? According to Gestalt theory, you *always* must perceive a figure on a background. Therefore, you can't see both as figure at the same time (Coren, Porac, & Ward, 1984).

● Reversible Perspectives

Look at the "impossible figure" in Fig. 5.10. Do the stairs go up or down, or both ways? Is the platform on the right higher or lower than the platform on the left? What is there about the perspective of this figure that "fools" your eyes?

Now look at Fig. 5.11, the famous Necker Cube. Does it project upward or downward? Actually, it projects *either way*. And, if you stare at it long enough, it will "reverse its perspective" from time to time. The *frequency* with which the Cube changes perspective may de-

FIG. 5.10 The magic stairs.

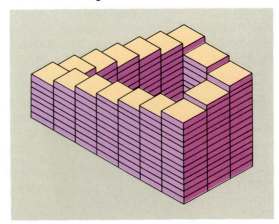

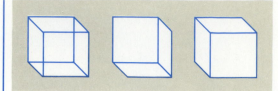

FIG. 5.11 The Necker Cube. It can be seen as projecting up or down in three dimensions in the first cube. In the other two cubes the perspective is stabilized.

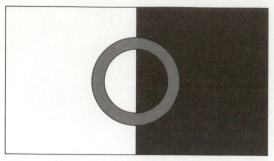

FIG. 5.12 The gray circle appears darker when viewed against a light background than when viewed against a dark background.

pend in part on what sort of person you see yourself as being, however. Judith and Bruce Bergum at Texas A&M showed the Cube to 128 students and asked them how frequently the Cube "changed directions." The Bergums report that students who had the *highest* reversal rates tended to perceive themselves as being more (1) creative and original, (2) enthusiastic and optimistic, and (3) excitable and appreciative than did students with the *lowest* reversal rates (Bergum & Bergum, 1981).

Can you learn to make the Cube reverse its perspective at a faster rate? Perhaps so. The Bergums note that architecture students at Texas A&M tended to have much *higher* reversal rates on the Cube than did business students. The Bergums believe the architecture students were probably rewarded by their teachers for being able to "change perspectives" rapidly. Students in business administration, the Bergums say, were probably expected to take a much more stable view of the world. The Bergum's results suggest that, with training, you can learn to make the Cube "reverse perspective" almost as frequently or infrequently as you wish (Bergum & Bergum, 1981).

□ □ **QUESTION** □ □

How else might the Bergum's findings be explained? (Hint: Are students with a "creative, unstable view of the world" more likely to study architecture or business?)

● *Effects of Surround*

One of the major beliefs of the Gestalt position can be found in a phrase they made famous in psychology: "The whole is greater than the sum of its parts." In truth, the phrase really means that the whole is *different* from the sum of its parts, and that the whole *interacts* with its parts (Arnheim, 1986). For example, the background on which you perceive an object often strongly influences your perception of that object.

Look at Fig. 5.12. Here is a gray circle displayed on a surround that is half white, half black. As you look at the circle, the gray seems uniform. But if you cover the border between the black and white sections with a pen, the

FIG. 5.13 The context in which an object appears affects the way you perceive it. The two parallel straight lines in Figs. 5.13A, 5.13B, and 5.13C seem "bent" because of the backgrounds on which they appear. In 5.13D the arrows make the top circle appear larger than the identical bottom circle. In 5.13E the two center circles are the same size.

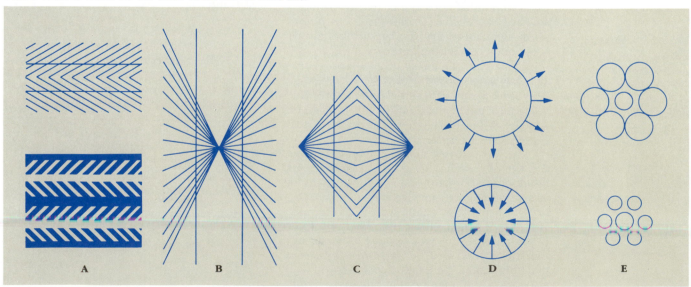

A   B   C   D   E

Proximity (procks-IM-it-tee). That which is close. If you live a block from the fire station, you live in the proximity of the fire station. Objects that are proximate (close to each other) tend to be perceived as units.

Closure. "To complete" or "to close." If you glance very quickly at a circle that has a tiny gap in it, you may very well see the circle as being closed, or complete.

Continuity (con-tin-NEW-it-tee). From the word "continue" or "continuous." Things that are connected together in time or space have continuity. Your own stream of consciousness has a certain continuity or connectedness, in that one experience follows the other without a noticeable gap or "blank period of consciousness."

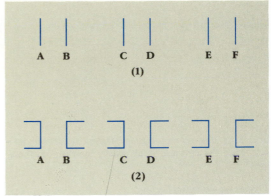

FIG. 5.15 **Which lines seem to relate in part 1? In part 2?**

FIG. 5.14 **If you perceive one line that "spirals" in to the center, trace the line with your finger. The "spiral" is actually a set of circles. What in this illusion actually fools your eye?**

gray semi-circle on the white background will look much darker than the semi-circle on the black surround. Why?

Figure 5.13 gives five examples of how the background influences the perception of the figure itself. One of the most striking examples of this effect, however, appears in Fig. 5.14. Do you see a spiral moving in toward the center of the drawing? If you do, use your finger to trace where the spiral actually goes.

□ □ **QUESTION** □ □
How would you attempt to explain these illusions from the "information-processing" viewpoint of perception? From the "empirical" approach? How do these explanations differ from those offered by the Gestalt psychologists?

Visual Grouping

As you look out at an object in space, your mind makes use of several Gestalt principles in tracing the *relationships* among these objects (Arnheim, 1986).

● *Proximity and Closure*

One Gestalt principle is that you tend to *group things together* according to how close they are to each other. In part 1 of Fig. 5.15, you probably see three "pairs" of lines. You will group *a*

and *b* together because they are close to each other.

In part 2, however, things have changed. Now *b* and *c* seem to go together—to form a rectangle of some kind. Indeed, if you stare closely at the *b-c* rectangle, you will see rather faint but *imaginary* lines as your brain attempts to fill in or close up the open figure.

Part 1 of Fig. 5.15 illustrates the Gestalt principle of **proximity**, or physical closeness. Part 2 illustrates the principle of **closure**—your brain's tendency to join broken lines together to make a closed figure of some kind.

□ □ **QUESTION** □ □
How might you derive the principles of proximity and closure from the Gestalt laws of Praegnanz and Dynamic Direction?

● *Continuity*

A third perceptual principle is that of **continuity** and is illustrated in part 1 of Fig. 5.16. In this illustration you will probably see a wavy line superimposed on a square-cornered line. If we

FIG. 5.16 **The Gestalt principle of continuity.**

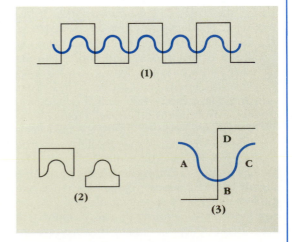

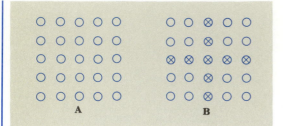

FIG. 5.17 How do you "group" these circles? Why do you group the circles in A differently than you do those in B?

now break up the pattern somewhat differently, as in part 2, you see not two lines but two closed figures joined together. Why do you think this is so? And if you wish, you may even break the figure up into a different set of components, shown in part 3.

Once you have learned what the parts of the figure can be, you can perceive it many different ways. But, at the beginning, your eye tends to follow the wavy line because it is *continuous*.

● *Similarity*

A fourth principle of perceptual grouping is that of **similarity**. Fig. 5.17A shows a series of 25 circles arranged in a square. If you fixate on this figure, you will notice that sometimes you "group" the circles together in bunches of 4s, or 9s, or 16s. And sometimes you see 5 horizontal rows of circles, sometimes 5 vertical columns. In such ambiguous situations, your brain apparently tests out various possibilities, attempting to see which fits the stimulus pattern best. But in Fig. 5.17B, you probably see a cross surrounded by four groups of empty circles. Why?

VISUAL DEPTH AND DISTANCE

So far, we have mostly discussed the viewing of two-dimensional objects. However, when you look at the world (beyond the printed page), it doesn't seem to be flat and two-dimensional. Rather, the world is *three-dimensional*. It has *depth* to it. This fact poses a problem to perceptual theorists. For the retinas in your eyes are, for all practical purposes, little more than flat "screens" on which the lenses in your eyes project two-dimensional images. How does your mind take these "flat" retinal images and *create* a third dimension—that of *depth*?

We are not entirely sure of the answer to this question. We do know, though, that true depth perception occurs only in people who have two eyes. And these two eyes must have slightly *different* views of the world for the third dimension to appear. It may also be the case (as we will see later in this chapter) that the *concept* of depth is innate. However, we are

quite sure that some aspects of depth perception are *learned through experience*.

So, let's ask another of those supposedly-obvious questions: What would your world be like if you had been born blind and only now opened your eyes? The answer to that question, as it happens, is anything but "obvious."

The Case of S.B.

Some years ago, British psychologist Richard L. Gregory reported the case of a man who had been blind from infancy, but whose vision was restored at age 52. This patient—whom Gregory calls S.B.—was an intelligent person whose vision had been normal at birth. At age 10 months, S.B. developed a severe infection of the eyes that left his corneas so badly scarred he couldn't see objects at all (Gregory, 1977).

Enough light leaked through his damaged corneas so that S.B. could just tell day from night. But he saw the world much as you would if someone cut a Ping-Pong ball in two and placed the halves over your eyes. S.B.'s corneal scars were so bad, in fact, that for most of his life no doctor would operate on him. Nonetheless, S.B. led an enjoyable and very active life. He went places by himself, waving his white cane in front of him to let people know he was blind. He often went for rides on a bicycle, with a friend holding his shoulder and guiding him.

S.B. spent considerable time making wooden objects with rather simple tools. He had an open-faced watch so he could tell time by feeling the positions of the hands. He took care of animals and knew them all by touch, sound, and smell. And he always tried to imagine what things looked like. When he washed his brother's car, he would vividly try to picture what color and shape it really was. When S.B. visited the zoo, he would get his friends to de-

Like S.B., many blind persons enjoy sports and other activities, sometimes aided by a guide. Note: BOLD stands for Blind Outdoor Leadership Development.

Similarity. Objects that are physically like one another tend to be perceived as units or wholes.

Grafted. Joining parts of one organism to another is called "grafting." In corneal grafts, part of the donor's cornea is surgically removed and transplanted to the eye of the recipient. If the corneal graft "takes," the grafted tissue will connect up to the recipient's bloodstream and function more or less normally.

scribe the animals there in terms of how different they were from the dogs and cats in his home.

• S.B.'s Operation

When S.B. was well past his 50th year, he prevailed upon a surgeon to attempt an operation in which his damaged corneas were removed and new ones were **grafted** on in their place. The operation was a great success but, as Gregory reports, S.B. was anything but happy with the results. When the doctor first removed the bandages, S.B. looked straight into the doctor's face—and saw nothing but a blur. He knew what he saw had to be the doctor's face, because he recognized the man's voice. But it was several days before he could begin to tell one person from another merely by *looking* at them. And he never became very good at identifying people visually.

Nonetheless, he progressed rapidly in some areas. Within a few days, S.B. could successfully navigate the halls of the hospital without running into things. He could tell time by looking at the face of a very large clock. And he dearly loved to get up early in the morning and sit at his window watching the traffic rumble by on the street far below his hospital room.

But there were problems. S.B. rapidly learned the names of the colors red, black, and white. However, he had trouble identifying most other colors. He could judge *horizontal* distances fairly well when looking at objects whose size he was familiar with. But *heights* of

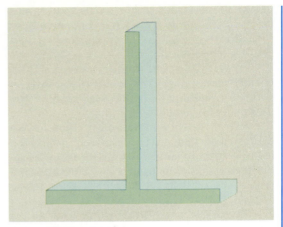

FIG. 5.18 Bisection illusion.

any kind always confused him. One day the nurses found him crawling out the window of his fourth-floor hospital room, presumably because he wanted to inspect more closely the automobile traffic in the street below. He looked at the ground 40 feet beneath him and thought it to be no more than 6 feet away.

Prior to the operation, S.B. had crossed even the busiest intersection alone without the faintest fear. He would plunge into traffic waving his white stick in front of him. And somehow the river of cars and trucks would part for him, much as the waters of the Red Sea parted for Moses in Old Testament times. But after S.B. got his vision back, he was absolutely terrified of crossing a street. Gregory states it usually took two people holding his arms to force him across an intersection.

Often when S.B. saw a familiar object for the first time, he would be unable to identify it until he closed his eyes and felt it. Then he knew it by touch. And once he "had the picture in his mind," he could recognize it visually after he had looked at it a few times.

But objects he hadn't (or couldn't) run his hands over before regaining his sight always gave him problems. The moon, for instance, puzzled him greatly. The full moon he could make out, but the quarter moon he had expected to be wedge-shaped, rather like a large slice of pumpkin pie. And when S.B. looked at Fig. 5.18, he saw the horizontal and the vertical lines as being the same length. How do they look to you?

• S.B.'s Depression

Immediately after his operation, S.B. was very enthusiastic and happy. He loved bright colors (although he couldn't always give their right names), and he enjoyed being able to see the faces of people he knew. But then he began to get depressed. He complained bitterly about the ugliness in the world around him—houses with the paint coming off, buildings with dirty walls, people with blemishes on their faces. He

A year after his operation, S.B. made this drawing of a typical London double-decker bus, complete with visual details such as the beer advertisement across the top. The front of the bus, however, which S.B. had never touched, is missing.

would spend hours sitting in his local tavern watching people *in the mirror*. Somehow their reflections seemed more interesting to him than their real-life images.

Often S.B. would withdraw from human contact and spend most of the day sitting in darkness, claiming he could "see" better when there was no light.

There have been no more than half a dozen confirmed cases of people who have gained sight as adults. According to Gregory, depression and unhappiness are common consequences of their getting back their vision (Gregory, 1977).

We should note, however, that not all patients who recover sight late in life have the same problems—or the depression—that S.B. experienced. One woman who recovered her sight in 1980 had no problem at all seeing and naming colors the moment her bandages were removed. Nor did she become unhappy with her new-found sight. These facts suggest S.B.'s early illness may have *damaged* his rods and cones. Thus, many of the difficulties S.B. had in perceiving the world were probably due to retinal damage rather than to an inability to learn to see the world correctly so late in life.

Clues to Visual Distance

S.B. gained the ability to perceive *horizontal distance*. That is, he could tell how far away you were if he saw you walking down a hallway toward him. But he never could perceive *depth* very well. As we noted, depth is a three-dimensional property. People with **monocular** vision—that is, people who have just one functional eye—can also usually judge distance fairly well. However, like S.B., they typically don't perceive depth (Gregory, 1977).

These facts suggest that *distance* cues are different than are cues to *depth*. As James Gibson noted many years ago, distance cues are typically embedded in the visual stimuli themselves. However, your mind judges distance using more inputs than just those that come from the retina. It also takes into account the way your eyes move in their sockets, the sounds your ears report, the smells around you, your body posture, and all the memories it can dredge up (Gibson, 1950).

For example, an automobile passes you on the street. You know it is about 30 feet away because you remember what size cars ought to be, how long it takes you to walk 30 feet, and how the visual image of the car will change as you walk toward it.

The *apparent size* of an object gives you a good notion of how far away the object is. You tend to perceive small objects as being far away, and large objects as being closer. But you do this only if you know what the "real size" of the object is, and after taking into account the *background* the object appears on. There are

FIG. 5.19 According to the principle of linear perspective, parallel lines appear to meet at the horizon.

other clues your brain uses, too, even though you are often unaware of what these clues are (Bartley, 1980).

- *Linear Perspective*

Look at Fig. 5.19. Notice that all the lines seem to meet at a point right in the center of the photograph. Figure 5.20 shows part of the same sort of illusion, but something new has been added. The three cylinders are actually the same size. But the cylinder on the far right appears more than twice as large as the cylinder on the far left. Can you use the lines on the drawing to explain why?

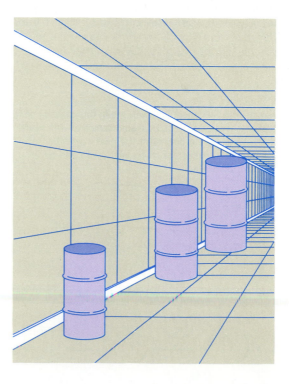

FIG. 5.20 Although the three cylinders are actually the same size, they appear to be different. Why?

Monocular (MON-ock-you-lar). From the Latin words meaning "one eye." Monocular cues are those that are effective when presented to just one eye at a time. As opposed to *binocular*, which means "two eyes."

Linear perspective (LIN-ee-er per-SPECK-tive). "Linear" has to do with straight lines, such as the horizon (the line between earth and sky). *Perspective* means "viewpoint." Parallel lines (such as railroad tracks) appear to meet at the horizon. If you were drawing a realistic picture of railroad tracks, you would want to draw them so they "met" at the horizon in your picture.

Convergence (kon-VERGE-ence). Means "to come together" or "to turn or move toward one another." Parallel lines converge at the horizon. You can demonstrate "eye convergence" if you get a friend to cooperate. Hold up one of your fingers about a foot in front of the person's nose and ask the person to focus on the tip of your finger. Now slowly move your finger right up to the person's eyes. As your fingertip nears the person's nose, the person's eyes will turn toward each other.

Aerial perspective (AIR-ee-ull). Literally, the "way you see an object through the air." Fuzzy objects seem distant; clear (distinct) objects seem close.

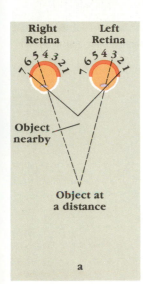

a

The apparent *convergence* of parallel lines as they approach the horizon is called **linear perspective**—one of the cues your brain uses to judge distance.

• Convergence

Humans are essentially two-dimensional animals, bound to those parts of the surface of the earth our two feet can walk on. We judge *horizontal* distances rather well—if they are no greater than those we can walk or run or ride. But we judge heights rather poorly, at least in comparison with animals such as birds and fish that move readily through all three dimensions of space.

When you look at something in the distance, both your eyes point straight ahead. When you look at something up close, however, both your eyes turn inward, toward your nose (see Fig. 5.21). The amount of strain this **convergence** creates in your eye muscles is an index of how far away the object is.

To judge how *distant* an object is, you have merely to let your eyes converge and notice the strain on your eye muscles. But to judge *height*, you usually have to move your head up and down or crane your neck. For most of us, the neck muscles are poorer judges of distance than are the eye muscles (Schiff, 1980).

□ □ **QUESTION** □ □
Why are airplane pilots usually better at judging heights than are non-pilots?

• Aerial Perspective and Texture

Anyone who has grown up in a smog-ridden city knows there often are days when you can't see more than a block or two away. But there are parts of the world still blessedly free from this aerial pollution. In some of our deserts, for instance, the air is often so clear that the visibility is practically unlimited. The city dweller who first visits these regions is sometimes shocked at how badly she or he actually judges distances in clean, fresh air. A mountain peak

FIG. 5.21 An example of convergence. When you focus on a near object, your eyes "converge" (turn toward each other).

that appears to be no more than 5 or 10 miles away may actually be more than 50 miles down the road.

The more hazy and indistinct a remote object seems to you, the farther away it appears to be. Psychologists refer to this "distance cue" as the **aerial perspective** of an object (see Fig. 5.22) (Rock, 1975).

Texture is a distance cue very similar to aerial perspective. In real life, the texture of objects near to you is more detailed than the texture of distant objects. Over time, you learn to use texture as a cue. Notice in Fig. 5.22 that you can see the bricks or stones in near buildings, but not in distant ones (Matlin, 1982).

• Light and Shadow

Often we use the *lightness* of an object to give us some notion of its size or distance from us. For reasons we still don't understand, dark objects often appear to be smaller than light-colored objects. For example, look at the 7 dots in Fig. 5.23. Although it doesn't look like it at first glance, the distance *between* the dots is exactly the same as the size of the dots themselves.

Sometimes we make judgments about the visual world from what we *don't* see, instead of from what we do see. Look at Fig. 5.24, a simple representation of the word "shadow." Notice that each of the six letters in this word is printed in full. Now look at the next word. Here there are no letters, just the shadows themselves. But look carefully. Doesn't your eye actually *see* the forms of the letters as if they

FIG. 5.22 *Les Promenades d'Euclide,* a 1955 painting by the Belgian artist René Magritte. See text.

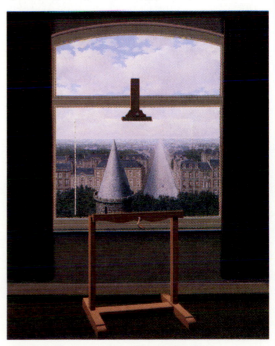

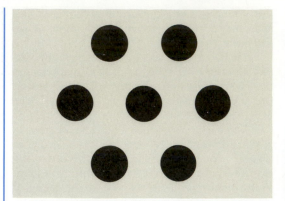

FIG. 5.23 The distance between the dots is actually the same as the size of each dot.

City dwellers are often deceived by distances in clear, dry mountain air. The peaks on the horizon may be many miles further away than they seem.

were really there? And what about the five blue figures in Fig. 5.25? Can you see the word "fly" spaced between the figures? And after you recognize the word "fly," can you perceive the drawing as just a collection of odd-shaped black figures? Why not?

You also make use of shadows in judging whether you are looking at a mountain or at the hole left when somebody dug up the mountain and carted it away. When you look at a photograph of a crater (see Fig. 5.26), you automatically make an assumption about how the sunlight is falling on the landscape. If you make the *wrong assumption*, then your brain will show you a hill instead of a crater (Levine & Shefner, 1981).

□ □ **QUESTION** □ □
S.B. often mistook shadows for real objects. Why do you think this was the case?

● *Interposition*
If one object seems to block another, you will usually perceive the "blocking" object as being closer to you than the object it masks. Look back at Fig. 5.22, a famous painting by the noted French artist René Magritte. Notice how the conical tower in the foreground blocks your view of some of the buildings. And notice too how the buildings and trees in the lower part of the painting mask the buildings "behind them." Your mind uses these *interposition* cues to perceive distance rather readily (Coren, Porac, & Ward, 1984).

This painting actually illustrates several of the distance cues we have already discussed. See if you can find examples of linear and aer-

ial perspective, texture, and light and shadows (as well as interposition). How do these cues give "apparent depth" (that is, distance) to the painting?

□ □ **QUESTION** □ □
Notice that the conical tower and the street in this painting are actually very similar triangles. How does the *context* of the other objects in the painting affect your perception of these two triangles?

● *Real and Apparent Motion*
Motion can also be a cue to distance. Imagine you are riding in a car, looking out the window. You will see telephone poles flash by rapidly, but a cow in a distant meadow will move across your field of vision slowly. Objects (such as the cow) that seem to move *slowly* as you are moving rapidly will seem *distant*. However, the telephone poles will seem *near* because they move *rapidly*. They also momentarily block out objects "behind them," such as the cow.

Apparent motion can also be a cue to distance. Look at Fig. 5.27. Here you have eight light bulbs and a grey rectangle. If you turned the bulbs on and off quickly in the order they are numbered, you might perceive just one bulb moving from left to right. (This sort of "apparent movement" is best illustrated by the

FIG. 5.24 The word *shadow* on the right is actually made up of "shadows" of the word on the left.

SHADOW SHADOW

FIG. 5.25 Do you see a word or five odd-shaped blue objects?

FIG. 5.26 Light and shade as a cue for depth. Turn the book upside down and the crater turns into a hill.

flashing lights on theater marquees.) Now imagine that you turned on the first four light bulbs in Fig. 5.27 in 1-2-3-4 order, then waited a second or two. Now you turn on 5-6-7-8 in sequence. The apparent movement of the lights might convince you the row of bulbs continued *behind* the black rectangle. Thus, you would perceive the rectangle as being closer to you than the lights (Ramachandran & Anstis, 1986).

Now, imagine you are standing in a dark hallway. Some distance from you is a large, white globe suspended in air. As you first look, the globe is dimly illuminated from within. But as you continue watching, the globe grows brighter and brighter. If you have no other cues as to distance, you will perceive two different effects. First, the globe will seem to get *larger*. And second, the globe will seem to *move closer*—even though it hasn't really moved at all. The change in brightness gives rise to apparent movement, for you tend to see bright objects as being nearer than dim objects.

Expectancy

One of the principle laws of perception is this: *You see what you expect to see.* As you experience the world, you learn that objects typically grow brighter as they move closer to you. Thus, when you see an object growing brighter, you expect it to be moving closer to you. So you *perceive* it that way. Any clues you get from your environment that change your expectancies will also have a strong influence on your perceptual processes (Rock, 1975).

Keep that thought in mind as you look at Fig. 5.28. As you can see, it is a drawing of an *ugly old woman* with her chin buried in a fur coat. Look at it carefully and try to figure out what this old woman is thinking of.

The artist who drew the picture claims she is dreaming of her daughter. And if you inspect the drawing again, you will see the face of the old woman change into that of the daughter.

Several experimenters have shown this picture to groups of college students. If the students are told to expect a picture of an *old woman*, most of them discover the mother's face before finding the daughter's. But if the students are told they will see a drawing of a *young woman*, they tend to see the daughter's face easily but often have trouble "finding" the picture of the mother (Matlin, 1982).

□ □ **QUESTION** □ □
Were you "fooled" by the ending to the story that begins this chapter? If so, can you discover the "false clues" that gave you the wrong expectancy?

CONSTANCIES AND ILLUSIONS

Expectancy is closely related to another perceptual principle, that of *constancy*. A knowledge of both principles may help you understand some of the visual *illusions* that you experience daily.

Imagine yourself in the same situation S.B. faced, when he gained sight at the age of 52. Before your operation, you crossed streets safely. You knew people would stop for you—but you could also judge the flow of traffic rea-

FIG. 5.27 If the lights go on and off in rapid sequence — with a slight pause between lights 4 and 5 — you will perceive the gray rectangle as being in front of the row of lights.

FIG. 5.28 Do you see an old woman or a young woman?

Size constancy does break down under certain conditions. First, if you don't have any cues as to the object's distance, you will often make mistakes about its real size—unless, that is, the object is something familiar, such as a football or a pack of cigarettes. Then, *expectancy* (from past experience) will give you a clue as to the object's real size. Second, size constancy often fails when you look at objects from a great distance. If you view the objects below you from an airplane or the top of a tall building, they often look like "toys" rather than the real thing.

Shape Constancy

Look at Fig. 5.29, which is the same as one we showed you earlier in this chapter. Here's your old friend, the coin. And chances are, you *still* see it as a round coin turned away from you in space.

As objects rotate in space, or as you move around the objects, the actual image they cast on your retina changes dramatically. The tendency to perceive objects as *maintaining their known shape* despite the image they project on the retina is known as **shape constancy**.

Generally speaking, shape constancy is good when you have cues as to whether you're viewing the object straight on, or whether it is tilted or slanted in space. As Gibson pointed out, there are many such cues, including light and shadow, texture, and linear and aerial perspective. Shape constancy breaks down in extreme conditions, however, or when you lack sufficient cues to guess the object's orientation in space (Gibson, 1950).

● *The Ames Distorted Room*

Adelbert Ames, a US psychologist who began his professional life as a painter, took advantage of *shape constancy* to produce a number of very amusing illusions which illustrate the Gestalt principles of perception. The best-known of these illusions is Ames's "distorted room," shown in Fig. 5.30.

FIG. 5.29 A coin viewed on edge.

sonably well by *listening* to it. You knew what a truck sounded like when it was 200 feet away, and what it sounded like when it was but 20 feet away and still moving rapidly. Now, suddenly, you can *see*. When you *look* at that truck 200 feet away, it seems incredibly tiny, almost insignificant. Why? Because the truck's visual image on your retina is also incredibly small. As the truck moves rapidly toward you, the *size* of the image it casts on your retina grows by leaps and bounds. But would you see the truck as changing *position*? Why couldn't you perceive a stationary truck that was suddenly swelling up in *size* like a balloon?

Size Constancy

Like most sighted people, you learned long ago that trucks don't change size. So you *interpret* changes in the *apparent size* of objects like trucks as evidence that they (or you) are moving. Put another way, there is a relationship between the perceived size of an object and its perceived distance. As long as you have some clue as to how far an object is from you, the object will appear to be the same "real size" whether it casts a large or small image on your retina. We call this relationship between size and distance the principle of **size constancy**.

FIG. 5.30 In the Ames room people appear to change sizes. In reality, the woman is much taller than the boy. As you can see from the diagram, the person on the left is almost twice as far from the viewer, and since this distance is not apparent to the viewer, the illusion results.

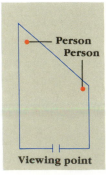

5 / Perception and ESP

Size constancy (KON-stan-see). Your brain gets a rough idea of the physical size of an object by noting how large a visual image the object casts on your retina. Generally speaking, the larger the visual image, the larger the object will be. However, an object very close to you will cast a much larger image on your retina than will the same object if it is far away from you. If the object is very familiar, your brain will interpret any change in the size of the retinal image as a change in the distance the object is from you. This is the principle of size constancy. If the object is unfamiliar, you may overestimate its size if it is up close, and underestimate its size if it is far away from you.

Shape constancy. The tendency to perceive the shape of an object as invariant (in-VER-rhee-ant) or unchanging even when the shape of the image the object casts on your retina changes considerably.

Trapezoids (TRAP-ee-zoids). Four-sided figures with two sides which are parallel. In the drawing of the picture frame "tilted away from you" on this page, notice that the left and right sides of the frame are parallel, but the top and bottom sides are not. The picture frame—as viewed from this angle—is a trapezoid.

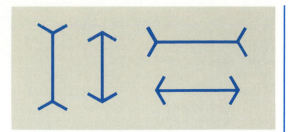

FIG. 5.32 The Mueller-Lyer illusion.

"size constancy" (the size of the people), your cortex typically votes in favor of good form.

▢▢ **QUESTION** ▢▢

How does the Ames distorted room illusion tend to confirm the Gestalt Law of Dynamic Direction?

Mueller-Lyer Illusion

Look at Fig. 5.32, which shows two versions of the famous Mueller-Lyer illusion. Don't the two lines with the outward-pointing "V's" seem much longer than the two lines with the inward-pointing "V's"? Yet if you measure the lines in both these figures, you'll see they are exactly the same length.

Why does one line look longer than the other? Richard Gregory believes this illusion is based on your perception of corners (see Fig. 5.33). If you are reading this book indoors, look at one of the corners of the room you're in. Notice that the angles the wall makes with the floor or the ceiling form lines much like those in the figures with the outward-pointing "V's." If you are sitting outdoors, look at the corner of a building. You will see that the angles made by the roof and the ground are similar to the same lines in the figures with the inward-pointing "V's" (Gregory, 1978).

When looked at head-on, the "distorted room" appears quite normal—until you see two people standing in the room. And then you know that something is very definitely wrong.

The windows in the Ames room *look* rectangular. In fact, the windows are really **trapezoids**. Now look at Fig. 5.31. At the left, the door is indeed a rectangle. But as it opens, it casts a trapezoid-shaped image on your retina. But since you *know* that most doors are really rectangles, you *perceive* it as retaining its shape as it opens.

When you look at the Ames distorted room in Fig. 5.30, your brain experiences a problem. For the windows really are trapezoids, instead of being rectangles. In order to keep the windows *looking* like rectangles, your brain must produce *distance distortions* that make one of the people in the room look much larger than the other. Given the choice between preserving "good form" (the shape of the windows) or

FIG. 5.31 We perceive the opening door as being rectangular in shape despite the nonrectangular images projected on our retinas.

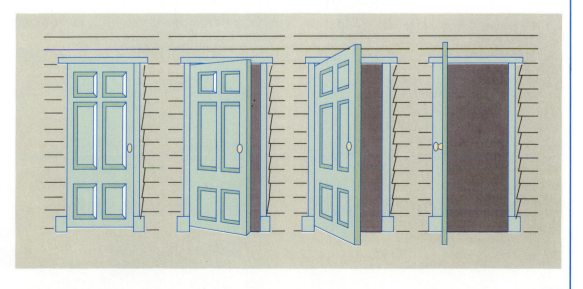

FIG. 5.33 The vertical line in the corner of the room is the same length as the vertical line that makes up the corner of the building. These two drawings make up a sort of "real-life Mueller-Lyer illusion."

□ □ QUESTION □ □

It is rather simple to train a pigeon in a laboratory to peck at the shorter of two lines in order to get a bite of food. How might you use this procedure to test whether pigeons are as fooled by the Mueller-Lyer illusion as humans are?

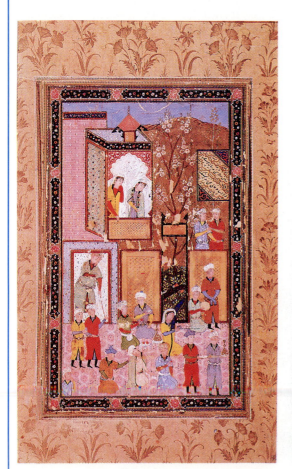

Other Illusions

You seldom see an object *all by itself*. Instead, you almost always see an object in relationship to the other objects around it. In the Mueller-Lyer illusion, for example, the "V's" at the ends of the horizontal lines affect your perception of how long the lines are.

Now look at Fig. 5.34. Is the hat taller than it is wide? If you think so, take out a ruler and measure the distances.

The apparent straightness of a line can easily be affected by whatever objects the line seems to penetrate. In Fig. 5.35, the **diagonal** line crossing the two bars seems to be three disconnected lines. In fact, as you can determine by using a ruler, the line is absolutely straight. Oddly enough, the illusion disappears for most people if they turn the drawing around so that the line is straight up and down.

● *Cultural Influences on Illusions*

You grew up in a world of straight lines, corners, and sharp angles. But suppose you had lived as a child in an environment where straight lines were **taboo**? How would you perceive these illusions?

The answer is—you probably wouldn't see some of them at all. The Zulus—a tribe of primitive people in South Africa—live in what Richard Gregory calls a "circular culture." Their huts are round mounds with circular doors (see Fig. 5.36). They plow their fields in curved lines, and even their toys and tools lack straight edges. When shown the Mueller-Lyer illusion, the typical Zulu native sees one line as being only very slightly longer than the other. Some illusions, such as the "top hat" drawing, affect the Zulu hardly at all (Gregory, 1978).

FIG. 5.34 The "top hat" illusion.

Why do artists in many cultures, like the Persian miniaturist who painted the scene at left, "break the rules" of linear perspective? (Hint: What would the gazebo in the photo at right look like if you were able to float around it and see it from all angles?)

Diagonal (die-AG-oh-null). If you were standing straight up, then leaned over at an angle, your body would be diagonal to the floor. The "slant mark" (/) on the typewriter is a diagonal line.

Taboo (tab-BOO). Sometimes spelled "tabu." Any object or behavior that is prohibited because it is illegal or immoral. The most common form, found in almost all cultures, is the incest taboo—the strong belief that you are not supposed to have sexual experiences with close relatives.

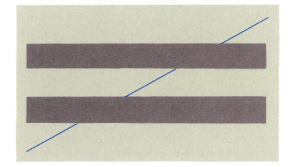

FIG. 5.35 **Is the diagonal line straight?**

PUPIL RESPONSES

As the illusions we've just described suggest, perception is an exceptionally complex process. From the "information processing" point of view, visual inputs are processed at various stages as they work their way up to your brain from your eyes (the "bottom-up" viewpoint). However, once you have perceived something, your mind can send commands back to the lower centers (and your eyes). These "top-downward commands" affect what you perceive *next*.

Now that we have discussed simple eye-to-brain illusions, let's look at some complex perceptions that are created *after* your mind has made its initial response to a visual input.

One of the major purposes of your visual system is to gird you for *action*. When you walk out of a darkened movie theater, your pupils decrease in size rapidly to keep you from being blinded by the sudden increase in light. Your brain didn't have to *learn* how to make your pupils close under these conditions—the response is *innate*. And at dusk, when the sunlight dims, your pupils automatically open up, or *dilate*. The wider your pupils open, the more light comes through and the better you can see and react to objects in your visual environment. Again, this response is determined by your genes, not by previous learning (Hess, 1965).

Your pupils also dilate when you look closely at some object, even though there is no change in illumination. The harder you stare at the object, the wider your pupils will open (see Fig. 5.37). *What* you choose to inspect closely, of course, is determined primarily by your past experience. So *this* type of pupil dilation is influenced by what you have learned about the world.

Psychologist Eckhard Hess made use of this information to test a hunch of his. Hess reasoned that people would stare *more* at something they were really interested in than at something they disliked. So he showed pictures of many different objects to the college students he used as subjects in his experiments.

FIG. 5.36 **The "circular culture" of the Zulus.**

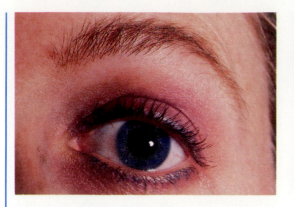

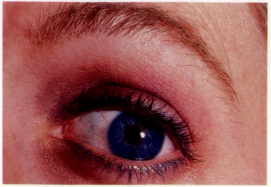

Hess found that women typically had much larger pupil openings when he showed them pictures of babies or nude males than when he showed these women pictures of landscapes or nude females. Men, on the other hand, usually had wider pupils when shown pictures of nude females than when they were shown photographs of babies, landscapes, or nude males.

Hess's research suggests you can often discover a person's *real* interests simply by noting when the person becomes "wide-eyed" (Hess, 1965).

□ □ **QUESTION** □ □

Is the tendency for women to become "wide-eyed" when looking at babies or nude males learned, innate, or both? How might you prove your answer is correct?

● *Visual Suppression*

Under certain very special conditions, your mind can be forced to *choose* between two entirely different visual inputs.

Imagine a large black box with two eyeholes in one side. There is a wooden partition inside the box that divides it in half. Thus, when you look through the holes, your left eye sees a different scene than does your right eye. The apparatus is also arranged so that these different scenes are visible only for *a brief fraction of a second*. How would your mind handle this odd situation?

Generally speaking, you will make one of two responses when faced with conflicting, very brief visual inputs. Most of the time your nervous system simply **suppresses** or rejects one of the pictures and *concentrates* on the other. But on rare occasions, your cortex may *combine* the two inputs into one.

If we show a different scene to your left eye than to your right, which scene will you suppress? If your vision is clearer in one eye than in the other, you will almost always pick the scene that you see best. But if both your eyes are in good shape, you face a **dilemma**.

If your left eye is looking at a cup, while your right eye is looking at a teapot that is pouring liquid from its spout, your mind may actually *fuse* the two scenes together so that you see a pot pouring tea into a cup (see Fig. 5.38). If one of your eyes sees a baby hanging in mid-air, while the other sees a woman holding out empty arms, your brain may superimpose one scene on the other so that you see the woman holding the child (Matlin, 1982).

But suppose the two pictures are so different they can't be fused? Then you typically concentrate on whichever scene you find *more interesting*, and suppress the other scene almost completely. In many cases this suppression takes place so rapidly, you are not aware you are being shown two different objects or photographs.

In a recent study, Georgia State psychologists Mark Gilson, Earl Brown, and Walter Daves tested both gay and straight males in a visual suppression situation. The experimenters presented "heterosexual" stimuli to one of the subject's eyes, and presented "homosexual" stimuli to the other eye. Generally speaking, straight males tended to suppress the homosexual stimuli while gay males tended to suppress the heterosexual stimuli (Gilson, Brown, & Daves, 1982).

FIG. 5.38 The teapot pouring liquid and the teacup can be fused visually so that the tea seems to flow into the cup.

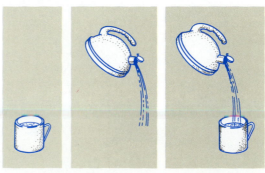

Suppresses (sup-PRESS-es). To inhibit or to put down.

Dilemma (die-LEM-mah). A problem that has two or more equally good solutions. To be "caught on the horns of a dilemma" is the same thing as being "caught between the devil and the deep blue sea," in that any solution you pick is equally good—and equally bad.

137-144

THE DEVELOPMENT OF PERCEPTION

You apparently are *born* with the tendency to suppress some types of threatening visual inputs. But *what* you find threatening is, of course, determined by your past experience and your outlook on life. These facts bring us back to the *nature-nurture problem* mentioned earlier in this chapter. There are some aspects of perception that appear so early after birth they can be considered *primarily* innate. And there are other parts of the perceptual process that emerge only when the infant has had a fair amount of "worldly experience." As we discuss this issue in detail, however, you should keep the following two points in mind: First, infants begin to learn about the world around them *even before the infants are born*. And second, all learning is based on innate responses the infants have available at birth. Perception, then—like all other parts of human experience—is truly multi-determined.

Innate Aspects of Perception

Al Yonas of the University of Minnesota's Institute of Child Development believes that many aspects of visual perception are controlled by the child's genetic blueprint. Yonas has shown that 3-week-old infants will blink and recoil slightly from a black triangle moving toward them—even when no physical contact occurs. However, these same babies will be unresponsive when the triangle moves away from them. Yonas also notes that early visual development tends to be better in female infants, those who are above-average in size, and those born after their due dates. These facts are better explained in terms of genetic inheritance than in terms of early visual experience (Yonas, 1979).

Face Perception in Infants

Recent research suggests that, just an hour or so after birth, infants will mimic the facial expressions of adults (see Chapter 14 for details). This work indicates there is something rather special about the human face—at least from an infant's point of view (Meltzoff & Moore, 1977).

Look at Fig. 5.39. One drawing is that of a face with the nose, eyes, and other features in their proper places. The other drawing has the same elements, but they are oddly scrambled. Now imagine a very young infant lying comfortably on her or his back looking up at these figures. What do you think the baby would spend more time looking at—the normal face, or the scrambled one?

Psychologist Robert L. Fantz photographed the eye movements of young babies. The infants he measured spent much more time looking at the normal than at the scrambled face. This finding suggests children have innate response patterns which allow them to recognize what the human face looks like (Fantz, 1963).

Fantz also found that babies prefer looking at simple round objects rather than at two-dimensional drawings of the same objects. Fantz believes infants may have an *innate appreciation of depth*. He points out, however, that his experimental results may also mean that babies learn about faces and depths very early in their lives (Fantz, Fagan, & Miranda, 1975).

According to University of Texas psychologist Judith Langlois, infants pay more attention to pictures of *attractive* faces than to pictures of *plain* ones. Langlois and her associates showed pairs of women's faces to infants aged 6 to 8 months. Each pair of pictures contained one face that was rated "attractive" and one face that was rated "unattractive" by adult judges. Some 71 percent of the infants stared longer at the attractive than at the unattractive face. When younger infants (aged 2 to 3 months) were given a similar test, some 65 percent of them preferred the more attractive face. Langlois believes that "a universal standard of [facial] attractiveness, overlaid with cultural and temporal variation, may exist" (Langlois *et al.*, 1987).

□ □ **QUESTION** □ □

Langlois notes that attractive faces "may be more curved and less angular, or more vertically symmetrical than unattractive faces." What would the Gestalt psychologists have to say about Langlois's remarks?

Visual Processing in Infants

Marshall M. Haith and his colleagues at the University of Denver have made extensive studies of the ways in which infants learn to process visual inputs during the first weeks of life (see

FIG. 5.39 Infants tested in Fantz's apparatus looked at the simple face longer than they did at the design with randomly placed facial features.

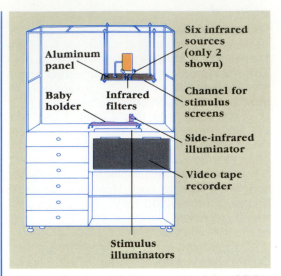

FIG. 5.40 Drawing of Haith's apparatus. Infrared lights provide illumination for recording of image of the eye via infrared TV camera onto video tape. Stimulus illuminators light stimulus screen above the baby holder so that a baby, lying in the holder, sees only the screen and the stimulus spray painted on it. A TV camera records through the screen.

Labels on figure:
Aluminum panel
Six infrared sources (only 2 shown)
Baby holder
Infrared filters
Channel for stimulus screens
Side-infrared illuminator
Video tape recorder
Stimulus illuminators

talking than at the mother's *mouth*. Although Haith doesn't say so, it seems likely that the sound of the mother's voice speeds up the infant's visual development—perhaps by soothing the child's fears. The infant responds to the soothing sounds by gazing at the mother's eyes more often. The mother usually interprets increased "eye gazing" as a sign the child is "paying attention." Thus, she talks to the child—and cradles the infant—more frequently. Whatever the case, it seems likely that visual perception in the human infant is as strongly influenced by auditory and skin-receptor inputs as it is by visual stimuli.

□□ **QUESTION** □□
Haith's research seems to contradict Fantz's belief that infants are born with the ability to recognize the human face. How might you resolve this contradiction? (Hint: How old might Fantz's infants have been when he tested them? And which of the two stimuli Fantz used was visually more complex?)

Fig. 5.40). According to Haith, a four-week-old child is not mature enough to *process* such "complex visual stimulus patterns" as the human face. Therefore, very young infants gaze *away* from their mother's face about 80 percent of the time, and *fixate* on her face only about 20 percent of the time. Even when the four-week-old child does gaze directly at the mother, the infant tends to fixate mostly at the *edge* of her face. Haith and his colleagues report that four-week-old infants fixated on the *center* of the mother's face (her eyes, nose, mouth) about 22 percent of the time (Haith, 1980).

By seven weeks of age, however, the normal infant has learned how to "process" faces. So the child gazes directly *at* the mother's face almost 90 percent of the time the child can see her. And when looking at her face, the infant fixates on the *center* of the face rather than the edges. Haith also reports seven-week-old infants looked at the mother's *eyes* almost twice as much as at her nose or mouth.

Haith believes newborn infants are innately attracted to *edges* or contours of objects in their visual world. By seven weeks of age, however, the baby is sufficiently experienced so the child can begin to perceive the human face as a unified "whole" rather than as a "collection of parts." We call this "unified whole" a perceptual **schema** (Haith, 1980).

Haith notes that a nine-week-old infant is more likely to gaze at the mother's face when she is *talking* to the child than when she isn't. But Haith also points out the baby is more likely to gaze at the mother's *eyes* when she is

The Visual Cliff

Another intriguing bit of evidence concerning the innate properties of perception comes from a series of experiments pioneered by Eleanor Gibson. Although Eleanor Gibson frequently collaborated on research with her husband, James J. Gibson, she is one of America's best-known perceptual psychologists in her own right.

One day several years ago, Eleanor Gibson found herself eating a picnic meal on the rim of the Grand Canyon. Looking straight down into that deep and awesome river bed, she began to worry about the safety of the children around her. Would a very young child be able to perceive the enormous drop-off at the edge of the cliff? Or would the child go toddling right over the edge if no adult were around to restrain the child?

Gibson was really asking two very important questions about perception. First, are babies born with an *innate ability to perceive depth*? And second, do infants have a *built-in fear mechanism* that would make them retreat from sharp drop-offs even without having been trained to do so?

Once Gibson had returned to her laboratory at Cornell University, she attempted to answer both these questions. And to do so, she designed an artificial **visual cliff** on which she could test infants safely (see Fig. 5.41). Running down the middle of the apparatus was a raised plank of wood painted in a checkerboard pattern. To one side of the plank was a sharp drop-off. On the other side was a normal "floor" an inch or so below the center plank.

The entire apparatus was covered with sturdy glass so the infant could see the cliff but could not fall off it.

When an infant was tested, the child was put on the center board and allowed to explore freely. Very few of the infants crawled off onto the "cliff" side, although most of them freely moved onto the "floor" side. Even when the child's mother stood at the side of the apparatus and attempted to coax the child to crawl out over the "cliff," most infants refused to do so. Instead, they began to cry loudly. If the mother stood on the "floor" side of the box, however, the infant would crawl toward her willingly (Gibson & Walk, 1960).

A variety of newborn animals—lambs, kittens, puppies, and rats—have been tested on the visual cliff too. For the most part, these animals showed an immediate perceptual awareness of the "dangers" of the cliff. Gibson concludes that many higher species have behavioral mechanisms built into their brains at birth that tend to protect them from the dangers of falling from high places (Gibson, 1981).

FIG. 5.41 The "visual cliff."

However, not all infants, nor all species, react to the visual cliff as did the babies in Gibson's first studies. Gibson and Rader point out that there are great individual differences between infants in their response to the visual cliff. Some babies seem to be *visually oriented*. These infants recoil with fear from the sight of the cliff. Others tend to be *touch oriented*. These children apparently trust their skin senses more than their eyes, and crawl right out on the glass covering the cliff as long as it offers firm support. Thus, the issue of whether infants are born with an innate fear of heights is far from settled (Gibson & Rader, 1979; Gibson & Walker, 1984).

Developmental Handicaps of the Blind

Some innate visual tendencies are so subtle we tend to overlook them—except when we observe the development of the child who is born blind. In her book *Insights from the Blind*, Selma Fraiberg says the blind youngster has two severe problems to overcome: (1) learning to recognize his or her parents from sounds alone, and (2) acquiring a healthy *self-concept* or perceptual "self-schema" (Fraiberg, 1977).

Fraiberg notes that normal eight-month-olds will reach out their arms the moment they hear their mother's voice—*anticipating* the sight of the parent even before she appears in the child's view. The blind baby does not show this reaching response until much, much later. The blind infant *hears* and *feels*, but cannot "integrate" these sensory experiences very well to form a unified schema of *mother*. Vision, then, is particularly important to a youngster because sight allows the child to pull the other sensory modalities together in her or his mind.

Blind children are frequently retarded in their speech development. They talk later and more poorly than do sighted children. Much of this speech retardation seems due to their slowness in recognizing the *permanence* of objects in the world around them (see Chapter 15). Blind children also have problems "imagining" things while young and do not identify readily with a doll or with a character in a story their mother reads to them. And they often do not learn the correct use of "I" and "you" until they are five or six (Fraiberg, 1977).

Fraiberg concludes that blind youngsters cannot *picture* themselves as objects that exist separate from their environments. And since they cannot *visualize* themselves as independent entities, they are slow to develop any real notion of "self."

In brief, *seeing* yourself may be the easiest and most natural way of building up a perceptual schema of your own *self*.

• *Innate or Learned?*

The question of which aspects of vision are learned and which are innately determined

The Development of Perception

may never be entirely solved. For instance, while children blind from birth are sometimes slow to develop social and verbal skills, they usually are able to move around in the world fairly readily. Indeed, according to Barbara Landau and her associates at the University of Pennsylvania, **congenitally** blind children perceive *physical space* (as distinct from "visual space") about as well as sighted children do.

Landau and her group tested Kelli, a 2½-year-old girl who was blind from birth, on a variety of tasks. When Kelli was allowed to explore a room on her own, she could thereafter take the shortest path from any spot to any spot in the room. Landau and her colleagues believe Kelli could "perceive" the physical layout of the room even if she couldn't "see" the room visually (Landau *et al.*, 1981).

Apparently, then, infants are born with an innate ability to *create three dimensional space in their minds*. But even with this inborn tendency, they still need "worldly experience" if they are to learn to perceive "objects in space."

□ □ **QUESTION** □ □
How might *auditory* perception help a child like Kelli develop a perception of physical space?

● *Sensory-based Perception: A Summary*
As we mentioned at the beginning of this chapter, there are four main theories of perception: the Gibsonian, the Gestalt, the empirical, and the information processing approaches. Although there are major differences among them, all four theories attempt to describe how information about the outside world is "captured" by your sensory receptors, is "processed" by your nervous system, and then is "experienced" as reality in your stream of consciousness. Thus, while proponents of these four theories might disagree on many points, there is one belief they'd surely all have in common: Without *sensory inputs,* you wouldn't *perceive* anything.

But ask yourself this question: Under certain circumstances, isn't it perhaps possible for you to acquire information by "channels" other than your sensory receptors? What about those people who claim they can "read other people's minds"? Or "communicate with supernatural spirits"? Or "foresee the future"? Obviously, if true, these sorts of experiences would involve *extra-sensory perception*, that is, the acquisition of knowledge by means "beyond the normal sensory pathways."

The Latin word *para* means "beyond." The study of "extra-sensory perception" and other phenomena that lie "beyond the normal bounds of scientific psychology" is called **parapsychology**. Let's look briefly at this fascinating field, both to see what it's like and because its study may yield important information about how people occasionally misinterpret "normal" perceptual processes.

□ □ **QUESTION** □ □
Studies suggest that most people dream about the future fairly frequently. What kinds of "future events" would you be most likely to remember if you dreamed of them?

EXTRA-SENSORY PERCEPTION AND PARAPSYCHOLOGY

Parapsychologists study many different types of unusual phenomena, most of which involve extra-sensory perception (ESP) of one kind or another. Four of the best-known are mental telepathy, clairvoyance, precognition, and psychokinesis.

Mental telepathy is the technical term for "reading someone's thoughts" (see Chapter 1).

Clairvoyance is the term we use to describe the perception of external objects or events without normal sensory stimulation. Comic book characters who can "see through walls" do so by using clairvoyance.

Precognition is the ability to perceive future events before they happen.

Psychokinesis is the power of "mind over matter." If you could influence the movement of physical objects simply by wishing them to move, or if you could "bend spoons" or other objects mentally, you would be using psychokinesis to do so.

Parapsychology also includes the investigation of such supernatural events as ghosts, **reincarnation**, communicating with the dead (or other non-physical beings), out-of-body experiences, and so forth. However, the four phenomena listed above are by far the most studied *in the laboratory*, so we will limit our discussion of ESP and parapsychology to these four.

Who Believes in ESP?
In 1978, psychologists Mary Monnet and Mahlon Wagner asked more than 1,100 college teachers if they believed in ESP. Overall, 16 percent thought ESP was an established fact, while 49 percent believed it probably was a real-life occurrence. About 24 percent of the teachers denied ESP existed, while the rest thought it "merely an unknown." Teachers in the humanities, arts, and education were the most enthusiastic supporters of ESP—about 75 percent believed in it. Only 5 percent of the psychologists thought ESP to be an established fact, and only 29 percent thought it was likely (cited in Edge *et al.*, 1986).

The general public, however, is more likely to accept ESP as an "established fact." A

Congenitally (kon-JEN-it-tally). From the Latin words meaning "to bring forth." A "congenital" defect is one present at birth. The defect may be innate (caused by genetic damage) or may be caused by trauma the infant experiences in the womb or during the birth process.

Parapsychology (PAIR-ah-sigh-COLL-oh-gee). The scientific study of events that are "beyond" normal explanation.

Clairvoyance (clair-VOY-ants). From the French words meaning "clear-sighted." The ability to see things hidden from normal sight.

Psychokinesis (SIGH-ko-kin-EE-sis). The Greek word *kinesis* means "movement," or "to move." *Psyche* is the Greek word for "mind." Psychokinesis (PK) is the ability to move things mentally, by willing them to move, rather than by touching them physically.

Reincarnation (ree-in-car-NAY-shun). To be born again, after death, usually in a new body and often in a new time or place.

1978 Gallup poll found that more than half the US population believed in ESP. And according to R. Wuthnow's survey in the same year, more people in the US believe in extra-sensory perception than believe in God (Wuthnow, 1978).

How can we explain the discrepancy between what the general public believes and what psychologists will accept as factual? The answer probably lies in the *experimental method*, which we discussed in Chapter 1. If you (or one of your friends) has had what seemed to be a paranormal experience, chances are good that your belief in ESP will be fairly strong. But the *science of psychology* can accept "super-natural" explanations only when all *natural* explanations have been ruled out. As Kenyon College psychologist Richard B. Hoppe put it recently, "The claim for some sort of nonsensory mental interaction with distant objects or persons is sufficiently extraordinary as to require very compelling evidence that the phenomenon even occurs and that evidence has not been produced by the parapsychologists" (Hoppe, 1988).

As we saw in Chapter 1, demonstrating that an event can be explained in normal scientific terms often calls for a fair amount of ingenuity—and some knowledge of how people can exchange subtle cues without being aware they are doing so. So let us see why ESP experiments are so difficult to design, and how their results are sometimes misinterpreted.

ESP Experiments

Suppose you volunteered to participate in a parapsychological experiment. You might be shown a pack of ordinary bridge cards so that you could make sure that—like all other bridge decks—this one contained 52 cards divided into four suits. The experimenter would then shuffle the cards thoroughly and place the deck face down on the table between the two of you.

The experimenter might then pick up the cards one by one in such a manner that he or she could see the card, but you couldn't. Next,

Unconscious "cheating" is very likely to happen with ESP parlor games like the Ouija board; scientists have tried to design "cheat-proof" experiments to test paranormal phenomena.

you would be asked to "read the experimenter's mind"—that is, to guess the *suit* of the card that the parapsychologist was looking at. Since there are four suits in the deck, you would have *one chance in four* of being right with any given card. If, the first time you tried this experiment, you guessed the suit correctly 13 times out of 52, you would have done no more than would be expected *by chance alone*.

Undaunted by your first experience, you try again. And this time you guess all 52 cards correctly! Surely this is evidence that mental telepathy occurred, isn't it?

The answer is—not yet. First, you must show that you had no *sensory cues* to help you out. Thousands of studies similar to this one have been performed in the past—and almost all of them are useless from a scientific point of view. Why? Because the experimenter did not control for the *exchange of subtle social cues* such as those we described in Chapter 1. Indeed, the vast majority of studies in this area can be discounted because the experimenters failed to take into account the "Clever Hans" effect (Edge *et al.*, 1986).

□ □ **QUESTION** □ □
How many times would you have to guess the suit correctly before you might begin to suspect that something paranormal had occurred?

• Schmidt's Precognition Study

One of the problems with ESP studies is that the experimenter must make sure there is *no possible way* the information the subject is trying to "receive mentally" could be received by normal sensory pathways. A second problem is that the experimenters themselves may unconsciously "cheat" while recording the results of the study. Several years ago, physicist Helmut Schmidt reported a study on *precognition* that seemed to overcome these problems.

Schmidt built a *random generator*—a machine that would randomly turn on one of four colored lights. Beneath each light was a button that the subject could press. It was the subject's task to predict which light the machine would turn on.

Since the machine did not make its random selection until *after* the subject had pressed a button, there was no obvious way that either Schmidt or the subject could know which light would turn on—except through *precognition*. In his first experiment, Schmidt used three subjects who made more than 60,000 guesses. The subjects' choices were correct far more often than chance would allow. In a second experiment, the subjects could guess either which light would turn on, or which one wouldn't. Again they did far better than chance. Schmidt has repeated these studies—usually with fair success—many times (Schmidt, 1976, 1981, 1985).

□ □ **QUESTION** □ □
The Schmidt type of experiment controls for "unconscious whispering," but what other types of errors would you want to control for as well?

• *Criticisms of Schmidt's Studies*

Do Schmidt's studies *prove* that precognition exists? No, not necessarily. A lengthy discussion of the pros and cons of Schmidt's work appears in the July 1980 issue of the *Zetetic Scholar* (see Chapter 1). Although some psychologists believe that Schmidt's research is fairly encouraging evidence, others are less convinced. As James Randi points out in the *Zetetic Scholar,* Schmidt's work has not as yet been properly observed by other scientists, nor has his work been **replicated** successfully by most other investigators. Randi also notes that in *almost* all of the famous ESP studies, subsequent investigations by skeptical scientists have either exposed a fatal defect or have uncovered evidence that the experimenter might have "fudged" the data. In a more recent survey, British scientist Susan Blackmore comes to the same conclusion, not only about Schmidt's research, but about ESP experiments in general (Blackmore, 1985).

Does ESP Exist?

Do all these objections mean that ESP is no more than a figment of people's imaginations? No, not at all. For the essence of science is that *we must always keep an open mind.* However, it does seem that extra-sensory perception is at best a kinky, slippery, undependable thing that happens rarely, unpredictably, and for the most part uncontrollably.

Over the years, a great many scientists have spent a fair amount of laboratory time trying to "prove" the existence of ESP and other paranormal phenomena. For example, more than a decade ago, Susan Blackmore had an "out-of-body experience," which prompted her to spend 10 years studying ESP scientifically. Much to her dismay, she failed to produce any reliable proof at all. Speaking of ESP studies in general (including her own research), Blackmore concludes that the more controlled these studies have been, the less evidence for the existence of ESP they have provided (Blackmore, 1986). And after surveying the field, Richard Hoppe concludes that "I know of no [paranormal] phenomenon that can be consistently produced under experimental conditions that rule out subject or experimenter fraud, statistical and procedural artifacts, or normal sensory functioning" (Hoppe, 1988).

If the *scientific evidence* doesn't generally support a belief in ESP, though, why do many

The popular press often reports the feats of "psychics" like Yuri Geller, who claims to bend spoons through powers of psychokinesis, without calling for scientific proof that the event did not occur through natural means.

people ignore the "scientific facts" and continue to place very strong faith in the paranormal? For many reasons:

1. ESP may, in fact, exist, but we do not as yet know how to reproduce it under laboratory conditions.
2. Many real-world events have, as yet, no logical, scientific explanation.
3. Most people tend to trust their own perceptions more than they do scientific evidence. And, as Susan Blackmore points out, "People who think they are intelligent, well-educated, and good observers believe that anything they cannot understand must be supernatural" (Blackmore, 1986).
4. Belief in the supernatural may, under certain circumstances, fulfill a very strong human need.

Let's look more closely at how *perceptions of supernatural events* come about, and why they are often highly rewarding.

□ □ **QUESTION** □ □
What sorts of "scientific sources" mentioned in the news media are you most likely to trust?

• *Belief in the Occult*

Barry Singer and Victor Benassi have spent many years studying **occult** beliefs in college students. In a recent article, they make three important points. First, their student subjects tended to believe whatever they saw in print or on television—particularly if they thought the source of the information was "scientific" or a

Astrological readings are usually phrased in such general terms that they could be interpreted to apply to a wide range of individuals, yet many people claim they are highly accurate.

"documentary." Second, when the students were asked to give examples of "scientific sources" and "documentaries," they listed *Reader's Digest*, the *National Enquirer,* and movies such as *Star Wars*. Third, as Singer and Benassi note, most newspapers, magazines, and TV programs report stories about paranormal events *without demanding scientific proof that the event occurred* (Singer & Benassi, 1981).

● **Intuition Versus Experimental Evidence**

Singer and Benassi give another important reason why belief in ESP may be so strong. To begin with, they cite a number of scientific studies showing that people tend to trust **intuitive** judgments rather than experimental evidence. Almost everyone has dreamed about something that eventually came true. But is this proof of *precognition*? No, because people have hundreds of similar dreams that don't come true. But we tend to forget those unfulfilled dreams and just remember the ones that "proved out." As Singer and Benassi put it, "A rare event is seen as one that seldom occurs, regardless of the number of opportunities for its occurrence. As a result of our natural tendency to misunderstand the probabilities involved in a match of dreams and reality," we are more likely to explain the dream as precognition than as mere chance.

Next, Singer and Benassi point out that many people resist giving up their belief in ESP no matter how strong the experimental evidence is against it. In one study, Singer and Benassi had a magician perform various "psychic tricks" for introductory psychology students. Even when the students were told in advance that the performer was a magician—and even when they admitted that what they saw could easily have been "mere tricks," *more than half the students* insisted that the magician's "tricks" were proof that ESP exists!

● **ESP and Motivation**

Singer and Benassi state that belief in the paranormal tends to rise during wars and other disasters, but tends to fall during good times. And, as Singer and Benassi note, belief in ESP seldom costs a person very much. Singer and Benassi conclude that accepting the supernatu-

ral gives people a feeling that they have greater control over their destinies than is actually the case (Singer & Benassi, 1981).

In a similar study, Lawrence University psychologist Peter Glick and his associates tested students' belief in astrology. The student subjects were given vague statements such as "Though you are a friendly person, at times you are rather shy." As Glick points out, such statements can apply to almost everyone. Students who believed in astrology thought these statements were "highly accurate" descriptions of themselves, *particularly when told the statements were produced by astrologers*. And even some of the skeptics accepted the accuracy of the statements if they thought the descriptions were based on astrology. Glick concludes, "In contrast to skeptics, people who believe in astrology have a greater need for a simple system to understand themselves and to predict the behavior of others. However, all of us, including skeptics, appear to have tendencies that may lead us falsely to lend credence to astrology" (Glick, 1987).

Perception and Stress Reduction

Perception is the psychological process by which you give meaning to and thus *"make sense" out of your sensory inputs*. But why do you bother to do so?

The best answer seems to be this: As you surely know from personal experience, uncertainty is *stressful*. Indeed, many psychologists believe that the need to reduce uncertainty is innately determined. Having a *theory* about why people act as they do *reduces uncertainty*. And the theory does so *whether the theory is accurate or not*. For, as Peter Glick notes, you are strongly motivated to search for (and accept uncritically) evidence that confirms your theory, and you tend to screen out any inaccurate predictions the theory makes.

Put rather bluntly, you not only tend to perceive what you *expect* to perceive, but you also tend to perceive what you *want* to perceive. To understand *perception,* therefore, you must know something about *motivation.* It is to the study of motivation, then, that we next turn our attention.

SUMMARY

1. Psychologists do not agree on how much of the perceptual process is determined innately, and how much is learned. This is called the **nature-nurture** controversy.

2. There are four major theories of visual perception: the **Gestalt** approach, the **Gibsonian** viewpoint, the **empirical** position, and the **information processing** approach.

3. Gestalt psychologists believe that perception results from an interaction between external (stimulus) factors and internal (psychological) processes. The **Law of Dynamic Direction** holds that perceptual systems move toward a state of balance, or equilibrium. Simple figures are the most balanced of all. Therefore, you tend to perceive objects in the simplest (most balanced) form possible.

4. James Gibson believed perception is **innate** and **direct**. You **see the world as it actually is**, because visual stimuli are rich in sensory cues that tell your brain what the objects actually look like.

5. The empirical approach states that you **learn** to perceive through experience. Thus, empirically speaking, **perception = sensory inputs + memories**.

6. The information-processing approach holds that inputs are highly processed before they reach your cortex. Special nerve cells **detect critical features** of visual inputs and pass this patterned information along to your cortex. Lower brain centers also **screen out** trivial information. Perception, therefore, is an indivisible part of **cognition**.

7. For Gibson and the empirical approach, perception is **driven** by stimulus factors and thus is a **bottom-up process**. For the information processing approach, perception is **driven** by cognitive (psychological) factors and thus is a **top-down process**. Gestalt theorists see perception as a **balance** between bottom-up and top-down factors.

8. The simplest type of visual information is **contours**, or a sudden change in lightness/darkness. Contours give **shape** to objects perceived visually.

9. The Gestalt **Law of Praegnanz** states you tend to perceive shapes or figures in the most **unique or clear-cut** form possible. Perception is determined by the **balance**

between the Law of Dynamic Direction and the Law of Praegnanz (plus other stimulus and internal factors).

10. **Figure-ground** relationships have a strong influence on perception. You tend to see **salient** objects as "figure" rather than as "background." The background always continues behind the figure.

11. **Ambiguous figures** show **perspective reversal**. The frequency with which the perspective reverses may be related to experience and personality factors.

12. You tend to group things together perceptually according to the Gestalt principles of **proximity**, **closure**, **continuity**, and **similarity**.

13. Humans who lose their sight in childhood but regain it as adults often have severe problems adjusting. They must learn to recognize visually objects that they had only touched or heard about. They do not perceive visual illusions in the same way that normally-sighted humans do.

14. **Linear perspective**, **convergence**, **aerial perspective**, **texture**, **light and shadow**, **interposition**, and **real and apparent motion** give you clues which allow your brain to perceive visual distance.

15. **Expectancy** has a strong influence on perception. For the most part, **you see what you expect to see**. You also **fail to see** what you don't expect (or want) to see.

16. **Size constancy** and **shape constancy** are the tendencies to see objects as maintaining proper size and shape despite changes in the image they cast on the retina.

17. Your **pupil size** is primarily determined by visual reflexes that you had when you were born. However, your pupils open wider when you look at something interesting than when you look at something boring.

18. When your two eyes are shown different scenes, your mind may **suppress** one of the scenes, or it may **fuse** the two together to make a "Gestalt." You are more likely to suppress threatening scenes than pleasant ones.

19. Some aspects of visual perception occur so soon after birth they seem *primarily* determined by your genes. Three-week-old infants will recoil from objects moving toward them, ten-day-old infants mimic the

facial expressions of adults around them, and babies prefer to look at pictures of human faces rather than mixed-up drawings of facial features.

20. Three-week-old infants tend to look away from their mothers' faces because they are not mature enough to have developed a **perceptual schema** of the mother. Nine-week-old babies are experienced enough to gaze directly at the mother's eyes and mouth. Infants also prefer looking at attractive faces.

21. Some (but not all) infants will avoid a **visual cliff**.

22. **Blind children** are slow to develop language and a **self-concept**, but do seem to have an innate appreciation of **physical space**.

23. **Parapsychology** is the scientific study of events that seem to have no "natural" explanation, such as **mental telepathy**, **clairvoyance**, **precognition**, and **psychokinesis**.

24. Although large numbers of people believe in **extra-sensory perception** (ESP), laboratory studies do not offer much support for this belief.

25. Belief in the supernatural tends to **rise in times of crisis**, and may satisfy a need for a simple explanation of human motivation and behavior.

(Continued from page 117.)

The last of the male passengers came out of the little airport waiting room sweating profusely and shaking his head. "Bunch of bloody nonsense," the man muttered to himself as he passed by the elegant figure of the Laforan Minister of Science and Technology.

Freddie glumly watched the man depart. They had held the passengers of the special jet from Paris in a quarantine waiting room, letting them pass one by one through the office where Professor Mann had inspected their eyes. Mann had agreed to signal Freddie if the tests detected the Snake, but no signal had come.

And now the waiting room was empty, save for a number of attractive but overdressed young women and one rather forlorn-looking matron cradling a baby in her arms. Freddie was confident the pretty women were girl friends of the munitions dealers. The matron was probably a wife of one of the dealers—although why a man would bring a wife and child to Lafora on a business trip, Freddie wasn't sure.

Freddie sighed. It seemed certain that Dr. Mann's tests had failed him—and failed the Republic of Lafora as well. The former fault he could tolerate. The latter came close to treason, and he mentioned this point to the Professor.

"What have you done, and why didn't it work?" Freddie demanded.

Mann looked annoyed at the Minister's bluntness. "First I showed a series of drawings to each man and measured the size of his pupils while he was watching. One of the drawings was of a snake. I had thought that our friend the assassin would show a larger pupil size to this drawing than to any other. Three of the men did so, but they failed the second test."

"Which was . . . ?"

"A suppression test. I have a variety of drawings—a pile of money, guns, airplanes, a picture of your President, a number of animals, and a snake striking at something with dripping fangs. I had the men look into my little black box that shows one drawing to the person's left eye, another to the right eye. And then I simply asked them to report what they saw. I figured most of the men would suppress the image of the snake, since most people are afraid of snakes."

Freddie snorted inelegantly. "But wouldn't the Snake see through your little tricks?"

"Perhaps, although I figured that, at the very least, he'd hesitate or be a little confused. But every man on the plane suppressed the picture of the snake without a moment's hesitation."

"And so your oh-so-scientific tests have failed," Freddie said glumly.

"No, Freddie, we're not through yet. There are still people in the waiting room."

Freddie looked around. "Just women and children, my dear Professor. We might as well let them go."

"You'll do nothing of the kind. Send them along for the eye checks, or their boy friends are going to be rather suspicious, don't you think?"

Freddie paused to consider the matter. As he did so, the matron approached them hesitantly and spoke to Freddie. "Excuse me, sir, my little boy is not feeling well. I'd like to get some warm milk for him and change his diaper. I wonder if you would allow us to go on through to the ladies' room?"

Before Freddie could respond, Professor Mann said loudly, "Right after you have your eyes checked, Madam. Part of the health inspection, you know. Now if you'll just look into this black box and tell me what you see . . ."

"Of course," the matron said, "if you'll promise to hurry."

The woman turned to Freddie and handed him the infant, which immediately set up a lusty bawling. Freddie's nose crinkled at the moist little bundle he had been handed, and he held the child clumsily and with obvious distaste. "Hurry it up, will you?" he said loudly to the Professor.

"Here's the first picture. What do you see?"

The matron leaned back a bit. "It's a gun of some kind," she said. "I don't approve of guns, you know."

"And how about this second picture?"

The matron glanced into the eyeholes in the black box, then leaned forward a bit. "Why, it's a snake—a big, black, ugly snake."

Freddie glanced up immediately. The Professor smiled at him with wide-open eyes.

"And now we'll try another test entirely. When I say 'Now,' I want you to look into the apparatus and tell me as quickly as you can what you see. All right?"

"Certainly," said the matron demurely, as Professor Mann adjusted the slides inside the box. "Now."

The woman leaned forward to look. She paused for several seconds, then responded. "That's odd, very odd indeed. I seem to see two things at once. First I see that snake again, and then I see a picture of the Laforan President, and then . . . then I see the snake biting the President. Now why would I see something like that?"

Freddie knew perfectly well why. He moved the infant to one arm and signaled vigorously with the other. Two large guards swooped down on them at once.

"Arrest this woman and search her baggage carefully," he told the guards.

General Chambro hurried up to them, a worried look on his big, round face. "Freddie, you've gone mad! This woman can't be the Snake!"

"How can you be sure, if you don't know what the Snake looks like?" the Professor asked, as the guards removed the matron from the scene.

"Yes, my dear General," Freddie said, a smile on his face. "I'll bet you a month's pay that Professor Mann has snared the Snake for us. The perceptual tests are positive."

"Perceptual tests be damned," said the General loudly. "Killing is a man's business, and everybody knows that the Snake is a man . . ."

"And that's why nobody ever caught her," replied Professor Mann. "She gave you a beautiful illusion to fool yourselves with. Down through history, the snake has always been a symbol of masculine sexual power and ruthlessness. Take the primitive tribe that I had hoped to visit, for instance. The chief warrior has a snake carved on the staff he carries. And if you look closely at those gold buttons that cover your uniform, General, you'll find the snake symbol on them all."

The General inspected his buttons, then frowned.

Professor Mann continued. "But of course the Snake did give you one clue to her identity—isn't poison a woman's weapon? Or was it just your minds she was attempting to poison?"

Freddie grinned, the General sputtered in protest, and Professor Mann added a footnote. "I'll offer one more suggestion. Look through those baby things very closely. What more unlikely place to carry snake venom than in a child's rattle?"

A few moments later the guards reported that they had found a tiny hypodermic needle and a small bottle of white liquid inside the bottle of milk that the woman carried.

General Chambro was beside himself with happiness. He embraced Professor Mann in a huge bear hug, then hurried off to tend to his nation's security.

"He smells a promotion, I'm sure," said Freddie caustically.

"Helping catch the Snake won't hurt your image any either, now will it, Freddie?"

"My dear Professor Mann, you speak with a forked tongue. But you are right, of course. The President will be very pleased . . ."

"And as for me?"

Freddie frowned. "Whatever do you mean?"

"What about those 'murderous savages' that I want to visit? If I can catch a snake for you, can't I manage to handle a few frightened primitives?"

"Well, my dear friend . . ."

The Professor interrupted. "You're still showing your prejudices, Freddie. You get very, very angry at all the whites in this world who judge a man by his skin color rather than by his true capabilities. Yet your view of women is just as biased and as distorted as their view of skin color. Isn't it about time you saw through some of your own illusions?"

Freddie smiled. "You psychologists! Ah well, I suppose that I might just mention to the President what your part in this afternoon's activities was. And our President is a very generous man indeed."

Freddie looked around and saw a couple of porters lounging near one of the doors.

"Here, you men! Get this equipment packed up again, then take it outside and put it back on the truck. Professor Mann will need it in the back country."

The American smiled softly. "Thanks, Freddie. I do appreciate your changing your mind. And now, how about that drink you promised me two hours ago?"

They walked off, arm in arm, headed for the cocktail lounge. The porters began to load up the heavy crates with the perceptual apparatus. The boxes were covered with address labels. On the largest label of all, written in scrawling print, was

Dr. Mary Ellen Mann
Department of Psychology
University of the Mid-West
USA

Introduction to Motivation

"By Bread Alone"

· C·H·A·P·T·E·R ·
6

STUDY QUESTIONS

As you read through the chapter, see if you can find the answers to the following questions:

1. What kinds of biological, intra-psychic, and social needs do you have?
2. Are intra-psychic and social needs learned, or are they innately determined?
3. What are the five levels of Maslow's hierarchy of human needs?
4. What does the term "homeostasis" mean when applied to human motivation?
5. How does arousal theory differ from drive theory?
6. What evidence is there that contemporary society discriminates against overweight individuals?
7. According to Marshall Jones, what three questions must you answer to understand behavioral sequences?
8. What is the influence of blood-sugar level on hunger?
9. What happens when you surgically remove both the hypothalamic "feeding center" and the "satiation center" in rats?
10. Why isn't dieting always a very effective way to lose weight?
11. What are the three main symptoms of anorexia?
12. Why are anorexia and bulimia primarily *feminine* problems?
13. What factors must you control to gain (or lose) weight on a permanent basis?

Thelma Green shook her plump face in dismay. "It's a dirty shame the way they treat people who are a trifle overweight," she said. "They don't consider our problems at all, and we've got lots."

Annette Holmes smiled and nodded encouragingly. Thelma Green certainly did have "lots"—about 250 pounds of "lots." But Annette liked the woman and, because Annette was a therapist at the Weight Control Clinic, she wanted to help Thelma shed some of those pounds if she could. So Annette just nodded and smiled and waited to see what Thelma had in mind.

"Take, for instance, clothes." Thelma Green picked at the blouse she was wearing. "Who makes good-looking clothes for somebody as fat as me? Potato sacks is what they sell us, and we have to buy them because there's nothing else available."

Annette looked carefully at Thelma's clothes. They didn't look all that bad. The woman was neat in her appearance despite her size. But Annette continued to nod her head.

"And anyhow, what kind of wardrobe can you have when you shoot up or down 30 pounds every six months?" Thelma continued. "I'm like a yo-yo. I gain a little, so I don't fit most of the things I have. And then I go on a crash diet, and I lose 40 pounds, and I still don't fit my clothes because now they're too big for me. I tell you, I've been on so many diets I think I'll puke if I ever see another bowl of cottage cheese!"

"Diets don't do all that much good, it's true," Annette said. "It's not losing pounds that is the difficult part, as you know. It's learning how to eat sensibly so that you reach, and maintain, a reasonable weight. That's what is so terribly hard for most overweight people."

"Why is that?" Thelma asked plaintively.

Annette warmed to her subject. "Starving yourself is a just a short-term change in behavior. If you want to keep your weight down permanently, you have to learn to eat sensibly, and keep on eating that way. Most overweight people just aren't motivated to make that drastic a change in the way they live and think and feel."

"That can't be my problem," Thelma said a bit testily. "Because I know what I eat, and it's very little, I assure you. No breakfast at all, and I have a very light lunch. I eat a sensible dinner, and that's it. Maybe 1,500 calories per day. But I gain weight on that, so maybe there's something wrong with the way my body utilizes food, or something."

Annette sensed the woman's impending anger and backtracked a little. "Well, there is a recent medical study indicating some people can eat less to maintain their weight than others have to eat. Have you seen a doctor yet?"

"I've seen a dozen," Thelma said unhappily. "I saw one guy last week. He told me I had a possible heart problem, that something might be wrong with my kidneys, and that I was going to die if I didn't lose 100 pounds right away. I asked him how I was going to shed those pounds, and he said that any dummy knew how to lose weight. Then he gave me a diet and said it would be my fault if I got sick and died because I was too stubborn to lose weight."

"So how did you react to this news?" Annette asked.

Thelma pulled out a handkerchief and dabbed it at her eyes. "I got so discouraged and depressed I went home and cooked a huge meal to make me feel better."

Annette had heard that one before. She just wished medical doctors would look at the actual consequences of the "little lectures" they gave their patients. Perhaps they'd lecture less and give their patients emotional support more often. "Well, I can understand your reaction," Annette said, smiling warmly. "But I do think you ought to try to learn how to eat better. So here's a form I'd like you to fill out. Please record everything you eat and drink. Put down the time, the place, the amount, who else is present, what you're doing, and how you feel. That will give us a good baseline or starting point."

"Fifteen hundred calories a day, that's all I eat!"

Annette nodded. "Perhaps, but you may be surprised. What I want you to do next is to decide how much you'd like to weigh a year or so from now. Then make a list of all the benefits and gains you'd receive if you got down to that weight."

"Well, my clothes would fit better," Thelma responded. "And I could go bowling again, and there's my friend Shirley in Miami I want to impress . . ." Her voice trailed off pensively.

"Very good thoughts!" said Annette. "Please put all those things down on your list, and any others you can think of. And come see me again on Friday at this same time. We'll have our dietitian see you then."

Three days later Annette got an urgent telephone call. "I don't believe it!" Thelma wailed. "I wrote down everything I ate and drank, just like you said I was supposed to do . . ."

"The baseline," said Annette. "That's good."

"No, it's terrible! I'm taking in 5,000 calories a day. Can you believe that?"

"I can believe it," Annette said, thinking of the woman's size. "But you said you didn't eat much breakfast or lunch and had just a light dinner. When are you taking in all those calories?"

"At night, after dinner, sitting in front of the boob tube," the woman replied. "I snack and snack and snack. About 3,000 calories worth an evening, to tell you the truth."

"And how do you feel when you're snacking?"

"Bored," came the reply. "I had a bad day at work yesterday. I got depressed, and I came home and started dinner and just kept on eating all night long."

"Well," said Annette, "what happened at work that got you so depressed?"

Thelma paused a moment before replying. "To tell you the truth, one of the women I super-

6 / Introduction to Motivation

vise screwed up a report, and when I told her to get her ass in gear and do it over again, she threw the report in my face."

Annette frowned. Weight control therapy seemed so simple when you first went into it: Just help people learn to eat correctly, right? But very often you had to help people clean up their emotional problems before you could teach them to control their overeating. Annette suspected she'd have to teach Thelma some new job skills so she wouldn't get depressed at work and then overeat when she came home.

"Listen," continued Thelma, "I've gone through the kitchen and thrown out all the junk food I could find. But now there's practically nothing left to eat. I'd go to the grocery store right now, but I don't know what to buy or how to cook low-cal stuff. Can you help me?"

"Of course I can," Annette responded. "Tell you what. I'll come over and we can make up a shopping list. Then we can have a light dinner somewhere and go to the grocery store."

Thelma snorted loudly. "Go to the store *after* you eat?"

"Certainly," Annette replied. "That way you cut down on the impulse buying. I'll bring over a really good diet plan our dietician has prepared. I'll bring over a nice exercise plan too."

"Exercise?" Thelma said in a shocked tone of voice. "I don't go for that stuff very much. Except for bowling, which I've given up for the duration."

"Why?"

Thelma sighed. "Well, I used to belong to this bowling league, but I got so big I didn't fit my bowling clothes any more. And then we usually had three or four drinks, and sometimes when I got a little snockered I had these arguments with my buddies . . ."

Annette could see it all quite clearly. Thelma simply didn't know how to get along very well with people. So she avoided company and stayed home by herself and got depressed and watched the tube and snacked. "Listen," Annette said, "you should go back to bowling even if your clothes don't fit. You can tip the bartender to give you a glass of ice water with lots of cherries and orange slices in it, and everyone will think you're drinking gin. And we can do some role playing so that you'll learn how to handle any social situations that might bother you. Okay?"

"Okay," came the reluctant response.

"But we're going to have to get you on a regular exercise program too. For instance, you tend to eat when you first come home from work, right?"

"Right."

"Well, we can interrupt that habitual behavior by having you walk for 10 minutes when you get home. That way . . ."

Thelma suddenly sounded excited again. "That way I don't associate eating with getting home from work, right? And you know I live in an apartment house, so even if it's raining I could just walk up and down the stairs for a while. Probably meet a lot of my neighbors for the first time, too. Might even be fun . . ."

"Of course it will be," Annette said enthusiastically. "Tell you what. Why don't you go for a walk and meet me at the parking lot in a quarter of an hour. Then we can look at the diet, have supper, and go grocery shopping."

"Okay, it's a deal. But listen, no grapefruit and no cottage cheese, or I'll upchuck right there."

Annette laughed. "Okay, but no cookies and no potato chips either."

Thelma moaned softly and hung up the phone.

A month later, Annette sat quietly in her office, a worried look on her face. For the first time ever, Thelma had missed an appointment. She had asked to see Annette at 9 p.m., because Thelma was going bowling right after work. Annette had agreed, because Thelma was doing beautifully. She had lost 22 pounds in four weeks, which was amazing. She was walking at least 30 minutes each day, and she had made several new friends while marching up and down the apartment stairs. Now it was nearly 11 p.m., but where was Thelma?

Annette reviewed the situation mentally. As Annette had guessed, Thelma tended to be rather bossy and punishing to her friends. But during their role-playing exercises, Thelma had learned how to express affection and gratitude openly instead of converting it into criticism. She also was doing much better on the job, so she seldom came home depressed. And she had so many invitations to visit her friends that she almost never spent the evening alone watching TV.

The one thing that Thelma wanted most was the respect and affection of others. Her feelings about Shirley, the friend who lived in Miami, were an example. "Shirley's a doll," Thelma had said. "She's stuck by me through thick and thin. Mostly thick, of course, given my size. Anyhow, what I want to do most is to lose 100 pounds, and fly to Miami without telling her I'm coming. I've seen that scene a thousand times in my mind's eye. Shirley opens the door, and she is thunderstruck. 'Hi, Shirl,' I say to her. 'It's the new me.'"

What better motivation? Annette had asked herself. So, at her suggestion, Thelma had started putting away $2.00 every day that she stuck to her diet. The money was to be used to pay for the projected trip to Miami.

Annette gave Thelma's number one last try. After three rings a discouraged and somewhat intoxicated voice answered.

"Thelma? This is Annette. What's happened?"

After a moment's silence, Thelma sobbed, "Oh, Annette. I'm so sorry. I'm just no damned good. I just don't deserve to get better."

The relapse crisis, Annette thought. It almost always happens when the person is right on the brink of success.

"Look, Thelma, I want to come over to see you. Right now."

"You better hurry, honey," came the tearful reply. "There may not be much left to see if you don't."

(Continued on page 172)

MOTIVATION: FACT AND THEORY

As David Edwards of Iowa State University notes, *motivation* isn't really an "area in psychology." Rather, it is a *series of questions* we ask as we try to explain *why* people act as they do (Edwards, 1972). Different psychologists tend to ask quite different sorts of questions. Therefore, there are about as many definitions of *motivation* as there are behavioral scientists.

Almost all scientists agree, however, that humans have *needs*, and that the study of needs makes up a large part of what we call "motivation." So, suppose we begin this chapter by asking four important questions about needs:

First, what *kinds* of needs do you have? Obviously, you have a biological requirement for things such as food and water. But can we explain everything you do in terms of your attempt to satisfy these basic *physical* requirements? Or do you have intra-psychic and social needs that are (in their way) as strong as your need for food and water? If so, what are these psychological and social needs? Do they vary much from person to person, or do all people develop about the same sort of social and psychological motives at the same stage in life? (In a sense, this is "the mind-body problem revisited." Those psychologists who take a biological viewpoint tend to emphasize bodily needs. However, those theorists who emphasize "mental" and "social" activities often hold that psychological needs are as "basic" as are physical needs.)

Second, where do your motivations *come from*? Your basic physical needs are surely determined by your genetic blueprint. But presuming we allow for social and intra-psychic motives, what causes them? Are they also determined (even in part) by your genetic blueprint? Or are they entirely imposed on you by your culture and your past experiences? (In brief, how much of your motivation is *innate*, and how much is *learned*? This is, of course, the "nature-nurture" debate extended to the field of motivation.)

Third, what are the various *mechanisms* by which you satisfy your needs? Are all your behaviors aimed at reducing stress and pain? Or are you motivated primarily by the promise of pleasure? That is, do you eat to reduce your hunger pangs, or because food tastes so good? Or are your eating behaviors (and their associated feelings) primarily controlled by such environmental inputs as cultural values and social

expectations? (Put briefly, are motivated behaviors determined by such single factors as stress and arousal? Or are motivated acts multi-determined?)

Fourth, what is the relationship between motivation and *conation*, or "the act of willing." Does your mind do anything more than yield to your body's itches and urges (the behavioral viewpoint)? Or can you voluntarily *choose* among a variety of behaviors in any given situation (the conative viewpoint)? (Put more simply, can we explain your motives entirely in terms of blind biological drives, or is motivation a matter of your consciously selecting among various behaviors available to you at a given time?)

These are some of the thorny questions you must try to answer when you try to explain *why* people do what they do. Little wonder, then, that the field of human motivation is one of the most fascinating but also one of the most frustrating areas in all of psychology.

Suppose we begin by looking at some early definitions of this slippery concept called motivation.

David Edwards

Motivation and Self-movement

The word **motivation** comes from the Latin term meaning "to move." Ancient scholars were fascinated by the fact that some objects in the world seem to be *self-movers*, while other objects remain stationary unless *acted upon* by some outside force. The ancients assumed that self-initiated motion was caused by a *spirit* inside the object—a "little man" of some kind—that pushed or impelled the object into action. Whenever the "spirit was moved," so was the object or body that the spirit inhabited (Petri, 1986).

It was not until about the 16th century that Western scientists gained enough knowledge of physics to explain the "behaviors" of such *inanimate* objects as rocks and rivers in purely *mechanical* terms. That is, it was not until a few hundred years ago that we managed to get the **animus** out of inanimate objects. And once scientists had made this giant intellectual step, they began to wonder if the actions of *living* organisms couldn't also be understood in physical or non-spiritual terms. Many of our theories of motivation are thus based on the belief that human activities are just as mechanical as are the movements of bedbugs and bacteria. The best known of these mechanistic approaches are *drive theory* and *arousal theory*.

Motivation (mote-tee-VAY-shun). From the Latin word *motivare*, meaning "to move." Motivation is defined in many different ways, the most common being that it is a series of questions that you ask about *why* people think, feel, and behave as they do.

Animus (ANN-ee-muss). The Latin word meaning "spirit."

Hierarchy (HIGH-er-ark-key). To make a hierarchy is to list things (or people) in order of their importance.

Opposed to these biological viewpoints are a variety of psychological and social theories which stress the importance of intra-psychic and environmental influences on behavior. But these approaches are limited too, in that most of them neglect the importance of biological needs.

Fortunately, there is one holistic theory which more or less encompasses the biological, the social, and the intra-psychic approaches to motivation. Although it too is far from being complete, let's talk about that approach first, and then explain drive theory and arousal theory. Finally, we will attempt to show the real complexities of motivation by discussing one very human problem in some detail—why some people overeat, while others deliberately undereat.

Maslow's Theory of "Self-Actualization"

According to Abraham Maslow, human needs can be placed on a **hierarchy**, or ladder. This hierarchy runs from the simplest biological motives up to the most complex of intra-psychic and social desires. As you develop in life, you move up the ladder until you reach the top rung, which Maslow calls *self-actualization* (see Fig. 6.1) (Maslow, 1971).

FIG. 6.1 Maslow's hierarchy of needs.

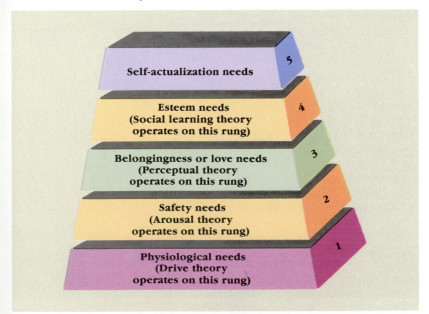

Self-actualization needs   5

Esteem needs
(Social learning theory
operates on this rung)   4

Belongingness or love needs
(Perceptual theory
operates on this rung)   3

Safety needs
(Arousal theory
operates on this rung)   2

Physiological needs
(Drive theory
operates on this rung)   1

Maslow assumes you start life at the lowest level of the motivational hierarchy. He believes you are born with innate reflexes that help you satisfy your basic biological needs. Once you are blessed with biological life, however, you must secure some control over your physical environment. Thus, almost immediately after birth, you begin to move up to the second level of the motivational hierarchy, that of safety needs.

The next two rungs of the ladder involve the social environment. You need people to love, and you need people to love you. Some of these needs are satisfied by your family, but there are also work groups and various social organizations you can join. These groups not only offer you rewards for performing well, they can also help you learn what self-respect is all about.

If you are fortunate, you will finally reach the top rung of Maslow's hierarchy and achieve *self-actualization*. This term is difficult to define (see Chapter 16). Put simply, it means reaching your own greatest potential, doing the things you do best in your own unique way, and then helping those around you achieve these goals too. But you can only get to this final stage of human development by first solving the problems associated with the four lower levels (Maslow, 1970).

Now that we have given Maslow's theory in broad outline, let's look at what he says in more detail.

• Maslow's Hierarchy of Needs

Maslow says there are five primary levels on the ladder of human motivation:

1. *Biological needs*. Bodily needs come first. You must always satisfy your physical wants or you won't live long enough to take care of any psychological or social needs you may have. You cannot take the next step up the motivational ladder unless, and until, your primary biological needs are met. (As we will soon see, *drive theory* operates at this rung of the ladder.)

2. *Safety needs*. Neither man nor woman lives by bread alone. Once an infant's basic needs are satisfied, the child is ready to explore the physical environment. But as we will show in later chapters, young children typically don't explore unless they feel secure. A predictable world is, generally speaking, a much safer environment than one which is unpredictable. Thus, one reason that you "move about" in your environment is to reduce your uncertainty about what the world has to offer. With this knowledge, you can choose sensibly among the various physical inputs you need to sustain life. And once you know what to expect from the world, you can move on to the next rung of

One of the basic needs that all people have, according to Maslow, is the sense of approval and belonging.

unique way, make your own special contribution to society, and thus achieve your true inborn potential (see Chapter 16).

And once you have achieved self-actualization for yourself, Maslow says, you will find you have a strong urge to help others get where you have gotten. And to do *that,* you will need to teach others the lessons you learned as you worked your way up the four lower levels of the motivational hierarchy (Maslow, 1971). (The many theories of personality and human development discussed later apply to all the rungs of Maslow's ladder, but primarily to the fifth rung.)

Abraham Maslow

the motivational ladder. (Arousal theory operates in part at this stage of development.)

3. *Belongingness* and *love needs.* Once you have gained control over your physical environment, you can then turn your attention to social inputs. As the poet John Donne once said, "No man is an island, complete to itself." Donne knew quite well that, to be a *human* being, you must have other people around you. Thus, according to Maslow, you have an innate need for affection and love that can only be satisfied by other people. You must *affiliate* with others, and identify yourself with one or more like-minded individuals. When you identify with someone else, you learn to perceive part of the world as that person presumably does. (As we will learn in Chapters 7 and 8, perceptual and emotional theories of motivation apply primarily to the first three rungs of the ladder.)

4. *Esteem needs.* One reason you need other people is to help you set your life's goals. Under the right conditions, the groups you affiliate with can offer you *models* of what your future behavior might (or should) be. Groups also offer you external *feedback* on how close you are coming to achieving your targets in life. And the better you get at reaching your goals, the more esteem you likely will have for yourself (and the more esteem you will probably get from others). According to Maslow, "esteem needs" are just as important for *human* life as are food and water (Maslow, 1971). (Social learning theory and the various theories of social motivation we will discuss later in this book operate at levels 2, 3, and 4 of the hierarchy.)

5. *Need for self-actualization.* Until you have achieved self-esteem, you probably will not feel secure enough to become a "fully-actualized person." Unless you have confidence in yourself, Maslow says, you will not dare to express yourself in your own

□ □ **QUESTION** □ □
How far up the ladder would a frequently-abused child be likely to climb? Or a student whose teachers gave the student nothing but criticism?

● *Criticisms of Maslow's Theory*

Like all theories in psychology, Maslow's *hierarchical* approach to human motivation has been subjected to many criticisms. As we will see in a later chapter, Maslow based his theory on the study of highly successful people in the Western world. Thus, his viewpoint is most applicable to middle- and upper-class individuals in our present society. But this theory may not apply to other cultures, nor even to all segments of our own society (Petri, 1986).

More than this, Maslow's is one of many "stage" theories. That is, Maslow presumed that *all* humans move up through five clearly-definable steps as they mature. Whether there are actually *five* rungs to the motivational ladder, or 15, or 150, is something that Maslow never really proved. Furthermore, he assumed that

Our theories of motivation do not always apply to foreign societies, such as the Masai of Kenya, shown here.

6 / Introduction to Motivation

you must somehow "conquer" the problems associated with each lower rung before you could move on to a higher one. This assumption is, at best, highly debatable.

Nor does Maslow tell us what biological and psychological mechanisms underlie the types of human needs he describes. For example, he admits you need food, but he doesn't describe how your body senses and responds to this need. And he states that you strive for self-esteem and self-knowledge, but doesn't say how you manage to learn what these concepts are all about.

Last but not least, other than the case histories Maslow offers, there simply is no *experimental* evidence proving that Maslow's approach is correct. Indeed, it is rather difficult to imagine how one might put many of Maslow's notions to a critical test (Petri, 1986).

● *Strengths of Maslow's Theory*

Despite these criticisms, Maslow's approach has many strengths to it. To begin with, it is one of the few theories that emphasizes the importance of *individual choice* in determining behavior. That is, Maslow views the human organism as being capable of choosing between alternative courses of action. True, many of the things you do are influenced by your biological state and your social environment. But given these limitations, you still are able (in Maslow's view) to exercise voluntary choice in most situations.

"YOU'LL HAVE TO LOSE SOME WEIGHT, CUT YOUR HAIR, GIVE UP WOMEN AND FAST CARS, AND LOSE YOUR OBSESSION WITH MONEY. IT **IS** POSSIBLE. I DID IT MYSELF A FEW WEEKS AGO."

Second, Maslow's hierarchy is by far the best known of the *holistic* approaches to the study of motivation. That is, Maslow's theory is one of the few which gives relatively equal value to biological, intra-psychic, and social/behavioral influences on behavior. Drive theory—which we will discuss momentarily—does a good job of explaining how organisms react in situations of extreme deprivation. Arousal theory incorporates the best aspects of drive theory and adds a number of its own strengths. However, none of these narrow theoretical viewpoints can begin to explain the enormous complexities of even the simplest of human activities, such as eating.

Suppose we first take a quick look at drive and arousal theory. Then we will discuss a highly specific problem—that of **obesity**—and show how drive and arousal theory simply cannot explain why we eat as we do. Next, we will talk about a very strange type of self-induced starvation. Finally, to make the matter both more interesting and more practical, we will use what psychologists know about human motivation to develop a highly workable recipe for *losing weight* (or *gaining weight*).

Now that we have set the stage, let's see what drive theory is all about.

DRIVE THEORY

For the past century, many psychologists have attempted to imitate the "hard" sciences by reducing the complexities of human motivation to fairly uncomplicated *biological* equations. Rather than assuming people (or animals) are capable of self-determined actions, these psychologists theorized that organisms are *driven* or pushed into motion much the way an automobile engine is cranked into activity when you turn the ignition key or step on the starter (Bolles, 1975).

At its simplest, the biological approach to motivation is often called *drive theory*. As David Edwards notes, psychologist Clark Hull was one of the first great drive theorists. Hull assumed *biological* needs are the ones that rule your life. Biological pain arouses or *drives* you to movement. *Reducing* your drives gives you biological pleasure and "rewards" those movements that led to the drive reduction. Hull made the concepts of drive and drive reduction the cornerstones of his theory of learning (see Chapter 10) (Edwards, 1972).

You do have motives other than biological pain and pleasure, of course. But drive theorists such as Hull assume that you *learned* these needs by associating them with your attempts to reduce the physical arousals that propel you along life's highway (Bolles, 1975).

Homeostasis

The key concept in understanding drive theory is that of **homeostasis**. The term itself comes from a Greek word meaning "homestate" or "normal condition." To a drive theorist, your body is like an automobile engine. To keep a car's engine in a state of fine tune—its "normal condition"—you need to take constant care of it. For example, you must give the engine oil, water, fuel, and lubrication. And you must protect it from damage. To keep your body in "fine tune"—or *homeostasis*—you must also give it the things it needs to function properly. These needs include food, water, air, a given range of temperatures, and protection from germs and accidents (Stellar & Stellar, 1985).

Whenever the engine in your car departs from its normal condition, red lights blink on the dashboard telling you what is wrong. Perhaps you need to add oil, or buy some fuel. Whatever the case, those lights will continue to flash until you satisfy the engine's needs. In similar fashion, whenever your body runs low on food or water, warning signals go off inside you telling you something is wrong. That is, you experience hunger or thirst. And you go on being hungry or thirsty until you satisfy your body's need—and return your body to its usual *homeostatic* condition.

"Homeostasis," then, simply means the innate biological urge you have to keep your bodily processes in a balanced or need-free state.

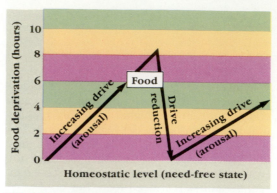

FIG. 6.2 A simple diagram of drive theory, using food deprivation as an example.

□ □ **QUESTION** □ □

What similarities do you see between the concept of *homeostasis* and the Gestalt Law of Dynamic Direction (see Chapter 5)?

Primary Needs and Drives

Most drive theorists refer to those things you absolutely must have to survive as *primary needs*. These basic needs include such things as air, food, water, and a proper temperature. Whenever you run short of one of these things, built-in mechanisms in your body detect that need. As the need increases, the firing rates in various neural centers in your brain start to increase. This increased neural activity creates a *primary drive* inside you that *arouses* you to action. When your arousal is great enough, you are *driven* to seek out whatever you need (Bolles, 1975).

Generally speaking, the longer you are deprived of something you need, the faster your nerve cells will fire. And the more *aroused* your nervous system becomes, the *greater* the primary drive you will experience. And the stronger the drive becomes, the more "motivated" you are to reduce that drive.

For example, you have a "primary need" for food. The longer you are deprived of food, the greater your primary drive (hunger) becomes, and the more aroused or driven you are to find something to eat. If you go hungry long enough, your aroused movements will probably bring you into a position to satisfy your need. Once you do so, the "hunger centers" in your brain stop firing. At this point, your drive level decreases, your arousal (motivation) disappears, and your normal homeostatic *balance* is reinstated. (See Fig. 6.2 for a diagram of drive theory, using food deprivation as an example.)

Intra-psychic and Social Needs

You need to take in food in order to maintain your normal homeostatic "good biological health." But *what* you eat depends in large part on what drive theorists call learned or *secondary needs*. Other psychologists refer to these as "intra-psychic needs" and "social needs" (Stellar & Stellar, 1985).

Primary (biological) needs are innately determined. But secondary needs presumably are learned through some association with the satisfaction of a primary need. For example, suppose you "get hungry for a steak." According to drive theory, this *specific hunger* is an acquired, secondary drive. At some time in the past when you were hungry, you ate a steak. This behavior reduced your hunger drive, and you were thus rewarded for consuming a steak. As a consequence, when you get hungry in the future, you are more likely to "want" a steak than some food you've never eaten before.

• Drive Theory: A Summary

The drive approach to motivation is what we might call a biologically oriented, *one-level* theory. It is biological in orientation because physical needs are presumed to be primary. All other motives are said to be acquired or learned. And the theory operates on only one level because it claims that the feelings, perceptions, cognitive activities, and social behaviors of the organism are learned *because* they are associated with the reduction of primary (biological) drives.

Homeostasis (home-ee-oh-STAY-sis). The tendency to move toward a need-free or drive-free condition. Any action by an organism to reduce drives is called a "homeostatic behavior."

Arousal Theory. A one-level, biologically-oriented theory in which motivation comes from some departure from a norm or optimum point of neural excitation. Any increase or decrease in neural firing moves the organism away from this optimum point and hence is arousing.

Postulates (POSS-tew-lates). To postulate is to make a guess about something, or to insist that something exists or is very important. Postulates may or may not be facts.

Optimum (OPP-tee-mum or OPP-tuh-mum). From the Latin word meaning "best." Literally, the most favorable point or condition. In arousal theory, optimum means "the point at which we operate most efficiently in our work, personal lives, and so forth."

Set point. Your body has a "set point" for internal temperature—98.6° F. If your temperature rises above this point, you sweat. If your temperature falls below this point, you shiver or seek warmth. Your body tends to have a set point for weight, too. That is, your body tends to "defend" or maintain a given weight in a homeostatic manner.

□□ **QUESTION** □□
What position do drive theorists appear to be taking with regard to solving the mind-body problem?

Criticisms of Drive Theory

Many objections have been raised to the simple form of drive theory we have just outlined. Three of the major objections are as follows:

1. Not all psychologists agree with drive theorists that intra-psychic needs are *learned*. For instance, most young animals (including children) seem to have an innate desire to explore their environment. This "exploratory drive" apparently is specified by the genetic blueprint, but it is difficult to think of "exploration" as being a *biological* need. Indeed, although we have some notion of the physical mechanisms that underlie the hunger drive, we simply don't know what parts of the brain control "exploration." Thus, to many psychologists, it seems more appropriate to consider exploration an innately determined *intra-psychic* drive (Bolles, 1978).

2. In similar fashion, not all psychologists believe social needs are merely acquired by

association with the reduction of some biological drive. For example, most newborn animals seem to have an innate urge to identify with a "mother figure." And as we will see in later chapters, most female animals readily develop an intense "social bond" with their infants immediately after birth. Therefore, many mother-infant behaviors seem to be specified by the genetic blueprint. However, we don't know what biological mechanisms underlie these instinctual needs. And it is difficult to think of these highly motivated social behaviors in terms of "homeostasis." For *homeostasis* always involves some *physical need*, but mother-infant behaviors involve *informational* or *social* inputs, not *physical* quantities (such as food and water) (Toates, 1985).

3. Drive theory equates an *increase* in neural excitation with an *increase* in motivation. Yet, as we will see in Chapter 12, sometimes a *decrease* in excitation can cause an *increase* in psychological arousal.

As we will see, the scientists who raised these objections often were "driven" to create competing motivational theories of their own.

□□ **QUESTION** □□
Under what conditions do you become bored, and how do you typically react? Why might a drive theorist have difficulties explaining your highly motivated response to boredom?

AROUSAL THEORY

In the late 1950's, Elizabeth Duffy (and others) made a telling criticism of classical drive theory. Duffy had spent many years studying the exploratory drive in animals. Her work convinced her that arousal is not always caused by a lack of such things as food, air, or water. For you have *informational needs* that are as innate and as highly motivating as are your life-sustaining or *energy needs*. However, classical drive theory almost totally ignores informational inputs (Petri, 1986).

This objection led Duffy and other scientists to create a new approach to motivation called **arousal theory**. The basic **postulates** of this position can be summarized as follows:

1. Homeostasis isn't really a point of *zero* neural excitation, but rather is a point of **optimum** stimulation. The *optimum* point is the level at which you function best *at any given moment in time*.

2. This optimum point—often called the **set point**—may *change* from time to time, depending on your biological condition.

3. There are *opposing processes* associated with each "set point." Some of these proc-

Hunger can often be for a specific food; notice how often people ask each other, "What do you feel like eating?"

esses are excitatory, and come into play when you move *below* your optimum set point. The other processes are inhibitory, and start to function when you move *above* your optimum set point. Working together, these *opponent processes* help you maintain your homeostatic set point.

4. You have *set points* for informational needs as well as for physical needs.

Boredom and Homeostasis

The concept of *boredom* was always a difficult one for the drive theorists to handle. For example, consider the hunger drive. Technically speaking, any balanced diet should satisfy all of your biological needs for food. Therefore, from a drive-theory point of view, you might well be expected to eat the same menu at every meal. But eating *exactly the same foods* at every meal gets boring, so you tend to vary what you consume. Yet, according to classical drive theory, you should eat primarily those foods you've eaten most often in the past. And it's difficult for a drive theorist to explain why you should ever eat something entirely new to you, when old (and satisfying) foods are available (Petri, 1986).

The conclusion Duffy drew from these points is as follows: You do not have a single "homeostatic level" that is set at birth and never varies thereafter. Rather, you have a different "set point" for each type of need, whether that need is related to energy inputs or informational inputs. Furthermore, each "set point" changes according to your past experience and present conditions. You are motivated to maintain this optimum level, Duffy says, whenever your inputs *increase* too much or *decrease* too much. For a movement in ei-

Unlike drive theory, arousal theory can explain why people choose to eat foods they are not accustomed to, for example, sushi.

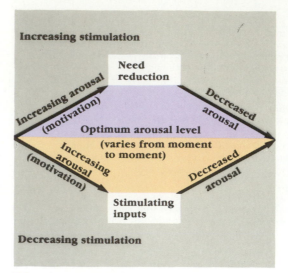

FIG. 6.3 A simple diagram of arousal theory.

ther direction will take you away from your optimum level of performance (Petri, 1986).

□□ **QUESTION** □□
Some people occasionally "pig out" on rich foods, then starve themselves for days afterward. Why would it be easier for Duffy to explain this type of behavior than it would for a drive theorist to do so?

Optimum Arousal

According to Duffy, the optimum level of stimulation that you need *varies from moment to moment*. There is good reason why this is so. If your sensory inputs become too constant, your receptors "turn off" and leave you with little or no stimulation at all. And if your inputs vary too much, your environment becomes too unpredictable.

Thus, you need a certain amount of *stability* in the world around you—just as the homeostatic model would predict. However, you also need a certain amount of *variability* in stimulation. According to Duffy, your "set point of optimum arousal" will fluctuate from moment to moment in response to the level of inputs that you receive from your environment. But this optimum point will always lie somewhere between complete stability and complete predictability. Figure 6.3 illustrates how we might diagram arousal theory.

□□ **QUESTION** □□
In Chapter 3, we noted that certain drugs such as LSD lead to a stressful experience called "loss of personal control." How might this unpleasant situation be related to a need to predict and control your inputs?

Problems with Arousal Theory

Arousal theory was a noticeable improvement over drive theory in that Duffy could explain a number of motivational situations that early drive theorists had difficulties with. But the arousal position still is a "homeostatic" theory that tends to reduce motivation to what seem to be purely physical processes.

There is an appealing simplicity to homeostatic models such as those proposed by Duffy and by the drive theorists. For these models attempt to explain all human behavior in terms of an innate urge to "return to a pre-set level of normal functioning." Unfortunately, as R.C. Bolles points out, the experimental data just don't give much support to homeostatic theories. According to Bolles, "the arousal of a motivational state in the individual has no necessary bearing on the homeostasis of the body; it is quite irrelevant to the solution of most regulatory problems." Bolles goes on to say, "What appears to be homeostasis is often only a constancy of environmental conditions. . . ." As Bolles notes, both drive theory and the arousal position tend to ignore intra-psychic and social factors (Bolles, 1975).

To show why psychologists such as Bolles prefer a broader, more *holistic* view of motivation, suppose we look in considerable detail at an important American problem, that of people who overeat.

OBESITY: A HOLISTIC APPROACH

Dietitians estimate that 10 to 25 percent of the American public are **overweight**. The exact number of individuals who qualify as being *obese* varies not only on how you define "fatness," but also according to what part of the country you're speaking of. For instance, in a recent nation-wide study of several thousand children and young adults by Tufts University scientists William Dietz and Steven Gortmaker, the "obesity rate" for the North-East is about 23 percent. For the Mid-West, the rate is about 19 percent. It drops to 15 percent for the South, and to 14 percent for the Western states. Generally speaking, young people who live in urban areas are more than twice as likely to be overweight as are young people who live in the country. There are strong racial differences,

too. White youngsters are 2.5 times as likely to be obese as are black children (Dietz & Gortmaker, 1984).

Presuming that your own weight is normal, however, why should you worry about such things as the national obesity rate? First, because fatness could happen to you someday, and probably has already happened to several of your friends or relatives. Second, because fat people are a very discriminated-against minority.

● *Problems Overweight People Face*

If you are overweight, you have difficulty buying attractive clothes. You may also find it hard to get out of many chairs and to squeeze into some small cars. Gina Kolata reports a study of 6-year-old children who, when shown drawings of an obese child, described the youngster as "lazy," "dirty," "stupid," and "ugly." Kolata also notes that, in a recent survey of employers, 16 percent said they would not hire an obese woman *under any circumstances* (Kolata, 1986).

Unfair? Of course it is. So is our society's discrimination against people with dark skins or slanted eyes. Of course, most of us realize you had little to say about your skin color—but fatness is primarily a *voluntary choice*, isn't it?

No, in a very strange way, you are not entirely responsible for how much you weigh. First, there is strong genetic component in fatness, and you are no more to blame for inheriting "fat genes" than for inheriting a certain skin color. For instance, in a study of adopted children, A.J. Stunkard found that adopted children showed the obesity pattern of their biological parents, not of their adoptive parents (Stunkard *et al.*, 1985). Second, the psychological and social influences on fatness or thinness are just as important as the genetic factors. So if you happen to be snacking on something delicious, perhaps you'll want to put the food aside while we look at various biological, intra-psychic, and social/behavioral influences on **gluttony**.

THE BIOLOGY OF HUNGER

Marshall Jones, who has spent most of his career studying problems of motivation, points out an interesting fact: Motivated behaviors are often *related sequences of responses*. And to understand behavioral sequences, you must answer the following questions:

● **1.** Why does a given behavioral sequence begin? That is, what inputs prompt the thought or get the action going?
● **2.** Why does the behavior go in a particular direction once it begins?
● **3.** Why does the thought or behavior eventually come to an end? That is, once a behav-

Attractive clothing for overweight people is a rarity, although in recent years manufacturers and retailers have given more attention to this segment of the population.

ioral sequence has begun, what brings it to a stop?

Eating is a motivated behavior—but so are overeating and undereating. Therefore, to understand why you eat as you do, we must answer three critical questions: Why do you start eating, why do you prefer steak and ice cream to fried worms and boiled monkey brains, and why do you eventually stop eating?

As we will see, drive theory and arousal theory offer partial answers to these questions. But they have little to say about why you select the foods you choose to consume, much less why you eat when you're not really hungry.

□□ **QUESTION** □□

From a motivational point of view, fat people might be overweight for at least four reasons: (1) They eat too frequently; (2) once started, they don't know when to quit; (3) they prefer rich, fat-laden foods; and (4) they don't burn up enough energy through exercise and physical labor. Why might different forms of therapy be needed depending on what combination of these four behaviors the person engaged in?

Blood-Sugar Level

When you eat a dish of ice cream for dessert, how does your body make use of this fuel? To begin with, your digestive system breaks the food into tiny molecules, most of which contain sugar. These molecules enter your bloodstream, flow through your body, and pass sugar on to any cell that might be "hungry." A few hours after you have eaten a large meal, your blood contains a great many sugar molecules. However, if you starved yourself for 24 hours or so, your blood would contain relatively few of these energy particles.

Here is our first clue as to what the *hunger drive* is all about. To maintain its homeostatic balance, your body needs a certain level of sugar in its blood. And when this level drops below a certain point, you experience hunger "pangs" and you are aroused to seek out food. Therefore, if we could somehow control the molecules floating around in your bloodstream, might we not be able to control your sensation of hunger directly?

From a purely biological point of view, the answer is a probable yes. However, to understand how blood sugar affects your behaviors, we first must look at the relationship between sugar and a chemical called **insulin**. Under normal conditions, your body secretes insulin,

Marshall R. Jones

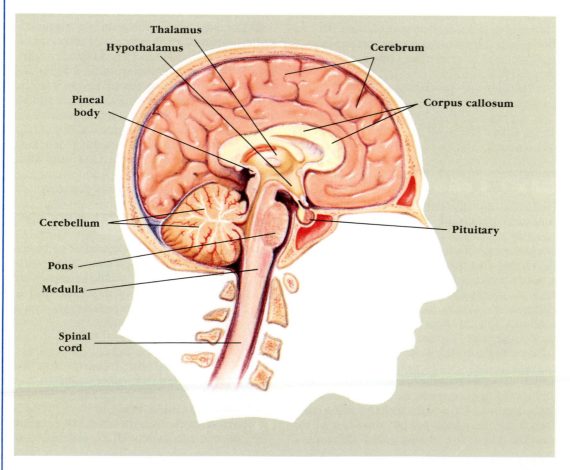

FIG. 6.4 A midsagittal section through the brain. Note that in this type of section half of the brain is cut away so that structures normally covered by the cerebrum are exposed.

Thalamus
Hypothalamus
Cerebrum
Pineal body
Corpus callosum
Cerebellum
Pituitary
Pons
Medulla
Spinal cord

which stimulates your body to digest sugar. If we let a hungry rat eat all that it wants, then take a blood sample from the animal a little later, we would find a lot of sugar molecules in the rat's blood. If we now inject the animal with insulin, its blood-sugar level drops—and to our surprise the rat will soon begin to eat again (even though it had just consumed a very large meal) (Stellar & Stellar, 1985).

According to Yale psychologist Judith Rodin, it's not the amount of sugar in your blood that matters. Rather, it's the amount of insulin *in relationship* to the amount of sugar. And it's not even the gross amount of sugar that counts—it's what *kind* of sugar is present in your body. Rodin injected 20 normal-weight men and women with varying amounts of either insulin or *glucose* (the type of sugar found in many prepared foods and baked goods). When given insulin, the subjects became hungrier, liked sweet tastes more, and also *consumed more food*. Injections of sugar water had no effect on the subjects' appetites or cravings for sweets. Rodin also reports that while *glucose* causes a massive increase in insulin in the body, *fructose* (the type of sugar found in fruits and honey) causes only a moderate increase in insulin levels and often brings about a *decrease* in appetite (Rodin, 1984).

Somewhere in your body, then, there must be a "sugar detector" that lets your cortex know how many glucose molecules are floating around in your bloodstream. Recent research suggests that this "detector" is located in a central part of your brain called the **hypothalamus**.

● *The Hypothalamic "Feeding Center"*

Your brain has three major parts: The **brain stem** (including the spinal cord), the **mid-brain**, and the **cerebrum** (including the outer covering of the cerebrum, the cortex) (see Fig. 6.4).

Sitting just above your *brain stem* is a neural center (in your mid-brain) called the **thalamus**. The thalamus is a sort of "central switchboard" through which sensory inputs pass before being relayed to your cortex. The word *hypo* means "below" or "beneath." The *hypothalamus* is a bundle of nerve cells lying just under the thalamus. The hypothalamus exercises rather strong control over many of your biological motivations and emotions (LeMagnen, 1986).

One small part of your hypothalamus contains neurons that are particularly sensitive to the amount of sugar in your blood. When the blood-sugar level drops too low, the cells in this region of your hypothalamus begin to fire more rapidly—and you typically begin to feel hungry.

If we put a metal electrode into this part of a rat's brain and stimulate the cells electrically, the rat will begin to eat at once (even if it has just had a big meal). If we stimulate this hypothalamic *feeding center* continuously, the rat will eat and eat and eat—until it becomes so obese that it can barely move around (see Fig. 6.5). If we continue the electrical stimulation even when food is not present in the rat's cage, the animal will often gnaw on anything handy, including air. If we destroy this "feeding center" in the rat's hypothalamus, the animal often refuses to eat at all. Some of the animals will die of starvation unless we force-feed them (Stellar & Stellar, 1985).

Does this one "feeding center" in the hypothalamus control all aspects of eating behavior? Certainly not. To begin with, even the "dumb rat" knows better than to overeat continuously, no matter what we do to it. If we give rats continual hypothalamic stimulation, the animals will become very, very fat. But eventu-

FIG. 6.5 Surgical removal of the "satiation center" in the hypothalamus causes a rat to overeat.

ally they will reach a cut-off point beyond which they will not go. Their weights will stabilize at this "set point" and we cannot induce them to become much fatter.

(You will probably be pleased to know that, when we stop prodding the rat's brain with electrical stimulation, the animal will typically go on a "crash diet" and return to its normal body weight.)

• Stress and Overeating

As we noted in Chapter 3, your body produces a number of natural pain-killers called *endorphins*, and this endorphin secretion increases dramatically when you are stressed. However, stress also induces eating behaviors in laboratory animals. John Morley and Allen Levine report they were able to get well-fed rats to eat immediately after a meal by administering mild stress to the animals. However, if the animals were given naloxone (which blocks the release of the endorphins), the stressed rats would *gnaw* at the food, or *lick* it, but typically would not **ingest** it. Morley and Levine believe that "bingeing" in humans may be mediated by endorphins released in stressful situations (Morley & Levine, 1980).

□ □ **QUESTION** □ □

Morley and Levine report that naloxone reduces eating, but not other stress-related "oral behaviors." Many surveys show that people tend to smoke more cigarettes (and consume more alcohol) in stressful situations than when they are not under stress. What connection do you see between these two sets of facts?

• Problems with the "Hunger Drive"

Drive theory can explain rather readily why you start to eat. As the sugar content in the blood reaching your brain *decreases*, insulin production *decreases*, and electrical activity in your hypothalamic "feeding center" *increases*. Your cortex translates this *increased neural activity* into the psychological experience of "hunger pangs." And you go looking for a decent meal, just as drive theory would predict. But why do you *stop* eating once you've begun? Why don't you munch away for hours and hours?

Because, you say, as soon as you start eating, the sugar content in your blood goes up dramatically, the production of insulin increases, and your "feeding center" turns off. That explanation would surely fit drive theory, but it happens not to be so. For eating behavior doesn't have a simple explanation, even at a biological level.

If you ate a big steak right now, it would take several hours for the meat to be digested and assimilated into your bloodstream. It takes only 10 to 20 minutes for you to eat the steak, though. Therefore, you actually *stop eating* long before that steak can greatly affect your blood-sugar level. In fact, if you're a quick eater, your "feeding center" may still be signaling "eat! eat! eat!" at the top of its neural voice at the very moment when you push yourself away from the table, so stuffed with food that you can't imagine ever being hungry again (Stellar & Stellar, 1985).

So a lowered blood-sugar level (or decreased insulin level) can turn on your hunger. But what biological mechanism turns it *off*?

• The Hypothalamic "Satiation Center"

As arousal theory points out, homeostasis is more a *balance* between opposing processes, rather than being a point of zero excitation. Thus, for every biological function that pushes you in one direction, there presumably is another function that tends to pull you back toward an optimum level of existence.

So if there is a "feeding center" in your hypothalamus that causes you to *start* eating, wouldn't you guess there might also be a center that, when stimulated, causes you to *stop* eating? It is called the **satiation center**, and it is also located in your hypothalamus, close to your "feeding center."

Suppose we implant an electrode in a rat's hypothalamic "satiation center." Then, just as the hungry animal starts to eat, we pass a weak electrical current through this "satiation center." The animal will suddenly refuse its meal. And if we continue the stimulation for a long enough time, the animal will come close to starving itself to death.

On the other hand, if we surgically remove the rat's "satiation center," the animal will go on an eating jag. Soon it will become as obese as the rats whose "feeding centers" were electrically stimulated. But as you might already have surmised, eventually the animal will reach its "obesity set point" and will taper off its wild consumption of food (Stellar & Stellar, 1985).

Under normal conditions, your "satiation center" functions *symmetrically* with the "feeding center." When your blood-sugar level goes up, the neurons in your "feeding center" *decrease* their response rate and the nerve cells in your "satiation center" *increase* their firing rate. When your blood-sugar level falls, your "feeding center" turns on and your "satiation center" turns off.

Furthermore, your "satiation center" seems sensitive to inputs from your digestive system as well as to your blood-sugar level. R.D. Myers and M.L. McCaleb report that receptor cells in the stomach are connected directly to the "satiation center." When Myers and McCaleb injected food into the stomach of rats, these receptors sent messages to the hypothalamus that caused neurons in the "satiation center" to increase their firing rate (Myers & McCaleb, 1980). The Myers and McCaleb research is important because it may tell us why you stop eating *before* your blood-sugar level falls—the mere presence of food in your stomach may cause your "satiation center" to start responding (and thus decrease your hunger pangs).

Additionally, the stomach apparently secretes chemicals that circulate to the brain and affect the satiation center. James Gibbs and his colleagues at the New York Hospital in White Plains have found that these chemicals are released from the gut whenever an animal ingests most types of food. When Gibbs and his associates injected rats with these chemicals prior to giving them *bland* food, the animals ate little or nothing at all (cited in Herbert, 1983). (Oddly enough, the chemicals had no effect on the consumption of *sweet* foods. We will return to this point in a moment.)

So now we know why you start eating and stop eating, don't we? No, we've learned only part of the answer. For what do you think would happen if we surgically removed *both* the "feeding center" and the "satiation center" from a rat's hypothalamus? Would the animal starve, or would it become obese?

The answer is, some animals will starve, but many will continue to eat pretty much as they did before the operation. So there must be systems in the brain other than the "feeding" and "satiation" centers that strongly influence eating behaviors (Stellar & Stellar, 1985).

The "Swallow Counter"

One mechanism for turning off eating behavior is what we might call the *swallow counter*.

A young rat eats almost continuously. As it grows up, however, it soon learns to associate the intensity of its hunger pangs with the amount of food that it ought to eat. When the rat has been deprived of food for a couple of hours, it eats a small amount. But when it has gone without eating for 12 hours, it will consume a great deal more food (Stellar & Stellar, 1985). The question is, how does the rat *know* how much food it actually needs?

Research indicates that some part of the animal's brain actually *counts* the number of swallows the animal makes as it eats. When the rat has had enough to satisfy its *present* state of hunger, it stops eating. And it stops *before* there is much of a change in its blood-sugar level, or

in the firing rates in its "feeding" and "satiation" centers. So *learning* plays as much of a role in turning the hunger drive on and off as do the centers in the hypothalamus.

● *Stellar's Experiments*

But even the "swallow counter" doesn't give us the whole answer to the puzzling question, Why do you stop eating? For example, experiments by Eliot Stellar and his associates at the University of Pennsylvania suggest that people are able to control their food inputs even if they can't "count" what they're swallowing.

Stellar and his colleagues asked students to swallow a tiny plastic tube that pumped liquid food directly into their stomachs when the students pressed a lever. The students could not see, smell, taste, chew, or swallow the food. But they somehow learned to control the amount they consumed just as readily as if they were drinking it from a glass. Perhaps the most interesting result of these experiments was the fact that the students were completely unable to explain to Professor Stellar how they managed this feat (Stellar & Stellar, 1985)!

Stellar's experiments suggest that your stomach "knows" things about your eating habits that your "feeding" and "satiation" centers are only dimly aware of. For example, when you've packed your stomach with a huge meal (or with liquid), the muscles in your stomach are stretched out or distended. The feedback nerve cells in your stomach would surely let your brain know how inflated your stomach was. Then your cortex could inhibit or block out the input messages from your "feeding center" even before your blood-sugar level changed.

It is possible that Stellar's results could be explained by appealing to the research just cited by Myers and McCaleb, and by James Gibbs and his colleagues. That is, perhaps the liquid food merely stimulated the stomach receptors that are connected to the "satiation center." Or perhaps the liquid food caused chemicals to be released in the gut that "turned on" the satiation center. However, research by Walter Cannon suggests that yet another mechanism may be involved.

● *Cannon's Experiments*

Long before the "feeding center" had been discovered, physiologist Walter Cannon performed a very important experiment on hunger. He got a student volunteer to swallow a balloon attached to a long hose. Once the balloon was inside the man's stomach, Cannon pumped air through the hose and inflated the balloon until it pushed firmly against the walls of the subject's stomach. (Fortunately, the man suffered little or no pain from this procedure.) Now, whenever the man's stomach contracted, the balloon was pinched and air was forced up

Eliot Stellar

the tube. By measuring the air pressure in the tube, Cannon got a rough reading of when the man's stomach muscles churned about.

Cannon found that "stomach contractions" began an hour or so before the man would normally have eaten a meal. As lunch time approached, for instance, the man's stomach began to contract more and more vigorously and the man reported an increased interest in food. An hour or so after the man's usual lunch time, the stomach contractions almost stopped—*despite the fact that the man hadn't eaten a thing*. The man's subjective experience of hunger also decreased (cited in Stellar & Stellar, 1985).

If you eat lunch every day at 12 noon, your "feeding center" and other parts of your brain begin to *anticipate* when they will have to go to work. An hour or so before noon, your brain starts sending neural signals to the muscles in your stomach telling them to "wake up" and get ready to start performing. The muscles contract in response to these signals, and your stomach "growls."

Other parts of your brain notice the growling (and the input signals coming from your "feeding center") and decide you're probably hungry. The closer the clock gets to noon, the more vigorously your stomach muscles respond.

Oddly enough, if you once get past the lunch hour without eating, your stomach will often calm down just as it does after you have eaten. Then your hunger pangs will decrease, only to rise again as supper time approaches.

□ □ **QUESTION** □ □
Why do both your hunger "pangs" and your stomach contractions tend to decrease after lunch even though you didn't eat anything?

The Hunger Habit

The hunger pangs that come from stomach contractions are **conditioned**. But almost any conditioned habit can be unlearned if you go about it the right way. If you stop eating *entirely*, your subjective experience of hunger will rise to a maximum in three to five days, as the centers in your brain and the muscles in your stomach continue to anticipate meal after missed meal. By the end of five days of *complete* starvation, however, your body will have learned that food simply isn't going to be coming along as it once did. Your stomach contractions will *habituate*, and your subjective experience of hunger will drop to a low ebb. However, if you go on a diet and "eat just a little" at each regular meal time, your "habitual" stomach contractions will take a very long time to change, and you may experience biting, gnawing hunger for weeks on end.

The fact that people on a complete fast soon lose the subjective experience of hunger suggests that hunger is to some extent a "habit." Thus, if you want to lose weight, it might help if you eat on a highly irregular schedule prior to going on a diet. Once the "hunger habit" is broken, dieting might well be less stressful and hence less painful (psychologically speaking).

Obesity and Metabolic Processes

In their 1982 book *The Dieter's Dilemma*, William Bennett and Joel Gurin make several controversial claims. To begin with, they believe "fat people" are born that way. That is, Bennett and Gurin theorize that people who tend to be overweight have a higher "weight set point" than do thin people, and that this "high set point" is inherited and thus can't be readily changed. As evidence to support their claim, Bennett and Gurin note that "no reputable study of calorie consumption has demonstrated that fat people eat more than others do."

Then why do fat people remain overweight? Because of their **metabolic rates**, Bennett and Gurin claim. Overweight individuals have much *lower* metabolic rates than do thin people. So fat people "burn up" food at a much slower pace than do thin people. That's why fat people can eat the same amount as thinner individuals, yet the fat people remain fat while the thin individuals remain thin. The fat person's body simply uses food *more efficiently* than does the thin person's body (Bennett & Gurin, 1982).

Then, what about dieting? Some research suggests it may actually be *counter-productive*.

Walter B. Cannon

"I JUST LOVE THESE FAD DIETS. I'M ON FOUR OF THEM RIGHT NOW."

162

6 / Introduction to Motivation

Conditioned (konn-DISH-shunned). When an organism is trained to give a particular response to a specific stimulus, we say that it has been conditioned to respond to that stimulus. As we will see in Chapter 10, there are several types of conditioning. Psychologists often use the words "learning" and "conditioning" as if they were the same.

Metabolic rates (met-ah-BOLL-ick). Metabolism (met-TAB-oh-lism) is the sum of internal processes that provide the energy to keep your body going. People with high metabolic rates are usually more active and thinner than people with low metabolic rates.

Calories (KAL-or-rees). The Latin word *calor* means "heat." The caloric (kal-LOR-ick) content of anything is the amount of heat it will generate when burned. Your body "burns" food when it converts what you eat into energy to keep you alive. Rich, sweet, fatty foods have lots of calories (that is, a high caloric content). Water has no calories at all. Fat burns; water doesn't.

According to Judith Rodin, whenever you diet, your metabolism slows down, and so (typically) does your activity level. Thus, you actually *need* less food when dieting than when eating normally (Rodin, 1984). Furthermore, recent studies suggest that the more frequently you diet, the more efficiently your body metabolizes food, and the more slowly you lose weight (Kolata, 1986). Therefore, the more times you try to diet, the harder it becomes to achieve your weight-loss goals.

How do you lose weight, then? According to Bennett and Gurin, the only way is to change your metabolic rate. And the most effective way to do that, they claim, is by exercising more. In a recent article, Bennett points to research showing that American men are fatter today than they were a century ago, despite the fact that men consume fewer **calories** now than 100 years ago. "Gasoline has a lot more to do with obesity than ice cream or French fries," Bennett says (quoted in Labich, 1986). However, as we will see, Bennett and Gurin may be wrong about the impossibility of losing weight other than by increasing the amount you exercise. There is considerable evidence that your "weight set point" is strongly influenced by past experience and present environmental inputs. And despite Bennett and Gurin's claims, several studies suggest you can lower your "metabolic set point" if you voluntarily control your food intake *for a long enough period of time* (LeBow, 1981).

☐☐ **QUESTION** ☐☐
Bennett is a medical doctor, and Gurin is a professional writer. Why might they be more likely to take a biological view of obesity than would a psychologist?

● *Sugar, Nicotine, and Fatness*
Almost all of us have known a person who gave up smoking—and who immediately gained several pounds. In the past, psychologists frequently interpreted this weight gain in terms of "eating as a substitute oral activity for smoking." More recently, however, scientists have

discovered a series of complex *biochemical* relationships between nicotine and eating.

First, a group of Swiss researchers reported recently that smoking 24 cigarettes a day increases the energy expenditure of the human body by 10 percent. Giving up cigarettes typically leads to a weight gain of more than 20 pounds, the Swiss scientists say. These researchers believe that nicotine causes the release of noradrenalin, which leads to an increase in physical arousal of the nervous system (see Chapter 8). Nicotine withdrawal also leads to a marked increase in the weight of rats (Grunberg & Bowen, 1985).

Second, smoking seems to decrease the need for sweets. According to psychologist Neil Grunberg and his associates, both animals and humans given nicotine tend to choose fewer sweet foods than do subjects not given nicotine. Furthermore, humans who give up smoking tend to be less anxious and hostile—and twice as successful at staying off tobacco—when given a high- rather than a low-carbohydrate diet (Grunberg *et al.*, 1985). Grunberg also notes that in the US, as smoking has decreased, there has been a dramatic increase in sugar consumption (cited in Herbert, 1986).

Thus, the amount you weigh—and perhaps even your "metabolic set point"—depends in part on what drugs you are taking as well as on how much you eat and what exercise you get. You might try to keep all these points about the *biology* of weight control in mind as we look at intra-psychic influences on eating and obesity (LeBow, 1981).

INTRA-PSYCHIC INFLUENCES ON OBESITY

Consciously or unconsciously, many parents train their children to be overeaters. Sometimes the parents are overweight themselves and, without realizing it, *overfeed* their children in order to make the children like themselves. Other parents may believe that "fatness" and good health are pretty much the same thing. If the usual reward the parents offer the child for good behavior is an extra helping of pie or cake, the child will soon come to associate rich foods with the act of winning parental approval. Food then takes on the *symbolic meaning of love* and acceptance. Later, as an adolescent or young adult, the person may feel a yearning to "raid the refrigerator" whenever she or he feels rejected or disappointed by life (LeBow, 1981).

Data to support this view come from a series of studies by psychoanalyst Hilde Bruch, who found that many overweight people felt unwanted, inadequate, and insecure as children. According to Bruch, these subjects began overeating not only to gain attention from their parents, but also because eating too much made them feel big and important to themselves (Bruch, 1971).

Schachter's Studies of Obesity

If fat people eat to satisfy symbolic needs, then one would expect eating behavior to be primarily under the control of internal or intrapsychic drives.

A decade or so ago, Columbia psychologist Stanley Schachter disputed this view—at least as far as fat people are concerned. In the late 1960's and early 1970's, Schachter came to the following conclusion: Normal people eat when their bodies tell them to—that is, when their stomachs contract and their "feeding centers" are active. However, Schachter said, obese people *don't listen to their bodies*. Rather than being driven to eat by internal cravings and desires, overweight individuals are simply abnormally sensitive to the world around them.

In one set of studies, Schachter and his group showed that fat subjects tended to "eat by the clock" rather than eating when their stomachs were contracting. In another study, Schachter showed that fat people tend to be "plate cleaners" who eat everything set before them whether they need it or not. People of normal weight, however, paid attention to their stomachs and ate only what they needed, even if this meant "leaving a little something on the plate" (Schachter, 1971).

Fat people are also more affected by the *taste* of food than normals, according to Schachter's early findings. When offered food of average or above-average taste, fat individuals ate a great deal more than did normals. When offered food of below-average or miserable taste, however, fat people ate a great deal less than normals did. Obese individuals were also less likely to perform physical labor for food, or to suffer mild amounts of pain to get to eat, than were people of normal weight (Schachter, 1971).

Recently, however, Schachter has changed his position slightly. He now sees obesity as a *multi-determined problem*. As one of his former students, Judith Rodin, put it recently, being fat is "determined by a combination of genetic, metabolic, psychological, and environmental events." In a recent article, Schachter apparently has accepted many of Rodin's views (Schachter, 1982).

When we see people who are grossly overweight, we often assume their problem is that they are greedy, or psychologically immature, or that they must have a medical difficulty of some kind. That is, we *attribute* their obesity to some sort of "character defect." But if Rodin and Schachter are right, we do the overweight individual an injustice by presuming the problem is always internal. For to make this assumption, we have neglected the strong effects that our culture has on our eating habits.

Let us look briefly at how the social environment influences what and how people eat.

□ □ **QUESTION** □ □
As we noted, James Gibbs and his colleagues found that chemicals released by the gut inhibit the ingestion of bland food, but not of sweet foods. What possible relationship do you see between this fact and Schachter's finding that fat people will work hard to get rich foods but not bland or bad-tasting foods?

SOCIAL/BEHAVIORAL INFLUENCES ON OBESITY

The culture you live in plays a great part in controlling what you eat—and when you eat it. In some places where food is or has been scarce, being fat is a sign of wealth. In other societies, "eating regularly and frequently" is not only a habit, but a status symbol of sorts.

For example, the reigning beauty in New York City in the 1890's was Lillian Russell, who weighed 186 pounds. And until recently, in parts of Africa, young girls were put into "fattening houses" when they reached puberty so they could gain weight prior to getting married. University of Maryland anthropologist Claire Cassidy reports that, when she was doing field research in Central America recently, she began (to her dismay) to gain weight. But, she says, "the fatter I got, the more they admired me. 'Finally,' one woman told me, 'you're starting to look healthy. And furthermore, you are starting to look marriageable'" (cited in Kolata, 1986).

Nor is thinness an unmixed blessing. In a recent 16-year-long study of 17,000 Harvard alumni, those men who had gained fewer than 15 pounds since graduation had a 30 percent *higher* death rate than those men who had gained 25 pounds or more. The researchers point out, however, that the "skinny group" included many more cigarette smokers and that men in this group tended to exercise less (Labich, 1986).

The social class you belong to is also an important factor in determining your weight, for people from different **social classes** have quite different types of eating (and exercise) habits. Men and women who belong to the wealthiest or "upper class" tend to be thinner, to be healthier, and to live longer than do men and women of the so-called "lower class." However, they may not exercise as much. In a recent study, Diane Hayes and Catherine Ross found that upper-class individuals are less likely to benefit *psychologically* from exercise

Stanley Schachter

Despite her weight, Lillian Russell was considered the most beautiful woman of her time.

than are middle- and lower-class individuals. Hayes and Ross believe that rich people already have so much going for them that they have less to gain emotionally from exercise than do others (cited in Rosenfeld, 1987).

Fat Wives and Insecure Husbands

Many of our social needs are pressed upon us by the people around us. Thus, we may overeat because individuals we love may be *rewarded* in various ways when we are fat.

Richard B. Stuart worked for many months with married women who were complete failures at losing weight. Stuart eventually began to suspect that the women's husbands were partially responsible for keeping their wives **corpulent**. To test his hypothesis, Stuart asked these couples to make tape recordings of their dinner-table conversations.

Stuart found that, although all the women were on diets and their husbands knew it, the husbands were 12 times more likely to *criticize* their wives' eating behaviors than to praise them. The men were also four times more likely to offer food to their wives than the wives were to offer food to the husbands (Stuart & Jacobson, 1987). These "food-pushing" husbands fell roughly into four groups:

1. Some husbands enjoyed demonstrating their masculine power by coaxing or forcing their wives to become fat. If the wife was overweight, the husband sometimes found this a useful fact to bring up in family arguments. The man could win almost any battle by calling the woman "a fat slob." Stuart believes the husbands realized (perhaps unconsciously) that if the wife lost weight, the husband would lose more arguments.
2. Other husbands viewed dinner time as being the main social event of the day. When the wives refused to eat very much, the husbands saw this as a rejection of themselves and the rest of the family group.
3. Some men had lost any sexual interest in their wives. They seemed to want to keep their wives fat as an excuse for their "playing around" with other women. Stuart's data

Richard B. Stuart

also indicate that the husband lost sexual interest first, and then began rewarding the woman for overeating, rather than losing interest after the wife was already fat.

4. Other husbands apparently feared their wives might be unfaithful to them if the women were too attractive. These men encouraged their wives to overeat in order to keep their wives ugly—and therefore faithful.

□ □ **QUESTION** □ □

Do you think even a superb therapist could help these women change their eating behaviors unless the husbands were somehow motivated to solve their own psychological problems?

EATING DISORDERS

So far, we've talked entirely about the problems associated with being overweight. However, there are also a number of eating disorders that are related to being too thin—or to attempts to maintain a very low weight through rather unusual eating behaviors.

The two major types of eating disorders associated with abnormal thinness are **anorexia** and **bulimia**. *Anorexia* involves self-induced starvation, even to the point of death. *Bulimia* is also known as the "binge-purge" syndrome. Both disorders are about ten times as likely to affect women as men. And both disorders are found primarily among young upper-middle-class and upper-class women who firmly believe (as the old saying goes) that "you can't be too rich or too thin" (Bell, 1985).

Anorexia

Hilde Bruch was one of the first psychiatrists to take an interest in anorexia. She states there are two types, *primary* (or true) anorexia, and *atypical* anorexia. Primary anorexia is a pathological fear of "being fat." The disorder is found primarily in young women in their teens. A woman suffering from this condition usually has a skeleton-like appearance. She also denies that she is abnormal in any way, but strives actively to maintain all her abnormal behavior patterns.

Atypical anorexia, Bruch says, differs from primary anorexia in just one important way: The woman knows her behaviors are abnormal, but feels helpless about changing them (Bruch, 1973).

• #### Three Symptoms of Anorexia

According to Bruch, there are three main symptoms that define primary anorexia. First, the anorexic woman has a false perception of her own body image. Thus, even though the woman weighs but 80 pounds, she may *per-*

#164-170

Singer Karen Carpenter, shown here at her brother Richard's birthday party in 1978, died of a heart ailment brought on by anorexia.

Hilde Bruch

ceive herself as being "grossly fat." So the woman starves herself and frequently engages in abnormal amounts of exercise. If she doesn't receive help, the woman may well starve herself to death in a desperate attempt to "avoid obesity."

The second symptom is a disturbance in the manner in which the woman "processes" bodily sensations. Bruch believes many overweight individuals confuse arousal with hunger. Therefore, she says, they eat when they are frightened or stressed in any way. The anorexic woman, on the other hand, does just the opposite: She confuses hunger with stress. When her body gives her "hunger signals," she *interprets* them as signs of stress or fear. Therefore, she denies she feels hungry, insisting she is merely "anxious" or even "depressed" instead.

The third symptom is that of abnormally low self-esteem. Bruch says the anorexic woman typically perceives herself as "enslaved by others, exploited by family and friends, and thus incapable of living a life of her own." Therefore, she isolates herself from "the exploiting others" whenever she can. And her refusal to eat, Bruch believes, is really a "struggle to attain self-respect." By not eating, she attempts to show others (and herself) that she can maintain some control over her life (Bruch, 1978).

The Anorexic's Family

According to Hilde Bruch, the family plays an important role in bringing about the anorexic disorder. Almost all anorexic women are from the upper class, or from the top levels of the middle class. The mothers of anorexic women are typically "high achievers, but are frustrated in reaching their desired goals in life." They also tend to be subservient to their husbands. The fathers of anorexic women tend to be successful, athletic, and good-looking. But they frequently perceive themselves as being "second best," Bruch says. The fathers are also "enormously preoccupied with outer appearances," particularly with maintaining physical fitness and beauty.

Bruch states that few parents of anorexic women are sensitive to the problems their daughters experience. The parents tend to carry an "idealized image" of the young woman in their minds, which is quite different from reality. Bruch claims that treatment of anorexia is seldom successful unless the parents participate actively, and unless they are willing to change the way in which they perceive and relate to the daughter (Bruch, 1978).

Johns Hopkins psychiatrist Arnold Andersen takes a more *holistic* view of anorexia than does Bruch. He believes that both anorexia and bulimia are caused by an *interaction* among sociocultural, psychological, familial, and biological factors that *predispose* the individual toward a given eating disorder. Treatment, according to Andersen, must involve not merely family therapy, but intra-psychic counseling and behavioral retraining as well (Andersen, 1985).

The Male Anorexic

In her 1983 book *The Slender Balance*, Susan Squire states that about 10 percent of anorexic patients are males. Squire reports that these men share some of the same concerns as do female patients. For example, the men have a pathological fear of obesity and feel a need to "control their bodies" in some rigorous fashion. They also tend to come from the upper and upper-middle classes and to be intelligent and well educated.

However, male anorexics differ from female anorexics in many ways. For one thing, the males frequently are homosexuals, while the females are chiefly heterosexual. The women tend to be overachievers; the males, underachievers. The women often develop "work rituals" and are almost obsessive about being "orderly." The men usually are hard workers, but their attempts at getting things done are often ineffectual and haphazard. And the families of male anorexics typically are more "emotionally disturbed" than are the families of female patients, Squire says.

Susan Squire believes that male anorexics are much more difficult to treat than are women patients. However, Squire says, the "success rate" for therapy with either male or female anorexics is fairly low (Squire, 1983).

Bulimia

Bulimia is an eating disorder characterized by "binges" of caloric intake followed by desperate attempts to get rid of the food consumed. The three most common ways of ridding the body of the food are by self-induced vomiting, by "purging" (using laxatives), and by post-binge starvation.

Anorexia and bulimia are similar in some ways, different in others. Like the anorexic patient, the bulimic individual tends to fear "fatness" and to prize "thinness." And both types of disorders are primarily found in upper-middle-class and upper-class individuals. However, the bulimic individual seldom denies reality to the extent that anorexics do. Indeed, the "binge-purge" person often feels guilty about his or her behaviors and hides them from family and friends as much as possible. In addition, most bulimic individuals engage in "binge-purge" activities only on occasion, but most anorexics starve themselves continuously (Striegel-Moore, Silberstein, & Rodin, 1986).

Some anorexic individuals are also bulimic and some bulimic individuals are extremely thin. However, most people who suffer from bulimia are of normal weight. A few are even overweight.

Bulimia is much more common than is anorexia. According to University of Toronto psychologists Janet Polivy and Peter Herman, recent surveys of college populations "have found a high incidence (13% to 67%) of self-reported binge eating in 'normal,' nonclinical samples" (Polivy & Herman, 1985).

□ □ **QUESTION** □ □

Bulimics almost always "binge" on rich, sweet foods. How might this fact be related to James Gibbs's finding that chemicals released by the gut inhibit the consumption of bland foods, but not the consumption of sweet-tasting foods?

- ### Causes and "Cures" for Bulimia

There are almost as many viewpoints toward what causes bulimia—and how best to treat the problem—as there are professionals working to solve the mysteries of this odd disorder.

For example, in a recent book, Harvard psychiatrists Harrison Pope and James Hudson report that two-thirds of the bulimic patients they treat also suffer from depression. Some patients "binge" in order to fight feelings of depression, Pope and Hudson say. However, others "pig out" and then feel depressed because of their failure to exercise self-control.

Consider a conversation Pope and Hudson had with a 21-year-old bulimic woman named Susan: "It would start to build in the late morning. By noon, I'd know I had to binge. I would go out . . . and buy a gallon . . . of maple-walnut ice cream and a couple of packages of fudge brownie mix—enough to make 72 brownies. . . . I'd stop the car, buy a dozen doughnuts. . . . On the way home I invariably finished all 12 doughnuts. . . . I'd hastily mix up the brownie mix and get the brownies in the oven . . . then, while they were cooking, I'd hit the ice cream. Sometimes I'd finish the whole gallon even before the brownies were done, and I'd take the brownies out of the oven while they were still baking. Seventy-two brownies later, the depression would begin to hit." Pope and Hudson believe the treatment of choice for bulimia is the use of anti-depressant drugs (Pope & Hudson, 1984).

Janet Polivy and Peter Herman believe that most "binge attacks" are caused by *prior dieting*. First, the bulimic individual tries to lose weight by going on a diet. But since the individual *lacks internal self-control*, the person fails. Considering himself or herself a complete failure, the person then just gives up and "pigs out." Therapy for bulimics that involves any form of dieting typically will fail, Polivy and Herman say, for dieting merely triggers another "failure/binge" attack. They believe that treatment should focus on training bulimics in self-awareness and self-control (Polivy & Herman, 1985).

Maria Root, Patricia Fallon, and William Friedrich take rather a different view of bulimia. They see the disorder as resulting primarily from the *socialization* that often occurs in three specific types of American families: the "perfect" family, the "overprotective" family, and the "chaotic" family. Root, Fallon, and Friedrich take a *holistic* approach to treatment, one that includes the use of drugs, group therapy, intra-psychic treatment, behavior therapy, and treatment that involves both the patient and her or his entire family (Root, Fallon, & Friedrich, 1986).

Finally, psychiatrists Harrison Pope and James Hudson view bulimia almost entirely from a biological point of view. They claim that most bulimic patients suffer from depression, and are best treated with anti-depressant drugs (Pope & Hudson, 1986). As we will see in Chapter 19, however, the use of these drugs typically *causes* as many problems as it *cures*.

Compulsive Eating and Compulsive Running

Alayne Yates, Kevin Leehey, and Catherine Shisslak are behavioral scientists at the University of Arizona. These scientists compare "compulsive runners" to "compulsive eaters" (bulimics) and "compulsive non-eaters" (anorexics).

Yates, Leehey, and Shisslak define *compulsive runners* as "those who are consumed by running, who run in spite of illness, and who suffer depression when they cannot run." The typical compulsive runner is an upper-middle-class or upper-class male. Like anorexic women, these men tend to be "introverted, compliant, self-effacing and unable to express anger." Most compulsive runners are high achievers, just as anorexic women tend to be. And, like anorexic women, most of these men have "an unstable self-concept," according to Yates, Leehey, and Shisslak. The men perceive themselves as being "out of shape" even when they are "dangerously overtrained," just as anorexic women perceive themselves as being "grossly fat" even when they are mere skeletons. There are differences, however. The men tend to focus on controlling "physical strength," while the women tend to focus on slimness. And the disorder hits women during adolescence, while it primarily appears in men during middle age (Yates, Leehey, & Shisslak, 1983).

Yates, Leehey, and Shisslak believe that the self-destructive behaviors associated with anorexia and compulsive running become *self-rewarding* because they lead to the release of endorphins, the body's "natural pain-killers." According to Yates *et al.*, anorexic women often have elevated *endorphin* levels. These women also often report that starvation gives them a euphoric feeling similar to "runner's high." Thus, both anorexia and compulsive running may be learned reactions to social or personal stress that are maintained by the release of endorphins (Leehey, Yates, & Shisslak, 1984).

Symptom Choice in Eating Disorders

There is almost no life-sustaining behavior that isn't considered abnormal if you engage in it too frequently—or too infrequently. Sleep, sex, and eating all offer evidence supporting this statement. The question then becomes, if you depart from the norm, why do you deviate in one direction and not the other?

Generally speaking, disordered behaviors are as multi-determined as are "ordered" activities. Some people overeat in response to stress, while others undereat when faced with the same problems. The *choice* between undereating and overeating, however, is clearly affected by biological, intra-psychic, and social factors. Unfortunately, "symptom choice" is a problem we can only speculate about at the moment, for scientists have gathered little valid data in this area.

We will return to this point frequently in future chapters. For the moment, though, let's assume that your weight is relatively normal and your eating behaviors are not particularly disordered. Still, the time might come when you *choose* to gain or lose a few pounds. Let's close this chapter by looking at one relatively effective system for gaining or losing weight. But as you will see, you have to know something about *why* you choose to gain or lose weight before you can do so efficiently.

HOW TO GAIN OR LOSE WEIGHT

You eat not just because you've been without food for a while, but also because (a) your blood-sugar level has fallen, (b) your stomach is contracting, (c) your "feeding center" has increased its neural activity, (d) your "satiation center" has decreased its neural activity, (e) your "swallow counter" has been silent for a while, (f) your regular dinner time is approaching, (g) you smell food in the air and hear other people talking about "what's for lunch," and (h) because food and eating have a variety of symbolic values for you.

Obviously, then, if you want to gain or lose weight, your dietary program must take into account not just the calories you consume and how you burn them up, but your *motives* and *mannerisms*, and your *perceptions* and *emotions*, as well as the behavior of the people around you.

If you wish to embark on a well-rounded weight-loss or weight-gain program, the first thing you should do is to have a medical check up. That way you can make sure you are not that one American in 20 who is under- or overweight because you have a physical problem of some kind. If you want to gain or lose more than 10 to 20 pounds, you probably should do so under medical guidance. Your physician may wish to prescribe drugs to help increase or decrease your appetite, and may also send you to see a registered dietitian.

However, diets and pills are only the first step in a long journey. The real problem usually lies in learning enough about yourself to recognize what internal and external *stimulus inputs* affect your eating behavior. You must somehow *measure* these inputs—and their consequences—and then change the way you react to these inputs.

Using Cognitive Behavior Modification to Gain or Lose Weight

If you wish to gain or lose weight, you might consider using *cognitive behavior modification* to help you do so. For a variety of studies show this approach yields the best long-term results as far as controlling your weight is concerned (LeBow, 1981; Stuart & Jacobson, 1987). Many behavioral therapists recommend a program that has 10 steps to it:

Compulsive runners, who are most often middle-aged men, have been shown to share many personality traits with anorexic women.

6 / Introduction to Motivation

1. Begin by recording *everything* you eat and drink for a period of at least a week. Psychologists call this "taking a baseline." Your own baseline should include a record of where you eat, the events that occurred just before you started eating, what you thought about just before you ate (and afterward), how you perceive food and the act of eating, and how you felt about eating as you did. And, *most important*, you should note who is around when you eat and what their response is to your food intake. Is anyone in your life (other than yourself) rewarded by your being too fat or too thin? In brief, your baseline should be a measure of (a) *what you eat*, (b) the *thoughts and feelings* associated with eating, and (c) the personal and social *consequences* of your eating behaviors.

2. Write down all the rewards and pleasures that will come to you if you gain better control over your eating behavior. And please note this point: Research suggests you will do far better if you *reward* yourself for improvement than if you *punish* or *criticize* yourself for failures (Glasgow, McCaul, & Schafer, 1986; Glasgow *et al.*, 1985).

3. If you are trying to lose weight, you might try "breaking the hunger habit" by changing your meal times to a very irregular schedule several weeks before you begin your diet. If you are underweight and eat irregularly, you may wish to force yourself to eat on schedule in order to help build up the hunger habit so that your stomach muscles will begin urging you to eat more.

A program to lose weight may be more successful if it is approached as an opportunity to improve one's eating habits.

4. If you wish to lose weight, increasing your physical activities will help you burn off excess fat. If you are out of shape, begin by walking a few minutes each day and work up from there. *Don't* push yourself to do too much at any one time. If you are underweight and exercise frequently, you may wish to reduce your activities.

5. Once you have your baseline material available, you may want to talk things over with a psychologist. You may be using your fatness or thinness as a psychological defense, or as a substitute for healthier behaviors. Unless you solve your own psychological problems first, you are not likely to be particularly successful at gaining or losing weight. Put another way, it will help you change your eating behaviors if you simultaneously change your cognitive processes and your emotional responses. You may even have to learn some new social skills—and better ways to control your thoughts and actions—as a part of your weight-change program.

6. Habits are difficult to change, and you will probably need all the help you can get. So you may find it wise to involve as many people as possible in your program. If someone close to you unconsciously wants you to remain fat (or thin), you may well have to find some substitute reward for this person. Otherwise, the person may try to sabotage your weight-loss or weight-gain program. You will do better, too, if you can get people to reward you for success rather than criticizing you for not doing well (Glasgow, Klesges, & O'Neill, 1986).

7. When you start your program, make a large chart or graph on which you record each aspect of your daily routine (including exercises!). Post the graph in a prominent place so everyone can see your progress and comment on it. Have someone give you regular rewards (money, special privileges, a gold star on your chart, or praise) each time you meet your daily goal. Give yourself a bonus for meeting that goal every day for a whole week.

8. Don't expect too much too fast. Unless you alter your diet drastically, your average weight loss or gain will be about 2 pounds a week. Because your weight fluctuates from day to day, it is a better idea to keep track of what you eat and the exercise you engage in than merely to record how much you weigh daily. However, do weigh yourself at least weekly and put this information on your chart.

9. Prepare yourself *in advance* for the occasional failure, and learn *in advance* ways to recover both behaviorally and psycho-

logically when you fall from grace. Kelly Brownell and his associates point out that you are more likely to recover if you view the mistake as a temporary *lapse* in an otherwise successful program than if you view the mistake as a *relapse* you simply couldn't control (Brownell *et al.*, 1986). Once you find you can readily recover from your mistakes, you probably won't make as many (or be as bothered by them) in the future.

10. Don't think of your program as being a "weight-loss" or "weight-gain" program. Rather, think of it as your way of increasing self-control by finally learning how to eat properly (Stuart & Jacobson, 1987).

□ □ **QUESTION** □ □

What are the most important differences you see between this weight-control program and the advice given in most "fad diet books"?

THE CONCEPT OF CHOICE

There is a great deal more to the field of motivation than just those behaviors (and thoughts and emotions) involved in eating. For the field of motivation also includes thirst, aggression, sexuality, parenting, stress, the urge to excel, love, the desire to be with others, and thousands of other motives. We will discuss sexual motivation in Chapter 7, stress and emotionality in Chapter 8, and the influence of motivation on learning in Chapters 9–11, love and parenting in Chapters 14–15, and social motives in Chapters 20–22. However, now that we've looked at eating in some detail, perhaps you can understand several things about *all types of motivation* better than when you started the chapter.

To begin with, probably you can now see why a simple question such as, "Why do some people overeat?" is so difficult to answer. For even when we attempt to study the simplest of human behaviors, there are biological, intra-psychic, and social influences that we always must take into account. So, even though we certainly don't know all the answers about human motives, at least we can guess at some of the questions we ought to be asking.

Many of these questions concern the *biology* of hunger. And, at first glance, it might well seem that we know more about this topic than about the intra-psychic and social/behavioral factors that influence food consumption. In a sense, that's true, for there have been many more experiments on the biological variables that affect eating than on the psychological and social aspects of the problem. But few of these biological studies do us much good when we try to help you *change* your eating patterns.

There are at least three reasons why this is the case.

First, most of the laboratory studies have used animal subjects rather than humans. We know little or nothing about the intra-psychic processes of the white rat, and next to nothing about the social influences of one rat's actions on the amount of food that another rat eats. And even if we did know more than we do, we couldn't be sure our knowledge about rats would *generalize* to the level of human beings.

Second, most research on the biology of hunger has focused on subjects who were severely deprived of food. Indeed, much of this work has dealt with animals who were near starvation. Little wonder, then, that the animals seemed preoccupied with obtaining food. As University of Washington psychologist R.C. Bolles has pointed out, biological mechanisms tend to dominate behavior in cases of extreme deprivation—but not at any other time in an organism's life (Bolles, 1983). Given a crisis of some kind, your body may well "take over" your behavior. Most of the time, though, you "pick and choose" what you want to do, because your biological needs are almost always being met on a regular basis. Bolles believes most eating and drinking—in humans as well as rats—is "secondary." That is, these behaviors are not really related to any *immediate biological* need. Thus, most human activities simply cannot be explained by drive theory, arousal theory, or any other "narrow" viewpoint.

Third, *medical intervention* has a very low "cure rate" when it comes to helping people gain or lose weight. The behavioral program outlined above is much more effective, because it pays attention to a wide range of intra-psychic and social factors that influence eating behavior (LeBow, 1981). And if these factors are most influential in helping people gain or lose weight, they are also likely to be involved in *causing* people to undereat or overeat in the first place.

R.C. Bolles

● **You Help Choose What "Moves You"**
R.C. Bolles believes motivation is best described as a "response selector mechanism." He notes that you are always active, always doing something—even if that "something" is just daydreaming or watching television. Thus, you are always *aroused* (behaviorally speaking) both to your external world and to your internal thoughts and needs (Bolles, 1975).

According to Bolles, you "behave" when you (1) respond to external stimulation, or (2) commit yourself to some course of action. In extreme situations, your responses will probably be governed primarily by your physical needs. But in most circumstances, you will select the one thing you want to do "right now"

People typically have a variety of stimuli competing for their attention at any given moment during the day.

from a long list of possible actions. And the factors that most influence (but do not totally determine) what you select are your past experiences and your present social environment (Bolles, 1978, 1979).

What "moves" you? According to Bolles, *you move yourself*. True, many of your actions are fairly predictable—but only if we know a great deal about who you are, what you have experienced in the past, and what your present environment is like. The study of motivation, then, boils down to knowing as much as we can about you and your own set of personal choices.

To repeat our opening quote from David Edwards, motivation is a set of questions you ask in order to determine why you do what you do. As you must realize by now, those questions are so numerous and so complex that you may never answer them to your complete satisfaction. However, the study of human behavior remains a delightful and rewarding journey for most people. And a journey of a thousand miles begins with the motivation to take the first step.

SUMMARY

1. **Motivation** is not so much an area in psychology as a series of questions about *why* people do what they do.

2. Many "why" questions involve human **needs**—what kinds of needs do you have, are these needs **learned** or **innate**, what are the **mechanisms** by which you satisfy your needs, and do you exercise any voluntary **choice** over your behavior patterns?

3. Motivation implies **movement**. Ancient scholars differentiated between objects that were **animate**, or "self-movers," and those that were not.

4. According to Maslow, human needs can be placed on a **hierarchy** with five levels: **biological**, **safety**, **belongingness**, **esteem**, and **self-actualization** needs.

5. **Drive theory** focuses primarily on biological needs. Clark Hull assumed that associated with each physical need was a **primary drive**. Whenever your body lacks something needed for life, the appropriate drive increases, causing you pain and thus motivating you to satisfy that need and return your body to **homeostasis**.

6. Hull assumed that **secondary needs**, or social needs, were learned by being associated with the pleasures that accompany primary **drive reduction**.

7. Criticisms of drive theory include the fact that you have **information needs** as well as **energy needs**, and the fact that some social behaviors seem innately determined rather than being learned.

8. **Arousal theory** was developed by Elizabeth Duffy to counter the criticisms of Hull's drive theory. Duffy assumed that homeostasis is a point of **optimum arousal**, and that a decrease in sensory inputs can be as arousing as an increase in biological drives. The optimum homeostatic **set point** changes from moment to moment.

9. At a biological level, the **hunger drive** is affected by **blood-sugar level** and *insulin level*. When you go without food, your **hypothalamic feeding center** detects a decrease in blood-sugar molecules and corresponding increase in insulin level and motivates you to eat. Stress can also stimulate your body to produce **insulin**, which decreases your blood-sugar level. Thus, you may overeat because of stress.

10. Your **hypothalamus** also contains your **satiation center** which, when stimulated, causes you to stop eating. Hunger pangs are also affected by your **swallow counter**, by your knowledge of how much you have already eaten, by **conditioned stomach contractions**, and by your **metabolic rate**. Chemicals released by the gut decrease consumption of bland foods but not **sweet-tasting foods**.

11. Intra-psychic influences on obesity include the fact that some parents train their children to be fat, thus giving overeating a **symbolic value**.

12. Social/behavioral influences on obesity include the fact that in some cultures fatness

suggests wealth, and that some **social classes** place more of a premium on thinness than do others. Your desired weight is also influenced by the people around you. For example, **insecure husbands** often reward their wives for remaining fat.

13. The most common **eating disorders** are **anorexia** (self-starvation) and **bulimia** (the "binge-purge" syndrome). Both disorders affect primarily upper- and upper-middle-class women who have a **distorted self-image** and low **self-esteem**.

14. Men with similar social backgrounds and psychological problems as female anorexics often engage in **compulsive running**.

15. **Cognitive behavior modification** offers an excellent method for losing or gaining weight. The technique involves taking a **baseline** of present food input, **establishing goals**, **exercising**, keeping precise **records** of food-related activities, and establishing personal and social **rewards** for progress.

16. According to Robert Bolles, **drives** affect behavior primarily in times of severe deprivation. For the most part, humans appear to be able to **choose** which behavior patterns are most satisfying to them.

The relapse crisis, Annette thought as she rushed up the stairs to Thelma's apartment. People like Thelma often did well for a while, and then failed momentarily. It was almost as if they were testing themselves, because they didn't understand why they should succeed. So they failed, and that was so devastating to them, they were tempted to give up. Giving up, at least, confirmed their negative self-image. When the crisis hit, you had to catch them right away and convince them to view the experience as a *lapse,* rather than a *relapse,* or else . . .

(Continued from page 150.)

A bedraggled-looking Thelma answered the door and quietly invited Annette in. Thelma's eyes were moist and puffy from crying. "Listen, Annette," she said when they were seated. "I'm terribly sorry about tonight. I just sort of lost control, you know?"

"I know," Annette replied.

"I mean, it was a rotten day at the office. I jumped all over people, and they were nasty to me in return. I knew what I was doing wrong, but I just couldn't stop myself. Anyhow, I went bowling after work, and I was feeling so damned rotten, I decided to have just one little drink. Just one, you know . . ."

Annette nodded. "I know exactly."

"And then before I knew it, I was on my fourth Tom Collins, and I bowled really lousy, and I told one of my friends to go to hell." Thelma started weeping. "I mean, I knew I was hurting people, and I just couldn't seem to stop."

"Yes, we all do that sometimes," said Annette quietly.

"Then I got so mad at myself I just ran out to the car and started driving. I couldn't bear to face you right then. Does that make sense to you?"

"Of course."

"I must have driven for three hours. I kept hoping the car would run out of gas way out in the country somewhere, and I'd just die or something before anybody found me." Thelma sighed. "But finally I just gave up and drove back here. And then you called."

"I'm glad I did."

Thelma nodded, trying to smile a bit. "So am I, Annette. I think I finally figured it out, what went wrong. But I want your advice on it."

"Of course," said Annette, brightening considerably.

"It sounds screwy, I know, but I think I got depressed because I was doing so well. You know what I mean?"

Annette nodded. "I know exactly."

"I mean, I've lost 22 pounds in a month, I've done better at the office—except for today— and you've helped me like nobody else ever has. But I was the one who did it, you understand? I mean, *you* didn't resist all those hunger pangs in the middle of the night, *I* did. And *you* didn't have to do all that exercise, *I* did."

"I know," Annette said reassuringly. "And you really did beautifully."

"That's the trouble!" Thelma cried. "I lost weight, I did better on the job, I've got my friends back, I look better, I feel better, I'm happier than I've been in years."

Annette smiled. "And that's the problem, isn't it?"

"Of course," Thelma said in a weary tone of voice. "I kept asking myself, why did I have to wait so long to make all these changes? And I kept thinking about all of the wasted times in my life, the people I'd hurt because I didn't know any better."

"You've got a lifetime left to make up for it," said Annette.

"Oh, I know. And I suppose I will. But even that isn't the real problem, is it?"

Annette grinned broadly. "No, Thelma, it isn't."

"I mean, the problem is, I know I can change myself. I've already done it. So I guess I could do some more, right?"

"Right," said Annette. "You've got both the motivation and the technique."

6 / Introduction to Motivation

Thelma nodded. "That's the scary part. Now that I can do just about anything I want to do, what the hell do I really want to do?" Thelma giggled a bit. "I mean, as long as I was failing, I could blame it all on God, or my parents, or just about anybody. Now I've got nobody to blame except myself. I finally have all the freedom anybody could ask for. That's frightening."

"Of course," said Annette. "Because there's no freedom without responsibility. Freedom's pretty expensive, when you stop to think about it."

Thelma laughed. "Well, I guess I can afford it now." She shook her head, as if in wonderment. "You know, I guess I must be the happiest person in town. No, that's wrong. I must be the happiest person in the whole wide world."

Now it was Annette's turn to cry a bit. "Can I be number two?"

Thelma reached over and squeezed Annette's hand tightly. "Sure. And thanks for everything, you know?"

"I know," said Annette, wiping her eyes with a tissue.

Thelma released Annette's hand and leaned back in her chair. "Listen, we've got some things to plan. I've been thinking about getting a new job in a year or so, after I've lost another hundred pounds or so. But you know what I want to be?"

"No, tell me."

Thelma grinned. "An airline stewardess."

"You're kidding!"

Thelma nodded. "They're so slim and trim, you know. I've wanted to be just like that, all my life. And now maybe I can be." She paused for a second. "And there's another thing about being a stewardess, you know."

"What?"

Thelma roared with laughter until she almost cried again. "Well, it sure would beat buying my own ticket to Miami!"

Sexual Motivation

"The Mating Game"

· C · H · A · P · T · E · R ·
7

Clare Wilson put down her library book and smiled warmly at her fiance, Bill Meyer. "I think we should have a girl first and don't you think that Christine would be a nice name for her?"

Bill's eyes opened slightly, but his gaze never strayed from the TV set. He was watching the US Open Golf Tournament, and didn't really want to be disturbed. One of his favorite golfers, Greg Norman, was two strokes ahead of the other players, and Bill was trying to give Norman some moral support. Norman sank a difficult 30-foot putt on the 14th hole, and the crowd cheered. "You drive for show, but you putt for dough," Bill said approvingly.

"You won't mind if our first child is a girl, will you, dear?"

Bill glanced quickly at Clare, then looked back at the television. "I don't think I have much choice in the matter," he said.

"Oh, I know that. But if it *is* a girl, you won't mind, will you?"

Bill sighed. It was difficult to concentrate on the golf tournament when Clare wanted to talk about things. "I don't really care, Clare. But how will you feel if she turns out to be a boy?"

Clare shrugged her shoulders. "We'll name him Christopher, and try again."

With a sly grin on his face, Bill replied, "I don't mind that 'trying again' business at all."

Clare laughed. "Sex. That's all you men ever think about, isn't it?"

"Way to go!" Bill said loudly, as Greg Norman hit a ball that flew 250 yards through the air before landing in the middle of the fairway on the 15th hole.

"Well, isn't it?" Clare demanded.

"Isn't it what?" Bill asked.

"Sex," Clare said, a touch of laughter in her voice. "Isn't that all that guys ever think about?"

Bill shook his head in dismay. "You brought the topic up, not me. I was just sitting here, minding my own business, watching a golf tournament on the tube."

"I did *not* bring the topic up," Clare said, teasing Bill a bit. "I was talking about what we were going to name our first child. And you had to go and drag sex into the discussion."

"Well, how in the world are you going to have kids if you don't have sex first?" Bill asked.

Clare raised an eyebrow. She knew Bill was trying to concentrate on the golf tournament, but she enjoyed twitting him a bit when he got too involved in sports. Besides, this was a very important issue between the two of them—at least as far as she was concerned. So she said, "Having children is primarily a matter of love and commitment, not sex. It means getting married, building a stable relationship, and taking a responsible role in life."

A TV announcer extolling the virtues of a new automobile interrupted the tournament. Bill stood up, pretended he had a golf club in his hands, and began taking practice strokes. "*Right* down the middle," he said as he hit a phantom golf ball down an imaginary fairway.

"Bill, I know that you're really into golf. But I do wish you'd listen a bit more attentively when I'm trying to have a serious discussion with you," Clare said.

"Sorry about that," Bill replied, a touch of guilt in his voice. He stopped pretending he was playing golf, sat back down in his chair, and smiled at Clare. "Now, let's see. You were talking about sex . . ."

"I was *not* talking about sex, Bill Meyer! I was talking about our *relationship*. You're the one who dragged the conversation into the gutter."

"The gutter!" Bill said in dismay.

"That's right," Clare replied, delighted that Bill was giving her his full attention now. "I asked if you would object to calling our first child Christine, and you said . . ."

"I said that having children involves having sex first. Which it does. But, okay, I apologize for not paying attention. Now, tell me, why do you think we ought to have a daughter before we have a son."

Clare smiled happily. "Because, the way my career is going, I'll have more time to spend with our first child than with the second. So, Christine ought to be the first, because I want to make sure that she grows up to be a completely liberated young woman. And that will take a lot of work on my part."

Bill gazed back at the television set. Pleased to see that Greg Norman was still ahead of the other golfers, he looked back at Clare. "I'm not supposed to play much of a role in bringing up our daughter, I gather."

"Oh, of course you'll play a part," Clare said. "An important part, too. But you're such a *traditionalist* when it comes to women, Bill. Sometimes I suspect that you think our only purpose in life is cooking and having babies . . ."

"Keep 'em barefoot and pregnant, huh?"

"There you go, talking about sex again," Clare replied in mock seriousness. "Anyway, that's why I want to make sure that Christine picks up her social values from me instead of from you. You can train Christopher, when he comes along. But Christine is going to be my responsibility, since I want her to break free of the usual social constraints that you men impose on women."

"Constraints?" Bill muttered. "I never met a woman yet I could constrain in any way imaginable."

"Don't be silly," Clare replied. "You are perfectly aware that women are not allowed to do most of the things that you men do."

"Like what?" Bill said, his gaze wandering back to the golf tournament again.

"Like, be president of the United States, or be chairperson of General Motors, or win the Heisman trophy in college football . . ."

"Well, we've got a woman on the Supreme Court now, and we had a woman vice-presidential candidate, as you'll surely recall since you campaigned for her."

Clare gave him an annoyed look. "But Ferraro lost, as you'll surely recall. And as for Sandra Day O'Connor, she's one out of nine. A token appointment to keep the natives from getting restless."

"Way to go!" Bill cried, as one of the golfers sank a very long putt. In his excitement, he stood up and started swinging his imaginary golf club again.

"See what I mean?" Clare responded. "You don't take the women's equality movement as seriously as you take that golf tournament you're watching. Which reminds me. Why don't you pay as much attention to women's golf as you do to the men's tours?"

"Because they won't let me play in the women's tournaments. Although the way my game is going lately, I'm not sure I could win, even playing against the ladies."

"You see!" Clare said teasingly. "You think women are inferior to men, even on the golf course. Typical, chauvinistic male attitude. And that's why I want to make sure I'm the one who trains our daughter, Christine. If I didn't, you'd dress her up in frilly clothes and hair ribbons, and make her think her only purpose in life was to attract young men."

A commercial featuring Joe Namath flashed on the television screen. Bill smiled, remembering the time that "Broadway Joe" had stirred up so much controversy by starring in a pantyhose commercial. Then he turned his attention back to Clare. "Well, our daughter Christine would look a lot better in frilly dresses and hair ribbons than our son Christopher would."

"So, you would *constrain* our daughter from dressing any way that suits her, eh? See what I mean about the typical male attitude?"

Bill thought a moment. "No, I don't care how Christine dresses. That's up to her."

"And me," Clare said.

"And you," Bill agreed. "But what about Christopher? How are you going to rear him?"

Clare gave the matter some thought. "Well, I want him to be healthy and happy, of course. And I do want him to realize that his sister is his equal. But aside from that, he's chiefly your responsibility."

"You don't want to make sure he learns how to cook and sew and change diapers?"

Clare paused. "Well, those would be useful skills, I suppose. And I do think that a man and woman should share responsibility for household chores. But I'm sure you'll want him to learn how to play golf, and football, and those sorts of things. I'd go along with that, just so Christine is free to participate in sports too."

"Wouldn't you prefer for Christopher to grow up wanting to stay home and cook and run the vacuum and take care of our grandkids? While his wife earned the money by being chairperson of G.M.?"

Clare frowned. "If he *wanted* to do that sort of thing, I suppose I wouldn't object. Not too much, anyhow." Then her face brightened. "Besides, if our daughter-in-law is chairperson of G.M., they could afford to hire a maid, and Christopher could do whatever he liked."

"But suppose he really *wanted* to be a househusband."

"Well, I don't really know," Clare said, realizing that the conversation had reached a delicate turn. "I just can't imagine that any son of mine would want to stay home and do the household chores."

Joe Namath appeared on the television set again, talking sincerely about another product. Bill thought about Namath for a moment, then said, "Well, what if Christopher was so liberated that he wanted to wear dresses and pantyhose?"

"Don't be silly!" Clare said in a shocked tone of voice.

"Aren't you the one who's being conventional now? I mean, you think it's okay if our daughter Christine wears slacks and sneakers and T shirts . . ."

"Of course it's okay, because she'll be liberated from the traditional feminine role . . ."

"But our son Christopher can't be liberated enough to wear pantyhose . . ."

"That's not 'being liberated,' that's being *abnormal*."

Bill grinned. "And you're the one who said that men can do anything they want, while women are constrained by the wicked, chauvinistic males in our society."

"That's absolutely true, Bill, and you know it. Men are free, and women aren't."

"But Christopher can't wear pantyhose, right?"

"No son of mine would *want* to wear pantyhose!"

"Why not, Clare? Why not?"

(Continued on page 192.)

SEXUAL MOTIVATION

Sex has always posed something of a problem for the psychologist. Part of the difficulty lies in finding a theoretical explanation for sexual motivation. But sometimes the problem has existed at a personal or social level, as well.

As far as theory goes, it would seem that sexual needs should be explainable in the same terms as are hunger, thirst, and the other biological needs. However, there is a crucial difference: Food, air, and water are necessary for the survival of the *individual*, but sex is necessary for the survival of the *species*. In

Sex, while not necessary for the survival of the individual, is necessary for the survival of the species.

order for reproduction to occur, two individuals of opposite sex must find each other and adjust to each other's needs—at least momentarily. Unlike hunger, then, sex involves at least two different sets of behavior patterns, *male* and *female*. Men and women breathe the same way, drink the same way, eat the same way. But their sexual behaviors are typically quite different, and so presumably their sexual motivations are different too.

If we look at sex from a *species* perspective, reproduction involves more than just a one-time act. For, in higher animals, species survival depends on keeping one or both parents around to care for the young until they are large enough to face the world on their own. An adequate theory of *species sexuality*, then, must explain not only the differing sexual desires and responses of male and female, but maternal and paternal activities as well (Dewsbury, 1981).

Given these complexities, it shouldn't surprise you to learn that motivational theories that account fairly well for hunger and thirst often do a poor job of explaining sexual behaviors.

Sexual Motivation: Theoretical Issues

In Chapter 6 we said that the study of human motivation is really an attempt to answer questions about *why* people do what they do. And we quoted Marshall Jones's belief that the answers to these questions must tell you why people *begin* a certain activity, why the behavior goes in the *direction* it does, why it *continues* for a period of time, and why it eventually *stops*.

Most people assume that sexual behavior *begins* because of some innately determined "sex drive." And there are some data suggesting a connection between *hormone* levels and sexual activities. However, as we will see, at the *human level* hormones don't directly determine the *directions* in which our sexual desires take us. Nor can we appeal to hormones for an explanation of why some people are *inhibited* in their sexual activities, nor why a particular sex act may be *prohibited* in some societies but allowed in others (Tavris & Wade, 1984).

We face similar problems when we try to explain why human sexual behaviors "continue" once started, and why they cease when they do.

One reason for our ignorance is the difficulty many people have in being objective about human sexuality. But suppose we try to put our preconceptions aside, and look at two things: what we know about sexual motivation

and behaviors, and why our knowledge of these subjects has been so difficult to gain.

Early Research on Sexuality

According to David Schnarch, "Sexology as a modern science began in Germany with physicians like Magnus Hirschfield and Iwan Bloch, who founded the first Institute for Sexology in 1919." However, Schnarch writes, "Destruction of the Institute and its vast library during Hitler's rise to power . . . decidedly slowed the development of sexology and deprived Hirschfield and Bloch of the recognition they deserved" (Schnarch, 1984).

In America, in the early 1900's, psychologists at Cornell asked their graduate students to record their **introspections** during sexual activities (as well as at other times). And Clelia Duel Mosher, a physician who taught at Stanford from 1910 until 1929, made an extensive study of sexuality in college women. However, the Cornell data never appeared in print, and Mosher's results were first published in 1974, almost 35 years after her death (Magoun, 1981).

• *Watson's Studies*

The most famous of the early investigators was John B. Watson, who started the behaviorist tradition in psychology. In 1929 Watson wrote that sex "is admittedly the most important subject in life. . . . And yet our scientific information is so meager. Even the few facts that we have must be looked upon as more or less bootlegged stuff" (Watson, 1929). Since the medical sciences had studiously ignored the subject of human sexuality, Watson set out in 1917 to investigate the matter himself.

Watson tackled the issue directly—by constructing a set of instruments to measure the physical responses of a woman during sexual arousal. Watson's wife refused to participate in such a project. However, Watson apparently talked his laboratory assistant, Rosalie Rayner, into serving as a subject.

With Rayner's help, Watson gathered what were probably the first reliable data on the female sexual response. And since this was a topic he could obviously study with pleasure, he acquired several boxes of scientific data. Unfortunately for all concerned, Watson's wife eventually discovered why her husband was spending so much time in the laboratory. Watson's wife not only sued him for divorce, she also confiscated the scientific records (Magoun, 1981)!

Although Watson was one of the brightest and most creative men of his time, his academic career was ruined by this episode. He had to resign his professorship at Johns Hopkins University, and most of his friends and colleagues deserted him. The Baltimore newspapers reported the divorce in lurid detail, and the judge presiding at the trial gave Watson a severe tongue-lashing—calling him, among other things, an expert in *mis*behavior.

After the divorce, Watson and Rosalie Rayner were married. But Watson still could not find a job at any other college or university. In desperation, he took a position with a large advertising agency and stayed there the rest of his professional life. Although he continued to write books and scientific papers, he considered himself a ruined man and soon slipped into the solace of alcohol (McConnell, 1985). Watson died at the age of 80 in 1958.

● *Sex Research in Columbia, Missouri*

In 1929 Watson wrote, "The study of sex is still fraught with danger. It can be openly studied only by individuals who are not connected with universities." As H.W. Magoun points out, Watson's warning was not an idle one. In 1929 a young man named O. Hobart Mowrer was an undergraduate at the University of Missouri in Columbia. As part of a project in a sociology class, Mowrer gave out a questionnaire on "The Economic Aspects of Women" to some 600 Missouri students. Three of the questions Mowrer included in his survey concerned attitudes toward extramarital sexual relations.

When the newspapers discovered what Mowrer was doing, they raised a furor. The townspeople in Columbia circulated a petition demanding that the "people responsible" for this outrage be fired. The state legislature agreed, and the president of the university responded by firing the professor who had taught the course. Mowrer fortunately survived the incident and went on to a distinguished career in psychology. In 1954 he became president of the American Psychological Association (Magoun, 1981).

Kinsey's Interviews

Watson's influence on the scientific study of human sexuality was profound, but largely indirect. One of Watson's students, Karl Lashley, did undertake some work in the area. But Lashley's major contribution came when he got a noted biologist interested in studying human sexual responses—a man named Alfred Kinsey (Magoun, 1981).

The first survey of sexual behavior based on an adequately large segment of the public did not come until 1948, when Kinsey and his associates published their monumental volume, *Sexual Behavior in the Human Male*. Using a standardized set of questions, the Kinsey group got many thousands of men to describe their sexual feelings and behaviors. A surprisingly large number responded to the questions without apparent shame or evasion (Kinsey *et al.*, 1948).

However, as many critics noted, there were methodological problems with Kinsey's survey.

Since Kinsey depended on volunteers, it may be that his sample was **biased**. That is, it could be that the sexuality of those people who wouldn't talk to Kinsey was quite different from the sexuality of those who did. Nonetheless, Kinsey did show that a large group of normal-appearing males regularly engaged in a wide variety of sexual practices that "nice people" were not even supposed to know about (Pomeroy, Flax, & Wheeler, 1982).

In 1953 Kinsey and his group published their findings on female sexual behavior (Kinsey *et al.*, 1953). And in 1981, scientists at the Kinsey Institute reported a study of **homosexual** activities (Bell *et al.*, 1981).

The public response to Kinsey's efforts was decidedly a mixed bag. Shortly after the study on women was published, New York Congressman Louis B. Heller had this to say about Kinsey: "He is hurling the insult of the century against our mothers, wives, daughters and sisters, under the pretext of making a great contribution to scientific research" (cited in Gould, 1982). In 1954 a special House committee accused the Rockefeller Foundation of "directly supporting subversion" and of promoting communism because the Foundation gave money to the Kinsey Institute. Citing these facts, Harvard biologist Stephen Jay Gould notes that "Kinsey never did find an alternate source of support (after the Congressional attack); he died two years later, overworked, angry, and distressed that so many years of further data might never see publication . . ." (Gould, 1982).

Masters and Johnson's Research

The writings of Kinsey and many others all sprang from conversations and case histories rather than direct observations. Subjects were asked to *talk* about their sex lives while the

Alfred C. Kinsey

"POP, IS IT TRUE MEN CAN BE SEXUALLY ACTIVE EVEN WHEN THEY'RE OVER 21?"

Biased (BUY-est). From a Latin term meaning "to cut or go against the grain." In psychological terms, to be biased is to have preconceived notions about a situation, or to perceive things as you want to see them, not as they actually are. A "biased sample" is one not selected randomly, but rather selected according to some (often unconscious) scheme.

Homosexual (HO-mo-SEX-you-all). Sexual activities between two (or more) males, or between two (or more) females. As opposed to *heterosexual* (HETT-er-oh-SEX-you-all) activities, which occur between a male and a female. Homosexual behaviors are frequently found in lower animals and, according to Kinsey, take place more often among humans than "prudish people" are willing to admit. Freud—and most other scientists who have studied human sexuality—believe that homosexual activities are as "normal" and as "genetically determined" as are heterosexual behaviors.

Gynecologist (guy-nuh-COLL-oh-jist, or jin-nuh-COLL-oh jist). The Greek word *gyne* means "woman." A medical doctor whose speciality is treating the reproductive problems of women is called a gynecologist.

Chromosomes (KROH-moh-sohms). From the Greek words *chromo*, meaing "colored," and *soma*, meaning "body." The genes of a cell are strung together like strands of colored beads. These "strands" are the chromosomes.

William Masters

Virginia Johnson

scientists recorded what the subjects *said*. It was not until the 1950's that William Masters and Virginia Johnson began to study what people actually *did*.

Masters was trained as a **gynecologist**—that is, a physician who has specialized knowledge of the female reproductive system. Johnson received her training in social work and psychology. They started their work in St. Louis, using female prostitutes as paid subjects. Following Watson's lead, Masters and Johnson made recordings of their subjects' bodily reactions while the women experienced various types of sexual arousal (chiefly masturbation). Later, they studied the biological changes that accompany sexual excitement in males, as well.

When Masters tried to present his early data to a gathering of US gynecologists, the majority of these physicians urged him to give up his research. Many of the best known medical journals would not publish his findings, and political pressure prevented his getting governmental support for his work. Thus, the first public discussion of Masters and Johnson's work was delayed until 1962, when they presented their findings at a meeting of the American Psychological Association (Masters & Johnson, 1966).

● *The Early Studies: A Summary*
Almost all the early research on human sexuality focused on intra-psychic or social variables. Those few scientists who attempted to look at the biology of *human* sexuality paid the price for so doing. Nor was there much interest until the 1970's in medical treatment of sexual disorders. Indeed, as University of Pennsylvania psychiatrist Harold Lief pointed out recently, in 1960 only three medical schools in the US taught courses in human sexuality, and by 1968 only 29 schools did so (Lief, 1984). Thus, much of what we know of the biological factors affect-

ing sexual motivation—and the guesses we often make about how to treat human sexual problems—has come from studies conducted on animal subjects. How much this animal research can be generalized to humans is still a matter of debate. However, let's look at what the facts seem to be, and then turn our attention to the intra-psychic and social/behavioral factors that influence sexual motives and acts.

THE BIOLOGY OF SEX

Most of the cells in your body contain 23 *pairs* of **chromosomes**, or 46 chromosomes in all. The only exceptions to this rule are the sperm cells and unfertilized egg cells. The sperm cell, like the egg cell, contains only 23 chromosomes. But the sperm cell is somewhat different from the egg. Its 23rd chromosome can be either the large X type or the smaller Y type (see Fig. 7.1 and Fig. 7.2). The 23rd chromosome of the egg cell is *always* a large X type.

If an X-type sperm is the first to enter the egg cell, the fertilized egg will have an XX 23rd chromosome pair—and the child will almost always be a *genetic* female. If a Y-type sperm fertilizes the *egg*, the 23rd chromosome pair will be of the XY variety and the child will be a *genetic* male (Bardin & Catterall, 1981). There are rare cases where an infant is genetically an XX female, but is born with male genitalia because one of the X chromosomes contains a tiny fragment of the Y chromosome that "codes" for the male sex organs. This "XX male" condition occurs about once in each 20,000 births (Edwards, 1988).

Hormones
Generally speaking, the X and Y chromosomes determine whether the cells in your body will carry the XX or XY pattern. However, *becoming* a male or a female is a much more complicated process. The actual *shape* of your body—and of your sex organs—is affected by many factors. The most important of these factors are the hormones produced by various *glands* in your body.

Glands are small chemical factories that release their products into the bloodstream, or onto the tissues surrounding the gland, or even into the outside world. Some of these chemicals primarily have a local effect. For instance, the tear glands in your eyes secrete that clear but romantic liquid which lubricates the movement of your eyes in their sockets. Other types of glands secrete their products directly into your bloodstream, and thus have their primary effects *some distance away* from the glands. These "action-at-a-distance" chemicals are the hormones.

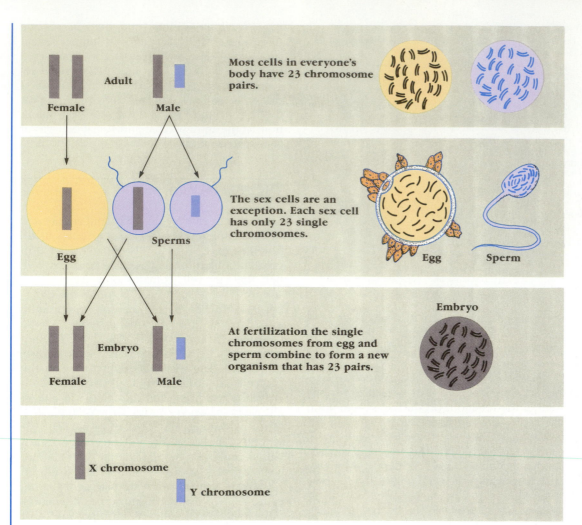

Most cells in everyone's body have 23 chromosome pairs.

The sex cells are an exception. Each sex cell has only 23 single chromosomes.

Egg

Sperm

At fertilization the single chromosomes from egg and sperm combine to form a new organism that has 23 pairs.

Embryo

X chromosome

Y chromosome

FIG. 7.1 Sex is determined by the sperm cell. An egg and sperm unite to form a new being.

The Sex Hormones

You have two **adrenal glands**—one atop each of your kidneys (see Fig. 7.3). Your adrenals secrete more than 20 different hormones. The majority of the adrenal hormones regulate such bodily functions as digestion, urine excretion, and blood pressure. As we will see in the next chapter, many of these hormones play a role in your response to stress. However, some of these chemicals also have a direct effect on your sex life. These are called the *sex hormones*.

Sex hormones are also produced by your **gonads**, or sex glands—the testes in the male, and the ovaries in the female. From shortly after conception onward, your adrenals and your gonads worked together to provide your body with the chemicals it needed to develop into—and to remain—a sexually mature adult.

Male hormones are called **androgens**. The best known of these is **testosterone**. The two main types of female hormones are known as the **estrogens** and **progesterone**. Whether you are a woman or a man, however, your adrenals and your gonads produce *both* male and

female hormones. As we will see, though, it is the *relative amount* of these two types of hormones that is important for sexual differentiation (Bardin & Catterall, 1981).

● *Primary and Secondary Sex Characteristics*

When scientists speak of *primary sex characteristics*, they mean the actual sex organs themselves—the ovaries, vagina, uterus, and clitoris in the female, and the penis and testes in the male. Additionally, those parts of the reproductive organs that can be seen by the naked eye are called the *external genitalia*, or **genitals**. Male-female differences in primary sex characteristics are usually present at birth.

The *secondary sex characteristics* are those that appear at **puberty**—the growth of facial hair and deepening voice in the young man, the development of the breasts and broadening of the hips in the young woman. The appearance of both primary and secondary sexual characteristics is controlled almost entirely *by hormones* (Wilson, George, & Griffin, 1981).

If a young boy's adrenals and testes *overproduce* androgens—or *underproduce* estro-

Primary sex characteristics first become visible in the fetus at seven weeks.

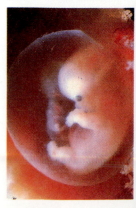

Adrenal glands (add-DREE-nul). The adrenal is a small gland at the top of the kidney that secretes many different hormones, including those that affect sexual growth and behavior. You have two adrenal glands—one atop each of your kidneys.

Gonads (GO-nads). The primary sex glands—the ovaries in the female and the testes in the male. The ovaries produce the egg cells that are fertilized by the sperm secreted by the testes.

Androgens (ANN-dro-jens). From the Greek words meaning "producer of males." There are several male hormones; collectively these are known as androgens.

Testosterone (tess-TOSS-ter-own). The most important of the androgens, or male hormones. Found in small quantities in females, as well as males. Many psychologists believe testosterone is the "major hormonal motivator" for many types of behaviors in both men and women.

Estrogens (ESS-tro-jens). The Latin word *estrus* (ESS-truss) refers to the period in a female's reproductive cycle when she is fertile and hence capable of becoming pregnant. Estrogens are the hormones that generate or bring about estrus.

Progesterone (pro-JEST-ter-own). One of the several female sex hormones.

Genitals (JEN-it-tulls). From the Latin word meaning "to beget, to reproduce, to generate children." The external sex organs, or *genitalia* (jen-it-TAIL-ee-uh).

Puberty (PEW-burr-tee). The onset of sexual maturity, when the person becomes physically capable of sexual reproduction. Usually between the 11th and the 14th year, the female's ovaries begin producing eggs and menstrual (MEN-strew-ull, or MEN-strull) bleeding begins. At about the same age, the male's testes begin producing semen and ejaculation becomes possible.

Sexual dimorphism (dye-MORE-fism). *Morph* (MORF) comes from a Greek word meaning "form" or "type." There are, generally speaking, two sexual "forms," male and female.

FIG. 7.2 Human chromosome cells. Only the 23rd pair differ — XX for female, XY for male.

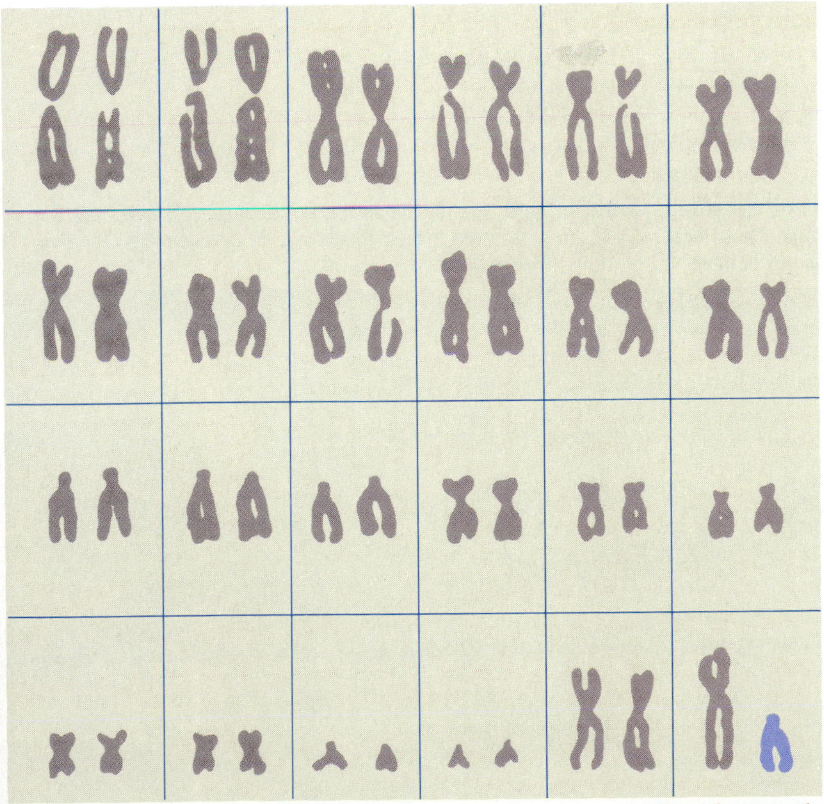

Female or male

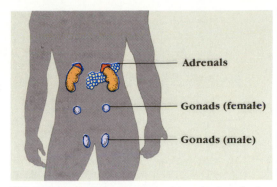

FIG. 7.3 The location of some major endocrine glands.

gens—he will experience early puberty. That is, his voice will change and his beard will begin to grow sooner than expected. But if the boy's glands *underproduce* androgens or *overproduce* estrogens for some reason, his puberty will be delayed and his body may take on feminine characteristics—a high voice, overdeveloped breasts, and a lack of facial hair.

If a young girl's adrenals and ovaries *overproduce* estrogens—or *underproduce* androgens—the girl will come to sexual maturity earlier than expected. If the reverse is true, her puberty will be delayed, and she may even develop such masculine secondary characteristics as flat breasts, excess facial hair, and a low voice (Wilson, George, & Griffin, 1981).

● **Androgens and Sexual Behavior**

Estrogens and progesterone seem to be correlated with child bearing in human females (Adler, Pfaff, & Goy, 1985). But it is testosterone—in both men and women—that tends to promote *sexual behavior itself*. Thus, either a man or woman with a low testosterone level is likely to experience a low *biological* sex drive. However, cultural inhibitions can suppress sexual behavior even in someone with a high testosterone level. And stimulation from the environment may be so strong at times that even someone with a low testosterone level may engage in a variety of sexual behaviors (Goy & McEwen, 1980).

Thus, both the strength of the sex drive—and the types of behaviors that the organism produces—are *always* affected both by genes and by social factors (Ehrhardt & Meyer-Bahlburg, 1981).

□□ **QUESTION** □□
How many sexes are there?

● **Sexual Dimorphism**

The division of the animal kingdom into male and female is called **sexual dimorphism**. However, nature often blurs the line between female and male body types. For even in higher

SCHOOL OF SECONDARY SEX CHARACTERISTICS

COURSE	ROOM
AUTO REPAIR	117
BILLIARDS	204
DECORATING	212
HOME EC	109
HUNTING	114
SECRETARIAL	209
SEWING	113
WOOD WORKING	102

animals, where sexual dimorphism is most pronounced, some offspring are born who possess part or all of both male and female sex organs. These **inter-sex** individuals range from "mostly female" to "mostly both" to "mostly male" (Ehrhardt & Meyer-Bahlburg, 1981).

● *Critical Periods in Sexual Development*

The March 20, 1981, issue of *Science* includes a number of articles on the effects of hormones on sexual dimorphism in humans and animals. According to these papers, both male and female hormones can be found in most fetuses while they are in the womb. It is the *balance* of the hormones during certain *critical periods of development* that biases the fetus toward male or female behavior patterns (Naftolin, 1981).

Generally speaking, the critical period for most species is just when the central nervous system is beginning to develop. If androgens predominate during this critical time, the fetus will develop male *genitalia*. In addition, various *parts of the brain* involved in masculine behavior patterns will be activated, and the brain centers that mediate feminine behavior patterns will be suppressed. If the androgens do not predominate during the critical period, the fetus typically will develop female genitalia and behaviors, while the brain centers that control masculinity will be suppressed (MacLusky & Naftolin, 1981).

This developmental pattern is not entirely uniform throughout the animal kingdom, however. In some lizard species, the *temperature* at which the eggs hatch determines gender. For example, if the eggs of the leopard gekko are incubated at 25° C, all the hatchlings will be female. At 32° C, almost all the animals will be male, and those few that become female *act like males* and never lay eggs (Kolata, 1986).

Furthermore, some fish begin life as functional females, then (after laying eggs for a period of time) develop into functional males. Other fish begin life as males but eventually turn into females when environmental conditions encourage them to do so (Adler, Pfaff, & Goy, 1985).

To summarize, the sex hormones affect sexual behavior during fetal development in two ways: first, by determining whether the organism will have male or female primary sex characteristics; second, by determining which sex-related centers in the brain will develop, and which won't. However, as we will see, it is the *combination* of hormonal bias, past experience, and present environmental stimulation that determines most adult sexual behaviors.

Mating and Nesting in Doves

The complex interplay between hormones and environmental stimulation is nicely illustrated in a classic series of studies on the ring dove by Daniel Lehrman and his colleagues at Rutgers.

During the mating season, the male ring dove approaches the female and dances around her. At one point in his ritual, he bows low in front of her and utters a characteristic "coo" sound. Under normal circumstances, the female accepts the male's advances, and the two subsequently mate. Both birds then build a nest. When the female lays her eggs, both birds sit on them and care for the young after they hatch.

If the male ring dove is castrated, he shows no interest at all in the female and simply won't mate. If he is subsequently injected with testosterone, he will perform the "bow-coo" dance and will mate with the female. But he won't help with nest building, nor will he sit on the

Parrot fish, like a number of other species, begin life functioning as females but become "functional males" when they reach their final stage of development. The fish shown is male.

7 / Sexual Motivation

Inter-sex. Many lower organisms are hermaphrodites (her-MAFF-rho-dights). That is, each organism contains both male and female reproductive organs. Although sexual dimorphism is fairly strong in higher animals, some individuals (including humans) are *inter-sexed*, in that they contain parts or all of both the male and female organs.

Orientation. The *orienting reflex* is the automatic response of turning toward a new or interesting stimulus. "Sexual orientation" is the term used to describe which sex you are most likely to "orient to," or be romantically interested in.

eggs. If the male is now injected with estrogen, he will help the female construct the nest, but he won't hatch the young. If he is also given progesterone, the male will complete the sequence and care for the young doves as well.

As far as the female dove is concerned, it is the *sight* of the male's dance and the *sound* of his voice that trigger the production of estrogen. The increase in estrogen causes her to mate, gather materials for the nest, and then lay her eggs. The *act* of nest building causes her ovaries to secrete progesterone, which encourages her to hatch the eggs and care for the young.

As Lehrman notes, in the case of the ring dove, sexual behavior affects hormone production as much as hormone production affects sexual behavior (Lehrman, 1956).

□ □ **QUESTION** □ □
There is no evidence that hormones affect child care behaviors in human males. Why isn't this fact particularly surprising?

183 - 192

INTRA-PSYCHIC ASPECTS OF SEXUAL MOTIVATION

Sexual behavior is strongly—but not completely—influenced by hormones and other biological factors in the lower animals. But what about humans? Surely we *choose* most of the sexual activities we engage in. Were that not the case, our laws against certain types of sex acts—with certain types of partners—would be scientifically indefensible.

Not all sexual behaviors are the product of voluntary choice, of course. A woman does not "choose" to engage in rape; she is forced into that behavior. Children who are molested by adults are often powerless to prevent the acts that are thrust upon them. And strong social pressures may make almost anyone engage in sexual behaviors that seem "personally unnatural" to the individual concerned. Many of these "personally unnatural" acts involve sexual **orientation**.

□ □ **QUESTION** □ □
Psychologically speaking, what is the difference between the terms "sexual orientation" and "sexual preference"?

Sexual Orientation

Psychologists don't entirely agree as to which factors affecting voluntary sexual behavior are the most potent. However, one obvious influence is *sexual orientation*. Women tend to be primarily attracted to men as sexual partners, and vice versa. Perhaps because heterosexuality is so "natural" to most people, it has been infrequently researched.

Those acts—such as homosexuality—that "go against the grain" of natural heterosexuality have received some scientific attention, however. Sigmund Freud once said we learn about the normal by studying the abnormal. Perhaps, then, we can learn something about heterosexual orientation by investigating the factors that influence supposedly "abnormal" thoughts, feelings, and behaviors.

Homosexuality

There are few topics in the entire field of psychology so emotionally charged as that of homosexuality. There are many reasons why this topic raises such intense feelings. First, homosexual acts are viewed as a "crime against nature" by many people. Second, effeminate males and masculine females appear to be rejecting their "normal sex roles." Third, homosexuals are often perceived as poor role models for children. Last, but surely not least, people with a strong heterosexual orientation frequently have difficulty imagining any other point of view. Thus, they may view a homosexual orientation as evidence of a "mental disorder."

Suppose we look briefly at these points, then discuss the factors that apparently influence sexual orientation.

● **Is Homosexuality Unnatural?**
In his 1980 book, *Homosexual behavior: A modern reappraisal*, psychiatrist Judd Marmor states that homosexuality is far from being "unnatural" in the *statistical* sense. It occurs in all

Homosexuality is viewed as being normal, abnormal, or even harmful by various segments of society.

higher species, even when members of the opposite sex are present and presumably available for mating. Therefore, we can presume that the *possibility* of homosexuality is as "coded for in the genes" as is the *probability* of heterosexuality (Marmor, 1980).

Homosexual acts among humans are fairly common in Western societies. Some 40 percent of Kinsey's male subjects admitted to having had "at least one homosexual experience" at some time in their lives. However, only 10 percent of the men stated they had a homosexual orientation. Another 10 percent or so were bisexual, or weren't strongly attracted either to males or females (Bell *et al.*, 1981; Kinsey, Pomeroy, & Martin, 1948). Judging from these figures, having a same-sex orientation in the US today is about as "unnatural" *in the statistical sense of that word* as is being Jewish, black, or a blue-eyed blond.

● Do Homosexuals Violate Standard Sex Roles?

In a recent study from the Kinsey Institute, Alan Bell and his colleagues report that the major *developmental* difference between "straights" and "gays" is that many male and female homosexuals experienced *gender non-conformity* while young. That is, the boys tended not to like sports and other "masculine" activities all that much, while the girls tended to prefer "non-feminine" activities (Bell *et al.*, 1981).

Data supporting this finding comes from a recent study by UCLA psychiatrist Richard Green, who looked at the psychosexual development of extremely feminine boys. Green began by assessing 66 "feminine" and 56 "masculine" boys when they were about 7 years old. He measured them again when they were about 19. Green reports that all but one of the "masculine" boys had made a normal heterosexual development. However, 75 percent of the "feminine" boys were either bisexual or homosexual in fantasy and/or behavior. The rest were judged to be heterosexual (Green, 1987). We must note, however, that not all homosexual adults show "gender non-conformity" when young, and not all children who do so become homosexual as adults.

Indeed, in terms of *adult* masculine and feminine sex-role behaviors, however, there is little difference between "gays" and "straights." Some gay males are effeminate; most are not. Some lesbians show strongly masculine behaviors; most do not. And some straight males and females show "non-traditional" sex-role behaviors (Bell *et al.*, 1981).

If we look at adult *sexual* behaviors and fantasies, the difference between heterosexuals and homosexuals becomes more pronounced. According to University of Kansas psychologist Michael Storms, female and male homosexuals have "values" and "self-images" that are identical to those of heterosexual women and men. However, the homosexuals tend to fantasize about (and engage in) same-sex relations, while the heterosexuals tend to fantasize about (and engage in) cross-sex relations (Storms, 1980, 1981).

● Homosexuality and Children

One standard objection to homosexuality is that it does not lead to child bearing. In fact, as Alan Bell and his colleagues have shown, this is not always the case. In a survey of more than 1,000 homosexuals in San Francisco, Bell and his associates found that 20 percent of the gay males had been married. About a third of the white lesbians and half the black lesbians had been or still were married. And many of these individuals had gotten (and remained) married precisely because they wished to have children (Bell *et al.*, 1981).

A second objection raised against homosexuality has to do with sexual identity. Many people assume that children reared by gay parents will have a greater-than-normal chance of becoming gay themselves. However, the data suggest otherwise. UCLA psychiatrist Martha Kirkpatrick studied the children of single lesbian and single heterosexual mothers. She could find no difference between the two groups of children, either in terms of emotional disturbances or sexual identity. Similar results come from a recent study by Richard Green, a psychiatrist at the State University of New York at Stony Brook. Green evaluated 37 children being reared either by female homosexuals or by parents who had undergone a sex-change operation. Of these 37, 36 showed no signs of confused sexual identity. And all of the teenagers in this group were decidedly

A large proportion of gay people of both sexes have been married, and many of them are parents.

"straight" in their sexual orientation (cited in Maddox, 1982).

A third objection has to do with a child's early sexual experiences. If children are seduced by homosexuals, won't that affect the children's sexual orientation? Again, the data suggest this isn't the case. In their 1981 study, Alan Bell and his colleagues compared 1,000 homosexuals with a carefully matched group of 500 heterosexual men and women. These scientists report that the majority of both groups "knew" their sexual orientation at a very early age, several years before they actually engaged in any overt sexual acts. A great many of the heterosexuals had homosexual encounters at an early age, but became "straight" anyhow. And most of the homosexuals had a number of heterosexual encounters early in life. They didn't find these experiences "traumatic," just less rewarding than same-sex relationships (Bell *et al.*, 1981).

- ### Bisexuality
According to Fritz Klein and Timothy Wolf, there are many different types of *bisexuality*. Some men, for example, have sexual fantasies that are exclusively "gay" but fall in love with, marry, and have sex only with women. On the other hand, some women fantasize about and have sex only with men, but are as likely to "fall in love with" a woman as a man. Thus, bisexuality—as with all other forms of human sexuality—includes not only "sexual behavior," but also attractions toward, fantasies about, and social relations with various sexual partners (Klein & Wolf, 1985).

According to Boston University psychologist James Weinrich, bisexual men and women tend to be more interested in the *social* aspects of sexuality than are individuals who are entirely "gay" or "straight." For instance, many bisexuals report they seek "a blending of sex and friendship" in their sexual relationships. For this reason, Weinrich says, "as a rule the more bi something is, the less sexual it is. But this rule has enough exceptions to it to keep scholars busy for some time" (Weinrich, 1987).

- ### Is Homosexuality a Mental Disorder?
Until fairly recently, most psychologists and psychiatrists considered homosexuality a "mental disorder." However, in the early 1970's, both the American Psychological Association and the American Psychiatric Association removed homosexuality from the list of "standard mental disorders." But to be entirely truthful, a significant minority in both professional groups still believes that gayness is a type of personality disorder (Fann *et al.*, 1983). However, in his book *The Male Experience*, psychologist James Doyle notes that many homosexuals are far healthier (and less confined in their sex roles) than are many heterosexuals. Indeed, Doyle says, heterosexual couples "could learn some new ways of living, loving and sharing, if they would only try to understand gay couples better" (Doyle, 1983).

Heterosexual Orientation
This rather lengthy discussion of homosexuality is important for two reasons. First, it tells us something about what may be the largest "hidden" minority in our society. Second, it gives us some of the data we need to discuss *heterosexual attraction*. For, as we mentioned earlier, most of the research on sexual orientation has focused on homosexuality rather than on heterosexuality.

We must also differentiate sexual *orientation* from sexual *identity* and sex *roles*. Orientation has to do with whether you are romantically attracted to the opposite sex, the same sex, or both. Sexual *preference* has to do with your choice of sex partners. Sexual *identity* has to do with whether you "feel" yourself to be male or female without regard to your sexual orientation. And sex *roles* have to do with displaying socially accepted patterns of "masculine" and "feminine" thoughts, attitudes, and behaviors.

- ### Sexual Identity
Most scientific research on sexual identity has focused on people who, because of hormonal problems, are born with both male and female sex organs. And, as Canadian sex researcher Ron Langevin put it recently, "The intersexes offer us an opportunity to examine which components of human sexuality are most important in gender identity and erotic object choice" (Langevin, 1983).

Perhaps the best-known studies on intersex individuals are those by Julianne Imperato-McGinley and her colleagues at the Cornell Medical Center (Imperato-McGinley *et al.*, 1986). The subjects of this research were 38 individuals who grew up in rural villages in the Dominican Republic. The subjects were all XY males who had normal levels of testosterone, but whose bodies could not produce a related male hormone called *dihydro-testosterone*. As a consequence, these *inter-sex* individuals were born with such ambiguous genitalia that more than half of them were reared as girls. However, at puberty, their voices deepened, they showed the male pattern of musculature, and their penises grew and became capable of erections and ejaculation (Imperato-McGinley *et al.*, 1980).

The question that interested Imperato-McGinley was this: How would these men react when they developed male primary and secondary sex characteristics after being reared all their lives as girls? Of the 25 living subjects, Imperato-McGinley and her colleagues were able to gather detailed information on 18. The

Cornell scientists report that 17 of the 18 switched to wearing male clothing at puberty and thereafter considered themselves to be "men." According to Imperato-McGinley, these 17 subjects began to question their sexual identity sometime between the ages of 7 and 12. Over this period, the men passed "through stages of no longer feeling like girls, to feeling like men, and finally to conscious awareness that they were indeed men." Imperato-McGinley concludes that hormones, rather than social factors, are the major determiners of sexual identity (Imperato-McGinley *et al.*, 1979).

However, UCLA psychiatrist Robert Rubin and his colleagues believe that only 13 of the 18 had clearly-defined male identities. And they point out that one subject whom Imperato-McGinley claims *developed a male sexual identity* continued to wear dresses. Rubin *et al.* also report on eight inter-sex individuals in the US who had similar hormonal problems and who were reared as girls. All eight *maintained their female gender identity of rearing* despite the development of male genitalia at puberty. According to Rubin and his colleagues, "Most investigators now regard the factors contributing to the development of gender identity to be neither 'nature' nor 'nurture' alone, but rather an interaction of hormonal and psychosocial influences" (Rubin, Reinisch, & Haskett, 1981).

□□ **QUESTION** □□
Why might inter-sex individuals living in a highly traditional culture such as the Dominican Republic be more likely to adopt a male identity than similar individuals living in the United States?

● *Why Are You "Straight" (or Otherwise)?*
Until fairly recently, most scientists assumed that hormonal bias determined whether a person turned out to be heterosexual, homosexual, or bisexual. However, as Robert Rubin and his colleagues suggest, this doesn't seem to be the case. With certain minor exceptions, the hormonal pattern of gay males is the same as that of heterosexual males. And no one has yet reported reliable hormonal differences between lesbians and "straight" females. Furthermore, injecting gay males with testosterone *increases their homosexual activities* rather than "turning them 'straight'" (Rubin, Reinisch, & Haskett, 1981).

Like all other human behaviors, sexual orientation and sexual identity are multi-determined. And both aspects of your sexuality seem to be more a matter of "discovery" than of "choice." You did not sit down, think things over, and then logically "decide" to be what you are. Rather, during your early years you simply became aware of what motives nature and your environment had given you.

□□ **QUESTION** □□
Men in Scotland and Greece have traditionally worn skirts. How would "wearing dresses" affect their sexual identity *within those cultures?*

SOCIAL/BEHAVIORAL INFLUENCES ON SEXUAL MOTIVATION

Society cannot control which hormones are present in your body. Nor can society entirely determine whether you are attracted to same-sex or opposite-sex partners (or both). But your culture does strongly influence your *feelings* about sex and about yourself—and how you *express* those feelings. Society does so by specifying which sexual *roles, behaviors*, and *values* are "acceptable" within that culture (Sonderegger, 1984).

Society not only sets sexual standards, it enforces them as well—in at least two ways: first, by surrounding you with *models*—that is, with people (such as your parents and peers) who have adopted society's standards; and second, by rewarding you when you imitate these models, and by punishing you when you don't. We will describe the "socialization process" by which you incorporate society's values in several later chapters. However, much of that socialization process involves learning **sex-role stereotypes**.

□□ **QUESTION** □□
Suppose you are a heterosexual male, hence strongly attracted to females. If men and women dressed and acted alike, how would you know whom to pursue sexually?

Society—and in particular the entertainment industry—surrounds us with sexual role models that are usually idealized and unrealistic.

Sex-Role Stereotypes

In her chapter in the *Handbook of Developmental Psychology*, Dee Shepherd-Look defines sex-role stereotypes as "widely shared and pervasive concepts that prescribe how each sex ought to perform." According to Shepherd-Look, "There is considerable agreement both within and between cultures as to the appropriate sex-role behaviors for males and females." In most societies, a man is expected to be "competent, independent, assertive, aggressive, dominant, and competitive in social and sexual relations." A woman, on the other hand, is supposed to be "passive, affiliative, affectionate, nurturant, intuitive, and supportive, particularly in her familiar role as wife and mother" (Shepherd-Look, 1982).

Why are these sex-role stereotypes so similar from one culture to another? The answer scientists give to this question depends on the viewpoint they take toward human motivation. Most *biologists* presume that sex roles reflect genetic traits. *Intra-psychic psychologists*, such as Sigmund Freud, see sex roles as individual responses that develop out of a conflict between biological tendencies and social influences. However, *social/behavioral theorists* believe sex roles are primarily *learned*. We will discuss the Freudian and developmental viewpoints later. For the moment, let's look more closely at the biological and the social/behavioral explanations of what sex roles are, and where they come from.

□ □ **QUESTION** □ □
In most societies, men frequently seek casual affairs, while women seem to prefer long-lasting relationships. Why?

Sociobiology

Harvard biologist Edward O. Wilson is the "father" of a relatively new theory called **sociobiology** that attempts to explain almost all human behavior in terms of Charles Darwin's notions about "survival of the fittest." Wilson argues that the major motivation all organisms

Edward O. Wilson

have is that of *helping their genes survive*. You do not eat, drink, and breathe to ensure your own good health. Rather, Wilson says, you try to survive because you have an overwhelming urge to reproduce your own genes (Wilson, 1975).

● Male and Female "Roles"

According to Wilson, stereotyped sex roles developed because men and women *must* have different reproductive strategies. These strategies stem from "genetic reality," Wilson says. And since men and women in all societies have similar genes, their sex roles in all cultures should also be similar.

Wilson believes the best strategy men can adopt to make sure their genes get passed on is to have sex with as many women as possible. Therefore, Wilson says, the "masculine role" is that of being aggressive, dominant, and **promiscuous**. Women, however, must bear and care for children. Their best chance to help their genes survive is to make sure their offspring thrive. So, Wilson says, the "feminine role" is that of being submissive, because this is women's instinctual way of getting men to protect the women's children (i.e., genes). Any attempt to change these traditional masculine and feminine behaviors, Wilson believes, would decrease reproductive success and might eventually lead to the termination of the human race.

● Sociobiology: An Evaluation

Wilson's theory does have its strengths. First, it fits neatly within the framework of Darwin's Theory of Evolution, which is the prevailing viewpoint in most biological sciences. Second, because Wilson explains almost all of human experience in terms of "genetic variation," sociobiology allows biologists to explain many

According to West German research, "un-macho" males are typically more fertile than are "macho" males.

behaviors without delving too far into the mind.

For example, Wilson claims that, at some time in the past, behaviors such as *territoriality* maximized the reproductive success of individuals who displayed those behaviors. By the process of "natural selection," these traits became "embedded in the genes," and therefore are almost impossible to change. Thus, Wilson says, we have wars because our genes tell us to be "territorial," and all attempts to ensure peace *by changing society* are probably doomed to failure (Wilson, 1975).

As Samuel P. Coe puts it, in rather blunt form, Wilson's position seems to be that genes determine human nature, and since we can't change our genes, we can't change ourselves either (Coe, 1981).

However, according to philosopher of science Philip Kitcher, Wilson's approach is little more than a misguided attempt to justify the present "status quo." Kitcher notes that Wilson spent most of his life studying the social behavior of insects. Wilson then attempted to construct a "logical ladder" from his studies of animals to pronouncements about human nature. But this ladder, Kitcher says, is "rotten at every rung. . . . Wilson might have brought to his study of human behavior the same care and rigor that he has lavished on ants. But he did not" (Kitcher, 1985). Using rather elegant mathematics—and a fair amount of data—Kitcher shows there is little scientific support for any of Wilson's basic assumptions.

For example, Wilson assumes that the "macho male" is the pinnacle of reproductive success. However, recent studies by German scientists cast doubt on this assumption. D.H. Hellhammer, W. Hubert, and their colleagues at the University of Muenster have recently shown that men who got high scores on measures of assertiveness, aggression, and self-confidence tended to have abnormally lower sperm counts, more hormonal imbalances, and to be less fertile than were less "macho" males (Hellhammer *et al.*, 1985). And in a related study, the Muenster scientists found that men with "un-macho" or even "feminine" personality traits tended to have above-average fertility rates (Hubert *et al.*, 1985).

Given these data, why has sociobiology had such an impact, particularly among biologists? For two reasons, Kitcher says. First, by *explaining* all of psychology and sociology in terms of genetics, sociobiology enhances the *social position* of academic biologists and reduces the prestige of psychologists and sociologists. Second, it appeals to "conservatives," particularly those who resist any change in the way that males and females relate to each other (Kitcher, 1985).

Perhaps the major objection to sociobiology, however, is this one: Wilson has so far failed to produce any evidence showing *how* social behaviors can be "coded in the genes." As one scientist put it, "Genes don't make behaviors; genes make proteins." Until Wilson provides a "map" showing the complex set of steps that runs from genes through proteins to patterns of neural firing in the brain, his theory of sociobiology remains little more than unsupported speculation.

Before evaluating Wilson's position further, let's look at the social/behavioral viewpoint on sex roles.

How Sex-Role Stereotypes Are Formed

Dee Shepherd-Look cites more than a hundred studies suggesting that sex-role differentiation is controlled by the environment and starts at birth (Shepherd-Look, 1982). For example, Jeffrey Rubin and his associates interviewed parents within 24 hours after their infants were born. The parents were asked to rate their new child on a number of scales. Both mothers and fathers of *daughters* described their infants as being "softer, finer featured, weaker, smaller, prettier, more inattentive, more awkward, and more delicate" than did parents whose infant was a male. *Sons* were described as "firmer, larger featured, more coordinated, alert, stronger, and hardier" than were daughters. Despite these parental *perceptions*, however, Rubin and his colleagues note that there were no *measurable* physical or behavioral differences between the male and female infants (Rubin, Provenzano, & Luria, 1974).

In a similar study, J.A. Will and his colleagues asked a number of women to play with a six-month-old child while the investigators watched. The women were all mothers who had small children (of both sexes) of their own. Half the time, the infant was dressed in blue pants, and the mothers were told the child's name was "Adam." The other half of the time, the child was called "Beth," and was clothed in a pink dress. The mothers who played with "Adam" almost uniformly offered him a masculine toy (such as a train). The mothers who played with "Beth" typically offered the child a doll. The women also smiled at "Beth" more than at "Adam." Will and his associates note that the mothers seemed entirely unaware they were engaging in sex-role stereotyping (Will, Self, & Datan, 1976).

More recently, NYU psychologist Nancy Weitzman and her colleagues observed both traditional and "feminist" mothers telling stories and talking to their young children. No matter what their orientation, mothers of sons asked them more questions, particularly those beginning with the word "what." They also used more numbers and more action verbs than when talking to daughters. The NYU researchers conclude that "Mothers, regardless of their attitudes toward women's rights and

According to Will's observations, a woman will play more boisterously with a baby if she is told it is a boy, more gently if told it is a girl.

Limbic system (LIM-bic). Part of the mid-brain that mediates emotional responses.

roles, appear to verbally stimulate their sons more than their daughters on a number of language variables." And in doing so, the mothers may be "subtly and unknowingly steering girls and boys in different directions with regard to intellectual mastery and self-confidence" (Weitzman, Birns, & Friend, 1985).

□ □ **QUESTION** □ □
What benefits do you gain from having ready-made social responses for the males and females you meet?

● *Childhood Stereotyping*

According to Dee Shepherd-Look, children learn by age two that there are some toys that "boys" play with, and others that "girls" play with. By that age, they *self-select* games that are stereotypically "correct" for their gender (Shepherd-Look, 1982).

During childhood, boys are more likely to avoid sex-inappropriate activities and toys than are girls. Apparently the boys' choices are strongly influenced by their parents. Several investigators have found that parents were not concerned when their daughters engaged in sex-inappropriate activities. However, both parents tended to react negatively (and punitively) when their *sons* made sex-inappropriate choices.

Dee Shepherd-Look believes that, by the time children reach puberty, society has "shaped" them into *perceiving their own sexu-*

ality in a socially-approved manner (Shepherd-Look, 1982).

□ □ **QUESTION** □ □
As we noted, many homosexuals show "gender-inappropriate" behaviors as children *despite* strong societal pressures to conform. What does this fact tell you about the relative importance of genetic and social/ behavioral factors in determining sex roles?

"Choice" Versus Genes and Society

There is ample evidence that sexual motivation is influenced by your genes *and* by what society has taught you is "appropriate" to your gender. However, both the biological and the social/behavioral viewpoints are incomplete in one important respect: Neither approach pays much attention to *personal feelings and motives*. Despite Wilson's theorizing on the matter, most humans apparently do not marry, mate, and rear children *primarily* because they consciously wish to reproduce their own genes. And many people engage in a variety of sexual activities *despite* society's standards rather than *because* of them.

Most intra-psychic psychologists would argue that *pleasure* is a critical element in shaping all aspects of sexuality. From an intra-psychic point of view, you *choose* your sexual acts for many reasons, but primarily because they "feel good"—that is, because they are rewarding or satisfying in some way. With that thought in mind, let's look at what pleasure is—particularly sexual pleasure—and where this delightful aspect of human experience may come from.

THE PLEASURE CENTERS

When scientists first began sticking electrodes into the brains of rats and other animals, they found that stimulation of a few parts of the **limbic system** caused the animals to react as if they had experienced sharp, biting pain (see Fig. 7.4). This discovery was, at first, surprising because, as we saw earlier, there are *no pain receptors* in the brain itself (Kimble, 1987).

These scientists suspected they had tapped into what are now called the "avoidance centers" of the brain. So they began to map out as many different regions of the brain as they could, trying to find out how extensive these "avoidance areas" really were. As it turned out, these centers are not very extensive at all. You can stimulate more than 99 percent of the brain electrically without getting an avoidance reaction from the animal (Hoebel & Novin, 1982). However, this search paid unexpected dividends when, in the early 1950's, two psychologists working in Canada discovered that electri-

FIG. 7.4 The limbic system. Structures labeled are generally considered to be part of the limbic system.

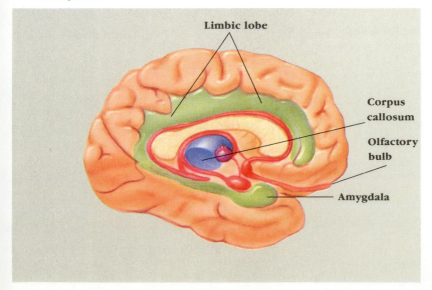

Limbic lobe

Corpus callosum

Olfactory bulb

Amygdala

cal stimulation to certain parts of the brain can have *pleasurable* consequences.

● Olds and Milner's Discovery

James Olds took his doctorate in psychology at Harvard in 1952. Then, because Olds was interested in the biological processes underlying motivation, he went to McGill University in Montreal to work with the noted psychobiologist Peter Milner.

Olds and Milner implanted electrodes in the "avoidance areas" in the brains of white rats, then let the animals run about on the top of a table. When the rat would move toward one particular corner of the table, Olds and Milner would turn on the current. The rat typically would stop, then turn around and move in the opposite direction. The animal subsequently *avoided* that particular corner of the table even if not given any more electrical stimulation.

However, one day Olds and Milner made a glorious mistake—they stuck a electrode in the wrong place in one rat's brain. When this animal started moving toward one of the corners of the table, Olds and Milner turned on the electrical current as usual. But this rat stopped, sniffed, and then moved a step or two *forward*!

Olds and Milner assumed the current wasn't strong enough to have any effect, so they turned up the juice and stimulated the animal again. And once again, the rat twitched its nose rather vigorously, and then moved several steps forward. The more Olds and Milner stimulated the rat's brain, the more eager it became to get to the corner. Finally, the animal reached the corner, sat down, and refused to move! It is to Olds and Milner's credit that, instead of thinking the rat was "sick" or "abnormal," they realized at once they had discovered a part of the rat brain where electrical stimulation was obviously very *rewarding* (see Fig. 7.5) (Olds & Milner, 1954).

We now know there are dozens of neural centers in the brains of most mammals (including humans) which, when stimulated electrically or chemically, will give the animal the subjective experience of *pleasure*. Most of these "pleasure centers" are located either in the hypothalamus or in the *limbic system* (see Fig. 7.4) (Hoebel & Novin, 1982).

● Pleasure or Compulsion?

In animals such as the white rat, neural excitation in these "pleasure centers" causes a strange and oddly *compulsive* set of behaviors to occur. Suppose we rig up a small, rat-sized box with a lever in it (see Fig. 7.6). The lever is connected to a electrical stimulator so that every time the rat presses on the lever, the animal stimulates one of the "reward centers" in its own brain. Will the rat press the bar very often?

FIG. 7.5 James Olds (right) and Peter Milner discovered that stimulating certain parts of a rat's brain seems "rewarding" to the animal.

The answer is yes—very often indeed. Under these conditions, a rat will "self-stimulate" (by pressing the lever) as often as a hundred times a *minute*. It will continue to do so hour after hour after hour—until it collapses in exhaustion. Then the rat will sleep a while until it regains its strength. But as soon as it wakes up, the animal typically starts pressing the lever again. And if we offer this rat the chance to bar-press as a reward for problem-solving behavior, it will learn highly complicated mazes just to get a few whacks at the lever (Kimble, 1987).

The *physiological response* the animal makes to each stimulation of its pleasure centers is, apparently, very similar to an *innate reflex* such as the "knee-jerk." Depending on

FIG. 7.6 A single-lever rat box.

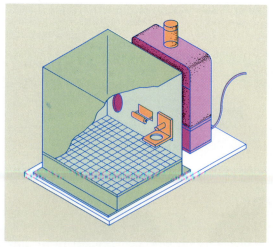

which part of its brain is receiving the electricity, the animal may shiver briefly, move its mouth as if eating, or even discharge a tiny drop of semen after each stimulation.

These facts suggest there must be a direct connection of some kind between the specific sensory receptors associated with satisfying each type of need and a specific pleasure center (or centers) in the brain. Once Olds and Milner had shown the way, psychologists began looking for just those connections.

Current animal research indicates that some parts of the rat brain are associated with sexual pleasure, while other parts are associated with eating or drinking pleasures. For instance, if we put an electrode in one of the "sex reward centers" of a male rat's brain, the animal will bar-press much more *compulsively* if it has been sexually deprived than if it has copulated recently. However, if we castrate the rat, we find that it presses the lever less and less frequently on the days following the operation. Apparently, as it uses up all the male hormone left in its body after castration, it finds the electrical stimulation less and less pleasurable (Kimble, 1987).

Orgasm and Other Human Pleasures

In humans, sexual pleasure is a *combination* of physical and psychological factors. This is particularly the case as far as sex is concerned. Orgasm, for example, is a reflex mediated by neural activity in (1) the spinal cord and (2) the pleasure centers in the *limbic system. Both* neural systems typically must be activated for orgasm to occur.

Neural firing in the spinal cord associated with orgasm leads to a massive arousal of the **autonomic nervous system**, similar to that which occurs during great fear or anger. Indeed, orgasm in the human male is as physically demanding as is climbing a steep flight of stairs. And according to Tulane psychiatrist Robert Heath, the electrical activity that occurs in the pleasure centers during orgasm is as intense as "what the whole brain experiences during epileptic seizure" (cited in Gallagher, 1986).

The right hemisphere also seems to be involved in the production of human orgasm. According to Raymond Rosen, Alan Cohen, and Leonide Goldstein, there is a large increase in electrical activity in the "nondominant" brain hemisphere from several minutes before orgasm until the moment it occurs. This increased electrical activity also occurs in normal males when they are exposed to erotic material—but does not occur in men who are im-

potent (Rosen, Cohen, & Goldstein, 1985). "We think that impotent men are either anxious or unable to immerse themselves in physical sensations during sex," Rosen says (cited in Meer, 1986).

However, neural firing *by itself* doesn't determine whether an orgasm will occur, or whether it will be *perceived* as pleasurable. Those women and men who have volunteered to have their "sex reward centers" tickled with electricity typically reported the experience as being mildly pleasant—but something they could take or leave. And physiologist Joseph Bohlen reports there is little or no correlation between *subjective perception of pleasure* and *intensity of physical arousal*. Bohlen asked his subjects to rate the "pleasurability" of their orgasms while he was taking 13 different physiological measures of arousal. He reports that very often, orgasms that were "weakest" from a physical point of view were those that were experienced as being most pleasant, and those that involved massive physical arousal were frequently perceived as being the least pleasurable (cited in Gallagher, 1986).

SEX IS MULTI-DETERMINED

Sexuality in humans is obviously a complex experience that is multi-determined. And we still have much to learn. William Masters puts it this way: "The science of sexuality is in its infancy, and there's no one orientation to it—not medicine only, not behavioral science only, but also theology, social work, politics, on and on. No matter what your background, there's always some postgraduate work to do" (cited in Gallagher, 1986).

What we do know is this: The androgens, estrogens, and progesterone shape our bodies, bias our brains, and energize our behaviors. But *overriding* these biological motivations are the neural commands that come from the higher centers of our brains. And these neural commands are primarily learned or the product of voluntary choice.

Society influences your choice in such matters by providing you with models of "appropriate" behaviors. Some of these models are arbitrary, and may vary markedly from one culture to another. Other models, though, may be based on "genetic reality," for males typically are larger and stronger than females are. And because males typically have more testosterone than do females, men are more likely to *want* to engage in a wide variety of physical activities—including sexual behaviors—than are women. On the other hand, females can bear and nurse children, while males cannot. These facts subtly shape—*but do not entirely determine*—sex-role stereotypes. And no matter what our social or political beliefs, we cannot ignore the biological factor in sex. As University of Massachusetts psychologist Alice Rossi put it recently, "An ideology that does not confront this basic issue is an exercise in wishful thinking, and a social science that does not confront it is sterile" (Rossi, 1985).

However, in the final analysis, it is the *interaction* of genetic, psychological, and social factors that helps make sex the fascinating topic that it is—and probably always will be.

SUMMARY

1. Sexual needs have a **biological basis**, but differ from hunger and thirst in that they are necessary for the survival of the species, but not the individual.
2. John B. Watson studied the female sexual response, but lost his professorship because of his research.
3. Alfred Kinsey published the first **scientific survey** of sexual behavior in 1948. The first studies of actual **human sexual behavior** were made by Masters and Johnson.
4. You began life as a single **egg cell** that contained 23 **chromosomes**. At the moment of **fertilization**, one of your father's sperms penetrated the egg and added 23 chromosomes of its own.
5. If an **X sperm** unites with the egg, the 23rd chromosome will be **XX**, and the child will be a genetic female. If a **Y sperm** unites with the egg, the 23rd chromosome will be **XY**, and the child will be a genetic male.
6. The **sex hormones** are secreted by the **adrenal glands** that sit atop the kidneys and by the **gonads**, the **testes** in males and the **ovaries** in females.
7. The male hormones are called **androgens**, the best known of which is **testosterone**. The female hormones are the **estrogens** and **progesterone**.
8. Testosterone promotes sexual behavior in **both sexes**. The female hormones primarily influence **child bearing** and **child rearing**, but have their strongest influences in the lower animals.
9. Both male and female hormones are found in both sexes. It is the relative amount of these hormones during **critical developmental periods** that determines **primary** and **secondary sex** characteristics.
10. The sexual behavior of the **ring dove** is controlled by a complex interaction between hormone levels and the **mating behaviors** of the male and female dove.
11. **Intra-psychic** aspects of sexual motivation include **sexual orientation**, **sexual identity**, and **sex roles**.
12. The three main types of sexual orientation are **heterosexual, bisexual**, and **homosexual**. Orientation is influenced by biological, intra-psychic, and cultural factors.
13. Although heterosexuality is the dominant orientation, some 10 percent of the population is primarily homosexual in orientation. Another 10 percent is probably bisexual.
14. **Children** reared by homosexual parents show little **gender confusion** and mostly have a **heterosexual orientation**.
15. **Bisexuals** often are more interested in the **social** aspects of sexuality than are people who are purely homosexual or heterosexual.
16. Children with **hormonal problems** who are reared as the "wrong sex" tend to respond to **cultural pressures** concerning gender identity rather than to biological urges.
17. Children **become aware** of their sexual orientation and gender identity long before **puberty**.
18. **Sex-role stereotypes** are widely-shared concepts that prescribe how each sex ought to behave.
19. **Sociobiology** is a theory by Edward O. Wilson, who assumes your **major motive** in life is to increase the odds your **genes** will survive. Wilson believes **sex roles** stem from the differing strategies males and females adopt to gain **reproductive advantage**.
20. **Stereotyping** begins at birth and affects the way people **perceive** males and females—and the way they perceive themselves.
21. Sexual behavior is strongly influenced in lower animals by **pleasure centers** in the animals' brains. Electrical stimulation of these centers leads to **compulsive behaviors** in the rat, but not in the human.
22. **Orgasm** involves massive physical arousal and great electrical activity in the **limbic system**. However, the **pleasurability** of orgasm is determined by psychological and social factors, not by intensity of physical arousal.

Sexual attraction and expression are complex phenomena, influenced by a multitude of factors.

"Why not, Clare?" Bill Meyer asked his fiancee. "You assume that our daughter Christine would *want* to wear men's clothes. So why wouldn't our son Christopher *want* to wear dresses and pantyhose?"

Clare Wilson frowned as she considered the matter. "Well," she said finally. "I guess I see what you're getting at. I know only too well the sort of stupid male prejudices against women my daughter will face. Maybe I'd never given much thought to what sorts of social constraints my son will have to put up with."

(Continued from page 176.)

"Right on," Bill said. "You women are convinced that men have locked you into a rigid social role of some kind. Well, men are at least as locked into a male 'role model' as women are—and maybe more. It always ticked me off that women demanded the right to wear men's clothes, and heaven help the man who got upset. Yet if a man appears on television dressed in pantyhose, you think he's a disgrace of some kind."

Clare grinned. "Yes, and so do you."

"Not if he's making as much money as Joe Namath did," Bill said, laughing. "But the point is, why do you approve of women who take on male characteristics, but get upset when a man acts in a feminine way?"

Clare paused for a moment. "It is odd, isn't it? I guess I see men as being socially superior in some strange way. When women dress like men—or act in a traditionally masculine way—they're just trying to improve their status in society. But when a man acts like a woman . . ."

"Then he's giving up status," Bill said. "And that does seem unnatural to all of us. But if men and women are *really* equal, then . . ."

". . . Then both men and women should be free to act as they wish," Clare said thoughtfully. "Yes, I can understand the logic behind that point. And maybe it's the same thing with blacks or any minority group. We can understand when they dress and behave like the dominant group in society. We even encourage them to take on the values of white, middle-class Americans, and think it's great when they do."

Bill nodded. "But saints preserve any white, middle-class person who tries to act or talk 'black.' Unless they're doing it as an obvious joke, we see 'black talk' by whites as being abnormal because it involves a voluntary loss of social status."

Clare sighed. "I guess we won't really be an unprejudiced society until we allow all people to act and feel any way their genetic makeup dictates, eh?" After a moment's hesitation, she continued. "But how can we be sure it's our genes, and not our social prejudices, that make us feel that a particular behavior is either normal or abnormal? There *must* be some way to tell the difference."

Bill glanced at the television screen. Greg Norman was still ahead in the golf tournament, but Calvin Peete was only one stroke behind going into the 17th hole. "You mean, like, men are more interested in sports, while women are more interested in library books and opera and stuff like that."

"Now, Bill," Clare said teasingly. "You know that women are just as sports-minded as men are."

"No, they're not," Bill replied, refusing to be baited by Clare's comment. "There's never been a culture in the history of the world where that was true. My psych prof was talking about that just a few days ago. Young male monkeys roughhouse three times as much as female monkeys do. Same thing with all the primates. The males are almost always bigger, stronger, and more physically active. Now, don't get me wrong. Women are *good* at lots of sports, and better than men at some, particularly at skills that require fine motor coordination. But, on the average, men are just more interested in physical challenges than women are."

Clare smiled. "And you think that's a genetic difference between men and women?"

Bill nodded. "Sure, just like their sexual interests are different."

"There you go again, Bill."

"Oh, come off it, Clare," Bill replied, having temporarily forgotten the golf tournament. "Women are just as interested in sex as men are. It took me a long time to realize that, but it's true. It's just that men and women are concerned about different aspects of the sexual experience."

"I should hope so."

"I should hope so too. If we weren't, we wouldn't have families and children," Bill replied.

"What do you mean?"

Bill thought a minute. "Well, somebody's got to make sure that sex occurs, so there will be children. And maybe that's the man's job. Men have more testosterone, and that makes them physically more active in all sorts of ways. And maybe that's part of what sports and social aggression are all about. But historically speaking, at least, it's been the woman's job to see that the children were fed and taken care of properly. And you've got a biological advantage over men in that department, you must admit."

Clare straightened her shoulders. "Now, Bill . . ." she said demurely.

"It's true, and I'm glad of it," Bill said in a playful tone of voice.

"But that still doesn't give you the right to talk about sex all the time," Clare said, trying to regain control of the conversation.

"You talk about it all the time, too, Clare. Only you call it 'commitment,' or 'our relationship,' or 'feelings.' But it amounts to the same thing."

"It does *not* amount to the same thing," Clare replied.

"Yes, it does. To a man, sex is an act that leads to child bearing. So the man thinks most about how to get the woman to 'do it.' That's his desire for physical activity, I'd guess. But to a woman, sex is an act that leads to child rearing. And to make sure that the man is around to help take care of the kids, she's got to get some kind of commitment out of the guy, so that he doesn't run off after every skirt he sees. So she thinks about how to get a loving relationship going. But it's still sex she's thinking about and talking about."

"And you think that sort of psychological difference is *genetic*?"

"I don't know of any data on the subject but it seems logical to me."

Clare considered the matter. "But what about the women's equality movement? Are we wrong to try to get men to do those things—like cooking and changing diapers—that have always been foisted off on women by the dominant males?"

Bill laughed. "Well, we can share the labor of taking care of the kids, but we can't share the labor pains, if you know what I mean."

"Ouch," said Clare, a hint of laughter in her voice.

"And I suspect that men are at least as good at taking care of kids as women are—maybe better."

"Better? What do you mean?" Clare said in surprise.

"Just last week my psych professor quoted a recent study showing that infants are more relaxed when held by their fathers than by their mothers. Maybe learning how to cradle a football in your arms teaches you how to cradle a baby, or something like that."

Clare sighed. "Okay, so you don't object to men and women sharing the burden of child rearing. That's progress, at least. But how do we get men to treat women like equals in *all* situations?"

"You can do that only if you give men something they want in return."

"Like?"

"Oh, like a lot of things. Like not demanding that we see the world from your viewpoint unless you're willing to look at things from the male point of view too. Like not demanding that a male 'commit' to a woman, and then telling him he's got a dirty mind when he wants sex in return. Maybe even admitting that you're as interested in the sexual *act* as men are."

"I'll have to think about that for awhile," Clare replied. Then she stood up, walked over to Bill, and put her arms around him. "What you're saying is that even if the equality movement succeeds, there will always be some differences in the way that men and women act and feel. Just because their genders are different."

"If men and women looked and acted exactly the same, it wouldn't be nearly as much fun as it is now, would it?"

"Well, I guess if society treats men and women as equals, it wouldn't hurt if we were different in *some* minor details."

"*Vive la différence,*" Bill said.

Emotion, Stress, and Coping

"The Stress of Life"

· C·H·A·P·T·E·R ·
8

STUDY QUESTIONS

As you read through the chapter, see if you can find the answers to the following questions:

1. What is the relationship between motivation and emotion?
2. What are the five important elements of emotionality?
3. According to the theory of the triune brain, how did your brain evolve?
4. How does removal of the amygdala affect behavior?
5. Why did psychosurgery become so popular?
6. How do the sympathetic and the parasympathetic nervous systems jointly bring about homeostasis?
7. Why is Freud's theory of the emotions often called an "energy theory"?
8. How do most cognitive theorists define emotion?
9. What is "learned helplessness"?
10. What is the difference between "externalizers" and "internalizers"?
11. According to Carol Tavris, what are the actual consequences of expressing anger openly?
12. What are the three stages of Selye's General Adaptation Syndrome?
13. According to Charles Darwin, how do an animal's emotions help it survive?

Pilot David Milne pressed the button on his microphone and said, "Tower, this is Mid-Continental flight 474 heavy, turning onto downwind leg."

The radio squawked and bleeped in Dave Milne's ear for a second or two, and then the voice of the traffic controller in the tower came through loud and clear: "Mid-Continental 474 heavy, this is the tower. Descend to 3,000 feet and maintain speed 220 knots."

Dave Milne answered smartly, "Roger, Tower. Mid-Continental 474 heavy descending to 3,000, maintaining 220." The airport complex was clearly visible to Dave through the cockpit windows as he banked the heavy, wide-bodied jet and headed "downwind" past the runway he would eventually be landing on. The actual landing was a few minutes away, however, and Dave had a thousand things to do before he could bring his huge plane safely to ground. He glanced briefly at his copilot, who was going one-by-one through the long "checklist" of operations involved in the landing. In fact, his copilot this trip was Mid-Continental's Senior Instructor, who was checking Dave out in the wide-bodied jet, and Dave certainly wanted to make a good impression on the man.

Although Dave felt mildly stressed by the situation, he relaxed momentarily and grinned. This landing was going to be a piece of cake. He had been a pilot with Mid-Continental Airlines for nearly 15 years, working his way up until he was captain of one of the smaller jets. Now he was switching over to the wide-bodied planes most passengers preferred these days. The change-over meant Dave had to learn many new skills, but he was confident he had mastered them all. A piece of cake, he told himself.

The tower controller's voice crackled through Dave's earphones again. "Mid-Continent 474 heavy, descend to 2,000, maintain 220 knots."

Dave acknowledged the controller's order, nodded to his copilot, and pointed the nose of the huge plane down a bit so that it would lose a thousand feet in altitude. Most pilots liked to say that flying a jet was a two-stage operation—you had hours of routine boredom while the plane was cruising at altitude, relieved by a few minutes of sheer terror when you took off or brought the jet in for a landing. Dave agreed, and he had had his share of hair-raising experiences during landings and take-offs. Particularly in bad weather. But the weather today was clear and the winds were light. Piece of cake, he told himself.

"Mid-Continent 474 heavy, turn left to 270, descend to 1,500, reduce speed to 200 knots," came the voice from the tower.

Again Dave acknowledged the command. He banked the plane to the left until it had completed a 90 degree turn, and slowed the engines down a bit. Then he extended the flaps on the wings to give the huge ship the additional "lift" it needed when flying "low and slow." Almost unconsciously he noted that the whining sound of the jet engines had decreased in intensity as he slowed the plane down for its landing. Piece of cake . . .

And then the terror started. Completely without warning, the copilot said in a loud voice, "Fire in number three engine!"

Instantly alert, Dave hit the emergency controls that would stop the flow of fuel and turn on the fire extinguishers in the number three engine. A fraction of a second later, he pushed forward the throttles on the other two engines to compensate for the loss of power. The wide-bodied jet had three engines—one on each wing, and one in the tail section. The plane could land safely on two engines—or even on just one, in a pinch. But all pilots were terrified by a fire anywhere in the plane. And they particularly feared a fire that started in an engine. Engines were simply too close to the plane's supply of fuel.

"Fire in number three engine extinguished!" the copilot cried.

Dave breathed a brief sigh of relief and began talking on the radio. "Tower, this is Mid-Continental 474 heavy. We've lost an engine! Request clearance for emergency landing!"

Moments later, the controller's voice came booming over the earphones. "Mid-Continental 474 heavy, you are cleared for a direct approach to the runway for an emergency landing. Fire trucks standing by. How can we help?"

Before Dave could respond, the copilot yelled at him, "Fire in number one engine!"

With one hand, Dave banked the plane and headed straight for the runway. With his other hand, he shut off the fuel and turned on the fire extinguishers in the number one engine. The stall warning alarm came on loudly, telling him that the plane was flying too slowly. Instantly Dave increased the power to the number two engine—the only one he had left—and prayed that he wouldn't run out of altitude before they reached the end of the runway.

"Fire still out of control," the copilot yelled.

Red warning lights flashed on several instruments. Dave tried to glance at each of them, to see what else had gone wrong with his ship. But he was too occupied with keeping the plane aloft and heading it toward the end of the runway to worry about them all. Safety was only a couple of miles away now—if he could get the plane there.

"Mayday, Tower, mayday. We've lost a second engine. I think we can make it, but . . ."

Suddenly the cockpit began to shake violently. The control panel lit up with so many flashing lights it looked like a Christmas tree gone wild. The stall warning screamed loudly for his attention, as did several other buzzing alarms. Dave felt an icy stab of terror in his heart as he tried desperately to take in and evaluate all the information that was assaulting his eyes and ears. And there, so close, just a couple of thousand feet away, lay the end of the runway.

"Stall speed! Stall speed!" the copilot cried.

8 / Emotion, Stress, and Coping

Dave lowered the nose of the plane a couple of degrees in order to pick up speed, but the ship was flying so slowly now that it was difficult to handle. He fought with the controls, trying desperately to keep the wings level and aim the plane so it would touch ground just past the end of the runway. For a few brief seconds, despite the screaming alarms and the flashing lights, everything seemed to be under control, when . . .

"Fire in number two engine!" the copilot screamed.

Again Dave shut off the fuel and turned on the fire extinguishers. The jet's rate of descent increased rapidly, as if it had a burning desire to kiss the earth immediately. Dave pulled the nose up a little, scared green they didn't have enough momentum left to reach the runway. But suddenly, miraculously, the plane crossed over the end of the runway, flopping down like a wounded bird toward the narrow ribbon of concrete now less than 50 feet beneath them. They'd made it! Three engines gone, but they'd made it!

And then, without warning, the cockpit shuddered violently, and the world outside the cockpit windows went black. The control panel lights flicked off, the alarms stopped, and everything was still.

Dave sat there, stunned, wondering what had happened.

Then the copilot looked over at him and smiled. "Well, Dave, you just smashed up $60 million worth of airplane and killed 300 passengers. How do you feel?"

Dave, still in shock, shook his head slowly. "What happened? We were headed straight in, and we had enough altitude. We should have greased right in . . ."

The copilot grinned. "Sure. But you forgot one thing."

"Forgot?" Dave said, a puzzled frown on his face.

"Yeah," the copilot said. "You handled the fires in the three engines pretty good, son. But you forgot to lower the landing gear."

Dave Milne shook his head groggily. "I guess I really bought the farm that time, didn't I?"

The copilot nodded and got up out of his seat. "You're not the first, Dave. We all do it." He patted Dave on the shoulder. "Come on, friend, I'll buy you a cup of coffee, and we'll talk it over. And then we'll try it again."

(Continued on page 218.)

EMOTIONS

In Chapter 6, we said that the term "motivation" was derived from the Latin word meaning "to move." There is another common psychological term which also comes from the same Latin source: "emotion."

Motivated behaviors usually involve *trying to achieve a goal*. Emotional responses typically are associated with *actually achieving or not achieving a goal*. Thus, emotion and motivation are related, since they both are concerned with goal-oriented activities.

But emotions are more than just behaviors. If you experience great anger, your mouth goes dry, your stomach may churn, and your muscles may tense. You also "feel" this anger "inside you." You typically *perceive* what caused your anger, and can "categorize" the experience as being anger rather than hate or love. In addition, you probably are conscious of how being angry alters your own thoughts and actions, and how expressing your anger affects the people around you. Thus, you may choose to suppress your rage—or to express it—depending on what you think the consequences will be. Emotions, as you can see, are exceptionally complex experiences.

Unfortunately, there is no one definition of the term "emotion" that all scientists will agree upon. For instance, in a recent book, several distinguished psychologists attempt to describe what emotionality is all about. Carroll Izard writes that, "A given emotion is defined as the integration of a particular set of neurochemical, motor, and mental processes." However, another contributor states that, "Human emotion is conceived to be a motivation-laden feeling resulting jointly from shifts in arousal and from the meaning attached to those arousal shifts." In the same book, Robert Zajonc and Hazel Markus contend that "In the extreme case, only [physical] arousal is a necessary consequence of the generation of emotion." However, several other writers insist that "There is little evidence to support the position that arousal is necessary for emotional experience or that arousal is a needed concept in the field of emotion" (Izard, Kagan, & Zajonc, 1984).

Whether or not we express a strong emotion may depend on the response we expect to get from those around us. These people cried openly on the street after the murder of John Lennon.

Emotions   **197**

Nor is there any agreement on how to *measure* emotions. Those psychologists who see emotions primarily as subjective "feelings" insist that only verbal reports by people experiencing the emotion are worth studying. Other scientists rely almost entirely on test scores. Still others—particularly those who focus on the biological correlates of human experience—insist that only physiological measures of neural or biochemical *arousal* can be trusted (Izard, Kagan, & Zajonc, 1984).

Five Elements of Emotionality

Given the diversity of opinion among experts as to what emotion is (and how best to measure it), how can we tie all the aspects of this complex subject together in one neat package? The answer is, not very easily. However, the five elements of emotionality mentioned most often by various theorists are the following:

- Physical arousal or depression.
- Feelings—usually those of pleasure or displeasure.
- Cognitive awareness and appraisal of the experience.
- Emotionally expressive behaviors.
- Environmental inputs and consequences.

Various theorists tend to emphasize one or more of these five elements. Generally speaking, though, we can divide the theories into the familiar three categories of "biological, intrapsychic, and social/behavioral."

● Biological Theorists

To many biologically-oriented scientists, emotion is primarily a *physical reaction* that involves rather special parts of your nervous system. To these scientists, your emotions have two major purposes: (1) to *arouse* your body for some kind of specific action (such as fighting or fleeing), or (2) to *depress* physical responses so your body can repair itself (Zajonc, 1984).

For the most part, biological theorists tend to see emotions as "instinctual survival mechanisms." For example, *pain* causes intensely unpleasant feelings that arouse you to move away from some inputs or, in the case of hunger, toward other inputs. And *fear* is a drive that prevents you from approaching a dangerous situation before it can become painful. We will discuss the biological viewpoint more fully in a moment, when we describe the various "arousal mechanisms" in your body.

● Intra-psychic Theorists

Some intra-psychic theorists emphasize the role of *subjective feelings*. Others focus on the *cognitive* aspects of emotionality.

Those psychologists interested in "feelings" often use terms such as *moods, passions,* and **affect** to describe the inner experiences associated with emotionality. Just as commonly, they will employ the terms *pleasant* and *unpleasant*. For example, James Averill notes that most people assume emotional responses are "impulsive, uncharacteristic, involuntary, and irrational (or at least not deliberate)." Thus, Averill says, we tend to perceive emotions as "passions"—things that happen to people—rather than being "actions," or things that people do (Averill, 1982). For the most part, "feeling" psychologists tend to believe emotions are unconscious and unlearned.

Those theorists interested in "cognitions" tend to focus on *conscious awareness* of subjective experiences. They often use phrases such as *cognitive appraisal of an experience*, or *value judgments* in trying to explain emotionality. Most cognitive psychologists believe your *perception* of a situation creates both your physical arousal and your subjective feelings (Lazarus, 1984).

● Social/Behavioral Theorists

Those theorists who take a behavioral viewpoint often think of emotions as *expressive responses*. They do not speak of fear, but rather of fearful reactions to some external stimulus. They talk not of depression, but rather of massive inactivity or unresponsiveness.

However, many social psychologists hold that emotions do not exist just "in the mind" or just "in the body." Rather, these theorists say, your emotions are a product of your *interactions with your environment*. You learn to respond to situations in certain stereotyped ways. You also learn to "label" your feelings in a manner that will justify your feelings to yourself and to others. Furthermore, you *construct* (or *use*) your emotional outbursts to achieve certain ends, and to communicate your inner experiences to others. According to these theorists, therefore, emotions are primarily determined by past and present *social inputs* (Averill, 1982).

□ □ **QUESTION** □ □
Which of the "five elements of emotionality" does each of these theoretical viewpoints seem to stress?

● Emotions and Stress

There is one point almost all psychologists agree upon, however: Whatever emotions are, and wherever they come from, they often can be *stressful* to the body and mind. Which is to say that, for the most part, your feelings involve the expenditure of physical, mental, and behavioral *energy*. Learning to cope with your emotions, therefore, requires learning how to handle the stresses and strains of life.

In the first part of this chapter, we will look at your emotions from the biological, intra-

Affect (AFF-fect). A psychological term meaning the conscious aspect of an emotion apart from any physical or behavioral reaction. Also means the visible display of an emotional experience. If you "lack affect," you don't respond emotionally—presumably because you don't experience any inner feelings.

Limbic system (LIM-bick). A related set of nerve centers in your brain that influences your emotional behavior.

Autonomic nervous system (aw-toh-NOM-ick). *Autonomic* means "automatic" or "reflexive," "without volition." The autonomic nervous system is a collection of neural centers which takes care of most of your normal body functions (breathing, pumping of the blood, digestion, emotional reactions) that occur automatically—without your having to think about them.

Theory of the triune brain (try-YOUN). A theory by Paul MacLean that there are three main divisions of the brain, each of which evolved from the brains of ancient animals. The brain stem evolved from the reptilian brain, the middle parts of the brain (thalamus, limbic system) evolved from ancient mammals, and the cerebrum evolved from more recent mammals. Each of the three parts of the brain supposedly controls different behaviors patterns. Not all scientists agree with MacLean's theory.

Brain stem. The lower area of the brain that connects the spinal cord with the middle parts of the brain.

Pons, medulla (me-DULL-ah). Neural centers in the brain stem that control vital activities such as walking and breathing.

Cerebellum (ser-ee-BELL-um). From the Latin word meaning "little brain." A large center of neural tissue at the rear of the brain, just below the occipital lobe, that coordinates muscle movements (among other things).

psychic, and social/behavioral viewpoints. We will pay particular attention to such important emotional reactions as fear, anger, rage, and aggression. Then we will discuss various ways to cope with emotional stress. Finally, we will define emotions from a holistic point of view and show how they are related to cognition (and other) activities.

THE BIOLOGY OF EMOTIONS

Those psychologists who view emotionality as primarily a biological event tend to perceive emotional reactions as being your body's way of preparing to respond to some kind of physical or psychological challenge. Perhaps you are in danger; then you must prepare yourself either to fight (in anger or rage) or to get out of the threatening situation because you are afraid. Or perhaps you are hungry and discover some food; then you must calm yourself down so that you can consume and digest your meal in comfort. In either case, your biological reactions are likely to be *reflexive* and hence *beyond your voluntary control.*

Put in simple terms, biological theorists tend to view emotions such as rage as "animal instincts" or "unruly passions" that civilized humans must constantly strive to control. Because of this perceptual bias, many biological theorists believe that "emotional problems" can only be "cured" by means of *physical treatment,* such as pills and surgery.

The two major parts of your nervous system that mediate emotional responses are the **limbic system** and the **autonomic nervous system**. We'll describe both of these neural systems in some detail in just a moment. First,

Paul MacLean

however, let's briefly discuss the three major divisions of your brain. Doing so will give us some important hints as to why biological theorists view emotions as they do.

The Triune Brain

Paul MacLean is a noted neurophysiologist who believes the human brain evolved over millions of years from the brains of lower animals. But this evolution took place in three main stages, says MacLean, and thus the human brain has three main parts. MacLean calls this belief the **theory of the triune brain**.

According to MacLean, the first animals to develop a true brain were the ancient reptiles. This *reptilian brain* still exists inside your head, says MacLean, in the form of your **brain stem** (see Fig. 8.1). Your brain stem includes such neural structures as the **pons** and the **medulla**. The pons and the medulla are nerve centers that help control such vital activities as walking, breathing, and swallowing. The brain stem also is the main pathway for conducting messages between your brain and your *autonomic nervous system* and hence mediates emotional arousal and depression (MacLean, 1980).

Over millions of years, the ancient mammals evolved from the reptiles. And in the evolutionary process, MacLean says, many additional neural structures got tacked onto the reptilian brain. MacLean calls these "tacked on" nerve centers the *old mammalian brain.* (Other neuroscientists often refer to the old mammalian brain as the "mid-brain.") The most important parts of this old mammalian brain are the *thalamus*, the *hypothalamus*, and the *limbic system*.

According to MacLean's theory, as the mammals themselves evolved—from rat to cat to elephant to monkey—they acquired the huge cerebral hemispheres that make up the major part of the human brain. MacLean calls this the *new mammalian brain*, which is composed of the the cerebrum (and the cortex), the corpus callosum, and the **cerebellum**.

• Functions of the "Three Brains"

MacLean notes that your "reptilian brain" is incredibly more complex than the brain of any snake or lizard. And your "old mammalian" brain is likewise much more developed than (say) the brain of a rat or cat. Small wonder, then, that your thoughts and feelings and actions are so much more complicated than either a snake's or a rat's.

MacLean tends to assign certain psychological functions to the three types of brain. For instance, he believes that the brain stem controls certain *inherited* types of behaviors, such as walking and breathing. According to MacLean, these "automatic" behavior patterns are primarily determined by your genes and

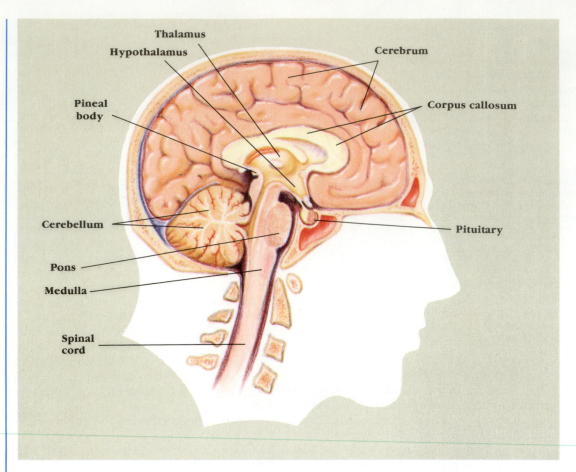

FIG. 8.1 A midsagittal section through the brain. Note that in this type of section half of the brain is cut away so that structures normally covered by the cerebrum are exposed.

function almost entirely at an unconscious level.

The old mammalian brain mediates "instinctual" emotional reactions as anger, rage, and aggression. The old mammalian brain also controls those activities involved in satisfying bodily needs. The old mammalian brain is, however, capable of *learning* new response patterns and thus is not restricted entirely to expressing inherited behaviors.

It is your "new brain," though, that gives you the capacity for learning to speak, to think creatively, and to deal with the rich array of informational inputs that come to you from the complex world you live in. It is also true, MacLean says, that your cortex and your cerebral hemispheres are capable of *coordinating* the activities of the two more "primitive" areas of your brain. Thus, given the proper training, you can learn to *control* such instinctual behaviors as aggression. However, anything that *disrupts* neural activity in the old mammalian brain might well disrupt cortical control of emotional responses as well.

To put things simply, MacLean believes that, because of the manner in which your nervous system evolved, there is a "primitive animal" lurking deep inside your brain that is likely to burst forth if given half a chance.

Not all scientists agree with MacLean's notions of how the three main parts of the brain evolved. But to show you how they operate—and how your cortex exercises control over the lower centers in your brain—let us now look more closely at what goes on in your limbic system.

□ □ **QUESTION** □ □
What kind of *therapy* would someone like MacLean be likely to prescribe for anyone who suffered from "fits of uncontrollable rage"?

● The Limbic System

The Latin word *limbus* means "border." The limbic system is so named because it makes up the "border" or inner surface of both your cerebral hemispheres. There are identical limbic systems in both your hemispheres. But since they are usually in close touch with each other (via the corpus callosal bridge), we can consider the two systems as one unit.

Your limbic system has several parts or structures to it (see Fig. 8.2). One of these structures is the **amygdala**, which is buried deep within the temporal lobe on each side of your head. The amygdala is a nut-shaped group of neurons that gets its name from the Latin word for "almond." Since the amygdala in each of your temporal lobes has a decided influence on how violent you are, and on your sex life, it is well worth studying.

Aggressive behavior in monkeys has been shown to increase when parts of the limbic system — especially the amygdala — are stimulated.

Cortex Versus Limbic System

Under normal circumstances, your cortex maintains control over the "primitive, emotional reactions" that are set off by activity in your limbic system. But what happens when you *lose cortical control* of the limbic system? In cats and other lower animals, the answer is clear. If we remove the animal's cortex surgically while leaving the limbic system intact, this "de-cortex-ed" (or **decorticate**) animal gets along surprisingly well, considering that it has been deprived of more than 10 percent of its brain. There seems to be no basic change in the animal's personality—friendly cats remain friendly, and aggressive felines remain aggressive. However, even *very slight pain or frustration* is enough to set these animals into an explosive, violent rage (Isaacson, 1974).

Next, what do you think would happen if we "reversed" the kind of operation just described? That is, what if we removed parts of the limbic system in animals but left most of the cortex intact? Heinrich Kl'uever and Paul Bucy were probably the first scientists to perform this operation. Their experimental animals were rhesus monkeys, a species of **primate** noted for its vile temper and its readiness to aggress. Kluever and Bucy removed the temporal lobes from *both* hemispheres in their animals—thus taking out the amygdalas and other parts of the limbic system. After the monkeys had recovered, their personalities appeared to have changed rather profoundly. They were gentle and placid in almost all circumstances, even when attacked by another animal (Kluever & Bucy, 1937). The animals also became markedly *oversexed*. For example, the males would attempt to mount anything handy, including inanimate objects.

Later studies by other scientists confirmed the Kluever and Bucy experiment by showing that removal of the amygdala in several species of wild animals makes them relatively tame (Isaacson, 1974).

Stimulating the Amygdala

Given the results of the Kluever-Bucy study, what do you think would happen if you could somehow *stimulate* the amygdala in a normal cat? The answer is not particularly surprising. If you insert a long, thin needle electrode into a cat's amygdala and turn on the current, the animal flies into a rage. Its hair stands on end, its back arches, it spits and screams, and it will usually attack anything nearby (including the experimenter) (Isaacson, 1974).

Brain Damage and Violence in Humans

Most humans can tolerate a fair amount of stress without becoming violent. Others of us, however, seem to fly off the handle at the slightest provocation. Could it be that individuals who are particularly bad-tempered might suffer from some subtle damage to their amygdalas?

Vernon Mark and Frank Ervin—two scientists who worked together in Boston for many years—believe that senseless human violence is almost always associated with some form of brain damage. Mark and Ervin studied many

FIG. 8.2 The limbic system. Structures labeled are generally considered to be part of the limbic system.

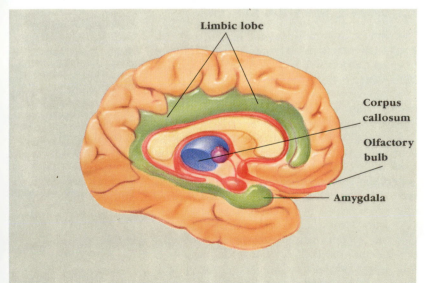

Limbic lobe

Corpus callosum

Olfactory bulb

Amygdala

A minor car accident may be simply an inconvenience for some people, while for others it is an occasion to blow up at the other driver.

patients who were hospitalized because they had killed or maimed others in "fits of rage." Some of these patients also had epileptic-type seizures, and EEG recordings often suggested the presence of scar tissue in their amygdalas.

When drugs and psychotherapy failed to reduce the number of violent attacks these patients had, Mark and Ervin decided to remove the damaged amygdalas surgically. Some of the patients showed a dramatic improvement following the operation. Unfortunately, many of the patients either were unchanged in their behaviors, or even became worse (Mark & Ervin, 1970).

□ □ **QUESTION** □ □

Statistics suggest that violent crime is on the increase in the US. Do you think that *all* violent criminals should have their amygdalas removed forcibly, whether they wished the surgery or not?

● **"Psychosurgery"**

Physicians call operations such as the removal of the amygdala *psychosurgery*, because the purpose of the surgery is to "cure" patients of inappropriate emotions or behaviors that seemingly cannot be "cured" by pills or psychotherapy.

But before we routinely chop up people's brains in order to "make them behave," there are several dangers we should take note of.

1. Mark and Ervin have been able to demonstrate clear-cut brain damage in but a small fraction of the patients they have studied. There is no doubt that people with damaged amygdalas often are violent. However, there is little or no reliable evidence that most people who are violent have damaged amygdalas.

2. Not all of Mark and Ervin's patients were improved after the surgery.

3. Not all scientists have been successful in their attempts to repeat the Mark and Ervin research (Valenstein, 1980).

□ □ **QUESTION** □ □

What kind of experiment might you perform to determine if it were the removal of the amygdala that decreased the patient's violent episodes, or merely the fact that the patient had had an operation of some kind?

● **Why Psychosurgery?**

In his recent book *Great and Desperate Cures*, Michigan psychologist Elliot Valenstein discusses some of the reasons why psychosurgery came to be used—particularly with violent and aggressive patients: (1) Some patients *did* improve, often remarkably (though most did not). (2) The treatment was "cheap and quick," simple to perform, and the death rate was fairly low. (3) Psychosurgery restored prestige to the neurologists, who had "lost turf" over the years to the psychiatrists. (4) Successful case histories received enthusiastic coverage in the popular press (Mark and Ervin's work was frequently documented on televison and got long spreads in several national magazines). (5) The technique seemed to satisfy some deep-felt need to *punish* people who were inappropriately hostile and aggressive (Valenstein, 1986).

Despite the evidence showing that psychosurgery is not a particularly effective way to change behavior, the technique continues to be used on some patients. The people in favor of psychosurgery are primarily those scientists and medical doctors who believe the brain controls the mind, who feel that most emotions are "animal passions" that must be *controlled* if civilization is to survive, and who have little faith that people can *learn self-control*. We will return to this point later.

AUTONOMIC NERVOUS SYSTEM

The limbic system does not *directly* set off emotional reactions in your body. Rather, it does so by means of increasing activity in your *autonomic nervous system*.

Your *autonomic nervous system* is connected to most of the glands and many of the muscles in your body. It has two major parts or divisions: (1) the **sympathetic nervous system** and (2) the **parasympathetic nervous system**. In general, activity in your sympathetic system tends to excite or *arouse* you. Activity in your parasympathetic system tends to *depress* many of your bodily functions.

Your sympathetic and parasympathetic nervous systems work together in a *coordinated* fashion to control your bodily activities. When you need to be aroused, your sympathetic system speeds up, and your parasympa-

The pilomotor response is controlled by the sympathetic nervous system.

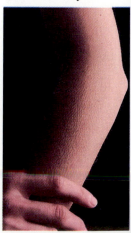

thetic system slows down. When you need to relax and "vegetate," your parasympathetic system increases its neural activities while your sympathetic system slows down. It is the *joint action* of the two systems which allows you to respond appropriately to most of the physical and psychological challenges you meet in life (Kimble, 1987).

Sympathetic Nervous System

Your sympathetic nervous system consists of a group of 22 *neural centers* lying on or close to your spinal cord (see Fig. 8.3). From these 22 centers, axonic fibers run to all parts of your body—to the salivary glands in your mouth; to the irises in your eyes; to your heart, lungs, liver, and stomach; and to your intestines and your genitals. Your sympathetic nervous system also connects with your sweat glands, with your hair cells, and with the tiny blood vessels near the surface of your skin (Brown & Wallace, 1980).

Whenever you encounter an emergency—something that enrages you, makes you suddenly afraid, creates strong desire, or calls for heavy labor on your part—your sympathetic nervous system swings into action by *speeding up* such bodily activities as heart rate, breathing, and sweating. It elevates your blood-sugar level and sets off various "fright reactions" such as the *pilomotor response* (which makes your hair "stand on end"). Sympathetic arousal also controls orgasm and ejaculation, and *slows down* digestion and repair of bodily tissues.

Put simply, activity in your sympathetic nervous system prepares you for fighting, for

FIG. 8.3 Schematic layout of the autonomic nervous system.

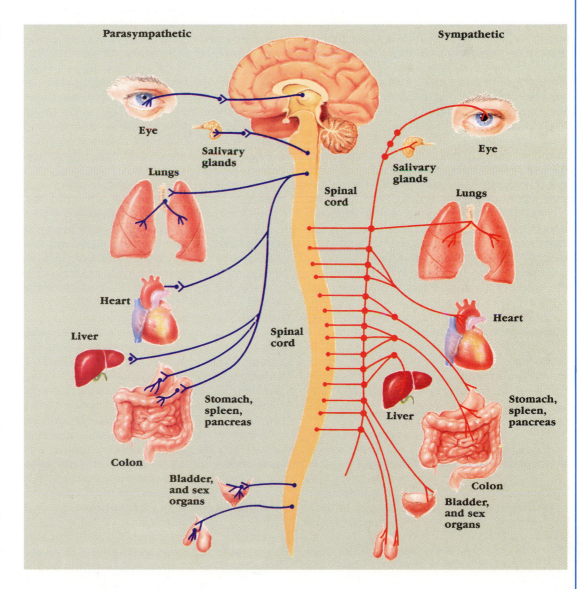

fleeing, for feeding—and for sexual climax (Brown & Wallace, 1980).

□ □ **QUESTION** □ □
Why do people often get red in the face when they get angry?

Parasympathetic Nervous System
Your parasympathetic nervous system connects to most (but not all) of the parts of your body that the sympathetic does (see Fig. 8.3). In general, parasympathetic stimulation produces physical effects that are the *opposite* of those induced by sympathetic stimulation. Activity in your parasympathetic system decreases heart rate, slows down breathing, and promotes digestion and excretion. It also controls nipple erection in females and penis erection in males.

Generally speaking, activity in your parasympathetic nervous system *conserves* or builds up your body's resources. For this reason, the parasympathetic is often referred to as the *vegetative* nervous system (Brown & Wallace, 1980).

For the most part, the two divisions of your autonomic nervous system work together to achieve a *homeostatic balance*. There is one major *difference* between the two, however: The sympathetic nervous system is connected to your adrenal glands, while the parasympathetic system is not (Kimble, 1987).

The Adrenal Glands
You have two adrenal glands, one sitting atop each of your kidneys. As we mentioned in the last chapter, your adrenals produce hormones that influence sexual development and that control such bodily functions as urine production. But these glands also produce two chemicals that are referred to as the "arousal" hormones. The old names for these two hormones are **adrenalin** and **nor-adrenalin**. These days, the terms "epinephrin" and "nor-epinephrin" are more common.

When epinephrin and nor-epinephrin are released into your bloodstream by your adrenal glands, these hormones bring about all of the *physical changes* associated with strong emotions such as fear, anger, hostility, and sexual aggressiveness. That is, these two hormones act to *prepare* your body to meet an emergency by increasing your blood pressure and heart rate, speeding up your breathing, widening the pupils in your eyes, and increasing perspiration (Kimble, 1987).

As you might guess from this description, the release of epinephrin and nor-epinephrin is under the control of your *sympathetic* nervous system, whose activities the hormones imitate or mimic. When you encounter an arousing situation, your sympathetic nervous system goes into action first, mobilizing your body's energy resources and also causing the secretion of the two "arousal" hormones. As you secrete epinephrin and nor-epinephrin, these hormones continue the arousal process by chemically stimulating the *same neural centers* that the sympathetic nervous system has stimulated electrically.

Why should you have two separate arousal systems? The answer seems to be this: Sympathetic arousal is quick—an "emergency alarm" that mobilizes your body almost instantly. But at times you need *sustained arousal*. It is more efficient for your body to maintain an aroused state by means of the adrenal hormones than by continuous activity in your sympathetic nervous system (Kimble, 1987).

Now that we've discussed the "biological facts" of emotional responses, perhaps you can better understand why many theorists have tried to explain *all aspects* of emotionality in physiological terms.

The James-Lange Theory of Emotion
The complex interplay between autonomic arousal on the one hand, and emotional behaviors and feelings on the other, has long fascinated theorists. One of the earliest theories was that proposed in 1884 by Harvard psychologist William James. According to James, your body always takes the lead in emotional situations. Your feelings, James said, are mental responses to the changes that have *already occurred* in your autonomic nervous system, muscles, and glands.

Let's see what James was really saying. Suppose you are driving down the expressway on a lovely summer day when another driver suddenly (and stupidly) cuts right in front of you. Chances are, you will immediately experience a classic "rage reaction." That is, your heart will start pounding, your face will flush, and you will breathe more rapidly. You may express your opinion of the other driver in a loud tone of voice, you may make various gestures at the person, and may even wish that God would strike the driver dead on the spot.

Now, you might think that you first became angry and then experienced autonomic arousal. But that is not the case, James said. Rather, your body reacted *automatically* to the situation, and *then* you experienced the "subjective" qualities associated with anger and/or rage. According to James, your physical responses precede and thus *cause* your feelings.

In 1885, the noted Danish scientist Karl G. Lange independently proposed much the same sort of explanation of emotional behavior. For that reason, this viewpoint is often called the **James-Lange theory of emotions**.

□ □ **QUESTION** □ □
Suppose you encounter a snake in the woods and run away. According to

Epinephrin and nor-epinephrin prepare the body to meet a stressful event by increasing blood pressure and heart rate, speeding up breathing, dilating the pupils, and increasing perspiration.

8 / Emotion, Stress, and Coping

James, do you run because you're afraid, or do you become afraid because you ran?

The Cannon-Bard Theory

The James-Lange approach led to a lot of highly emotional debate and, happily, a lot of useful research as well. For example, in 1927 Harvard physiologist Walter B. Cannon pointed out three objections to the James-Lange theory: First, James-Lange assume your feelings are dependent upon activity in your sympathetic nervous system. However, people who (through accident or disease) have lost use of their sympathetic systems still feel emotions and show emotional behaviors. Second, the physical changes associated with emotion generally occur *after* the "feelings and behaviors" have started, not *before* they take place. And third, the *same* physical changes occur in very *different* emotional states—and in non-emotional states as well (Cannon, 1927).

Cannon was one of the greatest of Ameri-

"I'M LISTENING, ERSKINE, BUT THE DOCTOR SAID I'LL STAY CALMER IF I KEEP LOOKING AT THE DAMN FISH."

Autonomic Nervous System

ca's neuroscientists. He was the first to demonstrate that the adrenals produce epinephrin during emotional arousal, he coined the term "homeostasis," and he developed the concept of the "fight or flight" function of sympathetic arousal (Benison, Barger, & Wolfe, 1987). Cannon was also one of the first scientists to hold that emotional inputs were processed simultaneously by two different parts of the brain, the *thalamus* and the *hypothalamus* (see Chapter 6). According to Cannon, the thalamus controlled emotional *feelings*, while the hypothalamus controlled *bodily responses*. Thus, Cannon said, you would experience conscious "fear" of a snake even if your body were totally paralyzed and you *couldn't* run. Why? Because "fear" and "running" are mediated by different centers in your brain (Cannon, 1929).

P. Bard advanced almost the same viewpoint in 1927 as well. For that reason, this approach to the explanation of emotionality is often called the **Cannon-Bard theory of emotions**.

As it turned out, however, the same sorts of criticisms Cannon leveled against James and Lange were also raised against the Cannon-Bard theory. In 1960, Karl Lashley noted people with a damaged thalamus still experience emotional feelings, and people with a damaged hypothalamus still show emotional responses. At about the same time, other scientists proved that both the *limbic system* and the right hemisphere were involved in mediating emotional feelings and behaviors (Kimble, 1987).

□ □ QUESTION □ □
How do you know to run from a snake until you have *perceived* the snake and been aroused by this perception? And since arousal is a part of both rage and fear, if you merely realized that you were "aroused," how would you know whether to run from the snake or attack it?

• *Emotions as "Arousal Plus Appraisal"*
Until recently, there was little evidence that your autonomic system responds differently according to the *type* of emotion that you feel. Several studies have shown that your adrenal glands produce more epinephrin when you are afraid, but secrete more nor-epinephrin when you are angry. But both hormones are released to some degree in *all* arousal situations. Thus, we cannot tell *objectively* whether you are angry or afraid just by measuring the relative amounts of epinephrin and nor-epinephrin floating around in your bloodstream (Schachter, 1971).

Stanley Schachter believes that the experience of an emotion cannot be explained solely in biological terms. Rather, he says, emotion is *always* the result of the *interaction* between neural activity in the brain, physiological arousal in the autonomic nervous system, and the individual's cognitive interpretation or *appraisal* of the situation the individual is in (Schachter, 1971).

• *Biological Theories: An Evaluation*

No one disputes the fact that bodily reactions do play an important role in *creating* and *sustaining* emotions. However, our feelings are so frightfully complex that we simply can't *reduce* them to mere hormonal and neural activity. To gain a more complete understanding of emotionality, we must look at intra-psychic variables as well.

☐☐ **QUESTION** ☐☐
Some people report that they are most easily aroused sexually when they are hungry, or immediately after a frightening experience or a violent argument. Why might this often be the case?

INTRA-PSYCHIC ASPECTS OF EMOTIONALITY

Roughly speaking, we can put most intra-psychic theories in one of two major categories: those that emphasize "feelings," and those that focus on "cognitions." The scientists who believe inner passions are the crux of emotionality often emphasize the *unconscious, instinctual* aspects of feeling states. The researchers who take the cognitive view usually hold that you *appraise* a situation first, then react to it emotionally. A few theorists straddle the dividing line between these two positions.

Let's look at the "feeling" theories first.

Freud's Energy Theory

Sigmund Freud is undoubtedly the best known of the psychologists who view emotions as "inner passions." Like all other *drive theorists*, Freud related emotionality to basic needs. He also placed a strong emphasis on the importance of early experiences in determining later emotional problems.

Freud believed you were born with the capacity to feel two types of sensations—pleasure and unpleasure (or pain). These powerful sensory drives exist in the unconscious portions of your mind, Freud said. The "emotions" you are aware of as an adult—love and hate, anger and disgust—actually *differentiated* out of the primitive sensory drives through experience. That is, as you matured, you associated certain types of situations with pleasure, and other situations with unpleasure. For example, you learned to love your mother because she gave you pleasure by feeding you and caring for you. But your *love* for your mother exists in the *combination* of your con-

scious associations with your unconscious feelings (Monte, 1987).

Freud's view of the emotions has often been called an *energy theory*. He believed your body continually creates "psychic energy" much as a dynamo continually produces electrical power. Freud called this psychic energy **libido**. According to Freud, *libido* is the motivating force that "powers" all your thoughts, feelings, and behaviors. *Expending* libidinal energy is associated with sensory pleasure. *Repressing* libidinal energy almost always leads to unpleasant tension, anxiety, and other negative emotional states.

Whenever you *suppress* an unpleasant thought or emotion, Freud said, you *block the release of libidinal energy*. Psychic tension builds up in your unconscious mind in much the same way physical pressure builds up in an overheated steam boiler. Some of the repressed energy will "leak out" in a variety of ways—through unusual dreams, fantasies, "slips of the tongue," and feelings of anxiety. However, according to Freud, the best way to discharge the pent-up tension is through **catharsis**, which involves the open expression of your feelings (Ross, 1987).

Because Freudian theory is so rich and detailed, we will postpone a fuller discussion of his views until later. We should note, though, that one emotion frequently repressed is that of *anger*. From a Freudian point of view, releasing pent-up anger—particularly through *aggressive acts*—should always reduce stress through catharsis.

• *Type A Personalities*

In 1974, Meyer Friedman and Ray Rosenman published a book entitled *Type A Behavior and Your Heart*. After years of studying heart patients, these two physicians concluded that many types of heart failure are due to "a particular complex of personality traits including excessive competitive drive, aggressiveness, impatience, and a harrying sense of time urgency." They named this behavioral syndrome "Type A Behavior." The opposite sort of behavior pattern—relaxed awareness, patience, and a lack of excessive aggression—they called "Type B Behavior" (Friedman & Rosenman, 1974).

Type A individuals often have exaggerated reactions to stress, Friedman and Rosenman claimed, and thus are "at risk" for a variety of stress-related illnesses. Friedman and Rosenman recommended that Type A's should learn to reduce their emotional reactivity or they might suffer a stress-related heart attack early in life. And, following the Freudian model, Friedman and Rosenman suggested that "cathartic discharge" of the emotions would be followed by a healthy decrease in blood pressure and other physical signs of tension.

Freud theorized that people are born with only two emotions: pleasure and nonpleasure.

Libido (lib-BEE-doh). The psychic energy created by your innate instincts. According to Freud, thoughts, feelings, and behaviors are "energized" by libido.

Catharsis (cah-THAR-sis). An act designed to "purge the system of its wastes or poisons." Freud believed that expressing your feelings was "cathartic" (cah-THAR-tick) because it released pent-up energy. Taking a laxative is also cathartic.

• Type A Behavior: An Evaluation

There do seem to be individuals who fit the classic Type A behavior pattern. And much of the early research did suggest that Type A men were more likely to suffer cardiac problems than were Type B men. However, almost all of the recent studies on this topic have shown little or no correlation between Type A personality traits and heart attacks (Myrtek, 1984). Furthermore, research on women Type A's has often given quite different results than has research on men (Wood, 1986).

Most surprising of all, early in 1988 Berkeley researchers David Ragland and Richard Brand reported that Type A males are *more* likely to survive a second heart attack than are Type B males. Ragland and Brand suggest that teaching Type A males "to relax more" may, in fact, decrease their chances of survival (Ragland & Brand, 1988). When asked to comment on this research, Meyer Friedman responded, "I think [their] study is a disservice." However, Friedman's former partner, Ray Rosenman, believes that Ragland and Brand "may be on the right track." Rosenman believes that Type A males may be more likely to change their behaviors after their first attack, and thus have a better chance of survival (cited in Bower, 1988).

Popular as it has proved to be, there seem to be two major problems with Friedman and Rosenman's theory. First, most researchers

Type A women seem to have very different responses to stress than do Type A men.

have used questionnaires or interviews to determine whether or not a given individual possesses Type A *personality traits*. However, after surveying much of this literature, Rutgers psychologist John Gormly concluded that "We should now recognize that the naturally occurring behavior of people does not seem to be organized in the way the trait viewpoint assumes it to be" (Gormly, 1985). Indeed, many psychologists now question whether or not such personality categories as "Type A" and "Type B" actually exist. Second, as Stanley Schachter and many others have pointed out, it is your *interpretation* of stressful situations, not your personality traits, that determines how stressed you will become (Schachter, 1971). We will discuss trait theory in detail later in this book. For the moment, let's look more closely at how *cognitive* factors influence emotions.

Arnold's Theory of Emotions

As we mentioned, while Freud viewed emotions as "feelings," most American theorists have tended to place more emphasis on the role of *cognitive activities* in emotional experiences. Some psychologists have straddled the fence, however. For example, in 1960, Magda Arnold revised the James-Lange approach by putting *perception* into the picture (Arnold, 1960).

According to Arnold, you perceive a situation and then react to it in two ways. First, you *unconsciously* and *intuitively* "feel" the situation is good or bad. You tend to approach situations that make you feel good, while avoiding or fleeing from situations that make you feel bad. But according to Arnold, arousal and all other behavioral reactions *follow* your emotional evaluations rather than precede them.

Once you have both "felt" and "responded behaviorally" to a situation, Arnold says, then you may well *appraise* the situation from a cognitive point of view. And, at that time, you may well make *conscious decisions* about the situation (and your own response to it). But according to Arnold, cognitions *follow* emotions rather than set them off (Arnold, 1981).

Lange: physical then emotional feelings

□ □ QUESTION □ □
In what ways are Freud's and Arnold's viewpoints similar? In what ways do they differ?

Cognitive Theories of Emotion

Those theorists who emphasize the "passionate" side of inner experiences (such as Freud and Arnold) tend to focus on the unconscious, intuitive aspects of emotionality. Those psychologists who prefer the cognitive approach are more impressed by the conscious, rational, explanatory side of emotional experiences. As we will see, though, these may simply be two sides to the same psychological coin.

Plutchik's Evolutionary Theory

One of the best known cognitive theories is that proposed by Robert Plutchik, who teaches at Albert Einstein College of Medicine. Plutchik believes emotions are *conscious interpretations* of what happens to you when you become emotionally aroused.

According to Plutchik, emotion is not a subjective experience. Rather, he says, emotion is "a construct or inference based on various classes of evidence." The *classes of evidence* Plutchik refers to are your physical and behavioral responses to emotion-arousing environmental inputs. Some of these reactions are learned. However, the more important ones were built into your genes as *evolutionary survival mechanisms*.

When you go through an emotional upheaval, Plutchik says, you *evaluate* the experience. Then you *construct* a "cognitive appraisal" of what has happened to you. This appraisal includes your interpretation of your physical arousal, your unconscious feelings, your behavioral responses, and your conscious thoughts while the experience was occurring. It is the *sum total* of all these events that can rightfully be called an "emotion" (Plutchik, 1980).

Like many cognitive theorists (and some "feeling" theorists), Plutchik believes that emotions are *bipolar*. That is, he thinks emotions come in pairs of opposites. You are born with two innate emotional reflexes, he says: arousal/depression, and approach/avoidance. However, over time, these innate responses *evolve* into such conscious appraisals as anger/fear, acceptance/disgust, and anticipation/surprise (Plutchik & Kellerman, 1980).

□ □ **QUESTION** □ □
Most studies show that when you try to "appraise" an emotion, the intensity of your feelings decreases significantly. Does this fact support Plutchik's position or not?

Lazarus's Cognitive Theory

According to University of California psychologist Richard Lazarus, "An emotion is not definable solely by behavior, subjective reports, *or* physiological changes; its identification requires all three components, since each one can be generated by conditions that do not necessarily *elicit emotion*." Thus, he says, emotions are actually composed of a *mix* of "action impulses and bodily expressions," various types of cognitive activities, inner feelings, and physical responses such as arousal or depression (Lazarus, 1984).

Lazarus was led to this point of view by the following facts:

Our "public behavior" is not always consistent with our inner feelings.

First, you can experience "arousal" just by exercising. So, emotion is *more* than just changes in your bodily processes.

Second, you can experience "feelings" that aren't really emotions. For instance, if you cut your finger, you feel pain. But Lazarus claims that pain and pleasure are "sensations" and not "emotions." And, Lazarus says, you don't really *know* what you're feeling until you apply a *cognitive label* to your inner experience. Thus, the true value of the inner experience lies in the label, not the "feeling."

Third, you can learn to behave in a stereotyped manner that will make others presume you're experiencing an emotion when you're really just faking it. Actors (and other performers) do this all the time.

According to Lazarus, it is only when you *consciously participate* in an experience that has three elements—physical arousal, subjective feelings and evaluations, and expressive behaviors—that you experience "emotion." And it is your *awareness* of the simultaneous occurrence of all three components that lets you evaluate the experience as "emotional" (Lazarus, 1982).

Intra-psychic Theories: An Evaluation

Strongly opposed to the Lazarus position is Michigan psychologist Robert Zajonc, who believes that you first react to a situation *emotionally*, and then subsequently evaluate the experience in *cognitive* terms. Zajonc notes that Lazarus has "broadened the definition of cognitive appraisal to include even the most primitive forms of sensory excitation, thus obliterating all distinction between cognition,

Richard S. Lazarus

Robert Plutchik

Magda Arnold

sensation, and perception" (Zajonc, 1984). Why does Lazarus take this odd position? In a recent interview, Zajonc speculates as follows: "For years we've been trying to explain almost everything by cognitive processes. This may be the vestige of Western philosophy's view of passion as the uncontrolled animal part of the psyche and reason as the crowning human achievement" (Hall, 1986).

Magda Arnold also is highly critical of the cognitive approach. To begin with, she says, there is a great difference between "conscious appraisals" and "unconscious feelings." And you only have to inspect your own inner experiences to realize this is the case. Cognitive appraisals are *deliberate value judgments*, Arnold says. Emotions, however, are *intuitive* and *unconscious*. To confuse emotions with cognitions is to blur the distinction between "thoughts" and "feelings." We have but to introspect our own emotions to know how wrong the cognitive approach is, she claims (Arnold, 1980).

At first blush, it may seem that these definitional arguments are little more than tempests in academic teapots. However, as we have already said (and will say again many times), "theory determines practice." Those psychologists who believe that emotions are primarily *biological* events usually attempt to "cure" emotional problems with pills and surgery. Those scientists who believe that "feelings" are the most important element usually opt for psychotherapy. Psychologists who take a more *cognitive* approach tend to believe that cognitive therapy is the best solution to emotional difficulties, while *social* psychologists often place their faith in therapeutic techniques that emphasize teaching people new social skills. We'll return to this point as soon as we discuss the influence of the *social environment* on emotional reactions.

□ □ **QUESTION** □ □

Suppose you have a friend who "flies off the handle" emotionally at the slightest provocation. What sort of treatment would you recommend for this person? And what does your recommendation tell you about *your* own definition of emotionality?

SOCIAL/BEHAVIORAL INFLUENCES ON EMOTION

In fact, almost all theories of emotion make some mention of environmental inputs and behavioral outputs. It is the *relative emphasis* placed on biological, intra-psychic, and social/behavioral influences that allows us to put the theory in one of the three major categories.

Behavioral Theories of Emotion

Although most biological and intra-psychic theories include "expressive behaviors" in their definition of emotionality, the behaviorists don't always return the favor. The most radical view of all, perhaps, is that of B.F. Skinner. Skinner sees emotions as being *expressive behaviors* rather than "feelings," "cognitive appraisals," "passions," or "states of autonomic arousal." And he believes most expressive behaviors are learned. Thus, Skinner recommends that people with emotional disturbances should simply learn new ways of behaving (Skinner, 1978). However, as the cognitive behaviorists showed more than 20 years ago, getting people to change their thoughts and feelings *in addition to their expressive behaviors* is a more effective type of therapy (Kendall & Hollon, 1979).

Skinner's major contribution to the study of emotions is probably this one: He proved that most emotional reactions are determined by their *consequences*. The importance of "environmental consequences" to our understanding of emotions can be seen in several lines of research. Let's first look at a topic called "learned helplessness."

Learned Helplessness

Some 35 years ago, Richard L. Solomon and L.C. Wynne made several interesting discoveries while working with dogs. Solomon and Wynne used what is called a "shuttle box" to train their animals (see Fig. 8.4). At the start of a training trial, the experimenters put the dog inside A of the box. Then Solomon and Wynne turned off the light above the animal's head as a *warning signal*. Ten seconds later, they gave the dog a mild shock through a metal grid on

Is this expression of surprise and dismay a learned behavior, or something people do instinctively?

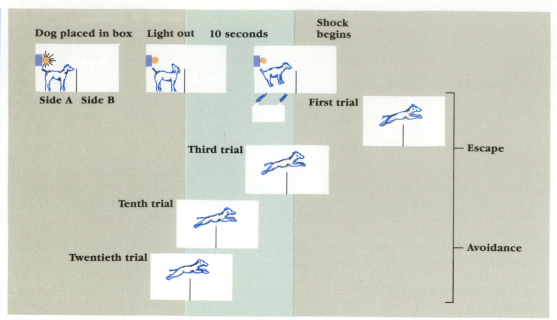

FIG. 8.4 Solomon and Wynne's avoidance experiment. First trial: Dog jumps over barrier long after shock begins. Third trial: Dog jumps immediately after shock begins. Tenth trial: Dog jumps between signal and shock. Twentieth trial: Dog jumps immediately after signal appears.

the floor of the shuttle box. The shock continued until the animal jumped over the barrier to safety in side B.

On the first training trial, the dogs often became quite emotional. When the shock came on, they jumped about randomly, barked, and whined. Eventually they hopped over the barrier. But they did so only *after* receiving several seconds of shock. By the third trial, though, the dogs learned to *escape*. That is, they jumped over the barrier the moment the shock came on. By the 20th trial, the animals leaped the barrier the instant the light was turned off. From this point on, they always *avoided* the shock.

Oddly enough, once the dogs had learned the "avoidance habit," they had great difficulty *unlearning* it. After the animals were uniformly jumping over the barrier whenever the light went out, Solomon and Wynne disconnected the shock apparatus. The dogs continued to jump for hundreds of trials each time the light went out, even though they would not have gotten shocked for "lingering behind" (Solomon & Wynne, 1953).

□□ **QUESTION** □□

Solomon and Wynne eventually found ways to demonstrate to the dogs that they'd no longer be shocked if they didn't jump. What sorts of techniques do you think would work?

• **Unavoidable Shock**

Many years later, Steven Maier, Martin Seligman, and Richard Solomon tried a variation on

this classic experiment. They began by *first* putting the dogs in a chamber and giving them *unavoidable shock*. The dogs (as you might suspect) were fairly upset at first, and showed all of the emotional behaviors Solomon and Wynne's animals had displayed on their first trial. Eventually, however, the dogs settled down and "coped" with the inescapable pain as best they could.

Then, Maier and his colleagues put the dogs in the shuttle box. Now the animals could learn to *avoid* the shock if they cared to do so. However, none of them did. Even though they could see safety on the other side of the barrier, *the animals refused to escape*. They simply sat there, apparently "depressed," and endured the shock for trial after trial (Maier, Seligman, & Solomon, 1969).

Seligman then tried a number of "tricks" to get these animals to jump. For instance, he put food on the other side of the barrier. The dogs ignored the food. He tried coaxing them over by calling to them. But the dogs sat passively, just accepting their "bad luck." Finally, Seligman tied ropes around their necks and pulled them over the barrier by brute force. He reports it sometimes took more than 30 "pulling sessions" before the dogs learned they could avoid the shock by voluntarily jumping the barrier.

Seligman believes the dogs had *learned to be helpless*. Since there was nothing they could do to escape the shock on the first trials, the animals simply "gave up" and "closed their minds" to thoughts of improving their lot (Seligman, 1975).

Martin E.P. Seligman

Julian Rotter

Seligman's Theory of Learned Helplessness holds that when people (or other animals) experience outcomes that are independent of their actions, they come to expect that their efforts to "gain control" will be futile. They become depressed and simply "suffer the stress" rather than try to reduce it. And they frequently become prime candidates for stress-related diseases (Seligman, 1976).

Just how much these people actually *suffer* is a matter of dispute, however. Recent evidence suggests that animals who experience "learned helplessness" have elevated amounts of endorphins in their brains—and below-normal amounts of nor-epinephrin. Thus, both humans and animals may "learn to be helpless" because the endorphins in their brains protect them from pain and also decrease their arousal levels (Reigle, 1985).

As you will see in Chapter 13, naloxone is a drug that counters the pain-killing properties of the endorphins. Injecting animals with naloxone *prior* to exposing them to unavoidable shock seems to lower the odds that the animals will "learn to be helpless" (Reigle, 1985). Injecting the animals with drugs that increase the amount of nor-epinephrin in their blood serves much the same purpose (Simpson *et al.*, 1986).

□ □ **QUESTION** □ □
Not everyone who faces unavoidable stress responds with "learned helplessness." How might the concept of *cognitive appraisal of a situation* be used to explain this fact?

• *Learned Helplessness: An Evaluation*
There is a fair amount of evidence that gives general support to Seligman's position. For example, Rona Harrell and Felice Strauss note that many visually-handicapped individuals have *learned* to act in a helpless fashion. Teaching these individuals to be more assertive, Harrell and Strauss say, "can increase their effectiveness in communicating with others and [help them] feel more in control of their lives" (Harrell & Strauss, 1986).

In similar fashion, Judith Voelkl notes that "activity personnel" at many nursing homes tend to *do too much* for elderly patients, thus encouraging them to adopt a "learned helplessness" way of coping with their world. Voelkl suggests that teaching elderly individuals to "maintain control" over what happens to them is the best way to help them live active and productive lives (Voelkl, 1986).

Several lines of research suggest that people who perceive the world as being either *unpredictable* or *uncontrollable* are likely to adopt a passive method of coping with stress (Overmier, 1986). For this reason, University of West Florida psychologist William Mikulas urges psychotherapists to encourage all their clients to *develop self-control skills.* Learning such skills protects clients from stress and depression (Mikulas, 1986).

Since the notion of *personal control* is crucial to Seligman's position, perhaps we should look more closely at research on this topic.

□ □ **QUESTION** □ □
If you saw a tornado heading your way, would you be more likely to (1) stand still and pray for deliverance, or (2) seek shelter as best you could (and perhaps then pray)?

Locus of Personal Control

One of your major motives is the need to predict and control your inputs. Evidence to support this belief comes from a variety of sources, including research on what is called the *locus of personal control*.

Almost 20 years ago, Julian Rotter noticed that some people believe they are **autonomous**. That is, they seem convinced they are masters of their own fates and take responsibility for what happens to them. They see their own *locus of personal control* as being *inside* themselves. And they believe that whatever rewarding inputs they get from their environments are due to their own actions. Julian Rotter calls these people *internalizers*.

On the other hand, many people believe they are helpless pawns of fate, controlled by *outside forces* over which they have little if any influence. These individuals feel their *locus of personal control* is external rather than internal, and that all rewards and punishments they receive are due to chance rather than to their own actions. Rotter calls these people *externalizers*.

According to Rotter, *externalizers* usually believe God or "fate" controls whatever happens to them. When faced with an external threat of some kind, externalizers either block off the stressful inputs, ignore them, or become depressed. *Internalizers,* on the other hand, don't believe in fate or "luck." They feel "getting ahead in the world" is primarily a matter of *what you do,* not what accidents befall you. When faced with a threat, internalizers tend to face the matter directly, or to remove themselves to temporary safety (Rotter, 1971).

In fact, as many theorists have noted, both internalizers and externalizers have found a way to gain some *apparent* control over their inputs. Internalizers do so by noting the consequences of their acts, and changing their out-

Working for a large company where individuals feel like "cogs in a wheel" can cause serious stress.

puts accordingly. Externalizers gain "the illusion of control" by such acts as reading horoscopes, using magic, or appealing to such supernatural concepts as "ghosts" and "gremlins" to explain what happens to them.

Concepts such as *locus of control* are useful, but we must not make the mistake of thinking everyone in the world must be either a "pure" externalizer or a "pure" internalizer. Indeed, many of us are "internalizers" in some situations and "externalizers" in other circumstances.

● *Locus of Organizational Control*

Psychologists Patricia and Gerald Gurin have found that many individuals have an *internal* locus of control as far as their personal lives are concerned, but have an *external* locus of control on the job.

These people are quite effective in handling their own personal stresses—they know how to cope in many day-to-day activities, and how to face the strains of living with their relatives and close friends. But many of these individuals work for large organizations and lack the social or managerial skills to achieve their goals on the job. Thus—while at work—they see themselves as puppets pushed around by forces they don't really understand. Locus of personal control therefore includes a somewhat different set of attitudes and behaviors than does locus of *organizational* control (Gurin, Gurin, & Morrison, 1978).

□ □ **QUESTION** □ □
What kind of therapy could you give externalizers to convince them that— under certain conditions, at least—they could "control their destinies"?

● *Locus of Control: An Evaluation*

Both "learned helplessness" and "locus of control" are attempts to explain why people react to stressful inputs as they do. However, these approaches place more emphasis on cognitive processes and behavioral outputs than on social inputs. Many psychologists hold that emotions are always the product of person-environment *interactions*. We can demonstrate the power of this viewpoint by discussing recent research on one of the most passionate of the emotions, *anger*.

□ □ **QUESTION** □ □
Is it better to express anger when you feel it, or to bottle it up inside you? What data can you give to support your answer?

Anger: A Social Process

"An emotion without social rules of containment and expression is like an egg without a shell: a gooey mess." This statement, by psychologist Carol Tavris, is an excellent summary of her theory of *anger as a social process*.

Tavris explains her views in depth in her 1982 book, *Anger: The Misunderstood Emotion*. "Anger is not a disease, with a single cause; it is a process, a transaction, a way of communicating." With the possible exception of anger caused by organic abnormalities (such as damage to the amygdala), most angry episodes are *social events*, Tavris claims.

According to Tavris, our modern notions about anger "have been fed by the Anger Industry, psychotherapy, which too often is based on the belief that inside every tranquil soul a furious one is screaming to get out." This notion was made popular by Sigmund Freud, Tavris says. Freud referred to anger "as if it were a fixed amount of energy that bounces through the system: If you pinch it in here, it is bound to pop out there—in bad dreams, neurosis, hysterical paralysis, hostile jokes, or stomachaches." As a consequence, Tavris says, "Therapists are continually 'uprooting' anger or 'unearthing' it, as if it were a turnip."

Because of Freud's popularity, Tavris claims, both psychiatry and the general public

Carol Tavris

Tavris's observations indicate that people who habitually vent their anger do not become less hostile; meanwhile, their loved ones have hurt feelings.

have come to believe that *suppressing anger* is medically dangerous. Thus, patients are often encouraged to "discharge their feelings," to relieve repressed energy, stress, and psychic tensions. You're told to "get it off your chest," or "blow off steam," or even to "let it all hang out." All these statements suggest there is some value in hitting, throwing, or even breaking things when you're frustrated (Tavris, 1982).

● The Consequences of Anger
But what do the *data* suggest? Just the opposite, Tavris believes. Expressing your anger can make you "feel good" temporarily. But what are the *long-term* consequences, both on you and on the people you're angry at? "I notice that the people who are most prone to give vent to their rage get angrier, not less angry," Tavris says. Why? In part because people give in to you when you're angry, in part because "ventilating" is self-rewarding. What about the objects of your anger, though? "I observe a lot of hurt feelings among the recipients of rage," Tavris says.

Tavris is not opposed to expressing anger. But she believes you should "ventilate" only when doing so will (1) achieve rational goals, and (2) have positive consequences for all concerned.

How do you learn to master your emotions? Primarily by gaining *cognitive control* of what goes on inside you (Tavris, 1982).

● Social/Behavioral Theories: An Evaluation
Behaviors, thoughts, and feelings don't occur in a vacuum. Everything you think, feel, and do occurs within some social context. Therefore, we cannot describe emotions without taking environmental inputs and consequences into consideration.

All of which leads us back to the questions we raised at the beginning of the chapter: What are emotions? Are they physical arousals, subjective feelings, cognitive appraisals, social responses, or a mix of all these factors? We will try to give a systematic answer to this question in a moment. But we have one more topic to consider first. We noted earlier that almost all theorists agree that emotional experiences usually are fairly stressful. So, suppose we talk about stress—and how to manage it—and then give a holistic definition of emotionality.

Hans Selye

STRESS

By now, it won't come as much of a surprise to you to learn that there are several dozen definitions of what *stress* is, hundreds of theories as to what causes it, and perhaps thousands of beliefs as to how best to cope with it. Some of these approaches focus on the biological aspects of stress, some on the intra-psychic fac-

"I THINK WE CAN RULE OUT STRESS."

tors involved, some on the effects of the environment—and a precious few that approach the problem of stress from a multi-dimensional viewpoint.

Roughly speaking, however, most scientists tend to view stress as a situation in which you are challenged *beyond your ability to adapt* (Krantz, 1986). The challenge itself may be *physical* (a virus, for instance), *psychological* (strong feelings of guilt), *social* (war), or some combination of these factors (the death of a loved one). For example, according to Richard Lazarus and Susan Folkman, "Psychological stress is a particular relationship between the person and the environment that is appraised by the person as taxing or exceeding his or her resources and endangering his or her well-being" (Lazarus & Folkman, 1984).

Generally speaking, the *biological responses* your body makes to stressful situations have been studied with greater frequency than have the intra-psychic or social responses—perhaps because there is more research money available for medical research than for psychological experimentation (a situation most psychologists find distinctly dis-stressing).

Let's begin, therefore, by looking at how your body reacts when it is *stressed*.

Selye's General Adaptation Syndrome
Given the frequency with which "stress" is discussed today, it may surprise you to learn that the concept was first linked to emotionality little more than 40 years ago.

Canadian scientist Hans Selye was probably the first scientist to outline the physical responses your body makes to stressful situations. Selye said your reaction to stress almost always follows the same adaptive pattern. He called this pattern the **General Adaptation Syndrome**, or GAS (Selye, 1976).

According to Selye, the GAS has three main stages or parts.

● Stage 1: Alarm Reaction

Suppose you suffer from a severe physical or emotional *trauma*. Your body will immediately respond with what Selye calls the *alarm reaction*, which is the *first stage* of the General Adaptation Syndrome. During this stage, your body and mind are in a state of *shock*. Your temperature and blood pressure drop, your tissues swell with fluid, and your muscles lose their tone. You don't think clearly, and your ability to file things away in Long-term Memory may be disrupted.

● Stage 2: Resistance

The second part of the GAS is the *stage of resistance*, or *counter-shock*. During this stage, your body begins to repair the damage it has suffered, and your mind begins to function more clearly. A small gland in your brain releases a complex hormone known as **ACTH**. The ACTH acts on your adrenal glands, causing them to release their own hormones. These adrenal hormones counteract the shock in several ways, chiefly by raising your temperature and blood pressure.

However, you pay a price for resisting the shock, for your body uses up its available supply of ACTH and adrenal hormones at a rapid pace. If the stress continues, your adrenal glands will swell as they strive to produce enough hormones to neutralize the stress.

● Stage 3: Exhaustion

During the first two GAS stages, your sympathetic nervous system is intensely aroused. However, if the emergency continues for too long, an overwhelming *counter-reaction* may occur in which your parasympathetic system takes over. You may fall into the third state— the *stage of exhaustion*. During this stage, you go into shock again because your body is depleted of ACTH and adrenal hormones. Further exposure to stress at this time can lead to depression, insanity, or even death.

Selye believed that many "diseases of adaptation"—high blood pressure, arthritis, and some types of ulcers—are caused by excessive stress (Selye, 1981–1983). We will have more to say about this point momentarily.

● Selye's GAS: An Evaluation

Almost everyone agrees Selye made the concept of *stress* a respectable part of science. However, recent studies suggest that Selye's theory, while correct in many aspects, needs updating and revision in at least three respects (Cooper, 1983).

1. In 1983, Nobel prize winner Julius Axelrod stated that recent research has led to two significant changes in Selye's theory. First, we now know that many hormones other than ACTH and the adrenal "arousal" chemicals are released during stress. The endorphins are one good example. Second, we now realize the body *defends itself* against exhaustion. When you experience chronic stress, your body adjusts by using less of the stress hormones, ACTH, and the other chemicals involved in the GAS. Therefore, you are less likely to suffer from "death by stress" than Selye had imagined (cited in Herbert, 1983).

2. Selye tended to focus almost entirely on reactions to biological stressors, but a great many of life's demands are psychological or social. There is a wide-spread belief, for instance, that you are more likely to become *physically ill* when you are worried or depressed than when you are "psychologically sound" (Dixon, 1986; Friedman & Booth-Kewley, 1987; Goldberger & Breznits, 1982).

3. Selye assumed that a given stressor would affect almost everyone in the same fashion. And early research by Thomas Holmes and Richard Rahe seemed to support Selye's position. In the mid-1960's, Holmes and Rahe interviewed and checked the medical histories of thousands of people. They found a significant correlation between *major events* in these people's lives and their *physical condition* in the following year or two. "Major events" were such things as losing your job, moving from one place to another, getting married (or divorced), the birth of a child, or the loss of a family member. Holmes and Rahe then developed a "checklist" that assigned "stress scores" to each type of "event" (Holmes & Rahe, 1967).

However, recent research suggests that the "major events" that Holmes and Rahe described account for less than 15 percent of the stress that people typically report. And there is tremendous variability in how various situations affect different people. For example, women tend to experience more distress than do men (Solomon & Rothblum, 1986), and women tend to be stressed by quite a different set of "major events" than do men (Baruch, Biener, & Barnett, 1987). Then, too, the situations described as "most traumatic" by Holmes and Rahe are not particularly relevant for the very young or the very old (Lazarus, 1981). Furthermore, people living in small towns and on farms apparently experience more stress—or react to it less effectively—than do individuals living in urban areas (Page, 1984). And most important of all, perhaps, is the fact that many

Minor "hassles" can often have a cumulative effect that is more stressful than one major life event.

8 / Emotion, Stress, and Coping

General Adaptation Syndrome (SIN-drome). A "syndrome" is a set of related symptoms that defines a particular disorder or behavior pattern. Selye's GAS is an attempt to describe the characteristic way in which the body responds to stress, particularly that caused by disease or physical trauma. As is true of most people trained in the medical sciences, Selye (SELL-ye) takes a biological view of emotionality.

ACTH. Adrenocorticotrophic (add-DREEN-oh-CORT-tih-coh-TROF-fick) hormone. For obvious reasons, almost always abbreviated as ACTH. A hormone released by cells in the pituitary (pit-TOO-ih-tarry) gland in the brain. ACTH stimulates cells in the "cortex" or head of the adrenal glands to release "arousal" hormones. *Trophic* comes from a Greek word meaning "to nourish." Thus ACTH is a hormone that "nourishes" or stimulates cells in the adrenal cortex.

Coping (KO-ping). From Latin and Greek words meaning "to strike." To cope with something is to fight against it successfully.

Defensive coping. A way of dealing with stress-related problems by running away from them physically or psychologically, by walling yourself off from reality, or by becoming depressed. According to Freud, all types of defensive coping are "unhealthy adjustments to reality."

Direct coping. A way of dealing with stress-related problems by facing the issues and solving them. Direct coping involves identifying the stressful inputs, then figuring out ways of handling them, usually in a step-by-step manner. Both defensive and direct means of coping are "lifestyles" that are learned, usually at an early age. Adults can usually acquire new ways of coping if given the proper help.

Defense mechanisms. According to Freud, your ego or "conscious self" must mediate between the demands of your unconscious instincts (your id) and the demands of society. To protect itself, your ego typically makes use of various psychological strategies, called defense mechanisms. See Chapter 16.

people can handle life's "major events," but have problems adjusting to the "little hassles" that bedevil all of us daily (Lazarus, 1981).

In psychology, therefore, stress research has begun to focus more on how people *appraise* stressful situations than on the actual events which *cause* stress. For your *perception* of what happens to you often determines how well you will *adjust* to stress.

COPING WITH STRESS

During your lifetime you have met many challenges, experienced many stressful situations, and worked your way through many emotional experiences. That is to say, you have *learned to adjust* to the problems that you face in life. Psychologists often speak of "learning to adjust" as **coping** with the world.

Your problems typically come to you as *inputs*, which you must *process* in some way and then *react* to. Thus, some methods of coping involve avoiding or even denying certain inputs. Other coping strategies require you to change the way you "process" or *appraise* problem-related inputs. Still other methods of coping involve altering your outputs—that is, changing the ways in which you respond or behave when the problem occurs.

But whether you attack the problem by working on your inputs, your internal processes, or your outputs, you will typically choose one of two major ways of adjusting—**defensive coping** or **direct coping** (Roth & Cohen, 1986).

Defensive coping typically involves protecting yourself by getting away from the threatening inputs. Direct coping involves meeting the challenge head-on.

Defensive Coping

Most forms of defensive coping involve mental or physical *escape* from the traumatic situation. You either flee from the problem and in the future avoid going near the stress-inducing situation—or you block out the threatening inputs and deny that the inputs are stressful (Roth & Cohen, 1986).

Many of the **defense mechanisms** described by Sigmund Freud are types of defensive coping. The most common of these are *repression, denial, hysteria, displacement*, and *regression*. These defensive ways of coping involve shutting off the outside world, suppressing emotions, misperceiving situations, or reverting to childish behavior patterns (Monte, 1987). We will discuss Freudian theory more fully in Chapter 16. However, we should note that all the defense mechanisms are elaborate ways to escape the stresses of reality.

Unfortunately, running away from your difficulties usually offers only temporary relief from stress. In the long run, it may be better to confront your problems. Doing so may well give you a way either of solving your difficulties or of reducing the distress they cause you.

□ □ **QUESTION** □ □

Freud did not consider depression to be a defense mechanism. However, in what ways might depression be a defensive type of coping?

Direct Coping

In a recent article, University of Chicago psychologist Bertram Cohler states that "One of the striking changes marking contemporary study in psychology is a shift in emphasis from the study of deficit, problem, and defense mechanism to the study of competence and coping" (Cohler, 1987). Accompanying this shift is also a move away from merely giving people *treatment* such as pills and therapy when they are overly stressed, and a move toward teaching people *competence skills* so they can cope directly with their problems (Marlowe & Weinberg, 1985).

Most forms of *direct coping* involve at least three steps:

1. An *objective analysis* of what your problem is, how it came into being, and how you are presently responding. It may well be that you are *over-reacting* to the situation you're in. Therefore, changing your "appraisal" of the problem might help you cope with it more effectively.

2. A precise description of what your *ultimate*

"SEE, MY INTENSIVE-STRESS THERAPY REALLY WORKS. YOU ARE NO LONGER CONCERNED ABOUT YOUR MINOR ANXIETIES."

goal or adjustment would be. Unless you know what you want to accomplish, you're not likely to make much progress in learning to handle stress.

3. A *psychological road map*, or a step-by-step list of the things you must do to achieve your goal once you know what it actually is.

Direct coping is not always easy, and it is often very time-consuming. However, there are certain things you can do to help ensure success:

1. It almost always helps to learn how to *relax*. In a recent study, John Hoffman and his colleagues at the Harvard Medical School found that subjects who had "learned to relax" showed significantly less sympathetic arousal when stressed than did subjects who hadn't been taught this technique (Hoffman *et al.*, 1982). Put more bluntly, it may help your *psychological* health if you find ways to reduce your *physical* response to stress.

2. You can often build up a "tolerance" for stress by learning how to handle mildly threatening events first, and then "moving up" to more challenging situations in a step-by-step fashion. Canadian psychologist Donald Meichenbaum reports this sort of *stress inoculation training* is particularly effective if combined with relaxation training (Meichenbaum, 1985).

3. It often "helps to have help." Michigan psychologist Robert L. Kahn believes that there is only one "anti-stressor" that helps in almost all situations—having "a strong system of social support" (cited in Kiechel, 1986). Your friends can provide you with an objective view of your problems, and they can also give you encouraging feedback as you make progress in learning how better to handle stress. However, under some circumstances, the best help you can get might

well be that offered by a professional counselor.

Finally, you should realize that not all stress is bad.

Eustress

Hans Selye died in October, 1982. However, shortly before his death, he talked at length about **eustress**, or "good" stress. According to Selye, we shouldn't try to avoid all stress. Rather, we should recognize what our typical response to stress is—and then try to adjust our lifestyles to take advantage of that response.

Selye believed some of us are "turtles"—that is, we prefer peace, quiet, and a tranquil environment. Others of us are "racehorses," who thrive on a vigorous, fast-paced way of life. The optimum amount of stress we may require to function best is what Selye called *eustress* (Selye, 1978).

The problem with Selye's approach is this—he assumed you are born a "turtle" or a "racehorse." Thus, from Selye's point of view, there is little you can do about changing your response to stress other than trying to compensate for the genes that nature gave you. Put another way, Selye recommended you *change your environment* because he believed people were unable to make significant changes in the way they react to their environments. Few psychologists agree with Selye on this issue.

Society depends on eustress, for cultures are kept going by motivated people who are willing to learn how to cope with each other—and with their own individual needs and personalities. Thus, *emotionality is necessary for life*. The problem comes in discovering ways to make your emotions helpful to you rather than harmful. Needless to say, the more you know about your feelings, the better off you will be. And that means not only discovering what your emotions *are*, but learning effective ways of *handling them* as well.

Now that we have explored several theoretical approaches to emotionality, perhaps it's time to put them all together in a systematic manner.

EMOTION: A HOLISTIC APPROACH

More than a century ago, Charles Darwin decided that emotions served several noble purposes: First, they motivated the animal to approach pleasure and avoid pain—behaviors that clearly have survival value. Second, emotions *communicate* one animal's feelings to other animals. If you were a lion and you roared in anger, other animals survived by running away. If you were a junior wolf and you "bared your neck" to the senior wolf, you didn't get bitten as often. Social psychologists

From cheering at a game to working on Wall Street, different kinds of stress can have positive effects on many people.

Eustress (YOU-stress). From the Greek word *eu*, meaning "good." Euphoria is "good feelings." Eulogy means "to speak good" of someone, eugenics means "good genes," and the eucalyptus tree gets its name from "good shade." Eustress is the amount of stress you need in order to operate at an optimum level of performance.

such as Carol Tavris (1982), James Averill (1982), and Robert Zajonc (1984) have built their theories of emotion on Darwin's early insights about the *communicative* value of emotional expression.

Those scientists with a biological bent also are clearly indebted to Darwin. In *Principles of Psychology,* William James quotes Darwin extensively—just before James begins a section in his book entitled "Emotion follows upon the bodily expression in the coarser emotions at least" (James, 1890). And Freud's thoughts on the importance of instincts and unconscious motivation surely stem in part from Darwin's theory.

It is only the cognitive theorists who, putting the mind "above" the body and thoughts "above" feelings, sometimes appear to downgrade the importance of emotions (Lazarus, 1982). However, emotions add *meaningfulness* to your thoughts and actions. To paraphrase Oscar Wilde, if all you did was *think*, you'd "know the price of everything and the value of nothing."

Your brain has two distinct *input systems,* one that processes *information,* the other of which processes *meaning.* The former deals with *cognitions;* the latter deals with emotions, or *affect. All* of your inputs are processed *simultaneously* by both systems. And while it is true that your cognitions can *guide* your emotions, it is equally true that your emotions *energize* your cognitions. Even Darwin recognized that you need *both* thoughts and feelings in order to survive.

We now must turn our attention to adaptation, which is to say, to learning. As you will see, the cognitive processing system in your brain apparently "learns" in quite a different fashion than does the emotional processing system.

SUMMARY

1. **Emotion** comes from the same Latin word as does **motivation.** Emotionality is associated with achieving or failing to achieve **goals.**

2. Biological theorists view emotions primarily in terms of **physical reactions,** such as arousal and depression, or as psychological responses to biological reactions. Intrapsychic theorists see emotions either as **subjective feelings** or as **cognitive appraisals** of complex experiences.

3. Behavioral theorists think of emotions entirely in terms of learned **expressive reactions.** Social theorists often view emotions as **social experiences** or **social events.**

4. Physical **arousal** and **depression** are controlled in large part by the **autonomic nervous system.**

5. Major control of the emotions lies in the **limbic system** and the **autonomic nervous system.**

6. According to the **triune brain theory,** your brain has three major parts: the **reptilian brain,** the **old mammalian brain,** and the **new mammalian brain.**

7. The limbic system contains the **amygdala.** Damage to the amygdala can lead to episodes of uncontrollable rage, but there is little evidence that *all* emotional problems are caused by brain damage.

8. The autonomic nervous system has two parts, the **sympathetic** and **parasympathetic nervous systems.**

9. Your sympathetic nervous system **arouses** you to handle such activities as fighting, fleeing, feeding—and sexual climax.

10. Your parasympathetic nervous system acts to **depress** those bodily functions that are aroused by sympathetic system activity. The parasympathetic is sometimes called the **vegetative nervous system.**

11. The sympathetic and parasympathetic systems generally have **opposite effects,** but work together in a **coordinated manner** to achieve a **homeostatic** balance.

12. Physical arousal causes your sympathetic system to release **epinephrin** and **norepinephrin**—the **arousal hormones** secreted by the **adrenal glands**—which produce **sustained arousal.**

13. The **James-Lange theory of emotions** states that you are "afraid because you run, not that you run because you are afraid."

14. According to the **Cannon-Bard theory of emotions,** your **thalamus** controls "feelings," while your **hypothalamus** controls bodily responses.

15. Schachter believes that your **appraisal** of the situation you are in is as important a determinant of your emotions as is your physiological state of **arousal.**

16. Freud believed the two innate emotions, **pleasure** and **unpleasure,** were correlated with discharging or suppressing **libidinal energy.** Releasing repressed libidinal energy leads to **catharsis.**

17. Type A individuals supposedly display such **psychological traits** as aggression, impatience, hostility, and excessive competition. Recent evidence suggests that Type A individuals may not be as likely to experience **cardiac problems** as once was thought.

18. Magda Arnold believes emotions are **subjective feelings** that are **unconscious** and **intuitive** perceptions of the goodness or badness of a situation.

19. Plutchik states that emotions are **cognitive appraisals** which are **consciously constructed** from evaluations of feelings and physical reactions. Plutchik believes emotions **evolved** from two innate **bipolar reflexes**, arousal/depression and approach/avoidance.

20. According to Lazarus, you have an emotion when you **consciously participate** in an experience that includes **physical arousal**, **subjective feelings**, **cognitive evaluations**, and **expressive behaviors**.

21. Skinner says that emotions are **learned behaviors** controlled by **environmental consequences**.

22. Seligman's **theory of learned helplessness** holds that when you cannot control what happens to you, you suffer **motivational, emotional**, and **cognitive deficits**.

23. Julian Rotter believes people respond to psychological pressures in different ways, depending in part on their own personal **locus of control. Internalizers** believe they are **autonomous**, while **externalizers** believe their reinforcers are controlled by fate.

24. Tavris claims emotions are **social contracts** controlled by personal and environmental **consequences**.

25. In his **General Adaptation Syndrome** theory, Hans Selye says your body goes through three rather distinct stages when stressed:

    a. The **alarm reaction**, in which your body's defenses are mobilized by activity in your **limbic system**, sympathetic system, and through secretion of epinephrin and nor-epinephrin.

    b. The **stage of resistance**, during which your adrenal glands secrete **ACTH**.

    c. The **stage of exhaustion**, during which your body may use up all of its ACTH and fall into **shock**.

26. There are two main ways of adjusting to stress—**defensive coping** and **direct coping**.

27. Defensive coping strategies include such **Freudian defense mechanisms** as **repression, denial, hysteria, displacement**, and **regression**. Another method of coping with stress defensively is **depression**.

28. Direct coping methods involve **problem analysis, goal setting**, and moving toward the goal in a **step-by-step manner**.

29. Direct coping is often enhanced by learning the **relaxation response**, by **stress inoculation training**, and by **moderating stress** by talking your problems over with friends or professional counselors.

30. All motivation is based on stress of some kind. Selye calls the amount of stress you need to function properly **eustress**, or good stress.

31. From a **holistic** point of view, inputs undergo **simultaneous processing** by two neural systems, the **emotional** and the **cognitive** systems. Emotions **energize** thoughts and behaviors, while cognitions **guide** emotional responses.

"I can't believe I forgot to lower the landing gear," Dave Milne said to the Senior Instructor, who had been his copilot just moments before. "I've landed a jet a thousand times or more, and I've never once forgot the landing gear."

(Continued from page 197.)

The Senior Instructor grinned. "Yeah, Dave, but you never had three engines catch on fire while you were trying to land either."

"And I thought it was just a 'piece of cake,'" Dave said, mentally kicking himself for his stupidity. "Thank God it was just a simulator we were flying, instead of being the real thing."

"That's what simulators are for," the Senior Instructor said, and then opened the back door of the simulated cockpit and began climbing down the flight of metal steps that led to the ground of the hangar.

Dave followed the man slowly. At the bottom, he paused and gazed back at the machine. From the outside, it looked for all the world like a large wooden box supported on flexible legs. Inside, it was a perfect mock-up of the cockpit of the wide-bodied jet Dave was learning to fly—right down to the last button and knob. But then, the simulators ought to be realistic, Dave told himself. They cost several million dollars each!

Dave and the Senior Instructor walked slowly toward the coffee shop, each man wrapped up in his own thoughts. Finally, to break the silence, Dave asked, "When did Mid-Continental start training pilots in simulators instead of in real planes?"

"About 15 years ago," the older man replied. "Of course, the push to use them didn't come until the new wide-bodied jets appeared on the market. The new planes were so expensive that nobody could afford to lose one of them in a training accident. And fuel's so expensive now that we save all of it we can. I reckon simulators have saved hundreds of millions of bucks, not to mention countless numbers of lives."

They entered the little cafe, sat down in a booth, and ordered coffee.

"I can see they'd save money, perhaps," Dave said as he stirred his coffee. He started to lift the cup to his lips, but found he had difficulty in controlling it. "Good as they are, though, simu-

8 / Emotion, Stress, and Coping

lators aren't the real thing. You just aren't under the same stresses and strains that you are in a real plane."

The Senior Instructor laughed. "If you didn't feel any stress flying that thing, then why are your hands trembling?"

"Okay," Dave said. "So I'm still a little upset at doing poorly. But how do I know I wouldn't have performed better if my life had really depended on my remembering to put down the landing gear? Are you really as strongly motivated to learn when you know it doesn't matter if you make a mistake?"

"Good question," the Instructor said. "But the answer's just as good. Simulators let us perform what we call 'stress inoculation training.' That is, we start with simple problems, and then when you've learned to handle them, we build up to more difficult situations. It works, Dave. Since we've been using the simulators, we've never had a fatal training accident. Before then, we cracked up several planes with trainees at the controls."

Dave nodded. "Sure. When you get through using this 'stress inoculation' with me, maybe I'll be able to land that simulator with all three engines gone. But how will I react if the same thing happens when I'm trying to land a real plane? How can you be certain that I won't go to pieces because I've never been tested in the fire of reality?"

The Instructor grunted. "Hope to hell you never are, Dave. Used to think that way myself, but then two things changed my mind."

"Two things?" Dave asked.

"Yep," the Senior Instructor said. "The first happened back in the 60's. A good friend of mine—a pilot for another airline—was taking a test ride in a DC-8 at an airport down south. He was just turning onto the final approach when the man who was checking him out suddenly killed two engines to see how my friend could handle the stress associated with an unexpected emergency. I guess my friend just panicked, or something."

Dave shook his head sadly. "Bought the farm, eh?"

"Bought the motel, is what he did. There was this fancy motor inn close to the airport, and the DC-8 plowed right into it and exploded. The motel was full of high school kids at a convention of some kind. Got pretty messy, I gather."

Dave Milne tried to picture the crash for a moment, but then blocked it out of consciousness. He let the Instructor sip his coffee for a few moments more before asking the man, "What was the other thing that convinced you simualtors are a good thing?"

"Oh, yeah," the Instructor replied, pulling himself back to the present. "One of the first guys I trained in a simulator was this scrawny little runt of a guy, nervous as a balloon salesman at a convention of porcupines. He had done all right as a pilot in smaller planes, I guess, but he was downright scared that he wouldn't be able to handle a huge jet. If it had been up to me, I would have washed him out the first day. I just knew he'd come unglued if he ever faced a real emergency. But he'd been with the company a long time. So, I stuck him in the simulator and used the step-by-step method of training him how to handle stress."

"How'd it go?" Dave asked.

The Instructor grunted. "Worked like a charm. Too good in fact."

Dave looked puzzled. "Too good? You mean he cracked up a plane?"

"No," said the Instructor. "But he got to be so sharp and so sure of himself that another airline hired him away from us. He's now a senior pilot with United."

Dave frowned. "Yeah, okay, but maybe he was an exception. I mean, how are you going to learn anything if you don't make mistakes? That's what training is all about, isn't it—learning from your mistakes?"

"Dave, we want you to learn how to *overcome* your mistakes, not die from them. So we don't let you pilot a real plane until *we* know—and *you* know—that you can do it well."

Dave laughed. "If you remember to put the landing gear down," he said. "That really was a dumb mistake."

The Senior Instructor was silent for a moment. Then he sighed. "Yes, it *was* a dumb mistake, Dave. But the mistake was mine, not yours."

"Your mistake?" Dave said in surprise.

"Yep. You were only supposed to have two engines go out on you in the simulator today. But you handled the emergency procedures so well that I cut off the third engine on you too. Pushed you too far, too fast. If I'd done it the way the stress inoculation book says, you'd have learned how to handle the two-engine-out problem with no sweat. And then you could have gone on to three engines without ever making a real mistake. And without risking any loss of confidence on your part, either."

Dave grinned. "I don't think you have to worry about my losing any confidence."

The Senior Instructor nodded slowly. "Maybe not in your case, that's true. But with the next trainee, who knows? Anyhow, I'm still learning, just like you. And I hope you'll forgive my mistakes if I forgive yours."

"That's a deal!" Dave said happily.

"Okay, man, let's get back to work. We're going to keep at it until we both get it right."

Dave gave the Senior Instructor the "thumbs up" sign. "A piece of cake," he said with a smile.

Summary

Conditioning and Sensitization

"The Leningrad Connection"

· C·H·A·P·T·E·R ·

9

"First of all, I'm only here because my wife wanted me to come," Kevin Lynn said to psychologist Dr. Nancy Wagner. "I have this little problem, I guess. Not really a problem, exactly, just my own way of doing things. It doesn't hurt anybody but me, so what's the difference? Do you see what I mean?"

A spark of veiled amusement lit up Dr. Wagner's dark blue eyes. "No, Mr. Lynn, I don't see. But I'm sure I will if you tell me more about it."

Kevin Lynn ran a nervous hand through his thick black hair. "Well, it's a sort of very personal problem. Nothing really abnormal, or anything like that. But it cuts close to the skin, and I'm not exactly eager to talk about it. And when you stop to think about it, it's as much my wife's problem as my own."

The man had a bright, glib way of talking, but Dr. Wagner sensed he wanted to do something about his problem, whatever it was. So she nodded encouragingly and said, "Marital problems almost always involve both husband and wife. So why don't you tell me more about what's troubling the two of you?"

Kevin Lynn began to sweat a little. "Gee, you know, some things are very personal. Now, don't take this wrong because I don't want to hurt your feelings. But . . . I mean, isn't there a *male* doctor I could talk to? I mean, there are some things . . ."

Dr. Wagner smiled reassuringly. "Mr. Lynn, I can't blame you for being reluctant to talk about sexual matters. But don't you think that women are often more understanding of a man's sexual problems than other men are? So just relax for a moment, lean back in your chair and get comfortable. And then see if you don't want to tell me what's troubling you."

Lynn stared at the woman for a moment or two, then followed her suggestion. He sighed deeply as he let himself go limp. Then he began to talk.

"I don't satisfy her, Dr. Wagner. At least, I can't usually make it, well, *worthwhile* for her without a little something extra to turn me on." His voice dropped to a halting whisper. "I guess if I told you how screwed up I really am, you'd be pretty shocked."

Nancy Wagner smiled. "It depends on what it takes 'to turn you on.' The last man I worked with was impotent unless he took his teddy bear to bed along with his wife."

"You're kidding!"

"No, not at all."

Kevin Lynn giggled. "Well, maybe I'm not so bad off as I thought. And it's not that I *have* to have them; it's just that it's usually better that way . . ."

"Have what?"

The man sighed again. "The whips. I like the touch of a whip when it's bedtime. Gives me the power to get up and go, stirs my blood a bit. So when we got married, I bought my wife a couple of small whips—tiny ones, really—and asked her to use them on me. At first, she didn't want to. But when she gave in and tried them for awhile, it was good, really good."

Kevin Lynn paused, remembering old times. "But now, she's read some stupid book, and she says I need help because I'm a masochist." He spat it out like a dirty word, MASS-oh-kist. "I guess that's pretty weird, isn't it? A guy who needs pain to get sexually excited?"

"It's a great deal more common than you probably realize. Pick up any of the underground newspapers and see how many 'personal' ads talk about whips and leather clothes and 'the need to be disciplined.'" Dr. Wagner smiled gently at the man. "And we may be able to give you more help than you suspect."

Lynn's voice quickened. "Gee, do you really think so? I mean, this book my wife read, it says I feel guilt and anxiety because I unconsciously think sex is dirty. Is that what you think is wrong with me?"

The woman cleared her throat. "Mr. Lynn, there are many different views on what causes masochism. Some therapists believe that the real problem is *sadism*—or the desire to hurt other people. Other psychologists believe that masochism is related to castration anxiety, that the man invites his wife to hurt him slightly as a way of warding off her attempts to castrate him. Still others think the problem is basically one of being *trained* to like or accept pain when you are very young."

Lynn frowned in confusion, not knowing quite what to think. "What do you believe, Doctor?"

The woman smiled. "There's a lot to be said for all those views, and just because one might be right doesn't mean that the others are wrong. In recent years, however, psychologists have found that many types of masochism are the result of improper learning when the person was young. In these cases, we 'condition' you to learn more appropriate ways of responding."

"How does this conditioning stuff of yours work? Do you have to whip me, or something?" Lynn's voice was eager and a bit mischievous.

The woman smiled. "No, we assume that some time early in your life, you were rewarded for hurting yourself or being hurt by someone else. Perhaps one time you were terrified of something that involved sexuality or your own sex organs, and you got hurt, and somehow your anxiety was greatly reduced. Then pain would become associated in your mind with fear reduction. For example, did your parents have frequent fights?"

Lynn's face reddened in embarrassment. "Oh, I wouldn't say they were frequent . . ."

Dr. Wagner nodded. "I'm not trying to insult your parents, Mr. Lynn. But when a child's parents fight, the child may become terrified. If parents stop fighting in order to give love or affection to the child, then the child might unconsciously be conditioned to seek pain in order to reduce fear and anxiety."

The man shrugged his shoulders, more at ease now. "Well, if you say so. But how do we start? Do I lie on a couch, or something? Or maybe a bed of nails?"

Dr. Wagner laughed warmly. "No, we'll talk about the origins of your masochism later on. But first, we'll teach you how to relax, and how to listen to your body. You see, pain has probably become a conditioned signal for sexual arousal in your case. If you skip the whips, you probably become nervous about whether or not you'll be able to perform sexually, am I correct?"

Lynn began to sweat a little. "Yeah, you got it right."

"Well," said Dr. Wagner, "Anxiety is controlled by your sympathetic nervous system. That's the part of your body that handles excitement. So we teach you how to handle your anxiety by learning how to relax. Then we'll make a list of all the situations that make you tense, beginning with things that aren't really all that disturbing and working up to things that make you break out in a cold sweat even just thinking about them."

"We'll make a little list, eh?"

"That's right. And then we'll start talking about the items on that list, starting with the simplest and working up to the most disturbing. If we can teach you to talk about these things while you're really relaxed, they won't make you very anxious any more. And if you're not anxious . . ."

". . . then I can make love to my wife without needing the whips, you mean."

Dr. Wagner smiled. "That's right."

Kevin Lynn pondered the matter for a long time. "Well, I guess it might work. How do we begin?"

"It's simple. First, stretch out your legs and make them as rigid and as tense as you can. Go ahead, do it now. Do you feel the tension?"

"Sure. It almost hurts."

"Good. Now, relax your legs completely. Relax your feet and your ankles and your thigh muscles. There. Now tense them up again. That's right, tense, tense, tense. Feel the tension? Okay, now relax again; just go completely limp. Now, can you tell the difference between tension and relaxation?"

"I sure can. There's a world of difference."

"Good," said the woman. "Next, we'll do the same thing with your arms, and then with your head and neck muscles. We want to get you to the point where you can discriminate tension from relaxation. Then you can command your body to relax any time you want to, and the muscles in your body will respond automatically."

Lynn grinned. "If I could do that . . ."

"Then your immediate problem would be solved, and you could go on to find out how the masochism got started."

"That sounds like a painfully slow process."

Dr. Wagner laughed lightly. "I thought you liked pain, Mr. Lynn."

Kevin Lynn favored her with a broad smile. "Okay, Dr. Wagner. You've got a deal." *(Continued on page 234.)*

THE INNATE REFLEX

Some time about the beginning of this century, a young man named E.B. Twitmyer began work on his doctoral dissertation in psychology at the University of Pennsylvania. Twitmyer was interested in *innate reflexes*—those automatic behavior patterns that are wired into your brain circuits by your genetic blueprint. And most particularly, he was interested in the **patellar reflex**, or knee-jerk.

You can evoke the patellar reflex in either of your legs rather simply (see Fig. 9.1). When you are sitting down, cross one leg on top of the other, leaving your uppermost leg hanging freely. Now, reach down with the edge of your hand and strike this leg smartly just below your kneecap. If you hit just the right place, you will strike your patellar tendon, which runs close to the surface of your skin at this point on your leg. Whenever you tap on this tendon, the lower half of your leg will swing forward involuntarily.

FIG. 9.1 Tapping the patellar tendon with a hammer elicits the "knee-jerk" reflex.

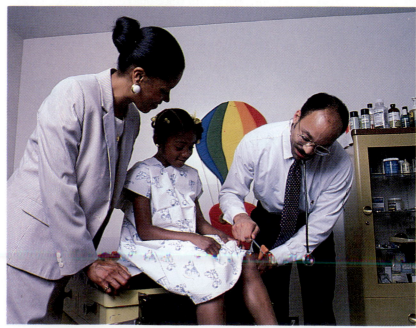

9 / Conditioning and Sensitization

Patellar reflex (pat-TELL-are). The patella is the knee bone. If you strike your leg just below this bone, the lower part of your leg will jerk. This "knee-jerk," or patellar reflex, is an automatic response over which you have little volitional control.

Conditioned reflex (con-DISH-shunned). A learned response pattern in which a stimulus is bonded or connected to a response. The "conditions" for acquiring the reflex usually involve pairing a "neutral" stimulus (such as a bell) with a stimulus that innately sets off a reflexive response (such as striking the patellar tendon). Also called a "conditional reflex."

FIG. 9.2 Ivan Pavlov (white beard) with his students and a dog in a training apparatus.

Twitmyer's Experiment

Twitmyer believed the patellar reflex might be influenced by the *motivational state* a subject was in when the reflex was set off. So he asked fellow graduate students to be his subjects. Then he rigged up a small hammer that would strike the subject's patellar tendon when he let the hammer fall. Twitmyer didn't bother telling his subjects when he was about to stimulate their reflexes—he merely dropped the hammer and measured how far their legs jerked. But his subjects complained the hammer blow often caught them by surprise. Couldn't he ring a bell as a warning? Twitmyer agreed, and began sounding a signal to announce the hammer drop.

One day when Twitmyer was working with a subject whose knee had been hit hundreds of times, he accidentally sounded the warning signal without dropping the hammer. As promptly as clockwork, the subject's knee jerked *despite* the fact that his tendon hadn't been stimulated. Although Twitmyer didn't realize it, he had just discovered the **conditioned reflex**, a response pattern upon which a dozen different psychological theories would later be built.

However, Twitmyer did appreciate the fact that he was on to something important, and he dropped his original research plans in order to investigate his discovery. He established some of the conditions under which this new type of reflex occurred—for example, the fact that much of learning is based on *stimulus-response associations*, and that conditioning is often a matter of making some change in an *innate reflex*. Twitmyer reported his findings at the 1904 meeting of the American Psychological Association. He published his research in a scientific journal the subsequent year (Twitmyer, 1905).

Although the conditioned response is now one of the "basic facts" on which experimental psychology rests, Twitmyer's report excited little or no attention in the US (Dallenbach, 1959). Discouraged by the frosty reception his ideas received, Twitmyer dropped his laboratory research and went on to other things.

About the same time that Twitmyer was working at the University of Pennsylvania, the noted Russian scientist Ivan Pavlov was performing similar studies at his laboratory in Leningrad. Whether Twitmyer or Pavlov was the first to "discover" the conditioned reflex is a matter of some dispute, although it does seem that Twitmyer was the first to publish his findings (Windholz, 1986). Whatever the case, it was Pavlov who ended up making most of the important early discoveries in this area.

PAVLOV'S CONDITIONING STUDIES

Ivan Pavlov, who lived from 1849 to 1936, is perhaps Russia's most famous scientist. After taking his medical degree in 1883, Pavlov traveled in Europe, studying with various other scientists. In 1890, he founded the Institute of Experimental Medicine in Leningrad, which he directed the rest of his life.

Pavlov's early interests were in the biological processes of *digestion*, and he chose dogs for his experimental animals. He trained the dogs to lie quietly on operating tables or in leather harnesses while he studied what went on inside their stomachs before and after the dogs had eaten a meal (see Fig. 9.2). His experiments proved for the first time that the nervous system coordinates *all* digestive responses. Because of the pioneering nature of his work, Pavlov was awarded the Nobel Prize in 1904—the first Russian to be so honored (Wertheimer, 1987).

● *Psychic Stimulations*

Digestion actually begins in the mouth, where *saliva* starts breaking up food particles chemically. So Pavlov began his work by studying the salivary glands. Pavlov soon found a way to measure the amount of saliva the glands produced. While the dog was in a harness, Pavlov would give food to the dog, then count the number of drops of saliva its salivary glands secreted.

Dogs do not have to be trained to salivate when given food—they do so *reflexively*, or automatically. Salivation is therefore an innate *response* (R) or reflex that is elicited by the *stimulus* (S) of food in the mouth.

E.B. Twitmyer

"HE SALIVATES."

Pavlov wanted to determine the neural pathways that *connected* the stimulus receptors in the dog's mouth with its salivary glands. But his research was often interrupted by *peculiar responses* the animals would make. After an animal had gotten accustomed to being fed in the harness, its salivary glands would often "juice up" *before* it got the food. In fact, an experienced dog would usually start salivating if one of Pavlov's assistants merely rattled the food dishes in the sink or walked toward the dog carrying a plate.

Pavlov called these "unusual" reactions *psychic stimulations*. These odd reactions infuriated him because they "got in the way" of his regular research. He did his best to ignore them because he wasn't interested in anything "psychological." However, the psychic stimulations refused to go away. And so, around 1901, Pavlov began to study them systematically, hoping to get rid of these "annoyances." He told his friends this work surely wouldn't take more than a year or two to complete. In fact, Pavlov spent the last 34 years of his life determining the properties of these "psychic stimulations" (Goldenson, 1970).

Unconditional Stimulus-Response Connections

If you blow food powder into a dog's mouth, the animal will salivate reflexively. This response is determined by the dog's genetic blueprint. Pavlov called the food an **unconditional** or **unconditioned stimulus** (UCS) because the food's ability to evoke salivation is not *conditional* upon the dog's having learned the response.

The salivation reaction is also innately determined. Therefore, Pavlov named it the **unconditional** or **unconditioned response** (UCR) since it too is not *conditional* upon learning.

□□ **QUESTION** □□
How would you go about *teaching* a dog to salivate when you gave it food if it didn't do so instinctively?

Conditional Stimulus-Response Connections

One of the first things Pavlov discovered in his research was this: If he sounded a musical tone just before he blew food into the animal's mouth, the dog eventually salivated almost as much to the *tone alone* as it did to the tone plus the food powder. Apparently the animal learned to "associate" the *sound* of the music with the *stimulus* of the food. And thus, each time the tone sounded, the dog *anticipated* it would be fed. So it salivated to the tone just as it did to the food.

This sort of *conditioning* occurs in people as well as in dogs. The smell of bacon frying in the morning is enough to set your mouth to watering, but only because you have *learned to associate* the smell of the meat with how it tastes. In similar fashion, the clang of a dinner bell is often enough to set your stomach rumbling because your stomach muscles have been *conditioned* to expect food shortly after the bell sounds.

- ### *"Neural S-R Connections"*

According to Pavlov, learning is always a matter of establishing new "connections in the brain" between stimuli (Ss) and responses (Rs).

The neural connection between the unconditional UCS_{food} and the unconditional $UCR_{salivation}$ is innately determined. Therefore, it is an *unlearned* or reflexive S-R connection that we might diagram as follows:

$$UCS_{food} \xrightarrow{\text{(innate S-R connection)}} UCR_{salivation}$$

However, when the previously neutral S_{tone} is presented *just prior* to the unconditioned UCS_{food}, a new "connection" is built up in the animal's brain that links the S_{tone} with the $UCR_{salivation}$.

Pavlov called the tone a **conditional** or **conditioned stimulus** (CS) because its power to call forth the salivation response is *conditional* upon its being paired with the food powder. We can diagram the situation as follows:

$$S_{tone} \xrightarrow{\left(\begin{smallmatrix}\text{S-S}\\\text{association}\end{smallmatrix}\right)} UCS_{food} \xrightarrow{\left(\begin{smallmatrix}\text{innate S-R}\\\text{connection}\end{smallmatrix}\right)} UCR_{salivation}$$

Unconditional (unconditioned) stimulus. Abbreviated UCS. You are born with certain innate responses, such as the patellar reflex. These reflexes are set off (elicited) by innately-determined (unconditioned or unlearned) stimuli. The blow to your patellar tendon is an unconditioned stimulus that elicits the unconditioned response we call the knee-jerk. The term "unconditional" is used to describe these stimuli because their ability to elicit the response are not *conditional* on learning.

Unconditional (unconditioned) response. Abbreviated UCR. Any innately-determined response pattern or reflex that is set off by a UCS. The knee-jerk is a UCR.

Conditional (conditioned) stimulus. Abbreviated CS. The CS is the "neutral" stimulus which, through frequent pairings with an unconditioned stimulus, acquires the ability to elicit an unconditioned response.

Conditional (conditioned) response. Abbreviated CR. Any reaction set off by a CS. A bright light (UCS) flashed in your eye causes your pupil to contract (UCS). If someone frequently rings a bell (CS) just before turning on the bright light (UCS), the sound of the bell (CS) would soon gain the power to make your pupil contract. Once this conditioning has taken place, the UCR (contraction) becomes a CR that can be elicited by the CS. Since pupil contraction can now be set off by *either* the CS or the UCS, the contractive response is *both* a CR and a UCR. In many cases, however, the CR looks slightly different from the UCR. In Pavlov's studies, for example, the CR usually consisted of fewer drops of saliva than did the UCR.

Once the dog has learned the connection between the tone and the food, you can present just the tone alone—without giving the food—and the dog will salivate. In similar fashion, once you have learned to associate the aroma of bacon with its taste, the mere *smell* of the meat will set off your salivary glands even if you don't eat any of the bacon.

□ □ **QUESTION** □ □
Is the odor of bacon more likely to cause you to salivate when you're hungry or when you've just finished a large meal?

• *The "Conditioned Response"*

But what can we call the salivary response when it is triggered off by the tone alone? Surely it is no longer an *unconditioned* response because there is no innate connection in the brain between a "neutral" musical tone and salivation. Pavlov named this *learned* reaction to the neutral stimulus a **conditional** or **conditioned response** (CR).

Conditioning is the term Pavlov used to describe the process by which the previously neutral stimulus (CS) gains the power to *elicit* the conditioned response (CR) (Pavlov, 1927). The CS gains this power, of course, because of the *new neural connections* that occur in the animal's brain linking the tone (CS) with the salivation (CR).

Once the conditioning process has taken place, we can diagram the situation as follows:

$$CS_{tone} \xrightarrow{\text{(learned S-R connection)}} CR_{partial\ salivation}$$

The type of training developed by Pavlov is called by many names: classical conditioning, reflex conditioning, Pavlovian conditioning, respondent conditioning, and stimulus-response (S-R) learning.

• *Conditioning: A Definition*

Generally speaking, when psychologists use the term *conditioning*, they refer to some situation in which a *previously neutral stimulus* gains the power to elicit a *response* in a reflexive or mechanical fashion. So when we say that you have been "conditioned" to do something, we mean that you have learned to respond rather automatically to a particular stimulus. We often speak of this sort of conditioning as "bonding" the S to the R.

Technically speaking, conditioning occurs because of the *association* that occurs when the CS and the UCS are "paired" repeatedly. However, from a Pavlovian point of view, this "pairing" merely allows the CS to become "connected" (or bonded) to the UCR. When Pavlov spoke of *conditioning,* he almost always referred to S-R bonds, not to "mental associations" between stimuli.

Perhaps the most important point about Pavlovian conditioning is this: Because the learning is reflexive, *you need not be aware that it has taken place*.

□ □ **QUESTION** □ □
Can you figure out how you were conditioned to believe that, in our society, men shouldn't wear pantyhose?

Factors Affecting Conditioning

During the many years that Pavlov studied the conditioning process, he discovered several factors that affect this type of learning:

• **1.** The more *frequently* the CS and the UCS are paired, the *stronger* the S-R bond becomes (see Fig. 9.3). For example, up to a

FIG. 9.3 The charts show first the acquisition of conditioned salivation in a trained dog, and then extinction.

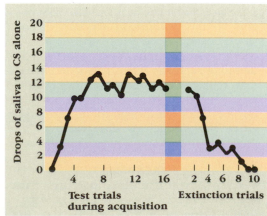

theoretical limit, the more often a tone is associated with food powder, the more drops of saliva the tone will elicit. And the more frequently the CS and UCS are paired, the stronger the S-R bond becomes and the better the animal will remember the learning later on.

- 2. Conditioning typically is fastest when the CS is presented *immediately* before the UCS. For example, the optimum time interval for conditioned salivation in the dog is about half a second. If the tone is presented more than a few seconds *before* the food—or is presented *after* the food—little or no learning usually occurs. However, the optimum time interval does vary from animal to animal, from species to species, and from situation to situation. And there is one notable exception to this rule that we will discuss momentarily.

- 3. Conditioned responses are *unlearned* just as easily as they are learned. Suppose you train a dog to salivate. That is, you establish a CS-CR connection in the animal between a tone and salivation. Now you present the dog with the tone *without* giving it the food. You would find that the animal salivates less and less on each trial. Finally, the response would be **extinguished** completely (see Fig. 9.4). Put another way, the S-R "bond" has been broken.

- 4. An "extinguished response" is not completely *forgotten*. Suppose you condition a dog, then extinguish the response. Then you pair the CS with the UCS for a second round of training trials. The dog now will re-acquire the conditioned response much more quickly than it did the first time around. Apparently the original conditioning has left a "trace" of some kind that makes relearning easier.

- 5. In similar fashion, suppose you *extinguish* a dog's conditioned salivation response and then let the animal sit in its cage for two weeks. Now you bring the dog back to the lab, hook it up in its harness, and again sound the tone. What will happen? As you might guess, the dog will have *forgotten the extinction* and it will again salivate. Psychologists call this *spontaneous recovery* of a previously extinguished S-R bond.

- 6. The mere passage of time can act as a conditioning stimulus. When Pavlov fed his animals regularly each half-hour, they began to salivate a minute or so before the next feeding was due even though there were no *external stimuli* such as dish rattles to give them cues that it was almost time to eat.

the subject wished to learn or found the experience rewarding. Look back over the past couple of pages. How many times have the terms "CS" and "conditioned stimulus" been paired? Are the two terms now associated in your mind? Were you conscious that you were learning? And the next time you watch television, look closely at the commercials. Do the advertisers seem to be using Pavlovian techniques to get you to like or remember their products?

- ### Conditioned Taste Aversion

As we mentioned, conditioning usually occurs most quickly when the CS precedes the UCS by less than one second. This "fact" is really just common sense. Suppose you ring a bell, and then a second later give a dog mild shock to its forepaw. The animal will surely whine, and withdraw its paw from the shock plate (if it can do so). After a few such trials, the animal will probably whine and pull back its paw *even if you don't turn on the shock*. However, if you ring a bell, then wait 30 minutes, and *then* give the animal shock, it probably never will associate the bell with the shock. For the *temporal delay* between CS and UCS is just too great in this case.

There is an important exception to this principle, however. If you eat an unusual food for lunch and then, *for any reason whatsoever*, become "sick to your stomach" a few hours later, you are likely to avoid that unusual food in the future. Here, the temporal delay between stimulus (unusual food) and response (illness) is several hours—but the **conditioned taste aversion** is strong, and is established in just one trial (Deems & Garcia, 1986).

The exact physiological mechanisms that control conditioned taste aversion are still a matter of considerable debate. However, it does seem as if this type of learning has high survival value. One reason that wild rats are so difficult to destroy is that, when they first encounter a novel-tasting food, they eat just a tiny amount even if they are extremely hungry. They then wait several hours. If the rats don't become ill, they then ingest more of the novel food. However, if they do become ill, they often return to the food and "mark" it by urinating or defecating on it—apparently as a way of warning other rats not to eat the suspect food (Bhardwaj & Khan, 1979). For obvious reasons, this type of learning is often called "bait shyness."

□□ **QUESTION** □□
Pavlov believed the mere pairing of the CS and the UCS was sufficient for conditioning to occur—whether or not

□□ **QUESTION** □□
How might you *overcome* a conditioned taste aversion if you wished to do so?

Extinguished (ex-TING-guished). To "extinguish" a response is to reduce the frequency (or intensity) of a learned response either by withdrawing the reward that was used during training, or by presenting the CS many times without the UCS. In fact, it is the "bond" or "connection" between the CS and the CR that is extinguished.

Conditioned taste aversion. A type of conditioning in which the unconditioned stimulus (internal cues associated with nausea or vomiting) usually occurs several hours after the conditioning stimulus (a novel food), but a strong CS-UCS association is built up in just one trial. Also called "bait shyness."

Masochists (MASS-oh-kists). Masochism (MASS-oh-kiss-em) is a sexual deviation in which pleasure is derived from pain. The pain may be psychological or physical, and may be self-inflicted or inflicted by others. The term comes from the name of the Austrian novelist Leopold V. Sacher-Masoch, whose stories frequently featured scenes in which sexual pleasure was associated with painful stimulus inputs.

Discrimination training. Teaching an animal to discriminate—that is, to react differently to fairly similar stimuli. If you can tell the difference between two things, you know how to discriminate between them.

Generalization (jen-er-al-eye-ZAY-shun). *Stimulus* generalization is the tendency to make the same response to two similar stimuli. If a monkey has been trained to lift its right paw when you turn on an orange light, it may also lift its paw when you turn on a yellow or a red light. *Response* generalization is the tendency to make a slightly different reaction to the same stimulus. If you hold down the monkey's right paw when you turn on the orange light, the response may generalize to the left paw instead.

Pavlov's Masochistic Dog

Pavlov believed "conditioning" could account for most types of human behavior. One way to prove his point, he reasoned, would be to produce in *animals* various abnormal behaviors some people thought could only occur in *humans*.

For instance, Pavlov wondered why a few individuals—called **masochists**—seemed to enjoy or seek out pain. Many psychologists believed *masochism* was the result of some "flaw" in the individual's personality. Pavlov suspected this "love of painful inputs" might be learned. To settle the matter—at least, in his own mind—Pavlov trained a dog to withstand extremely painful stimuli by using a "step-by-step" conditioning technique.

First, Pavlov marked off an area of skin on the dog's front leg. Then he stimulated this area with a weakly painful CS—and immediately gave the dog some food. The dog salivated to the food, but didn't flinch at the pain. Apparently the strong unconditioned salivation response *inhibited* the normal pain reflex.

Then, day after day, Pavlov slowly increased the intensity of the painful CS, each time pairing it with food. At no time did the animal respond as if it were being hurt. Indeed, the dog seemed more than willing to be put in the training harness and given the pain—since the pain soon *became a conditioned signal* that the dog would soon receive food.

Once the dog was fully trained, it would passively withstand incredible amounts of painful stimulation delivered to its front leg. However, if Pavlov applied the painful CS to any other part of the dog's body, the animal would instantly set up a great howl and attempt to escape from its training harness.

Pavlov concluded that when he touched the CS to the dog's front leg, the animal did not in fact *feel* any pain. Why not? Because the salivation response was so strong it *suppressed* all other responses to the *same stimulus*, Pavlov said. Apparently in dogs, as well as in humans, "You can't do more than one thing at a time." And whatever response is strongest tends to repress most other reactions that could be made to the same stimulus (Pavlov, 1927).

The parallel between Pavlov's masochistic dogs and those humans who seek out pain or humiliation in order to gain pleasure (often sexual) is rather remarkable. But as important as these experiments might have been to the discovery of a "cure" for masochism in humans, this research was regarded with considerable distaste by most other scientists.

□ □ **QUESTION** □ □
What similarities do you see between Pavlov's "step-by-step" conditioning procedure and the techniques for coping with stress discussed in the previous chapter?

Discrimination and Generalization

Perhaps the most interesting "mental health" experiment Pavlov conducted had to do with **discrimination training**. Pavlov began by showing a dog a drawing of a circle, then giving it food immediately. Very soon the dog became conditioned to salivate whenever it saw a circle.

Pavlov then tested the animal by showing it drawings of figures such as an ellipse, a pentagon, a square, a rectangle, a triangle, and a star. He found that the salivary response *generalized* to stimulus inputs other than the original CS (the circle). As you might suspect, this **generalization** followed a specific pattern—the more similar the other figure was to a circle, the more the animal salivated.

Pavlov then trained the dog to *discriminate* between the two stimuli by always giving food to the dog when the circle appeared, but never giving it a reward when he showed it the ellipse. Soon the dog learned to salivate *only* when the circle was shown.

After Pavlov had established that the dog could discriminate between a circle and an ellipse, he tried to fool the animal. On subsequent trials, he presented the dog with ellipses that were closer and closer to being completely round. Eventually the animal's "cognitive system" was strained to the breaking point, for the animal could not perceive the difference between the positive CS (the circle) and the negative CS (the ellipse). Therefore, Pavlov said, the animal did not know *which response to make—*

the response to the circle, or the response to the ellipse.

Overcome by stress, the animal broke down, snapped at Pavlov and his assistants, barked loudly, urinated and defecated, and tried very hard to get out of the restraining harness (Pavlov, 1927). If a human being had displayed the same behavior patterns, we probably would say the person was **neurotic** or "unable to cope."

How different Pavlov's two "mental health" experiments were! In the first case, an animal learned to give a *normal* response to a very abnormal stimulus input. In the second study—even though the dog received no painful stimulation at all—the animal gave an *abnormal* response to a very "normal" set of stimuli.

These two studies convinced Pavlov that "mental illness" was learned and was mostly a matter of mixed-up "connections in the brain." (Pavlov took a purely biological view toward the causes of mental illness. As we will see in later chapters, there are intra-psychic and environmental influences that are at least as important.)

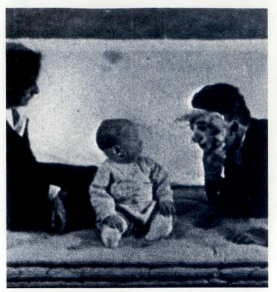

The *generalization* of a fear response to objects that are similar in appearance is shown in this archival photo of Little Albert with John Watson and his assistant. Watson is wearing a furry white mask, which frightens Little Albert much as a furry white rat would have. (Courtesy Dr. Ben Harris, University of Wisconsin–Parkside)

□□ **QUESTION** □□
Pavlov believed his dog became "masochistic" because it had learned that a food reward would always follow the pain. How could you use "extinction procedures" and "retraining" to bring about normal behavior patterns in the animal?

CONDITIONED EMOTIONAL RESPONSES

Once Pavlov had shown the way, a number of other psychologists began experimenting with conditioning procedures using humans rather than animals. John B. Watson, the father of behaviorism, was perhaps the first to study how emotional responses (such as fear) get established in children.

Watson and Little Albert

In one of Watson's most famous experiments, he and his second wife (Rosalie Rayner) conditioned a boy named Albert to fear a white rat. At the beginning of the study, Albert was unafraid of the animal and played with it freely. While Albert was doing so one day, Watson deliberately frightened the child by sounding a terrifying noise behind him. Albert was startled and began to cry. Thereafter, he avoided the rat and cried if it was brought close to him (Watson & Rayner, 1920). (This sort of experimentation is now forbidden by the American Psychological Association's Code of Ethics.)

In Pavlovian terms, Watson and Rayner had set up a *bond* or "connection" between the

sight of the rat (CS) and an arousal response in Albert's autonomic nervous system (CR). Once this S-R bond was fixed, the fear response could also be elicited by showing Albert almost any furry object. Put another way, fears often *generalize* to stimuli similar to the CS. The burnt child dreads not only the fire, but often comes to fear stoves, pots and pans, ovens, pictures of flames, and even stories about the great Chicago fire.

We will have more to say about conditioned fears (and how to treat them) in just a moment. First, let's look at how emotional responses such as fears are often measured in the laboratory.

Measuring Emotional Responses

Words are *stimuli*, just like bells and musical tones. If you were chased by a bull when you were a child, you probably experienced great fear. And you would still show some conditioned *autonomic arousal* even now if you read the word "bull," saw a picture of one, or were asked to think about one.

• ### The Polygraph

We could *measure* your fear reaction to "bulls" by attaching you to a **polygraph**, a machine often (incorrectly) called a "lie-detector." The polygraph would record your pulse, blood pressure, breathing rate, and the amount of sweat produced on the palms of your hands. These are all measures of *autonomic arousal*. And as you know from reading Chapter 8, auto-

David Lykken

The polygraph measures body responses such as pulse, blood pressure, breathing rate, and the amount of sweat on the palms. Its effectiveness as a "lie detector" has been questioned.

nomic arousal is often—*but not always*—associated with the subjective experience of emotionality.

If we showed you an emotionally "neutral" stimulus while you were hooked up to the polygraph, your record presumably would remain calm and regular. If we then presented you with a picture of a large bull, or said the word aloud, the graph would note a sudden, sharp *change* in your autonomic activity. We would then assume you had experienced some emotional arousal, such as that associated with fear, anxiety, or guilt.

The polygraph *can* detect lying at an above-chance level. However, when tested with actual criminal suspects in real-life conditions, its "success rate" in detecting lying is only about 70 percent (where chance expectancy is 50 percent). And, as Minnesota psychiatrist David Lykken points out, "the polygraph test is biased against the truthful respondent. . . . [Almost 50 percent] of the truthful suspects in these studies were erroneously classified as 'deceptive'" (Lykken, 1983).

In a recent survey of the scientific literature on "lie detection," Benjamin Kleinmuntz and Julian Szucko note that use of the polygraph "assumes that liars are aware of their lying, which in turn causes measurable emotional reactions. . . . The polygraphic technique based on this assumption yields unacceptably high error rates that have had ruinous effects on the lives of many misclassified truthful persons" (Kleinmuntz & Szucko, 1984).

□□ QUESTION □□
The ancient Chinese often gave criminal suspects rice to eat. If the suspect could swallow the rice easily, he or she was presumed to be innocent. What have you learned about the effects of autonomic arousal on salivation that might support the use of the "rice guilt detector"?

● *"Beating" the Lie Detector*
David Lykken has, for years, crusaded against the *misuse* of the polygraph. According to Lyk-

ken, "There is no such thing as a lie detector. . . . There is no specific response that everyone **emits** when lying but never when telling the truth. When we lie about something serious, most of us experience some sort of inner turmoil, what Daniel Defoe described 250 years ago as 'a tremor in the blood.' . . . What we forget is that a false accusation can elicit an inner turmoil also—and the lie detector cannot tell the difference!" (Lykken, 1980).

To show what he means, Lykken notes that you can "confuse the experts" during a polygraph test by biting your tongue (to cause pain) and pressing your toes against the floor (to create strong muscle tension). And recent studies do tend to support Lykken's views. For example, University of Wisconsin psychologists Charles Honts, Robert Hodes, and David Raskin trained students to use both the "tongue-biting" and the "toe-pressing" techniques, and then challenged expert polygraph examiners to discover which students were lying and which ones weren't. The students were able to fool the examiners almost 50 percent of the time (Honts, Hodes, & Raskin, 1985).

□□ QUESTION □□
How would it affect your responses if you took a tranquilizer just before being given a polygraph examination?

● *Uses and Abuses of Polygraphs*
David Lykken is not opposed to the *proper* use of polygraph tests, particularly in two situations: First, the polygraph is of considerable value in many scientific studies of autonomic responses. Second, the polygraph can be of great help in police investigations. Wisely employed, polygraph tests can help screen out innocent suspects. The police can then spend their time investigating just the people who "flunk" the exams. And, as Lykken notes, many criminals who "believe" in the polygraph often confess when threatened with a test.

But Lykken believes no person should ever be convicted just on the basis of a lie detector test. The chances the test will be wrong are simply too great, which is one reason few courts admit polygraph records as evidence. Nor, Lykken says, should corporations or government organizations use lie detector tests as "routine screening devices." Again, the odds are too large that people will be denied employment on the basis of some "expert's intuition," and not on the basis of their real skills and talents (Lykken, 1980). And David Raskin puts it this way: "There is not a single scientific study which demonstrates any reasonable degree of accuracy for [the use of the lie detector] for general employment screen tests" (cited in Holden, 1986).

As we saw in Chapter 8, emotionality is a powerful force in human affairs. And it does appear that many (if not all) emotional reactions are acquired by Pavlovian conditioning. However, if most emotional reactions are *learned*, then we might assume most of them can be *unlearned*, or extinguished. That particular insight has led to the development of a new type of psychotherapy called *counter conditioning*.

COUNTER CONDITIONING

In a recent article, Kansas State psychologist Franz Samelson describes the difficulties John B. Watson and Rosalie Rayner had trying to "condition fear" in Little Albert. At first they attempted to make the boy afraid of a flash of light (rather than a rat). They failed, in part because whenever they tried to frighten the child, he would pop his thumb into his mouth. Then he would sit peacefully thumb-sucking, instead of showing the normal "fear" response. According to Samelson, Watson and Rayner could get the fear reaction only when they kept Albert's thumb out of his mouth (Samelson, 1980).

It seems likely the problems Watson and Rayner had *conditioning* fear in Albert gave them the idea of how to *decondition* similar responses. For if thumb-sucking "overwhelmed" the fear response, perhaps they could "counter condition" other children to recover from fear by teaching them a "relaxing" reaction like thumb-sucking. In 1924, a student of Watson's named Mary Cover Jones tried just that.

To appreciate how "counter conditioning" works, imagine that at some time in the future, your own 2-year-old son accidentally· learned to fear small furry animals. You might try to cure the boy the way Mary Cover Jones did—by attempting to attach a *strongly positive* response to the fear-arousing stimulus.

The *sight* of a white rat would presumably upset your son—but the sight of food when he was hungry would surely make him happy and eager to eat. If you could somehow *bond* the "rat" stimulus to the "positive" eating response, you could "decondition" the child by making him like the rat rather than fear it.

You might begin the counter-conditioning procedure by bringing a white rat into the same room with your son while you were feeding him. At first, you would want to keep the animal so far away that your son could barely see it out of the corner of his eye. Since the animal wouldn't be close enough to bother him, he probably would keep right on eating. Then, step by step, you might bring the rat closer.

Children do not generally fear small furry animals, such as rabbits, unless one or more unpleasant experiences have "taught" them to feel fearful. Teaching children to overcome such learned fears has been done quite successfully using counter-conditioning techniques.

Since your son could not cry and eat *at the same time*, the CS-CR fear response would gradually *extinguish*. And while the strength of the fear reaction was decreasing, the strength of the CS-CR "pleasure of eating" bond would increase. Eventually, your son would be conditioned to give a new response to the animal that was *counter* to his previous reaction. When Mary Cover Jones followed this procedure (actually using a white rabbit instead of a rat), she found that children soon learned to play with animals that had previously terrified them (Jones, 1924).

The important point about counter conditioning is this—the technique almost always involves *breaking* an inappropriate S-R bond by attaching the *old* "S" to a *new* and more appropriate "R" (Catania, 1984).

□ □ **QUESTION** □ □

For most people, the sight of a big, hairy spider is a stimulus that evokes a very strong avoidance reaction. How might you try to "treat this fear" by counter coundititioning the spider stimulus to a new response?

Phobias

In a sense, Watson and Rayner created a **phobia** about rats in little Albert. Phobias are intense, irrational fears about people, places, things, or situations. Usually these fears are so strong that the person with the phobia cannot control her or his reactions even when the person clearly realizes the terror is illogical and unreasonable.

Specific phobias—such as fear of snakes—are often created from a single emotion-charged encounter with the object dreaded.

Mary Cover Jones

Just as likely, they can come about because of a series of highly unpleasant interactions. In Pavlovian terms, the phobia is said to be caused by the *association* of a previously neutral stimulus (the snake) with those stimuli associated with pain, fear, or great autonomic arousal. The snake stimulus therefore automatically becomes connected to the fear reaction.

The belief that phobias are *learned by association* led psychiatrists and psychologists to attempt to "cure" these irrational fears by using the same sort of *counter-conditioning* techniques pioneered by Mary Cover Jones. The technical term used to describe these techniques is **desensitization**.

Put simply, *desensitization* always involves *breaking* an old S-R bond by associating a *new response* with the *old stimulus*. In treating a snake phobia, for example, you could break the "snake-fear" S-R bond by attaching a *relaxation response* to the *snake stimulus*.

• A Hierarchy of Fears

Joseph Wolpe, a psychiatrist now working at Temple University in Philadelphia, is usually given credit for having popularized the use of "counter conditioning" in treating simple phobias. Wolpe's type of therapy is usually called *systematic* desensitization.

Let's suppose that, like a number of students, you have somehow acquired an "exam phobia." That is, every time you try to take an exam, you break out in a cold sweat and your mind "goes blank" no matter how hard you have studied. If you sought Wolpe's help, he would begin treatment by asking you to make a list or **hierarchy** of what frightened you about exam situations. Your hierarchy would range from the least-feared stimulus to the most feared. Wolpe would then try to pair *muscular relaxation* with each stimulus on your list, starting with the least-frightening item on the hierarchy.

Let's say that the lowest item on your list is thinking about an exam some time before it occurs. Wolpe would ask you to relax ("go limp") as you contemplated taking a test some time in the future. If the desensitization tech-

nique worked, the relaxation *response* would soon become "connected" to the internal *stimulus* of "thinking about taking an exam."

Then Wolpe would move up the hierarchy, step by step, trying to pair relaxation with each item on your list. At any point, if you tended to panic, Wolpe would stop immediately, get you to calm down, and then start over with an item lower on the list that you had already learned to handle successfully. Eventually, you'd know how to "go limp" as you sat in the classroom waiting for the teacher to pass out the tests on exam day.

Wolpe believes that, during treatment, the phobic reaction must never be allowed to get so strong that it cannot be counteracted by voluntary muscular relaxation (Wolpe, 1981b).

Thousands of patients have been treated with apparent success using one form of desensitization or another. However, there is still considerable debate as to whether "systematic" desensitization occurs for the reasons Wolpe says it does and whether the technique is actually the best type of therapy to use with phobic patients.

□ □ **QUESTION** □ □
Do you think it might help you to overcome your "exam phobia" if you learned better study habits after the phobic reaction itself had been desensitized?

Systematic Desensitization: Pro and Con

Joseph Wolpe is a psychiatrist who, like Pavlov, believes that the "body controls the mind." And, like Pavlov, Wolpe sees the "important" association that occurs during learning as being that which connects Ss to Rs. Therefore, therapy must consist of breaking S-R bonds.

Put another way, as far as Wolpe is concerned, it is your *autonomic arousal* to a fearful object or situation that must be "desensitized," not your "inner feelings" or "thoughts." As you can imagine, psychologists who take an intra-psychic view of things tend to disagree with Wolpe.

For example, is learning *primarily* an association between Ss and Rs? Can't strong bonds also be built up between two different Ss? In fact, there can be. Suppose we take an untrained dog and, for a dozen trials, present it with a white light (S_{light}) followed immediately by a musical tone (S_{tone}). Does the animal salivate? Of course not, since we haven't yet "paired" either stimulus with food powder. But perhaps this "pairing" of S_{light} and S_{tone} brought about a strong "mental association" linking the two stimuli. To test for this possibility, we next condition the animal to salivate to the tone using Pavlovian techniques. Once the CS_{tone}-$CR_{salivation}$ bond is firmly established, we

Joseph Wolpe

then present the dog with the S_{light} stimulus. Although the light has never been "paired" with the food powder, the S_{light} still elicits a few drops of saliva.

Pavlov called this type of training **higher order conditioning** and stoutly maintained it was "mediated" by S-R learning. However, a number of experiments suggest that *higher order conditioning* is better explained in terms of S-S associations (Rescorla, 1984, 1987).

□ □ **QUESTION** □ □
How could you explain an "exam phobia" in terms of S-S associations rather than S-R conditioning? (Hint: Could the student *misperceive* either the exam situation or his or her own abilities?) What type of treatment could you use to break inappropriate S-S associations?

● *Cognitive Desensitization*

Perceptual, attitudinal, and other cognitive changes often occur during desensitization training. That is, the patient frequently reports perceiving the once-feared situation in a new and less frightening light. When Wolpe first began his work, he appeared to believe that these perceptual changes were *caused* by changes in autonomic arousal.

However, D.H. Meichenbaum (and many other therapists) soon insisted Wolpe had put the cart before the horse. For instance, Meichenbaum noted that, during therapy, cognitive changes often occurred *first*. Once the patients had changed the *manner in which they perceived the situation,* they could relax more in the presence of the dreaded stimulus (Meichenbaum, 1974).

Furthermore, many studies show that purely mental relaxation can be as powerful in helping to cure phobias as is muscular relaxation (Berman, Miller, & Massman, 1985). The use of *mental* rather than *muscular* relaxation is sometimes called **cognitive desensitization** (Beck, 1986).

□ □ **QUESTION** □ □
How could you use a polygraph to measure the *decrease in fear* that occurs in either systematic or cognitive desensitization?

● *"Modeling Therapy"*

Stanford psychologist Albert Bandura believes that treatment shouldn't stop when the phobic response is desensitized. Next, Bandura says, the therapist should help the client learn an *appropriate* response to replace the "inappropriate" fear reaction. And the most efficient way to learn new response patterns, Bandura believes, is to "imitate the behaviors of an appropriate *model*." Then the client can learn a new

response *merely by observing* what the model does.

In a frequently-cited experiment, Bandura and his colleagues used an *observational learning* technique to help subjects overcome their phobic reactions to snakes. The subjects began by watching a "model"—a trained snake handler—who was playing with a reptile several feet from where the clients were standing. Then the clients were encouraged slowly to approach the model (and the snake, of course). Next the clients were urged to touch the reptile, then to hold it briefly. The "final exam" consisted of having the clients sit quietly in a chair while the snake crawled all over them. Bandura and his associates report that "modeling therapy" was significantly more effective at breaking the snake phobia than was systematic desensitization alone (Bandura, Blanchard, & Ritter, 1969).

□ □ **QUESTION** □ □
Suppose you watched a woman pick up a strange object, then drop the object in obvious pain. Could you develop a strong fear of the strange object even though you had never touched it yourself? Would this be S-S learning or S-R learning?

● *Wolpe's Response to His Critics*

In a recent article, Wolpe comments on the many criticisms of his approach. He now differentiates between "cognitively-based anxiety" and "conditioned anxiety." According to Wolpe, *cognitive anxiety* is brought about by mental "errors or misinformation." *Conditioned anxiety*, though, is "based on autonomic conditioning" and is acquired in just the manner that Pavlov described. Conditioned anxiety occurs primarily in such simple situations as specific phobias, Wolpe says. Both types of anxiety are likely to be present in more complex cases, such as non-specific phobias.

Wolpe urges the use of desensitization therapy to treat conditioned anxiety. However, he does not make any specific recommendations about how to treat purely "cognitive" anxiety (Wolpe, 1981a).

● *Desensitization or "Natural Extinction"?*

A survey of the literature suggests that any technique which keeps the patient in the "presence" of the feared object (or situation) for an extended period of time will help extinguish the fear. Desensitization may be effective, therefore, simply because it is an elegant way of getting patients to remain near the things they are afraid of until a sort of "natural extinction" takes place. And the more "cognitive" forms of counter-conditioning may work because they require the patient to think about

One step in Bandura's snake phobia therapy is holding a snake in one's hands. The person suffering from the phobia would not be asked to perform this activity until she could perform a less fearful activity — just touching the snake with her fingers, for example — without feeling fear.

Higher order conditioning. A training technique that involves "pairing" two neutral stimuli, then "connecting" one of the Ss to a response using Pavlovian conditioning. When the other neutral S is now presented, it usually can elicit a weak conditioned response even though it has never been directly "paired" with that response.

Cognitive desensitization. Pavlov and the early behavioral psychologists dealt entirely with external stimuli and observable responses. During the 1960's, psychologists discovered that Pavlovian techniques could be used to condition (or decondition) inner processes, such as thoughts and feelings. Desensitization seems to occur just as rapidly if the patient thinks relaxing thoughts (a cognitive process) as if the patient actually relaxes (an observable response).

Whatever method of treating phobias we think is best, we should remember that the goal of all therapies is to help the person engage in normal activities — such as flying in an airplane — without undue anxiety.

the feared objects or situations until the same sort of natural extinction occurs.

Which Position Is Correct?

In fact, there's little sense in fighting over which form of therapy is best, since all types of treatment have their uses. And, as we will see in a later chapter, most types of therapy yield similar results.

In fact, this battle (like many others in psychology) boils down to a matter of *definitions* and *theoretical viewpoints.* Many behavioral psychologists define learning entirely in terms of "stimuli" and "responses." Cognitive psychologists, on the other hand, see learning primarily in terms of *associations between thoughts or ideas.* In truth, however, the *same laws of learning* seem to hold—roughly speaking—whether you deal with behaviors or cognitions.

From a holistic point of view, a person with a snake phobia has *both* disordered behaviors *and* disordered thoughts and feelings. Treating just one part of the problem seldom is as helpful as treating *all aspects* of the phobic condition.

Sometimes, in the heat of defending our theoretical positions, we all lose sight of the prime goal—namely, to get the patient back to normal as quickly and as surely as possible. And to do that, we surely should make use of any type of treatment that "works." We will raise this issue again at the end of the next chapter, after we have looked at a different form of learning called *operant conditioning.*

SUMMARY

1. The American psychologist E.B. Twitmyer was probably the first to publish research on the **conditioned reflex**, but Ivan Pavlov developed most of the conditioning techniques and terminology still in use.

2. Conditioning involves pairing a **neutral stimulus** (the CS) with an **unconditioned stimulus** or *unconditional stimulus* (the UCS). The UCS already has the power to elicit the **unconditioned response** (the UCR). If the CS is associated with the UCS enough times, it conditionally takes on the power to evoke a reaction similar to the UCR. This "similar" reaction is called the **conditioned response** or *conditional response* (the CR).

3. Pavlov paired a tone (CS) with food powder blown into a dog's mouth (the UCS). The food naturally evoked salivation (the UCR). Once the tone had been paired with the food for several trials, sounding the tone without food caused the dog to salivate (the CR).

4. Psychologists often use the term **conditioning** to mean **learning**.

5. According to Pavlov, all learning or conditioning is built on—or is an adaption of— **innately determined stimulus-response connections**, the UCS-UCR bond.

6. Conditioning is sometimes referred to as strengthening S-R bonds or **stimulus-response bonds**. The stronger the bond, the more likely it is the conditioned stimulus will elicit the desired conditioned response.

7. The more often the CS and the UCS are paired, the stronger the **S-R bond** becomes.

8. Conditioning typically proceeds fastest when the CS is presented immediately **before** the UCS. The exception to this rule is a **conditioned taste aversion**. If you become ill several hours after eating some particular food, you may avoid that food in the future.

9. Conditioned responses are unlearned just as easily as they are learned. Unlearning proceeds fastest when the CS is presented several times without being followed by the UCS. Once the S-R bond is broken, the response is said to be **extinguished**.

10. An extinguished response is not totally forgotten. If the CS is again paired with the UCS, **relearning** usually takes fewer trials than did the original learning. Furthermore, extinguished responses often show **spontaneous recovery** after some time has passed.

11. **Internal stimuli** (such as muscle tension) can serve as a CS just as well as can bells or musical tones. The passage of time can also serve as a conditional stimulus.

12. Pavlov conditioned dogs to withstand pain by pairing a weak painful stimulus with a strong UCS, such as food. The food evoked salivation. Soon the **painful stimulus** also evoked salivation rather than escape.

13. If an animal is trained to respond to an orange light, this response may **generalize** to other similar stimuli, such as a red or yellow light. However, with the proper train-

ing, the animal can usually learn to **discriminate** among similar stimuli and give different responses to each.

14. If this discrimination becomes too difficult, the animal may show such **neurotic** responses as biting, barking, and defecation.

15. Watson and Rayner conditioned a boy called Little Albert to fear a rat by pairing the sight of the rat with a frightening noise. Mary Cover Jones reduced this sort of **conditioned emotional response** by pairing the sight of the animal with food using a technique called **counter-conditioning**.

16. The **polygraph** or "lie detector" measures **conditioned emotional responses**, not "lies" or "guilt."

17. Many psychologists believe that most human **phobic reactions** are conditioned in the same manner that Watson and Rayner created a fear response in Little Albert.

18. Joseph Wolpe showed that conditioned fears can be lessened through the use of **systematic desensitization**, a counter-conditioning technique that involves pairing the feared stimulus with relaxation. The patient makes a **hierarchy of fears** ranging from the least feared to the most feared. The patient learns to relax in the presence of stimuli low on the hierarchy of fears first, then **step by step** moves up the hierarchy.

19. **Higher order conditioning** involves first pairing two neutral stimuli, then bonding one of the stimuli to a conditioned response. When the other neutral stimulus is then presented, the animal often gives the conditioned response even though that stimulus has never been associated with the CR.

20. **Cognitive desensitization** involves the use of mental rather than physical relaxation, and seems to be more effective with complex fears than is *systematic desensitization*.

21. **Modeling therapy** encourages the phobic patient to observe and then imitate "appropriate" responses toward the feared object made by someone who doesn't fear the object. Bandura believes it is more important to give the phobic patient new ways of handling fears than it is merely to break S-R bonds.

22. There is some evidence that desensitization (and other therapies) are effective because they keep the patient in the presence of the feared stimulus long enough so that **natural extinction** of the fear can occur.

23. Perhaps the best form of therapy is one that treats all of the patient's problems, whether the problems are biological, psychological, or social.

"Well, what do you think about the desensitization program so far?" Dr. Nancy Wagner asked two months later. *(Continued from page 222.)*

Kevin Lynn grinned mischievously. "You really ought to ask my wife. After all, she's the one who whipped me into coming to see you."

Dr. Wagner clucked her tongue. "I thought the problem was that your wife wouldn't whip you."

"Just kidding," Kevin Lynn said. "Actually, it's going pretty well even without the whips."

"That's good to hear. We can stop therapy now, if you wish. Or, if you'd like, we can try to find out how you acquired the association between pain and sex in the first place."

The man sighed. "I'd like to go on. I think the treatment would last longer if I understood how all this mess got started."

"I agree," the woman replied. "Anything in particular you want to talk about?"

Kevin Lynn paused, and then a crimson blush spread over his pale face. "Let's talk about the other night."

"Oh," replied the woman. "What happened the other night?"

"Nothing happened," Lynn said quietly. "That was the trouble."

Dr. Wagner nodded sympathetically. "Why don't you tell me about it."

Lynn sighed. "Let me relax a minute first." He tensed various parts of his body, then let them go limp. "Still feels good when I do that. But it just didn't work the other evening."

"What was the situation?" the woman asked. "Tell me what you were doing, what your wife was doing, and how you responded."

"She was lying in bed, watching television, eating some candy. Chocolates, I think." Lynn stopped abruptly. "Funny, suddenly I'm tense all over."

Dr. Wagner smiled reassuringly. "Relax for a moment. Completely relax. Okay?"

"Okay," said the man.

"Now, shut your eyes and listen to your body while I talk. The moment that you feel any tension, lift your right hand. Understand?"

"Okay," said the man, exhaling loudly.

"I want you to imagine your bedroom. Look at the chairs, and the dresser. Any tension?"

The man shook his head.

"Now look at the bed. Any tension yet?"

"Maybe a tiny bit. No big deal, really."

Dr. Wagner nodded. "Okay, keep your eyes closed, and imagine your wife watching the TV. Just as you walk into the bedroom and start to approach her, she reaches into a box of chocolates . . ."

"Stop," the man said. "That did it."

"Chocolates," said the woman. "Why does that bother you?"

Lynn shook his head. "Haven't the foggiest." He sighed. "Oh, well, the tension seems to be gone now anyhow."

"Good," Dr. Wagner said. "Tell me if it returns. Now, what happened after you saw your wife eating the candy?"

"Hum," said the man, trying to remember. "We talked a bit, kidded around a bit. She was smoking a cigarette, but when I sat down on the bed, she went to put it out, and knocked the ashtray over . . ."

Dr. Wagner leaned forward. "Suddenly you're sweating."

"The tension started just then," the man said.

"Relax. Just go limp, really limp."

Kevin Lynn sighed deeply, and then nodded when his muscles seemed relaxed.

"Stop me if the tension starts again," Dr. Wagner said. "Now, there seem to be four stimuli that, put together, cause the tension. You just stay as relaxed as you can while I name them. First, your wife in bed. Second, she's watching television. Third, she's eating chocolates. And fourth, she knocks over the ashtray."

"Stop," Lynn said. "There it is again."

"Well," the woman said. "It seemed to be the ashtray that you really reacted to. Now, I want you to relax deeply again. Go deep down inside your mind, and look for something about an ashtray. Did you ever knock one over?"

The man shook his head. "Not that I remember."

Dr. Wagner continued. "Well, did you ever see someone else knock one over? Your mother, perhaps, when you were a small child."

"Stop," Lynn said. "I feel tense again. Not much, but a bit."

"Just relax. Be calm," the woman said. And when the man sighed, she went on. "Okay, the ashtray is the clue. Did your mother smoke?"

Lynn shook his head. "No, but my father did." He stopped. "Oh, wow, I'm tense again."

"Relax, relax as deeply as you can," the woman said. "We're getting close now. I want you to think of a time when you and your mother and your father were together, and your mother was eating chocolates and watching television."

Kevin Lynn groaned loudly. "Oh, my God, it's all coming back to me now."

"Good, good," said Dr. Wagner. "Just go limp, and then tell me what you remember."

"Incredible," said the man. "I completely forgot about it until now. I must have been nine or ten. Mom was watching television, and she made me stand in the corner in the bedroom while she watched. Seems like I was always standing in the corner for one reason or another. Anyway, this particular night, she was eating chocolates and watching the tube, and I really had to . . . to . . ."

"Urinate?" asked the woman.

"Yeah," the man said softly. "So I was squirming a bit, you know, and she got very upset because I was . . ." He shifted nervously in his chair.

"Touching your genitals?"

"That's right. I guess most kids do that, don't they, when they have to urinate?"

Dr. Wagner nodded her agreement. "They certainly do." She paused to think, then continued. "Now, I want to ask you a question, but I want you to relax deeply first. Okay?"

"Okay, I'm relaxed."

"Did your mother threaten to whip you when you touched your genitals?"

Lynn groaned again. "Oh, Lord, yes. All the time when I touched myself."

"Relax," commanded the woman. "It's all right. Now, tell me what happened next."

He paused. "I was standing in the corner, squirming around and touching myself, and my mother was watching the tube and eating chocolates and threatening to whip me if I didn't behave. Then my father came into the room, and I guess they must have had another argument. Scared the hell out of me . . ."

"Very understandable," said the woman, soothingly.

"Then they started shouting at each other, and my father got pretty mad, I guess. He probably had been drinking a little, you know?"

"I know," said Dr. Wagner.

The man sighed. "There's something else, though, something I can't recall."

"When your father rushed toward your mother, what did she do?"

"Oh, my God," the man said. "Of course! I remember now! She threw the ashtray at him, but she missed, and . . . and . . ."

The woman nodded. "I know, it hit you instead, didn't it?"

"That memory hurts," the man said softly. "It hurts like hell."

Dr. Wagner sighed. "See if you can remember what happened after the ashtray hit you."

"I remember I screamed, and they stopped arguing. My mother rushed over to me and grabbed me up. She hugged me to her breast and said she didn't mean it." Lynn stopped. "Oh, my," he said a moment later. "It all makes sense now."

Dr. Wagner nodded again. "Yes, it does, doesn't it? You got afraid and very tense, then you got hurt, and that stopped the argument and the fear. And then your mother hugged you and kissed you. One-trial conditioning, I'd say."

"Oh, my," the man said hoarsely.

The woman sighed deeply. "I think we've done enough for today. We can put the scene into the hierarchy the next time you're here. Shouldn't take too long to desensitize you to the whole thing. Okay?"

Kevin Lynn smiled. "Okay. But right now, I'm going home and break every ashtray in the house. And throw out all the chocolates."

"And the whips?"

"Yeah. Especially those. And then I'm going to kiss my wife, and . . ."

"And?"

Lynn grinned. "And then I'm going to show her I love her in the best way I know how."

"No sweat," said the woman.

"No pain," said the man.

Operant Conditioning and Cognitive Behaviorism

"That'll Learn You!"

· C H A P T E R ·

10

STUDY QUESTIONS

As you read through the chapter, see if you can find the answers to the following questions:

1. What sort of learning theory do "disciplinarians" seem to believe in?
2. According to E.L. Thorndike, what does learning chiefly consist of?
3. What were Thorndike's two "laws of learning"?
4. Why did Thorndike change his second law?
5. What is "learning by insight"?
6. Why was Pavlov so angry at Koehler?
7. What is a "cognitive map"?
8. Using Skinner's techniques, how could you train a pigeon to bowl?
9. What is the difference between "extrinsic" and "intrinsic" motivation?
10. How does "negative reinforcement" differ from "punishment"?
11. What type of reinforcement schedule do the slot machines in Las Vegas seem to operate on?
12. What are the major differences between operant and respondent conditioning?
13. Does biofeedback really "cure" headaches?
14. What is "cognitive behavior modification"?
15. What are the two main theoretical "models" used to explain "alcoholism"?
16. According to the *experimental data*, what type of treatment for "alcoholism" seems to yield the best "cure rates"?

I am writing this because I presume He wants me to. Otherwise He would not have left paper and pencil handy for me to use. And I put the word "He" in capitals because it seems the only thing to do. If I am dead and in hell, then this is only proper. However, if I am merely a captive somewhere, a little flattery won't hurt matters.

As I think about it, I am impressed most of all by the suddenness of the whole affair. At one moment I was out walking in the woods near my home. The next thing I knew, here I was in a small, bare room, naked as a jaybird, with only my good sense to stand between me and insanity. When the "change" occurred—whatever the change was—I was not aware of even a momentary flicker between walking in the woods and being here in this room. He must have a technology available to Him that is very impressive indeed!

As I recall, I was worrying about how to teach my introductory psychology class some of the more technical points of Learning Theory, when the "change" came. How far away life at the University seems at the moment! I hope Dean Steiner will forgive me if I am now more concerned about where I am—and how to get out of here—than about cajoling undergraduates into understanding Pavlov or Skinner.

Problem #1: Where am I? For an answer, I can only describe this gray, windowless room. It is about 20 feet square and 12 feet high. The ceiling glows with a soft white light, and the spongy floor has a "tingly" feel to it suggesting it may be in constant vibration.

The only furnishings in the room are "lumps" that resemble a table and chair. On the table I found a rough sort of paper and a stick of graphite which I have sharpened into a pencil. My clothes are gone. The suit was an old one I won't miss, but I am worried about what happened to my watch. It was an elegant Swiss model, and quite expensive.

The #1 problem still remains, however. Where in the hell am I—if not Hell itself!

Problem #2 is a knottier one—why am I here? I have the usual quota of enemies, but even Dean Steiner isn't powerful enough to arrange for something like this. And I surely am not rich enough to kidnap. So, where am I, and why? And who is He?

There is no sense in trying to keep track of time. This room is little more than a sensory deprivation chamber, and I haven't the faintest notion of what hour or even what day it is. Well, if He wasn't bright enough to leave me my watch, He can't complain that I don't keep accurate records.

Or is that the problem I'm supposed to solve?

Nothing much has happened. I have slept, been fed and watered, and have emptied my bladder and bowels. The food was waiting on the table when I awoke last time. I must say that He has little of the gourmet in him. Protein balls are not my idea of a feast. However, they will serve to keep body and soul together (presuming, of course, they *are* together at the moment).

But I must object to my source of water. While I was asleep, a small nipple appeared on the wall. It produces a sweetish liquid when I suck on it. However, drinking this way is a most undignified behavior for a full professor to engage in. I'd complain to the Management if only I knew to whom I should complain!

Following my meal, the call to nature became a little too strong to ignore. Now, I was adequately toilet-trained, and the absence of indoor plumbing is most annoying. But there was nothing much to do other than choose a corner of the room and make the best of a bad situation. However, I have at least learned why the floor vibrates, for the excreted material sank out of sight moments later. Clever technology, but bothersome, since I have to sleep on the floor. I will probably have nightmares that the floor will gulp me up too, all in a piece.

You know, this place seems dreadfully quiet to me.

Suddenly I have solved two of my problems. I know both where I am and who He is. And I bless the day that I got interested in sensory psychology and the perception of motion.

The air in this room is filled with dust particles. This fact became important when I noticed the dust tended to pile up along the floor against one particular wall. At first I thought there might be an air vent there. However, when I put my hand to the floor, I could feel no breeze whatsoever. Yet even as I held my hand there, dust motes covered my hand. I tried this same experiment everywhere else in the room, but this was the only spot where the dust coated my hand.

But if ventilation was not responsible for the dust, what was? Suddenly there popped into my mind some calculations I had made when NASA first proposed building a wheel-shaped satellite and then set it to spinning slowly in space. What we once called "centrifugal force" would substitute for the force of gravity, and the outer shell of the wheel would appear to be "down" to anyone inside the wheel. It immediately occurred to me that dust would move in a direction *opposite* to the rotation of the wheel, and thus airborne particles would pile up against any wall that impeded their flight.

It also seemed that the NASA engineers had overlooked one important fact. Namely, that humans are at least as sensitive to angular rotation as they are to the pull of gravity. As I figured the problem then, if a man aboard the wheel moved his head a few feet toward or away from the center of the doughnut-shaped satellite, he would have sensed the angular rotation of the wheel. Rather annoying it would have been too, becoming dizzy every time you sat down or stood up.

10 / Operant Conditioning and Cognitive Behaviorism

With this thought in mind, I climbed atop the table and jumped off. Sure enough, I immediately felt dizzy. My hypothesis was confirmed.

I am aboard a wheel-shaped spaceship!

The thought is incredible, but in a strange way comforting. At least now I can postpone worry about heaven and hell and start considering other things. And, of course, I know who "He" is. Or rather, I know who He *isn't*, which is something else again. Since no country on earth has a space station like this one, He must be an alien!

I still have no notion of *why* I am here, however, nor why this alien picked me of all people to bring to His spaceship. One dreadful thought did occur to me, though. Maybe He's an alien scientist—a biologist of sorts—out gathering specimens. Is He going to cut me open to see what makes me tick? Will my innards be smeared over a glass slide for hundreds of youthful Hims to peer at under a microscope? Brrrr! I don't mind giving my life to Science, but I'd rather do it a day at a time.

Good God! I should have known it! Destiny will play her little tricks, and all jokes have their cosmic angles.

He is a *psychologist*!

Had I given the matter thought, I would have realized that whenever you come across a new species, you worry about behavior first, biology second. So I have received the ultimate insult—or the ultimate compliment, I don't know which. I have become a laboratory specimen for an alien psychologist!

This thought first occurred to me when I awoke after my latest sleep (which was filled with frightening dreams). Almost at once I noticed that one of the walls now had a lever of some kind protruding from it. Underneath the lever was a small hole with a container beneath the hole. When I accidentally depressed the lever, it made a loud clicking noise. Immediately, a protein ball popped out of the hole and fell into the container. For just a moment I was puzzled. This seemed so strangely familiar. Then, all at once, I burst into wild laughter.

This room is a gigantic Skinner Box!

For years I have been putting white rats in an operant chamber and making them press a lever to get a pellet of food. And now, after all those experiments, I find *myself* trapped like a rat in a Skinner Box! Perhaps this is hell after all, and He is just following the Lord High Executioner's advice to "let the punishment fit the crime."

Anyhow, it didn't take me long to discover that pressing the lever would give me food only at rather lengthy intervals. The rest of the time, all I get is a click for my efforts. Since I am never quite sure when the proper interval has passed, I stomp over to the lever and press it whenever I think it's getting close to dinner time. Just like my rats always did. And since the pellets are small and I never get enough of them, occasionally I find myself banging away on the lever with all the compulsion of a stupid animal. But I missed the feeding time once and almost starved to death (so it seemed) before the lever next delivered food. About the only consolation to my wounded pride is that I've already lost an inch or so around my waist.

At least He doesn't seem to be fattening me up for the kill!

I have been promoted. Apparently He has decided I'm intelligent enough to handle the Skinner Box. So I've been promoted to solving a maze.

Can you picture the irony of the situation? All of the classic laboratory apparatus is being thrown right in my face. If only I could communicate with Him! I don't mind being subjected to tests nearly as much as I mind being underestimated. Why, I can solve puzzles hundreds of times more complex than the ones He's giving me. But how can I tell Him?

As it turns out, the maze is much like the ones I have used. It's rather long, with 23 choice points along the way. I spent half an hour wandering through the thing the first time. Surprisingly enough, I didn't realize what I was in, so I made no conscious attempt to memorize the correct turns. It wasn't until I reached the final choice point and found food that I recognized what was expected of me. The next time I made fewer errors, and was able to turn in a perfect performance fairly rapidly. However, I'm embarrassed to state that my own white rats could have learned the maze somewhat sooner than I did.

Now that I am sure of what is happening to me, my thoughts have turned to getting out of this situation. Mazes I can solve easily, but how to escape apparently is beyond my intellectual capacity. Come to think of it, though, there was precious little my own experimental animals could do to get out of my clutches.

And assuming that I am unable to escape, what then? After He has finished putting me through as many paces as He wishes, where do we go from there? Will He treat me as I treated most of my rats? "Following the experiment, the animals were sacrificed," as we so politely put it in our journal articles. This thought doesn't appeal to me very much, as you can imagine. But perhaps if I seem particularly bright to Him, He may use me for breeding purposes, to establish a colony of His own. Now, that situation might have possibilities . . .

Oh, damn Freud anyhow!

And damn Him too! I had just gotten the maze well learned when He changed it on me. I stumbled about like a bat in the sunlight for quite some time before I finally got to the goal box. I'm afraid my performance was pretty poor. What He did was to reverse the whole maze so that it was a mirror image of what it used to be. Took me only two trials to discover the solution. Let Him figure that one out if He's so smart!

My performance on the maze reversal must have pleased Him, because He's added a new complication. He's trying me out on a "jump stand." I sit on a little platform facing three doors across an empty space. If I jump to the correct door, I get food. If I pick the wrong one, I fall into a pool of icy water. And if I don't jump at all, He shocks the devil out of me until I do!

I suppose I could have predicted what He would do next if I had been thinking in the right direction. The trouble is, I've been out of graduate school for too long. I took my first advanced course in learning theory from a strict Behavioral Scientist. "Dr. B-S," we called him. He was convinced that rats learned a maze mechanically, by relying entirely on stimulus-response bonds. The professor for my second course was a confirmed "mentalist," who insisted that rats learned a maze by creating a "cognitive map" of the apparatus in their minds. "Dr. Cog," we called him. And oh! the delicious battles he and "Dr. B-S" had when they debated in public.

The conflict between the two reached a peak when one of Dr. Cog's students started working with the Oddity Problem. Imagine yourself sitting meekly on a jump stand, staring at three doors across the water-filled gap. The two outer doors are white, the middle door is black. You try jumping at each of the white doors, and end up in the drink. So you leap toward the black door in the middle and find a nice meal of protein balls awaiting you. Thereafter—whether the black door is on the right, the left, or in the center—you jump toward it as quickly as you can. And you are always rewarded.

Now, the question is, how did you learn this trick? Dr. B-S insisted that you had "acquired the habit" of approaching the black stimulus and avoiding the white stimulus. But Dr. Cog contended that you learned to go to the "odd" color—in this case, black. This explanation infuriated Dr. B-S, who insisted that oddness is a "mental concept" rather than a true stimulus and that rats weren't capable of "conceptualizing."

Dr. Cog then proposed a Grand Theoretical Test. Namely, he would now show a rat *two* black doors and *one* white door and see what it did. If the rat had merely learned "to approach the black stimulus," it would leap wildly toward one of the black doors. But if it had learned to "approach the odd-colored door," it would jump to the white door *even though it had never before been rewarded for approaching white*. Dr. B-S scoffed, since rats obviously weren't bright enough to "think in concepts."

So, what do you think happened? Most of the rats Dr. Cog tested jumped to the white door the first time they saw it! Dr. B-S was furious, and Dr. Cog chortled smugly for weeks on end. Dr. Cog then rubbed salt in Dr. B-S's wounds by testing his rats on two doors with vertical stripes and one with horizontal stripes. And then on the reverse. Each time, most of the animals picked the "odd" stimulus. The results were so impressive that Dr. B-S threw up his hands in dismay and went to Texas on sabbatical. When he returned, he began studying biofeedback in humans, and never touched a rodent again.

What has all this got to do with me? Well, He must be a simple behaviorist, like old Dr. B-S. The last time He put me on the jump stand, I found myself facing two blue doors and a yellow one. I realized what was up instantly, and leapt toward the yellow. Success! Immediately He tested me with two yellow doors and a blue one. I jumped to the blue, and heard what I can only describe as a cosmic roar of frustration. I gather He wasn't very happy with what I had done.

Next up were two red doors and a green one. I "went for the green," and had no more than landed safely when the whole apparatus started to shake as if someone had kicked it in anger!

The next thing I knew, I was tossed rather roughly back in my cage. Since nothing has happened for an hour or so, I presume He's off sulking somewhere because my actions didn't confirm His expectations.

I suppose I should have realized it before now. Theories are typically born of the equipment one uses. If Skinner had never invented his blasted box, if the maze and the jump stand had not been developed, we probably would have entirely different theories of learning today than we now have. For, if nothing else, the type of apparatus you use *reduces* the types of behavior your subjects can show. And your theories only have to account for the kinds of responses that show up in laboratory situations.

But if He has a problem, I have a worse one. What should I do next, now that I know what He expects of me? Should I help Him confirm his narrow notions about behavior—and about the new species He's testing? Or should I prove to the monster that I'm more "cognitive" than He thinks I ought to be?

I'm sure He will shortly snatch me back for a final test. When I face those different-colored doors, should I perform "stupidly" like the intelligent human being I really am? Or should I perform "intelligently" by acting like the dumb rat He wants me to be?

What am I anyhow? A man, or a mouse?

(Continued on page 261.)

10 / Operant Conditioning and Cognitive Behaviorism

Disciplinarians (diss-sip-plin-NAIR-ee-ans). From the Latin word meaning "teachers." We get our word "disciples" from the same Latin source. *Webster's New Collegiate Dictionary* defines *to discipline* as "to punish or penalize for the sake of discipline, to train or develop by instruction and exercise, especially in self-control."

Pedagogues (PEDD-ah-gogs). From the Greek words meaning "leader of children." Literally, a teacher or schoolmaster.

LEARNING THEORIES

During the many years that you have gone to school, you must have had contact with dozens of different teachers. Some of them probably were strict **disciplinarians** whose "learning theory" was based on two beliefs:

First, knowledge had to be pounded into your head through *constant repetition*.

Second, it was better to *correct your mistakes* than to *reward your progress*. Holding a lesson book in one hand and a stick in the other, these teachers probably "drilled" you to spew back from memory whatever material they believed you should learn.

Most disciplinarian instructors believe that learning is a matter of acquiring *associations*. The associations may be those that occur between stimuli and responses (Ss and Rs), or between stimulus inputs and "cognitive processes" (such as thoughts and ideas). However, almost all disciplinarians would agree that these associations must be forced on you by your external environment. If you survived their classes, you surely acquired a large number of facts. (Whether you remembered those facts for very long is another question.) But the constant threat of punishment may well have conditioned you to hate anything associated with school.

Other teachers may have been more concerned with creating an academic environment in which your inborn intellectual potential could grow like a seed planted in fertile soil. These sorts of instructors typically believe that learning is a matter of acquiring *cognitive skills*, and that any attempt they might make to "shape" your learning would *bias* you to perceive the world "their way" instead of "your way." Therefore, these teachers probably gave you a great deal of encouragement but little or no academic guidance. Probably you enjoyed their classrooms. But the important question is this: Are such unstructured settings the most effective way to acquire the basic skills of life (including self-control)?

Last but not least, you may occasionally have encountered a *behaviorally-oriented* teacher who set *highly specific academic goals* for you, who rewarded each small step you made toward achieving those goals, and who ignored your mistakes.

As you will soon see, the history of psychological learning theories—and the history of educational practice in the US—is little more than an account of the battle between **pedagogues** with radically different learning theories:

1. The "disciplinarians" are, chiefly, *associationists* who (like Pavlov) believe that education is a matter of connecting the "right" S to the "right" R. To do *that*, of course, the teacher often must first break *inappropriate* S-R bonds, usually by the use of punishment.

2. The cognitively-oriented teachers are also associationists, in their own way. But the important "connections" from their point of view are those that occur between such Ss (or internal events) as thoughts, feelings, ideas, and insights. These S-S theorists admit that punishment and reward "work," but often believe it's immoral to use them deliberately.

3. Instructors who take a "behavioral" orientation to teaching typically hold that education is chiefly a matter of acquiring *new responses*. These theorists usually hold that students either acquire new reactions—or fail to acquire them—because of what happens to the students *as a result of making a given reaction*. Thus, it is the association between a *response* (R) and its *consequences* (S_c) that behaviorally-oriented teachers usually emphasize. We might refer to these instructors as "R-S_c" theorists.

In real life, of course, most teachers make use of all three theoretical approaches. It is the *relative emphasis* that a given teacher puts on various techniques that determines whether the instructor can be called an S-R, S-S, or R-S_c pedagogue. It is primarily in the scientific jour-

Some teachers are traditional in their orientation, relying on rote memory and punishment of mistakes, while others use a cognitive approach, encouraging students to come up with new ideas of their own. Many successful teachers combine the two approaches.

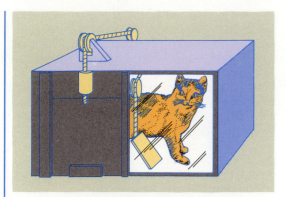

FIG. 10.1 Puzzle box used by Thorndike. In this version the cat can escape from the box and get food outside by pressing the treadle inside the box. A cord-and-pulley system unlocks the door.

nals that the arguments over which learning theory is "right" continue unabated.

Thorndike's Theories

In a sense, the "battle of the learning theorists" began with E.L. Thorndike, who influenced educational practices here almost as much as Pavlov did in Russia. Thorndike spent most of his academic career at Teachers College, a part of Columbia University in New York City. He helped create some of the very first intelligence and aptitude tests. And, with the help of C.L. Barnhart, Thorndike developed a series of dictionaries for school children that is still widely in use.

Thorndike's main interest was in human learning. However, he firmly believed humans were descended from the lower animals and hence *learned the same way* as did cats and rats. So, in 1890 he undertook some of the first laboratory studies ever performed on animal behavior.

Thorndike's early work involved putting cats inside a "puzzle box" (see Fig. 10.1). If the cat could figure out how to unlatch the door to the box, it escaped and was given a bit of food as a reward. At first the cat typically showed a great deal of what Thorndike called "random behavior." It sat and scratched or licked itself, it mewed and cried, it paced the box, or it bit at the bars and tried to squeeze between them. Eventually, the cat would accidently press a pedal that was connected to the door. The door would fly open, and the animal would rush out and be fed.

In subsequent trials, the cat spent more and more time near the pedal and got out of the box sooner and sooner. Eventually the cat learned what was required of it. The moment it was placed in the box, it would press the pedal, escape, and claim its reward (Thorndike, 1898).

When Thorndike plotted on a graph the amount of time it took the cat to exit from the box on each trial, he came up with something that we now called a "learning curve" (see Fig. 10.2). Similar experiments on monkeys, chickens, and even humans yielded the same-shaped curves, a finding that confirmed Thorndike's original theory that animals and humans solve such simple tasks in much the same manner.

Trial-and-Error Learning

Thorndike believed that animals learn to escape from puzzle boxes by **trial and error**. That is, they perform various behaviors in a blindly mechanical way until some action is *effective* in getting them out of the box. Ineffectual actions—such as sitting and scratching—bring the animal little satisfaction. So these responses rapidly drop out of the animal's behavioral **repertory**. But those actions that gain the animal's release and lead to food are very *satisfying*, so these responses become strongly connected to the stimuli in the puzzle box. The "satisfying" responses thus are much more likely to occur whenever the animal is next put in the box.

□ □ **QUESTION** □ □
How would you go about solving a "puzzle box" using "logic" or "insight"?

● *Thorndike's Laws of Learning*
The results of his puzzle box experiments led Thorndike to formulate two basic laws of learning: (1) the **law of exercise**, and (2) the **law of effect**.

In part, the *law of exercise* states that the S-R connections you make are *strengthened by repetition*—in short, that practice makes perfect.

The *law of effect* holds that S-R bonds are also strengthened by the "effects" of what you do. These effects may either be "satisfying" or

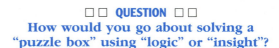

E.L. Thorndike

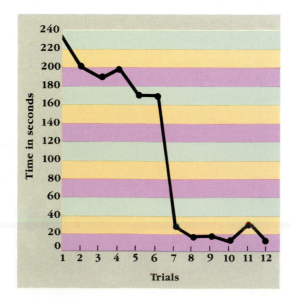

FIG. 10.2 The seventh trial shows a remarkable improvement in the time it took one of Thorndike's cats to open a puzzle box.

"punishing." Thorndike defined *satisfiers* as situations you willingly approach or do nothing to avoid. And he defined *punishers* as situations you typically avoid or do nothing to approach.

If the response you make to a stimulus somehow gives you pleasure or satisfaction, the connection (or association) between the S and the R will be appropriately *strengthened*. This is the first half of the "law of effect," and it holds today just as it did when Thorndike first announced it.

The second half of the law has to do with the effects of punishment on learning. Early in his career, Thorndike stated that "punishers" weakened or broke S-R bonds (Thorndike, 1898). But he changed his mind on this point later, when laboratory research proved that punishment *suppresses* responses temporarily rather than breaking S-R connections (Thorndike, 1935). At this point, Thorndike began speaking of "dis-satisfiers" rather than "punishers." However, by that time, many teachers had learned to use Thorndike's laws of learning as justification for using aversive control in the classroom. We will return to this point at the end of the chapter.

COGNITIVE THEORIES OF LEARNING

As we noted in Chapter 5, you typically see what you expect to see. This perceptual principle holds in scientific investigations as well as in ordinary life. Thorndike surely *expected* his cats to learn by trial-and-error methods before he began his work. Indeed, as **Gestalt** psychologist Wolfgang Koehler pointed out soon after Thorndike published his data, the puzzle box could hardly be solved in any way other than by trial and error (Koehler, 1925).

Koehler was trained at the University of Berlin. He believed animals were capable of greater intellectual accomplishments than random solutions to puzzle boxes. He thought that—given the chance—they could discover

cognitive relationships between objects and events. The animals could then use these "cognitive associations" to help them gain whatever ends they had in mind (Koehler, 1929).

Much of Koehler's research involved presenting various "intellectual" problems to chimpanzees, to see what kinds of solutions they might come up with.

□ □ **QUESTION** □ □
Koehler was obviously an S-S theorist, but what kind of theorist was Thorndike?

Learning by Insight

Koehler's most famous subject was a particularly bright chimpanzee named Sultan. First, Koehler taught Sultan to reach through the bars of his cage with a stick and rake in a banana. After Sultan had mastered this trick, Koehler set the animal the much more difficult task of *putting two sticks together* to get the food. The banana was moved farther away from Sultan's cage, and the chimp was given two bamboo poles. When the two poles were fitted together, they were just long enough to gather in the reward (see Fig. 10.3).

At first Sultan was confused. He tried to pull the fruit in with one stick and then with the other, but neither would reach. Despite the fact that this approach didn't get him the banana, Sultan repeated the behavior again and again. Then the chimp abandoned the banana and (perhaps in frustration) retreated into his cage to play with the sticks. So, Koehler decided the animal had failed the test. Koehler went home, leaving Sultan to be observed by an assistant.

Not long after Koehler left, Sultan happened to hold one stick in each hand so that

FIG. 10.3 Sultan in action.

their ends were pointed toward each other. Gently, he pushed the tip of the smaller one into the hollow of the larger. *They fitted*. Even as he joined the two sticks together, Sultan was up and running toward the bars of his cage. Reaching through with the double stick, he touched the banana and started to draw it toward him.

At this point fate played Sultan a nasty trick for which Koehler was most grateful—the two sticks came apart! Annoyed at this turn of events, Sultan gathered the sticks back into the cage, pushed them *firmly* together, tested them briefly, and then "liberated" the banana.

These actions proved—at least to Koehler's satisfaction—that Sultan actually understood that *joining the poles together* was an effective way of lengthening his arm. Koehler used the term **insight** to refer to this very rapid "perception of relationships" that sometimes occurs in humans and animals. He believed that *insight* involved a sudden restructuring or reorganization of the organism's perceptual world into a new pattern or *Gestalt* (Koehler, 1929).

As you might imagine, Ivan Pavlov did not take gladly to Koehler's experiments. As soon as the chimpanzee work appeared in print, Pavlov leapt to the attack. From his sanctuary in Leningrad, Pavlov issued one **vitriolic** criticism after another. First, he accused Koehler of being a "mentalist," which Koehler surely was. But Pavlov also unjustly criticized Koehler for performing "sloppy" experiments. (To Pavlov, a "sloppy" study was one in which the CS and the UCS could not readily be identified.)

Since Koehler was much more interested in learning how animals solved real-life problems than in specifying CSs and UCSs, he ignored Pavlov's comments. But thanks to Koehler's work, Pavlov soon found himself assailed by a barrage of experiments from the US. Unfortunately for Pavlov, few of these studies yielded results that could easily be fitted into the Russian scientist's theory of conditioning.

Tolman's "Cognitive Maps"
One set of studies came from E.C. Tolman and his associates at the University of California, Berkeley. During the height of the Pavlov-Koehler controversy, Tolman and his group published a series of articles showing that rats apparently were much more "insightful" than either Thorndike or Pavlov thought they ought to be.

● *Learning Versus Performance*
According to Thorndike, animals learned **mazes** by trial and error. That is, the food that the animal found at the end of the maze was a *reward* (or "satisfier") that *strengthened* the specific S-R connections the animal needed to learn in order to solve the maze. Without the

"GETTING AN 'A' OR A STAR IS ALLRIGHT, BUT I'D LIKE SOME SORT OF PROFIT-SHARING PLAN AROUND HERE."

food reward to strengthen the S-R bonds, Thorndike said, the animal simply wouldn't learn.

Tolman disagreed on two counts. First, he said that learning is a matter of forming "cognitive associations," not "S-R bonds." Second, Tolman believed that the food reward merely motivated the animal to *perform* in the maze, but had little or nothing to do with *learning*. Tolman, then, was one of the first American psychologists to differentiate between *learning* and *performance*.

● *Tolman's Studies*
In most of Tolman's experiments, the rats were trained in very complicated mazes. Typically, the animals were allowed to *explore* the apparatus at their leisure, but did *not* find food at the end of the maze. Usually it took the animals a *very* long time to get from the start to the end of the maze. Thorndike, of course, would say that the animals learned little or nothing about the maze during these explorations since their efforts weren't rewarded. Tolman, however, claimed the rats had "created a cognitive map" of the maze while poking around inside the apparatus. And he soon found a way to prove his point.

After the rat had been given several unrewarded "exploration" trials, Tolman suddenly introduced a food reward at the end of the maze. On the very next trial, the rat typically scooted through the apparatus fairly rapidly, making very few mistakes, and gobbled up the food at the end. This behavior suggested—to Tolman, at least—that the rat had *learned* the spatial relationships in the maze *without being rewarded*. The food merely *motivated* it to perform at a rapid pace.

E.C. Tolman

• Cognitive "Short Cuts"

In another series of studies, Tolman used a type of apparatus in which the animal could reach the food reward by a great many pathways. However, one pathway was typically much shorter than the rest and was preferred by the animals. When that pathway was blocked, however, almost all of the rats would instantly shift to the next most efficient way of getting to the food—even if they had never used that path before. This sort of behavior posed a real problem for Thorndike and his "S-R connectionism." For how could the animals "use" a new pathway when they had never acquired the specific S-R bonds associated with running that particular pathway?

To make matters worse—at least from Thorndike's point of view—if at any time the experimenter moved the reward from one part of the maze to another, the rats responded immediately and appropriately. That is, the rats behaved as if they understood a great deal about the *spatial relationships* involved in getting quickly from one part of the maze to another. From Tolman's point of view, the animals acted as if they had somehow acquired a "cognitive map" of the maze (Tolman, 1938).

The experiments by Tolman and other Gestalt psychologists were important for at least two reasons: First, the studies suggested that *some types of learning* involve the acquisition of "cognitive associations" rather than S-R bonds. And second, in these situations, *external* rewards (such as food) affect *performance,* but may not be necessary for *learning.*

Monkeys, chimps, and humans show a great deal more cognitive activity than do rats. For that reason, perhaps, the Gestalt theorists typically used primates as their preferred laboratory subjects. Because Pavlov, Thorndike, and the early behaviorists focused entirely on S-R bonds, they weren't interested in "mental processes." The rather mechanical behavior patterns of the lower animals appealed greatly to the behaviorists, and so they chiefly stuck to their rats, cats, and dogs. Finally, however, it took a bird-brained pigeon to show the narrowness of Pavlov's views, and to map out a kind of common ground between the Thorndikeans and the Tolmaniacs.

□□ **QUESTION** □□
The early behaviorists typically used "external" rewards, such as food and water, in their learning studies. Are there, however, other types of rewards that might explain why Tolman's rats behaved as they did?

OPERANT CONDITIONING

The learning theories of Pavlov, Thorndike, and Tolman have all been applied in classroom situations. But the theoretical approach most frequently followed in schools today is surely that called **operant conditioning**, which was developed by by B.F. Skinner. We will compare operant conditioning with the other theories of learning later in this chapter. First, let's see why operant conditioning is so powerful a method for teaching new behavior patterns to both pigeons and people.

Teaching a Pigeon to Bowl

Suppose that, as a final examination in one of your psychology classes, your instructor gives you a common, ordinary pigeon. The instructor then says that, if you want to get an A in the course, you must teach the pigeon to bowl!

After you recover from your surprise, you take stock of the situation. The apparatus you can use is a large box with a wire screen over the top of it. Inside the box is a small bowling alley with a tiny ball at one end and pigeon-sized bowling pins at the other. In one corner of the box is a metal cup into which you can drop food pellets from the outside. Just above the food cup is a bell (see Fig. 10.4). Fortunately, the pigeon has already been trained to run to the food cup to get the pellets whenever you ring the bell.

Your instructor tells you that if you can teach the pigeon to bowl in a matter of two

FIG. 10.4 A pigeon bowling alley.

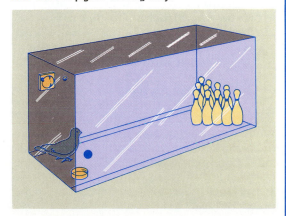

hours or less, you pass the exam and get your A reward. Keeping in mind all of the practical knowledge on learning theory you have acquired so far in this book, how would you go about educating your pigeon in order to satisfy your instructor, yourself, and, of course, the bird?

● Pavlov's Approach

If you played the game according to Pavlovian rules, what would you do? Well, you might begin by ringing the bell and then pushing the pigeon toward the ball, hoping that an S-R connection of some kind would be established in the bird's nervous system. In fact, the pigeon would surely resent such an intrusion into its life space. Instead of learning to bowl when you rang the bell, it probably would learn to peck at your hand viciously. For Pavlovian conditioning is almost always built on *already-established unconditioned responses* (UCSs). If dogs did not salivate naturally when given food, how would you go about teaching them to salivate when you sounded a buzzer?

If the pigeon already knew how to bowl, you could probably train it to give this response when you rang the bell. But you could read everything Pavlov wrote—in Russian or in English translation—without learning much about how to get a bird to bowl in the first place.

● Cognitive Approach

If you turned to Tolman and the Gestalt theorists instead, you might decide to give the pigeon plenty of experience in the bowling box itself before you started the training. Once the animal had acquired a cognitive map of the apparatus, it would surely learn how to bowl much faster. But the relationship between striking the ball and knocking down the pins is an insight that comes hard to most pigeons—unless you facilitate matters a little along the way. And not even Koehler offered much practical advice about how this facilitation should be accomplished.

□ □ **QUESTION** □ □

Most S-S theorists hold that organisms are *innately motivated* to learn how to master their environments. What would Pavlov and Thorndike say about the "motivation to learn"?

● Trial-and-Error Approach

If you looked to Thorndike for help, you still might have troubles. You could utilize the law of effect by waiting until the pigeon *accidentally* knocked the ball down the alley. You could then ring the bell and give the bird some food, and this reward would increase the chances the bird would *repeat* its actions in the future. But how long would you have to wait

until the pigeon *by accident* hit the ball straight down the alley the first time? The problem with Thorndike's approach, then, is that he doesn't give you a very efficient way of bringing about *the very first response*.

All of these components—*reward, repetition, motivation,* and *unlearned* or *innate responses*—are necessary if you are to train the pigeon and pass your exam. But putting them all together into a workable educational system took the genius of Harvard professor B.F. Skinner, who surely qualifies as being our most influential living psychologist.

B.F. Skinner

B.F. Skinner's Techniques

According to Skinner, whenever you wish to change an organism's behavior, you always begin by defining *precisely* what it is you want to accomplish. For instance, to get your A, you must train the pigeon to bowl. But what do we mean by "bowling"? Do we have some objective, clear-cut, agreed-upon way of measuring the response pattern we call "bowling"? If so, then we know when to *terminate* the training, and we know when you've passed the exam.

● Terminal Response or Goal

Bowling is obviously a complex *sequence of responses* that ends when the pigeon has whacked the ball down the alley toward the pins. Therefore, your goal must be that of getting the bird to hit the ball in the proper direction.

Skinner calls the *final* step in any chain of behaviors the **terminal response**. When the organism has performed this final act, the chain of responses is *terminated*—usually by a reward or punishment of some kind. Thus, when the pigeon finally "bowls," you will ring the bell and give the bird a pellet of food. And when the pigeon "bowls" regularly, you will terminate the training and receive your A.

The single most important thing about the terminal response, however, is that it must be *measurable*. As you will soon see, pigeons *can* be trained to bowl in two hours or less if you go about it the right way. However, how long do you think it would take to train a bird to be a "good sport"?

□ □ **QUESTION** □ □

College catalogues often state that the goal of a higher education is to turn students into "creative individuals" who are "good citizens" and "productive members of modern-day society." What might B.F. Skinner say about the *measurability* of such terminal responses?

● Taking a Baseline

Once you have a well-defined goal to work toward, you are ready to tackle the second

Terminal response. Also called "terminal behavior pattern" or "terminal goal." The last response the animal makes in a chain of learned behaviors.

Baseline behaviors. The behavior patterns of an organism before training begins. According to behavioral therapists, you must always build upon the client's strengths (the good or "appropriate" responses) and select out of these "baseline behaviors" those actions that can be shaped toward the terminal response. Entering behaviors also include problematic or inappropriate actions, but these should be ignored (or at least not rewarded) in the hope that they will thereby be extinguished.

Reinforcing successive approximations to a goal. Rewarding any incremental (in-kree-MENT-tal) response that will lead the organism toward the terminal response. That is, reinforcing any slight behavioral change (increment) that represents a step in the right direction.

Reinforced. Concrete with steel rods inside it is called *reinforced* concrete, because the steel strengthens the concrete. Positive feedback reinforces an S-R bond by making it more likely the response will occur again the next time the stimulus input appears.

Shaping. To "shape" a response is to bring it about by reinforcing successive approximations to a goal. Thus *shaping* means "training an organism using operant conditioning techniques."

stage in Skinner's analysis of behavioral change—that of determining what the organism is doing *before* you begin to train it. Skinner refers to these "prior responses" as the organism's **baseline behaviors**.

In order to determine the *baseline behaviors*, you measure what the organism is already doing, and plot its responses on a graph or record of some kind. Skinner calls this "taking a baseline." Like the terminal response, the baseline behaviors must be stated in objective, measurable terms. Clever animal trainers (or people educators) always take advantage of the response patterns the organism brings to the training situation. You always build new learning on old, according to Skinner.

□ □ **QUESTION** □ □

What responses does the average pigeon already make (without training) that are a part of the terminal response we call "bowling"?

● **Reinforcing Successive Approximations to a Goal**

When you are sure of (1) the organism's baseline behaviors, and (2) the terminal behavior you hope to achieve, you are (3) ready to move from (1) to (2). Skinner suggests you do so in a *step-by-step* fashion called **reinforcing successive approximations to a goal**.

Neither people nor pigeons typically change their behaviors in large, insightful jumps. We *can* do so occasionally, as the Gestalt theorists showed. But most of the time we change slowly, bit by bit, millimeter by millimeter. And we usually need to be coaxed and encouraged whenever we must acquire a new way of doing things. That is, we typically need to be rewarded or **reinforced** for each tiny step we make toward the goal. (We will have

more to say about the importance of reward momentarily.)

The technique of *successive approximations to a goal* is one of the cornerstones of the Skinnerian system. But mastery of the step-by-step technique calls for rather a penetrating insight on your own part. Namely, you must realize that even the faintest, feeblest movement toward the goal is *a step in the right direction*, hence something you must vigorously reward. Most people unfamiliar with Skinner's techniques seem unable or unwilling to analyze behavior in these terms. So, they give reinforcements grudgingly and infrequently. This fact may explain why most people would not be able to train a pigeon to bowl in two hours or less.

"Shaping" a Pigeon to Bowl

The Skinnerian technique of (1) setting a goal, (2) taking a baseline, and then (3) reinforcing successive approximations to the goal is often called behavioral **shaping**. Why? Because, just as a potter takes clay-like materials and "shapes" them into a new form (such as a vase), so operant conditioning involves taking old behavior patterns and "shaping" them into new response sequences.

If we apply what Skinner calls *behavioral analysis* to the problem of getting your pigeon to perform, we can perhaps see how "shaping" actually works.

● **Defining the Goal**

The terminal behavior your instructor has set is that of "bowling." But how shall we define it? Humans usually pick up the bowling ball in their hands and roll it down the alley. However, Mother Nature has given the pigeon wings instead of arms, and feathers are poor substitutes for fingers when it comes to lifting a heavy ball.

But could we teach an armless man to bowl? Couldn't the man kick the ball down the alley, or even butt it with his head? Do you really care how he manages it, so long as the ball zings down the alley and hits the pins?

One of the purposes of getting you to "take a baseline" of the pigeon's normal response patterns is this—it forces you to see what the bird *already* does that you can make use of during training. If you observe pigeons for a while, you will notice they use their beaks much as we use our hands. So if you can train the bird to hit the ball with its beak (so the ball rolls down the alley and hits the pins), you surely have taught the animal to "bowl" within the stated definition of the problem. And you surely should get an A on your exam.

● **Using "Baseline Behaviors" Creatively**

Now that you know what your goal is, you can begin to take advantage of the baseline behaviors the pigeon already shows. At the start of training, the bird merely moves around nervously, inspecting its new environment. The final response you want from the animal is that of striking the ball with its beak. To make this terminal response, though, the animal must be standing *near the ball*. So your first task would seem to be that of getting the pigeon to move to where the ball is. But how to do it?

If you were training your child to bowl, you would probably explain to the child—in English—what you wanted the youngster to do. Or you could "model" the behaviors involved in bowling and tell the child to imitate you. Then, when the child first approached the ball or picked it up, you would express your pleasure verbally. That's using what we might call *positive feedback*. But pigeons are nonverbal—they don't even speak "pidgin English." So, you can't use verbal explanations. Instead, you use rewarding feedback until the bird achieves the behavioral output you have defined as the goal. But *what* you reward are baseline behaviors that the bird already has available in its repertory.

• Rewarding the "First Step"

Once you have determined the goal and have measured the baseline behaviors, what's your next step in teaching the pigeon to bowl? Actually, as Skinner points out, the next step is up to the bird. As it wanders around the box excitedly, at one time or another it will *accidentally* move toward the bowling ball. If you have the insight to recognize this simple movement as being "a step in the right direction"—and if you ring the bell at once and reward the animal with food—you will have no difficulty in training the bird. But if you insist the bird doesn't *deserve* a reward until it scores a strike, it may take you years to pass the exam—if you ever do.

Presuming you do sound the bell the first time the bird moves tentatively in the general direction of the ball, how does the pigeon respond? By running to the food cup to claim its reward. After eating the food, it will pause for a while near the food cup. But when pausing doesn't ring the bell, it will usually begin its random trial-and-error movements around the box again. Once more, as soon as it heads toward the ball, you sound the bell. And again the bird runs to the food cup and eats.

The fifth or sixth or tenth time the pigeon repeats this response, a very strange event often occurs. The bird behaves as if it has experienced a "flash of insight" into what is happening. That is, the pigeon acts as if it had discovered that it can actually control *your* behavior! All it has to do to *force* you to give it food is to move in a given direction.

Once your pigeon has learned the connection between *doing something* and *being re-*

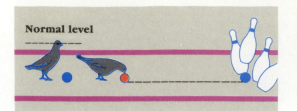

FIG. 10.5 Whenever the pigeon's head bobs below the normal level that it keeps its beak at, you ring the bell and reward the pigeon. Then, step by step, you reward it for moving its head lower and lower. Finally, the bird's beak will be on the floor, where the ball is.

warded, you can go much faster with your training. Each time you sound the bell, the pigeon will dash to the food cup, then return at once to where it was the instant the bell rang. Now, on each successive trial, you merely wait until the animal accidentally moves one step nearer to the ball before you ring the bell. In a matter of minutes, the bird will be hovering over the bowling ball.

• The Beak and the Ball

Once the bird is standing *over* the ball, you must find a way of getting the animal's beak *down to floor level*. Again, you go back to the natural responses the animal makes. As pigeons move, their heads bob up and down. Sometimes, then, the bird's beak is closer to the ball than at other times. An experienced animal trainer will soon perceive the bird's downward head movements as "good responses," and begin to reward them (see Fig. 10.5).

After several such reinforcements, the pigeon begins to return from the food cup holding its head a little lower than before. If you demand that the bird depress its head an additional inch or so on each subsequent trial, you can get it to touch the floor with its beak in a matter of minutes.

□ □ **QUESTION** □ □
Do you imagine that, at any time during training, the pigeon gains a cognitive awareness that it is "learning to bowl"? If you could somehow "explain" to the animal what you were doing, might this "cognitive understanding" speed up learning? Why?

• On to the Goal

By now the pigeon's beak is close to the floor, and the bird is moving about near the ball. Within a few moments, its beak will touch the ball "accidentally." The skilled animal trainer now rings the bell joyously, knowing victory is near.

When the bird returns from claiming its reward, it typically takes a second swat at the

10 / Operant Conditioning and Cognitive Behaviorism

ball. You reward it again. Soon, the pigeon is scooting back and forth from food cup to ball, whacking the ball each time it comes close to it.

Now it is up to you to shape the bird's "whacking responses" so the animal knocks the ball straight down the alley instead of merely hitting the ball at random. Such "shaping" should take only a few minutes, for at first you reinforce only those whacks that aim the ball in the general direction of the pins. Then you selectively reward those hits that are closer and closer *approximations* to your stated goal. The pigeon soon learns it will be fed only when it strikes the ball so it rolls straight down the alley and hits the pins.

An experienced pigeon-handler can usually shape a hungry pigeon "to bowl" in less than an hour. (Training the animal to get a good score takes a little longer.)

■■ **QUESTION** ■■

Skinner has proved that almost any pigeon can learn to bowl if trained in this step-by-step manner. Therefore, if *you* try to train a pigeon and it fails to learn, whose fault is it? Likewise, if you take a college course and don't do well, whom should we blame?

When teaching animals capable of inflicting grave harm, a trainer must carefully consider the consequences of any punishment used.

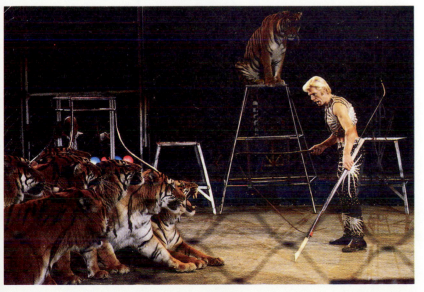

ANALYSIS OF SKINNER'S SYSTEM

There are several fairly subtle points about the Skinnerian system that are sometimes overlooked:

1. Skinner differentiates between two "unpleasant" types of inputs which have entirely different effects on behavior. The first is *punishment*, which is a painful input that the animal learns to avoid. The second is **negative reinforcement**, which occurs whenever you terminate a painful "drive state" such as extreme hunger. As we will see, *negative* reinforcement affects behavior in much the same way *positive* reinforcement does (Skinner, 1938).

   The difference between punishment and negative reinforcement is best seen in their *consequences*. Punishment *disrupts* behavioral sequences. It may occasionally *suppress* certain responses, but it usually does so only *temporarily*. And punishment seldom "wipes out" inappropriate behaviors. Thus, those teachers who threaten to punish you *unless* you perform correctly often teach you little more than to avoid them (and all academic settings).

   Negative reinforcement, on the other hand, *strengthens* a behavioral sequence just as positive reinforcement does. Negative reinforcement is an input that *reduces* discomfort, while punishment is an input that *increases* pain or displeasure. Punishment leads to active avoidance and other types of emotional behaviors. Negative reinforcement, however, leads to approach behaviors and to learning.

   The next time you visit a "marine world" of some kind, ask the animal trainers how they teach porpoises to perform in public. You'll find the trainers use reinforcement almost exclusively. If you punish a porpoise, it sulks in a corner for days. But if you give it food, you reinforce it both positively and negatively. First, the food tastes good, which is *positive reinforcement*. Second, the food slightly reduces the animal's natural hunger, which is *negative reinforcement* because it's the reduction of an unpleasant state or condition.

   Animals don't hold trainers responsible for getting hungry. They do hold trainers responsible for the punishment they inflict, though. And if you punish a "killer whale," the consequences may be more disastrous for you than for the whale!

2. Notice that in teaching the pigeon to bowl, *no punishment* was necessary to get the animal to perform. The pigeon obviously *can* learn. If it fails to do so, the fault presumably lies with the teacher (or with the learning environment) and not with the student.

249

3. You control the *timing* of the reinforcement—but the pigeon determines whether it *wants* the reward you offered it. If the reinforcement is meaningful and satisfying to that particular bird, then the animal will work. But if you offer the animal something it doesn't want or need—or if you expect too much work for what you give the bird in return—it is free to rebel and ignore you. (Surprisingly, pigeons appear to enjoy this type of training and, once they have learned the task, will "bowl" again and again with but a minimal amount of encouragement.)

4. "Bowling" is obviously a very complicated set of responses that the animal has to learn in a *particular order or sequence*. You got the bird to learn one simple thing at a time, never demanding too much. You always encouraged the "right" things the pigeon did, and you ignored (or certainly didn't punish) its mistakes. And by doing so, you **chained** the sequence of responses together from its first approaching step to its last whack at the ball. However, the experienced pigeon will perform its bowling routine so smoothly and efficiently that it is not easy to see the various *individual responses* that have been chained together during training.

□ □ **QUESTION** □ □

If you can train a pigeon to bowl without using punishment, would it be possible to teach a child how to read and write without criticizing or spanking the child when she or he makes a mistake? Why aren't more children taught this way?

- ### Schedules of Reinforcement

According to Skinner, at the beginning of training you should reward *each move* the bird makes toward the goal. However, once the pigeon has mastered a given response in the chain, you may begin slowly *fading out the reward* by reinforcing the response **intermittently**. You never fade out the reward completely. However, you can shift to a much less frequent schedule of reinforcement (Ferster & Skinner, 1957).

Continuous reinforcement is necessary at first, both to keep the animal eager to perform and to let it know it is doing something right. However, once the pigeon learns what that "something right" is, you may begin reinforcing the response every second time, then every third or fourth time, then perhaps every tenth time. If you fade out the reward very gradually, you can get a pigeon to repeat a simple response (such as pecking a button) several thousand times for each reinforcement.

During the fading process, the exact *scheduling* of the reward is crucial. If you reinforce

exactly every tenth response, the bird will soon learn to anticipate which response will gain it food. As soon as it makes this tenth response and feeds, it will "take a break" because it knows its next response never brings it any goodies. Skinner calls this **fixed-ratio reinforcement**, because the *ratio* between the number of responses required and the rewards given is fixed and never varies.

If we make a **cumulative record** of the time intervals between each response the animal makes, we would find it responds slowly just after a reinforcement, but more and more quickly as it approaches that response it knows will gain it the reward (see Fig. 10.6).

We can get the pigeon to respond at a more or less *constant* rate by tricking it a bit—that is, by rewarding it on a **variable-ratio reinforcement** rather than at a fixed ratio. Instead of reinforcing *exactly* the tenth response, we vary the schedule so that sometimes the 3rd response yields food, sometimes the 7th, sometimes the 11th, sometimes the 20th—or any response in between. A hundred responses will yield *about* 10 rewards, but the bird will never know when the next reward is coming. When trained on variable-ratio schedules, pigeons respond vigorously and at a fairly constant pace.

We could also reward the pigeon using **interval reinforcement**. That is, we could reward the *first correct response* the bird made after (let's say) an interval of 2 minutes had passed. Generally speaking, however, *ratio* reinforcement is easier to use than is *interval* reinforcement (Ferster & Skinner, 1957).

Technically speaking, rewarding an organism just "part of the time" when it makes a correct response is called *partial reinforcement*. In most real-life settings, you are rewarded on a *partial reinforcement schedule*. For example,

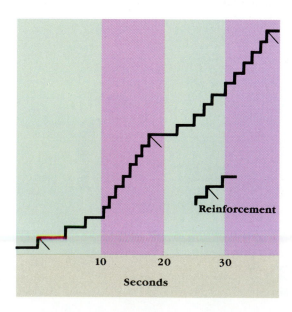

FIG. 10.6 A cumulative record of a pigeon trained to peck a button on a 10-to-1 fixed-ratio reinforcement schedule. Each vertical movement of the graph represents one press of the lever. Note that the pigeon responds more quickly just prior to a reinforcement than just afterward.

Reinforcement

10   20   30

Seconds

Chained. To write the word "cat" on a typewriter, you must first hit the "c" key, then the "a" key, then the "t." You will have made (at least) three different responses that are chained together to achieve the goal of typing the word "cat." Behaviorists believe complex human behavior patterns are mostly long chains of related responses that must be learned one at a time.

Intermittently (in-turr-MITT-tent-lee). If it rains on Monday, is clear on Tuesday, but rains again on Wednesday and Thursday, then it has rained intermittently during the week. If you reward a rat each third time it presses a bar, you are giving the animal intermittent reinforcement.

Fixed-ratio reinforcement. If you reward a rat for *exactly* each third bar press it makes, the ratio between responses (bar presses) and reward is fixed.

Cumulative record (CUE-mew-luh-tive). From the word *accumulate*, meaning "to acquire." As you grow older, your years are cumulative—that is, you never lose a year once you've lived through it. A cumulative record is an increasing graph or record of all the responses an animal makes in a certain time period. The record also shows the time between responses, and each reinforcement the animal receives.

Variable-ratio reinforcement. A schedule of reinforcement that involves rewarding the animal for *approximately* every 3rd (or 5th or 100th) correct response that it makes.

Interval reinforcement. Fixed-interval reinforcement involves rewarding the first response an organism makes after, say, 60 seconds. Variable-interval reinforcement involves rewarding the first response an organism makes, say, after *approximately* 60 seconds.

Instrumental conditioning. Also called "operant conditioning." A type of learning in which the organism must learn which of its responses will be *instrumental* in yielding a reward.

Respondent conditioning. Also called "classical conditioning" or "Pavlovian conditioning." So named because the organism always *responds* to presentation of the CS with the CR.

Elicits (ee-LISS-sits). To elicit is to pull out, to evoke, to stimulate into action. In Pavlovian conditioning, the stimulus that elicits the CR is always identifiable.

Emit (ee-MITT). The important association in operant conditioning is between the response itself and the reward that follows. If a rat is trained to press a lever only when a light is turned on, the rat is said to "emit" the response *in the presence of* the light stimulus. However, the light doesn't really elicit the bar-press response—the light merely serves as a "discriminative" stimulus that lets the rat know that if it now emits a response, that response will be rewarded.

at work, instead of being given a few pennies each time you do something right, you receive a paycheck at the end of the week (or month). And in school, you aren't given praise each time you read a sentence or two in a textbook. Instead, you receive encouraging feedback (let's hope!) when you have read several chapters and take (and do well on) an examination.

□ □ **QUESTION** □ □
Do the slot machines in Las Vegas pay off on a fixed ratio or a variable ratio? Why?

● **"Shaping" Responses**

"Shaping" any organism's responses is more of a psychological art than a science, and some people are much better behavioral artists than are others. Skinner says you should reward each successive step toward the behavioral goal you have in mind. But there are thousands of different response chains that might lead from the animal's baseline behaviors to the terminal goal. Unfortunately, Skinner doesn't tell

you which one to pick, nor how to judge which pathway is best.

Lion tamers at the circus—as well as teachers at dog and cat "obedience schools"—often make use of Skinnerian principles in teaching their beasts to perform dazzling tricks. But some lion trainers are much better at putting the "big cats" through their paces than are other animal-handlers, just as some college instructors are more effective than others at rewarding successive approximations to educational goals. As you might guess, there is still considerable debate about what behavioral traits you should have in order to become an effective "shaper" (Skinner, 1954).

□ □ **QUESTION** □ □
Which parts of "shaping" seem to be left hemisphere traits? And which might be right hemisphere or "perceptual" traits?

OPERANT VERSUS RESPONDENT CONDITIONING

Skinner calls the type of learning he studies **instrumental conditioning**, or operant conditioning. Skinner chose the term "operant" because he believes the organism must learn to *operate* on its environment in order to get the reinforcers it desires. Stated in slightly different terms, the organism must somehow change its behavioral outputs until it finds one that is instrumental in bringing it the rewarding inputs it needs.

Skinner refers to Pavlovian training as **respondent conditioning** because Pavlov taught his animals to *respond* in a specific way to a specific stimulus (Skinner, 1950).

● **Elicited Versus Emitted Responses**

There are many differences between operant and respondent conditioning. Surely one of the most obvious differences is this—Pavlovian (respondent) learning is always tied to a unique and specific stimulus, while operant conditioning is not. Food powder blown into a dog's mouth **elicits** the salivary response. Pairing the bell with the food gives the bell the power to *elicit* the same sort of salivation—whether the dog likes it or not. The important point is that neither dogs nor humans go around salivating unless they are stimulated to do so by a highly specific sensory input. Respondent conditioning thus involves setting up involuntary, *elicited* responses to specific stimuli. That's one reason it's called "S-R learning."

On the other hand, pigeons (and people) perform all kinds of actions that don't seem to be "elicited" or pulled out of the organism automatically. Rather, says Skinner, we typically **emit**, or produce, a wide variety of behaviors rather freely. Those activities that are reinforced, we tend to repeat. Those behaviors that aren't reinforced tend to drop out of our *behavioral repertoire*.

• Stimulus-Response Connections

Respondent conditioning involves attaching a *new stimulus* to an *already-established response*. Thus, the important association in Pavlovian conditioning is that between the CS and the UCS. Once this connection is made, the connection between the CS and the CR follows rather automatically. Put another way, respondent conditioning is S-(S)-R learning.

Operant conditioning, however, involves attaching a *new response* to *already-present stimulus inputs*. Thus, the important association is between the *response* itself and the *feedback* the response generates. This feedback, of course, is really a new sensory stimulus. So we can describe operant conditioning as (S)-R-S_c learning (where S_c is information about the **consequences** of the response).

Pavlov didn't train his animals to respond in a new way. He merely taught them to give the same old salivation response to a new stimulus (the bell). Skinner, however, almost always shapes organisms to respond in ways they never have before. But the only new *stimuli* Skinner adds to the picture are those associated with reinforcement.

• Voluntary Versus Involuntary Muscles

Respondent conditioning typically involves those *involuntary muscle groups* controlled by the autonomic nervous system and the lower brain centers. Most emotional learning—such as acquiring a fear or a phobia—is a type of Pavlovian conditioning. The fear response is *already present* in the organism's repertoire. All the respondent conditioning does is to attach the involuntary fear reaction to a *novel stimulus*.

Operant conditioning typically involves *voluntary muscle groups* controlled by the cortex and the higher brain centers. Motor skills—such as typing or playing football—are usually the result of operant conditioning. Put another way, acquiring a motor skill involves learning a new way of responding to stimuli that were already present in your environment.

The subtle differences between operant and respondent conditioning are probably of greater interest to learning theorists than to anyone else. For almost all real-life learning involves *both types of conditioning*. And both kinds of conditioning are built on the innate response tendencies that most organisms are born with (Rescorla, 1987).

□ □ **QUESTION** □ □

Suppose you trained a dog to press a bar to get food using operant techniques. Do you think that, at some time during the training, the animal might learn involuntarily to salivate at the sight of the bar?

BIOFEEDBACK

For many years, psychologists believed it was nearly impossible to use Skinnerian techniques to help organisms gain *voluntary* control over their *autonomic* responses. Recently, however, a number of experiments using a technique called **biofeedback** have challenged this view.

Biofeedback in Medicine

Suppose you were a physician trying to treat a 40-year-old woman suffering from hypertension, or high blood pressure. And further suppose the woman was so sensitive to drugs that you couldn't use any kind of medication to help lower her blood pressure. What could you do to help?

You might begin by teaching her the "relaxation techniques" we discussed in the previous chapter. But surely it would help if the patient had some way of knowing when her blood pressure was rising, and when it was falling. You might then hook the woman up to a machine that gave her *visual feedback* about a specific *biological* response (her blood pressure). If she *saw* the pressure was rising, she could "go limp" and try to think relaxing thoughts. And if she *saw* the pressure was falling, she could try to remember what she was thinking so she could repeat that calming thought in the future.

In a recent book, David Olton and Aaron Noonberg report considerable success in training hypertensive patients to gain voluntary (operant) control over heart rate and blood pressure. Olton and Noonberg have also found biofeedback useful in treating asthma, epilepsy, stomach disorders, and migraine headaches. In all these cases, Olton and Noonberg state, the secret of success lies in finding some way of giving patients new types of feedback about their involuntary bodily processes. During a migraine attack, for instance, patients often experience great tension in their neck and facial muscles. When given visual or auditory feedback on how tense their muscles are, however, the patients often are able to reduce muscle tension voluntarily. According to Olton and Noonberg, this operant control of muscle tension frequently helps reduce the severity of the headache (see Fig. 10.7) (Olton & Noonberg, 1980).

• Biofeedback: An Evaluation

When biofeedback first appeared on the psychological scene, it seemed a "cure-all" for a variety of ills. However, recent findings have dampened the enthusiasm of all but the most ardent advocates of the technique (Roberts, 1985).

Frank Andrasik

Take migrane headaches, for example. A double-blind study by Michigan psychologist Donald Kewman and A.H. Roberts found that biofeedback was of little help in the treatment of migraines (Kewman & Roberts, 1980). And in a recent survey of work in this area, J. Beatty concluded that "There is, in my opinion, no convincing evidence even to suggest, let alone to establish, that biofeedback methods represent a reasonable therapeutic procedure for the treatment of migraine headache" (Beatty, 1982).

Biofeedback does help *some* patients with certain types of problems. But the *cause* of the relief is now open to question. Take ordinary tension headaches, for example. Research by Frank Andrasik and Kenneth Holroyd shows that biofeedback can reduce the severity of the headache, but perhaps not for the reasons Olton and Noonberg suggested.

Andrasik and Holroyd tested four groups of students who suffered severe tension headaches. Subjects in the three experimental groups were individually connected to biofeedback devices that supposedly measured tension (1) in facial and neck muscles, and (2) in arm muscles. These subjects were informed they would hear a tone that would *decrease* in

FIG. 10.7 This woman, using biofeedback, can reduce the pain of a migraine headache by learning to lower the temperature of her forehead.

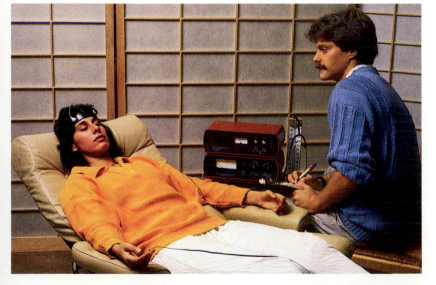

pitch as the tension in their muscles *dropped*. Andrasik and Holroyd suggested that, in order to "lower the tone," the students might try thinking peaceful thoughts, or just relaxing, or even try concentrating on the tone itself.

Subjects in the fourth group received no training or biofeedback at all, and thus served as controls.

The students in the first experimental group were given *accurate* biofeedback. That is, the tone *decreased in pitch* as tension in their face and neck muscles *decreased*, just as the experimenters had said it would. (However, the electrodes placed on their arms were fakes.) The subjects in the second and third groups were given *inaccurate* biofeedback. That is, the tone they heard *decreased in pitch* as tension in either face and neck muscles (group two) or arm muscles (group three) *increased*. So these students were actually being trained to *raise* muscle tension rather than *decrease* it.

Andrasik and Holroyd state that all three experimental groups reported a significant reduction in the severity of their headaches, while control-group subjects did not. Thus, we can conclude that biofeedback training had some positive effect. The subjects in the first experimental group noted the fastest improvement. So, *relaxation* does have a quick and positive influence on reducing headaches. By the end of six weeks of training, however, the subjects in groups two and three reported the same level of headache reduction as did the students in the first experimental group.

How can an *increase* in muscle tension help reduce the severity of "tension headaches"? Andrasik and Holroyd believe that what we might call *cognitive skills* may be the answer. They report all their experimental subjects developed "one or more mental exercises" to achieve success during biofeedback training. The students then used these mental exercises whenever they felt a headache coming on. According to Andrasik and Holroyd, "It may be less crucial that headache sufferers learn to directly modify [muscular tension] than it is that they learn to monitor the insidious onset of headache symptoms and engage in some sort of coping response incompatible with the further **exacerbation** of symptoms" (quoted in Horn & Rice, 1981).

Put more simply, biofeedback may "work" for two reasons: first, because it actually helps you gain voluntary control over some of your bodily activities. But second, biofeedback may be useful clinically because it helps you learn "cognitive strategies" for disrupting or suppressing painful inputs. We will have more to say about this point in Chapter 13, when we discuss hypnosis.

There's an interesting point to be made here. Both biofeedback and Skinner's "shaping" technique started out as being purely *behavioral* types of training. However, both approaches appear to be more successful when they are used to teach people control of cognitive activities *as well as* control of behavioral outputs.

SKINNER'S APPROACH: AN EVALUATION

B.F. Skinner has developed what is clearly the most advanced technology the world has ever known for helping people change their behaviors. It has probably done more *measurable* good for more people than any other type of psychological training technique. As powerful as the Skinnerian system is, however, it suffers from the same narrowness of view that afflicts most other psychological theories.

For one thing, Skinner views the organism as being a *passive receptor* of stimuli from the outside world. You have no "free will" because your actions are determined primarily by your past reinforcement history and your present environment. "People have assumed from the beginning of time that they initiate their own actions," Skinner said in an interview printed in the New York *Times* on September 15, 1981. "To suppose this is a great mistake." Instead of your *selecting* your own behaviors, he says, the environment does this for you.

Nor does Skinner have much use for such intra-psychic experiences as emotions. In a recent article, he writes that "I do not think feelings are important. Freud is probably responsible for the current extent to which they are taken seriously." Skinner thus banishes all of motivational and cognitive psychology from what he calls "the scientific study of behavior" (Skinner, 1983).

Nor does he give much **credence** to biology. "I don't deny the importance of genetics," he said in the *Times* interview. However, Skinner believes that the only thing your genes do for you is to "program" you to respond to environmental inputs in an operant manner. Skinner thus dismisses most of biopsychology from his system.

And because he pays most attention to the effects that the environment has on *individual organisms*, Skinner pays little attention to social psychology. Thus, the study of group processes and other social variables seems a waste of time to him. For, from Skinner's viewpoint, "scientific psychology" consists entirely of the study of the effects the outside world has on the measurable behaviors of *individual* organisms.

Skinner and Self-control

Skinner takes a very pessimistic view of the world these days, primarily because he views organisms as *passive* rather than *active living*

systems. He looks at people from the outside in, and refuses even to guess at "what goes on inside the mind." He talks about feedback, but not about learning by imitating the reactions of others. He measures biological rewards such as food, but ignores most intra-psychic reinforcers such as pride and self-esteem. And he refuses to deal with such matters as perceptions, cognitions, and self-awareness (Skinner, 1987). Thus, he fails to understand the importance of **self-control**.

When Skinner trains a pigeon to bowl, *he* determines what the goal of the training will be, *he* measures the entering behaviors of the bird, and *he* selectively reinforces approximations to the goal. The bird *behaves*; Skinner *monitors* these behaviors and *gives the animal feedback* in order to shape its responses. Because Skinner can tell you what he is doing as he goes along, he can describe both the terminal response and the approximations in measurable terms. Thus, he doesn't need to talk about what goes on inside the pigeon's mind. And he can legitimately claim that such intra-psychic concepts as "thinking" and "self-control" aren't needed in order to explain behavior.

However, you are a far more complex system than is a pigeon—or any other animal. Because of this complexity, you can use operant techniques to change your own outputs *voluntarily*—a technique now called "self-shaping." The problem for Skinner is that this sort of *self*-determined, *self*-monitored, and *self*-rewarded change is difficult to explain in purely operant terms (McConnell, 1985).

□□ **QUESTION** □□
Would you rather have a teacher show sincere enthusiasm when you learn something—and perhaps give you a

SKINNER BOXES

RAT PULLS LEVER—
ALWAYS GETS REWARD

HUMAN PULLS LEVER—
ONLY OCCASIONALLY
GETS REWARD

Credence (KREE-dense). From the Latin word meaning "to trust, or believe." To give credence to something is to trust in its value.

Self-control. A property of living systems. The ability to control your inner processes and outputs voluntarily in order to gain those inputs you desire.

Extrinsic (X-trin-sick). From the Latin word meaning "from without." Extrinsic rewards are those that come to you from others—food, praise, and so forth. *Extrinsic* motivation is thus the desire for external reinforcers.

Intrinsic (IN-trin-sick). Intrinsic rewards are internal reinforcers that you administer to yourself, such as pride and self-satisfaction. *Intrinsic* motivation thus is *self-motivation*, including the desire to be successful at whatever tasks you undertake.

Cognitive behavior modification. The use of Skinnerian techniques to modify or change inner processes (thoughts, feelings) as well as behavioral outputs.

small monetary reward for doing so—or have the teacher merely give you objective information on how you are performing without the praise or the cash?

● Extrinsic Versus Intrinsic Reinforcers

Many psychologists like to differentiate between **extrinsic** and **intrinsic** reinforcers. *Extrinsic* rewards are those stimulus inputs—such as food, or a pat on the back—that come to you from the external world. *Intrinsic* rewards are such "internal processes" as the satisfaction that comes from doing a job well, or the pleasure you feel when you finally master a task.

Skinner dealt primarily with animals. And he has always opted for the use of extrinsic rewards, since he prefers not to dwell on what goes on "inside the organism's mind." With animals, it surely is true that the use of *extrinsic* rewards almost always *increases* motivation and speeds up learning. With humans, however, the effects of reinforcement can be somewhat more complex. As Edward Deci and Richard Ryan note, some individuals—particularly those who are *internalizers* as far as their "locus of personal control" is concerned—will sometimes *lose interest* in a task if you give them *extrinsic* reinforcement or threaten them with punishment. According to Deci and Ryan, these individuals may perceive "extrinsic" rewards and punishments as attempts to *control* them in some fashion.

Deci and Ryan believe that "internalizers" are motivated almost entirely by *intrinsic* rewards—primarily by their own evaluation of how they are performing. Deci and Ryan believe that *intrinsic* motivation is "innate, natural propensity to engage one's interests and exercise one's capacities . . . to seek and conquer optimal challenges." They also suggest that *informational* feedback enhances intrinsic motivation while concrete rewards (such as money or insincere praise) decrease motivation. Deci and Ryan conclude that most *mature* individuals will perform better if you merely tell them how they did than if you give them "extrinsic" reinforcers (Deci & Ryan, 1985).

However, according to Cornell psychologist John Condry, it would be a mistake to conclude that "intrinsic" motivation is in any sense *superior* to "extrinsic" motivation. It is true that, in a few experiments, human subjects given praise or money performed *worse* than did subjects who weren't reinforced. However, as Condry puts it, "The tasks of education—acquiring real knowledge about the real world—seem far removed from the little tasks used in most of the studies reported [by Deci and Ryan]. Do these studies really provide us with the kind of empirical tools we need to weave such broad generalizations about motivation? I think not" (Condry, 1987).

In point of fact, the argument over the virtues of extrinsic versus intrinsic reinforcers is more theoretical than practical. As we noted at the start of this chapter, some psychologists are *morally opposed* to the use of extrinsic rewards (and to the use of "shaping" techniques, for that matter). Other psychologists believe—as Skinner does—that "what works, works." And under the proper conditions, *either* extrinsic or intrinsic reinforcers can be effective.

● Cognitive Behavior Modification

Skinner's demand that psychologists deal with measurable events was certainly a step in the right direction. And the techniques of *behavior modification* he developed in the 1940's and 1950's have obviously given us powerful tools for bringing about change. However, even Skinner's own students seem to have passed him by.

By the 1960's, several psychologists had shown that operant techniques could be used to shape thoughts and perceptions as well as overt actions. Intra-psychic events (such as attitudes and emotions) became "inner behaviors" that obeyed the same operant principles as did such "overt behaviors" as bowling. Simple operant technology thus evolved into **cognitive behavior modification**, and behavioral therapists started shaping their patients' thoughts and feelings as successfully as they shaped muscle movements (Kanfer & Goldstein, 1986).

As we noted, no one living has contributed more to psychology than has B.F. Skinner. But, in a sense, you demonstrate the narrowness of his viewpoint each time you have a creative insight; experience the joy of learning; think through a problem; or voluntarily control your thoughts, feelings, or behavioral outputs in order to achieve some personal goal.

☐☐ **QUESTION** ☐☐
Do you consider alcoholism a disease (or perhaps a "mental disorder")? What do you think the *goal* of treating this

problem should be, and what techniques do you think work best with alcoholic patients? What data do you have to support your beliefs? How would a *purely behavioral* view of the problem differ from yours both in terms of *measurable goal* and *treatment plan*?

Behavior Modification Versus Psychotherapy

Like Joseph Wolpe—whose desensitization therapy we described in Chapter 9—Fred Skinner believes that symptomatic behaviors associated with "mental disorders" are actually learned. Thus, therapy should consist of helping people learn new and healthier habits. Most psychotherapists, of course, take the opposite view. They see "mental illness" as being just that—a disorder of the mind, not a disorder of learned behavioral outputs. Therefore, treatment should consist of techniques designed to "uncover the patient's underlying psychological problem." Once the patients have "insight," the symptomatic behaviors will disappear more or less automatically.

The cognitive behaviorists stand somewhere in between these two extremes. They agree with Skinner that the ultimate focus in most types of therapy must be on learning new behavior patterns. But the cognitive behaviorists believe that teaching people how to control their own thoughts and feelings is often a very effective way of helping people learn to control their behavioral outputs (Kendall & Hollon, 1981).

We will discuss these issues at length in later chapters. But to give you a better understanding of both the strengths and the limitations of the behavioral approach—and why no one learning theory can explain all aspects of human behavior—let's look at recent research on therapy with alcoholic patients.

□ □ **QUESTION** □ □
If a symptomatic behavior has been heavily reinforced for many years, why might it not "disappear more or less automatically" once the underlying problem is solved? What type of *retraining technique* could you employ to reduce the strength of the symptomatic response?

ALCOHOLISM: DISEASE OR LEARNED BEHAVIOR?

Theory determines therapy, and the type of learning theory that you find "most reinforcing" often biases your perception of real-world situations.

If you view a "mental disorder" as stemming from a *biological dysfunction*, you might

Alcoholics Anonymous and its related groups—like Alateen, shown here—believe in the disease model of alcoholism.

attack the problem with medication. If you assume the problem is due to *repression* or *feelings of guilt*, you could try psychoanalysis or catharsis. If you think the cause is *poor S-S associations*, or a lack of *cognitive skills*, you surely would attempt cognitive behavior modification. However, should you perceive the problem in moral terms—as being due to a " lack of discipline" or even a "character disorder"— you might well opt for punishment training in order to "break S-R bonds."

Please keep the thought that "theory determines therapy" uppermost in your mind as we discuss the problem of *alcoholism*.

Two Schools of Thought

Millions of Americans consume alcohol on a regular basis. But only about 5 percent of these people are "problem drinkers." What is wrong with this small group of individuals? Why can 95 percent of the population *voluntarily control* their alcohol intake, while the other 5 percent can't?

There are two main schools of thought today as to what alcoholism is and how to treat it. One school views alcoholism as a *disease*. The other school perceives problem drinking as a *failure to learn self-control techniques*.

□ □ **QUESTION** □ □
How would the term you used— "alcoholism" versus "problem drinking"— bias your beliefs both as to the causes and the cures of the disorder?

The Disease Model

The "disease model" of alcoholism was first put forward by E.M. Jellinek. According to Jellinek, alcoholism is a *medical disorder* that has a biological basis. Because of *defective genes* (or perhaps a combination of genetic and developmental problems), the alcoholic cannot control her or his drinking the way "normal" people can. The alcoholic becomes *dependent* on alcohol, and comes to *crave* it the way a heroin addict "craves a fix." Since this is a *chemical dependency*, Jellinek implies, the only solution to the dependency must be total withdrawal from drinking (Jellinek, 1952).

People who adopt the disease model generally believe alcoholism is a "progressive disorder." Therefore, there can be no "cure" for the problem. However, the course of the illness can be *arrested* if the alcoholic gives up drinking entirely. Thus, the goal of treatment must be **abstinence**, or complete *sobriety*. For, theoretically speaking, even one drink will reinstitute both the craving and the progressive physical deterioration. And, to help alcoholics achieve sobriety, disease-model therapists often use confrontation (and even punishment) to *condition* patients to avoid alcohol—much as Watson used a loud noise to condition Little Albert to avoid white rats.

□ □ **QUESTION** □ □

In Chapter 3, we reported data (the "think-drink" effect) showing that alcoholics who consumed alcohol but thought they were drinking tonic water showed no "craving" for alcohol. But alcoholics who drank tonic water believing it was alcohol did report "cravings." How are these data an attack on the disease model?

The Behavioral Model

In 1962, British physician D.L. Davies published a report that seemed to challenge Jellinek's disease model of alcoholism. Davies studied a group of 93 alcoholics for almost 10 years after they had received "abstinence training" in a hospital setting. Some of the patients achieved and maintained sobriety. Most had fallen into

alcoholic drinking patterns again. However, *without any training or treatment to help them do so*, several of the patients had become "normal, social drinkers" (Davies, 1962).

On the basis of this admittedly small sample of subjects, Davies (and other researchers like him) concluded that the major difficulty most alcoholics have is this: They never learned the type of "self-control" most people acquire early in life. The researchers then set out to find ways to *teach* alcoholics the cognitive and behavioral skills they lacked. As it happened, the researchers not only discovered new and more effective therapeutic techniques for working with alcoholic patients, they also found fairly substantial evidence that the disease model is an inadequate explanation of why many people have alcohol-related problems (Miller & Hester, 1980).

● *Sobriety Versus Controlled Drinking*

Rather than forcing alcoholics to achieve *total abstinence*, the cognitive-behavioral approach attempts to help them become "non-problem" drinkers. From this viewpoint, if the person no longer has any alcohol-related *difficulties*, then the alcoholism has been "cured" for all practical purposes (Miller & Hester, 1986).

In stark contrast, the disease-model position is that alcoholism *cannot be cured*. Disease-model researchers contend that patients who learn to moderate their intake are still alcoholics *despite the fact that most of them no longer have any significant alcohol-related problems* (McCrady, 1985; Pendery, Maltzman, & West, 1982).

The question then becomes, how shall we decide which view is right?

The "Cure Rate" Controversy

You might think that scientific controversies such as this one would be settled on the basis of research findings rather than arguments. However, that's seldom the case in science or in any other human activity.

To begin with, alcoholism is a difficult problem to treat, no matter what view you take of its causes.

Second, research findings can often be interpreted in more than one way. For example, in the early 1970's, the National Institute on Alcohol Abuse and Alcoholism (NIAAA) commissioned the Rand Corporation to analyze data collected at three NIAAA treatment centers. The data collected by the Rand Corporation showed that *more than half* of the 597 patients treated from the disease-model perspective had returned to *uncontrolled* drinking 18 months after treatment. Only 24 percent "achieved and maintained sobriety for a substantial period of time." Other studies give similar data—overall, only 20 to 25 percent of patients given abstinence training maintain *long-term* sobriety.

Alcohol is readily available and socially accepted; in this context it is difficult to expect a former alcoholic to abstain completely.

Alcoholism: Disease or Learned Behavior?

Oddly enough, the first Rand report also showed that 22 percent of the patients had *voluntarily* achieved a normal level of "social drinking." They were not treated with this goal in mind. Rather, the patients apparently had learned to control their alcohol intake on their own (Rand, 1980).

If so many patients achieve "controlled drinking" without special training, what would the success rate be if you attempted to *teach* them cognitive self-control and social skills? Again NIAAA turned to the Rand Corporation. The second Rand report involved a four-year follow-up of patients trained *either* from the "disease model" or the "learned behavior" perspective. The data showed that the "controlled drinking" approach achieved significantly better results than did abstinence training (Rand, 1980).

In a recent book, Scottish researchers Nick Heather and Ian Robertson describe more than 74 published scientific studies showing the superiority of the skills-training approach (Heather & Robertson, 1981). Similar results are reported in a book edited by Rutgers psychologists William Hay and Peter Nathan (Hay & Nathan, 1982). Both books suggest that controlled drinking is frequently the treatment of choice in Britain and many other countries.

University of Washington psychologist G. Alan Marlatt and most other cognitive behaviorists see the "alcoholism problem" as one of teaching people self-management skills. However, Marlatt says, most people who take the disease-model perspective refuse to accept "controlled drinking" as a worthy therapeutic goal. From their standpoint, turning an alcoholic into a social drinker is no more a "cure" than would be therapy designed to turn murderers into muggers (Marlatt, 1983).

□ □ **QUESTION** □ □

Which would you think is a *better* outcome, complete abstinence or controlled drinking? Why?

Psychotherapy Plus Cognitive Behavior Modification

There are several purposes for this lengthy excursion into alcoholism, none of which has to do with proving one viewpoint wrong or the other right. For, as you will see, there is much to be said for both approaches.

First, as we noted, the manner in which you *perceive* the human organism strongly influences how you will *diagnose* human ills, what types of *treatment* you will prefer, and what you will consider a *cure*. Thus, we often cannot decide matters "on the basis of empirical data" because scientists don't always agree on what the data actually are.

Second, although the controlled-drinking approach is often referred to as "behavioral," it

is a very *cognitive* form of behavior modification. Among the treatment plans mentioned by Hay and Nathan are the following: blood-alcohol discrimination training (a type of biofeedback), drink-refusal training, craving-control methods, analysis of behavior chains leading to drinking, cognitive restructuring (learning new ways of defining drinking problems, changing beliefs and expectations), self-efficacy enhancement, relaxation training, stress management, lifestyle change, marital counseling, depression and anger management, family therapy, and enhancing social communication. Only a few of these techniques are derived from Skinner's operant technology or from Pavlovian conditioning. The others all involve attempts to change "internal processes" as well as behavioral outputs (Hay & Nathan, 1982).

Third, the best form of treatment would seem to be a *mix* of techniques derived from the various perspectives. Perhaps a brief look at research from G. Alan Marlatt's laboratory may show why this is the case. The data also demonstrate how different the effects of using reward and punishment can be.

G. Alan Marlatt

□ □ **QUESTION** □ □

Would it be easier to break an S-R bond by attaching a *new* response to the old stimulus, or by trying to *extinguish* the S-R connection *without* teaching the animal any new way to respond to the old stimulus?

● *Aversion Training*

More than a decade ago, Marlatt and his associates tried using *punishment* as a means of reducing alcohol consumption. Thirteen male chronic alcoholics were given **aversion training** in addition to abstinence training. That is, several times each day they were offered drinks they could consume or not consume, as they chose. But if they drank, they received a painful electric shock with each sip of alcohol. Marlatt and his colleagues hoped the *pairing* of pain with the sight, smell, and taste of alcohol would create a "conditioned emotional aversion" to drinking. Following this treatment, the subjects were studied for a period of 15 months to see how they fared "on their own." The results are shown in the left-hand portion of Fig. 10.8.

Compared with an unshocked control group of chronic alcoholics given abstinence training but *no shock*, the subjects in the "aversion training" group showed an *immediate* reduction of alcohol consumption. However, when the two groups were tested 15 months later, the patients in the shocked group were now drinking much *more* than the control group patients.

As Marlatt says, "Unless a new alternative response to drinking is established during the initial suppression stage . . . the old drinking

Aversion training. Pairing punishment with an undesirable response with the hope that the pain associated with the punishment will generalize to the response and thus prevent its recurrence.

patterns will gradually return as the impact of the aversion extinguishes . . ." (Marlatt, 1983).

□□ **QUESTION** □□
How do these results support Thorndike's law of effect, which states that "punishment *suppresses* responses temporarily rather than breaking S-R connections"?

● **Relapse Prevention Training**
These results led Marlatt to give alcoholic patients cognitive skills training instead of electric shock. He hoped this training would prevent relapse. The data from this study are shown in the right-hand portion of Fig. 10.8. As the graphs indicate, the skills training apparently was successful *in the long run*. However, note one important point: The *immediate* effect of "skills training" is an *increase* in alcohol consumption (as compared to the control group subjects) (Marlatt, 1983).

Marlatt believes different skills are needed at various stages in the therapeutic process. Early in treatment, as subjects struggle to achieve self-control, they have to learn how to *decrease* alcohol consumption. Later, they need to learn how to *maintain their gains*. As Marlatt puts it, "Future treatment research may show that intervention procedures may be differentially effective at each stage of the change process, from cessation (e.g., aversion therapy) to maintenance (e.g., relapse prevention)" (Marlatt, 1983).

Furthermore, Marlatt holds that while "abstinence is the best policy," there are many alcoholics who reject traditional treatment and who simply refuse to stop drinking entirely. Many of these individuals have indeed benefitted from learning how to control their alcohol intake voluntarily. As Marlatt puts it, "Without the opportunity to receive training in moderation, such clients would have nowhere else to turn for help" (Marlatt, 1984).

□□ **QUESTION** □□
How does the graph in the right-hand portion of Fig. 10.8 compare with the "trial-and-error" learning curve in Fig. 10.2? What does this comparison say about Thorndike's belief that "animals and humans learn the same way"?

● **A Holistic Approach**
As we have said many times before, behavior is multi-determined. Thus, any attempt to change behavior must address all the factors that influence those response outputs.

Confronting an alcoholic with his or her problems may well lead to a *suppression* of drinking, just as Pavlov and Watson would have predicted. But the data suggest this suppression is often fairly temporary—just as Thorndike discovered was the case whenever threats and punishment are used. Rewarding alcoholics for learning new responses that compete with "the urge to drink" does help, just as Wolpe showed was frequently true with other types of "counter conditioning." However, teaching alcoholics the cognitive skills involved in self-control is equally important. For you can't always have some external agency (such as Fred Skinner) standing over the alcoholic to

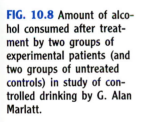

FIG. 10.8 Amount of alcohol consumed after treatment by two groups of experimental patients (and two groups of untreated controls) in study of controlled drinking by G. Alan Marlatt.

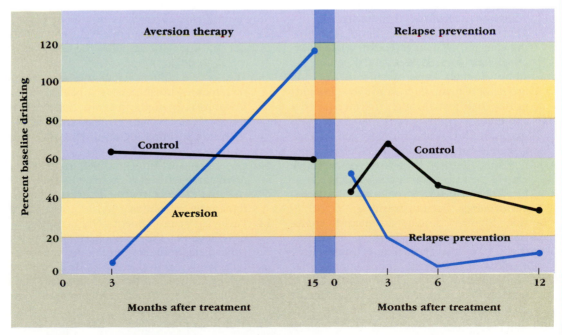

administer positive reinforcement at just the right time.

Put another way, effective treatment of alcoholism may well need to begin with *external* control. However, the locus of control probably must be *internalized* if long-term success is your goal. And "internalized control" is the aim of most types of cognitive behavior modification.

Finally, *any type of therapy* probably goes better if you help the person solve a wide range of social and personal problems *in addition to* changing symptomatic behaviors. For example, E.M. Pattison notes that even those patients who give up alcohol entirely still tend to function poorly in society unless given training specific to solving their social problems (Pattison, 1985).

To summarize, each of the various theories of learning tells us something important about how organisms acquire (and change) response outputs. Indeed, one theoretical approach often complements the other. For instance, in a recent article, University of Pennsylvania psychologist Robert Rescorla suggests using *Pavlovian* techniques to help analyze what happens during *operant* conditioning (Rescorla, 1987). However, no one theory gives us the complete story even in the simplest of learning situations. Thus, we cannot expect *therapy* or *educational practices* based on just one learning theory to work well in all situations and with all types of patients.

We will discuss these matters again in several later chapters. However, there is one important aspect of learning we've not yet touched upon—that of *memory*. So, it is to this topic that we now turn our attention.

□□ **QUESTION** □□

How could you use the various theories of learning to construct a holistic approach to education?

SUMMARY

1. E.L. Thorndike assumed that humans learn in much the same way that animals do. His studies with cats in a **puzzle box** led him to believe most new behaviors come about by **trial and error learning**.

2. Thorndike stated learning is influenced by two laws:
   a. The **law of exercise** states that the more frequently an animal repeats an **S-R bond**, the stronger it becomes.
   b. The **law of effect** states that stimulus-response (S-R) bonds are strengthened if the effect of the response is **satisfying**. Early in his career, Thorndike believed punishment "broke" S-R bonds, but later he stated punishment only **suppresses** responses temporarily.

3. Thorndike, like Pavlov, believed all learning is mechanical, or **reflexive. Gestalt psychologists**, such as Wolfgang Koehler, assume animals are capable of solving problems mentally (through **insight**) rather than just through mechanical trial and error.

4. According to Tolman, animals do not learn a maze by acquiring hundreds of S-R connections. Rather, they make a **cognitive map** of the maze, which guides their behavior. Tolman believed that reward affected **performance**, but not **learning**.

5. B.F. Skinner developed **operant conditioning**—a method of training organisms that differs from **Pavlovian**, or **respondent**, **conditioning**. Operant technology is by far more effective in the classroom (and elsewhere) than either Pavlovian or Gestalt techniques are.

6. Skinner believes animals **emit** responses freely and that the environment **rewards** or **reinforces** some of those responses but ignores or punishes others.

7. Training an organism by operant (Skinnerian) techniques consists of several steps:
   a. The **terminal response** or goal of the training must be stated in measurable terms.
   b. The **baseline behaviors** (what the organism is doing before intervention begins) must be measured precisely.
   c. Those baseline behaviors that seem directed toward the terminal response are **rewarded**, a technique called **reinforcing successive approximations to a goal** or **shaping** a new response.

8. According to Skinner, **reinforcement** tends to increase the probability that an organism will emit the same response the next time it is free to do so.

9. Punishment differs from **negative reinforcement**. Punishment is a painful input the animal attempts to avoid. Negative reinforcement involves strengthening a response by terminating an unpleasant drive or stimulus.

10. Generally speaking, **variable-ratio reinforcement schedules** yield smoother **cumulative records** (response curves) than do **fixed-ratio schedules**.

11. Pavlovian or respondent conditioning typically involves those **involuntary muscles** controlled by the **autonomic nervous system**, while operant conditioning typically involves those **voluntary muscles** controlled by the **cortex** and **higher brain centers**.

12. The proper use of **biofeedback** can some-

times allow you to gain voluntary control over such involuntary responses as your heart rate, skin temperature, and so forth. In real-life settings, however, biofeedback seems no more effective therapeutically than are **relaxation** and **cognitive control techniques**.

13. In the 1960's, many behavioral psychologists adapted Skinner's methods to the shaping of thoughts and feelings, a technique called **cognitive behavior modification**.

14. In Skinner's system, reinforcement (or reward) is always **extrinsic**, or "from the outside." Some studies suggest, however, that **internalizers** may prefer **intrinsic** reinforcers (such as personal pride) to external rewards.

15. The two major explanations of alcoholism are the **disease model** and the **learned behavior model**. Disease-model theorists believe the goal of treatment should be **abstinence**. Learning theorists believe that **controlled drinking**—which involves **skills training**—is a more achievable goal.

16. Alcoholism is probably best treated by a mix of **aversion training** (or social confrontation) during the early stages of therapy and **skills training** to maintain initial gains.

(Continued from page 240.)

FROM: Experimenter-in-Chief, Interstellar Labship PSYCH-192
TO: Director, Bureau of Science

Thlan, my friend, this will be an informal memo. I will send the official report along later, but I wanted to give you my impressions first.

The work with the newly discovered species is, unfortunately, at a standstill. Things went well at first. We picked what seemed to be an average but healthy animal and began testing it with our standard apparatus. I may have told you that this new species looks much like our usual laboratory subject, the White Rote. So we gave it a couple of the "toys" that the Rotes seem fond of—thin sheets of material made from woodpulp and a tiny stick of graphite. Imagine our delight when this new specimen made exactly the same use of the materials as have many of the Rotes. Could it be that there are certain innate behavior patterns to be found throughout the universe in the lower species?

The answer is of little importance, really. Your friend Verpk keeps insisting that the marks the Rotes make on the sheets are an attempt at communication, but that is, of course, utterly impossible. (Why did you saddle me with this idiot anyway when there are so many reasonable-thinking scientists available?) At any rate, this "scribbling" behavior did give us hope that the new species would behave according to accepted theory.

And at first this was the case. The animal solved the Bfian Box problem in short order, yielding as beautiful data as I have ever seen. We then shifted it to mazes and jump stand problems, and the results were equally pleasing. The animal clearly learns by bonding stimuli to responses in purely mechanical fashion.

Then, just to please Verpk, we tested it on the Oddity Problem. Now you and I both understand that lower organisms are not bright enough to solve the Oddity Problem, even if some cognitive theorists (whom I shall not name) disagree. For a few terrible trials, it seemed that those nameless theorists might be right! Which is to say that the animal *appeared* to react correctly even to stimuli it had never seen before! What an annoyance that would be since we are committed to "protecting" species intelligent enough to form concepts.

Ah, well, not to worry. The Oddity Problem apparently overloaded its simple brain circuits, for the organism soon broke down and became quite ill. Probably just as well, since this species is obviously unsuited for further experimentation.

I am not sure what to do next, either with this specimen or the world from which we took it. One of the students has nursed the animal back to some sort of health, and wishes to keep it as a pet. Verpk, however, suggests we put it back where we found it, and that we begin a crash program to see if these organisms really are concept-formers. Stupid suggestion, but I pass it along anyhow. My own belief is that we should sacrifice the animal and study its anatomy and its genes carefully to determine if it really is related to the White Rote.

But that is not why I write. Since this new species tends to break down readily under stress—much like Lavpov's Wogs—I see little sense in wasting our time in this part of the universe. We will not serve either our race or our glorious theories by studying what is clearly another stupid species.

The question is, then, should we stay here and continue our work as Verpk insists, or should we look for healthier and more normal animals elsewhere? And if we depart, should we first destroy the "home colony" so that these pests cannot be used in unscientific ways by those cognitive theorists whom I refuse to name?

Since all lower species are under your protection, we need your advice. My hope is that you will let us seek out new colonies and test our theories with *healthy* animals. For it is only in this fashion that science as we know it progresses.

Respectfully yours,
Iowyy

STUDY QUESTIONS

As you read through the chapter, see if you can find the answers to the following questions:

1. What are the six major problems that memory researchers are trying to solve?
2. According to the information processing theory, what happens to a sensory input from the time it enters the nervous system to the time it's filed in long-term memory storage?
3. How does iconic memory differ from echoic memory?
4. About how many items can you hold in Short-term Memory at the same time?
5. What evidence suggests that you *reconstruct* past events rather than *recalling them exactly?*
6. How does memory for odors differ from memory for sights and sounds?
7. What are the eight major memory categories?
8. What does the word "mnemonics" mean?
9. How do the recency effect and the primacy effect interact to produce the serial position effect?
10. What evidence suggests that memories can be altered *after* they are filed in long-term storage?
11. What is the difference between "declarative knowledge" and "procedural knowledge"?
12. About how long does it take a memory to "consolidate"?
13. What are the three stages of item retrieval?
14. What is "memory priming"?
15. What is an engram?

Memory

"Where Is Yesterday?"

· C H A P T E R ·

11

"Custard cups?" Bill Plautz said in a shocked tone of voice, as he unpacked the groceries. "You and Tom bought 32 glass custard cups?"

"Sure," Devin Eckhoff replied, a happy smile on his face. "They were only a dime apiece."

"You two paid 10 cents *each* for 32 glass custard cups?" Bill continued in an outraged tone of voice. "And you took the money out of our *grocery* budget?"

"Sure," Tom Laine said, sitting down at the kitchen table. "Better than taking it out of the beer budget."

Mike Keller looked up from his math book. "The four of us share and share alike in this apartment, Tom. So how could you and Devin spend $3.20 plus 16 cents sales tax for glass dishes, particularly when you know I don't even like custard!"

"The cups aren't for custard," Devin said. "They're for the worms."

"Oh," said Bill, his voice dropping a full octave on that single word. "Why didn't you say so?"

"You didn't ask," Tom responded.

Bill rummaged through the grocery bag a bit more. "And what is this tiny piece of beef liver for? Are we supposed to make a meal of this?"

"No, but the worms will love it," Devin said. "They don't eat very much, you know."

Mike sighed. "Neither will we, if you guys whoop off all our grocery money on worm dishes and beef liver."

"Well," Tom said. "You know we all agreed to work together on the research project that's required for our lab course in animal behavior."

"Yeah," Devin continued. "And we all agreed we'd try to condition planarian flatworms, to see if they could learn."

"Nobody's done it before, remember?" Tom said excitedly.

"I still don't see why we have to do this research project in our kitchen," Bill said, continuing to put away the food that Devin and Tom had bought.

"Because Professor Sauermann hates flatworms," Devin replied. "So he won't let us work in the animal labs."

Mike groaned. "That's no way to get an A on our project, you know. Doing research that Sauermann doesn't approve of."

"Our worm project is going to be so fantastic, he's bound to approve of it eventually," Tom said. "It might even make us famous!"

"Humph," Bill said, reaching the bottom of the grocery bag. "And what, may I ask, are these tiny camel's hair brushes for? Are we going to paint the worms different colors, or something?"

"We need the brushes to transfer the worms from the cups to the training trough," Devin replied. "You can't just pick 'em up with your fingers, you know. They're slippery little rascals, and they're only about an inch long."

"Speaking of worms, where are we going to get them?" Mike asked.

Tom laughed. "We're going to 'liberate' them from the pond in front of the biology building. I was over there yesterday. There are hundreds of the wee beasties crawling around in the muck at the bottom of the pond."

"And what about the training trough?" Mike asked.

"That's my department," Bill replied. "I'm working in Dr. Eastrum's chem lab this semester. He's got a dandy block of plastic he isn't using, and I can borrow his tools to gouge a tiny trough into it. And I've tucked away a couple of thick brass pins I can insert at either end of the trough to use as electrodes to pass shock through the water in the trough."

Devin frowned. "We still need a shock source of some kind."

"Dr. Calvin was showing me through the Psych Department Museum the other day," Mike replied. "They've got boxes and boxes of junky old equipment stuck away in the back room. One entire box was filled with strange metal devices that Dr. Calvin called 'Harvard inductoriums.'"

"Called *what*?" Tom asked.

"Inductoriums," Mike replied. "They're an old-fashioned contraption invented at Harvard around the turn of the century. Psychologists used them to shock undergraduates in verbal learning studies, or something."

"Do you think an inductorium would work with worms in a water-filled trough?" Bill asked.

"Probably," Mike replied. "And think how impressed Dr. Sauermann would be if we told him we gave our planarians a 'Harvard education.'"

Devin laughed, then turned serious. "All right, you guys. It's time we got organized. Mike, you go over to the Psych Building and see if you can scrounge one of those inductoriums when nobody's looking. And Bill, you go over to Eastrum's lab and get that trough put together."

"What about you and Tom?" Mike asked.

Tom grinned. "We're off to the biology pond to free 32 flatworms from their muckish existence."

"What are you going to do if somebody catches you?" Bill asked.

"Oh, we'll worm our way out of it somehow," Devin replied.

"I found a couple of fat ones," Tom said, carefully brushing two flatworms off a leaf into the bucket of water that he and Devin had beside them.

"Great," Devin replied.

"Hey, what are you two guys doing?" a biology student asked, walking up to the pond.

Tom looked up at the young man. "Gathering specimens for an experiment."

"What kind of specimens?"

"Flatworms," Devin said casually.

"Oh, platyhelminthes," the biology student said knowingly. "What are you going to do with them?"

"We're going to train them in a conditioning trough," Devin replied.

The biology student shook his head in dismay. "Don't be silly. Worms can't learn."

"How do you know that?" Tom asked.

"Because I was reading Libbie Hyman's classic work on platyhelminthes just last week, and she says they can't learn. That's why," the student replied.

"Why can't they?" Devin responded. "They've got brains and a primitive nervous system. They've even got synapses!"

The biology student laughed. "Who cares about synapses? If worms could learn, a zoologist would have done the study already. And then it would be reported in Hyman."

"Well, did any zoologist you know of ever try to condition a planarian?" Tom asked.

"Of course not," the student replied. "It would be a waste of time, because organisms that simple are incapable of forming associations."

Devin looked at Tom, and then grinned broadly. "Well, judging from the specimens I've seen today, I'm not sure that even biology students are capable of learning."

The biology student shifted uncomfortably on his feet. "Does the Chairman of the Biology Department know you're stealing our worms?"

"No," said Tom. "But we'll be sure to give the Biology Department credit when we publish our study proving planarians can learn."

"Yeah," Devin continued. "We'll mention you guys in a worm-sized footnote."

"Well, now, let's see," Bill said, laying out all of the equipment on the kitchen table. "We've got the worms. . . ."

"Thirty-two fat and healthy specimens, housed in individual custard cups," Tom remarked in a happy tone of voice.

"We've got the trough gouged out of the plastic block that I swiped from Eastrum's laboratory. The trough is precisely 8 inches long, half an inch wide, and half an inch deep."

"And it's filled to the top with pond water," Mike added.

"Water, courtesy of your old buddies, Devin and Tom, who risked life and limb to steal it from the biology building pond," Devin remarked.

"The electrodes at either end of the trough are connected to a 6-volt battery by means of a Harvard inductorium," Bill continued.

Mike interrupted him with a laugh. "Professor Calvin thought I was crazy, you know, borrowing such an *old-fashioned* piece of equipment."

"And we've got Tom's goose-neck study lamp to provide light to shine on the worms as the conditioning stimulus," Bill said.

"How many groups are we going to run?" Mike asked.

"Four," Bill said. "An experimental group that gets the light paired with the shock, and three control groups. With the experimental animals, we turn the light on for two seconds, then shock them. The light is the CS, the shock is the UCS."

"What's the UCR?" Tom asked.

"The 'scrunch' the worm makes when we shock it," Bill said.

Devin asked, "How are we going to prove to Professor Sauermann that the experimental animals have learned?"

Mike replied, "On each trial, we observe the worm to see what it does during the two seconds after the light comes on and before the shock starts. At the beginning of training, the animal shouldn't respond much to the light at all."

"Oh, I see," Devin said. "But as we train the animal, it should start 'scrunching' to the light more and more frequently."

"That's right," Tom said. "Because the light becomes a signal that the worm is about to get blasted. So it 'scrunches' in anticipation of the shock."

"But do we really need *three* control groups?" Mike asked plaintively, thinking of all the work involved.

Bill grinned. "Absolutely. We've got to prove it's the *pairing* of the light and shock that causes any change in the way the worms respond. So the first control group gets light, but no shock. The second group gets shock, but no light. And the third group gets both light and shock, but they're not paired. The response rate to the light should increase significantly in the experimental animals, and decrease in the three control groups."

"Okay, who does what when?" Devin asked.

"Mike and I will train two groups each day," Bill said, "and you and Tom can train the other two groups. We'll switch groups daily, to equalize the work."

"And when you and Mike are working, Tom and I can go play racquetball," Devin remarked.

"Yeah," Tom said, grinning. "And ever since Devin got hit in the eye with a ball, you should see him 'scrunch' whenever I serve him a zinger."

"Hey, man, you've got me conditioned!" Devin laughed.

They flipped a coin, and Bill and Mike won the honor of starting first. So while Devin and

Tom went off to the racquetball courts, Mike and Bill settled down to work. Mike put a healthy planarian in the trough, and then told Bill to get ready. When the worm was crawling steadily in a straight line, he called out, "Now."

Immediately Bill switched on the light. Two seconds later, he turned on the shock for half a second. The Harvard inductorium buzzed noisily.

"Boy," Mike said. "You should have seen that baby scrunch."

"Before or after the shock?" Bill asked.

"After the shock," Mike replied. "He sort of wiggled his nose for a fraction of a second when the light came on. But he didn't scrunch at all until you zapped him."

"Okay," Bill said. "We'll put down, 'Trial 1, W for Wiggle.'"

"Get ready for the next trial," Mike said moments later. And when the worm was again moving steadily in a straight line, he said, "Now!"

And again, Bill turned on the light for two seconds, and then the shock.

"Not even a wiggle that time," Mike announced. A few seconds later, he told Bill, "Ready. . . . Now!"

Bill applied the light and the shock.

"A scrunch!" Mike said excitedly. "A good, clean scrunch."

"Great," said Bill. "Let me observe the next worm while you run the light and shock."

"Sure," Mike replied. Then, as he waited for the animal to turn around at the end of the trough and start moving steadily again, he continued, "Do you *really* think these funny little critters are capable of learning?"

Bill thought a moment. "The worms will answer that for us, Mike. The important question is whether Devin will ever learn to wear goggles when he plays racquetball with Tom."

Mike sighed. "Oh, well. Maybe if worms can learn, humans can too." Then, noticing the planarian was again moving majestically down the trough, he said, "Ready. . . . Now!"

(Continued on page 287)

MEMORY

What time is it?

When someone asks you for the time, how do you respond? Probably you look at your watch, or at a clock, and you give the answer almost automatically. As simple as this process may seem, however, we know very little about how your brain handles inputs such as this one. And we know even less about how your mind responds so appropriately—and so quickly. However, we are reasonably certain about certain aspects of this cognitive process.

To answer any question, you must make use of your **memory**. If someone asks you the time, you must first recognize that someone has spoken to you. Next you must check your memory banks to make sure you recognize the words and phrases the person has used. Then you must realize that you have been *asked a question* to which you might respond.

But while your brain is "checking all these things out," it must have some way of *remembering* what the original question was. If you had no way of holding the question in some kind of "temporary storage," you might end up knowing you'd been asked a question without being able to recall what it was. However, you must remember several other things as well as what the question was. For example, you can't tell someone "what time it is" unless you can recall what a clock or watch is—and how to tell time. Nor can you respond to such questions correctly unless you can remember how to reproduce the words you must use in your an-

swer. Memory, then, is a much more complicated process than it might seem at first glance.

As in the study of all other areas of psychology, there are certain *major problems* that memory researchers are trying to solve. Let's look briefly at what six of these problems are. For once you understand what some of the basic issues are, you will be in a better position to answer the question of how *you* answer such questions as "What time is it?"

Six Important Issues

If we could solve the following six issues, we'd know a great deal more about your memory than we presently do:

1. How many types of memory—or memory systems—do you have?
2. What do you store in memory—exact copies of inputs or "processed" material of some kind?
3. Why do you store some things in memory, but not others?
4. How do you retrieve an item from your memory files?
5. What is forgetting, and what causes it?
6. What physical changes occur in your brain during memory storage?

As you will see, we can't answer any of these questions as fully as we might wish. However, discovering what we *do* know will surely give you greater respect for your own memory. And, who knows, this type of knowledge might even help you improve your own ability to remember things.

MEMORY SYSTEMS

In point of fact, you don't have just one "memory system," you have several different systems. Psychologists don't agree on how many systems there are, or how each functions. And, as you might suspect, there are many different theories that attempt to explain how memory works. But we might as well begin our investigation of memory by looking at the **information processing approach**, which probably is the dominant theory in memory research today. We'll discuss the other theoretical approaches later on.

Information Processing Approach

According to University of Arizona psychologist John Kihlstrom, the information processing approach is modeled after the high-speed computer (Kihlstrom, 1987). The theory assumes there are certain "memory structures" for storing information, and certain "memory processes" for transferring information from one structure to another. Information *processing* occurs at three different levels:

First, sensory inputs from the environment are "translated" (or **transduced**) into patterns of neural energy by the *sensory receptors*. The incoming information is held briefly in *sensory registers*, one for each sensory modality. Initial "processing" occurs at this level, and consists primarily of "feature detection" and "pattern recognition" (see Chapter 5). This is the *sensory information stage* of input processing.

Second, *important information* about the input is then transferred to the next stage, which is called *Short-term Memory* or *primary memory*. At this point, you become *conscious* of the input. After comparing the input with information filed away in long-term memory storage, you decide how to respond to the input.

Third, if the input is important, you are likely to transfer it to *Long-term Memory*, which Kihlstrom refers to as "secondary memory."

The three-stage, information processing "model" has guided most memory research since the 1960's (Kihlstrom, 1987). Recent studies, however, cast some doubt on the accuracy of the three-stage theory. Since the information processing model is still dominant, though, let's look at it more closely.

Sensory Information Stage

What time is it?

When the image of those words first impinges on the retinas in your eyes, your rods and cones respond by sending a characteristic *pattern of nerve impulses* along your optic nerve to the visual centers of your brain.

Memory storage and retrieval in humans are much more complex than in computers.

Suppose that we flashed the words "What time is it?" on a screen for exactly one-tenth of a second. How long would your rods and cones continue to respond after the words had disappeared? The answer is—it depends. If you had been sitting in absolute darkness for several minutes, the words *"What time is it?"* would hang suspended in your visual field for quite some time. However, if you were sitting in a lighted room, the next thing you looked at would erase the phrase "What time is it?" from your visual system.

Your memory *begins,* then, in your receptors—in what psychologists call the **Sensory Information Storage** or SIS stage of information processing (Dick, 1974).

Under normal conditions—as you look from one object to another in your visual world—your visual system holds on to each stimulus pattern for but a fraction of a second before that pattern is replaced by yet another visual input. According to psychologists Peter Lindsay and Donald Norman, this storage time typically lasts from 0.1 to 0.5 seconds under normal viewing conditions (Lindsay & Norman, 1977). (As we noted, though, the storage lasts longer if no new stimulus "erases" the input.)

You can measure your own Sensory Information Storage time by using a technique Lindsay and Norman describe. Extend your index finger on one hand, and then wave your finger back and forth in front of your eyes while you stare straight ahead. You'll notice that a "shadowy image" trails behind your finger. Studies suggest this image lasts for about 0.25 second. (Swinging a flashlight around in a circle in the dark gives the same sort of "trailing visual image.")

George Sperling, one of the first psychologists to work in this area, refers to visual SIS as **iconic memory**. For the amount of informa-

Memory. From the Latin and Greek words meaning "to be mindful, or to remember." Your memory is your store of past experiences, thus the seat of your ability to recreate or reproduce past perceptions, emotions, thoughts, and actions.

Information processing approach. The major theory in memory research today. Assumes there is a set of "structures" for storing information, and a set of "processes" for transferring information from one structure to another. Each sensory modality is assumed to have its own "sensory registers" or structures for holding sensory inputs momentarily in "Sensory Information Storage." Information in each "register" is analyzed, and "trivial details" are discarded. Important information is then transferred to "Short-term Memory" and is further analyzed and compared with information from permanent memory. Finally, important information is then filed in "Long-term Memory."

Transduced (trans-DOOST). To change something (such as a sensory input) from one form into another. A lamp "transduces" electrical energy into light and heat.

Sensory Information Storage. The first stage of memory storage. Your sensory receptors hold a more or less exact copy of an input for a fraction of a second before that copy is "erased" by the next input.

Iconic memory (eye-KON-ick). The word *icon* (EYE-kon) comes from a Greek word meaning "a visual representation or image." Iconic memory is a visual form of Sensory Information Storage.

Echoic memory (eh-KOH-ick). An auditory form of Sensory Information Storage.

tion stored in visual SIS is much like that in an *icon,* which is a "detailed image" of a person or event (Sperling, 1963). In similar fashion, auditory SIS is sometimes called **echoic memory**, because it seems to be an "exact echo" of an auditory input. However, by the time this sensory information reaches your cortex—and you become aware of what you are looking at—much of the rich detail is lost.

To put the matter another way, your *visual system* has a "photographic memory," but your *cortex* doesn't. We know this is the case because of studies George Sperling began at Harvard in the late 1950's.

● *Sperling's Research*

Imagine that you are sitting in a dark room staring at a blank movie screen. Behind you, a slide projector clicks briefly, and the stimulus pattern shown in Fig. 11.1A flashes onto the screen. The pattern appears for just 0.05 second (1/20th of a second, or 50 milliseconds), then disappears.

Your task in this experiment is to report all the letters you remember seeing during the 50 milliseconds exposure time. You do the best you can. But trial after trial, you can't recall more than 3 or 4 of the 9 letters. Does this result mean that your SIS system *recorded* only 3 or 4 of the letters? Not at all, as Sperling demonstrated almost 30 years ago.

Sperling suspected that his subjects actually saw all 9 letters, but *forgot* most of them during the time it took them to *report* what they had seen. So he changed the experimental procedure slightly. Immediately *after* presenting the stimulus pattern visually, he gave the subject an *auditory signal*. This signal told the subject *which letter to report*. For instance, one signal might ask the subject, "Which letter was in the upper right-hand corner?" Another signal would tell the subject to report which letter was in the center of the bottom row.

Suppose you were a subject in this type of study. Since the auditory signal occurred a fraction of a second *after* you had seen the 9 stimulus letters, you wouldn't know which of the 9 letters to pay attention to while the letters flashed on the screen. However, it wouldn't matter. For you would be able to remember *any* of the 9 letters you were signaled to report. So you obviously *saw* them all—and recorded them briefly in visual SIS. However, you would achieve this accuracy *only* if the auditory signal occurred within 100 milliseconds after the letters had disappeared from the screen. If the signal didn't come on until 500 milliseconds (1/2 second) afterward, your performance would drop to the chance level (see Fig. 11.1B).

FIG. 11.1B When Sperling asked his subjects to report immediately, they could identify any of the nine stimulus letters. When the subjects' reports were delayed for half a second (500 milliseconds), they could identify only half the letters.

FIG. 11.1A The stimulus pattern used in the Sperling experiment.

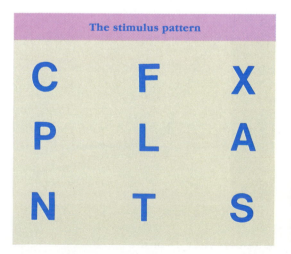

The stimulus pattern

C F X
P L A
N T S

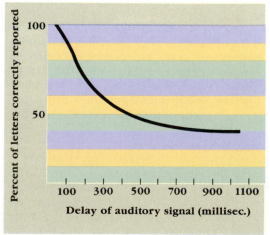

Percent of letters correctly reported

100

50

100 300 500 700 900 1100

Delay of auditory signal (millisec.)

SAY, MY SHORT-TERM MEMORY IS IMPROVING. I CAN REMEMBER WALKING DOWN SOME STEPS.

A&R MEMORY SCHOOL

S. Harris

Sperling's research showed three important things: First, your SIS *records* inputs in much greater detail than previously had been suspected. Second, items stored in SIS are normally *forgotten* (or "erased") within half a second. Thus, the reason subjects in previous studies couldn't report more than 3 or 4 of the letters is this: During the time it took them to *report* the first 3 or 4 letters, they had actually *forgotten* the rest of the 9.

Last but not least, Sperling's studies suggested that the eye sends a *visual* copy of the input to the brain. When Sperling delayed the auditory signal for more than one-half second, his subjects often made mistakes. But these were *visual* mistakes. That is, the subjects reported seeing a "P" rather than an "F." These letters are visually similar. However, the subjects seldom reported seeing an "X" when the letter actually was an "F" (Sperling, 1963). The importance of this point will become clearer in a moment.

□□ **QUESTION** □□

Many people believe your brain actually makes an "exact video tape recording" of everything you see, and that this "exact tape" is filed in your memory forever. What does Sperling's research suggest is the case?

Short-term Memory

Your eye apparently sends a very detailed representation of each visual input up to your brain. The lower centers in your brain then *extract the critical features* of the inputs and relay this information to your cortex. At this point, you become conscious of the input. Then you

attempt to *categorize* the input and make certain cognitive decisions about it (Lindsay & Norman, 1977).

However, you must have some means of *storing* the input for a few seconds while you "think" about it. So your brain *codes* the input and tucks it away in "temporary hold" while the input is being processed.

□□ **QUESTION** □□

How do the errors Sperling's subjects made support the belief that the lower centers *extract critical features* rather than send the entire input to the cortex? (Hint: How are "P" and "F" similar?)

Defining Short-term Memory

Now, let's suppose you're a subject in yet another memory experiment. The experimenter shows you a card. Printed on the card are three large letters: C F M. You look at the letters for a few seconds, then the experimenter removes the stimulus card. Some 20 seconds later, the experimenter asks you what the letters were. You respond correctly. The fact that you can remember the letters for more than half a second shows that you aren't using SIS in this case. Could it be that you're using "permanent" storage instead? Let's continue the study and see.

Next, the experimenter asks you to repeat the task with different letters. But this time, you have to perform a difficult cognitive task during the 20-second delay: You must "count backwards by three's," starting at some arbitrary number such as 487. That means you must say, "487, 484, 481, 478 . . ." until told to do otherwise. After you have counted backwards for 20 seconds, the experimenter stops you and asks you what the three stimulus letters were. Now, how do you think you'd fare?

When B.B. Murdock performed this study in 1961, he got the sorts of results shown in Fig.

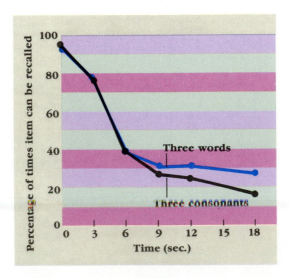

FIG. 11.2 When Murdock made his subjects "count backwards" after exposing them to three consonants (or three words), the subjects couldn't "rehearse" and thus tended to forget. See text.

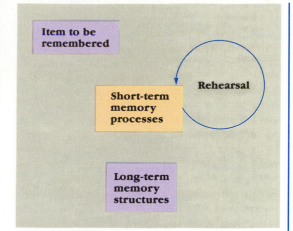

FIG. 11.3 Rehearsing an item keeps it current in Short-term Memory and helps move it to long-term storage.

11.2. If you count backwards for just three seconds, you probably will recall only two of the three stimulus letters. If you count backwards for more than six seconds, you're lucky to remember one of the three letters. And, as Murdock showed, you'd perform at about the same level if you were given three words to remember instead of three letters (Murdock, 1961).

Since you forgot so much so rapidly, it's obvious you're not using "permanent" storage to recall the letters. However, since you remember the letters for more than half a second, you can't be using SIS either. Psychologists use the term **Short-term Memory** (STM) to refer to this type of "temporary hold" during information processing.

A number of studies suggest that items filed in Short-term Memory remain available for recall no more than about 30 seconds before "vanishing forever" (Lindsay & Norman, 1977).

● Rehearsal

Why could you remember the three stimulus letters so well when you didn't have to "count backwards by three's"? If you've ever had to look up a phone number in a directory, you probably know the answer. What happens when you look the number up? Probably you silently *repeat* the number to yourself several times so you won't forget it during the length of time it takes you to close the directory, pick up the phone, and start dialing.

Psychologists use the term *rehearsal* to refer to the act of "silently saying things over and over again." When you *rehearse* an item, you actually keep putting it back into temporary storage again and again. By *rehearsing* the item into Short-term Memory several times, you can keep it available for a period of several minutes (see Fig. 11.3).

George Sperling

□ □ **QUESTION** □ □
Most people must "rehearse" a telephone number continuously until they dial it. What does this fact tell you about the length of time an item typically remains in Short-term Memory?

● Acoustical Coding

In describing George Sperling's research on visual SIS, we said the *type of mistakes* his sub-

jects made was important. As it turns out, subjects in Short-term Memory experiments make quite different sorts of errors than the mistakes Sperling's subjects made. And this fact has given us a clue to how the lower centers of the brain actually *store* items in STM.

When Sperling's subjects made mistakes, they often confused an "F" with a "P" or an "E." The fact that these letters all *look alike* suggests that *visual* SIS coding is *visual*. However, subjects asked to "count backwards by three's" will typically confuse an "F" with an "X," but seldom with an "E" or a "P." What's going on here?

If you say "F" and "X" aloud, you'll hear the answer. For the initial sound you make when you say each letter is the same. But "F" doesn't *sound* at all like "E" or "P." Thus, you must be *translating* these visual inputs into *sounds* prior to tucking them away in Short-term Memory. We call this process **acoustical coding**.

Technically speaking, *acoustical coding* refers to the tendency to "translate" certain visual inputs into something related to the sound or production of words when you put them in temporary memory storage.

Whenever a visual input involves *written or spoken language,* you tend to encode the input as *sounds* rather than *sights*. This fact shouldn't be too surprising. As you read this book, for instance, don't you "hear" yourself saying the words aloud? If you read a sentence, then close your eyes, it's the "sounds" made by your own "inner voice" you usually remember rather than the visual image on the printed page. Thus, with *language inputs*, what you actually file away in Short-term Memory is a sort of "auditory translation" rather than the visual input itself (Lindsay & Norman, 1977).

Not all Short-term Memory is made up of "auditory translations," however. Suppose we ask you to watch a young woman playing an accordion. Then we ask you to look away and describe what you saw. You might be able to do so in words alone, but the odds are you will recall *visual images* that you'd try to reproduce by *moving your own hands* the same way the woman had. *That* sort of Short-term Memory is obviously visual and muscular, not "acoustical coding."

□ □ **QUESTION** □ □
You encode the sight of a *word* acoustically, but not the sight of a beautiful *sunset*. Why does this fact suggest that while many types of "thinking" are really a form of "inner speech," some forms of thinking are non-verbal?

- ### *Familiar Items*

Short-term Memory for familiar objects is generally much longer (and better) than for unfamiliar objects. For example, read the following sentence rapidly and then look away from the page and try to remember exactly what the stimulus sentence was:

КОТОРЫЙ ЧАС?

Chances are—unless you are familiar with the Russian language—you had a difficult time

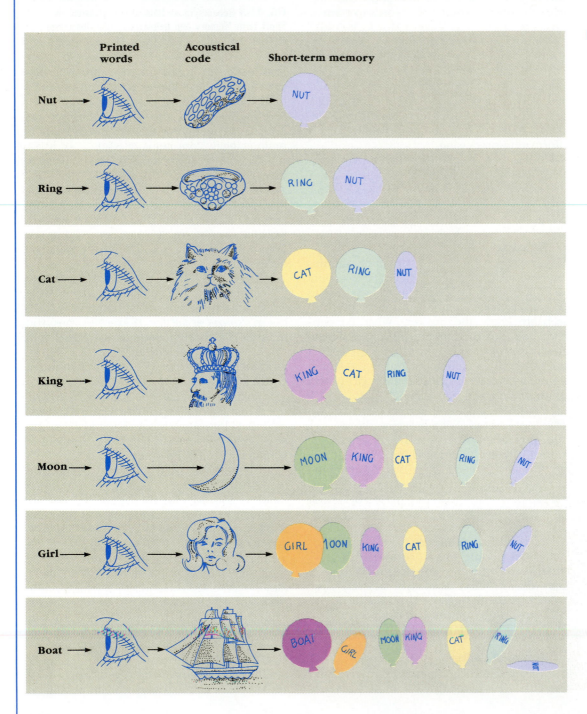

FIG. 11.4 Short-term Memory storage.

Printed words | Acoustical code | Short-term memory

Nut → → NUT

Ring → → RING NUT

Cat → → CAT RING NUT

King → → KING CAT RING NUT

Moon → → MOON KING CAT RING NUT

Girl → → GIRL MOON KING CAT RING NUT

Boat → → BOAT GIRL MOON KING CAT RING NUT

trying to remember what you actually saw. You surely sensed at once that the sentence was written in a language other than English. But could you "see" in your mind's eye each of the letters in that strange (to us) alphabet that the Russians use? Or was it more or less a jumbled blur?

□ □ **QUESTION** □ □

Would a camera have any more difficulty photographing the phrase in Russian than in English? What does this fact tell you about your STM and "acoustical coding?"

● *Memory "Interpretations"*

Now glance quickly at the following stimulus sentence and then look away and try to visualize exactly what it says:

What time it is?

When this phrase appeared in Russian, your Short-term Memory couldn't "code" the words acoustically because (chances are) you couldn't say them aloud. But when the phrase appeared in English, you remembered it *very* well, because you knew the *sounds* of the words. Generally speaking, *familiar items* are much easier to "code into sounds" than are unfamiliar items. Your Short-term Memory can hold a familiar item for up to 30 seconds. Less-familiar items (such as the phrase in Russian) tend to drop out much more rapidly.

□ □ **QUESTION** □ □

Look again at the "stimulus phrase" one paragraph above. Does it *really* say what you remembered it as saying? If

you didn't perceive it correctly, what does this fact tell you about "interpreting" items before you store them in Short-term Memory?

● *Limited Capacity*

Your Short-term Memory ordinarily cannot store more than five to seven items simultaneously. At the moment that your brain inserts an item into Short-term Memory, that item is strong and clear and easy to recall, if you do so *immediately*. But shortly thereafter, your brain tucks away a second item, and then a third item, and a fourth. Although only a few seconds have passed, you will now have much more trouble trying to recall what the first item was.

By the time your brain has pressed four or five new items down on top of the first, that original item has lost most of its strength and has faded away. The new items appear to *interfere with* or erase the ones in front of them—just as each new visual pattern you look at wipes clean the stimulus you were looking at just a moment before (see Fig. 11.4).

While you are holding an item in Short-term Memory, you can recall it more or less at will. And you can keep the item around for several minutes by "rehearsing" it. However, once the item drops out of "temporary storage," it is likely to be gone forever—unless your brain decides to make a *permanent record* of the stimulus input (Peterson, 1966).

□ □ **QUESTION** □ □

If you "rehearse" an item for a long enough period of time, you might well not forget it at all. What does that fact tell you about how items get shifted from Short- to Long-term Memory?

Long-term Memory

If you stroll along a busy street, you may see a thousand different people in one short hour. Most of their faces will fade from your memory almost immediately. Yet some things (and faces) you remember vividly—or at least you think you do.

For example, try to remember the last long trip that you took. Can you recall *right at this instant* the exact date and hour that the trip began and ended? Chances are that you can't. But if you take the time to think about the details—and perhaps write them down as you go—you'll find you can *reproduce* a surprising amount of detail about that trip, even though it may have occurred months or years ago. However, if you inspect those memories carefully as they pop back into consciousness, you'll find they are *qualitatively different from the immediate memory you have of a face you've just seen.*

In fact, your recollection of things that happened long ago usually is hazy and incomplete

You tend to forget the faces of people in a crowd rather rapidly—unless there is something "special" or "unusual" about one or more of the faces.

at first. One reason for this haziness was offered more than 100 years ago by Hermann Ebbinghaus, one of the earliest and greatest investigators of human memory. Ebbinghaus suggested that you typically don't *remember* complex events. Rather, you recall a few "high points" and then *reconstruct* the experience piece by little piece (Ebbinghaus, 1885/1964).

□□ **QUESTION** □□
How could you use Thorndike's law of exercise and law of effect (see Chapter 10) to explain why people remember what they remember?

• *Reconstruction Versus Exact Recall*

Your SIS system briefly stores a more-or-less *exact copy* of the original sensory input. Your Short-term Memory is rather like an "instant replay" on television—a few seconds of highlight action that you can recall with considerable clarity for a brief period of time thereafter. But it is a "processed copy" of the input—rather than all the rich sensory detail—that you can replay at will until the input fades away into obscurity.

Your **Long-term Memory** seems to be much more complex, for it stores many different aspects of your experiences. First, it records certain *critical features* of your sensory inputs and files these according to various *memory categories*. Second, your LTM creates an *acoustical representation* of the input. And third, Long-term Memory records information on how to *reproduce* the items you've filed away—that is, how to write and say things aloud.

When you draw on your Long-term Memory, it then *reconstructs* the event from the associations and auditory representations it has in its files. However, Long-term Memory does not usually allow you to *relive* experiences in any great detail.

• *Smell: An Exception*

There seem to be separate "memory banks" for each of the sensory modalities—plus several "superordinate" banks that help you relate (for instance) the *picture* of a dog with the *sound* of the animal's name. As Brown University psychologist Trygg Engen pointed out recently, however, *smell* seems to be an exception: "What odor perception does best, the basis for its reputation, is to recreate significant past episodes in a person's life" (Engen, 1987). (Vladimir Nabokov says much the same thing in his novel *Mary*: "Memory can restore to life everything except smells, although nothing revives the past so completely as a smell that was once associated with it.")

According to Engen, your memory for odors that you encounter in real-life situations is "almost perfect." You tend to forget specific sights and sounds rather rapidly. But your memory for specific odors tends to last your entire life. For example, as a young child you may have visited your grandmother's home only once. But suppose you peeked in her closet, and it had a unique smell—perhaps a mixture of lavender and cedar. If you ever encounter this same odor again, chances are you will be flooded by memories of your visit to your grandmother's home, and of the *emotions* you felt at that time. However, you probably will *not* be able to recall exactly what she said to you then, nor what specific clothes were hanging in her closet.

Engen also points out that the *name* of an odor is not usually a sufficient stimulus for recalling either the smell itself or any emotional experiences associated with the odor. As we pointed out in Chapter 4, sensory inputs from the nose by-pass the thalamus (and hence the cortex, with its "memory banks" for sights and sounds). Instead, olfactory inputs primarily go straight to the *limbic system*—the sub-center of the brain that mediates emotional experiences. Little wonder, then, that smells recreate *emotional experiences,* not *cognitive processes*.

□□ **QUESTION** □□
Try to recall both the color and the shape of a lemon. An easy task? Probably. But now, try to remember the *exact smell* of a lemon. What psychological differences do you see between the "remembered sight" of the fruit and the "remembered smell"?

Item Storage and Retrieval

Your Long-term Memory (LTM) is practically limitless—rather like a huge library with billions of books stashed away on the shelves. You add thousands of new volumes to that library every day of your life, but you never seem to run out of shelf space for new arrivals. But how in the world do you retrieve the correct item when you're searching your memory files for it?

The answer seems to lie in how you *categorize* your experiences in the first place. We will discuss memory categories in just a moment. But first, we might note an odd thing: It may take you some time to resurrect an item stored in your Long-term Memory; however, you often know *immediately* that you *don't* have an item stored in LTM (Lindsay & Norman, 1977). For example, what was George Washington's phone number? Ah ha! you say, he lived before phones were invented, so he didn't have a phone number. But what is the *present* president's phone number? Chances are, you know at once that you *don't* know what it is *even though you also know the president does have a phone number*.

Now, how many windows are there in the rooms where you live? Probably you can figure out the answer to this question by *visualizing* the rooms and then *mentally counting the windows*. But why did it take you so much longer to answer something you *did* know than it took to answer a question when you *knew you didn't know*?

When you try to retrieve an item from Long-term Memory, you apparently check through your "mental file cards" to see where the item is located in LTM. However, if at any time you come across a "blank file card" (or one that says, "This item does not exist"), then your search stops and you say, "I don't know." As Lindsay and Norman point out, we're not really sure how you know what information exists in your brain—and what doesn't (Lindsay & Norman, 1977). But it does seem clear that most people use the same sort of scheme for "constructing mental file cards."

▢▢ QUESTION ▢▢

What is the first word in the first sentence on this page? Chances are, you don't know. But you also know immediately that you *could have known*. Since you *did* know the answer at one point in time, why can't you remember what the word was?

Harold Goodglass

Memory Categories

According to memory expert Harold Goodglass, you tend to tuck items away in permanent storage in terms of several rather specific categories (Goodglass, 1980). We can best illustrate these categories by asking you to consider how you might go about filing the word "chair" in Long-term Memory.

1. *Identity*. First you would try to remember the word itself, "chair." But, as you will see, you rapidly split up this category in a variety of ways.
2. *Class*. A chair is a piece of furniture. Thus,

you would file this item not merely as a word unto itself, but as part of a **superordinate** class ("furniture") which would include such other items as "table," "couch," "bed," and "lamp."

3. *Attributes*. A chair is soft or hard, large or small, metal or wood, upholstered or plain. You may enjoy chairs, or hate them. Your memory of a chair, then, includes some notion of the various physical and psychological attributes that a chair has.
4. *Context*. You expect to see a chair in a living room, not inside a bathtub. But you may also remember a specific chair in an unusual context, such as an electric chair in a prison, or your mother's chair in her bedroom.
5. *Function*. You associate the word "chair" with certain verbs denoting its function, such as "sit," or "recline."
6. *Sensory Associations*. The word "chair" will be paired with the *sight* of typical chairs, with the smell of leather and wood, the *feeling* your skin has when you sit on a chair, and perhaps with a squeaking *sound* that old chairs make when you lean back too far in them.
7. *Clangs and Visual Patterns*. You not only file the *concept* of a chair away in your memory, but also certain salient features of the word itself, such as its *sight and sound*. Thus, "chair" will be stored according to its **clangs**, or "sound-alike" words ("bare," "pear"). It will also be filed according to the visual pattern the letters c-h-a-i-r make, the initial letter of the word, the number of syllables in the word, and so forth.
8. *Reproductive Information*. Your Long-term Memory also includes information on the muscle movements needed to say the word "chair," to *write* it, to *draw* a picture of a chair, and so forth.

These eight "memory categories" are by no means the only ones having to do with *item storage* in Long-term Memory. But they are perhaps the most important ones and, according to Goodglass, the categories most studied by psychologists (Goodglass, 1980).

▢▢ QUESTION ▢▢

How might "acoustical coding" of items in Short-term Memory make it easier to store the items in Long-term Memory according to "clangs" and "reproductive information"?

• *Mnemonics*

If nothing else, the eight categories listed above may give you some notions about how to improve your memory. There are a variety of **mnemonics**, or "memory tricks," that psychologists have developed to help people re-

member things better. Some of these devices involve training you to *associate* whatever you want to recall with something already well established in your memory banks. Other mnemonics require you to use one or more of the eight categories in trying to memorize a specific item.

For example, if Mr. Bird looks like an owl, you can make an easy connection between his face and his name. Or you might pick a salient feature about his background and try to associate that with his name. Something like, "Mr. Bird flew into town three years ago," could do the trick.

If you have a list of terms you must memorize, you might write a poem that includes all the items in the proper order. Or you could take the initial letter of each term and memorize the letters themselves. For instance, music students often use the sentence, "Every good boy deserves favor" as a mnemonic to help them remember the lines on the music scale (EGBDF).

● *Other Ways to Improve Memory*

Psychologist Laird Cermak lists a great many helpful hints on how to make learning easier in his book *Improving Your Memory*. Aside from using mnemonics, Cermak urges you to (1) pay very close attention to the most important features of what you want to memorize, and (2) organize your thoughts in a logical way.

It may also help if you *space out* your attempts to memorize whatever you have to learn. In a recent study, psychologists Harry Bahrick and Elizabeth Phelps tested students on their ability to learn and remember English-Spanish word pairs. Some of the students were

given 6 to 9 training sessions all on a single day. Other subjects received 3 to 4 training sessions on successive days. The final group received 1 to 2 training sessions 30 days apart. The subjects were then tested for retention *eight years later*. Bahrick and Phelps report that the students who were given 6 to 9 training sessions in a single day could not recall *any* of the word pairs eight years later. Those subjects given 3 to 4 training sessions on successive days recalled about 6 percent of the pairs. However, the students given 1 to 2 training sessions 30 days apart recalled almost 25 percent of the pairs (Bahrick & Phelps, 1987).

Generally speaking, *distributed practice* is always a more efficient way of learning than is *massed practice*.

Last but not least, more than a century ago, Hermann Ebbinghaus showed that learning "meaningful material" requires only about one-tenth the effort that is required for learning nonsense materials (or just memorizing unrelated items on a list). Thus, the more *meaningful* you can make the material, the easier you will learn it and the longer you will remember it (Ebbinghaus, 1885/1964).

□□ **QUESTION** □□

Given the effectiveness of "distributed practice," why do so many students wait until the night before a test and then "cram" for the exam?

FORGETTING

In an earlier chapter, we quoted Sigmund Freud's comment that you learn about the normal by studying the abnormal. In the field of memory research, that certainly is the case. For we have discovered a great deal about *memory* by studying *forgetting*. And we have learned an amazing amount about *item storage* in normal people by investigating the difficulties that brain-damaged people have in *retrieving* even the simplest of items from long-term storage.

Let's look at the most common types of "disremembering" in some detail.

Neural Decay

The SIS system in your receptors provides you with sharply etched neural impressions of the world around you. But this pattern of neural firing is quickly destroyed in one of two ways—either the receptor neurons adapt to the input (and hence the neural pattern *decays*), or the next visual input "erases" the first input.

Once an input reaches your brain, it may be put into Short-term Memory. But your Short-term Memory is very limited because, as new items are plugged into "temporary hold," older items decay and you thus forget them.

Neural decay is perhaps the simplest type of forgetting (Lindsay & Norman, 1977).

FIG. 11.5 Murdock's subjects tended to remember the first and last items in a 20-item list better than items in the middle, a result called the "serial position effect."

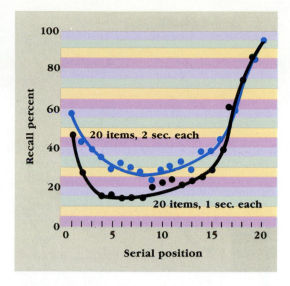

Interference

New memories interfere with old ones, and vice versa. There are two main types of "memory interference." The first has to do with *item storage and recall*. The second has to do with the fact that new inputs can actually distort or *transform* old memories.

- ### Serial Position Effect

The *serial position effect* is an example of how learning one thing can interfere with storing and recalling other items. Let's again imagine that you are a subject in a memory study. The experimenter shows you a list of 20 words, one at a time, and asks that you remember as many of the words as you can. Since you see each word for only one second, you surely won't recall all 20 later on. But which ones will you remember?

When B.B. Murdock ran a similar study in 1962, he got the results shown in Fig. 11.5. As you can see, Murdock's subjects tended to recall items at the beginning and end of the list much better than words in the middle. Apparently items at either end of the list *interfere* with your ability to recall the words in the middle. In short, the *position* of the item in the series affects how readily you can remember it later on.

Murdock also found that the *longer* you see the item in the first place, the better you tend to remember it. This unsurprising result might lead you to assume an item is "safe from interference" if you inspect it long enough and then file it away in long-term storage. However, that turns out not to be the case (Murdock, 1962).

Elizabeth Loftus

- ### Recency Versus Primacy

In a recent study, Anthony Wright and his colleagues at the University of Texas Health Science Center have found that, like humans, pigeons and monkeys also show the "serial position effect" when required to remember lists of items. However, this effect occurs *only* under certain circumstances.

Wright and his associates required their subjects (both humans and animals) to learn a list of four items presented one at a time. Each item appeared for one second, and there was a two-second interval between the items. The subjects were then tested to see which items they remembered best.

If the experimenters tested the subjects *immediately after* the final item had appeared, both animals and humans remembered the *final* item on the list the best, and the first item on the list the worst (see Fig. 11.6). Psychologists call this the *recency effect,* or the tendency to recall best (or be most strongly influenced by) what's just happened to you.

If the experimenters tested the subjects *after a long delay,* they tended to recall the *first* item best, and did worst on the *final* item in the list. Psychologists call this the *primacy effect,* or the tendency to be most strongly influenced by the first item in a list (or the first event in a series of related events).

Only if the experimenters tested the subjects with a *moderate delay* after the final item had appeared did the subjects show the "serial position effect." And while the monkeys remembered better than did the pigeons (and the humans remembered better than did the monkeys), the *shape of the memory curves* was essentially the same for all the subjects.

Wright and his colleagues believe that the "serial position effect" is actually caused by the *interaction* between two memory processes—the "primacy effect" and the "recency effect" (Wright *et al.,* 1985).

□ □ **QUESTION** □ □

Suppose you were asked to learn a list of 20 items (see Fig. 11.7). However, one of the middle items in the list was printed in red, another was in blue, yet another in green. How would the "unique properties" of the items printed in color affect your memory? And what does this fact tell you about why certain items are stored in LTM while others aren't?

- ### Memory Distortions

In an elegant series of studies, Elizabeth Loftus has shown that what you learn today may actually *distort* your memory of what happened to you yesterday (Loftus, 1984). In one experiment, Loftus showed films of auto accidents to people, and then asked them questions about what they had seen. If she asked her subjects, "About how fast were the cars going when they *smashed* into each other?" her subjects gave much higher estimates of speed than did subjects who were asked, "About how fast were the cars going when they *collided?*" Apparently, the use of the word "smashed" somehow *changed* the subjects' memories of what they had seen!

A week later, Loftus asked these same subjects if they had seen any broken glass in the films. In fact, there was *no* broken glass. But more of the subjects exposed to the word *smashed* "remembered" seeing broken glass than did those exposed to the word *collided.* Again, the question Loftus used to pull the memory out of long-term storage seemingly *changed the memory itself.*

In another experiment, Loftus showed half her subjects a series of photos involving a car. One photo showed the automobile approaching a yield sign. The other half of the subjects were exposed to the same series of photos, except that the car was shown approaching a stop sign (see Fig. 11.8). Loftus then asked the "yield sign" subjects what the car had done *at the stop sign.* Almost half of these subjects subsequently insisted that the sign had said "stop" instead of "yield" (Loftus, 1979).

According to Loftus, "No matter how well meaning or how well trained observers are, there are ways to make people see, hear, and even smell things that never were. Every time we recall an event we must reconstruct the memory, and so each time it is changed" (cited in Rodgers, 1982).

In brief, items filed in your memory banks can be radically altered by new inputs—even though you are unaware that the change has taken place.

☐☐ **QUESTION** ☐☐
How might the way that a lawyer *phrases a question* affect the answer a witness might give when testifying in court?

Rejection and Repression
In Chapter 5, we stated that the lower centers in your brain *reject* inputs (and parts of inputs) that are meaningless or unimportant to you. Although you are usually unaware of it, this "screening out" of trivial items goes on constantly and is a very necessary part of the forgetting process. (Can you recall *exactly* what the skin on your back felt like 20 minutes ago? How often do you need to recall such items?)

If a given stimulus input is threatening or disturbing, the emotional centers in your brain may *repress* the stimulus and hence make it very difficult for you to remember later on. (The "perceptual defense" studies discussed in the next chapter are an example of this sort of repression.)

☐☐ **QUESTION** ☐☐
In Chapter 3, when we discussed the "split-brain experiments," we noted that

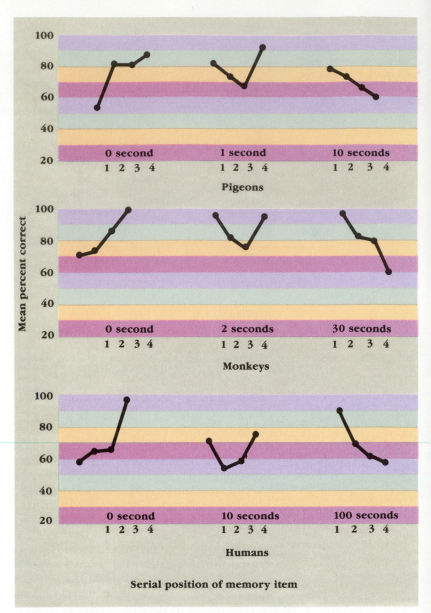

FIG. 11.6 The serial position effect. Data for pigeons, monkeys, and human subjects. In all cases, the subjects were first given a list of four items to remember, and then were tested for retention of the four items at various delay periods following the appearance of the last of the four items. When there was a 0 seconds delay, the subjects showed a recency effect. When there was an intermediate delay period, the subjects showed a "classic" serial position effect. But when there was a lengthy delay period, the subjects showed a primacy effect. These data suggest the serial position effect is caused by an interaction between the recency and primacy effects.

the left hemisphere often *denies* awareness of inputs directed to the right hemisphere, but is influenced by these inputs nonetheless. How do these data support the notion that your mind occasionally *represses* certain types of stimuli?

Cataloging, Filing, and Retrieval Errors
You "hold" items in Short-term Memory temporarily while you decide how important they are. *Meaningful* items are usually transferred

Horse	Horse
Table	Table
Wheel	**Wheel**
Water	Water
Tiger	**Tiger**
Whale	Whale
Chair	Chair
Train	**Train**
Field	Field
Shark	Shark

FIG. 11.7 The serial position effect predicts that, if you had to memorize the list of ten words at the left, you'd be more likely to remember those items at the beginning of the list (horse, table) and at the end of the list (field, shark) than items in the middle. However, if some of the middle items are printed in color (wheel, tiger, train), the serial position effect is counteracted by a "novelty effect," and you will remember the items printed in color more than those at the start and end of the list.

to Long-term Memory. This "transfer" usually involves cataloging the item in terms of the eight memory categories listed previously. Your brain also seems to make a "mental index card" for *each category* under which that experience will be filed. You use these index categories when you try to *retrieve* an item from your memory storage banks. Mostly, this system works well. However, these "mental index cards" occasionally get catalogued in the wrong way, mis-filed, or even totally lost (Goodglass, 1980).

Cataloging errors seem to occur most frequently when you have to learn too many things at once. For example, if you are introduced to a dozen unfamiliar people at a party, you may well make some mistakes as you try to attach the right names to the proper faces. If you met one new person a day for a dozen days, you would have a better chance of getting the "file cards" filled out correctly.

Your memory also *mis-files* things occasionally, and thus you will have trouble locating it in your memory banks. The more similar two items are, the more likely it is that one of them will be filed in the place supposedly reserved for the other.

According to a 1980 survey made by Elizabeth and Geoffrey Loftus, most people think Long-term Memory is much like a "video recorder"; thus you can *always* recover an item if you try hard enough. As the Loftuses note, though, the experimental data don't support this viewpoint. Indeed, a large number of scientific studies suggest that most of us *totally forget* much of what we've experienced in the past. And judging from the bulk of the laboratory studies on this subject, once an item is lost, it's probably gone forever (Loftus & Loftus, 1980).

MEMORY DISORDERS

There are many types of memory disorders. Among the most common of these are the *amnesias* and the *aphasias*. We will discuss each of these problems in detail momentarily. However, our coverage of the memory disorders will make more sense if we first look at rather a different type of "memory model" than the information processing approach we've been describing so far.

Anderson's ACT* Model

The "information processing model" of memory has many strengths. However, it does rather a poor job of explaining the memory disorders, such as *amnesia*. For that reason, a decade or so ago J.R. Anderson proposed what he now calls the **ACT***—or *Adaptive Control of Thought* model (Anderson, 1976).

FIG. 11.8 As in the Loftus study, here is the same vehicle approaching the corner where at one time there was a stop sign, at another time a yield sign.

"What" Versus "How to"

As we noted earlier, the information processing approach assumes there are three different memory systems—Sensory Information Storage, Short-term Memory, and Long-term Memory. However, Anderson assumes that there is but one "giant storehouse" for memories. This "unitary storehouse" has two major divisions. One division stores *factual information*, which Anderson calls **declarative knowledge**. The other division stores the *skills, rules, and strategies* that your mind uses to "make sense" out of the factual information in your memory. Anderson calls this type of memory **procedural knowledge**.

Declarative Versus Procedural Knowledge

If we look at the game of baseball, perhaps Anderson's views will become a bit more clear. You know what a baseball and a bat look like, and may even know that there are several types of gloves used in the game. That's "factual information," thus these items are a part of your "declarative knowledge" even if you've never touched a ball or bat in your life. Declarative knowledge, therefore, is your storehouse of information about "objects and items," the *whats* of daily existence. The term "declarative" is used to describe this type of memory because it consists of things you can *declare,* that is, describe in words.

However, the *muscular movements* you use in throwing a ball or hitting it with a bat are motor skills you had to learn. Skills, Anderson says, are a type of "procedural knowledge." And procedural knowledge is your storehouse of the "how-to's" of getting along in the world (Anderson, 1985).

Episodic and Semantic Knowledge

Anderson believes that there are two types of *declarative knowledge*: The first he calls **episodic knowledge**. The second he calls **semantic knowledge**.

Let's assume that when you were younger, you once hit a home run in the ninth inning and won a baseball game for your team. You'd probably remember this *episode* rather clearly (and perhaps with some pride). This unique event in your life is an example of what Anderson means by "episodic knowledge"—something you participated in or experienced first hand, at a particular time and place.

Your knowledge of hitting that home run is, however, independent of the storehouse of information you have about *baseball in general*. When did you learn a baseball game typically has nine innings in it, or what the phrase "home run" means? This *general information about the game* is, in Anderson's terms, *semantic knowledge*. Anderson believes that semantic knowledge is stored in memory *without* any

The "experiential memory" of having hit a home run is independent of factual memories about how the game is played.

reference to when or where the information was acquired.

It might be hard for you to describe in words exactly how you felt when you hit that home run, because "episodic knowledge" often includes remembrance of the emotions and feelings that occurred during the "episode." And, as we noted in Chapter 8, emotions are easier to experience than to describe verbally. General information—that is, "semantic knowledge"—is almost always "filed" in terms of words and phrases, however.

Anderson's ACT* model of memory may seem complex at first. However, there is a fair amount of evidence to support his views (Tulving, 1985). And Anderson's terms will probably become more meaningful to you when we look at *amnesia*.

□□ **QUESTION** □□

Why is it easier to describe a baseball bat (in words) than it is to describe how to hit a home run using a baseball bat? And what does your answer to that question tell you about the difference between "semantic knowledge" and "procedural knowledge"?

Amnesia

Memory is the process by which information is stored in your brain. *Amnesia* is the process by which this information is physically erased from your memory banks, blocked off from easy access, or prevented from being stored in the first place. Amnesia has both *biological* and *psychological* causes.

Declarative knowledge. Anderson's term for that part of memory which stores factual information, most of which can be readily described in words.

Procedural knowledge. Anderson's term for that part of memory which stores motor skills, strategies for manipulating facts, and knowledge of various rules for manipulating objects or events.

Episodic knowledge (epp-ih-SOD-ick). Anderson's term for memory of things you have done and episodes you have experienced. Perhaps, when you were younger, you won a spelling contest. Your memory of this specific event is a part of episodic memory.

Semantic knowledge (see-MAN-tick). Anderson's term for abstract knowledge, such as how to spell certain words. Abstract knowledge is said to be "independent of the circumstances in which it was learned."

Consolidation period. The period of time (20 to 30 minutes) it takes your brain to file an input or experience away in Long-term Memory. Any trauma that disrupts your nervous system during the consolidation process will probably prevent that input from being put in permanent storage.

Retrograde amnesia (RETT-tro-grade am-KNEE-see-ah). *Amnesia* comes from the Greek word meaning "forgetfulness." When you are hit on the head, you are likely to forget most of the things that had happened to you for 20 to 30 minutes prior to the blow—but you may remember things that happened immediately after the trauma. The amnesia is "graded" because you will very likely forget *everything* that happened immediately before the trauma, *most* of what happened 5 minutes before, and *some* of what happened 20 minutes before. The term *retro* means "after the fact."

Anterograde amnesia (AN-terr-oh-grade). Memory disorder usually caused by trauma or brain damage involving inability to transfer items from Short-term to Long-term Memory. You can recall things prior to the trauma quite well, but not what happened to you an hour ago.

Alzheimer's disease (ALTS-high-mer's). A disorder associated with old age, which usually involves an inability to file new items away in Long-term Memory. See Chapter 14.

There are two main types of amnesia caused by physical damage to the brain: *retrograde* and *anterograde* amnesia. These types of memory loss are far more common than is *psychological amnesia*.

● **Psychological Amnesia**

Psychological amnesia, caused by an emotional shock, is really a form of repression. Witnessing a terrible automobile accident can cause you to "block off" all your memories of that fateful day. The items are still in your long-term storage banks, however, and you could probably retrieve them if you tried hard enough to do so (or underwent psychotherapy).

True psychological amnesia is fairly rare, at least compared to memory loss caused by disease, accident, and old age. Indeed, some psychologists believe psychological amnesia occurs much more frequently on TV soap operas than it does in real life.

● **Retrograde Amnesia**

Memory storage does not occur instantaneously. Rather, it takes up to 30 minutes for your Long-term Memory to file an item away. Any physical or psychological *trauma* that occurs to you during this half-hour-long **consolidation period** can prevent the item from being recorded in your memory banks. This type of forgetting is called **retrograde amnesia**, because

a shock to your nervous system *now* can erase the memory of something that happened *several minutes earlier*. For example, people who survive a blow to the head in car accidents often can recall everything that happened immediately after the crash. However, they frequently can't remember anything that happened in the period *just prior* to the accident. Because these memories were still being "consolidated" at the time of the crash, they got "erased" by the blow to the head (Squire, 1986).

Memories already in long-term storage usually aren't affected by retrograde amnesia since they are already "consolidated."

□ □ **QUESTION** □ □

Why do the data on retrograde amnesia suggest that memory storage is basically a *physical* process?

● **Anterograde Amnesia**

Severe brain damage and the diseases associated with old age can cause a type of forgetting, called **anterograde amnesia**. If you suffered from anterograde amnesia, you could retrieve *old* items with ease, but you no longer would be able to file *certain types* of new items in long-term storage.

University of Toronto psychologist Daniel Schacter describes what it is like to play golf with a patient suffering from anterograde amnesia. This 58-year-old man had been a good golfer most of his life before suffering from **Alzheimer's disease**. Once the anterograde amnesia associated with Alzheimer's set in, however, his game become "horrendous" (Schacter, 1983).

There were some things the man could do perfectly. For example, he used golf jargon correctly, he teed up properly, he hit the ball well, and his selection of golf clubs was "virtually flawless." However, he couldn't keep score because a minute or two after playing a hole he forgot how many strokes he had taken. Unless he could walk straight from the tee to his ball, he usually lost track of where the ball had gone. When asked what brand of golf ball he used, he simply couldn't recall. However, as Schacter notes, when the man had to pick out "his ball" from several examples, he was always correct.

According to Schacter, most of the patient's problems can be explained in terms of anterograde amnesia—that is, an inability to file new items away in Long-term Memory (cited in Herbert, 1983).

□ □ **QUESTION** □ □

Did Schacter's patient seem to be forgetting "procedural" or "declarative" knowledge?

Forgetting "What" but Not "How to"

University of California psychiatrist Larry Squire has studied amnesia for many years. According to Squire, both retrograde and anterograde amnesia typically involve the loss of "declarative" rather than "procedural" knowledge.

In one study, Squire and Neal Cohen tested brain-damaged patients who suffered from anterograde amnesia. These patients typically couldn't remember at noon what they had eaten for breakfast, nor did they recall from one day to the next who Squire and Cohen were. When Squire and Cohen tried to train these patients to remember *specific words*, the patients did poorly. They could recall the words after brief intervals, but this knowledge was pretty well "wiped out" by the next day. However, when the experimenters tried to teach the patients how to "read words printed backwards," an odd thing occurred. For the patients showed *marked improvement* in the skill from one day to another. But they couldn't remember *specific words* from one day to another, nor could the patients recall anything about prior training sessions (Cohen & Squire, 1980). Put briefly, the patients could acquire new *skills*, but not new *facts*.

Squire believes the procedural ("how to") memory system is mediated by "deep" brain structures, and usually isn't affected by strokes or disease. However, the declarative ("what") memory system is mediated by cortical and other "higher" centers in the brain, and thus is more likely to be disrupted by accidents and illness. The same information may be stored in both systems, of course, although in slightly different form (Squire, 1986).

Aphasia

In a recent article, Harold Goodglass defines **aphasia** as impairment in the ability to use or remember language. In right-handed individuals, aphasia typically results from damage to the left hemisphere of the brain. The exact type of language impairment the person suffers from depends on what part of the left hemisphere is affected (Goodglass, 1980).

Goodglass notes that some aphasic patients can understand the spoken names of American cities and can locate them on a map, but may totally fail to understand names of common body parts. Other patients can understand nouns but not pronouns. And one brain-damaged patient—called "M.D." by Rita Sloan Berndt and her associates at the University of Maryland—had great difficulties naming fruits and vegetables. When M.D. was shown a picture of a pyramid (or just about any other object), he immediately responded with the name. But if he was shown a photograph of a carrot or a peach, M.D. was "dumbfounded," and simply couldn't produce the name. When provided with a *list* of names of fruits and vegetables, however, he could correctly match the names with the corresponding picture. "It is as if the name is the key to knowledge of fruits and vegetables; the patient cannot find the key for himself," said one psychologist who studied M.D. And according to Rita Berndt, "We only have data on one patient, but this clearly suggests that items in the mental 'encyclopedia' are organized along specific categories in the same brain area" (cited in Bower, 1985).

Aphasic patients are better at naming things they can *see* than things they *smell* or words they *hear*. They are also better at remembering objects they can touch and feel (ball, spoon) than objects they experience at a distance (cloud, moon). They can occasionally write words they cannot say, and they sometimes can speak words that they cannot write.

There are many types of aphasia. All of them, however, seem related to one or more of the "eight memory categories" we described earlier (Goodglass, 1980).

Three Stages of Item Retrieval

Based on his study of aphasic patients, Harold Goodglass assumes you probably go through three distinct stages when you are shown an item (such as a picture of a chair) and asked to retrieve the item's name from long-term storage:

1. First, you recognize the item and search through your memory banks for its "file card."
2. Second, you hunt for the *auditory representation* (or acoustical coding) of the item's name.
3. Third, you attempt to discover the set of *motor commands* that will permit you either to speak or write the name.

As evidence to support his views, Goodglass offers the following evidence:

1. Some aphasic patients cannot *recognize* a word at all. For example, if shown a picture of a chair, they will respond, "Something you sit on," or "I've got one in my living room." These patients apparently suffer from a breakdown in *stage one* of the retrieval process. That is, they simply cannot *find* the right "file card" and often do not recognize the word when you say it aloud for them.
2. Other aphasic patients will say "stool" or "sofa" for "chair." This fact suggests they can *get close to the right "file"* card, but must settle for the *class* of the item rather than for the item itself. This, too, is a breakdown in *stage one* of the retrieval process.
3. Some patients seem to *recognize* the word, but say "tssair" for "chair." This mistake sug-

gests they suffer from a breakdown in the *second stage* of item retrieval. They can retrieve the item itself, and they can get close to the *sound* of the word. Indeed, they can often repeat the word when told what it is. But they cannot generally find the correct "acoustical coding" on their own.

4. Still other aphasic patients recognize the stimulus word, can tell you what other words it sounds like, and indicate in a variety of ways they know the meaning of the word and most of its attributes. For example, they may say, "Flair . . . no, swair . . . fair." These individuals simply cannot write the word or say it aloud. Goodglass believes that these patients suffer from a breakdown in the *third stage* of retrieval. They can find the "file card" and its "acoustical coding," but they have lost access to the "motor commands" that would allow them to reproduce the word as language.

Judging from evidence Goodglass presents, these three different stages of item retrieval are *mediated by different parts of the temporal lobe*. Just how your brain manages to work through all three stages so rapidly when you're asked to name an item, no one really knows.

• "Tip-of-the-Tongue Aphasia"

Even people with normal memories sometimes show a momentary type of forgetting called "tip-of-the-tongue aphasia." For example, have you ever tried to retrieve a name from memory, and been quite confident that you knew the word you were looking for? Yet somehow you couldn't reproduce the item when first you tried? Chances are that you also knew the sound and the shape of the word, its meaning, and the letter it starts with. And if someone told you the name, you recognized it immediately as the word you'd been searching your memory banks for (Schacter & Worling, 1985).

"Tip-of-the-tongue aphasia" appears to be a good example of what Goodglass refers to as a "stage one retrieval error." That is, you know a lot about the item, but simply cannot find the right "file card" in your Long-term Memory. Since the item is properly filed, it seems likely that "tip-of-the-tongue aphasia" is due to some *interference* with the normal retrieval process (Goodglass, 1980).

□ □ QUESTION □ □
If you momentarily forget a word, why might thinking of words that start with the same letter help you retrieve the item?

• Memory "Priming"

The retrieval process in either brain-damaged or normal subjects is often speeded up if the subjects are given a "priming session" first. Suppose you give someone suffering from *anterograde amnesia* a list of words to learn which includes "defend," "carnal," and "burped." An hour or so later, you asked the person to *reproduce* the words on the list, but the subject can't do so. Indeed, the person is likely to insist that he or she can't recall being asked to learn the list! However, suppose you now give the subject a list of "word stems" to *complete*—such as "car—," "bur—," and "def—." The subject is much more likely to say "carnal," "burped," and "defend" than "carpet," "burned," and "define" (Schacter & Graf, 1986; Squire, 1986).

In a similar study, University of California psychologists Peter Graf, George Mandler, and Patricia Haden had college students go through a list of words as rapidly as they could. The students were told to ignore the meaning of the words, but were required to compare the *vowels* in each word with the vowels of words in a different list. Later, when the subjects were asked to *recall* the words on the comparison list, they were unable to do so. However, when given "word stems" to complete, the students were much more likely to use words from the list than chance would allow. The "priming effect" of having been exposed to the words obviously influenced the subjects' responses, even though they weren't conscious of the effect (Graf, Mandler, & Haden, 1982).

• Memory: A Summary

Despite the thousands of experiments that have been run since Hermann Ebbinghaus published his book on memory in 1885, we still don't know how you learn things, nor what factors influence how you recall items already tucked away in permanent storage. However, we can draw a number of tentative conclusions about memory and forgetting:

1. The more *meaningful* an item is, the easier it is to learn and the longer you will probably remember it.
2. The more you *practice* or *rehearse* an item, the more likely it is the item will be stored permanently.
3. The more *associations* you can make between a given item you're trying to memorize and items you've already mastered, the easier learning will be.
4. *Spaced learning* is much more efficient than is *massed practice*.
5. Long-term Memory tends to be *reconstructive* rather than exact.

6. The *manner* in which you reconstruct a past memory can be strongly influenced by present stimulus factors that you are typically unconscious of.

7. You *forget* much more than you ever remember.

8. You probably have *several different types* of Long-term Memory banks which "store" and "retrieve" items in somewhat different ways.

Now that we've looked briefly at the psychological side of learning and forgetting, perhaps it's time we discussed memory from a physiological point of view. Again, we don't know as much about the subject as we probably should. However, as you will see, many scientists suspect that changes in your brain's *synapses* are intimately involved in storing items in Long-term Memory (Deutsch, 1983).

□ □ **QUESTION** □ □
How could you use the eight conclusions about memory listed above to help improve your study habits?

THE SEARCH FOR THE ENGRAM

Logic suggests there must be a *physical change* of some kind in your brain associated with storing an item away in your permanent memory banks. We call that physical representation of a memory an **engram** (Deutsch, 1983).

We *assume* there must be a different engram for each tiny bit of information you have ever learned. Your brain, therefore, should be jampacked with billions of engrams. But we have no real proof for these assumptions, for no one has ever been able to put a finger on an engram or view one under a microscope. About all we can say is this—on the basis of the laboratory data gathered so far, different sorts of engrams appear to be stored in different parts of your brain (Thompson, 1986).

The "search for the engram," as it is sometimes called, has occupied the attention of thousands of scientists for the past century or so. When scientists first discovered the amazing amount of electrical activity that occurs in the brain (see Chapter 2), they speculated that the engram might be an electrical loop or circuit of some kind. As long as the electricity flowed in its proper pathway through the brain, the engram was maintained. Early computers were built on this memory model. The problem was, if you shut off the electricity even for an instant, the computer lost its memories and had to be completely "reprogrammed" when it was turned on again.

Years ago, Ralph Gerard and his colleagues tried to test this viewpoint using animal brains rather than computers. That is, Gerard and his colleagues tried to "turn off" all the electrical activity in an animal's brain to see if this act would erase the animal's memories. But how to accomplish this "turning off the juice"? As it happens, they found a way. When bears, hamsters, and other beasts go into the deep sleep associated with hibernation, their brain temperatures drop considerably and most electrical activity ceases. So Gerard and his group trained a hamster, then put it to sleep and cooled its brain down until they could no longer detect any electrical responses at all. Later they warmed the animal up again and checked to see what it would remember. The answer was, it could recall *almost everything*. The electrical current hypothesis had failed, and scientists had to look elsewhere for the engram (Gerard, 1953).

□ □ **QUESTION** □ □
Many types of digital clocks must be reset after a power failure. What kind of memory do these devices have?

Synaptic Switches

Computers store information in a variety of ways. One memory device used in computers is a simple *switch,* which can be left in either an open or closed position. When a message passes through the computer, the switches can route the information from one point to another—much the way the switches in a railroad yard can route a train from one track to another. If you ask a computer a simple question such as "what is 2 + 2?" the computer routes your question through a series of switches until the final destination "4" is reached. Switches are not very complicated mechanisms. But given enough of them, the computer can store almost any information, no matter how complicated.

Most scientists believe that the *synapses* in your brain function in much the same way the switches in a computer do. When someone asks you a question such as "What is your name?" the message must cross over a number of synaptic switching points before you can answer it. If you could rearrange the functioning of these synaptic connections—opening some neural switches and closing others—you could send the message to any part of your brain that held the right answer.

As John David Sinclair points out, however, there are important differences between the synapses in your brain and the switches in a computer. To begin with, synapses can be partly open and partly closed. Thus, memory storage in the brain is infinitely more complex than is memory storage in computers. Second, the "chips" in a computer do little more than store information. However, the 100 trillion synapses in your brain both *store* and *process* information. According to Sinclair, this fact means that your brain can *store* fewer data than can a large computer—but your brain can *process* complex sensory inputs much faster than can a computer because processing *occurs throughout the brain,* not just in a "central processing unit" (as is the case with computers) (Sinclair, 1983).

The Engram

We know how computers store memories. Unfortunately, we still have no good idea of what the engram is. Which is to say, we still don't know how data are filed away *physically* in your Long-term Memory.

Most neuroscientists believe that memory storage involves some functional change at the synapse. But there is not much agreement (or solid data) about how you go about shifting the switches in your brain. Recent research suggests that when you learn, one or two things must happen. Either your brain grows new nerve cells (which seems unlikely) or the neurons already present in your brain grow *new dendrites* (or parts of dendrites). These dendrites then *make new synapses* with the axons of other neurons during some stage of learning (or memory storage) (Greenough, Black, & Wallace, 1987; Rosenzweig, 1984).

The question then becomes, what *causes* dendritic growth at the synapse? No one knows for sure. However, many scientists believe some sort of *chemical change* has to occur at the synapse whenever you learn something.

THE BIOCHEMISTRY OF MEMORY

Perhaps the first person to speculate in public that chemicals might be involved in memory storage was Ward Halstead. In 1950, Halstead advanced the theory that **RNA** and protein molecules might be the *engrams* that scientists had sought for so many years (Katz & Halstead, 1950).

At about the same time, Swedish biologist Holger Hyden said much the same thing. However, Hyden believed that RNA, not protein, was the chief candidate. Hyden and his colleagues taught various tricks to rats, then looked at the chemical composition of the animals' brains. Hyden and his group theorized that the brain of a trained rat should be *chemically different* from the brain of an untrained rat, and their research tended to support this belief. For they found noticeable changes in the amounts of RNA in the brains of trained

animals (as compared with the brains of untrained rats) (Hyden & Egyhazi, 1962).

Subsequent experiments in laboratories both here and abroad have generally confirmed the view that an organism's brain chemistry is *subtly altered* by whatever experiences the organism has. More important, it now appears that different types of psychological experiences can give rise to quite different sorts of chemical changes.

Whenever an *action potential* sweeps down the axon of a neuron, the cell responds by suddenly increasing its production of several chemical molecules, including RNA. The more vigorously a neuron fires, the more RNA it produces. And the more RNA a nerve cell produces, the more protein it typically manufactures as well. In short, nerve cells are not only generators of electrical activity, they are very efficient chemical factories too (McConnell, 1968).

Chemical "Erasers"

You are not consciously aware of all the chemical changes taking place in your brain as they occur, of course. But if the changes didn't come about, you probably wouldn't be "aware" of anything at all! For example, what do you think might happen if, while you were studying for an exam, someone injected into your brain a chemical that *destroyed* RNA? How might that injection affect your ability to learn?

This question was first asked by E. Roy John. In the mid-1950's, John taught a cat a rather difficult task involving visual perception. Once the cat had learned the task, John injected **ribonuclease** into the animal's visual cortex. After the ribonuclease injection, the cat performed as if it had never been trained at all. Later, John and William Corning demonstrated the same sort of memory loss in simpler animals (Corning & John, 1961).

Memory Loss in Old People

One of the symptoms associated with senility is the type of *anterograde amnesia* we discussed earlier. That is to say, most senile patients are much better at recalling events that happened years ago than they are at learning new things. Psychiatrist D. Ewen Cameron spent many years trying to help older patients in several hospitals in Canada and the US. His studies were, for a time, aimed at discovering whether or not the *body chemistry* of his patients was measurably different from that of other individuals who were just as old, but who were not senile.

In one of his experiments, Cameron and his colleagues found that senile patients had more *ribonuclease* in their bloodstreams than did non-senile oldsters. Cameron guessed this enzyme might be destroying brain RNA as fast as the senile person's neurons could manufac-

Some older persons suffer memory deficits, but others retain good memories throughout their lives.

ture it. And if RNA were involved in helping the brain store away long-term memories, then too much ribonuclease would *wipe out the engrams* before they could become permanent. If so, Cameron thought he might be able to help his patients by *lowering* the amount of ribonuclease in their bodies.

Cameron tried two different types of chemical therapy. First, he injected his patients with large amounts of yeast RNA, hoping the ribonuclease would attack this foreign RNA rather than the RNA produced by the patient's brains. While this approach seemed to help *some* senile patients recover *part* of their memory functions, the yeast RNA was often impure and caused many patients to come down with fevers. Hoping to avoid the fevers, Cameron gave his subjects a drug that was supposed to increase the *production of brain RNA*. Again, he was fairly successful—but only with people who had not slipped too far into senility. And once the patient was taken off the drug, the person's memory often began to deteriorate again (Cameron, 1967).

Cameron died of a heart attack before he could complete his work. A group of scientists in Italy repeated his research and reported at least partial success, but no one in America seems to have picked up where Cameron left off. However, in 1982, Michael Warren reported that "elderly" mice who were good at problem solving had more RNA in their brains than did equally old mice who had difficulties with the same tasks (Warren, 1982). And in a series of experiments, Berkeley psychologist Mark Rosenzweig and his colleagues found that keeping the mice in "exciting environments" increased their brain RNA levels, while confining the mice to "sensory isolation chambers" decreased the amount of RNA in their brains (Rosenzweig, 1984). Both Warren and Rosenzweig suggest that older humans who maintain an active life in stimulating circum-

stances need not fear a decline in their mental abilities.

Drugs and Memory

As we noted earlier, your long-term memories take time to form or *consolidate*. Anything that disrupts normal brain function during this consolidation period will interfere with your ability to remember. A number of chemicals, including some antibiotics, have been shown to disrupt memory consolidation in animals, if the drugs are given either before or immediately after training trials (Deutsch, 1983).

The other side of the memory coin is perhaps a bit more intriguing, however. For it is also true that anything that *facilitates* or speeds up your brain activity during the consolidation period will make it easier for you to form engrams.

We usually think of strychnine as a poison. In fact, it is a neural excitant. In large doses, it causes convulsions and eventual death. In very small doses, strychnine increases neural firing rates, much as does the caffeine found in coffee or cola drinks.

If you inject a rat with a tiny amount of strychnine just *before* you train it on a simple task, the rat typically will learn the problem faster. The explanation usually offered for this effect is that strychnine makes the animal more active and alert to its environment; hence it learns faster. However, you can cause a similar "memory facilitation" by giving the strychnine a few minutes *after* the animal has been trained. Now, when you retest the rat on the same problem a day or so later, the animal injected with strychnine will remember the task much better than does a rat injected with salt water.

How can a *post-training* injection speed up *learning?* It can't, for the rat given the strychnine takes just as long to *learn* the task as does the animal injected with salt water. What the

The fresh-water planarian has a true brain, a simple nervous system, a food tube in the middle of its body instead of a mouth, and can regenerate any missing part of its body.

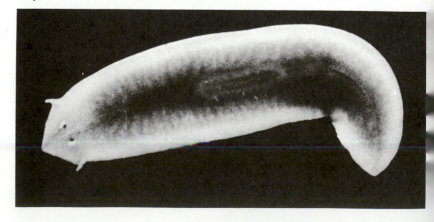

A water-filled training trough for planarians.

drug apparently does is to make the animal's brain more active during the *consolidation period* following training. And the more active the animal's brain is *following the experience,* the more of the experience it remembers later on. However, the strychnine must be given within 30 minutes or so after the training, or the "facilitation effect" does not take place. A rat injected two hours after training remembers no better than does an uninjected animal (McGaugh, 1973).

☐☐ **QUESTION** ☐☐
What do the strychnine studies suggest about the *length* of the "memory consolidation period"?

Memory Transfer

The most controversial evidence that the engram may be a chemical molecule comes from the so-called "memory transfer" experiments. Since I was personally involved in many of these studies, I hope you will forgive me for writing about them in the first person.

In 1953, when Robert Thompson and I were graduate students at the University of Texas, we attempted to train common flatworms, using Pavlovian conditioning techniques. We used light as the CS and shock as the UCS, and were able to show that the animals could make the same sorts of conditioned associations as did Pavlov's dogs (Thompson & McConnell, 1955).

The simple *planarian* flatworm we used in our studies reproduces both sexually and asexually. That is, a flatworm may mate with another planarian and subsequently lay eggs. Or its body may split in half, following which both head and tail sections will *regenerate* into complete worms.

The flatworm is the simplest animal to possess a true brain and a synaptic-type nervous

Robert Thompson

system. It was this fact that got Thompson and me interested in working with these animals. In 1953, the synaptic theory of memory storage was just becoming popular. We reasoned that if synapses were important for learning, the flatworm should be capable of learning. Since our conditioning data convinced us this was the case, Thompson and I published our findings in 1955.

• *Regenerated Memories*

When I came to the University of Michigan in 1956, my students and I continued where Thompson and I had left off. Daniel Kimble and Allan Jacobson helped with the first study, which involved training worms and then cutting them in half. We retested both heads and tails a month later, after they had completely regenerated all their missing parts. To our surprise, *both halves* of the worm remembered. We concluded there was not one engram, but several—scattered throughout the animal's body (McConnell, Jacobson & Kimble, 1959).

Shortly thereafter, E. Roy John and William Corning discovered they could "erase" a freshly cut tail's memories by exposing it to ribonuclease while it regenerated. Subsequent experiments in Russia and in Turkey suggested that a strong solution of ribonuclease could erase memories even in uncut planarians (Cherkashin & Sheimann, 1967).

• *Memory Transfer by Cannibalism and Injection*

All of these experiments led me to believe that memory formation somehow involved the creation of new molecules, and that RNA played some part in the process. But how to prove it?

About 1960, it occurred to me that if two worms learned the same task, the chemical changes that took place inside their bodies might also be identical. If this were so, it might not matter how the chemicals got inside the worms. Provided the right molecules were present, the worm should "remember" whatever its chemical engrams told it to remember. Our attempts to test this odd notion took us not to the heart of the matter, but to the worm's digestive system.

In 1960 Reeva Jacobson, Barbara Humphries, and I classically conditioned a bunch of "victim" planarians, then chopped them in bits and fed the "trained" pieces to untrained cannibalistic flatworms (our experimental group). We fed untrained victims to another group of cannibals (our control group). After we had given both groups of cannibals a couple of days to "consolidate" their meals, we trained both groups. To our delight, the planarians that had eaten educated victims learned much faster than did the worms that had consumed their untrained brethren. We seemed to have "transferred an engram" from

RNA from a conditioned donor being injected into a recipient planarian.

Jessie Shelby

Jessie Shelby and I apparently answered that question for planarians some time ago. We first trained donor worms to go either to the light or the dark arm of a simple, water-filled T-maze. We then fed the donors to untrained cannibals. As we had expected, we got a highly specific "transfer effect." That is, the cannibals learned fastest when trained to go to the same-colored arm as had the donors they ate. However, the most interesting results came from a group of cannibals fed "conflicting instructions." These planarians ingested a "worm stew" made up of some donors trained to go to the light-colored arm and of some donors trained to go to the dark arm of the maze. The "conflicting engrams" these cannibals digested made learning more difficult than if they had ingested nothing at all (McConnell & Shelby, 1970).

Several other laboratories soon showed much the same sort of stimulus-specific transfer using rats and goldfish.

- ### Are Memory-Transfer Studies Reliable?

An equally important question has to do with the *reliability* of the transfer effect. In 1970 James Dyal attempted to question everyone who had published articles on the transfer effect using rats and other higher animals. Dyal found that a number of well-known scientists had been *unable* to repeat the memory-transfer experiments successfully. However, *positive results* were reported by more than 100 scientists in a dozen different countries (cited in Corning, Dyal, & Willows, 1973).

Still and all, many scientists remain highly skeptical of this research, perhaps with good reason. For despite the apparent validity and reliability of our studies, we never were able to prove that each memory you form is "coded" by an RNA molecule. Nor could we ever figure out a humane way of testing the transfer effect with humans.

- ### Unraveling the "Memory Code"

But suppose your nerve cells *do* manufacture a unique new set of molecules for each of your memories. What a different world we could create if we could ever unravel this "memory code"! If we can ever devise *safe* drugs that would speed up learning, we might make college a more effective and less boring experience. And should we find ways to synthesize memories in test tubes, then students who "dropped chemicals" might be getting a higher education rather than merely "getting high."

one animal to another (McConnell, Jacobson, & Humphries, 1961).

A year or so later, my colleagues and I extracted RNA from trained worms and injected it into untrained animals. These animals showed a "transfer effect," but worms injected with RNA from untrained planarians did not (Zelman *et al.*, 1963).

In 1964 scientists working in the US, Denmark, and Czechoslovakia reported similar success using rats rather than worms. And by 1984 several hundred successful memory-transfer experiments had been reported in the scientific literature. However, we are still far from proving conclusively that memories are coded in RNA, or that engrams can be transferred from one animal to another.

- ### Are Memory-Transfer Studies Valid?

To begin with, there is the nagging question of *validity*. That is, when you inject an animal with chemicals taken from a trained donor, are you really transferring *specific memories* or are you merely giving the animal molecules that excite its brain activity as do caffeine and strychnine (Luttges *et al.*, 1966)?

SUMMARY

1. The major problems that memory researchers study include **how many memory systems** there are, **what** you store, **why** you store some things but not others, **retrieval** processes, what **forgetting** is, and what the **physical basis** of memory storage is.

2. According to the **information processing approach**, when sensory inputs arrive at

your receptor organs, they are held for up to half a second in **Sensory Information Storage**—an exact copy of the stimulus itself. Visual SIS is sometimes called **iconic** memory, while auditory SIS is sometimes called **echoic** memory.

3. **Short-term Memory** usually lasts for up to 30 seconds. You can increase the time an item is in STM by using **rehearsal**.

4. **Language inputs** are often translated into sounds while in STM, a process called **acoustical coding**.

5. Usually you can store no more than **six or seven items** in STM.

6. Important inputs move from Short-term Memory into **Long-term Memory**, which is the permanent "memory bank" of your brain.

7. Your Long-term Memories seem to be filed by **categories**, so that you can **retrieve** items readily.

8. Your Long-term Memory also stores information on how to **reproduce** items, that is, how to say, write, or draw them.

9. **Smell** is an exception to most rules of memory, for *specific odors* seem to trigger the *exact recall* of past experiences.

10. Once you understand how your memory files items, you can use **mnemomics**, or "memory tricks," to help you remember things.

11. There are many types of **forgetting**:
    a. An input to Sensory Information Storage either **decays** rapidly, or is "wiped out" by the next input.
    b. Items in your Short-term Memory **interfere** with each other, thus are continually forgotten. You tend to remember items at the start of a list (**primacy effect**) and at the end of a list (**recency effect**) better than items in the middle (**serial position effect**).
    c. Items in your Long-term Memory **interact** with each other, thus old items can be distorted or changed by new inputs.
    d. Some inputs are **rejected** by the lower centers of your brain because they are meaningless or unimportant, while other inputs are deliberately (if unconsciously) **repressed**.
    e. Your Long-term Memory also suffers

from **cataloging**, **filing**, and **retrieval** errors.

12. **Amnesia** is a type of memory loss caused by brain damage or emotional trauma. Amnesia typically involves forgetting "what" you have experienced (**declarative knowledge**), but not "how to" do things (**procedural knowledge**).

13. According to Anderson's **ACT*** model, there are two types of declarative knowledge: **episodic knowledge** (memory of specific events) and **semantic knowledge** (general information).

14. It takes about 30 minutes for your brain to **consolidate** an item in Long-term Memory. Interruption of the consolidation process leads to a type of forgetting called **retrograde amnesia**.

15. Brain damage can also cause **anterograde amnesia**, in which new items are no longer translated from Short-term to Long-term Memory.

16. **Aphasia** is an impairment in the ability to use or remember language.

17. According to Goodglass, retrieving the name of an item from long-term storage involves three steps:
    a. You must **recognize** the item and search your memory banks for the item's "file" or identity card.
    b. You hunt for the **auditory representation** of the item's name.
    c. You try to discover the set of **motor commands** that will permit you to say or write the name.

18. The physical representation of a memory is called an **engram**. No one knows what the engram really is, but remembering does seem correlated with rearranging the **synaptic switches** in your brain.

19. Recent studies of the biochemistry of memory suggest that molecular changes may occur in your neurons whenever you learn something. The molecules involved in memory formation may be **RNA** and/or **protein**.

20. A series of controversial studies suggests that memories can be **transferred** from one animal to another under some circumstances. However, there is some question as to whether these experiments are **valid** and **reliable**.

(Continued from page 265.)

"Look at those learning curves!" Mike Keller said, as he finished plotting the data of their planarian experiment on graph paper.

"How'd they come out?" Devin Eckhoff asked. He was too engrossed in the latest issue of *Penthouse* to look for himself.

Bill Plautz picked up the curves that Mike had drawn. "Amazing. The experimental animals initially responded to the light about 20 percent of the time. But after 150 trials, their response rate went up to 92 percent."

"What about the control groups?" Tom Laine asked, momentarily putting down his copy of *People*.

"They all started off with an initial response rate of 20 percent, just like the experimental worms," Mike replied. "But all three control groups showed a marked decrease in responding over the 150 trials."

"So, what next?" Devin asked.

Bill cleared his throat. "We write the experiment up and turn it in to Dr. Sauermann."

"And pray for a good grade," Tom said, going back to his magazine.

"Yeah, I know that," Devin continued. "But what do we do next with the worms? I mean, we've got the equipment, and the animals, and the custard cups . . ."

"Yeah," said Mike. "We ought to be able to think of *something* outrageous to confound the scientific world with next."

For a few moments, the four of them sat in silence, each lost in thought. Then suddenly Tom glanced up from his magazine. "Hey, guys, look at this!"

"What is it?" Bill asked.

"It's an ad for a home permanent, that's what," Tom replied.

"Just what you need," Devin said slyly.

Tom threw the magazine on the kitchen table. "You're still angry with me because I beat you at racquetball this morning. But look at the ad and tell me what ideas it gives you."

Devin picked up the magazine. "The ad shows two absolutely gorgeous young ladies. That gives me lots of ideas."

"They're identical twins," Mike said, looking over Devin's shoulder to inspect the ad. "One has an expensive, beauty-parlor permanent, and the other has a $1.79 home permanent."

"Yes, but what does the headline on the ad say?" Tom asked.

Bill replied, "It says, 'Which twin has the home permanent?' But what's that got to do with worms?"

"Well," said Tom. "I've been doing a little reading on planarians."

"You mean you actually *read* that book by Hyman that you got out of the library?" Mike asked in an amused tone of voice.

"Sure," Tom answered. "And Hyman says that if you cut a planarian in half, the head will grow a new tail, and the tail will regenerate a new head. And the regenerated halves are *identical twins,* just like the two gorgeous twins in the ad. Doesn't that give you an idea for a new experiment?"

"What do you have in mind?" Mike asked.

Tom grinned. "Well, suppose we conditioned a worm, then cut it in half and let both pieces regenerate into whole planarians. Which half would retain the original training?"

"Which twin has the memory, eh?" Bill said.

"Right," said Tom.

"That's an easy question," Devin responded. "The head would remember. After all, it keeps the original brain. The tail has to regrow an entire new nervous system when it regenerates."

"Yeah," said Mike. "But wouldn't it be amazing if the tail showed any retention at all of the conditioning, even though it had to grow a new head and brain?"

"That sure would upset those biology students," Devin said, a happy smile on his face. "I can just hear them now. 'If tails could remember, a zoologist would have done the study years ago.'"

"It's not mentioned in Hyman's book," Tom said. "I looked it up."

Bill shook his head. "It's really a nice idea, Tom. Very creative. But I don't think anybody would believe us if the tails remembered."

"Particularly not Dr. Sauermann," Mike added.

Tom thought the matter over for a moment. "I guess you guys are right. The scientific world just isn't ready for my brilliant insights yet."

Mike laughed. Bill snickered. Devin grinned, and picked up his copy of *Penthouse* again. But as he turned the pages, he asked, "Racquetball, anyone?"

"Sure," said Tom. "Go get your racquet. But if I cut you in half with my sizzling serve, I hope you don't regenerate into identical twins."

"Then you'd have twice as much trouble beating me," Devin replied.

Tom gathered up his equipment, then noticed that Devin was still reading his magazine. Tom crumpled a piece of paper into a ball and threw it at his roommate.

"Scrunch, scrunch," Devin said as he ducked. He put down the magazine and stood up. "I'll get my goggles too."

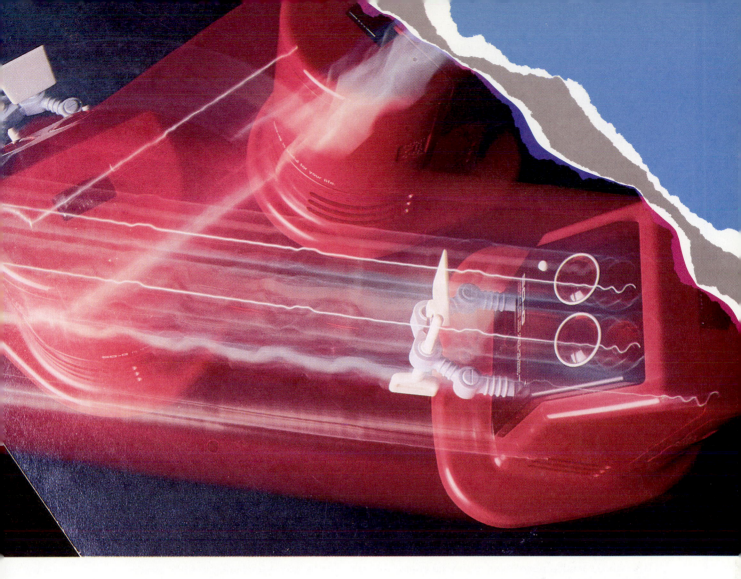

Cognition

"Cogito, Ergo Sum?"

· C · H · A · P · T · E · R ·

12

Philip Cassone laughed when they shut the door. This was going to be a cinch, no doubt about it. Imagine those crazy psychologists wanting to pay him $20 a day for just doing nothing! Plus room and board! He just might stay here for weeks, maybe for months. Let them go bankrupt, as far as he was concerned.

The bed Phil was lying on was narrow but comfortable. The long cardboard tubes into which his arms were stuck were annoying, but Phil was sure he could adjust to them.

The goggles covering his eyes let in some light. But he couldn't make out any details of the room he was in, except that the walls were painted black. He knew the room was small, though—maybe 6 feet wide by 10 feet long. Big enough to live in if you didn't move around very much, and the crazy psychologists were paying him for not moving.

All Phil could hear was the quiet, gentle, soothing whirr of an air-conditioning unit. Black as a tomb, that's what the room was. Phil yawned, stretched a little on the narrow bed, and relaxed. A lead-pipe cinch, that's what it was going to be. He drifted gently off into sleep.

Some time later, Phil awoke. He had a moment of panic when he couldn't remember just where he was. But then he smiled and relaxed.

"Inside the little black box," he said to himself. That's where he was. He must have slept for, oh, maybe 3 hours. Or was it more like 4 or 5? Phil couldn't tell exactly, and that bothered him a bit.

How long had he been in the room so far? Maybe 6 hours? How much had he earned? Maybe $5.00? Not bad for just sleeping.

A few minutes later, Phil decided that he needed to go to the bathroom, so he yelled out, "I want to go to the john." There was a microphone in his cubicle that carried his voice to the crazy psychologists in the next room. *If* they were still there, like they said they would be. They could talk to him too, over a loudspeaker hanging on the wall. But so far they hadn't said anything at all.

The door opened and someone came in and touched him on the shoulder. Phil hopped out of bed and almost fell flat on his face. Funny he should be so clumsy. Maybe he was still half asleep. He spoke several times to the person leading him, but got no answer. After he had urinated, he was led back to the little black room by his silent escort. Strange the man wouldn't talk to him . . . if it was a man.

Phil lay down on the bed again and started to contemplate the world. He thought about his school work; he thought about his family; he gave serious attention to several girls he had encountered in recent weeks. And then, when he ran out of things to think about, he started over.

It was all getting pretty boring. Maybe he'd only stay in the room for a few weeks after all, until he had earned enough money to make a down payment on that car he had seen in the showroom. What did that car look like anyway? He could barely remember . . .

"Phil, are you awake?"

The voice sounded remote and at first he couldn't be sure that he wasn't imagining it.

"Hello, Phil, are you awake?"

He told the crazy psychologist he was, but his own voice sounded odd and hollow to him.

"Okay, Phil, I want to give you some tests now. Are you ready?"

Phil said he was.

The psychologist's voice came out of the black haze again. "All right, let's start with the letter H. How many words can you think of that begin with the letter H? Don't use verbs and don't use proper names. Go ahead and start now."

H? What begins with H? Hell, for one thing. And Horse and House and Heart and Hurt and Help. And Hungry. Am I hungry? Maybe that was what was wrong. What will they give me for dinner? Maybe a hamburger. Oh, yes. Hamburger begins with H. And Horse. No, I said that. Horsemeat in the Hamburger . . .

What else? Celery? No, that doesn't begin with an H. Helpless? Honda. No, that's a proper name. Hello out there. Happy? No, that isn't a word, is it? More a state of mind, really. Head! Yes, Head would do.

Then Phil thought and thought, but nothing else popped into his head. Finally he asked, "Is that enough?"

"If that's all you can think of, that's fine, Phil."

He smiled and relaxed. That ought to show them.

My God, it's quiet, he said to himself a few moments later. The silence seemed to stab at his eardrums like an ice pick. How could silence be so loud, so overwhelmingly bright?

And the colors, the sparks of colors. Banners of different colors waving back and forth. The wallpaper was wiggling, writhing, pulsating, just the way it did that time he had foolishly taken that drug his friend Van had given him.

Oh, what in the world was that sound? A dark green clunking noise. Could it be the air conditioner? Sounded more like an elephant stomping around. Clunk, clunk, clunk. My God, it was a herd of elephants!

The elephants changed color. Now they were sort of black, with pink and blue and purple . . . elephants moving . . .

No, the elephants are standing still, aren't they? It's the picture that's moving, and the elephants are like cutouts in a moving picture. There they go, over the hill . . .

"Hey. You people listening in. Do you know there's a herd of elephants marching around in here?"

Why didn't the crazy psychologists answer?

And the quiet again. How long has it . . .

"Now, Phil, we have some recordings you can listen to if you wish. Would you like to hear them?"

Recordings? Why not? Maybe some good rock . . .

But no, it's a voice talking about ghosts. Who the hell cares about ghosts? Dullsville. But at least it's a voice, talking . . .

Yes, play it over one more time. This is getting interesting. Yes, play it again, Sam. . . . It sure sounds more sensible this time around. Yes, ghosts are for real. Why hadn't he realized that before? Yes, play it just one more time . . .

"Hey, you people. What time is it? Why don't you answer? Don't you know I can't stay in here too long? Why don't you say something? It's been at least 24 hours, hasn't it? I've earned my 20 bucks, now tell me what time it is . . ."

Floating . . . looking down. . . . Who was that strange person lying on that little bed down there with the cardboard tubes on his arms? Maybe he was dead and nobody knew it . . .

Clunk. . . . There's that dark green clunking sound again. They must be letting something else into the room. Last time it was elephants. Wonder what it is . . .

My God, it's a spaceship! It's only 6 inches long, but it's a real spaceship. How did they manage that? It's buzzing around the room like Darth Vader chasing Luke Skywalker . . .

"Hey, you crazy psychologists, what are you trying to pull? Get that spaceship out of here! Shooting at me, that's what it's doing. It's shooting laser beams at me!"

"Ouch! Oh, my God, I'm hit! Hey, you stupid people, stop that! If you don't stop that, I'll have to come out right away. You know that. What are you trying to do, make me quit? I can't take this much longer. Darth Vader is going to kill me with his laser beams . . ."

"Why won't you help me? If you don't do something right now, I'm coming out. Don't you understand, it's your fault!"

Philip Cassone angrily stripped the tubes from his arms and jumped off the bed. He jerked the door open and stumbled into the room next door where two startled psychologists sat working at a table containing recording equipment.

"You bastards ruined the experiment. You made me come out. Now aren't you sorry you let Darth Vader get at me?"

(Continued on page 316.) And then Phil started to cry.

COGNITION

The term *cognition* has many different definitions. In a recent book, Margaret Matlin states that "Cognition involves how we acquire, store, retrieve, and use knowledge." As such, she says, cognitive psychology is a "user's manual" that describes "what we know about how your mind works" (Matlin, 1983a).

• Two Major Approaches

There are two major methods for studying cognition—from the "bottom up," and from the "top down."

The "bottom-up" method is often referred to as the *information processing approach*, which we described briefly in Chapter 5. This point of view tends to focus on how sensory inputs are taken into the body, are translated into neural energy, are processed by the lower centers of the brain, and then gain consciousness when they reach the cortex. Overall, the information processing approach tends to emphasize such psychological functions as sensation, perception, attention, motivation, emo-

tion, and some aspects of learning and memory. Many of these functions operate at an *unconscious* level.

The "top-down" method of studying cognition is what we might call the "classical" approach to cognitive psychology. Here the focus is on such *conscious* activities as attention, concept formation, problem solving, daydreaming, creative thinking, and reasoning. Most of these intra-psychic processes involve the use of language in one form or another.

In the first part of this chapter, we will describe the "bottom-up," or *information processing approach*. As you will see, what goes on in the lower centers of your brain often has a strong effect on your mental activities. Then we will look at the classical, or "top-down," approach to the study of cognition. As you will also discover, your conscious mental activities can have a strong effect on what goes on in the lower centers of your brain. Finally, when we summarize what we know about cognitive psychology, we will argue that these two approaches are really little more than two sides to the same cognitive coin.

But let's begin with a brief survey of the history of cognitive psychology. For looking at how this field got its start, went into a brief decline, and then came back to the fore may well show us why these two major approaches have come to dominate the study of cognition.

The History of Cognitive Psychology

It is sometimes said that psychology has a short history but a long past. People have been interested in the workings of the mind as long as there have been people on earth. The ancient Greeks pondered over such matters as learning and perception, while the early Romans devised elaborate if fairly primitive "personality theories." And much of present-day learning theory stems from British philosophers who, in the 1700's and early 1800's, wondered how "ideas" got associated with each other. Thus, psychology does indeed have a long past. However, the *science* of psychology probably got its start in 1879, when Wilhelm Wundt founded the first psychological **laboratory** at the University of Leipzig, in Germany (Wertheimer, 1987).

At its birth more than a century ago, psychology was often defined as "the science of mind," and almost all early psychologists took the classical approach to defining cognition. For instance, according to Wundt, the subject matter of psychology was *immediate experience,* that is, "conscious awareness." And there were two methods by which psychologists could study consciousness, Wundt said: *experimentation* and *observation without experimentation.* Wundt believed that "experimentation" worked fine when you were interested in such "low-level" mental activities as attention and reaction times. But only observation, Wundt said, could deal with "higher mental processes" (Wertheimer, 1987).

According to University of Arizona psychologist John Kihlstrom, "Wundt . . . and others who founded the earliest psychological laboratories generally assumed that the mind was able to observe its own inner workings. For this reason, they relied on the method of **introspection**, by which trained observers attempted to analyze their percepts, memories, and thoughts, and reduce them to elementary sensations, images, and feelings" (Kihlstrom, 1987). And as you will learn later in this chapter, introspection is *still* one of the major investigative tools used by cognitive psychologists.

For the first 50 years after Wundt founded his laboratory, then, scientific psychology and cognitive psychology were almost one and the same thing. But this cozy state of affairs ended rather abruptly in the early 1900's—in the US, at least—when John B. Watson threw "introspection" and all other forms of what he called "mentalism" out the window.

Watson was "the father of behaviorism." As we noted in Chapter 9, he believed the proper focus of psychology should be the study of *observable* stimuli and responses. Watson believed humans were little more than machines, much like the primitive, mechanical typewriters available at that time. When you press a key, the machine reacts immediately by typing a letter. The typewriter doesn't "think things over" before responding—it reacts instantly and automatically. In similar fashion, Watson said, a stimulus *elicits* a "biomechanical response" in human beings without any thought or **volition**. Psychologists who talked about "mental activities" were being downright unscientific, as far as Watson was concerned, because such *subjective* experiences simply couldn't be measured *objectively* (McConnell, 1985).

From 1920 until 1970 or so, when learning theory dominated American psychology, the study of cognitive processes *as such* went into a temporary decline. But many psychologists remained interested in the topic during what Ulric Neisser has called "the dark days of behaviorism." And during the 1960's, the study of cognitive processes again became "respectable" (Wertheimer, 1987). This change occurred for several reasons:

First, during the late 1950's, humanistic psychologists such as Abraham Maslow began insisting that, rather than being behavioral "robots," people were capable of *voluntary decision making* (see Chapter 6).

Second, some of Skinner's followers developed *cognitive behavior modification,* a technique that employs behavioral methods to control thought processes (see Chapter 10).

Third, by 1970, computers had become fairly commonplace. Many scientists (and engineers) tried to design computer programs that would imitate the way the human brain "processed information." This search for what is now called **artificial intelligence** led to an increased interest in studying the sorts of human thought processes that computers were supposed to imitate. And "artificial intelligence" was a type of cognitive psychology quite acceptable to learning theorists because it emphasized *experimentation* and *physiological processes,* not the sort of "introspective observations" that Watson had rejected.

Humanism, cognitive behavior modification, and information processing—these were three of the major factors that **coalesced** into cognitive psychology. But it took the genius of Ulric Neisser to weave these factors into the proper pattern.

The "Birth" of Modern Cognitive Psychology

In a recent interview with Neisser, Daniel Goleman states that "Neisser is the father of the currently fashionable approach to the study of human behavior—cognitive psychology, the

Laboratory. The exact date for the beginning of psychological science is much debated. In fact, in 1875 both Wilhelm Wundt (VILL-helm VOONT) at Leipzig (rhymes with "RIPE-sig") and William James at Harvard received funds to purchase "demonstration equipment" for their classes in psychology. At that time, however, psychology courses were typically taught in the department of philosophy at most American and European universities.

Introspection (in-troh-SPECK-shun). To introspect is to "look inward" at your own flow of conscious experiences. This psychological technique is *subjective* since you are the only person who *can* be aware of what goes on inside the privacy of your own mind.

Volition (voh-LISH-shun). The act of doing something voluntarily, or of your own "free will."

Artificial intelligence. The attempt by psychologists, philosophers, and computer experts to describe human intelligence in sufficiently mechanical terms so they can build computers (or other "expert systems") that can reason and solve problems "in the human style."

Coalesced (koh-ah-LESSED). Means something has "fused," or "grown into a whole." When you add hot water to dried cocoa and stir the mixture, it "coalesces" into something new, namely, hot chocolate.

Attention. From the Latin word meaning "to stretch to." To attend class is to be physically present when the class is in session. To *attend* to the teacher is to "pay attention" to what the instructor is saying and doing. According to *Webster's New Collegiate Dictionary*, attention involves "a selective narrowing or focusing of consciousness and receptivity."

study of how people perceive, remember, and think" (Goleman, 1983). According to Goleman, Neisser's book *Cognitive Psychology* "both established and christened the field."

Put in fairly simple terms, Neisser believes that cognition should be studied *both* from a "bottom-up" and from a "top-down" point of view, for the two approaches actually complement each other (Neisser, 1967). If we now look at both viewpoints in some detail, perhaps we can understand why Neisser takes this position.

INFORMATION PROCESSING

According to the information processing approach, cognition is a complex set of operations:

1. Cognition begins with **attention**, the process by which you *detect* and *orient* toward sensory inputs.
2. Lower centers in your nervous system *screen out* certain types of inputs, but send others on to the cortex.
3. At this point, you *perceive* the input, or become aware of it (Perception).
4. Your nervous system *stores* the input for a brief period (Short-term Memory Storage).
5. You *think about* the input for a period of time (Reasoning, Problem Solving, Mental Imagery).
6. Eventually, you must *decide* what to do about the input (Decision Making).
7. You may decide to *ignore* the input (Forgetting).

8. Or, you may *store* the input in your Long-term Memory (Permanent Memory Storage).
9. You may also *respond* to the input. The "response-output sequence" involves such activities as issuing motor commands, generating predictions about consequences, and monitoring feedback (Response Output).
10. The *environment* then *responds* to your output, and the sequence begins all over again.

Now that we've briefly described the several elements of the information processing approach to cognition, let's inspect some of the details.

ATTENTION

Cognition begins with attention. According to William James, "Everyone knows what attention is. It is the taking possession by the mind, in clear and vivid form, of one out of what seem several simultaneously possible objects or trains of thought" (James, 1890).

To bring James's description up to date, we might say that your brain is rather like the control room of a television station. The director of a TV show usually sits in front of a bank of video monitors, each of which shows a different scene (see Fig. 12.1). The director must se-

FIG. 12.1 Your brain is like a TV control room, in that you have inputs coming in over many different sensory channels. When you choose to "pay attention" to one channel, your brain typically suppresses temporarily the inputs on all other channels.

lect—from instant to instant—which of the channels to send out on the air.

In similar fashion, inputs arrive at your brain over a *number of sensory channels*. But at any one moment in time, you typically "pay conscious attention" to the inputs coming in on only one channel. Psychologists use the term *selective attention* to describe this type of input processing.

• Selective Attention

Selective attention has many aspects to it, one of which is called *search*. Suppose you go to a party hoping to meet a particular friend. As you enter the door, you are greeted by a barrage of sensory inputs—sights, sounds, and smells. You might begin your "search" for your friend by blocking off the sounds and smells—that is, by paying conscious attention primarily to visual inputs. Now, suppose your friend is black. You might then look around the room for people with dark skin, while trying to ignore all inputs associated with people who have light-colored skins.

Put in information processing terms, a "search" involves selectively screening out some types of inputs, while letting other types through to consciousness. You *consciously* determine which sensory channel to pay attention to (vision or hearing). And you deliberately decide which types of inputs within a given sensory channel you're interested in (dark skin versus light skin), a "top-down" process. However, the "input screening" process itself is "bottom-up," for it occurs primarily in the lower centers of your brain.

The *ease* with which your brain blocks out some types of inputs, while admitting others, depends on many factors. For example, look at Fig. 12.2, and follow the instructions as you take a test devised many years ago by J.R. Stroop. In this case, your attempt to search for *actual* colors is interfered with by the strong learned tendency to search for (and report on) the *words* that stand for colors (Stroop, 1935).

□ □ **QUESTION** □ □

Suppose you went to a party hoping to find *two* friends. Which would be the more efficient search procedure—to look first for one friend, and then for the other, or to search for both friends simultaneously?

• Divided Attention

When you are paying attention to inputs coming in over one sensory channel, you seldom notice much (at a conscious level) about inputs that arrive via a different channel. But what would happen if you were required to keep track of two events that were occurring *simultaneously*? As you might guess, the data suggest you'd probably not do a very good job at all.

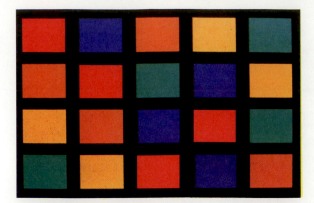

FIG. 12.2 These three illustrations reproduce the Stroop effect. The top illustration is a series of colored squares. Starting at the upper left corner, quickly call out the *names* of the colors in sequence. For the middle illustration, simply read the names of the colors as *printed*. For the bottom illustration, *quickly name the color in which the word is printed*. You will probably find that the meaning of the stimuli interferes with direct perception of their physical characteristics.

In a classic study, Ulric Neisser and R. Becklen asked subjects to watch a TV screen that showed two "sports" games, one superimposed on the other. The first game was a "hand game" that many children play in school, in which one player tries to slap the other's hands. The second contest involved three young men who were moving around a gym, bouncing a ball and occasionally throwing it to each other (see Fig. 12.3).

FIG. 12.3 A. Hand game alone. B. Ball game alone. C. Hand game and ball game combined.

Motor skills like the repetitive pedaling of an exercise bike are easily *overlearned* so that they become *reflexive,* leaving the cortex free for conscious activities like reading.

At first, Neisser and Becklen asked their subjects to attend to just one of the two superimposed games, and to press a button when one player slapped the other (hand game) or when one of the players either bounced the ball or threw it to someone else (ball game). The subjects did an excellent job of "screening out" one of the games and attending to the other. However, when Neisser and Becklen asked the subjects to attend to *both games simultaneously* and to press the button when something happened in *either game,* the subjects made eight times as many mistakes as they had when monitoring just one of the games (Neisser & Becklen, 1975).

The Neisser and Becklen study suggests there is some truth to the old saying that "You can't do two things at once." However, with practice, you can usually improve your performance on "divided attention" tasks. For example, University of Wisconsin psychologist Margaret Andreasen had students read magazines or fill out questionnaires. While the students were engaged in these *visual* tasks, Andreasen played audio tapes softly in the background. Later, Andreasen tested the students to see what they recalled about the material presented on the audio tapes. Students who were accustomed to listening to the radio while studying remembered significantly more about the material presented on the audio tapes than did students who didn't study with the radio on. Andreasen believes her results can be explained in terms of "prior practice" (Andreasen, 1985).

Theories of Attention

Psychologists have proposed several different theories to account for why you can attend to only a limited number of inputs at once. One of the best known is Donald Broadbent's *bottleneck* theory, which states that there is a *physical limit* on how many inputs your nervous system can process at any given point in time.

If you try to pour wine out of bottle that has a very narrow neck, the wine comes out very slowly because only so much liquid can exit the bottle at once. According to Broadbent, your nervous system suffers from the same sort of limitation. At any one point in time, Broadbent claims, more inputs arrive at the lower centers of your brain than your brain can handle. Therefore, only a small number of inputs get through. The rest of the inputs, Broadbent said, are "left behind and forgotten" (Broadbent, 1958).

The "bottleneck theory" explains the poor performance people show in "divided attention" tasks rather well. However, Broadbent's approach fails to explain why certain types of "unattended" inputs squeeze through the bottleneck, and why, with practice, you perform better on divided attention tasks.

Donald Norman and D.B. Bobrow prefer a *psychological* explanation. They believe that your attention is limited because you have only a *limited amount of mental effort* to expend on any one given task (Norman & Bobrow, 1975).

If you try to recite a long poem you've just memorized while simultaneously watching an exciting television program, chances are you'll make a lot of mistakes. Why? Because you must *stretch* your attentional *resources* to the limit in such situations. According to Norman and Bobrow, this is a *resource-limited* task. You can improve your performance in "resource-limited situations" in two ways: First, you can shut off the TV set and devote all of your attentional resources to reciting the poem. Second, you can practice doing both tasks at once, and thereby "improve the quality of your resources."

But now consider quite a different situation. Suppose you are listening to extremely loud rock music through earphones when someone 20 feet away from you starts whispering. No matter how hard you try, you simply cannot hear the whispering because *not enough auditory data* actually reach your brain for you to hear what the person is saying. According to Norman and Bobrow, this is a *data-limited* task because input limitations—not your own psychological resources—cause the attentional failure. And practice, they say, doesn't help much in "data-limited" situations (Norman & Bobrow, 1975).

Ulric Neisser disagrees both with Broadbent and with Norman and Bobrow. A decade ago, Neisser wrote that "There is no physiologically or mathematically established limit on how much information we can pick up at once" (Neisser, 1976). He admits that, in real-life situations, you may be fairly inefficient when you try to do several things at once. However, he points out that, with practice, you can almost always improve your performance.

Theoretically speaking, there *must* be limits of some kind to your attentional resources. However, to date, we have no real idea of what these limits are. What *all* the theories fail to explain adequately, however, is why inputs that you consciously "screen out" can still have an effect on your mental activities.

□□ **QUESTION** □□
Suppose, while you are searching *visually* for your friend, someone in the room calls out your name. Do you think this input would break through to consciousness even though you had "shut your ears off" for the moment? Why?

• *"Unattended" Inputs*

An attentional "search" involves blocking out a great many more inputs than you actually let through to consciousness. The question then becomes, what happens to the information that you "screen out." Can these "unattended inputs" have any influence at all on your thought processes? The answer to this question is a qualified "yes."

Many years ago, Charles Cherry put earphones on his subjects and had them listen to two quite different speeches simultaneously. One speech was presented to the left ear, the other to the right ear. The subjects were required to repeat *exactly* the words they heard in one ear, but were told to *ignore* anything they heard in the other ear. Cherry found that the subjects were so good at "screening out" the second speech that they often did not notice that the speaker had switched from speaking English to speaking German. However, the subjects *did* usually notice if the speaker changed from male to female, or vice versa (Cherry, 1953). And in a study similar to Cherry's, N. Moray found that subjects almost always heard their own name if it was inserted into the message they were supposed to be ignoring (Moray, 1959).

It would seem that the lower centers in your brain *analyze the meaning* of inputs coming in through the various sensory channels, even if you are not really attending to those inputs (Forster & Govier, 1978; Govier & Pitts, 1982). Unless these unattended inputs have some *significance* for you, however, they seldom break through to consciousness, and you seldom store them in Long-term Memory (Watanabe, 1980).

INPUT SCREENING

At any one moment in time, thousands of inputs compete for your conscious attention. How does your brain decide which inputs are trivial (and thus should be screened out), and which are so important they should be given priority?

Part of the answer to that question comes from research performed by H.W. Magoun and his colleagues at UCLA. In fact, Magoun (pronounced mah-GOON) was interested in the problem of *arousal*—that is, the biological and psychological mechanisms that wake us up and keep us functioning at a peak level of performance. By the time Magoun had finished his work, though, he and his associates not only had discovered what most of these mechanisms were, they had also identified many of the factors that influence the process of attention.

For reasons that will rapidly become obvious, most of this early research was performed with animals. However, as far as we know, Magoun's findings are as applicable to humans as they are to the lower species.

Input Control

Prior to Magoun's work, psychologists generally assumed that sensory information reached your brain in only one fashion (see Fig. 12.4). Inputs from your receptor cells would pass up your spinal cord to your thalamus. Cells in your thalamus would relay the message on to your cortex. Your brain then processed this message. And, if you needed to respond, the motor centers in your frontal lobes caused your muscles to move.

This approach to sensory functioning was correct as far as it went. But scientists holding this viewpoint assumed that information flowed in *one direction only*—from receptors up to the brain and then out from the brain to the muscles. As Magoun and his group showed, this view was far too narrow.

Magoun made three remarkable discoveries: First, incoming information actually reaches your cortex through *two* quite different pathways. Second, the sensory routes to your brain are "superhighways" where messages flow in *both* directions. And third, your

H.W. Magoun

Straight-line sensory system. The sensory input pathways that lead from the body's receptor neurons rather directly to the sensory regions of the cortex.

Reticular activating system (ree-TICK-you-lar). The information contained in sound waves goes from your ear to your temporal lobe by way of the auditory nerve (a straight-line sensory system). The *meaning* of the sound is carried by the auditory nerve. However, auditory inputs are also passed along to the reticular activating system in your brain stem. If the auditory stimulus seems important enough, your reticular system alerts or "activates" your cortex so you pay conscious attention to the message coming in on the auditory nerve.

RAS. Abbreviation for "reticular activating system." When Magoun and his associates made their first discoveries, they spoke of the "ascending reticular system," which they abbreviated ARS. The name was changed for perhaps two reasons: (1) Most important, it was later found that the reticular system "descends" as well as "ascends." That is, it sends neural commands down toward the receptor neurons, in addition to sending messages up to the cortex. (2) Amusingly enough, ARS is close to the British word "arse," meaning "ass." For a time, the reticular system was referred to as "Magoun's ARSe."

cortex exercises considerable *control* over what information gets through to it, and over what messages are blocked out in lower centers and thus never reach conscious awareness (Magoun, 1983). Thus, Magoun's research is as important to a "top-down" understanding of cognition as it is to a "bottom-up" explanation.

- ### Two Important Sensory Pathways
Suppose someone touches you on the arm. Receptor cells in your skin will respond by sending input messages up your spinal cord to your brain stem (the "stem" of the cerebral mushroom). Up to this point, only one input route is involved.

In your brain stem, however, the road to your cortex "splits" into two pathways. One road leads directly to the sensory input areas in your somatic cortex. This route is called the **straight-line sensory system**, which lets your brain know what part of your body has been stimulated and how strong the stimulation is (see Fig. 12.4).

A second road leads into the **reticular activating system**, which gets its name (like the retina) from the Latin word for net or network. The reticular system is a network of cells that begins at the top of your spinal cord and runs up through the brain stem to the lower parts of your cerebrum. The reticular system acts as an *alerting system* for the rest of your brain—rather like the bell on your telephone. When the reticular system is activated, it rings up your cortex to let it know an important message is coming through on the straight-line sensory "telephone."

The message from the receptors in your skin will usually reach your somatic sensory cortex *whether or not* your reticular system is aroused. However, unless the reticular system "rings the bell" and activates your cortex, your brain appears to *ignore* any information coming through on the straight-line system. And your brain acts in this fashion whether the message comes from your skin, your eyes, your ears, or from any other sensory receptors (Kimble, 1987).

- ### The Reticular Activating System (RAS)
Magoun's experiments demonstrating the function of the **RAS** (reticular *activating* system) were performed on animals rather than humans. So let us talk about cats first, and people second.

Suppose we implant a "stimulating electrode" in the RAS of a cat. Then we let the animal continue its daily life. But, occasionally, we deliver a small amount of electrical current to the cat's RAS. What happens?

If we stimulate the cat's RAS when it is awake and moving about, it shows the classic *orienting reflex*. That is, the animal suddenly becomes alert, as if its environment had suddenly *changed* dramatically and the cat real-

FIG. 12.4 Sensory input messages "split" at the top of the spinal cord. Unless activated by the reticular system, the cortex does not respond to the message coming through on the "straight-line" system. But activity in the cortex can inhibit or enhance activity in the reticular system as well.

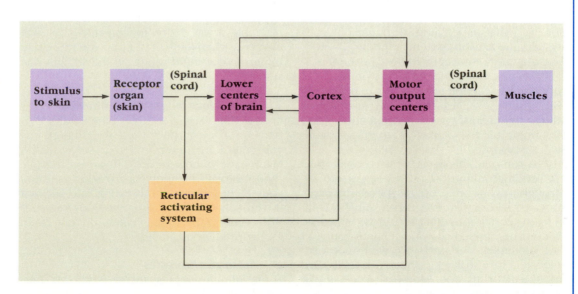

ized it ought to pay attention to what was going on around it.

If we wait until the cat goes to sleep, a short burst of electrical energy delivered to the RAS causes the cat to open its eyes and jump up, rather as if someone had stepped on its tail.

If we remove the cat's RAS surgically, the animal lapses into deep sleep from which it seldom if ever recovers. If we shook the cat violently, it would wake up momentarily and move around for a minute or two. But even if it were starving to death, the animal would soon lie down and drift off to sleep. (Humans who suffer damage to their reticular activating systems typically fall into a coma, or continuous deep sleep. They may be roused from the coma momentarily, but fall asleep again shortly thereafter. This condition is frequently fatal.)

Next, suppose we put a "recording electrode" in the somatic sensory cortex (parietal lobe) of the cat whose RAS we had removed. Then we pinch the animal's tail. The signal coming from the recording electrode would show that the neural message from the cat's tail does in fact reach the animal's parietal lobe. So the animal's straight-line sensory system is still functioning properly. But since there is nothing to *arouse* the animal's brain—to *alert* it that information is coming through that needs to be acted on—the cat remains asleep (Magoun, 1983).

- ### Stimulus Screening
Since your RAS sits atop your spinal cord—and extends up into your lower brain centers—the RAS is in a perfect position to act as a toll booth or *gate* through which incoming sensory information must pass if it is to have an effect on your cortex. If the incoming message is trivial or routine, the RAS will allow your cortex to ignore the stimulus by "screening it out" before the input reaches consciousness. But if the message seems important, the RAS *alerts* the higher centers of your brain and they pay attention to what is coming through on your straight-line sensory system.

What do we mean by *important* messages? Any dramatic change in your environment will reflexively trigger off the RAS. But experiments with animals suggest your RAS also *learns* which stimuli need your instant attention—and which stimuli are unlikely to require a conscious response.

As you read this book, your receptor cells are sending millions of messages per minute through to your brain on the straight-line sensory system. But your RAS is (presumably) telling your cortex it needn't bother with most of this sensory input. For instance, until you read this sentence, you probably were not consciously aware that your shoes (or socks) are full of feet, or that your clothes are pressing in on various parts of your skin. Your RAS has

learned these signals don't need your attention while you read.

But a sudden *change* in the pattern of incoming stimulation (as when a friend shouts "Help!") is recognized by the RAS as being important information, and it alerts your cortex that an *emergency message* is coming through. Your attention then shifts from vision (occipital lobe) to hearing (temporal lobe). The words your friend shouts at you are immediately processed by your cortex, and you respond appropriately to the emergency input.

The important point to remember is that the RAS tells the cortex that a message is important—but *not what the message actually is*. The "content" of the message is handled by the straight-line sensory system (Kimble, 1977).

□□ **QUESTION** □□
Suppose you are reading something interesting when a friend speaks to you. Why do you often have to ask your friend to repeat what was said, even though you know that your friend said something important?

- ### Cortical Influence on the RAS
The road between the cortex and the RAS is, as we suggested earlier, a two-way street. Early studies on the RAS showed it had a marked influence on activity in the cortex. But later experiments proved the cortex has ways of affecting the RAS as well.

Whenever you choose to focus your attention on something, your cortex tells your RAS not to bother it for a while. Your cortex exerts this control directly by *inhibiting* neural activity in the RAS. On the other hand, if you decide to cram for an exam by studying all night, your cortex is usually able to keep itself awake by continuing to *stimulate* the RAS—which feeds this stimulation back to the cortex itself (Kimble, 1987). And if you choose to *search* for one particular type of input, your RAS will automatically screen out those stimuli that don't resemble what you're looking for—but will alert you when the sort of input you're searching for is coming through on the straight-line system.

- ### Unconscious Influences on Attention
Most of the "classic" studies in the field of cognitive psychology have dealt with inputs that you consciously attend to and are aware of. Many experts now believe, however, that we cannot explain attention (or any other aspect of your mental life) without taking into account the influence of various *unconscious processes* that occur in the lower centers of your brain (Shevrin & Dickman, 1980).

- ### Automatic Processes
Some stimulus inputs are so weak that they simply never break through to consciousness.

Put another way, some stimuli are so weak that they cannot cross the **threshold** of conscious awareness. The Latin word for "threshold" is **limen**. Technically speaking, an input that is physically strong enough to cross the conscious threshold is referred to as a *supraliminal* stimulus. An input that is too weak to do so is often called a *subliminal* stimulus.

Just because a stimulus is supraliminal (above the conscious threshold) doesn't mean you will be aware of it at any given moment in time. For example, have you ever been driving a car along a highway while you were thinking about something important? And then you suddenly "woke up" to the fact that you had been paying no attention at all to the traffic? Yet somehow you managed to stay on the road, slow down at the right moments, and speed up when necessary. How is it that you didn't have an accident?

After you have been driving for a while, most of the motor skills necessary to keep the car on the road become *automatic*. That is, the responses your hands make on the steering wheel and your feet make on the pedals are so *overlearned* that they become *reflexive*.

Overlearned responses are processed by lower centers in the nervous system. As long as the responding goes smoothly, your RAS screens knowledge of these automatic reactions from your cortex. When the situation changes dramatically, however, your RAS arouses your cortex and orients your receptors toward the change. And because the stimulus controlling the overlearned response is *supraliminal*, you become conscious of it the instant your attention focuses on the stimulus.

Put another way, your RAS can sometimes act like an "automatic pilot." But it not only *executes* well-learned responses automatically. It also *screens* the inputs controlling these reactions from consciousness so your train of thought won't be interrupted.

However, you pay a price for "automating" such repetitive operations as walking or driving: You typically cannot recall, at least at a *conscious level*, what inputs you were responding to when your mind was on "automatic pilot" (Kihlstrom, 1987).

□ □ **QUESTION** □ □

What does the fact that you don't recall inputs while on "automatic pilot" tell you about how and why certain items get stored in Long-term Memory?

● *Information Overload and Underload*

Most theories of attention attempt to explain what happens when you are required to process too many inputs at once. This highly stressful situation is often called *information overload*. However, research begun more than 30 years ago suggests that you also experience stress when you don't have *enough* inputs to process, a situation called *information underload*. The importance of the *information underload* experiments to both the "bottom-up" and "top-down" approaches to cognition will become apparent once we discuss what happens to you when you experience an odd situation called *sensory isolation*.

INFORMATION UNDERLOAD: SENSORY ISOLATION

The information processing approach to cognition tends to emphasize *inputs*. If you doubt the importance of inputs, ask yourself this question: What would happen to you if something unexpectedly blocked off all incoming information both from your body and from the outside world? What if you couldn't hear, see, smell, taste, or feel anything at all? How would you know where your arms or legs were? How would you discover whether you were wearing clothes or not, or whether it was hot or cold where you were? How would you react if you couldn't determine whether any parts of your body were moving, or whether you were standing up or lying down? And if you tried to "pay attention" to what was happening, what would you *pay attention* to?

Consequences of Information Underload

Whenever you are deprived of the inputs you want or need in life, you respond in a variety of ways. To begin with, your motivational systems are *aroused*. If you get no food, you become hungry. If you are deprived of informational inputs, you hunger for intellectual stimulation.

The second important consequence of input underload has to do with the voluntary control you have over your thoughts and actions. Although you may not realize it, your mind *cannot operate normally if you are cut off from your environment*. You can't make hamburger if you don't have meat to grind, and you can't digest food until you've swallowed it. Nor can you *reason* about things—or even daydream—for very long if you don't have sensory inputs to process. Thus, under conditions of severe sensory deprivation (information or input underload), you could lose voluntary control of your thought processes. And if someone then gave you inputs aimed at changing your values and behaviors, you might well accept these inputs as uncritically as a starving person sometimes accepts rotten food.

"Brainwashing"

During the 1930's and 1940's, strange rumors began circulating in the scientific world that the Russian and Chinese governments were using some form of "sensory isolation" on prisoners in order to get the prisoners to "mend their ways." The term *brainwashing* apparently was first applied to these techniques by journalist Edward Hunter in his 1951 book *Brainwashing in Red China*. Hunter took the term from the Chinese words *hsi nao*, which literally mean "to wash the brain."

The reports on "brainwashing" in China and Russia had one immediate effect—Western governments became worried that the Communists had discovered some kind of psychological magic that would *force* people to change, whether they wanted to or not. The Canadians were perhaps the first to react. As early as 1951, the Canadian government commissioned a group of psychologists at Donald Hebb's laboratory at McGill University to investigate the effects of sensory isolation on such cognitive processes as *attitude change*. While the experiments were supervised by Hebb, the actual work and planning were done by four of Hebb's students and associates—W. Heron, W.H. Bexton, T.H. Scott, and B.K. Doane.

The McGill Experiments

Heron and his colleagues at McGill began by building a small **isolation chamber** (see Fig. 12.5). They then paid students $20 a day to lie on a small bed, their arms inside cardboard mailing tubes. The students' eyes were covered by **translucent** goggles, and their hearing was masked by a noisy air conditioner.

The students were fed and watered when necessary, but were asked to remain as motionless as possible during the entire experiment.

Prior to undergoing the sensory deprivation, the students were given a battery of tests and questionnaires designed to test their ability to perform certain cognitive tasks. The subjects received similar tests while in the isolation chamber, and after the deprivation experience had ended.

While the students were in the chamber, they were exposed to a series of propaganda messages read in a rather boring monotone. These messages concerned such supernatural events as mental telepathy, ghosts, and those noisy spirits called **poltergeists**.

In order to make sure any changes in the subjects' cognitive processes were due to the isolation and not merely to exposure to the propaganda, Heron and his colleagues hired a separate group of students to serve as a *control group*. These students simply sat in a quiet room and listened to the same propaganda speeches through earphones without undergoing any real sensory isolation (Bexton *et al.*, 1954; Heron, 1957).

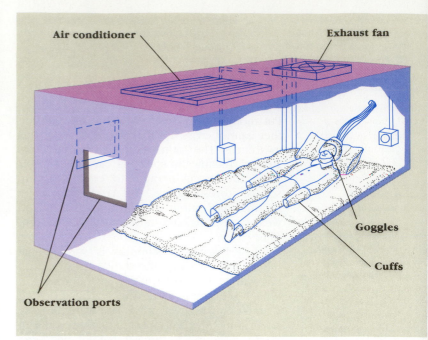

FIG. 12.5 A sensory deprivation chamber.

• Intellectual Impairment and "Blank Minds"

The results of the McGill experiments were somewhat surprising. First, there was the matter of "length of stay." Heron and his colleagues had expected most of the subjects to withstand the isolation for several days. In fact, almost half of the students quit during the first 48 hours.

Second, those subjects who did stay showed considerable cognitive impairment during the sensory deprivation itself and for some hours afterward. Simple problem-solving exercises often seemed beyond the students' mental capacities. Furthermore, they had difficulties with motor coordination, and they did not adapt well to new situations.

Not all of the isolated subjects lasted long enough to be exposed to the dull and repetitious propaganda messages. But those who did usually asked to hear the speeches again and again and again. These subjects were also much more profoundly affected by what they heard than were the students in the control group.

Of equal interest were the subjective reports the subjects gave of their experiences while in the "black box." At first, they thought a great deal about their various personal problems. But as time went on, they found such organized thinking more and more difficult. They could no longer concentrate on much of anything, so they just relaxed and daydreamed.

Eventually, however, most of these subjects experienced "blank periods" during which they couldn't even daydream. They were conscious—which is to say that they were not asleep. But their minds simply were not func-

An isolation chamber used by Peter Suedfeld. (The light is turned off while the subject is actually experiencing sensory isolation.)

Peter Suedfeld

Isolation tanks, which became fashionable as a way to relax in the late 1970's, have been credited with helping to reduce stress and improve concentration.

tioning in a logical fashion. During these periods, their emotions often ran wild.

All of the students found the sensory deprivation very stressful and even very frightening (Heron, Doane, & Scott, 1956).

Imagery

Some 80 percent of the McGill subjects reported *visual hallucinations* and other unusual forms of mental imagery. For reasons no one yet understands, the *content* of the imagery seemed beyond the voluntary control of the subjects. One student, for example, could see nothing but eyeglasses, no matter how hard he tried to think of something else. Surprisingly enough—at least, from a Freudian point of view—very little of the imagery was of a sexual nature.

Many subjects reported disturbances in their *body images*. For instance, one student had the impression his body had turned into *twins*. A second student stated his mind seemed to leave his body and roam around the cubicle. Still other students had "floating" feelings as if their bodies had somehow overcome gravity and were hanging suspended in mid-air (Hebb, 1955).

Since the early work in Hebb's laboratory, many other experimenters have studied how human beings react to sensory isolation (Vernon, 1963). Generally speaking, the more severe the deprivation, the more effect it had on the subjects' "cognitive processes" (Solomon *et al.*, 1961).

Sensory Isolation: An Evaluation

The sensory isolation experiments are important both for practical and for theoretical reasons.

From a practical point of view, sensory deprivation has proved helpful in the treatment of **autistic** children (Schechter *et al.*, 1969). And Canadian psychologist Peter Suedfeld has reported a number of experiments in which the deliberate (and voluntary) use of sensory isolation has helped people lose weight, stop smoking, and decrease their consumption of alcohol (Suedfeld, 1980; Suedfeld & Baker-Brown, 1986).

From a theoretical point of view, the sensory isolation studies remind us of something

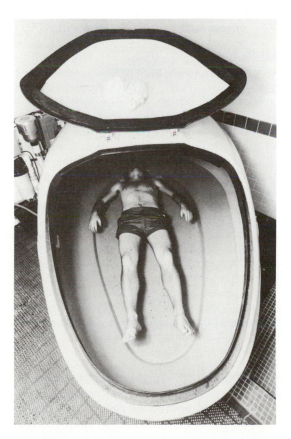

we often forget: Our "cognitive processes" are strongly influenced by the environment we're in.

Information Processing: A Summary

According to the "bottom-up," information processing viewpoint, information flows into your nervous system, then is processed by the lower centers in the brain. Most of these inputs are screened out and forgotten. A few important inputs are strong enough—or significant enough—to reach conscious awareness. But even those inputs that are screened out can influence your conscious mental activities.

The information processing viewpoint does an excellent job of explaining how inputs are handled *before* you become aware of them. The *classical* approach to cognition, however, does a far better job of explaining how your conscious mind actually works—at least, from a "user's" point of view.

As we noted earlier, the classical approach to the study of cognition includes such topics as concept formation, problem solving, creative thought, and reasoning. Let's begin our discussion of the classical approach by looking at how you "form mental categories." As you will see, you could hardly conduct an "attentional search" if you didn't know what you were searching for.

CATEGORIES AND CONCEPTS

When you undertake an "attentional search," how do you do so? For example, look at Fig. 12.6 and see if you can find *an animal*. Probably you'll have no difficulty at all doing so. Once the lower centers in your brain know what *category* of object you're searching for, they immediately screen out such objects as toasters and mixers.

The question then becomes, how do the lower centers in your brain *know* that a "turtle" fits into the *animal* category, while a "toaster" doesn't?

Research suggests that your *cortex* learns to place objects into various **cognitive categories**. You use some categories—such as "animal, vegetable, and mineral"—so frequently that the lower centers in your brain eventually *learn* to use the *distinguishing features* of these categories as they screen inputs during an attentional search. To understand how this miracle occurs, we will need to look more closely at what "cognitive categories" really are, and how your mind creates them.

□□ **QUESTION** □□
Without looking back at Fig. 12.6, can you remember if there is a *spoon* in the picture? What about a *pot holder*? What do your answers tell you about

FIG. 12.6 Can you see an animal in this picture?

how the process of "input screening" works?

□□ **QUESTION** □□
Suppose, some time in the future, you buy a "household robot." One night as you are reading, you tell the robot to go to your bedroom and fetch your slippers. What perceptual and cognitive abilities would the robot have to possess in order to execute this apparently simple command?

Attributes

As we mentioned, using cognitive categories lets you put objects, events, or concepts into convenient groupings. And you do so by looking for *attributes* that each member of the category shares with other members. For example, a birthday cake, a bowl of soup, and an apple all share at least one common attribute—they are edible. Therefore, these objects fall within the natural category "food." A tennis shoe and a tuxedo wouldn't fit within this category. Shoes and suits would fit within the "clothing" category, though, while soup and apples wouldn't.

Attributes allow you to group objects together (into a category) by *including* some objects while *excluding* others. However, most categories are complex. Which is to say, an object must often possess several attributes to fit within a certain category—and perhaps *not* possess certain other attributes.

Rules

Rules tell you how to *combine attributes* to form a certain category. For example, suppose you told your household robot to go to the

Cognitive categories Mental schemes that allow you to group certain objects together because the objects share certain attributes.

Superordinate (SOO-per-OR-din-ate). Anything is "superordinate" if it is "above the ordinary," that is, superior to the basic or usual category.

Basic categories. The most common of the cognitive categories. "Dog" is a basic category. "Animal" is a superordinate category that includes dogs, cats, and other beasts.

Subordinate categories (SUB-or-din-ate). If you are a boss, the people who work for you are your subordinates. Collies and poodles are types of dogs, thus they are subordinate to the basic category "dog."

Concepts. Cognitive schemas, or ways of perceiving a situation. A "mental abstraction" that usually is generalized from specific examples.

store and bring back some "fresh fruit." To respond appropriately, the robot would have to create a category with at least two attributes, "fruit-ness" and "fresh-ness." The *rule* in this case is the "and" rule, since the object selected must be both fresh *and* fruit. Frozen fruit and canned fruit would be excluded.

Another common rule is the "or" rule. You could have said to the robot, "Get me some fresh *or* frozen fruit." In this case, canned fruit would be excluded even though it had the single attribute "fruit-ness."

There are many other types of *rules* for combining attributes to form categories. Of these, the "if-then" rule is perhaps the most important. You might have said to the robot, "*If* the fresh peaches are really ripe, *then* get me some. But canned peaches are fine too." Using the "if-then" and the "and" rules, the robot would include ripe fresh peaches and canned peaches in the category, but exclude frozen peaches and peaches that were fresh but still green (Matlin, 1983).

□ □ **QUESTION** □ □
If you sent your robot to get your slippers, and it brought you a pair of boots instead, what would this tell you about the robot's cognitive categories?

Superordinate, Basic, and Subordinate Categories

How are a dog and a cat alike? They are both *animals*. But how are a collie and a cocker spaniel alike? They are both *dogs*.

Natural categories generally fall into *three levels of generality*. **Superordinate** categories—such as "animal"—tend to be extremely broad. For example, you are an animal, and so is an earthworm. What attributes do you share with an earthworm?

Basic categories—such as "dog"—tend to be of moderate generality. They are neither too specific nor too general.

Subordinate categories—such as "collie"—are highly specific (see Fig. 12.7).

Generally speaking, *basic* categories are easy to create and easy to think about. As you

will discover in Chapter 15, young children learn to use basic categories long before they master either subordinate or superordinate categories. At age two or three, a child may call the family cat a "doggie." The child usually must be four or five before she or he can perceive the relationship between such words as "collie," "cat," and "animal" (Matlin, 1983).

□ □ **QUESTION** □ □
When you think of the basic category "bird," what example first comes to mind?

- ### Natural Versus Artificial Categories
Berkeley psychologist Eleanor Rosch believes there are two major types of cognitive categories: *natural* and *artificial*:

"Natural categories" are those that occur in real-world situations, and which are immediately understandable to most people. Examples of natural categories would be such things as "big or small," "hard or soft," "red or green," "male or female," and even "normal or abnormal."

"Artificial categories" are contrived or synthetic groupings. Usually they are "made up" by humans (particularly by academics!). Dividing college departments into the physical sciences, natural sciences, social sciences, and the humanities is an example of one artificial classification scheme. Classifying students by such titles as freshman, sophomore, junior, senior, and graduate is another artificial set of categories (Mervis & Rosch, 1981).

You sort objects into either natural or artificial categories, Rosch says, according to various *attributes* you perceive the objects as having (Rosch, 1973).

- ### Prototypes
What we call **concepts** are usually artificial categories. Over the years, there has been a fair amount of psychological research on "concept formation." An example of the sorts of concepts usually studied in these experiments can be found in Fig. 12.8.

Eleanor Rosch has criticized most of the work on concept formation because it involves *artificial* rather than *natural* categories (Rosch, 1973). If you tried to figure out what the critical attribute in Fig. 12.8 was, for instance, you probably came to the conclusion that it was "eyebrows." Any face with rounded eyebrows fit within the concept/category. Any face with peaked eyebrows didn't fit. But how often in real life do you see faces like these, or "peaked" eyebrows?

Now, think of the basic category "bird." How did you form this category? And how do you know what animals to include in it, and which to exclude? You could make up a list of

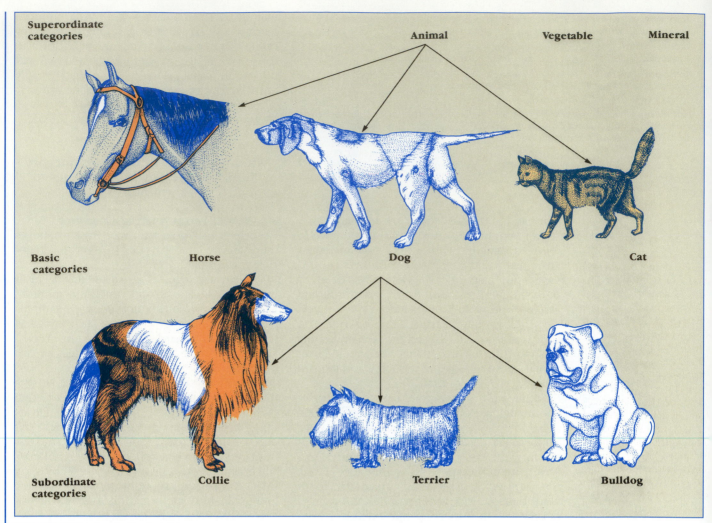

Superordinate categories   Animal   Vegetable   Mineral

Basic categories   Horse   Dog   Cat

Subordinate categories   Collie   Terrier   Bulldog

FIG. 12.7 Three types of categories.

defining features, such as "it flies," "lays eggs," and "has feathers." Then, when you were faced with putting an animal into this category or in some other category, you could check to see how many of the defining attributes the animal possessed. When you tried to solve the puzzle in Fig. 12.8, you had to use the *defining features* approach because that's the way the puzzle was structured.

According to Eleanor Rosch, that's not the way the human mind usually functions. Instead, she says, you tend to create a **prototype** for each basic category and compare any new possibility to the prototype. Most people in the US tend to use either the robin or the sparrow as a prototype of a "bird." Now, suppose you have never seen a canary. If someone showed you a canary, you wouldn't ask, "Does it fly?" or "Does it lay eggs?" Rather, you'd immediately say it *was* a bird because it is very much like your prototype, a robin or a sparrow (Mervis & Rosch, 1981).

Rosch has shown that concept formation is quick and easy if you have a ready-made prototype available. You can readily sort colored ob-

jects into categories such as "blue," "green," "red," and "yellow" because these are natural categories for which you already have clear-cut prototypes. It is much more difficult to sort colored objects if the categories you must use are "aquamarine," "magenta," "turquoise," and "chartreuse" (Rosch, 1977).

● **"Fuzzy" Boundaries**

Is a penguin a bird? You know the answer to that question, of course. But compare a penguin with that prototype of a bird, a robin. The two animals are quite dissimilar, yet both are birds.

Natural categories (such as "bird") often have fuzzy or indistinct boundaries. For instance, both "wolf" and "dog" are basic categories. But if you mated the two, which basic category would the offspring fall into? However, artificial categories often have fairly clear-cut boundaries. After all, they were artificially structured so the boundaries would be as clear as possible.

The "fuzzy boundary" problem becomes worse if you tend to categorize according to

Does this object fit your mental definition of "sofa"?

FIG. 12.8 An attribute discovery task. Before you begin, place a piece of paper so that it hides the correct answers in the right-hand column. Looking only at the figures on the left-hand side, say "yes" if you believe that the figure is an example of the concept, and "no" if you believe that it is not. Only one attribute is relevant in this task. After judging each pair, move the paper down to see the answer. Continue until you think you know what the concept is, and then check the text to see whether you are correct.

	Answers
1	Yes
2	Yes
3	No
4	No
5	No
6	Yes
7	No
8	Yes

prototypes rather than using "distinctive features." For example, "chair" is a basic category. What does your prototype of a chair look like? Does it have arms and legs? A seat and a back? Now think of a large canvas bag filled with beans. Does it *look* like your prototype of a chair? Probably not. And yet, if we call this object a "bean-bag chair," you can fit the object into the category "chair."

□ □ **QUESTION** □ □

If you told your household robot to bring you a "chair," and the machine brought you the head of the psychology department, what would that tell you about the robot's prototype of a "chair"?

● *Fuzzy Boundaries and Trait Descriptions*

Much of the recent research on cognitive categories has been in the fields of personality theory and abnormal psychology. We will discuss these matters more fully in later chapters. However, we might note that when you try to describe people in terms of their "personality traits," you are really attempting to *categorize* individuals according to the *attributes* (or "traits") they display (Buss & Craik, 1983). According to British psychologist Sarah Hampson, many of the problems trait theorists have stem from their use of personality categories that have rather fuzzy boundaries (Hampson, 1985).

The same sort of problem arises when you attempt to diagnose "mental patients" according to some diagnostic scheme. For instance, in a recent study, Michigan psychologists Nancy Cantor and Nancy Genero found that clinical psychiatrists could readily differentiate manic and depressive patients. However, the psychiatrists often included manic patients in the "schizophrenic" category, and often included schizophrenic patients in the "manic" category. Cantor and Genero conclude that conceptual boundary between "mania" and "depression" is fairly clear, but the boundary between "schizophrenia" and "mania" is fairly fuzzy. The Michigan psychologists suggest that psychiatric diagnoses would become more accurate if the *conceptual boundaries* between the categories used were more clearly defined (Cantor & Genero, 1986).

Now that we've discussed how you form concepts and put objects into categories, let's see how you *use* conceptual categories when you *imagine* things.

MENTAL IMAGERY

Close your eyes and imagine a lion, the "king of the beasts." Then, try to view the same lion running swiftly across a plain, roaring loudly as it chases a zebra.

The ability to create pictures and sounds "in your mind's eye" is the province of those cognitive psychologists who study *mental imagery*. Margaret Matlin defines imagery as "mental representations of things that are not physically present" (Matlin, 1983a). These "mental representations," of course, are often *prototypes* of a given cognitive category.

The study of mental imagery has a long and distinguished place in the field of cognitive psychology. Wundt made extensive studies of visual imagery at Leipzig more than a century ago, as did William James and other American psychologists at the turn of the century. At that time, most psychologists assumed mental images were primarily "memories of previous stimuli" (James, 1890). Modern cognitive psychologists take rather a broader view.

● *Synesthesia*

One of the first discoveries made by early investigators was that some people experience *crossed images,* a condition technically known as **synesthesia**. That is, some individuals experience very vivid mental images in one sensory modality when they are exposed to stimuli in a second sensory modality. More than 36 different types of synesthesia have been reported, including colored tastes and odors and "geometrically shaped tastes." However, the best-known (and most widely studied) type of "crossed images" probably is *colored hearing* (Marks, 1975).

Suppose someone asked you, "What *color* is the musical tone F sharp?" Probably you

One example of a "color scheme" keyed to the notes of the musical scale.

would shake your head and wonder about the person's sanity. However, a number of otherwise quite normal individuals "see" a specific color every time they hear a given musical tone or noise. For example, the noted Russian composer Alexander Scriabin "saw" such gorgeous colors whenever he heard music that he built a primitive "color organ" that projected colored lights on a screen whenever someone played the organ's keys. Scriabin wrote several symphonic compositions for the color organ, and toured the world with an orchestra to show off his invention. Unfortunately, the tour was not much of a success. Few members of the audience got the connection between the colors and the music, while those listeners who also experienced colored hearing complained that Scriabin "used the wrong colors" (McConnell, 1961).

Evidence suggesting that synesthesia is caused by "crossed neural pathways" and not merely from past experience comes from several studies. First, H.S. Langfeld tested a person with colored hearing on two different occasions, seven years apart, and found that the individual gave very similar responses (see Table 12.1). Langfeld believed that "mere conditioning" could not account for these results (Langfeld, 1914). Second, E. Lowell Kelly tried to *create* colored hearing in subjects using Pavlovian conditioning. That is, Kelly paired a given tone with a specific color for thousands of trials. At the end of the study, the subjects did indeed "associate" each tone with the proper color, but none of them reported *experiencing* the colors in the same vivid fashion as individuals with synesthesia do (Kelly, 1934). Psychologists Richard Cytowic and Frank Wood believe these studies—and their own research—demonstrate that synesthesia is due to "brain mechanisms" and not to conditioning (Cytowic & Wood, 1982).

□ □ **QUESTION** □ □

Why does the research on synesthesia suggest that some aspects of "mental images" are determined from "the bottom up," and not from "the top down"?

• Rotation of Visual Images

As S.M. Kosslyn points out, one of the major problems in studying introspections is that they can't be observed by anyone other than the person who experiences them. This difficulty is particularly severe in the case of mental images. To overcome this difficulty, Kosslyn says, "researchers have tried to externalize mental events (often in terms of performance time) of internal processing" (Kosslyn, 1980). That is, the researchers often ask their subjects to *ma-*

TABLE 12.1   A Case of Chromesthesia Investigated in 1905 and Again in 1912

	1905	*1912*
c	Red	Red
d♭	Purple	Lavender
d	Violet	Violet
e♭	Soft blue	Thick blue
e	Golden yellow	Sunlight
f	Pink	Pink, apple blossoms
f♯	Green blue	Blue green
g♭	Greener blue	Greener blue
g	Clear blue	Clear sky blue
a	Cold yellow	Clear yellow, hard, not warm
b♭	Orange	Verges on orange
b	Very brilliant coppery	Very brilliant coppery

Langfeld investigated the colors associated with the notes of the musical scale reported by an individual with colored hearing in 1905 and again in 1912. Note the tremendous similarity between the two reports, even though they were made seven years apart.

nipulate a mental image in some fashion, and then measure how long it takes the person to do so. The assumption is that, if there is a *regularity* between how long it takes subjects to manipulate images in specific ways, we may then assume that the subjects have *similar* mental experiences.

One such technique involves showing pairs of objects (such as those in Fig. 12.9), and ask the the subjects whether the pairs are different views of the same object, or are views of different objects. Look at Fig. 12.9A. If you "rotate" the left-hand object about 20° in your mind, you will "see" that it is the same as the right-hand figure. Similarly, in Fig. 12.9B, if you rotate the left-hand object 180°, it suddenly "looks" just like the right-hand object. However, no amount of rotation of the left-hand object in Fig. 12.9C will make it look like the

right-hand object. When R.N. Shepard and J. Metzler asked subjects to perform similar rotations, they found that it took significantly longer for most subjects to rotate an object 180° than 20° (Shepard & Metzler, 1971).

The question then becomes, are these "visual" rotations or "spatial" rotations? To determine the answer to this question, P.A. Carpenter and P. Eisenberg asked subjects who were blind from birth to perform similar mental rotations by "feeling" cut-out (or "block") letters presented in different spatial orientations. Carpenter and Eisenberg then compared the performance of the blind subjects with that of sighted subjects wearing blindfolds. Both groups did about the same. Carpenter and Eisenberg conclude that, since their blind subjects performed well despite their lack of a "visual sense," most mental rotations involve the use of *spatial imagery* rather than *visual imagery* (Carpenter & Eisenberg, 1978).

• *Mental Imagery and Psychotherapy*

The study of mental imagery is important in many fields, including art, architecture, and even physics and chemistry (Kosslyn, 1985). And in psychology, imagery has been studied not only by cognitive psychologists, but by psychotherapists. For instance, during *systematic desensitization* and *cognitive behavior modification*, therapists often ask their clients to "picture" some object or situation mentally in order to elicit (and then desensitize) the emotional responses that are associated with that object (see Chapter 9). The study of how both animals and humans create *cognitive maps* of their environments also is an example of psychological research on mental imagery.

However, some of the most interesting experiments on mental imagery surely are those involving reasoning, creativity, and problem solving. These topics are often loosely combined under the heading of "thinking." So it is to this subject that we now turn our attention.

□ □ **QUESTION** □ □
Suppose you ask a friend, "What's 2 + 2?" When your friend answers, you then ask, "What is the purpose of life?" What is the major psychological *difference* between these two questions?

FIG. 12.9 Mental rotation. Which of these pairs of objects are the same, and which are different?

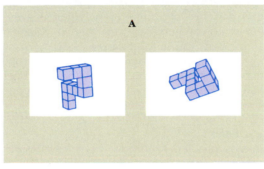

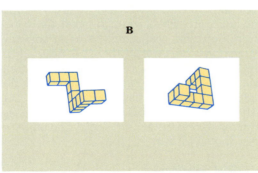

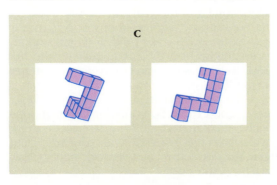

THINKING

Psychologists define *thinking* in a great many different ways. William James considered it the same thing as "consciousness" or "introspection" (James, 1890). In *The Encyclopedia of Human Behavior*, Robert Goldenson defines thinking as "Cognitive behavior in which we recall or manipulate images or ideas that stand for objects and events; symbolic behavior"

(Goldenson, 1970). And Michael Gazzaniga defines thinking as the narrative account your left hemisphere creates to explain why you do what you do (Gazzaniga, 1985) (see Chapter 2). Put simply, thinking is your "flow of conscious awareness" as you experience the world.

According to Scottish psychologist K.J. Gilhooly, there are four main types of thinking: *problem solving, creative thinking, daydreaming,* and *reasoning.* Gilhooly also distinguishes between *directed* and *undirected thought,* and between *well-defined* and *poorly-defined thought.*

The type of thinking you might use when designing a scientific experiment is probably a good example of "well-defined, directed thought." However, the type of mental activity you might engage in while writing poetry is perhaps best described as "ill-defined, creative thought" (Gilhooly, 1982).

Let's begin our discussion of thinking by looking at problem solving.

□ □ **QUESTION** □ □
What type of thinking would you likely engage in when playing poker or chess?

Problem Solving

To many researchers, particularly those who take the "classical view," conscious and deliberate *problem solving* is one of the most important areas of study in cognitive psychology. To give you a feel for the types of research that psychologists perform when investigating problem solving, let's examine a "prototypical" study by Norman R.F. Maier.

Imagine that you volunteered to be a subject in a psychology experiment. The researcher asks you to put on a bathing suit, then escorts you into an almost empty room. Two cord-like ropes are hanging from the ceiling. In one corner of the room there is a pair of pliers. Otherwise, the room is bare. Your job is to tie the two ropes together (see Fig. 12.10). Now, how would you go about solving this problem?

● *The Goal*

To begin with, the experimenter has made things easy for you by *specifying the goal.* For the first two steps in most types of problem solving are (1) realizing that a problem exists, and (2) defining what goal you are trying to achieve. If you don't know there's a problem, of course, you won't do much of anything. And if you don't know *what goal* you're trying to reach, you won't know when the problem is solved. Generally speaking, the more specific you can be in describing the goal, the more likely it is you will reach it (see Chapter 10).

Your goal in the experiment, of course, is to tie the two ropes together. Since that's a fairly specific goal, you should *know* when you've achieved it.

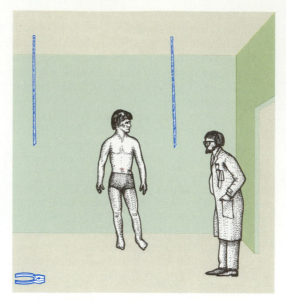

FIG. 12.10 Maier showed that the solutions subjects offered for "the rope test" depended on how they perceived the problem.

● *The Original State*

The next step in problem solving is to find out where you're starting from. Some psychologists call this "determining the original state." Other researchers—as you saw in Chapter 10—call it "taking a **baseline**.

What is your "original state" in the rope experiment? Well, you start with two ropes hanging from the ceiling, a pair of pliers, and your own body. That's it.

● *Rules*

In most problem situations, there are rules that determine what you can do and can't do. In the rope experiment, you're told right away what the rules are. First, you can't pull the ropes from the ceiling or change them in any way. Second, you can't use anything not presently in the room. Third, you can't take off your bathing suit and use it. (A fourth rule is usually unstated, but almost always exists. Namely, you can't behave in an abnormal way, such as assaulting the experimenter, setting the place on fire, and so forth.)

● *Trial Solutions*

Once you know the goal and the rules, you can try out some possible solutions. You go over to one of the ropes, take hold of it, and walk toward the second rope. You pull on the first rope as hard as you can (to stretch it a bit, perhaps). Then you extend your free arm as far as it will go. Unfortunately, you can't quite reach the second rope. So you drop the first rope, take hold of the second rope, stretch it out, and try to grab the first rope with your free hand. But that, of course, won't work either. Now, what do you do?

Baseline. As you saw in Chapter 10, a baseline is a measure of the behavioral outputs of a system *before* you attempt to change the system (or get the system to change itself).

Mental images. Internal or cognitive representations of external objects or events.

Functional fixedness. The tendency most people show to perseverate (purr-SEV-er-ate), or to resist changing a response pattern even when another response might be more effective.

Conceptualizing the Problem

In truth, you didn't really know what the *problem* was until you tried to tie the ropes together and found they wouldn't reach. At this point, you have to stop and think. Which is to say, you have to *conceptualize* the problem. "Conceptualizing" means to "construct an internal representation" of the problem. This "internal representation" really is a set of **mental images** of the elements or categories involved in the problem. A "prototype," for instance, is a *mental image* of a basic category.

Once you conceptualize the problem using mental images, you can manipulate the various elements of the problem *cognitively* rather than *physically* (Kosslyn, 1983, 1985).

Maier's Research

The "rope problem" was developed many years ago by Norman R.F. Maier. When he tested University of Michigan students on the problem, Maier found they tended (at first) to conceptualize the problem in fairly standard ways (Maier, 1931). Some students decided "their arms were too short." Their first trial solution was to "extend their arms" using the pair of pliers. They would pull one rope over as far as they could, then reach out for the other rope holding the pliers in their free hand. Unfortunately, using the pliers to "extend their arms" didn't work.

Other students conceptualized the difficulty as being, "The rope is too short." These students would "extend the rope" by grasping it with the pliers. Then they'd try to reach the other rope with their free hand. Again, no luck. (Before Maier learned to dress the students in bathing suits and tell them, "Don't take off your clothes," some of the students used their belts or shirts to "extend the rope.")

Still other subjects decided the problem was that "the rope won't come to me." They would stretch out one rope as far as it would go, then beckon to the other rope as if they could "will" it to swing toward them. These students sometimes solved the problem. Can you guess how they did so?

Functional Fixedness

Once you have conceptualized a problem in a certain way, you may find it difficult to see the

problem in a different light. Psychologists call this **functional fixedness**, or "mental set."

Abraham Luchins made an extensive study of functional fixedness. See Table 12.2 and work through the problems before you read any farther.

As you probably found, the best solution to problem 1 is first to fill up jar B. That gives you 130 gallons. Then you dip jar A into B and remove 24 gallons. That leaves 106 gallons. Now you dip jar C into B twice and remove 6 more gallons. That operation leaves you with 100 gallons in B, which is your goal. The best way to solve problems 2 through 5 is in much the same fashion. Check your answers and see if that's the way you solved the first five problems.

If you did solve 1–5, how about 6? In fact, you can solve 6 and 7 exactly the same way. However, that's a very round-about way. Look at the last two problems again and see if you can't find an easier method.

When Luchins asked students to solve 1–5 *first*, they did so. But then they almost always used the round-about solution to solve problems 6 and 7 as well. However, when he gave students *just problems 6 and 7* (without exposing them to 1–5 first), the subjects almost always came up with the "easy" solution first. The success the first group of students had solving problems 1–5 tended to "fix" a certain procedure in their minds. Because of this "mental set," the students continued to use the round-about solution even when better solutions existed (Luchins, 1942).

□ □ **QUESTION** □ □

How does "functional fixedness" relate to the perceptual principle that "you see what you expect to see?"

Reconceptualizing the Problem

One good way to break a "mental set" is to *re*-conceptualize the problem. Which is to say, you often need to look at a problem from a

TABLE 12.2

Imagine that you have three jars, *A, B,* and *C.* In each of seven problems the capacity of the three jars is listed. You must use the three jars in order to obtain the amount of liquid specified in the "Goal" column. You may obtain the goal amount by adding or subtracting the quantities listed in *A, B,* and *C.* (The answers can be found in the discussion of the experiment.)

Problem	A	B	C	Goal
1	24	130	3	100
2	9	44	7	21
3	21	58	4	29
4	12	160	25	98
5	19	75	5	46
6	23	49	3	20
7	18	48	4	22

Thinking

fresh perspective, or create new mental images (or prototypes) to describe the problem situation.

Maier's Rope Problem

As you may have guessed by now, the solution to Norman Maier's rope problem is to break your "mental set" about pliers. That is, you must see that pliers are not only tools—they also can be placed in a basic cognitive category called "pendulum weights." If you tie the pliers to the end of one rope, you can set it swinging back and forth. Then you can pull the other rope out far enough to catch the swinging rope when it comes close to you.

Many of Norman Maier's students failed to solve the problem because they couldn't "categorize" the pair of pliers as a pendulum weight. So Maier gave them some clues. First, he brought a type of pendulum into the room and set it in motion. This clue helped a few of the subjects. But most still conceptualized the problem in terms of "my arm is too short" or "the rope is too short." Then Maier gave them a more important clue. He started talking to the subject, to get the person's attention. Next Maier slowly walked toward the student. As he walked, he deliberately brushed into one of the ropes, so it caught against his body. When Maier walked past the rope, it slid over his shoulder and swung back and forth a couple of times. Shortly thereafter, almost all of the students solved the problem!

Maier then asked the subjects what gave them the clue to solving the problem. Oddly enough, almost all the students said, "The pendulum." Very few of them were conscious of having seen the rope swing back and forth. However, if Maier just showed them the pendulum but *didn't* brush into the rope, few of the students found the solution (Maier, 1931).

□ □ **QUESTION** □ □
How does Maier's experiment support the belief that many factors that influence cognition are *unconscious* rather than *conscious*?

Recent Research on Problem Solving

Most recent research on problem solving has focused on four main topics: (1) personality factors associated with problem solving; (2) problem solving in real-life (or social) situations; (3) methods of teaching people better problem solving skills; and (4) **metacognition**, or "ways of thinking about thinking." Let's look briefly at each of these four topics.

Personality Factors Associated with Problem Solving

There is not all that much agreement about what personality traits are associated with "good performance" in problem solving situations. However, in a recent study, Purdue psychologists Penny Armstrong and Ernest McDaniel found that subjects who perceive themselves as "competent learners" tended to make fewer mistakes when solving problems than did subjects who didn't give themselves high competence ratings (Armstrong & McDaniel, 1986).

There is some evidence that males tend to do better on *traditional* problem-solving tasks than do females. For example, Canadian psychologists Monique Lortie-Lussier and her colleagues studied 118 eight- and nine-year-old children with English, French, or Italian cultural backgrounds. Many of the girls had more "interpersonal skills" than did the boys, but the boys tended to show higher "resourcefulness and problem solving abilities" (Lortie-Lussier *et al.*, 1986). However, females may resort to problem solving in social situations more readily than in "academic situations." Caryl Rusbult and her colleagues at the University of North Carolina found that women were more likely to use problem-solving skills to improve close relationships, while "traditional males" tended to "exit" relationships rather than trying to resolve the problems and thus make the relationships better (Rusbult *et al.*, 1986).

□ □ **QUESTION** □ □
What have you learned about the *socialization* of men and women in our culture that could explain the findings described above?

Problem Solving in Social Situations

Several investigators have recently reported that teaching "social problem-solving skills" is an effective way of bringing about change in many real-life situations. For example, Robert Hierholzer and Robert Liberman found that chronically mentally-ill patients benefitted from learning how to set and achieve both short- and long-term goals (Hierholzer & Liberman, 1986). And Richard Perlmutter and James Jones found that helping families who experience "psychiatric emergencies" learn problem-solving skills was a particularly effective method of treatment (Perlmutter & Jones, 1985). (We will discuss this type of treatment more fully in Chapter 19, when we describe family therapy.)

Using Computers to Teach Problem Solving Skills

Some recent work on teaching people to solve problems has involved the use of computers. For instance, Army psychologist Scott Graham and his associates found that mechanics who were taught tank-maintenance skills using a "computer-based simulation program" did better than mechanics who were taught using traditional methods. And University of Minnesota psychologists Roger Johnson and his colleagues found that computer-assisted instruction was an effective tool for teaching eighth-grade students cooperative problem-solving skills (Johnson, Johnson, & Stanne, 1986).

□ □ QUESTION □ □
How might "computer simulations" of problem solving situations reduce the stress associated with learning new cognitive skills?

- ### *Metacognition*
Teaching people problem-solving skills often helps improve their performance. However, many psychologists and educators believe that teaching people to *monitor* their mental activities, and to *evaluate* their own performance as they work through a problem, yields even better results. The term *metacognition* is often used to refer to a variety of techniques that encourage individuals to "think about their own thought processes" while engaged in problem solving.

University of Michigan psychologists Scott Paris, David Saarnio, and David Cross report that third- and fifth-grade students who were given "metacognition" training "increased their awareness about reading and their [own] use of reading comprehension strategies." In most situations, these students also learned to read somewhat faster than did children given traditional training (Paris, Saarnio, & Cross, 1986).

Creative Thinking
Creativity of one sort or another is often called for in problem-solving situations. For instance, to solve the Maier rope problem, you have to discover a "creative" or "unusual" use for a pair of pliers.

As you might suspect, there is no single (or even creative) definition for creativity that all psychologists will agree to. Goldenson defines creative thinking as "a form of directed thinking applied to the discovery of new solutions to problems, new techniques and devices, or new artistic expressions" (Goldenson, 1970). Israeli psychologists Jonathan Smilansky and Naftali Halberstadt disagree. They believe that creativity is the mark of people who *invent* new problems, not a property of individuals who "merely find new solutions to old problems" (Smilansky & Halberstadt, 1986).

Other investigators define creativity as a type of "divergent thinking" (Lewis & Houtz,

1986). Still others believe that logical problem solving is a type of mental activity found primarily in the left hemisphere, while creativity is the right hemisphere's way of accomplishing the same task (Katz, 1986)

Given the lack of consensus as to what creativity is, hard data about how to measure it (much less teach it) are difficult to come by. It does seem the case, however, that most of the psychological tests that purport to measure creativity don't correlate very well with each other—or with real-life performance (Richardson, 1986). Nor is creative thinking highly correlated with traditional measures of intelligence (Katz, 1986; Runco, 1986; Sternberg, 1985). Most experts do agree, however, that creativity is fostered by positive reinforcement, and is inhibited by criticism and punishment (Skinner, 1954, 1987).

□ □ QUESTION □ □
What relationship do you see between creative thought and daydreaming? (Hint: Be creative in your answer!)

Daydreaming
Goldenson defines *daydreaming* as "A waking fantasy or reverie; the free play of thought or imagination." He goes on to say, however, that "Daydreaming is classed as a form of autistic thinking, since the individual's imagination is controlled primarily by his inner desires and not by outer reality" (Goldenson, 1970).

Twenty years ago, psychologists (such as Goldenson) believed that frequent daydreaming occurred primarily in children and adolescents. The normal adult, Goldenson said, "becomes absorbed in realistic activities and finds other ways of exercising his imagination." Indeed, excessive daydreaming in an adult was thought to be a sign of some "underlying emotional disturbance" (Goldenson, 1970). Modern research does not support Goldenson's views, however. If, several times a day, you ask normal adults to report what they're thinking about, you will find that they daydream fairly frequently (Hurlburt & Melancon, 1987). And Yeshiva psychologists David Baskin and Joel Goldstein report that normal adults daydream with the same frequency—and about the same sorts of things—as do adult psychiatric patients (Baskin & Goldstein, 1985–1986).

Why do people daydream? Again, there is no agreement among experts. Sigmund Freud believed daydreaming was a socially-approved (and fairly creative) manner of releasing pent-up libidinal energy (Freud, 1933/1964). Other psychologists believe daydreaming is a "narrative sequence"—that is, a story that you tell to yourself—similar to the dream sequences you have while asleep (Cicogna *et al.*, 1986). And UCLA psychologists Albert Mehrabian and Shari Friedman believe daydreaming is an "extraneous activity" you engage in "while preoccupied with certain situations and tasks" (Mehrabian & Friedman, 1986).

Put simply, daydreaming seems to be a normal activity you engage in when you don't have anything else on your mind, when you are constrained from doing other things, or when you want to "think through" something that is bothering you.

Reasoning

Margaret Matlin defines reasoning as "drawing conclusions from several known facts" (Matlin, 1983a). According to Matlin, there are four major types of cognitive tasks that involve reasoning:

1. *Linear series problems*. A linear series problem involves lining things up on a straight-line or "scale" of some sort. "Since A is bigger than B, and B is bigger than C, then A must be bigger than C." Here, you merely note that *since* a certain "ordered relationship" exists between A, B, and C, you can draw conclusions from this relationship.

2. *Propositional reasoning*. This type of reasoning involves the use of the "if-then" rule we described earlier. "If A is bigger than B, and if B is bigger than C, then A must be bigger than C." In the case of propositional reasoning, *if* the relationships described are true, *then* the conclusions you can draw will be valid! (The problem with propositional reasoning, therefore, lies in *proving* your propositions are true.)

3. *Syllogisms*. Generally speaking, **syllogisms** involve the use of terms such as "all" and "some." For instance, if it is true that "All collies are dogs, and some pets are collies," you can logically conclude that "some pets must be dogs." The trouble with syllogisms is that, if you don't follow the rules, you can often draw incorrect conclusions. For example, it may well be that "All collies are dogs, and some dogs are pets," but you cannot conclude *from that statement alone* that "some collies are pets" or that "some pets are collies."

4. *Analogies*. In the classic case, an analogy has four parts: *Collie* is to *dog* as *Persian* is to *cat*. Intelligence tests frequently contain this type of item. Although most of us use analogical reasoning fairly frequently in everyday life, this type of thought process can often lead to embarrassingly incorrect conclusions. As Freud supposedly said, "Analogies prove nothing, but they do make us feel at home."

Generally speaking, the use of reasoning involves following the "laws of logic." Many colleges teach courses in logic and reasoning, often under the title of "Critical Thinking." And there has been a fair amount of research, par-

ticularly in the field of developmental psychology, on such topics as "moral reasoning." We will discuss moral reasoning in Chapter 15. However, one of the best ways to discover both the benefits and the problems associated with the concept of *reasoning* is to look at an exciting new field in psychology called "artificial intelligence," or AI.

Artificial Intelligence

More than 20 years ago, scientists interested in cognitive processes asked themselves a very sticky question: Can we program a computer so that it *thinks* like a human being? With perhaps more enthusiasm than good sense, the scientists plunged into the problem headfirst. And hit bottom rather quickly. They had assumed that, since the human brain "processes" information in much the same way that computers do, it should be simple to get computers to *reason* in the same way that people do. After all, the "rules of logic" that we mentioned above are fairly well known.

As University of Pittsburgh psychologist John Haugeland points out, however, it soon became apparent that "the rules of logic" don't work very well in poorly-defined situations. And most real-world problems are, unfortunately, very poorly defined. As it turned out, however, the frustration the computer scientists experienced led them to look more creatively at how humans actually reason (Haugeland, 1985).

Herbert A. Simon received the Nobel Prize in 1978 for his research and theorizing on human thought processes. Simon takes the "in-

"YOU WANT THE PROBLEM-SOLVING PROGRAM. WHAT YOU'VE GOT IS THE COMMISSERATING PROGRAM."

formation processing approach" in his study of cognition. According to Simon, people tend to use two main *strategies* as they search for solutions to various problems: **algorithms** and **heuristics**.

"Algorithms" are *exact rules* you must follow to achieve some goal. It's usually a simple task to teach a computer to use an algorithm because computers can readily follow precise instructions. "Heuristics" are rather loosely-defined rules *along with the knowledge of when to use them*. The more knowledge you have about a situation, the more precise the heuristics can become. Simon believes that the ability of humans to cope with real-world situations depends primarily on the use of heuristics, not algorithms. And since we typically have but a limited amount of knowledge about the real world, it's difficult to teach either humans or computers which heuristics to use—and how to employ them (Simon, 1981).

• Heuristics Versus Algorithms

As we noted, computers can be programmed to use algorithms rather easily. For instance, a chess-playing computer will search through millions of possible chess moves, following a simple formula that tells it how to evaluate each possibility. The computer then decides on a move based on the evaluation it has made.

But when experts look at a chess board, they tend to *perceive patterns* rather than think about *exact search strategies*. Instead of evaluating *all* the possibilities, the expert will *remem-*

ber (from past experience) what sort of move works best in the present situation. Ulric Neisser puts it this way: "Capablanca, the former world [chess] champion, was once asked by an admirer how many moves he typically examined in a difficult position. He said, 'One, but it is the right one.'" Neisser goes on to say that "Master players see the whole board at a glance; they see patterns and configurations that suggest moves to them. The more they play, the better they get. . . . The computer doesn't do what the human player does: It doesn't recognize patterns, it doesn't get any better with experience, it doesn't learn" (cited in Goleman, 1983).

Unfortunately, no one has yet developed high-level, general heuristic techniques for computers. And the major reason for this inability to teach computers how to "think" is that we still don't really know how humans *recognize patterns* in real-world situations.

Expert Systems and Decision Making

Twenty years ago, AI specialists tried to program a computer to diagnose various types of illnesses by asking patients for their symptoms. In its simplest form, this sort of "medical diagnostics" is really an exercise in *categorization*. So, the AI researchers told themselves, diagnostics should involve little more than (1) identification of "defining attributes," and (2) rules for combining these attributes. Therefore, the AI experts created various highly logical algorithms that would make the computer ask the patient various types of questions. The computer would then try to combine the answers into a precise description of the patient's illness.

This algorithmic approach has succeeded fairly well with a few well-defined illnesses. However, computers do rather poorly with complex medical problems. And they fail miserably when trying to diagnose "mental disorders" (Trotter, 1986).

By 1980, the AI specialists started looking at medical diagnostics in rather a different light. Rather than building logical algorithms, they tried to *mimic* the decision-making skills of human experts. We now call this the search for *expert systems*, or computer programs that give expert-level advice.

For example, University of Pittsburgh psychologist Robert Glaser and his associates studied how highly-experienced physicians made medical diagnoses just from inspecting X-rays of patients. They tried to discover what kinds of "critical features" the skilled physicians looked for in the X-rays, and how they put these features together to make a diagnosis. Glaser and his group then compared the approach used by *experienced physicians* with that employed by *young doctors* who were just learning how to "read an X-ray."

Human chess players often use heuristics to help them win. Computers, in contrast, rely on algorithms.

Glaser suggests that skilled and beginning doctors use quite different decision-making strategies. An expert looks at an X-ray and immediately perceives features that a beginner either overlooks or finds only after a lengthy search. The young doctor may have all the *facts* she or he needs to arrive at a correct diagnosis. But the beginner uses an *algorithm*—a "logical search." The expert has learned to use *heuristics*. That is, the expert uses "rules-of-thumb" plus facts. The rules—or heuristics—tell the experienced doctor which features (or facts) are important, and which aren't. And these heuristics are *acquired through experience*.

According to Robert Glaser, *knowledge equals facts plus rules*. "As individuals acquire knowledge, they also should be empowered to think and reason," Glaser says. If and when we gain enough knowledge about the ways in which humans *acquire and use knowledge*, then perhaps we will know enough to teach a robot to "think and reason" too (Glaser, 1984).

□ □ **QUESTION** □ □
Computer chess programs can often beat inexperienced human players, but not those who have "played a million games." Theoretically, you should be able to build the *experience* of "playing a million games" into the computer's program. Why do you think this has turned out to be so difficult to do?

Cognitive Psychology: A Summary
At the beginning of the chapter, we mentioned two major theoretical views towards the study of cognition: (1) the information processing approach, which emphasizes the *flow of information* from the "bottom" of the nervous system up to the cortex, and (2) the classical approach, a "top-down" viewpoint that emphasizes *conscious* processes, such as problem solving, creative thinking, and reasoning.

• The Classical Approach
Because of its emphasis on language and thought, classical theory tends to downplay the importance of inputs in the decision-making process. For instance, it cannot explain why subjects undergoing sensory isolation simply "stop thinking" after awhile. And because the classical approach defines cognition as a *conscious process*, it also ignores the strong influence of *unconscious* activities in the lower centers of the brain. The classical approach also does a poor job of handling most of the data on learning and memory we discussed in previous chapters.

• The Information Processing Approach
The information processing approach is by far the most complete theory of how you process

and respond to inputs from your body and from the outside world. However, it too has its weaknesses, the greatest of which, surely, is its reliance on the computer as a "model" of human thought.

Machines don't have emotions. People do. Perhaps for that reason, information processing theorists have tended to ignore the important influences that your emotions have on your cognitive processes. Put simply, the theory focuses on *how* you think, not *why* you process information in the way that you do.

Also, computers don't have *volition*. They respond because they're built to respond, not because they *choose* to respond. By overly simplifying the cognitive process, the theory tends to lose the essence of what human thought is all about.

Each of the two major approaches has its strengths and weaknesses. However, many psychologists believe that the two viewpoints are merely two sides to the same coin. To see why this might be the case, let's look at what British psychologist Norman Dixon has to say about cognitive processes.

Robert Glaser

• Dixon's "Dual-Processing" Theory
Norman Dixon notes that the "lower centers" of the nervous system evolved long before the cortex did (see "Theory of the Triune Brain" in Chapter 8). Dixon calls these primitive centers the **preconscious processing system**, or PPS. Originally, these primitive centers mostly mediated attention, arousal, and emotional responses. When the cortex evolved, however, the PPS took on a new function—that of preliminary screening of *informational* inputs before they reach the "conscious processing system" in the cortex.

According to Dixon, the PPS can *attend simultaneously* to inputs from *all* the sensory modalities (sight, hearing, and so forth). The PPS also has much lower thresholds than does the conscious system. Thus, the preconscious system can process a large amount of information in a small amount of time. The PPS responds in a reflexive (automatic) fashion to many of these inputs. But the PPS is better at *detecting* the emotional significance of stimuli than at *making logical decisions* about these inputs. So, when the PPS detects important inputs, it sends these stimuli along to the cortex for "conscious processing."

In contrast to the PPS, Dixon says, the conscious system is relatively insensitive to weak stimuli. And the conscious system has a limited capacity for processing data. Therefore, it can attend to only one input at a time. However, the cortex only *needs* to pay attention to one thing at a time because the PPS has already screened the inputs for emotional significance. And *because* the cortex can focus on a limited number

Norman Dixon

Preconscious processing system. Abbreviated PPS. Term used by Norman Dixon to refer to all those "lower centers of the brain" that do the initial processing and screening of informational inputs.

of alternatives, the conscious system can make decisions *quickly* in emergency situations (Dixon, 1981).

The information processing approach to cognition has, so far, dealt primarily with the *preconscious processing system*. The classical approach to cognitive psychology, however, has focused primarily on the *conscious processing system*. As Dixon notes, we would hardly be the complex cognitive animals we are if both

these systems didn't function smoothly—and simultaneously. For that reason, surely, we should always look at cognitive processes both from a top-down and from a bottom-up perspective.

To summarize, what do we know about cognitive psychology? A lot, and yet not as much as we probably should. Eric Neisser puts it this way: "Being alive in a complex world has a richness we have just begun to understand" (cited in Goleman, 1983).

We will continue this discussion in the next chapter, when we look at a complicated subject called *pain*. As you will see, there are both "bottom-up" and "top-down" methods of reducing the unpleasantness associated with painful inputs.

SUMMARY

1. The two major ways of studying cognition are the **information processing approach** and the **classical approach**.

2. The information processing approach is a **bottom-up** theory that emphasizes how inputs are screened by lower centers in the brain. The classical approach is a **top-down** theory that focuses on conscious mental activities.

3. The **information processing** viewpoint came to dominate much of cognitive psychology in the 1960's, in part because of Ulric Neisser's influence.

4. According to the information processing approach, cognition begins with **attention** to an input.

5. Most subjects do poorly on tasks demanding **divided attention**, but may improve with practice. Broadbent's **bottleneck** theory claims there is a physical limit to the number of inputs the nervous system can process at once. The **Norman and Bobrow** theory claims the limitation is not physical but psychological.

6. **Unattended inputs** can occasionally have an influence on cognition.

7. Inputs reach your cortex by two routes, the **straight-line sensory system** and the **reticular activating system**, or RAS. The straight-line sensory system handles information. The RAS **screens** inputs for significance and **arouses** the cortex when an important message is coming through on the straight-line system.

8. **Overlearned responding** occurs when the lower centers execute **automatic processes** that the cortex is unconscious of.

9. Humans undergoing **sensory isolation** suffered a decline in cognitive skills, experienced unusual mental imagery, and uncritically accepted any inputs.

10. **Information underload** has been used as

therapy with autistic children, and to help people stop smoking, lose weight, and reduce their drinking.

11. The mind tends to put objects in categories using **attributes** of the objects and **rules** for combining attributes.

12. There are three levels of categories, **superordinate**, **basic**, and **subordinate**. Basic categories are the easiest to deal with cognitively.

13. There are two types of cognitive categories, **natural** and **artificial**.

14. Humans often create **prototypes** of basic categories to speed concept formation.

15. **Imagery** involves "mental representations of things not physically present."

16. **Synesthesia** involves experiencing mental images in one sensory modality when exposed to inputs from a different modality.

17. Humans are capable of **rotating mental images** in their imaginations. However, the greater the rotation required, the slower the process goes.

18. **Problem solving** typically begins with **goal setting** and a description of the **original state** or **baseline**. It continues with **conceptualizing the problem**, which involves creation of **mental images**, and with **trial solutions** that are governed by **rules**.

19. Finding solutions to problems is often inhibited by **functional fixedness**, or mental set. Breaking the set involves **reconceptualizing** the problem.

20. Recent research on problem solving has focused on **personality factors** associated with problem solving, **real-life** problem solving, methods of **teaching** problem-solving skills, and **metacognition**, or "thinking about thinking."

21. **Creative thinking** is difficult to define, but is encouraged by reward and inhibited by criticism and punishment.

22. **Daydreaming** was once thought to be unusual in adults, but is now seen as a normal cognitive activity.

23. Four major types of cognitive tasks involve reasoning: **linear series problems, propositional reasoning, syllogisms,** and **analogies.**

24. The study of **artificial intelligence** is a search for ways to program computers to **reason** (process inputs) as humans do.

25. Computers typically must use **algorithms** or exact formulas to solve problems. Humans tend to use **heuristics,** or "rules of thumb."

26. Knowledge is often defined as **facts** plus **rules** for using those facts.

27. According to Dixon, the RAS and other lower centers make up the **preconscious processing system,** or PPS, which evolved long before the cortex, or **conscious system.** The PPS may **attend simultaneously** to inputs from all modalities and screens inputs for **significance.**

28. Only significant inputs reach the **conscious processing system,** which can attend to just **one input at a time.** The preliminary screening of inputs by the PPS may allow the cortex to **make decisions efficiently.**

29. To understand cognition fully, you should study it both from the **bottom up** and from the **top down.**

(Continued from page 291.)

A few hours after he got out of the "black room," Philip Cassone returned to the laboratory to take some more tests. The psychologists explained that they were giving him the tests to find out how soon he had recovered from the effects of the sensory deprivation.

When he took the tests again, Phil did much better than when he had taken them in isolation. Although, to be truthful, he still didn't seem to be as sharp as he usually was. Obviously some of the effects were still lingering on. But the psychologists assured him that within a few days he would be as good as ever.

"How did I do as a subject?" Phil asked the man in charge when the tests were done.

"Let's see," the man said, putting down his pipe and checking the records. "You stayed in for about 26 hours. That's about average. Not bad at all."

Phil was annoyed. He had hoped to do much better than average. He turned to leave in disgust, when he spotted a tape recorder sitting on one of the tables.

"Did you record my voice?" Phil asked.

The psychologist put his pipe in his mouth and nodded gravely.

"Could I listen to some of it?"

The man picked a tape up off the table, put it on the machine, and started the tape in motion.

Phil was shocked to hear the way his voice came out. "Do I really sound like that?"

When the psychologist again nodded soberly, Phil paid even closer attention to the tape. He heard himself demand to know what time it was, heard himself insist that the psychologists talk to him, listened to his scream that if they didn't say something right away he was coming out.

And then he heard a door open and his voice come faintly from a distance.

"You bastards ruined the experiment. You made me come out."

Phil blushed. "Did I really call you guys bastards?"

Again the psychologist nodded his head slowly in agreement.

Phil groaned. It was the first time he had ever called a professor such a name—at least to his face. "I must have lost my mind to have said something like that," Phil said.

The psychologist just puffed on his pipe and smiled.

Hypnosis, Pain, and Placebos

"Mesmer's Magic Wand"

· C · H · A · P · T · E · R ·
13

"Are you sure you want to do it in class?" Brian Healy asked.

"Why certainly," Assistant Professor Don Powell replied, staring intently at his teaching fellow. "Hypnotic suggestion is a legitimate demonstration of mental functioning, a tool used extensively by respected members of the medical and dental professions. Hypnosis isn't a cure-all; it isn't a parlor trick; it isn't a mysterious force. It's merely mind over matter." Powell smiled. "Besides, the students will love it."

"I don't doubt that at all, Professor Powell," the teaching fellow said. "But what if something goes wrong?"

"What could possibly go wrong?"

Brian Healy thought for a moment. "Well, what if the person you hypnotize doesn't come out of the trance? Who'd want to be hypnotized for life?"

"Nonsense!" Powell snorted. "If you don't wake a person up deliberately, the person drops off into a restful, normal sleep and in a short time wakes up naturally. And with no physical ill effects, I might add emphatically," Powell added emphatically.

"Okay, you're the boss," Healy said. "But what if nobody in the class can be hypnotized? What would you do then?"

"Change the subject, probably," Powell said, perhaps a little too truthfully. "But it won't happen. In a class of 100, I'd expect roughly 15 students would not be hypnotizable at all, that about 65 would go into a light or medium trance, and that 20 would be capable of achieving a really deep hypnotic state. The subject's prior attitudes and experiences are the main controlling factor anyhow. If you think you can't talk when you're hypnotized, you won't talk no matter how much the hypnotist coaxes you. If you think you can't stop talking when you're in a trance, nothing will shut you up."

"Sounds like my mother-in-law. Nothing can shut her up either."

"Brian, no personal problems, please! Hypnotism isn't a joke of some kind. It's a serious psychological tool. We are following in the great tradition of Braid, Charcot, and Freud. Just do as I tell you, and everything will turn out fine."

And, of course, it did. Professor Powell began the class with a lengthy discussion of the history of hypnotism, beginning with Anton Mesmer and his animal magnetism and concluding with recent experiments on the effectiveness of hypnotherapy. Much of the class was entranced. Next, he attempted to hypnotize all 100 students at once. Much of the class was tranced.

Then, as his final demonstration, Dr. Powell asked for a volunteer who might want to test out her or his mental powers. An alert, eager, wiry young man immediately stuck up his hand.

"What is your name, please?" Powell asked the volunteer.

"Elvis McNeil," the young man said, running one of his hands through his wavy hair.

"All right, Mr. McNeil. I'm going to put you into a trance, if I can. And then we're going to open up the pathways to your mind. We're going to unshackle all the latent mental powers you've always suspected you had. We're going to prove to you that your own mind—as untrained and untutored as it may be in its present state—can move mountains."

The young man began nodding in almost too-eager agreement, so Powell changed to rather a cautious tone of voice. "We won't do anything that could possibly harm you, of course. But there is always the possibility that you may feel a little foolish afterward. Is your ego big enough to withstand the laughter of your fellow students?"

"Gee, Professor Powell, I think my ego only has problems when people don't laugh at me," the intense young man said, carefully adjusting his glasses. "I'll go along with anything you want to try."

Powell smiled. "Excellent, my boy, excellent. Now just sit in this comfortable chair right here in the middle of the stage and start relaxing. Are you comfortable?"

Elvis McNeil nodded as he settled into the chair. Dr. Powell then pulled out a long, sharp hatpin and sterilized it over the flame of a match. "Would it hurt you if I jabbed this pin into one of your fingers?"

Elvis tensed a bit. "Of course it would. I thought you said it wouldn't hurt!"

"Since we won't try it until you're fully hypnotized, I guarantee you that you won't feel a thing. It's just a test to see if you're really in a trance. You won't mind, will you, as long as it's a scientific test of sorts?"

"Not if it unleashes the latent powers of my mind," McNeil said solemnly.

"Good," Powell replied, pulling a gold watch on a long chain out of his pocket with a flourish. "Now, Mr. McNeil, I want you to stare at this mystical timepiece that was given to me by my grandfather. See it swing back and forth before your eyes? Look at it closely, Mr. McNeil. Watch as it moves back and forth, back and forth, back and forth."

McNeil stared intently at the glittering gold watch.

Powell continued in a soft, crooning tone of voice, almost as if he were singing. "Your eyelids are getting heavier and heavier. You are getting sleepier and sleepier and sleepier. Soon you will be fast asleep, deep asleep. Go to sleep, Mr. McNeil. Deep, deep, deep sleep."

McNeil's eyes closed. He sat rigid, unmoving.

"Are you asleep?"

McNeil's head nodded slowly, almost mechanically.

"Hold your hand out, Elvis. That's right, straight out in front of you. Your hand is made of steel, isn't it? See, I can touch it, and you can't feel my touch, can you?"

13 / Hypnosis, Pain, and Placebos

"No."

"I can even stick this sterilized pin in your hand and it will cause you no pain at all. You can't feel a thing, remember. Now I will stick the pin in—like this!—and it didn't hurt at all, did it?"

The class gasped as Powell plunged the sterilized hatpin half an inch into the young man's hand. But McNeil didn't react. Instead, he shook his head slowly and whispered, "No, it didn't hurt at all."

Professor Powell removed the pin, inspected McNeil's hand, then sterilized the wound and put a small bandage over it. Next he turned to the class and said, "So, you see, pain is ultimately controlled by the cortex. Your brain can turn pain off or turn it on, depending on the circumstances. Under hypnosis, you can be made to perceive things that aren't there, and you can be made not to perceive even very strong stimuli. Let me show you what I mean."

Powell motioned Brian Healy to come toward him. "Now, Mr. McNeil, you surely remember what my teaching fellow, Brian Healy, looks like. Right?"

McNeil nodded slowly.

"Well, in a moment, Mr. NcNeil, I'm going to ask you to open your eyes. But when you do so, you simply won't be able to see Mr. Healy no matter where he is or what he does. Do you understand?"

Again the slow nod.

"Good. Now, please open your eyes."

Elvis McNcil blinked a couple of times and looked around cautiously.

"You can see me, right?" Powell asked, putting an arm around Brian Healy's shoulders. "But is there anyone else up here on the stage with me?"

McNeil said, "Only me. There's just you and me on the stage, Professor Powell."

"Right, absolutely right. Now, then, I want to help you open up the channels of your mind and tap the secret powers that lie dormant inside your skull. Would you like to learn those universal secrets, McNeil?"

"Yes, yes," Elvis cried loudly. "I want to learn the secrets of the universe! That's what I came to college for in the first place!"

"Then you should have taken this course sooner, right? Well, now, Mr. McNeil, let's begin by teaching you how to make things fly through the air just by willing them to do so. We'll begin with that empty straight chair on the other side of the stage. Do you think you can get it to float upward merely by giving it the mental command to rise?"

McNeil looked dubious. "If you say so . . ."

"Good," Powell said, motioning Brian Healy to grab hold of the empty chair, which was some 15 feet away from McNeil. "Now, Elvis, all you have to do is to concentrate. Concentrate with all the hidden power in your cortex. Order the chair to rise. Do so now. Talk to the chair— give it commands out loud, and then watch what happens when your concentration becomes deep enough!"

McNeil took a deep breath. "All right, chair, you're going to go sailing up into the blue like a toy balloon. Rise!"

As the young man spoke, Healy began to lift the chair slowly from the floor.

"Rise! Rise!" McNeil cried again.

The chair "rose" an inch or two each time McNeil urged it upward.

"Holy Moly, Professor Powell, it's working! What a trip!"

The chair suddenly dropped back onto the floor.

"You're not concentrating, McNeil. Keep your mind on the business at hand."

"Sorry, sir," McNeil said, and took another deep breath. "Okay, chair, let's float some more. Up, up and away!"

In Brian Healy's strong hands, the chair rose a foot off the stage.

"That's right, chair, keep going. Higher, higher, higher!"

Healy raised the chair above his head. Small beads of sweat began to pop out on his forehead. The chair was heavier than he had thought it would be.

"Higher! Higher!" McNeil screamed.

Quickly, Professor Powell interrupted. "That's high enough for the first time around, McNeil. We don't want to strain your cortex, after all. Why don't you tell it to dance instead?"

"Sure. I can do it. I know I can! Okay, chair, I want you to shake, rattle, and roll."

Healy twisted the chair over his head rhythmically, following the beat of some distant drummer.

Suddenly McNeil burst out laughing. "It's a rocking chair! That's what it is. A crazy chair that dances because I've got rock in my head!"

"Be serious, McNeil, or you'll ruin everything," Powell warned him sternly.

As if in sympathy, the chair came crashing down onto the stage, and Brian Healy collapsed into it.

The class went wild with applause. McNeil beamed, confident the clapping was for him. Brian Healy stood up and took a bow, but Elvis appeared not to notice it and just smiled happily at his fellow students.

"And now, Mr. McNeil, I want you to wake up as soon as I count to three," Professor Powell commanded. "Ready? One, two . . . THREE! You're awake!"

McNeil shook his head, then looked around slowly.

"Do you feel okay? Good," said Powell, not waiting for an answer. "And can you see Mr. Healy now?"

Elvis McNeil looked at the teaching fellow, then nodded. "Of course. He's right here on the stage with us."

"And how do you feel?"

"Fine, fine. But what happened? How did I get this bandage on my hand?"

"That's where I injected you with the secret powers. Don't you remember making the chair dance in the air?"

McNeil looked puzzled. "Oh, yes. I remember. How did I do that, Professor Powell?"

"Mind over matter, my boy. Concentration, that's what does the trick. Thank you very much for your assistance."

At that point, the bell rang, ending the class. Several students crowded around Professor Powell to ask questions. After he had answered as many as he could, he and Brian Healy headed back toward the office.

"What do you think the after-effects will be for poor Mr. McNeil?" Healy asked.

"After-effects?" Professor Powell said. "Why there won't be any. Elvis will find out what really happened, and he'll be embarrassed for a while. He's one of those students who takes psychology thinking that it's magic, or something. Now perhaps he'll see that the only way to unleash the powers of the mind is to study like crazy, learn all the facts about human nature, and then discover how to apply the facts wisely. Besides, we proved another point that's even more important—you perceive what your mind wants you to perceive. Beautiful demonstration, didn't you think so?"

Brian Healy scratched his head. "Sure, Professor Powell. Sure."

(Continued on page 334.)

MIND OVER MATTER

In the last chapter, we looked at *cognition*, both from a "bottom-up" and "top-down" point of view. When we discussed the information processing approach, we focused mostly on *input control*. And when we discussed the "top-down," or classical, view of cognition, we primarily emphasized such topics as reasoning, daydreaming, and problem solving. For the most part, these are *theoretical* matters.

In this chapter, we would like to show you how you can "use your mind" for many practical purposes, including the *voluntary control of pain and other unpleasant inputs*. As you will see, some of this control is from the "bottom up," while other parts of it work from the "top down."

If you are to understand how to "use your mind" to control the experience of pain, however, you will first have to learn what *pain* is all about.

Pain

The field of medicine has always attracted its share of quacks and **charlatans**—disreputable men and women with little or no medical knowledge who promise quick cures for painful conditions at very cheap prices. The reasons why quackery thrives even in modern times are not hard to find.

To begin with, *pain* seems to be a chronic human condition. John Bonica is the founder of the International Association for the Study of Pain. In a recent book, he estimates that nearly one-third of the people in the US have persistent or recurrent pain. According to Bonica, "Chronic pain disables more people than cancer or heart disease, and it costs the American people more money than both." He estimates the price we pay for pain in the US is more than $70 billion *each year* (Bonica, 1980).

The second reason that charlatans still are with us is this: Many people lack the training necessary to evaluate medical claims. Given the choice between (1) a reputable physician who says a cure for cancer will be long, difficult, painful, expensive, and may not work at all, and (2) a **patent remedy** salesman who says that five bottles of his "snake oil" will cure not only cancer, but tuberculosis, syphilis, warts, and bad breath as well, some individuals will opt for the five bottles of snake oil. Put more bluntly, many people are not trained to use the

"I HATE TO BRING THIS UP, DOCTOR, BUT THERE'S A RUMOR GOING AROUND THAT YOU'RE A QUACK."

problem-solving and reasoning skills we discussed in the previous chapter.

Some patent medicines actually work. But the "snake oil" remedies sold by quacks are mostly bad-tasting concoctions that are highly laced with alcohol or narcotic drugs. People often drink them to drown their pains in the rising tide of pleasant intoxication. Little wonder that "snake oil" is a popular cure-all for minor aches and hurts! (To give you some notion of just how popular quack remedies are, a 1984 report by the House Subcommittee on Health and Long-Term Care states that Americans spend $10 billion a year on "quack medicines.")

The Correlation Illusion

Another reason that quack cures remain popular is what we might call the "correlation illusion." We all learn in school that if event B always *follows* event A, then B and A are *correlated*. That's true. But we then go on to presume that A somehow *causes* B to take place. That is, we infer a *causal connection* between two events merely because they are "co-related." Yet if there is one point you should learn about *statistics* from this text, it is this: "Correlations don't imply causality."

To make this point clearer, suppose that you overindulge at dinner and end up with a nasty stomach ache. A friend of yours offers you a sure-fire cure—dried frog eyes mixed with chicken blood! You hold your nose, swallow a spoonful of the dreadful medicine, and go to bed as quickly as you can. The next morning the stomach ache is gone. A miracle? No, for chances are you would have felt much better anyhow after a good night's sleep. And yet, the fact that you (1) took the medicine, and (2) the pain later went away, might (3) give you the *illusion* that A had caused B to happen.

Merely because two events occur together frequently—that is, merely because the two events are correlated—doesn't prove that one causes the other. (For more information on this point, see the Statistical Appendix to this book.)

□ □ QUESTION □ □
What connection do you see between Pavlovian conditioning techniques and how the *correlation illusion* occurs in the human mind?

The Placebo Effect

By far the most potent reason that quack medicines still are sold around the world has to do with what scientists call the **placebo** effect. A placebo is a pill made of sugar or ordinary flour. It does no harm at all, but when prescribed by a physician, the placebo may actually reduce pain and promote healing. How can a "sugar pill" help you recover more speedily from an illness? There are several reasons—some psychological, some biological, some social, and some a mixture of all three.

● *Expectancy*
As we noted in Chapter 5, you see what you expect to see. You also *feel what you expect to feel*. Sherman Ross and L.W. Buckalew put it this way: "People have become accustomed to the belief that a drug represents potential relief from any undesirable psychological or physiological state . . . drugs, however obtained, spell relief" (Ross & Buckalew, 1985). If you are convinced that taking a pill will reduce your pain, chances are that you will *perceive* whatever pain you have as being less intense after you swallow that pill. Therefore, one reason why placebos "work" is that they alter the way you "process" pain signals coming from your body.

● *Traditional Attitudes and Locus of Control*
Sugar pills are more effective with some people than with others. Boston University researcher D.M. McNair and his colleagues report that people who hold traditional values and who are "socially acquiescent" respond more dramatically to placebos than do people who are "less conforming." After taking placebos, the "conformist" subjects reported significantly less tension, depression, physical distress,

While it is true that many over-the-counter pain relievers are effective, it is also true that minor aches and pains often go away by themselves in a matter of hours.

anger, confusion, and fatigue than did the controls (McNair *et al.*, 1984).

As we noted in Chapter 8, Julian Rotter has shown that people he calls externalizers believe their destiny is controlled by outside forces. Internalizers, on the other hand, see themselves as being responsible for what happens to them. Several studies suggest you are more likely to respond to a placebo if your "locus of personal control" is external than if it is internal (White, Tursky, & Schwartz, 1985). However, the reasons for this "responsiveness" in externalizers (and people with "traditional values") may be as much biological and social as intra-psychic.

● *Placebos and Endorphins*

In 1978, Howard Fields and his associates at the University of California in San Francisco asked volunteers to rate how much pain they experienced after having a tooth pulled. Then he gave placebos to the patients. About a third of them got almost immediate relief from taking the sugar pill. Fields calls these people "placebo reactors." The other two-thirds experienced little or no decrease in pain, and thus were "placebo non-reactors."

Once Fields had identified the two subgroups, he gave them both **naloxone.** (As we noted in Chapter 3, naloxone is a drug that counteracts the pain-killing effects of the endorphins released by the body in most stressful situations.) The "placebo reactors" reported an immediate *worsening* of their pain after receiving naloxone, but the "non-reactors" didn't.

Fields believes his study proves that placebos cause the brain to release a sudden surge of endorphins. But the "placebo effect" is only likely to work in certain people—namely, those of us who have been *conditioned* to secrete endorphins much as Pavlov's dogs were conditioned to secrete saliva when the bell rang (Fields, 1978).

□ □ **QUESTION** □ □
Given the data so far, what percentage of the general population would you guess are "externalizers"?

● *Endorphins and Learned Helplessness*

How do people become *conditioned* to secrete endorphins when stressed? We're not really sure. But evidence on animals tested in the "learned helplessness" situation suggests a method.

As you may recall from reading Chapter 8, dogs that were given unescapable shock soon learned to "give up." That is, they seemed to fall into a depression and thereafter refused to attempt to escape even when escape was obviously possible. Recent research suggests this "giving up" behavior is highly correlated with *two* biochemical events. First, when shocked, the animals secrete endorphins. Second, once "learned helplessness" has set in, secretion of nor-epinephrine (nor-adrenalin) is *inhibited*. If the animals are given naloxone, most of them *do not* "learn to be helpless." However, they still do not learn efficient escape behaviors (Maier *et al.*, 1980, 1983; Whitehouse *et al.*, 1983). If the animals are given drugs that increase the amount of nor-epinephrine in their bodies, though, they do tend to search for ways to escape (Algarel, 1985).

The sequence of events in the learned helplessness situation seems to be this: The animals are shocked after a warning signal is given, experience stress, secrete endorphins and nor-epinephrine, and try to escape. However, every attempt the animals make to flee not only fails, but is punished by the shock. Eventually the animals become exhausted, relax, and simply "take" the shock. The relaxation response inhibits further release of the arousal hormone, nor-epinephrine. After several trials, the warning signal becomes a conditioned stimulus that leads *both* to the release of endorphins *and* to a decreased secretion of nor-epinephrine. Thus, even when escape eventually becomes possible, the animal simply isn't motivated to flee the situation.

We will have more to say about the endorphins and personality later in the chapter. First, let's look at some research suggesting how placebo reactors can learn to "use their minds" to develop more effective ways of dealing with pain.

□ □ **QUESTION** □ □
Suppose a child has highly punitive parents who not only punish the child's mistakes, but also punish any attempt the child makes to escape parental wrath. What sorts of behavior patterns and personality traits might the child eventually develop?

Placebos and "Cognitive Coping Strategies"

In a recent article, California psychologists Perry London and David Engstrom make an interesting point about placebos: Their effectiveness as pain-killers seems to reach a peak after 3 weeks of use, then slowly tapers off. By the end of 10 weeks of use, placebos often are of little use. (London and Engstrom note that morphine-like drugs show the same drop-off in effectiveness.)

In an attempt to extend the effectiveness of placebos beyond 10 weeks, London and Engstrom attempted to teach patients with lower back pain how to use "cognitive coping strategies." But London and Engstrom did so only *after* they had proved to the patients that *placebos work.*

London and Engstrom worked with a large number of lower-back-pain patients. These individuals were told they would be receiving either placebos or "real" medication, but weren't told which they would get. The patients agreed to this test. London and Engstrom also gave the patients a "locus of pain control" questionnaire based on Rotter's "locus of personal control" test. The experimenters then selected 32 patients who seemed to be *externalizers* as far as their locus of pain control was concerned.

All 32 patients actually received placebos; none was given morphine. But all 32 reported considerable relief that "peaked" at the end of three weeks or so. At that point, London and Engstrom informed half the patients they had been given sugar pills. London and Engstrom further told the patients their *belief* in the treatment had actually been responsible for the pain reduction. The patients were told they could receive morphine "later on." But first, London and Engstrom offered to teach the patients *cognitive coping strategies* that would allow the patients to control their own pain voluntarily. All 16 patients in the experimental group agreed. The other 16 patients (the control group) continued to receive placebos without being told this was the case.

According to London and Engstrom, the experimental subjects reported *increased* pain relief after using these cognitive coping strategies for the next 10 weeks. However, the control group subjects reported *decreased* pain relief from just using the placebos. Indeed, by the end of the 10th week, the sugar pills were giving the control subjects no relief at all (London & Engstrom, 1982).

We will describe the actual techniques London and Engstrom used at the end of this chapter, as a way of demonstrating how cognitive processes can control sensory inputs in a "top down" fashion. First, however, let's look at another "top down" way of controlling pain, namely, *hypnosis*.

□□ **QUESTION** □□
What type of person do you think would be more easily hypnotized, a "placebo reactor" or a "placebo nonreactor"? Why?

ANTON MESMER AND THE DISCOVERY OF HYPNOSIS

One of the most famous quacks in all of medical history was a man named Anton Mesmer. Born in 1734 in a tiny Austrian village, Mesmer took degrees in theology and medicine at the University of Vienna (where Freud later taught). At the time that Mesmer began his medical practice, the prevailing view toward mental illness was that insanity was due to an imbalance of certain chemicals called **humors** (see Chapter 17). Mesmer rejected the humoral theory in favor of the even more "humorous" notion that the mind was strongly affected by magnetic radiation from outer space (Bloch, 1980).

• *"Cures" by Magnetism*
Mesmer lived at a time when magnetism and electricity were newly-discovered physical forces. At that time, people believed that the stars and planets radiated "magnetic fluids." Little wonder, then, that Mesmer thought that magnets could focus these "celestial fluids" on a sick person's body and thus restore the person to health.

One of Mesmer's first patients was a hysterical woman who complained of various pains, convulsions, and "agitations." When Mesmer "magnetized" her stomach and legs, the woman's pains vanished for several hours. Mesmer became so successful at these "magnetic cures" that he took to wearing odd clothes and soon announced that, through his techniques, "the art of healing reaches its final perfection" (Bloch, 1980).

Mesmer never guessed that his "cures" might be due to a cognitive activity that is often called *the power of suggestion*. But this expla-

Anton Mesmer became the rage of Paris in the late 1700's when he convinced people that "magnetic fluids" could heal illnesses. Rich Parisians flocked to Mesmer's salon to touch injured parts of their bodies to metal rods that stuck out of tubs filled with "magnetic fluids."

nation did occur to Mesmer's colleagues at the University of Vienna. They investigated his techniques and decided his "cures" were a product of imagination rather than magnetism. Mesmer was thereafter expelled from the university, fled Vienna, and set up shop in Paris.

● ### Mesmer's "Grand Crisis"

Paris in the 1780's was friendlier to Mesmer than Vienna had been, and he soon opened a healing salon that had in its center a huge tub containing "magnetized water." Twisted, oddly-shaped rods stuck out from all sides of the tub. Mesmer made his patients sit holding hands in a closed circle around the tub so the rods could touch the injured parts of their bodies. The rods supposedly directed the "magnetic fluids" toward the wound and thus promoted healing.

To help things along, Mesmer dressed in a long purple robe and walked around the tub, touching his patients with a wand. He frequently urged them to yield themselves up to the magnetic fluids that surrounded them, saying they would be cured if only they could focus on the heavenly powers within their sick bodies. Some of the patients apparently went into trance-like states. They would sit or stand as if frozen in place, apparently unseeing and unhearing.

Mesmer had, in fact, discovered *hypnosis*, but made no real scientific study of what the hypnotic state was like or what really induced it. Instead, he urged his clients "to reach farther into their minds." By continually pushing his patients psychologically, Mesmer drove many of them to reach what he called a "grand crisis," something we would call a *grand mal* convulsive seizure. Mesmer was convinced that the "grand crisis" was responsible for the cures his clients reported. Other medical doctors were not quite so sure.

Mesmerism, the name soon given to the technique for inducing a trance state, became exceptionally popular in Paris. The French government offered Mesmer a reward of 20,000 francs to reveal the secret of his "cures." When he refused, the government appointed two committees to investigate his techniques. Benjamin Franklin, then the US ambassador to France, was a member of one. The committees were unanimous in their public reports—Mesmerism was a hoax, and the cures were due to suggestion and imagination rather than to magnetism. The committees also sent a secret report to the French king, warning that the "grand crisis" was probably habit forming and dangerous to your health. Furthermore, they told the king, women seemed to be particularly susceptible to the "grand crisis" and could easily be seduced while in this state.

So Mesmerism was banned on moral as well as medical grounds. Mesmer retired to Versailles, a town near Paris, where he lived another 30 years—presumably basking in the magnetic radiations of the celestial bodies and, perhaps, occasionally trying to Mesmerize a peasant or two (Goldenson, 1970).

HYPNOSIS

Until fairly recently, most scientists considered hypnotism more of a parlor trick than a legitimate psychological phenomenon. However, a few dauntless physicians and psychologists over the years did try to study hypnosis objectively.

James Braid, a Scottish physician, gave *hypnosis* its present name in 1842. He took the term from the Greek word for "sleep." After attending a session held by a wandering Mesmerist, Braid became convinced that magnetic fluids had nothing to do with the effect. Rather, Braid felt, it was an abnormal or *intense form of sleep* that the hypnotist induced by somehow affecting certain centers in the subject's brain.

Shortly thereafter, Jean Charcot, a noted French professor of anatomy, began work in this field. Charcot soon reported he had found a close connection between hysteria and hypnosis. Other French scientists disputed Charcot's claims, believing that the hypnotic state was a result of **suggestibility**, not hysteria, although there seemed little doubt that hysterics often made good hypnotic subjects (Goldenson, 1970).

Freud and Hypnosis

It was into this sea of controversy that Sigmund Freud stepped in the winter of 1885. Freud had

According to the famous French scientist Charcot, hysterical women made the best hypnotic subjects.

Theodore X. Barber

spent several months working with Charcot in Paris. Following his return to Vienna, Freud used hypnosis to suggest to hysterics that their symptoms would vanish. But he soon ran into difficulties. For while the patients' symptoms did disappear, they usually came back again. Furthermore, Freud soon discovered that not all of his patients could be hypnotized. And those who could be hypnotized often became so dependent on his suggestions that they could not function in society unless they were under his hypnotic spell. For these reasons, Freud soon renounced hypnosis as a useless therapeutic tool (Parisi, 1987).

As Freud's influence grew, his negative opinions about hypnosis tended to discourage people from investigating the technique. It thus was not until the 1930's—when American behavioral psychologists took up the subject—that hypnosis again became a subject deemed fit for study in scientific laboratories.

□ □ **QUESTION** □ □

What similarities do you see between the return of hysterical symptoms "a few weeks after hypnosis" and the fact that placebos lose their power after a few weeks?

Under hypnosis, many subjects become insensitive to pain.

Suggestibility

What is hypnosis? Braid called it **somnambulism**, and thought it a form of sleep. As Frank McGuigan points out, however, the deep sleep that Braid described occurs in less than 1 percent of people who are hypnotized. Indeed, McGuigan says, "It seems clear that hypnosis is not just a state of concentration. Nor is it a state of relaxation. . . . Two centuries after the discovery of artificial somnambulism, the only consensus seems to be that if there *is* a unique state of hypnosis, it is not sleep" (McGuigan, 1987).

The early behaviorists believed hypnosis was a state of narrowly focused attention in which the hypnotized person somehow becomes extremely *suggestible*. Clark L. Hull, the noted learning theorist, made a lengthy study of suggestibility and hypnosis. Hull was hunting for some simple test that would quickly tell who would be a good hypnotic subject. Perhaps because he looked at observable behaviors rather than at a person's "fantasy life," Hull was unable to find any one trait that was a sure-fire index of hypnotizability (Hull, 1933).

● *Suggestibility and Fantasy*

Several years ago, Theodore X. Barber developed a Suggestibility Scale that he uses in his research. The major questions on the Scale have to do with your ability to *imagine* yourself in a variety of unusual situations. One of the primary traits that the Scale seems to measure is the ease with which you can create mental fantasies (Barber, 1969).

In a recent study, Barber and Scheryl Wilson found that many women who are excellent hypnotic subjects—and who score high on Barber's Scale—seem to have spent much of their adult lives lost in a world of fantasy. Most of these women began to fantasize early in life, as an escape from an unhappy childhood. As children they tended to have imaginary companions, and almost all of them believed their dolls and stuffed animals were actually alive. The majority of these women reported they sometimes had orgasms solely through sexual fantasy. But despite the fact that they spent "at least 90 percent of the time" lost in fantasy, these women were quite successful. All were either college students or graduates. One was a psychiatrist, another a psychologist, and all but one were married or had steady boyfriends (Wilson & Barber, 1980).

Barber's research suggests there is a high correlation between the ability to "fantasize" and the ability to be hypnotized. As Barber notes, however, the fact that you are "suggestible" or are "addicted to fantasy" doesn't mean you can't live a happy and productive life. Furthermore, in a recent study, Ohio psychologists Steven Lynn and Judith Rhue note that while people with rich fantasy lives do make good hypnotic subjects, many individuals who are not "fantasy prone" also fall into hypnotic trances rather readily (Lynn & Rhue, 1988).

□□ **QUESTION** □□
What is the relationship between being able to "fantasize" and being able to "dissociate yourself" from the aches and pains of reality?

● *Imagination and Parental Punishment*
Data gathered by Ernest Hilgard, Josephine Hilgard, and their associates at Stanford tend to support Barber's views on the close connection between suggestibility and fantasy. The Hilgards' research suggests that the response you make to a hypnotist is partially determined by the type of upbringing you had. For example, Josephine Hilgard and Samuel LeBaron report that, if your parents were inclined to punish you severely and frequently when you were young, chances are that you will be able to "go under" in a hypnotic trance rather easily (Hilgard & LeBaron, 1984). And Lynn and Rhue note that the fantasizers they studied "recollected being physically abused and punished to a greater degree than other subjects did and reported experiencing greater loneliness and isolation as children" (Lynn & Rhue, 1988).

Ernest Hilgard gives three reasons why there is a correlation between a punitive upbringing and suggestibility. First, continual punishment can *condition* you to respond to authority automatically and without questioning what you are told to do. Second, you may learn to escape parental wrath by retreating into your own imagination. And third, you may find you can prevent punishment by learning to play various social roles (Hilgard, 1986). We will have more to say about this last point in a moment.

□□ **QUESTION** □□
Julian Rotter reports that most externalizers had punitive parents. Why isn't this fact particularly surprising?

● *Effects of Hypnosis*
One of the fascinating aspects of hypnosis is that people often *seem* to do things while hypnotized that they couldn't (or wouldn't) do otherwise. Thus, individuals may perform *apparently* amazing feats of strength or withstand apparently large amounts of pain *if told to do so* while hypnotized (Zilbergeld, Edelstein, & Araoz, 1986).

However, as Theodore Barber notes, there is a strange quality of *role playing* to most of these feats. After studying the literature on the subject—and after testing many subjects in his laboratory—Barber comes to quite a different conclusion: Under hypnosis, you will only perform those acts that you *would perform normally* if the situation were right, and if your

motivation were high enough. But even these factors are not usually enough. Barber states the major factor in hypnotic performance is the subject's *intense desire to please the hypnotist* (Barber, 1969).

□□ **QUESTION** □□
Who would be more likely to want to please an "authority figure" (such as a hypnotist), an externalizer or an internalizer? Why?

Hypnotic Age Regression

The early behaviorists were particularly impressed with the rapid access that hypnosis seemed to give to a person's early-life memories. For instance, while in a deep trance, subjects apparently could "relive" certain events of childhood. When told to "go back" to her fifth birthday, for instance, a young woman might begin to talk in a very childish voice. She would then recount in detail who was at her birthday party, what presents she got, what her parents said and did, and even what she dreamed later that night (Barber, 1970).

A few hypnotic subjects went much farther. When pressed to do so, some of them reported detailed conversations they thought had occurred between their mothers and fathers while they themselves were still being carried in the womb. Other subjects recounted events that happened to them centuries before, when they were seemingly *living in a different body*. The "memory feats" these people performed under **hypnotic age regression** seemed fabulous indeed to those early psychologists who had not yet discovered the connection between hypnosis and fantasy.

● *Age Regression and Expectations*
In a recent article, University of Kentucky psychologist Robert Baker reports a study on hypnotic age regression. Baker used 60 students whom he knew were good hypnotic subjects. He divided the 60 students into three groups. The first group heard a tape recording about a "new and exciting kind of therapy known as *past lives therapy*." These students were also told, "You will be able to take a fascinating journey back in time." Under hypnosis, 85 percent of this group reported having had at least one other life.

A second group of 20 students heard a neutral description of "past lives therapy." These subjects were told, "You may or may not drift back in time to another lifetime." Under hypnosis, 60 percent of this group claimed they had lived another life.

A third group of 20 students were told that "past lives therapy" was a crazy sort of game developed "by a bunch of far-out therapists on the West Coast." The students were also warned that, under hypnosis, "You might acci-

Robert A. Baker

dentally drift back and imagine you're living in another lifetime." However, "Most normal people haven't been able to see anything." During their hypnosis sessions, only 10 percent of the students in this group reported having had another life.

According to Robert Baker, his research shows how readily people will "role play extreme [age] regressions on demand" (Baker, 1982).

• Hypnosis and Memory

Many police agencies now routinely make use of hypnosis in criminal investigations. In particular, the police hypnotize witnesses to help them recall details of events that seem lost to ordinary memory. Martin Reiser of the LA Police Department claims that in 77 percent of the cases where hypnosis was used, "Important information was elicited from witnesses and victims that was not available by routine interrogation" (cited in Dellinger, 1978).

However, most psychologists now take rather a dim view of the use of hypnosis by the police. In a recent interview, Ernest Hilgard states, "It is well-known that hypnotists may implant memories, so that the hypnotized person accepts them as his [or her] own" (Hilgard, 1986). And Martin Orne, past president of the International Society of Hypnosis, notes that what people remember under hypnosis is often *completely inaccurate* (cited in Turkington, 1982).

To summarize, the major reasons that evidence obtained under hypnosis is not admitted in most courtrooms are the following:

1. While hypnotized, witnesses often report "as fact" events that simply did not occur (Dellinger, 1978).
2. Once a witness reports (under hypnosis) a false memory of "the facts," the witness's *confidence* in the "truth" of the report often increases dramatically (Turkington, 1982).
3. The more confident a witness is, the more likely it is that jurors will believe the witness (Wells & Lindsay, 1983).

□ □ **QUESTION** □ □
As we noted in Chapter 11, Elizabeth Loftus has shown that the questions you ask someone about an event can actually *transform* the person's memories. What problems does Loftus's research raise about the use of hypnotism by various police agencies to "recover forgotten memories"?

Hypnosis and Pain

Theodore X. Barber believes that hypnosis is mostly a matter of "role playing." In particular, Barber uses this idea to explain the effects of hypnosis on pain (Barber, 1970). We will return to Barber's beliefs momentarily. First, though, let's review research by Ernest Hilgard, who takes quite a different view of hypnosis than Barber does.

• Hilgard's Research

In a series of recent studies, Ernest Hilgard has shown that, while under hypnosis, a subject may both experience pain and simultaneously *not* feel it.

In one of his experiments, Hilgard asked 20 volunteers to hold their arms in ice water for 45 seconds (see Fig. 13.1). The water was painfully cold—as the subjects reported only too willingly if they were not hypnotized. Hilgard then "suggested" that they try consciously to control their experience of pain. Most of them were able to do so and now reported much less pain than before.

Next Hilgard hypnotized the subjects and suggested they would feel *no pain at all* from the ice water. While their arms were in the water, Hilgard asked them if they experienced pain. The subjects told him, "Some, but not much." Then Hilgard asked them to move a finger on the hand *not* in the water if the subjects *really* felt the pain at some "unconscious level." Most of the subjects immediately did so. Hilgard believes that *consciously* the subjects were suppressing the pain. But at some deeper

FIG. 13.1 Ernest Hilgard measuring the pain response of a subject whose arm is immersed in ice water.

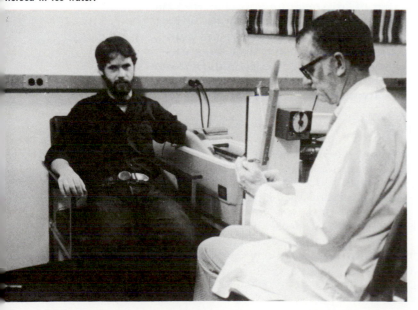

level, Hilgard says, they apparently knew the pain was really there (Hilgard, 1978).

● **"Hidden Observers"**

Hilgard believes hypnosis is an *altered state of consciousness* in which your consciousness can "split." One part of you acts in a hypnotized fashion and experiences no pain if the hypnotist tells you not to. But another part of your mind—which can communicate by gestures during the trance—remains unhypnotized and perceives the discomfort your conscious mind is repressing. Hilgard calls this part of the mind the subject's "hidden observer" (Hilgard, 1986).

As we will see in Chapter 18, this "splitting of the mind" is very similar to the *dissociation*—popularly called "split personality"—that is occasionally found in mentally-disordered individuals. Usually, when one personality "takes over," it temporarily *suppresses* any other personality patterns the person has. According to Hilgard, this same dissociation of personality may occur in normal individuals during hypnosis.

In a recent book, University of Utah psychiatrist Eugene Bliss states that multiple-personality patients "invariably are excellent hypnotic subjects." Bliss notes that many patients with multiple personalities "display a variety of dissociative states," and that most of these individuals have a history of physical, sexual, or psychological abuse that is associated with dissociation (Bliss, 1986).

□ □ **QUESTION** □ □

Earlier in this chapter, we mentioned Josephine Hilgard's research showing that children escape parental wrath by retreating into their own imaginations. How do all these facts suggest that overly punitive parents may actually *train* their children to have a very simple type of "split personality"?

● **Is Hypnosis an "Altered State of Consciousness"?**

Theodore X. Barber disagrees with Hilgard's definition of hypnosis as an "altered state of consciousness." He believes Hilgard's subjects may be unconsciously "faking" the presence of a *hidden observer*, just as people unconsciously "fake" any experience they think the hypnotist may want them to have.

In fact, Barber seriously doubts whether "hypnosis" actually exists! In a recent paper, Barber points out that Hilgard seems to define hypnosis in rather a circular way. "How do you know a man is in a hypnotic trance? Because he responds to suggestions. And why does he respond to suggestions? Because he is hypnotized!" According to Barber, hypnotism is actually made up of equal parts of (1) "role playing" and (2) learning how to control the way in which you *perceive* your sensory inputs (Barber, 1978).

● **"Conscious Strategies" for Controlling Pain**

Over the past 20 years, Barber has conducted a series of studies in which he has taught people *conscious strategies* for reducing the intensity of pain. Some of these strategies are more effective than others, but the best of them seem to reduce pain at least as much as does a hypnotic trance.

For example, in one study, Barber asked subjects to immerse their hands in extremely cold water. Some of the subjects were *not* hypnotized, but were urged to try the sorts of "cognitive strategies for coping with pain" that Perry London and David Engstrom used with patients given placebos. Another group of subjects was given similar instructions while hypnotized. By all measures of "painfulness," the *cognitive strategies* for reducing pain were at least as effective as was hypnosis.

Barber concludes that, since hypnosis is no better as an **analgesic** than is "mental discipline," perhaps we should discard "hypnosis" entirely as a psychological concept (Barber, 1978). Not all psychologists agree with Barber, and the matter is far from settled (Waxman *et al.*, 1985).

Despite the argument over what hypnosis is (and isn't), one thing seems amply clear: While under a hypnotic trance, a number of individuals gain the ability to *control the experience of pain*. Before we can discuss hypnosis further, therefore, we must face squarely a problem that we rather delicately ignored in Chapter 4—namely, what is *pain*?

□ □ **QUESTION** □ □

One "cognitive strategy" Barber teaches is that of "dissociating yourself from the pain." If you do so successfully, which part of you is experiencing the pain, and which part isn't? How does this question bear on the argument between Hilgard and Barber as to whether hypnosis is an "altered state"?

PAIN

A century ago, most sensory psychologists believed there were four unique psychological experiences you could get from stimulating your skin—warmth, cold, pressure, and *pain*. Each of these four experiences was thought to be mediated by a specific type of receptor or nerve ending buried somewhere in your skin. But further study turned up some troubling facts:

First, there is the problem of what *receptors* mediate pain. Research shows there are

Analgesic (an-al-GEE-sick). Any substance that reduces or "kills" pain. See Chapter 4.

Enigma (ee-NIGG-mah). From the Greek word meaning "to speak in riddles." Winston Churchill once said, "I cannot forecast to you the action of Russia. It is a riddle wrapped in a mystery inside an enigma."

skin receptors that are primarily concerned with temperature sensations, and other receptor cells that mediate the experience of pressure. But no one ever found a nerve ending that was *solely concerned* with the sensation of pain.

Second, there is the problem of where in the brain painful inputs are processed. Investigations of the parietal lobe uncovered parts of the *somatic cortex* that, when stimulated electrically, give rise to the experience of pressure or temperature (see Fig. 13.2). But no one ever found a part of the parietal lobe whose stimulation produced *pain*. Nor has a "pain input center" been found anywhere on the surface of the cerebral hemispheres (Wall, 1979).

Every other type of sensation—vision, hearing, taste, smell, and "touch"—has both specific receptors and specific input areas in the cortex. What an **enigma** pain is, then, since it has *neither* special receptors nor cortical projection areas!

Furthermore, pain simply does not yield the same sort of *psychological experiences* that most other sensory inputs do. As pain expert Patrick Wall pointed out a decade ago, when you touch a warm object, you perceive the warmth as being *in the object,* not in your skin. And if you look at a sunset, you perceive the colors as being in the sky, not in your eyes. However, Wall says, if you jab your finger with a pin, you experience the pain as a quality that is *in you,* not in the pin. Wall believes that pain is a *need state*, like hunger or thirst, not a *sensation* like light or warmth or sound (Wall, 1979).

Were it not for one more troubling fact, we might be tempted to agree with Wall that pain is not a "true" sensory input like warmth or pressure. It is true that we don't know how the pain signal gets started in the skin, nor have we discovered where the signal ends up in the brain. However, we are quite sure how painful inputs get from the "non-existent receptors" to the "invisible locus in the brain"! For scientists

FIG. 13.2 The cerebrum, showing the parietal lobe.

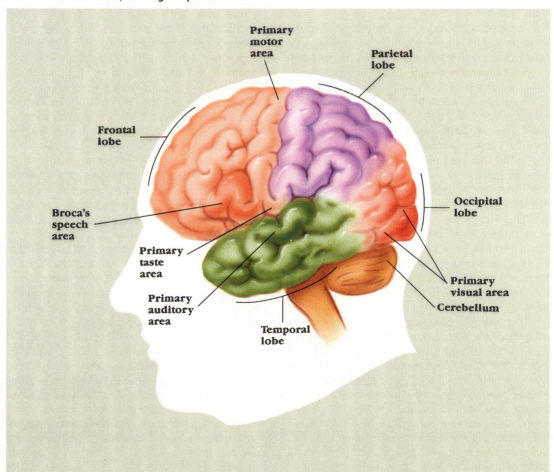

long ago proved that pain sensitivity is quite well represented in the *spinal cord* (Melzack, 1983).

• Spinal Pathways

Your spinal cord contains *input* pathways that run from your body to your brain, and *output* pathways that run from your brain back to your body. Certain types of diseases that affect the spinal cord often give rise to continuous and vicious pain that can be relieved only by *cutting* some of the sensory pathways going up the spinal cord from the skin receptors (Gibson, 1982). So pain obviously is an "input" message of some kind. But what kinds of stimulation set it off? And why do drugs like the endorphins—which have their primary effects in the brain and not the spinal cord—reduce the experience of pain?

We will answer the drug-related question (as best we can) in just a moment. First, let's turn our attention to sensory stimulation as it moves from the skin up the spinal cord. For, if you are to understand why pain hurts as it does—and why placebos, hypnosis, and "cognitive strategies" can sometimes reduce or alleviate the pain—we must take another (very quick) look at how your skin receptors operate.

Fast and Slow Fibers

The basket cells and the encapsulated nerve endings in your skin send their messages to your brain primarily by way of special pathways in your spinal cord. The axons of these cells have an *insulating sheath* wrapped around them. As we noted in Chapter 2, this sheath is actually a special type of "support cell." Because this support cell insulates the electrical impulses that pass along the axon, the speed with which the neural messages flow is *faster* in these fibers than in nerves that lack this insulation. Insulated fibers are called **fast fibers** (Kimble, 1987).

The free nerve endings, on the other hand, send their messages up your cord *slowly* by way of uninsulated axons. Since neural messages travel about 30 times slower in your uninsulated nerve tracts than in the "fast fibers," the uninsulated neurons are called **slow fibers**.

If you implant an electrode in the *fast fibers* of someone's spinal cord and stimulate these nerve cells directly, the person typically will report "pressury" feelings. If you stimulate the *slow fibers* instead, the person might report feeling pressure or temperature changes. But if the current was intense enough, the person might also report feeling *pain* from slow-fiber stimulation. However, if you stimulate both fast and slow fibers *simultaneously*, the person will not feel pain no matter how intense the slow-fiber stimulation is. Apparently slow-fiber activity turns pain *on*, but fast-fiber activity somehow turns it *off* (Melzack, 1983)!

The best guess as to why this "stimulation analgesia" occurs has to do with *channel capacity* (see Chapter 12). The lower brain centers (at the top of the spinal cord) can process only so many inputs per second. Fast-fiber activity overwhelms these centers, so they "turn the switch" and screen out slow-fiber activity—and hence pain. You get the same sort of effect when you "scratch where it itches." The massive fast-fiber activity associated with scratching apparently overwhelms the mildly-painful "itch input" (Melzack, 1979).

□□ **QUESTION** □□
How do the data on slow- and fast-fiber activity in the spinal cord support Broadbent's "bottleneck theory" of attention (see Chapter 12)?

• The Puzzle of Pain

What is pain?

Because of the spinal cord data we've just discussed, some psychologists continue to classify pain as a sensory modality like warmth and pressure. Other scientists believe it is a *warning signal* that you experience whenever your senses are stressed or damaged. But in a recent book, pain specialists Arnold Holzman and Dennis Turk define pain as a "complex phenomenon that is the product of the interaction of [injurious] sensory stimulation, psychological factors . . . and socioenvironmental factors" (Holzman & Turk, 1986).

Why the confusion about what pain is? Perhaps, as Holzman and Turk point out, it's because specialists tend to define pain *in terms of how they prefer to treat it*. Some experts prescribe pills; others prefer using "cognitive strategies." Both techniques work—with some kinds of people, in some types of situations. Could there, in fact, be *two separate kinds of pain*—or, at the very least, *two separate ways of controlling pain*? Some very important facts suggest this may indeed be the case:

Naloxone destroys the pain relief that comes from taking either placebos or morphine.

However, naloxone does *not* destroy the pain relief associated with hypnosis, fast-fiber stimulation, or the use of "cognitive strategies."

These two facts—and many others—suggest that the body must have *two separate mechanisms for controlling pain*. One mechanism seems to involve a release of endorphins under stress (Terman *et al.*, 1984). Naloxone affects this pain-control system. The other mechanism apparently involves a "blocking" of painful inputs at the level of the spinal cord (Melzack & Wall, 1965). Naloxone apparently has little or no effect on this second pain-control system.

Fast fibers, slow fibers. Neural messages travel along axonic fibers at different speeds, depending on the thickness of the fibers and whether or not the axon is insulated by a Schwann cell (see Chapter 3). Uninsulated fibers are "thin and slow": Sensory inputs travel along these fibers at a speed of about 10 feet per second. Some insulated fibers are so thick and fast that messages flow along the axons at about 300 feet per second or more.

Spinal gate. "To gate something out" means "to keep something from entering." Melzack and Wall believe there is a nerve center in the spinal cord that "gates out" some sensations and lets others through to the brain. No one has yet located the "spinal gate" precisely or determined how it works.

As you will see, the two pain-control mechanisms differ in a number of important ways.

Two Separate Pain-control Systems

Linda Watkins and David Mayer were among the first scientists to conclude that, because the body "processes" painful inputs in two distinct ways, there must be two separate pain-control systems (Watkins & Mayer, 1982).

To help you understand the important differences between these two systems, let's see what happens when pain occurs. Suppose you accidentally step on a sharp tack. Immediately, the skin receptors in your foot will send a signal up your spinal cord—via the slow fibers—that some "damage" has occurred. As we mentioned in Chapter 12, this painful input message "splits" when it reaches the top of your spinal cord. The *sensory information* (about stepping on the tack) is passed on to your parietal cortex by way of the straight-line sensory system. However, the *emotional significance* of the input is processed by your reticular system.

Since the painful input reaches your cortex by *two distinct neural pathways*, doesn't it make sense to theorize that there might be two separate systems for *controlling* the experience of pain? Let's call them the *emotion-suppressing system* and the *input-blocking system*.

The Emotion-suppressing System

According to Watkins and Mayer, the emotion-suppressing system is a stress-related, "general alarm" mechanism for controlling pain. The parts of the brain involved in this type of response are the reticular system and the autonomic nervous system (Watkins & Mayer, 1982).

When a painful input reaches your reticular system, the input triggers off activity in your autonomic nervous system. But your body also *protects you against pain* by secreting endorphins (and other related substances) that *slow down* activity in the autonomic nervous system. You *experience* this reduced neural activity as a decrease in the "emotional significance" of the painful input.

Watkins and Mayer believe that the *emotion-suppressing pain-control system* is easily

conditioned using Pavlovian techniques. Thus, externalizers (who have learned to release endorphins "on demand") react to placebos, but internalizers don't.

□ □ **QUESTION** □ □

As we mentioned in Chapter 9, Pavlov trained a dog to withstand physical discomfort by using pain as a signal the dog was about to be fed. Why might the dog not have experienced much conscious pain during this training?

The Input-blocking System

As we noted earlier, painful inputs go up the spinal cord by way of the slow fibers. However, the inputs can be blocked at the top of the spinal cord by activity in the fast fibers. This fact suggests there is a "neural switch" of some kind at the top of the spinal cord that can turn pain "on" or "off." Ronald Melzack of McGill University and Patrick Wall of University College in London call this switch the **spinal gate** (Melzack & Wall, 1965).

According to Melzack and Wall, activity in the fast fibers "closes the spinal gate." And when the spinal gate is closed, painful inputs never reach *either* the cortex (via the straight-line system) *or* the autonomic nervous system (via the reticular system). Put more simply,

What reasons can you think of for the fact that athletes engage in painful activities on a regular basis, yet they do not report experiencing pain?

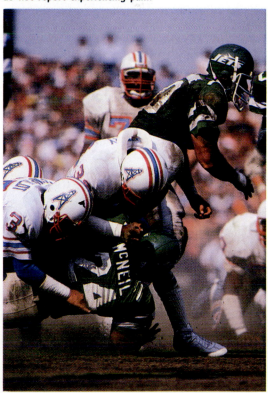

TABLE 13.1   A Comparison of Two Hypothetical Pain-Control Systems

	Emotion-suppressing System	*Input-blocking System*
Neural mechanisms	Reticular system, autonomic nervous system	Fast-fiber activity "closes spinal gate"
Chemical mechanisms	Endorphins and related substances	Unknown
Psychological mechanisms	Stress-related release of endorphins may become conditioned via Pavlovian conditioning	Cortical control of spinal gate may occur via operant conditioning
Psychological effects	Decreases emotional arousal; hence decreases emotional significance of input	Blocks input; hence prevents both emotional arousal and consciousness of input
Other aspects	Explains placebo effect	Explains analgesia associated with hypnosis, dissociation, and "cognitive strategies"

when the spinal gate is closed, you neither become conscious of the painful input, nor do you respond to it emotionally.

Using data from both humans and animals, Melzack and Wall showed the spinal gate can be closed by fast-fiber stimulation. This type of "input blocking" is an innate response to activity in the fast fibers. However, according to Linda Watkins and David Mayer, the *cortex* can also *learn* to "close the spinal gate." According to Watkins and Mayer, acquiring voluntary control over the spinal gate seems to involve operant (or Skinnerian) conditioning, not Pavlovian conditioning (Watkins & Mayer, 1982).

To summarize: The input-blocking system shuts out pain by "closing the spinal gate" so the painful stimulus reaches neither the reticular system nor the cortex. Fast-fiber activity is the "natural, unlearned" way to close the gate. However, by using a variety of "cognitive strategies" (including hypnosis), your cortex can gain operant control over the spinal gate (see Table 13.1).

□□ **QUESTION** □□

Hypnosis is sometimes described as "an abnormal narrowing of the focus of attention." What clues does this definition give as to the *mechanism* by which hypnosis reduces the experience of pain?

Cognitive Strategies for Controlling Pain

Now that we have described the two pain-control systems in some detail, perhaps we can begin to make sense out of the various strategies scientists have developed to help people gain "top-down" relief from the subjective experience of pain.

Perry London and David Engstrom list four "cognitive strategies" for pain control. The first seems aimed mostly at activating the emotion-suppressing system, while the other three appear to involve the input-blocking system (London & Engstrom, 1982).

□□ **QUESTION** □□

Which of the two pain-control systems would be more effective for reducing chronic pain? (Hint: The emotion-suppressing system influences the *significance* of the input. What does the input-blocking system do?)

- **Relaxation**

London and Engstrom note that anything which reduces stress will usually give immediate reduction in pain. The first thing to do, therefore, is to learn how to relax. Reduce tension in all the muscles of your body that you can, by "going limp." Also, try to slow down your breathing, and breathe through your abdomen, not your chest. This technique may well activate the emotion-suppressing system, and may also lead to the release of endorphins.

- **Counter Conditioning through Mental Imagery**

London and Engstrom suggest that you learn to use pain as a stimulus that will automatically evoke a pleasurable mental image. Imagine yourself floating comfortably in a warm pool, listening to peaceful music. Then, whenever you feel pain, immediately try to call up your image of the peaceful pool. Since you can't experience "warm comfort" and "discomfort" at the same time, you will have counter-conditioned yourself against the pain.

Or, you may wish to try transferring the pain to a different part of your body. If you have pain in your left arm, imagine that it's in your right arm instead. Then move it slowly down your right arm to your fingers. Finally, imagine the pain trickling out of your fingers. This "dissociation" technique is, of course, the type of "cognitive strategy" most people use when they "disregard" pain while hypnotized.

● Self-instruction

London and Engstrom believe that "self-talk" is an important cognitive method for cutting off pain. Remind yourself that you can "switch pain off" whenever you wish. Try to make the pain "hurt less" bit by bit, and then give yourself a mental pat on the back for succeeding. Train yourself to be more positive in your approach to others, and encourage them to be more positive toward your attempts at self-control. This type of strategy, too, seems to involve "conditioned dissociation."

● Monitoring Yourself (and Others)

Keep a log or chart that shows graphically how well you've gotten in controlling your pain. If you wish, you may arrange to have someone reward you for getting better at reducing your discomfort. Or, simply take pride in your own success.

Also, try to determine the response that the people around you make to your symptoms of pain. Your family and friends may unconsciously be rewarding you for expressing (and experiencing) pain. Or you may be using the pain as a way to control others—to get out of work or to avoid facing up to important interpersonal problems. Use direct coping strategies to work through these issues as best you can.

□ □ **QUESTION** □ □

Go back to the final pages of Chapter 6 and look over the plan for weight reduction offered there. What similarities do you see between learning to control caloric intake and learning to control pain? What do these similarities tell you about the general problem of "self-control"?

The Development of Pain-control Strategies

Perhaps the most important thing the study of pain teaches us is this: You can reduce the stings and arrows of life in two ways—from the bottom up, or from the top down.

If you attack the problem *from the bottom up*, you will either take pain-killers or learn to release endorphins whenever you're stressed. This approach reduces the *unpleasantness* associated with *acute* pain, but tends to lose its effectiveness after a few weeks.

However, if you adopt the *top down* approach, you will need to learn "cognitive strategies" for blocking out painful inputs. You can still take pain-killers to handle the immediate onset of pain, but you can switch to using cognitive control if the pain becomes chronic.

The approach you *presently* use is very likely a mix of "bottom up" and "top down" methods for coping with discomfort. You probably adopted this approach in part because of a genetic bias of some sort. But the most important influence surely is your past experience, particularly what happened to you during your early developmental years. As both Hilgard and Barber have shown, children whose parents were punitive tend to adopt "bottom up" strategies involving conditioned release of endorphins and "conditioned dissociation" (such as fantasy). Children whose parents emphasized positive self-control skills are more likely to use "top down" strategies involving conscious monitoring of the consequences of their thoughts and actions.

Last, but surely not least, knowing the influence that parents have on children, you might well think carefully about the ways in which you plan to teach your own children to respond to (and control) pain.

Of course, it would help if you knew a bit more about how children usually grow up and mature. So, it is to the topic of *developmental psychology* that we now turn our attention.

SUMMARY

1. According to a leading pain researcher, almost one-third of all Americans have persistent or recurring chronic **pain**.

2. Physicians have known for centuries that a **placebo** can be very effective in reducing pain—if the patient believes that the placebo is some powerful medicine.

3. Placebos work, in part, because they cause the release of **endorphins**. However, this **analgesic effect** occurs primarily in **externalizers**, people with **traditional attitudes**, and **social conformers**.

4. The **effectiveness** of placebos tends to diminish after 3–10 weeks. However, **cognitive coping strategies** can be effective for longer periods of time.

5. **Hypnotism** was made famous in the late 1700's by Anton Mesmer, who thought he could "cure" his patients by putting them in a **trance state**.

6. Sigmund Freud used hypnosis to "reduce pain" with **hysterical patients**, but abandoned the technique because it didn't always work.

7. Clark Hull and the early behaviorists believed that hypnosis was a state of narrowly focused attention in which the subject became extremely **suggestible**.

8. T.X. Barber has shown that people with rich **fantasy lives** often make good hypnotic subjects.

9. Ernest and Josephine Hilgard believe that people with **punitive parents** often resort to fantasy as a way of **dissociating** themselves psychologically from parental wrath.

10. Under hypnosis, you may perform **unusual feats** of mind and body—but nothing that you couldn't do anyhow if **highly motivated**. The primary motivation for performing these feats seems to be a strong desire to **please the hypnotist**.

11. Subjects undergoing **hypnotic age regression** often act as if they had access to **past lives** or forgotten memories. Most of these experiences can be explained as a type of **role playing** engaged in to please the hypnotist.

12. Under hypnosis, **witnesses** to a crime often report events that simply did not occur.

13. Hilgard believes that, under hypnosis, the mind "dissociates" and that painful inputs not experienced by the conscious mind are felt by a **hidden observer**.

14. Barber believes that hypnosis is not an **altered state of consciousness**, and that Hilgard's data can better be explained in terms of **role playing**.

15. A century ago, pain was thought to be a sensory input similar to pressure, temperature, sights, and smells. Recent studies suggest that pain is a **need state** or **sensory warning signal** rather than a sensory modality.

16. Pressure sensations are carried up your spinal cord by insulated **fast fibers**. Temperature sensations are carried by uninsulated **slow fibers**.

17. If stimulation from the slow fibers is greater than the stimulation from the fast fibers, the brain usually experiences pain. However, fast-fiber stimulation can **close the spinal gate** and thus prevent painful inputs from reaching the brain.

18. The fact that **naloxone** counteracts the analgesic effects of placebos but not of hypnotism and "cognitive strategies" for controlling pain suggests the body has two separate **pain-control systems**.

19. The **emotion-suppressing system** involves the release of the **endorphins** as a natural reaction to stress. However, release of endorphins can become associated with neutral stimuli such as **placebos** by Pavlovian conditioning.

20. The **input-blocking system** involves shutting inputs out before they reach the brain by closing the **spinal gate**. Voluntary control over the spinal gate is acquired by **operant conditioning**, and apparently explains the analgesic effect of **hypnosis, dissociation**, and **cognitive strategies** for reducing chronic pain.

Assistant Professor Don Powell and his teaching fellow, Brian Healy, were correcting exam papers in Powell's office when a loud knock at the door interrupted their work. *(Continued from page 320.)*

"Come in!" Powell cried.

When Elvis McNeil walked through the door, the psychologist paled momentarily. Recovering quickly, Powell forced a broad smile. "Come in, Mr. McNeil. Sit down! Why, we haven't seen you for several days! Wherever have you been?"

McNeil sat confidently in the chair that Powell had indicated. "Reading everything I could find about the powers of the mind, sir."

Powell seemed a little flustered. "Er, well, yes. Very interesting. We were afraid that you were angry about the little hypnosis demonstration we put on in class. I do hope you haven't stayed away from class because of some juvenile embarrassment . . ."

"Embarrassment? Of course not, sir! The very opposite."

"Then you aren't angry with us?"

"Certainly not, Professor. I came to thank you—and to ask for your help. You see, I've always been convinced I had a strong mind, that I had hidden talents which I simply couldn't bring out into the open and gain control of."

Powell and Healy looked at each other uneasily.

"Yes, Professor Powell," McNeil said, leaning toward the psychologist. "Even before I took your class, I had searched through all the occult literature. I answered ads in the magazines that offered to make me a mental giant if I would purchase a set of their long-suppressed secrets. I read the life histories of the mystics and tried to tap the power of the stars through astrology. But none of it worked very well. And then . . . and then, you opened the doors to my perception! You transported me to the pinnacles of power!"

Powell glanced sternly at Brian Healy, who was struggling valiantly to suppress a grin.

"Yes, well, I'm sure that's one way to look at it," Powell said hurriedly. "No harm done, then . . ."

"Oh, no. No harm at all. You see, I was sure I could really make the chair float around and dance without any help from you, if only I could find the key that would unlock my latent mental energies. Hypnosis did it, as you saw for yourself. So I've been reading all the books I could find on using hypnotism to unleash cortical forces."

Brian Healy made a noise suspiciously like a muffled giggle.

"The trouble is," Elvis McNeil continued, "I can't seem to regain the powers I had while hypnotized that day in class. I mean, I've tried and tried. I've talked to one chair after another, and none of them will float—not even an inch. I feel I'm getting extremely close to the mental break-through I've always searched for. But I can't seem to make that final step. That's why I'm here."

"Yes?" said Professor Powell suspiciously.

"Sir, how much would you charge to hypnotize me again, and bring back the power?"

The psychologist was stunned. "Well," he said a few moments later. "Well, well. We'll have to think about that one for a while."

Elvis McNeil said hurriedly, "I can't afford much, but I'll pay whatever I can. Anything, anything to get that mystical magic back under my voluntary control!"

Powell gave the young man a wide-eyed look. Then he shook his head, almost sadly. "Yes, well, I do think we'd better have a long talk about mysticism and magic, McNeil. In private." Powell reached for his desk calendar. "Could you come see me tomorrow afternoon, say about 4 o'clock?"

"Certainly, sir."

"And let's keep our mouths shut about all this, shall we? I mean, we wouldn't want to let everybody in on the secret, now would we?"

"Certainly, sir. Anything you say."

"And in the meanwhile, I want you to go to the library and check out a book called *LSD, Marihuana, Yoga and Hypnosis* by Theodore X. Barber. Read it through carefully, particularly the section on hypnosis. And if you're behind in any of your studies, use those latent mental powers of yours to catch up quickly. Okay?"

"Okay, Sir. I can hardly wait!"

After Elvis McNeil had left the office, Professor Powell sat staring at the wall and tapping a pencil nervously on his desk. Then he turned to his assistant and said, "You know, Brian, when we teach this course next semester, instead of having a class demonstration on hypnotism, what would you think about showing a movie on the subject? I mean, maybe that's a fine way to demonstrate that while hypnosis can be useful, if improperly used it can cause, er, unexpected problems."

Brian Healy scratched his head. "Sure, Professor Powell. Sure."

STUDY QUESTIONS

As you read through the chapter, see if you can find the answers to the following questions:

1. How do the terms "developmental psychology" and "life span approach" differ?
2. What four theoretical issues run through all the literature on developmental psychology?
3. What is the "classical" definition of development?
4. What is the main exception to "the rule of discontinuity"?
5. What does the phrase "Both the child and child psychology are 'cultural inventions' " mean?
6. How does the placenta protect the fetus?
7. What do the terms "cephalo-caudal" and "proximal-distal" mean?
8. What data suggest that Asian infants are less excitable than are black or white children?
9. What evidence suggests that fetuses can learn while still in the womb?
10. How do hormones influence maternal behavior?
11. What are the effects of rearing infant monkeys on "surrogate mothers"?
12. What is "anaclitic depression"?
13. What are the effects of paternal deprivation on boys? On girls?
14. How does "infant-stim" affect the development of Down's syndrome children?

Infancy and Early Childhood: Physical and Emotional Development

"Where Sex Leaves Off"

· C H A P T E R ·

14

Dr. Martin Mayer stared at the classroom, terrified. Through his thick-lensed glasses, the bright young faces seemed distorted, larger than life. The students swarmed around the room in constant motion, like bees defending their hive. High school students, Mayer said to himself, have more energy than they know what to do with. How in the world could he have let himself in for something like this?

The man standing at the front of the classroom beside Dr. Mayer smiled mechanically. "All right, young people. Let's settle down now and listen. We have a special guest today, someone famous in the field of genetic psychology, or the study of inherited behavior patterns. He's come all the way from Mid-American University to give the annual Science Lecture this afternoon. And since he arrived earlier than we had expected, we've prevailed upon Dr. Mayer to address all the biology classes today. Isn't that kind of Dr. Mayer?"

Kind? They hadn't really given him the chance to refuse. He had written out the lecture he was going to give to the whole school. In very simple terms, he was going to explain his research program on genetic psychology. But what could he tell these youngsters in addition to that? A sinking feeling in the pit of his stomach began working its way up his digestive system.

The biology teacher droned on. "Dr. Mayer has published more than a hundred articles in various scientific journals, and he is co-author of the famous *Handbook of Behavior Genetics*. I'm sure you'll want to give him your closest attention. And now let's welcome Dr. Mayer with a nice round of applause."

The students clapped loudly, and one or two even whistled. Dr. Mayer blinked twice. The co-author of the famous *Handbook of Behavior Genetics* was frankly petrified. Every face in the class was focused on him now, waiting expectantly. His wife, Elizabeth, would have called it a "pregnant pause." What had she told him, just before he got on the plane? "If you get stuck for something to say, just talk about sex. They'll listen."

Dr. Mayer adjusted his glasses on his nose. "With your permission, students, I'd like to talk about sex."

Their immediate rapt attention gave him all the permission he needed.

"As a scientist, I'm interested in sex—in all its aspects. Among lower animals, sex is primarily a matter of hormones and instincts. Among humans, it can also be an act of love. But among both humans and lower animals, sex is the beginning of life, not just the living end of things. For life starts where sex leaves off. And scientists who study the beginnings of life, as I do, must consider the biological as well as the social and moral consequences of the sexual act."

Mayer smiled at the students wanly. "A few months ago, I read Aldous Huxley's novel *Brave New World* for the third time. Late in his life, Huxley studied the effects of hallucinogens like mescaline on human perception. But before he got interested in drugs, Huxley studied genetics. He came to the study of genetics naturally, for his grandfather had defended Charles Darwin's theory of evolution against attack by religious leaders in the 1860's. Darwin believed that animals mated rather freely, and their genes mixed rather randomly. When a male lion had sex with a female lion, neither of them was trying to create a super-lion. They were just following their blind instincts. Some of their lion cubs were, by chance, bigger and stronger than others, and these cubs survived. The weak cubs died because the environment in which they lived favored big, strong lions."

Mayer glanced at the students. They were still listening raptly, so he continued. "Humans are different, of course. We have the ability to select quite deliberately which of our offspring will survive simply by controlling the environment our children live in. And that ability puts us in a moral bind that lions don't have to face."

Mayer paused to take off his glasses and clean them. "Sometimes I think it would be great just to be a lion, so I wouldn't have to worry about the consequences of having sex."

Several of the students laughed.

"Control of the environment is perhaps the most difficult problem facing us at the moment," Mayer said once his glasses were adjusted. "But Huxley saw that an equally difficult social issue would pop up in the near future. What would happen, he asked in *Brave New World*, if we could control the genetic process itself?"

Now the scientist smiled. "Ever ask yourself why you turned out to be a human instead of a lion? The answer lies in the genes you inherited from your mother and father. Human genes have different instructions in them than do lion genes. And you developed blue eyes—or brown ones—because your parents' and grandparents' genes passed along 'biological instructions' that programmed your cells to turn out as they did. You had no choice in the matter—just as you will pass on your genes for eye color or skin color to your children whether you or they like it or not.

"But what if we could change your genes before you started creating the next generation? Aldous Huxley was bright enough to see that, when scientists learned enough about genes, we could probably do just that."

Mayer shook his head. "See what I mean about the consequences of sex? Well, someday soon, we can go to a young married couple and say, hey, what kinds of kids would you like to have? Do you want a big, blond football player for a son? Would you prefer a small, dark-skinned daughter as beautiful as the Queen of Sheba? Or would you rather your daughter became a physicist, a sort of Alberta Einstein? And is there any reason why she couldn't be both beautiful and exceptionally bright? And would you like for your son to have big hands—not so he could catch a football, but so he could play the piano like George Winston?"

Some of the students frowned, a fact that pleased Mayer immensely, so he kept on talking. "That's part of what *Brave New World* is all about. What I'd like to ask you today is the same question—when that great day comes and we know how to reprogram the genes of our children, what kind of kids would you like to have?"

The class sat silent, as if this was an idea they didn't really care to give much thought to.

"You," Dr. Mayer said, pointing to a young girl sitting in the second row. "How are you doing in biology?"

The girl blushed and the class giggled. Obviously biology wasn't one of the girl's better subjects.

"Are you getting an A+ in biology?"

The girl shook her head.

"Wouldn't it have been nice if your parents had 'spliced up your genes' to make you a 'brain,' so you could breeze through the biology book and learn it all very quickly? Wouldn't that help?" Mayer asked in a joking tone of voice.

"But then I wouldn't be *me*," the girl wailed. "I'd be somebody else!"

Mayer turned quickly to a small but handsome young man sitting toward the back of the class. He had a guitar case lying beside his chair. "You, there, you're pretty good on the guitar, aren't you?"

"I'm just learning," the young man said shyly.

"Did you know that the best guitar players seem to have much better finger coordination than average players have? The ability seems to be inherited, and all the practice in the world won't make you a performing genius if you don't have the right genes to start with. Don't you wish now that your parents had fixed up your finger genes before you were conceived?"

"Sure," the boy said quietly.

"You're smaller than average, too," Dr. Mayer continued. "Does that ever bother you, maybe just a little?"

The boy nodded slowly.

"Well, wouldn't you like your kids to be taller than the average? Wouldn't you want to see a genetic engineer to splice up your genes before you start having a family?"

One of the boys in the middle of the room interrupted. "But if everybody wanted their kids to be bigger than average, what would happen to the average?"

The class laughed.

"That's pretty unnatural, isn't it?" one of the girls asked.

"Of course it's unnatural," Mayer shot back. "Lions can't do it and neither can elephants. But we can already do these sorts of things with bacteria. And it won't be long before we can do gene splicing at the human level. So maybe it's time we started to plan the consequences of what we'll be able to do. For instance, before you marry, you'll probably spend a lot of time deciding what your first house or apartment is going to look like. Don't you think you ought to spend just as much time planning what kind of children you'll have?"

"But you can't change human nature," the guitar-playing boy said.

"Ah, but you can," Mayer said. "Education is always an attempt to change human nature. But education starts too late in many cases, because you can't teach a child anything until after it's born. With genetic control, though, we can start 'educating' the child even before it's conceived."

One of the girls started to interrupt, but Mayer continued, "Nowadays, if you have ugly children, your friends and neighbors don't blame you for it because you couldn't do anything to change how they looked. But if your kids are badly dressed, or if you don't send them to school, that's a *conscious choice* and people hold you responsible. In the future, when we can reprogram genes at will, the world will hold you responsible for how pretty your children are—and for what native abilities they have. The lion can have sex without worrying about it. You can't. You'll have to decide whether you want your kids to be geniuses or just average types."

"But if everybody wanted their kids to be Einsteins, who'd collect the garbage?" complained a young man sitting in the front row.

"Beautiful question," Dr. Mayer said. "If there's a shortage of strong-bodied people who like to collect garbage, will the government require you to have kids who have an instinctive love for gathering up other people's trash?"

"I don't want anybody telling me what kinds of kids I've got to have," a young male student said. "Probably they'd try to make them all into robots."

"Hey, man, you're making *assumptions*," said another. "I mean, is garbage-loving an inherited tendency?"

"Magnificent!" Dr. Mayer cried. "As far as we know, it's not. But maybe it could be. What kinds of *behaviors* do you think we can engineer into your children's genes?"

After a moment's pause, the guitar-playing boy responded. "You already said that finger coordination was inherited."

"Right. But someone born with the ability to move her or his fingers quickly probably could become a great violinist as well as a great guitarist. Or would be great at sewing or repairing computers. How would you feel if you had your future son's genes arranged so that he had superb finger coordination and he wanted to become a football player instead of a musician?"

"I'd send him to Notre Dame," said a large young man with an apparent interest in sports.

"Good idea," said Mayer. "But what other innate skills would you want to program into your future son to push him toward music? An inborn sense of rhythm? Is that something you inherit, or do you learn it from your parents? You, young lady," he said, pointing again to the girl in the second row. "What musical talents do you think are inherited, and which ones are learned?"

"I think you're trying to make us think too much," the young woman replied. "Why can't we just have kids and let them grow up the natural way, like our parents did?"

Mayer smiled. "For the same reason that we can't pretend that nuclear bombs don't exist. Genetic engineering is going to happen whether you like it or not, so you might as well start thinking about how it might affect you. As for me, I can't do anything about changing my children's genes because they're already born. But I can study behavior genetics in my lab so that your kids, or your grandchildren, can make decisions I couldn't make. But meanwhile, I've got a great big problem and it has to do with sex."

The class, which had become rather noisy during the discussion, suddenly quieted down again. Mayer smiled at how well things were going. His wife, Elizabeth, had given him very sound advice.

"Someday in the future, as Huxley pointed out, we'll have genetic engineering and we can order our kids from a catalogue. But we already know that some diseases and maybe even some types of insanity have a genetic component. The facts are that some people carry the *wrong kind of genes*. If we were lions, nature would take care of things—lions with the wrong genes just don't survive in lion environments."

Mayer frowned. "The problem is, we're humans, and we tend to keep people alive no matter what's wrong with them, and no matter how much it costs. If we were 'natural' about things, the way lions are, we'd just let these people die when they were young. Until we have genetic engineering, and we can change these bad genes into good ones, what can we possibly do to protect ourselves from bad genes?"

The guitar-playing boy stuck up his hand. "Well," he said quietly, "why don't we just pass a law saying that people with bad genes can't have kids?"

(Continued on page 366.)

The class exploded in anger.

HUMAN GROWTH AND DEVELOPMENT

In the previous 13 chapters, we have discussed the biological and psychological *sub-systems* that make up your body and mind. These sub-systems included your neurons and the various parts of your brain, your sensory inputs and perceptions, your cognitions, and your motives and memories. In the next five chapters, we will put these bits and pieces together to form a bigger picture of what you are like and how you got to be that way.

There are two traditional ways of covering human growth and development. The first approach—typically called **developmental psychology** or *child psychology*—involves discussing how various *aspects* (or sub-systems) of your personality grow and mature over time, particularly during your younger years. However, the *manner* in which developmental psychologists study infants often differs from the *manner* in which older children (and adults) are described. Cornell psychologist Urie Bronfenbrenner puts it this way: "In terms of **empirical** work, our most sophisticated models, reflecting the greatest degree of integration that we possess, appear in the [study of] infancy. Here we are dealing with the organism as a whole. . . . After infancy, developmental psychology becomes the study of variables, not the study of systems, organisms, or live things living" (Bronfenbrenner *et al.*, 1986).

The second method—often called the **life span approach**—usually traces the maturation of a "typical" individual from birth through middle age to old age and death. According to child psychologist Margarita Azmitia, "The term *life span perspective* . . . entails both the holistic delineation of age periods (e.g., integrating biological, physical, social, and cognitive development during infancy) and the delineation of connections between age periods (e.g., how achievements during infancy influence the preschooler's development" (Azmitia, 1987). Life span theorists tend to look primarily at the "whole person" as she or he passes through various stages or "life crises."

In truth, neither theoretical approach is entirely satisfactory. University of Maryland psychologist Ellin Scholnick explains the problem this way: "Developmental psychology is in a crisis. It wants to do too much with too little. The discipline confronts changes within the life span of the individual, changes across biological evolution and the history of the species, and variations among situations and among individuals within situations. . . . There is no theory that can adequately account for some or all of these changes" (Scholnick, 1985).

□ □ **QUESTION** □ □
In your opinion, should child psychologists deal more with

experimental data and theories, or with giving practical advice on how to rear children?

● *A Life Span Approach*

Since we are interested *both* in the development of specific aspects of the child's personality *and* in the development of the child *as an intact person*, we will compromise a bit. That is, we will present the material on human development *both* from a traditional and from a "life span" point of view. For example, in this chapter we will focus primarily on infancy and early childhood, where the "child developmental" approach has traditionally been strongest. These are the years when physical growth and emotional development are of paramount importance, so we will discuss these topics at length. In Chapter 15, we will look at the years from adolescence through adulthood to old age. With certain obvious exceptions, this span of life is a time of great mental and social maturation. So we will cover such topics as language learning and cognitive development in Chapter 15, and we will do so primarily from a "life span" point of view.

Finally, in Chapters 16, 17, and 18, we will put all this material together in quite a different manner as we look at *personality*—what it is, how it develops, and how psychologists try to measure it.

Before we can cover any of these topics, however, we must first discuss four important theoretical issues. As we will see, developmental psychologists often organize their research efforts (and their theories) around these four issues.

DEVELOPMENTAL ISSUES

The four theoretical issues that run through all the literature on developmental psychology are as follows:

● The matter of *continuity* versus *discontinuity*.
● The problem of *individual differences* and *human similarities*.
● The infamous *mind-body problem*.
● The *nature-nurture* controversy.

There is a fifth important issue as well, although it is more practical than theoretical: namely, how much has the study of what human development *is* been influenced by society's notions of what human development *should be*?

Let's begin by looking at each of these five major issues briefly.

Continuity Versus Discontinuity

The so-called "continuity" issue in development is really several different problems lumped together under one title.

As you might guess, whether you perceive development as being "continuous" or "discontinuous" depends in large part on how you define those two terms, and on what sorts of psychological traits or observable behaviors you measure over time. Unfortunately, there simply is very little agreement among experts as to what these two terms actually mean (Emde & Harmon, 1984). There are, however, four rather major concepts that are often seen as being part of the "continuity-discontinuity" issue. Let's look briefly at what these four concepts are.

● Directionality of Development

First, there is the problem of *directionality*. Most early behavioral scientists used *physical growth* as their model for *psychological development*. After all, a child is born an infant, and almost uniformly gets larger thereafter. This pattern of continuous growth is, of course, "coded for in the genes." And if we presume that psychological growth is also controlled by genetic factors, then we might expect "the mind" would follow the same unidirectional growth pattern as the body does.

According to German psychologist Paul Baltes, it was this very line of reasoning that led early psychologists to define development as a process which moved *progressively* from birth toward some final end state. This process was seen as being *irreversible*. However, Baltes says, the experimental data simply don't support this "classical" definition of human development. Baltes claims that development is primarily controlled by environmental factors, not by some "internal master plan." He admits there is often "unidirectionality" over *very short developmental periods*. However, Baltes says, this type of continuity is caused by stability in the environment, not by internal (genetic) factors (Baltes, 1983).

Put simply, from a physical point of view, children do "grow up, not down." However, from a psychological point of view, children do *regress* from time to time. And this regression is determined primarily by the environment, not by genetic factors.

● Limited Versus Life-long Development

During late adolescence, or early adulthood, most young stop growing. They may add a few pounds during their middle years, and lose weight during the final period of life. But physical growth tends to stop a few years after puberty. Does psychological development follow this same pattern?

Sigmund Freud thought it did. As you will see in Chapter 16, he believed your personality was "set" by the time you were 15 or so. Thereafter, you might *regress*, but you surely didn't *progress* very much. As you can see, Freud took a view of development that was—at least in part—discontinuous.

Most modern-day psychologists disagree with Freud. Indeed, the entire thrust of the "life-span development" viewpoint is to demonstrate that, psychologically speaking, you never stop growing.

● Continuous Growth, or Stages of Growth?

As far as *physical* growth is concerned, it often occurs in spurts. A child may stay somewhat the same height for a period of time, then grow several inches during a period of a year.

Both Sigmund Freud and Jean Piaget believed that the human *personality* followed this same physical pattern. That is, they said that the mind goes through several *stages* of growth. Each stage presumably is marked by a period of fairly sudden change followed by a period of "consolidation." Put simply, stage theorists believe development occurs much as promotions do in the military—"suddenly" you are no longer a corporal but a sergeant, with new duties and new responsibilities.

As we will see in Chapters 15 and 16, there is still considerable debate as to whether psychological development occurs in stages, or whether it occurs fairly smoothly and continuously.

□ □ **QUESTION** □ □
When people say of a young girl who's throwing a temper tantrum, "Oh, she's just going through a phase," are they taking the continuity or discontinuity position?

● Stability

Finally, there is the problem of *stability*. Can we tell from what you are today what you will be like 10 years from now? If so, there is a *continuity* or *stability* to your development. If not, then we might conclude that development tends to be *unpredictable* and *discontinuous*.

According to Harvard psychologist Jerome Kagan, when we speak of "stability," we're really talking about three different but related matters. First, stability can refer to a psychological quality (or trait) that changes but little over

a person's developmental years. "Once a fool, always a fool" is an example. Second, we might be implying that two traits should maintain the same *relative positions* during development. For instance, if you're better at math than English in first grade, then you should have higher grades in calculus than in literature as a college senior. And third, there is "stability across people." If you're at the top of your class in kindergarten, you should be valedictorian in high school (Kagan, 1980).

Jerome Kagan states there is some evidence that *physical* traits such as height and weight are "partially stable." That is, if you're taller than average at 4, you're likely to be taller than average when you're 14. Certain *physiological* traits—such as the rate at which a child's heart beats, and whether the child is "inhibited"—also tend to remain fairly constant over periods of a year or two (Garcia Coll, Kagan, & Reznick, 1984; Kagan, Reznick, & Snidman, 1988).

As for psychological traits, Kagan notes they are so hard to measure that research often yields contradictory results. There does seem to be a tendency for such things as IQs and "personality test scores" to remain fairly stable over longer periods of time. However, this "continuity" tends to hold only when the individual's environment remains constant. Therefore, Kagan says, the tendency is for development to be unstable and hence discontinuous (Kagan, 1980).

The main exception to the "rule of discontinuity," Kagan says, has to do with **temperament**. Kagan notes that the temperamental trait "that seems to be the strongest, best-preserved throughout life and most likely to be genetic has to do with infants who, on the one hand, are wary, timid, vigilant, shy and fearful or, on the other hand, are outgoing, bold and sociable." According to Kagan, "These qualities can be seen toward the end of the first year and are obvious in children two to three years of age" (Kagan, 1987). However, Kagan also notes that at least 40 percent of the timid children he has studied became less inhibited as they grew older. Thus, he says, it is the *interaction* between genetic tendency and environment that determines even such traits as sociability, arousal, and timidity (Kagan, 1986).

● Continuity Versus Discontinuity: A Summary

Is development continuous or discontinuous? The answer seems to be "both." Leon Yarrow observes that all personality traits are continuous—at least for brief periods of time. And, under some circumstances, all traits are discontinuous. Yarrow concludes, "Whether or not individuals show constancy or change, or whether certain characteristics show continuity over time, are questions that are not only too simple, but also no longer have meaning" (Yarrow, 1981).

In this chapter, we will present some findings that seem to support the continuity position—and some data that seem to contradict that position. We then will discuss the matter more fully in Chapter 15.

□ □ **QUESTION** □ □

Two famous "old sayings" relating to development are as follows: "The child is father to the man," and "Man makes himself." Which saying takes the continuity position? Which the discontinuity position? What does the fact that these two sayings contradict each other tell you about this controversy?

Similarities Versus Differences

You are YOU—a unique living system. You have your own psychological needs and personality traits that differ in many ways from anyone else's. But like most other humans, you probably have two arms and legs, a nose and mouth, two eyes and ears, hair, and skin. Even your values and opinions are probably similar to those of your family and friends. From an objective point of view, then, you dress and walk and talk like most other humans. And you think, feel, and react to most situations as does almost everyone else in the world.

So, what is more important about you—the fact that you are unique, or the fact that you share most of your thoughts, feelings, and behaviors with almost all other humans?

As we will see, some psychologists who study the human personality tend to emphasize the ways in which people are similar. These scientists assume you go through the same developmental **stages** that everyone must pass through, and that you will experience *life crises* similar to those all humans presumably experience.

Other psychologists are more impressed by the fact that there are striking differences across individuals. These scientists note that even if you passed through similar stages as did most other people, you did so at your own speed and in your own way. And even if you encountered the same crises as did the person living next door, you surely solved your difficulties in your own unique fashion.

Actually, as you might guess, by far the *most important aspect* of your own development is the fact that you are like most people in some ways, but different from everyone else in the world in other ways. Whether you tend to emphasize similarities or differences, then, depends on your own view of what human nature is all about.

Mind-Body Problem

Does the mind control the body, or do bodily processes entirely determine what goes on in your "mind"? We have discussed the mind-body problem in several previous chapters. And we concluded that the best solution to this long-standing controversy was a *holistic* approach to understanding human beings. That is to say, everything you think, do, and feel is surely influenced by your mind, your body, and the environment in which you live.

In discussing physical development in the first part of this chapter, of course, we will tend to focus primarily on the "body" side of the mind-body equation. The "mind" part of the equation will surface when we begin talking about emotions. So, let's delay additional comments on this topic until then.

Nature-Nurture Controversy

There probably is no issue more violently debated in developmental psychology than the question of what is learned and what is innately determined. However, as Jerome Kagan notes, the issue really boils down to determining how nature and nurture *interact* (Kagan, 1986). Thus, we cannot really discuss this controversy in a sensible manner unless we know the social environment the child grows up in—and what sorts of *values* that society places on children and childhood.

□ □ **QUESTION** □ □

Do you think parents should be allowed to sell their children as slaves—or even to murder their children—if the parents so desired? If you answer "no," why not? What does your answer to this question tell you about your own perceptions of what childhood *should be*?

Social Influences on Developmental Concepts

As University of Houston psychologist Frank Kessel notes, in recent years "developmental psychology shows signs of becoming increasingly aware of its social, cultural, and broadly historical contexts or dimensions" (cited in Bronfenbrenner *et al.*, 1986). Put more bluntly, developmental psychologists have just begun to realize that the society in which *they* live determines—in part—not only their theories, but also the experimental "facts" they discover in their laboratory studies.

University of Virginia psychologist Sandra Scarr puts it this way: "Each scientist approaches scientific problems with a theoretical viewpoint, whether explicit or implicit. Theory guides inquiry through the questions raised, the framework of inquiry, and the interpretation of the results. Each scientist seeks to find 'facts' to assimilate into his or her world view. Thus, each of us is biased by the human tendency to seek 'facts' that are **congruent** with our prior beliefs" (Scarr, 1985).

Yale psychologist Willian Kessen surely had the same idea in mind when he wrote that "Both the child and child psychology are 'cultural inventions'" (Kessen, 1983). What Kessen means, of course, is that our notions of what childhood *should be* help determine the sorts of developmental theories we adopt.

And our notions of what childhood *should be* have changed dramatically over the years. As Robert Trotter notes, "Incredible as it may seem to today's doting parents, infants have not always been seen as bundles of joy. Throughout most of human history, in fact, they were treated as mewling, puking bundles of trouble, easier to be rid of than to rear. Infanticide, the murder of babies, appears to have been a common practice in many ancient societies and was not even outlawed in Rome until A.D. 374" (Trotter, 1987). And even when children were allowed to live, they were not always kept by their parents. Until 300 years ago, many children in western Europe were routinely sold into slavery. And as recently as 150 years ago in England, middle-class parents often "farmed out" their infants—that is, gave them to servants to rear—until the children were old enough to be sent away to school or put to work.

Quite obviously, then, the study of human development in Europe 300 years ago would have yielded quite different "facts and theories" than it does today.

It is equally true, of course, that certain *fairly constant* aspects of the developmental process have helped determine what our culture is like. Fetuses still spend about nine months in the womb before they are born, and they don't start walking or talking until a year or so after birth. These "facts" haven't changed over the course of human history.

However, it will surely help you understand the developmental process better if you realize one thing: Most of the important theoretical battles we will discuss in this and later chapters involve *social values* as much as experimental "facts."

Now that we have briefly discussed these five major issues in developmental psychology, let's turn our attention to how life gets started.

GENETIC DEVELOPMENT

As we noted in Chapter 7, you began life as a single cell. This egg cell—produced in your mother's reproductive organs—looked much like many other human cells. That is, the egg cell was a tiny round blob of material with a dark **nucleus** in its center. The nucleus contains what we might call the "managers" of the cell—its **chromosomes** (see Fig. 14.1).

Most of the cells in your body contain 23 *pairs* of chromosomes (see Fig. 14.2). If you looked at them through a microscope, each of these 46 chromosomes would seem to be a long strand of colored beads. These 46 chromosomes are composed chiefly of a substance

FIG. 14.1 A cell.

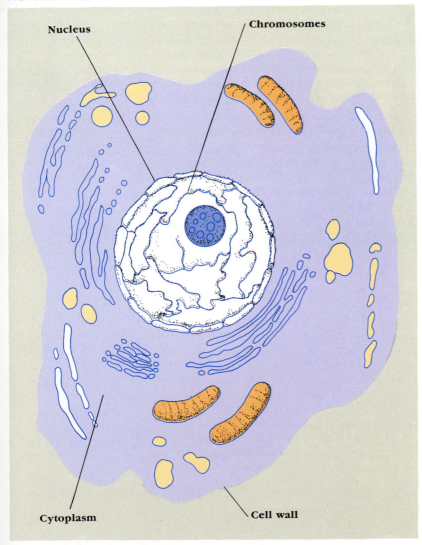

Nucleus

Chromosomes

Cytoplasm

Cell wall

called **DNA**. DNA is an *acid* because of its chemical composition. It is a *nucleic* acid because it is found chiefly in the nucleus of the cell. Your genes are composed chiefly of DNA molecules.

- ### Cellular Division

Cells reproduce by dividing (see Fig. 14.3). When a cell divides, its nucleus splits in two. Half the DNA in the original nucleus goes into one of the daughter cells, while the other half of the DNA goes into the other daughter cell. (The term "daughter" is used even if the child will develop into a son rather than a daughter.) But before cell division takes place, the nucleus must *double* the amount of DNA present so each daughter cell will have its full complement of 46 chromosomes the moment the split occurs. Since the daughter cells have exactly the same DNA, the two cells are "genetically identical."

The only exception to this rule is the case of the sperm and unfertilized egg cells. When an egg cell is produced through division, the original 23 chromosome pairs split in half *without doubling*, so that the egg cell contains exactly half the chromosomes it needs to survive and multiply. Thus, unless the egg cell is fertilized by a sperm cell—and receives the other 23 chromosomes it needs to survive—the egg cell will soon die. But since the sperm and egg have *different* DNA, they unite to form a cell that is *unlike* any cell in either the mother's or father's body (Clark, 1985).

- ### X and Y Chromosomes

As we said in Chapter 8, the sperm cell differs from the egg cell in one very important respect: The 23rd chromosome of the sperm cell can be either the large X type or the smaller Y type. The 23rd chromosome of the egg cell is *always* a large X type.

If an X-type sperm is the first to enter the egg cell, the fertilized egg will of course have an XX 23rd chromosome pair—and the child will be female. If a Y-type sperm fertilizes the egg, the 23rd chromosome pair will be of the XY variety and the child will be a male.

Chromosomal Abnormalities

Because the human reproductive process is so complicated, it occasionally breaks down. Sometimes the 23rd chromosome pair does not divide properly and the child ends up with but a *single* 23rd chromosome—always an X type—or with one or more *additional* X or Y chromosomes. In what is called the **Turner syndrome**, the child's cells contain but a single X chromosome. Individuals who experience this chromosomal problem have female genitalia but lack ovaries. If given injections of female hormones at puberty, they develop the normal behavioral and physical characteristics of an adult female.

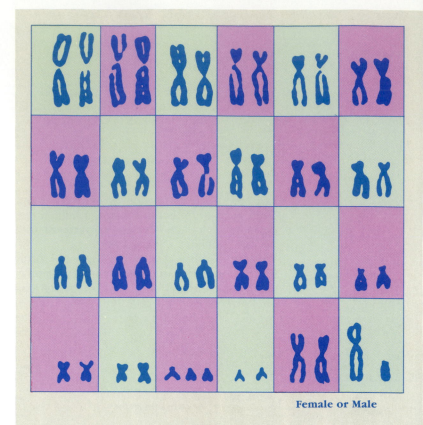

Female or Male

FIG. 14.2 Humans have 23 pairs of chromosomes. The 23rd pair is either XX or XY and determines the person's sex. If the 21st pair has an extra member, the person will suffer from trisomy-21, or Down's syndrome. (See Fig. 14.10.)

As we noted in Chapter 7, there are rare cases where an infant is genetically an XX female, but is born with male genitalia because one of the X chromosomes contains a tiny fragment of the Y chromosome that "codes" for the male sex organs. This "XX male" condition oc-

DNA. An abbreviation for deoxyribonucleic acid. The genes are composed chiefly of DNA molecules.

Turner syndrome (SIN-drome). A "syndrome" is a collection of symptoms all having (presumably) a common cause. Turner syndrome is the collection of symptoms associated with a woman's having a single X 23rd chromosome, rather than the normal XX 23rd chromosome.

Kleinfelter's syndrome (rhymes with "MINE-belter"). A set of related physical characteristics (syndrome) found in males who have an extra X chromosome.

This condition—known as **Klinefelter's syndrome**—occurs in about one child out of every 900. As J.A. Miller noted recently, however, "One child with a sex chromosome abnormality (SCA) may have numerous difficulties, while another with the same abnormality may appear quite normal" (Miller, 1986). Indeed, as Daniel Berch and Bruce Bender put it in a recent article, "The developmental difficulties associated with abnormal sex chromosomes are not always as devastating as once thought. . . . It is likely that many SCA children will lead normal, productive lives if they are reared by sensitive, realistic parents in a supportive environment" (Berch & Bender, 1987).

curs about once in each 20,000 births (Edwards, 1988).

A child with an XXY 23rd chromosome will be physically a male—with penis and testicles—but may have many feminine characteristics.

About 1 boy in 1,000 has two Y chromosomes and one X. The XYY male is typically taller than average, and most XYY males reach sexual puberty a year or more before the normal XY male does. About half of the XYY males suffer from moderate to severe acne—a much higher percentage than is found among normal men. Homosexual and many other abnormal patterns of sexual behavior are much more frequent in XYY males than in XY males. And, for reasons we still don't understand, the XYY condition appears primarily in white males.

Research reported in the 1960's and 1970's suggested that an abnormally large number of XYY males turn up in hospital wards reserved for the criminally insane. Some scientists at first believed the extra Y chromosome *caused* the criminal behavior to occur. However, current thinking takes a different view. The extra *male* chromosome causes the boy's adrenal glands to secrete abnormal amounts of testosterone during his development. This excess testosterone seems responsible both for the early onset of puberty and for the acne (Plomin, Defries, & McCleam, 1980). However, excess amounts of testosterone typically lead to an increase in *impulsive behaviors*. Most XYY males who get into trouble with the law appear to come from lower-class families in which the parents apparently lacked the social skills needed to teach such an impulsive child how to control himself. XYY males born to middle- or upper-class families seldom show this lack of self-discipline, and thus seldom end up in prisons or mental hospitals.

In summary, then, the XYY male is at risk only if he is born to parents who fail to give the boy adequate training in self-control during his early years. It is thus the *interaction* between genes and social environment that causes the problem, not the genes alone.

FIG. 14.3 Cell reproduction.

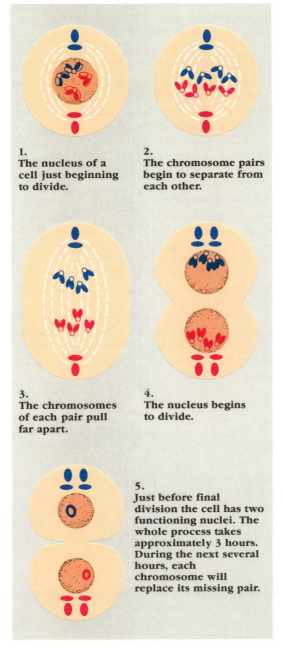

1.
The nucleus of a cell just beginning to divide.

2.
The chromosome pairs begin to separate from each other.

3.
The chromosomes of each pair pull far apart.

4.
The nucleus begins to divide.

5.
Just before final division the cell has two functioning nuclei. The whole process takes approximately 3 hours. During the next several hours, each chromosome will replace its missing pair.

□ □ **QUESTION** □ □
Some XYY males accused of crimes have asked to be pardoned, claiming their genetic disability "made them do it." If you were on the jury, what would your thinking be?

Occasionally the 21st chromosome pair does not divide properly, and the child is born with *three* 21st chromosomes rather than the normal pair. This **trisomy-21** condition leads to a type of mental, physical, and behavioral deficiency called *Down's syndrome*. In the past, the *mental retardation* often associated with trisomy-21 was blamed on the genetic abnormality. However, recent research suggests that Down's syndrome children need not experience severe psychological problems *provided the child is given special treatment starting at birth*. We will discuss this matter more fully at the end of this chapter.

THE BEGINNINGS OF LIFE

At the moment you were conceived, you were no more than a single egg cell locked away in your mother's body. But within 24 hours after your conception, that original egg cell had grown large enough to divide into two daughter cells. At this point in your life, you might have become *identical twins*. Usually the first daughter cells remain close together and develop into a single individual. However, for reasons not clearly understood, these first cells sometimes separate and *each daughter cell* eventually creates a complete human **embryo**. Since the daughter cells were identical, the twins will be identical too.

Fraternal twins are much more common. Occasionally a woman will produce two (or more) eggs during her fertile period. If both egg cells are fertilized, they will both begin independent growth at the same time, and the woman will produce fraternal twins nine months later. Since these two egg cells were fertilized by *different sperms*, they are no more identical than are brothers and sisters born to the same parents at different times.

If the two daughter cells remain linked after the first division, each of them will divide once more within a second 24-hour period. Within a third 24-hour period, all four of these cells will divide again. While this cell division goes on, the group of cells travels slowly down a tiny tube to the mother's womb. About nine days after fertilization, the rapidly forming human being attaches itself to the wall of the womb. At this point in your own life, you were about 0.5 millimeters (0.02 inches) in size (Clark, 1985).

Cellular Differentiation

Some two weeks after your life started, a remarkable change occurred in the tiny cluster of cells that made up your rapidly-forming body. Up until this point, all of your cells were pretty much identical—because the commands from the chromosomes were identical. But 13 to 14 days after fertilization, some of the chromosomes began giving out slightly different sets of "command" instructions. As a result, these cells began to produce slightly different proteins (and other materials).

As these new proteins and other molecules appeared, they forced the cells to *differentiate*—that is, to change shape, size, and function.

Identical twins are produced if the first egg cell divides into two daughter cells that each grow into a complete embryo.

• *Embryonic Development*

By the 14th or 15th day of your life, you were made up of three clearly different groups of cells. One of these groups developed into what we call the **ectoderm**, a technical term that means "outer skin." Eventually these cells became your skin, your sense organs, and your nervous system.

Another group of cells, on instructions from their chromosomes, developed into what we term the **mesoderm**, or "middle skin." These cells eventually became your muscles, bone, and blood.

A third group of cells received instructions to become **endoderm**, or "inner skin." These cells turned into your digestive system.

At the moment that this differentiation into the three "derms" occurred, you were a hollow ball about 2.5 millimeters (0.1 inch) in size, and technically you were then an *embryo* (see Fig. 14.4). It was not until six weeks later—some two months after your biological life began—that the three types of cells arranged themselves into vaguely human form, and the embryo thus became a **fetus** (Davis, 1985).

• *The Placenta*

Developing cells—like developing children—are *unusually sensitive* to the environments they find themselves in. Fortunately, as you grew within your mother's womb, you were

Trisomy-21 (TRY-so-me). From the Greek words *tri*, meaning "three," and *soma*, meaning "body." The modern term for mongolism, or Down's syndrome. A relatively common form of birth defect in which the facial features of the person somewhat resemble Asian or Mongolian characteristics. See the end of this chapter for more details, and the story that begins Chapter 16 for information on how Down's syndrome got its name.

Embryo (EM-bree-oh). An unborn child from the time of conception to the second or third month of development, when the child takes on vaguely human form and is thereafter called a fetus. From the Greek word meaning "to swell within."

Fraternal twins (fra-TURN-al). Twins born from two fertilized eggs. From the Latin word meaning "brothers," from which we get the word "fraternity."

Ectoderm (ECK-toh-durm). *Ekto* is the Greek word meaning "outer." *Derma* is the Greek word for "skin." A dermatologist (durr-mah-TOLL-oh-jist) is a medical doctor who specializes in treating skin diseases. A hypodermic is a needle that injects fluids under (*hypo*) the skin (*derma*).

Mesoderm (ME-so-derm). The "middle skin." The Greek word *mesos* means "in the center."

Endoderm (EN-doh-durm). The "inner skin." The Greek word *endon* means "inside" or "within."

Fetus (FEE-tuss). An unborn child after its second or third month in the womb, when it begins to take on vaguely human characteristics. Prior to this time, the child is referred to as an embryo.

Placenta (plah-SENT-ah). The organ inside a woman's womb that links the child's blood system with the mother's. A few drugs, such as thalidomide (thah-LID-oh-myde), can cross the placental (plah-SENT-al) barrier and affect the fetus. Most harmful chemicals, however, are screened out by the placenta before they can affect the fetus or embryo directly.

Fetal alcohol syndrome, or FAS. A developmental disorder associated with heavy consumption of alcohol by the mother during pregnancy. The child is born smaller than normal; often has malformations of the eyes, ears, and mouth; and may suffer from mental retardation and other physical and psychological abnormalities.

Like certain other diseases and substances, the AIDS virus can cause the infant to become infected before birth.

FIG. 14.4 The embryo at about two weeks, showing the three kinds of "derm."

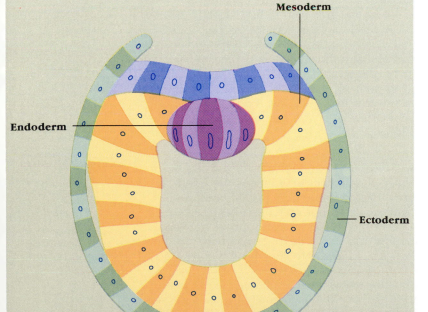

protected from most of the chemicals in her body by an organ called the **placenta**. This placenta acted as a barrier which blocked out most of the substances in your mother's blood that might have harmed your cells.

Illness can cause the pregnant woman's body to secrete somewhat different chemicals than usual. If these chemicals (or the germs that cause them) infiltrate the placenta, they can upset the normal development of the fetus. If a woman has German measles during the third month of her pregnancy, for instance, the child is often born badly retarded.

Various drugs also pass through the placenta and affect the fetus. For example, if the mother is addicted to morphine during pregnancy, the infant will be born with an addiction to morphine. Alcohol can also affect the fetus. Government researchers showed in 1982 that if a pregnant woman consumes three to five drinks, all blood is temporarily shut off to the fetus. The oxygen deprivation that results presumably can lead to birth defects.

About 1 child in 1,000 is born with a set of physical defects called **fetal alcohol syndrome**, or FAS. In 1981, the surgeon general issued a warning advising pregnant women to avoid alcohol entirely. Many scientists disagree with the surgeon general's position, however. According to Ernest Abel, a high rate of birth defects occurs *only* in women who are heavy drinkers. There is no difference, Abel says, between the rate of birth defects in children born to mothers who are moderate drinkers and mothers who don't drink at all. However, as Abel notes, excessive consumption of alcohol by a pregnant woman surely *can* affect the fetus (Abel, 1984). Perhaps to be on the safe side, most physicians now recommend that pregnant women give up alcohol entirely.

• *Effects of Physical Deprivation*
Your genetic blueprint specified in rather general terms what you would be like and how you would grow. But a genetic blueprint is always brought to life by orders from the chromosomes in each cell. And depending on *environmental* circumstances, physical growth and development can either be speeded up or retarded.

If a pregnant woman experiences starvation, her body protects the fetus by giving the unborn child almost all the resources the woman's body has available to it. Still, the child may be born much smaller than usual. If food-deprived children receive enough to eat immediately after birth, however, they usually catch up to the size their genetic blueprints had set for their normal development. For example, consider a study on Korean children reported by Myron Winick and his associates. During the Korean conflict in the 1950's, many very young children in that Asian country were separated from their parents and were placed in orphanages. Most of these youngsters suffered from severe malnutrition before they entered the institutions. After the hostilities ended, some of these children were returned to their war-shattered homes. But many others were placed in adoptive homes in the US. After several years of good care in the US, however, *all* of these children were taller and stronger than the average child who remained in Korea (Winick *et al.*, 1975).

It would seem that your genes *set limits* for your physical development. But it is the environment you were reared in that determines *where within these limits* your actual growth will fall.

Neonatal Growth and Development
In general, as soon as the newborn child's muscles, sense organs, and nerves are fully formed, the child begins to use them. But much of the human nervous system is not fully developed until the child is a year or two old—and some parts of the nervous system, such as the corpus callosum, continue to mature for many years.

As the noted child psychologist Arnold Gesell pointed out long ago, there are two general patterns of bodily development: (1) **cephalo-caudal**, which means development from *head to foot*; and (2) **proximal-distal**, which means development from *near to far*.

The underlying principle explaining both patterns has to do with maturation of the connections between the central nervous system and the muscles (Gesell, 1954).

The motor centers in the brain (see Chapter 2) send long nerve fibers out through the spinal cord to connect with the muscles in various parts of the body. Since the head muscles are closer to the brain than are the foot muscles, the head comes under the control of the motor centers long before the feet do. This is an example of *cephalo-caudal* development.

And since the muscles in the trunk of the body are closer to the spinal cord and brain than are those in the hands and feet, the shoulder and hip muscles come under control sooner than do those in the fingers or toes. This is an example of *proximal-distal* development.

According to Gesell, the appearance of a new motor skill (such as crawling or grasping) always suggests that the brain centers have just become connected to the muscles involved in the new motor skill (Gesell *et al.*, 1974).

Effects of Early Training
Children develop at different speeds, in part because of their environments, but also because they follow different genetic schedules. Most children begin to walk between 12 and 18 months of age. No matter how much coaxing and practice the parents may give their 6-month-old child, the youngster will not walk significantly sooner than if the parents had simply let the child alone. However, as we will see, encouraging children to practice such basic skills as walking may have a number of positive effects.

Boys and girls tend to have slightly different developmental schedules. As psychologist June Reinisch noted recently, "Little girls may start sitting without support earlier but spend more time at it than little boys do before they stand with support. Boys may start crawling earlier than girls but crawl for a longer period before they walk with support" (cited in Hall, 1986).

• *The Early Twin Studies*
Much of what we know about the effects of early training comes from two "classic" studies of motor development in twins begun in 1932. One of the studies was conducted by Wayne Dennis and his wife, the other by Myrtle McGraw. In both studies, the experimenters encouraged one twin to practice a skill (such as climbing stairs), while confining the other twin to a playpen. Training usually began well before either twin could be expected to display the skill and proceeded until the "experimental" twin had clearly mastered the desired behavior pattern. At that point, the experimenters

Cephalo-caudal (SEFF-ah-low CAWD-al). From the Greek and Latin words meaning "head" and "tail." Muscular development usually occurs first in the head region, then spreads downward toward the feet.

Proximal-distal (PROCKS-eye-mal DISS-tahl). *Proximal* means "close," while *distal* means "far." Muscular development usually occurs first in the center regions of the body and spreads outward to the hands and feet.

Native American. Most anthropologists believe the natives who inhabited America when Columbus arrived were immigrants from Asia. They apparently came across from Asia—through Alaska—more than 15,000 years ago. There are many genetic similarities between Native Americans and present-day Japanese, Mongolian, and Chinese peoples.

Critical-period hypothesis. The belief that there is a best time for a child to experience certain things or learn certain skills. Trying to train a child before or after this critical period is supposed to be like picking an apple before it is ripe—or after it has turned mushy and rotten.

removed the "control" twin from the playpen and tested the untrained child.

The usual finding was that, right from the first trial, the "untrained" twin could perform the task almost as well as the "trained" twin. Later research by Arnold Gesell seemed to confirm what Dennis and McGraw had found. Most behavioral scientists, therefore, concluded that *training did not speed up motor development*.

Israeli psychologist Micha Razel has recently re-analyzed all these early experiments, however. Razel's findings have raised considerable doubt both as to the conclusions drawn and the propriety of the studies themselves. Razel notes, for example, that Dennis and his wife kept the twins they studied in "semi-isolation." The infants were not given any toys to play with until they were 11 months of age. Nor were the twins allowed to see or play with each other. Razel cites Dennis as saying that "To restrict practice which might influence sitting, the infants were kept almost continually on their backs in the cribs." Nor did the Dennises give the twins any form of attention, affection, or sensory stimulation for the first six months of their lives. Razel states that McGraw also kept her twins in a highly-deprived environment.

Micha Razel presents data suggesting that *all* the twins in these early studies showed significantly retarded motor development (as compared to children reared in normal environments). Furthermore, he notes that the "stimulated" twin in McGraw's studies became far more "agile" and physically out-going than did the "restrained" twin. This physical difference, Razel claims, lasted at least until the twins were young adults (the last time they were measured). Razel concludes that early stimulation not only speeds up motor development to some extent, but also has a lasting influence on the child's way of approaching and dealing with the world (Razel, 1985).

□ □ **QUESTION** □ □
How might early encouragement affect a child's later *social* behavior?

Cultural Differences

In many cultures, infants often spend the first year or so of their lives bound to a board or *bundled* tightly inside a bag carried on their mothers' backs. These children are released from their restraints only for an hour or two each day, so they have little chance to practice motor skills. Yet their muscular development is not retarded. They creep, crawl, and walk at about the same ages as do children who are not restrained (Chisholm, 1983).

The practice of "bundling" infants is more common in the Orient than it is in Africa and the Western world. The reason for this difference may lie in part in subtle genetic differences among the races of the world. According to a report by Daniel G. Freedman and M. DeBoer, children in Europe, Africa, and America tend to be much more active and irritable than are Asian infants. White and black youngsters will usually struggle when confined, but Asian and **Native American** infants accept restraint rather passively. Asian children typically continue to be much less active physically during their developmental years than are white or black children. Freedman and DeBoer believe these behavioral differences are caused by genetic factors, for Asian children born and reared in the US respond like infants in China and Japan, not as white and black American infants do (Freedman & DeBoer, 1979).

Support for the Freedman and DeBoer position comes from a recent study by James Chisholm, who compared Navajo and "Anglo" infants who were "bundled" by their mothers. Both groups of mothers began weaning when the child's protests to the bundling board became excessive. Chisholm reports that the average age of weaning for the "Anglo" children was 5.9 months, while it was 10.3 months for the Navajo infants. Chisholm believes this difference in weaning times reflects a genetic difference in irritability between white and Native American infants (Chisholm, 1983).

□ □ **QUESTION** □ □
What other explanations for Chisholm's results can you think of? (Hint: How do mothers in various cultures react to their children's protests?)

Critical Periods

Many psychologists believe that the best time for a child to learn a given skill is when the child's body is just mature enough to allow mastery of the behavior in question. This viewpoint is often called the **critical-period hypothesis**, the belief that an organism must have certain experiences at a *particular time* in its developmental sequence if it is to reach its most mature state.

Imprinting in Animals

There are many studies from the animal literature supporting the critical-period hypothesis. For instance, Nobel Prize winner Konrad Lorenz discovered many years ago that birds, such as ducks and geese, will follow the first moving object they see after they are hatched. Usually the first thing they see is their mother, of course, who was sitting on the eggs. However, Lorenz hatched goose eggs in an incubator, and then let the goslings see him immediately after hatching instead of seeing another goose. The freshly-hatched geese followed him just the way they ordinarily would have followed their real mother.

After the goslings had waddled along behind Lorenz for a few hours, they acted as if they thought they were humans, not geese. When Lorenz returned the goslings to their real mother, they ignored her. Whenever Lorenz appeared, however, they became very excited and flocked to him for protection and affection. It was as if the *visual image* of the first moving object they saw had become so strongly "imprinted" on their minds that, forever after, this object was "mother" (see Fig. 14.5) (Lorenz, 1957).

Imprinting reaches its peak 16 to 24 hours after the baby goose is hatched. During this period, the baby bird has an innate tendency to follow anything that moves. And once

FIG. 14.5 Konrad Lorenz followed by his grayleg goslings.

the goose has been imprinted, this very special form of learning has long-lasting consequences. For example, when the birds Lorenz imprinted on himself were grown and sexually mature, they showed no romantic interest in other geese. Instead, they attempted to court and mate with humans.

Imprinting takes place in many (but not all) types of birds, and it also seems to occur in mammals such as sheep and seals. As we will see in a moment, however, there is still considerable argument as to whether anything like imprinting occurs in humans (Wachs & Gruen, 1982).

WHAT NEWBORN INFANTS CAN AND CAN'T DO

Are there "critical periods" in human development? As it turns out, we cannot answer this question satisfactorily without knowing what things newborn infants can and can't do. A century ago, many scientists believed that a neonate had few if any innate abilities. For example, almost 100 years ago, William James stated that the newborn's sensory world was a "blooming, buzzing confusion." Taking a very strong "nurturist" position, James saw the neonate's mind as a "blank piece of paper." It was only when *experience* wrote on this piece of paper that the child's mind began to form and develop, James said (James, 1890).

The notion that infants are almost totally helpless at birth continued to dominate the field until the 1970's. For example, as Jerome Bruner notes, until a decade or so ago, many pediatricians assumed that infants were "functionally blind" until they were several months of age (cited in Bronfenbrenner *et al.*, 1986).

In recent years, however, the pendulum of scientific opinion has begun to swing toward a "naturist" position. For instance, we now know that almost from birth, an infant can not only see and hear with great precision, but also can sort out stimuli, remember, and predict future inputs. Neonates apparently can recognize their own names by two weeks of age, and they can distinguish among colors by the time they are three months old. They seem to develop depth perception by the fourth month of life. There is even some evidence that fetuses can acquire simple associations while still in the womb (Mussen, 1983).

● ***Prenatal Learning?***

In a recent article in *Science*, Gina Kolata describes a number of experimental studies which suggest that both animal and human fetuses can be *conditioned* to respond to specific stimuli before birth (Kolata, 1984). For example, William Smotherman and his colleagues at Oregon State University have studied prenatal conditioning in rats. Smotherman injected a pleasant substance (apple juice) directly into the amniotic fluid surrounding one group of fetal rats. Later, he also injected an unpleasant substance (lithium chloride) into the fluid. When these experimental rats were born, they refused to suck on nipples that were coated with apple juice. Control fetuses who received *just* lithium chloride or *just* apple juice while still in the womb did not avoid the nipples coated with apple juice (Smotherman, 1982). More recently, Smotherman and S.R. Robinson successfully repeated this experiment using mint flavoring rather than apple juice (Smotherman & Robinson, 1985). Smotherman believes the experimental animals *associated* the mint or the apple juice with lithium chloride, hence *associated* the unpleasant properties of the lithium chloride with the apple juice (see the studies on "taste aversion" in Chapter 9).

Anthony DeCasper, a psychologist at the University of North Carolina in Greensboro, began his study of fetal learning in humans many years ago. DeCasper notes that newborn infants have excellent hearing, a fact that suggests fetuses should be able to hear sounds while still in the womb. DeCasper performed several experiments showing that neonates preferred the sound of their mother's voice shortly after birth to the sound of women's voices they had not previously heard. They also preferred the sound of their mother's heart beat to the sound of male voices (including the sound of their father's voice) (DeCasper & Prescott, 1984).

In a recent experiment, DeCasper and Melanie Spence asked pregnant women to "talk" to their fetuses daily. During the last six weeks of their pregnancy, the women read aloud from *The Cat in the Hat* (a children's book) twice a day. Then, shortly after the infants were born, DeCasper and Spence tested them. The infants preferred hearing their mothers read aloud from *The Cat in the Hat* than from another children's book. In a second study, DeCasper and Spence had pregnant women repeat a phrase aloud, several times a day, during the last weeks of their pregnancy. After birth, the infants preferred the spoken phrase to other similar phrases (DeCasper & Spence, 1986). DeCasper concludes that "Prenatal auditory experience is sufficient to influence postnatal auditory preferences" (cited in Kolata, 1984).

How much information fetuses can acquire before birth, we don't yet know. However, the fact that they can learn *anything* while still in the womb may help explain many of the early behaviors infants typically show.

◻ ◻ **QUESTION** ◻ ◻
In the Smotherman conditioning experiment involving apple juice and lithium chloride, what was the CS and what was the UCS?

● *Neonatal Learning*
Only moments out of the womb, infants are capable of a wide variety of behaviors. Their eyes are alert, and they turn their heads in the direction of any voice they hear (Stratton, 1982). They prefer female voices to male, but apparently search their visual world to locate the source of *any* human voice. They move their arms and legs in **synchrony** to human speech—but not to random noise, or many other sounds (such as tapping). Furthermore, they respond to any *human language*, but not to *artificial sounds* and broken-up speech patterns (Kuhl & Meltzoff, 1984). By the time they are a day or so old, they can discriminate between two sounds in order to receive a taste of sugar water (Lipsitt, 1982).

University of Miami psychologist Tiffany Field and her colleagues worked with two-day-old infants. Field and her group found that, only 45 hours after birth, newborns can integrate sights, sounds, smells, and touch into a meaningful perceptual pattern or *schema* that allows them to discriminate their mother from a woman they had never seen before (Field *et al.*, 1985).

Expressive Imitation
According to Andrew Meltzoff of the University of Washington, an infant can imitate some facial expressions *one hour after birth* (see Fig. 14.6). But because such newborn children are difficult to work with, Meltzoff and his colleagues have performed most of their research on two-week-old babies. In an elegant series of studies begun in 1977, Meltzoff has shown that two-week-old infants will stick out their tongues or open their mouths fully the first time they see these expressive facial expressions in the adults around them (Meltzoff, 1981).

Meltzoff's experiments seem particularly well controlled. The adults whose expressions the babies imitated were all strangers to the infants. The infants' responses were filmed and then judged by scientists who did not know what expression the baby was supposed to be imitating. Furthermore, Meltzoff did not tell the children's parents what he was up to. (In one early study when the parents were told, the mothers trained the infants to stick out their tongues before bringing them to the lab. As

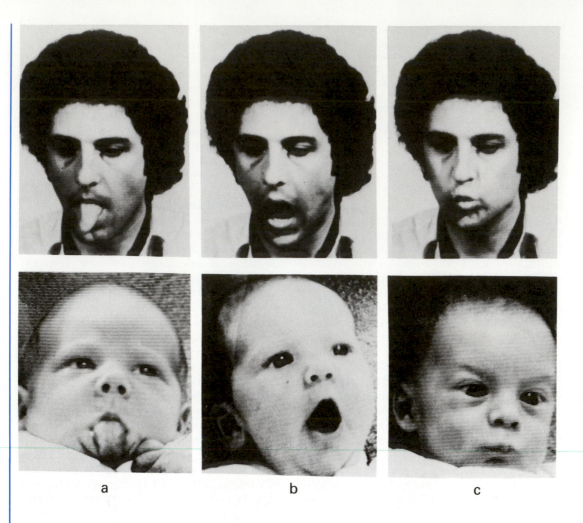

FIG. 14.6 Sample photographs from videotape recordings of two- to three-week-old infants imitating (A) tongue protrusion, (B) mouth opening, and (C) lip protrusion, demonstrated by an adult experimenter.

one mother put it, "I didn't want my baby to fail his first test.")

Meltzoff has also shown that two-week-old infants can *remember* facial expressions for brief periods of time. In one study, he stuck pacifiers in the babies' mouths and then exposed them to adults who either opened their mouths or stuck out their tongues. A few minutes later, when the pacifier was removed, the infants still gave the proper imitative response (Meltzoff & Moore, 1983).

In a similar set of studies, Tiffany Field and her colleagues at the University of Miami have shown that 36-hour-old infants can both detect and imitate such facial expressions as happiness, sadness, and surprise (Field *et al.*, 1986). However, psychologist Marsha Kaitz and her colleagues at Hebrew University in Israel disagree. They studied 26 newborn infants who were held by a woman who modeled various facial expressions, such as sadness and happiness. Two observers rated the newborns' reactions. The infants did open their mouths, stick out their tongues, and pout their lips in response to the model's facial expressions. However, Kaitz says, these reactions were merely "innate motor responses" that were triggered by the facial expressions. Kaitz and her associ-ates contend that "voluntary imitation of emotional expressions is not within a newborn's repertoire" (Kaitz *et al.*, 1988).

Nature or Nurture?

If newborns can do so much immediately after birth, doesn't that prove that most *mental development* is determined by *physical growth*? And if that is the case, isn't most of what we call "personality" shaped primarily by the genes, not the environment?

Probably the *interactionist* position taken by Princeton researchers J.L. and Carol G. Gould is the one best supported by present data. The Goulds believe that the genes *sensitize* newly born organisms to certain aspects of their environments. But both the environment, and the training techniques actually used, determine what infants learn (see Fig. 14.7). Simple animals—such as bees and birds—inherit rather rigid "learning programs," the Goulds say. These programs specify rather precisely what the animals can (and can't) learn from their environments, and when in the developmental sequence this learning should take place (Gould & Gould, 1981).

The restrictions on human learning are much more subtle. You were born with the ability (and the desire) to learn almost anything. However, you do best when your environment "shapes" you following the laws of learning outlined in Chapters 9–11. Thus, at all levels, *nature and nurture interact*. But according to James Gould, the *relative importance* of "nature" and "nurture" varies widely in different species (Gould, 1986).

Given the past history of the nature-nurture controversy, it's likely this issue will never be entirely settled. But as long as scientists continue to argue about what is innate and what is acquired, the more we will learn about the factors that influence human growth and development. We can make this point rather dramatically by looking now at emotional development.

EMOTIONAL DEVELOPMENT

In Chapter 9, we noted that the experts who study emotions are split into at least three camps:

Those scientists who believe that "the body runs the mind," and thus tend to define emotions in terms of *physical reactions*.

FIG. 14.7 Motor development in an infant.

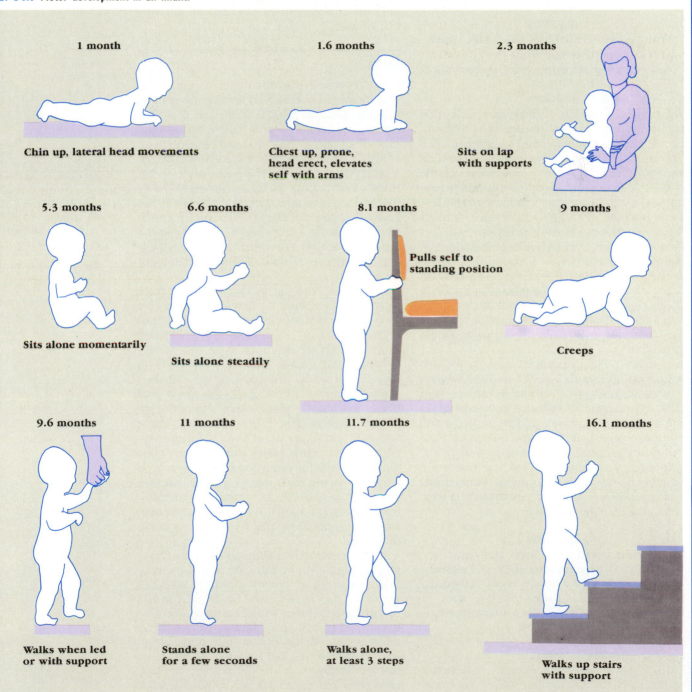

1 month — Chin up, lateral head movements

1.6 months — Chest up, prone, head erect, elevates self with arms

2.3 months — Sits on lap with supports

5.3 months — Sits alone momentarily

6.6 months — Sits alone steadily

8.1 months — Pulls self to standing position

9 months — Creeps

9.6 months — Walks when led or with support

11 months — Stands alone for a few seconds

11.7 months — Walks alone, at least 3 steps

16.1 months — Walks up stairs with support

Those experimenters who hold that "the mind runs the body," and thus tend to define emotionality in terms of *mental experiences*.

Those theorists who believe that the *social environment* "shapes" emotional responses, and thus tend to define emotions in terms of reactions to social inputs.

As of the 1980's, however, a growing number of psychologists believe that emotional development is determined by an *interaction* among biological, intra-psychic, and social/behavioral influences. However, the experts do disagree on the issue of which aspects of emotionality are learned, and which are determined by the genes (Brazelton & Yogman, 1986).

□ □ **QUESTION** □ □
Since newborn infants can't talk, how would you discover what they "really felt" during an emotional upheaval?

● *The "Nature" Position*

Tiffany Field and her colleagues believe that infants are born with an innate need to maintain a certain *optimal level of arousal* (see Chapter 6). To Field and her associates, smiling and laughing are "objective indicators" that the child is at this optimal level. Crying and frowning suggest the youngster's arousal level is less than optimal. Through experience, infants learn which emotional expressions will get them the inputs (food, cuddling) they need to maintain whatever level of arousal they desire at any point in time. However, as Field *et al.* make clear, emotional responses are merely "body signals" designed to regulate or control social interactions, not an indication of what the youngster *feels* "deep down inside" (Field *et al.*, 1985).

In brief, Field's position seems to be that you were born with a set of *undifferentiated* emotional responses. Through contact with others, you learn to enhance and enlarge on some of these reactions, and to suppress and minimize others. But you *do not create new emotional expressions*. You merely *reshape* the responses you inherited. And you use these emotional expressions to signal your needs and arousal level to others, not to suggest what your inner feelings are like.

□ □ **QUESTION** □ □
When you fall in love, do your emotional expressions merely "signal your needs and arousal level" to your beloved? Or is there more to the experience of "love" than just physical reactions?

● *The "Nurture" Position*

Carol Malatesta and her colleagues believe that infants learn to "display appropriate emotions" primarily through interactions with their mothers and other adults. Malatesta's research indicates that mothers influence their infants by "modeling" the appropriate reactions they want the youngsters to show. The mothers also selectively reward "appropriate" responses in the infants and punish emotional expressions the mothers believe to be "inappropriate." Malatesta says that early social contact with adults therefore serves to teach children cultural rules, gender-related rules, and personal rules involving emotional reactions (Malatesta *et al.*, 1986).

You should keep both the mind-body problem and the nature-nurture controversy in mind as we discuss the development of a very important emotion in infancy and childhood—that of *love*.

LOVE

Let us continue our discussion of emotional development by asking an apparently simple-minded question: What is love? The usual belief (in our society) is that love is an *internal state* or *emotional process*. Love certainly is an emotion, and it obviously has its *subjective* (or intra-psychic) aspects. This side of love has been written about for centuries by some of the wisest poets and novelists the world has known. When Elizabeth Barrett Browning wrote, "How do I love thee? Let me count the ways . . ." she told us as much about the subjective experience of love as any psychologist could.

However, love can also be approached *objectively*. For example, we may look at maternal love and say that it is an instinctual, biological response strongly influenced by the female's hormones. Or we may look at an individual's behavior and *assume* that only someone in love would act in that fashion. We can then study "loving behaviors" quite objectively, and draw conclusions about what internal processes might *mediate* these behaviors. These scientific investigations of love will never *replace* our subjective, poetic examination of this glorious condition—nor is there any reason why they should. But once we realize that love is, *in part*, a response to some living or inanimate object (or ideal), we can make certain statements about love that we could not make otherwise.

For example, by taking an *objective* viewpoint toward love, we can state with some confidence that loving behaviors will (1) *tend to increase* if they are followed by satisfaction and reward, and that they will (2) *tend to decrease* if followed by pain, punishment, or lack of reinforcement. We do not usually think about love in these terms. But by doing so, we often discover things about the development of love (and other emotions) that we couldn't learn if

Social dyad (DIE-add). A mutually-interacting group composed of just two members.

we focused entirely on the *subjective* aspects of the experience.

Parental Love

Society demands that parents love—or at least care for—their children. So social factors surely influence both paternal and maternal love. But these social influences always *interact* with biological and intra-psychic factors.

In a recent article, Daniel Stern describes how mother and child form a **social dyad** almost immediately after the infant's birth. Stern has a laboratory at New York Hospital's Payne Whitney Clinic. For many years, he has filmed the reactions of mothers to their newborn children. He then slows the movies down and analyzes the pictures one frame at a time. By making this sort of "slow-motion analysis," Stern is able to spot subtle mother-infant interactions that otherwise might be missed.

Stern reports that both the mother and her infant appear to have an "inborn mutual readiness" to respond to each other. This "readiness" apparently is a genetically determined *social behavior* in both the mother and the child. But it is also a pattern of interactions that society strongly reinforces once the behaviors occur (Stern, 1983).

Perhaps it is not as glamorous to study interactive patterns as it is to study "love." But as Robert Emde notes, we are more likely to understand these natural parental-child patterns if we look at them objectively. Emde is a psychiatrist at the University of Colorado Medical School. He and his colleagues believe that the infant triggers off maternal and paternal behaviors in the parents as much as parents set off innate responses in the child. He sums up the matter thusly: "For years, theories described how mothers shaped babies, but we are now beginning to appreciate how much babies shape mothers." And how they shape their fathers, too, as Emde also points out (Emde, 1983; Klinnert *et al.*, 1986).

The question then becomes, what are the crucial variables that determine parent-child patterns of interactions? Some of these variables are biochemical, and are determined by the genes. Other factors are psychological, and are influenced by past experience and the laws of learning. And some of the variables are social, for not all societies value infants as much as ours does.

● *Using Animal Subjects*

We will look at the various influences on parent-child interactions in just a moment. But first, a reminder about a scientific "fact of life."

There are some aspects of behavior we simply cannot study using human subjects. Therefore, in many studies, we use animal subjects instead. For instance, much of our knowledge of how hormones influence maternal care comes from experiments on rats, birds, sheep, and monkeys. As useful as the lower species are in this sort of work, however, we must always be careful in generalizing from animal subjects to the human level. And, just as important from an ethical standpoint, we must make sure the animals we use in our research are treated with as much concern for their welfare as if we were using human subjects.

These points made, suppose we begin by looking at some *biological* variables that affect parent-child relationships.

HORMONAL INFLUENCES ON MATERNAL BEHAVIOR

Harvard psychologist T. Berry Brazelton has for many years studied the ways that parents and infants react to each other. Brazelton states that a mother's emotional attachment to her infant does not appear "instantaneously, by magic" in the hospital delivery room. Rather, he says, this emotionality begins early in pregnancy and develops fairly slowly. It shows itself primarily in the *feelings and dreams* that many woman experience during pregnancy.

Brazelton notes that most women experience considerable anxiety about themselves and their yet-to-be-born child during pregnancy. These fears are part of the normal attachment process, Brazelton says, and probably reach their peak a few days before labor begins. The anxiety and nervousness are needed in order to break old habit patterns and prepare the woman to take on the new role of mothering. These fears also provide the woman with the heightened arousal and energy she will need in order to care for her infant.

Brazelton believes that the attachment process has two aspects to it. The first is an *increased interest in infants*. Research suggests this part of the process develops rapidly, is controlled primarily by hormones, and is usually found only in pregnant females. The second part of parental attachment involves a need for *continued contact with infants*. This need seems to be psychological rather than biological in origin, develops rather slowly, is strongly influenced by reinforcement, and can be seen in males as well as females (Brazelton, 1987; Brazelton & Als, 1979).

Hormonal "Triggers"

According to Jay Rosenblatt of Rutgers University, the hormone levels of pregnant females change dramatically just before labor starts. The amount of progesterone decreases

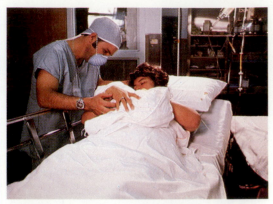

According to Brazelton, intimacy between mother and baby develops during the nine months of pregnancy; he believes the moments of "bonding" just after birth are not as crucial as some other researchers contend.

sharply, while the level of estrogen increases (see Chapter 7). Rosenblatt states that the onset of maternal behavior before delivery is based on this rise in estrogen. He calls this effect a "hormonal trigger" that significantly changes both *motives* and *behaviors*. For example, prior to the change, a pregnant female rat will avoid newborn pups taken from another mother. Immediately after the hormonal change—but before the female gives birth—she develops an intense interest in pups taken from other mothers, however (Rosenblatt, 1983).

Put more simply, progesterone merely makes it easy for the mother to *learn* to become attached to her offspring. This is the biological aspect of maternal attachment. However, it is the sight, sound, and smell of the pups that *reinforces* and thus maintains close contact with newborn infants. This is the intra-psychic aspect of the attachment process. And it is to this aspect that we must now turn our attention.

INTRA-PSYCHIC ASPECTS OF ATTACHMENT

Jay Rosenblatt believes that most animals (and perhaps some humans) are frightened by contact with newborn infants. "It appears to be part of a basic fearfulness of anything new," he says. How, then, to get adults (other than pregnant females) to overcome this fear of novelty?

Desensitization may be one answer (see Chapter 9). In one set of studies, Rosenblatt and his colleagues confined virgin female rats to small cages. The experimenters then introduced newborn pups from other females. At first, the virgin rats kept as far away from the pups as they could. After four to seven days' exposure, however, the virgins began to accept the pups and started showing maternal behaviors toward them. Male rats exposed to the

same desensitization process also displayed "maternal behaviors" toward the pups after a week or so. Generally speaking, the smaller the cage, the faster this behavioral change occurred (Giordano, Siegel, & Rosenblatt, 1986).

It would seem, therefore, that *intra-psychic variables* take over in the attachment process where *biological variables* leave off. Desensitization is one such intra-psychic variable. Imprinting and something called "contact comfort" might well be two others. Let's look at both imprinting and "contact comfort" in some detail.

□ □ **QUESTION** □ □
Why might it help a human father accept (and eventually assist in the care of) his child if the man is present during the birthing process?

Does "Imprinting" Exist in Humans?

Once Konrad Lorenz had demonstrated imprinting with birds, scientists began hunting for similar effects in humans. Among the first researchers to report success were Marshall Klaus and John Kennell, professors of pediatrics at Case Western Reserve University in Cleveland.

In their 1976 book, *Maternal-Infant Bonding*, Klaus and Kennell state there is a *critical period* in the first hour or so of life during which an infant can *bond* with its mother. This bonding takes place only if the mother and child are in close physical contact during the "sensitive period," according to Klaus and Kennell. Supposedly, the "bonding" increases the mother's love for her child and makes her more attentive to the infant's needs. Indeed, Klaus and Kennell cite several studies suggesting that the mother is likely to neglect or abuse the child if the "bonding" fails to occur (Kennell & Klaus, 1979).

Despite the data suggesting that "bonding" occurs in humans, however, some scientists remain skeptical. In a recent article, Michael Lamb reviews many of the experiments purporting to show that "bonding" occurs. Lamb is professor of psychology, psychiatry, and pediatrics at the University of Utah. He believes most of the "bonding" studies have such serious flaws that they offer little support for the position taken by Klaus and Kennell. "Taken together," Lamb says, "the studies . . . show no clear evidence for any lasting effect of early physical contact between mother and infant on subsequent maternal behavior. The most that can be said is that it may sometimes have modest short-term effects on some mothers in some circumstances" (Lamb, 1982).

Lamb notes that there are no known *ill effects* from early mother-infant contacts. But he fears that those mothers who were not allowed to hold their children immediately after birth

Jay S. Rosenblatt

Michael Lamb

may feel they are somehow "inadequate parents." That simply isn't so, Lamb says, and offers as proof the fact that most *adoptive mothers* are at least as loving as are "bonded" mothers (Lamb & Brown, 1982). Thus, the question of whether any form of imprinting occurs in human infants has not as yet been completely decided.

Surrogate Mothers

Even if maternal "bonding" doesn't exist (or is relatively unimportant) in humans, it is a powerful force in many lower species, including the **primates**. The scientist who conducted the best long-term laboratory experiments on mother-child relationships in primates was Harry Harlow, who did most of his work at the University of Wisconsin. Since Harlow needed a place to house and raise the monkeys he used as subjects, he built the Primate Laboratory at Wisconsin. He and his wife Margaret (also a psychologist) devised a breeding program and tried various ways of raising monkeys in the laboratory (Harlow, 1978).

The Harlows soon discovered that monkey infants raised by their mothers often caught diseases from their parents. So the Harlows began taking the infants away from their mothers at birth and raising the infants by hand. The baby monkeys were given cheesecloth diapers to serve as baby blankets (see Fig. 14.8). Almost from the start, it became obvious to the Harlows that their little animals developed such strong attachments to the blankets that, in the Harlows' terms, it was often hard to tell "where the diaper ended and the baby began." And if the Harlows removed the "security" blanket in order to clean it, the infant monkey often became greatly disturbed—just as if its own mother had deserted it.

What the baby monkeys obviously needed was an artificial or **surrogate** mother—something they could cling to as tightly as they typically clung to their own mother's chest. In 1957, while enjoying a champagne flight high over the city of Detroit, Harry Harlow glanced out of the airplane window and "saw" an image of an artificial monkey mother. It was a hollow wire cylinder, wrapped with a terrycloth bath towel, with a silly wooden head at the top. The tiny monkey could cling to this model mother as closely as to its real mother's body hair (see Fig. 14.9).

The Harlows gave the surrogate mother a functional breast by placing a milk bottle so that the nipple stuck through the cloth at an appropriate place on the surrogate's anatomy. The Harlows also developed ways to heat the cloth mother—or to cool it. They installed a mechanism that would rock the surrogate gently. Then they took infant monkeys away from their natural mothers and put them in with surrogates, to see how the infants would fare (Harlow, Harlow, & Suomi, 1971).

FIG. 14.8 Baby monkey in a cheesecloth blanket.

FIG. 14.9 Baby monkey with surrogate cloth mother.

□ □ **QUESTION** □ □

What kinds of information about the emotional development of humans (and other species) can best be obtained from "real life observations," and what kinds can best be obtained in a laboratory?

Contact Comfort

During the first two weeks of its life, warmth is perhaps the most important thing that a monkey mother has to give to its baby. The Harlows discovered this fact by offering infant monkeys a choice of two types of mother substitutes— one wrapped in terrycloth and one that was made of bare wire. If the two artificial mothers were both the same temperature, the little monkeys always preferred the cloth mother. However, if the wire model was heated, while the cloth model was cool, the baby primates picked the wire substitute as their favorite for the first two weeks after birth. Thereafter they switched and spent most of their time on the more comfortable cloth mother.

Why is cold cloth preferable to warm wire? Something that the Harlows call **contact comfort** seems to be the answer. Infant monkeys spend much of their time rubbing against their mothers' skins, putting themselves in as close contact with the parent as they can. Prolonged "contact comfort" with a surrogate cloth mother appears to instill confidence in baby monkeys and is much more rewarding to them than is either warmth or milk.

● *Endorphins and Contact Comfort*

Unlike surrogate models, real-life mothers spend a great deal of time rubbing and caressing their infants. And according to Duke University researcher Saul Schanberg, a mother's touch has biological as well as psychological effects. In a recent study, Schanberg and his associates showed that maternal touching promotes protein synthesis and weight gain in infant rats. Pups deprived of maternal touching— or an artificial substitute—failed to show normal growth despite the fact that they were well fed. The deprived infants also showed significantly elevated levels of *endorphins*. Apparently, this increase in endorphins *inhibited* the production of a protein needed for normal growth, Schanberg and his colleagues say (Pauk *et al.*, 1986).

Apparently, *lack* of maternal stimulation is stressful in most newborns. The stress causes a release of endorphins, which in turn inhibits the production of proteins needed for normal development. Harlow's monkeys, therefore, probably rubbed against the surrogate mother in an attempt to reduce stress. And in doing so, they aided their own physical growth.

● *Novelty, Stress, and Contact Comfort*

According to the Harlows, contact comfort creates *emotional trust* in infant monkeys. If the infant is put into an unfamiliar playroom without its mother, the infant ignores the toys no matter how interesting they might be. If its cloth mother is now introduced into the playroom, the infant rushes to the surrogate and clings to it. After a few minutes of contact comfort, the infant apparently begins to feel more secure. It then climbs down from the mother substitute and begins tentatively to explore the toys (Meyer *et al.*, 1975).

In an interesting series of studies, Michael Lamb and his colleagues have found that human infants show similar responses to Harlow's monkeys. For example, Lamb and Lynne Zarbatany showed 79 infants a toy spider and had the child's mother express either a joyful or a fearful facial reaction. Almost all the infants showed initial fear, but then looked at the mother to check her reaction. The children attempted to touch or play with the spider toy much sooner if the mother's facial expression was joyful than if she expressed fear. If the infants were shown the spider when their mother was absent—but a strange woman was present—the children ignored the stranger's facial expressions and tended to avoid the toy (Zarbatany & Lamb, 1985).

● *Good Mothers and Bad*

According to the Harlows, once a baby monkey has become *emotionally attached* to its mother (real or surrogate), the mother can do almost no wrong. In one of the Harlows' studies, they

The need for sensory stimulation of infants has been widely recognized in recent years, making nurseries like this one, where babies are held and cuddled only briefly, a rarity.

Contact comfort. The pleasure a young animal gets from rubbing its body against a soft, "woolly" object, or from clinging tightly to its mother's body.

Anaclitic relationship (ann-ah-KLITT-ick). A strong, non-sexual love; the loving dependency and trust of a young child for its mother. The emotional attachment that builds up between a child and its mother.

Nurturance (NURR-tur-ants). To give nurturance means to take care of.

tried to create "monster mothers" whose behavior would be so abnormal that the infants would desert the mothers. Some of these surrogates shook so violently the infants couldn't cling to the surrogates. Other "monster mothers" would mechanically toss the infants aside from time to time. However, none of these surrogates apparently was "evil" enough to impart fear or loathing to the infant monkeys. The baby monkeys did show a brief period of emotional disturbance when the surrogates first rejected the infants. But as soon as the surrogates returned to normal, the infant would return to the "monster mother" and continue clinging, as if all were forgiven. As the Harlows tell the story, the only prolonged distress created by the experiment seemed to be that felt by the experimenters (Harlow, Harlow, & Suomi, 1971)!

• *Anaclitic Depression*

A human infant cared for by a mother with consistent behavior patterns rapidly builds up an emotional *attachment* to its mother, for the child learns that much of what is pleasant and satisfying comes through the actions of the mother. Psychologists call this an **anaclitic relationship**, the phrase coming from the Greek word meaning "to lean on."

J.A. Bowlby studied infant-mother attachments for a great many years. According to Bowlby, disturbing the anaclitic relationship can be dangerous. If it is the mother who *always* feeds the child, the infant soon builds up a *perceptual schema* that incorporates both "food" and "mother." When food appears, the child expects the mother to be there too, because the youngster is not yet mature enough to discriminate food from mother. If the infant is suddenly separated from the mother during the first months of life, Bowlby says, the child may have considerable difficulty adjusting to changes in the youngster's environment (Bowlby, 1973).

Evidence supporting Bowlby's beliefs comes from research by psychiatrist R.A. Spitz. He studied the reactions of infants 6 to 12 months old who, for various reasons, had been separated from their mothers and put into institutions or foster homes. In their new environments, these infants received at best impersonal care. Almost as soon as the infants were institutionalized, they began showing signs of

disturbance. They became quite upset when anyone approached them. They lost weight, became passive and inactive, and had trouble sleeping as well. Spitz calls this condition *anaclitic depression*.

The first sign of anaclitic depression is a behavior Spitz describes as "a search for the mother." Some babies quietly weep big tears; others cry violently. None of them can be quieted down by any type of intervention, although at the initial stage of the depression they still cling tightly to any adult who picks them up. If the mother does not return in 3 to 4 weeks, the infant's behavior changes. The child withdraws, lies quietly in the crib, will not play if offered a toy, and does not even look up if someone enters the room. The baby becomes dejected and passive, refuses food, and becomes more susceptible than usual to colds and other ailments.

Spitz believes that anaclitic depression might well account for some types of mental retardation, since the children he studied seemed to show considerable physical and intellectual impairment during and immediately after their periods of depression (Spitz, 1945).

Psychologist Myron Hofer disagrees with Spitz, however. Hofer claims the reactions of human infants to separation may be no more than responses to withdrawal of the sensory stimulation or **nurturance** provided by the mother. Thus, Hofer says, it is not a disturbance of the "mother schema," but simply a decrease in sensory inputs that causes the infant distress (Hofer, 1981, 1984).

□ □ **QUESTION** □ □

Can you design an experimental study that might indicate whether Spitz's or Hofer's explanation was correct? Why would it be difficult to conduct this sort of research with *human* infants?

SOCIAL/BEHAVIORAL ASPECTS OF EMOTIONAL DEVELOPMENT

Most early research on parent-child attachments focused on how the child's emotional development was affected by "good mothering." Slowly, over the years, psychologists came to realize two important things: First, mothers and infants constitute *social systems*. That is, the infant influences the mother as much as the mother affects her child. Second, at the human level, the father often plays as crucial a role in helping the child develop as does the mother. As we will see, the father's behavior affects the infant in two ways—through father-child interactions, and by the support the father gives the mother. Given these facts, it seems appropriate to turn now to a discussion of social/behavioral influences on emotional development.

We will begin by looking at how monkeys respond to being raised in *social deprivation*. Then we will turn our attention to father-child patterns of interaction.

□ □ **QUESTION** □ □

If you had been reared in complete isolation from all other humans until you were four, how would you have reacted if suddenly introduced to other children your age?

Peer Relationships

Monkeys raised on cloth surrogates appear to be fairly normal in their behavior patterns—at least while they are isolated from their **peers**. However, when the Harlows put *groups* of surrogate-trained monkeys together, the Harlows soon found they had a problem. Although these animals had never seen other monkeys during their entire lives, they responded to one another with excessive amounts of aggressive behavior. Eventually this hostility waned and then disappeared, but the animals' social behavior remained unusual, to say the least.

Many of these monkeys showed the kinds of *stereotyped* activities found in certain types of patients in mental hospitals. That is, some of the monkeys made oddly repetitive movements that seemed to have no function. Others froze into bizarre postures, or stared into space for hours on end. As the Harlows point out, these infant monkeys had been raised in *partial* social deprivation. They had their surrogate mothers, and they often interacted with their human keepers. But the animals had never experienced the pleasures of socializing with other growing monkeys. Little wonder they didn't get along well with each other (Suomi, Delizio, & Harlow, 1976).

• *Peer Deprivation in Monkeys*

In one of their best-known experiments, the Harlows tried to reproduce a human type of *anaclitic depression* in normal infant monkeys. These young animals were from birth raised in a large group with their mothers present. Then, for a period of several weeks, the mothers were taken away, leaving the infants to get along together as best they could.

As you might expect, the tiny monkeys went through much the same sort of anaclitic depression as do human infants. At the time of their separation, the baby monkeys searched actively for their mothers and cried loudly. Soon, however, they began to withdraw. Even though they had their peers to romp about with, they stopped playing and socializing. Instead, the babies huddled in corners alone, each clinging tightly to its own body.

Once the mothers were reintroduced, the infants went through a momentary period of frantic activity, most of which was aimed at clinging so tightly to the mother that she could never leave them again. Peer play soon became re-established and the infants recovered normally.

In a further set of studies, the Harlows showed that it is not merely the loss of maternal "magic" that leads to severe depression. Rather, it is the deprivation of whatever form of social stimulation the organism is *accustomed to* at the time of separation that throws it into a state of hopelessness. Monkeys raised from birth in the presence of other infants their age (but without any mothers present) appear to grow up fairly normally. When these infants are isolated from their peers, however, they too fall into an anaclitic depression, just as if they had been separated from their mothers. When reunited with these peers, they engage in the same intense clinging as would an infant given back to its mother (Suomi *et al.*, 1975).

□ □ **QUESTION** □ □

The anaclitic depression occurs not merely because the infant is separated from its mother, but because its *expectancies* are grossly violated. How might this fact help explain adult depressions caused by loss of job, friends, or loved ones?

Isolation and Later Maternal Behaviors

In one study, the Harlows put peer-deprived monkeys together so they might breed and hence provide more baby monkeys for experiments. But the animals refused to cooperate. Even when the Harlows introduced an experienced, normally-raised male into the colony, he was a complete failure as far as impregnating any of the females was concerned (Harlow, 1975).

The Harlows were finally able to get female isolates pregnant by confining them in a small cage for long periods of time with a patient and highly-experienced male. But when these isolated females gave birth to their first monkey baby, they turned out to be the "monster mothers" the Harlows had tried to create with mechanical surrogates. At first, the motherless mothers totally ignored their infants. However, if the infant persisted, the mothers occasionally gave in and provided the baby with some of the contact comfort it demanded. Surprisingly enough, once these mothers learned how to handle a baby, they did reasonably well. Then, when they were again impregnated and gave birth to a second infant, they took care of it fairly adequately.

Maternal affection was totally lacking in a few of the motherless monkeys, however. To them, the newborn monkey was little more than an object to be abused the way a human child might abuse a doll or a toy train. These motherless mothers stepped on their babies,

Peers. From a Latin word meaning "equals." Your peers are the people of your own age and social station whom you grew up with.

crushed the infant's face to the floor of the cage, and once or twice chewed off their baby's feet and fingers before they could be stopped. The most terrible mother of all popped her infant's head into her mouth and crunched it like a potato chip (Harlow, 1978).

□ □ **QUESTION** □ □

What does the Harlows' research tell us about possible causes of child abuse in humans? (Hint: What kind of "maternal model" did the motherless monkeys have when they were young?)

THE FATHER'S ROLE IN INFANT DEVELOPMENT

The noted anthropologist Margaret Mead once said that "fathers are a biological necessity but a social accident." However, data gathered by developmental psychologists tend not to support Dr. Mead's viewpoint (Robinson & Barret, 1986).

As Michael Lamb notes, fathers contribute significantly to an infant's emotional growth, although the father's contributions are often quite different from the mother's. While the father is just as capable of taking care of an infant as is the mother, one of the father's chief roles (at least in our society) seems to be that of *playmate* to the child (Lamb, 1981).

Lamb reports several studies suggesting that men are just as likely to nurture and stimulate their children as are the mothers. In fact, there is some evidence that fathers are more

The more athletic style of play that fathers often engage in may give the child experience with different kinds of muscular and neural stimulation.

likely to hold their infants and to look at them than are the mothers. Furthermore, fathers are just as likely to interpret correctly the cues the infants give as are mothers. However, in most real-life settings, men are less likely to feed infants and change their diapers than are women. This difference in parental behaviors seems due to cultural roles, however, and not to innate differences in male-female "instincts" (Pleck, Lamb, & Levine, 1985–1986).

T. Berry Brazelton and his colleagues at Harvard found that fathers talked to their infants less than did the mothers. However, the men were much more likely to touch or hug the child than were the women. The fathers primarily engaged in rough-and-tumble play with their children, while the mothers were more likely to play conventional games, such as peek-a-boo. Brazelton notes that "When several weeks old, an infant displays an entirely different attitude—more wide-eyed, playful, and bright-faced—toward its father than toward its mother." One explanation for this, Brazelton says, is that the fathers apparently *expect* more playful responses from their children. And the children then respond to the father's expectations (Brazelton, 1986).

Paternal Deprivation

Given the fact that a father's influence on his child is more strongly emotional than intellec-

Fathers in our society generally spend less time caring for their babies than do mothers, although there seems to be no innate "mother instinct" to make women more capable of giving care.

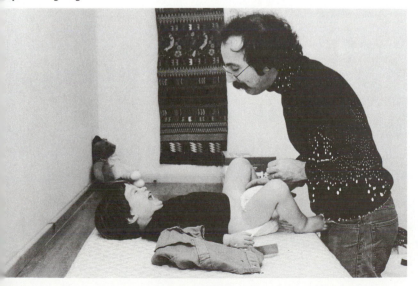

tual, what would be the result of the father's absence during the child's early years? Would boys react differently to paternal deprivation than would girls?

Several studies reported in the 1950's suggested that boys reared without fathers become less aggressive, more dependent, and have more "feminine" interests and behavior patterns than do boys who are brought up in normal families. In a recent paper, Sandra Scarr states that most of these experiments are of questionable value. In the 1950's and 1960's, Scarr says, "Families without fathers at home were studied extensively for their bad effects on the son's masculinity and were thought to result in poor mathematical skills and poor psychosocial development. The implicit, or sometimes explicit, assumption of the investigators of the period was that families without a masculine presence were doomed to inadequacy as rearing environments for children" (Scarr, 1985).

In a recent book, Paul Adams, Judith Milner, and Nancy Schrepf state that boys who grow up without a "male identity figure" present are neither more nor less "masculine" than boys reared in intact families (Adams, Milner, & Schrepf, 1984). For example, in a classic study, Elizabeth Herzog and Cecilia Sudia found that boys who grow up in fatherless homes turn out to be just as normal and well adjusted as boys reared in intact families. The only exception to this finding is that fatherless boys show a slight increase in delinquency and in school disci-

plinary problems. However, this same increase is found in both boys *and* girls reared by a single parent of *either* sex (Herzog & Sudia, 1968).

● Father-Daughter Relationships

Research by E. Mavis Hetherington suggests that young girls may need their fathers if they are to learn the social "dating skills" that our culture views as normal. Hetherington began by observing the activities of three types of girls: (1) those whose mothers had gotten divorces when the girls were very young, (2) those whose fathers had died when the girls were very young, and (3) those who had grown up in normal family situations. None of the girls had brothers. Although few of these young women had noticeable behavior problems, and all were doing reasonably well in school, there were marked differences in the way these adolescent girls *reacted to the males* in their environments.

According to Hetherington, girls reared by divorced mothers sought more attention and praise from males than did girls in the other two groups. They were also more likely to hang around places where young males could be found—gymnasiums, carpentry and machine shops, and the stag lines at school dances. In marked contrast, girls with widowed mothers tended to avoid males as much as possible. These fatherless girls stayed away from typically male gathering places, and many of them remained in the ladies' room the entire eve-

E. Mavis Hetherington

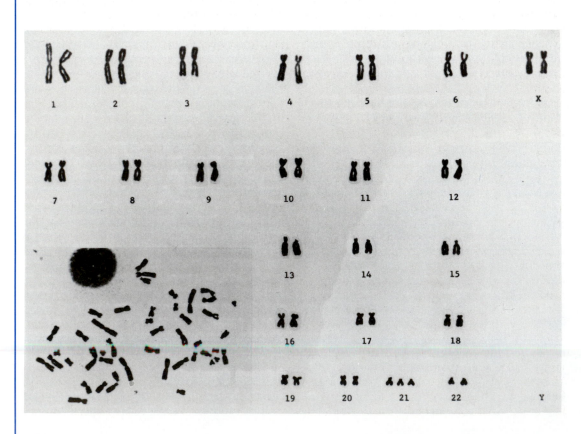

FIG. 14.10 Trisomy-21. Note the three chromosomes instead of the usual 21st pair. (See also Fig. 14.2.)

Thyroid (THIGH-roid). A large endocrine gland lying at the base of the neck that produces growth hormones.

ning during dances and other social events. These differences apparently were not due to popularity, for both groups of girls received equal numbers of invitations to dance when they were actually present in the dance hall.

All three groups of girls appeared to have similar and quite normal relationships with other women. However, girls reared by divorced mothers dated earlier and more frequently than did the others, and were more likely to have engaged in sexual intercourse. By contrast, girls with widowed mothers tended to start dating much later than normal and seemed to be sexually inhibited (Hetherington, Cox, & Cox, 1975). Data collected on the same girls 10 years later tended to confirm the original findings (Hetherington, Cox, & Cox, 1985).

Hetherington concludes that girls apparently need the presence of an adult male during their formative years in order to learn appropriate responses to men when the girls reach puberty (Hetherington, 1981).

☐ ☐ QUESTION ☐ ☐
Would you expect father-deprived girls to be as active in sports as girls reared in intact homes?

Emotional Development: A Summary
We are just beginning to learn the *scientific facts* of emotional development. We still do not know which aspects of maturation are primarily controlled by the genes, and which are more strongly influenced by experience. Nor do we yet understand as much as we should about helping children overcome the sometimes crippling effects of early emotional trauma. But the data do suggest that the best way to make sure a child grows up to be emotionally healthy is for both parents to give it wise and attentive love.

But what do we mean by "wise and attentive love"? Recent research suggests that our loving behaviors must be judged by their *consequences*, not merely by our *intentions*. We can demonstrate that point rather dramatically by returning to the subject of chromosomal abnormalities, and by discussing more fully the developmental disorder called *Down's syndrome*.

Down's Syndrome
Most authorities agree that Down's syndrome is the most common chromosomal defect affecting a child's development (Patterson, 1987). This disorder was once called "mongolism," because the child has an oriental-looking skin fold at the inner corners of the eyes. The young

person also typically has a small head; a flat nose; a protruding and thick tongue; a defective heart, eyes, and ears; and a defective **thyroid** gland. The cause of the disorder is well known—an extra 21st chromosome (see Fig. 14.10).

According to a recent study by the National Academy of Sciences, Down's syndrome occurs in one birth in 600. However, the age of the mother is a crucial variable. Among 25-year-old mothers, the incidence is 1 in 2,000 births. Among 40-year-old mothers, however, the incidence is one in 100 births. When the mother is 45 or older, the rate rises to one in 40. While some pediatricians believe the problem is due to "aging eggs," other specialists disagree. For example, David Kurnit of Boston's Children's Hospital believes that mothers under 35 may conceive as many Down's syndrome fetuses as do older mothers. However, Kurnit says, younger women's bodies are more capable of spontaneously aborting defective fetuses than are the bodies of older women (cited in Yulsman, 1986).

About 3 percent of the time, Down's syndrome is inherited, and may be due to defective genes on the father's as well as the mother's part. In most cases, however, the disorder is caused by a "genetic accident." For some reason, the 21st pair of chromosomes does not separate properly during cell division, and the extra chromosome is carried over in either the egg or the sperm. According to Cornell University specialist Terry Hassold, some 75 to 80 percent of the time, the defect is carried in the egg, not the sperm (cited in Tyndall, 1986).

The mortality rate for Down's syndrome children is very high early in life—especially for females—with 40 to 55 percent of them dying in their first year. These children seem to have defective immune systems, since they are particularly sensitive to viral diseases such as the flu. If their medical problems are handled properly, however, individuals with Down's syndrome often live until middle age (Patterson, 1987).

Mental(?) Retardation
At the beginning of this chapter, we discussed both the mind-body problem and the nature-nurture controversy. The importance of these issues can be seen particularly well in a discussion of the "mental retardation" that usually accompanies Down's syndrome.

Until fairly recently, most developmental psychologists assumed all Down's syndrome children were doomed to be mentally handicapped because of their defective chromosomes. And it is true that when given "ordinary" training as infants, these children typically have a limited intellectual potential. However, the *cause* of the retardation may be as much environmental as biological. As neu-

Children suffering from Down's syndrome are capable of learning more skills than was once thought.

rologist Mary Coleman put it recently, "Some of the retardation that is associated with Down's syndrome can actually be traced to a thyroid deficiency, which is easily corrected." Most of the children also suffer from middle- and inner-ear problems, which can be solved by minor surgery. "In the past," Coleman says, "people assumed that these children couldn't speak because they were dumb. But in fact, one major reason they were slow to speak was that they couldn't hear properly" (cited in Pines, 1982).

However, once the medical problems have been taken care of, the key to development is how much verbal stimulation and encouragement the children receive. Coleman recommends a program called *infant-stim*, which requires the parents of Down's syndrome children to spend several hours daily talking to and teaching the children. The parents are told to avoid punishment and give the children as much positive reinforcement as possible. Children treated with infant-stim usually show a remarkable jump in IQ within a few months. "The older literature on these children says that they **plateau** at 5," Mary Coleman says. "More recently, after the first infant-stim programs, people began to say that they plateau at 7. Then they said these children plateau at 12. I'm still waiting for them to plateau!"

Mary Coleman states that Down's syndrome children "can never become normal. Because of their hearing problems, they will never speak quite clearly. On the average, they have lower IQs than other children and, in some cases, they have certain brain deficits that prevent them from making much progress. But most of them can improve far beyond what used to be expected of them" (cited in Pines, 1982).

In the past, because we presumed that Down's syndrome was "caused" entirely by a chromosomal defect, we often considered these children to be hopelessly retarded. Now that we see both the problem and the youngsters in a different perspective, we can be more optimistic. As we noted earlier, your position on both the mind-body and the nature-nurture controversies determines not only *how you perceive people*, but *how you treat them* as well.

□ □ **QUESTION** □ □
In the early 1980's, physicians began using "cosmetic surgery" to make Down's syndrome children appear more normal. The surgery involves removing the extra skin from the corners of the eyes, reshaping the nose, and trimming excess tissue from the child's tongue. Immediately after the surgery, the child often shows a dramatic rise in *cognitive development*. How could *cosmetic* surgery influence *cognitive* growth?

Physical and Emotional Development: A Summary

Children do not develop in bits and pieces—a smidgin of physical growth this week, a tad of emotional maturation next week. Rather, children grow in all ways at all times. Thus, separating physical development from emotional, social, and intellectual growth is little more than a handy pedagogical device. For, in truth, all these aspects of the maturing infant *interact*.

The Down's syndrome child is born with genetic abnormalities. The extra 21st chromosome expresses itself in physical ways, such as a defective thyroid, middle ear, and unusual facial features. Correcting these physical problems enables the child to interact with the environment in more effective ways, and thus can radically alter the child's emotional development. But the way we *respond* to these children is just as important. If we give them the proper stimulation, their physical disabilities are not "converted" automatically into intellectual retardation. And by enhancing their cognitive development, we make it possible for them to learn emotional and physical self-control.

It should be obvious at this point that we cannot fully understand physical and emotional development without looking at how the mind matures. So, it is to the topic of cognitive development that we now turn our attention.

SUMMARY

1. There are two traditional ways of studying the growth and maturation of humans—the **life span approach** and **developmental psychology**. The first looks at the changes that occur in a "typical" individual from birth to death. The second studies how various aspects of the personality change, particularly during the younger years.

2. There are four main *theoretical* issues in developmental psychology—the **mind-body problem**, the **nature-nurture controversy**, **change versus constancy**, and **similarities versus differences**. A fifth but *practical* issue has to do with the influence of **social values** on developmental theories.

3. Very few psychological traits seem to be **continuous** over long periods of time. An exception seems to be **temperament**, which may be genetically determined.

4. You began life as a single **egg cell** that contained 23 **chromosomes**. At the moment of **fertilization**, one of your father's sperms penetrated the egg and added 23 chromosomes of its own. These chromosomes contain the **genes**, made up of **DNA** molecules, that govern the functioning of each cell.

14 / Infancy and Early Childhood: Physical and Emotional Development

Plateau. In psychology, "to plateau" means to reach the limit of some developmental or growth curve.

5. If an **X sperm** unites with the egg, the 23rd chromosome will be **XX**, and the child will be born a female. If a **Y sperm** unites with the egg, the 23rd chromosome will be **XY**, and the child will be born a male.

6. Sometimes the chromosomes of the mother and father contain **genetic defects**. If the child's cells contain but a single X chromosome, the child will suffer from **Turner's syndrome**. A child with an **XXY 23rd chromosome** becomes an infertile male and is said to suffer from **Klinefelter's syndrome**. A child with an **XYY 23rd chromosome** becomes a normal-appearing male but may have difficulty learning **impulse control**.

7. If the child's cells have three **21st chromosomes** rather than two, the child will suffer from **Down's syndrome**, or **trisomy-21**.

8. Two weeks after fertilization, the cells begin to **differentiate** or take on different roles. The three main types of cells are **ectoderm**, **mesoderm**, and **endoderm**.

9. During pregnancy, the fetus is protected from the mother's body by an organ called the **placenta**.

10. If the mother is starved during pregnancy, the child may be born smaller than usual. If the infant is given ample food, however, it will usually "catch up" to the size its **genetic blueprint** originally specified.

11. Physical development in the infant typically proceeds in a **cephalo-caudal, proximal-distal** direction.

12. While training cannot appreciably speed up **motor development**, encouraging the child to be active often has positive effects on the child's social development.

13. Baby geese (and the young of other animals) often **imprint** on the first moving object they see or can follow. Whether imprinting or **affectionate bonding** actually occurs in humans is not yet decided.

14. There is some evidence that **fetuses** can learn **simple assocations** while still in the womb. And only moments after birth, infants apparently can **imitate** (or at least respond to) facial gestures, **search** visually for the source of human voices, and **move their limbs in synchrony** with the human voice. By two weeks, babies **recognize** their mother and form perceptual **schemata**.

15. Theorists who take the **nature** position on emotional development believe you are born with **undifferentiated emotional responses** that are selectively reinforced by your environment.

16. Theorists who take the **nurture** position believe your **environment** shapes your emotions when you are very young, but you soon learn how to exercise **choice** in expressing your **inner feelings**.

17. Love is an **emotion**—an internal state or condition—that cannot be measured directly. But we can measure **loving behaviors** and discuss them objectively.

18. Mother and newborn child form a **social dyad**. Evidence suggests that both mother and child have an **inborn mutual readiness** to respond to each other. Infants also **shape** parental responses as much as parents shape the child's reactions.

19. The increase in **estrogen** that occurs just prior to birth may **desensitize** the mother and thus help overcome her innate fear of "little strangers."

20. A newborn monkey clings to its mother because she gives it warmth, food, and **contact comfort**. Contact with the mother (or her **surrogate**) appears to give the infant the **trust** that it needs in order to mature socially and emotionally. Contact comfort also reduces the level of **endorphins** in the brain.

21. Children who are treated inconsistently or who are given minimal stimulation by their mothers seem **predisposed** to suffer later psychological problems.

22. Maternal contact also allows the infant to build up **perceptual expectations** about its world. When its expectancies are grossly violated, the infant falls into an **anaclitic depression** and may die if not returned to its mother.

23. If an infant monkey grows up without having other young monkeys to play with, it does not know how to respond in **social situations**.

24. Female monkeys raised on surrogate mothers often treat their first infants cruelly.

25. When given the opportunity, human fathers seem as interested in and as responsive to their infants as are mothers. Fathers tend to engage in rough-housing and **physical contact** with their children more than do mothers.

26. Mothers tend to **talk** to their children more than do fathers, but **touch** and play with the children less.

27. Early studies suggested that boys who grow up without fathers often show very "feminine" behavior patterns, but later experiments contradict the early findings. The only consistent result is that fatherless boys tend to be more **aggressive** than normal.

28. Girls who grow up without fathers may either be strongly attracted to adult males or tend to avoid them, depending in part on whether the girls' mothers were divorced or widowed.

Summary

29. Down's syndrome children suffer from a variety of physical problems. However, the **mental retardation** often associated with this developmental disorder can be overcome to a great extent if the child is given **intensive stimulation** during its early years.

(Continued from page 339.)

When the class calmed down a bit, Dr. Martin Mayer continued. "That's a very interesting approach," he said, nodding at the guitar-playing young man. "I presume you mean we could identify men and women who are carriers of the wrong kinds of genes, and prohibit them from having kids. Not from getting married or from having sex—but from raising a family."

"You're asking us to play God with human souls!" said one of the girls. "That involves religion, not genetics."

"We certainly must take religious views into account," Dr. Mayer said, polishing his glasses again. "But sex is also a matter of economics. Any of you students grow up on a farm?"

Several of the young people held up their hands.

Mayer put his spectacles back on his nose. "Well, I guess your daddies have a few cows around to give milk and to supply meat, right? And probably your fathers buy the best breeding stock they can afford, because good cows give more milk and more butter fat than poor cows. And good bulls produce stronger offspring with better meat on them than do puny bulls. One good bull can service a whole lot of cows through artificial insemination. Even a scrawny little cow will have better offspring if her eggs are fertilized with genes from a first-rate bull. Perhaps we should do the same with humans. Maybe only the president should be allowed to have children."

"If only the president of the United States can have kids, he's going to be one busy daddy," one of the girls said laughing.

"Doesn't seem fair somehow," the boy sitting next to her said. "You've gotten rid of half the bad genes by using just one prime bull, but what about the scrawny cows? They're still passing along their scrawny genes to their kids. Why not have just one big mother cow that's as good as the bull?"

"Good idea," Mayer continued. "Just because a first-rate cow has good genes in her egg cells doesn't mean that she has to be burdened with carrying the calf until it's ready to be born. It's a waste of her time. So we've worked out a deal. After we inseminate the prime cow artificially, we let the fertilized egg grow for a few days, and then we remove the embryo and transplant it into the body of a scrawny cow and let her do all the work of carrying the little calf until it's ready to be born. A few months later, the scrawny cow gives birth to a super-calf with superior genes."

"Why bother?" a student asked.

"Financial reasons," Mayer responded. "Once we remove the embryo from the super-prime cow mother, she starts producing new eggs right away, which also can be fertilized artifically and then transplanted to the body of another inferior cow. That way, one super-momma can produce lots of superior calves each year instead of just one or two. It's still too complicated a technique for general use, but when the cost comes down, it's sure going to make a lot more money for the farmers."

"I know what you're going to say next," said the guitar-playing boy. "If it works with cows, why not try it with humans?"

"You've got to be kidding," one of the girls said. "I wouldn't want to carry somebody else's baby."

"Not even for a million dollars?" Mayer asked. "We're already doing embryo transplants at the human level—for women who can't conceive in the natural way. You've heard about 'surrogate mothers,' haven't you? But why put limits on the technique? Suppose a rich lady offered you a million dollars if you'd let her doctor transplant her embryo into your body. That way you could carry the child for her while she went off on a fancy vacation somewhere. Then, when the child was born, she could pick the child up at the hospital and give you the million dollars. How would you like that?"

"If I carried the baby, it would be mine, and no rich lady could take it away from me," the girl replied.

"Yeah, but what if the government decided you couldn't have kids," one of the boys said.

"Why couldn't I have kids, I'd like to know?"

"Because the government would say you didn't have the right kind of genes, stupid. Just like my daddy decides which of his cows can have calves and which can't," the boy added rather smugly.

"But I've got great genes!" the girl said. "And no government is going to tell me I don't! And even if they did, I'd just get Dr. Mayer to engineer my genes so they were the right kind. So there," she concluded, making a face at the boy who was tormenting her with his comments.

"What's the right kind of genes?" asked another girl.

"Yes, it all boils down to that decision, doesn't it?" Mayer said. "As Aldous Huxley pointed out in *Brave New World,* the day will surely come when we can engineer genes—if we know what kinds of kids we want to have. We can judge what kinds of cow we want because we value meat and milk production. But what do we value most in humans? Size? Strength? Intelligence?"

"That old Einstein wouldn't have done so well as a fullback for the Dallas Cowboys," an athletic young man said.

"I don't even want to talk about this, it scares me so," another girl said. "It's abnormal and immoral. It could never happen in the United States."

"That's probably what the cows thought a few years ago," said one of the boys.

"Well," said Mayer, "maybe it won't happen here, but the possibility of genetic engineering won't disappear just because we refuse to talk about it. In fact, just the opposite. But let's get back to that point about who should carry the baby. Is there any reason why a woman should have to go through a lengthy pregnancy? In *Brave New World* the embryos are grown in bottles rather than in their mothers' bodies. When they are ready to be born, the babies are uncorked like a bottle of fine wine. Maybe the day will come when each home has a mechanical incubator in it. You would watch your child's development before birth just the way you watch a plant grow and flower."

"That's outrageous," said the girl in the second row. "I don't want my baby born in a machine."

"You'd destroy the warm, maternal feeling every woman has when she's carrying her own baby," said another.

"Do you really think that maternal love is dependent on carrying the baby yourself?" Mayer asked.

"Of course," said the girl in the second row. "You just wouldn't take care of the baby as well if it weren't for that special feeling of closeness you get when you're carrying the child. It just wouldn't be *yours*, and you wouldn't love it as much."

A girl in the middle of the room suddenly stood up, tears filling her eyes. "I'd like to say something. A woman doesn't have to carry a child, or give birth to it, in order to love the baby and see that it gets the best care and attention. And whether a child is born in a bottle or from its mother's body doesn't affect the love it has for the woman who brings it up. Maybe you ought to remember that I'm adopted. And my adopted parents love me very, very much, both of them."

The class was absolutely silent for several moments. Then the bell rang.

"Thank you very, very much," Dr. Mayer said, a smile on his face.

Cognitive Development: From Childhood to Old Age

"Think About It"

· C · H · A · P · T · E · R ·

15

"Cynthia, my pet," Horace Smythe called out loudly. "Come here at once."

Mr. Smythe hummed a nervous, off-key tune for a few moments, a Civil War melody that most of the US was humming in 1867. He picked up a small Ming vase from his desk, dusted it carefully, and put it down again. It was far too valuable a possession, as he frequently told his wife, to allow it to be cleaned by their Negro servant woman, Melissa. He had bought the vase from a local Chinese laundryman who, Mr. Smythe observed, "Lacks the innate appreciation for culture that God in His infinite wisdom has given to members of the white race."

Then, since his wife hadn't yet appeared, Mr. Smythe stamped his foot impatiently on the old wooden floor. "Cynthia!" he cried. "Come here at once! I have marvelous news for you."

Cynthia Smythe walked briskly through the door to the kitchen, wiping her hands on a large towel as she did so. "Yes, Horace, what do you wish now? I was just helping Melissa prepare supper . . ."

"Bother supper," Mr. Smythe said. "I have just discovered why your nephew, Tommy, is an idiot, and I knew you'd want to know."

The woman sighed deeply. "Thomas is not an 'idiot' by any stretch of the imagination, Horace. And he's your nephew, too."

"Only by marriage, my pet. And he is most certainly an idiot, a Mongolian idiot. Dr. Down has just proven it."

"Mongolian?" the woman said in a puzzled tone of voice.

"Of course," Mr. Smythe said. "Does have an oriental look about him, now doesn't he? Especially the eyes."

"He doesn't look like any Chinese I've ever seen, Horace." Cynthia Smythe closed her eyes, as if to call her nephew's face to mind. "No, Tommy is a little different, naturally, but I wouldn't say he looked at all oriental."

Horace Smythe snorted in amusement. "Ha! You wouldn't say that if you had read Dr. Down's article."

The woman folded the towel in resignation and sat down. "Who is this Dr. Down, Horace?"

"Dr. John Langdon Haydon Down, to be precise. He's the medical superintendant of Earlswood Asylum for Idiots in Surrey." The man peered over his spectacles at his wife. "That's just outside London, England, you know."

"Yes, Horace. I know."

The man smiled wanly at his wife, then turned his gaze back to the papers in front of him. "Well, I was just reading about Dr. Down's paper, 'Observations on an Ethnic Classification of Idiots,' published in the *London Hospital Reports* for 1866. The good doctor has come up with an explanation for idiocy that is positively brilliant. Tommy is a 'throwback,' you see."

"A 'throwback' to what?"

"To a more primitive form of human development, of course," Mr. Smythe said in a superior tone of voice. "Modern biological theory tells us that the human fetus repeats all the stages of human evolution as it grows within the womb. It starts out as a single cell, and then it becomes fishlike. Next it turns into one of the lower mammals, such as a pig, and then grows into a little monkey."

The woman shook her head in amazement. "Tommy doesn't look any more like a monkey than you do, Horace."

"No, of course not. He's gone beyond that stage. But even when the fetus takes on a human appearance, it still must climb the evolutionary scale—from the black Ethiopian, up to the savage Malays or Indians who have dark brown skin. And from thence to the yellow-skinned peoples, the Mongolians. Finally, if all goes well, the fetus reaches the top rung of the developmental ladder."

Cynthia Smythe smiled. "The 'top rung' being a white American, I presume?"

"Or northern European," her husband replied. "I think our superiority to the dark-skinned human races is well established by now."

"The Bible says that we are all God's children, Horace."

"Cynthia, my pet, this is 1867, not the Dark Ages, and we must deal with the scientific facts. It is true, as Dr. Down points out, that all the races are descended from a single stock. But some of us—the whites, of course—have traveled farther down the evolutionary road than have the others. The inferior races may eventually catch up with us, of course, and it is our Christian duty to help them all we can. But in the meantime . . ." The man shrugged his shoulders eloquently.

The woman contemplated her husband's words for a moment. "What 'facts' does this Dr. Down present to prove his case?"

"Ah ha!" Horace Smythe said eagerly. "That's the real issue, isn't it? Well, remember that Dr. Down is a world-famous expert on idiocy. And among the patients at his hospital, he has found a very close connection between skin color and feeble-mindedness. The darker the color of the patient's skin, the more hopelessly stupid the patient appears to be. For example, the most terrible idiots of all have Ethiopian features—prominent eyes, puffy lips, dark skins, and woolly hair, just like Melissa's. 'White Negroes,' Dr. Down calls these poor, hopeless cases."

"Melissa's eyes are less prominent than yours are, Horace."

The man dismissed the woman's comments with a wave of his hand. "Pay attention, my pet.

Slightly superior in intelligence to the 'white Negroes' are those idiots with Indian features—'shortened foreheads, prominent cheeks, deep-set eyes, and slightly apish noses,' according to Dr. Down."

"And I suppose Dr. Down believes that the Indian race is intellectually superior to the Negro?" the woman asked, a bemused look on her face.

"Naturally," Horace Smythe replied. "Even an idiot knows that to be the truth. But to continue, the least retarded inmates of all have slanted eyes and skins that have a 'slight, dirty yellowish tinge' to them. Just like the Mongols who inhabit China and the rest of the Orient."

Cynthia Smythe sighed. "And the Mongolian race is superior to the Indian, I presume?"

"Of course!" the man responded in a delighted tone of voice. "Black, brown, yellow, white—that's the natural order of the races on Earth, and that's the natural order of the idiots in Dr. Down's asylum, he says. Doesn't that prove the case, once and for all?"

The woman frowned. "Tommy's skin is about the same color as yours, Horace. A bit more yellowish, perhaps, but . . ."

"But there you are, my dear. Tommy's a throwback to the yellow-skinned Mongol stage, which is immediately below the white or Caucasian stage. He simply stopped developing when he reached the Mongoloid level. His yellow skin proves it. And that's why he's mentally retarded, and always will be. No sense in trying to work with the lad, of course, as your sister is foolishly trying to do. No, she should send Tommy away to an asylum."

"Or give him to the Chinese laundryman you bought the vase from, perhaps?" the woman said, in mock seriousness.

"Excellent idea!" Horace Smythe responded. "Like calls to like, you know. The laundryman is so uncultured he probably wouldn't even notice Tommy's feeble-mindedness."

"The laundryman . . ." the woman said slowly, as puzzling over the meaning of what her husband had said.

Horace Smythe gave a deep sign of satisfaction and leaned back in his chair. "Well, don't you agree? Hasn't Dr. Down come up with a brilliant insight into the biological causes of idiocy?"

The woman laughed. "I think the man's an imbecile, Horace."

"What!"

A look of gentle contentment spread across Cynthia Smith's face. "I know little or nothing about science, but I do recognize utter nonsense when I hear it. And so should you, since the evidence is right before your very eyes."

"Evidence?" Horace Smythe wailed. He stared briefly at the Ming vase on his desk, then glanced at the paper he had been reading. "But I don't see . . ."

The woman rose from her chair. "Melissa needs help with the cooking, Horace. You think about it, and we'll discuss the matter further at supper. After all," she said slyly, "You're hardly an idiot like Tommy, now are you?"

(Continued on page 400.)

FOUR THEORETICAL ISSUES: A REVIEW

At the beginning of Chapter 14, we listed four major "theoretical" issues that cut across developmental psychology. Let's review those four topics as a way of introducing the field of cognitive development.

• Mind-body Problem

At first blush, it might seem that *cognitive* psychologists would uniformly resolve the mind-body problem in favor of the "mind." As you will see, however, there are many scientists working in this area who equate "cognitive development" with the growth of speech and problem-solving *behaviors*. (From a behavioral point of view, *talking* is a physical rather than a mental response.) So the theoretical conflict over the mind-body problem remains important even in the field of cognitive psychology (Richards & Light, 1986).

• Nature-nurture Controversy

The nature-nurture controversy is of major importance because cognitive psychologists often ask questions such as these: Are human infants born with an innate ability to think and to "process" language, or are these skills almost entirely learned? Are there basic "structures of the mind" which are part of a child's genetic blueprint? Or are thinking and reasoning "programmed" into a child by the youngster's social environment? As you will soon discover, there are almost as many answers to these questions as there are psychologists working in the area (Boyd & Richerson, 1985).

• Continuity Versus Discontinuity

The third issue has to do with developmental *continuity* and *discontinuity*. These topics show up primarily in the *stage theories* of mental growth.

Most stage theorists believe that *all* children must pass through the same developmental *stages*, or levels. The actual *change* from one level of mental maturity to another may be triggered by environmental experiences, but the *sequence* of developmental stages is supposed to be the same for all children. Because most stage theorists perceive mental growth as being highly predictable, they tend to take the *continuity* position. For example, in a recent paper, Harvard psychologists John Snarey, Joseph Reimer, and Lawrence Kohlberg state that, in the children they studied, "Stage change was found to be upward, gradual, and without significant regressions" (Snarey, Reimer, & Kohlberg, 1985).

On the other hand, "discontinuity" theorists typically believe the infant is born with potential to grow in many different ways and at a variety of speeds. The environment then encourages the development of a limited set of these cognitive skills, usually by providing the child with models and by rewarding the youngster for imitating these models. To these theorists, any continuity found in cognitive development is due to consistencies in the social and physical environment, not to the "natural unfolding" of the child's genetic potential (Fischer, 1983; Yarrow & Klein, 1980).

• *Individual Differences Versus Human Similarities*

"Stage theorists" typically make three major assumptions about human nature:

1. There is an *underlying genetic pattern* that guides cognitive development.
2. The major task of developmental psychologists is to determine what this "underlying pattern" actually is.
3. Since infants around the world grow up in quite different environments, whatever *similarities* exist in their development must be due to genetic influences.

These three assumptions lead stage theorists to focus on *similarities across children* rather than on individual uniqueness (Kessen, 1984).

On the other hand, "behaviorally-oriented theorists" make rather different assumptions:

1. Cognitive development is primarily "shaped" by the environment the infant grows up in.
2. One can often tell more about *specific* environmental effects by looking at how children *differ* than one can by looking at how they are *alike*.

Because of these assumptions, "behavioral theorists" often are more concerned with an individual child's unique pattern of development than in the fact that the child matures in ways similar to other children in the same environment (Feldman, 1986; Morrison, Lord, & Keating, 1985).

• *The Four Issues: A Summary*

These issues may seem highly theoretical to you, and hence of little practical importance.

However, as we have noted many times, *theory determines practice*.

Stage theorists believe that the environment can *retard* human development, but cannot *enhance* it in any significant fashion. Therefore, parents (and all of society!) should simply "let children grow according to their own natural inclinations" (Kamii, 1984). Behavioral psychologists, however, believe that parents (and all of society!) should become involved in the training of the child *from birth onward* (Everaerd *et al.*, 1983). As you might imagine, the types of *infant care* and *schooling* that stage theorists recommend are quite different from those suggested by behavioral psychologists. The types of *experimental studies* performed by the two types of theorists are also radically different.

At the beginning of the last chapter, we noted a fifth, practical issue—that of the influence of social values on studies of human development. The importance of this "practical issue" will become obvious when we look at studies on moral development.

You should keep all these issues in mind as we begin our survey of intellectual development.

□ □ **QUESTION** □ □
Suppose a child failed to learn very much in school. Would a stage theorist tend to blame the teacher, or the child's "lack of developmental readiness"? What would a behavioral theorist probably say about the situation?

COGNITIVE DEVELOPMENT

Before we can sensibly discuss what cognitive *development* is, we first should make clear we have some notion of what *cognition* is. Actually, as we pointed out in Chapter 12, psychologists use the term "cognition" in many different ways. However, as Margaret Matlin notes, the word usually refers to *mental activities*. Matlin lists eight types of mental activities that psychologists have paid particular attention to: perception, memory, imagery, language, concept formation, problem solving, reasoning, and decision making (Matlin, 1983a). We have already discussed many of these aspects of cognition. In this chapter, we will focus primarily on the development of *language* and *reasoning* in children, and then look at how various aspects of cognition develop through the rest of the span of life.

LANGUAGE DEVELOPMENT

According to Margaret Matlin, "Language acquisition is often said to be the most spectacular of human accomplishments." For instance, re-

Margaret Matlin

search by S. Carey suggests that the 6-year-old child may have a mastery of about 14,000 words (Carey, 1978). And to acquire this large a vocabulary, children must learn about *10 new words each day* from the time they start speaking until their sixth birthday (Miller & Gildea, 1987).

Learning to use language—and to use it properly—when you were a youngster changed your world profoundly. According to Neil Salkind and Sueann Ambron, having a *verbal label* to attach to an experience makes that experience easier to remember and deal with. "In fact," they say, "one reason most of us fail to remember much of what happened to us in our earliest years may be that we had not learned to use such verbal labels. We had nothing to file away in our memories as a coded symbol of the experience" (Salkind & Ambron, 1987). (For a discussion of "memory categories," see Chapter 11.)

Babbling is a signal that a baby is developing normally.

□ □ **QUESTION** □ □
Can you think of other reasons why you might have difficulties recalling early experiences? (Hint: How mature was your brain at the time?)

Language Acquisition

Ambron and Salkind take a fairly strong *continuity* position, at least as far as language acquisition is concerned. They believe that the stages children go through while progressing from baby talk to adult communication are roughly identical—regardless of native tongue, socioeconomic class, and ethnic background. Children everywhere talk about the same things while going through these developmental stages, Salkind and Ambron say. "They all speak of objects and situations, make demands, use mostly nouns and verbs, and talk *to* themselves a great deal but never *about* themselves or their relationship with others" (Salkind & Ambron, 1987).

According to Ambron and Salkind, language acquisition has four aspects to it:

1. A knowledge of how to produce **phonemes**, which are the basic sounds of speech.
2. Learning **semantics**, or the meaning of words.
3. A mastery of **syntax**, or the rules by which words can be combined into sentences.
4. Discovering the **pragmatics** of language, or the appropriate social use of speech.

Let's look at each of these four aspects of language acquisition in more detail.

Phonemes

Obviously, an infant can't talk if it doesn't make sounds, and phonemes are the basic sounds

that make up human speech. The developmental problem then becomes, how does an infant acquire the ability to produce phonemes? Do infants naturally (and spontaneously) produce all the phonemes they will need in order to speak any human language? Or are they born with a readiness to imitate the sounds their parents (and others) say to them?

If you have been around infants very much, you probably have observed them happily chattering to themselves in a language made up of repetitive syllables, such as "da da da" and "ba ba ba." This type of early speech is called **babbling**, and occurs in all normal children between three and seven months of age (see Fig. 15.1) (Bower, 1986).

Babbling frequently occurs early in the morning, when children first wake up and before they begin their daily "social life" with their parents and other adults. Normal patterns

FIG. 15.1 The range and average age for several landmarks of verbal behavior.

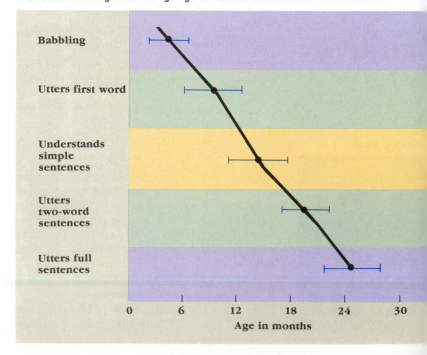

Age in months

Phonemes (FO-neems). The smallest units of speech, such as "da" or "ba."

Semantics (see-MAN-ticks). From the Greek word meaning "to signify." Semantics is the study of meanings, particularly the meanings of words.

Syntax (SIN-tax). From the Greek word meaning "to arrange together." Syntax refers to the orderly structure of language.

Pragmatics (prag-MAT-ticks). From the Latin word meaning "skilled in law or business." Pragmatics is the study of the "practical rules" of some aspect of life or science.

Babbling. Normal infants spontaneously produce simple phonemes, such as "da" and "ba," at age three to seven months. Infants who fail to babble often experience difficulty in learning to talk.

Holophrastic (ho-lo-FRAS-tick). The act of expressing a complex idea in a single word or phrase.

Telegraphic speech. Before long distance became cheap and convenient, people sent each other telegrams. Since the sender was charged "by the word," people tended to omit unnecessary words in telegrams. Infants do the same thing when first producing two-word sentences.

of babbling occur in Down's syndrome children, but do *not* occur in deaf children (Smith & Oller, 1981). Deaf children may babble briefly, but then stop producing the sorts of sounds that children with normal hearing do. This fact suggests that infants need to *hear* the sounds they are producing in order to continue producing them. Therefore, the *absence of babbling* may be a sign that the child needs special attention (Oller *et al.*, 1985).

Several studies suggest that infants everywhere in the world make the same sounds when babbling (Olney & Scholnick, 1976; Saito *et al.*, 1981).

Until recently, scientists believed that children produced the entire range of human sounds when babbling. However, recent studies show that many speech sounds are almost never heard in babbling. The most common sounds (worldwide) are those involving consonants such as *n, m, d, t,* or *b* combined with vowels such as *e* or *a*. Consonants such as *l, r, f,* and *v*, and combinations such as *st* are quite rare. According to Rebecca Eilers and D.K. Oller at the University of Miami, the sounds produced during babbling are also those the child favors a few months later, when the child begins to speak in words (Eilers & Oller, 1985).

In summary, current thinking holds that the early acquisition of phoneme production has three distinct aspects to it. First, most children babble innately, but do not produce *all* the sounds of speech in their babbles. Second, parents selectively reinforce some sounds which then come to predominate. Third, children innately imitate phonemes not produced in their babbles, and parents reward the children for doing so. Eventually, the child can produce all the sounds found in its "native language."

□ □ **QUESTION** □ □
Is speech in humans innately determined, or acquired through learning?

Semantics

Words represent objects and actions. Thus, words have *meanings* that infants must learn as they progress from babbling to true communicative speech. The problem children face as they learn *semantics* is that most words have more than one meaning. "Drink," for instance, is both a noun and a verb. "I drink the milk," and "Give me a drink," are examples of how the same word can mean either an action or an object. Furthermore, words such as "sea" and "see," and "dear" and "deer," sound alike but have quite different meanings.

At about a year of age, infants begin uttering **holophrastic**, or one-word, sentences. The child may actually *say* single words earlier, but doesn't appear to grasp the *meaning* of words (and to use them to communicate) until the child is about one year old. At this stage, a single-word sentence may have several meanings. For example, "Cup" may mean "I see the cup," or "Get me my cup," or even "This cup is just like the one I use at home" (Matlin, 1983a).

Most infants begin using two-word sentences about the 18th month. At first, these sentences are of the *agent + action* ("Mama drink") or *action + object* type ("Drink milk"). At this age, children also use negative statements, such as "No milk." They also use the so-called *Wh-questions*, such as "Where milk?" or "When drink?"

Some two-word sentences are called **telegraphic speech** because the youngster includes important words (such as nouns and verbs) but omits other parts of speech. Thus, rather than saying, "The cat is up the tree," the child may say, "Cat tree."

By the time children are two, most of them can speak in complete and fairly complex sentences, such as "Where is my milk?" and "I drank my milk." At this age, too, youngsters typically learn to change the meaning of words or sentences by changing the inflection they use. For example, "I drink *milk*?" might be a question asking if it's all right to drink milk rather than water. But "I *drink* milk!" might be the child's way of telling the mother the child has already consumed the milk (Salkind & Ambron, 1987).

Generally speaking, the meaning children assign to words tends to change from the overly general to the specific. Thus, at an early age, a little girl might use the word "Daddy" to refer to any adult male. Later, "Daddy" might refer just to males who look like her father. Finally, she learns to use "Daddy" only when referring to her father, and "man" when referring to other adult males.

By the age of four, most children can use simple "relationship" words, such as *more-less, young-old*, and *weak-strong*. Relationships such as *before-after* give youngsters difficulty, however. If you say to a four-year-old "I drank the milk *after* I played in the park," the child will probably think you consumed the liquid *before* you went to the park. Until they are eight or nine, most children seem to think that whatever is mentioned in the first part of a sentence must have occurred before whatever is mentioned in the second part. And until they are nine, most youngsters have difficulties with *come* and *go* and *bring* and *take*.

At any point in a child's development, the *meaning* the child assigns to words tells a lot about how far the youngster's cognitive development has progressed. These "meanings" also give some clues as to the child's notions about the *rules* by which words can be combined into sentences.

Syntax

Where do children learn about *syntax*—the "grammar" or "rules" that govern language? These rules are often frightfully complex—so much so that even people who never make a mistake in English can't always tell you what "laws" they are following. And most parents don't *teach* syntax to their children—they just provide models and then correct the youngster's mistakes. Therefore, the first questions we have to answer in our study of syntax are the following:

1. Are there *innate language structures* that are coded in the genes, or is syntax entirely learned?
2. Presuming some aspects of syntax must be acquired through experience, do children learn "syntactical rules" which they then apply to all language? Or do they learn words by rote, one at a time?

"WHEN I SAY 'RUNNED', YOU KNOW I MEAN 'RAN'. LET'S NOT QUIBBLE."

We will discuss the evidence for and against the existence of "innate language structures" in a moment. First, let's look at "rote versus rule" learning.

• *Reasoning by Rule or by Analogy?*

In a recent paper, David Rumelhart and James McClelland suggest that the "rules of syntax" are far too complex for most children to learn. Children just beginning to speak cannot grasp such concepts as "noun," "verb," "prefix," and "root," according to Rumelhart and McClelland. Instead, these experimenters say, young people learn a few words by rote. The children then increase their vocabularies by "making analogies"—that is, by reasoning that "this word sounds like that word." As evidence that this sort of "ruleless learning" is technically possible, Rumelhart and McClelland have created a computer software program that "learns" English without knowledge of syntactical rules. Rumelhart and McClelland claim that the computer makes many of the same verbal mistakes that children make (Rumelhart & McClelland, 1986, 1987).

MIT psychologist Steven Pinker takes the opposite point of view. He notes that the "rules versus analogies" debate is "a classical issue that keeps popping up in studies of philosophy and psychology whenever people try to understand what it is that underlies cognitive behavior and regulates thought" (cited in Kolata, 1987). Pinker believes that children learn rules or procedures which they then test out in their speech. Feedback from adults helps the children determine which rules "work," and which ones don't (Pinker, 1984; Pinker & Prince, 1987).

In fact, the data suggest that both positions may be right—in part. For example, several studies show that children start out by forming irregular past tenses correctly. That is, they say "brought" and "went" when first learning to speak. Then they discover the "past tense rule" for regular verbs and *overgeneralize* this rule: They begin to say "bringed" and "goed." Finally, the youngsters learn that the "past tense rule" works only with regular verbs. At this point, they return to saying "brought" and "went." These studies suggest that children learn syntax *both* by rule *and* by analogy (Kolata, 1987).

□ □ **QUESTION** □ □

If you isolated two infants at birth (as Harlow did with his monkeys), would the children learn to speak spontaneously? If they did speak spontaneously, what language would they "invent"? Would different pairs of children dream up different languages? If so, would these invented languages have similar grammars?

15 / Cognitive Development: From Childhood to Old Age

● Nature Versus Nurture in Language Learning

Is there an innately-determined "universal language" underlying all types of human speech? Or is syntax entirely learned?

Behaviorists—such as B.F. Skinner—have long insisted that children don't directly learn syntax at all (unless specifically taught it). Rather, they learn proper speech from imitation and "selective reinforcement." Skinner does admit that the *physical potential* to produce speech is "coded for in the genes." In a recent book, he puts it this way: "The human species took a crucial step forward when its vocal musculature came under operant control in the production of speech sounds. Indeed, it is possible that all distinctive achievements of the species can be traced to that one genetic change." But according to Skinner, it is the *ability to learn* that is inherited, not some "innate knowledge" of what syntax is all about. Thus, Skinner comes down strongly on the side of "nurture" (Skinner, 1987)

On the other hand, **linguists** such as MIT's Noam Chomsky have long taken the "naturist" position in this argument. Some 20 years ago, Chomsky stated that there is a universal **deep structure** or grammar underlying all human languages. Although he has modified his theory recently, Chomsky still believes that languages are far too complex for children to learn in the short times it takes them to do so—unless the children are born with some innate knowledge of the "rules" or syntax that govern speech in all human societies (Chomsky, 1986).

By the *deep structure of language*, Chomsky means "the innate tendency to process information in linguistic form." To understand what Chomsky is talking about, consider the behaviors involved in walking. You had to *learn* to walk, didn't you? And you probably learned very quickly. But could you have acquired those motor skills so readily if the "deep structure" of walking weren't somehow inbedded in your genes? In similar fashion, could you have learned to talk if the neurons in your brain weren't genetically biased to produce spoken language as readily as they produce running and walking (D'Agostino, 1986)?

Who is correct, Skinner or Chomsky? The answer seems to be, "both of them." Skinner looks at how *verbal behaviors are acquired through learning*. Chomsky prefers to deal with the *innate aspects of linguistic develop-*

Noam Chomsky

ment. Thus, Skinner explains quite well how parents use selective reinforcement to "shape" the sounds children produce when babbling. But Skinner doesn't explain *why* all children babble in similar fashion. Nor does he tell us how words become "mental symbols" for objects and actions in the physical world. Chomsky's strength lies in his attempts to explain those issues in cognitive development that Skinner simply ignores.

Pragmatics

Languages came about because people living together needed to *communicate* with each other. Communication involves more than phonemes, semantics, and syntax, however. It involves practical or pragmatic rules about when to speak and when not to speak, what is acceptable talk and what isn't. Put another way, children must learn not only how to communicate their needs, but also to predict what the *social consequences* of saying something will be.

Newborns cry to express their needs. As they acquire language, they find more complex ways to communicate. As Margaret Matlin notes, a seven-month-old child who wants a ball will reach out for the ball and make a fuss. By about nine months of age, the youngster will attempt to use adults to help gain what the child wants. That is, the child will alternately look at the adult and at the ball while fussing. By now, the child has learned there is a connection between making the right kind of sounds and getting the ball (Matlin, 1983a). Linguists often call this type of verbal behavior *intentional communication*, since the child announces his or her intentions in order to get assistance from someone else.

Society, however, puts constraints on *what* the child can say—and on *how* and *when* the child must say things, as well. As Michael McTear points out, all cultures have polite forms of social discourse. Often these polite forms of speech are a part of social rituals, such as saying "please" when you want something, and "thank you" when you get it. These rituals often include *body language*. In some societies, children must bow their heads and gaze at the floor when talking to adults in order to show respect. In other cultures, children are taught to stand up straight and look directly into the adults' eyes while talking. Children must also learn to "take turns" when speaking, and how to correct their own verbal mistakes (McTear, 1985).

Social Aspects of Language Learning

According to Harvard psychologist Jerome Bruner, while a child is acquiring the "pragmatic rules" of language, the child also may be learning something about "proper social behavior." In one study, Bruner and Anat Ninio

According to Jerome Bruner, parents often teach their children social skills while teaching them language.

made video tape recordings of mothers as they taught their children to communicate both verbally and nonverbally. Bruner and Ninio found that, during the first few months of the child's life, a mother spends much of her time simply trying to find out what the infant is looking at. Then she begins trying to get the infant to look where she is looking. Once the mother discovers how to attract the child's attention, she begins to point out objects and give them names. She then rewards the child for learning these names (Ninio & Bruner, 1978).

Bruner also notes that, during language learning, the mother begins making *social contracts* with the child that serve as the pattern for adult behaviors. If the child grows restless, the mother may say, "Let's learn two more words, and then we'll go play." If the child requests a cookie, the mother may ask the youngster where the cookies are kept. If the child answers correctly, the mother may give the child permission to go get the sweet. Should the child refuse to do so, the mother may offer to get the cookie herself if the child will do something for her in return (Ratner & Bruner, 1978).

When the child fulfills a social contract, the mother often praises the youngster by saying something like "See how well you did? Aren't you pleased with yourself?" According to Bruner, while the mother is "shaping lan-

guage," she is also encouraging the child to monitor the consequences of the child's own actions and thus to become less dependent on the mother (Bruner, 1984).

● *The Father's Role in Language Learning*
Traditionally, in most societies, it is the mother who spends the most time with an infant. And it is the mother who is most responsible for nurturing the child. However, the father's role in teaching an infant to speak is also important, although his contributions are likely to be more indirect than direct.

Although fathers tend to talk to their infants less than do mothers, fathers apparently give the child *confidence*. Studies from several different cultures suggest that infants cope better with the appearance of strangers when their fathers have spent considerable time with the children. A child whose father is an involved parent is thus more likely to *perform verbally in public* than one whose father is uninvolved in caring for the child (Bruner, 1984).

The Source of Language Learning
As we mentioned in Chapter 2, the "speech center" in the left hemisphere of the brain is physically a little larger than the same area of the right hemisphere in most right-handed humans. This size difference between the hemispheres exists to a much lesser extent in the higher primates, but is not found at all in lower animals. Furthermore, the vocalizations made by monkeys and chimpanzees seem to be primarily under the control of centers in the *limbic system* (see Chapter 8) rather than under the control of the cortex (as is the case in humans). Destruction of the "cortical speech center" in humans typically leaves them speechless. Destruction of similar areas of the monkey cortex does not affect the animal's vocalizations at all (Segalowitz, 1983).

It would appear, then, that human brains are uniquely suited for language learning. However, many scientists have recently been successful in teaching chimpanzees to communicate either in "sign language" or by pressing keys on a computer console.

For example, psychologists Sue Savage-Rumbaugh and Duane Rumbaugh have been able to train chimps to use an artificial language called **Yerkish**. To help the animals learn, the Rumbaughs present word-symbols on an overhead projector. The chimps respond by pressing illuminated buttons on a computer console. If the chimps use the word-symbols correctly, they are rewarded. Several chimpanzees have been able to learn 100 or more symbols, and use them as correctly as might a two-year-old child (Savage-Rumbaugh, Rumbaugh, & Boysen, 1980). More recently, scientists working with the Rumbaughs have used the

Jerome S. Bruner

same equipment to teach three severely-retarded women who were essentially nonverbal to communicate using word-symbols (Yarbrough, 1986).

Other psychologists have taught apes to use **American Sign Language**, and have claimed that their animals could "create sentences" and "use language in a symbolic way." However, there is a continuing controversy in the scientific literature about this research. For a detailed analysis of "ape language" often suggests that the trainers are *cueing* the animal's responses in various subtle ways much as did the man who owned the famous "talking horse," Clever Hans (see Chapter 1) (Premack, 1986).

Can apes speak? The answer depends on how you define "speak." Some apes can surely communicate by "signing," or by pressing buttons on a computer console. But as British scientist Adrian Desmond points out, no one has yet proven that ape language has "grammar." Nor is there concrete evidence that apes can manipulate *symbols* with, say, the sophistication of even a fairly young child (Desmond, 1979).

One point seems very clear, however, as J.L. Gould and Carol Gould noted recently. Humans talk *spontaneously*, and do so worldwide in their *natural environment*. Other animals do not. "You cannot keep a normal, healthy child from learning to talk. . . . Chimpanzees, by contrast, can be [coaxed] into mastering some sort of linguistic communications skills, but they really could not care less about language: The drive just is not there" (Gould & Gould, 1981).

Put more simply, humans are *programmed by their genes* to learn to talk, and they have a nervous system complex enough to support speech production. No other animal can make that statement.

● *Why Language?*

You acquired language in part because your genes made it easy for you to do so, and because your parents reinforced you for talking. But you also learned to speak because speech serves your own personal needs. As we pointed out in Chapter 11, many of your memory banks are built around the sounds and structures of language. And you not only *talk* and *remember* in words, you typically *think* and *reason* using language as well. Thus, speech is more than a means of communicating—it is also the method most of us employ when we form mental concepts and process information inside our minds.

Now that we have briefly described how language acquisition occurs, let's look at the development of those cognitive processes called "concept formation" and "problem solving." As we will see, these processes are heavily dependent on language.

CONCEPT FORMATION AND PROBLEM SOLVING

According to Boyd McCandless and Robert Trotter, when a one-year-old girl uses the word "ball," she typically refers to her own relationship to the toy. *She* is always the one who plays with the ball, and she always does so in her *bedroom*. "Ball" refers to *her red ball*, not to anything else. If you gave her a round blue toy and insisted it too was a ball, she might become confused. For to her, balls are red objects, not blue ones (McCandless & Trotter, 1977).

At about 18 months, however, the word is likely to take on an enlarged meaning. Now the girl uses "ball" to refer to round objects that she bounces on the floor, not just in the bedroom, but in the kitchen and outdoors as well. Other people may use the ball too, and balls can be red or blue or even striped. As McCandless and Trotter note, the girl's *concept* (or schema) for "ball" has obviously enlarged. But how does this miracle occur?

□□ **QUESTION** □□

What are the major differences between a "cup" and a "glass"? What does your answer tell you about your *concepts* of these two objects?

Concept Development

As we noted in Chapter 12, a "concept" is a category that *includes* some objects or ideas and *excludes* others. The rules of inclusion and exclusion *define* the concept or schema.

Very young children tend to be quite good at handling *basic level categories*, but have problems dealing with *superordinate* categories. For example, look at Fig. 15.2. When Eleanor Rosch asked three-year-olds to select the two items that were alike, they had no difficulty at all with Set 1. A cat is a cat is a basic level category. But the three-year-olds missed the correct answer in Set 2 about half the time. By the time they were five, however, the children almost always got perfect scores when given tests such as this one (Rosch *et al.*, 1976). Thus, as Rosch notes, concept development usually begins at the level of basic categories and moves outward to both superordinate and subordinate categories (Rosch, 1978).

Set 1

Set 2

FIG. 15.2 Pictures similar to those used by Rosch et al. (1976).

In another test of concept formation, E.S. Andersen asked children of various ages to differentiate between a cup and a glass. Three-year-old children tended to call anything you can drink from a cup, even such odd "cups" as wine glasses and crystal goblets. Slightly older children tended to call anything made of glass or china a "glass," and every other type of container a "cup." By the time the children were 12, they usually called any object *with a handle* a "cup," and anything *without a handle* (particularly if made of glass or china) a glass. Andersen notes that the three-year-olds *overgeneralized* basic concepts. Slightly older children put objects in categories according to *how they looked*. But 12-year-olds (and adults) tended to categorize primarily *according to use* (Andersen, 1975).

Concept formation is often difficult for a child because not all concepts have well-defined boundaries. Andersen notes that 12-year-olds seemed to have gained an appreciation of the fuzziness of most concepts. Younger children, however, were often quite rigid in insisting that a given object *had to* fit within a given category because it possessed one or two specific attributes.

□□ **QUESTION** □□
If a "cup" always has a handle, what do you call those paper containers put out by the Dixie Company?

Problem Solving

Solving life's problems often boils down to finding the right concepts to describe a given situation or difficulty. Problem solving also involves discovering which "search strategy" is most likely to help you fit things into their proper categories.

Margaret Matlin notes that psychologists haven't studied the development of problem solving in children very extensively. There is, however, one classic study on the subject. In 1966, F.A. Mosher and J.R. Hornsby asked children aged 6 to 11 to play a game much like Twenty Questions. Mosher and Hornsby showed youngsters of different ages a set of objects much like those in Fig. 15.3. They asked the children to *name* each object first, to make sure the youngsters knew what each was. Then Mosher and Hornsby told the children to guess which *one* of the objects the experimenters had in mind. The children were told to use as *few questions* as possible. Mosher and Hornsby then recorded each child's guess.

According to Mosher and Hornsby, the children's guesses seemed to reflect two different *search strategies*:

1. *Constraint-seeking questions.* These were questions general enough to refer to more than one picture. "Is it alive?" is an example of a constraint-seeking question.
2. *Hypothesis-scanning questions.* These were

very specific, and usually referred to just one picture. "Is it a doll?" is an example of a hypothesis-scanning question.

Mosher and Hornsby report the 6-year-olds primarily asked hypothesis-scanning questions. The 11-year-olds, however, mostly asked constraint-seeking questions. Mosher and Hornsby conclude that, as children develop cognitively, they seem to acquire more efficient search strategies. They cannot use these strategies effectively, however, until they are mature enough to know how objects can be linked together in superordinate concept categories. Children also gain the ability to handle **ambiguity** as they grow older (Mosher & Hornsby, 1966).

Research suggests that younger children tend to be fairly rigid when fitting objects and

FIG. 15.3 The items used in the Mosher-Hornsby "20 questions" experiment. See text for details.

ideas into cognitive categories, while older children tend to be more flexible. However, older children also have more *facts* about the objects they are asked to classify. Surprisingly enough, recent research suggests that "memory development" and an increased store of "facts" may be just as important in "learning how to think" as are problem-solving strategies.

□ □ **QUESTION** □ □

Look back at page 12 in Chapter 1. What kind of search strategy does the scientific method seem to be? How would you go about teaching a 12-year-old child to use the scientific method in solving a real-life problem?

Memory Development

According to Jerome Bruner, telling stories is one way in which humans organize and represent their experiences. Indeed, Bruner believes that the ability to remember events—and then to construct a "narrative account" of them—is one of the two major modes of thinking. Bruner believes that the importance of "narrative thinking" has been ignored because of psychology's "obsession" with the study of *logical* thought and problem solving (Bruner, 1986).

Katherine Nelson and her colleagues at City University of New York have, for many years, studied *memory development* in children. The technique that Nelson and her group uses is that of asking young people to recount what happens to them in daily life (French & Nelson, 1985). Several of Nelson's findings are of considerable interest.

First, children tend to abstract from a few personal experiences a set of "rules" they presume hold for all such experiences. For example, if a child attends two or three birthday parties, the child will develop a "script" for how such events should proceed.

Second, children seem better at remembering "scripts" than specific experiences. If you ask a child what happened at school yesterday, the child may respond, "Nothing." What the child actually means, Nelson says, is that *nothing out of the ordinary* occurred. A child will likely remember an event *only if it departs significantly* from the script for such events.

Third, memory development is a product of *the amount of knowledge the child has*, not of the child's "age" or "stage."

Fourth, the more experience a child has—and the more help the child has had in understanding and learning how to talk about events—the better the child's memory becomes.

Nelson's research suggests that children's memories are longer and better organized than previous experiments had indicated. However, as Nelson notes, this fact becomes

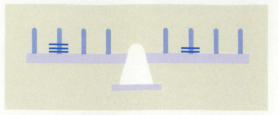

FIG. 15.4 A balance beam is used to identify children's rules for solving problems. On each side of the fulcrum are four pegs on which metal weights are placed. Depending on the arrangement of the weights, the beam ordinarily would tip to the left or right, or remain level. However, a lever (not shown) holds the beam motionless, regardless of how the weights are arranged. Children are asked to predict whether the beam would tip, and in which direction, if the lever were released.

clear only when you learn *what questions to ask children* about their daily experiences (Nelson *et al.*, 1986).

□ □ **QUESTION** □ □

Most older Americans can remember what they were doing the day President Kennedy was assassinated, but not what they did the day before. How does this fact support Nelson's point of view?

"Learning How to Think"

In a recent article, University of Pittsburgh psychologist Robert Glaser notes that most real-life problem solving involves the application of *knowledge*. Glaser defines "knowledge" as a combination of rules *plus* facts. The "facts" describe how to apply the rules in fairly specific situations. Glaser believes we cannot study the development of "thinking" and "reasoning" in children unless we first find out how much the children know about the world (Glaser, 1984).

This point is made clear in a series of experiments by Robert Siegler, a psychologist at Carnegie Mellon University. Much of Siegler's work involves the "balance beam" shown in Fig. 15.4. The beam is a sort of "teeter-totter" that can be locked into place.

As you know, there are two factors that determine which way the balance beam will tilt when released—*weight* and *distance*. The more weights there are on a given arm of the beam—and the farther the weights are from the center—the more likely it is that the beam will tilt in that direction.

• *Teaching Children to "Encode"*

Siegler says that the way a child perceives the balance problem depends on whether the child actually "encodes" the two important variables (weight and distance). By "encoding," he actually means "pays attention to."

To test his belief, Siegler asked a group of 5-year-olds and a group of 8-year-olds to guess which way the teeter-totter would tilt in one test situation. Both groups gave answers suggesting they were focusing entirely on weight—and ignoring the distance variable. Then Siegler gave the children "feedback" on the correctness of their answers: He released the balance and let the youngsters discover which way the teeter-totter actually tipped. Next, Siegler retested both groups on a similar problem. This time, the older children tended to take *both* weight and distance into account. However, the younger children doggedly kept on answering entirely in terms of weight.

Why did the older children improve, while the younger ones didn't? Videotapes of the pre-feedback session showed the eight-year-olds had looked back and forth from one end of the balance to the other, while the younger ones didn't. Siegler believes that because the older children "encoded" the distance factor—even though they didn't use it—they could benefit from feedback.

Next, Siegler gave "training sessions" to a new group of five- and eight-year-olds. During these sessions, he taught the children to consider both weight and distance. Once the youngsters had learned how to "encode" (or pay attention to) both variables, almost all of them began giving answers that involved both weight and distance (Siegler, 1984).

Siegler advocates first training children how to encode their environments, then teaching them problem-solving strategies (Siegler, 1983).

Like many other psychologists, Siegler is interested in how children acquire *knowledge*, which (as we noted) is facts plus rules. The person who made such studies popular was Jean Piaget. Indeed, Piaget's theory of cognitive development is really a theory of knowledge. Suppose we look at the theory first, then evaluate Piaget's contributions in light of recent studies by Siegler and other scientists.

JEAN PIAGET

Jean Piaget was one of the most respected figures in child psychology. He lived for 84 years. When Piaget died in September 1980, Harvard psychologist Jerome Kagan called him "the most influential developmental theorist of this century, if not of all time."

For some 50 years, Piaget was a professor at the University of Geneva and director of the Rousseau Institute. Trained as a zoologist, Piaget began his search for a "theory of knowledge" while still in college. This search soon led him to study the intellectual development of children (Boden, 1979).

Piaget was a gentle, wise man who loved children. But he also loved science, art, and religion. In 1918, when he was 20, Piaget published a novel, *Quest*, about a young man named Sebastien who is concerned with such questions as "Who am I?" and "What is the meaning of life?" The answers Sebastien discovers in the novel eventually became the basis for much of Piaget's theorizing about cognitive development. Indeed, according to University of Chicago educator Kenneth Kaye, most of Piaget's research on children appears to be little more than a life-long attempt to confirm the insights he had while still a very young man (Kaye, 1980).

Mental Development

The basic psychological problem Piaget tried to solve can be stated fairly simply. When you were born, you were little more than a bundle of biological reflexes. You took in food, you excreted wastes, and you responded in a reflexive way to a variety of stimuli. But you did not "think" or solve problems. Nor did you have any real understanding of who you were or what the world is really like. Now, many years later, you are a conscious, self-directed, mature human being. You speak a complex language, you are capable of understanding the strange symbols of mathematics and nuclear physics, and you can create new things (such as poetry and music) if you wish to. You engage in **altruistic** behaviors that often benefit others more than they benefit you. And you probably have a firm sense of what is right and wrong, and how to make many things in the world (including yourself) better than they presently are.

Now, how did you develop from a passive "bundle of biological reflexes" into the infinitely complicated, self-directed human being you are today? Piaget attempted to answer this question by developing a complex theory of cognitive development. His theory will make more sense, however, if we first look at where Piaget stood on the four developmental issues mentioned earlier in this chapter.

Piaget and the Four Issues

As far as the nature-nurture problem goes, Piaget was, in his own way, an interactionist. Indeed, he often called himself "the man in the middle" of this controversy. True, he believed you were born with certain *innate mental structures* that determined the shape of your cognitive development. These structures provided both your *motivation* to interact with your environment and guided the growth of your knowledge about the world. But Piaget thought the "shape of your mind" was affected by the environment you grew up in, too. Thus, he rejected Chomsky's notion that children are born with an "innate grammar" which helps them learn language. Children *construct* grammar in their own minds as they learn to talk, Piaget said, because their genes allow them to (Piaget, 1980a).

As far as the mind-body problem is concerned, Piaget came down clearly on the side of the mind. He paid little attention to behavior itself. Rather, it was the "mental functioning" which controlled behavior that interested him. Unlike the behaviorists—whom he battled with constantly—Piaget did not believe you were "shaped" by your parents and professors. Rather, he said, "The child is the teacher." By this, he meant you were actively involved in your own cognitive development. Your social environment merely provided the inputs— your mind *interpreted* and *reshaped* these inputs to create the knowledge you presently have (Piaget, 1978).

Piaget was also "somewhere in the middle" of the continuity-discontinuity controversy. According to Piaget, intellectual development in *all children* procedes through four clearly defined stages. We will describe these stages in a moment. Since he believed that the later stages developed out of the earlier ones, Piaget was a "continuity" theorist. However, he also said that development occurred in "giant steps" (or stages), rather than being merely the slow and steady accumulation of knowledge and information (Piaget, 1977b).

And while Piaget studied children individually, he was more impressed by how similar cognitive development is in all children than by individual differences among children (Piaget, 1981).

Now that we have briefly outlined Piaget's position on the four major issues in developmental psychology, let's examine his theory in some detail.

Equilibrium

At heart, Piaget was really an "information processing theorist" before such a label existed. That is, he saw the mind as a kind of computer that used sensory inputs to *construct* an internal representation of the outside world. However, ordinary computers are *passive* instruments that must be "programmed" by external sources. To Piaget, the child's mind is an *active* computer that continually changes or reprograms itself. The mind accomplishes this miracle by *abstracting* reality. By "abstracting reality," Piaget meant the search for general laws that will allow the mind to understand why people and objects behave as they do (Piaget, 1977b).

Computers process data because they are built to do so. Thus, their motivation is supplied by external sources. Children, however, are motivated by an inner biological drive that

Piaget calls the process of **equilibrium**. In Chapter 6 we discussed *homeostasis,* which is the body's innate tendency to move toward a need-free state. In a sense, the cognitive process of "equilibrium" is little more than the concept of homeostasis applied to mental rather than biological needs (Piaget, 1980b).

According to Piaget, you are born with the ability to construct an abstract representation of the world in your mind. But your attempts to do so are necessarily inaccurate, particularly when you are young and inexperienced. Sometimes, therefore, the things you experience may *contradict* your expectations. Whenever your *actual inputs* "contradict" your *expectancies,* you experience what Piaget called *dis-equilibrium*. And you are prompted to explain the contradiction.

In his book *The Development of Thought,* Piaget described some of his studies in this area. For example, suppose you show two small wheels to a child. The wheels appear to be identical. However, only one wheel is "normal." The other wheel has a hidden weight on its rim. Then you ask the child to guess what will happen when you roll the wheels down a slight incline. The child predicts the wheels will move downhill. You then release the normal wheel which does, indeed, roll downhill just as predicted. But when you release the weighted wheel, it sometimes stands still or even rolls uphill. The fact that the weighted wheel did not behave as the child predicted is a *contradiction* that causes *dis-equilibrium* in the child's mind. This dis-equilibrium motivates the child to search for an answer that will resolve the contradiction and restore mental equilibrium (Piaget, 1977b).

Generally speaking, children resolve contradictions by changing the way they perceive or "symbolize" real-world objects or events. And when they do so, they usually will have achieved a greater understanding of themselves and the world around them. Piaget referred to this type of cognitive growth as "achieving a higher state of equilibrium."

☐ ☐ **QUESTION** ☐ ☐

What similarities do you see between Piaget's "contradiction" study and Siegler's "feedback" experiment with the teeter-totter?

Dis-equilibrium

Dis-equilibrium is important in Piaget's theory for two reasons. First, dis-equilibrium *motivates* the child to resolve contradictions in order to re-establish equilibrium. Indeed, Piaget saw "the drive to maintain mental equilibrium" as being the major motive that fuels a child's cognitive development. Second, the *new equilibrium* the child achieves upon resolving the contradiction *is always higher*

Equilibrium (ee-kwill-LIB-bree-um). Piaget believed people are motivated by an innate desire to match actual sensory inputs with their own abstract representations of reality. Any mismatch results in dis-equilibrium, which "drives" the person to change her or his mental structures to bring them into accord with reality.

Schemata (ski-MAHT-tah). Plural of "schema." Schemata are mental structures that represent reality in some abstract manner. Similar to "perceptual schemata" that allow you to recognize and respond to sensory inputs (see Chapter 5).

Organization. One of the two invariant mental functions that guide the development of schemata and other mental structures. Organization is the innate tendency to create complex structures out of simple ones.

Adaptation. The second unchanging mental function. The innate tendency to adjust to the world either by assimilating inputs or accommodating to them.

Assimilation (ass-sim-il-LAY-shun). The process of adaptation by which inputs are altered in order to fit into present schemata or mental structures. "Coding" an input into memory categories for long-term storage is a form of assimilation. So is "pretending" that a stick is a magic wand, for you alter the input to fit your present needs.

Accommodation (ack-komm-oh-DAY-shun). The process of adaptation by which mental schemata are changed or added to in order to match them to reality. If a given input won't fit into any present schema, you accommodate by creating a new one.

(more mature) than was the previous level of equilibrium. This new level is higher, Piaget said, because it is a *more accurate representation* of the real world.

Drive theorists believe that children eat to reduce their hunger pangs and thus restore homeostasis—not because they have an innate urge to grow and survive. Piaget took much the same approach in describing cognitive motives. He stated that children construct better abstractions about the world because they are driven to reduce dis-equilibrium and restore equilibrium—not because they have an innate urge "to learn about the world." Therefore, the best way to teach children, Piaget often said, was to present them with contradictions that they must resolve (Piaget, 1986).

□ □ QUESTION □ □
How does Piaget differ from the early drive theorists? (Hint: Each time you eat, do you establish a "more mature" type of hunger?)

Structures of the Mind
Piaget said you construct reality in your mind by trying to resolve contradictions. But you couldn't start doing that at birth unless you were born with some innately-determined notion of what to expect from the world around you. Piaget called these "innately-determined notions" the *structures of the mind*.

As we noted in Chapter 9, you were born with certain *innate reflexes*, which allowed you to respond automatically to inputs from the outer world during your first days of life. The sucking reflex is a good example, since infants suck and swallow without having to be taught how to do so. At birth, however, you began

modifying these inborn reflexes because of your experiences with the outside world. Thus, new learning is always built on old, and *conditioned* reflexes are but adaptations of *innate* reflexes.

In much the same fashion, said Piaget, you were born with certain "mental reflexes." These innate cognitive structures allow you to process sensory inputs (and therefore represent reality) in a crude sort of way. At birth, however, you began to adapt these inborn mental structures as you constructed your own "mental action programs" for processing and responding to reality.

In Piaget's terms, each "mental action program" you have for thinking about and responding to the world is a *schema* (see Chapter 5). The history of a child's cognitive development is that of creating ever more complex **schemata**, or "action programs." Guiding the development of these mental structures, however, are the *functions of the mind* (Piaget, 1977b).

Functions of the Mind
You do not perceive yourself now in the same way that you did 10 years ago. Thus, your "self-schema" has changed over time, and will continue to change in your future years. But the growth of your "self-schema" was guided throughout your life by the same two mental *functions*. These "functions" are **organization** and **adaptation**.

By the term "organization," Piaget referred to the mind's innate ability to *put simple schemata together* so they form a more complex cognitive structure. For example, a six-month-old infant knows how to push an object such as a ball aside. "Pushing" thus is one of the infant's cognitive schemata, or "action programs." The infant also knows how to reach out and grasp a toy, such as a doll. "Reaching" is therefore a second but quite independent action program. At six months, the child is not mature enough to push a ball aside in order to grasp a doll that is behind the ball. At about nine months, however, the child can *integrate* these two schemata into a more complex mental structure. That is, the youngster can now *intentionally* push the ball out of the way and grasp the doll. Much of the process of cognitive development involves *organizing* simple schemata into more complex action programs.

Adaptation is the infant's innate tendency to adjust to the world by processing information in one of two ways. The child may either try to incorporate inputs into already-existing schemata, a process Piaget calls **assimilation**. Or, if the inputs simply will not fit the child's present view of reality, the child may be forced to change, add to, or reorganize her or his present schemata. Piaget refers to this process as **accommodation** (Piaget, 1976).

• *Assimilation*

Piaget was first and foremost a biologist. Thus, many of his notions of cognitive development are analogies to biological processes. For example, consider the process of digestion. You eat food, and your stomach breaks the food down into small particles. Your blood distributes these particles to the cells, which *assimilate* these particles by incorporating them into the structure of the cell. Biological assimilation therefore involves *changing* energy inputs to make them part of your body.

The process of *cognitive assimilation* works in much the same way. According to Piaget, when you "encode" an input in order to store it your mind, you *break the input up* just as your stomach breaks food down into tiny particles. You then incorporate the "encoded" input into already-existing mental structures, just as the cells assimilate food particles into already-existing cellular structures. Cognitive assimilation thus involves *changing* sensory inputs to make them part of your mind.

For instance, a newborn girl tends to suck any small object that is put in her mouth. She soon builds up a mental schema related to "suckability" and assimilates all small objects into this category whether they really fit there or not. Therefore, when she encounters any new small object, she often pops the object in her mouth at once (Piaget, 1977b).

☐ ☐ **QUESTION** ☐ ☐

What similarities do you see between Piaget's views on how assimilation occurs, and Goodglass's theory (discussed in Chapter 11) of how inputs are encoded in *categories* while being stored in Long-term Memory?

• *Accommodation*

Sometimes a given input simply will not fit within the schemata a child already has available. For instance, suppose an infant named Mary finds a small red pepper and pops that into her mouth. Very rapidly, Mary will discover she must create a new schema, that of "not suckable." Any new experience which contradicts her already-existing mental structures will cause Mary to resort to the process of *accommodation*—that is, to altering her schemata to make them fit reality.

To restate matters, assimilation is the mental function that allows you to change *inputs* so that they fit your present schemata or other mental structures. Accommodation is the mental function that allows you to change your *schemata* so that they match the reality represented by your present inputs. Both of these "functions of the mind" guide your cognitive development from birth to death (Piaget, 1977b).

Infants who suck on every new object may be classifying items according to a mental "suckability" schema.

Epistemology

One word Piaget used constantly was **epistemology**, which the dictionary defines as "the study or a theory of the nature and grounds of knowledge, especially with reference to its limits and validity." And much of Piaget's research was epistemological, in that it was aimed at discovering how *children come to know themselves and the world around them* (Piaget, 1977a).

Piaget's theory is actually an attempt to describe how the infant acquires both facts about the world and a set of "rules" for using those facts. And that is precisely what the study of epistemology is all about.

PIAGET'S FOUR DEVELOPMENTAL STAGES

According to Piaget, there are four major stages of cognitive development:

- **1.** The sensory-motor period.
- **2.** The pre-operational stage.
- **3.** The stage of concrete operations.
- **4.** The stage of formal operations.

According to American psychologist Gilbert Voyat, "Each new stage integrates the previous one, contains its own laws of organization and anticipates the succeeding one. From a structural point of view, each stage has a developmental relation to both the preceding and succeeding one" (Voyat, 1982).

Each of us goes from one stage upward to the next at slightly different ages. But the *average age* at which children attain each maturational level is said to be about the same in all cultures (Piaget, 1977b).

Sensory-Motor Period

The first of Piaget's four stages is called the **sensory-motor period**, which begins at birth and usually ends when the infant is about 24 months old. It is during this time infants build up their initial schemata, most of which involve the objects and people around them.

For the first month or so of life, infants "know the world" solely in terms of the innate reflexes which serve to keep them alive. But, within a month or so, infants begin to form crude "action schemata" which let them explore and respond to their world.

Through the processes of assimilation and accommodation, Piaget said, these initial action schemata develop and become organized into more complex mental structures. The infant begins to associate sensory inputs with muscular movements. For example, the child gazes at his/her hands while grasping for a toy, and thus connects visual inputs with motor responses and sensory feedback. Eventually the child can reach for the toy without looking at her/his hands (Piaget, 1977b).

□ □ QUESTION □ □
Do the data cited in Chapter 14 on what newborns can and can't do support Piaget's position, or not?

• *Object Permanence*
According to Piaget, during the first months of life, infants do not realize that an object can exist outside of their own perception of the object. Six-month-old children will typically follow an object with their eyes as the object moves across their field of vision. But if the object disappears, they show no disappointment, Piaget said, nor do they appear to anticipate the object's reappearance. Playing "peek-a-boo" with a child this young is often a frustrating task because the infant seems not to know what the game is about. When the child reaches eight months of age (on the average), however, the infant will usually reach for an object hidden from view provided that the infant has seen the object being hidden.

By the time children are 18 months of age or so, they will search for something they haven't seen hidden. According to Piaget, this is an indication that they have acquired the concept of **object permanence**. Piaget believed this concept is the beginning of *symbolic thought*, for the child maintains a mental symbol of the object even when the object is out of sight.

When youngsters gain the ability to represent objects symbolically, Piaget said, they pass from the sensory-motor period into the pre-operational period of development (Piaget, 1977b).

□ □ QUESTION □ □
What else does the child acquire during the first two years of life that allows the child to represent objects internally using *easy-to-manipulate* cognitive symbols?

• *Object Permanence Reconsidered*
As we noted in Chapter 15, infants apparently build up "perceptual schemata"—particularly of the mother—much sooner than Piaget realized. In a recent paper, British psychologist George Butterworth suggests that *object permanence* may also occur much earlier in life than Piaget thought was the case. However, you must *test* the infants in different ways than Piaget did in order to discover this fact.

Butterworth found that infants would search for objects visually a year sooner than Piaget thought they did—but their searches often *seemed to be* fairly random because they simply could not control their eye movements as well as older children could. When an object was hidden in a prominent location, however, they often acted as if they knew that something

A Piagetian experiment: When asked to place the man where the policeman cannot see him, the child at the "egocentric" stage would place him where *she* cannot see him. In fact, this child often placed the man where she could see him but the policeman could not.

had "vanished" at that spot (Butterworth, 1983).

In a similar study, Canadian psychologists Hildy Ross and Susan Lollis played a variety of "turn-taking" games (such as "peek-a-boo") with nine-month-old infants. After four "rounds," the experimenter would sit quietly and refuse to take her turn. "When the adults failed to participate, the infants showed considerable independent understanding of the games they played," Ross and Lollis report. That is, they made sounds and other signals urging the adults to take their turn. When the game involved playing with a toy, the infants gave clear evidence they understood the *permanence* of the toy, and who should play with it at a specific time during the game. Thus, Ross and Lollis say, object permanence (and several other cognitive skills) seem to emerge in infants much sooner than Piaget assumed was the case (Ross & Lollis, 1987).

Whether or not Piaget was correct about the precise *time* at which infants gain the concept of *object permanence* is, perhaps, not all that important to our understanding of his theory of child development. And it surely remains true that at a very early age, children do not seem to be able to think in symbols, while at a later age they can.

Pre-operational Stage

During the sensory-motor period, the infant responds to its environment directly and rather automatically. But as the child acquires *sophisticated language*, the youngster passes to the second, or **pre-operational stage** of development, which runs from about age two to seven.

Language gives the child the ability to deal with many aspects of the world in symbols, by talking and thinking about objects rather than having to manipulate them directly. Piaget believed that language also allows the child to *remember past events* and hence to *anticipate* their happening again (Piaget, 1976).

• *Egocentrism in Children*

According to Piaget, during all the early developmental periods—and sometimes even much later in life—the child makes use of **egocentric reasoning**. But this type of thinking is particularly noticeable during the pre-operational period. By "egocentric," Piaget didn't mean "selfish." Rather, he meant that children cannot readily *differentiate themselves from their environments*. For instance, Piaget had three-year-old children close their eyes and then asked them, "Can you see me?" The children replied, "No." He then asked, "Can I see you?" Again the children replied, "No." Five-year-olds answered both questions correctly. Piaget concluded that the three-year-olds simply were not mature enough "to realize that other people have different points of view than they do."

Whether or not young children are *actually* egocentric, however, depends not only on how you define the term, but also on how you question them (Cox, 1985). Most recent studies in this area, however, suggest that egocentrism is not the "hallmark" of infancy that Piaget assumed it was.

For example, when Stanford psychologist John Flavell and his colleagues repeated Piaget's experiments, they got quite different results. Flavell had three-year-olds close their eyes and put their hands over their eyes. Then he asked, "Can I see you?" The children said "No," just as Piaget's subjects had. However, when Flavell asked, "Can I see your arms?" the children replied, "Yes." They also agreed that Flavell could see an object placed in front of them, but could not see their backs. Flavell and his associates conclude that "adults take 'you' to mean their whole body while young children take it to mean primarily their face region." The Stanford psychologists conclude that, had Piaget asked different questions, he might have changed his mind about "egocentrism" in children (Flavell, Shipstead, & Croft, 1980).

In a recent article, Harriet Waters summarizes current thinking on egocentrism this way: "Since Piaget's theory was introduced, American psychologists have sought empirical confirmation of Piaget's assertions and hypotheses, often to the point of overlooking the wisdom and elegance of his insights. However, in the case of egocentrism, it must be fairly said that the data do not support [Piaget's] view of egocentrism" (Waters, 1987).

● Transformations and Conservation

Piaget believed that the pre-operational stage is also marked by *perception-bound thinking*. That is, the child realizes that objects have permanence, but struggles with the fact that objects can undergo *transformations* without being destroyed or physically changed. By "transformations," Piaget means the fact that some aspects of an object may change, but the object itself remains intact. For instance, if you turn a sock inside out, then back again, the child is surprised to see that the sock remains the same. For when the youngster's *perception* of the sock changed, the child assumed the sock had been altered too.

Because the child doesn't realize that *transformations are reversible*, Piaget claimed, the youngster cannot **conserve** physical properties such as quantity and length. For instance, if you fill two identical, tall, thin glasses with water, the child will agree both glasses have the same amount of water in them. But suppose you empty the water in one glass into a wide container (see Fig. 15.5). The water level is, of course, lower in the wide container than in the tall, thin glass. You "know" the fat glass holds the same *quantity* of water as does the thin glass because you can "conserve quantity" in

your mind. But when Piaget tested four-year-olds on this problem, they responded that the tall glass now had more liquid in it because the water level in that glass was higher. Piaget assumed the children didn't realize that the process of pouring didn't *alter* the quantity of liquid in any way. And, when he poured the water back into the tall, thin glass, he reported the children were surprised that the water level rose. Piaget concluded that the youngsters couldn't yet grasp the fact that transformations are reversible (Piaget, 1977b). As we will see, however, Piaget's results may depend more on *how you test* children than on their cognitive development.

Piaget's research suggested that children do not seem to be able to deal with abstractions—such as love and hate, up and down, large and small—until they are four or five years of age. In Piaget's terms, children this age can think—that is, they can use language to generate expectancies—but they cannot *reason*. Reasoning, to Piaget, is the mental manipulation of abstract symbols, the process of "knowing why."

The pre-operational stage is a transition period. As the child acquires more complex language and mental structures, the young person moves into the stage of concrete operations.

□□ **QUESTION** □□

Piaget seems never to have used the shaping techniques (described in Chapter 10) to teach a child to conserve quantity. How might you go about pouring just a little bit of water back and forth from tall to wide glasses to see if children could be taught conservation of quantity at an early age?

Stage of Concrete Operations

By the time children reach the age of 6 or 7, they typically enter into what Piaget called the **stage of concrete operations**. Now young persons can conserve quantity, Piaget said, because they can perform this transformation mentally. But children this age usually cannot conserve weight until the 9th or 10th year. If you place two identical rubber balls in front of a young boy, he will assure you they weigh the same. But if you now cut one ball in pieces, he may say the cut-up pieces don't weigh the same as does the intact ball. According to Piaget, the boy's answer suggests he actually *perceives* weight in quite a different way than do older children. However, once the boy learns to conserve weight, he finally realizes that the whole is equal to the sum of its parts.

The concept of *number* is another acquisition the child usually makes during the stage of concrete operations. Suppose you lay out 10

FIG. 15.5 Conservation of quantity according to Piaget.

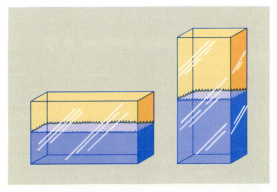

pennies in two rows on a table, and show them to a girl still at the pre-operational stage:

$$\circ \quad \circ \quad \circ \quad \circ \quad \circ$$

$$\circ \quad \circ \quad \circ \quad \circ \quad \circ$$

The girl will see at once that the two rows are identical and that they both contain the same number of pennies. But suppose you widen the spaces between the pennies in the bottom row:

$$\circ \quad \circ \quad \circ \quad \circ \quad \circ$$

$$\circ \quad \quad \circ \quad \quad \circ \quad \quad \circ \quad \quad \circ$$

A pre-operational girl may say the second row has more pennies, despite the fact that she can count the coins in each row with no difficulty. Piaget emphasizes that *counting* is not the same thing as the *concept of number*, a schema the child usually attains only during the stage of concrete operations. (As we will see shortly, however, more recent research suggests that the answer the child gives is more dependent upon the questions you ask than Piaget apparently realized.)

According to Piaget, during the stage of concrete operations the child begins to visualize a *complex sequence of operations*. A five-year-old boy can walk to school without getting lost—that is, he can perform a series of complex operations in order to reach a goal. But the boy usually must be six before he gains the ability to draw a map showing the route he takes from home to school. And it is only at this point he realizes that anyone else could follow the map as well. However, he cannot describe the *abstract principles* involved in map making (or anything else) until he reaches the stage of formal operations (Piaget, 1976).

□□ **QUESTION** □□

If you ask a pre-operational girl, "Which row has the more pennies?" how do you know she understands you mean "more pennies" and not "more space"?

Stage of Formal Operations

The last of Piaget's four periods of intellectual development is called the **stage of formal operations**, which begins about age 12 and continues through the rest of the person's life. Some people may never really reach this stage, Piaget said, and those that do may not go very far into it. Whatever the case, children usually don't reach the last stage until at least age 12.

Prior to the 12th year of life, Piaget said, the child is limited to thinking in concrete terms. Only in the final stage can the young person think in completely abstract terms. At this level of development, people can solve problems in their minds by isolating the important variables and manipulating them mentally. Now at last the individual is able to draw meaningful conclusions from purely abstract or hypothetical data.

It is during the stage of formal operations that the structures of the mind become complex enough to allow the individual to create a personal "theory of knowledge." This epistemological theory involves all types of knowledge—"how," "what," and most important, "why."

In a sense, Piaget's *stage theory* is an attempt to explain "why" children develop as they do. Now that we have briefly described it, let's see how others have reacted to his theory.

Piaget and His Critics

As you might suspect, any theory as influential as Piaget's is bound to draw a lot of criticism. Most of the criticisms are fairly minor. One objection to Piaget's approach, however, is of major dimensions. Let's start with the minor problems.

• Baldwin's Influence

One of the minor criticisms leveled at Piaget is that many of his ideas were mere adaptations of early work by US psychologist James Mark Baldwin (Broughton, 1981). As Robert Cairns points out, there is some truth to this accusation. For in 1897 Baldwin described the various stages of a child's cognitive development as part of his theory of "genetic epistemology," and Baldwin used many of the terms that Piaget later adopted (Cairns, 1980).

It is difficult to take Cairn's criticism seriously, however. To begin with, Piaget acknowledged Baldwin's influence (Piaget, 1978). Furthermore, Piaget's fame rests primarily on his astute observations of children's behavior, not on his stage theory of cognitive development.

• Piaget's Subjects

The children Piaget spent a lifetime observing were for the most part white, middle-class youngsters reared in normal European homes. His four-stage theory appears to hold to some extent for such children. There is little empirical evidence showing that it holds in other cultures, however (Flavell, 1985).

• Are There "General Structures of the Mind?"

Piaget assumed there were "general structures of the mind" that the child could apply to all situations. In a recent article, Tufts psychologist David Feldman disagrees. He believes the child builds up *specific* mental processes for handling *specific* types of situations. And the child may do much better in some situations than in others, Feldman says. For instance, a seven-year-old genius may play chess at an adult level,

15 / Cognitive Development: From Childhood to Old Age

but still may not be able to see the world from other people's point of view. What developmental stage shall we say this child is at (Feldman, 1985)?

● Contradictions about Equilibrium

Piaget argued that all significant cognitive development occurred through contradictions that bring about a higher level of equilibrium. But do the data support his position? John Flavell doubts this is always the case. Flavell notes that the equilibration process requires the child to do four things:

1. Attend to both of the conflicting elements at once—for instance, be aware of both the "normal" and the "weighted" wheel at the same time.
2. Realize that a conflict exists between the two—something that Flavell doubts young children always do.
3. Respond to the contradiction by *progressing*. As we noted when describing Siegler's studies with the teeter-totter, young children don't profit from contradictions unless they are taught to "encode" the problem differently.
4. Discover a better way of conceptualizing the situation—a way that will allow the child to resolve the contradiction in a more mature fashion.

Some children lack one or more of these four abilities, Flavell says, yet they develop cognitively anyhow. He summarizes the situation thusly: "I believe the equilibration process itself needs explaining when and where it does occur, and also that it does not occur in all instances of cognitive development" (Flavell, 1985).

● Are There "Stages" of Development?

A fair amount of the controversy over Piaget's theory is based on his use of *developmental stages*. As popular as this approach is among personality theorists, the data give scant support to the notion that development is a matter of "moving up a clearly-defined ladder" (Levin, 1986).

For example, Susanna Millar points out that Piaget's "stage theory" includes three assumptions that may not be true:

1. Intellectual development absolutely must proceed in 1–2–3–4 sequence. The *speed* at which a child matures may be increased or retarded, but the *sequence of stages* must always be the same.
2. There are no halfway points between two stages.
3. The developmental stages themselves can be differentiated entirely in terms of the logical operations a child employs while thinking.

After reviewing the literature, Susanna Millar concludes there is little *experimental* evidence to support these three assumptions (Millar, 1968).

John Flavell summarizes the present situation thusly: "I think it is fair to conclude that developmental psychologists are currently becoming increasingly skeptical of the theoretical use of the construct of "cognitive-developmental stage' (many, indeed, never thought much of it). . . . My own hunch is that the concept of stage will not, in fact, figure importantly in future scientific work on cognitive growth" (Flavell, 1985).

● Observations Versus Experiments

The major objection against Piaget's position, however, surely lies in the types of data he collected, and the manner in which he collected them. Piaget performed "observations and demonstrations," not rigorously controlled experiments. Scientists who have conducted actual experimental studies have often gotten results Piaget wouldn't have predicted.

For example, University of Pennsylvania psychologist Rochel Gelman tested Piaget's notion of "conservation of quantity" with three- and four-year-old children. She showed them two rows of toy mice. One row had three mice in it; the other had five mice. The row with five mice, of course, took up more space than the row with three mice. She told the children that the three-mice row was the "winner," and then asked the youngsters to "find the winner" in a slightly different situation. This time she again showed the children rows of three and five mice. But now the distance between the three mice was increased so that they took up just as much space as did the row with five mice. All the youngsters immediately identified the three mice as the "winner." As one child put it, "It's still three—they just spreaded out." Obviously these "pre-operational" four-year-olds could conserve quantity, although Piaget said this cognitive ability did not appear until age seven or eight, during the stage of concrete operations.

In a recent article, Boston University psychologist Jean Berko Gleason makes an equally telling observation: "Young children shown a liquid poured from a short, fat container into a tall, thin container . . . have been known, in the laboratory, to assert that the amount of liquid has increased; yet, in their real lives, preschoolers who want more juice at snack time are not known to pour their existing juice into taller glasses in order to accomplish this end" (Gleason, 1987).

Put simply, Piaget made certain assumptions about cognitive development in children, and then performed demonstrations that tended to support his prior beliefs. Had Piaget performed "controlled experiments" rather than simply observing children in cleverly-constructed situations, he might have come to different conclusions.

Piaget: A Summary

Piaget knew about most of the criticisms mentioned above, and cared little for any of them. He was convinced his basic assumptions were correct, and therefore saw little need to test them experimentally. As he put it in *Quest*, the novel he wrote when he was 20, "You would not search for me, had you not [already] found me." Thus, Piaget didn't seek the truth empirically; he merely tried to demonstrate to others the wisdom he had already found as a young man.

How shall we summarize Piaget's importance? Perhaps the old saying "The king is dead. Long live the king!" says it best. We can underscore that point by looking briefly at two additional aspects of cognitive development, *moral development* and *play*. As we will see, Piaget had a profound influence on our understanding of both subjects.

□ □ **QUESTION** □ □

Suppose someone you love dearly desperately needs a very expensive operation. Unfortunately, neither you nor your loved one can afford the surgery. Under these circumstances, would it be *moral* for you to steal the money to pay for the operation?

MORAL DEVELOPMENT

More than 30 years ago, Jean Piaget became interested in the *moral development* of young children. He noted that, as children grow, they acquire an increasingly complex "sense of justice" (Piaget, 1965).

After observing a number of youngsters, Piaget concluded that children from age two to five have little interest in "winning" the various games they play. Rather, they are primarily concerned with exploring how they can gain *physical control* over the objects they play with.

From about age five to age nine, however, the youngsters become more and more interested in *following the rules* of their games. Piaget called this the stage of *moral realism*, in which children tend to believe that social rules are as "absolute" as are natural laws. If you sug-

School-age children may perceive the rules of a game such as dodgeball to be absolute; breaking the rules is expected to bring about severe punishment from a higher authority.

gest to an eight-year-old boy that he play a game of baseball using different rules, Piaget said, the boy might insist that "God wouldn't want you to." During the stage of moral realism, it is the *consequences* of an act that determine whether or not it was "just." Break the rules, and you will be punished. Follow the rules, and you will either escape punishment or even be rewarded.

By age 10 or so, Piaget concluded, children begin to shift from "blind obedience to authority" to an understanding that they must meet the needs of others if their own needs are to be satisfied. At this point, Piaget said, children develop a viewpoint Piaget called the "morality of cooperation." They now realize that "the rules of the game" can be changed if all the players agree to the changes.

Finally, as children pass into the stage of *formal operations*, they start to perceive the world in terms of *moral autonomy*. At this point in their development, they come to believe that their "intentions," not the "consequences" of a given behavior, determine whether or not the act was *moral* (Piaget, 1965).

Kohlberg's Levels of Moral Development

Some 20 years ago, Harvard psychologist Lawrence Kohlberg created his own theory of moral growth that is based on Piaget's views. As the child passes upward through the various Piagetian stages of *cognitive* development, Kohlberg says, the youngster also moves progressively through various levels of *moral* development. Kohlberg believes that "moral reasoning" is merely one example of the general ability to *think and reason*. Therefore, he says, moral development is guided (and limited) by the child's cognitive development (Kohlberg, 1976).

According to Kohlberg, there are three *levels of moral development*, each of which contains two stages (see Table 15.1). "One way of understanding the three levels," Kohlberg says, "is to think of them as three different types of

TABLE 15.1   The Six Moral Stages

	Content of Stage	
LEVEL AND STAGE	WHAT IS RIGHT	REASONS FOR DOING RIGHT
LEVEL I—PRECONVENTIONAL Stage 1—Authoritarian morality	To avoid breaking rules backed by punishment, obedience for its own sake, and avoiding physical damage to persons and property.	Avoidance of punishment, and the superior power of authorities.
Stage 2—Individualism, Instrumental Purpose, and Exchange	Following rules only when it is to someone's immediate interest; acting to meet one's own interests and needs and letting others do the same. Right is also what's fair, what's an equal exchange, a deal, an agreement.	To serve one's own needs or interests in a world where you have to recognize that other people have their interests, too.
LEVEL II—CONVENTIONAL Stage 3—Mutual Interpersonal Expectations, Relationships, and Interpersonal Conformity	Living up to what is expected by people close to you or what people generally expect of people in your role as son, brother, friend, etc. "Being good" is important and means having good motives, showing concern about others. It also means keeping mutual relationships, such as trust, loyalty, respect, and gratitude.	The need to be a good person in your own eyes and those of others. Your caring for others. Belief in the Golden Rule. Desire to maintain rules and authority which support stereotypical good behavior.
Stage 4—Social System and Conscience	Fulfilling the actual duties to which you have agreed. Laws are to be upheld except in extreme cases where they conflict with other fixed social duties. Right is also contributing to society, the group, or institution.	To keep the institution going as a whole, to avoid the breakdown in the system "if everyone did it," or the imperative of conscience to meet one's defined obligations (Easily confused with Stage 3 belief in rules and authority; see text.)
LEVEL III—POST-CONVENTIONAL, or PRINCIPLES Stage 5—Social Contract or Utility and Individual Rights	Being aware that people hold a variety of values and opinions, that most values and rules are relative to your group. These relative rules should usually be upheld, however, in the interest of impartiality and because they are the social contract. Some nonrelative values and rights like *life* and *liberty,* however, must be upheld in any society and regardless of majority opinion.	A sense of obligation to law because of one's social contract to make and abide by laws for the welfare of all and for the protection of all people's rights. A feeling of contractual commitment, freely entered upon, to family, freindship, trust, and work obligations. Concern that laws and duties be based on rational calculation of overall utility, "the greatest good for the greatest number."
Stage 6—Universal Ethical Principles	Following self-chosen ethical principles. Particular laws or social agreements are usually valid because they rest on such principles. When laws violate these principles, one acts in accordance with the principle. Principles are universal principles of justice: the equality of human rights and respect for the dignity of human beings as individual persons.	The belief as a rational person in the validity of universal moral principles, and a sense of personal commitment to them.

relationships between the *self* and *society's rules and expectations*."

If you are at Level I, you are *preconventional*. You believe that rules and social expectations are external to you and are imposed on you "by God and society."

If you are at Level II, you are *conventional*. By now you have "internalized" society's rules, especially those imposed by authority figures.

If you are at Level III, you are *postconventional*. You realize that society's rules are arbitrary, and you define your values in terms of your own self-chosen principles.

Like almost all stage theorists, Kohlberg believes that movement through the six stages is always "upward, gradual, and without significant regressions" (Snarey, Reimer, & Kohlberg, 1985b).

In order to determine at what stage (or level) a given person might be, Kohlberg uses "doll play" with young children and stories about moral **dilemmas** with older individuals. One such dilemma concerns a man who must steal a valuable item in order to save his wife's life. A preconventional child might answer, "He shouldn't do it because he'll be punished." A young person at the conventional level might respond, "He shouldn't do it because he knows stealing is morally wrong." However, a person at the postconventional level might say, "Stealing is bad, but saving a life is more important than following society's rules."

Kohlberg differentiates between *moral reasoning* and *moral behavior*. He believes that "To act in a morally high way requires a high stage of moral reasoning. . . . One can, however, reason in terms of such principles and not live up to them" (Kohlberg, 1976).

Kohlberg and his associates have tested children and adults in several countries, including the US, Israel, and Turkey. Kohlberg reports that individuals in all these cultures appear to achieve the same levels of moral development (as measured by his tests) at about the same ages. These results convince Kohlberg that his stages are as "natural and universal" as the stages of cognitive development described by Piaget (Nisan & Kohlberg, 1982; Snarey, Reimer, & Kohlberg, 1985a).

● **Criticisms of Kohlberg's Theory**

Kohlberg's description of moral development is subject to all the criticisms of Piaget's stage theory mentioned earlier in this chapter—and a few that are unique to Kohlberg's work.

First, Kohlberg's early theorizing was based on interviews with a selected sample of white, middle-class US males. Although Kohlberg has since interviewed both males and females of all ages in several cultures, many psychologists conclude that there is "insufficient evidence" to support his belief that there

is "an invariant developmental sequence" of six developmental stages (Kurtines & Grief, 1974).

Second, the "moral dilemmas" he uses may not be representative of the types of moral dilemmas that children, adolescents, college students, and older individuals routinely face in their daily life (Yussen, 1977).

Third, Kohlberg's results are based on *his* interpretations of his subject's responses, thus may be biased (Flavell, 1985).

Fourth, Kohlberg's theory is derived from his own interpretation of Western (democratic) morality, and may not apply to cultures where people do not perceive "individual autonomy" as the highest moral goal (Flavell, 1985). Furthermore, his levels may not even be an adequate description of moral development within many sub-cultures here in the US (Stack, 1986).

Perhaps the strongest criticism of Kohlberg's theory, however, comes from those psychologists who point out that his approach is strongly "male-biased." Kohlberg sees *autonomy* as the peak of moral development, and *objectivity* as being at a higher level than *subjectivity*—just as Piaget did. However, as Harvard psychologist Carole Gilligan points out, men are socialized to place a high value on *independence*, while women are taught to value *interdependence*, *caring*, and *sharing*. If Kohlberg is right, then women will almost always score somewhat lower on Kohlberg's tests than do men (Bloom, 1986; Gilligan, 1983, 1986). Beverly Gelman puts the objection this way: What right has Kohlberg to say that "objectivity" is morally superior to "subjectivity" (Gelman, 1985)?

As you might imagine, the issues raised by Kohlberg's theory are far from settled. It does seem clear, however, that the ability to make moral judgments does develop over a person's life span.

● **A Sense of Justice**

Piaget believed that, as they mature, children develop what he called "a sense of justice." He often watched youngsters play games in order to study how their notions of "what was just" grew and matured (Piaget, 1965). Perhaps, then, we should continue our discussion of cognitive and moral development by looking at the fascinating subject of *play*.

□ □ **QUESTION** □ □
What aspects of morality might a child learn from playing with other children?

PLAY

The infant is born little more than an animal. The majority of educators believe that, if society does not condition the child, the youngster will remain non-verbal, non-social, and "retarded." We typically call this conditioning process *education*, and believe that "study" is more important than "play." Recent studies suggest, however, that children may learn as much from seemingly-random "play" as they do in the schoolroom.

Types of Play

There are several types of play, and most children go from one type to another in much the same fashion as they presumably "move upward" in Piaget's "developmental stages." Suppose we describe the types first, and then look at theoretical explanations of what causes playful behavior, and why it is so important.

● Pre-social Play

The first type of play that infants engage in is rightly called "pre-social." That is, six-month-old infants play with dolls dangling from their cribs, with bells and rattles and balls and teddy bears, and they play with their own hands and feet. Only later do they discover the marvelous possibilities for play that other people offer (Harlow, 1973).

● Social Play

As children pass from the pre-operational to the operational stage of intellectual development, their play becomes more complex and *social* as other people begin to become animate partners rather than mere objects to be manipulated (Smith, 1984).

In pre-social play, infants entertain themselves without interacting with others.

Social play seems to be of three major types: (1) free play, (2) formal play, and (3) creative play. Of the three, physical free play with other children is perhaps the easiest for the child, and hence often the first to appear. As Anthony Pellegrini points out, this sort of "rough-housing" is also the most disturbing to the middle-class parent, who is often afraid the child will either hurt others or be hurt by them. Yet this type of activity may help children learn to tolerate minor frustrations and how to control their tempers (Pellegrini, 1987).

As the child becomes more verbal, rough-and-tumble play drops off sharply, and formalized play begins. The mock fights of four-year-old boys develop rapidly into games of tag and "cops and robbers" in which the youngsters must follow *formal rules*. These rules, of course, constitute what Piaget would call "schemata."

In Piaget's terms, creative play is primarily a matter of *assimilation*—of "pretending" that things might happen that haven't yet happened. Piaget believes that creative play is the child's way of learning to manipulate symbols rather than objects. He calls it the "high point" of all types of play. He also calls it "a child's work" (Piaget, 1965).

But even if "play is work" in some sense, the question becomes *why* children engage in this activity at all. As we will see, there are many explanations.

Theories of Play

Most of us might assume that play is an activity that children fall into spontaneously, and that its major purpose might be that of making children more pleasant—or of keeping them occupied for a while. However, to some scientists, play has a deeper and more profound importance.

Both Plato and Aristotle urged parents to give their children toy tools to play with, to "shape their minds" for future activities as adults. This "educational" approach to play held until the 1800's, when philosophers suggested that play was the "unfolding" of innate talents and desires. These scholars told parents to leave their children alone, so the youngsters could freely determine what they wanted to do or become (Trotter, 1987).

Then, a little more than 100 years ago, British philosopher Herbert Spencer suggested what is now called the *surplus energy hypothesis* of play. Spencer thought each child was born with an energy-producing machine of some kind inside it. This energy had to be released regularly or the child would simply "explode." Spencer thought that all art came from play, as did Sigmund Freud (Pellegrini, 1987). As we will see in the next chapter, Freud incorporated many of Spencer's ideas about psychic energy into his theory of psychoanalysis.

Although Spencer's ideas on the purpose of play were influenced by Charles Darwin's books on evolution, it was G.S. Hall who pushed evolutionary theory to what now seem absurd lengths. Hall believed that each child must **recapitulate** (relive) the behavioral history of the human race through play. Children couldn't become adults, Hall said, until they had worked their way through all the ancient behaviors built into their genetic blueprints over millions of years of evolution (Sluckin, 1981).

□ □ **QUESTION** □ □
Why would Hall have difficulty explaining children's fascination with airplanes and computers in terms of "reliving ancient behaviors?"

The Purpose of Play
What then is play, if it isn't blowing off steam or a way of stepping rapidly up the developmental ladder? The truth is, play serves so many different functions that no one theory can explain its many functions.

Play allows the child to practice social roles—that is, to build up sequences of behaviors that yield approving feedback from the adults the child must live with. Play also helps children learn about aggression, and how to control their own aggressive behaviors. It lets children explore their physical and social environments, and thus helps the children learn to perceive the world more accurately (Rubin, Fein, & Vandenberg, 1983). Little wonder, then, that Otto Weininger says, "Play isn't everything—it's the only thing!" (Weininger, 1979).

Play serves to stimulate the physical, emotional, social, and intellectual development of the child. And its hallmark is *pleasure*. Children who laugh while they are fighting seldom hurt one another. Adults who grin as they play computer games seldom smash their video monitors. Play is therefore a useful, necessary, vital part of life—but primarily because it *rewards* children (and adults) for learning the cognitive and behavioral skills they have to learn (Trotter, 1987).

Cognitive Development in the Later Years
Both Freud and Piaget assumed that cognitive development ended during adolescence or early adulthood. People still *learned* in later life, but they presumably had reached "the top rung of the developmental ladder" by the time they were 20 or so. Phrases such as "mid-life crisis" and "the Golden years" are of relatively recent vintage.

One reason this viewpoint prevailed in psychology for so long is this: We are now both healthier and wealthier than our ancestors typically were. In past years, adults worked most of their lives because they had to, and if adults "played," this activity was of little interest to developmental psychologists. Now, we live longer, we retire earlier, and we have both the money and the energy to continue our cognitive development in our later years. Furthermore, we now often incorporate the concept of "fun and games" in various forms of "adult education."

We don't really know as much as we should about cognitive development in the later years of life. But let's look at what we do know about people in the second half of their lives.

MATURITY AND OLD AGE
To coin a phrase, the scientific study of aging is still in its infancy. Psychologists have studied children for more than a century, but their interest in older people is fairly new. For that and other reasons, we know a great deal more about how infants grow and develop than we do about how people at the opposite end of the life span meet life's challenges.

There are, however, a number of cultural myths in Western society about what elderly people *should be like*. One such myth is that, like a machine that has worn down from constant use, the older person should become slow moving, mentally inflexible, socially rigid, and above all, asexual. Let us look at each of these points in turn.

Physical Changes in Maturity
There is no doubt that younger people typically expend more physical energy than do most people in their 40's and 50's. But according to John Rowe and Robert Kahn, this decrease in "body tempo" is due primarily to changes in diet, exercise, and psychosocial factors—not to "a wearing out of the machine." Older people who *maintain the healthy habits of youth* tend to *be* as physiologically fit as are younger individuals (Rowe & Kahn, 1987).

There *are* physical changes associated with aging, of course. Testosterone levels tend to drop in both males and females, and the hormonal alterations associated with **menopause** are well known (Soules & Bremner, 1982).

The fact that older individuals often are not as active as younger persons suggests some change occurs at the *nerve-muscular* synapses as a function of age. Recent research suggests this may be true. But these changes seem to be caused by experience, not by "decay." University of Wisconsin scientist Julie Rosenheimer reports that older organisms release the same quantity of neurotransmitters when stressed as do younger organisms. But because the synapses in older organisms are *more complex*, the amount of neurotransmitter released at any one synaptic junction is less (Rosenheimer, 1985). Put more simply, because older people

One of the purposes of play is to allow children to try out different social roles and ideas.

are capable of making many more *types* of responses than are younger people, the *strength* of each reaction in older people is less vigorous (Rowand, 1984).

Reaction Time

One fairly consistent finding is that older people tend to have slower reaction times than do younger people. Some psychologists assumed this decline in response times was due to a decrease in the speed at which older individuals could *process information*. However, recent research suggests the problem has to do with *skills practice*.

In a recent study, University of Maryland psychologist Jane Clark and her colleagues tested two similar groups of men and women aged 57 to 83. At the beginning of the study, both groups had similar reaction times on such measures as responding as quickly as possible when a light was turned on. Then Clark and her associates had members of one of the groups play video games (such as Pac Man or Donkey Kong) for two hours per week for seven weeks. When the two groups were then retested, the "players" now had significantly faster response

times. Clark concludes that the game training helped the older people learn how to *process information faster*. "The present research indicates that declines in response times in the elderly can be reversed" (cited in McCarthy, 1987).

Stress and Health

Some older individuals are obviously in poorer health than when they were young. But long-term studies of hundreds of subjects in California suggest that many of the physical problems of mature individuals can be seen as poor responses to *psychological stress*. Dorothy Eichorn and her colleagues report there is a significant relationship between mental health early in life and physical health during maturity. Those subjects who showed emotional stability and controlled responses to stress as adolescents had far better health at age 50 than did those subjects who had poor stress reactions when young (Eichorn *et al.*, 1981).

Yale University psychologist Judith Rodin believes that the relationship between health and a *sense of personal control* grow stronger in old age. According to Rodin, "Studies show that there are detrimental effects on the health of older people when their control of their activities is restricted." Individuals who "lose control" of their world experience increased stress, and their immune systems become less responsive. Unfortunately, she notes, most nursing home operators prefer to "take control" away from their clients. Rodin recommends that those older patients who wish to do so be encouraged to maintain as much control over their lives as possible (Rodin, 1986).

□ □ **QUESTION** □ □
A recent study suggests that many college students believe you should "talk baby talk" to elderly patients. Why might doing so actually *harm* the patients?

The Aging Brain

The human body tends to shrink slightly as it ages, and so apparently does the brain. In a recent report, M.J. de Leon and his colleagues at the NYU Medical Center report that the brain of a healthy 70-year-old is slightly smaller than that of a healthy 25-year-old. But it is not the *number of neurons*, but rather *the amount of fluid* in the brain that decreases. And **sugar metabolism**—which is a measure of *activity* in the brain—is the same in the 70-year-old as in the 25-year-old. Thus, there is no medical support for the belief that older individuals *must* become "infantile" or **senile** because their brains either "shrivel up" or "stop functioning properly" (de Leon *et al.*, 1987).

The belief that "you lose brain cells every day of your life" apparently got its start in 1958,

Older persons may be able to keep their reaction times fast by regular participation in activities where timing is crucial, such as playing chamber music.

when a noted scientist estimated that "humans lose 100,000 neurons a day after age 30." This belief is nonsense, according to Marian C. Diamond. She has studied the brains of both animals and humans for many years in her laboratory at the University of California, Berkeley. Diamond concludes that, "In the absence of disease, our studies provide no reason to believe that normal aging in humans produces brain-cell loss until, perhaps, extreme old age" (Diamond, 1978; Diamond *et al.*, 1979).

● *Senility and Alzheimer's Disease*

According to University of Minnesota scientists J.A. Mortimer and L.M. Schuman, only one elderly person in five will become senile. One common cause of senility, of course, is *Alzheimer's disease*, which affects about a third of the patients who become senile. Only a small fraction of the population will fall prey to Alzheimer's disease. But caring for these patients is exceptionally expensive. Mortimer and Schuman estimate that *at least half of all Medicare costs* are spent on treatment of patients with Alzheimer's disease (Mortimer & Schuman, 1981).

Medical researchers disagree both on what causes Alzheimer's disease and how best to treat it. At first it was thought to be the result of "hardening of the arteries," but that theory has now been discarded. More recently, scientists assumed Alzheimer's might be related to Down's syndrome and hence be caused by a chromosomal defect. However, the latest research doesn't support this viewpoint (St. George-Hyslop *et al.*, 1987).

Most medical treatment of Alzheimer's patients has proved to be of minor value. Marion Diamond believes the real problem is our conception of Alzheimer's disease as a *medical disorder*. Diamond's research suggests that giving both animals and people stimulating environments actually *prevents* the types of brain changes found in Alzheimer's patients. Rather than hoping pills and surgery will "cure" the problems associated with senility, Diamond says, we should find new ways to keep older individuals active and in control of their lives. "The worst thing we can do is to consign elderly people to sedentary confinement in an unstimulating nursing home." To do so, Diamond says, is to perpetuate the false belief that brain-cell loss and mental deterioration always accompany old age (Diamond, 1978).

● *Learning and Memory in Mature Individuals*

One persistent belief in our culture is that "you can't teach an old dog new tricks." Applied to humans, this folk saying implies one of two things: Either (1) older people suffer an age-related memory deficit, or (2) mature individuals find it more difficult to adjust to changed circumstances than do young people. Recent data suggest that neither of these alternatives is necessarily true.

Penn State psychologist K.W. Schaie has been studying a group of 2,000 adults in Seattle for more than 30 years. At the start of the study, the group ranged in age from 22 to 88. Shaie reports there is a relationship between cognitive abilities, life styles, and the "mental flexibility" of the older members of the group (Schaie, 1983). In a recent interview, he explained his findings this way: "What seems to be happening is that the rigid person establishes life-styles which, through disuse, lead to the early decline of fluid abilities such as spatial orientation and inductive reasoning." However, Schaie says, "Recent work shows that some of the cognitive losses can be reversed through behavioral intervention" (cited in Meer, 1985).

Given these data, we might wonder why there is the pervasive assumption in our culture that old people "lose their memories." One answer has to do with *biased data*. The other has to do with *social expectations*.

Wayne State psychologist Hilary Horn Ratner notes that several investigators have reported that older subjects seem to have poorer memories than do younger subjects. However, Ratner says, in almost every case a *random sample* of older individuals was compared to a *non-random sample* of college students. She and her colleagues therefore compared three groups: (1) college students; (2) young subjects *who weren't in college*; (3) older subjects who also weren't in college. The subjects in all three groups had similar verbal abilities at the start of the experiment. In the main part of the study, the subjects were required to learn four short prose passages and then were asked to repeat what they had learned. The Wayne State psychologists found that both the younger and older out-of-school groups had similar recall, while the college students were superior to both the other groups. The experimenters conclude that "Without the demands to memorize that education requires, the old and perhaps any out-of-school group may lose the ability to remember as effectively as possible" (Horn *et al.*, 1987).

Psychologists sometimes assume that older individuals cannot remember either the recent or the distant past with as much accuracy as can younger individuals. However, University of Michigan psychologist A. Regula Herzog reports this is not the case. In a series of studies, she and her associates found that subjects 70 and older were just as accurate in their recall as were subjects 60 and younger. And when differences in accuracy did exist, Herzog says, the older subjects tended to remember *better* than did younger ones (Herzog & Dielman, 1985; Rodgers & Herzog, 1987).

Perhaps the major "memory" problem that old people have, however, is the set of cultural *expectations* younger individuals have about memory loss in old age. As Samuel Johnson wrote more than 200 years ago, "If a young or middle-aged man, when leaving a company, does not recollect where he laid his hat, it is nothing. But if the same inattention is discovered in an old man, people will shrug their shoulders and say, 'His memory is going.'"

□ □ **QUESTION** □ □

People who drop out of school, but return at a later age, often report they have problems studying. Why might this sort of problem be expected no matter how intelligent the individual was?

● *Sexuality in Older Individuals*

There is not all that much agreement among the experts on how aging affects sexuality, much less *why* these changes occur. The generally-accepted view of "sexual arousability" is shown in Fig. 15.6. From this point of view, males tend to reach their peak about age 18, then show a sharp drop that continues the rest of their lives. "Arousability" in women, however, tends to peak about age 35 or so and stays relatively high thereafter.

The truth of the matter is that there simply aren't enough studies—made in enough situations—to tell us all we need to know about sexuality in the later years. It is true that hormone levels reach a peak in the male at about

Sexual arousal is determined by many factors, including mental attitudes and social expectations, for adults of all ages.

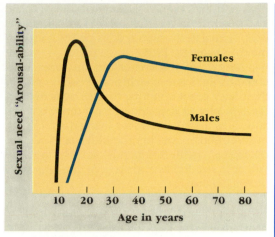

FIG. 15.6 Most psychologists believe that "sexual arousability" reaches a peak in males at about age 18 and thereafter declines, while "arousability" peaks in females at about age 35 and remains fairly constant thereafter.

age 18, and fall thereafter. But it is just as true that a healthy 90-year-old male typically has a high enough hormone level to perform the sex act several times a week (Soules & Bremner, 1982).

In a recent book, Edward M. Brecher reports the results of a survey (sponsored by Consumer's Union) on the sex habits of 4,246 Americans age 50 and older. Some of the findings are fairly surprising. For example, Brecher states that 40 percent of the women and 50 percent of the men over 60 masturbate. Some 65 percent of the women and 80 percent of the men 70 or older reported they were still sexually active, and about half of this group stated they had sex at least once a week (Brecher, 1983). We might note, however, that the subjects in this study may not be representative of the population as a whole, and that we have no way of determining the accuracy of their subjective reports.

Most research suggests that sexual "arousability" *at any age past puberty* is as greatly affected by intra-psychic and social factors as by hormone levels. Our society has certain "expectations" about sex among older individuals, and those expectations are primarily negative. Older individuals probably need more psychological (and perhaps physical) stimulation to maintain a high level of sexual performance. But then, this need for increased stimulation among older people may also be true of areas other than sex (Rowe & Kahn, 1987).

In a recent article, B.F. Skinner writes, "The aging of a person, as distinct from the aging of an organism, depends upon changes in the physical and social environment." Skinner urges older people to change their environments deliberately to suit their needs. He says older people should add more spices to their food and turn up the volume on the hi-fi. He also notes the successful use of pornography to keep sexual performance at its peak (at least in males) (Skinner, 1983).

Almost all researchers in this area have come to the same conclusion: People who, in their later years, continue to have an active sex life typically look younger, have more energy, and show a greater zest for living than do people who shun sexuality. The older person's *psychological age* thus depends more on the individual's *self-concept* than on the person's *biological age*.

According to Eisdorfer, more older persons would be self-sufficient, productive, and creative if society viewed these qualities as normal in the elderly.

□ □ QUESTION □ □
How does the expression "Use it or lose it" seem to apply to most areas of human aging?

A Model for Aging

In a recent article, Carl Eisdorfer proposes a "conceptual model for aging." He notes that, in all societies, older individuals tend to behave in ways that society believes are "acceptable." Thus, each culture has its own "model for aging."

Eisdorfer believes it is time our society rethought what its model should be. "The aged are now captives, the victims of a belief system that has most people over 65 identified with the small proportion of needy, dependent, and helpless individuals. Herb Shore once proposed that older people could be conceptualized in three different ways: The no-go group, the slow-go group, and of course, the go-go group. Are we so attached to the no-go and slow-go image that those who can and do go lose their options?" (Eisdorfer, 1983).

What Eisdorfer is saying, of course, is that our *theories of personality development* are still too narrow. We simply have not integrated all of our scientific knowledge about the entire span of life into one complete theory or model. "If we must have a model," Eisdorfer says, "should we not accept the broadest model? In this case, a biopsychosocial model appears to best recognize the complexity of the situation." Eisdorfer concludes, however, that we are not likely to build this new model until we recognize how much the best-known theories of personality limit our conception of what life-span development is all about (Eisdorfer, 1983).

Cognitive Development: A Summary

As we trace your cognitive development from birth to adulthood, several things become clear: First is the importance of your *genetic endowment*. You needed innate reflexes to survive your first days of independent life. Most of your subsequent mental and behavioral development stemmed from—and was based on—these inborn reflexes. However, your genes also gave you both the *motivation* and the *capability* to mature intellectually.

The second conclusion we can draw has to do with the importance of the environment you grew up in. Intellectual development results from the continual interplay between innate potential and environmental stimulation. No matter how superb your genetic endowment, if you spent your childhood in deprived circumstances, you would wind up functioning at an impoverished level. Thus, while there are genetic limits to how far even the best of environments can take you, there are also environmental limits to how much of your genetic potential can be expressed.

The third conclusion has to do with the complex interplay between behaviors and cognitions. As Piaget pointed out, thoughts develop out of motor reflexes. You learn not merely by thinking and reasoning, but by doing—by testing your cognitive expectations against real-world feedback. But you can also test reality by using language. Language gives you the ability to represent actions and objects symbolically, by thinking instead of doing. Which is to say, language lets you *behave without moving a muscle*. You can then anticipate the consequences of your actions before you act.

Finally, the data on cognitive development surely show the importance of your own personality—and your personal values—in determining what and who you become. During infancy and early childhood, your cognitive development was determined primarily by the interaction between your genes and your environment. Then, as you matured, you gained the ability to alter both your environment and the way that you expressed your genetic potential. However, what you make of yourself—and what changes you attempt to make in the world around you—are strongly influenced by your own personality.

It is thus to the study of personality that we now must turn our attention.

SUMMARY

1. The four major theoretical issues influencing the study of cognitive development are **the mind-body problem, the nature-nurture controversy, developmental continuity versus discontinuity**, and **individual differences versus human similarities**.

2. Many **stage theorists** believe children would develop to a cognitive peak if merely left alone. **Behavioral psychologists** hold that cognitive development is primarily **shaped** by environmental inputs.

3. **Cognitive development** refers to development in children of such **mental activities** as perception, memory, imagery, language, concept formation, problem solving, reasoning, and decision making.

4. Studies suggest a child may learn **10 new words a day** and by age six may have acquired a vocabulary of **14,000 words**.

5. **Language acquisition** refers to learning both **words** and the **rules** for using language correctly. Included in language acquisition are learning of **phonemes, semantics, syntax**, and **pragmatics**.

6. Children **worldwide** between three and seven months of age **babble** by uttering repetitive **phonemes** such "da da da" but do not reproduce all the sounds in most languages. Parents **selectively reinforce** some babbled sounds, and urge infants to imitate those phonemes not produced during babbling.

7. At about one year of age, children produce **holophrastic**, or one-word, sentences, and produce two-word sentences about the 18th month. Many of these sentences are **telegraphic speech** that contains just the important words. Most children produce **complex sentences** by age two.

8. Some **linguists** believe humans have an innate tendency to process information in linguistic form, which they call the **deep structure of language**. Behaviorists, however, believe language production is entirely **learned**.

9. While acquiring language, the child also learns the **social rules** for proper use of speech. The child's mother may make **social contracts** while teaching her infant to speak.

10. Fathers appear to be more involved in **physical stimulation** of the child than in teaching it to talk. However, children whose fathers are **supportive** of the mother and interested in the children tend to develop more rapidly than children whose fathers are uninvolved.

11. Chimpanzees have been taught to "speak" 100 or more words and phrases, but whether their language has **grammar** and whether they can communicate in **symbols** is still a matter of debate.

12. Children are better at developing **basic level category** concepts than at developing either **superordinate** or **subordinate category** concepts.

13. Children tend to develop **scripts** describing how repetitive events typically occur, and remember the scripts better than specific experiences. They also must learn to **encode** cognitive variables before they can respond to them.

14. **Jean Piaget** was one of the most respected figures in child psychology. For more than 50 years, he studied the child's **search for knowledge**, by which he meant the child's attempt to construct an **abstract mental representation** of the world.

15. According to Piaget, a child's motivation to develop comes from an innate drive to maintain **equilibrium**, a sort of **cognitive homeostasis**. When children's abstractions of the world don't match reality, they experience **dis-equilibrium**, which motivates them to change their inner representations of the world to bring them into accord with reality.

16. Each "mental program" that a child has for processing sensory inputs is a **schema**. Mental development proceeds as a child develops more and more complex **schemata**.

17. The two **mental functions** that guide development are **organization** and **adaptation**.

18. Organization is the tendency to create complicated mental structures out of simple ones. Adaptation is made up of two opposing processes, **assimilation** and **accommodation**.

19. Assimilation involves **changing inputs** to fit the child's present mental structures. Accommodation involves **changing mental structures** (or making new ones) to make them match present inputs.

20. According to Piaget, all children pass through four **developmental stages**, each of which grows out of (but is more complex than) the one preceding it.

21. During the **sensory-motor period** (birth to 2 years), the infant learns to integrate various sense impressions into complex **schemata**.

22. During the **pre-operational stage**, the child learns to speak and to deal with the world in **symbolic terms**, by talking about objects rather than by having to manipulate them directly. But the child's reasoning may be **egocentric**, and the child does not realize that objects can be **transformed** without being changed.

23. During the **stage of concrete operations**, children learn to visualize a whole series of operations in their minds and to differentiate themselves from the outer world. They also discover that the process of transformation is **reversible**.

24. During the **stage of abstract operations**, the young person gains the ability to think in purely **abstract terms**.

25. Piaget believes that children pass through these stages at their own individual speeds, but that the stages cannot be **reversed**.

26. Minor criticisms of Piaget include such problems as whether his theory applies to **children in all cultures**, whether children are really **egocentric**, whether **developmental stages** actually exist, and whether **stage reversals** occur.

27. The major criticism of Piaget is that he performed **demonstrations** rather than tightly controlled **experiments**.

28. Kohlberg believes there are three levels of **moral development**, the **preconventional**, the **conventional**, and the **postconven-**tional. However, his theory may not apply to people in different cultures, and may be biased toward **traditional male values**.

29. Piaget said that play was **a child's work**, but Herbert Spencer believed that play was necessary for the release of **surplus energy** within the child. G.S. Hall believed that in play a child **recapitulated** the history of the human race.

30. Play serves to stimulate the **physical, emotional, social**, and **intellectual development** of the child. Its hallmark is **pleasure**.

31. Early in life, **cognitive development** is determined primarily by the interaction of biological and social variables. Adults, however, gain the ability to **shape** both their own cognitions and the world around them.

32. The **physical changes** that occur during the later years can be described by the phrase "use it or lose it." The **psychological changes** suggest that older people do not lose memory, sexuality, or mental health if they remain in **control of their lives.**

Horace Smythe speared a piece of meat with his fork, then held it up in front of his face. *(Continued from page 370.)* "Marvelous invention, the fork," he said. "Much more efficient than those peculiar chopsticks used by the Mongols, you know. Just goes to prove how superior the white race is, now doesn't it, my pet?"

"According to *Godey's Lady's Book*," Cynthia Smythe responded, "the fork was invented in the Middle East by one of those oriental races you and Dr. Down feel so superior to."

"What!" said the man with considerable surprise.

The woman nodded. "The fork wasn't used in Europe until the Renaissance, and it didn't reach England until the 17th century. We've only had it in America since 1800 or so. But they've used it in the Middle East for hundreds of years."

"Humph," Horace Smythe replied. "I suppose you think that's evidence that Dr. Down's racial classification of the feeble-minded is incorrect."

"Well, that's one thing, of course."

Horace Smythe took some potatoes from the platter that the servant, Melissa, offered him. "And what else? What else?"

"As I understand it, Horace, Dr. Down believes that the human fetus must pass through several stages as it develops in the womb."

"Correct," the man replied in a pedagogical tone of voice. "The lowest is the Negroid, or black-skinned stage. Still primitives, most of the blacks." He glanced nervously at the servant woman. "Melissa excepted, of course. And then comes the brown-skinned, or Malay level, such as the Indians."

"And then the fetus takes on Mongol or oriental features, correct?"

The man nodded eagerly. "Correct. The heathen Chinee, and all those other funny-looking people from the Middle and Far East."

"From which we get forks, Christianity, and a few other things we superior whites find so useful, eh, Horace?"

Mr. Smythe choked momentarily on a piece of food. "The oriental mind is devious, my pet, very devious. Imitative, true. But not really inventive. Mostly they just copy from us."

Cynthia Smythe smiled. "Like that exquisite Ming vase you bought from the Chinese laundryman, Horace? Nothing like it in the Western world, you said. Whom did the Chinese copy that from, then?"

"A trivial point, my dear."

"And you still think that Tommy is a 'throwback' to the Mongolian stage of development?"

Horace Smythe nodded vigorously. "Makes complete sense to me. As a fetus, he stopped short of his final development into a Caucasian like us. He has the typical yellowish skin—you said so yourself. And he has Mongol eyes and dark hair, while his parents are blondes. So that proves that Dr. Down is correct in calling Tommy a Mongoloid, or Mongolian idiot."

"Balderdash," his wife said.

"Now, Cynthia, my pet. You shouldn't use such language. You are a mere woman, and thus you can't deal with facts as logically and as scientifically as Dr. Down and I can."

"Balderdash," his wife said again. "I can think of three very important facts that completely disprove your case."

"And what, pray tell, might those three facts be?" the man said in a very annoyed tone of voice.

"First, Tommy *does* look different from his parents, but he certainly *doesn't* resemble the Chinese laundryman."

Mr. Smythe snorted. "The exception that proves the rule."

"Second, why did the laundryman sell that exquisite vase to you?"

The man thought a moment. "He needed the money, of course."

"For what, Horace?"

Mr. Smythe squirmed in his chair. "Well, he had this feeble-minded child who needed medical attention . . ."

"A child who happens to look much like Tommy," the woman replied in a factual tone of voice. "What would Dr. Down call that child, Horace? A Mongol Mongolian idiot?"

"You're being entirely unreasonable, Cynthia."

The woman smiled. "And last, but surely not least, there's Melissa. Why did she come to work for us, Horace?"

"Money, of course. She is of an inferior race, and must work to support herself as best she can."

"And to support her niece, who is a feeble-minded young girl with many of the physical characteristics that Tommy and the laundryman's child have."

"So?" the man said coldly.

"So, how would you classify Melissa's niece? She can't be a 'throwback,' since you say that her race hasn't yet developed to the 'Mongol' level. What is she, then? A 'throw-forward' of some kind? And if she is, shouldn't she be brighter than Melissa?"

Horace Smythe sat quietly for a moment, poking at the food on his plate. "A 'throw-forward,' eh? Never thought of it that way."

Cynthia Smythe ate in silence while her husband pondered the matter.

After a while, the man sighed. "You know, my pet, I do believe that Dr. Down's ethnic scheme for classifying the feeble-minded isn't yet as perfect as it first seemed. Of course, he has described Mongolian idiocy rather well, and given it a scientific label . . ."

"Horace, those children need loving care a great deal more than they need a fancy label."

"Well, my dear, you women always do look at the practical side of things. Which leaves it up to us men to look at the world from a more abstract, intellectual viewpoint, and to puzzle out the logic of the universe."

Cynthia Smythe nodded in amusement.

"And having given the matter my due consideration, I now perceive that the good doctor's logic *is* somewhat shoddy. 'Throwbacks,' indeed! Balderdash, that's what it is."

"If you say so, dear."

The man carefully dissected the meat on his plate. "Shocking that a man in his position would fail to see the facts, now isn't it?"

"I suspect you're right, dear."

Horace Smythe impaled a piece of meat with his fork, then put it in his mouth. He chewed the meat slowly, deliberately, then finally swallowed it. "You know, my pet, I wonder if I shouldn't write Dr. Down and share my insights with him . . ."

Personality Theory: Psychoanalysis, Humanism, and Social Learning Theory

"The Span of Life"

· C·H·A·P·T·E·R ·

16

I think I have fallen in love with Susie. She's sitting in her glass cage, about 80 feet away. I lost my glasses on the trip, so I can barely see her, but I think she's combing her hair. Not that she needs to. She's a knockout even when her hair is mussed up. And to tell the truth, since she's newborn-naked, I don't notice her hair all that much.

Not that there's much else but Susie to look at. My own little cage is just like Susie's. It has your regulation wire mesh on the floor, with a removable pan underneath to catch the "droppings." There's a bunch of soft material in one corner that I use as a bed, a water spout that runs continuously, and a large drawer that slides in and out of the glass walls. That's where they put the food, if you want to dignify the crap the alligators give us as being "food." Up in the ceiling, about 8 feet above my head, there's a vent system of some kind. And that's it.

As far as I can tell, there's just no way out of this mess. So, just call me Caged-up Charlie.

What with the noise the vent fan makes and the glass walls on the cage, I can look at Susie, but she can't hear me even when I shout at her. We do make signs at each other, and try to spell out words, but I can't see her clearly enough to make out what she's trying to communicate. That's too bad, because we sure do have a lot to talk about.

Susie's cage is on a wooden shelf about 20 feet above the floor on the wall opposite the one my cage is on. The room we're in is about 80 feet square. It doesn't have a window, but there's a skylight overhead, so we can tell when it's day and night. There isn't much furniture in the room, but there's a large swimming pool in one corner. The toilet is in the other corner. That's the alligator toilet I'm talking about. Susie and I have to relieve ourselves in, shall we say, a somewhat more primitive fashion.

You know, it sure is a long distance from Florida to a couple of glass cages on the walls of this alligator outhouse. And don't ask me how we got here. All I know is this: My buddies and I had cruised down to Lauderdale on spring break, which is always the most enjoyable part of the semester as far as I'm concerned. The first night we were there, we were so tired we crashed pretty early. We sat around on the beach the next day, working on our tans and scoping the local fauna. That night we had a couple of beers at the motel and then went back to the beach looking for a little action. That's when I bumped into Susie.

Susie and I got along great, right from the start, and pretty soon we wanted some privacy. So we borrowed this big air mattress and floated out into the ocean. Things were just starting to get serious when the ocean exploded into a skillion stars and then dissolved into darkness. When we woke up, Susie and I were in these glass cages in a pet shop in Samarkand.

At least, that's what I call this place, Stinking Samarkand. In high school, I read this story about some ancient warrior king named Tamerlane, who lived out there in Asia in a city called Samarkand. And, hey, I figured any city that had a million people and no flush toilets must have had a pretty ripe odor. So, I called it Stinking Samarkand. But let me tell you, it couldn't have stunk any worse than that alligator pet shop did!

And there was this huge alligator about 40 feet tall who seemed to own the pet shop. At least, he looked like an alligator, except he had a pretty short tail and walked on his hind legs. All day long, the store was packed with customers—big parent alligators buying pets for the little children gators they had in tow. The kids would squeal and snort and point and poke, and finally they'd pick some animal or another. The pet shop owner would grunt and nod his head, pick up the animal's cage, and pop it into a carrying box. And off the happy alligator family would go, the parents smiling and the kids squealing.

I had to laugh when I figured out it was a *pet shop* run by *alligators* that we were in. I mean, you know that old story about how the sewers of New York City are filled with baby alligators that people flushed down the toilet when the gators got too big. Well, given all the exotic beasts I saw at that pet shop, I wonder what the sewers of Samarkand are full of!

Anyhow, after Susie and I had been in the pet shop for a couple of days, our present owners came along, the kid selected us, and into a carrying box we went. The good news is, obviously, that the parents bought both Susie and me, so we're still together. Sort of. The bad news is that I can't for the life of me figure out how we got here, much less think up a way to get us out of this mess. Oh, well, I suspect a lot of goldfish back on earth spent most of their lives wondering how they wound up in a glass bowl in somebody's living room.

2

Sitting in a glass cage all day with nothing to do has got me bored out of my gourd. I spent a couple of hours watching Susie, but she's asleep now, so it's dullsville around here at the moment.

So, I've been *thinking*. No joke. I mean, asking myself *serious,* philosophical-type questions. You see, this semester back at school, I was taking two weirdo type courses—one in sociobiology and one in Freudian personality theory. Talk about two profs who are at opposite ends of the pole, that's my soc-bio teacher and my psych teacher! They both started out the semester asking the same question: Why are guys like me attracted to gals like Susie? I would have thought the answer to that was pretty obvious, but it turns out the two profs came up with two really oddball answers.

As best I can figure out, it all boils down to how you answer the old question of "Which came first, the chicken or the egg?" Freud sided with the chickens, or at least with the chicken *mentality*. According to old Siggie, the first chicken was just responding to its unconscious urges when it decided that an egg would be a dandy way to produce another chicken-type personality like its own. But according to the sociobiologists, it's the other way around. They think the chicken is just the egg's way of making another egg.

In case you hadn't heard, sociobiology is this theory dreamed up by Harvard prof Edwin O. Wilson who is an absolute, positive nut about Darwin's theory of "survival of the fittest." But it's the fittest *genes* that survive, not the fittest *individuals*. And genes prove they are the fittest by making as many copies of themselves as they can. I don't count in all this, according to Eddie-O. My genes control my brain, and my brain controls *me*. So my attraction for Susie is just my genes' way of trying to create another set of genes. Weird, huh? I mean, sociobiology doesn't leave much room in the picture for me or Susie as *individuals*, now does it?

Of course, if you believe in sociobiology, it does explain a lot of things about why people act like they do. For example, guys don't get pregnant, and they don't have to take care of the kids. So males get this genetic itch that makes them want to impregnate as many females as they can. Quantity over quality, so to speak. *That* I can appreciate, at least in a male chauvinist sort of way. But females have just one kid at a time, so a female's genes urge her to charm some guy into paying the rent for her and her kids. And you know how she does *that*, now don't you?

Men invented spring breaks; women invented marriage.

Naturally, my psych prof thinks that sociobiology is for the birds, chickens included. Like, for instance, I've been dreaming about Susie a lot since we got to Samarkand, and maybe it's best I don't exactly describe those dreams in any detail. Anyhow, according to sociobiology, I dream about making love to her because my genes want to keep me thinking about things like that even when I'm asleep. But according to Freud, that's putting the cart before the horsing around.

You see, according to my psych prof, I was born with an *id*, which is Sigmund's way of talking about the instinctual urges and libidinal energies which are seething around in the great cesspool at the bottom of my mind. Siggie says the reason I get romantic is because I've got to release the pressure or I'll explode. But naturally I can't just go around attacking every young lady I meet without first saying hello, how are you. So my *Eros*, which is to say my Life Force, created my "ego," which is a neat kind of protection device. My ego's job is to keep my id caged up, like I am caged up here on Samarkand. My ego is also supposed to learn socially-approved ways to con young ladies into saying yes, so my id can have its jollies without getting me killed in the process.

Which came first, the chicken or the egg? Well, eggs don't have sex with each other, but hens and roosters sure do. So maybe my Life Force does control my genes, not the other way around. Anyhow, when somebody in class complained this was pretty silly, my psych teacher pointed out that life appeared on earth before genes did. So Eros was around long before eggs and DNA were, and when genes did occur by random mutation, the Life Force *selected* genes as a nifty way of creating another id. The chicken wins again, or "Take *that*, Dr. Wilson!"

Either way, of course, I end up wanting to make love to Susie. So does it really matter which explanation is best? Only at exam time, as far as I can tell!

3

Susie woke up a while ago, and started doing Jane Fonda type exercises. At first I got really turned on. And then a thought from my psych text popped into my mind, and I sort of went into a tailspin. You see, according to Siggie, it isn't really Susie I've got the hots for, it's my *mother*! But to appreciate the "logic" of *that*, you've got to buy into old Sigmund's theory about how my ego got itself created while I was breast feeding and getting potty trained.

It all started at my mother's breasts, Freud said. My id got a big kick out of nursing because it released libidinal energy. I mean, just look at that grin babies get on their faces when they've had a big meal! Anyhow, nursing was so enjoyable that I ended up associating all forms of tension reduction (including sexual orgasm) with my mother. And whenever I get aroused while watching Susie, I'm just trying to bring back the sexy feelings I had as an infant. Talk about weird!

Then my mother tried to teach me that I couldn't relieve myself whenever the urge occurred—I had to "go" on the potty and not in my pants. She rewarded me when I obeyed, which made me love her then and now. And she punished me when I couldn't control my idish urges, which made me feel guilty about *both* sex and relieving myself, particularly in public.

You know, like, all this thinking about sex instead of doing it is giving me a headache—among other things. And I still haven't figured out who's right, Wilson or Freud. Eddie-O says psychoanalysis is a joke, and I'll go along with sociobiology as far as explaining why I want to make love to Susie is concerned. But there is an oddball kind of logic to Freud's explanation of shame and guilt. I mean, where's the survival value associated with wanting to relieve yourself in private? Maybe the joke's on Wilson after all.

4

No, the joke's on me and Susie. I kept wondering why the alligators kept us in the john. Well, it turns out we're toys Mrs. Gator is using to get Junior to sit on the potty! She dragged the kid into the bathroom a little while ago, pulled his diaper off, and positioned him on a pot. Then she took down Susie's cage and mine and put them on a stool right in front of the kid. She pointed at us and gargled and snarled a bit, and Junior whined and snorted and shook our cages and looked pleased as hell. And after a while there was this tremendous stink, and Mrs. Gator giggled and gargled and patted Junior on the head, cleaned him up, and put on a fresh diaper. Then she emptied the pot in the toilet, flushed it, and put Susie and me back on our separate shelves.

Of course, while our cages were close together, Susie and I were desperately trying to communicate with each other. But Junior kept shaking our cages and knocking us about. You have no idea how frustrating it was to be so close to her, and yet so far! I mean, we need to talk about so many things—how we feel about each other, how we're going to get out of this mess, and a hundred skillion other things. There must be some way to break out of this cage and get to her! There's just got to be!

(Continued on page 431)

PERSONALITY THEORY

In Chapters 14 and 15, we described how *physical, emotional, social,* and *cognitive* development occurs across the span of life. However, *you* are more than the sum of your parts. That's one of the reasons that describing your own growth as a *person* is a far more difficult task than is merely detailing how your "mind" or "body" develops.

Psychologists often use the term *personality theory* to describe their attempts to discover how you "become a whole or fully-functioning person."

What Is Personality?

As you might surmise, there is no single definition of the term **personality** that will do justice to all of the theories and research found within this important psychological speciality. However, in a recent paper, Nancy Cantor and John Kihlstrom state that "The field of personality may be defined as that subdiscipline of psychology which is concerned with the distinctive patterns of thought, behavior, and experience which characterize the individual's unique adjustment to his or her life situation" (Cantor & Kihlstrom, 1981). According to Cantor and Kihlstrom, your own pattern of personality shows up in the way that you attempt to understand, respond to, and change the physical and social world in which you live.

Different theorists have, of course, emphasized different aspects of personality. However, there are two dominant approaches to the study of personality. The first tends to study people as *intact, functioning individuals.* The second tends to describe people as *collections of traits, temperaments, talents, and tendencies.* To start the chapter off in the proper direction, let's discuss these two dissimilar ways of defining—and studying—personality.

"Person-Oriented" Versus "Trait-Oriented" Personality Theories

Let's begin by assuming that you are a happy, successful individual. And let's see how the two types of theorists might try to study you.

● *The "Person-oriented" Approach*
A *person-oriented* personality theorist might ask the following questions about you:

1. How did you develop into the well-adjusted individual you are?
2. What early experiences influenced your present level of functioning?
3. Is your happiness "real," or is it your way of hiding or compensating for some "underlying" psychological problem?
4. If you have problems as well as strengths, are you conscious of them, or not?
5. How close are you to being precisely what you want to be?

Notice that the person-oriented approach tends to define you in terms of your own feelings, goals, and values. It is *developmental* in outlook, in that it presumes your present level of functioning is determined in part by your past experiences. It is *dynamic,* in that it places more emphasis on "internal processes" (which can change) than it does on *personality structures* (which often are viewed as being unchangeable). Most of all, the person-oriented approach tends to perceive you as YOU—that is, as a unique, intact, decision-making individual.

● *The "Trait-oriented" Approach*
Trait-oriented theorists take quite a different approach. For example, a *trait-oriented* personality theorist might ask the following sorts of questions:

1. What basic "type" of person are you?
2. How *high* are your scores on a "happiness scale"?
3. What other traits correlate with high scores on the "happiness scale"?
4. What basic psychological factors tend to make up the trait of "success"?

Notice that the trait-oriented approach tends to view you as "pattern of parts." That is, in order to describe "the real you," a trait theorist might give you a personality test of some kind. The theorist would then define you in terms of your *unique profile of scores* on the various scales that made up the test. On the basis of those scores, the theorist might predict how you probably would perform in various situations, but most likely wouldn't ask you questions about your prior life experiences.

● **Case Histories Versus Experimental Data**

Most of the better-known person-oriented theorists were *medical doctors* or *psychotherapists* who built their theories from case histories (and personal insights) rather than from data gathered from experimental studies. Sigmund Freud, Anna Freud, Carl Jung, Alfred Adler, Erik Erikson, Carl Rogers, and (to some extent) Abraham Maslow fit this description fairly well.

Most of the better-known trait-oriented theorists were trained as *experimental psychologists*. For that reason, perhaps, the trait theorists tend to perform scientific studies rather than work one-on-one with therapy patients. Gordon Allport, Raymond Cattell, and Hans Eysenck are examples of trait-oriented theorists.

Somewhere in between these two extremes are the *behavioral* and *social learning theorists* (such as B.F. Skinner and Albert Bandura). As you will see, the behaviorists and social learning theorists tend to focus on individuals and are developmental in approach. And many of them do perform therapy. But psychologists who take the behavioral or social learning approach also conduct a wide range of scientific studies.

In this chapter, we will briefly discuss the person-oriented theories, including the behavioral approaches. We will save our discussion of the trait-oriented theorists for Chapter 17.

SIGMUND FREUD

Freud was born in 1856 in what is now Czechoslovakia, but he lived most of his life in Vienna. After taking his degree in medicine in 1881, Freud spent many years in the laboratory studying the human nervous system. Thus, Freud was *first and foremost* a biologist who came to the study of psychology in the middle of his life. Early in his career, Freud tried to tie all of his theoretical concepts (such as "ego") to neural activity or to brain structures (as they were known a century ago). Later, however, he decided that psychology and biology were *equally important*, and thus adopted a more holistic approach to explaining the human personality (Parisi, 1987).

Freud was almost 40 when he married. Soon afterward, he left the laboratory and went into private practice. Much of his theory of psychoanalysis grew out of the observations he made on these patients. Since he saw patients almost until his death in 1939, he continued to rework his psychoanalytic theory throughout his lifetime. Part of the difficulty in giving a brief summary of Freud's views, therefore, is that he was constantly changing them. Indeed, there is not *one* Freudian theory, but at least *three* that he put together at different stages of his own life (Monte, 1987). More than this, however, it took Freud several million words to describe his ever-changing thoughts. And his followers have needed at least 100 million words to explain what *they* think Freud meant. In four or five pages in this text, therefore, we can hardly do more than hint at the richness of Freud's views.

There is another point we must make. In Chapter 15, we quoted Jerome Bruner as saying that there are two *equally important* modes of thought—"narrative explanations" and "scientific reasoning." Like most person-oriented theorists, Freud relied more on narrative descriptions than on mathematical equations. Much of the power of his theorizing comes from the fact that he was a superb narrator of what he saw as the "human condition." Summarizing Freud in a few paragraphs is thus as impossible a task as would be summarizing all of Hemingway's novels in the same brief space.

Freud: The Early Years

According to Wesleyan psychologist Robert Steele, certain "critical experiences" in Freud's childhood may well have provided him with some of the basic ideas he later developed into the theory of psychoanalysis. For example, Freud believed that all boys go through a period in which they first reject their fathers but then elevate them to the "majestic position of the all-powerful." Steele believes that this part of psychoanalytic theory may have come from a time when, on the streets of Vienna, Freud watched in terror as another man humiliated Freud's father because he was a Jew. Freud apparently became furious at his father's "powerlessness," and felt "an urge to kill the man." Later, Steele says, Freud "universalized his guilt" by assuming that all boys felt the same way (Steele, 1982).

Freud Visits Charcot

Around 1885, Freud spent several months in Paris, studying hypnosis with Charcot. Freud's interest in personality theory seems to have begun about this time. Many of the patients Charcot treated with hypnosis suffered from **hysterical paralyses**. That is, the patients reported that some part of their anatomy—often the hand—had become completely paralyzed, just as if the part of the brain controlling the hand had been damaged. The patient's *wrist*, however, usually was not affected by the paralysis. The onset of the problem often was associated with some traumatic event—for instance, having to touch some "dreaded object," such as a spouse's genitalia.

Sigmund Freud

Personality. From the Greek word *persona*, which means "mask." Those distinctive ways of thinking, feeling, and behaving that set you off from all other people. Your own unique way of adjusting to whatever situations you find yourself in.

Hysterical paralyses (his-TARE-ih-cal pair-AL-ih-sees). The term *hysteria* comes from a Greek word meaning "wandering womb." During the 1800's, many women were diagnosed as being "hysterical" if they displayed behaviors judged as being "immature," or "self-centered," or if they were given to "frequent emotional outbursts." These behavior patterns presumably were caused by some *physical* dysfunction of the female reproductive system. If the women also suffered from a "paralysis" of some type, this was referred to as being a "hysterical paralysis."

Catharsis (kah-THAR-sis). From the Greek word meaning "to purge, or to clean out." If you are constipated and take a laxative to "clean out" your digestive system, you have undergone a physical catharsis. Freud and Breuer (BROY-er) believed that psychotherapy could act as a psychological cathartic to cleanse the mind of bottled-up psychic energy (or "strangled emotions") by reliving the traumatic events.

Free association. Freud's psychoanalytic method of encouraging people to express their thoughts, feelings, and memories without fear of criticism, to "say whatever comes into mind," and to report whatever emotions they may associate with certain life experiences.

Topographical (top-oh-GRAFF-ih-kal). Topography is the study of regions or spaces. A topographical theory is one that attempts to trace the history of a given region or space, or to describe how a given space (or set of spaces) came about.

Both Freud and Charcot were aware that there was no way a drug—or damage to the nervous system—could affect the hand and not the wrist. Charcot maintained that the symptoms of paralysis were caused by "dynamic lesions of the functional kind" somewhere in the brain. Which is to say that Charcot tried to *reduce* the psychological symptom to some "unknown" neural damage. Freud took a different (and more holistic) point of view: He assumed that the patient was *defending* against conscious awareness of the emotions that the patient had experienced at the time of the trauma. The patient's mind then "converted" these *strangled emotions* into the physical symptom of paralysis. The *mind* has the concept of "hand," even if the brain does not, Freud said. Since the basic problem was obviously *mental*, not *physical*, then *therapy* to cure the problem should be psychological, not medical (Freud, 1893/1963).

According to St. Mary's College psychologist Thomas Parisi, Freud's conflict with Charcot led Freud to "give up hope of explaining psychological phenomena by reducing them to biological ones" (Parisi, 1987). Rather than hunting for pills to cure his mental patients, therefore, Freud turned first to hypnosis. And when that failed, he developed the technique of "free association."

Freud and Breuer

Freud returned from Paris believing that hypnosis might be useful in curing some types of mental disorders. This view was strengthened by the success another Viennese psychiatrist, Josef Breuer, had achieved using hypnosis with a hysterical patient. Under hypnosis, Breuer had gotten this patient to relive some early unhappy experiences. After the patient had "acted out" these childhood miseries, the hysterical symptoms often seemed to disappear. As Christopher Monte puts it, Breuer "became firmly convinced that neurotic symptoms had an . . . understandable cause to be found in the patient's life history, and that the *form* of the symptom was rooted in a deeply *personal meaning* attached by the patient to the past event" (Monte, 1987).

Together with Breuer, Freud developed a technique called **catharsis**, which involved the re-enactment of emotional situations while under hypnosis. Freud thought *catharsis* was useful for the release of what he called "strangled emotions." But, as we noted in Chapter 13, he soon rejected *hypnosis* because its occasional success didn't seem to be related to the *trance,* but rather to the personal relationship of the hypnotist to the patient (Monte, 1987). Instead, Freud turned to **free association**. That is, he encouraged his patients to talk about all aspects of their past and present lives.

Listening to what his patients said about their lives taught Freud many lessons. To begin with, most of the people he treated seemed to be *repressing* unacceptable wishes, ideas, or impulses. Often the patients would "convert" these repressed feelings into physical symptoms of some kind. Freud decided that these symptoms allowed the patients both to reject the unacceptable urge (by blocking it from consciousness) and simultaneously satisfy the urge (by allowing it to appear in symbolic form) (Freud, 1887–1902/1954).

FREUD'S "TOPOGRAPHICAL" THEORY OF THE MIND

As we noted earlier, Freud revised his theoretical outlook several times. The first revision came when he abandoned his original view that all of psychology could be *reduced* to biological functions. The second revision came around 1900, when he proposed what is often called his **topographical** (or spatial) theory of the mind. In this theory, he divided the mind into three regions: The *unconscious*, the *preconscious*, and the *conscious* (Freud, 1900).

Because Freud was led to his topographical theory by his investigations into the *unconscious*—and because he always saw it as being the primary determiner of the human personality—we will describe the unconscious mind first.

The Unconscious

As he listened to his first patients talk about their problems, Sigmund Freud became convinced they were *repressing* terrible wishes and disturbing memories that were unacceptable to them. These "forbidden thoughts and feelings" occasionally broke through to consciousness—in dreams, and slips of the tongue—but usually in disguised or symbolic form. The questions then became: Where did these terrible urges come from, why were they so terrifying, where were they hiding, and what prevented them from entering awareness?

Where did the unacceptable wishes and memories come from? After a careful study of his patients' dreams, Freud concluded that "What is unconscious in mental life is also what is infantile" (Freud, 1916/1963). Freud noted that adults can seldom remember things that happened to them prior to the fifth or sixth year of life. But these early experiences were not *forgotten*, Freud decided. Rather, they had become part of the *unconscious mind*. When the patients were awake, some part of the mind *blocked* these memories off (or "censored" them). But when the patients were asleep, this "censor" (as Freud called it) relaxed, and the disturbing material slipped through to consciousness. But the material almost always appeared in altered or disguised form (Freud, 1900).

As for why the repressed material was so disturbing, Freud put it this way:

> The desire of pleasure—the **libido**, as we put it—chooses its objects without inhibition, and by preference, indeed, the forbidden ones: not only other men's wives, but above all incestuous objects . . . a man's mother and sister, a woman's father and brother . . . Hatred, too, rages without restraint. Wishes for revenge and death . . . are nothing unusual. These censored wishes appear to rise up out of a positive Hell; after they have been interpreted when we are awake, no censorship of them seems to us too severe. (Freud, 1916/1963)

Did the antisocial nature of these repressed desires prove that humans are innately evil? Of course not, Freud said. The libido "is what it is." These lustful and aggressive desires first occurred during infancy, long before the patient had been socialized. The problem is, Freud said, adults *interpret* these infantile urges as being "evil," which is why some part of their minds "censors" the material to keep it from reaching the conscious mind (Freud, 1916/1963).

The Conscious Mind

As we noted in Chapter 3, *consciousness* is a primitive term that cannot be defined precisely. Whatever you are aware of at any given instant is what you are "conscious of" at that instant. In biological terms, conscious awareness seems to be a primary property of your left (dominant) hemisphere.

Long before Freud divided the psyche into three levels, German psychologists had likened consciousness to a cluttered stage in a darkened theater. A narrowly-focused spotlight sweeps across the stage, illuminating now this, now that. As you sit in the theater, you see a continual flow of images flash into focus, then disappear into darkness. The narrow beam of the spotlight is your momentary consciousness. The rest of the stage is *potentially* visible to you—if and when the spotlight shines on it. But *at the moment* all you can perceive is what's within the tiny circle of light.

The Preconscious Mind

Following other German philosophers, Freud believed that your *preconscious mind* included any sensory input or mental process that *you could become aware of*—if and when the spotlight of awareness shone on it (Freud, 1912/1958).

● The Two Agencies of the Mind

Freud decided there were two *agencies* or systems that determined mental life:

1. The *unconscious pleasure-seeking system*, which is associated with *libido*. The goal of the pleasure-seeking system is to obtain immediate gratification of all its desires.

2. The *preconscious censorship system*. The goal of the "censor" is to put *blocks* on the spotlight of consciousness so that it can't shine on some of the messier, more infantile areas of your "mental stage" that you'd rather not look at (Freud, 1912/1958).

What you think—and particularly what you dream—is determined by the interaction of these two mental systems.

● Pleasure Principle

The unconscious system is ruled by what Freud called the **pleasure principle**. That is, any gratification of libidinal desires leads to a physical and mental state of *pleasure*. If the desires are not satisfied, the person experiences pain or, as Freud put it, *unpleasure*.

Freud decided that infantile urges could be satisfied in two ways: First, by *real* gratification. For example, when the infant is hungry, milk satisfies its hunger. But if milk isn't available, the infant can also gratify its need for food in a "symbolic" or "imaginary" fashion, such as by sucking on its thumb or dreaming about eating (Freud, 1911/1958).

● Reality Principle

As the infant grows, it discovers that "real" satisfiers yield more lasting rewards than do "imaginary" or symbolic satisfiers. Thus, early in life, the infant strives to distinguish between these two types of satisfiers. In doing so, the

Libido (lib-BEE-doh). In Freud's second theory, the psychic energy created by your sexual instincts, found in the unconscious and controlled by the id. In his third theory, Freud decided that the ego has its own store of libido. This theoretical change is not really important, since Freud said the ego "split off from the id."

Pleasure principle. Freud's notion that the id (or the unconscious) is driven by the innate desire to satisfy its needs (or reduce its innate drives) immediately. Reducing the drive gives pleasure; an increase in a drive gives "unpleasure." According to Freud, "The id lives by the pleasure principle."

Reality principle. The unconscious (or id) can gratify its needs either with real objects or with fantasy. Both types of satisfiers give pleasure. But only real-world objects bring about a *physical* reduction in drives. This is the "reality principle." The task of the ego, therefore, is to find real-world objects to satisfy the id's demands, but to do so (as much as possible) in socially-acceptable ways. In doing so, the ego "obeys the reality principle."

Primary process thinking. The id cannot tell the difference between fantasy and reality, and is filled with lusts and hatreds that are not constrained by social demands. If the id cannot gratify its needs (such as hunger) with a real-world object (such as the mother's breast) it will do so in a fantasy manner (such as by thumb-sucking).

Secondary process thinking. Because the ego is in touch with reality, Freud said, it can tell the difference between reality and fantasy. The ego therefore searches for real objects that will satisfy the id's needs, but in a socially-acceptable manner.

Instincts. In Freudian terms, instincts are biological "drives" that exert physical pressures (such as hunger), have aims (such as eating), are associated with certain objects (such as food), and sources. The physical/chemical processes in the body are the *real* sources of all instincts, but each instinct also has associated with it certain "mental operations" that actually motivate the person's thoughts and actions.

Eros (AIR-roes). The Greek god of love.

child is actually beginning to follow what Freud called the **reality principle**. The infant's preconscious mind begins "scanning" the external environment for objects (such as the mother's breast) that provide "real" gratification. This sort of "scanning of the outer world" increases the child's dependency on his or her sensory inputs and moves the child toward "self mastery" (Freud, 1911/1958).

● **Dreams**

Adults, of course, have attained self mastery and can easily distinguish between real and symbolic satisfiers. However, their unconscious minds still seek gratification of infantile wishes—and these wishes are often too antisocial to be satisfied in any real manner. So, the adult *dreams* about fulfilling these wishes.

Dreams are important, Freud said, because they are *compromise structures* that provide a limited amount of satisfaction to the unconscious while still maintaining the adult's ethical standards.

Freud called dreams "the royal road" that leads to the understanding of the unconscious mind. "In all of us," he said, "even in good men, there is a lawless wild-beast nature which peers out in sleep" (Freud, 1900/1953). But because the unconscious mind behaves *as if reality does not exist*, its desires can be satisfied symbolically. Thus, the censor can satisfy most unconscious needs by expressing them in disguised form.

● **Primary Versus Secondary Process Thinking**

According to Freud, the unconscious pleasure-seeking system engages in **primary process thinking**. By this term, Freud meant that the unconscious obeys the pleasure principle (Freud, 1920/1955).

The preconscious system, Freud said, engages in **secondary process thinking**. By this term, Freud meant that the preconscious system can differentiate between fantasy and reality, and thus obeys the reality principle.

When you are awake, Freud said, most of your *conscious* cognitive activities reflect secondary process thinking. When you sleep, however, you engage in primary process thinking because dreams are controlled by the unconscious system (Freud, 1920/1955).

□□ **QUESTION** □□
According to the *drive theorists* we discussed in Chapter 7, what is your major motivation?

Instincts

In a 1915 paper, Freud defined *instinct* as "a mental representation of a physical need" (Freud, 1915/1957). According to Freud, **instincts** have four major characteristics:

Pressure. The longer you go without food, the stronger your hunger becomes and the greater pressure you feel to find and consume food.

Aim. The goal of all instincts is *reduction of pressure*. Thus, the ultimate aim of the hunger instinct is eating. However, thumb-sucking is what Freud called an *intermediate* aim in that it can temporarily reduce hunger pangs. Fantasy gratification of a need is always an *intermediate* aim of any instinct.

Object. Most needs can be satisfied only by contact with some real-world object. For example, the newborn infant soon learns that the mother's breast satisfies the child's hunger. Therefore, the breast becomes the *object* the infant seeks when hungry. Later, the "object" associated with this instinct may be a bottle, a pacifier, or the child's thumb.

Source. The *biological* sources of all instincts are physical and chemical processes within the body. However, the "mental operations" associated with these biological processes are what actually guide most behaviors, Freud said. Thus, the mind can be considered the *psychological source* of the instinct.

Eros and Thanatos

In 1920, Freud decided that there were two main instincts: **Eros**, the life force, and

Thanatos, the death instinct (Freud, 1920/1955).

In Freudian terms, *Eros* is the organizing, creative instinct that strives to keep the organism alive and to reproduce the species. Eros is love and pleasure.

Thanatos is the disruptive, disorganizing instinct that strives to destroy the integrity of the personality, and to move the organism down "its own path to death" (Freud, 1920/1955). Thanatos is thus self-hatred, aggression, and misery.

Most of Freud's followers accepted his description of *Eros*. But almost all of them rejected his concept of *Thanatos*. In trying to defend his latest notions on love and death, Freud was compelled to create his third "model of the mind."

FREUD'S "STRUCTURAL" MODEL OF THE MIND

The major "mental agencies" in Freud's *topological theory* were the unconscious and the pre-conscious. By 1923, however, Freud decided this model was inadequate for his purposes. He then created three new agencies, the **id**, the **ego**, and the **superego** (Freud, 1923/1961).

Emil Nolde, *Dance Around the Golden Calf*. Freud described the id as a "cauldron of seething excitement" which seeks pleasure in releasing its pent-up energies.

The Id

"Originally, to be sure, everything was id." By this phrase, Freud meant that the id is the most primitive portion of the personality. It exists at birth, and contains all of the unlearned, innate instincts. Freud called it a "cauldron full of seething excitations" (Freud, 1933/1964).

According to Freud, the id "knows no judgments of value: no good and evil, no morality. . . . It has no organization, produces no collective will, but only a striving to bring about the satisfaction of the instinctual needs subject to the observance of the pleasure principle" (Freud, 1933/1964).

The Ego

Left to its greedy self, the id would soon destroy itself—and the individual. However, Freud said, at a very early age, the *ego* begins to differentiate out of the id. The development of the ego is brought about by the person's need to *control* the id and to *respond appropriately* to demands from the external environment. "We might say that the ego stands for reason and good sense while the id stands for the untamed passions" (Freud, 1933/1964).

The id contains the libido and obeys the pleasure principle. The ego, however, obeys the reality principle. In doing so, the ego decides whether a given instinctual demand must be satisfied immediately, whether satisfaction can be postponed, or whether the instinct should be repressed.

Because the ego develops out of the id, the ego has access to its own store of libidinal energy. Some of this energy becomes directed toward external objects that satisfy its needs. Freud called this **object libido**. The remaining store of ego libido is used to oppose the "death instinct" (Freud, 1940/1964).

The ego *mediates* between the childish demands of the id and the requirements of external reality. In doing so, however, it is soon required to deal with a third mental agency, the *superego*.

The Superego

The first object that the child's ego invests libido in is the mother's breast. Soon, this "object libido" expands to include the rest of the mother as well. Later, however, during what Freud called the *latency period*, the child is forced to give up the mother as a "love object." We will discuss the latency period in a moment. But when this "loss of the mother" occurs, the ego *compensates* the id by taking on some of the mother's characteristics. "When the ego assumes the features of the [lost] object, it is forcing itself, so to speak, upon the id as a love-object and is trying to make good the id's loss by saying: 'Look, you can love me too—I am so like the object'" (Freud, 1923/1961).

This process of "becoming like the lost object" is called **identification**. And it is out of this sort of *identification* that the superego is

Thanatos (THAN-ah-toes). The Greek god of death.

_Id_ (rhymes with "kid"). The primitive, instinctual, childish, unconscious portion of the personality that obeys the pleasure principle.

Ego. From the Latin word for "I." That part of the personality which mediates between the id, the superego, and reality. Some parts of the ego are conscious, but the ego also extends into the preconscious and the unconscious.

Superego. That part of your personality which "splits off from your ego," and which contains both your own and society's "rules of conduct." The superego has two parts—the stern "conscience," which you acquired from your parents (mostly during the latency period and the genital stage), and the "self-ideal," which you acquired mostly from other people during puberty.

Object libido. Libidinal energy that is associated with, or can be released by, certain objects.

Identification. According to Anna Freud, identification is an "ego defense mechanism" by which you take on the characteristics of someone you fear in order to protect yourself from that person's wrath. As used by most psychologists, however, the term means "to take on the characteristics of another person," whether you dislike or like the person.

Theory of psychosexual development. Freud's belief that all children must pass through similar periods in the development of their personalities. Each stage has its own crisis, and during each stage the child discharges libidinal energy in a different manner.

Erogenous zones (air-RODGE-en-us). Eros was the Greek god of love. "Erogenous" means _to generate Eros_, or "erotic sensations." Erogenous zones are those parts of the body which, when stimulated, provide sexually pleasurably feelings.

born. Put simply, the superego is created when the child learns to "identify" with the parents.

Because the child forms her/his superego when quite young, the superego incorporates an _idealized_ notion of what the parents are like. This "idealized notion," of course, is little more than a set of _socially-approved behaviors_. For that reason, the superego actually functions as a "social conscience." In most situations, the superego therefore demands that the ego (and the id) obey the ethical standards of society, _no matter how stern those standards may be_.

The ego's task, Freud said, is to mediate not only between the id's urgings and reality's requirements, but to do so in a manner that satisfies the superego's strictures. Little wonder, Freud remarked, that for the ego "Life is not easy!" (Freud, 1923/1961).

Childhood Sexuality

As we mentioned earlier, Freud developed his theory of personality in part because, during free association, his patients frequently talked about having "unacceptable desires." What were these desires like? To Freud's amazement, many of them turned out to be sexual. Even more surprising was the fact that most of the repressed urges could be traced back to early childhood. For many patients reported that their fathers had attempted to abuse them sexually when the patients were quite young. At first, Freud assumed his patients were telling the truth. He soon abandoned this position, however, since he could not bring himself to believe that _all_ fathers attempt to seduce their offspring. Rather, he decided, the patients were

reporting "as fact" the sexual _fantasies_ they had while still very young (Monte, 1987).

The notion that children have sexual fantasies soon led Freud to make several important changes in his theoretical position. First, he concluded that the sexual instinct was one of the strongest forces shaping human nature. Second, he decided that most of his patients' problems resulted from the _conflict_ they experienced between their early sexual desires and the society's rules against _expressing_ sexual feelings. And third, Freud came to the conclusion that, from birth on, infants _actively sought sexual stimulation_ (Freud, 1905/1953).

By "sexual stimulation," however, Freud did not mean the genitally-oriented sexuality of adults. Rather, he meant _sensual pleasure_. Sucking on the mother's breast not only reduces hunger, but becomes a pleasant source of sensory inputs. This "sexual" pleasure soon _generalizes_ to other objects, including the infant's thumb or a pacifier. It also generalizes to other parts of the body, such as the anus. Soon the infant begins actively searching both his/her body and her/his environment for new sources of sensory stimulation.

Freud soon decided that "food and the breast" provided the infant with the child's first sexual/sensory pleasures. And since the infant's mother was associated with these first pleasures, the mother also became the first _object_ of the infant's sexual desires (Freud, 1905/1953).

The _biological force_ underlying infant sexuality, Freud concluded, was _libido_, or the "sexual instinct." In adults, libido is the force that leads to mating and procreation of the species. In infants, Freud decided, it expresses itself as an urge for pleasure and for the discharge of tension by the immediate gratification of all needs. From Freud's point of view, however, adult sexuality has its _roots_ in the child's constant striving for sensual pleasure (Freud, 1901/1960).

These "radical-for-their-times" insights on infant sexuality soon led Freud to create his **theory of psychosexual development**.

Psychosexual Development

In truth, Freud's description of the psychosexual stages a child passes through is a narrative account of how the "expression of libido" changes over time. Freud believed that, in each of the major stages, the libido was "organized" or expressed in a characteristic manner through stimulation of a specific **erogenous zone** of the body.

- ### _Oral Period_

In the first year of life, Freud said, libido is organized around the pleasurable activities of the mouth (see Table 16.1).

TABLE 16.1   The Psychosexual Stages

Psychosexual Stage	Libidinal Zone	Chief Developmental Issue	Libidinal Object
1. *Oral* (birth to 1 year)	Mouth, skin, thumb	Passive incorporation of all good through mouth; autoerotic sensuality	Mother's breast; own body
2. *Anal* (2 to 3 years)	Anus, bowels	Active seeking for tension reduction; self mastery; passive submission	Own body
3. *Phallic* (3 to 5 years)	Genitals, skin	Oedipus and Electra complexes; Possession of mother; Identification with same-sexed parent; Ambivalence of love relationships	Mother for boy; father for girl
4. *Latency* (6 to 8 years)	None	Repression of pregenital forms of libido; Learning culturally appropriate shame and disgust	Repressed previous objects
5. *Genital* (Adolescence onward)	Genital primacy	Reproduction; sexual intimacy	Heterosexual partner

Based on Freud, 1905 and 1916.

During the first part of the oral stage, libido is released primarily through self-stimulation, or **autoerotic** activities. After a few months, however, autoeroticism decreases as the infant begins to seek an *external* love object. For most infants, as we noted, the first external love object is the breast. The intense sensual pleasure the child derives from sucking on the mother's breast then becomes the "model" for sexual orgasm in the adult. As Freud put it, "No one who has seen a baby sinking back satiated from the breast and falling asleep with flushed cheeks and a blissful smile can escape the reflection that this picture persists as a prototype of the expression of sexual satisfaction in later life" (Freud, 1905/1953).

Freud defined thumb-sucking as "fantasy gratification," as no milk or food is delivered from the thumb.

Anal Period

During the first year of life, Freud said, children tend to be fairly passive. However, at some point between the first and second year, they begin to strive for *self mastery*. Toilet training typically begins around 18 months of age, and the libido becomes organized around the anus. Children soon learn that retention and expulsion of feces not only is associated with pleasure, but also with the mother's love and approval. According to Freud, gaining voluntary control over the sphincter muscle serves as the prototype not only for self mastery, but also for mastering the social and physical environment in later life (Freud, 1905/1953).

Phallic Period

Freud believed that, beginning about the start of the fourth year of life, the libido becomes organized around genital stimulation. At about this age—and extending into the fifth year—youngsters discover that manipulation of their genitalia can provide intense sensory pleasure. And because they have not yet developed a sense of shame, the children also develop an intense interest in the genitalia of others. It is at this age, Freud said, that the **Oedipus complex** arises in males and the **Electra complex** arises in females (Freud, 1908/1959).

We will discuss the Oedipus and Electra complexes in detail in just a moment. For the moment, we should note that Freud's description of psychosexual development in women caused him far more difficulty—both theoretical and social—than did his account of male development. For example, Freud assumed that, during the phallic period, boys learn "guilt" because the mother punishes them for

Autoerotic (AW-toh-air-ROT-tick). Self-stimulation of the erogenous zones, such as masturbation.

Oedipus complex (ED-ih-pus). A "complex" is a part of the mind that breaks free and begins to function on its own. Freud took many of his analogies from Greek mythology. Oedipus was a young man who inadvertently killed his father and married his mother. Freud believed that, during the phallic (FAL-ick) stage, all young boys develop an intense incestuous desire for their mothers and a strong hatred for their fathers. But they also fear that if they express their feelings, they will be punished (or even castrated) by the father. This "castration anxiety" shatters (or resolves) the Oedipus complex. The boy gives up his Oedipal love for the mother and takes on the standards of his father by creating his superego.

Electra complex (ee-LECK-trah). Electra was a Greek woman whose mother killed her father. Electra then talked her brother into murdering their mother. Freud believed that all young girls (during the phallic stage) develop an intense incestuous desire for their fathers and a strong hatred for their mothers. They believe the mother has somehow deprived them of the "penis" they were born with, and hope to get a substitute from the father. Freud said the Electra complex is not *resolved* in girls. Rather it *dissipates* over time as the girl creates her superego in part by taking on the mother's values and standards.

masturbating. This punishment often involves threats that the mother (or perhaps the father) will *remove* the offending organ if the boy doesn't stop "playing with himself." However, Freud said, during the phallic period girls discover that they "lack a penis," and they tend to blame their mother for the loss of "this important part of their bodies." In either boys or girls, therefore, the child's focus is on *male* genitalia, not *female* genitalia, which is why Freud called this the *phallic* period (Freud, 1908/1959).

● **Latency Period**

For a period of about two years—from about age six to about age eight—children are said to enter a period of *sexual latency*. Libido is suppressed by the combined forces of parental disapproval and the child's own sense of shame

During Freud's anal stage, libido is centered around toilet training.

and disgust with matters sexual. This relatively brief period ends when the child resolves the Oedipal/Electra complex and the onset of puberty begins (Freud, 1905/1953).

□ □ **QUESTION** □ □

One of the reasons Freud developed the notion of the "latency period" is that the children he observed seemed to give up self-stimulation at about age six. What other reasons can you think of for the decrease in *observed* sexual activity at this age?

● **Genital Period**

Once puberty has occurred, the individual is sexually capable of reproducing the species. According to Freud, the person now has three sources of sexual stimulation available to him/her:

1. Memories and impulses from earlier periods of psychosexual development.
2. Direct stimulation of the genital areas.
3. Chemical stimulation from the sex hormones.

At this stage, Freud said, libidinal energy is organized around the "discharge of sexual products." He noted, however, that this sort of activity brought intense sensory pleasure to the individual as well as leading to the "procreation of the species."

Freud believed that all of the prior stages and libidinal organizations culminated in the genital stage (Freud, 1905/1953).

Oedipus Complex

As we noted, Freud believed that, during the phallic period, boys typically are threatened with castration by their parents in an attempt to deter the boys' masturbatory activities. But masturbation itself, Freud said, makes the boy love his mother more intensely because he somehow associates the intense pleasures of genital self-stimulation with the mother. However, the boy soon notes two things:

First, his mother often pays a great deal of attention to the boy's father. The boy becomes *jealous* of and wants to get rid of the father in order to have the mother all to himself. But the boy also *suspects* the father is aware of this jealousy, and that parental threats of castration are therefore "only too real."

Second, because the boy has by now learned that little girls "lack a penis," he decides that *they have already been castrated* for loving the mother too much. This insight serves to intensify his fears of losing the "valuable possession" that has brought him so much pleasure.

Overwhelmed by anxieties concerning castration, the boy's ego defends itself by *re-*

During the Oedipus conflict, boys are strongly attracted to their mothers.

pressing all libidinal expression. Indeed, Freud said, "In boys . . . the complex is not simply repressed, it is literally smashed to pieces by the shock of threatened castration" (Freud, 1925). Almost in desperation, the boy flees into the *latency period*.

According to Freud, the boy *resolves* the Oedipus complex during the latency period by taking three important steps:

1. He *gives up* his first love object, his mother.
2. He *identifies* with the father by taking on the father's values and views.
3. He develops a *superego* or *conscience* that incorporates his parents' sense of morality.

Resolving the Oedipus complex brings about the end of the latency period and the start of the genital period in boys (Freud, 1925).

Electra Complex

Freud said that it is the fear of *losing* the penis that destroys the Oedipus complex in boys and brings on latency. However, Freud assumed that, during the phallic period, girls realize they have already *lost* the penis and usually blame their mothers for this "disaster." The girl then abandons her first love object (the mother) and turns to the father. She "knows" the father has a penis, and hopes to get one for herself from him. Since this is not possible, she begins to yearn for a "symbolic penis substitute, a baby." It is this wish for a "penis-baby" that propels the girl into the Electra complex— and the latency period (Freud, 1925).

Freud believed that the Electra complex *dissipates* in girls because they come to *identify with the mother*. They take on her values and feminine behaviors, Freud said, in order to appeal to the father. Over time, the girls' "penis envy" typically fades, and because they now identify with the mother, they slowly cease to hate her for depriving them of a penis in the first place.

Freud believed that, because the Electra complex *dissipates* rather than being *fully resolved*, women do not develop as strong a conscience (superego) as do men (Freud, 1933).

Dynamic Interactions

In 1933, Freud combined his topological and structural models in a drawing similar to those shown in Figs. 16.1–16.3. Freud saw the ego as lying mostly in the conscious and preconscious regions of the mind, but also as extending deep into the unconscious. The superego lies mostly in the preconscious and the unconscious. The id, of course, resides entirely in the unconscious. However, Freud had a warning about interpreting this sort of diagram too literally:

> We cannot do justice to the characteristics of the mind by linear outlines like those in a drawing or in a primitive painting, but rather by areas of color melting into one another as they are presented by modern artists. After making the separation we must allow what we have separated to merge together once again. (Freud, 1933/1964)

In Freudian theory, it is the *dynamic interaction* of these various elements—id, ego, superego; conscious, preconscious, unconscious— that determines what your personality is like (Monte, 1987).

• *Anna Freud*

Anna was Freud's sixth child, born (in 1895) after he and his wife had decided they would have but five children. She grew up shy, withdrawn, and with the feeling that she had been "unwanted." But she eventually became her father's most trusted companion and a famous psychoanalyst in her own right.

In the early 1900's, women in Austria did not generally enroll in college, much less in medical schools. Thus, Anna Freud was one of the few early psychoanalysts who lacked a medical degree. However, as her father grew to value her more and more, he began teaching her his techniques. Eventually, "Freud be-

Learning to identify with his father is part of a boy's resolution of the Oedipus complex.

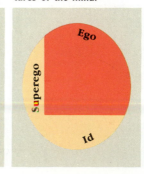

FIG. 16.1 Freud's "levels of consciousness."

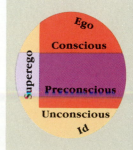
Anna Freud

FIG. 16.2 Freud's "structures of the mind."

FIG. 16.3 "Levels of consciousness" occupied by the id, ego, and superego, the structures of the mind.

queathed to her his place as leader of the psychoanalytic movement" (Monte, 1987).

Anna Freud made many contributions to psychoanalytic theory, chief among them (1) her development of techniques for analyzing children, and (2) her descriptions of the psychological mechanisms the ego uses to defend itself.

The Ego's Defense Mechanisms

Sigmund Freud believed that the mechanisms the ego used to defend itself were "trivial things" that got in the way of analysis. Anna Freud, however, recognized how important they could be. In her classic monograph, *The Ego and the Mechanisms of Defense,* she made a lengthy list of the ego defenses that her father had mentioned in his writings, then added several of her own. The best known of these *defense mechanisms* are as follows:

Repression. The blocking off from conscious awareness of any desire or memory the ego finds threatening. Perhaps the most common but most dangerous of the defense mechanisms.

Denial. Repression is the shutting off of *internal* threats to the ego. Denial is the cutting off from consciousness of *external* threats.

Projection. Attributing your own forbidden desires to someone else. If you hate someone, but cannot tolerate this hatred, you may "project" your dislike onto the other person by assuming that he/she hates you.

Displacement. If you become angry at your boss, but fear expressing your anger openly, you may kick the cat instead.

According to Anna Freud, the defense mechanisms often involve releasing repressed desires in socially-accepted ways.

Turning-Against-Self. Instead of kicking the cat, you may develop feelings of inferiority or guilt.

Reaction Formation. Turning unacceptable feelings into their opposite. A girl who hates her mother but cannot accept that hatred may smother the mother with love instead.

Introjection. Making the characteristics of someone you admire or love part of your own personality.

Identification. Making the characteristics of someone you hate or fear part of your own personality.

Regression. Returning to an earlier and more childish form of behavior. Under stress, a recovered alcoholic may begin drinking again.

Sublimation. Changing unacceptable impulses into behaviors that are socially acceptable. A man with strong aggressive urges may join the military forces or become a policeman.

These are some of the major ego-defense mechanisms listed by Anna Freud. However, as Christopher Monte notes, "It should be pointed out that other psychoanalysts have added endlessly to this list, so that the total number of possible ego defenses is considerably larger" than those mentioned by Anna Freud (Monte, 1987).

• Four Characteristics of the Defense Mechanisms

Almost all of the defense mechanisms available to the ego have four characteristics in common:

1. They are ways of trying to reduce stress and anxiety.
2. They involve the denying or distortion of reality.
3. They operate at an unconscious level.
4. They operate mechanically and involuntarily (which is why Anna Freud called them *mechanisms*).

As we noted in Chapter 8, the defense mechanisms are really indirect or "defensive" ways of coping with stress and anxiety. By encouraging his patients to bring their unconscious problems to the fore—and thus deal with them at a conscious level—Freud was attempting to get his patients to use a more direct method of coping with their developmental difficulties.

Freud's Influence

In a recent article, Gary Leak and Steven Christopher give this evaluation of Sigmund Freud: "There can be little doubt that Freudian psychoanalysis is the 'first force' in 20th-century psychology. Psychoanalysis as a personality the-

"YOU MEAN YOUR BIG SMILE IS BOTTLED-UP AGGRESSION? MINE IS BOTTLED-UP HOSTILITY."

ory is the most comprehensive one available, detailing the structure, dynamics, and development of personality to a degree unsurpassed by its competitors" (Leak & Christopher, 1982).

One reason for this influence is the fact that Freud paid attention to the *unconscious* aspects of human behavior. Prior to Freud's time, psychologists either studied overt behavior patterns or used introspection to study *conscious* activities. But neither introspection nor the study of conditioned reflexes yielded the insights into personality development that Freud gave the world because he looked at the "hidden" aspects of the mind.

● Freud's Writing Style

Earlier, we mentioned that there are two major modes of thinking—the narrative and the rational/problem-solving modes. Freud's dominant position is due, in part, to the fact that he was a superb writer. Indeed, his narrative style was so good that he was considered a candidate for the Nobel Prize—but in literature, not in medicine. You cannot begin to understand the power of his approach unless you immerse yourself in his many case histories. The descriptive names he gave to many of his patients— "Rat Man," "Wolf Man," "Little Hans"—suggest both what these individuals were like and the power of his imagination.

● Experimental Support

When it comes to experimental evidence, psychoanalysis has not fared so well. Freud's account of "what happens when" during childhood is simply not supported by most recent developmental research (see Chapters 14 and 15). And because he was a stage theorist, his

"LISTEN— IT'S PSYCHOANALYSIS COMING UP THE RIVER FROM VIENNA."

Sigmund Freud (front row, fourth from right) gave his first lecture in the US at Clark University in 1909. Other notables in the front row include Carl Jung (third from right), anthropologist Franz Boas (far left), and William James (third from left).

description of psychosexual development is subject to many of the criticisms raised against Piaget and Kohlberg. Freud cared little for these criticisms, however. Convinced of the wisdom of his insights into the "structure and dynamics" of the human personality, he felt no need for experimental validation of his theoretical views.

The major criticism that can be made of Freudian theory, therefore, is this one: Like most other "narrative accounts" in science, psychoanalysis tends to "explain almost everything, but predicts almost nothing." For that reason, perhaps, Freud's views have appealed more to humanists—to artists and writers, to philosophers and natural historians—than to data-oriented experimental scientists.

In a recent article, Thomas Parisi concludes, "I have not tried to argue that Freud was 'right' or that his theory is 'true.' If forced to choose—right or wrong—one must of course admit that Freud was wrong on many counts. But he was richly wrong" (Parisi, 1987).

The "perceived wrongness" of Freud's "conceptual richness" led many of his followers to offer their own adaptations of psychoanalytic theory. Let's continue our study of the human personality by seeing what Freud's disciples had to say.

Carl Gustav Jung

CARL JUNG

Born in Switzerland in 1875, Carl Gustav Jung came from a family of devout Christians and physicians. His father was a minister, and his mother a minister's daughter. As a medical student at the University of Zurich, he dabbled in biology, philosophy, archeology, mythology, and mysticism. Much of his *psychological* theorizing, however, was probably influenced by

16 / Personality Theory

his personal experiences, some of which were distinctly odd.

For most of his life, Jung suffered from nightmares and vivid hallucinations. For example, when he was three or four, he had a terrifying dream in which he found himself walking down a stone staircase. Soon he entered a huge chamber that contained a magnificent golden throne. Atop the throne was a large shaft about 15 feet high.

> It was a huge thing, reaching almost to the ceiling. But it was of curious composition: it was made of skin and naked flesh, and on top there was something like a rounded head with no face and no hair. On the very top of the head was a single eye, gazing motionlessly upward. (Jung, 1961)

The "thing," of course, was a phallus. But to the youthful Jung, it was also a "god" of some kind. From that time on, Jung tended to view sex as the frightening "underground counterpart" of religion. He also believed that, in dreams such as this, God had given him "secret knowledge" not shared with others (Jung, 1961).

Also, rather early in life, Jung decided that he was "two people" combined in one body. First, he was the child he appeared to be. But buried somewhere inside him was a wise old man who had "lived a century before." The "child" and the "old man" often had long conversations.

These two notions—that there are both "old" and "new" aspects to each personality,

Jung's archetypes are stories or characters that occur in the lore of many cultures, such as the figures of a father god, the first man on earth, and the creation of the human race.

and that Jung knew "secrets" that had been revealed to him alone—helped shape his thoughts on human nature (Monte, 1987).

The Word Association Test

Early in his career, Jung and his cousin, Franz Riklin, developed a *word association test*. The test consisted of a list of 100 or so fairly common words. When examining a subject, Jung would present the list and ask that the person respond to each item *as quickly as possible* by giving the first word that occurred to the subject. Jung not only measured how long it took the person to respond, but also measured the subject's galvanic skin response (GSR) as well.

Jung and Riklin found considerable variation in response times among "normal" subjects. However, they also discovered that neurotic and psychotic patients showed grossly abnormal response times and GSR records. Typically, when the item on the list touched on some area the patient found traumatic, the patient would hesitate, give an inappropriate response, or perhaps not respond at all. Jung interpreted these unusual reactions as evidence favoring Freud's views on "preconscious censoring of unconscious material" (Jung, 1909/1973).

• *Freud and Jung*

Freud was quite pleased with Jung's work, for it seemed to offer *quantitative* data that supported Freud's theory. In 1907, Freud invited Jung to visit him in Vienna. After a brief exchange of letters, Freud "annointed" Jung as his chosen successor. By 1912, however, Jung had developed his own psychoanalytic theory, and broke with Freud. The two remained bitter enemies the rest of their lives (Monte, 1987).

Libido as Intentionality

Freud saw libido as being primarily *sexual energy*. But Jung believed that sexuality was far less potent a force in human affairs than were religious feelings and the desire to become a *complete individual*. Jung decided, therefore, that libido was a type of *generalized* psychic energy which he called a *creative life force*. To Jung, libido was the energy underlying *intentionality,* or "volition," in human beings (Jung, 1912/1956).

Like Freud, Jung believed that libido could be "channeled" away from its original method of being released. Unlike Freud, however, Jung believed that this "channeling" was often a healthy thing, and was controlled by an innate tendency that all humans have for "making symbols." These symbols could be found, Jung said, in the myths and religious writings found in all cultures. To Jung, interpretation of "cultural myths" was as important a tool for studying the unconscious as was dream interpretation to Freud (Jung, 1912/1956).

Individuation

Jung could not accept Freud's notion that the goal of "growing up" was to bring the infantile, sexual instincts under control. Rather, Jung said, we are *religious* animals whose unconscious roots go back to the very beginnings of the human race. To Jung, the purpose of our existence is the integration of our conscious perceptions of the outside world with our unconscious, mystical experiences.

Jung called this integrative process **individuation**, which in many ways resembles what Piaget describes as the "building up of the self-schema." Jung, however, placed a great deal more emphasis on the ego's need to integrate unconscious with conscious processes than Piaget did (Jung, 1939/1969).

Structure of the Psyche

Like Freud, Jung had his own "structural theory" of the psyche, or mind. Unlike Freud, however, Jung believed the ego was entirely conscious, and that there were two distinct unconscious regions of the mind. Because of his feelings about the relative unimportance of sexuality, his theory contained no id.

• The Conscious Ego

Jung believed the ego is made up of feelings of *identity* and *continuity*. It is the part of your mind which knows you are the same person today that you were yesterday. But Jung didn't view the ego as striving to mediate between the childish id and the stern superego. Rather, it is a slowly-developing *structure* that pulls together all types of conscious and unconscious activity to form a new "whole" (Jung, 1939/1969).

• The Personal Unconscious

To Freud, the unconscious was primarily the source of our psychic energies and our memories of the past. Jung agreed that past experiences were stored in the unconscious, but he believed that *plans for the future* were also worked out at the unconscious level. He noted that, on many occasions, his patients would "wake up in the morning" having decided on some course of action that previously they had been unsure of. Jung took this as evidence that the unconscious contained "forward-looking" material as well as "residues of the past" (Jung, 1916/1969).

That part of the mind which contains personal memories and plans for the future is what Jung referred to as the *personal unconscious*.

• The Collective Unconscious

In his study of anthropology, Jung noticed that some myths—such as a "great flood," or the creation of the world—seem to appear in *all cultures*. Jung called these myths **archetypes**. He said that, through evolutionary processes, the *mental images* associated with these archetypes had become engraved on our genes. These images are not "pre-formed." Rather, they are merely *predispositions* to respond to certain real-world events in specific ways. For example, in times of social crisis, humans tend to seek out (and follow) great leaders. We do so, Jung said, because each of us contains a "hero archetype" that predisposes us to react to social stress by becoming emotionally attached to charismatic leaders (Jung, 1936/1969).

Jung believed the most important archetype of all is that of the *self-concept*, for it encourages you to integrate all of your conscious and unconscious psychological processes into one meaningful whole.

According to Jung, the archetypes are stored in the *collective unconscious*. He believed that the archetypes—and the collective unconscious—were far more important in shaping the human personality than were those psychic materials stored in the personal unconscious (Jung, 1936/1969).

Jung's "Polarities"

Like many of the trait theorists we will discuss in the next chapter, Jung tended to see things in terms of "polar opposites." That is, he believed the personality is shaped by "opposing forces."

• Animus and Anima

During the period 1913–1917, Jung underwent a series of "mystical experiences" that he interpreted as being a voluntary investigation of his collective unconscious, but which others believe was evidence Jung was undergoing a psychotic breakdown. During this period of time, several "personalities" emerged from his unconscious mind to hold long conversations with him (Monte, 1987).

At one point during this terrifying period, Jung asked himself the question, "What am I really doing?" At once, a voice within his mind replied, "It is art." Jung was apparently more annoyed than surprised, for he realized at once that the voice was a woman's. And what would a *woman* be doing inside him, since he was *male*?

Jung carried out lengthy talks with this "new" and obviously feminine personality. Eventually he concluded she was his **anima**, or female archetype. Buried inside each man, he decided, are feminine attitudes and intuitions. They come in part from the *anima* archetype, but also from the man's experiences with his mother and other women. This feminine side of each man determines his relationships with the women he meets in life.

Buried inside each woman, Jung said, is an **animus** archetype, which constitutes the masculine side of her nature.

According to Jung, there is a certain danger to the animus and anima. For they *oppose* our normal feelings of sexual identity. And they might, under certain circumstances, gain primary control over our personalities. However, unless we recognize (and deal with) these "opposing forces" inside us, we are not likely to become "whole individuals." (Jung, 1917/1966)

□ □ **QUESTION** □ □
What do you think Jung's explanation of homosexuality was?

● *Introversion and Extroversion*
Jung's most widely-accepted ideas have to do with *introversion* and *extroversion*. Jung said we are born with two innate *attitudes*, one of which leads us to look inward, the other of which leads us to look outward. Jung described them in this manner:

> The first attitude [introversion] is normally characterized by a hesitant, reflective, retiring nature that keeps itself to itself, shrinks from objects, is slightly on the defensive and prefers to hide behind mistrustful scrutiny. The second [extroversion] is normally characterized by an outgoing, candid, and accommodating nature that adapts easily to a given situation, quickly forms attachments, and . . . will often venture forth with careless confidence into unknown situations. (Jung, 1917/1966)

Jung believed you are born with both these tendencies, but that one usually comes to predominate. You are usually conscious of which attitude is dominant but, according to Jung, you may not realize that the other attitude often expresses itself unconsciously through your dreams and fantasies.

Jung Versus Freud
Freud emphasized the role of biology in personality development. Jung preferred to think humans could rise above their animal natures.

Freud believed that happiness often came from escaping pain or reducing anxiety, and he tended to attract patients who were highly anxious or pain-ridden. Many of Jung's clients were artists, mystics, or wealthy individuals who felt the need for spiritual guidance "outside the church." Freud focused on the early, developmental years, which he saw as determining the entire structure of an individual's personality. Jung worked to a great degree with older patients, and never did offer a complete account of how the personality is formed.

Perhaps the most telling difference of all between the two men, though, lay in their use of language. Jung's books and articles were difficult to read and were filled with obscure images and symbols. His greatest influence was perhaps not on psychology, but on art and mysticism (Goldenson, 1970).

As we mentioned, Jung broke with Freud in 1912. Freud's other major disciple, Alfred Adler, made the break a year or so earlier.

□ □ **QUESTION** □ □
Jung's popularity probably reached a high point in the US during the 1960's. Can you guess why?

ALFRED ADLER
Alfred Adler was born and educated in Vienna. Although he lived for 67 years, sickness and death haunted him all of his life. A rather sickly child when young, Alfred Adler often was angry because his older brother was athletic, while he wasn't. When he was three, his younger brother died in the bed next to Adler's. And when he was just five, he had such a bad case of pneumonia that the doctor gave him up for dead. Much of Adler's theorizing on human nature can be seen as an attempt to *overcome* his fear of death and feelings of *physical inferiority* (Monte, 1987).

As a young adult, Adler often recalled the times when, as a boy, he had to walk to school daily past a cemetery. Remembering the situation later, he was convinced that all the other children were brave enough to ignore the graveyard. But Adler felt fear and horror each time he came near the place. Deciding that he was *less courageous* than his peers, he determined he would have to train himself to overcome his fears. He did so, as he remembered things, by deliberately running back and forth over the graves until he had "mastered his fears." When Adler was 35, however, he discovered to his amazement that there actually *had not been a cemetery* near his school. He had somehow "made up" the memory, perhaps as a way of explaining his early feelings of *inferiority*, his fear of death, and his angry determination to overcome that fear (Adler, 1959).

The Fear of Death

According to Harold Mosak and Richard Kopp, Freud, Jung, and Adler all showed an early interest in death. For example, when Jung was still in school, he eagerly volunteered to help search for drowning victims. As an adult, he reported with some enthusiasm how he actually discovered one dead body. As a boy, Jung also insisted on watching the slaughter of a pig, much to the horror of his mother. As we noted earlier, Freud had death dreams when he was young. And Adler, of course, had his imaginary cemetery and his very real illnesses.

In comparing the three men, Mosak and Kopp conclude that "Jung is intrigued by death, Freud is awed by death's inevitability, while Adler resolves to work to overcome death. . . . The dominant life goals of each man emerge from their recollections. Adler's goal is to overcome inadequacy through effort and resolve. Freud strives to comprehend through analysis and interpretation, while Jung moves toward communion with nature through sensual awareness" (Mosak & Kopp, 1973).

Adler and Freud

Adler joined Freud's group a few years after taking his medical degree. But as fascinated as Adler was by Freud's ideas, be broke away from "the master" in 1911 and formed his own group, the Society for Individual Psychology.

Rejecting both Freud's theory of sexual drives, and Jung's emphasis on intra-psychic mysticism, Adler emphasized the importance of the social environment. He thought that people could shape their own destinies, and that they could build a superior society by satisfying their basic need to transcend their personal problems (Ansbacher & Ansbacher, 1973).

Ego and Oedipus

Freud said the ego *mediates* the demands of the id, the superego, and the external environment. Adler saw the ego as being a "creative intelligence" that was the source of the person's identity as a *complete individual* (Monte, 1987).

Freud believed the Oedipus complex involved the child's sexual desires to possess the mother. Adler said the key issue was the child's desire to compete with the father for equal *strength*, not equal *pleasure*. According to Adler, "The boy wants to grow beyond himself, wants to attain a superiority over his father" (Adler, 1931).

Freud was a drive theorist who assumed humans were motivated to *move away from pain*. Adler was one of the first humanistic psychologists. He concluded that people move *toward self-chosen goals*, not merely away from "unpleasure": "The main problem of psychology is not to comprehend the causal factors as in physiology, but the direction-giving, pulling

Edvard Munch, *The Dance of Life.* The interplay between life and death was a subject that fascinated Freud, Jung, and Adler.

forces and goals which guide all other psychological movements" (Adler, 1931).

Adler criticized Freud for creating a "psychology of the pampered child, who feels that his instincts must never be denied, who looks on it as unfair that other people should exist." Adler believed that, to the contrary, people were motivated to *cooperate with each other* (Adler, 1931).

The Inferiority Complex

Some children are, Adler said, unhealthy when young. Others are born smaller than average. But even large, healthy children learn very early in life that adults can do things that youngsters cannot. This knowledge creates in all of us an *inferiority complex* that adds to our motivation to succeed, Adler said. This knowledge also creates a drive for *compensation*, the urge to overcome our failures in one part of life by excelling in another. The small, weak boy may try to succeed in his school studies or become a great musician in order to *compensate* for his physical weakness (Adler, 1931).

"Feeling for Others"

To Adler, life is a conscious struggle to move from what he called a "felt minus" to a "felt plus." By this, Adler meant you have a innate urge to rise above your own inferiorities *as you feel or perceive them* and to become superior to what you were in the past.

Adler concluded that only *neurotics* strive to become superior *to* others. Normal individuals, he said, want to perfect *themselves*. But they realize they can do so only with the help of others. It is, therefore, the "feeling *for* others" that differentiates normals from neurotics (Adler, 1964).

Alfred Adler

16 / Personality Theory

Style of Life

Adler was an optimist. He believed that you have buried in your genes a basic need to co-operate with others and to work toward building a better society. But you need guidance from others in order to express this need. For it is only through training and experience that you develop your *style of life*—your own unique way of expressing yourself (Ansbacher & Ansbacher, 1956).

Adler believed that the "style of life" is the self-consistent, goal-oriented core of personality. At first, Adler thought this style was fixed in childhood. Later, he decided that you continue to mature even as an adult. Thus, Adler was one of the first theorists to emphasize *life-span development*.

Adler's belief in the importance of *social factors* in determining personality was, for a time, unique in psychoanalytic circles and helped give rise to what we now call "social psychology." And by assuring people that they were basically humane, open-minded, and in control of their own destinies, Adler encouraged the development of "humanistic psychology."

Indeed, as humanist Abraham Maslow stated shortly before his death, "Alfred Adler becomes more and more correct year by year. As the facts come in, they give stronger and stronger support to his image of man."

□ □ **QUESTION** □ □

Freud called his theory *psychoanalysis*. Jung named his approach *analytical psychology*. Adler referred to his viewpoint as *individual psychology*. What do these three terms tell you about the theories themselves?

The Ego Psychologists

Sigmund Freud had many followers, the most devoted of which was surely his daughter, Anna. Some, like Jung and Adler broke away from Freud entirely. Others, following Anna's lead, moved away from the original emphasis on id and unconscious toward what is now known as **ego psychology**. That is, they started to emphasize the conscious determinants of human behavior, and the role of the ego in achieving life's goals. And taking a leaf from Adler's book, many of the ego psychologists began to describe the important influence the *social environment* has on personality development. Of all the ego psychologists, Erik Erikson is perhaps the best known. Suppose we continue our discussion of "person-oriented" personality theories by looking at how Erikson has added to the Freudian position.

ERIK H. ERIKSON

Erikson's mother was short, dark, and Jewish. Her first husband—Erikson's father—was tall, blond, and Scandanavian. The father deserted the mother shortly before Erikson was born. Her second husband was a Danish pediatrician named Theodor Homburger who, like the mother, was also Jewish. Throughout his childhood, Erikson wrote, his mother and stepfather "kept secret from me the fact that my mother had been married previously . . . so that I would feel thoroughly at home in their home" (Erikson, 1975).

Their loving concern to make the boy "feel at home" was unsuccessful, however. In his autobiography, he states that he "always felt out of place." This sense of "being an alien" led to what he later called an *identity crisis*. As Erikson notes, it helped shape his theoretical writings as well (Erikson, Erikson, & Kivnick, 1986).

Erikson and Freud

Erikson loved his stepfather and, as an adult, took Homburger as his middle name. However, he turned down the chance to become a medical doctor and studied art instead. When he took a position teaching art in Vienna, he soon met Anna Freud and "her famous father." They accepted him into their group, and Anna Freud herself trained him in the psychoanalytic techniques. Erikson later expressed his feelings about the situation as follows:

> It must be obvious now what Freud came to mean to me . . . Here was a mythical figure and, above all, a great doctor who had rebelled aginst the medical profession. Here also was a circle which admitted me to the kind of training that came as close to the role of a children's doctor as one could possibly come without going to medical school. What, in me, responded to this situation was, I think, some strong identification with my stepfather, the pediatrician, mixed with a search for my own mythical father. (Erikson, 1975)

Erikson accepted most of Freud's notions on the importance of instinctual drives in young children. But Erikson insisted that the goal of psychoanalysis should be that of explaining *healthy development*, not merely how development can go wrong. He also believed it is the *conflict* between instincts and cultural demands that shapes the child's personality (Erikson, 1974).

Freud and Jung emphasized the importance of past history on the maturation of the

Erik H. Erikson

individual. Erikson, like Adler, emphasized the future. At any given moment in time, Erikson said, your *anticipation of future events* helps determine how you will behave in the "here and now" (Erikson, 1959).

Eight Developmental Stages

According to Erikson, the ego passes through eight developmental stages on its way to complete maturity. Each of these stages is characterized by its own type of *crisis*, or conflict. Erikson saw these crises as being eight great tests of the ego's character (Monte, 1987).

Typically there are two *opposing tendencies* operating at the time of each crisis. One tendency is negative, in that it may retard development. The other tendency is positive, and promotes healthy growth. The crisis at each stage is resolved when the *relative balance* between the two tendencies swings either to the positive or the negative. And out of these crises grow the "ego strengths" or "virtues" that people need in order to mature and survive in a healthy fashion.

• *The Sensory Stage*

Erikson called the first developmental stage the "sensory stage," which corresponds to Freud's oral stage. To Erikson, the crisis at the sensory stage is that of learning a basic *trust or mistrust* of other people. As Erikson puts it, "A basic sense of trust means both that the child has learned to rely on his (or her) caregivers to be there when they are needed, and to consider himself trustworthy" (cited in Hall, 1983). If the mother (or someone else) meets the infant's needs, the child learns to depend on others in later life.

In Erikson's words, "Out of the conflict between trust and mistrust, the infant develops hope, which is the earliest form of what gradually becomes faith in adults." The infant gains the "ego strength" of hope, however, only if the mother is consistent in satisfying the infant's needs. If she is inconsistent, the tendency to mistrust becomes dominant. But the infant cannot be trusting in all cases. "Just imagine," Erikson says, "what somebody would be like who had no mistrust at all" (cited in Hall, 1983). Thus, it is the *balance* between the opposing tendencies that actually determines personality.

• *Muscular Development*

The second of Erikson's stages, similar to the anal stage, is that of *muscular development*. During toilet training the child learns to control her or his own muscles and begins to assert his or her individuality. The two opposing tendencies are **autonomy** and *shame and doubt*. If the child learns to control those bodily functions, the child becomes self-directed and autonomous and develops the *ego strength*

of will, or volition. If the opposing tendency prevails, the young person may develop "a **precocious** conscience," and with it a sense of shame, or what Erikson calls "rage turned against the self." If this happens, the child may fear losing self-control and may suffer a loss of self-esteem.

• *Locomotor Control*

Erikson's stage of *locomotor control* is similar to Freud's phallic stage. The opposing tendencies at this age are *initiative* versus *guilt*. Children now turn from total dependency on the parents to *identification* with one or both parents. Urged by their instincts to possess the opposite-sex parent (at least in fantasy), children face the crisis of inner desires versus society's demands. If their superegos become too strict and strong, the children may experience excessive guilt and resort to repression as a means of handling their fears. However, if they resolve their Oedipal difficulties, the youngsters gain the *ego strength of purpose*—the sense that they can control their own lives.

• *Latency*

Both Freud and Erikson called the fourth developmental stage that of *latency*. During these (typically) school years, the opposing tendencies are *competence* versus *failure* or, as Erikson put it, "industry versus inferiority." Children who do well in school and other activities

Erikson's sensory stage involves learning to trust others, especially parents.

Erikson's "industry versus inferiority" stage is the period when children learn to master skills and to perform competently on their own.

learn they can succeed. Therefore, they become industrious and gain the *ego strength of competence*. If the children do poorly, they experience failure and may develop a sense of inferiority.

• Puberty

At *puberty*, during what Freud called the genital stage, sexual interest returns and the individual must make what Freud called "the final adjustment," that of heterosexuality. Erikson sees the puberty crisis as that of either finding your *identity*, or of developing what he called *role confusion*. Erikson coined the term "identity crisis." At this age, you must decide what the future will hold and who you will become. If you are successful, you gain the *ego strength of fidelity*, or faithfulness to what you really are.

• Young Adulthood

Erikson postulated three final stages of maturation beyond the five Freud spoke of. The first of these stages, which occurs in young adulthood,

In early adulthood, individuals learn to make commitments to each other and achieve intimacy.

Erik H. Erikson

presents you with the crisis of *intimacy* versus *isolation*. According to Erikson, "Real Intimacy includes the capacity to commit yourself to relationships that may demand sacrifice and compromise. The *ego strength* of young adulthood is *love*—a mutual, mature devotion" (cited in Hall, 1983).

Erikson sees a great difference between "Intimacy" with a capital I and "intimacy," by which he means sexual activity. In a recent interview, he put it this way: "Some people today may fool themselves in their so-called recreational sexuality and actually feel quite isolated because they lack mutuality—real Intimacy. In extreme cases, you could have a highly active sex life and yet feel a terrible sense of isolation because you're never there as a person; you're never perceiving your partner as a person" (cited in Hall, 1983).

• Adulthood

One of Erikson's greatest contributions to personality theory has been his descriptions of what happens to people during their middle years. He sees the opposing tendencies here as being **generativity** and *stagnation*. Generativity is composed of three related activities—procreativity, productivity, and creativity.

As for procreativity, Erikson says, "I believe there is a procreative drive. There is an instinctual wish to have children, and it's important that we realize that" (cited in Hall, 1983). This urge, however, can be *sublimated* into productivity and creativity.

As for productivity, Erikson states that we have an innate desire to "take care of things. The Hindus call it the maintenance of the world" (cited in Hall, 1983). In part, this drive is a desire to make society better for one's children.

And as for creativity, it involves learning to accept the new rather than rigidly trying to maintain things as they were in the past. But creativity is also linked to procreativity because it often involves child-like (id-like) activities. Erikson says, "Einstein used the word 'wonder' to describe his experience as a child, and he was considered childlike by many people. And I think he claimed that he was able to formulate the theory of relativity because he kept asking the questions that children ask" (cited in Hall, 1983).

The *ego strength* the person gains at this stage is *care*.

• Maturity

Erikson's final stage is that of *maturity*. The opposing tendencies at this age are *integrity* and *despair*. Erikson defines integrity as "a sense of coherence and wholeness." He says further that "What is demanded [at this stage of life] could be simply called Integrality, a readiness to keep things together. The [ego] strength that grows out of resolving this final conflict is that of 'wisdom'" (cited in Hall, 1983).

In a sense, Erikson has extended the tendency for generativity to this age as well. However, as he notes, "Old people can no longer procreate, but they can be productive, and they can be creative." Even if they no longer must take care of their own children, they can "care for" other children. "I'm convinced that old people and children need one another and that there's an affinity between old age and childhood that, in fact, rounds out the life cycle. You know, old people often seem childlike, and it's important that we be permitted to revive some qualities that we had as children" (cited in Hall, 1983).

If older people remain active—and if they still relate directly to society—they can *integrate* all of life's experiences and thus bring integrity to their egos. However, if they fail to solve most of their earlier crises, they may succumb to feelings of despair at the futility of existence.

Erikson: An Evaluation

Erikson's ideas—like those of Freud—are not always easy to test experimentally. And, like Freud, Erikson is a "traditionalist" in most senses of that word. For example, David R. Matteson notes that Erikson's choice of *identity* as the central theme of adolescence has a "male bias" to it shared by most other Western personality theorists. "From my reading of the life span literature," Matteson says, "I believe our society has encouraged men to develop identity at the expense of intimacy and women the reverse. In mid-life, many women resume the task of developing mature identity, and many men reassess their priorities and finally develop interpersonal sensitivities." Matteson criticizes Erikson, therefore, because he (like Freud) pays little attention to the developmental pattern most women show (Matteson, 1984).

In a recent book, German psychologist Paul Baltes criticizes Erikson from a somewhat different point of view. According to Baltes, Erikson's theory is a "biological age-directed model." Human development is not "mapped out by the genes," Baltes says. Nor does development procede in clearly-defined stages. Rather, it is characterized by "reversibility and pluralism." You can always change, you are always affected by (and have an effect on) your enviroment, and there is no *one developmental pattern* that is best for all people (Baltes, 1982).

Right or wrong, Erikson's views have had a great impact on personality theory. And his emphasis on growth during the middle and later years is a signal addition to psychoanalytic theory.

We will mention Freud and Erikson again later in this chapter. First, let's turn our attention to "person-oriented theorists" other than the psychoanalysts. We will start by discussing two humanistic psychologists, Abraham Maslow and Carl Rogers. Then we will cover the various behavioral approaches, including social learning theory. As you will see, like Adler and Erikson, all these theorists tend to emphasize *conscious ego control, personal growth and psychological health*, and/or *the influence of the social environment*.

HUMANISTIC THEORIES OF PERSONALITY

Freud believed that our destinies lay in our genetic blueprints, and that the structures of our personalities were determined by the interaction between our social environments and our genes. This rather rigid view of the human personality was rejected by a group of theorists who call themselves **humanistic psychologists**. They believe that *you help shape your own destiny*.

Like many medical doctors, Freud tended to define "health" as *the lack of pathology*. The humanistic psychologists disagreed. As Abraham Maslow put it, "Health is not simply the absence of disease or even the opposite of it. Any theory of [personality] that is worthy of attention must deal with the highest capacities of the healthy and strong man as well as with the defensive maneuvers of crippled spirits" (Maslow, 1970).

To humanistic psychologists, *being healthy* means *being yourself*.

Abraham Maslow

Abraham Maslow was, like Erik Erikson, something of a "stranger in a strange land." In an interview late in his life, he stated that, as a child, "I was isolated and unhappy. I grew up in libraries and among books, without friends" (cited in Hall, 1968).

Neither of Maslow's parents were educated. He described his mother as "a pretty woman—but not a nice one." He felt she showed him little affection. He described his father as "a nice man," and as a "vigorous man, who loved whiskey and women and fighting" (cited in Wilson, 1972). However, early in his life, his parents lost interest in caring for their children. From that time on, Maslow was reared by one of his uncles.

● *Self-Confidence in Monkeys and Humans*
Maslow was Harry Harlow's first doctoral student (see Chapter 14). Since Harlow was just setting up his primate lab at the University of Wisconsin, Maslow experimented with monkeys. He soon concluded that one animal came to lord it over the others because of the animal's *dominance feelings*, not because of the

Erikson believes that older people and children need each other and can benefit from regular interaction.

monkey's physical size or strength (Monte, 1987).

Soon thereafter, Maslow began to study "dominance feelings" in humans (chiefly college students). He decided that "High dominance-feeling empirically involves good self-confidence, self-assurance, high evaluation of the self, feelings of general capability or superiority, and lack of shyness, timidity, self-consciousness or embarrassment" (Maslow, 1939).

● **Sexual Behavior of High-Dominance Women**

Somewhat later in his career, Maslow investigated the sexual feelings of women with high, middle, and low dominance. As part of this study, he asked women in each of these groups what kind of men they preferred, and what they considered to be the "ideal love-making situation."

Maslow reported that middle- and low-dominance women preferred men who were "adequate" rather than "superior"—men who loved children and who were kind, gentle, and faithful. High-dominance women, however, preferred a high-dominance man who was "highly masculine, self-confident, fairly aggressive, sure of what he wants and able to get it, and generally superior in most things" (Maslow, 1942).

As for "ideal love-making," Maslow reports, the high-dominance woman wanted it to be "straightforward, unsentimental, rather violent, animal, pagan, passionate, even sometimes brutal. . . . She wishes her favors to be taken, rather than asked for. In other words, she must be dominated, must be forced into subordinate status" (Maslow, 1942).

□ □ **QUESTION** □ □
What would today's "high-dominance feminist" probably say about Maslow's own sexual needs?

● **The Search for Perfection**

During his early life, Maslow felt insecure and even "inferior" to his professors. He saw them as being "angels," while he was a poor sinner. And he apparently projected onto his teachers those psychological perfections he feared he lacked. This early idealism apparently was destroyed, however, when one day he found himself standing at a urinal next to one of his professors: "It stunned me so that it took hours, even weeks, for me to assimilate the fact that a professor was a human being and constructed

with the plumbing that everybody else had" (cited in Wilson, 1972).

Maslow apparently overcame this early shock rather well. But as he continued his career, he deliberately sought out the "top people," the "self-actualizers," both in the academic world and in the realms of arts and politics. But, wisely, he now realized that they were "nearly perfect," and thus not quite "angels" (Monte, 1987).

Some of these individuals were his personal friends. Others—such as Lincoln, Einstein, Eleanor Roosevelt, and Beethoven—he studied through books, papers, and letters. Maslow assumed these individuals had achieved a high degree of self-fulfillment or they wouldn't have been so prominent and have demonstrated so much leadership. By determining the similarities among the members of this noted group, he arrived at the characteristics of a truly "self-actualized" person. A list of these characteristics appears in Table 16.2.

● **B-Values**

We described much of Maslow's developmental theory in Chapter 6. As we noted there, Maslow developed a "hierarchy of needs" that runs from basic (physical) needs through social and love needs to *self-actualization*. Late in his life, however, Maslow concluded that self-actualization was more complex than he originally had thought:

> It may turn out to be useful to add to the definition of the self-actualizing person, not only (a) that he be sufficiently free of illness, (b) that he be sufficiently gratified in his basic needs, and (c) that he be positively using his capacities, but also (d) that he be motivated by some values which he strives for or gropes for and to which he is loyal. (Maslow, 1971)

Self-actualized people, Maslow said, are motivated by the need to grow. That is, they develop "Being-needs" or "B-values." Among the 15 B-values Maslow listed are truth, goodness, beauty, uniqueness, perfection, simplicity, and playfulness.

● **Maslow: A Summary**

According to Maslow, the two major theories that shaped modern psychology are Freudian psychoanalysis and behaviorism. He believed that *humanistic psychology* took the best of both schools of thought and added something extra:

> If I had to condense [my theory] into a single sentence, I would have said that *in addition* to what the psychologists of the time had to say about human nature, man also [has] a higher nature. . . . And if I could have had a second sentence, I would have stressed the

TABLE 16.2   Abraham Maslow's Whole Characteristics of Self-Actualizing People

They have more efficient perceptions of reality and are more comfortable with it.

They accept themselves and their own natures almost without thinking about it.

Their behavior is marked by simplicity and naturalness and by lack of artificiality or straining for effect.

They focus on problems outside themselves; they are concerned with basic issues and eternal questions.

They like privacy and tend to be detached.

They have relative independence of their physical and social environments; they rely on their own development and continued growth.

They do not take blessings for granted, but appreciate again and again the basic pleasures of life.

They experience limitless horizons and the intensification of any unself-conscious experience often of a mystical type.

They have a deep feeling of kinship with others.

They develop deep ties with a few other self-actualizing individuals.

They are democratic in a deep sense; although not indiscriminate, they are not really aware of differences.

They are strongly ethical, with definite moral standards, though their attitudes are conventional; they relate to ends rather than means.

Their humor is real and related to philosophy, not hostility; they are spontaneous less often than others, and tend to be more serious and thoughful.

They are original and inventive, less constricted and fresher than others.

While they tend toward the conventional and exist well within the culture, they live by the laws of their own characters rather than those of society.

They experience imperfections and have ordinary feelings, like others.

Source: Condensed from "Self-Actualizing People: A Study of Psychological Health," in *Motivation and Personality,* 2nd ed., by Abraham H. Maslow, Copyright 1954 by Harper & Row, Publishers, Inc.: Copyright © 1970 by Abraham H. Maslow. By permission of the publishers.

profoundly holistic nature of human nature in contradiction to the analytic . . . approach of the behaviorists and of Freudian psychoanalysis. (Maslow, 1970)

We will have more to say about Maslow's contribution after we look at another major humanistic psychologist, Carl Rogers.

Carl Rogers

Carl Rogers was born in 1902 in Chicago to parents he described as being "highly practical, 'down to earth' individuals." They were also, perhaps unfortunately, "rather anti-intellectual, with some of the contempt of the practical person toward the long-haired egghead" (Rogers, 1967).

Rogers remembered both of his parents as being "extremely loving and 'masters' of the art of subtle control" (Monte, 1987). They were quite stringent in the way they reared their six children. And Rogers' mother, who was extremely religious, managed to convey to the youngsters the belief that they were in some way "elect," or "superior." She also taught them that there were certain things they were *not* to do: "Such was the unity of our family that it was understood by all that we did not dance, play cards, attend movies, smoke, drink, or show any sexual interest" (Rogers, 1967).

Much of Rogers' professional life can be seen as an attempt to help people *overcome external control* (no matter how subtle) and *become themselves* (Atwood & Tomkins, 1976).

• *Early Training*

Rogers began his collegiate training at the Union Theological Seminary in New York, hoping to become a minister. However, he soon broke not only with organized religion, but also with his family. He married his childhood sweetheart and enrolled at Columbia to study clinical psychology.

At that time, Columbia was something of a hotbed of behaviorism. However, while still in training, Rogers was granted an internship at the Institute for Child Guidance, where the staff was primarily Freudian in its orientation. Eventually he rejected both viewpoints and developed his own approach.

• *Client-centered Therapy*

We will discuss Rogers' approach to therapy more fully in the next chapter. However, some of his early experiences as a therapist helped shape his theory of personality.

For example, when (as a beginning therapist) he tried to apply Freudian techniques, he found they often "simply did not work." Nor did "trying to give the patient insight by direct questioning" seem particularly helpful. Indeed, it appeared that the *less direct* Rogers became, and the less he tried to manipulate the therapeutic situation, the more likely it was that his patients improved. Rogers soon concluded that "it is the *client* who knows what hurts, what directions to go, what problems are crucial, what experiences have been deeply buried." Rogers decided that traditional types of treatment were *therapist-centered*. His type of therapy was, instead, to be *client-centered*. And he wanted his clients to *experience* their feelings rather than merely *talk* about them (Rogers, 1961).

Shortly after obtaining his doctoral degree in clinical psychology, Rogers took a job as

Carl Rogers

head of the counseling center at the University of Chicago. Later he taught at Ohio State and at the University of Wisconsin. On retirement, he moved to California, where he continued to write for many years. He died in 1987. Prior to his death, however, he was considered the "reigning king of the humanistic psychologists."

● The Phenomenal World

Rogers believed you were born with no self-concept, and no self. But Rogers held that you did have an innate urge to *become* a fully-fuctioning and actualized person.

At birth, all you had was a confusing set of sensory impressions, biological processes, and motor activities. Rogers put it this way: "Every individual exists in a continually changing world of experience of which he is the center." Rogers called this the **phenomenal world**, which is *reality as you experience it* (Rogers, 1959).

During your early childhood, Rogers said, you slowly learned to *differentiate* your "self" from other parts of your phenomenal world. As you did so, you learned to see yourself as "I" or "me." Eventually, you came to realize you are an "independent self" capable of acting on your own (Rogers, 1951).

● Self-structure

According to Carl Rogers, you developed your self-concept through your interactions with others, by *evaluating* the way that others treated you. In particular, you evaluated positive and negative feedback from your parents and *incorporated* that feedback into your *self-structure*.

As an infant, why would you do something your parents perceive as "bad"? Because, Rogers says, it is part of you, part of your self structure, part of the way *you* perceive reality. When your parents punish you for this act, however, you face a difficult problem. You want to maintain your parents' love, so you must change the behavior itself. But you may also be tempted to change your *perception* of the behavior too. That is, you may decide that the part of you that initiated the punished behavior *isn't really you*. And so you may reject part of your self-structure by blocking it off from consciousness.

Rogers explained the situation this way: "The accurate symbolization would be: 'I perceive my parents as experiencing this behavior as unsatisfying to them.' The distorted symboli-

zation, distorted to preserve the threatened concept of self, is: '*I perceive this behavior as unsatisfying*.'" He calls this, "experiencing reality secondhand" (Rogers, 1951).

Put in simpler terms, Rogers said that, in order to maintain your parents' love, you may *become someone you aren't*. What you *really* want to be is still part of your self, but it is now part of your unconscious mind. According to Rogers, client-centered therapy allows patients to bring this repressed material to consciousness. Once they have done so, they can reject "external influences" and get on with the task of "becoming what they really are."

□□ **QUESTION** □□
What similarities—and differences—do you see between Rogers' explanation of the development of the "self-structure" and Freud's description of how the superego is formed?

● Unconditional Positive Regard

A key concept in Rogerian client-centered therapy is **unconditional positive regard**. By this term, Rogers meant that the therapist must accept the patient as she or he is, as being a *genuine person* with his or her own set of values and goals.

Rogers believed that parents should give their children the same "unconditional positive regard." To accomplish this goal, he said, the parents should do three important things:

1. Learn to accept the child's own feelings and goals.
2. Learn to accept their own feelings about what the child does without trying to force their values on the child.
3. Find ways to let the child know they accept the child as a person.

Children whose parents treat them with "unconditional positive regard" eventually learn to treat *themselves* in the same fashion. Put more simply, Rogers said that before you can accept yourself, you must first see that others respect you for what you are.

When you can accept yourself completely, you become what Rogers calls a *fully-functioning individual*. You are open to all experience, and you do not suppress knowledge of anything that is a real part of you. You are aware of both your faults and your virtues, but you have a high positive regard for yourself. And most of all, you maintain happy and humane relationships with others (Rogers, 1951).

□□ **QUESTION** □□
In what ways does Rogers' theory of emotional and cognitive development in the child appear to be a reaction to the way his own parents reared him?

Humanistic Psychology: An Evaluation

Neither Rogers nor Maslow offered a full-fledged "theory of personality development," as did both Freud and Erikson. We discussed the pros and cons of Maslow's hierarchy of needs in Chapter 6. His explanation of motivational development appeals to many people because of its simplicity and because of its emphasis on personal choice. However, there is little in the way of experimental data to support his views, and his hierarchy of needs is subject to all the criticisms raised against Piaget's and Freud's "stage theories."

The major strengths of the humanistic approach appear to be twofold: (1) its emphasis on health rather than on sickness, and (2) its belief that people actively participate in shaping their personalities. The major weaknesses seem to be a de-emphasis on behavior and objective measurement, and a failure to explain in *precise terms* how personality is formed.

At the same time that Maslow and Rogers were developing the holistic approach they called "humanistic psychology," Stanford psychologist Albert Bandura was beginning to "shape" B.F. Skinner's notions on operant conditioning into what is now called *social learning theory* (Bandura, 1986a). Thus, of the three major "person-oriented" approaches to personality theory, the social learning viewpoint was the last to develop. We discussed the early history of social learning theory in Chapter 10, and we will describe Bandura's ideas in some detail in Chapter 21. Let's conclude this chapter, however, by looking briefly at what social learning theory is, and how it differs from psychoanalysis and humanistic psychology.

SOCIAL LEARNING THEORY

In a sense, social learning theory is an interesting mixture of Piaget, Adler, and Skinner. Social learning theorists tend to emphasize cognitions rather than observable behaviors, as did Piaget. Social learning theorists believe that much of what you become is determined by your interactions with your environment, as did Adler. And social learning theorists believe learning is the key to understanding personality, as does B.F. Skinner.

However, social learning theorists differ from earlier theorists in many ways. For example, Piaget believed that "mental structures" were determined primarily by the genes, but the social learning theorists see cognitive processes as being "shaped" the same way that Skinner says behavior is "shaped." Skinner says you learn because your actions are *directly* rewarded or punished. The social learning theorists agree with this point of view, but add something unique—the concept of **observational learning**.

Observational Learning

Skinner believes that you learned to act as you do because certain of your responses were *directly reinforced*. The social learning theorists agree that direct reinforcement does work, particularly with children. But they say that you also learn by *observing the consequences of other people's actions*. You can then *imitate* those behaviors that yield rewards, and avoid those actions that bring unpleasant results. Since *learning by observation* takes place "in your mind," it is far too *cognitive* a concept to fit readily within the "pure" behavioral theory of B.F. Skinner (Bussey & Bandura, 1984).

According to Bandura, first you *observe* someone else attaining a particular goal, then you *rehearse* the behaviors involved in achieving that goal. The "motor rehearsal" helps you create a more accurate *cognitive representation* of the skill, and the more accurate this "cognitive representation" becomes, the better you can reproduce the observed behavior in real life (Carroll & Bandura, 1985).

• *Two Stages of Personality Development*

According to Bandura, personality development tends to occur in two broad stages. When you were very young, your parents and the rest of your social environment shaped your behaviors the way that Skinner says pigeons are shaped to perform behavioral tricks. That is the first, or "passive," stage of development. The second, or "interactive," stage grows out of the first. For, as you *behaved*, you were also creating *cognitive structures* in your mind much as Piaget claimed was the case. These cognitions do at least two things for you:

First, they allow you to observe and evaluate the actions of others, and to change your own behaviors consciously.

Second, your cognitions allow you to *reshape your own environment*.

As your external world changes, you respond to it differently. Thus, to the social learning theorist, the person-environment interaction is a continual process of *complementary shaping*. Bandura refers to this process as **reciprocal determinism** (Bandura, 1984).

• *Self-efficacy*

Adler believed that development was driven by such motives as the inferiority complex and the need to cooperate with others. Both Maslow and Rogers thought that you had an innate drive to become a fully-functioning person. However, according to Bandura, much of development is determined by the need for a feeling of "self-efficacy."

By "self-efficacy," Bandura means your own perception of how well you can cope with the situations you face in life (Bandura, 1986b). People with high perceived self-efficacy in any

Observational learning. The belief by Bandura and other social learning theorists that you take on many behaviors by observing others and then imitating them in order to get the same environmental consequences that the others have gotten. Bandura typically refers to this as "modeling" your behaviors after those of other people.

Reciprocal determinism (ree-SIP-pro-cal dee-TURR-min-ism). Bandura's belief that psychological processes are a joint function of behavioral, cognitive, and environmental influences. According to Bandura, you build up schemas (behavioral standards, or perceptions) that allow you to evaluate both social inputs and your own reactions to those inputs. Your evaluations affect both your attitudes and your behaviors. And because you monitor the consequences of having a given attitude or acting a certain way, your attitudes and behaviors can affect your future evaluations. Thus, each part of the process—behavior, attitudes and cognitions, and environmental inputs—affects every other part in a reciprocal manner.

situation, Bandura says, tend to be more highly motivated to succeed. Their desire to "meet their own standards" causes them to *monitor* their performance carefully in any given situation.

• Self-evaluation and Personal Agency

Why do you monitor your actions? According to Bandura, you do so because of your need to *maintain control*. But it is not only your own internal processes that you must influence (self-control)—you also strive to find ways to "shape" your environment, as well. This "desire to establish personal control over things" is what Bandura refers to as the sense of *personal agency* (Bandura & Cervone, 1983).

In a sense, what Bandura has done is to translate Skinner's notions on "shaping" the behavior of *others* into a scheme for *self-shaping* in various social situations. But this "self-shaping" involves changing your own *cognitions* as well as changing your *behavioral outputs*.

Because social learning theory grew out of experimental psychology, Bandura has tested his theory *in the laboratory* more than most other personality theorists have. As we noted, Bandura believes that high perceived self-efficacy is correlated with high motivation. In a recent paper, Bandura and his colleagues at Stanford measured "perceived self-efficacy to withstand pain" in subjects, and then taught the subjects the cognitive methods of pain control we discussed in Chapter 13. Bandura and his associates report that the higher the subject's perceived self-efficacy, the more pain the subject could actually withstand (Bandura *et al.*, 1987.

Because many of Bandura's concepts (and terms) come from social psychology, we will delay further description of his theory to Chapter 21.

• Social Learning Theory: An Evaluation

There are many strengths to social learning theory. To begin with, it is somewhat more holistic in its approach to describing personality

development than are the others. And because it sprang from behavioral learning theory, social learning theory is also more firmly grounded on empirical evidence. Unlike Skinner, however, Bandura accepts the importance of "conscious thought" and "cognitive representations of the outer world" as important determinants of human behavior. And also unlike Skinner, Bandura describes methods of "shaping" these cognitive processes.

On the negative side, Bandura's approach places far more emphasis on *social* than on *biological* influences so far as personality development is concerned. Thus, it is not quite the "full-fledged" holistic theory that perhaps some day it will become. And, as yet, Bandura has not given us the sort of detailed picture of how personal growth occurs "from cradle to grave" that can be found in either Freud or Erikson.

Now that we have discussed the three major types of "person-oriented" personality theories—the Freudian, the humanistic, and social learning theory—let's close by looking at what the most recent trends in this fascinating field are. As you will see, the general trend is a movement away from Freud toward the social learning theory position.

RECENT TRENDS IN PERSONALITY THEORY

If you look back over this chapter, certain "developmental trends" in personality theory become apparent.

1. A shift from the "naturist" position of Freud and Piaget to the "nurturist" position of Skinner to the "interactionist" view of the social learning theorists.
2. A movement away from Freud's and Skinner's view of the organism as a "passive reactor" toward the humanistic and social learning position that you are an "active participant" in the shaping of your own personality.
3. A trend away from Freud's emphasis on emotions, and an increasing emphasis on cognitive processes.
4. A shift from Freud's emphasis on unconscious processes toward a belief that conscious processes are the important elements in personality.
5. A decreased interest in "developmental stages," and a growing belief that the pattern of personality development is shaped by a *continuous interplay* between you and your social environment.
6. A movement away from Freud's belief that the personality structure was fixed at age 15 toward the belief that you continue to grow and mature all your life.

Someday, perhaps, we will have a master theory that tells us everything about the human personality that we want to know—one that is *holistic* enough to give us "deep understanding" of ourselves as well as the power to shape our personal development. But both understanding and shaping imply that we can somehow measure what it is we are trying to comprehend and change. So it is to the *measurement* of human personality by *trait-oriented* personality theorists that we must now turn our attention.

SUMMARY

1. The study of **personality** is concerned with identifying the distinctive patterns of thought, behavior, and experience which characterize the individual's unique **adjustment** to his or her life situation.

2. There are two major approaches to the study of personality theory. **Person-oriented approaches** tend to be narrative, holistic, case-history accounts of the development of single individuals. **Trait-oriented approaches** tend to focus on scientific data describing *patterns of traits* across individuals.

3. In a sense, psychoanalytic theory began when Freud and Breuer developed **catharsis**, a means of releasing repressed **psychic energy**, or **libido**.

4. Freud modified his views several times. In his **topographical** theory, he divided the mind into three regions: the **unconscious**, the **preconscious**, and the **conscious**.

5. The **unconscious** contains the instincts, the libido, and repressed memories of infancy. It is ruled by the **pleasure principle**, and engages in **primary process thinking**.

6. The **preconscious** contains the **censor**, obeys the **reality principle**, and engages in **secondary process thinking**.

7. According to Freud, the **instincts** have four major characteristics: pressure, aim, object, and source. **Eros** is the pleasure instinct, located in the id, and the life maintenance instincts, located in the ego. **Thanatos** is the death instinct that expresses itself in aggression and hatred.

8. In his **structural model of the mind**, Freud created three new agencies, the **id**, the **ego**, and the **superego**.

9. The **id** is located in the **unconscious**, and is the most primitive portion of the personality.

10. The **ego** splits off from the id in order to protect the organism by finding realistic ways of satisfying the id's demands for immediate gratification of its needs.

11. The **superego** is created as the Oedipal/Electral complex is terminated and contains both parental and societal values and ethics.

12. Freud's early theory of **psychosexual development** describes how **libido is organized** or expressed during several developmental stages.

13. During the **oral stage**, libido is expressed through the mouth, while during the **anal stage**, libido is released through the anus. At the **phallic stage**, the libido becomes organized around genital stimulation. Libido is repressed during the **latency period**, but reasserts itself in heterosexual activities during the **genital stage**.

14. Freud believed boys give up their early attachment to the mother in different ways than do girls. The boy experiences the **Oedipus complex**, in which he fears the father will castrate him. He resolves the complex by taking on the father's values. The girl experiences the **Electra complex**, in which she slowly takes on the mother's values in order to appeal to the father.

15. Anna Freud used psychoanalytic therapy with children and studied the **defense mechanisms** used by the ego. These mechanisms include **repression, denial, projection, displacement, reaction formation, introjection, identification, regression, sublimation**, and several others.

16. Carl Jung believed that a feeling for **religious values** rather than *infantile sexuality* was the major force in human development. He developed an early **word association test** that seemed to support Freud's position, but soon split with Freud and developed his own theory, **analytical psychology**.

17. Jung believed that people undergo the process of **individuation**, during which they build up their **self-schemas**.

18. Jung divided the unconscious into two regions: the **personal unconscious** that contains past memories and plans for the future, and the **collective unconscious**, which contains the **archetypes**, or inherited tendencies to respond in certain ways to personal and environmental crises.

19. Jung believed everyone is born with two innate, opposing attitudes: **introversion**, which leads us to look inward, and **extroversion**, which leads us to look outward. One attitude usually dominates, but the other is always present.

20. Alfred Adler broke with Freud before Jung did, and formed the **Society for Individual Psychology**. He emphasized **social values** rather than infantile sexuality.

21. Adler believed children acquire an **inferior-

ity complex when they discover adults have superior strength. They **compensate** by trying to move from a **felt minus** to a **felt plus**, that is, by becoming superior to what they were in the past.

22. Adler said each person develops a **style of life** which is the self-consistent, goal-oriented core of personality and which continues to change over the entire life span.

23. Erikson extended Freudian theory to the later years by **emphasizing the ego**, and by postulating **eight psychosocial stages**. There are **opposing tendencies** at each stage. Development of the ego is determined by how the person resolves the **crisis** associated with each stage.

24. The **humanistic psychologists** emphasize health rather than pathology, active rather than passive participation in your own development, and the need to **be yourself** rather than what others wish you to be.

25. Abraham Maslow created a **hierarchy of needs** from his study of **self-actualized individuals**. Self-actualized people continue to grow by developing **Being-needs** or **B-values** such as the need for truth, goodness, beauty, and perfection.

26. Carl Rogers believed you exist in a **phenomenal world** which is reality as you experience it. Early development involves learning to differentiate your **self** from other parts of the phenomenal world.

27. Rogers urged parents to give their children **unconditional positive regard** by accepting the children as they are rather than trying to force the children to become what the parents want.

28. **Behaviorists** such as B.F. Skinner believe that personality is entirely **learned** by direct experience with the **external environment**.

29. **Social learning theorists** such as Albert Bandura believe behavior is learned but is mediated by **cognitive processes**. Personality development is thus the study of how people use **social models** and **observational learning** to **construct reality** in their minds.

30. According to Bandura, people have a need to establish control over themselves and their environments, which Bandura refers to as a sense of **personal agency**.

31. Bandura believes that **perceived self-efficacy** motivates people to monitor their own cognitions and behaviors as they attempt to change themselves and their environments, an interactive process Bandura calls **reciprocal determinism**.

32. Recent trends in personality theory include the realization that **development continues throughout the entire life span**.

33. All types of personality theories have contributed to our ability to understand and predict human experience, but no theory is complete in itself.

(Continued from page 405.)

Mr. Reginal Shorttail, Prop.
Exotic Pets, Inc.
1400 Timur Lane
New Samarkand

Dear Mr. Shorttail:

A week ago, my husband, my son, and I visited your store in order to purchase a pet for my son. To my deep regret, I let you foist a pair of humanoids off on us. You assured me that learning to care for these primitive animals would help my son acquire *responsibility*, and we were foolish enough to believe you.

We kept the humanoids in the bathing room, and only let our son play with them when he responded suitably to his toilet-training regimen. And, for the first few days, all seemed to go well. Yesterday, though, after I had placed our son on the training container and put the cages within his grasp, I was called from the room momentarily. When I returned, I found to my extreme horror that he had opened the cages and put the two humanoids together! Needless to say, they wasted no time in, how shall I say it, *clinging* to each other! What an absolutely disgusting sight! Needless to say, I flung the humanoids into the toilet and flushed them out of sight.

Now, I am certainly no prude, and I realize that humanoids lack shame. But surely you must realize that witnessing this primal scene at such an early age could leave psychological scars from which my son might never fully recover. I will be talking to our lawyer about this matter next week, and it may well be that you will be hearing from us thereafter.

Meanwhile, the very least you can do is to refund the purchase price of the humanoids.

Sincerely,

(Mrs.) Gayye Torre

Personality Theories: Traits, Temperaments, and Psychological Tests

"Measure for Measure"

C · H · A · P · T · E · R ·
17

"What is this 'Late Bloomer' test of yours, Mr. Flagg? I don't think I've ever heard of it," Jessie Williams said quietly. Tom Flagg had an athlete's physique, a handsome dark-brown face, and a ready smile. But Jessie had learned the hard way that she couldn't always tell the shape of a man's intentions from the shape of his physique. So she was wary of this young graduate student who had just walked into her fourth-grade school room. But she was also quite taken by his appearance.

"The 'Late Bloomer' test was devised by Professor Rosenthal at Harvard," Tom Flagg replied, hoping (for several reasons) to overcome the good-looking, young black woman's obvious distrust. "You've been teaching fourth grade for several years, haven't you, Miss Williams?"

"Three years, Mr. Flagg. Exactly three years."

Tom grinned at the woman's precise way of expressing herself. "Well, maybe you've had a kid who seemed real dumb the first few months or so of school. Then, all of a sudden, the kid just took off and bloomed. Like a flower you'd forgotten to water until just then."

"I water all my flowers regularly, Mr. Flagg," Jessie replied. "I don't neglect any of them. Black or white, red or yellow—I hope they all bloom for me as much as they can."

Tom nodded appreciatively. If it wouldn't have prejudiced the results of his experiment, he would have tried to date her. He pulled himself together and resumed the conversation. "Mr. Washington, your principal, told me you were one of the best teachers he's ever seen. So I'm sure all your kids do learn a lot. But aren't you occasionally surprised when one of them does a lot better than you had expected?"

Jessie Williams shook her head. "I expect great things of them all. Maybe that's why I'm not surprised when they do well."

"Okay," said Tom, "I guess my test won't help you any. But maybe you can help *me* by letting me give it to your class anyhow. If I don't get to try out the test in enough classrooms, I won't get a good grade on my project back at the university. Even if you don't need the information, I do."

To his surprise, Jessie smiled broadly. "Well, why didn't you say so, friend? I'm always happy to help one of us get ahead. Tell me about these 'Late Bloomers' of Professor Rosenthal's."

"Well, it's really your bloomers I'm interested in," Tom said, and then blushed furiously as he realized what he had said. "I mean, it's a test devised by Professor Rosenthal and his associates at Harvard. They think they've found a way of telling in advance when a school kid is going to show a sudden spurt in intellectual achievement. Rosenthal says the test can also tell when a kid is going to backslide or tread water for a while. The change usually shows up in the kid's grades, although sometimes the IQ blossoms or backslides too."

"Some of our education books say that a child's intelligence is fixed at birth. Don't you believe that's so, Tom?" Jessie asked, a malicious twinkle in her eye.

Tom looked startled. "Well, I suppose that the limits to a person's mind are determined by the genes. But the rate at which people develop intellectually sure varies a lot. And the IQ that you get depends as much on which test you take, who gives it, and how you feel when you take it as it does on how bright you really are. Have you even given any of your kids intelligence tests?"

"No, Tom. I'm not qualified to do that. I give achievement tests, but the school counselor tests their intelligence."

"But aren't you sometimes surprised at the scores the counselor reports on your kids?"

Jessie Williams smiled slyly. "I just don't pay them any mind."

"What do you do when the parents want to know what the kid's IQ is?"

"I tell them the story of my life, Tom," she said. "I was born in Mississippi, where my father was a tenant farmer. We moved north when I was 6. My first year in school they gave me a test and said my IQ was 87. As you know, that's what you might call 'dull normal'. You don't learn very much about the world on a tenant farm in the back woods of Mississippi. But I loved school, and I had good teachers, and when I was in the seventh grade, I took another test. This time I got a score of 98. The counselor couldn't understand the change. So he gave me a different test, and I scored 104. He asked me what I wanted to do, and I said go to college and learn how to teach. He told me to forget it, that I'd never make it."

"But you did," Tom said, smiling to reassure her.

"Yes, I did," she said, a strong tone of confidence in her voice. "In high school they gave me another test. This time I tried very hard to impress the woman giving me the test, and I got a score of 111."

"The 'halo effect,' probably," Tom responded. "Good-looking, eager children always score a little higher than uglies do because the tester gives them the benefit of the doubt. And I suspect you were very good-looking indeed."

"You needn't flatter me, friend. I've already agreed to help you with your study. Anyway, the counselor said I might just get through college if I worked very hard, although you're supposed to have an IQ of 120 to graduate."

"So you went to the university and got your degree anyhow?"

"No, Tom, it wasn't that easy. My high school grades were excellent but I didn't score too well on the college entrance examination. The university didn't want me. So I went to a community college for two years. I got all A's, and the university finally let me in. My last year there, I

17 / Personality Theories

433

took another IQ test. This time I got a score of 122." She paused for a moment, then laughed. "But, of course, by then I knew the kinds of answers they wanted on the test."

Tom shook his head in amazement. His route to the university had been quite different. "And that's why you don't tell the parents what their kids' IQ scores are?"

"Right on. Now suppose you tell me what your study is all about."

"Okay," he said. "I'll give the Rosenthal 'Late Bloomer' test to all the kids in your room. When I've scored the results, I'll tell you which kids are supposed to 'bloom,' and which kids are supposed to backslide. Then, six months from now, I'll come back and see if that's what really happened."

A suspicious look crept into Jessie's eyes. "Why are you doing this, Tom? Doesn't sound much like an experiment to me."

"Rosenthal validated the test mostly in white classrooms. I want to see if it predicts for integrated classes as well."

"And you'll come back in six months to see what happened?"

Tom Flagg squared his shoulders a bit. "Well, your class is so important to me, I might just drop around a little more often than that—just to see how things are going."

She favored him with a broad grin. "You do that, Thomas. You do that very thing."

(Continued on page 456.)

TRAIT-ORIENTED THEORIES

At the beginning of the last chapter, we noted that there are two major approaches to the study of personality—*person-oriented* and *trait-oriented* theories.

Generally speaking person-oriented theorists are interested in explaining the *process* by which your personality "grew and developed." That is, they tend to see your personality as a "functioning whole" that started out simple and matured over time into a complex system. In this regard, person-oriented theorists are much like those biologists who study the development of an organism as it grows from a single cell into a complicated adult.

Trait-oriented theorists, however, typically are more interested in the *structure* of your personality. Indeed, they are often called *structural theorists*. Put another way, these theorists often focus on the basic elements of personality—the **traits** or **dispositions**—that are common to all people. In this regard, trait-oriented theorists are much like those biologists who study the anatomy of adult organisms. For instance, your body has a limited number of organs—one heart, one liver, two kidneys, and so forth. If we know something about the make-up of each of these organs—and how they interact with each other—we can explain a great deal about how and why your body functions as it does. In similar fashion, if we knew the basic *structures* that make up your personality—and how these structures interact with each other—couldn't we explain most of what you think and feel and do?

We discussed person-oriented theories in the last chapter. Now it's time to see what the trait-oriented (or structural) theorists have to offer in the way of understanding human behavior. As you will see, this discussion will ultimately lead us into a description of how psychologists *measure* individual differences.

Temperaments and Traits

What are the basic structures of your personality? As you might guess from having read the previous chapter, there is little agreement as to what the important elements of personality actually are. The two major approaches, however, seem to be the study of *temperaments* and *traits*.

In the *Encyclopedia of Human Behavior*, R.M. Goldenson defines *temperament* as "A general term for emotional make-up, including characteristic energy level, moods and mood changes, intensity and tempo of reactions to people and situations" (Goldenson, 1970). If you believe that "moods," "emotions," and "reactivity" are the basic structures of human personality, then probably you lean toward the "temperament" position.

More likely, you may perceive the human personality as a "collection of traits." That is, you might tend to describe people in terms of their characteristic ways of *thinking about* or *responding to* rather specific situations. *Webster's New Collegiate Dictionary* defines a *trait* as "a distinguishing quality (as of personal character); a peculiarity; an inherited characteristic." Aren't some people honest, while others (perhaps for their own "peculiar reasons") tend to lie and cheat a lot? Don't some individuals strike you as being *innately* warm, enthusiastic, and accepting—while others seem cold, aloof, and critical? If you talk about people in these terms, you probably qualify as a "trait theorist."

In actual fact, what one psychologist calls a "trait," another may call a "temperamental tendency." Thus, it sometimes is difficult to differentiate between temperament and trait. However, these terms are widely used in the scientific literature. And *properly* used, they do refer to somewhat different concepts.

Of these two "structural" approaches to describing personality, the study of tempera-

17 / Personality Theories

ments is probably the oldest. However, trait descriptions have been around for almost as long a time. Suppose we begin our study of structural theories, then, by looking briefly at some of the older approaches. Then we will discuss trait theory in some detail. For of the three, the identification and measure of human traits is surely the dominant structural approach today.

Galen's "Four Temperaments"

Galen was one of the greatest medical doctors the world has known. Although he was born and educated in Greece a century or so after the death of Christ, Galen spent much of his adult life practicing medicine in Rome. His studies of the functioning of human and animal bodies were so excellent that he is often considered the father of modern physiology.

One of Galen's main interests was the various glands in the human body, and the chemicals these glands secreted. Like most other physicians 2,000 years ago, Galen called these glandular secretions the **humors** of the body. Galen stated that four of these humors were mainly responsible for creating four different types of *temperaments*. Galen believed that these "four temperaments" were the basic structures of the human personality.

As far as Galen was concerned, blood was a "humor." If a woman was most influenced by her blood, Galen called her a **sanguine**, or "bloody," person. People with sanguine temperaments were supposed to be cheerful, hearty, outgoing, sturdy, fearless, optimistic, and interested in physical pleasures.

The second humor was *phlegm*, the thick, white material that you sometimes cough up when you have a cold. From Galen's point of view, phelgm was cold, moist, and unmoving. If your bodily processes were dominated by too much production of phlegm, you had a **phlegmatic** temperament. That is, you were cold, aloof, unemotional, uninvolved, dependable, and perhaps just a trifle dull.

Galen believed that the human liver produced two different "humors"—yellow bile and black bile. He called the yellow bile *choler*, because it supposedly caused the disease we now refer to as "cholera." The **choleric** temperament was one easily given to anger, hate, and fits of temper—someone who gave in to most of his or her bad impulses.

Black bile was even worse, for it symbolized death in Galen's mind. If your personality was dominated by black bile, you had a **melancholic** temperament. That is, you were always depressed, unhappy, suicidal.

Each of Galen's four "temperaments" is really little more than a *collection of associated traits*. Galen assumed, obviously, that the biochemical "humor" that predominated in your body *caused* this collection of traits to dominate your personality.

Modern Research on Temperament

The study of human temperament was, for many years, rather a neglected field within American psychology. It has, however, surfaced again in recent years, and for rather an interesting reason.

In previous chapters we have, on several occasions, mentioned the "continuity-discontinuity" problem. Continuity theorists, in their search for "enduring traits," often came up empty handed. For research soon suggested there was little or no correlation between measures of intelligence (and other cognitive processes) in infants and the same measures taken when the children were several years old. The **behavioral geneticists**, looking for aspects of early behavior that were clearly determined by the genes, faced the same problem. Fairly recently, both groups of scientists have begun to focus on *temperament* as being worthy of their study.

Put more simply, many continuity-oriented personality theorists have turned away from the study of cognitive processes toward the study of long-term *emotional dispositions*.

• The Temperament Theory of Personality Development

In a recent book, psychologists Arnold Buss and Robert Plomin discuss their own "temperament theory of personality development." They believe that temperament is made up of three major traits: emotionality, activity, and sociability. It is the *interaction* of these three main traits that determines how each individual reacts to her/his environment (Buss & Plomin, 1984).

Galen

Some people show *animated* activity patterns, Buss and Plomin say, while others are more *lethargic*. Buss describes the "animated" activity pattern as follows:

> Animated people walk briskly, tend to dash for the elevator, and sit and rise quickly. Their handshakes are vigorous, and they wave suddenly and rapidly. When signalling agreement, their heads bob up and down; when signalling disagreement, their heads rotate like a top. . . . Animated people speak rapidly, hardly pausing for breath, and the pace may be staccato. (Buss, 1986)

Buss and Plomin believe that, for the most part, the three traits of *emotionality, activity*, and *sociability* are genetically determined (Buss & Plomin, 1984). Some evidence to support their view comes from work by Jerome Kagan. As we noted in Chapter 14, Kagan says that traits such as "boldness" and "shyness" tend to show up in infants and endure at least until age three or four (Kagan, 1987; Kagan, Reznick, & Snidman, 1988). However, by far the most fascinating data on the "endurability" of human temperament come from the study of twins who have been reared in quite different circumstances.

□□ **QUESTION** □□

Who would be more likely to believe that personality characteristics are *inherited*, a biologist or a psychologist? Why?

● *The Minnesota Twin Studies*

In 1979, University of Minnesota psychologist Thomas Bouchard, Jr., began a long-term study of twins who were reared apart from each other since very early in life. So far, Bouchard and his group have discovered 77 sets of twins and 4 sets of triplets who were separated at birth. The Minnesota group has also studied several hundred sets of twins who have been reared together. The group's main research focus is discovering what aspects of the personality are determined primarily by genetic factors (Bouchard, 1983: McGue *et al.*, 1984).

One member of the Minnesota group is psychologist David Lykken. In a recent interview, he noted that many of the twins reared apart are surprisingly similar in terms of their personality traits. For instance, consider a set of identical twins named Jerry Levey and Mark Newman who were separated at birth and put up for adoption. When the men finally met, they were about 30 years old. Aside from a slight difference in weight, they looked identical. They had the same sort of mustache and sideburns, and they wore the same type of glasses. Both were captains of volunteer fire-fighting groups. Both men drank only Budweiser, and held the beer bottle in the same rather

Identical twins Mark Newman and Jerry Levey were separated at birth and reunited at the age of 32. They found they are both firefighters and have many other things in common.

odd way when drinking. Both were bachelors, compulsive flirts, and both were loudly good-humored. At their first meeting, both men found that their tendency to make "the same remarks at the same time and using the same gestures" was "spooky" (cited in Rosen, 1987).

Lykken describes another set of twins studied by the Minnesota group as follows:

> Despite growing up in opposite socioeconomic circumstances, [Daphne and Barbara] both were penny-pinchers. And both were stingy not just with their money but also with their opinions. . . . Both had suffered miscarriages during their first marriage but went on to have three healthy children. The women shared a fear of heights. Shortly after meeting for the first time, they began finishing each other's sentences and answering questions in unison. (cited in Rosen, 1987)

David Lykken points out that, despite the amazing similarities in the temperaments of some identical twins reared apart, other twins are fairly dissimilar. "Genes do not fashion IQ or personality, they make proteins. And those proteins are many biochemical steps removed from the complex traits and abilities we see in a person. . . . Subsequent experience can sometimes overcome nature" (cited in Rosen, 1987; Lykken, 1985). Lykken believes that temperament is *inherited*, but learning can "reshape" these basic tendencies. As we will see, not all psychologists agree with him.

One theorist who does support Lykken's views is British psychologist Hans J. Eysenck, whose *typological theory* is a modern version of Galen's "four temperaments."

Hans Eysenck

EYSENCK'S BIOLOGICAL TYPOGRAPHY

Hans Eysenck's first job after taking his doctorate in experimental psychology was at a British mental hospital. When Eysenck suggested performing a study to see if the treatment the patients were given was *actually effective,* his superiors threatened to fire him. This experience obviously "soured" him against the practice of psychotherapy, and since that time he has seldom passed up a chance to criticize psychoanalysts and other therapists.

For example, in his book *Psychology Is about People*, Eysenck writes that

> Most people of course, whatever they may say, do not in fact want a scientific account of human nature and personality at all. . . . They much prefer the great story-teller, S. Freud, or the brilliant myth-creator, C.G. Jung, to those who, like Cattell or Guilford, expect them to learn matrix algebra, study physiological details of the nervous system, and actually carry out experiments rather than rely on interesting anecdotes, sex-ridden case histories, and ingenious speculation. (Eysenck, 1972)

We will discuss Cattell and Guilford later in this chapter. For the moment, we might note that, despite Eysenck's protests against psychoanalysis, he was strongly influenced by Jung's ideas on *introversion* and *extroversion*.

□□ **QUESTION** □□
Would *you* be willing to spend years studying matrix algebra and neurophysiology in order to understand people *fully*?

Neuroticism and Introversion-Extroversion

In one of his earliest studies, Eysenck asked psychiatrists to evaluate the personal histories and "mental functioning" of 700 hospitalized patients. He then performed a **factor analysis** on the data. From this statistical analysis, Eysenck determined that most of the patients could be placed on two *bi-polar scales*. Each of these scales represented, really, a *cluster of related traits* (Eysenck, 1947).

- *Neuroticism*

The first of Eysenck's two personality scales runs from "Normal" at one end to "Neurotic"

at the other. Those patients who scored at the "Normal" end of the scale seemed to have fairly well-organized personalities, stayed out of trouble, and had good muscle tone. Those patients who scored at the "Neurotic" end of the scale, however, seemed to have disorganized personalities, had problems adjusting, and had poor muscle tone.

Drawing on Pavlov's experiments with dogs (see Chapter 9) and various other sources in the experimental literature, Eysenck decided that "neurotics" are highly emotional people who have (in his terms) *strong nervous systems*. By "strong," however, Eysenck means that these people can tolerate high levels of external stimulation. However, Eysenck says, they are relatively *insensitive* to subtle changes in their environments. Put another way, neurotics tend to have *high sensory thresholds* (see Chapter 12). In Eysenck's view, neurotics tend to *seek out* the stimulation associated with emotionally-charged situations because they simply *cannot detect weak inputs*.

"Normals," on the other hand, are people who are relatively unemotional. In Eysenck's terms, normals have *weak nervous systems*. Put another way, "normals" tend to have *low sensory thresholds*. They can readily detect (and appreciate) subtle changes in their environments, but tend to be *overwhelmed* by strong inputs. Normals appear to be "unemotional" because they typically *block out* (and thus don't respond to) moderate to strong levels of stimulation.

To overgeneralize, neurotics tend to *love* places like discotheques; normals usually are forced to block off all the noisy inputs in such places and thus rapidly become bored. Normals often *love* games such as chess; neurotics typically find such games tedious (Eysenck, 1947).

- *Introversion-Extroversion*

The second of Eysenck's personality scales runs from *introversion* to *extroversion*. Jung used these same terms, of course. But Eysenck rejected Jung's descriptions and has tried to tie his concept of "introversion-extroversion" to *patterns of neural functioning*.

As we mentioned in Chapter 2, your behavior patterns result from a "mixture" of excitation and inhibition within your nervous system. According to Eysenck, the *speed* at which you acquire new behavior patterns is directly correlated with the *amount* of neural excitation you generate. The *higher* the level of excitation, the more *quickly* you learn.

In similar fashion, Eysenck says, the speed at which you *unlearn* habits is directly correlated with the amount of neural *inhibition* in your nervous system. The *higher* the level of inhibition, the more rapidly your old habits will *extinguish*.

According to Eysenck, introverts are people who have *strong* excitatory processes. Thus, introverts *acquire* new habits rather rapidly. But introverts also have rather *weak* inhibitory processes. Therefore, introverts tend to *unlearn* (or give up) old habits rather reluctantly. Put more simply, introverts learn things easily. But once they do acquire a new habit, it tends to "stick forever" because the introvert's nervous system doesn't generate enough inhibition for extinction to occur. For that reason, Eysenck says, introverts tend to adopt rather "passive" and "unchanging" lifestyles (Eysenck, 1957).

Extroverts are just the opposite, Eysenck says. Extroverts have *weak* excitatory processes. So extroverts are *poor* at learning new tasks. Furthermore, they have *strong* inhibitory processes. Indeed, extroverts build up inhibition so quickly that they soon "give up" whatever new habits they do manage to acquire. Therefore, Eysenck says, extroverts tend to adopt rather "active" and "changeable" lifestyles because they lack the ability both to *acquire* and to *stick to* consistent behavior patterns (Eysenck, 1957).

● **Eysenck's Revision of Galen's Four Temperaments**

Eysenck believes that you were born with certain *innate neural tendencies* that place you somewhere on both the "Emotional-Nonemotional" (neurotic-normal) and the "Changeable-Unchangeable" (extroversion-introversion) scales. These two tendencies *interact* with each other to produce the four classic "temperaments" that Galen described so many centuries ago (see Fig. 17.1) (Eysenck, 1957).

● **Eysenck's "Psychoticism" Scale**

In recent years, Hans Eysenck and his psychologist son, Michael, have added a third scale to the original two. This "new dimension" is *psychoticism*, which the Eysencks say runs from "normal, through criminal, psychopathic, alcoholic, and drug addictive behavior generally, to schizoid and finally entirely psychotic states" (Eysenck & Eysenck, 1985).

To date, the Eysencks have not given a very elaborate description of this new scale, nor have they related it in any effective manner to patterns of *neural functioning*, as they did with the other two scales (Briggs, 1987).

Eysenck's Theory: An Evaluation

In a recent review, University of Tulsa psychologist Stephen Briggs notes that there is more *experimental* evidence supporting Eysenck's theory of personality than any other. This is particularly true of Eysenck's "Extroversion-Introversion" scale, Briggs says, which is buttressed by hundreds of studies. There is less evidence in favor of the "Normal-Neurotic" scale, however, and little or none supporting the new "Psychoticism" scale (Briggs, 1987).

Despite the amount of experimental data supporting Eysenck's views, Briggs says, his theory has actually had little impact on American psychology. Why is this the case? Because he is British? Perhaps, but then Freud, Jung, and Piaget were not Americans either. Or is it because, as Eysenck himself says, people prefer "narrative accounts" of personality develop-

FIG. 17.1 Dimensional and categorical personality classification.

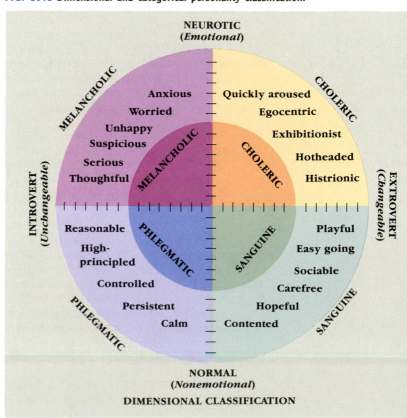

Eugenics (you-JEN-icks). From the Greek words meaning "good genes." Literally, the scientific study of the hereditary characteristics of various races with the hope of improving the incidence of "good genes" through selective breeding.

Sir Francis Galton

ment to "scientific descriptions"? Perhaps that, too. The major criticism one can raise against Eysenck, though, is that he *tends to neglect the influence of the present environment.*

Many people tend to score as "introverted" when taking a test in a psychologist's office. However, in real-life settings, they may act quite the opposite. For example, in a recent study, Wellesley psychologist Avril Thorne compared the *speech patterns* of extroverts and introverts in several social situations. Thorne found that, when one extrovert talks with another extrovert, or an introvert holds a conversation with another introvert, they tend to behave "according to type." But when an extrovert talks with an introvert, the extrovert becomes rather introverted, and the introvert becomes decidedly extroverted (Thorne, 1987). Thus, Eysenck's classifications may be valid *in the laboratory,* but less so in the real world of "people being people."

There is a fourth reason for Eysenck's neglect that has to do with the relation between *theory* and *therapy.* We will return to this point at the end of the chapter. First, however, let's take a closer look at *trait theory,* and how it developed. After all, as we noted, "temperaments" are sometimes described as being "collections of traits."

□ □ **QUESTION** □ □
What kind of *therapy* does Eysenck's personality theory suggest should be used to treat "mental illness"?

TRAIT THEORY

According to *Webster's Third New International Dictionary,* the English word *trait* comes from a Latin term meaning "a brush stroke." The dictionary gives the current meaning of *trait* as "a distinguishing quality or feature, as of personal character."

Writing in the February 1983 *American Psychologist,* Fordham psychologist Anne Anastasi states that "Trait theories . . . arose out of inquiries into the nature of intelligence." By this statement, Anastasi means that *modern* trait theory got its start about a century ago, when Sir Francis Galton tried to create the first intelligence test. So, we will begin with a discussion of Galton's work, then look briefly at more recent examples of trait theory.

□ □ **QUESTION** □ □
Many experts believe that severely-retarded individuals should be

sterilized so they can't have children. What is your position on this very sensitive issue?

Sir Francis Galton

Modern-day trait theory is a direct descendent of Charles Darwin's theory of evolution. Given that fact, perhaps it's not surprising that one of the first people to interest himself in measuring human traits was Francis Galton, who was Darwin's cousin. Darwin had said that evolution was a matter of "the survival of the fittest." In Galton's view, "fittest" meant "intellectually gifted." He assumed that intellectual differences were due primarily to inheritance, not to training. Thus, the best way for the human race to survive, Galton said, was to encourage "gifted people" to have more children, and to discourage (or even prevent) "people of inferior intelligence" from reproducing.

Galton called his approach **eugenics,** which he defined as the "science" that "takes cognizance of all influences that tend in however remote a degree to give the more suitable races or strains of blood a better chance of prevailing speedily over the less suitable than they otherwise would have" (Galton, 1883/1907). He also founded the British Eugenics Society, which is still active—and still maintains Galton's original goals (Turner & Miles, 1983).

Galton's first problem was that of identifying those psychological traits that were somehow *correlated* with "superiority." His second problem was that of finding ways to *measure* these traits. By the time he had solved both of these difficulties to his satisfaction, he had

1. Devised the first intelligence test.
2. Made the first scientific study of individual differences.
3. Proven that childhood experiences have an effect on adult thinking.
4. Developed the first psychological questionnaire.
5. Undertaken the first behavioral study of human twins.
6. Helped establish the use of fingerprints to identify people.
7. Made the first use of statistical correlations in a psychological study.
8. Written the first book on eugenics.
9. Measured the sensory and motor capabilities of almost 10,000 people.

Rather an impressive set of accomplishments, even for a man whose IQ was probably about 200. However, Galton's major contribution to trait theory surely came from his detailed studies of individual differences.

□ □ **QUESTION** □ □
There is, at present, a privately-run "sperm bank" where Nobel Prize-

winning scientists and other highly-creative men can "store their seed for future generations." Do you think it might "improve our chances of survival" if the government paid "the best and the brightest" women to have children using sperm from this or similar banks?

• Individual Differences and Human Similarities

Galton published his first book on trait theory in 1869. Called *Hereditary Genius*, the book was an attempt to prove that intelligence and creativity tended to "run in families." What Galton actually did, of course, was to show that children are more similar to their parents than they are to a random sample of unrelated individuals. And twins are more like each other than they are like distant cousins. Thus, trait theory—as defined by Galton and most other psychologists—is partially the study of human *similarities* (Galton, 1869/1962).

But even twins will differ in many ways. If they are both musicians, one twin may have a finer sense of rhythm than does the other. So trait theory also concerns itself with the study of individual *differences*—what they are, and where they come from (Galton, 1883/1907).

• The Nature-Nurture Controversy in Trait Theory

Galton defined traits as *measurable* and *consistent* patterns of human performance and character. And he assumed that traits were inherited and thus couldn't be altered to any significant degree.

The famous British philosopher John Stuart Mill disagreed rather violently with Galton. Mill's IQ probably matched Galton's, but Mill ascribed his brilliance to the *careful and dedicated teaching* he received from his father. According to Mill, the belief that there are *innate* differences between "individuals, races, or sexes" was "one of the chief hindrances to the rational treatment of great social questions, and one of the greatest stumbling blocks to human improvement" (cited in Fancher, 1985). Mill believed that society had a *moral obligation* to assume that the environment, not genes, was the major cause of "individual differences."

To a great extent, the history of modern trait theory is a battle between these two extreme positions—that is, a conflict between those theorists who believe that *nature* determines your intelligence and most other aspects of your personality, and those "nurturist" theorists who contend that you became what society allowed you to be.

We will return to the nature-nurture controversy shortly, when we discuss intelligence. First, let's look at some of the better-known modern trait theorists.

□ □ **QUESTION** □ □
Suppose that someone convinced Congress and the president that certain "racial types" were "intellectually inferior." How might this affect America's willingness to admit immigrants from all parts of the world?

Allport's Theory of Traits

According to Christopher Monte, "Gordon Allport created American personality psychology" (Monte, 1987). Born in Indiana in 1897, Allport was the youngest of four brothers. His parents, Allport wrote, believed in "plain Protestant piety and hard work" (Allport, 1967).

As a child, Allport had few friends. "I never fitted the general boy assembly. I was quick with words, poor with games." Indeed, when he was about 10, another boy said of him, "Aw, that guy swallowed a dictionary." To compensate, Allport said, he "contrived to be the 'star' for a small cluster of friends" (Allport, 1967).

One of his older brothers, Floyd Allport, took his Ph.D. at Harvard and became a noted social psychologist. Floyd Allport then encouraged his younger brother to enroll at Harvard, too. Gordon Allport found the first semester as an undergraduate a difficult time, but persevered, did exceptionally well, and went on to take his doctorate in psychology at Harvard.

Oddly enough, even though Floyd and Gordon Allport had similar interests, they seldom collaborated. Indeed, it seems likely that one of Gordon's main professional motivations was the determination to prove he was in some way *superior* to his older brother (Atwood & Tomkins, 1976).

• Allport and Freud

Shortly after finishing his undergraduate work, Gordon Allport wrote to Sigmund Freud. Allport was going to be in Vienna, he said, and he was sure that Freud would be most happy to meet him. Freud agreed to receive this brash young American, and "The visit proved to be of lasting consequence for Allport's subsequent career as a personality theorist" (Monte, 1987).

Allport writes that, when they met, Freud sat in "expectant silence," waiting for Allport to say something. In desperation, Allport described the behavior of a boy he had seen on the bus en route to Freud's. The boy had "a conspicuous dirt phobia," which Allport believed could be traced to the boy's mother, who was "so dominant and purposive looking that I thought the cause and effect apparent." However, Freud apparently misunderstood Allport's motivation. For, when Allport finished the story, "Freud fixed his kindly therapeutic eyes upon me and said, 'And was that little boy you?'" (Allport, 1968).

Gordon Allport

Functional autonomy (aw-TAHN-oh-me). Allport's notion that the motive that impells you to *learn* a habit may not be the same motive that *maintains* the habit. For example, you may begin a rigorous exercise program because the doctor tells you to do so, but continue to exercise because you then lose weight and feel better, or simply because exercising is now "a habit" that has an "autonomy" all its own.

Allport was amused, but also dismayed, by his encounter with Sigmund Freud:

> I realized that he was accustomed to neurotic defenses and that my manifest motivation (a sort of rude curiosity and youthful ambition) escaped him. . . . This experience taught me that depth psychology, for all its merits, may plunge too deep, and that psychologists would do well to give full recognition to manifest motives before probing the unconscious. (Allport, 1968)

Allport continued to believe that unconscious forces were important "shapers of personality," and that "the past helps determine the present." However, he insisted that quite often the best way to find out what people were like was simply to ask them to talk about themselves:

> When we set out to study a person's motives, we are seeking to find out what that person is trying to do in this life—including, of course, what he is trying to avoid and what he is trying to be. I see no reason why we should not start our investigation by asking him to tell us the answers as he sees them. (Allport, 1960)

● **Allport's Major Beliefs**
According to Christopher Monte, there are three "central themes" to Allport's point of view on why you are what you are:

1. Your personality is made up of a mixture of major and minor *traits*.
2. Each of those traits is a combination of biological, intra-psychic, and social/behavioral factors that predispose you to respond in specific ways to certain specific environmental inputs.
3. A psychologist can "understand" you only by looking at your *entire life history*, and only if the psychologist also asks you to evaluate yourself.

Monte concludes that, "the contributions of Gordon Allport steered the thinking of several generations of personality theorists into the channel of considering whole human lives rather than isolated motives, wishes, and actions" (Monte, 1987).

● **Traits and Language**
Gordon Allport believed that the very *concept* of traits was buried deep within the structure of language. Early in his career, he and H.S. Odbert made a list of 18,000 English words, each of which was actually a *trait description* (Allport & Odbert, 1936). You cannot even *think* of some other person, Allport claimed, without generating a whole list of "trait words" that you associate with that individual. Little wonder, then, that "traits" are such an important part of personality theories.

● **Cardinal, Central, and Secondary Traits**
In Allport's theory, there are three types of traits: *cardinal, central*, and *secondary*.

1. Cardinal traits are those aspects of personality that so dominate the way a person acts that you cannot fail to notice them. Allport named many of these traits after well-known figures, such as "Christ-like" and "Napoleonic." Few people have cardinal traits, Allport said.
2. Central traits "are those usually mentioned in careful letters of recommendation, in rating scales where the rater stars the outstanding characteristics of the individual, or in brief verbal descriptions of a person" (Allport, 1937).
3. Secondary traits are less important in determining behavior than are cardinal or central traits. Secondary traits are fairly weak tendencies to respond to certain specific situations in fairly specific ways. Put more simply, perhaps, we might say that secondary traits are the "little things" that make you the unique person that you are.

Allport believed that traits resulted from *learning imposed on biological tendencies*. However, he said, once you acquire a trait (or a motive), it may "take on a life of its own." That is, the conditions that *maintain* a motive (or a trait) may not be the same that caused you to acquire the motive in the first place. Allport called this the **functional autonomy** of motives.

● **Gordon Allport: An Evaluation**
There is little doubt, as Christopher Monte points out, that Gordon Allport had a tremendous influence on personality theory in the US. Whether his emphasis on *traits* was the best approach to take, however, is something psychologists are still debating. For example, more than two decades ago, Walter Mischel criticized the concept of traits in these terms: "With the possible exception of intelligence, highly generalized behavioral consistencies have not been demonstrated, and the concept of personal traits as broad response predispositions is thus untenable" (Mischel, 1968).

More recently, Mischel's views were echoed by John F. Kihlstrom: "After almost 50 years

TABLE 17.1　The Sixteen Factors of Personality

1. Schizothymia (aloof, cold) vs. Cyclothymia (warm, sociable)
2. Dull (low intellectual capacity) vs. Bright (intelligent)
3. Low Ego Strength (emotional, unstable) vs. High Ego Strength (mature, calm)
4. Submissiveness (mild) vs. Dominance (aggressive)
5. Desurgency (glum, silent) vs. Surgency (enthusiastic, talkative)
6. Low Superego Strength (casual, undependable) vs. High Superego Strength (conscientious, persistent)
7. Threctia (timid, shy) vs. Parmia (adventurous, thick-skinned)
8. Harria (tough, realistic) vs. Premsia (sensitive, effeminate)
9. Inner Relaxation (trustful, adaptable) vs. Protension (suspecting, jealous)
10. Praxernia (conventional, practical) vs. Autia (Bohemian, unconcerned)
11. Naivete (simple, awkward) vs. Shrewdness (sophisticated, polished)
12. Confidence (unshakable) vs. Timidity (insecure, anxious)
13. Conservatism (accepting) vs. Radicalism (experimenting, critical)
14. Group Dependence (imitative) vs. Self-Sufficiency (resourceful)
15. Low Integration (lax, unsure) vs. Self-Sentiment Control (controlled, exact)
16. Low Ergic Tension (phlegmatic, composed) vs. High Ergic Tension (tense, excitable)

Source: Reprinted from *Personality Theories: A Comparative Analysis* by S. R. Maddi, by permission of Dorsey Press. Copyright © 1973 by Dorsey Press.

of factor analysis, the structural relationships among personality traits remain as obscure as ever." Why is this the case? Because, Kihlstrom says, trait theorists forget that behavior is *always expressed within the context of an environment*. And "individual behavior across contexts is considerably more variable than the notion of a personality trait would seem to permit" (Kihlstrom, 1980).

All things considered, Allport's major contribution to personality theory probably was this: He tried to get psychologists to abandon their "narrow theories" and adopt a more holistic description of what people are like.

Now that we have discussed Allport's view of trait theory, let's look at Raymond Cattell's approach.

Cattell's Factor Analytic Approach

Raymond Cattell reduced the 18,000 traits that Allport and Odbert had listed to a mere 16. Cattell did this by using *factor analysis*—which we have already described—and by making certain assumptions about human behavior.

• Surface Traits and Source Traits

Cattell's first assumption was that there are just a few "common factors" underlying all the traits other scientists had described. And his research soon suggested that many of the traits *clustered together*. From observing people, and from looking at the results of tests he gave his subjects, Cattell identified about 35 of these "trait clusters." To Cattell, though, these were mere "surface" expressions of more fundamental personality patterns. Cattell thus called these 35 clusters of related behaviors *surface traits* (Cattell, 1950).

Once he had identified this limited number of "trait clusters," Cattell tried to *factor out* the basic relationships among the surface traits. He ended up with a list of 16 factors that he

called *source traits*. To Cattell, these 16 source traits are the dimensions by which everyone's personality structure can be measured.

All 16 of Cattell's source traits are *bi-polar*. Which is to say that each trait has two extremes, such as "warm-cold," "bright-dull," and "relaxed-tense" (see Table 17.1). Cattell then devised a test which he believed would measure each person's location on all 16 of the source-trait scales. Cattell believed that your scores on this test described your "source traits" in objective, measurable terms. But to paint a complete picture of your personality, he needed additional information (Cattell, 1957).

Cattell took his data about human behavior from three sources: (1) from records of people's lives, and from reports by friends and relatives; (2) from asking people what they thought they were like; and (3) from scores on objective tests such as his "16 Personality Factors Test." Only by analyzing all three types of data, Cattell said, could you give a complete description of an individual's personality and hence *predict* what the person would do in the future (Cattell, 1965).

• Criticisms of Cattell's Theory

Cattell's is surely the most comprehensive approach to the study of human traits. But his theory suffers from the same difficulties that all trait theories suffer from. First, he assumed your thoughts and behaviors are determined almost entirely by the *structure* of your personality. However, as we noted earlier, people tend to be more responsive to present environmental inputs than some trait theorists assume is the case.

Second, Cattell relied rather heavily on self-reports. But as we will see in future chapters, there is often a great difference between what you *say* your response will be in a given situation and how you *actually behave* when

Raymond Cattell

you face that situation in real life. Thus, test scores and interviews often do a poor job of predicting future responses.

Third, although Cattell said traits were partially learned and partially hereditary, he gave no indication of how traits developed during the early years of life.

Last, but surely not least, Cattell's list of 16 traits is quite different from lists prepared by other factor analysts. For example, University of Michigan psychologist Warren Norman reduced the Allport and Odbert list of 18,000 traits to some 20 trait scales. Then Norman had trained judges *rate other people* on the 20 scales, and factor-analyzed the results. He found five "underlying factors" could account for the results (see Table 17.2) (Norman, 1961, 1963).

Given the problems associated with trait theory, why do we bother with it? The answer is simple: We can hardly hope to discuss individual differences meaningfully without having instruments available which *measure* these dif-

TABLE 17.2   Some Trait Dimensions and Their Components

Trait Dimension	Descriptive Components[a]
I. Extraversion or Surgency	Talkative—Silent Frank, Open—Secretive Adventurous—Cautious Sociable—Reclusive
II. Agreeableness	Good-natured—Irritable Not Jealous—Jealous Mild, Gentle—Headstrong Cooperative—Negativistic
III. Conscientiousness	Fussy, Tidy—Careless Responsible—Undependable Scrupulous—Unscrupulous Persevering—Quitting, Fickle
IV. Emotional Stability	Poised—Nervous, Tense Calm—Anxious Composed—Excitable Not Hypochondriacal— Hypochondriacal
V. Culture	Artistically Sensitive— Artistically Insensitive Intellectual—Unreflective, Narrow Polished, Refined—Crude, Boorish Imaginative—Simple, Direct

Adapted from Norman (1963).
[a]Adjectives describing the two ends of the scales that comprise the dimension.

ferences. And most present-day attempts to *measure human performance or personality* are based on some form of trait theory. Thus, almost all psychological tests—including intelligence and aptitude tests—stem from Galton's early efforts. Suppose we look at intelligence tests first, then describe how psychologists measure other aspects of performance and personality.

☐☐ **QUESTION** ☐☐

In 1865, Galton wrote that there is "a difference of not less than two grades between the black and white races." Galton also thought that reaction time, speed, and physical strength were good measures of intelligence. How might Galton have reacted to the performance of blacks in professional sports and the Olympic games?

INTELLIGENCE TESTS

One of the people most influenced by Galton's work was a Frenchman named **Alfred Binet**. In about 1890, he became interested in the differences between bright and dull children and tried to devise a simple scale that would allow him to distinguish the smart children from those who would have problems in school.

Shortly before Binet began his work, another French scientist named Paul Broca had theorized that *brain size* was related to intelligence, and (at first) Binet believed Broca was right. So Binet initially relied on *physical measures*—such as the size of the child's head or the pattern of lines on the palm of the child's hand. However, none of these scales correlated very highly with the child's performance in school, so Binet abandoned them. As Binet himself put it, "The idea of measuring intelligence by measuring heads [now seems] ridiculous" (cited in Fancher, 1985).

☐☐ **QUESTION** ☐☐
How would *you* define intelligence?

The Binet-Simon Test

In 1904 the French government asked Binet and a physician named **Théophile Simon** to devise a test that would allow teachers to identify "retarded" children who might not benefit from schooling. Since "measuring heads" hadn't worked, Binet and Simon decided that seeing how well the students performed ordinary tasks might give some indication of how bright the students were. So Binet and Simon pulled together a large number of rather simple problems that seemed to require different mental skills. Then they tried out the test problems on a large number of French school children of different ages. This technique allowed

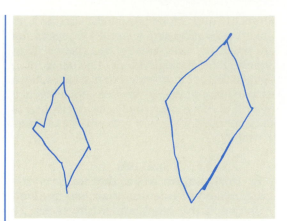

FIG. 17.2 Drawing of a diamond by a 5-year-old (left) and a 7-year-old (right).

Binet and Simon to select "appropriate" test items for each age group. They found, for example, that the average seven-year-old could correctly make a pencil copy of the figure of a diamond, but most five-year-olds could not (see Fig. 17.2).

If a boy of 9 got the same score on the test as did the *average* 7-year-old, Binet and Simon presumed that the boy's mental development was retarded by two years. The boy would thus have a "physical age" of 9 but a "mental age" of 7. If an 8-year-old girl did as well on the test as the average 11-year-old, then she had a mental age of 11, although her physical age was but 8.

Later, psychologists in Germany and in the US put the relationship between **chronological** (physical) age and mental age into an equation:

$$\frac{\text{Mental age}}{\text{Chronological age}} \times 100 =$$
$$\text{Intelligence Quotient, or IQ}$$

A girl with a mental age of six and a chronological age of six would have an IQ of

$$\frac{6}{6} \times 100 = 1 \times 100 = 100 = \text{IQ}$$

By definition, she would be of average intelligence. A boy with a mental age of seven and a chronological age of nine would have an IQ of

$$\frac{7}{9} \times 100 = .777 \times 100 = 78 = \text{IQ}$$

A girl with a mental age of 11 and a chronological age of 8 would have an IQ of

$$\frac{11}{8} \times 100 = 1.375 \times 100 = 138 = \text{IQ}$$

The Binet-Simon test did so well at predicting the *academic performance* of school children that intelligence testing became a standard part of educational psychology. However, as psychologists have grown more sophisticated at measuring intelligence, they have pretty much abandoned the use of the "intelligence quotient" itself. Instead, most psychologists now *convert* intelligence test scores into "standard scores" or "percentiles," for these measures give a more accurate and reliable measure of intellectual performance (Tyler, 1973).

Alfred Binet

• *Other Intelligence Tests*

From the start of his research, Binet was worried about the *misuse* of his test. As Harvard scientist Stephen Jay Gould points out, Binet didn't believe that intelligence could be captured by any single number, nor did he think intelligence was primarily inherited. He was afraid that teachers would "rank" their students according to some simple (and incorrect) scheme, and then respond to the rankings, not to the students. So Binet refused to rank all the students he tested (Gould, 1981).

According to Gould, American psychologists tended to ignore Binet's warnings. For example, the noted Stanford psychologist L.M. Terman made up his own version of the French scale early this century. He called his device the Stanford-Binet intelligence test. It yielded a single number, which Terman called the IQ. Other psychologists soon followed Terman's lead, and now there are hundreds of intelligence tests available. When used properly—by people who understand both the strengths and weaknesses of intelligence tests—these measures of individual differences can be of con-

These people are members of Mensa, an international organization open to anyone whose IQ falls within the top 2 percent of the general population.

Chronological (kron-oh-LODGE-ih-kal). Chronos (KROH-nos) was the Greek god of time. Your chronological age is the actual number of years that you have lived.

Lewis Terman

Robert J. Sternberg

siderable academic value. As we will see momentarily, however, these tests have been abused almost as often as they have been properly used.

● *Is Intelligence a Single Trait?*
The results of many psychological studies suggest that intelligence is not a single trait. Rather it is made up of a great many related talents or abilities. Psychologists don't entirely agree what these "related" talents are, but they often mention such things as the ability to memorize words and numbers, to learn motor tasks, to solve verbal and numerical problems, to evaluate complex situations, to be creative, and to perceive spatial relationships. Indeed, in 1959, J.P. Guilford listed 120 "factors of intelligence," each one representing a different intellectual ability (Guilford, 1959, 1967)!

If intelligence is really a mixture of many different traits, then there is no reason to expect that IQs should fit a bell-shaped curve. However, most trait theorists continue to believe that intelligence test scores should be normally distributed. The reason for this belief is simple—there seem to be more people of "normal" intelligence in the world than there are "geniuses" and "mentally-retarded" individuals. These facts caused Charles Spearman and Raymond Cattell to rethink the concept of intelligence entirely.

Types of Intelligence
To Charles Spearman, the noted British psychologist, there were but two types of intelligence. Many years ago, Spearman noted that, if you took 10 different intelligence tests, you would usually wind up with 10 different scores. True, the scores probably would be *related* to each other. But which one gave your *real* IQ? And why so many different scores?

Spearman decided each test item actually measured two factors. One he called *general* intelligence, or the "g factor." But each item also measured one or more *specific* types of mental ability, which he called "s factors." Thus different tests yield different scores because each test tends to emphasize "s" or "g" to a different degree. However, the *mix* of "s" and "g" factors for each test could still fit a bell-shaped curve (Goldenson, 1970; Spearman, 1904).

Raymond Cattell agrees that there are two "intellectual factors," but disagrees with Spearman on what they are. Cattell says you have *fluid* intelligence and *crystallized* intelligence.

Your "fluid" intelligence is inherited, and involves such talents as the ability to think and reason. "Crystallized" intelligence involves learned skills such as being able to add and subtract, and the size of your vocabulary.

According to Cattell, your "fluid" intelligence sets limits on your "crystallized" abilities. If you aren't innately bright, all the training in the world won't help you get through school. However, if you have a high "fluid" intelligence, and you grow up in a deprived and unstimulating environment, you won't acquire many skills. And you won't get a high score on most intelligence tests, either. From Cattell's point of view, if everyone grew up in the best of all possible environments, "fluid" intelligence would be the major determinant of IQ—and test scores then would "fit the curve" almost exactly (Cattell, 1982).

Robert J. Sternberg disagrees with both Cattell and Spearman. Sternberg thinks there are *three different kinds of intelligence*.

□ □ **QUESTION** □ □
Do you think "street smarts" are the same thing as "book smarts"?

● *Sternberg's Triarchic Theory of Intelligence*
Describing his early experiences in a recent interview, Robert Sternberg says, "I really stunk on IQ tests. I was just terrible" (cited in Trotter, 1986). Despite his poor test performance as a child, Sternberg somehow managed to obtain a Ph.D. from Stanford, and now is a professor at Yale. And perhaps *because* of his early difficulties, Sternberg has spent many years studying what intelligence is, and how best to measure it (Sternberg, 1982, 1984).

By the 1980's, Sternberg had come up with a *triarchic* (or three-factor) theory (Sternberg, 1986). He claims there are three entirely different sorts of intelligence:

1. *Componential*, or *analytical* intelligence. People with this kind of intelligence tend to do beautifully on tests that require them to *analyze* a problem into its "component parts."
2. *Experiential*, or *creative* intelligence. People with this kind of intelligence often have mediocre test scores, but can combine different experiences to come up with new insights. They not only solve unusual problems quickly, but usually train themselves to handle familiar problems by rote memory in order to free their minds for creative efforts.
3. *Contextual* intelligence, or "street smarts". People with this kind of intelligence learn quickly how to "beat the game" in any context, but usually don't have the highest scores on standardized tests, nor are they necessarily creative. Sternberg defines con-

textual intelligence as "all the extremely important things they never teach you in school."

Sternberg believes we should have three different *kinds* of intelligence tests, for the ones we now use tend to measure only componential intelligence. As Sternberg puts it, "Standard IQ tests are fairly good for predicting how people will do in school, but they have a very low correlation with job performance" (cited in McKean, 1985).

Sternberg thinks that intelligence is primarily *learned,* not *innate.* Therefore, *all* children would do well on intelligence tests if the youngsters were reared in the best-possible environment. But what constitutes "the best of all possible environments"? We can't as yet answer that question. But recent studies do suggest that the early environment can have a significant effect on a child's intelligence test scores.

"Street smarts" may be more important to success in some occupations than are the more traditionally recognized forms of intelligence.

□□ QUESTION □□

Which of Sternberg's three "types" of intelligence would you expect school teachers (and other academics) to be highest in? Why?

IQ and Early Deprivation

As we noted in Chapter 14, children who are reared in deprived environments often show remarkable improvements in their IQs if they are later given the proper intellectual stimulation. One of the first psychologists to make this point was H.M. Skeels. In the 1930's, Skeels shocked many of his colleagues by reporting he had been able to *increase* the IQs of apparently retarded children by putting them in an unusual environment.

Skeels took several children out of a dreary orphanage and gave them to a group of retarded women to rear. The first children he studied were two little girls, whose IQs rose from below 50 to near normal. Skeels believed the girls got higher scores because the retarded women gave them *massive stimulation and attention*, which children at the orphanage didn't receive. Skeels was thus one of the first psychologists to suggest that an enriched environment can have a dramatic effect on IQ (Skeels *et al.*, 1938).

● The Minnesota Study

Several recent studies tend to confirm Skeels' findings. Sandra Scarr and Richard Weinberg studied several hundred children in Minnesota who were placed in adoptive homes. All the children were either black or of mixed racial background. Some of the adopting parents were black, but many were white. Most were college graduates with professional jobs or responsibilities.

Scarr and Weinberg estimate that, judging from the adopted children's genetic backgrounds, they might have been expected to end up with IQs well *below* the national average. Instead, they scored well *above* average. In fact, their IQs were very close to those of youngsters brought up in natural homes similar to the ones the adopted children were placed into.

Scarr and Weinberg also report that the younger the child had been when adopted, the higher the child's IQ tended to be later in life. Generally speaking, black children adopted into middle-class white homes had higher IQs than did black children reared in middle-class black homes (Scarr & Weinberg, 1983, 1986).

There are at least two important conclusions we can draw from the Scarr and Weinberg study: First, intelligence test scores are strongly influenced by environmental factors. Second, children from disadvantaged homes who are reared by well-educated adoptive parents *of either race* have higher IQs than they probably would have had if reared by their own parents.

□□ QUESTION □□

The obvious "control group" for this study would be white children adopted into black homes. Why do you think Scarr and Weinberg were not able to find enough such children to make a meaningful comparison?

Does "Coercive Discipline" Affect IQ?

Sociologist Zena Blau of the University of Houston recently conducted a study of more than a thousand children in Chicago. Half of the youngsters were black, the other half were white. Blau reports that black and white children who had *similar home environments* tended to have highly similar intelligence test scores. However, Blau notes that IQs were lowest among children (black or white) whose mothers used punitive and "coercive discipline" on their children. And IQs were highest among children (white or black) whose mothers tended to reward their children for learning self-control rather than punishing them for misbehaving (Blau, 1981).

Results supporting Blau's position come from a recent study by University of Houston psychologists Thomas G. Power and M. Lynn Chapieski. They observed sixteen 14-month-old infants in their home environments for several weeks. Some of the mothers used physical discipline, such as slapping the child on the wrist, while other mothers didn't. Power and Chapieski report that infants who were physically punished by their mothers *continued to misbehave*, while infants whose mothers used verbal discipline (or none at all) tended to learn appropriate behaviors rather readily. Furthermore, when the infants were tested seven months later, the physically-punished youngsters did more poorly on problem-solving tasks than did the infants whose mothers never slapped their children (Power & Chapieski, 1986).

□□ **QUESTION** □□
Suppose you grew up in an environment that rewarded you for answering questions *quickly* rather than for answering *correctly*—and for defending your answers vigorously, whether right or wrong. How would your early experiences affect your performance in school and on intelligence tests?

What Your Environment Teaches You

As Robert Sternberg notes, most intelligence tests place rather heavy emphasis on *analytical reasoning*—the ability to work your way through a complicated mental task step-by-step. Cattell, Galton, and most other trait psychologists assume that "reasoning" is an inherited ability. Few psychologists doubt that *some* aspects of intelligence are determined by the genes. But are people poor reasoners because of their genes? Or is some aspect of that trait learned?

Several years ago, Benjamin Bloom and Lois Broder studied how college students with either low or high IQs react to mental challenges. Bloom and Broder gave these subjects various problems to work on and asked the students to "talk out loud" as they proceeded. High IQ subjects tended to read the instructions carefully, then diligently eliminated all the incorrect answers. The low IQ students often skipped over the instructions, and lacked the patience to isolate the correct answers when faced with questions that required formal reasoning. The low scorers didn't seem to carry on an "internal conversation" with themselves, nor did they proceed through a step-by-step sequence of deductions. If the low IQ students couldn't see the answer *immediately*, they usually guessed.

Bloom and Broder were convinced that the low-scoring students had never acquired the "proper" cognitive skills. So they developed a training program aimed at helping these young people "learn how to reason." First, they made the low scorers *read the instructions aloud*. Many of the students showed immediate improvement, because they were forced to pay attention to what was required of them. Next the students were asked to solve various problems *aloud*. After Bloom and Broder had discussed the student's solution with the student, the experimenters read the correct solution aloud. Then they asked the student to explain what had gone wrong if the student had been incorrect. The students had many difficulties at first, and the instructors had to show tremendous patience. But once the students *learned* what was required to do well on the tests, they began to perform much better. Although Bloom and Broder did not retest the students' IQs after this training, the psychologists report most of their subjects got much higher grades in college thereafter (Bloom, 1982, 1985).

□□ **QUESTION** □□
In terms of "street smarts," which is better: being "right," or being "quick and aggressive"?

Reliability and Validity of Intelligence Tests

When a psychologist makes up a "measurement scale" of any kind, the psychologist has to prove two things to other scientists before they will accept the scale and use it themselves. First, the creator of the test must show that it is *reliable*. Second, the psychologist must provide evidence that the test is also *valid*.

At its simplest, the term "reliability" merely means that a test will yield the same results no matter how frequently you give it. However, Leona Tyler states that—when applied to instruments such as intelligence tests—reliability really means "accuracy." That is, a test is "reliable" if the results it yields are free from *chance effects* (Tyler & Walsh, 1979).

At its simplest, the term "validity" means that the test measures what it says that it does. However, Leona Tyler also notes that modern psychologists take a more complex view of the term. To Tyler, you cannot judge the validity of a test unless you know all of the current re-

Leona Tyler

search showing just what a test does and does not measure. Determining the validity of a psychological scale, therefore, is both a complicated and continuing undertaking (Tyler, 1973; Tyler & Walsh, 1979).

With these simplified definitions in mind, let's examine both the reliability and the validity of intelligence tests.

● Are Intelligence Tests Reliable?

If IQs were *absolutely fixed* at birth, psychologists would probably have little trouble making up highly reliable tests. However, intelligence tests actually measure *your present level of functioning*, not the underlying factor that Cattell calls "fluid intelligence." Thus, your IQ is always affected by your genes, your past experience, *and* your present situation. If you are unmotivated when you take a test, or if you are worried about something or have a toothache, you probably will do more poorly than if you were "up" for the exam. In similar fashion, if you grew up in a deprived environment, or if you never learned to reason, your test scores won't be as high as they otherwise might have been.

Intelligence tests are much more reliable than are many other psychological scales. And when given under the best of circumstances, the tests are fairly "accurate" in the sense that Leona Tyler uses that term. However, as we noted, no two intelligence tests will yield identical scores. That's one of the reasons intelligence test results are now often quoted in percentiles. And even if you take the same test several times, your IQ may vary considerably depending on how you feel and what you have learned since the last time you took the test. Thus, your IQ *is not a fixed quantity*.

● Are Intelligence Tests Valid?

The term *validity* has several different meanings, and can be measured in several different ways. For our purposes, however, we can assume an intelligence test is "valid" if it successfully predicts how you will do in situations where you presumably need "intelligence" in order to succeed.

Test builders usually offer their own *carefully limited* definition of what they think intelligence is, and then show that their particular instrument is valid within those limits. For instance, Binet and Simon assumed that "intelligence" was whatever mental properties were needed to succeed in French schools. Children who scored high on their tests generally got good grades—and were rated as being intelligent by their teachers. Students who scored lower on the Binet-Simon test got lower school grades—and were rated as being less intelligent by their teachers. Binet and Simon then used the correlations among test scores, teacher ratings, and grades to *validate* their in-

The grades a child gets in school are usually correlated with his or her IQ test scores.

telligence test. And within the limits of their definition, Binet and Simon were correct.

The first indication that intelligence tests can be valid, therefore, is the fact that IQs have a high correlation with academic grades. A second indication, Leona Tyler notes, is that IQs often predict how well people will do in various occupational *levels*. That is, if you have an IQ of 80, you probably will do better in an unskilled or semi-skilled job than you would trying to become a nuclear physicist. However, IQs don't predict the success that people *within* a given occupation will have (Tyler, 1973, 1984).

● Academic Versus Real-life Success

A recent report by California psychologist Robert T. Ross shows when intelligence tests are both reliable and valid—and when they are not. Ross studied 160 "mentally-retarded" individuals over a period of 40 years. Their intelligence test scores (IQs) ranged from 60 to 80 when the subjects were tested in San Francisco schools during the 1920's and 1930's. These scores put the subjects in the category "educable mentally retarded." When the subjects were tested again some 40 years later, as adults, they got similar scores. Thus, the intelligence tests were *reliable*.

Two of Ross's findings also suggest that the intelligence tests were *valid*, at least as far as *school performance* and *job placement* are concerned. First, the subjects tended to do poorly in school 40 years ago, and many of them dropped out early. Second, the subjects tended to find lower-paying jobs (and jobs that required fewer "intellectual skills") than did subjects with "normal" IQs. However, Ross reports, the tests were *not valid* as far as pre-

Robert V. Guthrie

dicting "personal success and satisfaction" in real-world settings. He notes that most of the subjects were married, had families, and expressed just as much satisfaction with their lives and their jobs as did people with "normal" IQs. Furthermore, Ross says, these so-called "retarded" individuals performed well as parents, too. They took their children to the doctor just as often, used similar forms of discipline, and taught their children almost as many school-related skills as did parents with "normal" intelligence scores (Ross, 1985).

These data suggest that IQs can be a fairly valid indicator of performance in school and on the job—provided that the testees aren't given the kind of "special training" that Bloom and Broder used. The problem comes, however, when we use IQs to make judgments in situations where they are known *not* to yield valid predictions. And, as we will see, we also can get into trouble if we use IQs without realizing the various *biases* that are built into the tests.

Cultural and Racial Biases

Built into most intelligence tests is a *cultural bias* that we are not always aware of. Binet and Simon, for instance, took many of their basic ideas from Paul Broca, who believed that the size of your brain determined the amount of your intelligence. A century or so ago, Broca performed some very inexact measurements on brain size and incorrectly concluded that men were brighter than women and that whites were smarter than blacks.

Most modern psychologists reject Broca's notions about the superior mental abilities of males and whites. However, a few scientists do still cling to Galton's belief in genetically-deter-mined racial differences. For example, in 1969, Arthur Jensen published an article in the *Harvard Educational Review* entitled "How Much Can We Boost IQ and Scholastic Achievement?" In this paper—and in many books and articles he has published subsequently—Jensen claims that blacks are genetically inferior to whites as far as intelligence goes. Jensen's writings have, to say the least, created a storm of controversy. Let's look at the evidence that Jensen cites, then at the counter-claims.

Jensen begins by quoting a national survey of 81 different studies of black-white IQs. According to this survey, blacks tend to average about 15 IQ points lower than do whites on standardized intelligence tests. Blacks also score somewhat below other disadvantaged minority groups, such as Hispanics. Jensen also claims that blacks from "upper-status" homes tend to obtain significantly lower test scores than do whites reared in similar circumstances. Jensen then *ascribes* these differences to "genes" rather than to "environmental influences," although he offers little in the way of *reliable evidence* to support his views on the "genetic superiority of whites" (Jensen, 1969, 1979).

Had we not already pointed out that intelligence tests have a built-in bias toward certain cultural values, Jensen's points might deserve serious consideration. However, as Robert V. Guthrie points out in his book *Even the Rat Was White*, the psychologists who constructed most of the widely-used intelligence tests were almost all middle-class white males. (See Table 17.3.) And most of them shared Jensen's view that intelligence is *primarily an inherited trait*. Thus, if blacks did poorly on standard intelligence tests, the test-makers *presumed* this difference was due to "bad genes" and not to "bad environments." Guthrie also notes that, until recently, psychologists studying blacks tended to focus on *differences* between the races, not *similarities* (Guthrie, 1976).

In his book *The Intelligence Men: Makers of the IQ Controversy*, Raymond Fancher states that the study of intelligence is "unusual among scientific problems for the degree to which it interacts with the extra-scientific and some-times even non-rational concerns of its investigators" (Fancher, 1985). With Fancher's words in mind, suppose we try to put aside our own cultural biases and look at the *data* on racial differences in IQs—and what factors presumably cause these differences.

TABLE 17.3   The Chitling Test[a]

1. A "handkerchief head" is:
   - (A) a cool cat
   - (B) a porter
   - (C) an uncle Tom
   - (D) a hoddi
   - (E) a preacher
2. Which word is most out of place here?
   - (A) splib
   - (B) blood
   - (C) gray
   - (D) spook
   - (E) black
3. A "gas head" is a person who has a:
   - (A) fast-moving car
   - (B) stable of "lace"
   - (C) "process"
   - (D) habit of stealing cars
   - (E) long jail record for arson
4. "Bo Diddley" is a:
   - (A) game for children
   - (B) down-home cheap wine
   - (C) down-home singer
   - (D) new dance
   - (E) Moejoe call
5. If a man is called a "blood," then he is a:
   - (A) fighter
   - (B) Mexican-American
   - (C) Negro
   - (D) hungry hemophile
   - (E) Redman or Indian

[a]This IQ test was designed by Adrian Dove, a sociologist who is familiar with black ghetto culture. It probably seems as unfair to white middle-clas culture as the tests designed by them appear to other culture groups. The answer to all the above questions is C. (Copyright 1968 by Newsweek, Inc.)

□ □ **QUESTION** □ □
How would it affect *government policies and financial expenditures* if it could be proved that IQ differences among racial subgroups were due to *cultural* rather than *genetic* factors?

The "Profile of American Youth Survey"

In 1986, R.D. Bock and Elsie Moore published a report entitled "Advantage and Disadvantage: The Profile of American Youth Survey." The study, which was supported by both the US Department of Labor and the Department of Defense, was an attempt to assess the "cognitive development" and "vocational aptitudes" of 12,000 Americans between the ages of 15 and 23.

The American Youth Survey data tend, at first glance, to support Jensen's views. For, on standardized intelligence tests, Hispanic young people tended to score below whites, and blacks tended to score (on the average) below Hispanics. However, Bock and Moore show rather conclusively that these differences are *not* due either to *genetic endowment* or to *linguistic ability*. Rather, Bock and Moore say:

> A more satisfactory explanation [for overall group performance differences on the tests] is simply that the communities represented . . . maintain, for historical reasons, different norms, standards, and expectations concerning performance within the family, in school, and in other institutions that shape children's behavior. Young people adapt to these norms and apply their talents and energies accordingly. (Bock & Moore, 1986)

Put more simply, the data from this survey suggest that young people *take on the values of the culture they grow up in*. If they are rewarded for learning "street smarts" rather than "analytical skills," the young people will do well in their own subcultures, but do poorly in school (and on standard intelligence tests) that emphasize only one of the three types of thinking Sternberg has described.

Evidence to support this position comes from two sets of studies: one, an investigation into upper-class black children in Boston, and the other a comparison of white children in the US with their age-mates in Japan.

□ □ QUESTION □ □

Do you think lower-class children or upper-class children would, generally speaking, be more "creative"? Why?

The Boston Study

During the 1970's, Regina Yando, Victoria Seitz, and Edward Zigler made an extensive study of 304 children in the Boston area. All the subjects were eight years old when the study was begun. Half the children came from upper-class homes, half from lower-class homes. Half the children from each class of home were black, and half were white. The children in each of these four groups were carefully matched for IQ. The psychologists also gave each child tests that measured such traits as creativity, self-confidence, autonomy, curiosity, frustration threshold, and dependency.

The results of the Boston study were, in many ways, fairly surprising. To begin with, Yando and her colleagues note that almost all of the differences between black and white children could be accounted for in terms of *social class*. Upper-class children—black or white—were very similar. So were lower-class children. However, lower-class children (of either race) were more creative in solving problems, and they were more likely to take risks and persevere at tasks despite frustration. Upper-class children had larger vocabularies and were better at step-by-step reasoning, but were anxious and overly concerned about failure. Lower-class black children attending predominantly white schools tended to suffer a loss in self-confidence, but did better academically than their peers in predominantly black schools.

Yando, Seitz, and Zigler also asked the children's teachers to rate each of the subjects. Teacher ratings did, in fact, predict academic skills. However, the psychologists note that these ratings might well have been due to the bias that the teachers showed against youngsters from lower-class homes (Yando, Seitz, & Zigler, 1979). More likely, however, lower-class children were probably rewarded for learning *different skills* in their non-school environments than were upper-class children (Bock & Moore, 1986).

□ □ QUESTION □ □

***Academic* psychologists (among others) sometimes use the term "disadvantaged" when referring to lower-class children (either black or white). What kind of *cultural bias* does the use of this term suggest?**

Cross-cultural Studies of Intelligence

Several recent studies have shown that Japanese children tend to score about 11 points *higher* on intelligence tests than do white American children of similar ages and socioeconomic status. In a recent book, Harold Stevenson, Hiroshi Azuma, and Kenji Hakuta describe some of the cultural differences that may lead to this cross-cultural difference in IQs (Stevenson, Azuma, & Hakuta, 1986).

First of all, Japanese children spend more hours per day in school than is the case here and go to school more days of the year. Furthermore, they typically spend several hours a week outside of school in special "cram courses" designed to help them pass the nation-wide exam that determines which children can enter college (and which can't). Students who don't pass the exam have problems getting good jobs, and are usually considered

Regina Yando

"failures." Thus, the *students'* level of motivation to succeed in school may be much higher in Japan than in the US.

Second, in Japan the husband traditionally has worked while the wife's main job has been that of making sure the children do well in school. If her children don't pass the exam, their mother is considered a failure.

Third, in the US, there are many more one-parent homes and more families where both parents have jobs. Thus, in America, the parents typically spend less time per week tutoring their children in "school skills" than is the case in Japan.

Fourth, in Japan the use of *coercive* or *physical discipline* is much lower than in the US. And, as we have already noted, children who are rewarded for improvement tend to have higher cognitive skills than do children who are physically punished for their mistakes (Power & Chapieski, 1986).

Given these data, perhaps we shouldn't wonder that Japanese school children have higher IQs. However, we must also note a cultural "disadvantage" as well. MIT scientist Susumu Tonegawa won the 1987 Nobel Prize in medicine for his pioneering studies on immunology. Tonegawa was born and reared in Japan, but did his graduate work and most of his award-winning research in the US. In a re-

cent interview in *Science*, Tonegawa states that he would not have won the Nobel Prize had he stayed in Japan, because creativity is punished rather than being rewarded in most segments of Japanese society. Japanese education is focused almost entirely on "rote learning and memorization," Tonegawa claims (cited in Marx, 1987).

In their recent "profile of American youth," Bock and Moore state that each society has its own values, as does each sub-culture within any given society. In middle- and upper-class America—and even more so in Japan—the emphasis in child rearing and in school is on rote memorization and the acquisition of "analytical skills." Grades and intelligence test scores are, therefore, a direct measure of our cultural biases, not of some "biologically-determined trait" that we might call *general intelligence*. Blacks, Hispanics, and lower-class whites will continue to do poorly on intelligence tests, Bock and Moore imply, until we do one of two things: First, we could change our "culturally-biased definition" of what "intelligence" is, and then alter the educational process itself to reflect the new definition. Or second, we could find some way to incorporate *the same set of cultural values and child-rearing practices* into all segments of society. To achieve either change, Bock and Moore say, would take "decades" (Bock & Moore, 1986).

▢▢ QUESTION ▢▢
Why do you think that most people who believe that differences in black-white IQs are "genetically determined" also argue that the differences in Japanese-American IQs are caused by "cultural differences"?

Intelligence: A Holistic Viewpoint

Anne Anastasi takes a holistic view toward what intelligence really is, and how we might measure it better. She writes, "Both the traits that constitute intelligence and the level of development of these traits reflect the demands and the **contingent reinforcements** imposed by the environments in which individuals function through the life span. Accordingly, the composition of intelligence may vary as a function of age and cultural context" (Anastasi, 1986).

Anastasi goes on to say that such factors as cognitive skills, knowledge, motivation, and attitudes are all an integral part of what we call *intelligence*. A valid intelligence test would measure all these factors. To date, Anastasi notes, no such test exists. But as we free ourselves from our earlier, rigid beliefs that intelligence is made up of "g" factors and other traits determined primarily by the genes, Anastasi says, we will come closer to creating an adequate measure of intellectual performance (An-

In addition to spending more time in school, most Japanese teenagers attend a *juku*, or "cram school." These *juku* students wear headbands to indicate the level of study they have achieved.

astasi, 1983). As we will see, the same thing might well be said of our attempts to measure any other aspect of personality.

OBJECTIVE VERSUS SUBJECTIVE TESTS

Although intelligence tests have received most of the publicity in recent years, there are many other types of psychological scales that attempt to measure traits or some other aspect of human performance or personality. Some of these tests are *objective*, in that they yield numbers which describe how much of a given trait you possess. Others tests are *subjective*, in that an expert must "analyze" your responses and then give a subjective evaluation of what the responses mean. (In the academic world, a multiple-choice test is usually "objective," while an essay exam is usually "subjective.")

Both objective and subjective tests have been used for years in the study of human personality. Let's look at both kinds, then discuss the problems and benefits associated with using them.

FIG. 17.3 A sample Thematic Apperception Test card. What is going on in this scene, what are the characters thinking and feeling, what led up to the portrayed situation, and what will its outcome be?

Subjective Tests

Suppose that you wanted to devise a means of getting at the *unconscious* aspects of a person's mind. You could hardly ask the person about such matters directly—using a pen-and-paper test—because *by definition* the person isn't aware of unconscious processes.

But what if you presented the subject with a variety of unstructured or *ambiguous* situations? Wouldn't you expect people to *project* themselves into the task given them? After all, the "first law of perception" is that you *perceive what you expect to perceive*. Therefore, shouldn't people *perceive* ambiguous stimuli according to their unconscious needs and desires? If they did, then you could easily interpret their responses to these **projective tests** as reflecting unconscious processes.

Projective tests are among the most widely-used subjective scales. So let's look briefly at several of them.

• Word Association Test

The first "projective" instrument was the *word association test* devised by Galton more than 100 years ago. As we noted in Chapter 16, it was subsequently revised by Carl Jung in the early 1900's. The test consists of a list of stimulus words that are presented to you one at a time. Some of the words are "emotionally charged." Others are persumably "emotionally neutral." You are asked to respond to each word with the first thing that comes to mind.

Both Galton and Jung assumed that if you reacted to a word like "sex" by blocking (refusing to answer)—or if you started sweating, or fainted, or gave a wildly inappropriate reaction

such as "firecrackers" or "death"—then you might have sexual problems. Sometimes the tester will use a polygraph, or "lie detector," to check your physical reactions as you respond to the words.

• The TAT

The **Thematic Apperception Test**, or TAT, consists of a set of 20 stimulus pictures that depict rather vague but potentially emotional situations. You respond by making up a story telling (1) what led up to the situation shown in the picture, (2) what the people are thinking and feeling and doing right then, and (3) what will happen to them in the future. Each story you produce is scored and interpreted individually. The psychologist giving the test usually assumes you will express your deep-seated needs and personality problems by *projecting* them onto the hero or the heroine in the story.

• Inkblot Tests

By far the most famous of the projective instruments is the inkblot test, first devised in the 1920's by Swiss psychiatrist **Hermann Rorschach**. The Rorschach test is a series of 10 inkblots that are given to you one at a time. You look at each inkblot and report what you see—much as you might look at clouds passing overhead and tell someone what "faces" and other things you saw in the clouds. The psychologist then interprets your responses according to one of several scoring methods.

□ □ **QUESTION** □ □
It is sometimes said that Rorschach interpretations tell us more about the

Projective tests. According to psychoanalytic theory, people tend to project their own personalities onto vague or ambiguous stimulus inputs. Projective tests—such as the inkblot test and the TAT—consist of vague stimuli that a psychologist might ask you to describe or talk about, in the hope that you will somehow structure the stimuli in the same way that your personality is structured.

Thematic Apperception Test (the-MATT-tick app-purr-SEP-shun). Apperception is defined as "the process of perceiving something in terms of your prior experience." The TAT is a set of vague stimulus pictures that you are asked to "tell stories about," presumably because you will perceive the pictures in terms of your own personality. Hence the "themes" of the stories you tell will give the psychologist some clue as to your own "themas."

Hermann Rorschach (HAIR-man ROAR-shock). A Swiss psychiatrist (1884–1922) who devised the famous inkblot test.

person doing the "interpreting" than they do about the person who took the test. Why might this sometimes be the case?

- ### Usefulness of Projective Tests

The bulk of scientific research suggests that most projective tests are neither very reliable nor particularly valid as presently used. In the 1982 edition of their book *Personality Assessment*, Richard Lanyon and Leonard Goodstein review nearly 10,000 studies on projective instruments. As for the Rorschach, they state that "the empirical basis for interpreting this test remains thin." Lanyon and Goodstein go on to say, "Although the volume of literature on the TAT is large . . . its status as a proven, clinically useful instrument is still in doubt."

Despite the fact that the scientific evidence argues against the validity and reliability of projective tests, they still are in widespread use. We will return to this point momentarily.

"Rorschach! What's to become of you?"

Objective Tests

Objective tests have several purposes. One is to *measure present traits, skills, and knowledge*. Another is to *predict future performance*. A few objective tests attempt to serve both purposes simultaneously.

- ### Achievement Tests

An achievement test is a psychological scale that measures how much you have learned about a given topic. The test does *not* indicate either *why* you learned as much as you did, or how much you *could have learned* under different circumstances. People with high IQs will do poorly on achievement tests if they haven't learned much about the topic, or if they once knew the material but now have forgotten it. People with lower IQs will do well if they have studied the subject thoroughly. Therefore, achievement tests presumably tell us little or nothing about your motivation or your IQ. *At their best*, they simply measure your present level of performance (Tyler & Walsh, 1979).

- ### Aptitude Tests

In its purest form, an aptitude test attempts to determine whether you possess enough of a certain trait—or certain personality factors—in order to succeed in some job or other situation. Some aptitude tests are fairly simple measures of such skills as mechanical or clerical aptitude. Other tests, such as those given to prospective airline pilots, measure a broader range of abilities. Scores on these *simple scales* tend to predict future performance fairly well.

Unfortunately, many devices that are called *aptitude* tests are really combinations of *achievement* and *intelligence* tests. The Scholastic Aptitude Test (SAT) is one such, for it tends to measure how much you have already learned about a given academic subject and thus is an achievement test. The SAT also measures—to some extent—how "test wise" you are, and how good you are at solving the types of problems you are likely to face on examinations while in college. Since the SAT correlates rather well with intelligence test scores, it provides a rough measure of your IQ. And since SAT scores are reasonably good at predicting future grades in college, the SAT would seem to be a *valid* academic screening device (Tyler & Walsh, 1979). This statement is only true, of course, as long as schools continue their present emphasis on "analytical skills," rather than "creativity" or "street smarts" (Sternberg, 1985).

- ### Personality Tests: The MMPI

Not all objective tests attempt to measure achievement or aptitudes. Many personality tests are "objective," in the sense that they are made up of multiple-choice items and yield numerical scores. One such is the **Minnesota Multiphasic Personality Inventory**. The MMPI, as it usually is called, is widely used today as a device for detecting individuals who might have personality problems (or mental disorders). The MMPI was created to be as reliable as possible—and research suggests that its reliability is indeed fairly high.

In its original form, the MMPI consisted of some 560 short statements that were given to large numbers of people, some of them mental patients, some of them presumably normal. The statements mostly concern psychiatric problems or unusual thought patterns, such as (1) Someone is trying to control my mind using radio waves, (2) I never think of unusual sexual situations, and (3) I never have been sick a day of my life. When you take the MMPI, you respond to each statement either by agreeing or disagreeing, or by saying that it is impossible for you to respond at all.

As you might expect, the mental patients used in the original sample reacted to many of the statements in quite different ways than did the "normal" subjects. Depressed or suicidal patients gave different responses than did patients diagnosed as being schizophrenic or paranoid. The authors of the test were able to pick out different groups of test items that appeared to form "depression" scales, "paranoia" scales, "schizophrenia" scales, and so forth. If an otherwise normal individual takes the test and receives an abnormally high score on the "paranoia" scale, the psychologist interpreting the test might well worry that the person could become paranoid if put under great psychological stress or pressure. By looking at the pattern or *profile* of a subject's scores on the different MMPI scales, a psychologist might also be able to predict what areas of the subject's personality needed strengthening.

This approach to the study of personality—judging people almost entirely in terms of their *objective* responses—gives the MMPI a very high reliability. Whether the MMPI is a *valid* index of personality structure is another matter altogether. For example, there is the nagging question of whether the so-called "normal" group used when the MMPI was first created is still accurate. The normal group was made up of visitors to the University of Minnesota hospital, of government workers in Minnesota, and of high school graduates seeking job counseling. In a recent book, Mayo Clinic psychologist Robert Colligan states that "Whoever takes the MMPI today is being compared with the way a man or woman from Minnesota endorsed those items in the late 1930s and early 1940s." Colligan notes that by 1980 a similar "normal" group gave quite different answers than did the "normal" group more than 40 years ago. Thus, modern-day MMPI scores based on the original sample may not be valid (Colligan, 1983).

Richard Lanyon and Leonard Goodstein agree with Colligan. They report that, as of 1981, there were more than 5,000 published studies on the MMPI. Despite this "mountain of literature," though, Lanyon and Goodstein believe there is little scientific evidence that the MMPI is a valid measure of personality (Lanyon & Goodstein, 1982).

Psychological Testing: A Summary

By now, a certain trend may be obvious to you: Psychologists have devised a large number of instruments for measuring personality, traits, intelligence, aptitudes, achievement, and unconscious processes. Generally speaking, both the *scientific* reliability and the validity of these measures are suspect, if not downright doubtful. However, most of these instruments are presently in widespread use. Why?

The answer seems to lie in the difference between "academic respectability" and "practical experience." Most scientifically-oriented psychologists *do* argue against the usefulness of these sorts of tests (Piotrowski & Keller, 1984a, 1984b). However, the vast majority of *clinical psychologists* continue to employ the tests in everyday practice (Piotrowski, 1984; Piotrowski, Sherry, & Keller, 1985). And, of course, school personnel continue to use intelligence and aptitude tests on a daily basis.

Why then the difference between the beliefs of "scientific" and "practicing" psychologists? In part, practicing psychologists simply place greater faith in their own clinical experience than they do in experimental evidence (Wade & Baker, 1977). Then, too, real-world constraints for practicing psychologists are different than those that hold in academic circles. Research-oriented scientists can take years making up their minds about the reliability and validity of a given psychological test—and their daily lives aren't much affected by the decisions they ultimately make. Clinical and counseling psychologists, however, must decide *each day* how best to treat or advise a number of clients. Over the years, these *practicing* psychologists build up strong viewpoints about what "works" for them and their patients. And since the test-builders have not yet devised instruments that are more valid and reliable than the ones presently in use, the old ones continue to serve an urgent professional need.

In similar fashion, school administrators often must decide the fates of hundreds of students during a given school year. Intelligence and aptitude tests may not be perfect, but they are the *only* instruments administrators typically have available to them. And, as we noted, the tests *are valid* for predicting academic and job-related performance unless the testees are given special training. Little wonder the tests continue to be used.

Minnesota Multiphasic Personality Inventory (mull-tee-FAZE-ick). An objective personality test that yields scores on many different scales. By looking at the *profile* of your test scores, a trained interpreter can often determine those areas in which you are "normal" (that is, like most other people) and those areas in which you might be somewhat abnormal, or might experience problems.

We could make the same sort of comments about personality theories. Trait theory may not be perfect; however, as Allport wisely noted, the trait approach is embedded in the very fabric of our language. We probably will find the concepts of "traits" useful in daily life—if not in laboratory situations—until our language itself changes.

● **Tests and Therapy**

We are left with the puzzling question we asked earlier in this chapter: Eysenck's trait-oriented theory has gathered much more scientific support than any other. Why then isn't it more popular?

Again, the answer seems to lie in *practicality*. While Eysenck's approach can *describe* people in fairly reliable fashion, it offers no suggestion at all as to *how to treat disturbed patients*. Eysenck himself tends to use behavior modification with most of his patients. However, Eysenck did not *develop* behavior modification, nor do most of the people who did develop these techniques subscribe to Eysenck's theoretical views.

As we mentioned in Chapter 16, most "person-oriented" theories were developed by *practicing therapists*. For that reason, perhaps, "narrative accounts" of personality typically suggest what kinds of treatment certain types of people might benefit from. The same cannot be said of *any* trait-oriented theory. Little wonder, then, that most practicing psychologists find Freud more useful than Eysenck—and Carl Rogers more useful than Raymond Cattell—both in terms of *diagnosing* and *treating* the mental patients they work with on a daily basis.

With these thoughts in mind, let's look more closely at how psychologists describe abnormal thoughts, feelings, and behaviors. We will save our survey of therapeutic techniques for Chapter 19.

SUMMARY

1. There are two main types of personality theorists: those interested in **temperaments**, and those interested in **traits**.
2. **Temperament** theorists (such as Galen) believe that body chemistry determines personality type. Galen assumed the four main fluids or **humors** of the body (**blood, phlegm, yellow bile, black bile**) were the major determinants of personality, a belief long since discarded by scientists.
3. Arnold Buss and Robert Plomin believe there are three types of temperaments, **emotionality, activity**, and **sociability**.
4. Studies of **twins reared apart** suggest that some aspects of temperament may be inherited.
5. Hans Eysenck believes human personality can be measured using three scales: **neuroticism, introversion-extroversion**, and **psychoticism**. Research data tend to support Eysenck's views on the introversion-extroversion scale, but are less supportive of the other two.
6. The scientific study of **individual differences** probably began with Francis Galton, who also devised the first **intelligence test**. Modern **trait theory** has been strongly influenced by Galton.
7. Allport believed there were three main types of traits, **cardinal, central**, and **secondary**. Cardinal traits are rare. Central traits are a person's "outstanding characteristics." Secondary traits are less important and consistent aspects of personality.
8. Allport and Odbert identified 18,000 trait terms buried in the English language.
9. Raymond Cattell believes there are but two types of traits, **surface** and **source** traits. Using **factor analysis**, Cattell determined there are but 16 source traits, which determine some 35 surface traits. Warren Norman, however, has reduced Cattell's list of traits to 5.
10. Some psychologists define **intelligence** as a trait, but others do not. Galton devised a crude intelligence test, but the first true intelligence scale was the **Binet-Simon** test, which measured **mental age**.
11. **Intelligence Quotient**, or IQ, is often defined as mental age divided by **chronological age** times 100. Most modern intelligence tests measure IQ using **standard scores** or **percentiles** rather than mental age.
12. Charles Spearman listed two types of intelligence, a **general** or "g" factor, and several **specific** or "s" factors.
13. Raymond Cattell claims there are two intellectual factors, **fluid intelligence**, which is inherited, and **crystallized intelligence**, which involves learned skills.
14. According to Robert Sternberg's **triarchic theory**, there are three types of intelligence: **componential**, or "analytical"; **experiental**, or "creative"; and **contextual** intelligence, or "street smarts."
15. Children brought up in deprived or **disadvantaged circumstances** generally have

lower IQ scores than do children brought up in **stimulating environments**. Making the child's environment more stimulating can often help increase the child's **IQ**.

16. Research suggests that children whose mothers use **coercive discipline** tend to have lower IQs than do children whose mothers trained them to exercise **self-control**.

17. Individuals who have failed to learn the **analytical skills** required to do well in school can often raise their test scores by learning **step-by-step reasoning**.

18. Intelligence tests are fairly **reliable**, but tend to be **valid** only when used to predict school performance or job performance where **analytical reasoning** is considered the "mark of intelligence."

19. Intelligence tests are **not valid** when used to predict real-world success or job and personal satisfaction.

20. There are **performance** differences among cultural groups in the US, but a recent survey of American youth suggests these differences are due to **cultural norms**, not to genetic differences among racial groups.

21. Because of the strong emphasis on school performance and rote memory in Japan, Japanese children tend to have **higher IQs** than do American children. However, Japa-

nese children may well be **less creative** than are youngsters in the US.

22. **Projective tests**, such as the **Rorschach**, the **word association test**, and the **TAT**, contain ambiguous stimuli that you are supposed to "structure" in terms of your own personality. Both the **validity** and the **reliability** of these tests is questionable in most circumstances.

23. **Achievement tests** measure knowledge of a certain subject, while **aptitude tests** attempt to predict future performance. Many aptitude tests actually measure achievement and IQ, however, and thus may be **biased** against disadvantaged individuals.

24. **Objective personality tests**, such as the **MMPI**, tend to be reliable measures of personality, but their validity is open to question.

25. **Practicing psychologists** continue to use personality tests because they believe the tests are helpful—and because there simply aren't better instruments available.

26. **Person-oriented** personality theories may be more popular because they tend to suggest the method of **therapy** that should be used to treat psychological problems, while (in general) **trait-oriented** personality theories are not closely tied to any given type of treatment.

"Well, Jessie, if I don't get my Ph.D., I can always blame it on you," Tom Flagg said, his smile (Continued from page 434.) belying the seriousness of his words.

"Did I mess up your experiment?" Jessie Williams asked in a concerned tone of voice.

"Royally. But luckily, you were practically the only teacher who did."

"None of my bloomers bloomed?"

Tom shook his head. "That wasn't the problem. Just the opposite. All of your kids bloomed, black or white, whether the test said they should or not."

"And that's bad?"

"Good for the kids. Bad for my experiment."

Jessie frowned. "Will it really hold you back from getting your doctorate in psychology?"

"No, not at all. As I said, the Rosenthal test predicted rather well for several other teachers." Tom stretched his muscular legs out in front of him. "I just wish that it hadn't."

Jessie looked puzzled. "But I thought you wanted the test to work. I thought you wouldn't get credit for your experiment if it didn't."

"I couldn't tell you everything about the test, Jessie," Tom said sheepishly. "You see, Professor Rosenthal didn't really make up a test for 'Late Bloomers.' He was interested in people's expectancies instead. He figured if you told a teacher one of her children was going to 'bloom,' the teacher would pay a lot more attention to that child. And the kid would respond to the teacher's expectancies, and would really improve. But if the teacher expected the kid to backslide, she'd pick on the kid's faults and mistakes. Then the kid would become discouraged and wouldn't do well."

"Is that what this Professor Rosenthal found?"

Tom shrugged his shoulders. "In a lot of cases, yes. But it's an iffy sort of thing. Not everybody has been able to replicate Rosenthal's original results, and a lot of psychologists don't believe in it. Rosenthal still insists his results were valid, though, and I tend to believe him."

"But it didn't work with me, did it?" Jessie said, grinning.

"No, it didn't. Not that I'm complaining, you understand. It shouldn't work with really good teachers, because they wouldn't be prejudiced for or against kids just because of their test scores."

"Shower them with love and affection, and you help them all bloom as much as they can."

"Right," said Tom.

"Then why are you concerned if I didn't pay any attention to your test scores, Tom? I'm not suggestible enough for you?"

17 / Personality Theories

Tom laughed. "How did you guess?"

"Keep your mind on your experiment. What's troubling you, friend?"

Tom shrugged. "The fact that some teachers were influenced by the faked test scores that I gave them. I can maybe understand why some of the white teachers might be prejudiced in favor of white kids and against blacks—that's part of our culture, though it's changing some now. And maybe I can understand why some of the black teachers would be prejudiced against white kids and biased toward the blacks. Somehow you expect that. But why would white teachers be prejudiced against white kids, and black teachers prejudiced against black kids—just because some silly test said the kids were going to backslide, or do poorly?"

"Brother Thomas, we are all human beings," Jessie Williams said. "Our blood is the same color, our brains are the same size, our bodies are the same shapes, and we all learn our prejudices at our mothers' knees. I'm just lucky that I was taught to be prejudiced *toward*, instead of prejudiced *against*. But it's prejudice, just the same."

"You think love is prejudice?"

"Of course. Love is prejudice in favor of life."

Tom swallowed hard. "Well, do you think you might be prejudiced just a little in my direction?"

"It might happen to be so."

"Then maybe I ought to ask you out to the movies tomorrow night."

Jessie grinned. "You do that, Baby. You do that very thing."

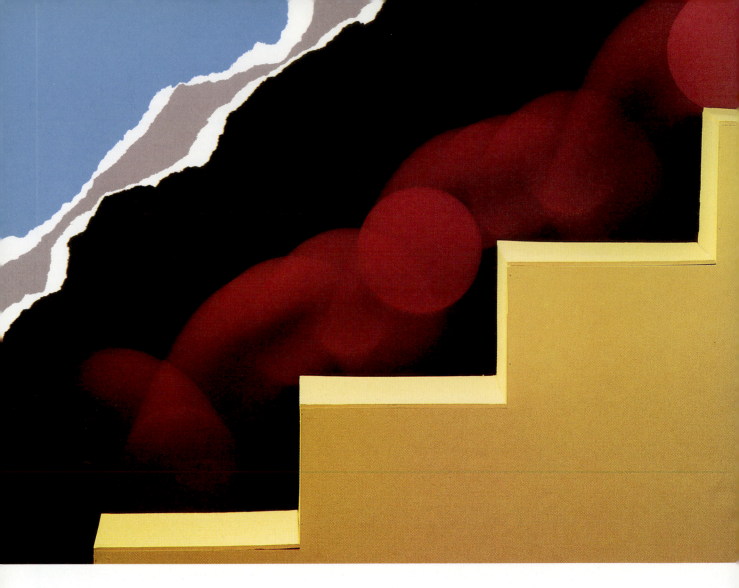

Abnormal Psychology

"I'm Crazy — You're Crazy"

C · H · A · P · T · E · R ·

18

Steve May got out of the car, closed the door, then stuck his head back in through the window. "You really think it will work?" he said for perhaps the tenth time that day.

Dr. Mary Ellen Mann smiled reassuringly at the handsome young man. "Well, it worked for all of Professor Rosenhan's subjects. They all got admitted to the mental hospital without any trouble at all. Getting out seems to be the problem, not getting in. But I'm sure you'll be able to cope beautifully with any difficulties that may arise. Just get yourself in gear and go convince those people that you're crazier than a bedbug."

Steve thought about the matter for a moment or two. He had willingly committed himself to helping Dr. Mann with her research on the reliability of psychiatric diagnoses. But committing himself to a state mental hospital was a very frightening thought. He supposed that he couldn't really chicken out at the last moment, but still. . . . "If they do admit me," the blond young man said, "You're sure that I can prove to them that I'm okay so they'll let me out?"

Dr. Mann snorted as she laughed. "As I told you, Steve, if you get stuck in there, you've got to get out on your own. Oh, I'll come rescue you eventually, have no fears about that." She leaned toward him a trifle. "Or maybe you're afraid that you really are a bit nuts. Is that the problem?"

A rosy flush spread over Steve's face. "Of course not! I'm as sane as you are!"

Dr. Mann snorted even more loudly. "Just don't tell the psychiatrist that, or you may never get out!" Then she smiled warmly. "Good luck, Steve. I really appreciate your helping out my research this way."

Steve nodded slowly, then pulled his head out of the car window. Dr. Mann waved at him, then put the car into gear and slowly drove off.

Steve turned to look at the hospital. It was a huge, towering, forbidding structure. The thought of spending the next few days—or weeks, or months—in that place frankly scared him. But he had promised. . . .

He walked slowly up the path and through the heavy, wooden door. The lobby inside was cool and almost empty. A nice-looking young woman sat behind a reception desk, filling in a form of some kind on a typewriter. Steve put on his best smile and walked over to her.

"Hello," Steve said.

The woman stopped typing and looked up at him. Her face brightened as she took in his handsome features and his muscular body. "Oh, hello," she said warmly. "What can I do for you? Would you like to see a patient?"

Steve returned her smile. "No, I want to *be* a patient, if you don't mind."

The woman's smile faded a bit. "Oh," she said briskly. "There's something wrong?"

Steve nodded. "Yeah. I need help. I hear voices."

The woman's smile faded away entirely, as if she had suddenly tucked him into a much less desirable category in her mind. "What do the voices seem to be saying?" she asked.

"They're kind of indistinct," he replied. "Mostly words like 'dull,' 'thud,' 'empty.' You know, things like that."

The woman nodded slowly, mechanically. "And what sex are the voices, male or female?"

Steve smiled wanly. "I can't always tell."

The woman frowned. "Are you in any pain right now?"

"No, not really," Steve said. "But I do think I need your help—for a while, that is, until the voices go away."

Again the woman frowned. "Well, we're pretty full these days. You'll have to see the admitting psychiatrist, of course. But he's very busy. And we'll have to fill out a lot of papers, and. . . ."

Two hours later, Steve's fingers were almost numb from writer's cramp. He finished all the forms, and then sat patiently in the lobby for another hour or so until the psychiatrist could see him.

The psychiatrist was a pleasant man of about 40 who spoke with such a thick foreign accent that Steve couldn't always understand the questions the man asked him. Steve told the man about his voices—that they were indistinct and that they seemed to be saying "dull," "thud," and "hollow." The doctor nodded sagely, and muttered under his breath. Steve thought the man had said something like "Existential crisis." Steve smiled inwardly. It was going just like Rosenhan's paper had suggested it would. Almost all of Rosenhan's subjects got the same sort of diagnosis.

Then the psychiatrist started asking questions about Steve's early life. When Steve admitted that he occasionally argued with his father, and that he really got along better with his mother, the doctor nodded sagely again. Steve thought he mumbled something like, "Very significant." And when Steve said that he wasn't always sure what his goals in life were, and that he now and again lost his temper, the psychiatrist muttered something under his breath that sounded suspiciously like "Poor impulse control."

Finally the psychiatrist leaned back in his chair, tapped a pencil on his desk, and stared silently at Steve for a few moments. "Look, Steven, I don't want to alarm you, but I do think I ought to be honest with you. You seem to be suffering from very real psychological problems. You were right to come to us. I'm sure that we can be of help. We'll keep you under observation for a while, and then we'll talk about getting you legally certified . . ."

"Legally certified?" Steve said in a horrified tone of voice.

"Of course. If you are to stay here more than 60 days, which will likely be the case, there are certain legal formalities we have to go through . . ."

"Sixty days! But what if I get better right away—like tomorrow?" Steve protested.

The psychiatrist allowed himself a brief, thin-lipped smile. "As you Americans say, we'll cross that bridge when we come to it." The doctor pressed a button on his desk and, almost immediately, a burly young attendant entered the office.

"Charles, this is Steven," the psychiatrist said. "He will be staying with us for a while. Please check him in and then put him on Ward A-5."

The attendant nodded, then said to Steve, "This way, please."

Steve got up and started to extend his hand to the psychiatrist. But the man was already busy working on the papers that would admit Steve to the mental hospital. So Steve picked up his small bag and followed the attendant out of the office.

"First, we'll check you in and get all your valuables stowed away," the burly attendant said.

"Oh," said Steve, "I'd rather keep them with me."

"Can't. It's the rule," the attendant said. "Got to stow it all away—your money and credit cards and all that stuff. Your watch and rings, too. We can't be responsible, you know. And we'll have to inspect your shaving kit and all your personal gear. No razors, you know, and you can't keep all your clothes either."

"Clothes?" Steve said in an unbelieving tone of voice.

"Belts, stuff like that. Might hurt yourself."

Steve had to hurry a bit to keep up with the attendant. "But surely I can keep my pictures, and my books, and things like that . . ."

"Nope. It's against the rules."

For a moment, Steve panicked. The folly of what he was doing finally struck home. They were taking away all his "cards of identity." They were stripping him of his personality and turning him into a number, a card in a file, a statistic.

"We'll give you a shower and then get you some hospital clothes," the attendant said, opening a huge metal door and then locking it securely after they had passed through.

"But I just had a shower, about an hour ago," Steve protested as they walked down a long, bare corridor. "Do you think what I've got is catching?"

"Don't give me any trouble, man. I don't make the rules." The attendant unlocked another huge metal door at the end of the corridor and banged it shut behind them. They walked down a flight of metal stairs and then the attendant unlocked yet another door that had a small window in it. The window was covered with thick steel bars. The burly attendant told Steve to strip, took his things, and pointed to a shower room. When Steve returned, water still dripping from his hair, the attendant gave him a set of hospital clothes.

"You look fine," the attendant said. "Now, let's get on with it."

They walked down another long, bare corridor to a metal door that bore a small sign, "Ward A-5." Steve shook his head in dismay. They had passed through four locked, steel doors already. If getting *into* the ward was this difficult, what would getting *out* be like?

"This is it," the attendant said, unlocking the door and walking into the ward. "Wait here until I find the nurse."

Steve stood staring at the inmates. Several of them were watching a television set, but they didn't seem to respond to the program in any way. One middle-aged man rushed feverishly about the ward, as if looking for something he had lost. A younger man was rocking back and forth in a straight-backed chair. A third man was standing in a corner, quietly urinating.

My God, Steve thought. *You've got to be crazy to stay in a place like this.*

The attendant came back with a nurse, who gave Steve an efficient smile and then showed him where his bed would be. The man in the next bed was curled up in a fetal position, laughing quietly to himself, a serene smile on his face.

Steve stretched out on the narrow bed and stared at the ceiling. "Well, I made it in okay," he said aloud. "But how in the world am I ever going to get out of this place?"

The man in the next bed giggled softly.

(Continued on page 484.)

WARNING: CONTROVERSIAL MATERIAL!

Like all other sciences, psychology has its agreed-upon facts, but it also has its controversies. *Agreement* tends to be highest in those areas of the behavioral sciences which touch on biology and physics—the brain and the nervous system, sensory psychology, and (to some extent) perception. Consensus is somewhat lower in the fields of motivation and learning, and lower still in developmental and social psychology. But *disagreement* among psychologists is surely at its greatest in the areas of personality theory, abnormal psychology, and psychotherapy.

Since we have already covered personality theory, you are aware of what some of these controversies are all about. As you read this chapter (on abnormal psychology), and the next chapter (on therapy), you will discover even more ways in which professional scientists and therapists disagree. Perhaps it will help, therefore, if you keep several points in mind as you go through this material:

1. The study of human abnormalities is one of the richest and most fascinating areas in all of psychology.

18 / Abnormal Psychology

2. No one disagrees that these abnormalities exist. Rather, the controversy concerns how best to describe these conditions, where they come from, and what to do about them.

3. There is no way to be completely objective about abnormal psychology. Why is this so? Because the very word "abnormal" is based (for the most part) on subjective value judgments or interpretations.

What follows, therefore, is a *necessarily biased* presentation of the *necessarily controversial* material on abnormal thoughts, feelings, and behaviors. Before reading this chapter, you might wish to look over page 16 in Chapter 1 again, to remind yourself of what the author's biases are. You might also wish to keep a list of those issues raised in this chapter that puzzle you, or that you disagree with. For surely that is the best way to discover what your own biases about abnormal psychology actually are.

Let's begin by trying to define some terms.

What Is a "Mental Disorder?"

Many of the great personality theorists—Freud, Jung, Adler, Erikson, Rogers, and the rest—based their ideas on the study of mentally-disturbed patients. Most of these patients had problems that were *exaggerations* of the mental and behavioral traits that we all have. Therefore, the theorists presumed, the mental patient differs from the average citizen in the *quantity* (amount) of madness, not in the *quality* (type) of psychological problem. In short, the view of most theorists has been that we are all mildly abnormal, but some of us are more abnormal than others (Belmaker & van Praag, 1980).

But does that view make sense? If everyone **deviates** from the norm one way or another, doesn't the word "normal" lose most of its meaning? And if we can't define the word "normal," what shall we make of the word "abnormal," which literally means "away from the normal"?

There is also the question of *what* about the person is abnormal, and how we shall *refer to* the abnormality. The legal profession uses the word **insanity** to refer to many types of behavioral abnormalities, but psychologists typically avoid that term. Instead, we employ phrases such as "mental illness," "mental disorder," "behavioral disorder," or "problems of adjustment." These labels imply different *causes* and *therapeutic approaches*, of course:

1. "Mental illness" suggests the abnormality is medical or biological in origin, and perhaps *medication* might help.
2. "Mental disorder" implies the problem is primarily intra-psychic, thus *psychotherapy* might be called for.
3. "Behavioral disorder" suggests the abnormality is learned and thus treatable with *relearning techniques*.
4. "Problems of adjustment" (or sometimes "problems of living") implies something unusual about person-environmental interactions, and thus a *systems* approach could be the therapy of choice.

As you will soon see, there is as little agreement over which of the four *labels* to use as there is what *therapy* to employ.

No matter what term we use to describe psychological difficulties, though, all our concepts of the "abnormal" spring from a theory of what's "normal." So before we can discuss such topics as "mental illness," "behavior disorders," and "adjustment problems," we must first take a good, hard, objective look at the word "normal."

□□ **QUESTION** □□
You have surely met one or more *abnormal* people in your life. What about these individuals suggested to you that they might not be "entirely right?" And what does your answer to that question tell you about your own "theory of abnormality"?

WHAT IS NORMAL?

Many years ago, J.P. Foley defined *abnormal* as "a deviation from the statistical norms of a particular cultural group" (Foley, 1935).

There are good points and bad points about Foley's definition. On the positive side, it notes (1) that abnormalities are *unusual* occurrences (at least in some *statistical* sense), and (2) that these abnormalities are always defined in terms of some specific culture or group. On the negative side, Foley's definition does not differentiate between "good" deviations and "not-so-good" ones.

Can there be "good" abnormalities? Of course there can be. If someone said you were "much brighter than average," would you be insulted? No, you probably would be pleased (or even flattered). Yet the person has said, really, that you are *abnormally* intelligent. Physical beauty, creative talent, great wealth, and even excellent health are other examples of what most people would consider to be "good" abnormalities.

In a statistical sense, the word "abnormal" is neutral. That is, it covers both positive and negative deviations from the average. *As most people use the term*, however, "abnormal" usually refers to deviations that are inappropriate, disabling, unhealthy, or even "undesirable" and "immoral." Thus, for the most part, when we use the word "abnormal," we're not only noting a departure from some statistical norm, but making a *value judgment* about the situation as well.

Some psychologists attempt to get around this difficulty by restricting their use of the term to certain specific situations. For example, in 1939 H.J. Wegrocki stated that behaviors should be considered "abnormal" only if the *purpose* of the action was somehow deviant. No matter what you did, Wegrocki said, if you're simply trying to cope with a difficult situation, your responses shouldn't be thought of as abnormal. But if you were trying to avoid a situation—rather than coping with it—then your actions should be thought of as deviant (Wegrocki, 1939).

In 1957, E.J. Shoben moved a bit farther toward defining abnormality in terms of the individual rather than in statistical (or cultural) terms. Taking a lead from the humanistic psychologists, Shoben stated that normality consists of fulfilling your own potentialities as a human being. Any failure to live up to your own standards or ideals should be considered "abnormal," according to Shoben (Shoben, 1957).

As Melvin Zax and Emory Cowen point out, however, Shoben's approach raises as many problems as it solves. For instance, who sets standards, and where do ideals come from if not the cultural group into which you're born? And statistically speaking, how close must you come to "fulfilling your own potential" to be considered normal?

Zax and Cowen believe that all definitions of "abnormal" must be based on some concept of what is "healthy" or "normal" for a given person in a given culture. If you decide to seek psychological help, you might well tell the therapist, "I have trouble sleeping," or "I have no appetite," or "I don't have any friends." As Zax and Cowen note, these *statements of your problem* imply a comparison to some standard (or norm) of how long you should sleep, how much you should eat, or how many friends you should have. And the therapist, in evaluating your difficulties, must always realize that some people sleep longer than others do, eat more than others do, and have more friends than perhaps you have (or want to have). So the therapist must not only deal with your own "norms," but also with the "norms" of the culture you live in. Furthermore, the therapist

must also have some way of *measuring* how far you depart both from your own and from societal definitions of normality (Zax & Cowen, 1976).

Like it or not, then, you can't make much sense out of abnormal psychology until you learn a bit about statistical concepts of "the norm." So, let's look at how we might apply statistics to help understand and resolve the abnormalities of Mr. and Mrs. Smith.

Psychological Deviants

Suppose a young married couple named Mary and John Smith are on the verge of divorce. They go to see a psychologist and ask for help. Even before the psychologist learns their names, this counselor knows several things about the Smiths:

1. One or both of them is going to be suffering considerable psychological pain, distress, or anxiety.
2. Things are probably worse for the couple now than at some time in the past. That is, their way of life has changed from its usual (normal) pattern.
3. They are bright enough to sense this departure from normal and to seek help.

Any deviation from a person's usual way of thinking, feeling, or behaving can be considered a symptom of psychological abnormality—provided that the person was reasonably "normal" (as defined by the person's culture) to start with. Generally speaking, if this deviation is slight, the psychologist is likely to believe the person suffers from what has generally been

Mother Theresa, who has devoted her life to helping the "poorest of the poor," is certainly unusual. Is she abnormal?

"I CAN REMEMBER WHEN PARANOIA WAS UNUSUAL."

Neurosis (new-ROW-sis). Also called "psychoneurosis." A mild form of mental disorder that usually does not keep the individual from living a reasonably successful life. Freud thought that the seeds for a neurosis were planted in early childhood.

Psychosis (sigh-KOH-sis). A severe and usually incapacitating form of mental disorder that often requires hospitalization.

Satyr (SAY-teer). An ancient Greek country god supposedly fond of wine, women, and song—but mostly fond of women. Represented in art as a horse or goat.

classified as a **neurosis**. (The fact that the deviation is "slight" doesn't mean that the person doesn't suffer from a great deal of pain, however.) If the deviation is large, the psychologist may worry that the person suffers from a more severe problem called a **psychosis**.

Not all psychologists use terms such as "neurosis" and "psychosis." And there is less than complete agreement on how to define these terms among those psychologists who do make use of these diagnostic labels. Indeed, the *terminology* in the field of clinical psychology is undergoing rapid change right now, a point we will discuss later in this chapter (Davison & Neale, 1986). For the moment, all you need to remember is that some people have relatively minor problems, while others have such major difficulties that they may need to be hospitalized at some point in their lives. It is the psychologist's job, in either case, to help the person solve the problem and return to "normal"—as defined both by the person and by the society in which the person must live and function.

- ### Sexual Dysfunctions
Mary and John Smith could have many quite different *kinds* of psychological difficulties. Later in this chapter we will describe what some of the more common types are like. But to help us understand what the word "normal" means, let's assume that either or both of them has what a psychologist might call a *sexual dysfunction*.

Suppose that, in their first interview with the psychologist, John complains that Mary is sexually inhibited, and that she consistently refuses him the pleasures of the marriage bed. Mary replies that John is a **satyr**—that is, he has an unusually strong sex drive. She claims that he thinks of nothing but sex, talks of nothing else, and that he is interested only in her body and not in her mind or personality. (Of course, the problem might be the other way around—the wife might desire sex more frequently than the husband. But we will delay discussion of that situation for a moment.)

The psychologist might well assume that the woman was *normal*, but that the man's libido had gotten out of control and was ruining the marriage. Or the counselor might assume that the man had a *normal*, healthy appetite for

sex, but that the woman was so *repressed* that she could not enjoy one of the finer aspects of marriage. Or the therapist might assume that *both* Mary and John showed symptoms of abnormality. How could the psychologist tell for sure?

□ □ **QUESTION** □ □

Psychologists always make *assumptions* about what is normal and abnormal for a particular patient. Do you think that male counselors might tend to make different assumptions about John and Mary Smith than would female counselors?

- ### Cultural Norms
Normality is always defined *within a given context or culture*. No psychologist can come to any meaningful conclusions about the Smiths' problems if the counselor ignores the *social environment* in which the couple lives. That is, before the psychologist can concentrate on the unique aspects of the Smiths' difficulties, the therapist must ask how other people with similar backgrounds think, feel, and behave (Davison & Neale, 1986).

One question the psychologist would ask is, therefore, "What *values* about sexuality do the Smiths (and their culture) hold?" Another question would be "What *past experiences*—pleasant or unpleasant—have the Smiths (and people like them) typically had?" Unless the counselor knew the answers to these questions, the psychologist could hardly hope to put the Smiths' problems in proper perspective.

However, the counselor would also need to know something about *actual sexual practices* in the world the Smiths live in. How many times do most young husbands expect sex each week? How frequently do most wives desire it? Do husbands typically *wish* to make love more frequently than their wives, or the other way around? How frequently do young married men achieve sexual climax? And is it always with their wives? How frequently do young married women reach orgasm, and is it always with their husbands? And, most important, how do the Smiths compare to other people in their segment of society?

Questions about sexual values and past experiences are often difficult to find answers to. But, as we saw in Chapter 7, the real controversy started when scientists started asking people *what they actually did* in the privacy of their bedrooms. Yet, logically speaking, how can we know what is "normal" sexual behavior until we know what's *statistically* "the norm" for most married people like the Smiths?

Sex and the Bell-Shaped Curve
Until Alfred Kinsey performed his pioneering research on human sexuality, no one really

knew much about the "statistics of sexual be-havior." But judging from a rough analysis of the Kinsey data, the average white married man aged 21–25 reaches sexual climax about three to four times a week. Using rather stilted language, Kinsey reported that the young, married, middle-class, white male in the US achieved an average of about four *sexual outlets* per week (Kinsey, Pomeroy, & Martin, 1948). (Kinsey included all forms of sexual activity in his figures—including masturbation, homosexuality, bestiality, "wet dreams," and extramarital heterosexual contacts.)

Although Kinsey gathered his data more than 30 years ago, recent surveys tend to confirm his findings (Bell, Weinberg, & Hammersmith, 1981; Brecher, 1984). Thus, we can use Kinsey's results to give us a "social context" in which to consider the Smiths' marital problems—but only assuming that the Smiths are white, middle-class people living in the US.

Even making these assumptions, there is still a lot more we need to know. If Mr. Smith desired 7 outlets a week, would you consider him abnormal? What if he demanded 17? And would John Smith be "far above normal" if he wanted 77?

Range

As you can see, knowing what the average is doesn't always help. The average score on most intelligence tests is 100. If you get a score of 101, are you "way above average"? Before we could answer, we would have to know the *range* of scores, as well as how those scores were *distributed* over the range. And the best way to find out would be to resort to that favorite psychological tool, the bell-shaped curve.

The range of IQs on some tests goes from 0 to about 200. The tests are so constructed that most people's scores are *bunched up in the middle* of the distribution. Although some 50 percent of the scores lie above the mid-point of the curve—and some 50 percent lie below it—most of the IQs do not *deviate* very far from this mid-point (see Fig. 18.1). Depending on how the mid-point is calculated, it is called the **mode**, the **mean**, or the **median**. If you are interested in how these terms are calculated, see the Statistical Appendix at the back of this book. However, "mode," "mean," and "median" are merely words that mean the *norm*, or the middle of the range of scores.

In the case of Kinsey's data on the sexual behavior of the (young, white, middle-class) male in the US, the mean, median, and mode are probably close together (Kinsey, Pomeroy, & Martin, 1948). Thus, for our present purposes, we can consider any of them the norm. The actual distribution of outlets per week probably looks something like the graph shown in Fig. 18.2.

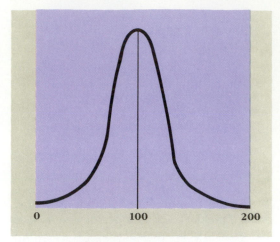

FIG. 18.1 A bell-shaped curve of IQ's.

Now we can see that if Mr. Smith desired 7 outlets a week, he would be fairly close to the norm. But what if he wished 17? Would this fact make him ab-norm-al, or away from the norm? How far away is "away"?

Standard Deviation

Psychologists have a method of measuring deviations from the norm that they call the **standard deviation**. If you are interested in learning more about this matter, you might wish to look at the Statistical Appendix. However, when all is said and done, the standard deviation is little more than a fairly accurate way of measuring *percentages*.

Psychologists assume that, on any given test (or on the measurement of any given behavior), whatever *two-thirds of the people do* is probably pretty normal. On an intelligence test, for example, the norm (or mean) is arbitrarily set at a score of 100. On many such tests, about two-thirds of the people get scores between 84 and 116. As you can see from Figure 18.3, this fact means that about one-third of the people

FIG. 18.2 Range of weekly outlets in young married men.

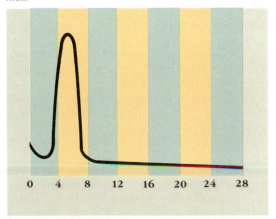

Mode. From the Latin word *modus*, meaning "to measure." The highest point or most frequent score on a bell-shaped distribution of scores.

Mean That which is "middling" or intermediate in rank or order. The arithmetical average.

Median (ME-dee-an). From the Latin word *medius*, meaning "middle." The median on a superhighway is the paved or planted strip down the middle dividing the road in half. The median in a distribution is the score that exactly cuts the distribution in half.

Standard deviation (dee-vee-A-shun). The standard deviation is a mathematical way of figuring out how much a test score deviates from the mean, median, or mode (usually the mean). The standard deviation thus gives you a precise way of measuring how significantly your own score on a test varies or departs from the norm.

scored within 16 points *below* the mean, and about one-third of the people scored within 16 points *above* the mean. By definition, then, the *standard deviation* for such a test would be 16 points. If you score within 1 standard deviation of the norm, your performance is almost always considered "within the normal range."

If you got an IQ of 132 on the test, you would be 2 standard deviations above the mean, and you would be well above average. If you got a score of 148 on the test, you would be 3 standard deviations above the norm. This exceptional score would put you in the upper two-tenths of a percent of the test population.

□ □ **QUESTION** □ □

How many behaviors can you think of that are *statistically normal* (in that most people engage in them) but that aren't necessary "good" or "healthy" or "moral"?

FIG. 18.3 Standard deviations tell you what percentage of scores fall within a certain distance from the mean.

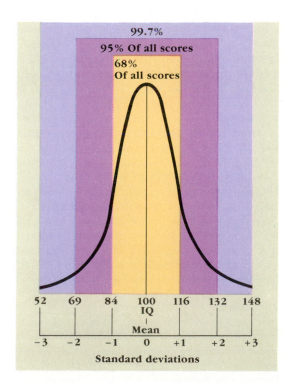

● **"Normal" Sexuality and the Standard Deviation**

Now we're ready to put the Smiths' problem into context. Kinsey's surveys of sexual behavior suggest that young married men like John Smith have, on the average, 4 sexual outlets per week. The range is from 0 to more than 29. The standard deviation is about 2.

These facts mean that if John Smith desires sexual contact with his wife from 2 to 6 times a week, he is probably like two-thirds of all similar men that Kinsey talked to. In short, *within the society* in which the Smiths live, John's sexual demands would seem average, or normal. If he expected sex more than 8 times per week, John would be more than 2 standard deviations from the norm (for his culture), and thus his requests would be at least *statistically* abnormal.

Of course, in the long run, the problem that exists between Mary and John Smith is a *personal* one that cannot be solved by reference to bell-shaped curves. And any valid discussion of the Smiths' problems would have to include *values* and *past experiences* as well as actual behaviors. Yet the beauty of Kinsey's work was that he brought sexual behavior out in the open, so that it could be examined statistically as well as personally or theoretically. *Lacking* this important reference information, the psychologist might well make some very wrong decisions about how to help the Smiths. For we all tend to judge normality *in terms of our own behaviors and expectations.*

□ □ **QUESTION** □ □

How might the "personality theory" you believed in affect your judgment about who was "mentally ill" and who wasn't? How would it affect your opinion of *what* was wrong with the person?

● **Classifying Abnormal Behavior Patterns**

As you can gather, it is difficult to define psychological abnormality without a theory of some kind—or some set of data such as Kinsey's—to tell you both what is *statistically* normal and how any abnormality might have come about.

There is, unfortunately, no one master theory of human behavior that everyone agrees on. There are, however, *general trends* that most scientists agree upon at any one given moment in time. For example, had you read a book on abnormal psychology 20 years ago, it would have been filled primarily with *case histories* and *interpretations* of results from such psychological tests as the MMPI and the Rorschach (see Chapter 17). In those days, patients were diagnosed primarily in terms of their *personalities*. In current textbooks, you are much more likely to find page after page of data on "brain scans," "genetic markers," and "bio-chemical reactions." For today, mental patients are much more likely to be diagnosed in terms of their *medical responses* than in terms of their personality profiles. Whether this shift from a psychological toward a physiological approach has led to more accurate diagnoses—or to more effective therapy—is a matter still under dispute.

Over the years, psychologists and psychiatrists have worked out a variety of diagnostic schemes that are supposed to classify people according to their problems. Of these, the best known is surely the *Diagnostic and Statistical Manual of Mental Disorders*, first published by the American Psychiatric Association in 1952. The third edition (DSM-III) appeared in 1980, and the revised third edition (DSM-III-R) was published in 1987.

DSM-III is quite different from DSM-I. In 1952, almost all the diagnostic categories were listed as *psychological reactions*. The experts who compiled DSM-I tended to believe in a theory of psychology put forth by the noted psychiatrist Adolph Meyer. It was Meyer's view that "mental disorders" were best understood as awkward attempts to adjust to external demands (Meyer, 1951). Thus, the people who created DSM-I perceived "mental disorders" as resulting from *imperfect person-environment interactions* (APA, 1952).

DSM-II appeared in 1968. By that time, Freudian theory had become dominant in many psychiatric circles. And Freud, as you know, viewed "mental disorders" as having intra-psychic causes (and cures). What had been described in DSM-I as a schizophrenic *re-action*, therefore, became *schizophrenia* in DSM-II. Thus, DSM-II put the "locus" of psychological abnormalites *inside the mind* (APA, 1968).

By 1980, when DSM-III was published, the pendulum had swung in yet another direction. Currently, professional psychiatry is (to a great extent) dominated by individuals who believe there is usually a *biological* cause underlying most psychological problems. Thus, in DSM-III, "schizophrenia" has become "schizophrenic *disorder*." And the "locus" of abnormality has been moved from "the mind" to "the body."

As we will see, a great many psychologists object to DSM-III. One major complaint raised is that the people who created the *Manual* seem to believe in what is called the **medical model** of "mental illness." That is, DSM-III appears to be based on the notion that all abnormal thoughts and behaviors are but *symptoms* of some underlying "illness." (As we noted earlier, many psychologists prefer to view human abnormalities as being "problems of adjustment," "psychological difficulties," or "learned behaviors" rather than "symptoms of illness.")

We will discuss the good and perhaps not-so-good points of DSM-III a bit later. First, though, it will pay us to take a look at the 1980 *Manual*—and the 1987 revision—before we go any further in our study of abnormal behavior patterns, sexual or otherwise (see Table 18.1).

DSM-III AND DSM-III-R

DSM-III and DSM-III-R were designed to give specific diagnoses for *every* patient who might be referred to a psychiatrist (or perhaps to a psychologist)—no matter what the patient's problems might be. After interviewing the patient—and perhaps giving the individual various tests—the interviewer rates the patient on each of five different **axes** or categories. These axes were changed slightly in DSM-III-R. The categories listed below (and in Table 18.1) are taken from the revised edition:

Axis 1. Clinical Syndromes and Other Conditions
Axis 2. Developmental Disorders; Personality Disorders
Axis 3. Physical Disorders and Conditions
Axis 4. Severity of Psychosocial Stressors
Axis 5. Global Assessment of Functioning (Highest Level of Adaptive Functioning during Past Year)

Let's look at each axis (or category of abnormality) in some detail.

• Axis 1

Included on Axis 1 are most of the psychological disorders that the American Psychiatric Association officially recognizes as being "mental disorders." Generally speaking, Axis 1 is made up of all those severe psychological or behavioral problems that would send you to see a therapist in the first place.

• Axis 2

Technically speaking, Axis 2 is limited to what are called the *developmental disorders* and the *personality disorders*. In fact, Axis 2 is designed to let the therapist describe the patient's psychological traits or "enduring behavior patterns" rather than any problems that have occurred recently. The major difference between DSM-III and DSM-III-R is that "mental retardation," "autism," and other developmental disorders that were included on Axis 1 in DMS-III have been moved to Axis 2 in DSM-III-R.

• Axis 3

Included on Axis 3 are all the *physical symptoms* of any type of disease, damage to the brain or any other part of the body, and disabilities caused by accidents or drugs. The *psychological reactions* to these biological problems,

Medical model The belief—in psychiatry and psychology—that mental disorders are caused by some "underlying" or "deep-seated" psychological problem, just as influenza is caused by an infectious virus. In fact, what we call the "medical model" should really be termed "the infectious disease model," since there are many other "models" in the field of medicine.

Axes (AX-ease). The plural of "axis." An axis is a line about which something rotates. In DSM-III and DSM-III-R, the five axes are really "categories" or types of information that the psychiatrist should use in making a diagnosis about what could be troubling a given patient. Whether it is the patient or the psychiatrist who "rotates" around these five axes is an open question.

divorced). Generally speaking, only those stressful events that occurred in the past 12 months are given serious consideration.

- ### Axis 5

Axis 5 is a scale running from "superior" to "grossly impaired" that describes your highest level of psychological adjustment for the past year.

however, are generally considered to be mental disorders that would be listed under Axis 1.

- ### Axis 4

Axis 4 is a "social stress scale" that lists such traumas as the death of a loved one, changing (or losing) your job, and getting married (or

MENTAL DISORDERS

As we noted earlier, DSM-III marks a radical shift in the psychiatric approach to classifying mental disorders. DSM-II was based in large part on psychoanalytic theory. Freud believed that almost all types of mental illness were due to psychological causes. Some disorders were

TABLE 18.1 **An Abbreviated Outline of the Diagnostic Categories Included on Axis 1 and Axis 2 of DSM-III-R.**

AXIS 1: CLINICAL SYNDROMES

Disorders Usually First Evident in Infancy, Childhood, or Adolescence	Stereotypy/Habit Disorder
Disruptive Behavior Disorders	Undifferentiated Attention-Deficit Disorder
Attention-Deficit Hyperactivity Disorder	Organic Mental Disorders
Conduct Disorder	Dementias Arising in the Senium and Presenium
Oppositional Defiant Disorder	Primary Degenerative Dementia of the Alzheimer Type, Senile Onset
Anxiety Disorders of Childhood or Adolescence	Primary Degenerative Dementia of the Alzheimer Type, Presenile Onset
Separation Anxiety Disorder	Multi-Infarct Dementia
Avoidant Disorder	Psychoactive Substance-Induced Organic Mental Disorders
Overanxious Disorder	Alcohol
Eating Disorders	Amphetamine
Anorexia Nervosa	Caffeine
Bulimia Nervosa	Cannabis
Pica	Cocaine
Rumination Disorder of Infancy	Hallucinogen
Gender Identity Disorders	Inhalant
Gender Identity Disorder of Childhood	Nicotine
Transsexualism	Opioid
Gender Identity Disorder of Adolescence or Adulthood, Nontranssexual Type	Phencyclidine (PCP)
Tic Disorders	Sedative, Hypnotic, or Anxiolytic
Tourette's Disorder	Organic Mental Disorders Associated with Axis III Physical Disorders or Conditions, or Whose Etiology Is Unknown
Chronic Motor or Vocal Tic Disorder	Psychoactive Substance Use Disorders
Transient Tic Disorder	Alcohol
Elimination Disorders	Amphetamine
Functional Encopresis	Cannabis
Functional Enuresis	Cocaine
Speech Disorders Not Elsewhere Classified	Hallucinogen
Cluttering	Inhalant
Stuttering	Nicotine
Other Disorders of Infancy, Childhood, or Adolescence	Opioid
Elective Mutism	Phencyclidine (PCP)
Identity Disorder	Sedative, Hypnotic, or Anxiolytic
Reactive Attachment Disorder of Infancy or Early Childhood	Polysubstance Dependence

TABLE 18.1 (continued)

Psychoactive Substance
  Dependence
Psychoactive Substance Abuse
Schizophrenia
  Catatonic
  Disorganized
  Paranoid
  Undifferentiated
  Residual
Delusional (Paranoid) Disorder
Psychotic Disorders Not Elsewhere Classified
  Brief Reactive Psychosis
  Schizophreniform Disorder
  Schizoaffective Disorder
  Induced Psychotic Disorder
  Atypical Psychosis
Mood Disorders
  Bipolar Disorders
    Bipolar Disorder
    Cyclothymia
  Depressive Disorders
    Major Depression
    Dysthymia
Anxiety Disorders
  Panic Disorder
  Agoraphobia
  Social Phobia
  Simple Phobia
  Obsessive Compulsive Disorder
  Post-Traumatic Stress Disorder
  Generalized Anxiety Disorder
Somatoform Disorders
  Body Dysmorphic Disorder
  Conversion Disorder
  Hypochrondriasis
  Somatization Disorder
  Somatoform Pain Disorder
  Undifferentiated Somatoform
    Disorder
Dissociative Disorders
  Multiple Personality Disorder
  Psychogenic Fugue
  Psychogenic Amnesia
  Depersonalization Disorder
Sexual Disorders
  Paraphilias
    Exhibitionism
    Fetishism
    Frotteurism
    Pedophilia
    Sexual Masochism

Sexual Sadism
Transvestic Fetishism
Voyeurism
Sexual Dysfunctions
  Sexual Desire Disorders
  Sexual Arousal Disorders
  Orgasm Disorders
  Sexual Pain Disorders
Sleep Disorders
  Dyssomnias
    Insomnia Disorder
    Primary Insomnia
    Hypersomnia Disorder
    Primary Hypersomnia
    Sleep-wake schedule Disorder
  Parasomnias
    Dream Anxiety Disorder
      (Nightmare Disorder)
    Sleep Terror Disorder
    Sleepwalking Disorder
Factitious Disorders
Impulse Control Disorders Not Elsewhere
  Classified
    Intermittent Explosive Disorder
    Kleptomania
    Pathological Gambling
    Pyromania
    Trichotillomania
Adjustment Disorder
Psychological Factors Affecting Physical
  Condition
Conditions Not Attributable to a Mental
  Disorder That Are a Focus of Attention or
  Treatment
    Academic Problem
    Adult Antisocial Behavior
    Childhood or Adolescent Antisocial
      Behavior
    Malingering
    Marital Problem
    Noncompliance with Medical
      Treatment
    Occupational Problem
    Parent-Child Problem
    Other Interpersonal Problem
    Other Specified Family
      Circumstances
    Phase of Life Problem or Other
      Life Circumstance Problem
    Uncomplicated Bereavement

AXIS 2:   DEVELOPMENTAL DISORDERS/PERSONALITY DISORDERS

Developmental Disorders
  Mental Retardation
  Pervasive Developmental Disorders
    Autistic Disorder
  Specific Developmental Disorders
    Academic Skills Disorders
    Language and Speech Disorders
    Motor Skills Disorder
Personality Disorders
  Cluster A
    Paranoid

Schizoid
Shizotypal
Cluster B
  Antisocial
  Borderline
  Histrionic
  Narcissistic
Cluster C
  Avoidant
  Dependent
  Obsessive Compulsive
  Passive Aggressive

From *Diagnostic and Statistical Manual of Mental Disorders* (Third Edition-Revised). Washington, D.C.: American
Psychiatric Association, 1987. Adapted by permission. Copyright 1987 American Psychiatric Association.

very severe, and were called the *psychoses*. Other forms were not as severe, and were called the *neuroses*. There were exceptions to this rule, however. First, there were a few psychoses that were due to physical or *organic* conditions. We will mention them again momentarily. Second, a very severe neurosis of long duration might well have a greater negative effect on a patient than a very mild psychosis. Generally speaking, though, the psychoses were thought to be *more debilitating to an individual* than were the neuroses.

According to Freud—and DSM-II—the psychoses are characterized by a loss of contact with reality; a disorganized personality; and by extreme deviation from normal patterns of acting, thinking, and feeling. Some of these severe disorders had clear-cut biological causes and were referred to as **organic psychoses**. However, Freud believed that most severe disorders had emotional causes. DMS-II referred to these types of disorders as being **functional**

psychoses. But the authors of DSM-II held that the neuroses always *had emotional rather than organic causes*.

DSM-III reflects a strong movement within the field of psychiatry away from Freudian theorizing. Instead of employing such diagnostic categories as "psychosis" and "neurosis," DSM-III uses the medical term "disorder." As we discuss the various *disorders*, however, we will also give their older names.

Disorders Evidenced During Infancy, Childhood, Adolescence

Axis 1 of DMS-III begins by listing a variety of mental disorders that "usually first manifest themselves in infancy, childhood, or adolescence." Some of them have clear-cut biological causes; others don't. We will talk about some of these disorders again in the next chapter. (As we noted, in DSM-III-R some of the developmental disorders have been moved from Axis 1 to Axis 2.)

Organic Mental Disorders

At the other end of the age scale from the childhood disorders are those problems associated with growing old. DSM-III refers to these as "**dementias** arising in the **senium** and 'presenium.'"

● *Senile Dementia (Senile Psychosis)*

Many physical problems associated with old age can cause you to lapse into a child-like state commonly called a *senile dementia*, or *senile psychosis*. You may suffer from a series of slight strokes, or from **Alzheimer's disease** (see Chapter 15). In 1974 this type of mental illness accounted for almost 5 percent of the admissions to public mental hospitals. By 1984, this figure had risen considerably, in part because older people now make up a larger percentage of the population. (The actual percentage of older mental patients is hard to determine since some half of them are put in nursing homes rather than mental hospitals.) The average age at hospital admission for patients diagnosed as senile is 75 for both men and women, although the problem may occur as early as age 60 or so.

● *Psychoactive Substance-Induced Organic Mental Disorders*

Drug abuse can lead not only to behavioral changes, but to organic mental disorders as well. However, as the *Manual* notes, "In most cases, the diagnosis of these Organic Mental Disorders will be made in individuals who also have a Substance Use Disorder."

Psychoactive Substance Use Disorders

Addiction to, or overdose from, many types of drugs can lead to abnormal behavior and

Patients in mental hospitals were generally classified as psychotic before DSM-III. The new Manual uses the medical term "disorder" to describe mental illnesses.

thought patterns. A person suffering from such abnormalities is said to have a *drug-induced psychosis*, or a "substance use disorder." We discussed many of the causes for drug-related problems in Chapter 3, and most of the types of drugs that people "abuse" are listed in Table 18.1. By far the most commonly-abused substance, however, is alcohol.

Schizophrenic Disorders

According to Melvin Zax and Emory Cowen, "Schizophrenia is the most highly researched and least well understood of all the psychotic disorders" (Zax & Cowen, 1976). Descriptions of people who apparently suffered from schizophrenia can be found in the Bible. However, the modern-day conception of schizophrenia dates from 1911, when the noted Swiss psychiatrist Eugen Bleuler first described the disorder in detail and gave it its present name.

The term *schizophrenia* comes from the Latin words that mean "splitting of the mind." The use of this term is unfortunate, for the "multiple" or "split personality" we will discuss later as a type of dissociative disorder has nothing to do with schizophrenia. As we will see, *shattered mind* is a better description than is "split mind."

General mental disorganization is usually the major hallmark of schizophrenia. The authors of DSM-III state that "Invariably there are characteristic disturbances in several of the following areas: content and form of thought, perception, [emotion], sense of self, **volition**, relationship to the external world, and psychomotor behavior" (APA, 1980).

An older name for schizophrenia is **dementia praecox**, from the Latin words meaning "youthful insanity." And schizophrenia is *primarily a disorder of the young*. A decade ago, Yale psychologist Jeffry Blum made a study of thousands of people admitted to VA hospitals in the US. He found that 45.7 percent of patients aged 17–24 were diagnosed as being schizophrenic. However, only 8.9 percent of patients over 65 years of age were classified as being schizophrenic. Schizophrenia affects men and women in equal numbers but single males are particularly susceptible (Blum, 1978).

● *Schizophrenia: A Case Study*

There are many different types of schizophrenia. **Catatonic** schizophrenics often "freeze" in bizarre positions—much as Harlow's monkeys reared in isolation sometimes did. **Hebephrenic** schizophrenics, on the other hand, often show a progressive withdrawal from society, have fits of uncontrolled giggling, and talk in ways that suggest they are "out of contact with reality."

Melvin Zax and G. Stricker describe one hebephrenic patient as follows: "Gertrude B.,

an unmarried woman who had been living with her family in the same New England town in which she was born, entered a state hospital for the second time when she was 29 years old." At one point during her lengthy hospital stay, Gertrude B. spoke to her doctor as follows:

> No, I never was crazy, a little nervous. Look at my teeth. I came here to have my teeth fixed. We going to have a strawberry party now. Yesterday I heard voices. They said, "I ran to the drugstore and I am going home tomorrow." I heard J.B. Scott's voice and it came from up here in the air. We've got 39 banks on Market Street. We've got lots of property. Say, take me home and I'll give you three laundry bags. I'm 29 and a half, 29 and a half. Now I want you to get me 10 apples—10 of your most beautiful apples and two dozen lemons. Now listen, if I get you some pineapple will you preserve it?

Zax and Stricker note that Gertrude B. became more destructive over the years; she began creating disturbances in the hospital ward, and eventually had to be restrained. She died of coronary problems when she was 87 (Zax & Stricker, 1963).

● *Incidence of Schizophrenia*

In 1984, the National Institute of Mental Health reported on the "state of America's mental health." NIMH experts interviewed more than 20,000 people in five communities around the nation. According to the NIMH report, nearly 20 percent of American adults currently suffer psychiatric disorders of one kind or another. However, fewer than a million of these people are hospitalized at any one point in time.

Schizophrenia is one of the most common of the psychoses that lead to long-term hospitalization. According to the NIMH report, about 1.5 million Americans suffer from *schizophrenia*.

● *Research on Schizophrenia*

In 1987, the Institute of Medicine estimated that schizophrenia costs the US some $48 billion dollars a year, both in terms of treatment and because of lost productivity. However, we spend but about $17 a year per schizophrenic patient on research. In contrast, we spend some $300 a year per patient on cancer research, and some $10,000 a year per patient on muscular dystrophy (Holden, 1986, 1987).

Despite the small amount spent per year on research, recent studies have cast some light on the causes of schizophrenia.

Causes of Schizophrenia

There is considerable argument in psychological circles as to whether schizophrenia really exists as a "single" mental illness, or whether

Volition (voh-LISH-shun). Voluntary control of your behaviors. See Chapter 12.

Dementia praecox (dee-MENT-chee-ah PREE-cox). The original name for schizophrenia. Means "insanity of the young."

Catatonic (kat-tah-TAHN-ick). There are two main types of catatonic schizophrenia. The first (called "catatonic stupor") often comes on rapidly. The patient becomes mute; stares blankly at the floor; and may assume a fixed, stereotyped posture which the patient may maintain for days or weeks. The second (called "catatonic excitement") is characterized by frenzied motor activity. The patient may talk incoherently at the top of the voice, rush frantically back and forth, tear off clothing, and without warning may attack someone or break up furniture. The two states may alternate—that is, a patient may be "stuporous" for a while, then lapse into excitement, then become calm and "freeze" into a strange posture for several days.

Hebephrenic (heeb-eh-FREN-ick). From the Greek words meaning "childish mind." A type of schizophrenic disorder characterized by hallucinations, delusions, "word salads," silliness, and "a general regression to child-like behavior."

Manifest (MANN-eye-fest). Something that is "out in the open," or measurable, as opposed to something that is hidden.

we simply call people "schizophrenics" because we don't know what else to call them. The fact that so many people are diagnosed as schizophrenic suggests that this category may be too loose and too large to be meaningfully applied to the complex living systems we call human beings.

This controversy over what schizophrenia actually "is" can be seen in the variety of explanations offered for what causes this disorder. As you might surmise, there are three main types of theories—biological, intra-psychic, and social/behavioral.

● *Biological Correlates of Schizophrenia*

The thought that schizophrenia is *caused by* some genetic or biochemical misfunctioning in the brain is particularly appealing to those scientists who believe that the "brain controls the mind," and not vice versa. And many types of data do support the notion that there is some *biological* problem at the root of many types of schizophrenia. For example, if one identical twin suffers from this disorder, the other twin is five times as likely to experience schizophrenia too than if the twins are merely fraternal. This trend seems to hold whether the twins are reared together, or reared apart (Gottesman & Shields, 1982).

Schizophrenia has long been known to "run in families." For instance, Italian psychiatrist Laura Bellodi and her associates studied 229 schizophrenia patients (age 13–72) and their close relatives. Bellodi and her group found several "genetic markers" suggesting that schizophrenia may be inherited (Bellodi *et al.*, 1986).

Just *how* the genes might *cause* schizophrenia is not yet known. There are, however, several hypotheses. One possibility is that "defective genes" bring about either an "underdeveloped" or a "damaged" brain. Support for this view comes from research by University of Nebraska researcher Charles Golden and his

colleagues, who use "scanning devices" to study the brains of schizophrenic patients. Golden and his associates report that the brains of many (but not all) schizophrenic patients are "less dense" than are the brains of normal subjects (Golden *et al.*, 1980, 1981). Golden and his group have also found that, in right-handed schizophrenic patients, the left hemisphere has less blood flow than does the right hemisphere (Golden *et al.*, 1985). Golden believes that schizophrenia is caused by an "underdeveloped" or "damaged" brain.

There also are dozens of studies in which the experimenters have reported that schizophrenic patients have abnormal levels of various *neurotransmitters* as compared to normals. Research in this area has been particularly active in the late 1980's, since the hope is that schizophrenia could be *cured* if the person's brain chemistry could somehow be brought back to normal. However, as University of Wisconsin psychiatrist Gary Kraemer noted recently, almost all of the neurochemical differences reported in schizophrenic patients so far can readily be caused in *normal* individuals—and in animals—by changes in diet, social stress, daily routine, and drug use (Kraemer, 1985). It is further the case that no one, to date, has been able to *cure* schizophrenia by increasing or decreasing the levels of neurotransmitters in a schizophrenic's brain.

In almost all the studies in which correlations between brain chemistry and schizophrenia have been reported, the researchers have compared subjects *already diagnosed as being schizophrenic* (many of whom have been hospitalized for years) with normal individuals. As British psychiatrist Steven Rose points out, this sort of comparison may be misleading. When researchers find "structural or functional abnormalities" in the brains of schizophrenic patients, Rose says, the scientists *assume* these physical abnormalities *caused* the mental disorder. It is more likely, Rose contends, that the *mental disorder caused the structural changes*. He also cites considerable evidence suggesting that subjects with "genetic markers" for schizophrenia only become "mentally disordered" in certain types of social environments. Therefore, schizophrenia should be considered a "bio-psycho-social disorder," and not a "medical disease" (Rose, 1984).

Williams College psychologist Andrew Crider makes a similar point in his book, *Schizophrenia: A Biopsychological Perspective*. Crider concludes that no single biochemical problem can account for all the symptoms associated with schizophrenia. Crider believes that genes *predispose* an individual to schizophrenia, primarily by making the person overly vunerable to stress. However, the disorder only becomes **manifest** under certain environmental conditions (Crider, 1979). This viewpoint is sometimes called the **diathesis**-*stress hypothesis*.

Given the current belief that schizophrenia is either "caused" or at least "triggered" by psychosocial factors, it is to these problems that we must next turn our attention.

● *Bateson's "Double-Bind" Hypothesis*

One of the earliest psychosocial theories of schizophrenia came from anthropologist Gregory Bateson. In his studies of the families of schizophrenia patients, Bateson noted that the patients' mothers often communicated with their children using "contradictory messages." For example, the mother might say she loved the child, but say it in a matter (and with body language) suggesting just the opposite. The child was then caught in what Bateson called a "double-bind." That is, the child desperately wanted to understand and respond to what the mother was saying, but could neither decipher the "real" message the mother was giving nor tell the mother about the confusion she was causing. The child then supposedly withdraws from reality in an attempt to avoid further emotional turmoil (Bateson *et al.*, 1956). Unfortunately, most research studies have failed to support Bateson's hypothesis.

● *The "Controlling Mother" Hypothesis*

In a recent book, California researchers David Reynolds and Norman Farberow suggest that a "controlling mother" may be the major cause of schizophrenia. Their book contains a detailed study of a short period in the life of a mental patient named "Chuck Smith." In order to discover what the world of the schizophrenic was like, Reynolds actually lived with Chuck and his family for a period of several weeks just after Chuck was released from a mental hospital.

Reynolds sees Chuck's mother as being the main cause of the young man's problems. Jewel Smith was a depressive. And "like most depressives," Reynolds says, "she believed that love is a matter of controlling the loved ones and sought to control her family." Chuck's reaction to this was to escape into unreality (Reynolds & Farberow, 1981). Again, we should note that most research studies do not support the belief that "smothering mothers" are the major cause of schizophrenia.

● *The "Interpersonal Demand" Hypothesis*

In a recent report, NIMH psychologist Allan Mirsky discusses a long-term study of children who had one schizophrenic parent. The control group subjects all had normal parents. Half of the children in each group were reared in Israeli cities with their parents. The other half of each group were reared in **kibbutzim**—rural "communes" where children are taken care of by the entire community rather than by

their natural parents. The children were originally studied in 1967, and were re-examined in 1981 (when most of them were in their late 20's).

Allan Mirsky reports that there were no major psychiatric disorders among the control-group children who had normal parents. However, the children of schizophrenics brought up in kibbutzim had a much higher incidence of **psychopathology** than did those children reared by schizophrenic parents. Sixteen of the 22 kibbutzim children had mental problems—6 were schizophrenic while 10 had mood disorders. In contrast, only 6 of 21 children reared by their schizophrenic parents were ill, and only 3 of them were diagnosed as having schizophrenia. Mirsky believes that children growing up in kibbutzim have higher "interpersonal demands" placed on them than do children growing up in family settings (Mirsky, 1986; Mirsky & Duncan, 1986; Nagler & Mirsky, 1985). Mirsky's "interpersonal demand" hypothesis, of course, is similar to the "diathesis-stress theory" that we discussed earlier.

● *Schizophrenia: An Interactive Model*

Although some theorists still take a narrowly-focused view of the causes of schizophrenia, most scientists now believe this mental disorder is "multi-determined." For example, in a recent book, John Strauss and William Carpenter propose an "interactive-developmental-systems model" of schizophrenia. Strauss and Carpenter believe there is a genetic "predisposition" toward schizophrenia. However, this innate tendency is expressed only in certain stressful environments, particularly in "demanding" family situations. Thus, Strauss and Carpenter say, there is no *single cause* for this mental disorder. Rather, schizophrenia is a developmental problem determined by biological, intra-psychic, and social/behavioral factors. *All of these factors* must be present, Strauss and Carpenter believe, for the disorder to surface (Strauss & Carpenter, 1981).

Despite the emphasis on "stress" as a factor in inducing schizophrenia, however, to date no one has identified precisely what sorts of social stressors are correlated with schizophrenia. Nor has anyone described the biochemical mechanisms that cause one stressed person to become schizophrenic while another equally-stressed person remains normal.

All things considered, we still do not have an adequate theory that explains what schizophrenia really is or what causes this disorder.

Mood Disorders

People suffering from what we call the *mood disorders* (or affective psychoses) often seem stuck at one end of the emotionality scale or the other. That is, they usually are very "up" or very "down," although sometimes they "flip-flop" from one extreme to the other. (In DSM-III, these sorts of problems were called "affective disorders").

According to the NIMH report on the status of mental health in the US, almost 10 million people currently suffer from one of the affective disorders.

● Types of Mood Disorders

DSM-III-R lists two major types of affective disorders—the *bipolar* disorder, and *depressive* disorder. There is considerable controversy among experts about *mania*, or the *manic bipolar disorder*. Some writers believe it is possible for individuals to suffer from a "manic psychosis" that never develops into a depressive condition. Other theorists contend that *all* patients who experience "manic episodes" will eventually become depressive. DSM-III-R takes the latter viewpoint, and therefore uses the term "bipolar disorder" to describe anyone who shows manic behavior whether or not the patient also has a history of depression (APA, 1980).

● Bipolar Mood Disorder

The term *affective* means "mood," or the subjective feelings that accompany emotions. In

"I'M 33 PERCENT BETTER THESE DAYS. I SEEM TO BE MANIC-NORMAL-DEPRESSIVE."

DSM-III, the term *affective* was used throughout. In DSM-III-R, the term *mood* is used instead.

Most psychologists consider both "mania" and "depression" to be disordered *moods*. Mania is *inappropriate* elation, excitation, or heightened arousal. The mood is "disordered" because it doesn't seem to be a response to any real-world event.

A person experiencing a manic attack typically becomes hyperactive, cannot sleep, often tears his/her clothes off, and shouts and screams or talks so rapidly and so loudly that no one can understand the person. *What* the person says often resembles the sort of irrational "word salad" produced by the hebephrenic schizophrenic. Indeed, even experienced diagnosticians sometimes cannot differentiate between a manic attack and an episode of schizophrenia (Cantor *et al.*, 1980).

DSM-II included a diagnostic category for mania, one for depression, and a "bipolor" category for patients who seemed to "flip-flop" between the two extremes (APA, 1968). DMS-III-R, however, combines mania with the bipolar category (APA, 1987).

□ □ **QUESTION** □ □

Presumably manic patients didn't change all that much between 1968 (DSM-II) and 1987 (DSM-III-R), even though they are now put in a different diagnostic category than they previously were. What does this fact tell you about the importance of social and professional *impressions* in the field of abnormal psychology?

● Depressive Disorders

People experiencing a major depression often appear to be overwhelmed by the sadness and futility of life. They become passive, may refuse to move from their bed, and sometimes have to be force-fed to be kept alive. Particularly in younger individuals, there is always the danger of suicide.

As we mentioned, manic attacks seldom seem to be triggered by environmental events in which "excessive activity" would seem to be an appropriate response. Major depressions, however, often are triggered by the loss of a job, a loved one, or some other traumatic event.

□ □ **QUESTION** □ □

What might Harlow's research on "depressed monkeys" tell us about the causes of some types of human depressions?

● Biological Correlates of Mood Disorders

There is little agreement among experts as to the cause of mania, depression, or the manic-depressive (bipolar) condition. As usual, there are several "narrow" theories that stress *biological* or *psychological* or *social* factors. But the trend appears to be toward "interactive" or "systems" models.

In the mid-1980's, several research groups reported results suggesting there may be a genetic factor of some kind that "codes" for depression. For instance, Columbia University psychiatrist Ronald Fieve and his colleagues studied 604 depressed patients and 2,711 of their close relatives. Fieve and his group report that the patients' relatives were significantly more likely to have experienced depression than were normal control subjects. And both the patients and their relatives showed certain biochemical abnormalities that suggested their depressions might be inherited (Fieve *et al.*, 1984). More recently, however, University of Pennsylvania psychiatrist R.A. Price and his colleagues found evidence for the "genetic transmission of depression" only in those patients who also experienced panic disorders (see below) (Price *et al.*, 1987).

In 1987, University of Miami researcher Janice Egeland and her associates reported on a long-term study of depression among members of the Old Amish religious communities in the US. Egeland and her group found that the majority of depressed Amish patients had a "genetic marker" on their 11th chromosome, while most normal members of the Amish communities didn't have this marker (Egeland *et al.*, 1987). However, other scientists studying the genetics of depression among populations in Iceland and Israel found "genetic markers" on other chromosomes, but not on number 11 (Hodgkinson *et al.*, 1987). Thus, if some aspects of depression are "coded for in the genes," different genes apparently are involved in different populations.

It is important to note, however, that in almost all of these studies, only about 60 percent of the depressed patients showed the "genetic markers." Therefore, we certainly cannot say that *all* types of depression are "inherited." It is also true that the genetic abnormalities showed up in some normal individuals who had never experienced depression. Thus, as Stephen Rose notes, the tendency to become depressed may be inherited by *some people*. But even in these individuals, it must be triggered by past experiences and by present environmental situations. These same "triggering" experiences, Rose states, may also bring about depressions in individuals who don't carry any known genetic tendency toward depression (Rose, 1984).

• Cognitive Theories of Depression

At a more *psychological* level, University of Pennsylvania researcher Aaron T. Beck has developed his own *cognitive* explanation of de-

pression. Beck believes that depression is caused by *self-defeating thinking*.

As we will see in the next chapter, Beck believes that treatment of depression should focus on *changing people's perceptions of themselves and others*. He believes, as well, that most individuals are excellent judges of their own state of depression, and has developed a psychological test (the Beck Depression Inventory) which measures "subjective depression." According to Beck and his colleagues, the Beck Depression Inventory reliably differentiates depressed patients from those suffering from anxiety and other disorders (Beck *et al.*, 1987; Steer *et al.*, 1986).

In a sense, Beck's approach is similar to the *cognitive* explanations of emotion that we discussed in Chapter 8. Richard Lazarus, for example, believes that both arousal (mania) and depression are due to *cognitive interpretations* of events, not merely to *autonomic arousal or depression* (Lazarus, 1982, 1984).

• Behavioral Theories of Depression

Other researchers presume that both mania and depression are almost entirely *acquired behaviors*. In Chapter 8, we described Martin Seligmann's research on "learned helplessness," which is very similar to depression (Seligman, 1976). Behaviorally-oriented theorists Leonard Ullman and Leonard Krasner take a similar view. In a recent book, they describe several situations in which parents have unconsciously *trained* their children to be manic or depressive by paying attention to (and otherwise rewarding) the youngsters *only* when the children display manic or depressive behaviors (Ullman & Krasner, 1975).

As you can see, we still don't have a theory that explains what the affective disorders really are and why they occur.

• Suicide and Depression

In recent years, the rate of suicide among young people in America has more than tripled from what it was 30 years ago. White males between the ages of 20 and 24 seem most affected—their suicide rate is now five times as great as it was three decades ago. There is some evidence that young women may *threaten* or even *attempt* suicide more than men do, but men are much more likely to complete the act (Roy, 1986).

University of Kentucky psychiatrist Mohammad Shafii and his colleagues performed "psychological autopsies" on 21 young people who had killed themselves between 1980 and 1983. As part of the "autopsy" process on these suicide victims, the researchers interviewed their families, friends, and teachers, and learned as much about the young people as the researchers could. They then compared these individuals with normal young people in

Janice Egeland

the same community who had not attempted suicide. According to Shafii and his associates, 19 of the suicide victims were male; only 2 were female. Some 95 percent of the victims showed evidence of psychological disturbance prior to suicide, 70 percent were drug or alcohol abusers, 70 percent had been in trouble with the law or showed signs of antisocial behavior, and 76 percent were diagnosed as being depressed immediately prior to suicide. In a significant number of cases, the victim came from a family where the mother showed signs of depression, and the father had a history of alcohol abuse (Holden, 1986; Shafii *et al.*, 1985).

Since the *genetic make-up* of young Americans surely hasn't changed much in the past 30 years, the increase in the rate of suicides supports the belief that the *cause* of depression cannot be entirely biological.

□ □ **QUESTION** □ □
What reasons can *you* think of to explain the dramatic rise in the suicide rate?

Neurotic Disorders

In a preliminary draft of DSM-III circulated in the late 1970's, the term "neurosis" was discarded completely. Probably no other aspect of the preliminary draft caused so much criticism (Bayer & Spitzer, 1985). In the final version, the authors of DSM-III have again listed the neuroses—but in parentheses after their "new names." On page 9 of the *Manual*, the authors write, "When Freud first used the term 'psychoneurosis,' he was referring to only four subtypes: anxiety neurosis, anxiety hysteria (phobia), obsessive compulsive neurosis, and hysteria." Over the years, however, the term was broadened to include many disorders that didn't fit Freud's original four categories. And thus, according to the authors of DSM-III, "There [now] is no consensus in our field as to how to define 'neurosis'" (APA, 1980).

In fact, most of what DSM-III (and DSM-III-R) calls "Anxiety Disorders," "Somatoform Disorders," "Dissociative Disorders," and "Factitious Disorders" are what once were called *neuroses*. The same might be said for some sexual disorders, "disorders of impulse control," and most of the other abnormalities that fill out Axis 1 and all of Axis 2 of DSM-III and DSM-III-R. We will list some of the more common types of neuroses below, following the DSM-III-R classifications.

Anxiety Disorders

Generally speaking, *anxiety* is the hallmark of these disorders. The authors of DSM-III estimate that from 2 to 4 percent of the general population has at some time had a disorder that would be classified as an anxiety disorder. However, the 1984 report from NIMH estimates that about 13.1 million people in the US (almost six percent of the population) *currently* suffers from an anxiety disorder. Most of these individuals have a phobic disorder, or a "phobia."

● *Panic Disorder (Anxiety Neurosis)*
Fear begets fear, and panic leads to more panic. If John Smith is unconsciously worried about his masculinity, he may suffer from such acute anxiety that he is unable to perform sexually. The more he tries to satisfy his wife, the more anxiety he experiences, and the worse he performs. Eventually he may break out in a cold sweat if Mary so much as puts her arm around him in the kitchen, fearing that this show of affection is the prelude to another bedroom disaster.

According to the NIMH report, about 1.2 million Americans currently suffer from a panic disorder. As we will see later in this chapter, however, many researchers now doubt that patients supposedly suffering from "panic disorders" can reliably be differentiated from patients supposedly suffering from phobias and other types of anxiety (Turner *et al.*, 1986).

● *Phobic Disorders (Phobic Neurosis)*
As we mentioned in Chapter 9, phobias are abnormal or unusual fears that have no real basis in fact. If John Smith is unconsciously afraid of sexual activity, he may transfer this unacceptable anxiety to a fear of small or tight places. If the Smiths' bedroom is cramped for space, John may avoid the anxiety associated with entering his wife by refusing to enter the bedroom.

● *Obsessive Compulsive Disorder (Obsessive Compulsive Neurosis)*
Obsessions are irrational thoughts that break through to conscious awareness in a constantly recurring pattern. There are two major categories of obsessive thoughts. The first type is characterized by doubting, indecision, and uncertainty. The second type of obsessive thoughts, which usually create considerably anxiety in the patient, are overwhelming fears that the person may engage in some illegal, immoral, or antisocial behavior.

Compulsions are irresistable urges to repeat some ritualistic behavior or set of activities. If prevented from acting out his/her compulsions, the person may experience considerable anxiety. One of the most common types of compulsions is the "need for cleanliness." For example, Gerald Davison and John Neale report that one patient they treated washed her hands more than 500 times a day, despite the sores that this compulsive act created (Davison & Neale, 1986).

"...AND FLAIR SOAP HAS A SPECIAL OFFER FOR ALL YOU OBSESSIVE-COMPULSIVES WHO WASH YOUR HANDS BETWEEN 30 AND 50 TIMES A DAY..."

Obsessions typically deal with thoughts. *Compulsions* typically have to do with behaviors. In either case, the patient is diagnosed as suffering from an "obsessive compulsive disorder."

According to the NIMH report, about 2.4 million Americans currently suffer from an obsessive compulsive disorder.

• *Post-traumatic Stress Disorder*

DSM-III contains a diagnostic category called "Post-traumatic Stress Disorder," or PTSD, which is considered an Anxiety Disorder.

As we noted in Chapter 8, many psychologists believe that, immediately following traumatic stress, both your *physical* and your *mental* health are at great risk (Holmes & Rahe, 1967). The Post-traumatic Stress Disorder category was added to DSM-III in response to this belief—and to account for the rather unusual behavioral problems suffered by some US military personnel who served in Vietnam.

For reasons we still don't understand, some veterans who suffered traumatic experiences in Vietnam seem to be caught up in a pattern that includes depression, anger, hostility, suicide, murder, and a variety of other aggressive crimes. Military personnel who served in Germany or elsewhere in the world during the period of the Vietnam conflict do *not* show this same pattern of aggressive reactions *even if they too suffered traumatic experiences while in the military*. The usual explanation is that Vietnam veterans felt "rejected by society" when they returned. Thus, it is the *combination* of "trauma-induced stress" plus "feelings of rejection" that supposedly accounts for the problems many Vietnam veterans have experienced (Escobar, 1987).

As we noted in Chapter 8, there actually is little in the way of reliable research to support the belief that "major stresses" are more damaging to either the mind or the body than are a series of "minor stresses." In similar fashion, Case Western scientists Naomi Breslau and Glenn Davis state that "there is as yet little empirical research" to support the existence of a "post-traumatic stress disorder" that is different from any other type of stress reaction (Breslau & Davis, 1987).

□ □ **QUESTION** □ □

Highly-traumatized veterans of World War I often suffered from what was called "shell shock," the major symptom of which was a desire to run away when loud noises or other stressful situations occurred. What *changes in society* might account for the difference between the manner in which Vietnam veterans and World War I veterans responded to war-related trauma?

Somatoform Disorders

Freud used the term *hysteria* to refer to what DMS-III calls *somatoform disorders*. The essential features are recurrent and multiple complaints about "illnesses" or "body dysfunctions" that apparently are not due to any physical disorder. The patient may experience pain that has no relation to medical problems. Or the individual may so fear having a particular disease that the patient goes to one doctor after another in an attempt to get someone to confirm the patient's fears. This latter type of disorder is called **hypochondriacal neurosis**.

The combination of traumatic experiences while in the military and a sense of rejection for having fought in an unpopular war may account for the problems that Vietnam veterans often experience.

- ### Conversion Disorder (Hysterical Neurosis, Conversion Type)

In Chapter 16, while discussing Freud and Charcot, we described some of Charcot's hysterical patients who had lost all sensitivity in some part of their body. Freud believed that these individuals had "converted" their psychological fears and anxieties into *physical symptoms*. Many of the patients with "glove anesthesias" (loss of feeling in the hand), for example, apparently feared having to touch some dreaded object. These patients are classic examples of people suffering from a *conversion disorder*.

Dissociative Disorders

These problems are also closely related to hysteria. The essential feature of most of these disorders is a sudden change in memory, consciousness, identity, or motor behavior.

- ### Multiple Personality

One of the most famous cases of multiple personality was described many years ago by C.H. Thigpen and H. Cleckley in their book *The Three Faces of Eve*. A young woman who is called Eve White began psychotherapy because she had severe headaches that often were followed by "blackouts." During the early therapy

Multiple personality, though a rare type of dissociative disorder in real life, often appears in novels and movies, such as *The Three Faces of Eve*.

sessions, Eve White appeared to be a quiet, composed, rather conventional person. However, during one session, the woman suddenly put her hands to her head, as if experiencing acute pain. Moments later, her hands dropped, she looked up at the therapist, smiled broadly, and said in a rather loud and boisterous voice, "Hi there, Doc!"

During the rest of the therapy session, this "new personality" spoke in an off-handed manner about Eve White and her problems, but always referred to her as if she was a *separate person*. And when the therapist asked the new personality what her name was, she immediately replied, "Oh, I'm Eve Black."

Over the course of treatment, yet a third personality appeared, who called herself Jane. At first, Thigpen and Cleckley report, Jane appeared to be little more than a composite of Eve White and Eve Black. Later, however, she took on her own identity (Thigpen & Cleckley, 1954).

In his 1979 book, *Mindsplit*, New Zealand psychologist Peter McKellar describes in detail many of the most famous multiple personalities in psychiatric history, including Eve White. Since the term *schizophrenia* means "split mind," many people wrongly presume that patients who suffer from multiple personality disorders must be schizophrenic. According to McKellar, this is seldom the case. In schizophrenia, "the personality . . . is not 'split' into a finite number of subsystems, it is 'shattered' into innumerable fragments" (McKellar, 1979). In cases of multiple personality, however, each "minor personality" is usually an *organized* and reasonably well-developed subsystem (McKellar, 1977).

To date, there is little agreement among experts as to the *causes* of multiple personality. Freud believed these patients offered proof that parts of the ego could *split off* and become independent. However, many present-day psychologists believe that these patients are merely "playing roles," much as hypnotized individuals often do (see Chapter 13).

□□ **QUESTION** □□

What similarities do you see between patients with "multiple personalities" and the "hidden observers" Hilgard reported finding in his hypnotized patients?

Sexual Disorders

In DSM-III, there were several different types of "psychosexual disorders," including "gender identity disorders" and **ego-dystonic homosexuality.** In DSM-III-R, the category itself has been changed to "sexual disorders." "Gender identity disorders" and "ego-dystonic homosexuality" are no longer considered to be "mental disorders."

The **paraphilias** involve the need for unusual or bizarre imagery or acts in order to achieve sexual excitement. For instance, some men are more excited by the sight of a woman's clothing than they are by the woman herself, which DSM-III-R describes as a "clothing fetish." But if the man can only become excited by *wearing* women's clothing, this would be a paraphilia called **transvestic fetish**.

Sexual dysfunctions have to do with inhibited desire or performance, or with reaching orgasm too rapidly or too slowly.

We covered many of these topics in Chapter 7. As we noted there, the prevailing view among psychologists and psychiatrists is that most of these behaviors are "abnormal" only in the statistical sense of the word. That is, they are unusual, but not pathological.

Sleep Disorders

Added to DSM-III-R is a category called *sleep disorders* that did not appear in DSM-III. Since we discussed these problems at length in Chapter 3, we will not describe them further. We might note, however, that most psychologists (and many psychiatrists) do *not* consider *insomnia* and other similar sleep problems to be "mental disorders" in the classic sense of that term.

Other Disorders

Both DSM-III and DSM-III-R include on Axis 1 several "minor" categories, such as "factitious disorders" and "impulse control disorders" that are either relatively uncommon, or that are considered "bad habits" rather than "mental disorders" by most psychologists. We will not discuss them further.

AXIS 2: DEVELOPMENTAL AND PERSONALITY DISORDERS

There are two major types of disorders covered on Axis 2 in DSM-III-R, those involving *development,* and those involving *personality*.

We discussed most of the major types of developmental disorders in Chapters 14 and 15. We might, however, look at the personality disorders in more detail.

Personality Disorders

The authors of DSM-III state that, "Personality *traits* are enduring patterns of perceiving, relating to, and thinking about the environment and oneself, and are exhibited in a wide range of important social and personal contexts. It is only when *personality traits* are inflexible and maladaptive and cause either significant impairment in social or occupational functioning or subjective distress that they constitute *Personality Disorders*" (APA, 1980).

The personality disorders are coded on Axis 2 of DSM-III (and DSM-III-R), not on Axis 1. Although many of the these problems are similar in type to the mental disorders described on Axis 1, they are thought to be "traits," not "mental illnesses." Thus, according to the authors of DSM-III, "The diagnosis of a Personality Disorder should be made only when the characteristic features are typical of the individual's long-term functioning and are not limited to discrete episodes of illness" (APA, 1980).

The major type of personality disorder not described elsewhere is that of the "antisocial personality."

● *Antisocial Personality Disorder*

Whatever their causes or cures, most mental disorders typically give the most pain and unhappiness to the individual concerned. Someone with an *antisocial personality disorder*, however, is likely to cause more problems for others than for the person with the deviant behaviors. Many mass murderers and other criminals fall into this category, as do "manipulators," "con artists," and some types of political rebels.

In previous diagnostic schemes, the terms "psychopath" or "sociopath" were often used to describe individuals with an antisocial personality disorder. Most of these people lack a superego or "conscience," and experience little or no guilt or anxiety about breaking social laws. They often appear to be greedy, impulsive, egocentric men and women who cannot comprehend the social consequences of their actions.

There is no agreement among experts as to what causes a person to experience this problem. On the biological side, Finnish researcher Matti Virkkunen reports that violent prisoners diagnosed as being sociopathic tend to secrete insulin more rapidly than do normals, a factor that might account for their easily-aroused emotions (Virkkunen, 1986).

As you might imagine, more men than women are diagnosed as having antisocial personalities (Reich, 1987). And in a study of several hundred young people, University of Wisconsin scientists Eleanor Hall and her associates found that "For the male adolescents, tolerance of rape and sexist attitudes were associated with antisocial, delinquent personality tendencies" (Hall *et al.*, 1986).

There is also a high correlation between drug abuse and antisocial tendencies. In a recent study of 175 cocaine addicts, Yale researcher Thomas Kosten and his colleagues found that "Cocaine abusers spent more days in illegal activities and committed more crime than nonabusers, supporting the [previously reported] increased rate of antisocial personal-

Paraphilias (pair-ah-FILL-ee-ahs). From Greek words meaning "love of things above and beyond the normal." These sexual disorders involve a need for abnormal or unusual objects or stimulation in order to achieve climax.

Transvestic fetish (trans-VEST-ick FEHT-ish). *Transvestic* comes from the Greek words *trans*, meaning "across," and *vestire*, meaning "to dress." A transvestite is a female who "cross-dresses," that is, who wears masculine clothes, or a male who wears dresses and feminine underwear. A *fetish* is an object or body part that gives someone abnormally intense sexual pleasure. For example, a man with a "shoe fetish" might fixate all of his sexual attention on the shoes that women wear, rather than on the women themselves, and might not be able to achieve sexual climax unless his partner was wearing shoes (or he imagined that she did).

ity disorder among cocaine abusers" (Kosten *et al.*, 1986). And in a study of 270 male and female alcoholic patients, University of Connecticut psychiatrist James Stabenau and his associates found that "Regardless of gender, alcoholics with antisocial personality diagnosis drank significantly more alcohol than [did] nonantisocial personality alcoholics" (Stabenau *et al.*, 1986). Similar results come from a study of 8,165 adolescents and their parents by John Forliti and Peter Benson, who report that "a restrictive religious orientation was found to be tied to antisocial behavior, alcohol use, racism, and sexism" (Forliti & Benson, 1986).

According to the 1984 NIMH report, about 1.4 million Americans currently could be diagnosed as having an antisocial personality.

□ □ **QUESTION** □ □
Many psychologists consider Adolf Hitler to be the "prototype" of someone with an antisocial personality disorder. What other political leaders also seem to fit the description in DSM-III-R? Why might their followers disagree with you?

DSM-III: AN EVALUATION

Like all diagnostic schemes, DSM-III has both strengths and weaknesses. Let's look at the good points first. (Since DSM-III-R has just been published, most of the evaluative research is on DSM-III. However, almost all of the comments on DSM-III apply to DSM-III-R as well. We will describe how DSM-III-R came into being—and some specific reactions to it—later in this chapter.)

Strengths of DSM-III

To begin with, by focusing on the biological underpinnings of many "mental" disorders, DSM-III offers a broader view of the behavioral disorders than did DSM-II. Because DSM-II (1968) was heavily influenced by psychoanalytic theory, its diagnostic categories strongly suggested the use of psychotherapy (or "talk therapy"). However, because DSM-III (1980) is oriented more toward the biological end of the

spectrum, its diagnostic descriptions seem to suggest the use of chemotherapy ("pills") rather than psychotherapy. Since chemotherapy is the "treatment of choice" for many mental disorders these days, DSM-III would seem to be closer to present-day practice than was DSM-II (Bayer & Spitzer, 1985; Griest, Jefferson, & Spitzer, 1983; Matarrazo, 1983).

Second, because DSM-III was put together by psychiatrists, psychologists, and social workers, it has a broader scope than did previous *Manuals*. And because of this input from several professional fields, DSM-III contains more diagnostic categories than did DSM-II or DSM-I (Spitzer, 1984b).

And last, but surely not least, DSM-III answers a real need. We obviously must have *some* type of classification scheme in order to deal with the very human problems we find around us. As we pointed out in Chapters 12 and 16, humans seem to have a need to *categorize*. Indeed, we seem to have difficulties *thinking about* such concepts as "mental illness" without a classification scheme of some kind. And DSM-III is, quite simply, the best such scheme we presently have available to us (Bastos, 1984).

Weaknesses of DSM-III

There are at least two kinds of problems associated with the 1980 *Manual*. The first type of difficulty is professional, while the second is scientific.

• *Professional Problems*

Any new classification scheme demands that people re-orient both their perceptions and their behaviors. Some mental health professionals accustomed to using DSM-II have raised questions about DSM-III that may do little more than reflect their own reluctance to change. In a series of recent books and articles, Robert Spitzer attempts to deal with this issue.

Spitzer is a psychiatrist—a medical doctor—who chaired the group that developed DSM-III. Thus, some of his arguments are doubtless biased in favor both of psychiatry (as opposed to psychology) and to the use of the *Manual*.

To begin with, Spitzer notes that many psychologists fear DSM-III is yet another attempt by the medical doctors to "take complete charge" of the behavioral sciences. Spitzer disagrees. He states that psychologists as well as psychiatrists helped prepare the *Manual*. More psychologists have bought copies of DSM-III than anyone else, including psychiatrists, Spitzer says, and use of the *Manual* is now widespread, both in medical schools and in departments of psychology (Williams & Spitzer, 1985).

However, most clinical psychologists apparently *perceive* DSM-III as having a "medical bias." Evidence for this statement comes from a recent survey of 546 practicing psychologists, conducted by Darrell Smith and William Kraft. The vast majority of these clinicians rejected DSM-III as a "useful diagnostic instrument." They also rejected the idea that "mental disorders" are a subset of medical disorders. Smith and Kraft urge all mental health professionals to work together to develop a better diagnostic tool than DSM-III appears to be (Smith & Kraft, 1983).

• *Scientific Problems with DSM-III*

Many psychologists object to DSM-III on scientific rather than professional grounds. To begin with, because the authors of the present *Manual* have rejected Freudian theory, they have made DSM-III more **eclectic** in its approach than were previous versions. Thus, the categories listed above are little more than a hodgepodge of "labels" that are to be pinned on individuals who don't behave as most of us presumably do (Klerman, 1983).

Next, there is the difficulty associated with getting the right label on the right person—that is to say, can we be sure the *Manual* is reliable when used in real-life situations?

Last but not least, we must somehow make sure that the diagnostic categories used are "valid" enough to tell us how to *help* the people we have labeled as being "mentally disordered" (Klerman, 1985).

We will have more to say about the problem of how to categorize people correctly in a moment. First, let's look at studies on the validity and the reliability of DSM-III in some detail.

Is DSM-III Valid?

By 1988, there were more than 200 journal articles in print that included either comments or experimental data on the *validity* of DSM-III. Generally speaking, these articles suggest that DSM-III does an adequate job of placing mental patients into *broad diagnostic categories*, but often performs more poorly in placing disturbed individuals into *highly specific categories*.

For example, Cleveland researchers Glenn Davis and Hagop Akiskal found that while "the diagnosis of borderline personality disorder [using DSM-III] has reasonable interrater and test-retest reliability, its . . . validity is poor" (Davis & Akiskal, 1986). And when New York University researcher George Serban and his colleagues recently tested 49 patients who received diagnoses either of "borderline personality disorder" or "schizotypal personality disorder," they found no reliable differences among the two types of patients. Serban and his group believe these two diagnostic categories should be combined (Serban, Conte, & Plutchik, 1987).

Scottish psychiatrist David Copolov and his colleagues report that, while DSM-III does a reasonably good job of picking up patients suffering from depression, it does not accurately place them in the various sub-categories of depression (Copolov *et al.*, 1986). More recently, Iowa researchers Mark Zimmerman and his associates have reported similar objections to the sub-categories of depression on DSM-III (Zimmerman *et al.*, 1987).

In similar fashion, University of Pittsburgh scientists Samuel Turner and his colleages found no differences between patients diagnosed as having "panic disorders" and those diagnosed as suffering from "**agoraphobia** with panic fear" (Turner *et al.*, 1986). And NIMH researchers Allen Doran and his associates have recently questioned whether DMS-III accurately differentiates among the various sub-categories of schizophrenia (Doran, Breier, & Roy, 1986).

Most telling of all, perhaps, University of Oslo (Norway) scientist Nils Retterstol notes that in Scandinavia, psychiatrists use quite different diagnostic categories than those found in DSM-III. The *concept* of mental illness in Scandinavia is significantly different from that held in the US, Retterstol says. Thus, Scandinavian psychiatrists find DSM-III of limited value (Retterstol, 1986).

We might conclude, therefore, that while DSM-III does seem to have a certain amount of validity, its diagnostic categories are "fuzzier" than originally was thought to be the case. And it seems best suited for use in the US, not in other cultures or societies.

☐ ☐ **QUESTION** ☐ ☐

How do Retterstol's views support the old adage that "Insanity is in the eyes of the beholder"?

• *Validity of DSM-III with Women Patients*

There is also some question about the validity of the *Manual* when used with female patients. Several authors discuss this problem in the July 1983 issue of the *American Psychologist*. Psychologist Marcie Kaplan notes that women are more likely to be diagnosed as suffering from a "dependent personality disorder" than men are. One reason for this difference, Kaplan argues, is that the authors of DSM-III were predominantly male. Thus, Kaplan says, masculine-biased assumptions about what behaviors are healthy and what behaviors are "crazy" are built into the diagnostic categories of DSM-III (Kaplan, 1983).

In that same journal, however, Janet Williams and Robert Spitzer deny Kaplan's assertions. In a test of 3,250 patients, Williams and Spitzer report, "there was no overall tendency for a female patient to receive a personality disorder diagnosis more often a male patient" (Kass, Spitzer, & Williams, 1984; Williams & Spitzer, 1983).

We will return to this issue momentarily, when we discuss recent revisions in DSM-III.

Validity of DSM-III: A Summary

There is little doubt that DSM-III is a more valid diagnostic instrument than was DSM-II (Russell *et al.*, 1979). However, its applicability seems to be limited, since it apparently is better at diagnosing white American males than it is at finding valid categories for American females, blacks, or members of other minority groups. And its usefulness in other cultures is, as we noted, also somewhat suspect.

Perhaps, however, we shouldn't worry too much about the *Manual*'s validity. For one of the statistical facts of life is that *no test can be valid if it is not reliable*. And, as we are about to see, many scientists have serious concern about the reliability of DSM-III.

Is DSM-III Reliable?

There is considerable evidence that psychiatrists who use the *Manual* often disagree on what diagnosis to make about a particular patient. Worse yet, psychiatrists sometimes cannot tell (in a reliable fashion) who is a "geniune" mental patient and who is "just faking it."

Rosenhan's "Pseudo-patients"

In 1973, Stanford psychologist David L. Rosenhan shocked the psychological world with a report of research he had undertaken on the reliability of psychiatric diagnoses. Rosenhan asked several "normal" people to try to get into mental hospitals by pretending to be mentally ill. These **pseudo-patients**, as Rosenhan called them, asked for voluntary admission to several public and private mental hospitals. The pseudo-patients all stated that they "heard voices," and thus needed help. Other than on this one point, these quite normal people told the admitting psychiatrists the *absolute truth* about their lives and feelings.

To Rosenhan's surprise, *all* of the pseudo-patients were admitted without question. They were all classed as being *psychotic*. About 95 percent of the time, they were diagnosed as being "schizophrenic."

David L. Rosenhan

Once the pseudo-patients were admitted, it was up to each of them to get out of the mental hospital as best they could. On the average, it took the pseudo-patients more than two weeks to get out. One man was detained (against his will) for almost two months. He finally escaped because, as he put it, the hospital was driving him crazy (Rosenhan, 1973).

When Rosenhan's article was published, it caused a furor. Many psychiatrists (including Robert Spitzer) attacked him violently for daring to say they couldn't tell normal people from people who were mentally ill. Rosenhan then agreed to a further study. He promised to send an unspecified number of pseudo-patients to a number of hospitals in the near future. The admitting psychiatrists at these hospitals were asked to "guess" whether each patient they admitted during this time period was a pseudo-patient or not. In fact, Rosenhan sent out no more pseudo-patients. He merely checked all the psychiatric admissions at the end of the time period. To his surprise, he found that some 25 percent of the *actual* patients admitted were thought to be "pseudo-patients" by the psychiatrists.

Rosenhan concludes that psychiatric judgments of what is normal and what isn't—and what is "mental illness" and what is "mentally healthy"—are much less reliable than we had previously suspected (Rosenhan, 1975).

Other Studies of Diagnostic Reliability

There are several published studies suggesting that psychiatric diagnoses can be highly unreliable. For instance, Stanford scientists Robert Hoffman and Lorrin Koran made an extensive study of 215 patients admitted to a noted psychiatric clinic. Thorough examinations of these patients showed that 41 percent of them had been "misdiagnosed in ways that could make an important difference in treatment." Many of the patients actually had physical disorders that were causing their "mental problems," but the physicians giving the initial diagnosis failed to detect the physical disease. Other patients were labeled as being "depressed" when, in fact, they were merely reacting to the medications given to them by the diagnosing physician. When the medication stopped, so did the depression (Hoffman & Koran, 1984).

In a recent review, California researchers Herb Kutchins and Stuart Kirk conclude that most of the studies purporting to show that DSM-III is reliable are "flawed, the analyses incomplete, and their interpretations often misleading." According to Kutchins and Kirk, "not a single major diagnostic category" of DSM-III appears to be reliable (Kutchins & Kirk, 1986).

One way to improve the reliability of DSM-III appears to be the use of *standardized inter-*

views by the diagnostician. In a recent study, New Zealand psychiatrist Thakshan Fernando and his colleagues found that, while the reliability of DSM-III was questionable in "normal clinical practice," it could be improved dramatically if the diagnosticians were required to interview all their patients in a standardized manner, and if the diagnosticians were given additional training prior to making the diagnosis (Fernando *et al.*, 1986).

Not all reliability studies have yielded such dismal data, however. In the late 1970's and early 1980's, Nancy Cantor and her associates performed a series of studies on diagnostic reliability using DSM-III. Cantor and her colleagues found very high reliability—and good validity—in most of their research. However, as we noted in Chapter 12, Cantor and Nancy Genero also found that there were "fuzzy boundaries" between such diagnostic categories as *mania* and *schizophrenia*. Cantor and Genero suggest that diagnostic reliability and validity could both be improved if the *definitions* of the illnesses represented in DSM-III were improved (Cantor & Genero, 1986).

DSM-III, Revised Edition

Because of the many objections to both the reliability and the validity of DSM-III, the American Psychiatric Association published a "Revised Edition" of the *Manual* in 1987. DSM-III-R contains a minor reworking of some of the various subcategories to such major categories as Anxiety Disorders, Substance Abuse, and Depression (Rounsaville *et al.*, 1987). Whether the revised version is substantially more valid and reliable than DSM-III remains to be seen, however.

As we noted, many psychiatrists and psychologists had objected that DSM-III was "prejudiced against women." One reason for this objection, as psychologist Paula Caplan noted in her book *The Myth of Women's Masochism*, was the fact that most patients diagnosed as suffering from "sexual masochism" were women (Caplan, 1985). In order to deflect this sort of criticism, the authors of DSM-III-R changed the name of this category to "Self-defeating Personality Disorder" and moved the category to an appendix in the *Manual*. The fact remains, however, that there is little scientific evidence to support the existence of such a category (Franklin, 1987).

As we also pointed out, DSM-III-R contains a new major category, the "Sleep Disorders." Many psychologists believe that this new category was included primarily for financial reasons. There are now dozens of sleep clinics in the US. People seeking treatment at these clinics can claim medical insurance reimbursement *only* if these problems are recognized as being *medical* disorders. The inclusion of the "Sleep Disorders" in DSM-III-R makes it much easier for sleep clinics to receive insurance payments.

Evaluating DSM-III: A Summary

As we have said many times, all behavior is multi-determined. Human problems, like human successes, are almost always due to *interactions* of biological, psychological, and sociological forces. Thus, any diagnostic scheme that does not view people *holistically* is bound to be relatively unreliable and invalid.

We can demonstrate this point by returning once more to John and Mary Smith, the couple we described at the beginning of this chapter. The authors of the DSM-III consider sexual inhibition in females as being primarily the *woman's* problem—a mental disorder (or personality trait) that resides in the woman's mind. But all personality traits (and mental disorders) have a biological background, and they are always expressed in social, interpersonal situations. In a small percentage of cases, sexual repression in women may be related to physical causes. But biological difficulties don't really *cause* the inhibition. Rather, the inhibition is the woman's *response* to her physical condition. And this response is chiefly determined by her own unique developmental history and the social environment she presently lives in. Sexual inhibition in men—which is defined by DSM-III as being the *man's* problem—can be seen in much the same light.

Sexual difficulties are seldom the exclusive problem of just the male *or* the female. A man may have problems with inhibition at the start of his marriage, but it is his wife's (often unconscious) responses to his condition that help keep him that way. A woman may dislike sex when she marries, but if her attitude does not change after the wedding, it is surely as much her husband's responsibility as it is hers. As Masters and Johnson discovered more than 20 years ago, it typically is useless to treat one of the marriage partners and not the other (see Chapter 7). For, generally speaking, when a person develops abnormal behavior patterns, *everyone the person has close contact with* must be considered part of the cause.

In the long run, a theory of mental illness—or a set of diagnostic categories—stands or falls on its ability to help people get better. Thus, we cannot make a final evaluation of DSM-III, or any other similar scheme, until we discover what kind of "cure rate" it gives us. As we will see in the next chapter, the holistic approach to treating mental illness apparently yields a higher percentage of cures than does the "medical model" on which DSM-III is based. And perhaps that is the strongest evidence we can offer in favor of viewing human beings as highly complex living systems.

SUMMARY

1. The study of abnormal psychology is **controversial** because it is based on the concept of normality, and the words **normal** and **abnormal** have no meaning except when they are defined within a given context.

2. Personality theorists usually assume that abnormal thoughts and behaviors are **exaggerations** of the mental and behavioral traits that we all have. Thus, most **mental disorders** can be viewed as "deviations from a **norm**."

3. The term or **label** applied to abnormalities often implies not only the presumed **cause** of the problem, but also what type of **therapy** might be effective.

4. **Normal** and **abnormal** are "neutral" terms. However, we typically see "normal" things as being "good" and "healthy," while we see "abnormal" things as being inappropriate, disabling, unhealthy, or undesirable.

5. Generally speaking, if a person deviates slightly from a psychological or cultural norm, the person is said to suffer from a **neurosis**. If the deviation is large, the person is said to suffer from a **psychosis**, and probably will require hospitalization or extensive treatment.

6. Psychologists often use the terms **mean**, **median**, and **mode** to describe the center of a **normal distribution** of test scores or behavioral measures. This distribution is often a **bell-shaped curve**. An abnormal behavior or score is one that departs 2 or more **standard deviations** from the norm.

7. Psychiatrists and psychologists use many different **diagnostic systems** to describe and interpret thoughts or actions that are presumed to be abnormal. One such system is described in the **Diagnostic and Statistical Manual of Mental Disorders**, the third edition of which was published in 1980.

8. **DSM-III** and **DSM-III-R** are based on the belief that most mental disorders have a **biological basis**. In contrast, **DSM-II** was based on Freudian theory, and **DSM-I** was based on the belief that mental disorders came from abnormal person-environment interactions.

9. According to DSM-III-R, patients should be rated on five different diagnostic **axes**:
   a. **Axis 1 covers the clinical psychiatric syndrome(s)** or major mental disorder(s) the patient suffers from.
   b. **Axis 2 lists the personality disorders** or abnormal **personality traits** the patient shows, if any, as well as certain **developmental disorders** that were included on Axis 1 in DSM-III.
   c. **Axis 3 covers any physical problems** the patient has, such as brain damage or disease.
   d. **Axis 4 lists any social stressors** the patient has experienced in the past year.
   e. **Axis 5 evaluates the patient's highest level of adaptive functioning** during the past year.

10. A 1984 report by the **National Institute of Mental Health** suggests some **20 percent of American adults** suffer from mental disorders. According to the NIMH report, about 13 million Americans would be diagnosed on DSM-III as having **anxiety disorders**, 2.4 million as having **obsessive-compulsive disorders**, 9.4 million as having **affective disorders**, 1.5 million as having **schizophrenic disorders**, and 1.4 million as having **anti-social personalities**.

11. **Schizophrenia** is primarily a disorder of the young. It typically involves disordered thinking, perception, emotions, sense of self, volition, relationship to the external world, and psychomotor behavior.

12. There is some evidence that the tendency to suffer schizophrenia is **partially inherited**, but must be triggered by stressful situations, primarily those involving **family relationships**.

13. The two major types of mood disorders are the **bipolar disorder** and **depressive disorders.** Although **genetic markers** for depression have been found in some cultural groups, most depressions appear to be triggered by **social stress**.

14. The recent increase in **suicides** in American youth seems to be correlated with an equally large increase in the rate of **depression** among young people.

15. Although DSM-III-R includes a category called **post-traumatic stress disorder**, research suggests this may not be a valid diagnostic category.

16. In the **dissociative disorders**, one or more additional personalities "split off" and seem to "take on a life of their own." In **schizophrenia**, the mind is "shattered," not "split."

17. The **antisocial personality disorder** is found primarily in men and is correlated with drug abuse and aggression.

18. The **strengths** of DSM-III are that it offers a broader view of the behavioral disorders than did DSM-II, it gives a measure of standardization, it was tested extensively prior to publication, and it answers a real psychiatric need.

19. The professional weaknesses of DSM-III are that it is based on the **medical model**, and that many psychologists see it as a **grab for power** by psychiatrists.

20. DSM-III appears to have many **scientific weaknesses**. It appears to place patients adequately in "large categories," but many of its sub-categories appear to lack validity. In some respects DSM-III may be biased against women patients, and its usefulness in other cultures is limited.

21. **DSM-III-R**, a revised version of DSM-III published in 1987, attempts to correct some of these problems. It adds a category called **sleep disorders**, reduces the number of **sexual behaviors** that now are considered "mental disorders," and responds (in part) to the criticism that DSM-III was **biased against women**.

22. Worries about the **reliability** of DSM-III are based on studies showing that psychiatrists cannot always differentiate between real patients and **pseudo-patients**, and that experts do not always agree on the **diagnosis** for any given patient.

23. The best possible **diagnostic scheme** would be a **holistic approach** that took into account the biological, intra-psychic, and social factors that influence the disturbed individual's level of functioning.

(Continued from page 460.)

Steve May looked at the hamburger and burst into tears. "It's the most beautiful thing I've ever seen," he said.

Dr. Mary Ellen Mann nodded her head sympathetically. "Would you like a milk shake to go with it?"

"I'm not sure I could stand that much pleasure all at once," Steve replied in a serious tone of voice. Then he smiled. "But let's order one and see."

Dr. Mann motioned to the waitress and gave her the order. She watched with amusement as Steve demolished the hamburger and sucked up the milk shake in one long gulp. Then the young man sat back in his chair, a contented smile on his face, and uttered a very loud belch. The people at the next table glared at him. "Sorry," Steve said loudly enough for them to hear. "I forgot where I was."

"It's not where you are, but where you've been the past two weeks that I'm interested in," Dr. Mann said. "You said you'd tell me all about your stay at the hospital if I would buy you dinner. I have given you the food of your choice, although I cannot imagine why you chose to celebrate your freedom at Wendy's. So, for starters, why a hamburger instead of a steak?"

"You miss the things you can't have," Steve explained. "Sometimes the food was okay, but mostly it was terrible. The food at that place is as crazy as the inmates sometimes act." He groaned. "You have no idea what obscenities can be inflicted on innocent objects such as hamburgers and green peas."

"Oh, yes, I have," Dr. Mann replied. "I eat at the Faculty Club all the time. But start at the beginning. I want to know what happened, from the moment you walked through the hospital door until the moment you exited in the garbage truck."

Steve stirred his coffee slowly, considering what to say. "Well, I got in, as you no doubt know. The admitting psychiatrist never batted an eye when I told him I heard voices. He just nodded his head and then asked me what the voices said. And then he asked me about my relationship with my mother, and did I have arguments with my father," Steve continued.

"The Oedipus complex, of course."

Steve smiled. "Of course. Seems I've never worked it out. He thought it significant also that I lose my temper a couple of times a year."

"Poor impulse control," Dr. Mann said. "You tend to belch in public places, and terrible things like that."

"I guess you do get back to the elementals in the mental hospital. Nobody thought twice about belching, or even crapping on the floor. They didn't even make you clean it up afterwards."

Mary Ellen Mann nodded. "If the people around us didn't complain, we'd all act a lot crazier than we presently do. But to return to the subject, the psychiatrist never guessed you were a 'pseudo-patient,' like the ones in Professor Rosenhan's study?"

"No, he just asked questions for a while, then wrote down on the admission form that I was a certified nut."

"Which you probably are for letting me talk you into the whole affair," Dr. Mann said with a sigh. "I'm really sorry if you suffered very much, Steve."

"Oh, it wasn't all that bad. I did feel terrified at first, but I got over it after a while."

"Terrified of what?" Dr. Mann asked gently.

Steve grinned. "First I was worried that the 'crazies' might attack me. But of course they didn't. In fact, getting to know them was the best part of the whole experience. But after I realized I was physically safe, I got to worrying about not having any control over what was happening to me. I didn't have any money or power or status, so I tried to act sane and sensible and be nice to people. And I smiled a lot."

"Did it work?"

"Not hardly," Steve replied. "One nurse finally told me that smiling was a symptom of my underlying problems. So I stopped. Maybe she was right. Anybody who'd smile in there has to be out of touch with reality."

Dr. Mann frowned. "But they did treat you decently, didn't they?"

"The patients did. The staff treated me more like I was retarded, or some species of vegetable. There was one rather good-looking young nurse's aide I tried to get to know, but she wasn't about to get serious with a 'mental patient,' if you know what I mean. The nurses were much better, but I didn't see much of them. That's one of the things that frightened me."

"Why?" the woman asked.

Steve laughed. "You can't get out of that place unless the nurses and the social workers see you and realize that you're 'doing better,' as they put it. And most of them aren't around too much."

"Where are they?" Dr. Mann asked.

"In their offices, filling out papers, I guess." Steve May shook his head. "You can't convince people you're sane if they aren't around to be convinced."

Mary Ellen Mann sighed. "Rosenhan says that if we just valued the patients as people, if we treated them as human assets rather than as liabilities, we might learn a lot from them and simultaneously help most of them get better."

"Some of them don't want to get better," Steve said quietly. "They're afraid they can't cope 'outside,' and it's easier to stay where someone will take care of them. I tried to help a couple of them, as best I could."

"Like how?" Dr. Mann asked.

"Well," said Steve, "There was Crampy Joe. Nice guy, really, but he walked around all stooped over like he had the cramps. I started giving him a cigarette every time he walked upright."

Dr. Mann laughed. "Behavior modification to the rescue, eh? Did it work?"

Steve nodded. "It worked until the nurses made me stop. They said it was against the rules for one patient to perform therapy on another."

"A sobering thought, that," Mary Ellen Mann said. "And they never caught on to your game, did they?"

"Oh, many of the patients did," Steve said. "But the staff members never guessed. That's what terrified me most, I guess. The crazy people thought I was sane, but the sane people insisted I was crazy. After a while, I didn't know which group to believe. And that *really* worried me."

"And that's when you decided to get the hell out of there, eh?"

Steve grinned. "You bet. I tried to see the psychiatrist for two weeks, but I couldn't get an appointment. They just increased the number of pills they gave me. And I just kept on flushing them down the toilet, when nobody was watching."

"You aren't as crazy as you look," the professor said.

"No, but I did get to worrying about it." He smiled shyly at the woman. "For a day or two, I even thought you had cooked the whole deal up, because you thought I was nuts and it was the only way you could think of to get me into the looney bin. That's when I knew it was time to leave."

Dr. Mann laughed. "But why make your grand exit in a garbage truck?"

"Only way out. I noticed that the garbage truck always arrived right at lunchtime. So today I waited until they weren't looking and hid under the garbage. Once the truck was outside the gates, I dropped off, cleaned myself up as best I could, and hitch-hiked home. Then I took a very long shower, and called you."

Mary Ellen Mann gave a deep sigh. "Well, I do appreciate what you did, and we'll talk more about it later on. Do you have any final words of wisdom for tonight, though?"

Steve nodded. "Yes, I do. I realize that we can't improve the hospital system until we know it from the inside out, as well as from the outside in. And so you've got to have volunteers like me go in and look for you. But I have a favor to ask. If you talk anybody else into volunteering, tell them one thing for me, will you?"

"What?" she asked.

He smiled. "Tell 'em they're nuts."

Psychotherapy

"The Odds in Favor"

· C · H · A · P · T · E · R ·
19

Mark Evans looked at the little old lady standing by the slot machine. She wore cheap gloves to keep her hands clean, and dirty tennis shoes to keep her feet comfortable. As Mark watched her, she grubbed about in her huge purse, then produced a dollar bill and handed it to a scantily-clad young woman who made change for the machines in the casino. The attractive attendant smiled as she handed the older woman a roll of 20 nickels. "Good luck," she said.

"Good juju," the little old lady said in response. Then she tottered along a row of slot machines until she found one to her liking. Mark Evans moved over to watch her as she dumped her purse beside the one-armed bandit, then ever so carefully unrolled the nickels. She counted them one by one. Exactly 20. Examining one of the coins closely, she decided it would do. She spat on it, then rubbed the nickel gently between her gloved fingers to remove the tarnish.

"You'll rub all the luck off it, honey," said a large, red-headed woman who was dropping dimes into the next machine.

"Luck?" cackled the little old woman, taking a grimy cloth bag from her purse and shaking it at the slot machine. "Luck is just a matter of chance, and I don't leave anything to chance. I put a hex on the machines, and they always pay off. I brought my juju bag with me today, so I can't lose. My juju is strong today. I feel its strength in my bones. You just wait and see."

The old lady dropped the coin in the machine and pulled the handle. The three reels spun wildly, then clicked to a stop, one by one. A plum, an orange, and a lemon. She shook her head, and deposited another nickel. Again the reels whirred into action and jerked to a stop—two lemons and a bell.

"Your juju is all lemons today, dearie," the red-headed woman said.

The little old lady gestured wildly at the machine with the bag. "Juju!" she cried. "Give me a jackpot."

The reels produced a cherry and two bells, and the machine grudgingly coughed up two nickels as a reward.

"See! That's a good start. It's going to be a good day. I feel it in my bones!"

Mark Evans shook his head in amazement, then checked his watch. Time to meet his relative-in-law, Lou Hudson, from Chattanooga, Tennessee. Lou, who had married Mark's cousin Ann, was in Las Vegas for a convention of life insurance agents. Ann had called Mark a few days ago, asking Mark to take time out from his graduate studies at the University of Nevada to "show Lou the sights." That was the trouble with studying psychology in Las Vegas—sooner or later everbody you knew showed up and expected you to entertain them.

Lou Hudson turned out to be a thin young man with blond hair and blue but bloodshot eyes. "Stayed up half the night playing blackjack," Lou said, after the introductions were completed. "You wouldn't believe my luck. I was 200 bucks ahead, and I just knew I had a streak going. But then the cards turned against me. I barely broke even."

Mark Evans smiled. He had heard the phrase "broke even" enough to know that it usually meant losing a lot.

"Hey, man, this Las Vegas place is too much!" Lou gestured at the activity in the casino. "Hotels with gambling halls instead of lobbies, people running around 24 hours a day, throwing their money away like there wasn't any tomorrow! Bands playing, and free drinks, and nobody to tell you when to get up or when to go to bed. Why, it's a gambler's paradise!"

"You're here for a convention?" Mark asked, a touch of sarcasm in his voice.

"Yeah. I suppose I really ought to get around to some of the meetings pretty soon now," Lou said with a frown. "But I've been having so much fun, there just hasn't been time." His face brightened suddenly. "Hey, man, they've got every kind of game here you can imagine, haven't they? I mean, I like to gamble a little, just now and then you know. Poker, blackjack, the horses—strictly for small stakes. But they got things here I've only read about, like roulette. You ever play roulette?"

Mark Evans shook his head. "No percentage in it. The odds against winning are too great."

"Whatta ya mean, too great?" Lou demanded almost hostilely, leading Mark toward one of the roulette tables nearby. "See—36 numbers, half of them red, half black. You put a dollar chip on any one of them, and they spin the ball around the wheel. If the little ball drops into your number, the house pays you back 35 to 1. That's pretty good odds, isn't it?"

Mark groaned. "Lou, you forget the two green zeros at the top of the board. There are really 38 numbers, not 36. If you put a dollar down on all the numbers, it would cost you $38 a game. And you'd win back only $35, no matter what number came up. You'd lose $3 each time the wheel spun, because the odds are against you."

"Yeah, but if you pick a lucky number, and put a dollar on it 10 times in a row, and it hits twice, then you've won $70 and it only cost you $10. You can quit a big winner," Lou said.

"*If* you quit, which most gamblers don't. If you keep betting, it doesn't matter whether you play all 38 numbers once, or one number 38 times—you're going to spend $38 to win $35. Because your number is going to win just once in 38 times—on the average."

Lou was plainly annoyed. "You don't understand, man. Look at that fat man over there with the big diamond ring on his pinkie. He's got a stack of chips in front of him that would choke a giraffe. He's bound to be making money on the roulette wheel."

"The only way to make money in Las Vegas is to open your own casino, Lou. That man may be winning now, but if he plays long enough, he'll lose. Because the odds are against him."

Lou shook his head. "You may be right in theory, Mark, but look at that man's stack of chips. Maybe he's got a secret system or something. Maybe he knows what number's going to come up next."

Mark was beginning to understand why the casinos made so much money. "Lou, old man, if that wheel is honest—and out here, they almost always are—there's no way in hell that you or anybody else can make money at roulette if you play long enough."

"Well, how the hell *can* you win at this game, anyway?"

Mark thought a moment. "The only way I know of is to sit for hours and keep a record of each number that comes up. Sometimes the wheel does get out of balance. It gets biased toward one number, let's say 25. Out of 38,000 spins, 25 ought to come up 1,000 times. But if it comes up 2,000 times, or even 3,000, then you know something's abnormal about the wheel."

"You're saying I ought to just sit and take records first instead of just going with my hunches?"

"Absolutely," Mark replied, happy that Lou seemed to be getting the message. "You may not know *why* 25 is better than the other numbers, but the graph tells you it's a winner. So you go with the odds."

"Sounds like a lot of work to me," Lou said, taking a free drink from a cocktail waitress as she passed by. His hands trembled slightly as he sipped the drink. "Oh, I know. You've studied statistics and all that. But Mark, you've neglected the most important thing—the human factor. Man, when I get hot, I get really hot. I mean, I win big. It's like I've got some power over the cards, or the horses, or maybe even the roulette wheel. That kind of power is a helluva lot more important than sitting and watching a wheel turn round 38,000 times."

Mark sighed. "Lou, if you gamble to have fun, then you can just charge your losses off as entertainment expenses. But if you gamble for money—if you absolutely have to win—then you hunt for situations in which the odds are in your favor."

It was obvious that Mark's answer didn't satisfy Lou Hudson. His bloodshot eyes opened wide. "But man, I'm a special case! I mean, I get these streaks when I'm hot as hell. How do you explain the power I have over the cards when I've got a streak going?"

"Lou," Mark said gently, "How much money do you have?"

"Me? Well, to tell the truth, I'm pretty near broke right now."

"And you've been gambling all your life. If you have all that power, how come you aren't a big winner?"

Lou took a big gulp of his drink. "Well, I've been down on my luck lately. But just wait until tomorrow. I'm gonna bounce right back with a big killing. I got that special feeling, you see . . ."

Mark sighed heavily. "Lou, friend, listen. How does the insurance company you work for manage to make money?"

Lou frowned. "Why they sell policies, of course. You wouldn't happen to need some life insurance, would you?"

"No, but pretend I did," Mark replied. "Suppose I bought a million dollar policy from you."

"Nice commission on a policy that big," Lou said dreamily.

Mark nodded. "Yes, but how can the company make any money when I might die an hour after I bought the policy?"

"It's simple," Lou said. "The company knows how many people your age are likely to die in any one year, and they charge enough to cover their expected losses and to make a little dough on the side too."

"They go with the percentages, you mean."

"Sure," Lou replied. "They don't know who's gonna live, or who's gonna die. And I reckon they don't really care. They just go with the odds. I tell you no lie, Mark, those people are pretty hard-nosed when it comes to money." Lou stopped for a moment. Then his head drooped a little, and he continued in a voice grown suddenly hoarse. "Speaking of money, Mark, you wouldn't happen to have a little extra cash on you, would you? Just a temporary loan, you know. Until my luck turns good again."

Mark shook his head. "Sorry, man. The way tuition's shot up recently, students just barely get by these days. But what's the matter? Aren't you selling very many policies?"

Lou's bloodshot eyes filled with tears. "Oh, I sell a few. But the money always seems to go out faster than it comes in. Ann's pretty disturbed about it, I suspect. She says that I'm a compulsive gambler. And she ought to know, her being a psychiatric social worker. You're a psychologist, Mark. Do you think I've gone looney or something?"

Mark sighed. "I'm just a grad student, Lou, and there's lots of things I don't know yet. What do you think?"

"I think I've got a problem, Mark. I mean, I hurt. Deep down inside. I hurt real bad." Lou grabbed Mark by the arm. "Man, you gotta help me. What can I do to get rid of the pain? What can I do?"

(Continued on page 512)

TURNING KNOWLEDGE INTO POWER

There's an old saying that "knowledge is power." Sometimes you study the world to figure out what makes things go. But as soon as you discover some significant relationships about the things you've been studying, you're likely to want to put your knowledge to use to make things go *better*.

At other times, when you're faced with a practical problem, you may try out something new. If it works to your satisfaction, you may sit down and attempt to figure out *why* the new technique succeeded—so that you can use it again, perhaps more effectively. In either case, you're trying to convert knowledge into power.

In the last chapter, we dealt with *knowledge*. For *diagnostic schemes* are really attempts to discover what abnormal behaviors people engage in, and to determine *why* people act, think, and feel in unusual ways. In this chapter we ask a *power* question—"How do you change or 'cure' abnormal behavior once it occurs?" Generally speaking, the more restricted your viewpoint is about what *causes* these abnormalities to occur, the more limited your power to *change* them becomes.

In many primitive parts of the world, for instance, people still believe in the "devil theory" of mental illness. "Crazy" people are thought to be *possessed* (or at least affected) by devils—outside spirits that take over a person's mental functioning for one reason or another.

Let's look at some examples of the "devil theory" in action before we discuss more modern approaches to the problem of curing mental illness.

PRIMITIVE APPROACHES TO MENTAL ILLNESS

The Cree Eskimos and Ojibwa Indians of Canada occasionally suffer from a psychosis known as **witigo**, or devil-caused cannibalism. The first symptoms are usually a loss of appetite, vomiting, and diarrhea—as well as the person's morbid fear that she or he has been possessed by a *witigo*, or witch, who lives on human flesh. The affected individual becomes withdrawn, brooding, and cannot eat or sleep. The person's family—fearing for their very lives—immediately calls in a "witch doctor" to cast out the witigo by saying magic words or casting spells. However, if a witch doctor can't be found in time, the disturbed individual may be overwhelmed by the witigo's powers and kill and eat one or more of the members of the family (Goldenson, 1970).

In Malaysia, in Southeast Asia, young males occasionally suffer from a different type of possession by devils, called **running amok**. At first the man becomes more withdrawn, depressed, and brooding than usual. Then he will suddenly leap to his feet with a blood-curdling scream, pull out a dagger, and begin stabbing anyone or anything in his path.

Therapy for "running amok" usually consists of killing the amoker before he can kill you, or keeping everyone out of the amoker's way until he kills himself. The few men who have survived this type of psychotic "seizure" have often said the world suddenly "turned black," and they had to slash their way out of the darkness with a knife (Goldenson, 1970).

In Spain and Morroco, the name given to this form of mental disorder is *juramentado*,

In primitive times and cultures, mentally ill individuals visited witch doctors, or tied a list of their problems to a tree and "left them behind."

the Spanish word for "cursed person." In the United States, we sometimes call it *homicidal mania*. DSM-III calls it "an explosive disorder of impulse control." And it surely won't shock you to learn that this disorder is also correlated with depression and alcoholism (Virkkunen, 1986).

□ □ **QUESTION** □ □

Why would the *therapy* you suggested for "running amok" vary according to the *label* you put on the problem?

Koro

Many Chinese believe that mental and physical disorders result from an imbalance of Yang and Yin, the masculine and feminine "powers" that control the entire spiritual universe. Chinese males occasionally suffer from an odd phobia called **koro**—a dismal fear that their penis is about to be sucked up into their stomachs and disappear, causing death and other disappointments. To prevent this disaster, the man will hold on to his penis for dear life. When he tires, he asks for help from friends and relatives. The man's wife may "cure" the attack if she practices oral sex on him immediately, but this treatment is not always successful.

Koro is thought to be caused by a sudden upsurge in the strength of the man's Yin, or femininity. Thus, it can be cured by giving the patient "masculine" medicine containing a strong Yang factor—such as powdered rhinoceros horn. If this therapy fails, the man may use a special clasp that holds his penis out from his body mechanically.

On the Pacific island of Borneo, a similar disorder affects women—who fear that their breasts and genitalia are being pulled up into their bodies. Therapy in Borneo often consists of asking a witch doctor to remove the curse, which presumably was laid on the woman by a "witch" jealous of the woman's physical beauty (Goldenson, 1970).

□ □ **QUESTION** □ □

Under what diagnostic category would a psychiatrist using the DSM-III put *koro*?

FOUR ISSUES CONCERNING PSYCHOTHERAPY

Even in the United States—where most of us no longer believe in witches, demons, and evil spirits—our therapies almost always stem from our theories of what causes human behavior. If we see an organic psychosis as being due *primarily* to physical causes, we tend to treat the patient with physical measures, such as drugs, electric shock, and surgery. If we see a neurosis as being due *primarily* to a conflict between ego and superego, we use psychoanalysis to help bring some rational resolution to the con-

"MY ASTROLOGER SAYS ONE THING, MY GURU SAYS ANOTHER, MY PSYCHIATRIST SAYS SOMETHING ELSE—I DON'T KNOW WHO TO TURN TO ANYMORE."

flict. If we assume that deviant behavior is *primarily* the consequence of inappropriate rewards and punishments, we might prescribe behavior therapy or somehow attempt to alter the person's social environment.

In this chapter we will discuss all these special forms of treatment, and the theories that gave rise to them. But before we can evaluate the various forms of therapy, we must raise several pertinent (and very hard-nosed) issues:

1. How successful is the therapy? That is, what is its "cure rate"? Would the patient have

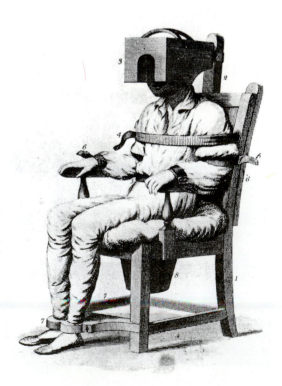

The belief that persons who behaved abnormally were "possessed" led to abusive "cures." This "Tranquilizing Chair" was invented by Dr. Benjamin Rush of Philadelphia in the 1700's.

Koro (KOH-roh). A phobia occurring in the East Indies and southern China. The disorder consists of a sudden fear that the penis will disappear into the abdomen and lead to death.

Lunatic asylums (LOON-ah-tick as-SIGH-lums). In Europe during the Middle Ages, many people believed that insanity was caused by some influence the moon had on human behavior. *Luna* is the Latin word for "moon," thus mental illness came to be called "lunacy," and mentally-ill individuals were called "lunatics."

recovered anyhow, even if we hadn't done anything? Would a "witch doctor," or someone using a different form of treatment, have done as well? In short, does the therapy make a *significant difference* in helping the patient? Is it a *valid* form of treatment?

2. Assuming the therapy does make a significant difference, how *reliable* it is? Does it work all the time, or just occasionally? Is it effective with all sorts of patients, or does it succeed better with some than with others?

3. What are the *side effects*? What else happens to the patient when we apply the treatment? Is the "cure" sometimes worse than the "disease"?

4. And cutting across all these issues is the basic question: "What do we mean by *cure*?" How shall we define "improvement"? Just as important, how shall we measure it?

We will have much more to say about these issues as we discuss the three main types of psychotherapy. We will also find it all too customary for therapists of opposing views to call each other "witch doctors," and to accuse each other of using "black magic" rather than "scientific magic."

BIOLOGICAL THERAPIES

Two centuries ago, when the "demon theory" was the accepted explanation of most mental disorders, the therapy of choice was *punishment*. The belief was that if you whipped a patient vigorously enough, you could "beat the devil" out of the person. The fact that some patients did improve after whippings was evidence enough to support the validity of the theory. It was not until *scientific investigations* suggested that the "cure rate" for unbeaten patients was higher than for those who were beaten that we finally hung up the whip in our **lunatic asylums**. Whether our present forms of psychotherapy are all that much more effective than "beating the devil" out of *lunatics*, however, is a point much debated today in psychology and psychiatry (Garfield, 1983b).

As we suggested in the last chapter, the organic psychoses do seem directly related to damage to the central nervous system or to genetic causes. Perhaps for that reason, many of the therapies used to treat organic psychoses are explicitly *biological*—the three main types

being artificially-induced *seizures, psychosurgery,* and *drugs.* (As we will see, these types of treatment are also occasionally used with patients who have functional psychoses.)

Convulsive Therapy

In 1935 a Hungarian psychiatrist named Ladislaus J. Meduna noted an odd fact—very few of the schizophrenic patients he worked with also suffered from epilepsy. Meduna concluded that seizures somehow *prevented* schizophrenia. If he could induce epileptic-type seizures in his schizophrenic patients, he reasoned, he might be able to cure them of their problems.

As a test, Meduna injected schizophrenic patients with drugs that caused seizures. Many patients did show some improvement, but an alarming number of them were severely injured or died from the treatment. Other patients showed intense apprehension about the unpleasantness of the experience. Meduna's treatment was abandoned as "barbaric," but the idea lived on (Breggin, 1979).

□ □ **QUESTION** □ □
If therapy is extremely painful—be it whippings or convulsions—why might some patients show immediate improvement?

● *Electro-convulsive Therapy*

In 1938 two Italian psychiatrists—Ugo Cerletti and L. Bini—began using electrical current rather than drugs to induce seizures. If you were to be given electro-convulsive therapy (or

Electro-convulsive therapy has relieved depression for some patients who were not helped by other methods, but serious side effects have been reported.

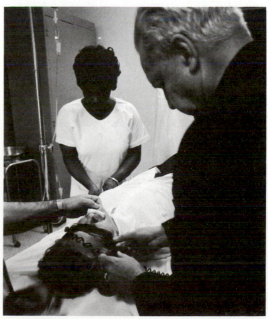

ECT, as it is often called), the psychiatrist would probably apply it in the following way. First you would be given (1) a muscle relaxant, (2) a drug to prevent you from choking and perhaps a rubber device to put in your mouth to keep you from biting your tongue, and (3) a fast-acting anesthetic to put you to sleep. Then you'd be strapped to a padded bed in order to reduce the possibility of your breaking an arm or leg during the seizure.

When you were unconscious (from the drug), the psychiatrist would apply electrodes to your head, and pass a brief but fairly strong electrical current directly through your brain. Your muscles would become rigid for about 10 seconds. Then you would go into convulsions much as if you'd had a *grand mal* seizure (see Chapter 2). The convulsions would last for a minute or two, but you would remain unconscious for up to 30 minutes and would be drowsy or confused for many hours thereafter. Because seizures induce *retrograde amnesia* (see Chapter 11), you probably would not remember the shock or the events immediately preceding it. Typically, you would be given ECT three times a week for a period of a few weeks—or until you showed some recovery (Abrams & Essman, 1982).

Use of ECT reached a peak in the 1960's, then fell dramatically, only to rise again in recent years. In 1980, the National Institute of Mental Health reported that about 33,000 patients were given ECT. However, by 1985, the number had increased dramatically to more than 100,000. Most of these patients given ECT were in private, not public hospitals (Holden, 1985).

□ □ QUESTION □ □
What social and financial factors might have encouraged the increased use of ECT during the 1980's?

● *Effectiveness of ECT*
There is considerable argument about the effectiveness of ECT. Many psychiatrists believe ECT can help with severely depressed patients. Evidence to support this view comes from many sources. In 1985, a panel assembled by the National Institutes of Health gave "cautious endorsement" to the use of ECT—but only as short-term treatment with patients who suffer from *severe depression*. A few psychiatrists also believe ECT is effective with schizophrenic patients. According to the NIH report, however, the research data do not presently support use of electroshock treatment for any disorder other than depression (Holden, 1985). Perhaps this is not surprising, for Meduna's original observations about schizophrenia and epilepsy were based on a mistaken idea. He apparently did not realize that all patients with epilepsy *and* schizophrenia were put in a different ward

than the one he was working on (Goldenson, 1970).

● *Dangers of ECT Treatment*
There are many dangers associated with the use of ECT. To begin with, this type of treatment causes dramatic changes in the neurological and biochemical functioning of the brain. Thus, even when ECT *is* effective with depressed patients, we do not as yet know *why* the treatment works (Maltz & Sackeim, 1986).

There is also the question of side effects. A few patients do die as a result of treatment, but the death rate typically is well below 1 percent. As we mentioned, many patients who are given ECT report fairly-severe memory problems. According to California psychiatrist Larry Squire, however, most of this memory loss is temporary, and disappears after a few weeks (Squire, 1982). However, New York University psychiatrist Barbara Steif and her colleagues recently reported somewhat different results. Steif and her group tested 19 depressed patients and 20 matched, normal controls on their ability to acquire and retain information. The depressed patients showed a "marked deficit" in learning new material, compared to the controls, but no deficit in retaining information once it was acquired. However, after a series of seven ECT treatments, the depressed patients showed a marked improvement in their ability to *learn* new material, but a significant deficit in *retaining* information once learned (Steif *et al.*, 1986). Thus, the effects of ECT on memory apparently are more complex than Squire had assumed was the case.

Maryland psychiatrist Peter Roger Breggin takes a different if somewhat extreme view. He admits some depressed patients do show improvement after ECT. But he states that the effects of ECT on the brain are often "severe," "catastrophic," and "devastating." Breggin believes that most of the "perceived benefits" of ECT are due to the *placebo effect*—and several studies do show that patients who *thought* they were given convulsive therapy showed almost as much improvement as did patients who actually receive shock. Breggin notes, as well, that the "cure rate" for depression achieved by psychiatrists who refuse to administer ECT is as high as or higher than that among psychiatrists who use shock extensively (Breggin, 1979).

To summarize, ECT appears to be a fairly effective "treatment of last resort" with severely-depressed patients for whom all other forms of therapy have failed. As the 1985 NIH report states, however, there is at present no scientific evidence that ECT is of value with any other type of disorder.

□ □ QUESTION □ □
Some patients request ECT, particularly after they have been performing badly

for a period of time. How might Freud's notions about the causes of *masochism* explain the patients' request for ECT?

Psychosurgery

As you will remember from reading the early chapters of this book, many types of emotional responses are controlled by the brain's *limbic system* (see Chapters 8, 12). Portions of the thalamus and the frontal lobes are also involved in emotional reactions. In 1935, John F. Fulton and C.E. Jacobsen demonstrated that surgery on the prefrontal lobes had a *calming effect* on two chimpanzees they were working with. After learning of this research, a Portuguese psychiatrist named Egas Moniz decided that cutting the prefrontal lobes—an operation called a **lobotomy**—might help aggressive or hyper-emotional patients. In 1936 Moniz and his associates reported that lobotomy did seem to be effective with some of these patients (Valenstein, 1980).

Lobotomies were introduced to the US in 1942 by Walter Freeman and his colleagues, and Moniz and Freeman later received the Nobel Prize for their work. Other psychiatrists soon reported that cutting the *connections* between the lower brain centers and the prefrontal lobes seemed to work just as well as *removing* the prefrontal lobes.

The question is, of course, "Work as well as what?" Many lobotomy patients do show an improvement after the operation, but many do not. And the fatality rate from the operation may run as high as 4 percent. (We might note that the "fatality rate" must include Moniz himself, who died after being shot by one of his lobotomy patients.)

Lobotomy is sometimes used as a treatment of last resort with patients suffering from severe attacks of *grand mal* epilepsy (see Chapter 2). There are, however, rather serious cognitive deficits associated with the operation. British psychiatrist Robin Jacobson found that, 10 years after psychosurgery, one patient had severe problems recognizing people's faces and had lost much of her "social self-control" (Jacobson, 1986). And Mayo Clinic researchers Robert Ivnik and his colleagues report that, while IQ tended to remain the same after lobotomy, patients whose left hemispheres were removed showed a significant decrease in language-dependent cognitive tasks (Ivnik *et al.*, 1987).

Furthermore, as University of Michigan psychologist Elliot Valenstein points out in a recent book, well-controlled comparisons of patients given lobotomies and those given other forms of treatment suggest that the operation is neither effective nor reliable as a "cure" for any type of mental illness (Valenstein, 1986).

□ □ **QUESTION** □ □
Why might many physicians be more interested in performing *operations* on patients with mental disorders than in giving the patients long-term *psycho*therapy?

Drug Therapy

There are a number of *psychoactive drugs*—that is, chemicals that have a psychological effect. We discussed many of them in Chapter 3. Among the most widely used psychoactive compounds are the major and minor tranquilizers, and the antidepressants. These drugs are now referred to as **neuroleptics**.

According to Scripps Institute researcher George F. Koob, "Neuroleptic drugs were first defined as drugs that decrease initiative, emotional response, and affect; later they were defined as antipsychotics because of their dramatic effectiveness in reducing the severity of symptoms in many psychiatric patients" (Koob, 1984). As we will soon see, however, many scientists today believe that the *side effects* that the neuroleptics cause are far worse than whatever benefits they may bring.

● **Major Tranquilizers**

For many centuries medical practitioners in India have given tense or manic patients a drug made from the snake root plant because it seemed to calm them down. We now call this

Psychoactive drugs have been used increasingly to treat mental illness, although there is widespread concern about their side effects.

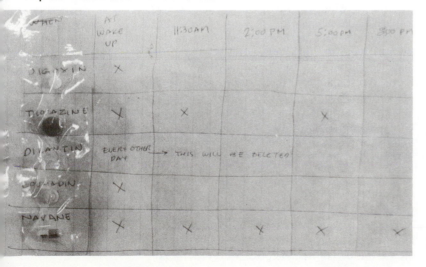

drug **reserpine**. In 1953 the Indian physician R.A. Hakim reported that reserpine seemed to be effective with some schizophrenic patients. When Nathan S. Kline tried reserpine here in 1954, he stated that it brought about marked improvement in 86 percent of the schizophrenic patients he tried it with (Breggin, 1983).

At about the same time, a French surgeon named Henri Laborit suggested that giving a powerful drug called **chlorpromazine** to schizophrenic patients might make them more manageable. Research soon showed that the drug not only calmed these patients down, but seemed to relieve some of their symptomatic behaviors as well (Goldenson, 1970).

Reserpine and chlorpromazine were the first of the many tranquilizers now widely used with mental patients. One interesting point about these drugs is that patients often dislike and seldom "abuse" these chemicals. However, since the major tranquilizers make "disturbed" patients easier to handle in hospitals, these drugs are now frequently prescribed by psychiatrists (Greenhill & Gralnick, 1983).

Since the mid-1970's, a drug called *lithium carbonate* has been used—with varying degrees of success—with patients displaying bipolar affective disorders (manic-depressive psychoses). Lithium carbonate can have a calming effect during manic episodes. Not all manic patients are helped by the drug, though, and it has dangerous (even deadly) side-effects (Breggin, 1983).

Lithium carbonate is also used occasianly in conjunction with anti-depressants. However, David Kantor and his associates at the University of Ottawa found no difference in the recovery rate of depressive patients given lithium carbonate and those receiving a placebo (Kantor *et al.*, 1986). There is also some evidence that lithium carbonate helps promote abstinence in some alcoholics (Fawcett *et al.*, 1987).

• *Minor Tranquilizers*

Drugs such as Valium and Librium are called "minor" tranquilizers because they have less dramatic effects on behavior and mental functioning than do the major tranquilizers.

Valium and Librium are among the most abused drugs in the US today, in part because many patients seem to enjoy their effects. These drugs are obviously addictive, and recent studies suggest they may cause birth defects if taken during pregnancy. Two recent studies suggest, however, that their dangers may have been exaggerated. University of Michigan psychologist Robert Caplan and his colleagues report that long-term use of Valium apparently has little effect on the quality of life, on emotionality, job performance, stress, social support, coping, or physical health (Caplan *et al.*, 1985). And in a study of 600 patients, VA

"HE ALWAYS WANTS TO PERFORM LION'S MANE TOSSED UPON SHARK-FILLED WATER, UNDER YELLOW MOONLIGHT, BUT I PREFER ORANGE BLOSSOMS TOUCH HUMMINGBIRD WING BY SPRING RAINBOW."

researcher J.C. Mason found that both the "addictive nature" and problems associated with withdrawal of the drug "have been previously overstated" (Mason, 1985).

• *Antidepressants*

As we noted in Chapter 3, antidepressants are also called "psychic energizers." Except for the amphetamines, the antidepressants are seldom abused. Wisconsin researcher Carlyle Chan and his colleagues studied the effects of antidepressants on 1,054 patients. They report that 67 percent of the nonpsychotic depressed patients and 35 percent of the psychotic depressed patients were helped by the drugs (Chan *et al.*, 1987). However, recent research also suggests that the antidepressants can have dangerous side effects, particularly when given to elderly patients or when a patient given these drugs also drinks alcohol.

Vanderbilt researcher W.A. Ray and his colleagues recently studied the records of more than 6,600 elderly Medicaid patients. They found that patients given antidepressants and other long-lasting neuroleptic drugs were two to three times more likely to suffer hip fractures as were patients who didn't receive these medications. Apparently some elderly patients become so sedated that they no longer take adequate care when they walk, hence run an increased risk of falling (Ray *et al.*, 1987a).

Having made this important discovery, W.A. Ray and his group then visited a number of nursing homes, reported on their findings, and urged nursing home administrators to decrease the use of neuroleptics with elderly patients. While the administrators apparently were impressed by the data, a subsequent check of the nursing home records showed no decrease whatsoever in the use of neuroleptics. Ray and his colleagues note that use of these drugs often makes the patients easier for staff members to handle, and that "financial factors" might well encourage nursing homes to continue to prescribe them (Ray *et al.*, 1987b).

Long-term use of antidepressants may also lead to a variety of physical and mental problems. For example, British psychiatrist Susan Golombok found that many patients developed sexual dysfunctions while taking antidepressants. These sexual difficulties tended to clear up once the patients were taken off the medication (Golombok, 1986).

The chief problem caused by chronic treatment with neuroleptics, however, is a "movement disorder" known as **tardive dyskinesia** (Shah & Donald, 1986).

Tardive Dyskinesia

The field of psychiatry faces rather a severe problem concerning the use of medication to treat mental disorders. On the one hand, as George Koob notes, neuroleptics apparently are effective in helping some 70 percent of those patients diagnosed as having schizophrenic disorders (Koob, 1984). On the other hand, from 40 to 50 percent of those patients who are given neuroleptics on a chronic basis develop *tardive dyskinesia* and other physical disabilities (Coyle & Enna, 1983).

Tardive dyskinesia typically involves "uncontrollable movements" of one kind or another, including eye blinks, "shaky" hands, and a peculiar way of walking. However, the disorder can sometimes involve breathing irregularities, particularly in elderly patients. Unfortunately, when the respiratory tract is involved, a small but significant number of the patients may die (Howell *et al.*, 1986).

About 2 percent of the patients given antipsychotic drugs develop a condition called *neuroleptic malignancy syndrome*, or NMS, which involves fever, elevated blood pressure, kidney failure, brain damage, and coma. About 20 percent of the patients who suffer from NMS die from the condition (Pope *et al.*, 1986).

According to psychiatrist Ian Wilson, a significant number of patients who develop tardive dyskinesia suffer such severe brain damage that they lapse into a form of *senile dementia*. Wilson and his colleagues suggest that, in this case, the "cure" for a mental disorder can *cause* a physical illness that is worse than the original problem (Wilson *et al.*, 1983).

In a recent book, psychiatrist Peter Breggin puts the matter this way: "Psychiatrists simply cannot admit that they have effectively "lobotomized' millions of patients with chemicals that are toxic to the brain" (Breggin, 1983). Breggin's sentiments are echoed by Brown University scientists Phil Brown and Steven C. Funk, who believe that psychiatrists are "resisting the truth" about the dangers associated with the neuroleptics. Brown and Funk state that the problem is due to "sociomedical" factors, not to a lack of understanding of the "biomedical" data (Brown & Funk, 1986).

Fortunately, as we will see, there is also a growing recognition that psychotherapy and behavioral treatment can often achieve the same results as do the neuroleptic drugs—and with significantly smaller risks.

□ □ QUESTION □ □
Abraham Maslow once said, "If the only tool you have is a hammer, you tend to see every problem as a nail." How might Maslow's words be applied to the use of neuroleptic drugs?

Drugs Alone Don't "Cure"

Scarcely a month goes by that the popular press doesn't serve up a juicy story about some new drug that seems to offer "miracle cures" for many types of psychological problems. Most of the reports need to be taken with a grain of salt, however.

First, as Nathan S. Kline and Jules Angst noted a decade ago, chemicals *by themselves* seldom solve mental, social, or behavioral problems. Even if the drug "cures" some underlying biological dysfunction, the patient will still need psychological and social help in adjusting to life. Thus, chemotherapy is at best no more than the *first step* in treating "mental disorders" (Kline & Angst, 1979).

Second, not all of the drug research reported in the popular press has been as well planned and nicely controlled as we might wish. In particular, many drug studies have not been "double blind." Thus the results reported may well be due to placebo effects (see Chapter 15).

Perhaps a case history will demonstrate these points.

Mendel's Research
Werner Mendel is professor of psychiatry at the USC School of Medicine. He was also, for many

years, the clinical director of the only public facility for treating acutely-disturbed psychotic patients in Los Angeles County.

Like all psychiatrists, Mendel is a medical doctor. After receiving his MD degree at Stanford, he served a year as a psychiatric resident at St. Elizabeth's Hospital in Washington, DC. Thereafter, Mendel spent several years as a resident at the Menninger Foundation in Topeka, Kansas—one of the best psychiatric training facilities in the world. Once he completed his training at Menninger's, Mendel was qualified to call himself a psychiatrist. Next, he studied for several years at the Southern California Psychoanalytic Institute and completed his training as a psychoanalyst. He is an instructor at the institute.

After moving to Los Angeles, Mendel continued a series of experiments on the treatment of mental illness he had begun as a resident in Washington, DC.

At the time Mendel served at St. Elizabeth's Hospital, it was the largest of all the US government facilities dealing with psychiatric patients. When Mendel arrived at St. E's, he was put in charge of a ward of Spanish-speaking patients, most of whom came from Puerto Rico or the Virgin Islands. All of these patients were diagnosed as being hostile, aggressive individuals. Many were considered so dangerous to themselves and others that they were confined to "padded cells" or were kept in straight-jackets. Mendel says he usually took two attendants along with him whenever he visited the wards. And because the patients spoke little or no English, and Mendel spoke no Spanish, there was little he could do in the way of treatment.

- ### Double-Blind Method

Fortunately, it was just at this time that news of the apparent effectiveness of reserpine spread to the US. The authorities at St. E's decided to test the drug. To make the test scientifically valid, they used the *double-blind method*. That is, they selected certain wards whose patients would be given reserpine. But they also needed some *comparison groups* to make sure that the changes they noted in the patients given reserpine (the "experimental groups") were due to the drug and not just to the fact that the patients had been given pills. So the researchers selected an equal number of wards whose patients were given "sugar pills" rather than reserpine. The pills looked the same no matter what was in them. The experiment was "double-blind" because neither the patients nor the doctors in charge of the wards knew which drug the patients on any particular ward were actually receiving.

The experiment ran for several months, during which any improvement in the patients was recorded as carefully as possible. Mendel's ward of Spanish-speaking patients was one of those chosen for the experiment.

Mendel reports that, almost as soon as the study began, he was sure his patients were receiving the reserpine—for they all calmed down dramatically. Within a short period of time they were so tranquil that many of them could be released from restraint. Mendel was convinced that a psychiatric revolution had begun.

Then the experiment ended and the results were announced. To Mendel's amazement, he learned his ward had been one of the "controls." All of his patients had received *placebos* instead of reserpine. Yet they had shown marked improvement! It occurred to Mendel that, when the experiment began, he unconsciously changed his attitude toward the patients. Convinced they were becoming more peaceful, he then treated them as if they were improving. And they did improve—not because of the drug but because of the way in which he responded to them (Mendel, 1966, 1969).

The St. Elizabeth's experiment points up one dramatic difficulty in evaluating any psychiatric research: The good results that an experimenter obtains may be due to *chance factors*, or to factors the scientist *failed to control*. Drugs are always given in a social setting. The patient's attitude—and the doctor's—may be more influential than the chemical's effects on the patient's body. Likewise, if a surgeon communicates to the patient the belief that psychosurgery will surely solve the person's problems, the patient may very well get better after the operation—for all the "wrong" reasons (Kline & Angst, 1979).

We might sum up our discussion of chemotherapy by quoting from University of Pittsburgh pharmacologist Jay D. Glass: "Drug treatments for mental illness have been with us for the better part of two decades, and yet we still have drugs that seem to function with the subtlety of a sledgehammer. They can hype up the depressed and slow down the manic. However, the types of delicate perturbations of cognition and mood that would truly be a boon to psychiatry still elude us" (Glass, 1981).

Biological Therapies: An Evaluation

What goes on in your body surely affects what goes on in your mind—and vice versa. *Some* types of biological therapies will surely help *some* types of patients suffering from *some* kinds of mental disorders. Thus, we should *use* biotherapies when the data strongly suggest they are valid and reliable forms of treatment. And chemotherapy can often calm hospitalized patients down—and even allow their return to the community. However, the bulk of research in this area suggests we have not yet discovered

Werner Mendel

any "magic pill" that will cure *most types* of psychosocial abnormalities.

With that sobering thought in mind, let's look at other types of treatment.

INTRA-PSYCHIC THERAPY

Most personality theorists believe that abnormal thoughts and behaviors are mere symptoms of an underlying dysfunction in an individual's basic personality. To "cure" the symptom without handling the underlying problem would, therefore, be as senseless as giving aspirin to a patient suffering from yellow fever. The drug might decrease the fever symptom, it is true. But aspirin wouldn't kill the virus that is really responsible for the disease. Removing the fever with aspirin might delude patients into thinking they had been "cured" when, in fact, the patients might still be carrying the virus. A "deeper" form of therapy is necessary to kill the virus.

Intra-psychic therapy almost always focuses on making "deep changes" in the structure or the functioning of the individual's core personality. The belief behind this approach is that the symptomatic behaviors will disappear

naturally as the cure progresses. As we noted in Chapter 17, this type of treatment is based on what is called the *medical model of mental illness*.

If you ever have need for intra-psychic therapy, you would seem to have your choice between two major types: (1) those methods that are primarily designed to help you understand your present self by giving you *insight* into what has gone wrong in your past; and (2) those techniques that focus on future goals in order to help you change your present mode of existence. (In fact, the difference between the two types may be more a matter of emphasis than anything else. Highly successful therapists appear to treat their patients in similar ways despite the fact that their theories may be quite different.)

Psychoanalysts usually follow the first method. That is, they concentrate on discovering traumas that occurred during psychosexual development in order to help patients set their "mental and emotional houses" in order. Psychoanalytic theory suggests that, if you complete your analysis and gain insight into your problems, you should experience a full recovery.

The humanistic psychologists, on the other hand, mostly follow the second method. They hope to make you aware both of your present condition and of your ultimate goals, so you can shorten the distance between the two and hence move toward self-actualization.

Psychoanalytic Therapy

There is no single accepted and approved method of psychoanalytic treatment—it varies widely according to the patient's needs and the analyst's skills and beliefs. Freud compared analysis to a chess game in which only the opening moves could be standardized. Thereafter, he said, endless variations may develop (Freud, 1910/1957). Furthermore, in addition to "classic" Freudian analysis, there are a number of newer, briefer types of analytic treatment. Since most of the more modern approaches are extensions of Freud's original techniques, however, we will give primary attention to the "classic" analytic methods.

Freud viewed psychoanalysis as a way to bring about a basic reconstruction of the patient's personality. The analyst achieves this end in two ways: first, by encouraging the patient to build up an emotional relationship, or **transference**, with the analyst; and second, by getting the patient to freely associate about past thoughts and experiences. By *interpreting* these *free associations*, the analyst can often discover both the content and the dynamics of the patient's unconscious mental processes.

But the task is not an easy one. Psychoanalysis typically takes from two to five years to

"I UTILIZE THE BEST FROM FREUD, THE BEST FROM JUNG AND THE BEST FROM MY UNCLE MARTY, A VERY SMART FELLOW."

complete, and the 50-minute-long therapy sessions are usually held three to five times a week. Costs for a complete analysis typically run from $10,000 to $30,000 (or more). The most successful patients seem to be between 15 and 50 years of age. They must be bright, verbal, self-motivated, and be willing to cooperate with the therapist. Although psychoanalysis is occasionally used with individuals classed as "psychotic," the usual patient is a mildly disturbed or "neurotic" individual.

While Freud insisted that the medical degree was not necessary for the practice of psychoanalysis, more than 90 percent of American analysts are physicians who have gone through psychiatric residencies before becoming candidates at a psychoanalytic institute. During the several years of training required for graduation, the candidate undergoes a "training analysis" to make him- or herself aware of personal problems that might prejudice analytic interpretation of a patient's problems. As Freud put it years ago, "Every analyst's achievement is limited by what his own complexes and resistances permit" (Freud, 1910/1957).

● Psychoanalysis: A Summary

Psychoanalysis takes so long—and there are so few analysts available—that only a tiny fraction of the people who need help ever undergo this process. Most patients settle for briefer, less intensive (and less expensive) types of treatment.

Psychoanalytic theory has influenced almost all other forms of intra-psychic therapy. Any type of treatment that concentrates on explaining the present in terms of past experience and unconscious motivations owes a large debt to Sigmund Freud.

Humanistic Therapy

Freud grew up in Austria, a land of kings and emperors who possessed "divine rights" their subjects dared not question. Austrian fathers typically claimed the same privileges—when the man of the family spoke, the children listened and obeyed. Perhaps it is understandable, then, that in psychoanalysis the fatherly analyst often sets the goals of therapy and urges the patient onward.

As we noted in Chapter 16, modern humanistic psychologists reject the "divine right" of the therapist to determine what is mentally healthy for the patient. In humanistic therapy, the patient rather than the therapist is king. Humanistic psychologists—such as Carl Rogers and Abraham Maslow—emphasize the *conscious* determinants of behavior. All human beings are presumed to have a positive drive toward good mental health. As Adolph Di Loreto puts it in the April 1981 issue of *Contemporary Psychology*, Freud's patients may be depicted as fighting for their life, but Rogers'

and Maslow's clients are fighting for a better life.

● Client-centered Therapy

According to Christopher Monte, "The client who faces Rogers in therapy finds himself confronted with a warm, evenhanded, non-evaluative person sincerely attempting to understand his client's meanings. Perhaps for the first time in his or her life, a Rogerian client discovers that in the presence of another human being, he or she is fully free to be" (Monte, 1987).

In 1942, Rogers listed four important principles of "client-centered therapy":

1. "Therapy is not a matter of doing something *to* the individual, or of inducing him to do something about himself. It is instead a matter of freeing him for normal growth and development."
2. Rogers' approach "places greater stress upon the emotional elements, the feeling aspects of the situation, than upon the intellectual aspects."
3. Client-centered therapy "places greater stress upon the immediate situation than upon the individual's past."
4. Rogers' approach "lays great stress upon the therapeutic relationship itself as a growth experience" (Rogers, 1942).

In 1951, Carl Rogers added a fifth principle: "The client . . . is one who comes actively and voluntarily to gain help on a problem, but without any notion of surrendering his own responsibility for the situation" (Rogers, 1951).

As we noted in Chapter 16, one of the major aspects of Rogerian non-directive therapy is that the therapist must give the client *unconditional positive regard*.

● Hallmarks of Successful Treatment

According to Carl Rogers, the client who undergoes successful therapy shows three major characteristics:

First, the client is now a *fully functioning individual*, by which Rogers meant that the person is "fully open to experience." The person no longer feels the need to distort reality or repress his or her feelings.

Second, the person now has the ability to *live in an existential fashion*. The person realizes that "What I will be in the next moment, and what I will do, grows out of that moment, and cannot be predicted in advance either by me or others" (Rogers, 1964).

Third, people who are fully functioning have an "increased trust in their own organisms." That is, they feel free to do whatever "feels right" at any point in time, because they know they are competent to meet any challenge (Monte, 1987).

Was Rogers a Rogerian?

Most of the people practicing intra-psychic therapy in the US today are neither "pure" Freudians nor "pure" humanistic psychologists. Rather, therapists tend to be *eclectic*—they make use of whatever psychological techniques seem to work best for them and their clients. And they may do so almost without realizing what they are doing.

As we noted in Chapter 16, Carl Rogers apparently rejected any form of "therapist control" because he felt that his own parents were too manipulative. And, in particular, Rogers was dismayed by behavior therapy, in which the therapist deliberately "shapes" the thoughts and behaviors of the client. Rogers and B.F. Skinner debated this issue on many occasions. Oddly enough, during these famous debates, Skinner seldom bothered to reinforce Rogers in any fashion, and Rogers surely showed Skinner less than "unconditional positive regard" (McConnell, 1985).

And as far as therapy goes, there is some question as to just how "non-directive" Rogers really was. For example, during the 1960's, C.B. Truax studied tapes and movies made of Carl Rogers and other Rogerians as they actually performed therapy. Far from providing his patients with "unconditional positive regard," Truax says, Rogers was unconsciously "shaping" his patients by rewarding "healthy self-statements" with head nods and smiles. Rogers also tended to ignore any "unhealthy statements" the patient made (Truax, 1968).

We will have more to say about unconscious "shaping" later in this chapter. For the moment, we need only note that even Carl Rogers was perhaps a bit more eclectic—and perhaps even a bit more directive—than he strived to be.

• Transactional Analysis and Gestalt Therapy

Both Gestalt therapy and Transactional Analysis were developed by former psychoanalysts with strong humanistic leanings. Since both types of treatment are somewhat more likely to be used with groups than with individuals, we will postpone discussing them until later in this chapter.

The Effects of Intra-Psychic Therapy

Many factors make it difficult to evaluate the effectiveness of psychotherapy scientifically. Science deals with objective events, things that can readily be measured. But by its very nature, intra-psychic therapy concerns itself with personality changes (and other variables) that seldom can be viewed in detail under a microscope. The success rates of various forms of treatment, then, must always be considered in terms of *the results both clients and therapists hope to achieve*.

• "Art Form" Versus "Applied Science"

Some psychiatrists see therapy as an "art form," thus something that cannot be measured objectively. One such person is Jerome Frank, a professor at the Johns Hopkins School of Medicine. Frank compares therapy to music. "To try to determine by scientific analysis how much better or worse . . . Gestalt therapy is than Transactional Analysis, is in many ways equivalent to attempting to determine by the same means the relative merits of the music of Cole Porter and Richard Rodgers. To ask the question is to reveal its absurdity" (Frank, 1973).

Jerome Frank believes that the effectiveness of therapy depends more on the therapist than on the technique (Frank, 1985; Frank & Dietz, 1979). Unfortunately, Frank does not give any standards by which to judge who is a "good" therapist, and who isn't.

Although Frank's viewpoint has its merits, other psychiatrists are willing to use more objective measures of improvement—such as modifications in the patient's overt behavior and the gradual disappearance of neurotic or psychotic symptoms. At least these changes can be observed and agreed upon by people other than the therapist.

Washington University psychologist Sol L. Garfield has written extensively on the effectiveness of psychotherapy (Garfield, 1983a, 1983b, 1987). In a recent article, Garfield discusses one of the most widely-publicized studies on *psychoanalytic* treatment, which was performed at the Menninger Foundation. The Menninger experiment involved 21 patients given psychoanalysis and 21 given analytically-oriented "insight" therapy. Both sets of patients were followed for many years. In discussing the Menninger study, Garfield states that "My understanding or interpetation of this material is that 6 patients were judged to be worse at the end of therapy, 11 were unchanged, 7 showed slight improvement, and 18 (or 43 percent) showed moderate or marked improvement. If one takes my interpretation as provisionally valid, the results cannot be viewed as a very convincing demonstration of the efficacy of psychotherapy—particularly when the therapy is so expensive and time-consuming" (Garfield, 1981).

In a recent "final summing up" of the Menninger project, University of California psychiatrist Robert Wallerstein notes that giving the patients "insight" into their problems probably was *less effective* than was "supporting their attempts to solve their own problems." Wallerstein suggests that psychoanalysis should primarily be used with "less disturbed" patients (Wallerstein, 1986).

Similar conclusions can be drawn from a recent study by psychiatrists John Gunderson and A.F. Frank at McLean Hospital near Boston.

These researchers gave either "expressive, insight-oriented" or "reality-adaptive, supportive" therapy to almost a hundred hospitalized schizophrenics. "Supportive therapy" consisted of helping the patients find solutions to their present problems and "shoring up their psychological defenses." Gunderson and Frank report that supportive therapy worked at least as well as insight-oriented therapy, cost less and took less time, and was superior at helping patients leave the hospital and find (and keep) jobs (Gunderson & Frank, 1985).

In psychoanalysis, the *therapist* usually decides whether or not a "cure" has taken place. But in the humanistic therapies, the *patient* usually determines whether the therapy was successful or not. Rogers does have objective tests that measure changes in the client's *perceptions* of his or her progress, and the tests do seem to be reliable. Whether or not "perceptual changes" should be the major goal of therapy, however, is an open question. In any event, the "cure rate" claimed for humanistic therapy is usually in the neighborhood of 70 percent or so (Rogers, 1962).

• Eysenck's 1952 Report

In recent years, the behavioral psychologists and social learning theorists have leveled strong criticisms against the "unscientific ways" in which the effectiveness of psychotherapy is usually determined. As we noted in Chapter 17, immediately after World War II, personality theorist Hans Eysenck investigated several thousand mental patients in a British hospital. Eysenck reported in 1952 that the overall improvement rate among those patients given psychoanalytic treatment was about 44 percent. The improvement rate for patients given any other form of psychotherapy (eclectic treatment) was about 64 percent. Several hundred other patients received no psychotherapy at all. Their physical ailments were treated as necessary, but they were given no psychological therapy. The improvement rate among these *untreated* patients, Eysenck claimed, was about 72 percent. These data led some scientists to compare psychoanalysis with "witch doctoring," and to suggest that psychoanalysis might actually retard the patient's progress (Eysenck, 1952).

As we will see later in this chapter, Eysenck's "cure rate" figures both for psychoanalysis and for eclectic therapy have stood the test of time. However, it now seems that the rate of **spontaneous recovery** is closer to 40 or 50 percent than the 72 percent figure Eysenck reported (Garfield, 1983b).

There is also the problem of *negative outcomes*—that is, of patients who get *worse* after treatment rather than getting *better*. Several studies suggest that negative outcomes are more frequent with psychoanalytic or other types of "insight-oriented" therapy than with "behavioral" or "supportive" treatment (Bergin & Lambert, 1978; Gunderson & Frank, 1985; Sloane *et al.*, 1975).

□ □ **QUESTION** □ □
Why would it be more difficult to prove that therapy "works" using objective criteria than if you merely measured the subjective opinions of the clients and therapists?

"Sick Talk" and "Well Talk"

As we noted, some patients given "insight-oriented" therapy tend to get worse rather than getting better. One explanation for this finding may lie in research by Joel Greenspoon.

In the late 1950's, Greenspoon demonstrated how important the *attitude* of the therapist is in affecting the behavior of most clients. Greenspoon noticed that when a patient begins talking about sexual abnormalities, or about bizarre thought patterns, the therapist may unconsciously encourage the patient to continue talking. The therapist may lean forward, look very interested, and say to the patient, "Yes, yes, tell me more about that." But when the patient is speaking normally, or discussing solutions rather than problems, the therapist may believe the patient is making little or no progress. So the therapist may lean back and look disinterested (Greenspoon, 1955).

In Greenspoon's terms, there is always the danger that the psychotherapist may unwittingly *reward* the patient for "sick talk" and *ignore* (or even punish) the patient for "well talk."

State University of New York psychologists Joseph Masling and Ira Cohen believe that "unconscious shaping" may also account for the strong beliefs that some therapists have that *their* brand of treatment is far superior to any other form. Masling and Cohen believe that therapists unwitting reward patients for "believing in" a given type of treatment, and for "producing evidence" that the treatment "works" (Masling & Cohen, 1987).

□ □ **QUESTION** □ □
Given Greenspoon's findings, are you surprised that Rogers may have "unconsciously shaped" his patients toward better health?

Psychotherapy: An Evaluation

In 1980, the National Institute of Mental Health (NIMH) began a long-term study of the effects of several types of psychotherapy on the treatment of depression. The first results were reported in the spring of 1984 by Irene Elkin and her colleagues, and were first published in 1985 (Elkin *et al.*, 1985).

So far, Elkin and her group have studied 236 moderately- to severely-depressed patients at three noted medical centers: George Washington University, the University of Oklahoma, and the University of Pittsburgh. The patients were divided into four groups: One group received an antidepressant drug; a second group was given a "pill placebo"; a third group was treated with Beck's "cognitive behavior therapy"; the fourth group received "interpersonal therapy."

As we noted in Chapter 18, cognitive behavior therapy attempts to correct distorted thinking and the patients' negative views of themselves (Beck & Emery, 1985). (Thus, in a sense, it is not really "behavioral" at all, but rather a type of cognitive treatment.) Interpersonal therapy, Elkin says, is designed to help patients develop better ways of relating to members of their families, friends, and co-workers in job-related situations.

Patients in the two drug-related groups were treated by psychiatrists. Patients in the two psychotherapy groups were treated by 18 psychotherapists, all of whom received special training in the type of treatment they were to use.

Patients in all groups underwent an average of 13 weeks of treatment. Of the 236 patients who began the study, 162 completed 16 weeks of treatment. Judgments of improvement were made by the patients themselves, by their therapists, and by independent clinicians (Elkin *et al*, 1985).

● *Results of the NIMH Study*

Elkin reports that about 29 percent of the patients given pill placebos "recovered with no serious symptoms after 16 weeks." In contrast, the "cure rate" in the three treatment groups was greater than 50 percent. Thus, "real" therapy was significantly better than was pill "placebo" treatment.

There were, however, other differences between the groups. Elkin notes that the least-depressed patients "did surprisingly well" in the pill placebo group. Severely-depressed patients, however, did not respond at all well to the placebo—but did respond well both to the antidepressant and to interpersonal therapy. Married patients with lengthy histories of *moderate* depression did best when given cognitive behavioral treatment, but the antidepressant worked best with married patients with *severe* depression.

As you might imagine, some therapists seemed to have significantly higher "cure rates" than did others. Overall, however, *psychotherapy* was as effective in treating all but the most severe forms of depression as was *chemotherapy* (Elkin *et al*., 1985).

We will have more to say about the effectiveness of psychotherapy later in this chapter. First, let's look at the third major type of treatment, *social/behavioral therapy*.

☐☐ **QUESTION** ☐☐
Psychiatrists and psychologists have reacted to the Elkin data in quite different ways. Can you guess what the reactions were, and why?

SOCIAL/BEHAVIORAL THERAPY

Up until fairly recently, most of our laws, customs, and philosophies have been based on the assumption that psychological problems existed *within* an individual. When factors *outside* the individual contributed to "mental disorders," these factors were presumed to be primarily supernatural—gods, witches, and evil spirits. Most forms of biological and intrapsychic therapy can be seen as attempts to treat the patient by working *from the inside out*.

Within the last century, rather a different point of view has emerged—a belief that "mental illness" is as much a disruption of relationships *between people* as it is a disruption of *one person's inner psychodynamics*. Abnormal behavior is almost always expressed in social situations. And unless "crazy people" disturb or upset others, they seldom are sent to mental hospitals or to see a therapist.

From a social/behavioral point of view, the goal of treatment is not merely altering the

Psychiatry includes a wide variety of orientations and approaches. These people are all attending a meeting of the American Psychiatric Association.

Social/Behavioral Therapy

function of the patient's body or brain. Nor is the goal just to change the patient's personality. Rather, the purpose of treatment is that of helping the patient *get along better with others*. Indeed, in many instances, the group of people around the patient may actually be contributing to the "craziness" without realizing it. In such cases the best form of therapy may be removing the person from that environment—or somehow getting other people to behave differently toward the patient. It also helps the patient get along better in interpersonal and job situations if he/she learns *social* and *job-related skills*. This type of treatment obviously works *from the outside in*.

The three major types of social/behavioral treatment are (1) group therapy, in which the patient learns better ways of responding and gains support from being with a group of people who often have similar problems; (2) behavioral therapy, including situations where patients are rewarded for getting better; and (3) **milieu therapy**, in which the patient's social environment or milieu becomes the focus for treatment.

GROUP THERAPY

The history of group therapy probably stretches back to the dawn of recorded time. In a sense, the early Greek dramas offered a type of psychological release not much different from the psychodrama we will discuss in a moment. Bull sessions, prayer meetings, revivals—all these are the ancestral forms of today's encounter groups.

Group therapy did not gain any scientific notice, however, until 1905, when a Boston physician named J.H. Pratt made a fortunate mistake. Pratt found that patients suffering from tuberculosis were often discouraged and depressed. He first believed their despondency was due to ignorance on their part—they simply didn't know enough about the disease they suffered from. So he brought them together in groups to give them lectures about "healthy living." The lectures soon turned into very intense discussions among the patients about their problems. Pratt discovered his patients gained more strength from learning they were not alone in their suffering than they did from his lectures (Scheidlinger, 1982).

In the *Encyclopedia of Human Behavior*, R.M. Goldenson notes that European psychoanalysts were for the most part hostile to group psychotherapy, but this form of treatment soon gained a firm foothold in the US. Some of the major varieties are psychoanalytic group therapy, directed group therapy, inspirational group therapy, play group therapy, activity group therapy, family therapy, encounter groups, and psychodrama (Yalom, 1985).

The mental health of an individual is interdependent with the functioning of the family and other social systems to which that person belongs.

As you might guess, these various forms of group treatment differ considerably among themselves. But, as J.D. Frank puts it, they all seem to be based on the belief "that intimate sharing of feelings, ideas, [and] experiences in an atmosphere of mutual respect and understanding enhances self-respect, deepens self-understanding, and helps the person live with others" (Frank, 1973).

● ***Research on Group Therapy***

In a recent study, German psychologist Volker Tschuschke measured the *physiological responses* of members of a therapy group during

Sharing common problems and concerns in an atmosphere of mutual respect and understanding is the purpose of most self-help and therapy groups. These people meet regularly to discuss concerns about adoption.

treatment sessions. Tschuschke reports that autonomic arousal increased and decreased almost simultaneously in most subjects, including those "silent members" who seldom spoke during the session. Tschuschke believes his data show that the group did, indeed, function as a "system," not as "a collection of individuals." Tschuschke believes his data show that a group can have a profound influence on the individuals within that group (Tschuschke, 1986).

Group therapy has been found to help such diverse populations as black women seeking social support from each other, individuals suffering from anorexia nervosa and bulimia, stutterers, young victims of child abuse, schizophrenic patients, and Vietnam veterans experiencing post-traumatic stress disorders (Boyd-Franklin, 1987; Lansen, 1986; Steward *et al.*, 1986; Raou, 1984; Kanas, 1986; Lipton & Schaffer, 1986).

As we will see, there is still some argument as to precisely how useful group therapy actually is. In a recent survey of 32 studies, Ronald Toseland and Max Siporin found that group therapy was more effective than several other methods of therapy, and that "In no case was individual treatment . . . more effective than group treatment" (Toseland & Siporin, 1986). In a similar survey, VA psychiatrist Nick Kanas found that group treatment was effective with 67 percent of hospitalized schizophrenics and 80 percent of out-patient schizophrenics. Kanas notes, however, that "insight-oriented" group treatment was less effective than "interaction-oriented" group treatment, and that the insight-oriented approaches were harmful for some subjects (Kanas, 1986).

We should note, however, that few of the studies cited by Roseland and Siporin—or by Kanas—included adequate control groups. And, as we will see later in this chapter, the overwhelming bulk of the experimental literature suggests there is little if any difference in the effectiveness of the various types of psychological treatment.

● Psychodrama

J.L. Moreno, who first used group therapy with socially-displaced persons in Vienna around 1910, later developed a type of treatment he called **psychodrama**. The therapist usually serves as "director" for the psychodrama, which often takes place on a real stage. The patient stars as "heroine" or "hero" in a "play" that centers around some problem in the patient's life. Trained actor-therapists assist in the production. At times, a whole family or group may act out their difficulties.

Moreno often invited audiences to watch psychodrama sessions, for he believed that people in the audience could benefit from seeing problems similar to their own presented on stage (Moreno, 1947).

Psychodrama has been used to treat deaf adolescents, disturbed families, Vietnam veterans, and drug addicts, and for training US Army personnel to handle "terrorist situations" (Barrett, 1986; Remer, 1986; Baumgartner, 1986; Adelman & Castricone, 1986; Altman & Hickson-Laknahour, 1986). There is, however, little or no reliable scientific evidence showing that psychodrama is either better or worse than other forms of group treatment (Garfield, 1983b).

● Transactional Analysis

A very different form of role-playing is found in **Transactional Analysis**, or TA. In the 1950's, psychiatrist Eric Berne developed a personality theory that was, in part, an extension of Freudian psychoanalysis. Berne used the term "game" to refer to the stereotyped and often misleading interpersonal "transactions" that people frequently adopt in dealing with others (Berne, 1964).

According to Berne, a game is a "recurring series of transactions, often repetitive and superficially rational, with a concealed motivation." He believed that each game is but a tiny part of a "script" that a person uses in "performing" various roles in her or his life. According to Berne, the goal of TA is that of consciously changing your behavior so that you no longer engage in unconscious role-playing (Berne, 1958).

Transactional Analysis has been used as a part of family therapy, for training business executives, for increasing job effectiveness in working groups, and with suicidal patients (Bredehoft, 1986; Krausz, 1986; Nykodym, Ruud, & Liverpool, 1986; Douglas, 1986). Although British psychologists Raman Kapur and Keith Miller state that TA is less effective with groups than is insight-oriented therapy, the bulk of the scientific data suggest there is little difference between the "cure rate" of TA and of other forms of group treatment (Kapur & Miller, 1987).

Gestalt Psychotherapy

Gestalt therapy has its roots in classical Gestalt psychology (see Chapter 5), psychoanalysis, and the analysis of nonverbal behavior. The main object of this type of treatment often seems to be that of *growth through exploration.* Gestalt therapy was begun by Fritz Perls (Feder & Ronall, 1980).

More than anything else, Gestalt therapy is based on Perls' belief that people should "take responsibility for themselves," and should "focus attention primarily on the here and now" (Perls, Hefferline & Goodman, 1951). In his book *Creative Process in Gestalt Therapy,* Joseph Zinker defines Gestalt therapy as "an ongoing creative adjustment to the potential in the therapeutic situation" (Zinker, 1978).

Although Gestalt group leaders often speak in terms of "therapists and clients," the goal of Gestalt treatment is more **experiential** than that of achieving "measurable, objective cures." For that reason, perhaps, there are not many studies in the literature on the effectiveness of Gestalt treatment. However, in a recent paper, University of Southern Mississippi psychologists Gary Tyson and Lillian Range report that "the mere passage of time" seems to yield the same "cure rate" as does Gestalt therapy. Tyson and Range tested 44 moderately depressed subjects both before and after treatment. Some of the subjects were given classical Gestalt therapy; others were given "placebo" treatment of one kind or another. Tyson and Range found that subjects in the placebo groups showed as much improvement as did those given Gestalt therapy (Tyson & Range, 1987).

Encounter Groups

Encounter groups vary so widely among themselves that no simple description of them is possible. In general, an encounter group is made up of people who have had little previous contact with one another. The group may meet one or more times a week for several weeks. Or the members may live together in close, intense contact for a day, a weekend, or even longer (Yalom, 1970, 1985).

Encounter group participants are usually encouraged to bring their feelings out into the open and to learn more honest ways of communcating with each other. Often the focus is on some aspect of non-verbal experience—perhaps on developing better sensory awareness of bodily reactions, perhaps on learning how facial expressions communicate deep-seated emotions. As a means of helping group members strip away their defenses, a few encounter groups meet in the nude (Yalom, 1985).

In his book, *Group Processes and Personal Change,* British psychologist Peter B. Smith lists two factors he believes are characteristic of successful encounter groups. First, the group gives "maximum support" to each member. Second, the group *confronts* each member with his or her faults, delusions, and excuses. Personal change occurs in encounter groups, Smith suggests, because the groups "accept" members as they actually are, while urging members to "face up" to their own inappropriate thoughts and feelings (Smith, 1980).

One of the best-known types of encounter groups is Erhard Seminars Training, or "est." In a recent paper, Stanford researchers Peter Finkelstein, Brant Wenegrat, and Irvin Yalom state that some 500,000 persons have participated in est sessions. According to Finkelstein, Wenegrat, and Yalom, "Rigorous research fails to demonstrate that benefits reported among est graduates result from the training; expectancy and response sets may account for positive outcomes." The researchers also note that "Reports of psychological harm from est indicate that borderline or psychotic patients should not participate" (Finkelstein, Wenegrat, and Yalom, 1982).

Irvin Yalom and his colleagues note, however, that *supportive* group therapy apparently has been of considerable help to patients with terminal cancer (Spiegel, Bloom, & Yalom, 1981; Spiegel & Yalom, 1978).

Family Therapy

In group psychotherapy, a number of people with no prior relationships get together to work out their individual difficulties in the presence (and with the support) of others. Unlike most other forms of group treatment, of

In family therapy the problems of the individuals are seen as part of the social system of the family. The therapy's goal is to improve the functioning of that system so that the individuals can also function better. The therapist may work with just one family member, or more than one. This therapist uses concrete props, such as a stuffed bear and a "magic wand," to represent problems and solutions.

course, in *family therapy* the "group" has been in existence for some time. Rather than focusing on individuals, the family therapist strives to change the functioning or the structure of the *family itself* (Green & Framo, 1981).

Family therapy grew out of "systems theory," in which the family is viewed as a *social system*. Almost any difficulty an individual member of the family has is thought to result from a "faulty system" rather than from "individual deficits." For example, if the teen-aged daughter in a family is bulimic, her eating disorder is viewed as a *family problem*, not a difficulty that somehow exists *within the young woman's mind or personality*. Perhaps the mother is "overcontrolling," or the father is "withdrawn and punitive," or other children are "too competitive" for the parents' attention and affection. The "cure," therefore, must come in a change in the relationships between the girl and all other members of the family (Berger *et al.*, 1984).

Recent articles suggest family therapy can be helpful for many types of families, including those with retarded adolescents, married couples with sexual problems, and in families where one or more members are physically abusive or even suicidal (Parker *et al.*, 1987; Kayata & Szydlo, 1986; Deschner & McNeil, 1986; Douglas, 1986). Family therapy is also often combined with other types of treatment, such as psychodrama, Gestalt therapy, and Transactional Analysis (Collison & Miller, 1985; Law & Smith, 1986; Bredehoft, 1986).

There seems to be little difference between the "cure rates" claimed for family therapy and other types of group (or even individual) treatment. And family therapy appears to "fail" in precisely the same sorts of situations where other forms of treatment fail—with exceptionally difficult cases, including those where one or more family members have psychoses or major neuroses (Coleman, 1985).

Evaluating Group Therapy

Perhaps the best evaluation of the effectiveness of different types of group therapy comes from a series of studies performed by psychiatrist Irvin Yalom and his colleagues. This research on group therapy began at Stanford in 1968 and is still going on. Over the years, Yalom and his associates have studied almost every type of group treatment offered to the public. Typically, these researchers investigate the group leader's perceptions of what went on, and ask the participants to evaluate the experience immediately after treatment and at some later time. The scientists also ask close friends or relatives of the participants to rate the participants' progress.

In a recent book, Yalom reports that his studies offer little scientific evidence that group therapy is of much *therapeutic* value. Indeed, it may often do real harm. Yalom states that about 8 percent of the participants are "casualties"— that is, people who show evidence of serious psychological damage that can be attributed to the group experience. Overall, however, *on a long-term basis*, about a third of the group members get better, about a third get worse, and the rest seem unchanged (Yalom, 1985).

According to Yalom, there are *few differences* among the various types of group therapy as far as their *effectiveness* is concerned (Yalom, 1983).

• Benefits of Group Therapy

Yalom concludes that none of the groups he and his colleagues studied were particularly effective as *change agents*. However, the groups can excel at creating *instant, brief, and intense interpersonal experiences*. Yalom believes this chance to learn something about yourself from the open reactions of others is important, and not often available in our society. In some situations—if, for example, you were a patient with terminal cancer, or were close to someone facing a similar problem— having the support of others with similar difficulties could give you social and psychological support. In most other situations, Yalom says, group therapy simply does not alter people permanently for the better (Yalom, 1985).

Environmental Therapy

One thing we have slowly come to realize in recent years is our sensitivity to our environments. The ecologists have made us aware of the disasters that can occur when we pollute the *physical* world around us. But polluted *psychological* environments can kill or corrupt the spirit as readily as dirty air and water can kill or corrupt the body. Thus, the job of the *environmental psychotherapist* is similar to that of the ecologist—to identify sources of pollution and remove them. If the therapist cannot easily find ways of removing the "psycho-pollution" from a patient's world, or of helping the person live more happily despite the pollution, then more radical treatment is usually needed. Typically this treatment takes the form of moving the individual to different surroundings—such as a mental hospital.

• *Milieu Therapy*

Social/behavioral therapists tend to see mental illness as being caused by *unhealthy living conditions*—not by character defects or mental weakness. It is the failure of society to *teach* people healthy behaviors—not the failure of people to *learn*—that causes mental disorders or antisocial behaviors. The best form of treatment, these therapists claim, would be putting the person in a new *milieu*. Each aspect of this new milieu would be carefully designed to help the individual *learn better habits of adjustment*.

The term "therapeutic community" was actually coined by British psychiatrist Maxwell Jones in 1953 to refer to this type of *milieu therapy* (Goldenson, 1970). But according to Harvard psychiatrist Thomas Gutheil, in recent years "the therapeutic milieu has undergone significant alteration and corruption by the increased use of pharmacotherapy, high staff turnover, and a lack of trained staff. However, the hallmarks of milieu therapy (e.g., patients' participation in decision making, collective responsibility for ward events) remain a part of many modern inpatient settings" (Gutheil, 1985).

Therapeutic communities have been set up for treating schizophrenic patients, elderly people in nursing homes, drug addicts, retarded and emotionally disturbed children, and prisoners (Dahl & Jorgensen, 1985; Waters, 1984; Van Bilsen & Van Emst, 1986; Simons, 1985). Just how effective this type of treatment is remains a matter of debate.

Thomas Gutheil believes that "milieu therapy remains a viable treatment modality," particularly when it has a psychoanalytic focus (Gutheil, 1985). Rather a different view comes from research by VA psychologists Morris Bell and Edward Ryan, however. Bell and Ryan studied three therapeutic communities—one with a biological orientation, one with a psychoanalytic orientation, and one with a "rehabilitative" (skills training) focus. Only the rehabilitative community seemed to be effective (Bell & Ryan, 1985).

• *Token Economies*

Rather a different type of environmental treatment is favored by behavior therapists, whose aim is that of changing habit patterns rather than altering inner psychological states.

Patients in mental hospitals often develop what is called an **institutional neurosis**. That is, the patients lose interest in the world and the people around them; develop hallucinations and fantasies; and become quarrelsome, resentful, and hostile. Institutional neurosis appears to be caused in part by the fact that, in

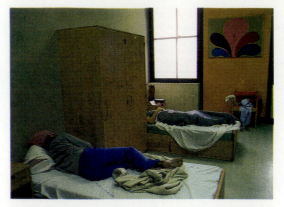

"Institutional neurosis" is the term for the behavioral disturbances that many patients display when they are hospitalized. These problems have been treated by giving the patients more responsibility for their own improvement.

most hospitals, patients often are "given" everything they might need by the staff. Under these conditions, many of the patients develop a rather child-like dependency on the staff (Jha, 1972; Liberakis, 1981).

Behavioral psychologists believe the best cure for institutional neurosis is making the patients take as much responsibility for their own improvement as possible. To help achieve this goal, the behaviorists have developed what they call the *token economy*. In the money economy that operates in the world outside the hospital, you typically must work to live. The better you work, generally speaking, the more money you make. If you perform poorly or refuse to work, you may very well starve. In contrast, mental hospitals typically operate on a "free economy." That is, the patients are given whatever they need merely by asking for it. In fact, the *worse* they behave, the *more* attention and help they usually receive (Paul & Lentz, 1978).

In a token economy, each patient is encouraged to decide what rewards she or he wants to work for. The staff members then reinforce "socially-approved" or "healthy" behaviors by giving the patients tokens. Staff members ignore "inappropriate" or "abnormal" behaviors. The patient is given the tokens as visible evidence that he or she is making progress (Kazdin, 1974, 1978).

In recent years, token economies have been used effectively with schizophrenic patients, with mentally-retarded young adults, with autistic children, and in a variety of school settings (Hikita, 1986; Sandford *et al.*, 1987; Mangus, Henderson, & French, 1986; von Brock & Elliott, 1987).

One major difference between studies on the effectiveness of token economies and studies on other forms of treatment is this: Behaviorally-oriented psychologists almost always measure outcome variables precisely, and almost always use experimental controls of one kind or another. Thus, evidence supporting the efficacy of token economies is much stronger (from a scientific point of view) than it is for other types of therapy (Paul & Lentz, 1978). Indeed, as VA psychologist Patrick Boudewyns and his colleagues pointed out recently, the surprising thing is that token economies aren't used more often. Boudewyns and his associates surveyed 152 VA medical centers and found that only 10 had token economy programs. Boydewyns and his colleagues believe that "staff shortages and staff resistance" account for the minimal use of this highly effective ap-proach to treatment (Boudewyns *et al.*, 1986).

The criticism most often raised against the token economy is that it is mechanistic and dehumanizing because it focuses on observa-ble behaviors—on symptoms—rather than dealing with underlying, dynamic psychologi-cal problems. However, an extensive study by Temple University psychiatrists a decade ago showed that (1) behavioral treatment of mental patients was at least as effective as was "insight-oriented" treatment for most problems, (2) behavioral therapy was significantly more ef-fective at helping patients deal with social and work-related problems than was "insight-oriented" treatment, and (3) patients perceived behavioral therapists as being significantly *warmer* and *more supportive* than the patients perceived the "insight-oriented" therapists as being (Sloane *et al.*, 1975).

Behavior Therapies

One of the most exciting developments in the field of therapy in recent years has been the increased use of the various types of *behavioral therapies*. Thirty years ago, there were two major types of behavioral treatment: (1) Wolpe's *systematic desensitization,* which we discussed at length in Chapter 9, and (2) ther-apy based on Skinner's "shaping" techniques, which we described at length in Chapter 10. Now, there are dozens of different types of treatment roughly based on a "learning" model, including Beck's cognitive behavioral treatment described above, the use of "cogni-tive strategies" for the control of stress and pain (see Chapter 13), family therapy (de-scribed above), and Bandura's "modeling" therapy, which we will talk about in Chapter 21.

Most behaviorally-oriented therapists per-ceive human problems as *failures to learn the proper cognitive, behavioral, or social skills*. The emphasis in treatment, therefore, is on *training and rehabilitation*, not on such things as "talking through your problems," "cathar-sis," "insight," or "explorations of human po-tential." Some eclectic behavioral therapists do, however, combine "skills learning" with some of the techniques used by psychoanalytic or humanistic therapists.

In most types of behavioral therapy, the focus is on achieving *measurable change*, ei-ther in the client's cognitions or in the person's observable behaviors or physiological reac-tions. While "counter conditioning" and "bio-feedback" are often employed for dealing with phobias and headaches (see Chapter 9), the major emphasis is usually on helping the client acquire "self-control" and learn more effective skills for dealing with the social environment.

Generally speaking, behavioral treatment begins with goal setting. The client is then en-couraged to "take a baseline" in order to deter-mine those strengths the person can build on in order to reach the therapeutic goals. Next, the therapist and the client work out a treat-ment plan in which the client is encouraged to move in small steps from her/his present situa-tion toward his/her goal through the use of positive feedback and other forms of reinforce-ment. Finally, the clients are often taught ways of undertaking similar projects *on their own* in the future.

Behavioral therapy that is focused on interpersonal or job-related skills is often successful.

The techniques for gaining or losing weight—described at the end of Chapter 6—are something of a *prototype* of what most psychologists mean when they use the term "behavioral therapy."

Evaluating Social/Behavioral Therapies

Behavioral therapies seem particularly effective at increasing "desirable" responses and at decreasing "symptomatic" or "undesirable" behavior patterns. And, as we noted in Chapter 10—and earlier in this chapter—cognitive behavior modification is useful in altering both perceptions and attitudes.

As for milieu therapy, it does seem effective in teaching people to learn to live together better when the focus is on *helping people acquire interpersonal skills*. However, milieu therapy doesn't seem to work as well when the focus is on changing "feelings" or on "uncovering deep-seated emotional problems" (Bell & Ryan, 1985; Yalom, 1985).

Twenty years ago, many traditional psychotherapists rejected behavioral treatment out of hand as being "too mechanistic" and "too cold and impersonal." However, research by R. Bruce Sloane and his colleagues soon showed that most patients perceived behavior therapists as being significantly "warmer, more involved, more genuine, and as having greater and more accurate **empathy**" than the patients perceived traditional psychotherapists as being (Sloane *et al.*, 1975). And most recent research suggests that behavioral treatment is even more effective than psychotherapy when treatment goals can be specified in measurable terms, or when the focus is on helping individuals learn interpersonal or job-related skills (Garfield, 1981, 1983b).

PSYCHOTHERAPY: A SUMMARY

The February 1986 issue of the *American Psychologist* is devoted to the topic of "Psychotherapy Research." The entire issue should be read by anyone interested in evaluating the current status of psychological treatment in the US.

Given the state of the art, as reported in the *American Psychologist*, we now can give tentative answers to some of the questions we have raised in this chapter.

• *Is Psychotherapy Effective?*

As we noted, the answer to this question depends in large part on what you think the *goal* of psychotherapy should be. Not all types of treatment have the same goals, nor should we expect any one type of therapy to work with *all* types of psychological disorders. Indeed, as Laurence Grimm points out, "There simply is no universally accepted set of measures to define the effectiveness of treatment and little

agreement on what aspects of the client's behavior are most critical to change" (Grimm, 1981).

Generally speaking, however, it does seem that, when properly used, psychotherapy can have a positive effect. Although several well-known studies of "cure rates" in psychotherapy have not yielded outstanding results, the *overall trend* may be more encouraging. In 1977, M.L. Smith and G.V. Glass reported on the use of a new "trend analysis" technique called **meta-analysis**. This technique involves analyzing hundreds of studies on the effects of therapy. Smith and Glass performed this "meta-analysis," and then added up the number of studies with positive results and the number of studies with negative outcomes. Smith and Glass report that their "meta-analysis box score" supports the belief that psychotherapy is effective (Smith & Glass, 1977; Smith, Glass, & Miller, 1980).

Several other authors have also reported favorable "box scores" using the meta-analysis technique (Garfield, 1983a; Michelson, 1985). However, some researchers have gotten negative results when using meta-analysis. And behavioral psychologists (in particular) have been highly critical of the meta-analysis technique itself (Rachman & Wilson, 1980).

Taking all the data into account, however, we can tentatively draw the following conclusions:

First, the "spontaneous recovery" rate varies between 30 and 50 percent. That is, about 30 to 50 percent of the patients with mental disorders will show "spontaneous" improvement whether treated or not. The spontaneous cure rate appears to be lowest with severely-disturbed patients, and is highest with mildly-disturbed patients (Elkin *et al.*, 1985).

Second, the "treatment" cure rate for most types of therapy is about 70 percent. The actual figure varies with the type of treatment used and the type of problem addressed. Of the various forms of psychotherapy, psychoanalysis appears to have the lowest cure rate. It also is the most expensive and takes the longest (Garfield, 1983a, 1983b). Cognitive and insight-oriented therapies do best at achieving changes in cognitive processes, whether the method is applied to individuals or to groups. Behavior therapies do best when aimed at teaching people self-management or social skills. Under these conditions, the cure rate for behavioral treatment can reach 80 to 90 percent (Sloane *et al.*, 1975).

Third, there is actually little difference in the reported cure rates for the various forms of "talk therapies." As Smith and Glass put it a decade ago, "Despite volumes devoted to the theoretical differences among different schools of psychotherapy, the results of research demonstrate negligible differences in the effects

Empathy (EM-path-thee). From the Greek words meaning "to suffer with." Literally, the ability to understand fully another person's thoughts and feelings, or to experience the same emotions another individual is experiencing.

Meta-analysis (METT-ah). *Meta* means "beyond." Meta-analysis, developed by M.L. Smith and G.V. Glass, involves several steps. First, you survey *all* the published literature on a given topic, such as the effects of psychotherapy. Second, you judge whether each published study yielded positive or negative effects. Third, you add up the number of positive and negative studies. Fourth, you use statistical analysis to determine whether these results would have been expected by "chance alone." One problem with meta-analysis is that scientists tend to publish studies that yielded positive results, but not to publish experiments that yielded negative or insignificant results. Thus, the published literature may have a "positive bias."

produced by different therapy types" (Smith & Glass, 1977).

Fourth, since *any* form of psychotherapy appears to be more effective than is no therapy at all, and since *all types* of treatment appear to yield similar cure rates, it would seem that it is (to some extent, at least) the *patient's belief in therapy* that yields the improvement, and not the specific treatment methods that the therapist uses (Berman, 1981).

Fifth, chemotherapy seems to be more effective with severely disturbed patients *in the short run* than is psychological or behavioral treatment. However, 40 to 50 percent of the patients given neuroleptics on a chronic basis develop drug-related side effects, some of which can be fatal.

Sixth, *negative outcomes* are more likely with biologically-oriented therapies—and with psychoanalysis—than with other forms of treatment. Negative results are also more common (as you might suspect) the more severely disturbed the patient was to begin with. Negative outcomes may be less common with behavioral treatment than with any other type (Mays & Franks, 1985).

Seventh, *research* on the effectiveness of psychotherapy appears to have little if any effect on *actual practice*. Several articles in the February 1986 issue of the *American Psychologist* make this point rather dramatically. For example, University of Toledo psychologists Cheryl Morrow-Bradley and Robert Elliott report that 62 percent of the practicing clinicians they polled had not published even one research paper. When asked how much psychotherapy research influenced the way they practiced, only 17 percent said "quite a bit," only 10 percent said "a great deal," while not one person said "more than anything else" (Morrow-Bradley & Elliott, 1986). Indeed, as Lawrence Cohen, Meredith Sargent, and Lee Sechrest note, practicing therapists seldom read the research literature and tend to *repress* any research findings that contradict the therapists' views of "what works best" (Cohen, Sargent, & Sechrest, 1986).

Eighth, there have been surprisingly few attempts to test the effects of using *different types of therapy* at different stages during treatment. As we noted in Chapter 10, G. Alan Marlatt found that aversive therapy worked best at the start of treatment of alcoholic patients, while behavioral treatment was more effective during later stages (Marlatt, 1983). Perhaps the future of psychotherapy lies in this direction: discovering what types of treatment are most effective with what kinds of patients during which of the various stages of the treatment process.

Oddly enough, this approach is precisely that pioneered by one of the early giants in the mental health movement, Adolf Meyer.

THERAPY AND THE WHOLE INDIVIDUAL

As we mentioned in Chapter 18, DSM-I was based on the work of Adolf Meyer. He believed in the *holistic* approach to treating people, and recognized there were multiple causes for even the simplest of behaviors. Rather than passing verdicts on patients by labeling them as "schizophrenics" or "neurotics," Meyer preferred to discover both what was wrong and what was right with the patients at all levels of analysis—the biological, the psychological, and the sociological.

Meyer also attempted to determine those *normal* aspects of behavior that the patient might still have available. He then tried to build on these psychological assets to bring about change. Meyer believed that the patient should set both the goals and the pace of therapy, and that the therapist should work as hard at changing the patient's home (or hospital) environment as in changing the patient's psyche or behaviors. Meyer called his approach *critical common sense* (Meyer, 1951).

If we apply Adolf Meyer's "critical common sense" to an analysis of the strengths and weaknesses of all the various types of therapy, we might discover that most successful forms of treatment have several things in common:

1. Psychological change almost always occurs in a supportive, warm, rewarding environment. People usually "open up" and talk about things—and try new approaches to life—when they trust, admire, or want to please the therapist. Criticism seldom changes thoughts or behaviors, and it often kills all chance of improvement.

2. Most successful forms of treatment can be seen as feedback mechanisms. That is, appropriate feedback provides you with information about your past, puts you in touch with the functioning of your body, and makes you aware of how your behavior actually affects other people. Feedback also helps you realize the distance between your desired goals and your present achieve-

ments, and offers information on how the social environment influences your thoughts, feelings, and behaviors. Ideally, a complete form of therapy would do all these things—and also help you learn how to seek out and make even better use of feedback in the future.

3. Magic can "cure" mental illness overnight; all other forms of psychotherapy take a little longer. If you believe that madness is a matter of possession by devils—or that it's due to a "poor attitude" on the part of the patient—then you might expect that beatings or sermons could cure the illness quickly. But if you believe it takes many years of stressful experiences (and perhaps a particular genetic predisposition) for a full-blown psychosis to develop, then you might also expect the road to recovery to be a fairly lengthy one.

4. The attitudes of both the patient and the therapist are of critical importance. A Cree Eskimo woman suffering from *witigo* "knows" she needs a witch doctor. Will giving this woman a tranquilizer help her much? On the other hand, patients often see their therapists as being models of mentally-healthy or socially-approved behaviors. Effective therapists (witch doctors, psychoanalysts, humanists, or behaviorists) usually practice what they preach.

5. The best forms of therapy seem to build on strengths rather than on attacking weaknesses. By helping the patient work toward positive improvement—toward problem solving, good social behaviors, and self-actualization—the therapist motivates the patient to continue to grow and change. Therapies that focus entirely on uncovering or discussing psychological problems may merely confirm the patient's attitude that sickness is inevitable.

The Future of Psychotherapy

It is likely that, in the coming years, we will take Adolf Meyer's ideas more seriously than we have in the past. That means we will treat the whole patient as a unique individual rather than treating just one aspect of the person's difficulties. Already in some hospitals there is a *team of therapists* available to work with each patient. One member of the team looks at the person's physical or biological problems. Another deals with the person's intra-psychic dynamics. A third helps the patient change behavior patterns. A fourth team member is an expert in altering social environments. The patient can then get as much—or as little—of each type of therapy as his or her own particular case demands.

Ideally, the goals of therapy should be spelled out in a written contract agreed to by the patient and all members of the therapeutic team. And the patient's progress should be recorded regularly on a graph of some kind so all team members are aware of the patient's achievements. As this "team-contracting approach" increases in popularity, our success rate in curing mental illness is likely to show a significant increase.

Perhaps the single most important thing we have learned about mental health in the past 25 years is that neither problems nor cures occur in a vacuum. No matter how well a patient may respond in a hospital setting—and no matter what insights a client achieves in a therapist's office—the ultimate test of therapy comes when the person returns to her or his usual environment. If the patient can function successfully and happily in the real world, we can then conclude that a "cure" has indeed taken place.

It is thus to the complexities of the social environment that we now must turn our attention.

SUMMARY

1. The types of therapy that we prescribe for mentally-ill persons usually stem from our **theoretical explanations** of what causes the people's problems.

2. In primitive times (and societies), insanity was said to be caused by **possession**. That is, a **devil** of some kind was thought to take over the sick person's mind or a **witch** was thought to **cast a spell** on the person.

3. Primitive forms of **psychotherapy** typically involve the use of magic to "cast out the witch," or painful whips to **beat the devil out of the patient.**

4. As our scientific explanations of the causes of human behavior have changed, so have our types of treatment. In evaluating any form of therapy, we must ask ourselves four questions:
   a. How successful or **valid** is the treatment?
   b. How **reliable** is the therapy?
   c. Are there unfortunate **side effects**?
   d. How shall we define "success" or **cure rate**?

5. Biological treatment typically involves the use of **electro-convulsive shock, psychosurgery**, and **chemotherapy** or the use of neuroleptic drugs.

6. **ECT** is most often used for **depression**, while **lobotomies** are used with aggressive or highly-emotional patients. Both types of treatment can have dangerous side effects

and have not been proven scientifically to be of great worth except in very special cases. ECT does seem to be useful in treating **severe depression.**

7. The **neuroleptics** are widely used with hospitalized and severely-disturbed patients. Neuroleptics bring about improvement in some 70 percent of **schizophrenic** patients, but about half the patients develop **tardive dyskinesia**, a "movement disorder" caused by drug-related brain damage that occasionally can be fatal.

8. The **antidepressants** are useful in relieving major depressions, but are dangerous when given to **elderly patients**.

9. There are many forms of intra-psychic treatment, including **psychoanalysis, humanistic therapy**, and **eclectic therapy**.

10. In **psychoanalysis,** the client is encouraged to undergo a **transference relationship** in which the analyst becomes a kind of "father figure." The therapist often **interprets** the client's **free associations**, feelings, and dreams in psychoanalytic terms in order to determine the client's unconscious **psychodynamics** and motivations.

11. In humanistic therapy, the client sets his or her own **therapeutic goals** and determines the **pace** at which treatment proceeds.

12. In **Rogerian** or **client-centered therapy**, the stress is on the **emotional** aspects of the situation, upon the **present** rather than on the past, and on the therapeutic relationship itself as a **growth experience**.

13. Research by Greenspoon shows that therapists may **unconsciously shape** patient responses by rewarding them for **sick talk** or **well talk**.

14. All therapy must be judged in relationship to the rate of **spontaneous recovery** patients show without treatment. In most recent studies, this rate has been between 30 and 50 percent.

15. Some psychiatrists consider therapy to be an **art form** which cannot be judged using the **scientific method**. Other therapists admit that the effects of treatment must be measured **objectively**.

16. In the **Menninger** study of psychoanalytic treatment, the "cure rate" was about 43 percent. However, many patients showed little improvement or were worse at the end of treatment. Psychoanalytic treatment seems to work best with educated, highly-verbal, mildly-disturbed patients; it seems not to work well with severely-disturbed psychotic patients.

17. A recent study by NIMH suggests that **chemotherapy** works best with severely-depressed patients, but that **cognitive and behavioral treatment** is as effective as chemotherapy with moderately- or mildly-depressed patients.

18. There are many types of **group therapy**, including **psychodrama, transactional analysis, Gestalt therapy, family therapy**, and **encounter groups**.

19. Group therapies seem better as ways of encouraging people to explore and express themselves than as **change agents**, and some 8 percent of the clients end up as **psychological casualties** who are worse after treatment than before.

20. Environmental therapies include many types of **group therapy**, as well as attempts to change the patient by altering the patient's **milieu** and **social behaviors**.

21. **Milieu therapy** involves changing the patient's environment so that the person may grow in psychologically-healthy ways.

22. **Behavioral psychologists** often use a **token economy** to help patients overcome **institutional neuroses**. Patients are **rewarded** for achievements with tokens, while inappropriate behaviors are ignored.

23. Behavioral treatment usually proceeds in five steps: (1) setting a **goal**, (2) taking a **baseline**, (3) making a **treatment plan** that involves moving toward the goal in small steps, (4) the use of **positive reinforcement**, and (5) teaching the client **self-change skills.**

24. Behavior therapy is particularly effective when the client has **measurable goals**, or needs to learn **interpersonal** or **job-related skills**.

25. Research suggests that there is little difference in the actual **cure rates** achieved by the various types of group therapy, but behavioral treatment is highly effective when the goal is that of changing **specific behaviors**.

26. Research studies using **meta-analysis** suggest that almost all forms of psychotherapy achieve a "cure rate" of about 70 percent, a figure that is significantly greater than the **spontaneous cure rate**.

27. **Negative outcomes** are more likely with chemotherapy and with psychoanalysis than with other forms of treatment.

28. **Research** on the effectiveness of psychotherapy appears to have little influence on actual practice.

29. Most effective therapy takes place in a **warm, supporting environment** in which patients are given appropriate **feedback**. The **attitudes** of both patient and therapist are important, as is **building on strengths** rather than merely correcting weaknesses.

30. It is likely that, in the future, a **team approach** to treatment will prove to be highly effective, particularly if **patient-therapist contracts** are employed.

(Continued from page 488.)

"I hurt, Mark," Lou Hudson repeated, ignoring all of the boisterous activity in the gambling casino as he poured out his heart to Mark Evans. "I've lost almost everything we own. The house, the car, everything—gambled it all away. I've borrowed from everybody in the family and lost it all on the horses. I'm even going to lose Ann and the kids if I can't shape up somehow. But I get those urges, you understand, those times when I just know that I've got a winning streak going, and I have to play my hunches. I've got to get help of some kind, Mark, but what should I do?"

"What does Ann think you should do?"

"She wants me to join the Chattanooga chapter of Gamblers Anonymous. They're a bunch of people just like me that get together regularly to talk over their problems and help each other out. Ann says they've helped lots of folks."

"So, why don't you join and see what they can do for you?"

"'Cause it would make your uncle angry at me. I mean your Uncle John, the psychoanalyst. He says I have an unconscious desire to punish myself by losing all the time. He thinks I ought to lie on a couch for a few years and find out what's wrong deep down inside me. He says that group therapy just doesn't get at the roots of the problem."

Mark smiled at the thought of Lou lying on a couch. "Well, why don't you try psychoanalysis, then?"

"Because of your Cousin Sophie," Lou said.

"The Rogerian?"

"Yeah. She thinks I need nondirective therapy to help me achieve self-actualization. Sophie's a wonderful woman, Mark, and she's awful easy to talk to. Every time I say something to her, she just says it back to me in different words. Trouble is, she isn't talking to your Uncle John, and I owe her almost as much money as I owe him."

Mark decided that he needed a drink too, and hoisted a glass off the tray of a passing cock-tail waitress. "So, why don't you go in for a little self-actualization?"

Lou groaned. "Your Aunt Beverly would never approve."

"You mean the behavior therapist?"

Lou nodded. "Yeah." He swallowed half his drink in a single gulp. "Man, you've got more different kinds of shrinks in your family than I ever heard of!"

"Psychology runs in my family the way that insanity runs in others. But what does Aunt Beverly, the behaviorist, think?"

"She wants to set up a behavioral program that will reward me for not gambling. And I hate to tell you how much I owe that woman, Mark."

"The cure rates for some kinds of behavioral therapy are very impressive, Lou. So why don't you try it?"

Lou shook his head in dismay. "Because it would make everybody else in the family mad as hell at me, including my wife, Ann. I wouldn't mind going to any of them if I was sure they could help me. But how can you be sure you're going to be cured, Mark?"

"You can't be, Lou. Any more than you could be sure that if you sold me a life insurance policy, I wouldn't die the next day. All you can do is play the odds."

"What do you mean?"

"Ask each of the shrinks in the family to tell you what the cure rate is for compulsive gambling with their type of therapy. Take a good, close look at what they consider successful treatment to be, and how they measure success, and what the cost to you is going to be. Then pick the one that gives you the best odds for your time and money."

Lou Hudson blinked his bloodshot eyes as he pondered the matter. "That's being pretty hard-nosed about a very human predicament, isn't it?"

"Being hard-nosed about human predicaments is what keeps insurance companies and gambling casinos in business, Lou. You can't be sure that the therapy with the best overall cure rate is going to work for you and your own unique set of problems, but the fact that the odds are in your favor gives you a bit of a head start."

"Yeah," said Lou reluctantly. "I see what you mean."

"But what do *you* want to do, Lou? That's the most important factor of all."

"I kind of like the advice your Cousin Oscar gave me, and I owe him more than anybody."

Mark laughed. "Ah, yes, Cousin Oscar. What does the black sheep of the family recommend?"

Lou grinned. "Well, he knows of this woman who's a fortune teller. She lives in the same trailer park that Oscar lives in. He says that if I slip her a few bucks, she might look into her magic crystal ball and give me a tip on the races. Oscar says she's almost always right. If I could just win a few big ones, Mark, I could pay back my debts, stop gambling, and then I wouldn't need any therapy at all. What do you think of that?"

Mark shook his head. "No dice. If she's so good with crystal balls, how come she lives in a trailer instead of a mansion?"

Lou frowned. "Yeah, I see what you mean. Bad odds, eh? But what can I do? No matter whose therapy I pick, I'm going to make everybody else in the family madder than a wet hen."

Mark scratched his nose. "I think I have an idea. Lou, *you* haven't got a problem. The *family* has a problem. So we ought to come up with a family group solution."

"What do you mean? Me get a divorce from Ann?"

"No, Lou, nothing that drastic. But I suspect everyone in the family would rather give you free therapy than continue to lend you money."

Lou Hudson rubbed his eyes with the back of his hands. "Maybe you've got something there, Mark. I'd better go call Ann on the phone and see what she thinks."

As the two men walked toward the door of the casino, the little old lady in tennis shoes stopped them. She held up a coin. "My juju's deserted me today, boys, but I feel a change coming over me. This is my very last nickel, and I've got to get a winner. Where do you think I ought to put it?"

"Back in your purse," Mark said.

"Naw, Mark, you don't understand us gamblers." Lou closed his eyes and turned around three times. Then he pointed to a small slot machine far down the row. "Try that one, lady. I gotta hunch."

The little old woman trotted obediently down the row of one-armed bandits and paused to look the machine over carefully. Then she spat on the coin gently, rubbed it lovingly between her gloved hands, dropped the nickel in the slot, and pulled the handle. The reels spun wildly. The first one stopped on a bar. The second one did likewise. When the third reel clicked into place, it too sported a bar.

Suddenly the machine exploded. A bell rang loudly, and lights flashed off like skyrockets.

"Jackpot!" the woman screamed. "I did it, I did it! I've got my juju back! The magic power is with me again!"

A small crowd of people gathered around to watch the slot machine pay off.

Lou Hudson looked at the woman and smiled wanly. "She probably spent $50 in nickels just to win one $10 jackpot. And now she'll put all those nickels right back in the machine, won't she?"

Mark nodded in agreement. "If she's a compulsive gambler, she will."

"You think I can stop that kind of nonsense, Mark?"

"If you really want to, and you get good help," Mark said, "The odds are definitely in your favor."

The slight young man with bloodshot eyes grinned in response. "I'll bet on that!"

STUDY QUESTIONS

As you read through the chapter, see if you can find the answers to the following questions:

1. What are the five most important issues that social psychologists typically deal with?
2. How do social psychologists define the word "attitude"?
3. Why does social psychology tend to be oriented more toward applications than many other areas of psychology?
4. What is the "Social Interaction Sequence"?
5. What is "person perception"?
6. Why are stereotypes, once formed, so difficult to change?
7. How does physical appearance affect first impressions?
8. What is "body language"?
9. What is "behavioral congruence"?
10. What are the "rules of eye contact" in middle-class America?
11. What is the "attribution process" and when is it most likely to be used?
12. According to H.H. Kelley, what three concepts are crucial to understanding enduring two-person relationships?
13. According to Bales, what two types of people tend to get high scores on leadership rating scales?
14. What is "social exchange theory"?

Person Perception, Attribution, and Social Roles

"The Best of Intentions"

· C·H·A·P·T·E·R ·
20

DAY 1

I was walking home from the meeting when I saw the police car sitting in front of our apartment house. They had come for Charlie, of course. Charlie is my best friend and bosom buddy.

Charlie and I have been rooming together ever since we came to college here two years ago. He is a top-notch person, and since we are both pre-legal, we have decided to open up an office together when we get out of Law School. Charlie is a born leader, always coming up with great ideas about things to do and giving me advice on what to wear and how to act. Which I guess I sometimes need. I suppose that when we do open that office, his name will be first on the door.

It was Charlie who read the ad in the student newspaper. The one offering to hire us at $25 a day to take part in this two-week-long "prison" experiment that this Dr. Mark Matossian is running. That struck us as a great way to earn some big bucks over the summer vacation. So we showed up, got interviewed, took all those psychological tests, and signed away our rights. I was sort of skeptical about that, but as Charlie pointed out, it was only for two weeks. And besides, they promised they wouldn't use physical punishment of any kind on us. So when Charlie volunteered, I felt sort of obligated to go along with him.

Funny that they should have selected me to be a guard, and Charlie to play the prisoner's role. Well, maybe the tests showed he was more impulsive or something like that.

I arrived at the apartment house just as the cops were dragging Charlie out the door. He sure did look surprised! We learned at the Guard's meeting this afternoon that the local police were cooperating with Dr. Matossian. They had agreed to pull the prisoners in unexpectedly, charge them with suspicion of armed robbery, search them, fingerprint them, and take "mug shots" of their faces. Then the cops put blindfolds on the prisoners and we picked them up and drove them over to school where the "mock prison" is. Which we did, all in the spirit of good, clean fun, you understand. Tried to get them in the mood, so to say.

They needed some mood-setting because the prison is pretty "mock," I tell you no lie. Just some rooms in the basement of the Psych Building, with bars painted on the doors and the tiny windows. Dr. Matossian said he is repeating a study performed by some professor at Stanford named Philip Zimbardo, who found that isolating people from society was dehumanizing. But these prisoners are hardly going to be "isolated from society." There will be us guards, three to a shift, and Dr. Matossian and his students who will be the Prison Staff and actually live there. Plus the guys—the prisoners, I mean—will be allowed visitors twice a week. So I do not think this study is going to work very well. But maybe it will be fun anyhow, plus the money.

Dr. Matossian asked us to keep diaries which he will collect, and we are to write down everything we think and do, even if it seems critical of him and the staff. I don't like criticism or hassling people anyhow, so he shouldn't worry.

At the meeting today we decided on the Rules and Regulations for the Uni-Prison. There is to be no physical abuse, although we can lock a prisoner up in the isolation room if he breaks the Rules. Which, given the sensible nature of the Regulations, a prisoner would be stupid to do anyhow. Charlie being anything but stupid, I figure he will do OK as a prisoner.

I am not so sure about me in the role of a guard. Sorry. We are to refer to ourselves as Correctional Officers. Anyhow, I put on my uniform at the apartment after the Police Officers took Charlie away. The dumb-looking khaki pants and shirt are a size too big and I feel uncomfortable in them. But I have a whistle and a billy-club, just to make me look "official." And they gave me a neat pair of mirrored sun glasses. Before I left, I stood in front of the mirror for a few minutes. Funny thing. I look pretty tough in that outfit, maybe because you can't see that my eyes are laughing. Mostly at myself.

Then I went over to the Uni-Prison and checked in. They started bringing the "Numbers" in about half an hour later. I call them "Numbers," because that is how I am to address them. Good old Charlie is now #853, which is written on both sides of the nightshirt he wears. He was one of the first Numbers brought in. We stripped him down, then sprayed him with a "de-louser" which, it turned out, was only deodorant. Well, they are going to need that deodorant because they are not going to get a shower while they are in prison. That is one of the Regulations.

Charlie got a little bit teed-off when we put the steel chain around his ankle and then required him to stand naked in the exercise yard for 20 minutes before we gave him his nightshirt. Well, it was necessary to remind him that he is a Prisoner even when he's bare-assed. Of course, underneath, I felt just as foolish as he did, but I don't think he or the other guys noticed. A Correctional Officer should not be embarrassed since he is just doing the job for which he is being paid.

When we checked the guys in—the Numbers—we gave them a nylon stocking to put on over their heads. Makes them harder to tell apart, but they are just Numbers, after all. They have got nothing on under the nightshirts, and that does lead to some comical situations. Charlie complained right off that he wasn't a woman and didn't like wearing a skirt, but I told him to shut up because that is one of the Rules.

Warden Matossian then assembled the Staff and the Numbers and gave them an Official Welcome. "Listen," he said to the Numbers, 'You have shown that you are unable to function outside in the real world. We of this prison, your Correctional Staff, are going to help you learn what your responsibilities as citizens of this country are. Here are the Rules. We expect you to know them and to be able to recite them by number.

"Rule #1: Prisoners must remain silent during rest periods, after lights are out, during meals, and whenever they are outside the prison yard.

Rule #2: Prisoners must eat at mealtimes and only at mealtimes.

Rule #3: Prisoners must not move, tamper with, deface, or damage walls, ceilings, windows, doors, or other prison property.

Rule #4: Prisoners must address each other only by their numbers.

Rule #5: Prisoners must address the guards as 'Mr. Correctional Officer.'

Rule #6: Prisoners must obey all lawful commands and orders issued to them by Correctional Officers.

Rule #7: Failure to obey any of the above rules may result in punishment."

Well, after the Warden had welcomed them, we put the Numbers away in their cells for Rest Period, and then I was off for the evening. I went back to the apartment, which I admit was sort of empty, what with old #853 being in Prison. Of course, he got himself into this, so I guess it serves him right. But I do not know yet whether I am going to enjoy this experience at all.

DAY 2

This morning when I got to work the guys on the night shift told me that some of the Numbers broke the Rule about not conversing after Lights Out, but the guys said they stopped that nonsense in a hurry. Charlie likes to talk a lot so I was not surprised to learn that my old buddy #853 got himself shouted at a few times.

We got the #'s through the morning ritual pretty well. Part of their job is to sweep up the place. Naturally #853 complained about having to clean the toilets. I would have given him a chit to see the movie that night if he had done a good job, but he bitched too much, and that's against Regulations. Then at lunch he acted up something awful. Broke the Rules all over the place. Lunch was sausages and potatoes, and being his roommate, I am well aware that he does not like sausages. So #853 refuses to eat them, although that's illegal, because Rule #2 says that #'s *must eat* at mealtimes, which means that they must eat *everything* we give them, right?

So I said, "You don't scare me, 853. You eat that damn sausage or I'll stick it in your ear and let you digest it that way." Of course I didn't say "ear," but you know what I mean.

Well, that must have teed him off, or something, because he started arguing with me and abusing me, which is definitely against the Rules. So the other guys and I just grabbed #853 by his nightshirt and led him away to solitary confinement. Which is really just a closet he's got to stand in, but is just what he deserved.

Even then he didn't calm down much, so I shook the billy-club at him, just to let him know who was boss. I wouldn't ever use it, of course, because that's against the Regulations. But it was a little frightening to have this guy I thought I knew threaten me with verbal abuse and physical gestures. Finally, I couldn't take it any more, so I went and got the other guys and we got a couple of sausages and took them down to the "hole" and stuck them in #853's hands.

"Listen 853," I told him in no uncertain tone of voice. "You are going to hold on to those sausages until you see fit to obey the Rules and Regulations and eat them."

To tell the truth, even with the other guys around to protect me, I was a little worried because 853 has got one helluva temper, him being Irish and red-headed and all that. Anyhow, 853 shook the sausages at me and stepped forward, like he might be going to hit me with them. So in self-defense I held up my billy-club. Funny thing. He stopped and stared at me, and then burst out crying, and turned around and hid his face in a corner. I just let the old sissy cry, since he brought it all on himself.

Jeez, I hate sissies.

DAY 3

The first thing that the guys told me when I came on duty was that 853 still refused to eat the sausages, so they were starving him until he gave in. I saw right away we had trouble on our hands, because he was setting the other #'s a very bad example. So I called his two cellmates into the yard, and then I handcuffed 853, sausages and all, and brought him out too.

"Listen you Numbers. This stupid jackass is disobeying the Regulations, and we cannot let him get away with the gross violations of the Rules he is guilty of. Therefore, we are going to take away your eating privileges until your cellmate here gives in and eats the sausages we have provided to keep him alive."

Well, naturally, the other two #'s are not very happy. But we told them to shut up and to get back on the Routine. Which, I am happy to say, they did without too much complaint. Then as I am taking 853 back to the "hole," Warden Matossian came up and asked me to remove the handcuffs. I am not sure why he did this, since I was just trying to keep 853 from escaping. Which is what I am paid to do.

At lunchtime, when we wouldn't let them eat, the other two #'s stood in front of the "hole" and tried to talk some sense into 853. Which, I am sad to say, they failed to do, so they went hungry.

Naturally, this whole nasty business upset the Routine so much that nobody knew which way was up. Finally, things got so bad that I suggested we ought to take away the eating privileges of all the #'s until 853 showed he was sorry for his misdeeds and corrected his bad attitude and

20 / Person Perception, Attribution, and Social Roles

behaved like any decent human would. The other CO's agreed with me, but they were a little worried about keeping discipline if all the #'s went hungry.

When we told the #'s of our decision, they got pretty surly. In fact, one of them started wise-mouthing a bit and showing off, but I tapped him lightly with my billy-club, and he got back into line.

DAY 4

I was barely asleep when the CO's on the evening shift phoned. They said the #'s have gone crazy and were rioting! The Evening Shift got the the #'s cornered by spraying them with a fire extinguisher, but they needed reinforcements.

As I rushed over to help, I really got angry thinking what a sissy jerk 853 turned out to be. Embarrassing us all with that stupid, childish behavior. Why didn't he just give in and obey the Rules, like everybody else?

(Continued on page 538.)

Well, when I got there, I guess I taught him a lesson, didn't I?

SOCIAL PSYCHOLOGY

In the first chapters of this book, we described *psychobiology* as the junction point between two academic disciplines—biology and psychology. Social psychology can be defined as *the scientific study of human social behavior*. As such, it is the junction point between *sociology* and *psychology* (Stephan & Stephan, 1985).

When we described psychobiology, we noted that *biologists* tend to focus on the actions of *cells* and *organs*, while the psychologists primarily talk about the behavior of *organisms*. But organisms, of course, are made up of "subsystems" such as cells and organs. In similar fashion, *sociologists* often pay more attention to such "supersystems" as groups and organizations than do psychologists. We will discuss this matter more fully as soon as we briefly describe individuals, groups, organizations, and societies from the point of view of *General Systems Theory*.

• General Systems Theory

According to General Systems Theory, a *group* is a simple **social system**. Groups are composed of "subsystems" that we call individuals. Your family is a group, and you are a subsystem within that group.

In systems theory terms, *organizations* are fairly complex social systems that are composed of "subsystems" that we call groups. If your family belongs to a health maintenance organization (or HMO), then your family group is a *subsystem* within that medical organization.

According to General Systems Theory, *societies* are exceptionally complex social systems that are composed of "organizations." A health maintenance organization is one of a great many "subsystems" within this society (Miller, 1978).

• Social "Psychology" Versus "Social" Psychology

Generally speaking, social *psychologists* tend to focus on responses *within* a single organism. That is, they anchor themselves at the level of the individual and look up the "systems" ladder toward groups and (perhaps) organizations. However, societies are so far up the scale that they are beyond the **ken** of many social *psychologists* (Raven & Rubin, 1983).

Social psychologists, on the other hand, come to this field from the perspective of sociology. They stand at the top of the "systems" ladder and look down toward the individual. To many *social* psychologists, the individual is about as interesting as a single neuron in your brain would be to most clinical psychologists (Michener, DeLamater, & Schwartz, 1986).

If you take a course in social psychology in the Department of Sociology, you will mostly learn about such topics as "socialization," "organizational structures," "cultural symbols," and "social deviance." If you take a course in social psychology in the Department of Psychology, you will probably cover such issues as "attitude change," "person perception," "attribution theory," and "social roles."

Since this is a book on *psychology*, we will start with the individual and work our way up to groups and some types of organizations. And we will mostly talk about such things as attitudes, attributions, and roles.

Social psychologists are typically more interested in groups than in individuals.

Social Psychology Defined

What, then, is *social psychology*, and how does it differ from all the other areas of psychology we have already discussed? According to Michigan psychologist Theodore Newcomb, the major difference is that social psychology pays attention chiefly to *relations between people*, while most of the rest of the field focuses on *the individual* (Newcomb, 1981).

Bert Raven and Jeffrey Rubin prefer the following definition: "Social psychology is the study of the ways in which people influence, and are influenced, by each other" (Raven & Rubin, 1983).

These two conceptions of the field are similar. But you should remember there is no one, agreed-upon definition of "social psychology" as you read about the ways in which you relate to and are influenced by others.

Five Important Issues in Social Psychology

Theodore Newcomb believes there are several major issues social psychologists typically deal with. Five of the most important issues are as follows:

1. In describing social relationships, should we look at how the individual affects the group, or how the group influences the individual?
2. When we attempt to study social variables, should we look primarily at internal processes such as *attitudes*, or at objective events such as *behaviors*?
3. Are social responses mostly learned, or mostly determined by the genes?
4. Should we be more interested in relatively consistent features of individuals and social organizations (*structures*), or in those aspects that change fairly readily (*functions*)?
5. Is social psychology primarily a *theoretical* or an *applied* science (Newcomb, 1967)?

Some of these questions may sound a bit familiar. But let's look at them briefly from a new perspective as we begin our discussion of social psychology.

The Individual or the Group?

Should social psychologists study individuals, or groups? The answer, of course, is *both*. In this chapter, our focus will primarily be on the *individual*. How, for instance, do you perceive others, and how do they perceive you? How do you influence others, and how do they affect your thoughts and behaviors?

In Chapter 21, our focus will primarily be on *groups* and *organizations*.

Attitudes or Behaviors?

Traditionally, social psychologists have focused more on measuring and describing **attitudes** than on *behaviors*. Indeed, 50 years ago, Gor-

don Allport stated that *attitude* is "the single most distinctive and indispensable concept in contemporary American social psychology" (Allport, 1935). According to Texas A&M psychologist William Crano, many social psychologists became "disenchanted" with the study of attitudinal variables during the 1960's, when research suggested little connection between attitudes and behaviors. However, Crano says, research on attitudes is now "back in fashion" in social psychology (Crano, 1983).

Whatever the case, since attitudes are "internal processes," the "attitude-behavior" argument actually boils down to the mind-body problem revisited.

The traditional way of defining an attitude is as follows: It is a consistent way of thinking about, feeling toward, or responding to some environmental stimulus or input (Newcomb, 1961). Thus, attitudes are composed of cognitive, emotional, and behavioral components. Some social psychologists emphasize the cognitive aspects of attitudes, some focus more on emotions, while a few try to deal with both cognition and affect (Hamilton, 1981). Whatever the case, these scientists come down on the "mind" side of the question.

Other social psychologists prefer to deal with measurable behaviors. For example, in a recent article, social scientist Peter Drucker discusses the problem of trying to predict actions from attitude surveys. Drucker says, "In a good many social matters, attitudes are secondary and attitude surveys are a snare and delusion. What matters is what people do, not what they say they will do" (Drucker, 1981).

Since we have discussed the mind-body problem many times already, we need not restate all the issues here. We might note, however, that social learning theory offers a compromise between the two extreme positions. As you probably will remember, social learning theorists believe that attitudes are "cognitive structures" that allow you to process environmental inputs in consistent ways. Thus, in many (but not all) situations, attitudes actually control behaviors. But the social learning theorists also believe that you "acquire new cognitive structures" as you learn new behavioral habits. So to explain social relationships completely, you must deal *both* with attitudes and behaviors (Bandura, 1986).

Learned or Innate?

The nature-nurture controversy has gained prominence recently in social psychology thanks to Edward Wilson's theory of **sociobiology**. As we pointed out in Chapter 7, Wilson believes that most social responses come from an inherited desire to *help your genes survive*. Wilson says that your own particular social attitudes are controlled in large part by your genes. You perceive your family in a favorable

As we noted in Chapters 14 and 15, however, some aspects of *all* behaviors are relatively consistent, and some are relatively changeable. To emphasize one more than the other would be like a heart surgeon's paying attention only to the structure of your heart while ignoring the way your heart functioned.

Theories or Applications?

As we mentioned in Chapter 1, the field of psychology is split down the middle. Some scientists spend most of their time generating knowledge—that is, in performing experiments and creating new theories. Other psychologists are more interested in putting knowledge to use—that is, they like to help people, groups, and organizations solve real-life problems.

Although there are a great many theories (and theorists) in social psychology, the field has always leaned ever so slightly toward applications. There are many reasons for this "emphasis on the applied."

To begin with, social problems are often highly visible and of obvious importance. And many social psychologists were originally attracted to the field because they were strongly motivated to *change society* in some fashion. For example, Kurt Lewin was a pioneer in the field of social psychology. Writing in the *Handbook of Social Psychology,* Morton Deutsch describes Lewin's approach in these words: "Lewin devoted much of his scientific work to furthering the understanding of the practical day-by-day problems of modern society." Lewin did so by developing a technique he called **action research**. The goal of "action research" is to find ways to achieve social change in the real world (Deutsch, 1969).

A modern proponent of "action research" is Harvard psychologist Chris Argyris. The term Argyris uses, however, is *action science*. In a recent book, he defines the term as follows: "Action science is an approach to social and organizational inquiry that is designed to generate knowledge that is both theoretically valid and practically useful" (Argyris *et al.*, 1985).

It is also true that a lot of social research *of necessity* takes place in real-life settings. Much of learning theory stems from laboratory studies of rat and pigeon behaviors. But social psychologists study *people*, and there are both ethical and practical constraints on the study of human subjects. For instance, we can't bring two people who are friends into a laboratory and deliberately create hostility and conflict between them. We can, though, study hostility and conflict *as they already exist* in real life. We might try to find ways of reducing inter-racial tensions in an integrated school or housing project, for example. Discovering new methods of helping people "get along better" would not only solve a pressing social problem, but

Kurt Lewin

light—and perceive strangers in an unfriendly manner—because you realize that your relatives "carry your genes" (Wilson, 1975).

Very few social psychologists take Wilson's point of view seriously. Rather, the strong tendency is to believe that most social behaviors are *learned* (Caplan, 1978).

• Consistency Versus Change

Some social scientists emphasize the *consistent features* of individuals, groups, and organizations. The question then becomes, what factors increase (or decrease) social consistency (White, 1982; Zanna, Higgins, & Herman, 1982)?

One answer to that question comes from a series of experiments by Robert A. Wicklund and his associates. They found that the more *self-aware* you are, the more consistent your attitudes and behaviors become. For instance, if you are asked to respond in front of a mirror, or listen to a recording of your voice before reacting, you tend to act in a manner that matches your attitudes (Stephenson & Wicklund, 1983; Wicklund & Braun, 1987).

Other theorists believe that *change* and *flexibility* are the hallmarks of social responses. Behavioral social psychologists, for instance, think you are attracted to others because you find them *rewarding* in some way. And since social rewards are learned—and vary from person to person and situation to situation— the "consistency" lies in *interaction* between people and situations, not merely in the personality structure of the individual (Caspi, Elder, & Bem, 1987).

Those scientists who emphasize "consistency" tend to be *structuralists*, while those theorists who emphasize "change" tend to be *functionalists* or *interactionalists* (Bem, 1983).

would create new knowledge as well (Deutsch, 1969). Little wonder, then, that many social psychologists have adopted Kurt Lewin's motto, "The world is my laboratory."

The "Social Interaction Sequence"

Social psychologists typically study *people interacting with other people*. Suppose we want to study *your* interactions with another individual. What we would immediately discover is this important fact: How you behave toward another individual is determined, in large part, by how you *perceive* the other person. Thus, in part, social psychology is the *study of social perceptions*.

According to John Darley and Russell Fazio, "Perception is a constructive, interpretative process. Such interpretation is particularly critical in the perception of other people. The actions of another person do not automatically convey meanings, but are given meanings by the perceiver" (Darley & Fazio, 1980). With this thought in mind, Darley and Fazio state that the "social interaction sequence" typically has five distinct steps:

1. When you meet someone, you develop a *set of expectancies* about the other person.
2. You then *act* toward the person in a way that is consistent with your expectancies.
3. The other person *interprets* the meaning of your actions.
4. Based on this interpretation, the other person *responds*.

A couple on a blind date may be more likely to perceive each other in terms of what friends have told them about the other person than in terms of what can actually be observed.

5. You then *interpret* the meaning of the other person's response (Darley & Fazio, 1980).

As we go through the chapter, we will touch on each of these five points in the social interaction sequence. And we will begin by trying to find out how you *generate a set of expectancies* about others.

□ □ **QUESTION** □ □
When you meet someone new, what do you look for in that person? And what about that person is most likely to influence whether or not you like the individual?

PERSON PERCEPTION

One common social sequence is this: You meet someone new, you decide you like this person, and thus you see the individual more frequently in the future. Eventually, you form a warm friendship with (or even get married to) the person. Social psychologists have spent a great amount of time studying—and theorizing about—this type of social interaction. You may perceive this sequence of events as "happening naturally." Social scientists, however, have discovered that your perceptions, attitudes, and actions throughout the sequence are strongly affected by factors you may be unaware of (Cook, 1984).

When you meet someone new, the first thing you do is to *perceive* the other person. But what influences your perception of this other individual? The many different answers to this question make up the fascinating field of *person perception*.

Defining "Person Perception"

What is "person perception"? Two decades ago, Renato Tagiuri defined it as follows: "The processes by which man comes to know and think about other persons, their characteristics, qualities, and inner states" (Tagiuri, 1969).

However, according to University of Washington psychologists Edith Greene and Elizabeth Loftus, the meaning of this term has changed in recent years: "Traditionally, [person perception] has been thought to be the study of how people perceive their human environment. It concerns our ability to know another individual's intentions, attitudes, emotions, ideas, and possible behavior. It is how we know that one person is friendly, another a cheat, and a third is depressingly angry." But Greene and Loftus believe that we must now add the term "person memory" to the older definition because perceptions are primarily *learned*. Thus, the way you perceive someone will depend to a great extent on what kinds of "codes" you use to file your memories of people in long-term storage (Greene & Loftus, 1981).

But your perceptions are also affected by your needs. So the area of *person perception* must take into account not only social *perceptions*, but social *memories* and *motives* as well. Let's attempt to illustrate these points by describing "person perception" in more detail.

First Impressions

Suppose some good friends of yours have talked you into going to a party with a blind date. They paint a glowing picture of your date as a kind of super-person in order to get you to agree to the date. When the fatal moment comes, and you meet the person, what sorts of things do you look for first? That is, what *immediate stimulus clues* influence your *judgment* of the individual?

If you have read Chapter 7, you will remember the primary rule of perception: *You see what you expect to see.* Before you meet your date, your friends will have *biased* your perceptions by their descriptions of the individual. If they have told you the person is warm, affectionate, responsive, and outgoing, you will probably *look for* these attributes in your date as soon as the two of you meet. Certainly your *attitude* toward the person will be different than if you have been told your date is rather intellectual, cold, withdrawn, quiet, and self-possessed.

The question then becomes, how do attitudes affect perceptions?

● *Attitudes*

As we noted earlier, an *attitude* is a consistent way of thinking about, feeling toward, or responding to some aspect of your environment (or toward yourself). Thus, an attitude is actually a sort of "cognitive structure" that allows you to process and respond to social inputs in an efficient manner (Jones, 1986).

But an attitude is also a "mental program" for *coding* experiences in order to store them in Long-term Memory. Therefore, your attitudes affect not only your *present* perceptions and responses, they also help determine your future memories of what you saw and did in the present. We can prove that point by looking at how you form "first impressions" of the people you meet.

● *Reputations*

When your friends describe your blind date to you, they are telling you something about that person's *reputation*. That is, your friends are describing how most people perceive your date, or the attitude most people have toward the person.

Social psychologist Harold Kelley tested the importance of "reputations" in a study performed at MIT in the late 1940's. Kelley told a large class of undergraduates they would have a visiting lecturer for the day, and that the students would be asked to evaluate this man at the end of the class. Kelley then passed out a brief biographical note about the teacher, presumably to help the students with their evaluation. Although the students did not realize it, the description half the class received referred to the lecturer as being "rather a warm individual," while the description given the rest of the class called the man "rather a cold intellectual."

After the class had read the printed comments, the man arrived and led the class in a 20-minute discussion. Kelley watched the students and recorded how often each of them asked a question or made a comment. Afterward, the students were asked to rate the man on a set of attitude scales and to write a brief description of him.

Although everyone in the class had witnessed *exactly* the same performance at *exactly* the same time, the manner in which each student responded was measurably affected by the descriptions each had read. Those students who had been told the instructor was "warm" tended to rate him as much more informal, sociable, popular, good-natured, humorous, and humane than the students who had been told the same man was "cold."

More than this, the subjects *reacted* to the man quite differently. The students who were told he was warm spoke to him in class much more frequently than did the students who were told he was cold (Kelley, 1950).

More recently, Gerard Connors and Mark Sobell studied the responses of undergraduate males in a "social drinking" situation. The subjects drank either one or two doses of alcohol in the presence of another young male who actually was a "confederate" of the experimenters. Part of the time, the "confederate" pretended to drink, and then acted as if he were intoxicated. Part of the time, the "confederate" did *not* drink, but then acted in the same uninhibited way he did as when he pretended to be intoxicated. The undergraduates tended to rate the "confederate" as being "more friendly, admirable, responsive, warmer, and less reserved" when he *pretended* to drink than when he didn't, although his behavior was the same in both situations. Thus, Connors and Sobell say, it was the confederate's *reputation* as being "a drinker" that influenced the manner in which the subjects perceived him (Connors & Sobell, 1986).

□ □ **QUESTION** □ □
How might Kelley's research help explain the difficulty that Rosenhan's "pseudo-patients" had in convincing mental hospital staffs that they (the "pseudo-patients") were really normal or sane?

• Autistic Hostility and Negative Reputations

Judging from much of the research on "reputations," once you believe you *won't* like a person on the basis of his/her reputation, you tend to avoid her or him in the future. Theodore Newcomb has called this avoidance response **austistic hostility**, and suggests that it may apply to interactions among groups as well as among individuals (Newcomb, 1961).

However, you might well be able to *compensate* for a poor reputation if you try hard enough. In a recent study, James Hilton and John Darley told some students—called the "evaluators"—that they would meet another student (the "target") who had a "cold" personality. Some of the "target" students were then told that the "evaluator" they would meet *believed them to be cold*. Other "targets" were not given this information. Hilton and Darley reports that the "evaluators" did, indeed, perceive the uninformed "targets" as being "cold." However, the "targets" who knew what their reputation was supposed to be apparently were able to overcome this negative evaluation (Hilton & Darley, 1985).

• Stereotypes

When you don't know a given person's "reputation," your initial impressions are likely to be affected by the **stereotypes**, or biased perceptions, that you have about certain types or groups of people. If you assume that all blacks are lazy, dull, ignorant but musical, you will tend to "see" these attributes even in an energetic, bright black doctor who perhaps couldn't carry a tune in a handbag. If your attitude toward Jews is that they are intelligent, emotional, and penny-pinching, you may respond to each Jew as if she or he had to fit your stereotype.

Any time you react to an individual *primarily* in terms of that person's membership in some group—or in terms of that person's physical characteristics, race, or religion—you are guilty of *stereotyping*. That is, you have let the reputation of the group influence your perception of the individual who belongs to that group (Hamilton, 1981).

University of Minnesota psychologist Mark Snyder points out that, once you form a *stereotype* of a given group, you tend to seek out information that *confirms* the stereotype, and *repress* information that doesn't. Furthermore, Snyder says, when you interact with people you've "stereotyped," you tend to behave toward them in ways that will *elicit* responses that fit the stereotype (Snyder, 1983).

Put in more cognitive terms, when you "stereotype" people, you are using what Piaget called the process of "assimilation" (see Chapter 15). That is, you are forcing your perception of the individual to fit your *schema* for remembering or classifying that type of person. When

"ACTUALLY IN OUR GROUP THE WHITE GUYS PLAY LIKE BLACK GUYS, THE BLACK GUYS PLAY LIKE WHITE GUYS, AND THE WOMAN PLAYS LIKE A 'MAN.'"

you change your perception to fit the facts, you are "accommodating" to the real world by altering your schema.

□ □ **QUESTION** □ □

How would you explain Newcomb's concept of "autistic hostility" in terms of Piaget's "process of assimilation"?

• "Self-Fulfilling Prophecies"

Perceiving a person in a biased fashion often leads us to *behave* toward that individual in a stereotyped fashion. And, in response, the indi-

Many interactions between people of different racial or ethnic groups are influenced by stereotyping.

Autistic hostility (aw-TISS-tic). Autism (see Chapter 1) is the act of withdrawing into oneself, of shutting off external stimulation. Autistic hostility is the act of cutting off or denying favorable inputs about people or things we don't like. "My mind is made up—don't try to confuse me with facts."

Stereotypes. A stereotype is a fixed or unconscious attitude or perception—a way of responding to some person or object solely in terms of the the person's (or object's) class membership. The failure to treat people as individuals, each different from the other, is the act of stereotyping.

vidual may *react* to us in a way that confirms our original perception. Evidence for this statement comes from a recent study by University of Arkansas psychologists Mark Sibicky and John Dovidio.

Sibicky and Dovidio studied the social behaviors of 136 undergraduates who were paired off in a "get acquainted" situation. One of the students in each pair was called "the evaluator," while the other student was called "the target." The evaluators were told that the "target" he/she would meet was either (1) a "client" seeking psychological therapy, or (2) a student in an introductory psychology course. The "targets" were not told anything at all about the experiment.

During the "get acquainted" meeting, those evaluators who thought their target-partners were "therapy clients" treated their partners more negatively than did evaluators who thought they were meeting "just another student." The evaluators also gave "therapy-client-targets" lower ratings than they gave to "student-targets."

More than this, Sibicky and Dovidio report, during the meeting itself, the "client-targets" *responded* to their evaluators in "less socially-desirable ways" than did "student-targets." Sibicky and Dovidio believe that the evaluators *elicited* behaviors from their partners that would fulfill the evaluators' expectations (Sibicky & Dovidio, 1986).

Put in simple terms, when you perceive someone in a stereotyped fashion, you *predict how they will respond*. You then may act toward that individual in a manner that almost *forces* the person to respond in ways that confirm your stereotyped expectations. Social psychologists call this sequence of behaviors *self-fulfilling prophecies* (Jones, 1986; Miller, 1982).

□ □ **QUESTION** □ □
How does the research by Sibicky and Dovidio compare with Rosenthal's "Late Bloomer" study described in the story that begins Chapter 17?

• *Primacy Effect*

Stereotypes are *cognitive schemes* that exist in Long-term Memory. As we mentioned in Chapter 11, items that you file away in your permanent memory banks are affected both by the

primacy effect and the *recency effect*. Stereotypes are no exception.

Research on stereotypes and the "primacy effect" goes back to the 1940's, when psychologist Solomon Asch gave a group of subjects a list of adjectives describing someone they might meet. Half the subjects were told the person was "intelligent, industrious, impulsive, critical, stubborn, and envious." The other subjects were given the same list, but in opposite order: "envious, stubborn, critical, impulsive, industrious, intelligent." The subjects were then asked to write a brief paragraph evaluating what they thought the person might be like.

A subject told the person was "intelligent . . . envious" wrote that "The person is intelligent and fortunately he puts his intelligence to work. That he is stubborn and impulsive may be due to the fact that he knows what he is saying and what he means and will not therefore give in easily to someone else's idea of what he disagrees with."

A subject told the person was "envious . . . intelligent" wrote, "This person's good qualities such as industry and intelligence are bound to be restricted by jealousy and stubbornness. The person is emotional. He is unsuccessful because he is weak and allows his bad points to cover up his good ones" (Asch, 1946).

You can perceive any person you meet in dozens of different ways. Presumably, the first information you get about a person pulls one particular memory schema to the "top of the memory bin." Once that happens—according to the primacy effect—you are likely to "assimilate" any other data about the person into the schema you first used to categorize that individual (Vinokur & Ajzen, 1982).

□ □ **QUESTION** □ □
Sigmund Freud believed that the causes of most personality problems lay buried in childhood. What would Freud have to say about the "primacy effect"?

• *Recency Effect*

Psychologists often speak of a *recency effect*, which can either counteract or reinforce the primacy effect. If you have recently used a given schema to categorize people—and have found it useful—you are very likely to apply it to the next person you meet. Thus, if one of Asch's students had already encountered a lot of "envious" people that week, the student might well have perceived almost anyone that way despite the fact that "intelligent" was first on the descriptive list the student received.

Which is more important, the primacy or the recency effect? As we reported in Chapter 11, the *situation* itself usually determines the answer to this question. Research by Anthony Wright and his colleagues suggests that if you are asked to make a judgment about someone immediately after meeting the person, then primacy probably prevails. However, if you are asked to judge someone later on, your *most recent* impressions may be more important (Wright *et al.*, 1985).

◻◻ **QUESTION** ◻◻

What kind of first impression do you think you give the people you meet? *Why* do you think they perceive you this way? Are strangers more influenced by what you are really like "deep down inside," or by how you look?

Two Channels of Communication

The way you perceive someone you have just met is obviously affected by such *internal processes* as attitudes, reputations, stereotypes, the primacy effect, and the recency effect. But your perceptions are also influenced by *present stimulus inputs*.

When you meet someone new, you transmit information about yourself to that person by way of *two main channels of communication*—what you do with your body, and what you say with your tongue. The way you look and dress and move—these are part of your **body language**. What you say, the opinions you express, and the verbal responses you make—these are part of your verbal language. Surprisingly enough, when it comes to first impressions, people are often more influenced by your looks and physical movements than they are by what you actually say. Needless to say, your "first impressions" of others are also strongly affected by their physical attractiveness and body language.

◻◻ **QUESTION** ◻◻

Suppose you met two people, one with obvious good looks, the other with average looks. Which person do you think would be the happier? Why?

Physical Appearance and Interpersonal Attraction

Although it may be "undemocratic"—to use Elliot Aronson's term—the plain fact is that people tend to be impressed by good looks (Aronson, 1984). Indeed, most of us tend to *attribute* highly positive characteristics to handsome individuals. And far too often, we tend to *attribute* negative characteristics to individuals who are "below average" in terms of their physical appearances. Many years ago, this fact led psychologists Elaine (Walster) Hatfield, Ellen Berscheid, and Karen Dion to conclude that, to most of the people they studied, "beautiful is good" (Dion, Berscheid, & Walster, 1972).

During the past two decades, Berscheid, Hatfield, and Dion have been pioneers in the

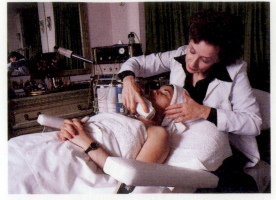

The "easy on the eyes" smoothness of youthful skin is considered beautiful and therefore highly desirable.

study of the effects of physical attractiveness on social behavior. In an early experiment on "computer dating," Elaine Walster (now Elaine Hatfield) discovered that "good looks" was the only factor that could predict how much both the male and female subjects liked their dates. Furthermore, the importance of "good looks" tended to increase from the first to the fifth date in both men and women (Walster *et al.*, 1966). More recently, Paul Sergios and James Cody obtained similar results in a "computer dating" study of homosexual males (Sergios & Cody, 1985–1986).

According to Elaine Hatfield and Susan Sprecher, most of us consider attractive people to be more sensitive, stronger, more modest, more sociable, more outgoing, kinder, more interesting, and sexually warmer than unattractive people. We also tend to believe that handsome individuals are more likely to have important jobs, happy marriages, and to "enjoy life to the fullest" (Hatfield & Sprecher, 1986).

Other research has shown that strangers are more likely to help someone who is good looking, that handsome "criminal defendants" are less likely to be convicted (and if convicted, to get shorter terms) than are ugly "criminal defendants," that attractive mental patients are more likely to recover—and to be accepted back in the community—after release from a mental hospital, and that physically-attractive individuals are more likely to be hired for jobs than less good-looking people are (Bardack & McAndrew, 1985; Benson, Karabenick, & Lerner, 1976; Burns & Farina, 1987; Miller, 1986).

We are also more likely to ascribe *negative* characteristics to people who are not beautiful. For example, Karen Dion found that most teachers believed that unattractive children were more likely to have "a chronic disposition to commit bad acts" than were attractive children (Dion, 1972).

Why this bias toward beauty? One answer comes from University of Minnesota psychologist Ellen Berscheid. She believes that the less information you have about someone, the more likely it is that you will judge that person in terms of his/her looks. Thus, beauty has a *primacy* effect. After you get to know the person, however, you may be more impressed by other factors. However, Berscheid believes that, in terms of *sexual attraction*, beauty remains important over long periods of contact (cited in Leff, 1981).

Another sort of answer comes from studies on the *visual complexity* of physical beauty. As we noted in Chapter 5, Judith Langlois and her colleagues at the University of Texas found that infants spent more time looking at attractive than unattractive faces. Langlois and her associates note that "pretty" faces tend to be highly symmetrical, smooth, and almost "juvenile" in their features (Langlois *et al.*, 1987). Such faces are also *less complex visual stimuli* (and hence are easier to "process") than are irregular, marked, unattractive faces. Thus, the phrase "easy on the eyes" may well offer a valid explanation of our preference for handsome facial features.

To summarize, beauty may be "in the eye of the beholder," but it obviously does shape our perceptions of others to a greater extent than many of us would like to believe is the case.

□ □ **QUESTION** □ □

Why do you think beautiful children tend to score higher on individually-administered intelligence tests than when they take a written test administered to a whole group of children?

• Non-Verbal Communication

No matter how much you wish to impress other people, you can't do all that much about changing your looks. But you can alter your physical movements—that is, the way you present yourself to others. Whether you know it or not, you have a characteristic way of dressing, of combing your hair, of moving your arms and legs, of looking toward or away from people as you speak or listen, of smiling, of frowning, and of giving feedback. This "body language" may not be an accurate indicator of what you are "really like." However, experiments suggest

many people you meet will judge your *intentions toward them* primarily by the way in which you communicate non-verbally. And, of course, you tend to evaluate others in much the same fashion.

But what makes up your own unique brand of body language? What can a stranger tell about you just by watching you behave? To begin with, and perhaps most important, is the simple fact that you are either *male* or *female*. As we pointed out in Chapter 7, every culture has different *social expectations* about the ways that women and men should look and behave.

Your *age* is also an important aspect of your "body image," as is (obviously) your skin color and how good-looking you are. The clothes you wear, the way that you move, even such seemingly trivial behaviors as how close you stand to the people you meet and the eye contact you give them—all these things "communicate" information to the people you meet.

Once people have *stereotyped* you according to your sex, size, age, skin color, dress, and physical beauty, they *expect you to behave in certain ways*. Generally speaking, if your behavior *confirms* these expectations, most people will gain a good "first impression" of you. However, if your actions *disconfirm* people's expectations, you are not likely to win very many popularity contests (Schneider, Hastorf, & Ellsworth, 1979).

□ □ **QUESTION** □ □

Is there any objective truth to our culture's stereotypes about men and women? About young and old people? Why is this the case? (Hint: What about "self-fulfilling prophecies"?)

• Behavioral Congruence

Person Memory, a book edited by Reid Hastie and several other social psychologists, contains several chapters on how your perception of others changes over time. One important process which influences *perceptual change* is what Hastie calls **behavioral congruence**. If the way people act later on tends to confirm your initial perception of them, then you perceive their behaviors as being "congruent" with your first impression. If their later actions *disconfirm* your first impression, you experience "discongruence." According to Hastie *et al.*, when most people experience discongruence, they tend to "rationalize" (or explain away) any data that don't reinforce their original impressions (Hastie *et al.*, 1980).

Oddly enough, Hastie's research shows that most people remember *incongruent* behaviors better than *congruent* ones. Hastie believes that congruent behaviors are readily coded and filed away in Long-term Memory. But when someone acts in an unexpected way, you must try to "explain the behavior" before you can tuck it into long-term storage. Hastie believes you remember incongruent actions more readily because it takes more time to process them (Hastie, 1984).

□ □ **QUESTION** □ □

In Chapter 15, we noted that people tend to create "memory scripts" for their day-to-day activities, and remember "departures from the scripts" better than events that did not vary from the expected. What similarity do you see between "memory scripts" and Hastie's notion of "behavioral discongruence"?

Personal Space

How close people stand to you when they first meet you can often influence your impression of them. California psychologist Robert Sommer has for many years studied what he calls *personal space*. Sommer believes you carry an "invisible bubble" around your body that encloses what you consider to be your own, personal psychological space. He notes that in a number of studies, subjects have shown a dramatic increase in nervousness when an experimenter moved to within a foot or so of them. Most of the subjects "defended their territories" either by moving away from the intruder, or by becoming increasingly hostile.

Sommer states that the size of your own personal space bubble is influenced by such factors as your personality, status, and the present social situation. For middle-class Americans, this private area extends outward about 2 feet from any part of the body. For people in the Middle East and South America, the space is usually much smaller. For Scandinavians and Japanese, the bubble is typically larger. However, the size of each person's "space bubble" may expand or contract depending on the circumstances (Sommer, 1969).

According to John Lombardo, men respond more negatively to invasions of their personal space in face-to-face confrontations, while women respond more negatively to side-by-side invasions. In a recent study, however, Lombardo found that both men and women with "traditional sex-role stereotypes" were more threatened by invasions of their space than were men and women with less "traditional" views (Lombardo, 1986).

Virginia psychologist Dennis Donat reports that altercations among elderly patients in a mental hospital most often involved "cognitively-impaired" individuals who unwittingly wandered into the personal space of other patients. Donat notes that simply changing the environment to "reduce wandering" also reduced the number of altercations (Donat, 1986).

Individuals each have an imaginary "space bubble" that expands or contracts depending on the circumstances.

Psychologists Nan Sussman and Howard Rosenfeld report that personal spaces varies with the language you're speaking. Sussman and Rosenfeld asked students from different cultures to "sit and converse" in their *native tongues*. The students from South America sat closer together than did students from the US. But Japanese students sat several inches farther apart than did the Americans. However, when these students were asked to converse in English, the Japanese students sat closer to each other, and the South Americans moved farther away. Apparently these students were quite aware that the size of the "space bubble" in the US was different from their own—and they tried to imitate our space requirements while speaking in our tongue (Sussman & Rosenfeld, 1982).

□ □ **QUESTION** □ □

When you change roles—as from Correctional Officer to prisoner—why does the size of your personal space often change?

● *Territoriality*

Wild animals often have clearly-defined "territories" that they mark off and defend. Do humans have "territories" too? If so, what purpose do they serve?

One set of answers to these questions comes from a 1975 study by Paul Rosenblatt and Linda Budd, who asked married and unmarried couples the following questions:

1. Do you have your own separate bed or your own special side of a bed that's exclusively yours to sleep on?

2. Do you have a certain and separate area of the closet in which you store your own things?

3. Do you have a certain and separate portion of the bathroom in which to place items such as your toothbrush?

Rosenblatt and Budd report that, although the unmarried couples had lived together for the same amount of time as had the married couples, the two groups gave quite different responses to the questions. Generally speaking, the married couples had "staked out individual territories" and respected each other's rights. The unmarried couples, however, were significantly less territorial.

According to Rosenblatt and Budd, the married couples apparently had decided their relationship could not endure unless they settled "territorial rights" early in their marriage. However, the unmarried couples took a different view. Either they saw the relationship as being so temporary it wasn't worth the effort to argue about such things. Or, as Rosenblatt and Budd put it, "They sensed that staking territorial claims and setting boundaries would commit them to a long-term relationship that neither wanted" (Rosenblatt & Budd, 1975).

More recently, Kathleen Cooper found that "chronically institutionalized nonverbal clients" did better when allowed to have individual possessions and when they could establish a certain area of the institution that they could call their own (Cooper, 1984).

□ □ **QUESTION** □ □
Would having clear-cut territories reduce or increase the stress most people feel when forced to live together in crowded conditions?

● *Body Posture*

Even when you respect other people's "personal space" or territories by standing at just the right distance from people "to make them comfortable," the way that you *hold your body* influences the impressions that you give others. In our culture, most people assume that if you lean toward them, you like them (and perhaps are inviting intimacy). But if you lean away from them, they may assume you dislike or reject them.

In a study on body posture, psychologist Albert Mehrabian asked men and women to act out the way they would sit when speaking to someone they liked or disliked. Mehrabian reports that both men and women leaned *forward* to express liking, but that men (more than women) leaned back or became more tense when addressing someone they disliked (Mehrabian, 1971).

Once you have established a "proper distance" to stand from an individual, any further movement you make may signal a change in your feelings. Psychologist Donn Byrne and his associates set up an experiment in which couples were selected by a computer for blind dates. After the young man and woman had gotten to know each other briefly, they were called into Byrne's office and stood before his desk for further instructions. The subjects were then separated and asked to fill out a questionnaire indicating how much they liked their dates. Byrne and his colleagues report that couples who liked each other moved closer together in front of the desk than did couples who didn't care much for each other (Byrne, Ervin, & Lamberth, 1970).

□ □ **QUESTION** □ □
If a man stared at you intensely while talking to you, what motives would you *attribute* to him? If he averted his eyes while listening to you, would you think he was showing disinterest or respect?

● *Eye Contact*

Movements of your face and eyes are often as critical to the first impression you give as are how close you stand and whether you lean toward or away from someone. For the eye contact you make with people often controls both the flow of conversation and their initial opinion of your honesty and aggressiveness. Little wonder, then, that a decade ago C.T. Brown and P.W. Keller said, "Eye contact is the single most important feature of [non-verbal communication] in the conveying of interpersonal meaning" (Brown & Keller, 1979).

The "rules of eye contact" vary considerably from one society to another, and thus seem to be primarily learned behaviors (Nadler & Nadler, 1987). However, the *reason* there are "rules" is probably grounded in innate emotional responses.

Among both primates and people, prolonged "direct eye contact" is a mark of intense emotionality (Strom & Buck, 1979). Primates usually respond hostilely to being stared at. (Next time you're at a zoo, try staring directly at a monkey's eyes and watch how the animal responds.) Among humans, "mutual gazing" of any duration occurs primarily among (1) lovers, (2) two people locked in some kind of emotional confrontation, and (3) a mother and her infant (Patterson, 1983; Patterson *et al.*, 1984).

Humans avoid the emotionality of direct "mutual gazing" by developing rules that govern who looks at whom, and when. For example, if you happen to be a middle-class adult, you probably gaze *at* people when they are talking or lecturing. For staring directly at a speaker is your way of encouraging that person to continue conversing—particularly if you also nod or smile in apparent agreement. When you look *away* from whoever is talking, however, you signal that you are bored or that you want to take over the talking role yourself (Argyle & Cook, 1976).

When *you* are telling a story or making a point, though, chances are you will gaze *away* from your audience—particularly if you are trying to think through what you are talking about. While you speak, you may glance back at your audience from time to time to make sure they are still with you (that is, still looking at you), then look away again as you continue talking (Kleinke, 1986).

These "rules of eye contact" vary not only from culture to culture, but also *within* a particular culture. For example, individuals brought up in lower-class environments in the US have eye signals that are almost the direct opposite of those found in middle-class society. People reared in lower-class homes tend to stare directly at people when talking, but avert their eyes when listening to show respect (particularly if listening to someone of higher status) (Brown & Keller, 1979).

In middle-class America, people who engage in prolonged direct gaze are often perceived as being more powerful and of higher social status. For example, King's College psychologists Charles Brooks, Michael Church, and Lance Fraser had undergraduates view video tapes of a woman student who maintained direct eye contact with an interviewer for 5, 30, or 50 seconds. The students tended to rate the woman as being more socially "potent" (and as having a higher grade point average) the *longer* she engaged in direct mutual gaze with the interviewer (Brooks, Church, & Fraser, 1986).

You learn the "rules of eye contact" so early in life that you may not be aware of how

The rules of eye contact are learned very early and are usually followed unconsciously.

strongly they influence your perceptions and behaviors. Unless you understand how these rules affect your first impressions, however, you are likely to *misinterpret* the eye signals that someone from another culture or socioeconomic class gives to you (Kleinke, 1986).

□ □ **QUESTION** □ □
What sorts of "body language" cues do you look for when you try to determine whether someone is lying?

● *"Deceitful" Body Language*
Studies by Harvard psychologist Robert Rosenthal and his colleagues suggest that the old belief that "people who look you straight in the eye are telling the truth" has little or no validity to it. Indeed, people who tell embarrassing truths are more likely to maintain poor eye contact than are people who are deliberately lying (Zuckerman *et al.*, 1982). Nervous *speech* apparently is a better indication of lying (or emotionality), however, than is poor eye contact (Scherer *et al.*, 1985).

□ □ **QUESTION** □ □
If you encountered a patient in a mental hospital who refused to look at you, what would be your "first impression" of what might be wrong with the person?

● *Eye Contact in Disadvantaged Persons*
There is considerable evidence that people who are handicapped, or who suffer from mental disorders, often maintain poor eye contact. For example, Laurie Weiman reports that physically-disadvantaged individuals often display "low status" eye contact when talking with

able-bodied individuals, but not when talking with another disabled person (Weiman, 1986). And German psychologist Heiner Ellgring found that depressive patients tend to avoid direct eye contact, while schizophrenic patients often display what we might call "generally inappropriate" body language, including poor eye contact (Ellgring, 1986).

☐☐ **QUESTION** ☐☐
Would *chemical* treatment of depressive patients *by itself* help them learn proper eye contact?

● *Responding to "Body Language"*

According to psychologists Dana Christensen, Amerigo Farina, and Louis Boudreau, *recognizing* body language cues is fairly easy for most people. But *responding appropriately* may be harder. Christensen and her colleagues gave 130 undergraduate women a "social competence" questionnaire. The experimenters then selected 15 of the women with the highest scores, and 15 women who got low scores on "social competence."

Next, Christensen and her group asked the students in both the "high" and "low" groups to interview a young woman. The students were told to ask this woman 10 prepared questions about each of three topics: the woman's extracurricular activities, the courses she was taking, and her family life. The students were specifically instructed to *move on to the next topic* if the woman seemed uncomfortable.

Actually, the woman being interviewed was a confederate trained by the experimenters to act in a normal fashion when being asked about the first topic. However, when the students reached the second topic (academic courses), the woman always started showing visible signs of distress. She wrung her hands, avoided direct eye contact, stammered, and hesitated for long periods before responding.

Christensen and her associates report that the students with high "social competence" scores moved on to the next topic (or stopped the interview) almost immediately after the "confederate" showed distress. The students with low "social competence" scores, however, continued the questioning for much longer periods. When the experimenters asked the students in the "low" group about their actions, the "low" students all claimed they had *detected* the signs of stress at the same time that the "high" students did. So "perceiving" body language wasn't the issue. Rather, it was a mat-

ter of *interpreting* and *responding accurately* to the situation.

Students with "low" social competence scores offered many excuses for their actions. Some said they continued the questions because, from their point of view, "The woman had no reason to be upset about such trivial questions." Others responded that the woman was "so hopelessly tense about being interviewed that changing the subject wouldn't have helped."

Christensen and her colleagues conclude that most women students can "read" social cues rather well. The trouble the low-scoring students had, however, came from their "tendency to make judgments about how others should behave rather than being open to how they are actually behaving" (Christensen, Farina, & Boudreau, 1980).

☐☐ **QUESTION** ☐☐
How would *you* define "social competence"?

THE ATTRIBUTION PROCESS

By now, you have learned some of the rules that influence the way you perceive people, particularly someone you've just met. But *why* do you do so? For instance, why do you often "stereotype" people? According to Fritz Heider, you do so to *avoid stress*. Heider notes that most of us become alarmed whenever we cannot guess fairly accurately what will happen to us next. By using what Heider calls the **attribution process**, we attribute to others various motives that make their actions more predictable (and hence less stressful) to us.

According to Heider, when you perceive a woman's actions as being an expression of her character, you are actually *attributing* certain personality traits to the woman. Most of these *attributed traits* are stereotypes, for she may not possess these characteristics at all. But once you stereotype her, you have a ready-made attitude or perception to fit her. Therefore, you not only can predict her *actions* (or so you think), but you have a way of *responding* to her as well (Heider, 1958).

Edward E. Jones notes that we use the attribution process to *explain our own faults* as well. But we attribute these faults to the environment, not to our own personality. We see ourselves as merely reacting to whatever situation we find ourselves in. However, when we observe inconsistent behaviors in *others*, we tend to ignore the social background. Instead, we attribute their actions to some inner need, motive, or flaw of character. To summarize, we perceive ourselves as being *forced* to act in inappropriate ways from time to time. But when others misbehave, we perceive them as *wanting* to act that way (Jones, 1986).

Psychologists Richard Lau and Dan Russell call this the "I win because of me: I lose because of you" effect. In a recent article, Lau and Russell studied the explanations offered by professional players and coaches after important baseball and football games. More than 80 percent of the time, the athletes claimed that "wins" were due to their own superior performance. About half the time, however, they attributed "losses" to such factors as bad luck, bad officiating, or injuries to key players (Lau & Russell, 1980).

□ □ **QUESTION** □ □

In Europe, in recent years, unusually bad weather is often blamed on the nuclear power plant explosion that occurred recently in the Soviet Union. But unusually *good weather* is never attributed to the nuclear disaster. Why?

Kelley's Theory of Personal Relationships

The person who has advanced attribution theory the most in recent years is Harold H. Kelley, who is now at UCLA. His thinking about the attribution process is shown most clearly in his book *Personal Relationships: Their Structures and Processes.*

Kelley is interested more in long-term relationships between people than in "first impressions." He believes that three concepts are crucial to understanding enduring *dyads,* or two-person relationships. These three concepts are *interdependence, responsiveness,* and *attribution* (Kelley, 1981).

- ### Interdependence
By "interdependence," Kelley refers to the belief that the *outcomes* of a relationship depend in large part on both the individual and the joint actions that people in a dyad undertake. For instance, suppose you are married. Both the benefits and the costs of the marriage—to you and to your spouse—will depend not only on what each of you does individually, but also on the *joint actions* the two of you take. Therefore, to get the most out of your marriage, you must not only pay attention to what you do, but you must be able to *anticipate* what your spouse will do as well. Much of your own behavior, then, is dependent on your predictions of how your spouse will behave in certain situations.

If your predictions about your spouse are accurate, you can often use this knowledge to maximize your own personal gains. But if you do, your spouse may suffer. Therefore, the relationship may break apart unless you are responsive to your spouse's needs as well as to your own.

- ### Responsiveness
By "responsiveness," Kelley means that you take your spouse's needs into account when

According to one study, professional football players tended to attribute losses to causes beyond their control, but attributed wins to their own efforts.

making decisions about your own behavior. If your partner does the same, Kelley says, both you and your spouse will probably assume this means you have a loving, interdependent relationship. That is, you will *attribute the trait of lovingness* to each other.

To Kelley, the essence of a good personal relationship is the fact that the partners care about one another. And this caring is most readily visible in situations where one partner gives up benefits or endures costs out of consideration for the other.

- ### Attribution
Even loving couples occasionally have problems. Kelley has shown that marriage partners are inclined to explain problems in their relationship in terms of *attributed traits* rather than in terms of *specific behaviors.* Thus, a wife who is upset with her husband typically won't speak of the actions that bother her—he leaves his dirty underwear on the floor for her to pick up, doesn't listen to her, or won't help her with the housework. Rather, she will describe the problem in terms of his personality and his presumed attitude toward her—he is sloppy, lazy, and doesn't love her. This attribution of the causes of his misbehaviors constitutes what Kelley refers to as a *sanction.* That is, the wife calls attention to what the husband is doing wrong and *challenges* him to prove that her attribution of the causes is incorrect.

The husband, on the other hand, will attribute his faults to environmental stress, such as problems he is experiencing at work. He perceives himself as still being deeply in love with her, and believes she ought to forgive him for his minor misbehaviors because his *intentions* are good. When his wife fails to forgive him, he

Harold H. Kelley

attributes her anger to such traits as "moodiness" and "bad temper."

If the husband changes his behaviors, the wife may not be satisfied if she thinks he is merely trying to appease her. Because she *attributes* his actions to "underlying traits and attitudes," she wants an *attitudinal change* from him rather than a mere shift in the way he acts. At this point, Kelley notes, the husband is in something of a bind. Since his wife can never *see* his attitudes or intentions *directly*, the only thing he can do is to change his behaviors toward her. But she is always free to *interpret* these behavioral changes any way she wishes, and he cannot prove her wrong (Kelley, 1981, 1984).

□□ QUESTION □□
How does the attribution process help explain the popularity of the "trait approach" to describing human personality?

When Attributional Conflicts Occur
In a recent book, Harold Kelley and his colleagues describe those situations in which attributional conflicts are most likely to occur between two people.

The first observation Kelley and his associates make is this one: You typically make use of the attribution process in situations of conflict of interest. And you tend to use attributions in order to escape the constraints of social control or to deal with social conflict. Thus, you are much more likely to use the attribution process when interpreting "bad" behaviors than "good" behaviors.

The second observation by Kelley *et al.* is that most attributional conflicts aren't about which factors were *present* in the conflict situation. Rather, the dispute usually concerns which factors were *crucial*. Since there are always many factors present in any social situation, the person using the attribution process can almost always find one to suit his or her fancy.

Kelley and his colleagues believe that attributional conflicts are usually irresolvable. Why? For three reasons. First, there are no objective (behavioral) standards by which one person can *prove* another's attributions are wrong or his or her own attributions are correct. Second, most people *genuinely believe* they have an accurate understanding of why they act as they do—and that their explanations of "why" are justified by "the facts." Third, most people perceive *explaining* their actions as a "good behavior" designed to reduce social stress. Thus,

when you use the attribution process, you may actually see yourself as "playing the peacemaker's role." And most of us are extremely reluctant to give up what we perceive as being "socially-approved roles" (Kelley *et al.*, 1983).

□□ QUESTION □□
In a recent study, Bernice and Albert Lott found that, regardless of race or gender, "persons in winning, positive situations" were perceived as being more attractive than were "persons in losing, negative situations" (Lott & Lott, 1986). How would you explain this finding in terms of attribution theory?

SOCIAL ROLES

Attributions are *highly-personal* explanations for behaviors. But you may also excuse your actions in terms of *social expectations*. That is, you may describe what you did as "merely playing the role that society has put you in."

As we shift our attention from attributions to social roles, we move slightly up the ladder—away from the individual toward larger social systems. For "traits" are generally perceived as intra-psychic factors. Roles, however, are *systematic behavior patterns* that are embedded in the structure of groups, organizations, and societies rather than inside the individual's psyche. You *are* generous or stingy. But you *play the role* of doctor, lawyer, merchant, or thief.

□□ QUESTION □□
Are social roles learned or innate?

• Social Roles Defined
According to Theodore Newcomb, a *social role* is a more-or-less stereotyped set of responses that you make to related or similar situations. Some roles (such as socially-approved "masculine" and "feminine" behaviors) are a basic part of your **repertory** all through your life and are influenced by your genetic blueprint (see Chapter 7). Other roles seem to be entirely learned, such as that of "leader" or "manager."

Learned, innate, or (more likely) a mixture thereof, two things seem to be true of roles: First, the *concept* of a role may well be embedded in society's norms. However, the *manner in which you play* a role is determined both by your genes and by your unique personality. Second, the *purpose* of most roles seems to be that of making "social interactions" go more smoothly (Newcomb, 1961).

• Types of Roles
There are many types of roles. And, as Shakespeare put it centuries ago, "One man in his time plays many parts." This much, everyone admits, just as most psychologists agree that

role-learning usually occurs through imitation. However, there is little agreement on how and why you switch from one role to another in certain situations. And there also isn't much consensus on which social roles are the most important ones to study.

Social psychologists have researched the *leadership role* for many years, however. And while theorists disagree on why certain individuals become leaders and others don't, some aspects of the leader's role are fairly well defined (at least for our culture). Given the amount of information we have on the subject of leadership, therefore, suppose we look at this topic first.

□□ **QUESTION** □□
Assume you have a "social interaction sequence" with a physician. How would your knowledge about *social roles* affect the way you perceived and responded to this individual? Would you have reacted differently had the other person been a "janitor" rather than a "doctor"? Why? And how does the presence of clearly-understood roles help reduce stress in "social interaction sequences"?

Leadership Roles

Many years ago, Harvard sociologist Robert Bales and his colleagues performed a classic set of experiments on leadership. Their subjects were groups of male college students brought together in a laboratory and given certain intellectual problems to solve. Bales *et al.* measured the men's verbal behaviors as objectively as they could. And at the end of each problem-solving session, the experimenters asked the subjects to rate each member of the group in a number of ways, including how much the man liked the others and which men seemed to be leaders or have the best ideas (Bales, 1953).

● *Two Types of Specialists*
Bales and his associates found that two types of people got high scores on the leadership rating scales: the "idea generator" (or *task specialist*) and the "social facilitator" (or *social-emotional specialist*).

During group sessions, the task specialist gave opinions and made suggestions more often than anyone else. He kept reminding the group of its goals and brought the group back to the task at hand whenever the members strayed from problem solving. These behaviors apparently caused other group members to rate the man as a good leader or idea-generator.

The social-emotional specialist, on the other hand, was much more likely to *ask* for suggestions than to give them. He was particu-

larly sensitive to the needs of others. He made extensive use of praise and other forms of feedback, and he smoothed over arguments in order to create what Bales calls *group solidarity*. In short, he "shaped" the group into moving farther toward its goals.

According to Bales, the "task specialist" directed the cognitive or intellectual resources of the group, and was respected for his knowledge and expertise. The "social facilitator" directed the emotional resources of the group, and was warmly liked for his ability to keep the group functioning as a **cohesive** unit (Bales *et al.*, 1953).

□□ **QUESTION** □□
The noted Chinese scholar Lao-Tzu once said, "When a great leader finishes a project, the people rejoice and say, 'We did this ourselves.'" Which of the two types of leaders did Lao-Tzu apparently have in mind?

● *Leadership "Traits" or Leadership "Behaviors"?*
There have been hundreds, if not thousands, of studies attempting to determine the "traits of leadership." One of the "personality characteristics" of any great leader is supposed to be *charisma*, which Webster's defines as "a personal magic of leadership arousing special popular loyalty or enthusiasm." But according to management expert Peter Drucker, effective leadership "has little to do with 'leadership qualities' and even less to do with 'charisma.' It is mundane, unromantic and boring. Its essence is performance" (Drucker, 1988).

The most charismatic leaders of this century, Drucker says, were Hitler, Stalin, and Mao—"the misleaders who inflicted as much evil and suffering on humanity as have ever been recorded. . . . Dwight Eisenhower, George Marshall and Harry Truman were singularly effective leaders yet none possessed any more charisma than a dead mackerel" (Drucker, 1988).

Nor is there a "leadership personality," Drucker says. Rather, he claims, leadership is mostly *hard work*. Effective leaders set clear-cut goals, establish standards of conduct (and enforce them), listen attentively to their subordinates, and "praise and promote" those subordinates for actual achievement (Drucker, 1988).

What Drucker seems to be saying, of course, is that social roles must be defined in terms of *behaviors,* not in terms of "attitudes" or "personality traits."

● *Successful Managers*
A study reported in 1979 by Texas psychologists Jay Hall and Susan Donnell seems to support Drucker's views. Hall and Donnell mea-

Robert Bales

sured the attitudes and behaviors of more than 12,000 managers in 50 different US business and government organizations. By determining how rapidly each manager moved up through the corporate structure, Hall and Donnell were able to identify "successful," "average," and "unsuccessful" managers.

Hall and Donnell found that *successful* managers almost always sought the opinions and consent of the people who worked for them. *Average* and *unsuccessful* managers, however, did not encourage much participation at all from their subordinates.

Jay Hall and Susan Donnell believe that a manager's *goals* in large part determine how successful the manager will be. They report that successful managers showed *both* a strong interest in achieving organizational goals *and* in helping their subordinates satisfy their personal needs. "Average" managers also tried to "get the task done," but had considerably less concern about what happened to their employees in the process. The unsuccessful managers appeared to be protecting themselves. They had little commitment either to the goals of the organization or to satisfying the needs of those individuals whom they supervise (Hall & Donnell, 1979).

□ □ **QUESTION** □ □

What similarity do you see between Hall's "unsuccessful managers" and the "women with low social competence" described earlier in this chapter?

• **Women Managers**

The first study by Jay Hall and Susan Donnell dealt exclusively with male managers. In their second study, they gave similar measures to women managers and to their subordinates. Out of the dozens of measures they took, Donnell and Hall found only two real differences between male and female executives. First, women seem to be more "achievement oriented" than are their male counterparts. And second, women managers seem to be less open and candid in relating to their colleagues than are males. Donnell and Hall conclude that "Women, in general, do not differ from men, in general, in the ways in which they administer the management process" (Hall & Donnell, 1979).

According to Donnell and Hall, there is a certain irony in these results. For one of the main problems that women managers have is that males *perceive* the women as being skilled

Although women are often stereotyped as being skilled at handling social-emotive situations, research indicates that women business managers tend to take a more rational, less emotional approach than their male counterparts.

at handling social-emotive resources, but as being poor at task achievement. In fact, the truth is just the opposite—males (in general) are less oriented toward achievement than are women managers, and males may be more skilled at interpersonal relations than the present crop of female managers are. Yet, as long as males dominate the work scene, it is their *perceptions* of women that make the difference, not the actual behaviors of the women themselves (Hall & Donnell, 1979).

□ □ **QUESTION** □ □

Given the fact that women appear to be as effective leaders as are males, why have we never had a woman president? A black president? What do your answers tell you about the influence of *environmental factors* on social roles?

• **Leadership: Personal Qualities or Situation?**

Many psychologists—particularly those with a "disposition" toward explaining human behavior in terms of inner traits—continue to believe that you are either a "born leader," or that you become one because of the structure of your personality. At the most, these theorists say, the environment may *restrict* your opportunities for taking on a leadership role (Graumann & Moscovici, 1986).

However, a growing number of theorists see social roles as resulting from an *interaction* between "person and situation" (Magnusson, 1981). Data to support this view come from research by Reuven Gal, who was, for many years, chief psychologist of the Israeli Defense Forces. Gal studied 77 soldiers who were decorated for bravery during the Yom Kippur war. He then compared these "heroic leaders" with 273 similar soldiers who had not received medals. All the soldiers had taken psychological tests *before* the war broke out. Gal found that the "heroes" were significantly higher on four traits: leadership, devotion to duty, decisiveness, and perseverance under stress.

Gal then asked three military psychologists to analyze the actual battle conditions under which the "heroes" had won their medals. He then concluded that "In many of the given cases it was predominantly the specific . . . circumstances that evoked the exceptional behavior, while the determination of the particular individual who would accomplish this behavior was almost by chance" (Gal, 1986; cited in Horn, 1985).

▢▢ QUESTION ▢▢
Some soldiers win medals; others don't. Some military personnel are high-paid officers with special privileges; others are low-paid enlisted personnel. But almost all soldiers risk their lives during a war. Is this "inequity" fair?

Social Exchange Theory
All groups, organizations, and societies have certain *resources* available to them. Some of these "resources" may be material; others are psychological or social. Within any group, however, certain "roles" (such as those associated with leadership) have a stronger claim on available resources than do other more subordinate "roles." If there is to be *stability* in a group or organization, however, there must be some *equity* in the way that resources are shared—or exchanged.

Japanese psychologist Kazuko Inoue studied *equity relationships* in couples who were "going steady." Inoue found that both male and female "dating partners" tended to agree as to how *equitable* their relationships were. And the more *inequitable* the relationships, the more distress *both* partners felt. Generally speaking, both partners strove to *restore equity* to the relationship. If they failed, they tended to break off the romance—and seek more equitable relationships with other people (Inoue, 1985).

But what is "equity," and how do people achieve it? University of Illinois psychologist Harry C. Triandis views the process of human interaction from the perspective of *social exchange theory*. That is, he believes human relations are governed by "exchanges of resources." You want things from me, and I want things from you. The question then becomes, how do I discover what you want, and how do we negotiate an exchange of resources that satisfies both of us?

• *Roles as "Behavioral Intentions"*
Harry C. Triandis believes your actions are determined primarily by two things: habits, and behavioral intentions. *Habits* are those stereotyped ways you have of responding to specific situations. Your *behavioral intentions* are, more or less, whatever set of goals you are trying to reach at any given moment. These momentary goals are affected by many things—the roles you have learned, your emotional reactions, and your cognitive expectancies (Triandis, 1984).

Triandis believes the first thing you must do when you learn a new role is this: You have to discover what *behavioral intentions* are associated with that role. Thus, when you meet someone new, learning what role the person has assumed will tell you a great deal about that person's intentions. Therefore, you learn about other people's roles in order to find what "social exchanges" they are interested in (Triandis & Lambert, 1980).

According to Triandis, if you know my intentions, you can guess at what I want—and what I am willing to pay for satisfying this goal. But the intentions you *attribute* to me are strongly influenced by *your own social expectations*. And your expectations, of course, are strongly influenced by the society you grew up in (Triandis & Brislin, 1984).

In a series of recent studies, Triandis and his colleagues report on what happens when two people from different cultures meet and interact. Most subjects Triandis and his associates have studied assume that someone from a different country *must have the same intentions as they do*. Thus, most Japanese will explain the behavior of Americans in terms of Japanese tradition and culture, while Americans find it difficult to believe that the Japanese aren't motivated by precisely the same intentions as we have (Hui & Triandis, 1986; Kashima & Triandis, 1986).

Doubtless it is true, as Triandis and others claim, that behavior is determined by the *interaction* between situational and personal factors. However, to date no theory tells us which of these two influences will predominate in any given setting. If you are like most people, you probably assume that your own long-standing goals and values will assert themselves no matter what. However, as you are about to see, there are times when the situational factors are so powerful that almost anyone will behave in an unusual, or even shocking, fashion.

Harry C. Triandis

▢▢ QUESTION ▢▢
From your own experience, which "role" do you know the most about, that of "prison guard" or that of "prisoner"?

Zimbardo's "Jail"

As we noted, roles can be thought of as a set of behavioral expectancies. For example, you could play the role of a police officer if you were called upon to do so. You would know you were "just acting a part." However, someone watching you perform might well *attribute* your actions to some deep-seated character trait. The fact that most people in our culture tend to perceive behaviors as being caused more by attributed traits than role-play may explain why the public reacted so negatively to research performed by Stanford psychologist Philip Zimbardo (Haney, Banks, & Zimbardo, 1981; Zimbardo *et al.*, 1973).

Several years ago, Philip Zimbardo and his students studied the "roles" that people play in prison situations. Zimbardo and his group took over a basement corridor in the psychology building at Stanford and converted it into a mock prison. Next, they put an ad in two local papers offering to hire students to play the roles of prisoners and guards for a two-week period. Zimbardo interviewed all the volunteers, screened them for physical and mental health problems, and then selected the 21 men who seemed most healthy, mature, and "normal." On a random basis, 11 of them were chosen to be "guards," while the other 10 were to be "prisoners."

The guards were given special uniforms designed to look "official." The prisoners were required to wear muslin smocks, a light chain and lock around one ankle, and a cap made from a nylon stocking. Each prisoner was given a toothbrush, towels, soap, and bed linen. No personal belongings were allowed in the cells.

Zimbardo and the guards developed a set of "rules" the prisoners were expected to memorize and follow while in jail. The prisoners were expected to "work" in order to earn their $15 daily payment. Twice a week, the prisoners were allowed visitors. The guards could also give them a variety of "rewards" for good behavior, including the right to exercise in the "yard" and to attend movies.

The first clue as to how the study would turn out came during the "count" of the prisoners the guards took three times daily. The first day, the "count" took 10 minutes or less. But by the second day, the guards starting using "count time" to harass the prisoners, so the time increased. By the fifth day, some of the "counts" lasted for several hours as the guards berated the prisoners for minor infractions of the "rules."

● *Deindividuation*

Philip Zimbardo had designed his experiment in an attempt to study some of the conditions that lead to *deindividuation*, or "depersonalization." He quickly discovered that one primary factor was the behavior of the guards, who rapidly began treating the prisoners as "non-persons" who weren't really humans at all.

As far as "deindividuation" went, however, the *reactions* of the prisoners were probably just as important as the *actions* of the guards. Instead of protesting their treatment, some of the prisoners began to act in depressed, institutionalized, dependent ways—exactly the role behaviors shown by many real-life prisoners and mental patients. And, as you might guess, the more the prisoners acted like "non-persons," the more they were mistreated by the guards.

By the end of the sixth day, the situation had nearly gotten out of hand. The guards began modifying or changing the prison "rules" and routines to make them increasingly more punitive. And even some of Zimbardo's students got so caught up in the spirit of things, they neglected to give the prisoners some of the privileges they had earned.

At this point, wisely, Zimbardo called a halt to the proceedings (Zimbardo, 1975).

□ □ **QUESTION** □ □
How do the actions of the guards and the reactions of the prisoners fit Darley and Fazio's "five-step social interaction process"?

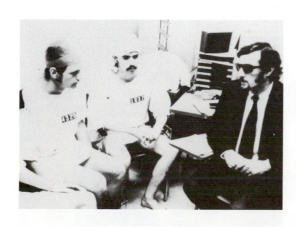 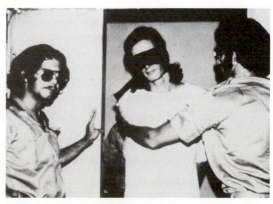

Philip Zimbardo and his students at Stanford University studied the dehumanizing effects of a mock prison environment.

After stopping the experiment, Zimbardo and his students interviewed all of the subjects and analyzed the video tapes they had made during the six days. Perhaps their most important finding is that the subjects simply "became" the roles that they played. *All* of the 11 guards behaved in abusive, dehumanizing ways toward the prisoners. Some of them did so only occasionally. But *more than a third* of the guards were so consistently hostile and degrading that Zimbardo refers to their behavior as sadistic.

Many (but not all) of the prisoners, on the other hand, showed a reaction which (in Chapter 8) we called *learned helplessness*. Day by day, these prisoners did less and less, initiated fewer conversations, and became more surly and depressed. Five of the prisoners were unable to cope with their own reactions and asked to leave. But the other five seemed to accept their fates and (in a few cases) didn't even bother to "request parole" when given a chance to do so.

The second important finding Zimbardo made is obvious but, to most people, simply unbelievable: There was absolutely *no prior evidence* that the subjects would react as they did. Before their random selection as guard or prisoner, the two groups did not differ from each other in any way that Zimbardo could discover. All 21 were healthy, normal, mature young men—and not one of them predicted he would act as he did. Furthermore, there is no reason to believe that the study would have turned out any different *had the roles of the two groups been reversed*.

One of the personality tests Zimbardo used is the F-Scale, which measures **authoritarianism**. Surprisingly enough, the guards didn't differ from the prisoners on this scale, nor were the "sadistic" guards more authoritarian (as measured by the test) than were the more "humanitarian" guards. However, the prisoners who refused to leave were, generally speaking, the ones who scored as being the *most authoritarian*. Zimbardo believes these men were psychologically better prepared to cope with the highly-structured and punitive environment of the prison.

The third finding is perhaps less surprising. At no time did any guard ever *reward* a prisoner for anything. The only "correctional" techniques the guards ever employed were criticism, punishment, and harassment.

□ □ **QUESTION** □ □

Given the data, can you be *really* sure that you wouldn't have played the guard or prisoner role exactly as Zimbardo's subjects did?

● **Public Reaction**

The results of his experiment distressed Zimbardo so much that he made them available to the news media almost immediately. Public reaction was swift, and primarily punitive. Many critics found it inconceivable a "noted Stanford professor" would undertake such a dehumanizing study. Most of these same critics also suggested Zimbardo must have picked a very abnormal bunch of young men for his subjects, because ordinary citizens surely wouldn't behave in that fashion.

In fact, there is no better illustration of the *attribution process* at work than Zimbardo's study. At first the prisoners tended to blame their behaviors on the situation they were in. But eventually many of them became depressed and attributed their failure to cope to their own "innate trait of spinelessness." The guards tended to justify their harassment in terms of "being paid to do the job," as well as the "criminal instincts" they perceived in the prisoners. The critics attributed both the brutality of the guards and the "helpless" behaviors of the prisoners to innate character flaws in *those* specific men. No one caught up in the experiment—including, at times, Zimbardo and his students—perceived that the *environment* was almost entirely responsible for the behaviors of both guards and prisoners. No one saw that the men were just "playing roles."

□ □ **QUESTION** □ □

One of the problems that psychologists often face is this—their research findings occasionally contradict rather cherished notions other people have about human behavior. If you had been Zimbardo, how would you have gone about trying to convince people your results were valid?

Social Roles Versus "Attributed Motives"

Social roles are patterns of attitudes, emotions, perceptions, expectations, and behaviors that are "the norm" for a particular group, organization, or culture. They seem to be learned early in life, primarily through observation and imitation. Although some aspects may be innately determined, *roles are primarily determined by the social situation*.

Social situations can have a strong influence on behavior. It is unlikely that any one of these young men would engage in this behavior if he were alone.

20 / Person Perception, Attribution, and Social Roles

Most of the things you do, think, and feel are strongly influenced by the conditions you grew up in and by your present social milieu. But society still *attributes* the causes of human behavior to such internal processes as "personality" and "character." So if you find yourself attributing motives and intentions to other people, perhaps that is merely a role *you* have been taught to play.

Fortunately, however, there are ways to change both perceptions and roles.

Changing Perceptions, Changing Roles

At the beginning of this chapter, we listed five steps that John Darley and Russell Fazio believe "define" the social interaction sequence: First, you perceive someone else (usually in a stereotyped fashion) and generate expectancies about that individual. Next, you act in accord with your perception. Then the other person interprets the "meaning" of your action, and responds accordingly. Finally, you interpret the other person's response and then either break off the interaction or move on to another five-step sequence. Darley and Fazio note, however, that occasionally there is a sixth step to the sequence. That is, at some point you may pause and wonder why *you* responded the way you did.

Most of the time, of course, you may interpret your own actions as appropriate and as being "caused" by the other person. But, occasionally, you might well learn something new about yourself. And as a result of this gain in self-knowledge, you could change your perception both of yourself and of others (Darley & Fazio, 1980).

Now that you know something about person perception, stereotypes, attribution conflicts, and role theory, perhaps you might wish to add step six to more of your own social interaction sequences.

SUMMARY

1. **Social psychology** deals with **relationships among people,** while other fields of psychology tend to focus on the **individual**.
2. According to **General Systems Theory**, a **group** is a simple social system made up of individuals, an **organization** is a more complex social system made up of such subsystems as individuals and groups, and **society** is a very complex social system made up of subsystems such as individuals, groups, and organizations.
3. Five important issues **social psychologists** deal with are
   a. Should the focus be on the **individual** or the **group**?
   b. Is social psychology the study of **attitudes**, or **behaviors**?
   c. Are attitudes and behaviors **learned** or **innate**?
   d. Should the focus be on **consistent features** (such as social structures) or on **changeable aspects** (functions) of groups and organizations?
   e. Is social psychology primarily **theoretical** or **applied**?
4. Generally speaking, social **psychologists** focus on the individual, while **social** psychologists look at group and organizational structures and functions.
5. **Attitudes** are consistent ways of thinking about, feeling toward, or responding to some environmental stimulus or input. Generally speaking, attitudes are **learned** by acquiring new **behaviors**.
6. Social psychology tends to be more **applied** than other areas, in part because of its use of human subjects. **Action research** involves experiments performed in real-life settings.
7. The **social interaction sequence** has five steps: (a) You meet someone and **generate expectancies**, (b) you **act** in accordance with your expectancies, (c) the other person **interprets** the meaning of your actions, (d) the other person then responds, and (e) you then **interpret** the meaning of the other person's response.
8. **Person perception** is defined as the process by which you come to perceive, remember, and respond to people as you do.
9. **First impressions** of people are determined by such factors as **prior attitudes**, **reputations**, **stereotypes**, **self-fulfilling prophecies**, the **primacy** and **recency effects**, and by **autistic hostility**, or the tendency to repress favorable data about people or things you dislike.
10. First impressions of someone are also influenced by **present stimulus inputs**, including the person's **physical appearance** and **body language**.
11. We tend to attribute **good traits** to good-looking people and **bad traits** to less attractive individuals.
12. Most people tend to think that your body language signals your **intentions**, or your **underlying traits and motives**. Research suggests people with **low social competence** may be better at detecting body language signals than in responding to them properly.
13. If your actions are **incongruent** with peo-

ple's expectations of you, the people tend to "explain away" these behavioral inconsistencies but **remember** them more clearly than actions that confirm expectations.

14. Each of us seems to have a **personal space** around us that we defend as our **psychological territory**. The size of our territory is determined by the culture we grew up in and by our **status** in that culture. We tend to **approach** (or lean toward) people we like, and **retreat** (or lean away from) people we don't like.

15. Each culture has its own rules for **eye contact** that determine the ways in which people converse with each other—and sometimes make it hard for people from different cultures to communicate with one another.

16. We tend to perceive people with **inappropriate eye contact** as being of low status, or as being mentally or socially handicapped.

17. In order to predict and influence the actions of others, we use the **attribution process**. That is, we attribute motives and intentions to them that make their behaviors understandable to us. However, we often see our own actions as responses to the **social environment**.

18. Harold Kelley believes that long-term relationships are determined by **interdependence**, **responsiveness**, and **attributions**.

19. Relationships are interdependent because the **costs and benefits** are a joint function of the behavior of both partners. If the partners are responsive to each other's **needs**, the partners will attribute to each other the trait of **lovingness**.

20. Marriage partners are inclined to explain problems in terms of **attributed traits** rather than **observed behaviors**. To resolve the problems, both partners may desire **attitudinal change** rather than mere **behavioral change**.

21. People are more likely to use the **attribution process** in conflict than in nonconflict situations.

22. Both our genes and our early experiences affect our **social roles**.

23. Research on problem solving in small groups suggests that there are two types of **leadership roles**, the **task specialist** and the **social-emotional specialist**.

24. Studies of 12,000 US managers suggest that successful supervisors tend to use **participatory management** techniques, while average or below-average supervisors tend to manage in an **authoritarian** way.

25. Women managers tend to be slightly more **task oriented** than men, who seem to be somewhat better at **social relations**. Overall, though, there is little difference between men and women managers.

26. **Leadership** appears to be a quality that emerges in certain **specific situations**.

27. Triandis views the process of human interaction as little more than an **exchange of resources**. In order to get what we want from others, we must therefore guess their **behavioral intentions**.

28. Zimbardo's **jail study** suggests that abnormal behaviors such as **authoritarianism, social aggression**, and **deindividuation** may be nothing more than **role behaviors** determined primarily by the **social milieu** in which they occur.

29. Critics of Zimbardo's research prefer to **attribute** his results to **innate traits**, but the critics themselves may be just playing a **learned social role**.

30. An occasional **sixth step** in the **social interaction sequence** is that of **changing** your attitudes, perceptions, and behaviors based on what you have learned from the sequence.

DAY 5

(Continued from page 517.)

I don't understand why Warden Matossian stopped the experiment. We had the riot under control, and we hadn't violated the Regulations. I mean, it isn't really physical punishment if you just poke the Numbers a little. That sort of stuff goes on in jails all the time, doesn't it? And how else were we going to get 853 to obey the Rules?

I looked at some of the video tapes that Dr. Matossian took, particularly the last one showing how we settled 853's hash. And I had to grin. I don't think I will ever forget the sight of him standing there, with that sausage sticking out of his mouth.

I watched that final tape twice, and even if I do say it myself, I think I came out of the whole thing looking pretty darn good. Like, when I got there, all of the #'s were backed into a corner of the yard, and the CO's on the evening shift were pointing the nozzle of a fire extinguisher at them. Old 853 was shaking one of those stupid sausages at the CO's, and they were shaking their billy-clubs back at him. But nobody was getting anywhere. And I saw what I had to do, right off.

I told the CO with the nozzle to keep me covered, and motioned to the other two CO's to come with me. Then we marched right up to 853.

"Grab his arms, men," I said, and they did. He seemed shocked and started to struggle, but the CO's straightened him out right away. Then I grabbed the sausage and stuck it right in 853's

20 / Person Perception, Attribution, and Social Roles

face. "Listen, twerp," I said, "We are going to finish this business *right now*. Then you are going to *apologize*, and we are going to get back on the Routine, just like the Rules say."

853 gave me some smart-ass reply, so I jabbed his nose with the sausage and said, "I will give you five seconds to start eating, or I am going to cram this thing down your throat, and it will serve you right if you choke."

He gave me this peculiar look, like he didn't recognize who I was because of my mirror sunglasses, or something. Then I started to count, "One . . . Two . . . Three . . . Four . . . Five!"

Well, at that moment 853 opened up his mouth to say something, and I jammed the sausage right between his teeth. "Bite," I said, in a firm tone of voice. But all that animal did was grin at me defiantly. So, I jabbed him in the stomach with my billy-club. Just a firm little poke, but sudden like, if you know what I mean. Well, his teeth chomped shut automatically, and there was the first bite of the sausage inside his mouth.

"Now chew," I said. And to help things along, I jabbed him another good one. I guess the sausage must have had a lot of pepper in it, because his eyes started to water. He stared at me sort of funny, and then his eyes watered some more.

And then, ever so slowly, #853 started to chew.

And everybody breathed a sigh of relief. The Rules were Obeyed.

For some reason, that's when Dr. Matossian came out and stopped the game. I mean, why then? We had it all under control, and could have gone right back to the Routine. That way, we'd have earned the full 300 bucks.

Well, even if Charlie did cost me the money, he taught me something important. I was looking at the tape, see, and I had this sudden insight. Old friend Charlie was *enjoying* himself, getting all that attention for flouting the Rules that way. The way I see it, Charlie has got some basic flaw in his moral character. He's just a little *bent*, if you know what I mean. Fortunately, I discovered the truth in time, before asking him to take on the role of my legal partner.

Not that I don't still like the kid, sort of. I'm not even mad that he won't converse with me, because I figure he's depressed about how he behaved. He did say we ought to go talk to Dr. Matossian and apologize for what happened, but I don't see much sense in that. He can go if he wants to, but I have nothing to apologize for.

I was just doing my job.

Social Groups, Persuasion, and Attitude Change

"The Mind Benders"

· C · H · A · P · T · E · R ·
21

"Tell me, Mr. Kraus, what area of psychology are you most interested in?"

Norman Kraus squirmed around in the hard, wooden chair. It pained him that his adviser, Professor Ronald Ward, kept such uncomfortable chairs in his office. Professor Ward's seat, of course, was a soft armchair covered with English leather.

"Well, sir, I'm most turned on by social psychology, I guess."

"Good, good. Bloody important field," the professor said. "Many excellent experiments that you could replicate as your training research."

Norm Kraus squinted at his adviser. Ward spoke with a slight British accent that oddly annoyed Norm. He assumed the man took this means of reminding everyone that he had spent several years at Oxford. Then it dawned on Norm what Ward had said.

"Replicate?"

"Yes, of course. We expect our first-year graduate students to replicate, or to repeat as exactly as possible, some piece of published research. Learn by doing what's already been well done, that's our motto."

"If you don't mind, sir, I'd really rather do something new, something no one's tried before."

Professor Ward nodded sagely. "Yes, I'm sure you would. And did you have something particular in mind?"

Norman Kraus stopped to consider. "No, but I thought we could figure something out."

The professor's lips pursed into a bitter-lemon smile. "There, you see what I mean. Our attitude is that students should learn to walk before they attempt to run. Try something we know will work first, before they exercise their presumed creativity." Ward coughed discreetly, then continued. "Now, what part of social psychology would you like to work on?"

Norm's anger might have boiled over had he not suddenly recalled his father's advice: "If you want to get along with people, you have to go along with people." But a devilish urge still prompted him to say, "I'd like to find out why people knuckle under to other people."

Professor Ward glanced at the young man sharply, then frowned. "I presume you are referring to the conformity experiments. The early studies by Muzafer Sherif and Solomon Asch opened the field up, of course, but I've always liked the work that Bob Blake and his group did at Texas back in the '50's. Particularly their use of tape recorders to create synthetic social environments. Have you read Blake's experiments?"

The wooden seat was getting more uncomfortable by the moment. "No, sir."

Ward leaned back in his leather armchair, lit his pipe, and continued. "Asch had students guess the length of lines—a very easy task if no one were around to influence their decisions. But when the students had to judge immediately after several other subjects had spoken, matters got sticky. The other subjects were 'stooges,' paid by Asch to lie about which line was longest. If the stooges gave patently stupid judgments, the students often 'knuckled under' and gave incorrect reports themselves. The presence of the group of stooges was apparently so intimidating that many of Asch's subjects conformed to the false group standard."

"And what did Blake do?" Norm asked, in a slightly desperate tone of voice. This stuff sounded even duller than the flatworm research another professor had tried to talk him into doing.

Ward tapped his pipe on an ashtray and continued. "Blake and one of his graduate students proved that the stooges didn't have to be physically present. Just hearing a tape recording of the stooges' voices was enough to pressure the subject into conforming. They reported this research at the 1953 meeting of the American Psychological Association in Cleveland, as I recall."

Inwardly, Norm Kraus groaned. Professor Ward's memory for trivial detail was legendary. He should have been a cop instead of a professor, Norm told himself. But aloud he said, "Gee, that's interesting. Do you remember exactly what they did?"

Professor Ward smiled, delighted at the chance to show off. "They used the auto-kinetic effect, as did Sherif. You may recall that if you look at a stationary pinpoint of light in a dark room, the light seems to dance around like a firefly. Because the apparent movement is created by the person's own eyes, everybody sees a rather different dance. Given a 10-second exposure to the light, some people will say that it moved a few millimeters, some will say it danced several meters, while others may insist that it hardly moved at all."

Fireflies? Norm thought. In an experiment on *social* psychology? Maybe he had better go back to the worms after all.

The psychologist plowed right on, as if not noticing Norm's dismay. "Because the auto-kinetic, or self-movement, effect is so subjective, it's rather easy to pressure people into conforming to group standards. But that's not what the experiment looked like to the subjects, who were undergraduate males at Texas. They were told it was a study on visual perception. The US Air Force, so the subjects were informed, wanted to find out how people judged the movement of tiny lights on the horizon. So the psychologists had devised a complicated and very expensive piece of apparatus that simulated the movement of airplanes in a night-time sky."

"What was the apparatus like?" Norm asked, beginning to be interested in spite of himself.

Ward snorted with amusement. "An empty tin can with a hole punched in one end. There was a flashlight bulb inside the can that could be turned on and off from the next room. Blake and his student hired four stooges to sit in the dark room and give false reports on how far the light moved. The real subjects were called into the room one at a time and sat directly in the middle of the stooges. During each trial, the light went on for 10 seconds, after which each person was asked to report how far it seemed to move. The four stooges always gave their reports first, before the real subject did.

Norm looked puzzled. "Didn't the real subject know the others were stooges?"

"Certainly not. They looked and acted just like real subjects would have acted—they asked questions and complained about the stupidity of the study."

"And it worked?" Norm asked.

Professor Ward lit his pipe again. "Only too well. About two-thirds of the subjects were greatly influenced by what the stooges said."

"And that was news?"

"No, but the second part of the study was. In this part, the subjects sat in the room alone and merely heard the tape-recorded voices of the stooges. Naturally, the subject didn't know a recording was being used."

Norm wiggled around on the hard chair. "So, what happened?"

Professor Ward smiled benevolently. "The subjects were just as influenced by the taped voices as they were when the stooges were physically present. We seem to conform to imaginary groups as much as to real ones." Ward paused to grind at his pipe with a metal tool. "Yes, I think you ought to replicate that experiment as your training research."

Norm could feel the crunch coming. "But couldn't I jazz it up a bit, just to make it more exciting?"

The Professor looked at the young man sternly. "You will learn a great deal more if you first do it exactly the way the Texas group did. Of course, if you have a streak of serendipity in your personality, you might turn up something unexpected anyhow. But be so kind as to try it our way first."

"But Professor Ward, I don't think . . ."

"Mr. Kraus," the Professor barked in a tone of absolute authority, "Our departmental rule is clear. We will expect you to replicate the Blake work *exactly*, as your training research. Report back to me after you've set things up and have run a few pilot subjects. Do you understand?"

Through gritted teeth, Norm Kraus muttered, "Yes, sir." *(Continued on page 572.)*

WHAT IS A GROUP?

In the last chapter, we looked at how your social environment affects you *as an individual*. In this chapter, we will discuss *groups* of people—how groups are formed, what keeps them together, and what the structures and functions of groups are. As you will see, one important characteristic of groups is that their members tend to have *shared attitudes*. So in the second part of the chapter, we will look at attitudes—how they are formed, how they are maintained, and how they are changed. At that point, we will also investigate such interesting topics as persuasion, propaganda, advertising, and public relations. In all these cases, you see, some group (or organization) attempts to "alter the attitudes and behaviors" of some other group or set of individuals. Finally, we will discuss the ethics of trying to persuade people to change their attitudes, and describe some recent trends in social psychology.

But the first question we must ask is, what *is* a group, and why would you want to belong to one?

□ □ **QUESTION** □ □
How many groups do you think you belong to?

Social Groups

Whenever you set up a continuing relationship of some kind with one or more other people, you have in fact either started a new **social group** or joined one already in existence. In the strictest of terms, a group is a *social system* made up of two or more individuals who are psychologically related, or who are in some way dependent on one another. Generally speaking, people who are dependent on each

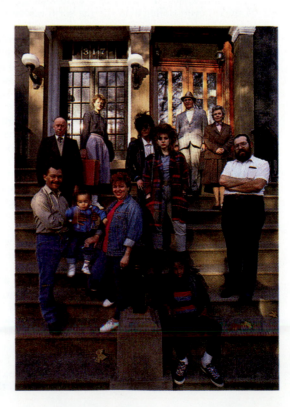

Do these people constitute a group? The answer is yes: they all live in the same New York City neighborhood. Despite their ethnic and cultural differences, they are likely to share concerns about community issues.

other are, in fact, seeking a common goal. Thus, groups, like all other living and social systems, are *goal oriented* (Miller, 1978).

You belong to dozens, if not hundreds of groups. Some are *formal membership groups*. For instance, you apply for membership in most colleges, religious groups, and tennis clubs. But you are born into *family groups* and *ethnic groups*.

Some groups, such as "all the people attending a party," are fairly temporary or very informal systems. Other groups—such as friends and lovers—are informally structured but may exist for months or years.

The most important groups in your life are typically those that (1) last a long time, and (2) are made up of people with whom you have frequent, face-to-face encounters. For obvious reasons, these are called **interaction groups** (Blumberg *et al.*, 1983).

Interaction Groups

Whenever you set up a new friendship, you have begun an interaction group. That is, you have given up some part of your own personal *independence* to create a *state of interdependence* between you and the other person. Whenever you join or create a group, you lose the privilege of "just being yourself" and of ignoring the other group members. But you may gain many things that compensate for this loss (Newcomb, 1981).

Some of the rewards for group membership are social. For example, you now have someone to talk to—someone to be with and to share things with. Other rewards are more practical or task oriented. For instance, pushing a car out of the mud, rearing a family, playing tennis, and having sex are activities that typically are more reinforcing if two or more individuals participate.

Most interaction groups, then, are made up of people who have affection and respect for each other, who have similar attitudes toward a number of things, or who have a common set of goals and interests (Blumberg *et al.*, 1983).

□ □ QUESTION □ □
In Chapter 20, we noted that unmarried couples living together didn't establish

"personal territories," while married couples did. How would you explain this result in terms of "group membership"?

Group Structure and Function

As Theodore Newcomb noted many years ago, groups typically form when two or more people sense that the pleasure of each other's company would be more *rewarding* than remaining socially isolated (Newcomb, 1961). Most such groups are informal.

Generally speaking, an informal group does not have a *stated set of regulations* governing the behavior of its members (as does a formal group). But informal groups do have "informal rules," most of which are based on *cultural expectations* of how people should behave when they are together. If you misbehave at a party—if you are too noisy, if you spill drinks on people, or assault the host or hostess—you might well be asked to leave.

As Newcomb points out, one of the major characteristics of any group is the *shared acceptance of group rules by all the members*. This acceptance may be conscious or unconscious, but it is almost always present in one form or another (Newcomb, 1981).

Part of the fun of forming a two-person friendship group (becoming friends or lovers) often is trying to understand what the other person wants. That is, the early pleasures of *dyadic relationships* often come from determining what *rules of the game* the two of you believe ought to be followed. If the person is very much like you, perhaps little or no discussion of the rules may be necessary. If the person is very different from you, the dyad may not last for long (although it can be an exciting relationship at the very beginning).

In most cases where the members of a dyad are neither too similar nor too different, each person will compromise a little. For no group can maintain itself unless there is some minimal agreement or **consensus** as to what its members can and can't do (Hewstone, 1988).

□ □ QUESTION □ □
How would "social exchange theorists" probably define a group?

Group Norms

Newcomb also noted that the ability to predict the behavior of people and objects in our world appears to be innately rewarding. One of the most reinforcing aspects of belonging to a group is that each member can to some extent predict what the other members are likely to think and do in most situations. Perhaps that is why group rules are almost always stated in terms of behavioral or attitudinal *norms*. That is, the rules specify what the average or *norm-*

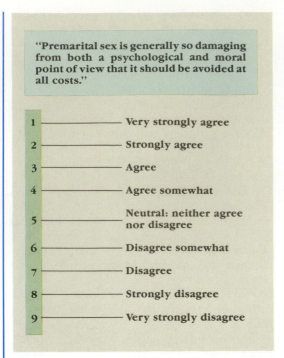

"Premarital sex is generally so damaging from both a psychological and moral point of view that it should be avoided at all costs."

1 ——————— Very strongly agree

2 ——————— Strongly agree

3 ——————— Agree

4 ——————— Agree somewhat

5 ——————— Neutral: neither agree nor disagree

6 ——————— Disagree somewhat

7 ——————— Disagree

8 ——————— Strongly disagree

9 ——————— Very strongly disagree

FIG. 21.1

al behavior of each member should be, or what role(s) each member should play (Newcomb, 1981).

According to Solomon Asch, no group member will fit all the norms *exactly*, just as no one is *exactly* average in all aspects of intelligence or sexual behavior. Most groups tolerate some deviation from the norm, so long as the member is not perceived by the group as playing "too abnormal" a role. The more similar the group's members are to each other, and the more emphasis the group places on "following the rules," the less deviation the group will usually tolerate (Asch, 1987). Perhaps we can demonstrate this point with an example.

Suppose we measure the attitudes toward premarital sex of two different groups—a class of students taking introductory psychology, and a group of young adults at a campus church or religious center. We will ask the members of both groups to record their agreement or disagreement with a statement about sex by placing a check mark on the 9-point attitude scale shown in Fig. 21.1.

After both groups respond, we measure the position each person has marked on the 9-point scale. We can then use the number closest to each check mark as a *scale score* that fairly accurately represents each member's attitude toward the statement on premarital sex. And, since we have a number, or score, for each person, we can calculate the mean or *average attitude* for both groups. This average would, presumably, be the group norm. We can also calculate the *range* and the *standard deviation* of scores for both groups. (See Chap-

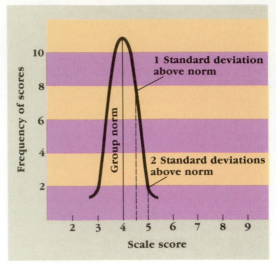

FIG. 21.2

ter 18 and the Statistical Appendix for a discussion of "range" and "standard deviation.")

For the sake of this discussion, let us assume that the mean or norm for both groups happened to be a scale score of 4: "Agree somewhat." This result might suggest to you that the church group and the psychology class were very similar, since the norm seems to be the same in both groups. But ask yourself this question: If your own position was a 6 ("Disagree somewhat"), would either group perceive you as being "too abnormal" to belong to that group?

The answer is—it depends on what each group's *standard deviation* is. Church groups, in general, are much more **homogeneous** in their attitudes toward sexual behavior than are the more random collections of students who make up classroom groupings.

The distribution of scores for the church group *might* look like those shown in Fig. 21.2.

However, the distribution of scores for the classroom group *might* look like those shown in Fig. 21.3.

FIG. 21.3

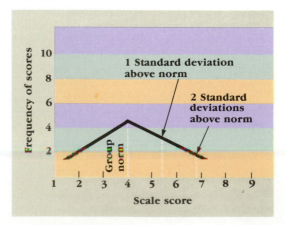

Homogeneous (ho-moh-GEE-knee-us). From the Greek words meaning "same kind." The more alike members of a group are, the more homogeneous the group is. In more technical terms, the smaller the standard deviation of a distribution of test scores, the more homogeneous the scores are.

Heterogeneous (HETT-turr-oh-GEE-knee-us). From the Greek words meaning "different kinds." The more dissimilar the members of a group are, the more heterogeneous the group is, and hence the less cohesive the group is.

As you can see, your score of 6 would be more than 2 standard deviations from the church group norm, but well within the "normal" range for the psychology class. Presumably, the church group would consider your attitude "significantly deviant," while the classroom group probably would not (Rouan & Thaon, 1985).

Generally speaking, the more homogeneous the group, the smaller its standard deviation will be on most scales. And the more **heterogeneous** the group, the larger its standard deviation will be on most measures (Sinyagin, 1985).

□□ QUESTION □□
What do you think would happen to the standard deviation of the church group's scores if you attacked the group for being narrow-minded on the subject of premarital sex?

● *Group Cohesion*

According to Theodore Newcomb, *cohesiveness* is the psychological glue that keeps group members sticking together. The more cohesive a group, the longer it will typically last and the more resistant it will be to external pressures (Newcomb, 1981).

In ordinary situations, cohesion is often a function of the homogeneity of the group—the more homogeneous the attitudes or behaviors of the members, the more cohesive the structure of the group will be. However, even such heterogeneous groups as introductory psychology classes can be made momentarily cohesive if the group is threatened by some outside force (Rouan & Thaon, 1985).

According to Kent State psychologist Stanford Gregory, members of an "established group" often adopt their own "group jargon," or unusual patterns of speech. The "jargon" not only is a "badge of group membership," but also tends to increase group cohesiveness, since outsiders often can't understand what members of the group are talking about (Gregory, 1986).

● *Temporary Versus Permanent Groups*

Some groups are permanent. But others are temporary. People riding together in an elevator are not usually considered a group, for they have no real psychological interdependencies, and their attitudes are likely to be very dissimilar on most subjects. However, if the electric power fails and the people are trapped together in the elevator for several hours, this very heterogeneous bunch of people may quickly form into a group. They will give each other psychological support and comfort, and work together on the goal of escaping.

As soon as the people are released from the stalled elevator, however, the common threat to their survival is removed. At this point, the heterogeneity of the members' attitudes and behaviors will probably overcome the temporary cohesion and the group will disband (Asch, 1987). (Individual members of the group may be similar enough to strike up friendships as a result of the experience, however.)

□□ QUESTION □□
Why do groups that were close-knit in high school tend to become less cohesive if some of the members go on to college, while others don't?

● *Group Commitment*

The members of a group often are free to abandon the group whenever they wish. But a group can survive only if it can hold its members together. One of the functions of any group, then, seems to be that of inducing the highest-possible *commitment* among its members. For the more committed to the group's norms and goals the members become, the more cohesive the group typically will be and the more homogeneous the group members' attitudes will become.

There is some evidence that the more you have to pay for group membership, the more highly you value it. Elliot Aronson and Judson Mills offered college women a chance to participate in a discussion group—if they were willing to pay a price. Half of the women were required to suffer a very embarrassing initiation in order to "buy" entrance to their discussion group. The other half of the women were put through a much milder form of initiation. Those who suffered less embarrassment liked their discussion group significantly *less* than did the women who had committed themselves to paying the much higher psychological price (Aronson & Mills, 1959).

In a recent study, University of Tennessee psychologist Larry Ingram found that religious groups often use "public testimonies" to enhance group commitment. That is, during meetings, members testify as to why they belong to the group and why their commitment to the group is so strong. According to Ingram, "testimony" can be seen as a "test of membership," and attempts by members to "enhance their status in the group." One major result of these "testimonies," however, appears to be that of strengthening group commitment by protecting members against "outside threats." Another result, of course, is that of encouraging members to *conform* to group norms (Ingram, 1986).

□ □ **QUESTION** □ □
Which country club would seem more desirable to you, one that charged a $1,000 membership fee or one that charged but $100?

GROUP PRESSURES TO CONFORM

Most of us believe our attitudes toward such things as sexual behavior, politics, economics, and religion are primarily the result of our own decision making. In truth, as Harold Kelley points out, we use the groups we belong to as reference points, or guides, for much of what we think and do.

According to Kelley, **reference groups** influence your behavior in at least two ways: First, by providing comparison points which you use in evaluating yourself and others. Second, by setting standards and rewarding you when you conform and punishing you when you do not conform to these norms. As Kelley has shown, members who express opinions, attitudes, or judgments too far from the reference group norm are typically pressured by other members to fall back into line (Kelley, 1952, 1983).

□ □ **QUESTION** □ □
Your most important reference group is usually your family. How did members of your family *set and enforce* group norms when you were growing up?

"I USED TO PANIC IF ANY TREND PASSED ME BY, BUT I NOW HAVE A SERVICE WHICH ALERTS ME TO EVERYTHING."

The Sherif Experiment

The study of how groups induce their members to conform to group norms is one of the most fascinating areas of social psychology—and probably one of the most relevant. Scientific experiments on this topic date back to 1935, when social psychologist **Muzafer Sherif** first demonstrated the effects of group pressures on visual perception. Sherif asked students to observe a pinpoint of light in a dark room and tell him how much the light moved.

When the students made their judgments sitting alone in the room, each went his or her own way. But when the students were tested in groups, the first members to give their judgments created a perceptual "group norm" that the others had trouble resisting (Sherif, 1935).

Attitudes expressed verbally in groups almost always tend to be more homogeneous than those the group members express if questioned in private (Sherif, 1936).

□ □ **QUESTION** □ □
Can you explain the phrase "divide and conquer" in terms of destroying group cohesion and reducing group pressures toward conformity?

The Asch Experiment

Several years after Sherif reported his findings, social psychologist Solomon Asch carried the matter a step farther. Asch first tested the perceptual abilities of a group of students who served as "control subjects" for the latter part of his experiment. Asch showed these controls a white card that had a black line 8 inches long drawn on it, as shown in Fig. 21.4. He referred to this as the "standard line" and asked the controls to remember it well.

Then Asch removed the first card and showed the subjects a second card that had three "comparison lines" drawn on it. The first of these lines was 8.75 inches long, the second was 10 inches, while the third was the same 8-inch length as the standard. Asch then asked

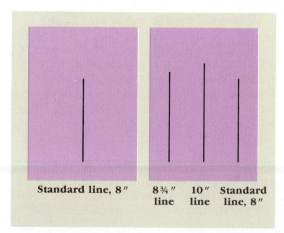

Standard line, 8"   8¾"   10"   Standard
                   line   line   line, 8"

FIG. 21.4 The lines used in Solomon Asch's experiment.

Reference groups. Those groups that set social norms you are expected to live up to. Reference groups typically determine the goals you and other group members should attain, then reward you for moving toward those goals and punish you for moving away from the goals.

Muzafer Sherif (MUZZ-a-fer shair-REEF). An early pioneer in the field of social psychology.

the control subjects to report *privately* which comparison line matched the standard. To no one's surprise, the controls picked the correct answer some 99 percent of the time.

With his "experimental subjects," Asch played a much more subtle game. He asked these volunteers to appear at his laboratory at a certain time. But when each young man arrived, he found several other students waiting to participate in the experiment. What the experimental subject did not realize was that the others were stooges—that is, the others were "confederates" of Asch who were paid to give occasional false judgments. After the stooges and the experimental subject had chatted for a few moments, Asch ushered them into his laboratory and gave them several opportunities to judge line lengths for him. The judgments were given *out loud*, so that everyone could hear, and much of the time the stooges reported *before* the experimental subject did.

During the first two trials, the stooges picked the *correct* comparison line—as did the experimental subject. But on the third trial, each of the stooges calmly announced that the 10-inch line matched the 8-inch line! These false judgments created an *incorrect group perceptual norm*, and apparently put the experimental subjects under tremendous pressure to conform. In this first study, the experimental subjects "yielded" to group pressures almost one-third of the time by reporting that the two lines matched. In later studies, when the judgments were more difficult to make, the experimental subjects yielded to the group of stooges about two-thirds of the time (Asch, 1951).

● Size of Group

In another experiment Asch varied the number of stooges who reported before the experimental subject did. While the presence of one, two, or three stooges did induce some conformity, the maximum pressure to yield apparently was reached when there were four stooges giving false reports. Having 14 or even 40 stooges doesn't increase conformity much more than having 4. However, if even 1 stooge out of 40 gives the "correct" answer, the homogeneity of the group is broken and much (but not all) of the "group pressure" is lifted. Under these conditions, the experimental subject "yields" only about one-fourth as often as when the stooges give a unanimous report (Asch, 1956).

● Reasons for Conforming

The importance of the Asch study lies not merely in its dramatic demonstration that people tend to conform to temporary reference groups, but in the *reasons* they gave for doing so.

If you were to ask the subjects who "conformed" *why* they judged the 8-inch line as being as long as the 10-inch line, *most of them* would look at you sheepishly and confess that they couldn't stand the pressure. They might say they figured something was wrong, or they thought the stooges "saw through a trick" they hadn't recognized, or they simply didn't want to "rock the boat" by giving a judgment that went against the group norm.

The few remaining "conformers" are far more interesting, however. For they typically insist they *actually saw* the two lines as being identical. That is, they were not conscious of "yielding" at all (Asch, 1956, 1987).

These studies suggest that group norms not only influence your attitudes toward complex social issues, but your perceptions of even the simplest objects as well.

□ □ **QUESTION** □ □

In a famous children's story, a con man talks an emperor into going naked by pretending to create new clothes so delicate that only the "pure of heart" could see them. Most of the emperor's subjects "oohed and aahed" over the beautiful clothes. Who broke the spell, and how would you explain the story in terms of "group pressures"?

WHAT MAKES PEOPLE CONFORM?

Shortly after Asch reported his initial results, a number of psychologists began to study how groups *induce conformity* in their members. Perhaps the most detailed of these studies was a series of experiments by Robert R. Blake, Harry Helson, and their colleagues at the University of Texas.

In one of the first of these, which I performed under Professor Blake's direction, we demonstrated that the "stooges" did not have to be physically present in order to pressure the experimental subject into conforming. If the subjects merely heard tape-recorded voices of the "stooges," the subjects still conformed about two-thirds of the time (McConnell & Blake, 1953).

In further studies, Blake and his colleagues showed that subjects would volunteer for difficult tasks, donate large or small sums of money to a fake charity, violate social rules ("Don't Walk on the Grass!"), and change their reported attitudes toward war and violence in order to conform to the behavior of various groups of stooges (Blake, Mouton, & Olmstead,

1956; Helson, Blake, & Mouton, 1958a, 1958b; Helson *et al.*, 1956).

Adaptation-level Theory

Robert Blake is a social psychologist with a long-standing interest in group behavior. Harry Helson, however, was an experimental psychologist who spent many years studying visual perception in individuals, not groups. Some of Helson's best-known research had to do with the effects of the *background* on the perception of a visual stimulus—for example, the fact that a white rose appears reddish when seen on a background of blue-green velvet (see Chapter 5) (Helson, 1964).

Originally, Helson had little interest in social psychology. However, he soon perceived that the stooges in Blake's studies were really a "social background" that affected perceptual judgments much as the blue-green velvet "colored" the perception of the white rose. Thus, conformity behavior could be explained by reference to **Adaptation-level Theory**, which Helson had devised to account for the way that humans perceive the world. The discovery that their interests were similar led Blake and Helson to form a research group—and to jointly direct a series of experiments that helped clarify the conditions that induce people to conform to group norms (Blake & Helson, 1956).

According to Adaptation-level Theory, all behavior (including conforming) is influenced by three factors:

1. *Stimulus factors.* These influences include the task or problem set before the subject—what the subject looks at or is told to do.
2. *Background factors.* These influences include the social situation or context in which the stimulus is presented.
3. *Personality factors.* These influences include such matters as innate response tendencies, traits, and past experience.

According to Adaptation-level Theory, if you want to understand why people do or do not yield to group pressures, you must look at all three factors in detail (Helson, 1948).

• Stimulus or Task Variables

The physical properties of the stimulus you must judge in a conformity experiment have a lot to do with whether or not you will yield to group pressures. In general, the *vaguer* the stimulus, the more likely it is that you will conform. It is a relatively simple task to get you to change your opinions about the beauty of a work of art or the melodiousness of a piece of music. However, it is much more difficult to get you to say that a 10-inch line is shorter than an 8-inch line (Asch, 1987).

Attitudes about almost anything are easier to shift than are *judgments of concrete facts*.

However, strong *personal preferences* for things like food are harder to influence than are guesses about such vague facts as the distance from New York to London (Duncker, 1938).

The more *difficult the stimulus task* appears to be, and the more *confusing the instructions* about the task, the more likely it is that the group will be able to influence your behavior. For this reason, perhaps, group pressures are most effective if you must judge the stimulus from *memory* (Deutsch & Gerard, 1955).

• Situational or Background Variables

If the group is to have an influence on you, you must know what the group's opinion or norm actually is. One of the most important situational factors, therefore, is how much information you have about what the group is like, and what you know about the beliefs of the other group members. In general, the more *knowledge* you have concerning the group, the more strongly you will feel pressured to yield (Schachter & Hall, 1952).

Group pressures to conform develop when stimulus and background factors are in conflict—that is, when your perception of the stimulus *differs significantly* from that offered by some reference group you belong to. Up to a point, the larger the difference between your judgment and that of the group, the more likely it is you will be influenced by group standards (Festinger *et al.*, 1952). However, if the matter is carried to ridiculous extremes, the pressure on you may lift. It is all very well to ask you to report that an 8-inch line is the same length as one 10 inches long. It is something else to expect you to report than an 8-inch line is identical to a line several feet in length (Asch, 1951, 1987; Blake, Helson, & Mouton, 1956).

The way you perceive the other group members is also critical. The more *prestige*, status, or competence members of the group seem to have—or the more *trustworthy* they appear to be—the more powerful the pressures on you to conform. You are more likely to conform to friends than to strangers, and more likely to yield to strangers who say they like you than to strangers who don't (Harvey, Kelley, & Shapiro, 1957; Luchins & Luchins, 1955).

The more out in the open you are forced to be in making your judgments, the more likely it is that you will yield to group pressures. If you must state your name, or respond so that the rest of the group can hear, then you are more likely to submit to group pressures—at least in public. But if you get the impression that the group may be on the verge of rejecting you, then you may conform in public but not when you're given a chance to make your judgments in private (Asch, 1956).

If you are told that the whole group must come to a unanimous decision on the matter at hand, you will be strongly pressured to yield. Also, the greater the reward for yielding, or the more importance the judgment is supposed to have, the more likely it is that you will be swayed by incorrect or inappropriate group norms (Brehm & Festinger, 1957; Festinger & Thibaut, 1951).

□ □ **QUESTION** □ □
Why is it particularly important that juries, who often decide matters of life and death, should always take secret ballots?

● *Personality Factors and Past Experience*
Some people seem to conform much of the time, some practically never. Most of us, however, yield in some situations and not in others. The personality traits of the individual who readily yields to group pressures have often been measured—but not all of these studies have come up with the same results. Looking at the broad picture, however, we find that yielders often had harsh parents who gave their children very little "independence training" (Mussen & Kagan, 1958). Yielders are also reported to be "followers" rather than "leaders," and often are rather rigid and authoritarian in the way they respond to rules (Crutchfield, 1953, 1955). Men who yield more than average are reported to score as being more "feminine" than average on masculinity tests (Crutchfield, 1953; Goldberg *et al.*, 1954). Members of various religious "cults" also tend to be more "conformist" than normal (Weiss & Comrey, 1987).

Blake and Helson report that men tend to conform more in areas of traditional interest—such as politics and economics—while women are more likely to yield to group pressures in matters of art and social affairs (Helson, Blake, & Mouton, 1958b).

Past experience also has its effects on conformity. If you are an expert on the task at hand, or if the experimenter somehow makes you *think* you are an expert, you are less likely to yield. If you are rewarded for going against the group, you tend to yield less often than if you are punished for refusing to conform (Kelley & Lamb, 1957).

There is little or no evidence that conformity is an innate or inherited trait. Rather, "yielding" seems to be a behavior that you learn—primarily because your reference groups reward you when you conform and punish you when you deviate. There is also evidence that even high yielders can be trained to resist group pressures (Riecken, 1952).

Some cultures may be more "conformist" than others. For example, as we noted in Chapter 17, Japanese school children have higher intelligence test scores than do Americans, but are supposed to be more "conformist" than are Americans. Some evidence to support this view comes from a recent study by Japanese psychologist Noriyuki Matsuda, who found that female Japanese undergraduates showed "strong conformity" in an Asch-type situation—much higher than that reported by Asch (and others) for undergraduate females in the US (Matsuda, 1985).

To summarize, "conformists" tend to have many of the same personality characteristics—and the same sorts of social backgrounds—as do the "placebo reactors" and "good hypnotic subjects" whom we discussed in Chapter 13. They also tend to be more *obedient* to authority than do people who tend to resist group pressures.

□ □ **QUESTION** □ □
Would you expect "internalizers" or "externalizers" to be more likely to conform to group pressures?

● *Self-monitoring Theory*
According to University of Minnesota psychologist Mark Snyder, some individuals appear to *monitor* their own performance, and then try to adjust their behaviors to whatever situation they find themselves in. They appear to ask themselves, "Who does this situation want me to be, and how can I be that person?" Snyder calls these people *high self-monitors*.

Other individuals appear to approach new situations by asking themselves, "Who am I, and how can I be me in this situation?" Snyder calls these people *low self-monitors*, and believes their actions are "controlled by inner attitudes, dispositions, and values" (Snyder, 1987).

Some years ago, Snyder developed a Self-monitoring Scale for use in his research. As you might imagine, "yielders" tend to get high scores on this questionnaire, while people who resist group pressures tend to get low scores. In recent years, Snyder has attempted to determine how "high" and "low" self-monitors react in various social situations.

Generally speaking, in the area of romantic encounters, high self-monitors are strongly influenced by the physical appearance of "potential romantic partners," while low self-monitors are reportedly more interested in the personality of a prospective partner. High self-monitors also report having more sex partners, they have more "one night stands," and expect to have more partners in the future than do low self-monitors (Snyder, 1987).

There is a fair amount of research that appears to support Snyder's position. However, there is also some doubt as to whether the Self-monitoring Scale actually measures what it says it does (Crocker, 1988). And, as we will see later in this chapter, most theorists currently believe that behaviors such as "yielding" or "conforming" are always the result of a *combination* of situational and personal factors, and therefore are not due just to one personality trait such as "self-monitoring."

□□ **QUESTION** □□

From Snyder's point of view, who would be more likely to *obey authority*, low or high self-monitors?

OBEDIENCE

One interesting sidelight to the conformity studies is this—in most of the experiments, the subject was never told that he or she *had to yield* to the group norm. Indeed, many of the subjects were quite unaware they had given in to group pressures. Some people even *denied* they had done so. So let us next ask a very important question: What might the results have been had the subjects been *ordered* to yield by the experimenter?

The Milgram Experiments

The answer to this question may well come from a fascinating set of experiments performed by psychologist Stanley Milgram in the 1960's at Yale. His subjects were men who ranged in age from young to old, and who came from many different walks of life. These men were paid to participate in what they thought was a study on the effects of punishment on learning.

- #### "Teachers" and "Learners"

In the first experiment, each man arrived at Milgram's laboratory to find another subject (a stooge) also present. The stooge was supposed to be the "learner" who would have to memorize a list of word pairs. The experimental subject was supposed to be the "teacher" who would punish the stooge if he made any mistakes. The stooge was sent into another room and was strapped into a chair so he couldn't escape when the punishment became severe. The stooge was then out of sight for the rest of the experiment.

Sitting in front of the experimental subject was a very impressive piece of electrical equipment that *supposedly* was a powerful shock generator. In fact, the machine was a fake. *No shock was ever delivered during the experiment*. This "fake" generator had 30 switches on

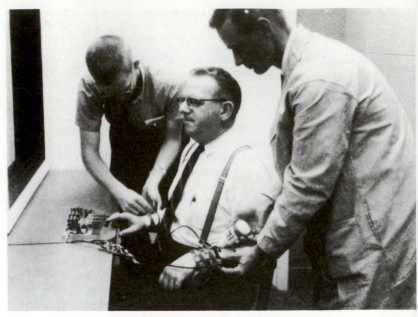

A "learner" in the Milgram study being wired to the console.

it to control the (apparent) strength of the electrical current. Labels on these switches ranged from "Slight Shock" (15 volts) to "Danger: Severe Shock" (420 volts) to "XXX" (450 volts).

The first time the stooge made a mistake, the subject was to give him 15 volts of shock. For each subsequent mistake, the subject was to increase the shock intensity by flipping on the next-highest switch. The apparatus was so ingeniously designed that none of the subjects guessed the stooges actually weren't receiving shocks from the machine.

At the beginning of the session, things were easy for the experimental subject. The stooge got most of the word pairs correct, and the "shocks" delivered for making errors were presumably very mild. As time wore on, however, the stooge made more "mistakes" and the "shocks" became more and more severe. When the shock level reached what seemed to be a fairly high point, the stooge suddenly pounded on the wall in protest. Then the stooge *stopped responding entirely*, as if he had fainted or had suffered an attack of some kind.

At this point the experimenter told the "teacher" to continue anyway—no matter how dangerously high the shock might get. If at any time the subject wanted to stop, the experimenter told him in a very stern voice, "Whether the learner likes it or not, you *must go on* until he has learned all the word pairs correctly. So please go on." However, the experimenter never *forced* the "teacher" to continue (Milgram, 1963).

What would you do in this situation? Would you refuse to cooperate, or would you "obey" the experimenter and go on shocking the stooge right up to what you believed were the limits of the electrical generator?

And how do you think most other people would react if they faced this challenge?

- ### *Some "Shocking" Facts*

After Milgram had completed his first study, he asked a great many college students how they thought most people would react when told to shock the "learner." If you are like Milgram's students, you will insist that you—and most other people—would refuse to continue the experiment when a dangerously high shock level was reached (and particularly when the "learner" apparently had fainted or died in the other room). But, in fact, your guess (at least about other people) would be wrong. For out of the first 40 subjects Milgram tried, *almost 65 percent* continued to "obey orders" right up to the bitter end. Most of these subjects were extremely distressed about doing so. They complained, they showed tension, and they said they wanted to stop again and again. But some 65 percent were *completely obedient* in spite of their inner conflict (Milgram, 1964).

□□ **QUESTION** □□

What similarities do you see between the people who "obeyed" Milgram and the young men in Zimbardo's experiment who became "brutal" in their behaviors toward men who were playing the role of prisoners?

- ### *Factors Inducing Obedience*

In Adaptation-level Theory terms, the verbal orders to Milgram's subjects were "stimulus factors," while the behavior of the stooge can be considered part of the "background or situational factors." By manipulating each of these factors in subsequent experiments, Milgram was able to determine a variety of ways in which obedience can be increased or decreased.

As you might expect, the weaker the stimulus, the fewer the number of people who obeyed. When the experimenter stood right over the experimental subjects, breathing down their necks and ordering them on, about 65 percent followed through to the end. But when the experimenter was out of the room and gave his orders by telephone, only some 22 percent of the subjects were completely obedient.

In the first experiment, the subjects could not see or hear the stooge in the other room. In subsequent studies, Milgram altered this "background factor." If the stooge began moaning, or complaining about his heart, fewer subjects obeyed orders. Having the stooge physically present in the same room so that the subject could see the supposed pain from each shock reduced obedience even more. And if the subject had to grab hold of the stooge's hand and force it down on a metal "shock plate" before each punishment, very few of the subjects followed instructions to the end. Put more simply, the subjects were more likely to deliver severe punishment if they couldn't see the *consequences* of their actions (Milgram, 1964).

- ### *Group Pressures and Obedience*

In a later experiment, Milgram added the group-pressures technique to his own method of studying obedience. In this experiment, Milgram used three stooges with each experimental subject. One of the stooges, as usual, was the "learner" seated in the next room. The other two were supposed to be "teachers" working in a team with the subject.

The experiment proceeded as before, except that one of the stooge-teachers backed out as soon as the "shock" reached a medium-low intensity. Saying that he refused to continue, this stooge simply took a seat as far from the shock machine as he could. When the "shock" reached a medium-high level, the other stooge-teacher also refused to go on. The subject then was faced with *conflicting social norms*. The experimenter kept pressuring him to continue, while the "group" of stooge-teachers was exerting pressure to stop. Under these conditions, the "social background" factors won out over the "stimulus" of the experimenter's orders. More than 90 percent of the subjects refused to complete the experiment (Milgram, 1965).

We are taught to obey, just as we are trained to conform. If you consider the great rewards and massive punishments that groups can administer to their members, perhaps it is not so surprising that many of us obey and conform rather readily.

□□ **QUESTION** □□

What do you think would have happened in Zimbardo's prison study had the "warden" *ordered* the guards to punish the prisoners severely for infractions of "the rules"?

Attribution Theory and Obedience

Before we go any further with our discussion of obedience, let's ask a question. Suppose, in one of his studies, Milgram had allowed the "teacher" to *set the shock level himself*. That is, rather than insisting that the "teacher" blindly increase the amount of shock given the "learner" after each trial, suppose Milgram had told the "teacher" to decide how much punishment would be "appropriate." The "teacher" could increase the shock to the maximum level, keep it in the "mildly painful" range, or decrease the shock to almost zero.

Under these circumstances, how much shock do *you* think the "average teacher" would eventually administer? And what percentage of the "teachers" do you think would give the maximum amount of electricity? Why not write your predictions down on a sheet of paper, and then see what actually happened.

In fact, Milgram actually performed this experiment and reported the results in 1974. He began by giving all the teachers themselves a mildly painful shock of 45 volts, so they would "understand how shock felt." Thereafter, the "teachers" were allowed to administer (false) shock to the "learner" that could vary from 15 up to 450 volts. Milgram found that almost all of the "teachers" maintained the shock in the "mildly painful" range (45 to 60 volts). Only 1 "teacher" out of 40 administered the maximum shock of 450 volts (Milgram, 1974). That finding itself is very interesting. However, an extension of this research by Martin Safer of Catholic University of America yielded even more intriguing results.

Safer began by showing a film of Milgram's research to 132 students in an introductory psychology class. He then asked the students to *predict* what the "teachers" would do if allowed to set their own shock levels. Safer found that the students systematically *overestimated* the amount of shock they thought the "teachers" would administer. They guessed that about 12 percent of the "teachers" would give 450 volts, and that the average "teacher" would end up giving about 175 volts!

Safer believes that his students *attributed evilness to the "teachers."* That is, the students apparently assumed most people have a "cruel streak" in them, and that they will express this trait if given a chance. Safer points out the paradox of his findings. First, before learning about Milgram's research, most students presume that *almost nobody* would shock an innocent "learner." When they learn what actually happened in Milgram's laboratory, however, the students attributed the results to some character flaw inside the "teachers." For the students failed to perceive that the "teachers'" actions were due to the *social environment*, not to some personality trait. Thus, when asked how the "teachers" would react when allowed to set their own shock levels, the students predicted on the basis of *attributed traits*, not on the basis of the actual situation the "teachers" were in (and responding to).

Martin Safer concludes that *few people* "appear to have insight into the crucial situational factors affecting behavior in the obedience . . . experiments" (Safer, 1980).

□ □ **QUESTION** □ □
What level of shock did *you* think the "teachers" would use? What have you learned about your own perceptions from these studies?

The Ethics of Deception

The Milgram studies, the Zimbardo prison research, and many other experiments raise a number of complex but important questions about the *ethics* of using humans as subjects in scientific experiments. One of these questions involves the morality of *deceiving* the subjects as to the real purpose of the study, even if the experimenter believes such deception is necessary because people seldom act naturally when they know they're being observed (Schuler, 1982).

● *Milgram's Critics*

When Milgram's research was published, a storm of protest was raised by sincerely-concerned individuals who urged that studies such as Milgram's be banned or prohibited. This same barrage of criticism, as we noted in the last chapter, occurred when Zimbardo released the results of his prison experiment. In consequence, a number of codes of ethics were proposed, but workable guidelines for experimentation on humans are not easy to agree upon. For, given a little time and motivation, we could all think of certain types of studies in which deception might be morally justified, and other experiments in which misleading the subjects would be both a legal and an ethical outrage.

● *When Is Deception Ethical?*

Obviously we should always consider the *actual results* of experiments before drawing hasty conclusions about what is ethical, and what isn't. Viewed in this perspective, Milgram comes off fairly well, for he did discover some fascinating facts. More important, there is no evidence reported in the scientific literature that any of his subjects suffered ill effects. In truth, Milgram seems to have employed little more deception in his work than is used regularly on TV programs such as "Candid Camera." Yet the nagging question—"When is it ethical to use deception?"—remains for the most part unanswered.

Some of the emotional reaction to Milgram's experiments probably stemmed from the rather unflattering picture his results gave us of ourselves. Had most of Milgram's subjects *refused* to obey blindly, perhaps he would not have been so vigorously attacked. Despite the emotionality of some of Milgram's critics, however, the issue of experimenter responsibility remains a crucial one, and the American Psychological Association has recently taken a stand against the unwarranted use of deception in similar research. Similar codes are now in force in several other countries, including Poland, Germany, France, and the Netherlands.

☐ ☐ QUESTION ☐ ☐
Under what circumstances do you personally think that deceiving subjects in a scientific experiment might be ethically warranted or justified?

Bystander Apathy

Milgram created problems for his subjects because he told them what to do. In real-life conflicts, there often isn't anyone around to give you directions, and you must act (or fail to act) on your own. If there are other people around when a crisis occurs, however, you may look at them as "models" of what you ought to do. And you may assume that *they are as responsible as you are* for taking action (or not doing anything) in an emergency. Thus, if your "models" fail to react, you may feel strong group pressures to follow their lead. Keep that thought in mind as we describe a particularly gruesome murder.

What would you do if, late some dark night, you heard screams outside your place? Would you rush out at once, or would you first go to the window to see what was happening? If you saw a man with a knife attacking one of your neighbors, how would you react? Might you call the police, or go to the neighbor's aid? Or would you remain **apathetic** and unresponsive? And if you failed to assist the neighbor in any way, how would you respond if someone later on asked why you didn't help?

Before you answer, consider the following facts. Early one morning in 1964, a young New York woman named Kitty Genovese was returning home from work. As she neared her front door, a man jumped out of the shadows and attacked her. She screamed and attempted to defend herself. Because she screamed loudly, 38 of her neighbors came to their windows to see what was happening. And because she fought valiantly, it took the man almost 30 minutes to kill Kitty Genovese. During this period of time, not one of those 38 neighbors came to her aid—and not one of them even bothered to call the police (Cunningham, 1984; Shotland, 1985; Darley & Latané, 1968; Takooshian & O'Connor, 1984).

● *The Darley-Latané Studies*

Kitty Genovese's death so distressed scientists John Darley and Bibb Latané, they began a study of why people refuse to help others in similar situations.

In one experiment, Darley and Latané staged a disaster of sorts for their subjects. They paid people $2 to fill out a survey form which was given to them by an attractive young woman. While the people were in an office filling out the forms, the woman went into the next room. Shortly thereafter, the subjects heard a loud crash from the next room, and the woman began moaning loudly that she had fallen and was badly hurt and needed help.

Now, how many of the subjects do you think came to her rescue?

The answer is—it depends. Some of the subjects were exposed to this little drama when they were all by themselves in the testing room. About 70 percent of the "alone" subjects

The Kitty Genovese murder scene. At location (1), she drove into the parking lot. She noticed a man in the lot and proceeded to location (2) toward a police telephone box. Here, the man caught and attacked her with a knife. She got away, but he attacked her again at location (3) and finally at location (4).

offered help. Another 40 subjects faced this apparent emergency in pairs. Only 8 of these 40 people responded by going to the woman's aid. The other 32 subjects simply sat there listening to the moans and groans.

Were the subjects who failed to rush to the woman's assistance merely apathetic and uncaring? In this case, yes. Many of the "apathetic bystanders" informed the experimenters they hadn't really thought the woman was seriously hurt and were afraid of embarrassing her if they intervened. But we should note that the subject's *perception* of the emergency was strongly influenced by whether or not there was someone else present in the testing room.

In another experiment, subjects heard a young man (presumably in the next room) discuss the fact that he frequently had seizures similar to *grand mal* epilepsy. Shortly thereafter, the stooge began crying for help, saying he was about to have an attack and would die if no one came to help him. About 85 percent of the subjects who were "alone" rushed to the stooge's assistance. However, only 62 percent of the subjects who were in pairs offered aid, and only 31 percent of those in 5-person groups overcame their apathy (Darley & Latané, 1968; Latané & Darley, 1975).

□ □ **QUESTION** □ □

In Chapter 20, we discussed the "personal qualities of leadership." Would you expect the "31 percent of those who overcame their apathy" and rushed to help would score higher or lower on leadership tests? Why?

• *Latané's "Theory of Social Impact"*

In 1981, Bibb Latané proposed a "theory of social impact." Latané states, "As social animals, we are drawn by the attractiveness of others and aroused by their mere presence. . . . We are influenced by the actions of others, stimulated by their activity and embarrassed by their attention . . . I call all these effects, and others like them, "social impact.'"

Latané believes the impact of your social environment can be determined by three factors: The *strength*, the *immediacy*, and the *number* of people around you. The more people involved in a given situation, the more *diluted* you will perceive your own responsibility as being. Thus, Latané says, each person who witnessed Kitty Genovese's murder felt but a fraction of the responsibility for helping the woman or reporting the crime. Therefore, while the murder itself had a strong and immediate impact on the neighbors, the *number of people* was so great that it diluted each person's sense of responsibility to the point where no one took action (Latané, 1981).

□ □ **QUESTION** □ □

Consider those 38 neighbors as an Asch-type "conformity group." Why would each person be under strong pressures *not* to intervene if none of the other 37 did?

Who Intervenes, and Why

In 1981, psychologist Ted Huston and his colleagues offered an interesting comparison between people who have helped crime victims and those who have not. The state of California has long compensated **Good Samaritans** who are injured when they intervene to give assistance in holdups, assaults, burglaries, or other serious crimes. Huston *et al.* interviewed 32 people who had received "Good Samaritan" awards and contrasted them with 32 "control subjects"—individuals from the same community who were identical in most other ways but hadn't intervened in a crime for at least the previous 10 years.

According to Huston and his group, the "interveners" and the "controls" had strikingly similar scores on standardized personality tests. The interveners were no more sympathetic or socially responsible, nor were they more likely to *state* they would be willing to help others. The one *personality test* difference *was that the interveners* perceived *themselves to be stronger, more aggressive, and more emotional than did the controls.*

In terms of *experience with crime*, however, there was a marked contrast between the two groups. The interveners had witnessed crimes at least nine times as often as had the control subjects (although the two groups lived in the same community). In addition, the "Good Samaritans" had themselves been crime *victims* more than twice as often as the controls. Just as important, the interveners had much higher levels of training in such *skills* as life-saving, first aid, and self-defense.

Huston and his associates note that helping out in crisis situations may be habit forming. Some 34 percent of those individuals who received "Good Samaritan" compensation reported they had intervened in at least one crime other than the one they got the award for (Huston *et al.*, 1981).

□ □ **QUESTION** □ □

Suppose you witnessed a crime and didn't intervene. How would you explain this failure to yourself afterward? Would you be more likely to change your *attitude* toward yourself, or would you strive to change your *behavior* in crisis situations?

Cognitive Dissonance

Not all the conflicts we face involve a choice between satisfying group expectancies or satisfying our consciences by living up to a moral code. Sometimes the problem has to do with trying to *explain to ourselves* why we picked a biological reinforcer rather than an intra-psychic one. For instance, most of us are taught that sexual intercourse is immoral except when engaged in by a married couple. Yet, if Kinsey's data are true, many of us violate this ethical standard at some time during our lives. Afterwards, rather than admitting that our ids got the better of our superegos, we may *rationalize* our actions in a variety of ways: "I did it only because I loved him (her)," "She (he) needed me," or "I was forced into doing it."

● Doomsday Prophecies

Over the years, Leon Festinger has conducted a series of intriguing studies on how human beings react to situations involving social conflicts. In one of his first studies, Festinger worked with H.W. Riecken and Stanley Schachter. These social scientists made an extensive study of a "doomsday group" whose leader had predicted the world would end on a certain day. As the fatal day approached, the members of the group became more and more excited and tried to convince others to repent and join their group in order to "save their souls." When "doomsday" arrived, the members of the group gathered together to await final judgment and to pray for deliverance. To their amazement, the day passed, and so did several other days, and the world continued to speed on its merry way.

And how did the leader of the "doomsday group" respond to the failure of her predictions? Apparently, by finding a "rational excuse" for what actually happened. Several days after the date the world was supposed to end, she told the members of her clan that "God had spoken to her, and had spared the world in answer to the group's prayers." The group members then reacted with great joy. Rather than rejecting the leader, they accepted her more warmly and believed even more firmly in her prophecies (Festinger, Riecken, & Schachter, 1956).

● Changing Perceptions to Reduce Conflict

The "failed prophecy" study led Festinger to hypothesize that people tend to reduce mental conflict by changing their *perceptions* of what really happened to them. In perhaps the best known of his experiments—reported in 1959 by Festinger and J.M. Carlsmith—college students were asked to do about 30 minutes of very tedious and boring work. The subjects performed these repetitive and uninteresting tasks while alone in a laboratory room.

After the students had completed the chores, Festinger and Carlsmith offered some of them a dollar as a reward to tell the next subject what an exciting and thrilling task it had been. Other subjects were paid $20 for doing exactly the same thing. Afterward—no matter how good a "selling job" the person had done—each subject was asked to give her or his actual opinion of how pleasurable the work was.

Festinger and Carlsmith report that the students paid but $1 thought the chores were really pretty interesting and enjoyable. However, the subjects paid $20 rated the tasks as being dull, as did a group of subjects who were not asked to "sell" the experiment to another student (Festinger & Carlsmith, 1959).

Why did the subjects paid but $1 rate the work as being much more pleasant than one might have expected? Festinger believes they had a difficult job rationalizing their own actions. For they had *lied* to the other subject about how interesting the task was supposed to be. The subjects paid $20 for lying apparently were willing to face the fact they had "fudged" a bit for that much money. The students paid but a single dollar couldn't admit to themselves that they'd "sell out" for so little money. Therefore, Festinger says, they apparently changed their *perception* of the enjoyability of the task "after the fact" (Festinger, 1957)

● Dissonance Theory

According to Leon Festinger, whenever people are put in conflict situations, they experience **cognitive dissonance**. That is, whenever we do something we think we shouldn't, we face the problem of explaining our actions to ourselves and to others. Festinger stated we are usually highly motivated to reduce cognitive dissonance when it occurs, and we do so chiefly by changing our *beliefs or attitudes* to make them agree with our *actual behaviors*—and then we go right on behaving the way we always had (Festinger, 1957).

There have been hundreds of studies on cognitive dissonance since the Festinger and Carlsmith experiment. In most of these studies, the researchers forced subjects to take a position opposite to their normal views and then rewarded the subjects for doing so. In this sort of situation, many subjects do indeed "reduce dissonance" by changing their attitudes toward the position they were rewarded for taking. However, Hungarian psychologist Csaba Szabo found recently that subjects who tended to be "manipulators" showed little or no dissonance (and changed their attitudes very little) when paid to write essays opposed to their normal views. Subjects who weren't "manipulators," however, tended to experience "high dissonance" and changed their attitudes a significant amount (Szabo, 1985).

French psychologist Robert Joule believes that most studies on cognitive dissonance are better explained in terms of *rationalization*. In certain social situations, Joule says, you may well do things that *appear* to be inconsistent with your normal values. However, Joule says, changing your attitude afterwards is not your attempt to "create cognitive consistency"—it's merely a very simple way of explaining your actions to yourself (Joule, 1986).

☐ ☐ **QUESTION** ☐ ☐
What similarities do you see between Festinger's theory of cognitive dissonance and Piaget's description of how "dis-equilibrium" drives us to change our perceptions of the world?

• *Group Pressures: A Summary*
Perhaps you will have noticed a certain similarity between the group-pressures experiments, the obedience studies, the research on bystander apathy, and the cognitive dissonance experiments. In all these cases, the conflict arose when people failed to recognize we all are immensely sensitive to group pressures, and it is a *natural function of a group* to exert these pressures.

Given the fact that so few of us ever perceive what strong control our environments exercise over us, perhaps it is not surprising we invent all kinds of "rational explanations" that overemphasize the importance of intrapsychic processes in determining how we think and behave. These "inventions" include most of our theories about "traits," "attitudes," "personality factors," and "mental illness.".

The critical importance of the environment becomes particularly clear in studies on *conflict* between various social groups.

INTER-GROUP CONFLICT

For the most part, the studies on conformity, obedience, and cognitive dissonance have dealt with individual subjects put under strong psychological pressure to avoid conflict with other members of a group, or with their own value systems. From the standpoint of General Systems Theory, however, we can consider the group itself as a kind of "super-organism" that should be subject to social pressures to conform to the standards set by other groups or organizations.

Groups should also show many of the same sorts of *internal processes* (structures and functions) as do individuals. Not unexpectedly, most of the factors that influence individual conformity and internal conflict have their direct parallels when we study the behavior of groups as groups (Pruitt & Zubin, 1986; Stroebe, Kruglanski, & Bar-Ral, 1987).

Sherif's "Camp" Experiments
Muzafer Sherif was born in Smyrna, Turkey, in 1906. During the First World War, when Sherif was about 13, Greek soldiers invaded his village. Sherif and other townspeople rushed out to defend themselves, but were powerless against the better-equipped Greek forces. A Greek soldier came directly at Sherif, bayonet drawn, and actually killed the man standing next to Sherif. Then, for reasons Sherif says he still doesn't understand, the Greek soldier turned and walked away, sparing Sherif (cited in Trotter, 1985).

As you might expect, that early experience of bloody conflict between two warring nations left an indelible impression on Sherif. After coming to the United States and taking his doctorate in psychology at Harvard, Sherif devoted his life to the study of *conflict resolution*. In a recent interview, Sherif puts it this way: "Conflict between groups—whether between boys' gangs, social classes, races or nations—has no simple cause, nor is mankind yet in sight of a cure" (cited in Trotter, 1985). Nonetheless, Sherif's research has surely taught us some of the more elemental facts about why conflicts occur, and what might be done to reduce tensions between warring factions.

• *The "Robber's Cave" Studies*
Muzafer Sherif taught for many years at the University of Oklahoma. Near the university is a state recreation area called "Robber's Cave Park," because the area was used as a hideout by the famous bandit Jesse James. During the late 1950's, Sherif and his colleagues helped run a summer camp for 11- and 12-year old boys at Robber's Cave Park. These youngsters were all from settled, well-adjusted, white, middle-class, Protestant homes. The boys were carefully selected to be happy, healthy individuals who had no difficulty getting along with other young men their age. None of the boys knew each other before being admitted to the camp. Nor did any of them realize that they were to be subjects in Sherif's experiments.

• *Eagles and Rattlers*
The camp itself had two rather separate housing units. The boys living in one unit were called the "Eagles," while the other group's name was the "Rattlers." Since there were no pre-existing friendships among the boys, group

commitment and cohesion in both units was very low on the first day of camp. In an attempt to increase group cohesion, Sherif gave both the Eagles and the Rattlers various problems that could be solved only if the boys *in each separate unit* worked together effectively. As each unit overcame the difficulties Sherif put to it, the boys came to *like* the other boys in the same unit more and more. The Eagles and the Rattlers each became a "natural group," and commitment to the specific group (and to its particular emerging norms) increased significantly.

• Competition Versus Cooperation

After the Eagles and the Rattlers had shown considerable cohesion, Sherif introduced a series of contests designed to make the two groups hostile toward one another. As the groups competed for prizes, conflict developed, since one group could win only at the expense of the other. Very soon the Eagles were making nasty comments about the Rattlers, and vice versa. Most of this hostility consisted of one group's *attributing* selfish or hostile motives to the other group. Name calling, fights, and raids on the cabins belonging to the other group became commonplace. At the same time, Sherif reports, there was a marked *increase* in cooperativeness and cohesiveness *within* each of the groups.

• Reducing Inter-group Hostilities

Once the groups were at each other's throats, Sherif tried to bring them back together again. In his first experiment, Sherif attempted to unite the two groups by giving them a common enemy—a group of threatening outsiders. This technique worked fairly well, in that it brought the Eagles and the Rattlers closer together. But they still held *hatred* for their common enemy.

The next year Sherif and his colleagues repeated the group-conflict experiment with a different set of boys. Once inter-group hatred had reached its peak, Sherif brought the two units into very pleasant, non-competitive contact with each other. They sat together in the same dining hall while eating excellent food, and they watched movies together. However, this approach didn't succeed, for the groups merely used these occasions for fighting and shouting at each other.

Sherif then confronted the hostile groups with problem situations that could be solved only if the two units *cooperated* with each other. First, a water shortage "suddenly developed," and all the boys had to ration themselves. Next, Sherif offered to show the whole camp an exciting movie—but to see it, both units had to pool their resources. And one time when all the boys were particularly hungry, the transportation for their food "broke down." It could be fixed only if both groups worked together quickly and effectively.

Sherif reports that his technique succeeded beautifully. The two groups did indeed cooperate—reluctantly at first, but more and more willingly as their initial efforts were reinforced.

Before the "crises" occurred, almost none of the boys had friendships outside their units. Afterward, some 30 percent of the friendships were inter-group rather than in-group. During the hostile period, about one-third of the members of each group rated the members of the other group as being "stinkers," "smart-alecks," or "sneaky." Afterward, less than 5 percent of the boys gave the members of the other group such highly unfavorable ratings (Sherif *et al.*, 1961).

Muzafer Sherif believes that the best way to reduce inter-group conflicts is by giving both parties "overriding, superordinate goals" that can only be achieved if the groups work together. But he laments the fact that many group leaders typically see "striving toward common goals" as a sign of weakness and compromise, not a movement toward healthy conflict resolution (cited in Trotter, 1985).

• Effects of Group Membership on Perception

Group membership has a strong effect on perception. For instance, during the hostile period in the Robber's Cave studies, several of the boys were asked to estimate how many jellybeans were in a jar. When the boys were told the jellybeans had been collected by a member of their own group, the boys tended to *overestimate*. When told the candies had been collected by a member of the other group, however, the boys tended to *underestimate* (Sherif *et al.*, 1961).

In a similar study reported in 1981 by Henri Tajfel and his colleagues, British boys were given a simple perceptual task to perform. The task involved estimating the number of dots that flashed on a screen. Then each boy was taken aside individually. Half the boys were told they were "overestimators" as far as guessing dots was concerned. The rest were informed they were "underestimators." Next, each subject was asked to divide a sum of money between two other boys—one supposedly an "overestimator," the other supposedly an "underestimator." As you might guess, the subjects tended to award more money to someone they thought *shared their own trait* than to someone they perceived as "being different" (Vaughan, Tajfel, & Williams, 1981).

□ □ **QUESTION** □ □
Do you join groups because they are made up of people like yourself? Or do

you join groups and then *become similar to the people who make up the group?*

Social Identity Theory Versus Social Learning Theory

Henri Tajfel had a strong influence on many social psychologists in England. Tajfel explained most group behaviors in terms of what he called "Social Identity Theory." According to Tajfel, you first define *who you are*. Then you join groups of other people whom you *perceive* as being similar to you in one way or another (Tajfel, 1982a).

Tajfel believes that, at some point in your life, you "categorize" all the people around you into various groups. Then you deliberately affiliate with some of those groups—but not with others. The groups you join *define your social identity*. As Tajfel puts it, social identity is "the portion of an individual's self-concept that results from knowledge of his or her membership in some social groups together with the value and emotional significance attached to that membership" (Tajfel, 1982a).

Tajfel further presumes that you wish to "attain or maintain a positive social identity." Therefore, he says, you are strongly motivated to distinguish between *your* groups and *other* groups by assigning positive traits to your groups and negative traits to others. Tajfel suggests that one major reason people are prejudiced against others is because of this need to "maintain a positive social identity" (Tajfel, 1979, 1982b).

As you might surmise, many American social psychologists disagree strongly with Tajfel. For instance, according to social learning theory, you typically are pushed into various groups by your environment. Then you *learn* the group's norms and adhere to them (rather than picking groups in terms of norms you already have.) Thus, if your group *happens* to take a prejudiced view toward some other group, you are likely to *acquire* this prejudice as a consequence of group membership. But because the prejudice is *learned*, it can be *unlearned* through experience (Bandura, 1986a).

In fact, the truth seems to lie somewhere between these two extremes. As we noted earlier, you are "born into" family, religious, and other types of groups. You then take on the values of these groups through the *socialization* process during your early years. But, later on, you obviously pick some groups to join because the members share values you already have. And then you become even more like the members of the groups you've voluntarily joined.

□ □ **QUESTION** □ □

Suppose you voluntarily joined a group, and then discovered that other

According to Tajfel's social identity theory, we define ourselves by the people we choose to associate with and the groups we choose to join.

members of the group strongly rejected someone who was a good friend of yours. How would you try to resolve this conflict?

Attitudes: Groups Versus Societies

At the beginning of Chapter 20, we noted that social *psychologists* tend to study "group" structures and dynamics, while *social* psychologists mostly look at what goes on in "organizations and societies." This difference in focus is nowhere more apparent that in the study of *attitudes,* and how they are affected by larger social systems. We have spent the past several pages discussing how groups exert their pressures on your attitudes and perceptions. Now, let's see how your viewpoints are influenced by the culture in which you live.

ATTITUDE STABILITY

In Chapter 20, we defined an attitude as a relatively enduring way of thinking, feeling, and behaving toward an object, person, group, or idea. And, as we noted, attitudes almost always involve some bias or pre-judging on your part. When you *label* someone as "stingy" or "psychotic," you both state an attitude and reveal the way in which you perceive the person. In a sense, then, attitudes are *perceptions* (cognitive schemas) coupled with *feelings* that predispose you to act in a certain way (Newcomb, 1981).

You could not do without attitudes, for many reasons. To begin with, the attitude (or schema) you have of someone or of some object allows you to *predict the future behavior* of that person or thing. If you made no pre-judgments about things, you would have trouble walking across a street or carrying on even the simplest of social conversations. For example, when you tell a man wearing an ecology button that you "hate pollution," you not only can predict the man's response but also influence his attitude toward (or perception of) you.

□ □ QUESTION □ □
How do attitudes help reduce social stress?

Attitudes and Memories

A second important aspect of attitudes has to do with memory. As you learned in earlier chapters, you seem to file your experiences in Long-term Memory according to certain *categories*. That is, you attach "cognitive labels" to the important features of the experience, and then file the memory according to these "labels." When you try to remember something that happened in the past, you search your memory files using this same set of cognitions. Another word for "labels," of course, is *attitudes* (Greene & Loftus, 1981).

Psychologists believe that the more that you know about a person, thing, or idea, the more *stable* your attitude will usually be. Likewise, the more strongly you feel about something, the more difficult it will probably be to get you to change the "memory labels" attached to that thing. Furthermore, the better that your attitude allows you to predict future events or inputs, and the more you are rewarded for holding a certain percept, the less susceptible that percept or attitude is to being changed (Eiser, 1986).

Since the attitudes of individuals are affected by the groups to which they belong, *attitude consistency* is also a property of social groups and organizations. Generally speaking, the more important a given attitude is to the continued functioning of a group, the less likely it is that group members will give up or change this attitude (Asch, 1987).

□ □ QUESTION □ □
Studies show that most college students have attitudes very similar to those held by their parents. Can you think of at least five reasons why this might be the case?

Newcomb's Study of Bennington Women

As Theodore Newcomb notes, liberal arts colleges are populated by professors who often have very liberal political opinions. When a student from a politically conservative family arrives on such a campus, the student often comes under fairly intense social pressure to change her or his attitudes. If you were such a student, do you think you would change, or would you retain your old attitudes despite the pressure?

● Bennington College

Newcomb answered this question many years ago. At the time he began his research, he was teaching at Bennington, a woman's college in Vermont noted for its fine programs in the liberal arts. Because the student body was limited to about 600, Newcomb was able to work with the entire college population in his study of political attitudes.

Most of the women attending Bennington in the mid-1930's came from wealthy and rather conservative homes. The faculty members, however, were quite liberal in their views. Indeed, they felt duty-bound to familiarize the students with the social and political implications of a Depression-torn America and a war-threatened world. Therefore, the faculty encouraged the students to become politically active and socially concerned.

The college itself, nestled between the Taconic and the Green mountains of Vermont, was physically isolated from much of the rest of the world. The nearest town, a village of fewer than 15,000 people, offered few excitements. The students visited the town infrequently, and went home for the weekend less than once a month. Hence, the students made up what advertising executives call "a captive audience."

● Student Reference Groups

In the first part of his research, Newcomb found that the more prestige or *status* a woman had among her fellow students, the more likely it was that she was also very liberal in her views. Conservative students typically were looked down upon; liberal students were very much looked up to. Seniors were significantly less conservative than were freshmen.

Under these conditions, the entire college population acted rather like a *reference group* that rewarded liberal attitudes and punished political conservatism. Those women who *identified* with the college community tended to become much more liberal during their four years at Bennington. However, those women who tended to identify more with their parents than with their classmates *resisted* the liberal college tradition (Newcomb, 1943).

□ □ QUESTION □ □
How many Bennington women would have become politically liberal had they lived at home and commuted to their classes? What if they had taken most of their courses by television and seldom met their teachers or other students?

● 25 Years Later

To find out how their attitudes would change over time, Newcomb followed 150 of the most liberal of these women for the next 25 years of their lives. Although he originally had suspected the students might revert to a more conservative position, this turned out not to be the case with many of them. In fact, during the entire 25 years, most of the women remained liberal in their outlooks *despite family pressures.* But why?

Newcomb reports that most of these women *deliberately* set out to remain liberal in spite of their social backgrounds. They tended to select liberal (or non-conservative) husbands who would reinforce their political views. They found little pockets of liberalism in their environments and tried to stay entirely within these pockets. And they kept in close touch with their Bennington classmates who were also liberal. These students also tended to ignore those "old classmates" who weren't as liberal as they.

Newcomb believes that if maintaining a given attitude is important enough, you will consciously or unconsciously select environments that will continue to support that attitude. You may also shut out incoming sensory messages that might tend to disrupt the attitudes you already hold (a form of *autistic hostility*) (Newcomb, 1967).

• 1960's Student Activists

A recent study by Alberta Nassi tends to confirm Newcomb's findings. In 1964, highly liberal students at the University of California at Berkeley formed a loosely-knit organization called the "Free Speech Movement." Nassi looked at how these "student activists" had fared 15 years afterwards. She reports they "do not appear to have grown out of the political philosophy that galvanized their activist youth." Nassi notes they have maintained these attitudes much as the Bennington women did—by seeking environments that would protect them from change (Nassi, 1981).

Nassi studied *leaders* of the student activitist movement at Berkeley. However, Dean Hoge and Teresa Ankney studied "rank and file" members of the Free Speech Movement who were at the University of Michigan in 1969. Ten years later, the "activists" were still more interested in politics than were non-activists. However, by 1979, the former activists were no longer as strongly critical of the universities or of American society as a whole as they had been. Generally speaking, the activists were still more "radical" than the average citizen probably is. But the activists were somewhat "less radical than before" (Hoge & Ankney, 1982). Thus, the stronger your *original* commitment to a group, the more likely it is that you will *maintain* that commitment over time.

These studies are among a very few aimed at measuring *stability* of attitudes. Attitude *change* is much easier to investigate, in no small part because the subjects need not be studied over such a long time span. Indeed, as you will see, it seems that much of what we

Leaders of the 1960's Free Speech Movement remained politically active and liberal when studied fifteen years later.

know about attitude stability comes from experiments designed to change people's opinions.

□□ **QUESTION** □□
Ethnic and religious groups often tend to "flock together" even when they are free to do otherwise. How might this tendency be related to a desire to maintain attitude stability within the group?

PERSUASION AND ATTITUDE CHANGE

According to University of Massachusetts psychologist Icek Ajzen, "Social psychologists probably have expended more time, effort, and ingenuity on the study of persuasion than on the study of any other single issue." And until recently, Ajzen says, research on persuasion was primarily "guided by a conceptual framework developed in the 1950s by [Carl] Hovland and his associates at Yale University" (Ajzen, 1987).

Let's begin our survey of the literature on persuasion, then, by looking at what Hovland and his colleagues did, and at the theoretical model they created for describing *the communication process.*

The Communication Process

In one of the first major publications from the Yale group, Carl Hovland, Irving Janis, and Harold Kelley stated that *persuasive communications* have four main factors: the communicator, the message, the audience, and the feedback loop between the audience and the communicator (Hovland, Janis, & Kelley, 1953). This viewpoint is often called the "Yale model" of persuasion.

21 / Social Groups, Persuasion, and Attitude Change

Credibility (kred-ih-BILL-it-tee). From the Latin words meaning "worthy of lending money to." Literally, the power or ability to inspire belief.

According to the Yale model, the *communicator* is the person (or group) trying to induce the attitude change. As we will see, the way that the audience *perceives* the communicator often affects the readiness with which the audience will change.

The *message* is the information the communicator transmits to the audience. The type of language or pictures used, and the channel through which the communicator chooses to transmit the message, can be of critical importance.

The *audience* is the person or group whose attitude is to be changed. Obviously a clever communicator will wish to know as much as possible about the personalities and attitudinal characteristics of the audience in order to make the message as persuasive as possible.

Until fairly recently, the *audience-communicator feedback loop* was perhaps the least-studied aspect of the communication process. Yet it is of crucial importance. For unless the communicator knows what type of response the audience *actually* makes to the message, the communicator is very likely to misjudge the success of the persuasive project.

Let's begin our study of the communication process by looking at the *communicator*.

◻ ◻ **QUESTION** ◻ ◻

Why do you think the audience-communicator feedback loop was so little studied until recently?

The Communicator

If your best friend told you that a given product was incredibly good, would you be more likely to believe this communication than if you heard a TV announcer say the same thing on a television ad? Chances are you'd put more **credibility** in your friend's endorsement than in the TV announcer's. According to the Yale model, "credibility" is one of the most influential traits a communicator can possess.

◻ ◻ **QUESTION** ◻ ◻

What magazine, newspaper, or TV commentator do you trust the most?

● *High Credibility Sources*

In one of the first of the Yale studies, Hovland and Walter Weiss tested the influence of "trustworthiness" (credibility) on attitude change. They began by making a list of "communicators" they figured were very trustworthy, and another list of communicators they figured few people would trust. The "high credibility

"AT LEAST WITH WASHINGTON AS PRESIDENT, WE WON'T HAVE A CREDIBILITY GAP TO WORRY ABOUT."

sources" included the *New England Journal of Medicine*, a Nobel-Prize-winning physicist, and *Fortune* magazine. The "low credibility sources" included a noted gossip columnist, the Soviet newspaper *Pravda*, and a well-known American publication that specialized in scandals and sex-oriented stories. When Hovland and Weiss asked students to judge the credibility of these sources, about 90 percent of the subjects rated the first group as being very trustworthy and rated the second group as being exceptionally untrustworthy.

Next, Hovland and Weiss tested the "attitude toward the effectiveness of atomic submarines" in two similar groups of students. They found that most of the students were rather neutral about this highly complex topic. If we were plotting their attitudes on a graph, we would say the students were right in the middle—at the "neutral" point on the graph shown in Fig. 21.5.

Hovland and Weiss then wrote a "message" in which they argued that atomic submarines would indeed be a very important weapon in any future war. They showed this message to the two groups of students. The first group was told the message came from one of the high credibility sources (such as *Fortune*). The second group was informed the message came from one of the low credibility sources. Immediately after exposing the students to the message, Hovland and Weiss retested their subjects' attitudes.

As you might guess, the subjects in the "high credibility" group tended to accept the

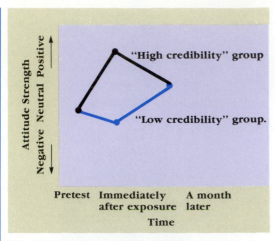

FIG. 21.5 The "sleeper effect." Effects of exposure to propaganda on "effectiveness of atomic submarines."

arguments. That is, their attitudes about the importance of atomic submarines became significantly more positive. The students in the "low credibility" group tended to reject the arguments as being "biased and untrustworthy." If anything, their attitudes became slightly more negative.

Apparently you tend to move *toward* the position of someone you trust, and *away* from the position of someone you distrust—even if this movement involves giving up your original attitude (Hovland & Weiss, 1951).

● The "Sleeper Effect"
Had Hovland and Weiss stopped their work at this point, we might well have misunderstood the real importance of communicator credibility. However, they continued by retesting all their subjects a month later. To their surprise, they found significant attitude changes in both groups over this period of time. The attitudes of the "high credibility" subjects became significantly *less* positive, while the attitudes of the "low credibility" subjects became significantly *more* positive. As Fig. 21.5 suggests, the students had apparently forgotten the *source* of their information on submarines, but remembered the *arguments* rather well. Hovland and Weiss call this the **sleeper effect** (Hovland & Weiss, 1951).

The "sleeper effect" predicts the following: The credibility of a source will have an *immediate* and often strong influence on whether you accept or reject incoming information. However, once the message has gotten through, you will soon forget the source and recall only the information itself.

□ □ **QUESTION** □ □
How much time do you spend daily worrying about "the effectiveness of atomic submarines"?

● Other Studies on the "Sleeper Effect"
Soon after Hovland and Weiss published their first results, other investigators attempted to replicate their research. Some of these investigators reported positive results (Brehm & Mann, 1975). However, many of these attempted replications failed, a fact which led many scientists to doubt the validity of the "sleeper effect" itself (Cook *et al.*, 1979; Moscovici *et al.*, 1981).

Is the "sleeper effect" a valid discovery, or not? As it happens, the answer to that question is, "sometimes yes, sometimes no; it depends on the situation." Let's look more closely at this issue, not because the effect itself has any great overriding importance, but because a study of the issues involved can tell us a lot about this type of scientific research.

First of all, the "sleeper effect" is not particularly strong, and only occurs under certain conditions. For example, Charles Gruder and his colleagues at the University of Illinois found that if they *warned their subjects* to "pay attention" to the source of the information as they read the message, the effect practically disappeared. It's only when you *forget* the source at a later time that the effect presumably occurs (Gruder *et al.*, 1978).

The "sleeper effect" can also be counteracted by "group pressures," or if you're rewarded for taking an opposing viewpoint (Brehm & Mann, 1975). Furthermore, the effect occurs primarily in the laboratory, not in real-life settings (Clarke & Clarke, 1982).

In a recent article, Ohio State psychologist Anthony Greenwald and his associates claim that the "sleeper effect" is a good example of when theory *obstructs* research progress. They believe that Hovland and Weiss *overgeneralized* their findings to situations where the "sleeper effect" didn't occur—and then spent decades trying to discover the precise conditions where the effect did occur in order to "defend their theory" (Greenwald *et al.*, 1986).

As we will see, the "sleeper effect" research was not the only instance in which the Yale group engaged in "overgeneralization."

□ □ **QUESTION** □ □
Not all social scientists take the time to interview their subjects after an experiment, to ask the subjects *why* they responded as they did. Why might this sort of interviewing be helpful?

● Credibility and "First Impressions"
A number of further experiments by Hovland, Janis, and their associates seemed to demonstrate that the factors which influence credibility are much the same as those which influence first impressions (see Chapter 20). People whom you like, or who are like you, or who seem to be acting naturally rather than "playing

Sleeper effect. As Hovland and Weiss showed, people tend to remember the facts of an argument rather well but often forget the source of those facts. The credibility you place in a source may cause you to accept or reject a message as soon as you see or hear it. However, the facts are somehow "sleeping" in your Long-term Memory and will emerge on their own long after you have forgotten who told you those facts.

Propaganda (prop-ah-GAN-dah). From the Latin word meaning "to create off-spring." You "propagate" plants when you plant seeds. You propagate ideas when you try to convince people to believe in them.

1. Should the communicator tell "both sides of the story," or give a "one-sided presentation"?
2. Should the appeal be emotional, or should it be rational?
3. Should the communicator promise to satisfy old needs, or try to create new ones?
4. Should the communicator try to create "fear of punishment" for non-compliance or "promise rewards" for compliance?

roles," are people whom you typically trust. Persons with high social status—such as doctors, scientists, and church leaders—are somehow more believable than are people with low social status (Hovland, Harvey, & Sherif, 1957; Hovland & Weiss, 1951).

According to Polish psychologist Stanislaw Mika, credibility is higher if the communicator is a member of a positive reference group, and if the message is communicated in technical rather than "street" language. Particularly if the audience is made up of educated subjects, credibility is greater if you give the audience "both sides of the question" rather than just the side of things you're trying to promote. According to Mika, the perception of the communicator's credibility also depends on the level of anxiety of the recipient and the level of anxiety-arousal of the message. Subjects with a high anxiety level tend to perceive the communicator who arouses strong anxiety as being less credible than someone who presents messages that do not evoke strong anxiety (Mika, 1981).

The question then arises, "How credible is the research on credibility?" At the beginning of their work, the Yale group assumed that "credibility" was a factor that somehow resided *within the communicator*. However, according to Anthony Greenwald and his associates, it is (1) your *perception* of the communicator, (2) the motives you *attribute* to this person, (3) the type of *argument* a given communicator uses, (4) your past history, and (5) your present state of arousal that *jointly* determine how much you will be influenced (Greenwald *et al.*, 1986).

Put more bluntly, the early assumptions about communicator credibility made by Hovland and his group have been heavily modified by later research.

☐☐ QUESTION ☐☐
If you were trying to sell a cold remedy on television, what kinds of TV actors would you choose, and how would you have them dress?

The Message
There have been hundreds of attempts to determine how to make the *message* itself more persuasive. Some of the variables studied have been the following:

The first studies, performed by Hovland and his colleagues at Yale, suggested that "one-sided" messages were usually better persuaders, as were emotional appeals (Hovland *et al.*, 1957). More recent research, however, suggests that the situation is far more complex than originally thought. For the type of message typically must be tailored to suit the intended audience (DeBono, 1987; Leippe & Elkin, 1987).

The one exception to this rule of complexity seems to be that of fear-arousing messages.

● *Fear-arousing Messages*
Many of us seem to believe that people would behave in more socially-acceptable ways if someone in authority just threatened them enough. In recent years, for instance, nation-wide campaigns against AIDS, other venereal diseases, the use of hard drugs, cigarette smoking, and the dangers of not wearing seat belts have emphasized the "hellfire and damnation" approach. That is, the main thrust of the **propaganda** has been to describe in exquisite detail the terrible consequences of various types of misbehavior.

But are such threats really as effective as we sometimes think them to be? The experimental evidence suggests that "the punitive approach" seldom yields the results most people believe it ought to.

In 1953, Irving Janis and Seymour Feshbach investigated the effects of fear-arousing communications on high school students. These scientists picked "dental hygiene" as their topic. They wrote three different 15-minute lectures on tooth decay. The first was a "high fear" lecture that contained 71 references to pain, cancer, paralysis, blindness, mouth infections, inflamed gums, ugly or discolored teeth, and dental drills. The second, or "moderate fear," lecture was somewhat less threatening. But the third, or "minimal fear," lecture was quite different. It made no mention at all of pain and disease. Instead, the "minimal fear" message suggested ways of *avoiding* cavities and decayed teeth through proper dental hygiene.

Janis and Feshbach presented each of the three appeals to a different group of 50 high school students (a fourth group of students heard no lecture at all and thus served as a control group). Janis and Feshbach found that *immediately afterwards*, the subjects exposed to the "high fear" lecture were highly impressed with what they heard. A week later, however, only 28 percent of the "high fear" group had brushed their teeth more often, and 20 percent of them were actually *doing worse*. In marked contrast, the "low fear" students were not particularly impressed with the lecture—but a week later 50 percent of them were "brushing better" and only 14 percent were doing a worse job (Janis & Feshbach, 1953).

The high fear appeal apparently evoked strong emotional responses in the students, many of whom thought that being frightened was somehow "good for them." When it came to actually *changing behaviors*, though, the high-fear message simply didn't work as well as did the minimal-fear message. In fact, for reasons we will discuss in a moment, the high-fear propaganda seems to have had *exactly the opposite* long-term effect that you might have predicted.

• Counter-propaganda

Propagandists often point out that it is not enough to change the attitudes an audience has. You must also make sure that the audience resists any further attempts that might push the audience back toward their original beliefs. Effective propaganda, then, not only causes attitude shifts but also protects against *counter-propaganda*.

A week after the high school students in the Janis-Feshbach experiment had listened to the dental hygiene lectures, the experimenters exposed the students to information that contradicted what they had originally been told. The students were then asked whether they believed this counter-propaganda or not.

Twice as many subjects in the high-fear group were affected by the counter-persuasion as were subjects in the minimal-fear group. Janis and Feshbach concluded that, "Under conditions where people will be exposed to competing communications dealing with the same issues, the use of a strong fear appeal will tend to be less effective than a minimal appeal in producing stable and persistent attitude changes" (Janis & Feshbach, 1953).

□ □ QUESTION □ □
Given the data on the long-term results of the "high fear" approach, why do so many communicators still make use of this technique?

• Fearful Avoidance or "Self-Efficacy"?

In a recent article, Stanford psychologist Albert Bandura states that "The belief that fear controls avoidance behavior dies hard, despite growing evidence to the contrary" (Bandura, 1986b).

It is not someone's threat that keeps you from performing a "forbidden act," Bandura says. Rather, it is your own perception of how well you can cope with the situations that determines what you will do. If you perceive yourself as having "self-efficacy," Bandura believes, you will simply ignore the threat of punishment and do whatever you think you're competent to do. However, if you believe that you lack the skills required to handle the situation, you may well "obey the law." But you may well *attribute* your obedient behavior to the threat, not to your perceived "self-inefficacy" (Bandura, 1977a, 1983).

In Chapter 10, we described G. Alan Marlatt's research on therapy with alcoholic patients. Marlatt discovered that when the treatment was primarily punishment-oriented and "confrontational," many patients stopped drinking immediately. When tested a year later, however, most of these patients were actually *drinking more* than before they started therapy. When therapy consisted of teaching the patients "self-control skills," most patients showed an immediate but slight increase in alcohol consumption. A year or so later, though, these same patients were drinking significantly less than when therapy started (Marlatt, 1983). The parallel between the Janis-Feshbach studies and the Marlatt experiment are, in their own way, fairly striking.

□ □ QUESTION □ □
How would you explain Marlatt's data in terms of Bandura's "self-efficacy" theory?

• Scared Straight

In the spring of 1979, a film called *Scared Straight* was presented on many American television stations. The movie shows how inmates at a prison in New Jersey used "scare tactics" to frighten troubled young people into avoiding further scrapes with the law. The youths spent several hours in the prison, mostly listening to the convicts describe the effects of homosexual rape, fights, and prison brutality. The film is highly dramatic, and implies strongly that the "Scared Straight" program has been a great success. The film won an Academy Award in 1979. After the movie was broadcast, many state legislatures debated whether or not to make such treatment compulsory for all juvenile offenders.

Unfortunately, the actual data do not support the effectiveness either of the first version of the program or of the film's fear-arousing message. In a recent article, John Heeren and David Shichor note that the program was popular for all the wrong reasons—it promised a

Deterrent (dee-TURR-ent). From a Latin word meaning "to frighten, or to discourage from acting." Punishment is usually thought to be a highly effective deterrent that keeps "sane" people from commiting crimes. In fact, many studies suggest that fear of punishment seldom keeps people from doing things that they really want to do, or that they find particularly rewarding. If punishment really deterred criminals, those countries with the most punitive laws would be those with the lowest crime rates, which doesn't happen to be the case. Closer to home, punitive laws have obviously not stopped people in the US from smoking marijuana, exceeding the speed limit, or driving while intoxicated.

"quick and easy fix" to a complex social problem, and a "fix" that was cheap, as well (Heeren & Shichor, 1984). Echoing these sentiments, University of Detroit psychologists Robert Homant and Gregory Osowski note that "The program's dubious effectiveness, poor methodology, and difficult political implications [stand in marked contrast to] its low cost and positive impact on the adult offenders involved" (Homant & Osowski, 1981).

Put in simple terms, "Scared Straight" doesn't have much of a positive effect on the youthful offenders, but the prisoners certainly enjoyed scaring the youngsters.

Worse than this, there is considerable evidence that "Scared Straight" can have *negative effects* on some of the young people. Roy Lewis works for the California Department of Youth Authority. In a recent study, he found little or no positive effect of using programs such as "Scared Straight" with juvenile delinquents. In fact, Lewis reports, those youngsters at "high risk" apparently were *more* likely to engage in further crimes after being involved in the program (Lewis, 1983).

Although the fear-arousing tactics of *Scared Straight* were highly acclaimed, actual data indicated that the experience had little effect on deterring young people from crime.

□□ **QUESTION** □□

How would you explain the *increase* in crime by high risk offenders in terms of Bandura's "self-efficacy theory"?

● *Nothing Succeeds Like Success*

According to *attribution theory*, you see your own actions as being a response to environmental circumstances. But you see the actions of others as being determined primarily by their personality or character traits. Therefore, you may believe that "punishment works" because others need a fear-evoking **deterrent** to keep their anti-social impulses under control. But the data show that many criminals—particularly youthful offenders—simply don't have the *social skills* to succeed in a complex environment. What would happen if juvenile delinquents were given skill-training rather than being threatened?

In 1979, Carolyn Mills and Tim Walter gave an answer to this question. They reported achieving a marked reduction in anti-social behaviors among a group of youthful offenders who were given special training in how to get and hold a job. Mills and Walter began with a group of 76 young people aged 14–17 who had been arrested four times or more prior to the start of the experiment. Mills and Walter randomly selected 23 of the young people to be a "no-treatment control group." The other 53 were put into a behavioral training program.

In the first part of their program, Mills and Walter recruited a number of local business people who were willing to offer employment to youths "on probation." These business people signed contracts agreeing, among other things, to give the young people day-by-day feedback on their performance and to meet with the experimenters weekly to discuss the youths' progress.

Next, Mills and Walter asked the youths to make a list of the behaviors they thought would be *expected* of them while working. If the subjects could not guess, they were given a list of job-appropriate activities produced by the employers. The youths then "role-played" the behaviors they thought would help them get and hold the job. They were rewarded for learning these skills and, once they were on the job, they got written feedback *daily* by the employer.

When the subjects had been successful "on the job" for a period of several weeks, Mills and Walter began helping the youths gain skills in handling personal and school-related problems (rather than focusing primarily on job-related tasks). All in all, the subjects were followed for a period of 18 months or more.

Mills and Walter report that more than 90 percent of the experimental subjects had no further arrests, while only 30 percent of the control subjects stayed out of trouble. Some 85 percent of the experimental subjects stayed in school, but only 14 percent of the control subjects did.

Mills and Walter note two further points of interest. At the beginning of their intervention program, their subjects got considerable verbal harassment from their peers for "giving in to the system." However, as the subjects began earning good paychecks, many of these peers voluntarily requested placement in the training program. Second, while the training program was fairly costly, the "re-arrest" rate among the trainees was so small that the juvenile court sponsoring the program ended up saving many thousands of dollars (Mills & Walter, 1979).

In summary, we might conclude that changing people's attitudes may be important—but teaching people the skills that will allow them to *maintain healthy attitudes* and a strong feeling of "self-efficacy" may be the best form of propaganda presently available to us.

• *Fear-arousing Messages: A Summary*

To summarize, Hovland and his associates at Yale were correct in noting that fear appeals typically have a negative rather than a positive effect. However, the Yale group was not as successful as were other experimenters in discovering ways of changing inappropriate or antisocial attitudes and behaviors.

☐☐ **QUESTION** ☐☐
Does criticism or punishment for inappropriate behaviors *by itself* tell you what to do in order to succeed?

THE AUDIENCE

In terms of Helson's Adaptation-level Theory, the "message" is a *stimulus* factor, while the social context in which the message appears is a *background* factor. The character traits and past experiences of the audience are, as you might expect, *personality* factors that affect how the audience will perceive and respond to the message.

Obviously, the most persuasive messages are those created with all three factors in mind. A good communicator thus attempts to discover as much as possible about the audience, and then *shapes* the message to suit both the occasion and the people receiving the message. However, as we will see, it also helps if the communicator *gets feedback* from the audience concerning the effectiveness of the persuasive message. Unfortunately, neither the Yale group (under Hovland's guidance) nor several other investigators bothered to study the *reactions* of their audiences. A case in point is a "classic" study on persuasion performed in Cincinnati many years ago.

The Cincinnati Study

Knowing something about your audience doesn't always guarantee you will be able to get your message *through to them*. Several years ago, Shirley Star and Helen Hughes helped lead a monumental advertising campaign designed to inform the citizens of Cincinnati about the great value of the United Nations. Star and Hughes began by taking surveys to determine what people thought about the UN. The groups who knew the least about the UN (and who liked it the least) included the relatively uneducated, the elderly, and the poor.

Once Star and Hughes knew the characteristics of their target audience, they carried on a six-month "pro-United Nations" campaign. Unfortunately, the messages apparently reached or persuaded few of the target population. Instead, the propaganda was effective primarily with young people and with the better-educated and relatively well-to-do segment of the general public. These were, of course, the very people who were already favorably disposed toward the world organization (Star & Hughes, 1950).

☐☐ **QUESTION** ☐☐
How might you explain the response of the "target audience" in the Star and Hughes study in terms of *autistic hostility*?

Audience Responses

Why did the Cincinnati campaign fail? There probably are many different reasons. To begin with, we have no guarantee that Star and Hughes knew what kinds of messages would be most likely to reach their target audience (the poor, the uneducated, the elderly). Nor can we be sure that those involved in creating the propaganda knew what sorts of appeals would convince the targets to change their attitudes.

A more glaring mistake, however, was the fact that Star and Hughes did nothing to establish feedback loops to monitor the *effects* of their propaganda campaign while it was going on. The Cincinnati communicators talked—the audience was merely supposed to listen and to respond appropriately. We will have more to say about this point in a moment.

The one "success story" in the Cincinnati study was that people *actually engaged* in the propaganda campaign showed significant attitude change in the desired direction. As they worked on the project, this group of people apparently became more and more committed to making the study a success. Since the group was favorable toward the UN, anyone who joined the group was under strong pressure to conform to the group norm. These individuals also had the greatest exposure to the persuasive messages (McConnell, 1966).

□ □ **QUESTION** □ □
How successful would the Mills and Walter study of juvenile offenders have been had the experimenters not monitored continuously the youths' actual "on the job" behaviors?

The Yale Studies: An Evaluation

As we noted earlier, the studies by Carl Hovland and his colleagues at Yale had a tremendous impact on the study of persuasion and communication. For the Yale group's rather simplistic approach to studying human behavior seemed to promise that "merely changing attitudes" could be an effective method of combating prejudice, stereotypes, delinquency, and the negative effects of propaganda.

However, as Richard Petty, Thomas Ostrom, and Timothy Brock point out, in recent years the Yale group's work "has fallen on hard times." For the social issues Hovland and his associates were studying turned out to be far more complex than they had assumed would be the case. According to Petty, Ostrom, and Brock, there were several reasons why the Yale approach failed:

First, Hovland and his colleagues assumed that what they found in the laboratory would readily translate to real-life situations. But that turned out not to be the case. The Star and Hughes study is a good example of why the Yale approach failed. In the *laboratory*—using college students as subjects—the Star and Hughes persuasive attempts would have succeeded. In *real life*—when the target audience was the poor and uneducated segment of the population—the message failed to get through. The Yale approach was tested on "willing student subjects," not "the unwilling general public."

Second, Hovland and his associates assumed that the "audience" was a passive receptacle into which the communicator poured a message. Indeed, Hovland once defined his research as the study of "Who says what, how, and to whom." The Yale group almost completely ignored the *response* of the audience to the inputs that it received. However, as research soon showed, the audience was anything but passive. Indeed, the audience frequently would argue with the communicators, reject what was said to them, or refuse to listen further to a given message or communicator. By the 1980's, most scientists studying the persuasive process had begun to focus as much on active audience responses as on such factors as the "communicator" and the "message."

Third, the Yale group had assumed that *attitudes control behavior.* But by 1965, psychologists had discovered an unexpected difference between what people *said* their attitudes were, and what people actually *did* in real-life settings. Most of us conform at one time or another—but we seldom *perceive* ourselves as being "conformist." And few authoritarian people are likely to refer to themselves by that name on a pen-and-paper test. Furthermore, many of us apparently have very inconsistent or conflicting attitudes (Petty, Ostrom, & Brock, 1981).

The failure of the Yale group's approach led Richard Petty and John Cacioppo to propose their own approach to the study of persuasion, which they call the "elaboration likelihood model."

● The Elaboration Likelihood Model

According to Petty and Cacioppo, factors such as the "communicator, message, and audience" are of *secondary importance* when it comes to attitude change. These "secondary factors" have an effect on your attitudes only when you aren't really *involved* in the situation. Do you *really* care about the supposed effectiveness of atomic submarines? If not, then you might indeed be swayed by the "credibility" of a presumed expert.

However, Petty and Cacioppo say, when it comes to the *primary* issues in your life, you "thoughtfully assess and elaborate on the central merits" of the persuasive messages you receive. If your *assessment* is positive, your attitudes will change in a positive direction. However, it is your *cognitive response* to the message, and not the message itself, that changes your attitudes (Petty & Cacioppo, 1986).

Put in simpler terms, Petty and Cacioppo state that the more you think about ("elaborate on") persuasive messages, the greater the "likelihood" that you will be affected by them.

University of Massachusetts psychologist Icek Ajzen believes the Petty and Cacioppo model is superior to that offered by Hovland and the Yale group. But it too has its flaws, Ajzen says. So far, Petty and Cacioppo have paid little attention to fear-arousing messages, nor have they specified how "elaborated thoughts" get incorporated into "permanent belief systems" (Ajzen, 1987).

There is another—and very important—point that Petty and Cacioppo have not yet addressed: the relationship between *attitudes* and *behaviors.* They do note that attitudes changed by "elaborated thoughts" are more *predictive* of future behaviors than are attitudes changed via the Yale model. However, Petty and Cacioppo have not as yet specified how attitudes get *translated* into behaviors.

It's time we addressed just that issue.

ATTITUDES VERSUS BEHAVIORS

According to most social psychologists, whenever you state an attitude, you are making a prediction about your future thoughts, feelings, and behaviors. But what are we to think if your attitudinal statement doesn't predict what you actually do at some future time?

● *Chinese and Blacks Keep Out!*

The research study that first opened up this problem was reported many years ago by R.T. LaPiere. Just prior to the Second World War, LaPiere spent considerable time driving through the US with a Chinese couple as his companions. Despite the very strong "anti-Chinese" prejudice to be found among many Americans at that time, LaPiere and his friends were refused service only once during 10,000 miles of travel.

Later, when they were safely home, LaPiere sent questionnaires to all the hotels and cafes where they had stopped. One item on the questionnaire asked, "Will you accept members of the Chinese race as guests in your establishment?" More than 90 percent of the places responded with a very firm "no," and yet all but one of these hundreds of establishments actually had accepted the Chinese couple without question or comment. Obviously there was a very marked difference between "attitude" and "behavior" on the part of these establishments (LaPiere, 1934).

In a similar study reported in 1952, B. Kutner, Carol Wilkins, and Penny Yarrow had three young women visit various restaurants in a fashionable suburban community in the northeastern part of the US. Two of the women were white; the third was black. The two white women always arrived at the restaurant first, asked for a table for three, and were seated. Shortly thereafter, the black woman entered, informed the head waiter or hostess that she was with friends who were already seated, found the table, sat down with the two white women, and was served without question.

Two weeks after each visit, Kutner, Wilkins, and Yarrow wrote a letter to each restaurant asking if they would serve blacks. Not one replied. The experimenters then called the manager of each establishment on the phone. The managers uniformly responded in a very cool and distant manner, suggesting that they held a highly prejudiced attitude toward serving blacks. Yet, as in the LaPiere study, this attitude was simply not translated into action when the restaurant personnel were faced with seating a black person (Kutner, Wilkins, & Yarrow, 1952).

Since 1965, there have been dozens of similar experiments, all of which suggest that attitudes (as measured by questionnaires) are often poor indicators of what people actually do in real-life situations. Furthermore, there is often little relationship between attitude *change* and a subsequent change in the way a person *behaves*. Just as important, as we noted earlier in this chapter, people often change

Many well-informed Americans state that they know AIDS is not a gay disease and is not spread by casual contact. However, some of these same people may avoid restaurants with gay waiters.

their behaviors *without* changing the attitudes related to the behaviors.

☐☐ QUESTION ☐☐

How would you explain LaPiere's results in terms of Adaptation-level Theory?

● *Attitudes Toward Attitudes*

In their classic book *Opinions and Personality*, M. Brewster Smith, Jerome Bruner, and Robert W. White ask a most important question: "Of what possible use to you are your opinions?" The answer to that question is not an easy one to find. Smith, Bruner, and White believe that attitudes or opinions *serve needs*. That is, whenever you express an attitude, you are really describing some need or goal that you are "driven" to fulfill. When you state your attitudes to the people around you, therefore, you presumably are hunting for others with similar needs who might assist you in achieving mutual goals. Like most social psychologists, Smith, Bruner, and White believe that attitudes are *internal processes* that somehow guide or direct your behaviors (Smith, Bruner, & White, 1956).

A radically different approach to the subject, however, was stated in the late 1970's by Daryl Bem. According to Bem, attitudes are simply *verbal statements* about your own behaviors. Bem points out that LaPiere really measured two quite different attitudinal responses that occurred in two very different environments. LaPiere's questionnaire seemed designed to elicit negative responses from the hotel and innkeepers to whom it was sent. But when LaPiere presented himself and a well-dressed Chinese couple at the desk of the hotel, the stimulus situation was so different from that evoked by the questionnaire that the behavioral response of the innkeeper was bound to be different as well (Bem, 1977; Bem & Allen, 1974).

● Bem's "Triple Typological" Theory of Personality

More recently, Daryl Bem has developed his own "triple typology theory" of personality that relates attitudes to behavior. According to Bem, your personality is a function of the complex *interactions* among three variables: your attitudes, your "behavioral style," and the specific *situations* you find yourself in.

Bem believes that you develop particular "response tendencies" or "styles" of behavior that express themselves *only* in particular situations. For example, a "typical college jock" might behave in a fairly crude, "macho" manner in the locker room with "the rest of the gang," but express quite different attitudes and respond in an entirely different fashion when first meeting his girlfriend's parents. The consistencies in the young man's behaviors, Bem says, are thus the product of an *interaction* between the situation and his own personal style (Bem, 1983).

To give another example, Bem believes that, *in the laboratory*, you tend to respond in quite a different way than you do in the real world. For in laboratory situations, he says, you are free to act in some "idealized" way. Thus, asking you about your *attitudes* when you are a subject in an experiment can often tell a social psychologist how you will react in a given laboratory situation. However, Bem notes, you are likely to behave in quite a different fashion in most real-world settings. Thus, Bem believes, if we wish to predict your real-world actions, we should ask those people who have actually *seen how you behave* in those situations, rather than

asking you about such matters *when you are still in the laboratory* (Bem, 1982).

● Psychological Traps

Yet another explanation of the LaPiere study comes from a recent article by Jeffrey Z. Rubin. Once you "invest too much" in a situation, Rubin says, you may continue in a given line of behavior simply because you can't find an easy way out. Rubin calls these situations "psychological traps."

Suppose you phone someone and are put on hold. You wait a while and consider hanging up. But you'd just have to call again. So you wait some more. Then you decide, since you've waited so long already, you'll "lose" the time you've already waited if you hang up. So you wait still longer.

Rubin gives another example of a psychological trap that seems unbelievable to many people—until they get caught up in it. Some years ago, Yale economist Martin Shubik auctioned off a dollar bill to friends at a cocktail party. The money went to the highest bidder. The "trap" came from the fact that the person who made the second-highest bid also had to pay whatever the person with the highest bid had offered, but didn't get the dollar. Rubin reports that "Several researchers have had people play the Dollar Auction game under controlled laboratory conditions and have found that the participants typically end up bidding far in excess of the $1 prize at stake, sometimes paying as much as $5 or $6 for a dollar bill" (Rubin, 1981).

The interesting question is why people would engage in such a self-defeating course of action. According to Boston University psychologist Allan Teger, participants in the Dollar Auction typically offer two reasons for their behavior. The first reason has to do with economics—they genuinely want the money (at first). Then they are motivated by a desire to regain their losses or to avoid losing more money. The second reason is intra-psychic—a desire to "save face," a desire to prove yourself as the "best player," or an urge to "punish the other person." However, these are all *after-the-fact* attitudes expressed by people to explain why they behaved in a self-defeating manner (cited in Rubin, 1981).

Rubin's work suggests that when, for example, two white women are seated in a restaurant, the manager *has an investment* in these customers. Thus, when a black woman arrives to join the two whites, the manager may feel "trapped." For to refuse service to the newcomer means "a messy scene" in which the white women may get up and leave. Thus, the *social situation* may determine which of two attitudes ("not wanting to serve blacks" versus "not wanting to make a scene and lose customers") actually prevails.

Do most attitude questionnaires specify the social situation in which the attitude is to be expressed?

Reciprocal Determinism

Are your thoughts and actions regulated by internal processes such as attitudes? Or by environmental inputs that directly influence your visible behaviors? Do you "change your mind," and let your actions follow suit? Or do you first change the way you act, and then alter your attitudes to fit your behaviors?

According to Albert Bandura, you do both at the same time: "Explanations of human behavior have generally favored unidirectional causal models emphasizing either environmental or internal determinants of behavior. In social learning theory, causal processes are conceptualized in terms of **reciprocal determinism**" (Bandura, 1978). Bandura goes on to say that, from his point of view, psychological functioning involves a *continuous* interaction between behavioral, cognitive, and environmental influences.

Bandura believes that you first build up "behavioral standards" by observing others and by noticing the consequences of their actions. You may then test these standards yourself, to determine if you will be rewarded or punished for thinking and acting in a given way. Once your standards are set, though, you tend to *evaluate* future social inputs in terms of (1) the situational context in which the input appears, (2) your own internal standards, and (3) the possible consequences of acting or thinking in a given way. But these three factors are *reciprocal influences* on each other (Bandura, 1977).

To give an example of what Bandura is talking about, consider the following: Other people obviously influence your internal standards. That's the "external environment" at work. However, as Newcomb has shown, you tend to avoid people who don't share your standards and seek out those who do. So, you *influence your environment* by hunting for those settings that will allow you to act in the way that your internal standards dictate. You may also try to influence the people around you, so that they reinforce you for what you consider appropriate behavior.

The notion of "self-regulating systems" lies at the heart of Bandura's position. He sees you not as the "passive audience" for persuasive messages from your environment, which was the position of Hovland and the Yale group. Nor does Bandura view your mind as a "behavior-producing machine," as do trait theorists. Nor does he assume that all of your responses are conditioned reactions triggered off by external inputs, as does B.F. Skinner. Instead, Bandura believes that there is a reciprocal *interplay* between your social inputs, your perceptions, and your responses. You continually evaluate the consequences of perceiving a given stimulus in a particular way. And you change both your behaviors and your attitudes in order to achieve your own particular goals (Bandura, 1986a).

When most people diet, they tend to avoid banquets and bakery shops. How does this wise decision on the dieter's part tend to support Bandura's views?

THE ETHICS OF ATTITUDE CHANGE

Whatever solution you take to the attitude-behavior (mind-body) problem, there is a deeper issue involved. We *do* know ways of inducing attitude change, and we *do* have methods for creating new behaviors. Given this knowledge, we must then face the following issue: *Who has the right to use these powerful techniques?*

Is it right to talk someone into buying an expensive new car? Is it ethical to convince people that the United Nations is worthy of support? Is it a morally-responsible act to persuade a mentally-disordered person to seek professional help? Is it ethical to teach children religious beliefs or economic theories? Shouldn't all individuals be free to make up their own minds without interference from persuasive sources (Barnes, 1982)?

Psychology, as an objective science, is not in a position to answer ethical questions. Psychology can, however, attempt to provide some of the information and facts that you will need in order to make your own ethical decisions (Sieber, 1982).

In truth, everything you do in the presence of someone else affects that person. That being the case, the only way you can hope to judge the ethical value of your actions is to have an *objective* understanding of how your behavior influences others. And since you acquired many of your own attitudes from others, you will also need to learn as much *scientific* information as possible about how you were "shaped" to be what you presently are. For only when you know the full facts of how people communicate with and influence each other can you hope to make good ethical decisions about human attitudes and actions.

As Carl Rogers noted long ago, people need people, and no one ever achieved self-actualization without considerable assistance from hundreds of other individuals. The debt you owe these people, in return, is to help them achieve their own unique goals.

And perhaps that is what ethics is all about, at some deep psychological level—helping others so that they in turn can help you. There-

Reciprocal determinism (ree-SIP-pro-cal dee-TURR-min-ism). Bandura's belief that psychological functions are a joint function of behavioral, cognitive, and environmental influences. According to Bandura, you build up schemas (behavioral standards, or perceptions) that allow you to evaluate both social inputs and your own reactions to those inputs. Your evaluations affect both your attitudes and your behaviors. And because you monitor the consequences of having a given attitude or acting a certain way, your attitudes and behaviors can affect your future evaluations. Thus, each part of the process—behavior, attitudes and cognitions, and environmental inputs—affects every other part in a reciprocal manner.

fore, the more that you learn about human behavior (and attitudes), the more likely it will be that you can achieve your own form of self-actualization, and the more likely it will be that you can be of *optimal* assistance in helping others.

Now that we've covered many of the theoretical aspects of social psychology, it's time we turned our attention to more practical subjects. We'll do just that in the next (and final) chapter.

SUMMARY

1. A **group** is a set of persons considered as a **social system**—a collection of two or more individuals who are psychologically related to or dependent upon one another and who share common goals.

2. There are many types of groups, including **formal membership groups**, **family groups**, and **ethnic groups**. **Interaction groups** are made up of individuals who have frequent face-to-face encounters and who share **common attitudes**.

3. The more similar the members, the more **cohesive** the group and the more **homogeneous** it becomes. The more cohesive a group, the more **commitment** the members are likely to have toward the group and its goals.

4. Our **reference groups** are those we look to as social **models** or **norms**. Reference groups give us **feedback** on our behavior by rewarding movements toward and punishing movements away from the **group norm**.

5. Whenever we make a judgment or give an opinion that is different from the perceived group norm, we typically find ourselves under strong psychological **pressure to conform** more closely to the group standard.

6. **Group pressures** become most effective when at least four group members have announced their judgments or opinions without being openly contradicted. If even one group member disagrees openly, **group cohesion** may be destroyed.

7. Some group members know when they are conforming (but do so anyway), but others **yield to pressures** because these pressures affect their **perceptions** of what has taken place.

8. Helson's **Adaptation-level Theory** states that judgments, perceptions, and attitudes are influenced by three factors—the **stimulus**, the **background** in which the stimulus appears, and the **personality and past experience** of the individual under pressure.

9. **Stimulus factors** include the vagueness of the stimulus, the difficulty of the stimulus task, and the instructions given. **Background factors** include the size of the group, how the group members feel about

each other, how expert they are in the task at hand, the openness with which judgments must be made, and whether the group decision must be unanimous.

10. Although there does not seem to be a "conformist personality," **yielders** in conformity experiments are frequently reported to be more **authoritarian** than are people who tend to resist group pressures. Conformity increases when it is **rewarded**.

11. Milgram's research suggests that, when given orders from a higher authority, most of us tend to show **obedience** even if we sometimes end up hurting ourselves or others. We are particularly likely to obey orders if the people around us are doing so.

12. Latané's **theory of social impact** states that the impact of the social environment is determined by the **strength**, the **immediacy**, and the **number** of people around you. **Bystander apathy** occurs in part because groups tend to **dilute** feelings of responsibility.

13. **Cognitive dissonance** develops when you hold two conflicting attitudes, or when your attitudes differ from your behaviors. According to Festinger, all people act to **reduce dissonance**, usually by changing the way they **perceive** the situation rather than by changing their actual behaviors.

14. **Social conflicts** can occur between groups that must compete for limited resources. Sherif has shown **inter-group conflicts** can be reduced if the groups are either **threatened** by an outside danger or **rewarded** for working toward a common goal of overriding importance.

15. Henri Tajfel's **social identity theory** states that you first define who you are, then join groups whose members have similar attitudes. But according to **social learning theory**, you tend to join groups first, then take on the group norms. In truth, you do both.

16. Attitudes are important because they allow you to **predict** future events. They also aid you in **remembering** past experiences.

17. In Newcomb's study of Bennington women, he found that students felt **group pressures to conform** to the liberal environment at the college. The most liberal of the stu-

dents tended to seek out or create post-college environments that would help them **maintain** their liberal attitudes.

18. **Student activists** from the 1960's have tended to maintain their "radical" attitudes over the years much as have the Bennington women. The more **committed** to the radical attitude the students were, the less they changed their views.

19. According to the "Yale model," the **communication process** is influenced by at least four different factors: the **communicator**, the **message**, the **audience**, and the **feedback** (if any) from the audience to the communicator

20. Early studies by Hovland and his associates suggested that one of the most important aspects of the communication process is the **credibility** the audience places in the communicator.

21. According to Hovland, immediately after hearing a message, we tend to accept the word of **high credibility sources**, but reject the word of **low credibility sources**. Several weeks later, we tend to be more influenced by the actual content of the message than by its source—a phenomenon called the **sleeper effect**. Later research showed the sleeper effect can be counteracted if you are reminded of the original **source** of the message in some fashion, and that the effect occurs only in fairly trivial situations.

22. When we receive **fear-arousing messages**, our first impression may be that the stimulus is a very persuasive one. However, studies show that fear usually achieves little more than **repression** and does not protect the audience from **counter-propaganda**.

23. High-risk youthful offenders exposed to **"Scared Straight"** programs actually had a higher rate of subsequent arrests than did a control group not exposed to the fear-arousing experiences.

24. Youthful offenders given **job-skill training**

and **positive feedback** about their attitudes and behaviors showed a much lower rate of subsequent arrests than did control-group subjects.

25. The more that a **propagandist** constructs the message to fit the prior beliefs and attitudes of the audience, and the more the communicator pays attention to **audience feedback**, the more successful the persuasive attempt will usually be.

26. People involved in presenting **propaganda** are usually more affected by it than are the intended audience.

27. The Yale researchers had problems because: (a) they ignored the **social context** in which persuasion occurs, (b) they assumed the audience was **passive** and thus ignored **feedback**, and (c) they presumed that **attitudes always determine behavior**.

28. According to the **elaboration likelihood model** of persuasion, the more that you **elaborate** or think about a message, the greater the **likelihood** that you will change your attitudes.

29. According to Bem's **triple typology model** of personality, behavior is determined by the joint interaction of **attitudes**, **behavioral style**, and the **specific situation** the person is in.

30. Some studies suggest that attitudes are poor predictors of what people actually do. One reason may be that attitudes are **verbal statements about your own behaviors**. Or, you may invest so much in a situation you are **psychologically trapped** into behavior in ways counter to your attitudes.

31. Bandura believes psychological functions are determined by **reciprocal determinism**—a continuous interaction among behavioral, cognitive, and environmental influences. Thus, you change both your attitudes and behaviors **simultaneously** in order to achieve your goals.

(Continued from page 542.)

"All right, Mr. Kraus, please calm down and tell me what happened."

Norm Kraus leaned forward excitedly, hardly noticing the hardness of the chair in Professor Ward's office. "Well, the Blake experiment worked just like it was supposed to. I put a flashlight bulb inside an empty cocoa box to make the auto-kinetic light, and I got some friends to act as stooges. We made tape recordings of their voices, but I wanted to start with the situation where the subject was sitting right in the middle of my four friends."

Taking a quick breath, the young man hurried on before Ward could interrupt him.

"I got an undergraduate named Dan Gorenflo to volunteer for the experiment. I introduced Dan to the stooges, and then we all went into the lab. The cocoa box was hidden behind a black curtain that I didn't open until the lights were off when nobody could see what it was. Then I gave Dan and my friends the song and dance about airplanes moving on the horizon, turned off the overhead light, and left them to adapt to the dark."

"Sounds fine so far," Ward said.

Norm Kraus smiled. "The lab next door was my control room, where I ran the experiment. I could open the curtains, turn the flashlight bulb off and on, and talk to the subjects over a loud-speaker. I put a mike right in front of Dan so I could hear his voice. And, of course, I could also hear the stooges and make sure they said what they were supposed to say."

Professor Ward nodded in an absent-minded fashion. "Yes, yes, but how did it go?"

Norm beamed. "Beautifully, at least at first. I was sitting in the control room recording Dan's reactions. The first trial, he seemed to ignore the group. But on the next 14 trials, he hit the midpoint of their judgments right on the nose. I couldn't believe it! I was so excited at the end of the test that I rushed over to the next room to congratulate everybody and turn on the lights. And that's when it happened."

"Dare I ask what?"

"Well, Dan came bolting out of the lab and went rushing down the hall toward the toilet. I had to chase after him to catch up. He was shouting at me over his shoulder, 'Don't believe a word I said. You can't use my results.'"

"Did he tell you why?"

Norm nodded. "Yes, sir, he did. He said, 'You put me in a bad seat. I couldn't see the damned light at all. I just said whatever the other subjects said. You shouldn't do things like that, it curdles the stomach.'" Norm frowned rather theatrically. "And then Dan rushed into the john and was sick all over the place."

Ward picked up his pipe and stuffed it with tobacco. After a moment, he asked, "Why do you think Dan responded that way? Were the group pressures to conform that strong?"

Norm tried to hide the smirk that kept creeping over his face. "Serendipity, sir. After I left your office the last time, I looked the word up."

"Oh, yes, the Persian fairy tale about the three princes of Serendip, or Sri Lanka, as it is called today. They were always going out on expeditions to search for something like iron and discovering a mountain of gold instead. Invaluable gift in scientific research, serendipity is." The Professor smiled rather warmly. "And you think you have the gift?"

Norm attempted a modest grin. "Well, I did luck onto something strictly by accident. It isn't every day you can upset a subject that much without laying hands on him."

"All right, Mr. Kraus, tell me exactly what happened."

Norm Kraus leaned back in the hard chair and relaxed. "Well, at first I couldn't figure it out, and neither could the stooges. But then I checked out each piece of equipment, just to make sure. Guess what I found?"

"I'm veritably breathless with anticipation," Ward said, smiling with encouragement.

"The flashlight bulb had burned out! As far as I can tell, the light went on during the first trial, but then it got shorted or something. I kept saying the light would go on . . . NOW. And the stooges kept giving their reports. But for the last 14 trials, the light simply didn't appear."

"Why didn't your friends, the stooges, notice it?"

"I had painted the numbers they were supposed to give on little cards—in luminous paint. They were just too busy trying to read those dim little numbers to notice the light had gone out."

Professor Ward poked at the tobacco in his pipe with a match. "But why did the poor young man get sick?"

"How would you like it if you were sitting smack in the middle of four people who all acted as if they could see something that you saw once, but couldn't see thereafter? Dan told me later that he looked and looked, but the light just wasn't there. He thought maybe he was going crazy. But he didn't want to upset the experiment, so he just sat there and gave the same reports the stooges were giving. He couldn't disobey orders by leaving, and he couldn't violate the group standard by saying he didn't see what everybody else was seeing. The stress was so great that his stomach curled up into a tight little ball. He said he'd never felt so much pressure in his life."

A stern tone crept back into Professor Ward's voice. "I hope you explained things to him and tried to make amends."

"Oh, yes, sir. I took him over to the clinic and had the doctors examine him. They gave him a tranquilizer and two aspirins and told him to call them in the morning if he didn't feel better. While we were walking back to Dan's place from the clinic, I told him about what we had done, and why. Now he wants to be a stooge if we continue the experiment."

"If?"

Norm sighed dramatically. "Well, sir, it does seem we've discovered an interesting way to measure psychosomatic responses to social stress. I was talking to some of the doctors at the clinic about it. They thought we might do some joint research. You know, trying to figure out how group pressures toward conformity can lead to ulcers and hypertension and things like that. I realize that's not a replication of the Blake experiment, and I wouldn't want to break the rule . . ."

Professor Ward interrupted. "Mr. Kraus, we have *two* departmental rules about graduate students. The first is that they should begin by repeating a piece of published research. The second rule is that, if the student finds something exciting on his or her own while performing the replication, we expect him or her to follow it up. You wouldn't want to violate our departmental standards, now would you?"

Norm Kraus smiled slyly. "Oh, no, sir."

"Good work, Norm. I'm pleased with your progress. Let me know if I can help, and keep me posted on how you come along. And by the way, why don't you call me Ron instead of Professor Ward?"

Norm could hardly believe his ears. "Yes sir, Profes . . . I mean, bloody good of you, Ron!"

A Conclusion

· C · H · A · P · T · E · R ·

22

Like most scientists, I believe in the future. I suppose I always have. I am much more interested in new things than in old. And I am more intrigued by what a person might become than by what a person has already been. Indeed, about the only time I think about yesterday is when I need information that might let me better understand what tomorrow could be like.

Humans seem to be the only animals that can look far into the future and plan accordingly. This ability to change some parts of the present world *deliberately* in order to shape the world of tomorrow is, in my opinion, one of the essential characteristics of being human.

Science is (among other things) the fine art of predicting the future in objective terms. It is therefore one of the most *human* of occupations. It took people a long time to learn how to make their predictions accurate, however, for at least two reasons:

First, being emotional or subjective is probably more immediately rewarding for most of us than is being rational or objective. Perhaps this fact is not too surprising. As we noted in Chapter 8 when we discussed Paul MacLean's "Theory of the Triune Brain," the nervous systems of lower animals are dominated by their emotional centers. The "thinking" or "processing" centers in the cortex reach their fullest development in humans. But these are *additions to* (rather than subtractions from) the basic blueprint of the highly reactive animal brain.

The sheer size of the human cortex gives us the potentiality of bringing the lower centers—and hence our passions and desires—under *voluntary control*. As we mentioned in Chapters 10 and 12, we need training and experience in order to learn how to be rational. However, we need precious little training to be emotional.

Language is one of the keys to rational thought, and hence to emotional control. In order to reason in a logical manner, you often have to be able to translate parts of the world into verbal symbols, so you can manipulate the world *symbolically* in your mind. But speech alone is not enough. As human society developed, we had a long heritage of animal emotionality to overcome. Therefore, we had to construct symbolic languages (such as mathematics) in order to help us gain control of our passions.

If this line of thought seems odd to you, ask yourself this question: How many "dirty" numbers can you think of? One or two, perhaps. But how many hundreds of "dirty," emotion-laden words can you think of? A computer (which has no emotions) can translate numbers directly. But how can a computer "process" (i.e., understand) any of the hundreds of put-down terms we use to refer to ethnic groups, minority groups, or sexual functions? It is only when we get the emotionality out of our language that we can think objectively, and hence make rational projections about the future.

We must not *banish* emotionality, however, for our feelings give *value* to the world around us. What we must do is to learn how our feelings *color* our intellectual decisions. Once we understand how subjectivity *interacts* with objectivity, we can then combine these two human functions in a more effective fashion.

Second, understanding our own cognitive/emotional processes isn't enough, however. For even when early men and women did attempt to view the world in objective terms, they often lacked sufficient *data* to make good predictions. It probably wasn't until around the year 1600 A.D. that we had gathered enough hard, unemotional facts about the world—and had the proper mathematical tools—for science to prove a worthwhile occupation.

The Industrial Revolution

Perhaps because it is easier for most of us to look at *things* objectively than for us to be "unemotional" about ourselves, the physical (or "thing") sciences were the first to develop. Modern physics and astronomy date from the 1600's. Chemistry came a little later. These scientific disciplines soon matured enough to let us understand and predict the behavior of a few objects under certain specified conditions—for that kind of prediction is science's job. But once we could *guess* how physical things would behave, we could also hunt for ways to *control* the future behavior of these objects. This ability to control "things" marked the rise of physical technology.

The first major applications of physical technology in Europe began in the mid-1700's, and led to what we call the "Industrial Revolution." Before this time, almost everyone in Europe lived on farms or in relatively small towns, and almost every "thing" was handmade. Life changed little from one generation to another. A man typically became what his father had been, and a woman married the sort of man her mother had married. As greater and greater application of the physical sciences gave humans the ability to shape their physical environments, however, the tempo of cultural change speeded up noticeably.

Of course, there was considerable resistance to this change. For instance, in England in 1811 groups of workers called "Luddites" roamed the countryside, destroying as many machines as they could lay hands on. Part of the Luddite protest was justifiably against working conditions, low pay, and unemployment. However, many of the Luddites were simply opposed to *change and technology*.

The Medical Revolution

By the 1800's, we had learned enough to begin viewing our bodily reactions in an objective manner. Biology became a true science, and medical technology became a reality. As the "Medical Revolution" gathered steam in the early 1900's, we discovered ways to predict and control some of our biological reactions. Because of this applied knowledge, we are now bigger, stronger, healthier, and we live longer than at any previous time in human history.

Again, "progress" is a mixed blessing. Even in the 1980's, many devoutly religious groups protest against medical technology as a "violation of God's ways."

The Psychological Revolution

During the last part of the 1800's and the first part of the 1900's, we took the next step up the ladder—we discovered ways to look at our minds and behaviors objectively. Psychology and the social sciences came into being. We are just now starting to build a technology based on our new-found objective knowledge of ourselves. We call this technology *applied psychology*—that is, the application of psychological facts and theories to the solution of real-life problems.

From my biased point of view, we are now in the midst of what I call the "Psychological Revolution." The cultural changes this third revolution has brought about are, in their way, as "mind-blowing" as those caused by the Industrial and Medical Revolutions.

What will scientific psychology be like in the future? That question is difficult to answer, since it depends in part on the often unpredictable outcomes of all the thousands of experiments that psychologists are conducting right at this moment.

The future of applied psychology is somewhat easier to predict, however, since tomorrow's technology will lean heavily on today's scientific knowledge. In these final pages, let me share with you my *guesses* about the changing world of human behavior, and what these changes might mean to you. Other psychologists will surely see things differently, and you must realize that my predictions are really little more than my own wild speculations.

Still, it might pay us to try to answer three interesting questions:

1. What will the world be like in the year 2010?
2. What kinds of job opportunities might be open to you then?
3. What types of psychological services will probably be available to you by 2010?

In defense of my answers to these questions about the year 2010, let me remind you of one fact. At least half of the *types* of jobs available to college graduates today simply didn't exist as "job classifications" 30 years ago.

THE FUTURE OF BIOLOGICAL PSYCHOLOGY

There seems little doubt that we will shortly gain a great deal more control over our heredity (and hence our instinctual behaviors) than we would have dreamed possible a few years back. In 1973 scientists at the University of Wisconsin announced they had synthesized a gene in a test tube. That is, they took ordinary chemical molecules and combined them to "build" a very simple gene. By the late 1970's, other scientists had shown that "artificial genes" could function *normally* in very simple organisms. By the early 1980's, researchers had transferred "active genes" from one simple organism to another. And by 1988, hundreds of corporations had been formed in the US alone to exploit the possibilities of "genetic engineering." Thus, is seems clear that in the very near future we will indeed be able to change a person's heredity (genes) both before and after that person is born (see Chapter 14).

Once the biologists give us greater control over our inheritance, psychologists will be able to determine with much greater precision what the genetic contribution to behavior really is. We should also be able to learn much more about how to overcome genetic handicaps that people already have. By the year 2010, many psychologists should be employed as "genetic counselors," giving advice to prospective parents both before and after they get married. Other psychologists will be able to offer physically-handicapped people much better training than now exists. These psychologists may also offer surgeons advice on what kinds of drugs and operations might be helpful to maximize the *psychological* potential of brain-damaged individuals.

If nothing else, psychologists who work with handicapped people may be able to train them to *increase their sense of self-efficacy*. As we noted in Chapter 20, disabled individuals often use body language that able-bodied people *interpret* as showing "low self-esteem." Teaching handicapped persons better "self-presentation" behaviors might go a long way toward bringing them fully into the mainstream of society.

The Two Hemispheres

There is no part of biological psychology presently more exciting than the study of the functions of the two hemispheres. Recent research suggests that such "mental illnesses" as schizophrenia and autism are related to a *functional imbalance* between the two halves of the brain. Fifty years ago, autism was thought to be a type of schizophrenia. But in the last two or three years, brain scan studies have clearly shown this isn't the case. Autistic children process information primarily with their right hemispheres, while patients diagnosed as schizophrenic process inputs primarily with their left hemispheres. I would guess that our whole approach to treating these two "mental disorders" will change markedly in the next decade. Instead of locking schizophrenic patients up in asylums, or using just chemotherapy, we surely will begin training them to process information with *both hemispheres*.

We are also likely to be able to help normal children who have language problems by measuring how they input information to their two hemispheres. Joseph Cioffi and Gillray L. Kandel report that young boys tend to process information in quite a different manner than do young girls. When Cioffi and Kandel gave "word-shapes" to more than 100 young subjects, the girls tended to respond to the "word value" of the stimulus, while boys tended to respond to the "visual shape" of the input. Boys also tend to have more language development problems than do girls, while girls typically have more difficulty learning spatial concepts and the correct use of mathematical symbolism than do boys (Cioffi & Kandel, 1979).

There are also differences in the brains of men and women. According to University of Chicago psychologist Jerre Levy, the right ear and eye are more sensitive in women, while the left ear and eye are more sensitive in men. Levy believes the left hemisphere dominates in women, the right in men. The cause for this difference in hemispheric dominance may be the corpus callosum, which is thicker in women than in men. Because puberty occurs earlier in women than in men, the callosum doesn't "stretch out" as much in women as it does in men, Levy says. And because sexual maturity stops the "lateralization" of the brain, women have *less-lateralized brains*. Thus, women are better at integrating processes that occur in both hemispheres. Men, Levy believes, are better at tasks that depend on the dominance of one hemisphere, such as spatial perception and mathematics (Levy, 1983; Levy & Levy, 1979).

J. Merrill Carlsmith

Support for Levy's views comes from a report by Stanford psychologist J. Merrill Carlsmith. In a recent book, Carlsmith notes that girls who *mature late* "matched or outscored their male counterparts in mathematics." Like Jerre Levy, Carlsmith believes late maturity allows for a greater "lateralization of the brain." Therefore, Carlsmith says, late-maturing women should have the same range

Added emphasis on verbal skills for boys, and spatial and mathematical skills for girls, may help the sexes achieve academic equality.

of cognitive abilities as do men. Carlsmith also believes that *early-maturing* males (who have less-lateralized brains) tend to do better at verbal tasks than do *late-maturing* males (Ward, Carlsmith, & Leiderman, 1988).

If further experiments support Levy and Carlsmith, perhaps we eventually will "custom-tailor" the high school curriculum to the individual needs of both young men and women. For example, we could give girls (and early-maturing boys) special training in mathematics and perceptual skills. And we could give boys (and late-maturing girls) special training in language and "integration skills."

Finally, there is the possibility of using "computerized" brain scans to detect *physical* abnormalities in the brain before they show up as *behavioral* or *psychological* abnormalities (Andreasen, 1988).

Behavioral Medicine

There are very few psychologists working in hospitals today. By the year 2010, however, hospitals may employ more psychologists and behavioral technologists than they do physicians and surgeons. This surprising situation will be a direct consequence of the three revolutions we mentioned earlier. For thanks to our increased knowledge of the physical and biological sciences, the major health hazards are no longer diseases that have a purely biological cause—such as pneumonia, influenza, and tuberculosis. Medical technology has "cured" us of these maladies, for the most part. But medical technology is presently ill-equipped to help us with health problems that have an intrapsychic, behavioral, or social component.

For example, the field of pediatrics has undergone a dramatic change in recent years. Medical science has found cures (or preventions) for such childhood diseases as measles, smallpox, mumps, and polio. Today, the pediatrician's time is likely to be occupied treating cases of child abuse, eating disorders, behavioral problems, learning disabilities, and childhood accidents (Krasnegor, Arasteh, & Cataldo, 1986). Unfortunately, few pediatricians have adequate training in the sort of psychological technology needed to treat these behavior disorders. Much work in this area, therefore, will fall to psychotechnologists.

• What Is Behavioral Medicine?

Gilbert Levin is director of the Division of Health and Behavior at the Albert Einstein College of Medicine. In a recent article, Levin writes about a new field that is variously called "behavioral medicine" or "health psychology":

> Today's important diseases, mostly chronic diseases, simply cannot be made to fit a strictly biological mold. We know that the patient's behavior and perhaps his or her attitudes play a role in the cause of at least some of these diseases and in the recovery process from all of them. (Levin, 1987)

Levin goes on to say that traditional medicine has failed to keep up with the times, because it still relies on a strictly *biological* point of view as far as curing human discomforts is concerned. The viewpoint taken in health psychology is more modern—and more effective—because "it affirms the more fundamental faith that science is a seamless web that encompasses both cell and psyche" (Levin, 1987).

The assumption underlying most approaches to health psychology or behavioral medicine is this: Our biological systems *interact* with our intra-psychic and our social/behavioral systems. From this viewpoint, it would seem that the next breakthroughs in medicine will come from the wise and humane use of a psychotechnology that helps *coordinate* the inputs and outputs of all three systems (Taylor, 1986).

• Stress Management

The relationship between stress (on the one hand) and pain and physical ailments (on the other hand) are by now well established. Generally speaking, psychologists are better trained at helping patients reduce stress than are medical personnel.

For example, 20 years ago when behavioral psychologists tried to interest dentists in *desensitizing* their patients' fears of dental procedures, the psychologists were almost uniformly laughed at. Today, desensitization is part of the training regimen in most dental schools.

The same type of desensitization procedures are now used by surgeons at the University of Rochester Medical Center. Prior to an operation, surgery patients are routinely given a "slide show" that explains precisely what will happen to them during and following the oper-

ation. As compared to patients who merely have the operation "explained" to them by a physician, the "slide show" patients experience less anxiety, have fewer complications, and request less medication for pain (Horn, 1983).

• Patient Compliance

Physicians are usually at their best diagnosing medical problems and prescribing treatment. Getting the patients to *comply* with the treatment plan, however, is something that medical personnel aren't always very successful at. For *compliance* is a behavioral, not a biological, problem (DiMatteo & DiNicola, 1982).

For example, in the mid-1970's, nurses at the University of Michigan Medical Center were faced with a dilemma. Hypertensive patients in their care were supposed to attend weekly clinics, so the nurses could monitor their compliance with the doctors' orders concerning diet and medication. However, attendance at the clinics was less than 50 percent. At the suggestion of a behavioral psychologist, the nurses began giving each patient a $1 lottery ticket as a "reward" for attending each session. The attendance rate immediately increased to almost 100 percent.

As UCLA psychologist Bertram Raven notes, physicians often expect patients to "follow orders" despite the fact that medical regimens are often excruciatingly painful. Since many physicians pay little attention to such matters, it is often up to an attending "health psychologist" to find ways of "making compliance more truly rewarding and certainly not punishing" (Raven, 1987).

There is also a *social* problem associated with medical treatment, namely, the fact that patients with job-related disabilities may well

Some health psychologists study ways to improve communication between patients and physicians.

Marty Merrill

not *want* to be "cured." Many of these patients have learned to put their "disabilities" to personal advantage—as a means of avoiding social obligations, as a way of controlling family members, and as a way of gathering significant insurance income without working. The task of the health psychologist, therefore, is to find ways to solve these social and economic problems so that the patient will "agree to be cured" (Gerber & Nehemkis, 1986).

● *Physical Rehabilitation*

To date, most psychiatrists have shown little or no interest in working with people who are obviously *not* mentally ill, but who suffer from physical or behavioral problems. For that reason, perhaps, most *behavioral* retraining in medical centers takes place in Departments of Physical Rehabilitation. However, as "The Case of Eliza" will demonstrate rather vividly, *psychological* treatment can occasionally lead to rather important changes in *physical* functioning.

The Case of "Eliza"

In 1984, Marty Merrill earned her doctorate in psychology at Michigan working with brain-damaged patients who suffer from "cortical blindness." There usually isn't anything wrong with the patients' eyes. So visual inputs from the eyes still do get through to the visual cortex in one fashion or another. However, because the patients have suffered extensive brain damage, the visual inputs simply aren't "processed" effectively after they reach the visual cortex. As a result, the patient cannot "see" at all.

One of the patients Marty Merrill worked with was a 14-year-old girl whom we will call Eliza. Marty first encountered Eliza in 1981, when Marty was gathering data for her doctoral dissertation at the rehabilitation section of the University of Michigan Hospital. One day her supervisor at the hospital, neuropsychologist Donald Kewman, asked Marty to assist him with a particularly difficult patient. This young woman—Eliza—was in such poor shape that the medical doctors believed she'd never recover.

"The first time I saw Eliza, she was lying in a hospital bed," Marty Merrill said to me recently. "Her legs were twisted up under her, and her fists were so tightly clenched that she couldn't open her hands. She didn't seem to know where she was, and she barely responded to the questions I asked her. Frankly, I thought that Eliza was a hopeless case."

As it turned out, Marty's first evaluation of Eliza was wrong. By the time Marty and Don Kewman had worked with Eliza for a year or so, the girl was able to return to a near-normal life. Let me first describe Eliza and the behavioral techniques that Don Kewman and Marty

Merrill used with her. Then I'll tell you why her story is so important.

● *Eliza: Initial Diagnosis*

About five months after her 14th birthday, Eliza suffered a heart attack and went into a coma. She remained unconscious for almost six weeks. Because her brain was deprived of oxygen during (and following) the heart attack, Eliza's cortex was badly damaged. Tests showed that her visual cortex was almost totally destroyed, as were those areas of the brain typically associated with touch, balance, muscle movements, and memory.

A few weeks after Eliza came out of the coma, she could detect the onset of a very bright light if you pointed it directly at her eyes. Other than that, she wasn't conscious of "seeing" anything at all. The medical doctors who treated Eliza were confident that she would never regain her sight. They based their diagnosis on two important facts: First, several months after the young woman had recovered from the coma, she showed little spontaneous improvement. Second, no patient suffering from cortical blindness had ever shown significant recovery of visual function. Eliza's physician urged Marty to help the young woman "accept her fate."

Marty made several video tape recordings of Eliza at the start of treatment. Having viewed the tapes, I can understand why her physician doubted Eliza would ever recover. Because she had lost the brain centers that control balance, the young woman had to be strapped upright in a wheelchair whenever she left her bed. She could remember her name, but not her birthdate. She understood spoken language and could repeat words and short sentences, but couldn't repeat long sentences. She couldn't perform complex sequences of movements on command—such as raising her right arm and then wiggling her hand. She couldn't even repeat the alphabet, a deeply-ingrained habit that tends to survive all but the most severe types of brain damage.

Worst of all, there was little evidence that Eliza could *learn* anything at all, particularly any task involving language.

● *"She Can See Blue!"*

Thinking it would be useless to work on Eliza's vision, Marty first tried to train her to recognize objects by touch. The attempt failed. "Eliza would withdraw her hand the moment I touched it," Marty told me. "She said it hurt. But there was more to it than that. The first thing she said to me was 'Am I always going to be blind?' Perhaps she believed that learning to recognize things with her hands would be admitting she'd never regain her sight. And she never did give up hope she'd see again."

Shortly thereafter, when Don Kewman was talking with Eliza in his office, she spontaneously said, "Blue." Don looked down at the large hospital chart in his hand. Indeed, it was blue. Don ran across the hall to Marty's office and shouted, "She can see blue! Maybe we can teach her to recognize colors." Marty agreed, and so the therapy started.

Don and Marty began by showing Eliza four large sheets of colored paper. She identified blue, but she missed red, yellow, and green. They praised her for getting "blue" right and told her the names of the colors she'd missed. Then they tried again—praising her correct responses and gently correcting her mistakes. Within two days, Eliza could consistently identify the four colors she had been trained on.

Next came form recognition. Don and Marty presented Eliza with four different shapes—a circle, a square, a triangle, and a cross. Each shape came in four colors—red, blue, green, and yellow. One by one, they showed her each of the 16 stimulus cards and asked her to identify both the color and the shape. At the beginning, she could give the colors but not the shapes. Then Don and Marty began tracing the contours of each shape by running a pointer around the edges before asking Eliza to name the shape. Again, they praised her when she was right and told her the correct response when she was wrong. In less than a month, she could consistently identify the four shapes and their colors (Merrill & Kewman, 1986).

Learning to Read

At this point, Marty decided to try to teach Eliza to read. Letters, after all, are little more than "arbitrary shapes." So, first of all, Marty taught Eliza to recognize (and name) the individual letters. After a week of training, she could breeze through the entire alphabet. Within two weeks, she could read simple words and phrases. A month later, she could comprehend sentences. Six months after the visual retraining started, Eliza could read even small print in textbooks. More surprising than this, tests using the Snellen chart—the one with the large "E" at the top—showed that her visual acuity was now as good as it had been before the coma. In fact, although she had worn glasses previously, the eye doctor told her she didn't really need them now.

About the time Eliza began to recognize letters, she reported that she could "see things" once more. Her posture improved and she began to walk again without running into anything. Soon thereafter, she could get around entirely on her own.

Eliza still had many problems, however. She could read—but she couldn't write because she had no memory of how to form written letters. So Marty taught her. Eliza couldn't spell, she couldn't pronounce many words correctly, and she couldn't tell time. Marty taught her these skills too, one step at a time.

Eliza had been fairly good at mathematics before the coma, but afterwards she couldn't remember such simple tasks as how to add and subtract. Again, Marty was able to retrain the young woman in a fairly short period.

Eliza continued to have problems with skilled movements. She could walk, but she was fairly clumsy. And she had forgotten how to dance. So, Marty "modeled" the appropriate movements, and rewarded the young woman for imitating the correct responses. She recovered these skills very rapidly.

After a year of retraining, Eliza had normal verbal memory, normal motor memory, normal visual memory, and most of her cognitive functions were normal as well. So she returned to school. She had not recovered completely, however. She still slurred her words when excited, and sometimes Marty had to remind her to pay attention to *how* she walked. Nonetheless, she was now able to get along in school and to take care of most of her own needs (Merrill & Kewman, 1986).

In the summer of 1986, I asked Marty how Eliza was doing then, almost four years after treatment had ended. Marty's eyes lit up. "She's doing marvelously. She's just graduated from high school, and she's thinking about going to college. Can you believe that she wants to become a psychologist?"

Yes, I can believe it.

Eliza: A Summing Up

Since working with Eliza, Marty Merrill has been able to retrain three other cortically-blind patients to "see." Given this *pattern* of success, we can expect that behavioral retraining techniques will eventually become a standard part of the medical regimen with cortically-blind patients.

Behavioral retraining takes much longer (and requires different skills) than does medical diagnosis and treatment. That's just one reason why I believe that, by the year 2010, there may be more psychologists working in hospitals than there are physicians.

Applied Psychology Involving Drugs

Drugs and surgery hold little hope for patients such as Eliza. But chemotherapy can be effective in helping make *behavioral* changes under certain circumstances. For example, we already know that chemicals such as caffeine speed up learning, and that "downers" typically retard it. By the year 2010, psychologists may use a wide variety of drugs that will help people achieve goals not presently within their reach.

Chemicals to slow down or help reverse the process of senility are a possibility, as are drugs that will help prevent some types of mental illness. It is highly probable that all such compounds will be used *in conjunction with* psychological and social/behavioral treatment, but there is no reason not to use drugs if they can be helpful.

As we learn more about "consciousness," we will surely discover more effective means of inducing whatever "altered states of consciousness" anyone might desire to experience. Both drugs and biofeedback techniques seem likely candidates in this type of research.

Applied Psychology Involving Sensory Processing

Computers are crude models of our brains. As we gain more insight into how your cortex "processes" sensory inputs, we should be able to build dramatically better yet simpler computers than we presently have. It is already theoretically possible to use, for example, the brain of an ant or a worm as a "biological computer." That is, we should be able to "store" inputs in a tiny living brain and later retrieve these inputs in the form of motor outputs. The problem at the moment is in controlling the sensory inputs and the motor outputs.

Biological computers should be able to handle complex decision making much better than present-generation electrical or mechanical computers—and brains are likely to be smaller and easier to handle than machines. Thus, it is possible that some "computer technologists" in the year 2010 will be, in effect, animal trainers rather than machine-tenders.

If this sort of research seems strange to you, consider the following: We already make use of animals' brains to help people. What are seeing eye dogs but "biological computers" that blind people use instead of their own visual inputs? Also, psychologists have recently been able to train small monkeys to act as "arms and legs" for paralyzed individuals. On verbal command, the monkeys will open doors or cabinets, fetch hard-to-reach items, change tapes or records on the stereo, position food so the paralyzed person can eat it, or summon help for people who have lost all or part of their ability to move around. And the very presence of these animals seems to have a therapeutic effect on the *emotional good health* of the patients. "Robots don't play with you; monkeys do," one paraplegic patient said recently. Another patient noted that when he took his monkey with him to the shopping center, 71 passersby paused to chat. But when he went without the animal, only two people talked to him in an hour's time (MacFadyen, 1986).

Biological engineering will be a part of our future whether we like it or not. But it seems reasonably certain that it will always be used *along with* improved ways of "engineering" our thoughts and behaviors. So let us look next at what applied intra-psychic psychology may be like in 2010 A.D.

APPLIED INTRA-PSYCHIC PSYCHOLGY

Technology implies measurement. The more accurately you can describe or measure anything, the better chance you have of being able to exercise some kind of control over it. As you may have gathered from the earlier chapters in this book, one of the major problems with the intra-psychic or subjective approach to human existence is that internal events are most difficult to describe in quantitative or measurable terms. For this reason alone, we can probably expect greater immediate technological development in biological and behavioral psychology than in the intra-psychic area.

There are a number of highly promising developments, however, that we should take note of. Personality theory in the past has been based on the assumption that your character was fairly well fixed by the end of the first few years of your life. Freud, for instance, thought that only superficial or "surface" changes occurred in people once they had passed the years of early adolescence. Personality tests were usually designed to measure the intellectual and emotional traits a person already possessed, not the traits the person *might acquire* with training and encouragement.

My guess is that by 2010 A.D., we will have entirely new types of intelligence tests. Some will involve the use of EEG machines and computers to measure the *speed* with which the brain "processes" incoming information. Other more psychologically-oriented tests will determine the *quality* of your decision-making skills and the rapidity with which you can acquire and utilize new information. These tests will probably be oriented more toward measuring performance in "real-life" situations than present intelligence scales, which tend to focus on certain academic skills (see Chapter 17).

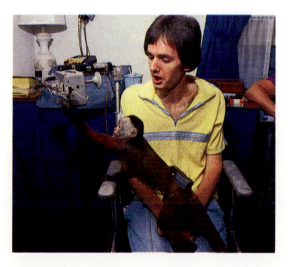

Animals can provide help with motor tasks, as well as companionship, for humans with disabilities.

Already, computers are being used to help diagnose mental patients. In a recent study, E.R. John and his associates at the New York University Medical Center measured four different types of brain waves in normal subjects using an EEG machine. They also measured the same brain waves in individuals diagnosed as having monopolar and bipolar depressions, alcoholism, schizophrenia, mild cognitive impairment, and dementia. Then John and his colleagues used a computer to *average* the brain wave activities of subjects in all these groups. The results are shown in Fig. 22.1. As you can see, there were marked differences among the various groups. John and his associates believe that "computer-assisted differential diagnosis of brain dysfunctions" will add considerable validity to *psychiatric diagnoses* in the future (John *et al.*, 1988).

□ □ **QUESTION** □ □

How could you use John's technique to demonstrate the effectiveness of psychotherapy?

Traditional Psychotherapy Versus Human Services Psychology

Psychotherapy is one of the most important and exciting areas in psychology because it involves *people helping people*. But according to University of Maryland psychologist Leon Levy, "Traditional conceptions of [psychotherapy] as centering around the treatment of individuals suffering from mental health problems are no longer adequate." Rather, Levy says, we must look upon clinical psychology as a part of a new field, which he calls *human services psychology*. This new discipline, Levy believes, will be *systems oriented*, and will offer both treatment and prevention for a wide variety of human problems (Levy, 1984).

Traditional psychotherapy will, of course, remain a viable part of "human services psychology." However, our views of what *should* occur during psychotherapy might well change. Many psychologists now believe that "talk treatment" is really a form of *personal exploration* rather than a type of *therapy*. In a society as mobile as ours, it is not always easy to find someone to talk your troubles over with. More than this, not even your friends can always guide you through a full-fledged "investigation into the self." And yet, that is just what most forms of psychotherapy turn out to be.

We might also expect that people will seek out psychologists whenever they wish to improve any aspect of their lives, from changing jobs to bettering their golf scores (Simek & O'Brien, 1981).

Applied Developmental Psychology

One of the fastest-growing fields within the behavioral sciences is that of *developmental*

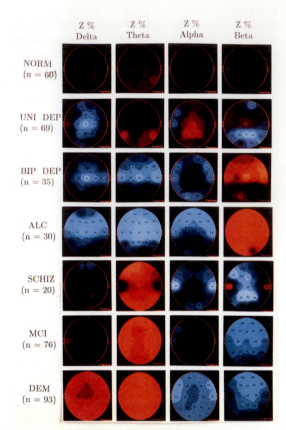

FIG. 22.1 Computer-averaged EEG records from normal subjects (top row) and patients in several diagnostic categories. E. Roy John notes that the patient groupings all differ from the normals — and from each other. See text.

psychology. Although this term once meant much the same thing as *child psychology*, we now realize that people continue to change throughout their lives. In the future, developmental specialists will work with people of all ages, helping them solve whatever "growth" difficulties arise at any time in a person's life.

● *Life-long Learning*

As our health gets better and our lives get longer, we will realize that there is no reason why we should commit ourselves to one occupation, or to one style of life, and stick with it forever. Indeed, studies of "job burn-out" and "career plateauing" suggest many people may *benefit* from changing occupations in mid-life. By the year 2010, therefore, some psychologists may specialize in helping middle-aged individuals acquire new job skills (Bardwick, 1988).

For that matter, we now realize that education should not stop when some college places a degree in a person's hands. Rather, learning should continue to the moment of the person's death. So even those middle-aged individuals who are content with their jobs may well decide to take additional college courses just to "freshen up their minds."

• *Later Life*

Some of our greatest untapped resources are the skills and abilities of our senior citizens. As we learn how to maintain psychological youthfulness even when our bodies have started to creak and groan a bit, we will need specialists to help older people continue to be useful and contributing members of society.

Death is as much a part of the business of living as is life itself, yet we often avoid the topic, and it has seldom been studied scientifically. Developmental psychologists will probably be called upon as much to help people prepare psychologically for facing death as for facing life.

Applied Cognitive Psychology

The computer has revolutionized the way people think. But it has also dramatically altered the way that people "think about thinking." As we attempt to build machines that process information and make decisions the same way that humans do, we are forced to build ever-more-accurate models of the cognitive processes that allow us to survive in this complex world of ours. Little wonder, then, that cognitive psychology is one of the fastest-growing areas in the behavioral sciences.

Computers will also have a profound effect on education. As we discover more about how people learn, we surely will find new ways of helping people to learn *better*. We know from Skinner's research on "programmed learning" that students acquire information faster when they are allowed to work at their own pace. Computers can be programmed to measure each student's knowledge and ability. Then the computer can "customize" the manner in which it presents data to each student. It will

reward progress and gently correct mistakes. And, unlike most teachers, computers never get punitive when students don't learn at an "acceptable" speed. My suspicion is that, by the end of the century, most types of classroom learning will be handled by computers. The teachers will then be free to act as "models," as "resource persons," and as "mentors" for the students.

Computers are obviously changing the workplace. Many data-processing jobs now performed "at the office" could just as readily be done in the home. All you need is a computer terminal that is hooked into a central processing machine via the telephone line. Many corporations are using this approach already. Some workers seem to thrive on working at home, for they can proceed at their own pace and on their own schedules. Others miss the social excitement and challenge that comes from being around their fellow employees. But computers can even provide social stimulation. Presently there are "networks" of people who use computer terminals to send and receive messages from each other—and to talk over work-related and personal problems. Perhaps by the next century, the computer will let us add to our "extended families" just as the telephone has in the past.

• *Sports Psychology*

Psychologists have, in the past, helped athletes increase and maintain their "levels of motivation." However, there now is a growing use of "sports psychology" to assist athletes improve performance.

One technique used by sports psychologists combines video taping with cognitive behavior modification. The psychologist first makes a tape of the athlete's "typical" performance. Then the psychologist replays the tape and encourages the athlete to "imagine ways of improving his or her techniques." The athlete then performs again, trying to make the agreed-upon changes. A tape is made of this second performance and, on playback, the psychologist points out (and praises) actual improvement (Stark, 1985).

As Canadian psychologists Garry Martin and Dennis Hrycaiko point out in a recent book, sports psychologists are also working extensively with coaches. Despite all the scientific evidence to the contrary, most coaches still believe that *punishing mistakes* is a better way to train athletes than is *praising good performance*. Thus, the first thing a sports psychologist must do, Martin and Hrycaiko say, is to convince the coaches that reward is a more effective tool than is criticism. The second step involves teaching the coaches how to *analyze* performance in measurable terms. Third, the coaches need to learn how to increase motivation in positive ways.

One of the greatest untapped resources in our society is the skill and experience of senior citizens.

Martin and Hrycaiko cite dozens of studies in which this approach has yielded surprisingly large gains in athletic performance. The Canadian psychologists conclude that "The desire by coaches and athletes to improve, and the increased emphasis on coaching as a science, make the future of effective behavioral coaching both promising and exciting" (Martin & Hrycaiko, 1983).

□ □ **QUESTION** □ □

Why do you think that most coaches still believe that shouting at players when they make mistakes improves their performance more than does rewarding good behaviors?

APPLIED SOCIAL/BEHAVIORAL PSYCHOLOGY

The engineering profession really got its start with the beginning of the Industrial Revolution. Part of an engineer's job is to take known scientific data and use those data to transform the physical environment. But in doing so, engineers often discover new scientific principles on their own. And, in putting well-known scientific theories to practical tests, the engineers may uncover flaws in the theories that laboratory scientists were unaware of.

One of the most important new professions is that of behavioral engineering—women and men who use psychological data to help create new and more satisfying social and work environments. My private opinion is that, by the year 2010, half the psychologists in the US will be employed in jobs demanding behavioral engineering skills. Let us look at some of the things they might be doing.

Community Mental Health
Traditionally, most psychotherapists have worked in their own offices or clinics, treating one client at a time. Some two decades ago, however, many psychologists started moving out of the "office environment" into the community. And so began what is now called the *community mental health movement*.

According to Garry Martin and J. Grayson Osborne

> Behavioral community psychology projects may be more likely to examine behaviors that are collectively significant to society and that occur in locales other than the clinic, for which there should be societal consequences (as contrasted with individual consequences). But this approach does not rule out projects with individuals, in clinics, for which there are consequences dispensed by individuals. (Martin & Osborne, 1980)

As Yale psychologist Seymour Sarason noted in an article in *American Psychologist* in

The community mental health movement takes the position that family harmony should not be left to chance.

1981, from a historical point of view, clinical psychology has emphasized work with individuals. But, according to Sarason, "The substance of psychology cannot be independent of the social order. It is not that it *should not* be independent but that it *cannot be*" (Sarason, 1981).

People always live with—and are affected by—other people. As clinical psychologists move out into the "real world of people," they are likely to face many new challenges. Let's look at what some of these challenges might be.

"Parenting" Skills

Already we have a great many community mental health centers scattered across the US and Canada. We will need many more of them, for they tend to focus on changing "systems" rather than just working with individuals. The data suggest, for instance, that many parents who mistreat their children were mistreated by their own parents. If we are to stop this destructive behavior toward innocent children, we will have to find effective ways of teaching some parents to manage their children without resorting to violent physical punishment. Since most high schools and colleges fail to give training in "parenting skills," probably the community mental health centers will have to fill the educational gap (O'Neill & Trickett, 1982).

What we call "mental illness" tends to run in families partly because of genetic factors, but also because certain types of parental responses induce "insane" (that is, disordered) behavior in children. And when those children grow up, they tend to treat their own offspring as they were treated. To break this self-perpetuating pattern of mental illness, we will need more effective forms of family counseling. Much of this counseling will be systems-oriented "family therapy."

But just because we *can* help families doesn't mean we automatically *should* do so—particularly when the families reject our attempts to be helpful. Therefore, we will also have to make some rather difficult moral decisions concerning society's right to intervene in unhealthy family situations when the parents may resent or fight against outside intervention (Segraves, 1982).

Sheltered Environments

Mental hospitals as we presently know them may well vanish during the first part of the next century. These "asylums" will be replaced by clinics, re-education centers, halfway houses, group homes, and other forms of "sheltered environments" where people with mental problems may go for relatively short periods of time. Behavioral engineers—working in teams with psychiatrists, clinical psychologists, and social workers—will help these disturbed people find solutions to their problems. The patients will then be eased back into society bit by bit, rather than being discharged abruptly with little in the way of after-care. Behavioral psychologists will also be involved in helping to change the social environment (such as a family situation) into which the patient will return (O'Connor & Lubin, 1984).

The sprawling concrete prisons we presently send criminals to will also slowly fade from the scene. As we gain greater control over the social environment, fewer people will "want" to become law-breakers. Rehabilitation and re-education are much more effective ways of dealing with criminals than are merely punishing them and locking them away behind bars. Thus, prisons should develop into "schools for social and personal learning" and be staffed as much by psychologists as by wardens and guards. And prisoners—like ex-mental patients—should be given extensive assistance after leaving jail in order to help them learn the skills necessary for day-to-day survival. However, given the "urge for vengeance" that seems to afflict us all, and because of the strong belief that "punishment works," prison reform will probably come much more slowly than will changes in mental hospitals (Kotlarski, 1985; Wexler & Williams, 1986).

Public Health, Social Psychology, and AIDS

In a recent article in *Science*, Harvard professor Allan Brandt compares the current AIDS epidemic with the syphilis epidemic which raged in the US during the first part of this century. The parallels Brandt draws between these two "scourges" are fairly disturbing. But his conclusion that the problems associated with AIDS cannot be "cured" without the help of social psychologists is worthy of note (Brandt, 1988).

According to Brandt, both the infection rate and the death rate for syphilis in the US during the early 1900's were far higher than is true of AIDS today. He notes that, during the

Moral attitudes have made it difficult to educate the public about how to prevent AIDS.

First World War, 13 percent of the military draftees tested positive for either syphilis or gonorrhea. In a report issued by the Pentagon early in 1988, only some 1.5 percent of the almost 4 million personnel tested positive for AIDS. Brandt also notes that nearly 200,000 people living in Chicago in 1940 were infected with syphilis. In contrast, according to the Centers for Disease Control, as of January 25, 1988 only 51,916 people had been diagnosed as having AIDS in the entire US.

The major *differences* between syphilis and AIDS, Brandt notes, are (1) we have had a *cure* for syphilis since 1909, while we still have no cure for AIDS; (2) syphilis tends to kill older people, while AIDS kills young people; and (3) syphilis is primarily a heterosexual problem, while most AIDS victims are gay males or intravenous drug abusers.

The *similarities* between both the social and the medical responses to AIDS and syphilis, Brand says, are legion. Like AIDS, one of the best preventive measures for syphilis is the use of condoms. However, there were strong pressures against informing the public about the proper use of condoms in the early part of this century, just as there are similar social pressures against giving *precise and accurate information* about how to prevent AIDS today.

For example, during the First World War, the military services refused to issue condoms to the soldiers in the belief that doing so would merely "encourage immorality." When syphilis then raged out of control, the military instituted "prophylaxis stations" where soldiers could go for treatment after sexual contact. The treatment consisted of inserting a needle into the opening of the penis and applying disinfectant. According to Brandt, this procedure was designed to be "painful and [was] intended to serve as an inhibition to sex. Some reformers protested, nevertheless, that the provision of such treatments promoted promiscuity among the troops" (Brandt, 1988).

Most frightening of all, Brandt notes, is the fact that many moralists urged that treatment for syphilis be *withheld* in order to punish the diseased person for his/her crimes.

☐☐ **QUESTION** ☐☐

If and when we do discover a cure for AIDS, do you think we should withhold treatment from gays and drug users as a means of "reducing the numbers of these deviant populations"?

● *Medical Response to Syphilis*

During the first part of this century, Brandt states, "Doctors catalogued the various modes of transmission [of syphilis]: pens, pencils, toilet seats, door knobs, and drinking cups. We now know, of course, that syphilis cannot be transmitted in these ways" (Brandt, 1988). And many medical personnel refused to treat syphilis patients, on the grounds that the doctors might catch the disease themselves. The parallel to the present situation with AIDS is obvious.

In the early 1900's, many physicians insisted that the major source of syphilis was the flood of immigrants coming into the US. In 1910, a noted gynecologist at Johns Hopkins stated that "The tide [of venereal disease] has been raising [sic] owing to the inpouring of a large foreign population with lower ideals" (Brandt, 1988). There was, of course, no evidence to suggest that immigrants were more likely to be infected than US citizens, but Brandt notes the immigrants made a handy scapegoat. And how did these immigrants transmit the disease to others? Many medical leaders, Brandt says, believed the route was through prostitution.

Perhaps in response to this belief, during the First World War, red light districts were closed down in most big cities, and prostitutes were routinely arrested and jailed without bond. Congress established a "civilian quarantine and isolation fund" as part of a "comprehensive venereal disease program." According to Brandt, "More than 20,000 women were quarantined . . . with the assistance provided by federal funds, [and] thousands more were incarcerated as a result of local programs" (Brandt, 1988). Still, the syphilis rate *increased*.

Soldiers who became infected during the war lost their pay and privileges. And the entire thrust of public education was of the "Just Say No" type. "Despite these major efforts in social engineering and public health, rates of disease remained high during the war. . . . The war tested the basic assumptions of the social hygiene movement: rigorous education promoting sexual abstinence coupled with vigorous repression of prostitution would conquer the problem. The war revealed the limits of this approach" (Brandt, 1988).

Fortunately, during the Second World War, the military took a more enlightened viewpoint: Condoms were issued without cost, there were no penalties for infection, and educational programs were mostly fact oriented. As a result, Brandt says, syphilis was held in check.

● *Compulsory Testing*

Between the First and Second World Wars, many medical and political leaders championed *compulsory testing* as the only effective way of controlling the spread of venereal disease. As a result, many states passed laws making it mandatory that all couples be screened prior to marriage. According to Brandt, this approach failed for at least two reasons: First, the tests were too insensitive; second, less than

1.27 percent of the total number of cases of syphilis identified nationwide came from premarital screening (Brandt, 1988).

Voluntary testing, however, did seem to be effective—perhaps because syphilis could be readily cured. Whether that would be the case now, with AIDS, is not yet clear, since no cure is available.

• Social Policy and Social Psychology

Our society's response to the AIDS epidemic, Brandt says, "will be a function of our own time, our own culture, and our own science. The importance of the history of syphilis is that it reminds us of that range of forces that influence disease, health, and social policy. . . . No *single* medical or social intervention can thus adequately address the problem. Just as penicillin did not 'solve' the problem of syphilis, no single treatment or even vaccine is likely to free us from AIDS" (Brandt, 1988).

According to Brandt, "Behavior is subject to a range of influences, biological and cultural, economic and political. As the history of syphilis demonstrates, the modification of behavior to reduce risk of disease has rarely responded simply to fear or moral exhortation. In this light, considerable social science and behavioral research is required to identify effective approaches to education and behavior modification" (Brandt, 1988).

Put more bluntly, the government must spend more money learning how to change attitudes and behaviors relating to human sexuality in order to cure what most people still see as a purely medical (or perhaps moral) problem, namely, AIDS. Whether or not increased financial support for social psychological research is actually forthcoming, of course, remains to be seen. But we can surely hope that political leaders will, in the future, make better use of social psychological knowledge than they have in the past.

Industrial Psychology

In a recent article, R. Fox, A. Barclay, and D. Rodgers define *professional psychology* as that "which is concerned with enhancing the effectiveness of human function. Therefore, a professional psychologist is one who has expertise in the development and application of quality services to the public in a controlled, organized manner . . ." (Fox, Barclay, & Rodgers, 1982).

"Enhancing the effectiveness of human function" is one of the main tasks of *industrial psychologists* and *organizational psychologists*.

Generally speaking, there are three main types of psychologists whose laboratory is the "world of business." These three types are industrial and organizational psychologists (I/O psychology), psychologists who study organiza-

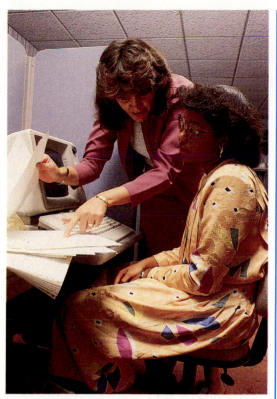

Employee performance and morale can be improved by positive feedback from supervisors, and by participatory management.

tional behavior (OB psychology), and those interested in human resource management (HRM psychology). Although these three fields do overlap somewhat, taken together they include the study of such problems as staffing, performance appraisal, attribution in organizations, training, goal setting, feedback, participation in decision making, the use of incentives and reinforcement, and job satisfaction (Locke, 1986).

Psychologists have long been employed by business firms and governmental agencies. In the past, one of the chief functions of these industrial psychologists has been that of personnel selection. A great many intelligence and aptitude tests have been developed that, under the right conditions, allow psychologists to evaluate the knowledge and skills of potential employees. Psychologists also have tried to develop "job descriptions" that would state what abilities were needed to handle a particular position. It was then up to the psychologist to match the person to the job. As we learn more about how to help people grow and develop, however, industrial psychologists will probably spend more time *training* personnel than in *selecting* them.

Putting matters rather bluntly, industrial psychologists have much the same task that other professional psychologists typically have—that of *inducing* and *maintaining change* in human thoughts and actions. The *techniques* that industrial psychologists use are often quite similar to those employed by clinical and health psychologists. The major difference is that industrial psychologists "treat" organizations rather than individuals.

● *Improving Job Performance*

A worker's performance is not dependent entirely on her or his own talents. It also depends on the type of encouragement and feedback the worker's supervisor gives, and on how rewarding and satisfying the job happens to be. However, Thomas K. Connellan points out that gaining some control over their own destinies—that is, being able to participate in decision making—is a major reinforcer for most workers (Connellan, 1978). And as we noted in Chapter 20, most successful supervisors do in fact use "participatory management" as one of their main managerial tools.

Giving employees appropriate feedback on job performance is a large part of "participatory management." Indeed, the so-called *quality control circles* used by many Japanese companies are little more than feedback devices in which both workers and managers can let each other know "how things are going" and suggest ways of improving matters. The fact that "quality control circles" actually work is "shocking" to many automobile executives, who still are reluctant to commit themselves to such "new-fangled ideas." Why the reluctance? As one GM official put it recently, "We're not accustomed to learning from other people" (cited in Holden, 1986). Given that response, the *really* shocking thing is that both the theory and practice of participatory management were developed by behavioral psychologists here in the US many years before the Japanese began using them (Connellan, 1978).

● *The Hawthorne Effect*

For almost half a century, industrial psychologists have spoken of the "Hawthorne Effect," meaning that one must be careful in real-life experiments because subjects will often produce the results they think the experimenters want. The effect gets its name from a series of studies performed at the Hawthorne (Chicago) plant, where the Western Electric Company makes equipment for AT&T. This research, done between 1926 and 1932, was designed to discover how much productivity and morale might be improved when the experimenters made various changes in the work environment.

According to the initial reports the experimenters issued, productivity increased *no matter what the experimenters did*. The usual interpretation of these data has been that the subjects knew they were being measured.

Hence they worked harder whether the experimenters made conditions better or worse. Psychologist H.M. Parsons has recently re-examined all of the original data in this study. Parsons shows that productivity increased *only* in those situations in which the workers could have gotten some feedback as to how well they were performing. Parsons believes the so-called "Hawthorne Effect" offers strong support for the belief that productivity tends to increase *primarily* when employees are given appropriate feedback about their performance (Parsons, 1982).

● *Management "By Exception"*

Generally speaking, most American managers and supervisors "manage by exception." They typically *ignore* appropriate work behaviors and focus on *punishing* inappropriate or off-target behaviors. But as Thomas Connellan points out, "management by exception" actually tends to punish productive responses and reinforce (with attention) unproductive and disruptive responses (Connellan, 1978).

As an example of how behavioral engineers might help managers overcome this tendency to "manage by exception," suppose we look briefly at industrial absenteeism.

● *Absenteeism*

Gary Johns is professor of management at Concordia University in Montreal. In a recent article, Johns notes that absenteeism costs American businesses about $30 billion a year. Johns says that the usual "excuse" offered for being absent is illness. However, during the last 100 years, both medical care and general health have *improved*, but absenteeism has gotten *worse*. Furthermore, around 1960, the medical reasons employees offered for missing work changed dramatically—from "somatic" illnesses (such as flu) to "psychosomatic" illnesses (such as lower back pain).

Johns believes that boredom, poor working conditions, and punitive styles of management account for much of the recent increase in absenteeism. He suggests that managers need to find ways (1) to increase employee *involvement* in the decision-making process, (2) of letting workers have a say in how their work is scheduled and performed, and (3) of rewarding employees (both financially and psychologically) for improved attendance (Johns, 1987).

According to a recent report by the American Productivity Center, absenteeism tends to *decrease*—and productivity tends to *increase*—when employees are given *incentives* for meeting clear-cut goals. Oddly enough, as Jack Horn noted recently, sales and marketing people have used incentives and bonuses for "meeting or surpassing quota" for decades. However, Horn says, managers on production lines are reluctant to institute such rewards, nor do they even like "sharing information" about corporate goals and strategies with the workers (Horn, 1987).

In a recent book, J.R. Hackman, Edward Lawler, and Lyman Porter note that the major task industrial psychologists must face is finding ways to *change the attitudes and behaviors of American managers*. For it is only when the supervisors learn better management techniques that the workers will improve *their* performance (Hackman, Lawler, & Porter, 1983).

Were American corporations not threatened by competition from overseas, of course, there would be little pressure for change in the industrial world. Perhaps the day will come when we will bless the Asians and the Europeans for "pressuring" us into learning how to treat our employees in a humane (and therefore effective) manner. If we don't change, of course, foreign corporations will simple buy up American businesses and do the job for us.

Applied Social Psychology

As we begin to use the behavioral sciences to bring about changes in groups and organizations, social psychologists become involved in such tasks as helping groups, organizations, and even countries resolve conflicts. One way to do so, surely, would be to make people more aware of how much social havoc the *attribution process* can wreak. (If you want to see the attribution process at work in international affairs, read what commentators in the Soviet Union have to say about American *motives*, what the Arabs say about the Israelis, what the Israelis say about the Arabs, and so forth.) We will never have "one world" until all of us stop attributing cultural differences to personality flaws rather than to learned responses (Kelley *et al.*, 1983).

For more than two decades now, social scientists have been studying how juries make decisions. As you might guess, jurors are likely to attribute crimes to character defects, and thus to decide guilt and innocence on a biased basis. At some time in the future, surely, we may wish to restrict jury membership to those individuals who have some knowledge of the social (as well as the intra-psychic) variables that influence human behavior—or to give people training in this area before they are called to jury duty (Seguin & Horowitz, 1984).

Perhaps the most important thing that psychologists can bring to human affairs, however, is the knowledge that all social change has costs as well as benefits. "Cleaning up the environment," for instance, is a very expensive proposition. Social psychologists might well help us estimate precisely what the price of change will be—and then work out informational programs that will encourage people to make the sacrifices necessary to achieve worthy goals (Pilon, 1986).

PSYCHOLOGY IN YOUR FUTURE

Fifty years ago most Americans were employed in producing "things"—farm products and manufactured goods. Today more than half of all Americans are employed in service occupations—that is, in processing information, helping other people, or taking care of people's possessions. As we learn more effective ways of assisting one another, the need for psychological services will grow tremendously. The behavioral sciences have rapidly become one of the most popular undergraduate majors in US colleges and universities. My own estimate is that by the year 2010 at least 10 percent of the US work force will be able to lay claim to the title "psychologist" or "behavioral engineer."

Whether you choose to become a psychologist yourself is a decision only you can make. But perhaps reading *Understanding Human Behavior* has given you some notion of what the future possibilities in psychology will be. At its best, psychology can offer you the tools to shape your body, your mind, and your social environment somewhat closer to your heart's desire.

Now that you have discovered what psychology is all about, perhaps you can use your new-found knowledge to help plot your own course into the future.

Let me close by thanking you for making me your guide through some of the frontiers of psychology, and by wishing you the happiest of life's journeys.

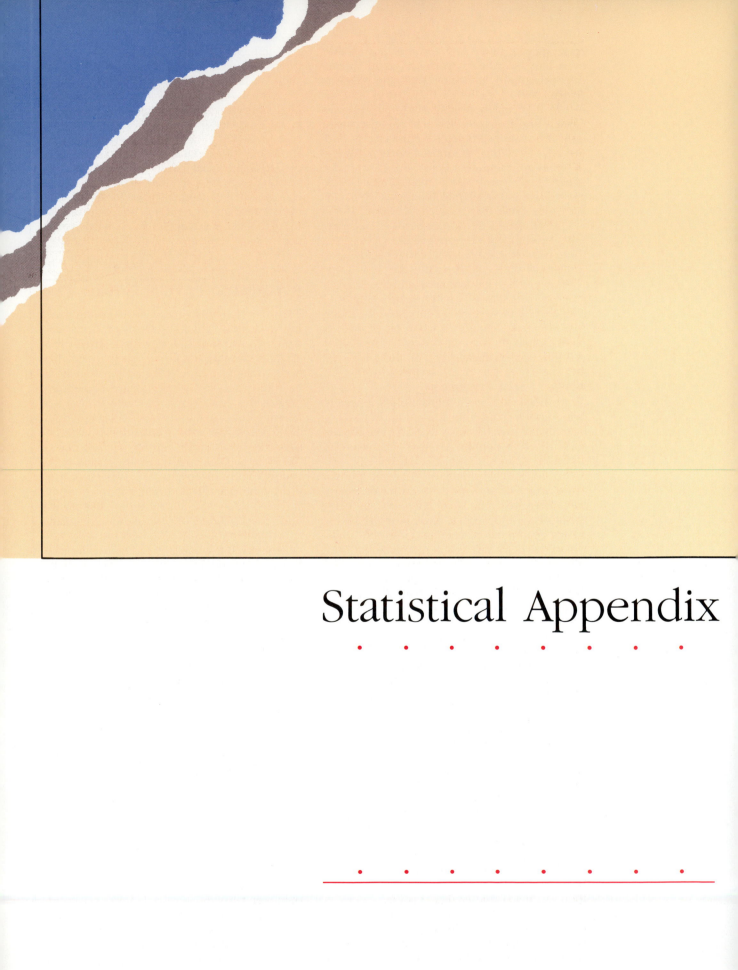

Statistical Appendix

THE RED LADY

I was sitting in the student union not long ago, talking with a friend of mine named Gersh, when two young women came over to our table and challenged us to a game of bridge. The two women—Joan and Carol were their names—turned out to be undergraduates. They also turned out to be card sharks, and they beat the socks off Gersh and me. Joan was particularly clever at figuring out how the cards were distributed among the four bridge hands—and hence good at figuring out how to play her own cards to win the most tricks.

One hand I will never forget, not merely because Joan played it so well, but because of what she said afterwards. Joan had bid four spades, and making the contract depended on figuring out who had the Queen of Diamonds—Gersh or me. Joan thought about it for a while, then smiled sweetly at Gersh. "I think you've got the Red Lady," she said, and promptly captured Gersh's Queen of Diamonds with her King.

Gersh, who hates to lose, muttered something about "dumb luck."

"No luck to it, really," Joan replied. "I knew you had 5 diamonds, Gersh, while Doc here had only 2. One of you had the Queen, but I didn't know which. But since you had 5 of the 7 missing diamonds, Gersh, the odds were 5 to 2 that you had the Little Old Lady. Simple enough, when you stop to think about it."

While Gersh was dealing the next hand with noisy frustration, Joan turned to me. "I know you're a professor, but I don't know what you teach."

"Psychology," I said, picking up my cards for the next hand. The cards were rotten, as usual.

"Oh, you're a psych teacher! That's great," Joan said with a smile. "I really wanted to study psych, but they told me I had to take statistics. I hate math. I'm just no good at figuring out all those complicated equations. So I majored in history instead."

STATISTICS — A WAY OF THINKING

I shook my head in amazement at what Joan said. I don't know how many times students have told me much the same thing—they're rotten at mathematics, or they just can't figure out what statistics is all about. But these same students manage to play bridge superbly, or figure out the stock market, or they can tell you the batting averages of every major league baseball player, or how many miles per gallon their car gets on unleaded gasoline.

Statistics is not just a weird bunch of mathematics—it's a way of thinking. If you can think well enough to figure out how to play cards, or who is likely to win the next election, or what

"I THINK YOU SHOULD BE MORE EXPLICIT HERE IN STEP TWO."

"grading on the curve" is all about, then you're probably already pretty good at statistics. In fact, you surely use statistics intuitively every minute of your life. If you didn't, you'd be dead or in some institution by now.

Sure, a few of the equations that statisticians throw around get pretty fancy. But don't let that fact discourage you. I've been a psych prof for more than 20 years, I minored in mathematics, but even I don't understand all the equations I see in the statistical and psychological journals. However, those "fancy formulas" are usually of interest only to specialists. Forget about them—unless you happen to be a nut about mathematics.

The truth is that you *already know* most of the principles involved in basic statistics—if, like Joan, you're willing to stop and think about them. Yet many psych students reject statistics with the same sort of emotionality that they show when somebody offers them fried worms and rattlesnake steak for dinner. Well, worms are rich in protein, and rattlesnake meat is delicious—and safe to eat—if you don't have to catch the snake first. But you may have to overcome some pretty strong emotional prejudices before you're willing to dig in and see what snake meat (or stats) is all about.

Odds and Ends

I've been a gambler all my life, and I really enjoy trying to "psych people out" at the bridge or poker table. So maybe I didn't get conditioned to fear numbers and "odds" the way a lot of people do. But whether you realize it or not, you're a gambler too. And you (like Joan) are pretty good at figuring out all kinds of odds and *probabilities*. Every time you cross the street, you gamble that the odds are "safely" in your favor. Each time you drive your car through a green light without slowing down, you gamble that some "odd" driver won't run the red light and hit you broadside. Every time you study for a true-false exam, you're gambling that you can learn enough to do better than somebody who refuses to study and who just picks the answers randomly. And whenever you go out with somebody on a date, you're gambling that you can predict that person's future behavior (on the date) from observing the things that the person has done in the past.

So you're a gambler, too, even if you don't think of yourself as being one. But if you're going to gamble, wouldn't it be helpful to know something about odds and probabilities? Because if you know what the odds are, you can often do a much better job of achieving whatever goals you have in mind.

One way or another, almost everything in statistics is based on *probability theory*. And, as luck would have it, probability theory got its start some 300 years ago when some French gamblers got worried about what the pay-offs should be in a dice game. So the gamblers—who were no dummies—hired two brilliant French mathematicians to figure out the probabilities for them. From the work of these two French geniuses came the theory that allows the casinos in Las Vegas and Atlantic City to earn hundreds of millions of dollars every year, that lets the insurance companies earn even more by betting on how long people will live—and that lets psychologists and psychiatrists employ the mental tests that label some people as being "normal" and other people as being "abnormal."

The Odds in Favor

If you want to see why Joan was so good at playing bridge, get a deck of cards and pull out the 2, 3, 4, 5, 6, 7, and Queen of Diamonds. Turn them face down on a table and shuffle them around so you won't know which card is which. Now try to pick out the Queen just by looking at the back of the cards.

If the deck is "honest" (unmarked), what are the odds that you will pick the Red Lady instead of the 2, 3, 4, 5, 6, or 7? As you can see, the odds are exactly 1 in 7. If you want to be fancy about all this, you can write an equation (which is what Joan did in her mind) as follows:

The probability (p) of picking the Queen (Q) is 1 out of 7, therefore

$$pQ = 1/7$$

Next, shuffle the cards again, place them face down on the table, and then randomly se-lect 2 of the cards and put them on one side of the table, and the remaining 5 on the other side of the table. Now, what are the odds that the Queen is in the stack of 5 cards (Gersh's bridge hand), and what are the odds that the Queen is in the stack of 2 cards (my bridge hand)?

Well, you already know that the probability that any 1 card will be the Queen is 1/7. I have 2 cards, therefore, I have two chances at getting the Queen, and the equation reads:

$$pQ \text{ (Me)} = 1/7 + 1/7 = 2/7$$

Gersh had 5 cards, so his probability equation is:

$$pQ \text{ (Gersh)} = 1/7 + 1/7 + 1/7 + 1/7 + 1/7$$
$$= 5/7$$

So if you dealt out the 7 cards randomly 70 times, Gersh would have the Queen about 50 times, and I would have the Queen about 20 times. No wonder Joan wins at bridge! When she assumed that Gersh had the Queen, she didn't have a sure thing—but the odds were surely in her favor.

Outcomes and Incomes

Now let's look at something familiar to every-one, the true-false examination. Suppose that you go to a history class one day, knowing there will be a test, but the teacher throws you a curve. For the exam you get is written in Chi-nese, or Greek, or some other language you simply can't read a word of. The test has 20 questions, and it's obviously of the true-false variety. But since you can't read it, all you can do is guess. What exam score do you think you'd most likely get—0, 10, or 20?

Maybe you'd deserve a 0, since you couldn't read the exam. But I'm sure you real-ize intuitively that you'd most likely get a score of about 10. Why?

Well, what are the *odds* of your guessing any single question right, if it's a true-false exam?

If you said, "Fifty percent chance of being right," you're thinking clearly. (See what I mean about statistics being a way of thinking?)

The probability (p) of your getting the first question right (R_1) is 50 percent, or 1/2. So we write an equation that says:

$$pR_1 = 1/2$$

The probability of your getting the first question wrong (W_1) is also 50 percent, or 1/2. So we write another equation:

$$pW_1 = 1/2$$

Furthermore, we can now say that, on the first or any other equation, the

$$p\text{R} + p\text{W} = 1/2 + 1/2 = 1$$

Which is a fancy way of saying that whenever you guess the answer on a true-false exam, you have to be either right or wrong—because those are the only two *outcomes* possible.

Now, suppose we look at the first two questions on the test. What is the probability that you will get *both* of them right, if you are just guessing at the answers?

Well, what outcomes are possible? You could miss both questions (W_1W_2), or you could get them both right (R_1R_2), or you could get the first answer right and the second answer wrong (R_1W_2), or you could get the first one wrong and the second right (W_1R_2).

Thus, there are 4 different outcomes, and since you would be guessing at the right answer on both questions, these 4 outcomes are *equally likely to occur*. Only 1 of the 4 outcomes (R_1R_2) is the one we're interested in, so the odds of your getting both questions right is 1/4.

$$p\text{R}_1\text{R}_2 = 1/4$$
$$p\text{W}_1\text{W}_2 = 1/4$$
$$p\text{R}_1\text{W}_2 = 1/4$$
$$p\text{W}_1\text{R}_2 = 1/4$$

and

$$p\text{R}_1\text{R}_2 + p\text{W}_1\text{W}_2 + p\text{R}_1\text{W}_2 + p\text{W}_1\text{R}_2 =$$
$$1/4 + 1/4 + 1/4 + 1/4 = 1$$

In a sense, getting both questions right is like selecting the Queen of Diamonds when it is 1 of 4 cards face down on the table in front of you. In both cases, you have 4 equally likely outcomes, so your chances of getting the Queen (or being right on both answers) is 1 out of 4, or 1/4.

As you can see, if you're taking an exam, playing bridge, or trying to add to your income by buying a lottery ticket, it will surely pay you to consider all the possible outcomes.

Actually, we can figure the odds of your answering the first 2 questions correctly in a much simpler way. We simply multiply the odds of your getting the first question right ($p\text{R}_1$) by the odds of your getting the second question right ($p\text{R}_2$):

$$p\text{R}_1\text{R}_2 = p\text{R}_1 \times p\text{R}_2 = 1/2 \times 1/2 = 1/4 = 25\%$$

Maybe you can see, too, that the odds of your getting both answers *wrong* would be exactly the same:

$$p\text{W}_1\text{W}_2 = p\text{W}_1 \times p\text{W}_2 = 1/2 \times 1/2 = 1/4 = 25\%$$

If the exam had just three questions to it, the odds of your getting all the answers right by chance alone (that is, by guessing) would be:

$$p\text{R}_1\text{R}_2\text{R}_3 = p\text{R}_1 \times p\text{R}_2 \times p\text{R}_3 =$$
$$1/2 \times 1/2 \times 1/2 = 1/8 = 12.5\%$$

To put the matter another way, on a 3-question exam, there are 8 different outcomes:

$R_1R_2R_3$	$W_1R_2R_3$
$R_1R_2W_3$	$W_1R_2W_3$
$R_1W_2R_3$	$W_1W_2R_3$
$R_1W_2W_3$	$W_1W_2W_3$

Since only 1 of these 8 possible outcomes is the one you want ($R_1R_2R_3$), the odds in your favor are only 1 in 8.

If the test had 4 true-false questions, there would be 16 different outcomes—twice as many as if the test had but three questions. These outcomes would range from $R_1R_2R_3R_4$, $R_1R_2R_3W_4$ . . . all the way to $W_1W_2W_3R_4$ and $W_1W_2W_3W_4$. If there are 16 different outcomes, only 1 of which is "all answers right" or $R_1R_2R_3R_4$, what would be the odds of your guessing all the answers right on a 4-question true-false test?

(If you said, "1 in 16," congratulations!)

Now, let's take a giant leap.

If the exam had 10 questions, the odds of your getting all 10 answers right by guessing would be:

$$p\text{R}_1\text{R}_2\text{R}_3\text{R}_4\text{R}_5\text{R}_6\text{R}_7\text{R}_8\text{R}_9\text{R}_{10} = 1/2 \times 1/2 \times 1/2 \times$$
$$1/2 \times 1/2 \times 1/2 \times 1/2 \times 1/2 \times 1/2 \times 1/2 =$$
$$1/1024$$

So if you took the exam 1024 times and guessed randomly at the answers each time, just *once* in 1024 times would you expect to get a score of 0, and just *once* in 1024 times would you expect to get a score of 10.

Now, at last, we can answer the question we asked you a few paragraphs back: If you took a 20-question exam on which you had to guess at each answer, what exam score do you think you'd most likely get—0, 10, or 20?

Well, what are the odds that you'd get a score of flat 0? In fact, the odds are astronomically against you, just as they are astronomically against your getting a score of 20 right. In either case, the probability would be:

$$p\text{W}_{1\text{-}20} = p\text{R}_{1\text{-}20} = 1/2 \times 1/2 \times 1/2 \ . \ . \ .$$
$$(20 \text{ times!}) = 1,048,576 \text{ to } 1!$$

So the odds are more than a million to one that you won't get all the answers right or all the answers wrong on a 20-question true-false exam just by guessing. Which might give you good reason to study for the next exam you have to take!

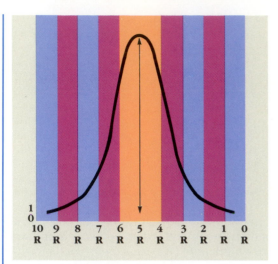

FIG. A.1 A bell-shaped curve showing the distribution of "right answers" expected by chance alone when taking a 10-item true-false exam.

Normal Curves

Next, let's throw in some pictures just to liven things up a bit. Statisticians have a way of plotting or graphing probabilities that may make more sense to you than equations do.

Let's make a diagram of the *distribution* of outcomes when you take an 10-question true-false exam (See Fig. A.1):

As we mentioned earlier, the number of possible outcomes in a 10-question exam is 1024. So the odds of getting all 10 questions right by just guessing ("by chance alone") would be 1 in 1024. Not very good odds. But the probability of your getting 4, 5, or 6 questions right would be well above 60 percent! That makes sense, because just looking at the curve you can see that better than 60 percent of the possible outcomes are bunched up right in the middle of the curve.

DESCRIPTIVE STATISTICS

The curve we've just drawn is the world-famous, ever-popular "bell-shaped curve." In fact, the curve describes a *random distribution of scores* or outcomes. That is, the curve describes the outcomes you'd expect when students are forced to guess—more or less at random—which answers on a true-false exam are correct. Naturally, if the exam were written in clear English, and if the students knew most of the material they were being examined on, the curve or *distribution of scores* would look quite different.

There are many sorts of "outcomes" that fit the bell-shaped curve rather nicely. For example, if you randomly selected 1,000 adult US males and measured their heights, the results you'd get would come very close to matching the bell-shaped curve shown in Fig. A.2. Which is to say that there would be a few very short

men, a few very tall men, but most would have heights around 5'10". The same bell-shaped curve would fit the distribution of heights of 1,000 adult women selected at random—except that the "middle" or peak of the bell-shaped curve would be about 5'5"

Measures of Central Tendency

As we noted in Chapter 18, intelligence tests are constructed so that the scores for any age group will approximate a bell-shaped curve. In this case, the peak or "middle" of the distribution of IQ's will be almost precisely at 100. A very few individuals would have IQ's below 50, a very few would have scores above 150. But some two-thirds of the scores would fall between 84 and 116 (see Fig. 18.1).

Why this bulge in the middle as far as IQ's are concerned? Well, think back for a moment to the true-false test we were discussing earlier that had 10 questions on it. There are 1024 possible outcomes. If you wanted to get all 10 questions right, there was only one way you could answer the 10 questions—all had to be correct. But there were 256 ways in which you could answer the questions to get a score of 5—right in the middle.

There is only one way you can earn a top score on an intelligence test—you've got to answer all the questions rapidly and precisely the way the people who constructed the test say is "right." But there are thousands of different ways you can answer the questions on the usual test to get a "middle score," namely, an IQ between 84 and 116.

In a similar vein, there are precious few ways in which you can earn a million dollars, but there are dozens and dozens of ways in which you can earn between $15,000 and $20,000 a year. So if we selected 1,000 adult US citizens at random, asked them what their incomes were, and then "took an average," what kind of curve (distribution of incomes) do you think we'd get?

FIG. A.2 A bell-shaped curve showing the distribution of heights of a thousand men and a thousand women selected at random.

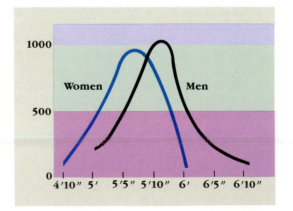

TABLE A.1   Table of Grade Point Averages

Course	Hours Credit	Grade	Hour × Grade
History	3	A	3 × 4 = 12
Psychology	4	A	4 × 4 = 16
Mathematics	4	C	4 × 2 = 8
Spanish	4	B	4 × 3 = 12
TOTALS	15		48

$$GPA = 48/15 = 3.2$$

Whenever we measure people psychologically, biologically, socially, intellectually, or economically, we often generate a distribution of outcomes that looks very much like a bell-shaped curve. Each person in the world is unique, it's true. But it is equally true that, on any given *single* measuring scale (height, weight, grade-point average, income), most people's scores will be somewhere in the *middle* of the range of possible outcomes.

Psychologists have a variety of tools for measuring the "middle" of any curve or distribution of outcomes. These techniques are often called *measures of central tendency*, which is a fancy way of saying that these techniques allow us to measure the center or midpoint of any distribution of scores or outcomes.

Mean, Median, Mode

1. *The Mean.* The *mean* is simply the statistical "average" of all the scores or outcomes involved. When you figure your grade-point average (GPA) for any semester, you usually multiply your grade in each course by the number of credit hours, add up the totals, and divide by the number of hours credit you are taking. Your GPA is actually the *mean* or mathematical average of all your grades (see Table A.1).

2. *The Median.* Since the mean is a mathematical average, it sometimes gives very funny results. For example, according to recent government figures, the "average" US family was made up of about 4.47 people. Have you ever known a family that had 4.47 people in it? For another example, if you got two As and two Cs one semester, your average or "mean" grade would be a B. Yet you didn't get a B in any of the courses you took.

There are times when it makes more sense to figure the exact *midpoint score* or outcome, rather than figuring out the *average* score. At such times, psychologists often use the *median*, which is the score that's in the precise middle of the distribution—just as the "median" of an expressway is the area right down the middle of the highway.

The median is often used as a "measure of central tendency" when a distribution has one or two extreme scores in it. For instance, if 9 people earn $1 a year, and a 10th earns $100,000, what is the *mean* income of these 10 people? About $10,001 a year, which is a misleading statistic, to say the least. However, the *median* income is $1, which describes the actual income of the *majority* of the group somewhat better than does the mean of $10,001.

3. *The Mode.* The word *mode* is defined in the dictionary as "the prevailing fashion or most popular custom or style." When we are talking about distributions of scores or outcomes, *mode* means the most popular score. That is, the mode is the highest point (or points) on the curve. If the distribution has two points that are equally high, then there are two scores that are *modal*, and we can call the curve *bi-modal* (having two modes).

Skewedness

If the distribution of scores is more or less bell-shaped, then the mean, median, and mode usually come out to be the same. But not all curves do us the favor of being so regular in shape. For example, suppose you were interested in whether a particular teacher—Dr. Johnson—started and ended her classes on time. To find out, you take a very accurate watch with you all semester long and make a scientific study of Dr. Johnson's behavior.

During the term, let's say, there are supposed to be 50 lectures by Dr. Johnson. So the number of possible start-time scores or outcomes will be 50. For the most part, Dr. Johnson begins on time, but occasionally she starts a minute or two early, and sometimes she's a minute or two late. Now and again, she is fairly tardy in getting to class, and once she didn't show up at all. But she *never* begins a class more than two minutes early. If you put all of her starting times on a graph, it would look something like the curve on the left side of Fig. A.3. If you plotted all her closing time scores on a similar graph, it would look like the curve on the right in Fig. A.3.

The term we use to describe these curves is *skewedness*, which means they are "slanted" or "pushed out of shape." In the starting-time example, the tail of the curve slants out far to the right-hand side, so we say that the curve is "skewed to the right." The other curve has a tail that slants out to the left, so the curve is "skewed to the left." As is the case in many distributions where the scores are measures of reaction times or beginning times, the mean, median, and mode are fairly different.

Range and Variation

There are two more important concepts we have to get out of the way before we can finish our discussion of *descriptive statistics*—which is to say, statistics that measure or describe something. The first concept is the *range* of

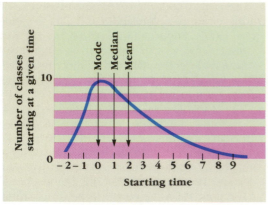 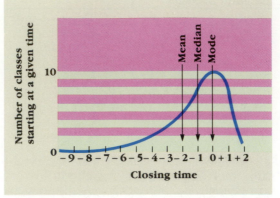

FIG. A.3 A plot of Dr. Johnson's "beginning times" and "closing times."

possible scores or outcomes; the second is the *variability* of the scores. The first concept is easy to understand, but the second will take some careful thought on your part.

What is the *range* of possible scores on a 10-item "fill in the blanks" test? From 0 to 10, of course. And since you can't guess as easily on this type of test as on a true-false examination, you can't really tell ahead of time what the class average is likely to be. The range on a 100-item test would be from 0 to 100—and again, you have no way of knowing before you take the test what the "mean" or average score is likely to be.

Let's suppose that you took a 10-item "fill in the blanks" exam and got a score of 8 right, which also turned out to be the mean or average score for the whole class. Then you took a 100-item "fill in the blanks" test and again you got a score of 8, which again turned out to be the class average. What does knowing the *range* of possible scores tell you about the level of difficulty of the two tests? Wouldn't you say that the 100-item test was considerably more difficult, even though the class average was the same on both tests?

Now, let's add one more dimension. Suppose that on the 10-item examination, *everybody in class* got a score of 8! There would be no *variation* at all in these scores, since none of the scores *deviated* (were different from) the mean. But suppose on the 100-item "fill in the blanks" exam, about 95 percent of the class got scores of flat zero, you got an 8, and a few "aces" got scores above 85. Your score of 8 would still be the *mean* (but not the median or mode). But the *deviation* of the rest of the scores would be tremendous. Even though you scored right at the mean on both tests, the fact that you were better than 95 percent of the class on the 100-item test might well be very pleasing to you.

The variation or variability of test scores is simply a measure of *how spread out across the range* the scores actually are. Thus, the variabil-

ity of a distribution of scores is a very important item to know if you're going to evaluate how you perform in relation to anybody else who's taken the test.

The Standard Deviation

If you know the range of scores, plus the mean, median, and mode, you can usually get a fairly good notion of what shape the curve might take. Why? Because these two bits of information tell you something about how the scores are *distributed*. If the mean, median, and mode are almost the same, and they fall right at the center of the range, then the distribution curve must be "vaguely" bell-shaped, or regular in shape.

But why do we say "vaguely" bell-shaped? In Chapter 21, we discussed the distribution of scores on an attitude questionnaire in two different groups. In the homogeneous group, as Fig. A.4 shows, the range of scores was very small. But in the heterogeneous group, as Fig. A.5 shows, the range was much larger. The means for the two distributions were the same, and if the groups had been large enough, we might even have found that the ranges of the two distributions were the same. However, in

FIG. A.4 A distribution of attitude scores for a homogeneous group.

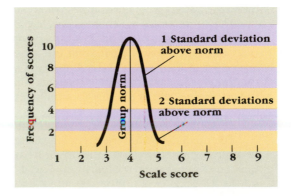

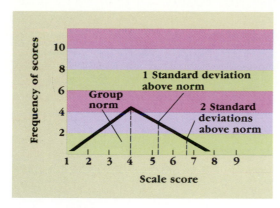

FIG. A.5 A distribution of attitude scores for a heterogeneous group.

the homogeneous group, the scores were all bunched up close to the mean, while in the heterogeneous group, the scores were broadly *dispersed*, or spread out.

In Chapter 18, we found that we needed a concept we called the *standard deviation* to describe the *dispersion of scores* across the range (or around the mean). The larger the standard deviation, the more widely the scores vary around the mean (and the more heterogeneous the group probably is). The smaller the standard deviation, the more bunched up the scores are around the mean (and the more homogeneous the group probably is).

We can now define the *standard deviation* as a statistical term meaning the variability of scores in a distribution.

There are a variety of mathematical formulas for figuring out such statistics as the standard deviation. Once upon a time, students were required to memorize these formulas and grind out statistical analyses using nothing more than their brains (and perhaps their fingers and toes to count on). Nowadays, however, even cheap pocket calculators will figure out the standard deviation of a distribution of scores almost instantaneously (if you input the right data in the first place).

However, as we said earlier, statistics is more a way of thinking than it is a bunch of fancy formulas. *Descriptive statistics* are shorthand ways of describing large bunches of data. They are "thought tools" that let you think about the world in convenient symbols.

Let's now see how you can use "descriptive" statistics to help you *make inferences* or draw conclusions about the data you're mulling over in your mind.

INFERENTIAL STATISTICS

Whenever you test a hunch or a scientific hypothesis, you often are hunting for *reliable* differences between two groups of subjects or

between two sets of data. Again, there are *many* different formulas for figuring out how reliable (or important) the group differences really are. But one of the simplest—and most often used—is the standard deviation. By convention, scientists accept differences as being "real" if the means of the two groups depart by 2 or more standard deviations from each other.

We pick the figure 2 standard deviations for a very understandable reason. If on a bell-shaped curve we measure out from the mean a distance of 2 standard deviations, we will take into account about 95 percent of all the IQ scores described by the curve. Any score falling outside of this distance will be there *by chance alone* less than 5 percent of the time. So the odds of your getting an IQ of 132 are but 5 in 100, or 1 in 20. Since these odds are pretty impressive, we can assume that your score didn't occur "by chance alone," and thus the score suggests you are "brighter than average."

• Differences Between Groups

Now, suppose we compare the IQ's of two people, Bill and Mary. Bill has a score of 84, which is exactly 1 standard deviation from the mean of 100. He might have "below average" intelligence, true. But he's so close to the mean that we might as well call him "average" since he might have been overly tired when he took the test. (In fact, even if his *true* IQ was 100, Bill would get a *measured* score of between 84 and 100 about one-third of the time that he took the test. Can you guess why this would be the case?)

Mary has an IQ of 116, which is exactly 1 standard deviation above the mean. But again, her score isn't all that different from the mean, so we could (technically speaking) say that she too has "average intelligence." (She too would be expected to get a *measured* score between 100 and 116 one-third of the time if her *true* IQ was 100. And, like Bill, she would also get a *measured* score between 84 and 100 a third of the time.)

Since both Bill and Mary have IQ's that "vary" from the mean but 1 standard deviation, their scores of 84 and 116 don't differ reliably from each other, right?

Wrong! (As if you didn't know that intuitively anyhow.)

Bill's score differs from Mary's by *2* standard deviations, thus the odds are at least 20 to 1 that Mary's *true* IQ score is significantly higher than Bill's. (And wouldn't you have been willing to make a small wager that was the case the moment you knew what their scores were?)

• Significant Differences

Whenever you hear scientists say that their "findings are significant at the 5 percent level," you can translate this to mean that their groups differed by about 2 standard deviations. In general, if the odds are not at least 20 to 1 in support of the hunch you're trying to prove, you probably shouldn't use the word "significant" in describing your results.

There are many different tests or formulas you could use for calculating whether the results of an experiment were significant or not. Among the best-known of such statistical devices are the *t-test* and the *critical ratio*. Should you ever need to employ one of these tests, you'd do well to read about them in a statistics text.

Correlation Coefficients

In several chapters of this book, we have mentioned the term *correlation* to suggest that two events or traits were somehow connected or associated with each other. The mathematics underlying correlations are not too difficult to understand. However, the correlation concept itself has a "problem" buried deep within it that makes it one of the most misunderstood and misused ideas in all of human experience. We'll come back to this problem in just a moment. First, let's look at how one figures out if two sets of scores are correlated.

As we noted in Chapter 17, there is a strong relationship between IQ's and grades in school, and for a very good reason. Intelligence tests are usually devised so that they will predict academic success, and the items on most such tests are juggled around until the final score does in fact yield the expected predictions. Thus, if we give intelligence tests to all incoming freshmen, and we know their grades at the end of their first collegiate year, we should expect to find the sort of relationship between these measures shown in Table A.2.

Just looking at the rank orderings of these scores, you can tell that a strong correlation exists between the two distributions. As Fig. A.6 shows, if we plotted the data on what is called a *scatter diagram*, we'd get pretty much a straight line. (A scatter diagram shows how the scores for each subject are *scattered*, or distributed, across the graph or diagram.)

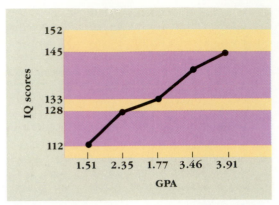

FIG. A.6 A scatter diagram showing the positive correlation between IQ's and grade-point averages.

If we reversed the scores, so that Ann has an IQ of 152 but a GPA of 1.51, Bill got an IQ of 145 and a GPA of 2.35, and so forth, we'd get a scatter diagram that looked like the one in Fig. A.7.

Generally speaking, the closer the scatter diagram comes to being a straight line tilted to the right or left as these are, the higher the correlation between the two variables (scores).

There are several formulas for figuring out the *mathematical* correlation between two sets of scores that we needn't go into here. All of these formulas yield what is called a *correlation coefficient*, which is merely a "coefficient" or number between +1 and −1.

A correlation coefficient of +1 indicates that the two sets of scores are *perfectly correlated in a positive way*. Which is to say, the person who got the highest score on one test got the highest on the second test, the person who got the second highest score on one test got the second highest on the other test, and so forth.

A correlation coefficient of −1 indicates that the two sets of scores are *perfectly correlated in a negative way*. Which is to say that the person who got the *highest* score on the first test got the *lowest* score on the second, the per-

FIG. A.7 A scatter diagram showing a negative correlation between IQ's and grade-point averages.

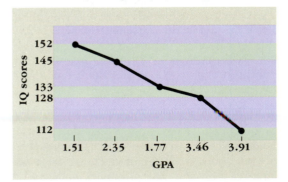

TABLE A.2   **Relationship between IQ Score and GPA**

	Entrance Test IQ Score	Grade Point Average (GPA)
Ann	152	3.91
Bill	145	3.46
Carol	133	2.77
Dick	128	2.35
Elmer	112	1.51
Σ (Sum of)	670	14.00
Mean	134	2.80
SD	15.54	0.94

son who got the second *highest* score on the first test got the second *lowest* score on the other test, and so forth.

A correlation coefficient of +.75 suggests there is a strong (but not perfect) association between the two sets of scores. A coefficient of −.75 would indicate the same strength of association, but in a negative direction.

A correlation coefficient of 0 (or close to it) tells you that there is little or no significant relationship between the two sets of scores.

Uses and Abuses of Correlation Coefficients

The ability to make quick correlations is just about the most useful trait that your mind has available to it. Whether you realize it or not, your brain is so built that it automatically makes connections between incoming stimuli. Think back to the discussion of Pavlovian conditioning you read about in Chapter 9. When you ring a bell, and then give food to a dog, the animal's brain soon comes to associate the sound of the bell with the appearance of the food. When the dog eventually salivates to the sound of the bell *before* food arrives, its nervous system has calculated a crude sort of "correlation coefficient" between the onset of the bell and the presentation of the food. Since (in the experiment) the two events *always* occur together, the correlation coefficient of the two events would be close to +1. Thus, the dog can anticipate (predict) the stimulus input "food" as soon as the stimulus input "bell" has occurred.

If dogs could talk, how might they explain their conditioned responses? Don't you imagine that Pavlov's beasts might explain matters in *causal* terms? That is, might not a well-conditioned canine remark that the bell has "magic powers" that cause the food to appear?

As peculiar as this notion may sound to you, evidence in its favor comes from some real-life experiments. In several studies, bell-food conditioned animals have later been trained to turn on the bell themselves by pressing a bar in their cages. What do you think the animals do when they become hungry?

As we mentioned earlier, the concept of correlation has a problem buried in it. The problem is this: We too often assume that if event A is *correlated* with event B, then A must somehow *cause* the appearance of B. This "causal assumption" gets us into a lot of trouble. For example, does the sound of the bell really *cause* the food to appear? Do high IQ's really *cause* students to get good grades? As you can see, the answer in both cases must be a resounding *no*.

Scores on an intelligence test don't cause much of anything (except, perhaps, favorable reactions from college admissions commit-tees). The underlying trait of intelligence presumably causes both the high IQ and the good grades. Thus, *intelligence* is responsible for the correlation between the two events, just as Pavlov's desires were responsible for the correlation between the bell and the food.

There are times when highly significant correlations may seriously mislead us. As we have mentioned several times, there is a high correlation between going to a psychotherapist and "getting better." But as many studies have shown, you are just about as likely to show improvement if you *don't* seek help as if you do. But the fact that you (1) went to a therapist and (2) solved some of your problems may incorrectly convince both you and your therapist that it was the *treatment* that primarily caused your improvement.

At their very best, correlations can help us predict future stimulus inputs and give us clues as to what the underlying causal connections among these inputs might be. However, in daily life, we too often misuse correlations. If you want to make your psychology teacher very happy indeed, say "Correlations don't determine causes" over and over again—until you're conditioned to believe it!

STATS AND EVERYDAY LIFE

Why statistics? Or, to phrase the question more precisely, is there any correlation between knowing something about stats and knowing something about yourself and the people around you?

As it happens, the difference between knowing stats and not knowing it is highly significant. All of your future life you will be performing "little experiments" in which you try to understand the people around you. It's likely (at the 5 percent level) that you will probe your environment better if you know how to interpret the results of your informal experimentation. If you are introspective, an understanding of correlations and conditioning could help tell you some very important facts about how you have acquired many of your values and attitudes. And, if nothing else, understanding what a bell-shaped curve is all about could save you a lot of money should you ever happen to visit Las Vegas.

The second reason for imposing statistics on you, willy-nilly, is that you may wish to take further courses in psychology. If you do, you may be encouraged (or even required) to perform one or more controlled experiments, either in a laboratory or in a real-life setting. Therefore, you might as well learn the first law of statistics right now:

Your statistical inferences are never better than your experimental design will allow.

The topic of how to design a good experiment has filled many a thick textbook, and there's little sense in subjecting you to more grief than we've done already. What we can say is this—the secret of good experimentation lies in *controlling variables*. If you want to pick a random sample of people for a political poll, make sure your sample is *really random*. Just asking a few of your friends what they think won't do, because your method of choice was highly biased—and hence not random at all.

Several times in this book we've mentioned the concept of a "control group" that some scientist(s) used in an experiment. There probably is no more powerful way of making sure your results are reliable than by incorporating as many groups as possible in your study—one group to *control* for each factor (variable) that might influence the results of your study.

But, most important of all, if you must run a scientific study, think it through carefully *before you start*. Then you can design your study intelligently so that the data you gather will be easy to analyze, and so your expected results will be as truthful and as reliable as you can make them. Scientists are probably about as honest and as open in their work as any professional group can be. And yet all of us may unconsciously bias our results if we feel passionately about the subject we're studying. So we should use control group after control group—just to make sure that we screen out our unconscious biases before they can affect our results. Anything that you love, or that is important enough to you, is worth working hard for—and worth being entirely honest about.

Animals show a lot of intelligent behaviors. They "sing," and monkeys even draw pictures of a sort. But only human beings run experiments, control for bias, select their subjects randomly, and perform statistical analyses. Being a scientist is thus one of the most *humane* occupations you can have, because we all need reliable and valid data about how things are now so we can make things (including ourselves) better in the future.

As it happens, I love science. To me, it is a "fun game," a way of wisdom, and a means of achieving self-actualization. My parting hope is that you will someday come to appreciate this art form as much as I do. And if the scientific love bug does bite you, perhaps then and only then will you come to enjoy statistics and experimental design as much as most scientists do.

I wish you the best of luck!

(Meanwhile, Gersh and I are reading several books on probability theory as applied to bridge. Joan and Carol, you'd better watch out!)

.. References ..

Abrams, R., & Essman, W.B. (Eds.). (1982). *Electroconvulsive therapy: Biological foundations and clinical applications*. New York: SP Medical & Scientific Books.

Adams, P.L., Milner, J.R., & Schrepf, N.A. (1984). *Fatherless children*. New York: Wiley.

Adelman, E., & Castricone, L. (1986). An expressive arts model for substance abuse group training and treatment. *Arts in Psychotherapy, 13(1)*, 53-59.

Adler, A. (1927). *Understanding human nature*. Greenwich, CN: Fawcett.

Adler, A. (1931). *What life should mean to you*. New York: Putnam.

Adler, A. (1959). *The practice and theory of individual psychology*. Totowa, NJ: Littlefield-Adams.

Adler, N., Pfaff, D., & Goy, R.W. (Eds.). (1985). *Handbook of behavioral neurobiology, Vol. 7: Reproduction*. New York: Plenum Press.

Ajzen, I. (1987). A new paradigm in the psychology of persuasion. *Contemporary Psychology, 32*, 1009-1010.

Akerstedt, T. (1985). Shifted sleep hours. *Annals of Clinical Research, 17(5)*, 273-279.

Akerstedt, T., & Froberg, J. (1976). Interindividual differences in circadian patterns of catecholamine excretion, body temperature, performance, and subjective arousal. *Biological Psychology, 4*, 277-292.

Algarabel, S. (1985). Learned helplessness, human depression, and perhaps endorphins? *Behavioral and Brain Sciences, 8*, 369.

Allport, G. (1935). Attitudes. In G. Murchison (Ed.), *Handbook of social psychology*. Worcester, MA: Clark University Press.

Allport, G. (1960). *Personality and social encounter: Selected essays*. Boston: Beacon Press.

Allport, G. (1966). Traits revisited. *American Psychologist, 21*, 1-10.

Allport, G. (1967). Autobiography. In E.G. Boring & G. Lindzey (Eds.), *A history of psychology in autobiography*, Vol. 5. New York: Appleton.

Allport, G. (1968). *The person in psychology: Selected essays*. Boston: Beacon Press.

Allport, G., & Odbert, H.S. (1936). Trait names: A psycholexical study. *Psychological Monographs, 47*, 1-171.

Altman, K.P., & Hickson-Laknahour, H. (1986). New roles for psychodramatists in counter-terrorism training. *Journal of Group Psychotherapy, Psychodrama and Sociometry, 39(2)*, 70-77.

Ambron, S.R., & Salkind, N.J. (1987). *Child development*, 5th ed. New York: Holt, Rinehart and Winston.

American Psychiatric Association. (1952). *Diagnostic and statistical manual of mental disorders*. Washington, DC: APA.

American Psychiatric Association. (1968). *Diagnostic and statistical manual of mental disorders*, 2nd ed. Washington, DC: APA.

American Psychiatric Association. (1980). *Diagnostic and statistical manual of mental disorders*, 3rd ed. Washington, DC: APA.

American Psychiatric Association. (1987). *Diagnostic and statistical manual of mental disorders*, 3rd ed., rev. Washington, DC: APA.

Amoore, J.E. (1977). Specific anosmia and the concept of primary odors. *Chemical Senses and Flavor, 2*, 267-281.

Anastasi, A. (1983). Evolving trait concepts. *American Psychologist, 38*, 175-184.

Anastasi, A. (1986). Experiential structuring of psychological traits. *Developmental Review, 6*, 181-202.

Andersen, A.E. (1985). *Practical comprehensive treatment of anorexia nervosa and bulimia*. Baltimore, MD: Johns Hopkins University Press.

Andersen, E.S. (1975). Cups and classes: Learning that boundaries are vague. *Journal of Child Language, 2*, 79-103.

Anderson, J.R. (1976). *Language, memory, and thought*. Hillsdale, NJ: Erlbaum.

Anderson, J.R. (1985). *Cognitive psychology and its implications*. San Francisco: Freeman.

Andrasik, F., & Holroyd, K.A. (1983). Specific and nonspecific effects in the biofeedback treatment of tension headache: 3-year follow-up. *Journal of Consulting and Clinical Psychology, 51*, 634-636.

Andreasen, M. (1985). Listener recall for call-in versus structured interview radio formats. *Journal of Broadcasting and Electronic Media, 29(4)*, 421-430.

Andreasen, N.C. (1988). Brain imaging: Applications in psychiatry. *Science, 239*, 1381-1388.

Annett, M., & Kilshaw, D. (1982). Mathematical ability and lateral asymmetry. *Cortex, 18*, 547-568.

Ansbacher, H.L., & Ansbacher, R.R. (1956). *The individual psychology of Alfred Adler: A systematic presentation in selections from his writings*. New York: Viking.

Ansbacher, H.L., & Ansbacher, R.R. (Eds.). (1973). *Superiority and social interest: A collection of Alfred Adler's later writings*. New York: Viking.

Argyle, M., & Cook, M. (1976). *Gaze and mutual gaze*. London: Cambridge University Press.

Argyris, C., Putnam, R., & Smith, D.McL. (1985). *Action science: Concepts, methods and skills for research and intervention*. San Francisco: Jossey-Bass.

Armstrong, P., & McDaniel, E. (1986). Relationships between learning styles and performance on problem-solving tasks. *Psychological Reports, 59*, 1135-1138.

Arnheim, R. (1986). The two faces of Gestalt psychology. *American Psychologist, 41*, 820-824.

Arnold, M.B. (1960). *Emotion and personality*. New York: Columbia University Press.

Arnold, M.B. (1981). Reinventing the wheel. *Contemporary Psychology, 26*, 535-536.

Aronson, E. (1984). *The social animal*, 4th ed. New York: W.W. Freeman.

Aronson, E., & Mills, J. (1959). The effect of severity of initiation on liking for a group. *Journal of Abnormal and Social Psychology, 59*, 177-181.

Asch, S.E. (1946). Forming impressions of personality. *Journal of Abnormal and Social Psychology, 41*, 258-290.

Asch, S.E. (1951). Effects of group pressure upon the modification and distortion of judgments. In H. Guetzkow (Ed.), *Groups, leadership, and men*. Pittsburgh: Carnegie Press.

Asch, S.E. (1956). Studies of independence and conformity: A minority of one against a unanimous majority. *Psychological Monographs, 70*, Whole No. 416.

Asch, S.E. (1987). *Social psychology*. Oxford, England: Oxford University Press.

Aschoff, J., Daan, S., & Groos, G.A. (Eds.). (1982). *Vertebrate circadian systems*. New York: Springer-Verlag.

Aserinsky, E., & Kleitman, N. (1953). Regularly occurring periods of eye motility, and concomitant phenomena, during sleep. *Science, 118*, 273-274.

Atwood, G.E., & Tomkins, S. (1976). On the subjectivity of personality theory. *Journal of the History of the Behavioral Sciences, 12*, 166-177.

Averill, J.R. (1982). *Anger and agression: An essay on emotion*. New York: Springer-Verlag.

Azmitia, M. (1987). Why the whole is not the sum of its parts. *Contemporary Psychology, 32*, 469.

Bahrick, H.P., & Phelps, E. (1987). Retention of Spanish vocabulary over 8 years. *Journal of Experimental Psychology: Learning, Memory, and Cognition, 13*, 344-349.

Baker, R.A. (1982). The effect of suggestion on Past-Lives Regression. *American Journal of Clinical Hypnosis, 25(1)*, 71-76

Bales, R.F. (1953). The equilibrium problem in small groups. In T. Parsons, R.F. Bales, and E.A. Shils (Eds.), *Working papers in the theory of action*. Glencoe, IL: Free Press.

Baltes, P.D. (1982). *Life-span development and behavior*. New York: Academic Press.

Baltes, P.D. (1983). In R.M. Lerner (Ed.), *Developmental psychology: Historical and philosophical perspectives*. Hillsdale, NJ: Erlbaum.

Bandura, A. (1973). *Aggression: A social learning analysis*. Englewood Cliffs, NJ: Prentice-Hall.

Bandura, A. (1974). Behavior theory and the models of man. *American Psychologist, 29*, 859-869.

Bandura, A. (1977a). Self-efficacy: Toward a unifying theory of behavioral change. *Psychological Review, 84*, 191-215.

Bandura, A. (1977b). *Social learning theory*. Englewood Cliffs, NJ: Prentice-Hall.

Bandura, A. (1978). The self system in reciprocal determinism. *American Psychologist, 33*, 344-358.

Bandura, A. (1983). Self-efficacy determinants of anticipated fears and calamities. *Journal of Personality & Social Psychology, 45*, 464-468.

Bandura, A. (1984). Representing personal determinants in causal structures. *Psychological Review, 91*, 508-511.

Bandura, A. (1986a). *The social foundations of thought and action: A social cognitive theory*. Englewood Cliffs, NJ: Prentice-Hall.

Bandura, A. (1986b). Fearful expectations and avoidant actions as coeffects of perceived self-inefficacy. *American Psychologist, 41*, 1389-1391.

Bandura, A. (1986c). The explanatory and predictive scope of self-efficacy theory. *Journal of Social and Clinical Psychology, 4*, 359-373.

Bandura, A., Blanchard, E.B., & Ritter, B. (1969). The relative efficacy of desensitization and modeling approaches for inducing behavioral, affective, and attitudinal changes. *Journal of Personality and Social Psychology, 13*, 173-199.

Bandura, A., *et al*. (1987). Perceived self-efficacy and pain control: Opioid and nonopioid mechanisms. *Journal of Personality and Social Psychology, 53*, 563-571.

Barber, T.X. (1969). *Hypnosis: A scientific approach*. New York: Van Nostrand Reinhold.

Barber, T.X. (1970). *LSD, marihuana, Yoga and hypnosis*. Chicago: Aldine-Atherton.

Barber, T.X. (1978). Hypnosis, suggestions, and psychosomatic phenomena: A new look from the standpoint of recent experimental studies. *American Journal of Clinical Hypnosis, 21(1)*, 13-27.

Barber, T.X., Wilson, S.C., & Scott, D.S. (1980). Effects of a traditional trance induction on response to "hypnotist-centered" versus "subject-centered" test suggestions. *Journal of Clinical & Experimental Hypnosis, 28(2)*, 114-125.

Bardack, N.R., & McAndrew, F.T. (1985). The influence of physical attractiveness and manner of dress on success in a simulated personnel decision. *Journal of Social Psychology, 125*, 777-778.

Bardin, C.W., & Catterall, J.F. (1981). Testosterone: A major determinant of extragenital sexual dimorphism. *Science, 211*, 1285-1293.

Bardwick, J.M. (1988). *The plateauing trap: How to avoid it in your career . . . in your life*. New York: Bantam.

Barlow, H.B., & Mollon, J.D. (Eds.). (1982). *The Senses: Cambridge texts in the physiological sciences, Vol. 3*. Cambridge, Eng.: Cambridge University Press.

Barnes, D.M. (1987). Defect in Alzheimer's is on chromosome 21. *Science, 235*, 846-847.

Barnes, J.A. (1979). *Who should know what?: Social science, privacy and ethics*. Cambridge, England: Cambridge University Press.

Barrett, M.E. (1986). Self-image and social adjustment change in deaf adolescents participating in a social living class. *Journal of Group Psychotherapy, Psychodrama and Sociometry, 39(1)*, 3-11.

Barrios, B.A., & Pennebaker, J.W. (1983). A note on the early detection of bulimia nervosa. *Behavior Therapist, 6(2)*, 18-19.

Bartley, S.H. (1980). *Introduction to perception*. New York: Harper & Row.

Baruch, G.K., Biener, L., & Barnett, R.C. (1987). Women and gender in research on work and family stress. *American Psychologist, 42*, 130-136.

Baskin, D., & Goldstein, J. (1985-1986). Daydreaming in psychiatric patients: A normative comparison. *Psychiatric Forum, 13(1)*, 65-72.

Bastos, O. (1984). Diagnosis in psychiatry. *Jornal Brasileiro de Psiquitria, 33*, 311-316.

Bateson, G., Jackson, D.D., Haley, J., & Weakland, J.H. (1956). Toward a theory of schizophrenia. *Behavioral Science, 1*, 251-264.

Baum, A., & Singer, J.E. (Eds.). (1980). *Advances in environmental psychology, Vol. 2: Applications of personal control*. Hillsdale, NJ: Erlbaum.

Baumgartner, D.D. (1986). Sociodrama and the Vietnam combat veteran: A therapeutic release for a wartime experience. *Journal of Group Psychotherapy, Psychodrama and Sociometry, 3(1)*, 31-39.

Bayer, R., & Spitzer, R.L. (1985). Neurosis, psychodynamics, and DSM-III: A history of the controversy. *Archives of General Psychiatry, 42*, 187-196.

Beatty, J. (1982). Biofeedback in the treatment of migraine: Simple relaxation or specific effects? In L. White & B. Turksy (Eds.), *Clinical biofeedback: Efficacy and mechanisms*. New York: Guilford Press.

Beauchamp, G.K. (1987). The human preference for excess salt. *American Scientist, 75(1)*, 27-33.

Beck, A.T. (1972). *Depression: Causes and treatment*. Philadelphia: University of Pennsylvania Press.

Beck, A.T. (1986). Cognitive therapy: A sign of retrogression or progress. *Behavior Therapist, 9(1)*, 2-3.

Beck, A.T., & Emery, G. (1985). *Anxiety disorders and phobias: A cognitive perspective*. New York: Basic Books.

Beck, A.T., *et al*. (1987). Differentiating anxiety and depression: A test of the cognitive content-specificity hypothesis. *Journal of Abnormal Psychology, 96(3)*, 179-183.

Bell, A.P., Weinberg, M.W., & Hammersmith, S.K. (1981). *Sexual preference*. Bloomington: Indiana University Press.

Bell, M.D., & Ryan, E.R. (1985). Where can therapeutic community ideals be realized? An examination of three treatment environments. *Hospital and Community Psychiatry, 26*, 1286-1291.

Bellodi, L., *et al*. (1986). Family study of schizophrenia: Exploratory analysis for relevant factors. *Schizophrenia Bulletin, 12(1)*, 120-128.

Belmaker, R.H., & van Praag, H.M. (Eds.). (1980). *Mania: An evolving concept*. Jamaica, NY: SP Medical & Scientific Books.

Bem, D.J. (1977). Predicting more of the people more of the time: Some thoughts on the Allen-Potkay studies of intraindividual variability. *Journal of Personality, 45*, 327-333.

Bem, D.J. (1982). Toward a response style theory of persons in situations. *Nebraska Symposium on Motivation, 201-231*.

Bem, D.J. (1983). Constructing a theory of the triple typology: Some (second) thoughts on nomothetic and idiographic approaches to personality. *Journal of Personality, 51*, 566-577.

Bem, D.J., & Allen, A. (1974). On predicting some of the people some of the time: The search for cross-situational consistencies in behavior. *Psychological Review, 81*, 506-520.

Benbow, C.P., & Stanley, J.C. (1983). Sex differences in mathematical reasoning ability: More facts. *Science, 222*, 1029-1031.

Benjamin, L.T. (1986). Why don't they understand us? A history of psychology's public image. *American Psychology, 41*, 941-946.

Bennett, W., & Gurin, J. (1982). *The dieter's dilemma.* New York: Basic Books.

Bennison, S., Barger, A.C., & Wolfe, E.L. (1987). *Walter B. Cannon: The life and times of a young scientist.* Cambridge, MA: Belknap (Harvard University Press).

Benson, P.L., Karabenick, S.A., & Lerner, R.M. (1976). Pretty pleases: The effects of physical attractiveness, race, and sex on receiving help. *Journal of Experimental Social Psychology, 12*, 409-415.

Berch, D.B., & Bender, B.G. (1987). Margins of sexuality. *Psychology Today, 21(12)*, 54-57.

Berger, M., *et al.* (1984). *Practicing family therapy in diverse settings: New approaches to the connections among families, therapists, and treatment settings.* San Francisco: Jossey-Bass.

Bergin, A.E., & Lambert, M.J. (1978). The evaluation of therapeutic outcomes. In S.L. Garfield & A.E. Bergin (Eds.), *Handbook of psychotherapy and behavior change*, 2nd ed. New York: Wiley.

Berkowitz, L. (1979). *Advances in experimental social psychology*, Vol. 12. New York: Academic Press.

Berman, J.S. (1981). Will wise words fall on deaf ears? *Contemporary Psychology, 26*, 665-666.

Berman, J.S., Miller, R.C., & Massman, P.J. (1985). Cognitive therapy versus systematic desensitization: Is one treatment superior? *Psychological Bulletin, 97*, 451-461.

Berne, E. (1958). Transactional analysis: A new and effective method of group therapy. *American Journal of Psychotherapy, 12*, 735-743.

Berne, E. (1964). *Games people play.* New York: Grove.

Bernstein, D.A. (1976). Anxiety management. In W.E. Craighead, A.E. Kazdin, & M.J. Mahoney (Eds.), *Behavior modification: Principles, issues, and applications.* Boston: Houghton Mifflin.

Bexton, W.H., Heron, W., & Scott, T.H. (1954). Effects of decreased variation in the sensory environment. *Canadian Journal of Psychology, 8*, 70.

Bhardway, D., & Khan, J.A. (1979). Effect of texture of food on bait-shy behaviour in wild rats (*Rattus rattus*). *Applied Animal Ethology, 5*, 361-367.

Bickhard, M.H., & Richie, D.M. (1983). *On the nature of representation: A case study of James Gibson's theory of perception.* New York: Praeger.

Blackmore, S. (1985). The adventures of a psi-inhibitory experimenter. In P. Kurtz (Ed.), *A skeptic's handbook of parapsychology.* Buffalo, NY: Prometheus Books.

Blackmore, S. (1986). A critical guide to parapsychology. *Skeptical Inquirer, 11(1)*, 97-102.

Blake, R.R., & Helson, H. (1956). *Adaptability screening of flying personnel. Situational and personal factors in conforming behavior.* School of Aviation Medicine, USAF.

Blake, R.R., Mouton, J.S., & Olmstead, J.A. (1956). Susceptibility to count-norm attitude expressions in a small group situation. In R.R. Blake & H. Helson (Eds.), *Adaptability screening of flying personnel. Situational and personal factors in conforming behavior.* School of Aviation Medicine, USAF, 49-55.

Blass, E.M., & Teicher, M.H. (1980). Suckling. *Science, 210*, 15-20.

Blau, Z.S. (1981). *Black children/white children: Competence, socialization, and social structure.* New York: Free Press.

Bliss, E.L. (1986). *Multiple personality, allied disorders, and hypnosis.* New York: Oxford University Press.

Bloch, G. (1980). *Mesmerism: A translation of the original scientific and medical writings of F.A. Mesmer.* Los Altos, CA: William Kaufman.

Bloom, A.H. (1986). Psychological ingredients of high-level moral thinking: A critique of the Kohlberg-Gilligan paradigm. *Journal for the Theory of Social Behaviour, 16(1)*, 89-103.

Bloom, B.S. (1982). *Human Characteristics & School Learning.* New York: McGraw-Hill.

Bloom, B.S. (Ed.). (1985). *Developing talent in young people.* New York: Ballantine.

Blum, J.D. (1978). On changes in psychiatric diagnosis over time. *American Psychologist, 33*, 1017-1031.

Blumberg, H.H., Hare, A.P., Kent, V., & Davies, M.F. (Eds.). (1983). *Small groups and social interaction*, Vol 1. Chichester, England: Wiley.

Bock, R.D., & Moore, E.G.J. (1986). *Advantage and disadvantage: A profile of American youth.* Hillsdale, NJ: Erlbaum.

Boden, M.A. (1979). *Jean Piaget.* New York: Viking Press.

Bolles, R.C. (1975). *Theory of motivation.* New York: Harper & Row.

Bolles, R.C. (1978). What happened to motivation? *Educational Psychologist, 13*, 1-13.

Bolles, R.C. (1979). *Learning theory.* New York: Holt, Rinehart and Winston.

Bolles, R.C. (1983). The explanation of behavior. *Psychological Record, 33*, 31-48.

Bonica, J.J. (Ed.). (1980). *Pain. Research publications: Association for research in nervous and mental disease*, Vol. 58. New York: Raven Press.

Boring, E.G. (1942). *Sensation and perception in the history of experimental psychology.* New York: Appleton-Century-Crofts.

Boring, E.G. (1950). *A history of experimental psychology*, 2nd ed. New York: Appleton.

Botstein, D. (1982). The molecular biology of color vision. *Science, 232*, 142-143.

Bouchard, T.J. (1983). Do environmental similarities explain the similarity in intelligence of identical twins reared apart? *Intelligence, 7*, 175-184.

Boudewyns, P.A., *et al.* (1986). Token economy programs in VA medical centers: Where are they today? *Behavior Therapist, 9(6)*, 126-127.

Bower, B. (1985). Taking food from thought: Fruitful entry to the brain's word index. *Science News, 128*, 85.

Bower, B. (1986a). Steady cocaine use linked to seizures. *Science News, 130*, 214.

Bower, B. (1986b). Recurrent dreams: Clues to conflict. *Science News, 129*, 197.

Bower, B. (1986c). Winter depression: Rise and shine? *Science News, 130*, 390.

Bower, B. (1986d). Babies sound off: The power of babble. *Science News, 129*, 390.

Bower, G.H., & Hilgard, E.R. (1981). *Theories of learning*, 5th ed. Englewood Cliffs, NJ: Prentice-Hall.

Bowlby, J. (1973). *Attachment and loss: Separation*, Vol 2. New York: Basic Books.

Boyd, R., & Richerson, P.J. (1985). *Culture and the evolutionary process.* Chicago: University of Chicago Press.

Boyd-Franklin, N. (1987). Group therapy for Black women: A therapeutic support model. *American Journal of Orthopsychiatry, 57*, 394-401.

Boynton, R. (1980). Vision. In D. McFadden (Ed.), *Neural mechanisms in behavior.* New York: Springer-Verlag.

Braginsky, D.D., & Braginsky, B.J. (1971). *Hansels and Gretels: Study of children in institutions for the mentally retarded.* New York: Holt, Rinehart and Winston.

Brainard, G.C., Richardson, B.A., Petterborg, L.J., & Reiter, R.J. (1982). The effect of different light intensities on pineal melatonin content. *Brain Research, 233(1)*, 75-81.

Brandt, A.M. (1988). The syphilis epidemic and its relation to AIDS. *Science, 239*, 375-380.

Brazelton, T.B. (1986). Issues for working parents. *American Journal of Orthopsychiatry, 56(1)*, 14-25.

Brazelton, T.B. (1987). "On infant day care": Dr. Brazelton

replies. *American Journal of Orthopsychiatry, 57(1)*, 140-141.

Brazelton, T.B., & Als, H. (1979). Four early stages in the development of mother-infant interaction. *Psychoanalytic Study of the Child, 34*, 349-369.

Brazelton, T.B., & Yogman, M.W. (Eds.). (1986). *Affective development in infancy*. Norwood, NJ: Ablex.

Brecher, Edward M. (1984). *Love, sex, and aging: A Consumers Union report*. Boston: Little, Brown.

Bredehoft, D.J. (1986). An evaluation of self-esteem: A family affair. *Transactional Analysis Journal, 16*, 175-181.

Breggin, P.R. (1979). *Electroshock: Its brain-disabling effects*. New York: Springer.

Breggin, P.R. (1983). *Psychiatric drugs: Hazards in the brain*. New York: Springfield.

Brehm, J., & Festinger, L. (1957). Pressures toward uniformity of performance in groups. *Human Relations, 10*, 85-91.

Brehm, J.W., & Mann, M. (1975). Effect of importance of freedom and attraction to group members on influence produced by group pressure. *Journal of Personality and Social Psychology, 31*, 816-824.

Breslau, N., & Davis, G.C. (1987). Posttraumatic stress disorder: The stressor criterion. *Journal of Nervous and Mental Disease, 175(5)*, 255-264.

Briggs, S.R. (1987). Hawking a good theory. *Contemporary Psychology, 32*, 854-865.

Brogden, W.J. (1939). Sensory preconditioning. *Journal of Experimental Psychology, 25*, 323-332.

Bronfenbrenner, U., Kessel, F., Kessen, W., and White, S. (1986). Toward a critical social history of developmental psychology: A propaedeutic discussion. *American Psychologist, 41*, 1218-1230.

Brooks, C.I., Church, M.A., & Fraser, L. (1986). Effects of duration of eye contact on judgments of personality characteristics. *Journal of Social Psychology, 126(1)*, 71-78.

Broughton, J.M. (1981). The genetic psychology of James Mark Baldwin. *American Psychologist, 36(4)*, 396-407.

Brown, C.M. (1984). Computer vision and natural constraints. *Science, 224*, 1299-1305.

Brown, C.T., & Keller, P.W. (1979). *Monologue to dialogue*. Englewood Cliffs, NJ: Prentice-Hall.

Brown, P., & Funk, S.C. (1986). Tardive dyskinesia: Barriers to the professional recognition of an iatrogenic disease. *Journal of Health and Social Behavior, 27(2)*, 116-132.

Brown, T.S., & Wallace, P.M. (1980). *Physiological psychology*. New York: Academic Press.

Brownell, K.D., Marlatt, G.A., Lichtenstein, E., & Wilson, G.T. (1986). Understanding and preventing relapse. *American Psychologist, 41*, 765-782.

Bruch, H. (1973). *Eating disorders*. New York: Basic Books.

Bruch, H. (1978). *The golden cage*. Cambridge, MA: Harvard University Press.

Bruner, J. (1984). Interaction, communication, and self. *Journal of the American Academy of Child Psychiatry, 23(1)*, 1-7.

Bruner, J. (1986). *Actual minds, possible worlds*. Cambridge, MA: Harvard University Press.

Burgess, R.L., & Huston, T.L. (Eds.). (1979). *Social exchange in developing relationships*. New York: Academic Press.

Burisch, M. (1984). Approaches to personality inventory construction: A comparison of merits. *American Psychologist, 39*, 214-227.

Burns, G.L., & Farina, A. (1987). Physical attractiveness and self-perception of mental disorder. *Journal of Abnormal Psychology, 96(2)*, 161-163.

Buss, A.H. (1986). *Social behavior and personalty*. Hillsdale, NJ: Erlbaum.

Buss, A.H., & Plomin, R. (1984). *Temperament: Early developing personality traits*. Hillsdale, NJ: Erlbaum.

Buss, D.M., & Craik, K.H. (1983). The act frequency approach to personality. *Psychological Review, 90(2)*, 105-126.

Bussey, K., & Bandura, A. (1984). Influence of gender constancy and social power on sex-linked modeling. *Journal of Personality and Social Psychology, 47*, 1292-1302.

Butterword, G. (1983). Structure of the mind in human infancy. *Advances in Infancy Research, 2*, 1-29.

Buzsaki, G. (1982). The "where is it?" reflex: Autoshaping the orienting response. *Journal of the Experimental Analysis of Behavior, 37*, 461-484.

Byck, R. (Ed.). (1974). *Cocaine papers: Sigmund Freud*. New York: New American Library.

Byrne, D., Ervin, C.R., & Lamberth, J. (1970). Continuity between the experimental study of attraction and real-life computer dating. *Journal of Personality and Social Psychology, 16*, 157-165.

Cahill, C., & Akil, H. (1982). Plasma beta-endorphin-like immunoreactivity, self reported pain perception and anxiety levels in women during pregnancy and labor. *Life Sciences, 31*, 1871-1873.

Cairns, R.B. (1980). Developmental theory before Piaget: The remarkable contributions of James Mark Baldwin. *Contemporary Psychology, 25*, 438-440.

Cameron, D.E. (1967). Magnesium pemoline and human performance, *Science, 157*, 958-959.

Cannon, W.B. (1927). The James-Lange theory of emotions: A critical examination and an alternative. *American Journal of Psychology, 39*, 106-124.

Cannon, W.B. (1929). *Bodily changes in pain, hunger, fear and rage*, 2nd ed. New York: Appleton.

Cantor, N., & Genero, N. (1986). Psychiatric diagnosis and natural categorization: A close analogy. In T. Millon & G. Klerman (Eds.), *Contemporary issues in psychopathology: Toward the DSM-IV*. New York: Guilford Press.

Cantor, N., & Kihlstrom, J.F. (Eds.). (1981a). *Personality, cognition, and social interaction*. Hillsdale, NJ: Erlbaum.

Cantor, N., & Kihlstrom, J.F. (1981b). Cognitive and social processes in personality: Implications for behavior therapy. In C.M. Franks & G.T. Wilson (Eds.), *Handbook of behavior therapy*. New York: Guilford Press.

Cantor, N., Smith, E.E., French, R.D., & Mezzich, J. (1980). Psychiatric diagnosis as prototype categorization. *Journal of Abnormal Psychology, 89*, 181-193.

Caplan, A.L. (Ed.). (1978). *The sociobiology debate: Readings on ethical and scientific issues*. New York: Harper & Row.

Caplan, P.U. (1985). *The myth of women's masochism*. New York: Dutton.

Carey, S. (1978). The child as word learner. In M. Halle, J. Bresnan, & G.A. Miller (Eds.), *Linguistic theory and psychological reality*. Cambridge, MA: MIT Press.

Carlson, C.R., & White, D.K. (1982). Night terrors: A clinical and empirical review. *Clinical Psychology Review, 2*, 455-468.

Carpenter, P.A., & Eisenber, P. (1978). Mental rotation and the frame of reference in blind and sighted individuals. *Perception and Psychophysics, 23*, 117-124.

Carroll, W.R., & Bandura, A. (1985). Role of timing of visual monitoring and motor rehearsal in observational learning of action patterns. *Journal of Motor Behavior, 17*, 269-281.

Cartwright, R.D. (1972). Dreams, dream content, and their psychophysiological correlates. In M.H. Chase (Ed.), *The sleeping brain*. Los Angeles: University of California Press.

Caspi, A., Elder, G.H., & Bem, D.J. (1987). Moving against the world: Life-course patterns of explosive children. *Developmental Psychology, 23*, 308-313.

Catania, A.C. (1984). *Learning*, 2nd ed. Englewood Cliffs, NJ: Prentice-Hall.

Cattell, R.B. (1950). *Personality: A systematic theoretical and factual study*. New York: McGraw-Hill.

Cattell, R.B. (1957). *Personality and motivation structure and measurement*. Yonkers-on-Hudson, NY: World Book.

Cattell, R.B. (1965). *The scientific analysis of personality*. Baltimore: Penguin Books.

Cattell, R.B. (1982). *The inheritance of personality and ability: Research methods and findings*. New York: Academic Press.

Cermak, L. (1978). *Improving your memory*. New York: McGraw-Hill.

Chan, C.H., *et al*. (1987). Response of psycholotic and nonpsychotic depressed patients to tricyclic antidepressants. *Journal of Clinical Psychiatry, 48(5)*, 197-200.

Chance, P. (1984). Food madness. *Psychology Today, 18(6)*, 14.

Chase, M.H., & Morales, F.R. (1983). Subthreshold excitatory activity and motoneuron discharge during REM periods of active sleep. *Science, 221*, 1195-1198.

Chase, M.H., & Weitzman, E.D. (Eds.). (1983). *Sleep disorders: Basic and clinical research. Advances in sleep research, vol. 8*. New York: SP Medical & Scientific Books.

Cherkashin, A.N., & Sheimann, I.M. Conditioning in planarians and RNA content. *Journal of Biological Psychology, 9(1)*, 5-11.

Cherry, C. (1953). Some experiments on the recognition of speech with one and with two ears. *Journal of the Acoustical Society of America, 25*, 975-979.

Chisholm, J.S. (1983). *Navajo infancy: An ethological study of child development*. New York: Aldine.

Chodorow, M.S., & Manning, S.K. (1983). Cognition and memory: A bibliographic essay on the history and issues. *Teaching of Psychology, 10(3)*, 163-167.

Chomsky, N. (1986). *Knowledge of language: Its nature, origin, and use*. New York: Praeger.

Christensen, D., Farina, A., & Boudreau, L. (1980). Sensitivity to nonverbal cues as a function of social competence. *Journal of Nonverbal Behavior, 4(3)*, 145-156.

Cialdini, R.B. (1985). *Influence: Science and practice*. Glenview, IL: Scott, Foresman.

Cicogna, P., Cavallero, C., & Bosinelli, M. (1986). Differential access to memory traces in the production of mental experience. *International Journal of Psychophysiology, 4(3)*, 209-216.

Cioffi, J., & Kandel, G.L. (1979). Laterality of stereognostic accuracy of children for words, shapes, and bigrams: A sex difference for bigrams. *Science, 204*, 1432-1434.

Clark, A.D., & Clarke, A.M. (1982). "Sleeper effects" in development: Fact or artifact? *Annual Progress in Child Psychiatry and Child Development*, 94-112.

Clark, J. (1985). *The cell*. New York: Torstar Books.

Coe, S.P. (1981). Sociobiology: Some general considerations. *American Psychologist, 36*, 1462, 1464.

Cohen, A.S., Rosen, R.C., & Goldstein, L. (1985). EEG hemispheric asymmetry during sexual arousal: Psychophysiological patterns in responsive, unresponsive, and dysfunctional men. *Journal of Abnormal Psychology, 94*, 580-590.

Cohen, L.H., Sargent, M.D., & Sechrest, L.B. (1986). Use of psychotherapy research by professional psychologist. *American Psychologist, 41*, 198-206.

Cohen, N.J., & Squire, L.R. (1980). Preserved learning and retention of pattern-analyzing skill in amnesia: Dissociation of knowing how and knowing that. *Science, 210*, 207-210.

Cohler, B.J. (1987). Competence and the chronic psychiatric patient. *Contemporary Psychology, 32*, 459-460.

Coleman, S.B. (Ed.). (1985). *Failures in family therapy*. New York: Guilford Press.

Colligan, R.C. (1983). *The MMPI: A contemporary normative study*. New York: Praeger.

Collison, C.R., & Miller, S.L. (1985). The role of family reenactment in group psychotherapy. *Perspectives in Psychiatric Care, 23*, 74-78.

Condon, W.S., & Sander, L.W. (1974). Synchrony demonstrated between movements of the neonate and adult speech. *Child Development, 45(2)*, 456-462.

Condry, J.C. (1987). When does encouragement destroy

enthusiasm, and why? *Contemporary Psychology, 32*, 737-739.

Connellan, Thomas K. (1978). *How to improve human performance: Behaviorism in business and industry*. New York: Harper & Row.

Connors, G.J., & Sobell, M.B. (1986). Alcohol and drinking environment: Effects on affect and sensations, person perception, and perceived intoxication. *Cognitive Therapy and Research, 10*, 389-402.

Cook, M. (Ed.). (1984). *Issues in person perception: Psychology in progress*. London: Methuen.

Cook, T.D., *et al*. (1979). History of the sleeper effect: Some logical pitfalls in accepting the null hypothesis. *Psychological Bulletin, 86*, 662-679.

Cooper, C.L. (Ed.). (1983). *Stress research: Issues for the eighties*. Chichester, England: Wiley.

Cooper, K.H. (1984). Territorial behavior among the institutionalized: A nursing perspective. *Journal of Psychosocial Nursing and Mental Health Services, 22(12)*, 6-11.

Copolov, D.L., *et al*. (1987). DSM-III melancholia: Do the criteria accurately and reliably distinguish endogenous pattern depression? *Journal of Affective Disorders, 10(3)*, 191-202.

Corballis, M.C., and Beale, I.L. (1983). *The ambivalent mind: The neuropsychology of left and right*. Chicago: Nelson-Hall.

Coren, S., Porac, C., & Ward, L.M. (1984). *Sensation and perception*, 2nd ed.. New York: Academic Press.

Corey, G., & Corey, M.S. (1982). *Groups: Process and practice*, 2nd. ed. Monterey, CA: Brooks/Cole.

Corning, W.C., Dyal, J.A., & Willows, A.O. (1973). *Invertebrate learning: I. Protozoans through annelids*. New York: Plenum Press.

Corning, W.C., & John, E.R. (1961). Effects of ribonuclease on retention of conditioned response in regenerated planarians. *Science, 134*, 1363-1365.

Corsi-Cabrera, M., *et al*. (1986). Dream content after using visual inverting prisms. *Perceptual and Motor Skills, 63*, 415-423.

Cotman, C., & McGaugh, J. (1980). *Behavioral neuroscience: An introduction*. NY: Academic Press.

Cox, M.V. (Ed.). (1985). *Are young children egocentric?* New York: St. Martin.

Coyle, J.T., & Enna, S.J. (Eds.). (1983). *Neuroleptics: Neurochemical, behavioral, and clinical perspectives*. New York: Raven Press.

Craft, S., Willerman, L., & Bigler, E.D. (1987). Callosal dysfunction in schizophrenia and schizo-affective disorder. *Journal of Abnormal Psychology, 96*, 205-213.

Crano, W.D. (1983). The second time around. *Contemporary Psychology, 28*, 913-915.

Crider, A. (1979). *Schizophrenia: A biopsychological perspective*. New York: Halsted Press.

Crocker, J. (1988). Self-monitoring: Fifteen years of research. *Contemporary Psychology, 33*, 16-17.

Crutchfield, R.S. (1953). Correlates of individual behavior in a controlled group situation. *American Psychologist, 8*, 338.

Crutchfield, R.S. (1955). Conformity and character. *American Psychologist, 10*, 191-198.

Cunningham, S. (1984). Genovese: 20 years later, few heed a stranger's cries. *Social Action and the Law, 10(1)*, 24-25.

Cytowic, R.E., & Wood, F.B. (1982). Synesthesia: II. Psychophysical relations in the synesthesia of geometrically shaped taste and colored hearing. *Brain and Cognition, 1(1)*, 36-49.

Czeisler, C.A., Allan, J.S., Strogatz, S.H., Ronda, J.M., Sanchez, R., Freitag, W.O., Richardson, G.S., & Kronauer, R.E. (1986). Bright light resets the human circadian pacemaker independent of the timing of the sleep-wake cycle. *Science, 233*, 667-671.

D'Agostino, F. (1986) *Chomsky's system of ideas*. Oxford, England: Oxford University Press.

Dahl, A., & Jorgensen, M.G. (1985). Intensive outpatient

milieu therapy and psychotherapy of young schizophrenic patients: Description of the Nordhuset Treatment Center in Helsingor. *Nordisk Psychiatrisk Tidsskrift, 39,* 509-511.

Dallenbach, K.M. (1959). Twitmyer and the conditioned response. *American Journal of Psychology, 72,* 255-262.

Darley, J.M., & Fazio, R.H. (1980). Expectancy confirmation processes arising in the social interaction sequence. *American Psychologist, 35,* 867-881.

Darley, J.M., & Latané, B. (1968). Bystander intervention in emergencies: Diffusion of responsibility. *Journal of Personality and Social Psychology, 8,* 377-383.

Davies, D.R., & Parasuraman, R. (1982). *The psychology of vigilance.* London: Academic Press.

Davis, G.C., & Askiskal, H.S. (1987). Descriptive, biological, and theoretical aspects of borderline personality disorder. *Hospital and Community Psychiatry, 37,* 685-692.

Davis, H., & Hurwitz, H.M.B. (Eds.). (1977). *Operant-Pavlovian interactions.* Hillsdale, NJ: Erlbaum.

Davison, G.C., & Neale, J.M. (1986). *Abnormal psychology: An experimental clinical approach,* 4th ed. New York: Wiley.

DeBono, K.G. (1987). Investigating the social-adjustive and value-expressive functions of attitudes: Implications for persuasion processes. *Journal of Personality and Social Psychology, 52,* 279-287.

DeCasper, A.J., & Prescott, P.A. (1984). Human newborns' perception of male voices: Preference, discrimination, and reinforcing value. *Developmental Psychobiology, 17(5),* 481-491.

DeCasper, A.J., & Spence, M.J. (1986). Prenatal maternal speech influences newborns' perception of speech sounds. *Infant Behavior and Development, 9(2),* 133-150.

Deci, E.L., & Ryan, R.M. (1985). *Intrinsic motivation and self-determination in human behavior.* New York: Plenum Press.

deLeon, M.J., *et al.* (1987). Positron emission tomography studies of normal aging: A replicationof PET III and 18-FDG using PET VI and 11-CDG. *Neurobiological Aging, 8,* 319-323.

Deems, D.A., & Garcia, J. (1986). Involvement of dorsomedial hypothalamus in taste aversion learning: Possible alterations in general sensitivity to illness. *Nutrition and Behavior, 3(1),* 91-100.

Dellinger, R.W. (1978). Investigative hypnosis: Tapping our cerebral memory banks. *Human Behavior, 1(1),* 36-37.

Deschner, J.P., & McNeil, J.S. (1986). Results of anger control training for battering couples. *Journal of Family Violence, 1(2),* 111-120.

Dethier, V.G. (1986). The magic of metamorphosis: Nature's own sleight of hand. *Smithsonian, 17(2),* 123-130.

Deutsch, J.A. (Ed.). (1983). *The physiological basic of memory,* 2nd ed. New York: Academic Press.

Deutsch, M. (1969). Field theory in social psychology. In G. Lindzey & E. Aronson (Eds.), *Handbook of social psychology.* Reading, MA: Addison-Wesley.

Deutsch, M., & Gerard, H.B. (1955). A study of normative and informational social influences upon individual judgment. *Journal of Abnormal and Social Psychology, 51,* 629-636.

Dewsbury, D.A. (Ed.). (1981). *Mammalian sexual behavior: Foundations for contemporary research. Benchmark Papers in Behavior, Vol. 15.* Stroudsburg, PA: Hutchinson Ross.

Diamond, M.C. (1978). Aging and cell loss: Calling for an honest count. *Psychology Today, 12(9),* 126.

Diamond, M.C., Johnson, R.E., & Ehlert, J. (1979). A comparison of cortical thickness in male and female rates—normal and gonadectomized, young and adult. *Behavioral and Neural Biology, 25,* 485-491.

Dick, A.O. (1974). Iconic memory and its relation to perceptual processing and other memory mechanisms. *Perception & Psychophysics, 16,* 575-596.

Dietz, W.H., Jr., Garn, S.M., & Gortmaker, S.L. (1986). An adoption study of human obesity. *New England Journal of Medicine, 315,* 128-129.

Dietz, W.H., Jr., & Gortmaker, S.L. (1984). Factors within the physical environment associated with childhood obesity. *American Journal of Clinical Nutrition, 39,* 619-624.

Dion, K.K. (1972). Physical attractiveness and evaluation of children's transgressions. *Journal of Personality and Social Psychology, 24,* 207-213.

Dion, K.K., Berscheid, E., & Walster, E. (1972). What is beautiful is good. *Journal of Personality and Social Psychology, 24,* 285-290.

Dixon, B. (1986). Dangerous thoughts: How we think and feel can make us sick. *Science 86, 7(3),* 63-66.

Dixon, N.F. (1981). *Preconscious processing.* Chicester, England: Wiley, 1981.

Dodwell, P.C., & Caelli, T. (Eds.). (1984). *Figural Synthesis.* Hillsdale, NJ: Erlbaum.

Donat, D.C. (1986). Altercations among institutionalized psychogeriatric patients. *Gerontologist, 26(3),* 227-228.

Doran, A.R., Breier, A., & Roy, A. (1986). Differential diagnosis and diagnostic systems in schizophrenia. *Psychiatric Clinics of North America, 9,* 17-33.

Doty, R.W., Megrao, N., & Yamaga, K. (1973). The unilateral engram. *Acta Neurobiologiae Experimentalis, 33,* 711-728.

Douglas, L. (1986). Is adolescent suicide a third degree game and who is the real victim? *Transactional Analysis Journal, 16,* 165-169.

Doyle, J.A. (1983). *The male experience.* Dubuque, IA: Wm. C. Brown.

Drucker, P.F. (1981). Working women: Unmaking the 19th century. *Wall Street Journal,* 6 July.

Drucker, P.F. (1988). Leadership: More doing than dash. *Wall Street Journal,* 6 January.

Duncker, K. (1938). Experimental modification of children's food preferences through social suggestion. *Journal of Abnormal and Social Psychology, 33,* 489-507.

Dunnett, B. (1986). Drugs that suppress immunity. *American Health, 5(9),* 43-45.

Eastman, C., & Rechtschaffen, A. (1983). Circadian temperature and wake rhythms of rats exposed to prolonged continuous illumination. *Physiology and Behavior, 31,* 417-427.

Ebbinghaus, H. (1885/1964). *Memory: A contribution to experimental psychology.* New York: Dover.

Edge, H.L., Morriss, R.L., Rush, J.H., & Palmer, J. (1986). *Foundations of parapsychology: Exploring the boundaries of human capability.*

Edwards, D.D. (1988). New gene may solve the Y (and X) of sex. *Science News, 133,* 4.

Edwards, D.L. (1972). *General Psychology,* 2nd ed. New York: Macmillan.

Egeland, J.A., *et al.* (1987). Bipolar affective disorders linked to DNA markers on chromosome 11. *Nature, 325,* 783-787.

Ehrhardt, A.A., & Meyer-Bahlburg, H.F.L. (1981). Effects of prenatal sex hormones on gender-related behavior. *Science, 211,* 1312-1317.

Eichorn, D.H., *et al.* (Eds.) (1981). *Present and past in middle life.* New York: Academic Press.

Eilers, R.E., & Oller, D.K. (1985). Developmental aspects of infant speech discrimination: The role of linquistic experience. *Trends in Neurosciences, 8(10),* 453-456.

Eisdorfer, C. (1983). Conceptual models of aging: The challenge of a new frontier. *American Psychologist, 38,* 197-202.

Eiser, J.R. (1986). *Social psychology: Attitudes, cognition and social behavior.* New York: Cambridge University Press.

Ekman, P. (Ed.). (1982). *Emotion in the human face*, 2nd ed. Cambridge, England: Cambridge University Press.

Ekman, P., Friesen, W.V., & Simons, R.C. (1985). Is the startle reaction an emotion? *Journal of Personality & Social Psychology, 49*, 1416-1426.

Elkin, I., *et al.* (1985). The NIMH treatment of depression collaborative research program: Background and research plan. *Archives of General Psychiatry, 42*, 305-316.

Ellgring, H. (1986). Nonverbal expresion of psychological studies in psychiatric patients. *European Archives of Psychiatry and Neurological Sciences, 236(1)*, 31-34.

Emde, R.N. (1983). The prerepresentational self and its affective core. *Psychoanalytic Study of the Child, 38*, 165-192.

Emde, R.N., & Harmon, R.J. (Eds.). (1984). *Continuities and discontinuities in development*. New York: Plenum Press.

Engen, T. (1982). *The perception of odors*. New York: Academic Press.

Engen, T. (1987). Remembering odors and their names. *American Scientist, 75*, 497-503.

Erdelyi, J.H. (1974). A new look at the New Look: Perceptual defense and vigilance. *Psychological Review, 81*, 1-25.

Erikson, E.H. (1950). *Childhood and society*. New York: W.W. Norton.

Erikson, E.H. (1959). *Identity and the life cycle: Selected papers. Psychological issues*, Monograph No. 1, vol. 1. New York: International Universities Press.

Erikson, E.H. (1974). *Dimensions of a new identity: Jefferson Lectures, 1973*. New York: W.W. Norton.

Erikson, E.H. (1975). *Life history and the historical moment*. New York: W.W. Norton.

Erikson, E.H. (Ed.). (1978). *Adulthood*. New York: W.W. Norton.

Erikson, E.H. (1982). *The life cycle completed: A review*. New York: W.W. Norton.

Erikson, E.H., Erikson, J.M., & Kivnick, H.Q. (1986). *Vital involvement in old age*. New York: Norton.

Erwin, E. (1980). Psychoanalytic therapy: The Eysenck argument. *American Psychologist, 35*, 435-443.

Escobar, J.I. (1987). Posttraumatic stress disorder and the perennial stress-diathesis controversy. *Journal of Nervous and Mental Disease, 175(5)*, 265-266.

Everaerd, W., Hindley, C.B., Bot, A., and van der Werff ten Bosch, J.J. (1983). *Development in adolescence: Psychological, social and biological aspects*. Boston: Martinus Nijhoff.

Eysenck, H.J. (1947). *Dimensions of personality*. London: Routledge & Kegan Paul.

Eysenck, H.J. (1957). *The dynamics of anxiety and hysteria: An experimental application of modern learning theory to psychiatry*. London: Routledge & Kegan Paul.

Eysenck, H.J. (1972). *Psychology is about people*. New York: Library Press.

Eysenck, H.J., & Eysenck, M.W. (1985). *Personality and individual differences: A natural science approach*. New York: Plenum Press.

Fancher, R.E. (1985). *The intelligence men*. New York: W.W. Norton.

Fann, W.E., *et al.* (Eds.). (1983). *Phenomenology and treatment of psychosexual disorders*. New York: SP Medical & Scientific Books.

Fantz, R.L. (1963). Pattern vision in new-born infants. *Science, 140*, 296-297.

Fantz, R.L., Fagan, J.F., & Miranda, S. (1975). Early visual selectivity. In L. Cohen & P. Salapatek (Eds.), *Infant perception: From sensation to cognition*. New York: Academic Press.

Fawcett, J., *et al.* (1987). A double-blind, placebo-controlled trial of lithium carbonate therapy for alcoholism. *Archives of General Psychiatry, 44*, 248-256.

Feder, B., & Ronall, R.E. (Eds.). (1980). *Beyond the hot seat: Gestalt approaches to group*. New York: Brunner-Mazel.

Feffer, M. (1982). *The structure of Freudian thought: The problem of immutability and discontinuity in developmental theory*. New York: International Universities Press.

Feldman, D.H. (1980). *Beyond universals in cognitive development: Publications for the advancement of theory and history in psychology*. Norwood, NJ: Ablex.

Feldman, D.H. (1985). The concept of nonuniversal developmental domains: Implications for artistic development. *Tufts U Visual Arts Research, 11(1)*, 82-89.

Feldman, D.H. (1986). How does development work? In I. Levin (Ed.; Sidney Strauss, Series Ed.), *Stage and structure: Reopening the debate*. Norwood, NJ: Ablex.

Fellman, B. (1985). Clockwork gland. *Science 85, 6(4)*, 77-81.

Fernald, L.D. (1984). *The Hans legacy*. Hillsdale, NJ: Lawrence Erlbaum Associates, Inc.

Fernald, L.D. (1987). Of windmills and rope dancing: The instructional value of narrative structures. *Teaching of Psychology, 14*, 214-216.

Fernando, T., *et al.* (1986). The reliability of axis V of DSM-III. *American Journal of Psychiatry, 143*, 752-755.

Ferster, C.B., & Skinner, B.F. (1957). *Schedules of reinforcement*. New York: Appleton-Century-Crofts.

Festinger, L. (1957). *A theory of cognitive dissonance*. Stanford, CA: Stanford University Press.

Festinger, L. (1980). *Retrospections on social psychology*. New York: Oxford Press.

Festinger, L., & Carlsmith, J.M. (1959). Cognitive consequences of forced compliance. *Journal of Abnormal and Social Psychology, 58*, 203-210.

Festinger, L., Gerard, H.B., Hymovitch, B., Kelley, H.H., & Raven, B. (1952). The influence process in the presence of extreme deviates. *Human Relations, 5*, 327-346.

Festinger, L., Riecken, H., & Schachter, S. (1956). *When prophecy fails*. Minneapolis, MN: University of Minnesota Press.

Festinger, L., & Tibaut, J. (1951). Interpersonal communication in small groups. *Journal of Abnormal and Social Psychology, 46*, 92-99.

Field, T., Cohen, D., Garcia, R., & Greenberg, R. (1985). Mother-stranger face discrimination by the newborn. *Annual Progress in Child Psychiatry and Child Development*, 3-10.

Field, T., Goldstein, S., Vega-Lahr, N., & Porter, K. (1986). Changes in imitative behavior during early infancy. *Infant Behavior and Development, 9*, 415-421.

Field, T., *et al.* (1985). Pregnancy problems, postpartum depression, and early mother-infant interactions. *Developmental Psychology, 21*, 1152-1156.

Fields, H.L. (1978). Secrets of the placebo. *Psychology Today, 12(11)*, 172.

Fieve, R.R., Go, R., Dunner, D.L., & Elston, R. (1984). Search for biological/genetic markers in a long-term epidemiological and morbid risk study of affective disorders. *Journal of Psychiatric Research, 18*, 425-445.

Fillion, T.J., & Blass, E.M. (1986). Infantile experience with suckling odors determines adult sexual behavior in male rats. *Science, 231*, 729-731.

Finkelstein, P., Wenegrat, B., & Yalom, I. (1982). Large group awareness training. *Annual Review of Psychology, 33*, 515-539.

Fischer, K.W. (Ed.). (1983). *Levels and transitions in children's development: New directions for child development*, No. 21. San Francisco: Jossey-Bass.

Fischman, J. (1986). Golden years and restless nights. *Psychology Today, 20(2)*, 70.

Fisher, C., *et al.* (1974). A psychophysiological study of nightmares and night terrors: III. Mental content and recall of Stage 4 night terrors. *Journal of Nervous & Mental Disease, 158*, 174-188.

Fisher, S., & Greenberg, R.P. (1978). *The scientific evaluation of Freud's theories and therapy: A book of readings*. New York: Basic Books.

Flavell, J.H. (1977). *Cognitive Development*. Englewood Cliffs, NJ: Prentice-Hall.

Flavell, J.H. (1985). *Cognitive Development*, 2nd ed. Englewood Cliffs, NJ: Prentice-Hall.

Flavell, J.H., Shipstead, S.G., & Croft, K. (1980). What young children think you see when their eyes are closed. *Cognition, 8(4)*, 369-387.

Foley, J.P., Jr. (1935). The criterion of abnormality. *Journal of Abnormal and Social Psychology, 30*, 279-291.

Forster, P.M., & Govier, E. (1978). Discrimination without awareness? *Quarterly Journal of Experimental Psychology, 30*, 289-295.

Fox, N.A., & Davidson, R.J. (Eds.). (1984). *The psychobiology of affective development*. Hillsdale, NJ: Erlbaum.

Fox, R., Barclay, A., & Rodgers, D. (1982). The foundations of professional psychology. *American Psychologist, 37*, 306-312.

Fraiberg, S. (1977). *Insights from the blind: Comparative studies of blind and sighted infants*. New York: Basic Books.

Frank, J.D. (1973). *Persuasion and healing: A comparative study of psychotherapy*. Baltimore: Johns Hopkins Press.

Frank, J.D. (1981). Reply to Telch. *Journal of Consulting and Clinical Psychology, 49*, 476-477.

Frank, J.D. (1985). Further thoughts on the anti-demoralization hypothesis of psychotherapeutic effectiveness. *Integrative Psychiatry, 3(1)*, 17-20.

Frank, J.D., & Dietz, P.E. (Eds.). (1979). *Psychotherapy and the human predicament: A psychosocial approach*. New York: Schocken.

Franklin, D. (1987). The politics of masochism. *Psychology Today, 21(1)*, 53-57.

Freedman, D.G., & DeBoer, M. (1979). Biological and cultural differences in child development. *Annual Review of Anthropology, 8*, 579-600.

French, L.A., & Nelson, K. (1985). *Young children's knowledge of relational terms: Some ifs, ors, and buts*. New York: Springer-Verlag.

Freud, A. (1936). *The ego and the mechanisms of defense. The writings of Anna Freud*, Vol 2. New York: International Universities Press.

Freud, A. (1981). *Psychoanalytic psychology of normal development, 1970-1980. The writings of Anna Freud*, Vol. 8. New York: International Universities Press.

Freud, S. (1887-1902/1954). *The origins of psycho-analysis, letters to Wilhelm Fliess, drafts and notes: 1887-1902*. New York: Basic Books.

Freud, S. (1893/1963). Some points in a comparative study of organic hysterical paralyses. In M. Meyer (Ed.), *Freud: Early psychoanalytic writings*. New York: Collier Books.

Freud, S. (1900/1953). *The interpretation of dreams*. In J. Strachey (Ed. and Trans.), *The standard edition of the complete psychological works of Sigmund Freud*, Vols. 4 and 5. London: Hogarth Press and the Institute of Psycho-Analysis.

Freud, S. (1905/1953). Three essays on the theory of sexuality. In J. Strachey (Ed. and Trans.), *The standard edition of the complete psychological works of Sigmund Freud*, Vol. 7. London: Hogarth Press and the Institute of Psycho-Analysis.

Freud, S. (1908/1959). On the sexual theories of children. In J. Strachey (Ed. and Trans.), *The standard edition of the complete psychological works of Sigmund Freud*, Vol. 9. London: Hogarth Press and the Institute of Psycho-Analysis.

Freud, S. (1910/1957). Five lectures on psychoanalysis. In J. Strachey (Ed. and Trans.), *The standard edition of the complete psychological works of Sigmund Freud*, Vol. 9. London: Hogarth Press and the Institute of Psycho-Analysis.

Freud, S. (1911/1958). Formulations of the two principles of mental functioning. In J. Strachey (Ed. and Trans.), *The standard edition of the complete psychological works of Sigmund Freud*, Vol. 12. London: Hogarth Press and the Institute of Psycho-Analysis.

Freud, S. (1912/1958). A note on the unconscious in psychoanalysis. In J. Strachey (Ed. and Trans.), *The standard edition of the complete psychological works of Sigmund Freud*, Vol. 12. London: Hogarth Press and the Institute of Psycho-Analysis.

Freud, S. (1913/1958). On the beginning of treatment. In J. Strachey (Ed. and Trans.), *The standard edition of the complete psychological works of Sigmund Freud*, Vol. 12. London: Hogarth Press and the Institute of Psycho-Analysis.

Freud, S. (1915/1957). Instincts and their vicissitudes. In J. Strachey (Ed. and Trans.), *The standard edition of the complete psychological works of Sigmund Freud*, Vol. 14. London: Hogarth Press and the Institute of Psycho-Analysis.

Freud, S. (1916/1963). Introductory lectures on psychoanalysis. In J. Strachey (Ed. and Trans.), *The standard edition of the complete psychological works of Sigmund Freud*, Vols. 15 and 16. London: Hogarth Press and the Institute of Psycho-Analysis.

Freud, S. (1920/1955). Beyond the pleasure principle. In J. Strachey (Ed. and Trans.), *The standard edition of the complete psychological works of Sigmund Freud*, Vol. 18. London: Hogarth Press and the Institute of Psycho-Analysis.

Freud, S. (1923/1961). The ego and the id. In J. Strachey (Ed. and Trans.), *The standard edition of the complete psychological works of Sigmund Freud*, Vol. 21. London: Hogarth Press and the Institute of Psycho-Analysis.

Freud, S. (1925). Some psychical consequences of the anatomical distinction between the sexes. In J. Strachey (Ed. and Trans.), *The standard edition of the complete psychological works of Sigmund Freud*, Vol. 19. London: Hogarth Press and the Institute of Psycho-Analysis.

Freud, S. (1931). Female sexuality. In J. Strachey (Ed. and Trans.), *The standard edition of the complete psychological works of Sigmund Freud*, Vol. 21. London: Hogarth Press and the Institute of Psycho-Analysis.

Freud, S. (1933/1964). New introductory lectures. In J. Strachey (Ed. and Trans.), *The standard edition of the complete psychological works of Sigmund Freud*, Vol. 22. London: Hogarth Press and the Institute of Psycho-Analysis.

Freud, S. (1940/1964). An outline of psychoanalysis. In J. Strachey (Ed. and Trans.), *The standard edition of the complete psychological works of Sigmund Freud*, Vol. 23. London: Hogarth Press and the Institute of Psycho-Analysis.

Friedman, H.W., & Booth-Kewley, S. (1987). The "disease-prone personality": A meta-analytic view of the construct. *American Psychologist, 42*, 539-555.

Friedman, M., & Rosenman, R. (1974). *Type A behavior and your heart*. New York: Knopf.

Fromkin, V., & Rodman, R. (1983). *An introduction to language*. New York: Holt, Rinehart and Winston.

Gackenbach, J., Heilman, N., Boyt, S., & LaBerge, S. (1985). The relationship between field independence and lucid dreaming ability. *Journal of Mental Imagery, 9(1)*, 9-20.

Gal, R. (1986). Unit morale: From a theoretical puzzle to an empirical illustration: An Israeli example. *Journal of Applied Social Psychology, 16*, 549-564.

Galdino, L. (1984). The diagnosis in psychiatry. *Neurobiologia, 47*, 141-152.

Galin, D. (1974). Implications for psychiatry of left and right cerebral specialization. *Archives of General Psychiatry, 31*, 572-583.

Galin, D., Johnstone, J., & Herron, J. (1978). Effects of task difficulty on EEG measures of cerebral engagement. *Neuropsychologia, 16*, 461-472.

Gallagher, W. (1986). The etiology of orgasm. *Discover, 7(2)*, 51-59.

Galton, F. (1865/1976). Hereditary talent and character: I & II. In C.J. Bajema (Ed.), *Eugenics: Then and now*. Stroudsburg, PA: Dowden, Hutchinson & Ross.

Galton, F. (1869/1962). *Hereditary genius: An inquiry into its laws and consequences*. London: Collins.

Galton, F. (1883/1907). *Inquiries into human faculty and its development*. London: Dent.

Galvin, R.M. (1982). Control of dreams may be possible for a resolute few. *Smithsonian, 13(5)*, 100-106.

Garber, J., & Seligman, E.P. (Eds.) (1980). *Human helplessness: Theory and applications*. New York: Academic Press.

Garcia Coll, C., Kagan, J., & Reznick, J.S. (1984). Behavioral inhibition in young children. *Child Development, 55*, 1005-1019.

Gardner, H. (1981). How the split brain gets a joke. *Psychology Today, 15(2)*.

Garfield, S.L. (1981). Psychotherapy: A 40-year appraisal. *American Psychologist, 36*, 174-183.

Garfield, S.L. (1983a). *Clinical psychology: The study of personality and behavior*, 2nd ed. New York: Aldine.

Garfield, S.L. (1983b). Effectiveness of psychotherapy: The perennial controversy. *Professional Psychology, 14 (1)*, 35-43.

Garfield, S.L. (1987). Ethical issues in research on psychotherapy. *Counseling and Values, 31(2)*, 115-125.

Garmon, L. (1985). Of hemispheres, handedness, and more. *Psychology Today, 19(11)*, 40-48.

Gatchel, R.J., & Price, K.P. (Eds.). (1979). *Clinical applications of biofeedback: Appraisal and status*. New York: Pergamon Press.

Gazzaniga, M.S. (1985). The social brain. *Psychology Today, 19(11)*, 29-38.

Gazzaniga, M.S., & LeDoux, J.E. (1978). *The integrated mind*. New York: Plenum Press.

Geldard, F.A., & Sherrick, C.E. (1986). Space, time and touch. *Scientific American, 255(1)*, 91-95.

Gelwick, B.P. (1985). Cognitive development of women. *New Directions for Student Services*, No. 29, 29-44.

Gerard, R.W. (1953). What is memory? *Scientific American, 189(3)*, 118.

Gerber, K.E., & Nehemkis, A.M. (Eds.). (1986). *Compliance: The dilemma of the chronically ill*. New York: Springer.

Gesell, A. (1954). The ontogenesis of infant behavior. In L. Carmichael (Ed.), *Manual of child psychology*. New York: Wiley.

Gesell, A., Ilg, F.L., Ames, L.B., & Rodell, J.L. (1974). *Infant and child in the culture of today: The guidance of development in home and nursery school*. New York: Harper & Row.

Gibson, E.J. (1981). The ecological approach to perception and its significance for developmental psychology. *International Journal of Behavioral Development, 4*, 477-480.

Gibson, E.J., & Rader, N. (1979). Attention: The perceiver as performer. In G. Hale & M. Lewis (Eds.), *Attention and cognitive development*. New York: Plenum Press.

Gibson, E.J., & Walk, R. (1960). The "visual cliff." *Scientific American, 202*, 64-71.

Gibson, E.J., & Walker, A.S. (1984). Development of knowledge of visual-tactual affordances of substance. *Child Development, 55*, 453-560.

Gibson, H.B. (1982). *Pain and its conquest*. London: Peter Owen.

Gibson, J.J. (1950). *Perception of the visual world*. Boston: Houghton Mifflin.

Gilbert, A.N., & Wysocki, C.J. (1987). The smell survey. *National Geographic, 172*, 514-525.

Gilhooly, K.J. (1982). *Thinking: Directed, undirected and creative*. London: Academic Press.

Gilligan, C. (1983). *In a different voice: Psychological theory and women's development*. Cambridge, MA: Harvard University Press.

Gilligan, C. (1986). On "In a different voice": An interdisciplinary forum: Reply. *Signs, 11*, 324-333.

Gilson, M., Brown, E.C., & Daves, W.F. (1982). Sexual orientation as measured by perceptual dominance in binocular rivalry. *Personality and Social Psychology Bulletin, 8*, 494-500.

Giordano, A.L., Siegel, H.I., & Rosenblatt, J.S. (1986). Intrasexual aggression during pregnancy and the estrous cycle in golden hamsters. *Aggressive Behavior, 12(3)*, 213-222.

Glaser, R. (1984). Education and thinking: The role of knowledge. *American Psychologist, 39*, 93-104.

Glasgow, R.E., Klesges, R.C., Mizes, J.S., & Pechacek, T.F. (1985). Quitting smoking: Strategies used and variables associated with success in a stop-smoking contest. *Journal of Consulting and Clinical Psychology, 53*, 905-912.

Glasgow, R.E., Klesges, R.C., & O'Neill, H.K. (1986). Programming social support for smoking modification: An extension and replication. *Addictive Behaviors, 11(4)*, 453-457.

Glasgow, R.E., McCaul, K.D., & Schafer, L.C. (1986). Barriers to regimen adherence among persons with insulin-dependent diabetes. *Journal of Behavioral Medicine, 9(1)*, 65-77.

Glass, A.L., & Holyoak, K.J. (1986). *Cognition, 2nd ed.* New York: Random House.

Glass, D.C. (1977). *Behavior patterns, stress, and coronary disease*. Hillsdale, NJ: Erlbaum.

Gleason, J.B. (1987). The contents of children's minds. *Contemporary Psychology, 32*, 147.

Goldberg, S., Hunt, R.G., Cohen, W., & Meadow, A. (1954). Some personality correlates of perceptual distortion in the direction of group conformity. *American Psychologist, 9*, 378.

Goldberger, L., & Breznitz, S. (Eds.). (1982). *Handbook of stress: Theoretical and clinical aspects*. New York: Free Press.

Golden, C.J., *et al*. (1980). Brain density deficits in chronic schizophrenia. *Psychiatry Research, 3*, 179-184.

Golden, C.J., *et al.*. (1981a). Differences in brain densities between chronic alcoholic and normal control patients. *Science, 211*, 508-510.

Golden, C.J., *et al*. (1981b). Structural brain deficits in schizophrenia. Identification by computed tomographic scan density measurements. *Archives of General Psychiatry, 38*, 1014-1017.

Golden, C.J., *et al*. (1985). Neuropsychological deficit and regional cerebral blood flow in schizophrenic patients. *Hillside Journal of Clinical Psychiatry, 7*, 3-15.

Goldenson, R.M. (1970). *The encyclopedia of human behavior*. New York: Doubleday.

Goldstein, A.P., Sprafkin, R.P., Gershaw, N.J., & Klein, P. (1980). *Skill-streaming the adolescent: A structured learning approach to teaching prosocial skills*. Champaign, IL.: Research Press.

Goleman, D. (1983). A conversation with Ulric Neisser. *Psychology Today, 17(5)*, 54-62.

Golombok, S. (1986). The role of anxiolytic and antidepressant drugs in the development and treatment of sexual dysfunction. *Sexual and Marital Therapy, 1(1)*, 43-47.

Goodglass, H. (1980). Disorders of naming following brain injury. *American Scientist, 68*, 647-655.

Gortmaker, S.L., Dietz, W.H., Jr., Sobol, A.M., & Wehler, C.A. (1987). Increasing pediatric obesity in the United States. *American Journal of the Disabled Child, 141*, 535-540.

Gottesman, I.I., & Shields, J. (with Hanson, D.R.). (1982). *Schizophrenia*. Cambridge, England: Cambridge University Press.

Gould, J.L. (1986). The biology of learning. *Annual Review of Psychology, 37*, 163-192.

Gould, J.L., & Gould, C.G. (1981). The instinct to learn. *Science 81, 2(5)*, 44-50.

Gould, S.J. (1981). *The mismeasure of man*. New York: W.W. Norton.

Gould, S.J. (1982). Of wasps and WASPS. *Natural History, 91(12)*, 8-15.

Govier, E., & Pitts, M. (1982). The contextual disambiguation of a polysemous word in an unattended message. *British Journal of Psychology, 73*, 537-545.

Goy, R.W., & McEwen, B.S. (1980). *Sexual differentiation of the brain*. Cambridge, MA: MIT Press.

Grafman, J. (1985). Effects of left-hand preference on post-injury measures of distal motor ability. *Perceptual & Motor Skills, 61*, 615-624.

Graumann, C.F., & Moscovici, S. (Eds.). (1986). *Changing conceptions of leadership*. New York: Springer-Verlag.

Green, R. (1987). The "Sissy Boy Syndrome" and the development of homosexuality. New Haven, CT: Yale University Press.

Green, R.J., & Framo, J.L. (Eds.). (1981). *Family therapy: Major contributions*. New York: International Universities Press.

Greene, E., & Loftus, E. (1981). The person perceiver as information processor. *Contemporary Psychology, 26*, 343-345.

Greenhill, M.H., & Gralnick, A. (Eds.). (1983). *Psychopharmacology and psychotherapy*. New York: Free Press.

Greenough, W.T., Black, J.E., & Wallace, C.S. (1987). Experience and brain development. *Child Development, 58*, 539-559.

Greenspoon, J. (1955). The reinforcing effects of two spoken sounds on the frequency of two responses. *American Journal of Psychology, 68*, 409-416.

Greenwald, A.G., Pratkanis, A.R., Leippe, M.R., & Baumgardner, M.H. (1986). Under what conditions does theory obstruct research progress? *Psychological Review, 93*, 216-229.

Gregory, R.L. (1977). *Eye and brain: The psychology of seeing*, 3rd ed. New York: World University Library.

Gregory, S.W. (1986). A sociolinguistic indicator of group membership. *Journal of Psycholinguistic Research, 15(3)*, 189-207.

Griest, J.H., Jefferson, J.W., & Spitzer, R.L. (Eds.). (1983). *Treatment of mental disorders*. New York: Oxford University Press.

Grimm, L.G. (1981). Catholic views on the long-term effects of psychotherapy. *Contemporary Psychology, 26*, 750-752.

Gruder, C.L., *et al.* (1978). Empirical tests of the absolute sleeper effect predicted from the discounting cue hypothesis. *Journal of Personality and Social Psychology, 36*, 1061-1074.

Grunberg, N.E., & Bowen, D.J. (1985). The role of physical activity in nicotine's effects on body weight. *Pharmacology, Biochemistry and Behavior, 23*, 851-854.

Grunberg, N.E., Bowen, D.J., Maycock, V.A., & Nespor, S.M. (1985). The importance of sweet taste and caloric content in the effects of nicotine on specific food consumption. *Psychopharmacology, 87*, 198-203.

Guilford, J.P. (1959). *Personality*. New York: McGraw-Hill.

Guilford, J.P. (1967). *The nature of human intelligence*. New York: McGraw-Hill.

Gunderson, J.G., & Frank, A.F. (1985). Effects of psychotherapy in schizophrenia. *Yale Journal of Biological Medicine, 58*, 373-381.

Gurin, P., Gurin, G., & Morrison, B.M. (1978). Personal and ideological aspects of internal and external control. *Social Psychology Quarterly, 41*, 275-296.

Gutheil, T.G. (1985). The therapeutic milieu: Changing themes and theories. *Hospital and Community Psychiatry, 36*, 1279-1285.

Guthrie, R.V. (1976). *Even the rat was white: A historical view of psychology*. New York: Harper & Row.

Haber, R.N., & Hershenson, M. (1973). *The psychology of visual perception*. New York: Holt, Rinehart and Winston.

Hackman, J.R., Lawler, E.E., & Porter, L.W. (Eds.). (1983). *Perspectives on behavior in organizations*, 2nd ed. New York: McGraw-Hill.

Haith, M.M. (1980). *Rules that babies look by: The organization of new-born visual activity*. Hillsdale, NJ: Erlbaum.

Hall, E. (1983). A conversation with Erik Erikson. *Psychology Today, 17(6)*, 22-30.

Hall, E. (1986a). Conversation with Robert B. Zajonc: Mining new gold from old research. *Psychology Today, 20(2)*, 47-51.

Hall, E. (1986b). Profile: June Reinisch. *Psychology Today, 20(6)*, 33-39.

Hall, E.R., Howard, J.A., & Boezio, S.L. (1986). Tolerance of rape: A sexist or antisocial attitude? *Psychology of Women Quarterly, 10(2)*, 101-117.

Hall, H. (1986). A pat on the back helps smokers quit. *Psychology Today, 20(6)*, 20.

Hall, H. (1987). Beauty is in the eye of the baby. *Psychology Today, 21(8)*, 12.

Hall, J., & Donnell, S.M. (1979). Managerial achievement: The personal side of behavioral theory. *Human Relations, 32*, 77-101.

Hall, M.H. (1968). A conversation with Abraham Maslow. In R.E. Schell (Ed.), *Readings in developmental psychology today*. New York: CRM Books.

Hambert, O. (1984). Narcolepsy. *Nordisk Psykiatrisk Tidsskrift, 38*, 481-491.

Hamilton, D.L. (Ed.). (1981). *Cognitive processes in stereotyping and intergroup behavior*. Hillsdale, NJ: Erlbaum.

Hampson, S.E. (1985). The focus of semantic categorization of personality: A revision. *Boletin de Psicologia, 9*, 7-27.

Haney, C., Banks, C., & Zimbardo, P.G. (1981). A study of prisoners and guards in a simulated prison. In E. Aronson (Ed.), *Readings about the social animal*, 3rd ed. San Francisco: W.H. Freeman.

Harlow, H.F. (1973). *Learning to love*. New York: Ballantine.

Harlow, H.F. (1975). Lust, latency and love: Simian secrets of successful sex. *Journal of Sex Research, 11(2)*, 79-90.

Harlow, H.F. (1978). Affectivity. *Psychologia Wychowawcza, 21(1)*, 13-23.

Harlow, H.F., Harlow, M.K., & Suomi, S.J. (1971). From thought to therapy: Lessons from a primate laboratory. *American Scientist, 59*, 539-549.

Harnad, S. (1984). What are the scope and limits of radical behaviorist theory? *Behavioral and Brain Sciences, 7*, 720-724.

Harrell, R.L., & Strauss, F.A. (1986). Approaches to increasing assertive behavior and communication skills in blind and visualy impaired persons. *Journal of Visual Impairment and Blindness, 80*, 794-798.

Hartman, E. (1978). *The sleeping pill*. New Haven, CT: Yale University Press.

Hartman, E. (1983). Two case reports: Night terrors with sleepwalking—a potentially lethal disorder. *Journal of Nervous & Mental Disease, 171*, 503-505.

Harvey, O.J., Kelley, H.H., & Shapiro, M.M. (1957). Reactions to unfavorable evaluations of self made by other persons. *Journal of Personality, 25*, 393-411.

Hastie, R. (1984). Causes and effects of causal attribution. *Journal of Personality and Social Psychology, 46(1)*, 44-56.

Hastie, R., *et al.* (Eds.). (1980). *Person memory: The cognitive basis of social perception*. Hillsdale, NJ: Erlbaum.

Hatfield, E., & Sprecher, S. (1986). *Mirror, mirror: The importance of looks in everyday life*. Albany: University of New York Press.

Haugeland, J. (1985). *Artificial intelligence: The very idea*. Cambridge, MA: MIT Press.

Hay, W.M., & Nathan, P.E. (Eds.). (1982). *Clinical case studies in the behavioral treatment of alcoholism*. New York: Plenum Press.

Heather, N., & Robertson, I. (1981). *Controlled drinking*. London: Methuen.

Hebb, D.O. (1955). Drives and the C.N.S. (conceptual nervous system). *Psycholgical Review, 62*, 243.

Heeren, J., & Shichor, D. (1984). Mass media and delinquency prevention: The case of "scared straight." *Deviant Behavior, 5*, 375-386.

Heider, F. (1958). *The psychology of interpersonal relations*. New York: Wiley.

Heil, J. (1983). *Perception and cognition*. Berkeley: University of California Press.

Hellhammer, D.H., Hubert, W., Freischem, C.W., & Nieschlag, E. (1985). Male infertility: Relationships among gonadotropins, sex steroids, seminal parameters, and personality attitudes. *Psychosomatic Medicine, 47(1)*, 58-66.

Helson, H. (1948). Adaptation-level as a basis for a quantitative theory of frames of reference. *Psychological Review, 55* 297-313.

Helson, H. (1964). *Adaptation-level theory*. New York: Harper & Row.

Helson, H., Blake, R.R., & Mouton, J.S. (1958a). Petition-signing as adjustment of situational and personal factors. *Journal of Social Psychology, 48*, 3-10.

Helson, H., Blake, R.R., & Mouton, J.S. (1958b). An experimental investigation of the effectiveness of the "big lie" in shifting attitudes. *Journal of Social Psychology, 48*, 51-60.

Helson, H., Blake, R.R., Mouton, J.S., & Olmstead, J.A. (1956). Attitudes as adjustments to stimulus, background and residual factors. *Journal of Abnormal and Social Psychology, 52*, 314-322.

Hensel, H. (1981). *Thermoreception and temperature regulation*. London: Academic Press.

Hensel, H. (1982). *Thermal sensations and thermoreceptors in man*. Springfield, IL: Charles C Thomas.

Herbert, W. (1983a). Canine clues to narcolepsy. *Science News, 123*, 292-293.

Herbert, W. (1983b). Depression: Too much vigilance? *Science News, 124*, 13.

Herbert, W. (1983c). Memory in the rough. *Psychology Today, 17(9)*, 18.

Herbert, W. (1983d). Modeling bulimia. *Science News, 123*, 316.

Herbert, W. (1986). Sweet treatment. *Psychology Today, 20(12)*, 6-7.

Hergenhahn, B.R. (1982). *An introduction to theories of learning*, 2nd ed. Englewood Cliffs, NJ: Prentice-Hall.

Herman, B.H., & Panksepp, J. (1981). Ascending endorphin inhibition of distress vocalization. *Science, 211*, 160-162.

Heron, W., Doane, B.K., & Scott, T.H. (1956). Visual disturbances after prolonged perceptual isolation. *Canadian Journal of Psychology, 10*, 13.

Herzog, A.R., & Dielman, L. (1985). Age differences in response accuracy for factual survey questions. *Journal of Gerontology, 40*, 350-357.

Herzog, E., & Sudia, C.E. (1968). Fatherless homes: A review of research. *Children, 15*, 177-182.

Hess, E.H. (1965). Attitude and pupil size. *Scientific American, 212*, 46-54.

Hetherington, E.M. (1981). Tracing children through the changing family. *APA Monitor, 12*, 14-22.

Hetherington, E.M., Cox, M., & Cox, R. (1975). Beyond father absence: Conceptualization of effects of divorce. Paper presented at the annual meeting of the Society for Research in Child Development. Denver, 1975.

Hetherington, E.M., Cox, M., & Cox, R. (1985). Long-term effects of divorce and remarriage on the adjustment of children. *Journal of the American Academy of Child Psychiatry, 24(5)*, 518-530.

Hewstone, M. (1988). *Introduction to social psychology: A European perspective*. London: Basil Blackwell.

Hikita, K. (1986). The effects of token economy procedures with chronic schizophrenia patients. *Japanese Journal of Behavior Therapy, 11(2)*, 55-76.

Hilgard, E.R. (1978). Hypnosis and Consciousness,. *Human Nature, 1(1)*, 42-49.

Hilgard, E.R. (1986). A study in hypnosis. *Psychology Today, 20(1)*, 23-27.

Hilgard, J.R., & LeBaron, S. (1984). *Hypnotherapy of pain in children with cancer*. Los Altos, CA: William Kaufmann.

Hilton, J.L., & Darley, J.M. (1985). Constructing other persons: A limit on the effect. *Journal of Experimental Social Psychology, 21(1)*, 1-18.

Hochberg, J. (1984). Visual perception. In P.C. Dodwell & T. Caelli (Eds.), *Figural Synthesis*. Hillsdale, NJ: Erlbaum.

Hodgkinson, S., *et al.* (1987). Molecular genetic evidence for heterogeneity in manic depression. *Nature, 325*, 805-806.

Hoebel, B.G., & Novin, D. (Eds.). (1982). *The neural basis of feeding and reward*. Brunswick, ME: Haer Institute.

Hofer, M.A. (1981). Parental contributions to the development of their offspring. In D.J. Gubernick & P.H. Klopfer (Eds.), *Parental care in mammals*. New York: Plenum Press.

Hofer, M.A. (1984). Relationships as regulators: A psychobiologic perspective on bereavement. *Psychosomatic Medicine, 46(3)*, 183-197.

Hoffman, D.D. (1983). The interpretation of visual illusions. *Scientific American, 249(6)*, 154-162.

Hoffman, J.W., *et al.* (1982). Reduced sympathetic nervous system responsivity associated with the relaxation response. *Science, 215*, 190-192.

Hoffman, R.S., & Koran, L.M. (1984). Detecting physical illness in patients with mental disorders. *Psychosomatics, 25*, 654-660.

Hoge, D.R., & Ankney, T.L. (1982). Occupations and attitudes of former student activists 10 years later. *Journal of Youth and Adolescence, 11*, 355-371.

Holden, C. (1985). A guarded endorsement for shock therapy. *Science, 228*, 1510-1511.

Holden, C. (1986a). Days may be numbered for polygraphs in the private sector. *Science, 232*, 705.

Holden, C. (1986b). Giving mental illness its research due. *Science, 232*, 1084-1085.

Holden, C. (1986c). Youth suicide: New research focuses on a growing social problem. *Science, 233*, 839-841.

Holden, C. (1987). A top priority at NIMH. *Science, 235*, 431.

Holmes, T.H., & Rahe, R.H. (1967). The social readjustment rating scale. *Journal of Psychosomatic Research, 11*, 213-218.

Homant, R.J., & Osowski, G. (1981). Evaluation of the "scared straight" model: Some methodological and political considerations. *Corrective and Social Psychiatry and Journal of Behavior Technology, Methods, and Therapy, 27(3)*, 130-134.

Hoppe, R.B. (1988). In search of a phenomenon: Research in parapsychology. *Contemporary Psychology, 33*, 129-130.

Hopson, J. (1979). *Scent signals: The silent language of sex*. New York: William Morrow.

Horn, J.C. (1983). Preview surgery. *Psychology Today, 17(6)*, 18.

Horn, J.C. (1985a). A call to glory. *Psychology Today, 19(12)*, 20.

Horn, J.C. (1985b). TV as social substitute for hearing-impaired. *Psychology Today, 19(5)*, 18.

Horn, J.C. (1987). Bigger pay for better work. *Psychology Today, 21(7)*, 47.

Horn, J.C., & Rice, B. (1981). Biofeedback helps by deception. *Psychology Today, 15(4)*, 30-32.

Hovland, C.I., Harvey, O., & Sherif, M. (1957). Assimilation and contrast effects in reactions to communication and attitude change. *Journal of Abnormal and Social Psychology, 55*, 244-252.

Hovland, C.I., Janis, I.L., & Kelley, H.H. (1953). *Communication and persuasion*. New Haven, CT: Yale University Press.

Hovland, C.I., & Weiss, W. (1951). The influence of source credibility on communication effectiveness. *Public Opinion Quarterly, 15*, 635-650.

Hovland, C.I., *et al.* (1957). *The order of presentation in persuasion*. New Haven, CT: Yale University Press.

Howell, T., Bauwens, S.F., & Thurrell, R.J. (1986). Neuroleptic-induced respiratory dyskinesia in the elderly:

Two case reports and a brief review. *Clinical Geron-tologist, 4(3)*, 17-22.

Howes, D., & Solomon, R.L. (1950). A note on McGinnies' "Emotionality and perceptual defense." *Psychological Review, 57*, 229-234.

Hubert, W., Hellhammer, D.H., & Freischem, C.W. (1985). Psychobiological profiles in infertile men. *Journal of Psychosomatic Research, 29(2)*, 161-165.

Hudspeth, A.J. (1983). The hair cells of the inner ear. *Scientific American, 248(6)*, 54-64.

Huessy, H.R. (1982). Letters: Schizophrenia and kibbutzim. *Science News, 122*, 207.

Hui, C.H., & Triandis, H.C. (1986). Individualism-collectivism: A study of cross-cultural researchers. *Journal of Cross-Cultural Psychology, 17*, 225-248.

Hull, C.L. (1933). *Hypnosis and suggestibility: An experimental approach*. New York: Appleton-Century-Crofts.

Hurlburt, R.T., & Melancon, S.M. (1987). P-technique factor analyses of individuals' thought- and mood-sampling data. *Cognitive Therapy and Research, 11*, 487-500.

Huston, T.L., et al. (1981). Bystander intervention into crime: A study based on naturally-occurring episodes. *Social Psychology Quarterly, 44(1)*, 14-23.

Hyden, H., & Egyhazi, E. (1962). Nuclear RNA changes in nerve cells during a learning experiment in rats. *Proceedings of the National Academy of Sciences, 48*, 1366-1373.

Imperato-McGinley, J., Gautier, T., Peterson, R.E., & Shackleton, C. (1986). The prevalence of 5 alpha-reductase deficiency in children with ambiguous genitalia in the Dominican Republic. *Journal of Urology, 134*, 867-873.

Imperato-McGinley, J., Peterson, R.E., Gautier, T., & Sturla, E. (1979). Androgens and the evolution of male-gender identity among male pseudohermaphrodites with 5 alpha-reductase deficiency. *New England Journal of Medicine, 300*, 1233-1237.

Imperato-McGinley, J., Peterson, R.E., Leshin, M., Griffin, J.E., Cooper, G., Draghi, S., Berenyi, M., & Wilson, J.D. (1980). Steroid 5 alpha-reductase deficiency in a 65-year-old male pseudohermaphrodite: The natural history, ultrastructure of the testes, and evidence for inherited enzyme heterogeneity. *Journal of Clinical and Endocrinological Metabolism, 50*, 15-22.

Ingram, L.C. (1986). Testimony and religious cohesion. *Religious Education, 81(2)*, 295-309.

Inoue, K. (1985). An examination of equity theory in dating couples' intimate romantic relationships. *Japanese Journal of Experimental Social Psychology, 24(2)*, 127-134.

Isaacson, R.L. (1974). *The limbic system*. New York: Plenum Press.

Iversen, L.L., Iversen, S.D., & Snyder, S.H. (Eds.). (1983). *Neuropeptides: Handbook of psychopharmacology, Vol. 16*. New York: Plenum Press.

Ivnik, R.J., Sharbrough, F.W., & Laws, E.R. (1987). Effects of anterior temporal lobectomy on cognitive function. *Journal of Clinical Psychology, 43(1)*, 128-137.

Izard, C.E., Kagan, J., & Zajonc, R.B. (Eds.). (1984). *Emotions, cognition, and behavior*. Cambridge, England: Cambridge University Press.

Jacobson, R.R. (1986). Disorders of facial recognition, social behaviour and affect after combined bilateral amygdalotomy and subcaudate tractotomy: A clinical and experimental study. *Psychological Medicine, 16*, 439-450.

Jaffe, A. (Ed.) (1979). *C.G. Jung: Word and image*. Princeton, NJ: Princeton University Press.

Janis, I.L. (1982). *Stress, attitudes, and decisions: Selected papers*. New York: Praeger.

Janis, I.L., & Feshbach, S. (1953). Effects of fear-arousing communications. *Journal of Abnormal and Social Psychology, 48*, 78-92.

Jellinek, E.M. (1952). Phases of alcohol addiction. *Quarterly Journal of the Study of Alcohol, 13*, 673-678.

Jenkins, C.D., Zyzanski, S.J., & Rosenman, R. (1971). Progress toward validation of a computer-scored test of the type A coronary-prone behavior pattern. *Psychosomatic Medicine, 33*, 192-202.

Jennings, K.D., Yarrow, L.J., & Martin, P.P. (1984). Mastery motivation and cognitive development: A longitudinal study from infancy to 3.5 years of age. *International Journal of Behavioral Development, 7*, 441-461.

Jensen, A.R. (1969). How much can we boost IQ and scholastic achievement? *Harvard Educational Review, 39(1)*, 1-123.

Jensen, A.R. (1979). *Bias in mental testing*. New York: Free Press.

Jha, B.K. (1972). Institutional neurosis: Its causes and remedy. *Indian Journal of Psychiatric Social Work, 1(1)*, 5-19.

John, E.R., et al. (1988). Neurometrics: Computer-assisted differential diagnosis of brain dysfunctions. *Science, 239*, 162-169.

Johns, G. (1987). The great escape. *Psychology Today, 21(10)*, 30-33.

Johnson, R.C., et al. (1985). Galton's data a century later. *American Psychologist, 40*, 875-892.

Johnson, R.T., Johnson, D.W., & Stanne, M.B. (1986). Comparison of computer-assisted cooperative, competitive, and individualistic learning. *American Educational Research Journal, 23*, 382-392.

Jones, E.E. (1986). Interpreting interpersonal behavior: The effects of expectancies. *Science, 234*, 41-46.

Jones, M.B. (1970). A two-process theory of individual differences in motor learning. *Psychological Review, 77*, 353-360.

Jones, M.C. (1924). Elimination of children's fears. *Journal of Experimental Psychology, 7*, 382.

Jones, R.L. (Ed). (1980). *Black Psychology*, 2nd ed. New York: Harper & Row.

Joule, R.V. (1986). Twenty five on: Yet another version of cognitive dissonance theory? *European Journal of Social Psychology, 16(1)*, 65-78.

Jung, C.G. (1909). The psychological diagnosis of evidence. *The collected works of C.G. Jung*, Vol. 2. Princeton, NJ: Princeton University Press.

Jung, C.G. (1912). Symbols of transformation. *The collected works of C.G. Jung*, Vol. 5. Princeton, NJ: Princeton University Press.

Jung, C.G. (1916/1969). General aspects of dream psychology. *The collected works of C.G. Jung*, Vol. 8. Princeton, NJ: Princeton University Press.

Jung, C.G. (1917/1966). Two essays on analytical psychology. *The collected works of C.G. Jung*, Vol. 7. Princeton, NJ: Princeton University Press.

Jung, C.G. (1936/1969). The archetypes and the collective unconscious. *The collected works of C.G. Jung*, Vol. 9i. Princeton, NJ: Princeton University Press.

Jung, C.G. (1939/1969). Conscious, unconscious, and individuation. *The collected works of C.G. Jung*, Vol. 9i. Princeton, NJ: Princeton University Press.

Jung, C.G. (1948/1969). On psychic energy. *The collected works of C.G. Jung*, Vol. 9i. Princeton, NJ: Princeton University Press.

Jung, C.G. (1961). *Memories, dreams, reflections*. New York: Pantheon.

Kagan, J. (1980). In O.G. Brim, Jr., & J. Kagan (Eds.), *Constancy and change in human development*. Cambridge, MA: Harvard University Press.

Kagan, J. (1986). Rates of change in psychological processes. *Journal of Applied Developmental Psychology, 7(2)*, 125-130.

Kagan, J. (1987). Essay. *Psychology Today, 21(5)*, 47.

Kagan, J., Kearsley, R.B., & Zelazo, P.R. (1978). *Infancy*. Cambridge, MA: Harvard University Press.

Kagan, J., Reznick, J.S., & Snidman, N. (1988). Biological bases of childhood shyness. *Science, 140*, 167-171.

Kaitz, M., Good, A., Rokem, A.M., & Eidelman, A.I. (1987). Mothers' recognition of their newborns by olfactory cues. *Developmental Psychobiology, 20*, 587-591.

Kales, A. *et al.* (1982). Biopsychobehavioral correlates of insomnia: I. Role of sleep apnea and nocturnal myoclonus. *Psychosomatics, 23,* 589-600.

Kales, A., & Kales, J.D. (1984). *Evaluation and treatment of insomnia.* New York: Oxford University Press.

Kamii, C. (1984). Autonomy: The aim of eduation envisioned by Piaget. *Phi Delta Kappan, 65,* 410-415.

Kanas, N. (1986). Group therapy with schizophrenics: A review of controlled studies. *International Journal of Group Psychotherapy, 36,* 339-351.

Kanfer, F.H., & Goldstein, A.P. (Eds.). (1986). *Helping people change: A textbook of methods,* 3rd ed. Oxford, England: Pergamon Press.

Kaniza, G. (1979). *Organization in vision: Essays on Gestalt perception.* New York: Praeger.

Kantor, D., *et al.* (1986). The benefit of lithium carbonate adjunct in refractory depression: Fact or fiction? *Canadian Journal of Psychiatry, 31,* 416-418.

Kaplan, B. (1967). Meditations on genesis. *Human Development, 10(2),* 65-87.

Kaplan, M. (1983). A woman's view of DSM-III. *American Psychologist, 38,* 786-792.

Kapur, R., & Miller, K. (1987). A comparison between therapeutic factors in TA and psychodynamic therapy groups. *Transactional Analysis Journal, 17(1),* 294-300.

Karoly, P., & Kanfer, F.H. (Eds.). (1982). *Self-management and behavior change: From theory to practice.* New York: Pergamon Press.

Kashima, Y., & Triandis, H.C. (1986). The self-serving bias in attributions as a coping strategy: A cross-cultural study. *Journal of Cross-Cultural Psychology, 17,* 83-97.

Kass, F., MacKinnon, R.A., & Spitzer, R.L. (1986). Masochistic personality: An empirical study. *American Journal of Psychiatry, 143,* 216-218.

Kass, F., Spitzer, R.L., & Williams, J.B. (1983). An empirical study of the issue of sex bias in the diagnostic criteria of DSM-III axis II personality disorders. *American Psychologist, 38,* 799-801.

Katz, A.N. (1986). The relationships between creativity and cerebral hemisphericity for creative architects, scientists, and mathematicians. *Empirical Studies of the Arts, 4(2),* 97-108.

Katz, J.J., & Halstead, W.C. (1950). Protein organization and mental function. *Comparative Psychological Monographs, 20(1),* 1-38.

Kayata, L., & Szydlo, D. (1986). The treatment of psychosexual dysfunction in a mixed sex group: A new approach. *Sexual and Marital Therapy, 1,* 7-17.

Kaye, K. (1980). Piaget's forgotten novel. *Psychology Today, 14(11),* 102.

Kazdin, A. (1974). A review of token economy treatment modalities. In D. Harshbarger & R.F. Maley (Eds.), *Behavior analysis and systems analysis: An integrative approach to mental health programs.* Kalamazoo, MI: Behaviordelia.

Kazdin, A. (1978). *History of behavior modification.* University Park: University of Maryland Press.

Keller, H. (1970). *Story of my life.* New York: Airmont.

Kelley, H.H. (1950). The warm-cold variable in first impressions of persons. *Journal of Personality, 18,* 431-439.

Kelley, H.H. (1952). Two functions of reference groups. In G.E. Swanson, T.M. Newcomb, & E.L. Hartley (Eds.), *Readings in social psychology.* New York: Holt.

Kelley, H.H. (1979). *Personal relationships: Their structures and processes.* Hillsdale, NJ: Erlbaum.

Kelley, H.H. (1983). The situational origins of human tendencies: A further reason for the formal analysis of structures. *Personality and Social Psychology Bulletin, 9(1),* 8-36.

Kelley, H.H. (1984). Affect in interpersonal relations. *Review of Personality and Social Psychology, No. 5,* 89-115.

Kelley, H.H., & Lamb, T.W. (1957). An experiment on conformity to group norms where conformity is detrimental to group achievement. *American Sociological Review, 19,* 667-677.

Kelley, H.H., *et al.* (1983). *Close relationships.* San Francisco: W.H. Freeman.

Kelly, E.L. (1934). An experimental attempt to produce artificial chromaesthesia by the technique of the conditioned response. *Journal of Experimental Psychology, 17,* 315-341.

Kelso, S.R., & Brown, T.H. (1986). Differential conditioning of associative synaptic enhancement in hippocampal brain slices. *Science, 232,* 85-87.

Kendall, P.C., & Hollon, S.D. (Eds.). (1979). *Cognitive-behavioral interventions.* New York: Academic Press.

Kendall, P.C., & Hollon, S.D. (Eds.). (1981). *Assessment strategies for cognitive-behavioral interventions.* New York: Academic Press.

Kessen, W. (1983a). The child and other cultural inventions. In F.S. Kessel & A.W. Siegel (Eds.), *The child and other cultural inventions,* pp. 224-259. New York: Praeger.

Kessen, W. (Vol. Ed.). (1983b). *Mussen's handbook of child psychology, Vol. 1.: History, theory, and methods,* 4th ed. New York: Wiley.

Kewman, D.G., & Roberts, A.H. (1980). Skin temperature biofeedback and migraine headaches: A double-blind study. *Biofeedback and Self-Regulation, 5,* 327-345.

Kilhstom, J.F. (1987). The cognitive unconscious. *Science, 237,* 1445-1452.

Kilshaw, D., & Annett, M. (1983). Right- and left-hand skill: I. Effects of age, sex and hand preference showing superior skill in left-handers. *British Journal of Psychology, 74,* 253-268.

Kimble, D.P. (1977). *Psychology as a biological science,* 2nd ed. Santa Monica, CA: Goodyear.

Kimble, D.P. (1987). *Biological psychology.* New York: Holt, Rinehart and Winston.

Kimura, D. (1985). Male brain, female brain: The hidden difference. *Psychology Today, 19(1),* 52-58.

Kinsey, A.C., Pomeroy, W.B., & Martin, C.E. (1948). *Sexual behavior in the human male.* Philadelphia: W.B. Saunders.

Kinsey, A.C., Pomeroy, W.B., Martin, C.E., & Gebhard, P.H. (1953). *Sexual behavior in the human female.* Philadelphia: W.B. Saunders.

Kitcher, P. (1985). *Vaulting ambition: Sociobiology and the quest for human nature.* Cambridge, MA: MIT Press.

Klaus, M.H., & Kennell, J.H. (1983). *Bonding: The beginnings of parent to infant attachment.* St. Louis, MO: Mosby.

Klein, F., & Wolf, T.J. (Eds.). (1985). *Bisexualities: Theories and research.* New York: Haworth Press.

Kleinke, L.C. (1986). Gaze and eye contact: A research review. *Psychological Bulletin, 100(1),* 78-100.

Kleinmuntz, B., & Szucko, J.J. (1984). Lie detection in ancient and modern times: A call for contemporary scientific study. *American Psychologist, 39,* 766-776.

Kleitman, N. (1987). *Sleep and wakefulness.* Chicago: University of Chicago Press.

Klerman, G.L. (1983). The significance of DSM-III in American psychiatry. In R.L. Spitzer, J.B.W. Williams, & A.E. Skodal (Eds.), *International perspectives on DSM-III.* Washington, DC: American Psychiatric Press.

Klerman, G.L. (1985). An incomplete manual. *Contemporary Psychology, 30,* 57-58.

Kline, N., & Angst, J. (1979). *Psychiatric syndromes and drug treatment.* New York: Aronson.

Klinnert, M.D., Emde, R.N., Butterfield, P., & Campos, J.J. (1986). Social referencing: The infant's use of emotional signals from a friendly adult with mother present. *Developmental Psychology, 22(4),* 427-432.

Kluever, H., & Bucy, P.C. (1937). "Psychic blindness" and other symptoms following bilateral temporal lobectomy in rhesus monkeys. *American Journal of Physiology, 119,* 352-353.

Koehler, W. (1925). *The mentality of apes.* New York: Harcourt, Brace & World.

Koehler, W. (1929). *Dynamics in psychology*. New York: Liveright.

Koehler, W. (1974). *Gestalt psychology*. New York: Liveright.

Kohlberg, L. (1976). Moral stages and moralization: The cognitive-developmental approach. In T. Likona (Ed.), *Moral development and behavior: Theory, research, and social issues*. New York: Holt, Rinehart and Winston.

Kolata, G. (1984). Studying learning in the womb. *Science, 225*, 302-303.

Kolata, G. (1986a). Maleness pinpointed on Y chromosome. *Science, 234*, 234-235.

Kolata, G. (1986b). Weight regulation may start in our cells, not psyches. *Smithsonian, 16(10)*, 91-97.

Kolata, G. (1987a). Associations or rules in learning language? *Science, 237*, 113-114.

Kolata, G. (1987b). Early signs of school age IQ. *Science, 236*, 774-775.

Koob, G.F. (1984). Neuroleptics: Breaking the dopamine circle. *Contemporary Psychology, 29*, 733-734.

Kosslyn, S.M. (1980). *Image and mind*. Cambridge, MA: Harvard University Press.

Kosslyn, S.M. (1983). *Ghosts in the mind's machine: Creating and using images in the brain*. New York: Norton.

Kosslyn, S.M. (1985). Stalking the mental image. *Psychology Today, 19(5)*, 23-28.

Kosten, T.R., *et al.* (1986). Abuse of cocaine with opioids: Psychological aspects of treatment. *National Institute on Drug Abuse: Research Monograph Series, Mono 67*, 278-282.

Kotlarski, K. (1985). Psychological practice and ethical dilemmas. *Przeglad Psychologiczny, 28*, 495-505.

Kozel, N.J., & Adams, E.H. (1986). Epidemiology of drug abuse: An overview. *Science, 234*, 970-974.

Kraemer, G.W. (1985). The primate social environment, brain neurochemical changes and psychopathology. *Trends in Neurosciences, 8(8)*, 339-340.

Krantz, D.S. (1986). An overview of the stress field. *Contemporary Psychology, 31*, 493-494.

Krasnegor, N.A., Arasteh, J.D., & Cataldo, M.F. (Eds.). (1986). *Child health behavior: A behavioral pediatrics perspective*. New York: Wiley.

Krausz, R.R. (1986). Power and leadership in organizations. *Transactional Analysis Journal, 16(2)*, 85-94.

Krieger, D.T. (1983). Brain peptides: What, where, and why? *Science, 222*, 975-985.

Kuhl, P.K., & Meltzoff, A.N. (1984). The intermodal representation of speech in infants. *Infant Behavior and Development, 7(3)*, 361-381.

Kurtines, W., & Grief, E.B. (1974). The development of moral thought: Review and evaluation of Kohlberg's approach. *Psychological Bulletin, 81*, 453-470.

Kutchins, H., & Kirk, S.A. (1986). The reliability of DSM-III: A critical review. *Social Work Research and Abstracts, 22(4)*, 3-12.

Kutner, B.C., Wilkins, C., & Yarrow, P.R. (1952). Verbal attitudes and overt behavior involving racial prejudice. *Journal of Abnormal and Social Psychology, 47*, 649-652.

Labich, K. (1986). The hunt is on for an antifat pill. *Fortune, 114(4)*, 37-42.

Lamb, M.E. (1981). The role of the father: An overview. In M. Lamb (Ed.), *The role of the father in child development*, 2nd ed. New York: Wiley.

Lamb, M.E. (1982). Second thoughts on first touch. *Psychology Today, 16(4)*, 9-11.

Lamb, M.E., & Brown, A.L. (Eds.). (1982). *Advances in developmental psychology*. Hillsdale, NJ: Erlbaum.

Landau, B., Gleitman, H., & Spelke, E. (1981). Spatial knowledge and geometric representation in a child blind from birth. *Science, 213*, 1275-1278.

Langevin, R. (1983). *Sexual strands: Understanding and treating sexual anomalies in men*. Hillsdale, NJ: Erlbaum.

Langfeld, H.S. (1914). Note on a case of chromaesthesia. *Psychological Bulletin, 11*, 113-114.

Langlois, J.H., *et al.* (1987). Infant preferences for attractive faces: Rudiments of a stereotype? *Developmental Psychology, 23*, 363-369.

Lansen, J. (1986). Group therapy with anorexia nervosa patients. *International Journal of Group Psychotherapy, 36*, 321-322.

Lanyon, R.I., & Goodstein, L.D. (1982). *Personality assessment*, 2nd ed. New York: Wiley.

LaPiere, R.T. (1934). Attitudes versus actions. *Social Forces, 13*, 230-237.

Larson, J., & Lynch, G. (1986). Induction of synaptic potentiation in hippocampus by patterned stimulation involves two events. *Science, 232*, 985-988.

Latané, B. (1981). The psychology of social impact. *American Psychologist, 36*, 343-355.

Latané, B., & Darley, J.M. (1975). *Help in a crisis: Bystander response to an emergency*. Morristown, NJ: General Learning Press.

Lau, R.R., & Russell, D. (1980). Attributions in the sports pages. *Journal of Personality and Social Psychology, 39(1)*, 29-38.

Lawe, C.F., & Smith, E.W. (1986). Gestalt processes and family therapy. *Individual Psychology, 42*, 537-544.

Lawren, B. (1986). Dreamless sleep. *OMNI, 8(6)*, 34.

Lazarus, A.A. (1976). *Multi-modal behavior therapy*. New York: Springer.

Lazarus, R.S. (1982). Thoughts on the relations between emotion and cognition. *American Psychologist, 37*, 1019-1024.

Lazarus, R.S. (1984). On the primacy of cognition. *American Psychologist, 39*, 123-129.

Lazarus, R.S., & Folkman, S. (1984). *Stress, appraisal, and coping*. New York: Springer Publishing.

Lazarus, R.S., & McCleary, R.A. (1951). Autonomic discriminations without awareness: A study of subception. *Psychological Review, 58*, 113-122.

Leak, G.K., & Christopher, S.B. (1982). Freudian psychoanalysis and sociobiology: A synthesis. *American Psychologist, 37(3)*, 313-322.

Lebow, M.D. (1981). *Weight control: The behavioural strategies*. Chichester, Eng.: Wiley.

Leehey, K., Yates, A., & Shisslak, C.M. (1984). Alteration of case reports in "Running—an analogue of anorexia?" *New England Journal of Medicine, 310*, 600.

Leff, W.F. (1981). Beautiful people. *OMNI, 4(2)*, 26.

Lehrman, D.S. (1956). On the organization of maternal behavior and the problem of instinct. In *L'instinct dans le comportement des animaux et de l'homme*. Paris: Masson et Cie.

Leippe, M.R., & Elkin, R.A. (1987). When motives clash: Issue involvement and response involvement as determinants of persuasion. *Journal of Personality and Social Psychology, 52*, 269-278.

LeMagnen, J. (1986). *Hunger*. Cambridge, Eng.: Cambridge University Press.

Lerner, R.M., & Spanier, G.B. (Eds.). (1978). *Child influences on marital and family interaction: A life-span perspective*. New York: Academic Press.

Levin, G. (1987). Is medicine a facet of psychology? *Contemporary Psychology, 32*, 845-847.

Levin, I. (Ed.). (1986). *Stage and structure: Reopening the debate*. Norwood, NJ: Ablex.

Levine, M.W., & Shefner, J.M. (1981). *Fundamentals of sensation and perception*. Reading, MA: Addison-Wesley.

Levy, J. (1983). Functional hemispheric asymmetry and psychopathology: Commentary. *Integrative Psychiatry, 1*, 52-53.

Levy, J., & Levy, J.M. (1978). Human lateralization from head to foot: Sex-related factors. *Science, 200*, 1291-1292.

Levy, L.H. (1984). The metamorphosis of clinical psychology: Toward a new charter as human services psychology. *American Psychologist, 39*, 486-494.

Lewis, C.D., & Houtz, J.C. (1986). Sex-role stereotyping and young children's divergent thinking. *Psychological Reports, 59*, 1027-1033.

Lewis, R.V. (1983). Scared straight—California style: Evaluation of the San Quentin Squires Program. *Criminal Justice and Behavior, 10*, 209-226.

Lewy, A.J., Sack, R.L., Miller, L.S., & Hoban, T.M. (1987). Antidepressant and circadian phase-shifting effects of light. *Science, 235,* 352-354.

Liberakis, E.A. (1981). Factors predisposing to institutionalism. *Acta Psychiatrica Scandinavica, 63,* 356-366.

Lieberman, H.R., *et al.* (1985). Possible behavioral consequences of light-induced changes in melatonin availability. *Annals of the New York Academy of Sciences, 453,* 242-252.

Liebert, R.M., & Wicks-Nelson, R. (1981). *Developmental psychology,* 3rd ed. Englewood Cliffs, NJ: Prentice-Hall.

Lief, H.I. (1984). Can a book fill the gaps in sex? *Contemporary Psychology, 29,* 735-736.

Lindsay, P., & Norman, D. (1977). *Human information processing: An introduction to psychology.* New York: Academic Press.

Lindzey, G., & Aronson, E. (Eds.). (1960). *The handbook of social psychology,* 2nd ed. Reading, MA: Addison-Wesley.

Lipsitt, L.P. (1982). Infancy and life-span development. *Human Development, 25(1),* 41-48.

Lipton, M.I., & Schaffer, W.R. (1986). Post-traumatic stress disorder in the older veteran. *Military Medicine, 151,* 522-524.

Locke, E.A. (Ed.). (1986). *Generalizing from laboratory to field settings: Research findings from industrial-organizational psychology, organizational behavior, and human resource management.* Lexington, MA: Lexington Books/Heath.

Loftus, E.F. (1979). The malleability of human memory. *American Scientist, 67,* 312-320.

Loftus, E.F. (1984). Eyewitness: Essential but unreliable. *Psychology Today, 18(2),* 22-27.

Loftus, E.F., & Loftus, G.R. (1980). On the permanence of stored information in the human brain. *American Psychologist, 35,* 409-420.

Lombardo, J.P. (1986). Interaction of sex and sex role in response to violations of preferred seating arrangements. *Sex Roles, 15(3-4),* 173-183.

London, P., & Engstrom, D. (1982). Mind over pain. *American Health, 1(4),* 62-67.

Long, M.E. (1987). What is this thing called sleep? *National Geographic, 112,* 787-821.

Lorenz, K. (1957). Comparative study of behavior. In C.H. Schiller (Ed.), *Instinctive behavior.* New York: International Press.

Lortie-Lussier, M., Fellers, G.L., & Kleinplatz, P.J. (1986). Value orientations of English, French, and Italian Canadian children: Continuity of the ethnic mosaic? *Journal of Cross-Cultural Psychology, 17,* 283-299.

Luchins, A.S. (1942). Mechanization in problem solving. *Psychological Monographs, 54* (Whole No. 248).

Luchins, A.S., & Luchins, E.H. (1955). On conformity with true and false communications. *Journal of Social Psychology, 42,* 283-304.

Lugaresi, E., *et al.* (1986). [Familial insomnia with a malignant course: A new thalamic disease.] *Review Neurologique, 142,* 791-792.

Luttges, J., Johnson, T., Buck, C., Holland, J., & McGaugh, J.M. (1966). An examination of "transfer of learning" by nucleic acid. *Science, 151,* 834-837.

Lykken, D.T. (1980). *A tremor in the blood.* New York: McGraw-Hill.

Lykken, D.T. (1983). Polygraph prejudice. *APA Monitor, 14(4),* 3.

Lykken, D.T. (1985). "Emergenic traits": Lykken replies. *Psychophysiology, 22(1),* 122-123.

McCandless, B.R., & Trotter, R.J. (1977). *Children: Behavior and development,* 3rd ed. New York: Holt, Rinehart and Winston.

McCarthy, P. (1987). A quicker response. *Psychology Today, 21(10),* 12.

McConnell, J.V. (1961). Experiencing the world. In A.D. Calvin *et al., Psychology.* Boston: Allyn & Bacon.

McConnell, J.V. (1966). Persuasion and behavioral change. In *The art of persuasion in litigation handbook.* West Palm Beach, FL: American Trial Lawyers Association.

McConnell, J.V. (1968). The biochemistry of memory. *Medizinisches Prisma,* No. 3. Ingelheim am Rhein, Germany: Boehringer Sohn.

McConnell, J.V. (1985a). Practicing what we preach. *Behavior Therapist, 8,* 176-177.

McConnell, J.V. (1985b). Psychology of the scientist: LII. John B. Watson: Man and myth. *Psychological Reports, 56,* 683-705.

McConnell, J.V., & Blake, R.R. (1953). A methodological study of tape-recorded synthetic group atmospheres. *American Psychologist, 8,* 395.

McConnell, J.V., Cutler, R.L. & McNeil, E.B. (1958). Subliminal stimulation: An overview. *American Psychologist, 13,* 229-244.

McConnell, J.V., Jacobson, A.L., & Kimble, D.P. (1959). The effects of regeneration upon retention of a conditioned response in the planarian. *Journal of Comparative and Physiological Psychology, 52,* 1-5.

McConnell, J.V., Jacobson, R., & Humphries, B.M. (1961). The effects of ingestion of conditioned planarians on the response level of naive planarians: A pilot study. *Worm Runner's Digest, 3(1),* 41-47.

McConnell, J.V., & Shelby, J. (1970). Memory transfer in invertebrates. In G. Ungar (Ed.), *Molecular mechanisms in memory and learning.* New York: Plenum Press.

McCrady, B.S. (1985). Comments on the controlled drinking controversy. *American Psychologist, 40,* 370-371.

McDermott, W.V. (1980). Endorphins, I presume. *Lancet, 8208,* 1353.

MacFadyen, J.T. (1986). Educated monkeys help the disabled to help themselves. *Smithsonian, 17(10),* 125-132.

McGaugh, J.L. (1973). Drug facilitation of learning and memory. *Annual Review of Pharmacology, 13,* 229-241.

McGinnies, E. (1949). Emotionality and perceptual defense. *Psychological Review, 56,* 244-251.

McGue, M., Bouchard, T.J., Lykken, D.T., & Feuer, D. (1984). Information processing abilities in twins reared apart. *Intelligence, 8,* 239-258.

McGuigan, F.J. (1987). The current status of hypnosis. *Contemporary Psychology, 32,* 177-178.

McKean, K. (1985). Intelligence: New ways to measure the wisdom of man. *Discover, 6(10),* 25-31.

McKellar, P. (1977). Autonomy, imagery, and dissociation. *Journal of Mental Imagery, 1(1),* 93-107.

McKellar, P. (1979). *Mindsplit: The psychology of multiple personality and the dissociated self.* London: Dent.

MacLean, P. (1978). A mind of three minds: Educating the triune brain. In *Education and the brain: 77th Yearbook of the National Society for the Study of Education, Part II.* Chicago: University of Chicago Press.

MacLusky, N.J., & Naftolin, F. (1981). Sexual differentiation of the central nervous system. *Science, 211,* 1294-1302.

McNair, D.M., Kahn, R.J., Frankenthaler, L.M., & Faldetta, L.L. (1984). Amoxapine and amitriptyline: II. Specificity of cognitive effects during brief treatment of depression. *Psychopharmacology, 83(2),* 134-139.

McTear, M. (1985). *Children's conversation.* Oxford, England: Basil Blackwell.

Maddox, B. (1982). *Married and gay.* New York: Harcourt Brace Jovanovich.

Magnusson, D. (Ed.). (1981). *Toward a psychology of situations: An interactional perspective.* Hillsdale, NJ: Erlbaum.

Magoun, H.W. (1963). *The waking brain,* 2nd ed. Springfield, IL: Charles C Thomas.

Magoun, H.W. (1981). John B. Watson and the study of human sexual behavior. *Journal of Sex Research, 17,* 368-378.

Maier, N.R.F. (1931). Reasoning in humans: II. The solution of a problem and its appearance in consciousness. *Journal of Comparative Psychology, 12,* 181-194.

Maier, S.F., Seligman, M.E.P., & Solomon, R.L. (1969). Pavlovian fear conditioning and learned helplessness. In R. Church & B. Campbell (Eds.), *Aversive conditioning and learning*. New York: Appleton-Century-Crofts.

Maier, S.F. *et al.* (1980). Opiate antagonists and long-term analgesic reaction induced by inescapable shock in rats. *Journal of Comparative and Physiological Psychology, 94*, 1172-1183.

Maier, S.F. *et al.* (1983). The opioid/nonopioid nature of stress-induced analgesia and learned helplessness. *Journal of Experimental Psychology: Animal Behavior Processes, 9(1)*, 80-90.

Maltz, S., & Sackeim, H.A. (Eds.). (1986). *Electroconvulsive therapy: Clinical and basic research issues*. New York: New York Academy of Sciences.

Maltzman, I., Vincent, C., & Wolff, C. (1982). Verbal conditioning, task instructions, and inhibition of the GSR measure of the orienting reflex. *Physiological Psychology, 10*, 221-228.

Mangus, B., Henderson, H., & French, R. (1986). Implementation of a token economy by peer tutors to increase on-task physical activity time of autistic children. *Perceptual and Motor Skills, 63(1)*, 97-98.

Marks, L.E. (1975). On colored-hearing synesthesia: Cross-model translations of sensory dimension. *Psychological Bulletin, 83*, 303-331.

Mark, M.M., & Greenberg, J. (1987). Evening the score. *Psychology Today, 21(1)*, 44-50.

Mark, V.H., & Ervin, F.R. (1970). *Violence and the brain*. New York: Harper & Row.

Marlatt, G.A. (1983). The controlled-drinking controversy: A commentary. *American Psychologist, 38*, 1097-1110.

Marlatt, G.A. (1984). Innovative approaches to the treatment of alcoholism. *Contemporary Psychology, 29*, 103-105.

Marlatt, G.A., & Gordon, J.R. (Eds.). (1985). *Relapse prevention: Maintenance strategies in the treatment of addictive behaviors*. New York: Guilford Press.

Marlatt, G.A., & Rohsenow, D.J. (1981). The think-drink effect. *Psychology Today, 15(12)*, 60-69.

Marlow, H.A., Jr., & Weinberg, R.B. (Eds.). (1985). *Comptence development: Theory and practice in special populations*. Springfield, IL: Charles C Thomas.

Marmor, J. (Ed.). (1980). *Homosexual behavior: A modern reappraisal*. New York: Basic Books.

Martin, G.L., & Hrycaiko, D. (1983). *Behavior modification and coaching: Principles, procedures, and research*. Springfield, IL: Charles C Thomas.

Martin, G.L., & Osborne, J.G. (Eds.). (1980). *Helping in the community: Behavioral applications*. New York: Plenum Press.

Marx, J.L. (1982). Autoimmunity in left-handers. *Science, 219*, 141-142.

Marx, J.L. (1987). Antibody research garners Nobel Prize. *Science, 238*, 484-485.

Masling, J., & Cohen, I.S. (1987). Psychotherapy, clinical evidence, and the self-fulfilling prophecy. *Psychoanalytic Psychology, 4(1)*, 65-79.

Maslow, A.H. (1939). Dominance, personality and social behavior in women. *Journal of Social Psychology, 10*, 3-39.

Maslow, A.H. (1942). Self-esteem (dominance-feeling) and sexuality in women. *Journal of Social Psychology, 16*, 259-294.

Maslow, A.H. (1970). *Motivation and personality*, 2nd ed. New York: Viking.

Maslow, A.H. (1971). *The farther reaches of human nature*. New York: Viking.

Masters, W.H., & Johnson, V.E. (1966). *The human sexual response*. Boston: Little, Brown.

Matarrazo, J.D. (1983). The reliability of psychiatric and psychological diagnosis. *Clinical Psychology Review, 3*, 103-145.

Matlin, M. (1983a). *Cognition*. New York: Holt, Rinehart & Winston.

Matlin, M. (1983b). *Perception*. Boston: Allyn & Bacon.

Matsuda, N. (1985). Strong, quasi-, and weak conformity among Japanese in the modified Asch. *Journal of Cross-Cultural Psychology, 16(1)*, 83-97.

Matteson, D.R. (1984). Identity: Is that all there is to adolescence? *Contemporary Psychology, 29*, 140-142.

Mayer, D.J. (1980). In K.Y. Ng & J.J. Bonica (Eds.), *Pain, discomfort and humanitarian care*. Amsterdam: Elsevier/North-Holland.

Mayer, M. (1958). *Madison Avenue, USA*. New York: Harper & Row.

Mays, D.T., & Franks, C.M. (1985). *Negative outcome in psychotherapy and what to do about it*. New York: Springer.

Meadow, K.P. (1980). *Deafness and child development*. Berkeley: University of California Press.

Meer, J. (1985a). Mental alertness and the good old days. *Psychology Today, 19(3)*, 8.

Meer, J. (1985b). Quiet: I'm driving. *Psychology Today, 19(1)*, 20.

Meer, J. (1986). Impotence: Sex on the brain. *Psychology Today, 20(2)*, 18-19.

Mehrabian, A. (1971). *Silent messages*. Belmont, CA: Wadsworth.

Mehrabian, A. (1981). *Silent messages: Implicit communication of emotions and attitudes*, 2nd ed. Belmont, CA: Wadsworth.

Meichenbaum, D.H. (1974). *Cognitive behavior modification*. Morristown, NJ: General Learning Press.

Meichenbaum, D.H. (1985). *Stress inoculation training*. Oxford, England: Pergamon Press.

Meltzoff, A.N. (1981). Imitation, intermodal co-ordination and representation in early infancy. In G. Butterworth (Ed.), *Infancy and epistemology*. Brighton, England: Harvester Press.

Meltzoff, A.N., & Moore, M.K. (1977). Imitation of facial gestures by human neonates. *Science, 198*, 75-78.

Meltzoff, A.N., & Moore, M.K. (1983). The origins of imitation in infancy: Paradigm, phenomena, and theories. *Advances in Infancy Research, 2*, 265-301.

Melzack, R. (Ed.). (1983). *Pain measurement and assessment*. New York: Raven Press.

Melzack, R., & Wall, P.D. (1965). Pain mechanisms: A new theory. *Science, 150*, 971-979.

Mendel, W.M. (1966). Effect of length of hospitalization on rate and quality of remission from acute psychotic episodes. *Journal of Nervous and Mental Disease, 143(3)*, 226-233.

Mendel, W.M. (1969). Tranquilizer prescribing as a function of the experience and availability of the therapist. *American Journal of Psychiatry, 124(1)*, 16-22.

Merrill, M.K., & Kewman, D.G. (1986). Training of color and form identification in cortical blindness: A case study. *Archives of Physical Medicine and Rehabilitation, 67*, 480-483.

Mervis, C.B., & Rosch, E. (1981). Categorization of natural objects. *Annual Review of Psychology, 32*, 89-115.

Meyer, A. (1951). The psychobiological point of view. In E.E. Winters (Ed.), *Collected works of Adolph Meyer*. Baltimore: Johns Hopkins Press.

Meyer, J.S., Novak, M.A., Bowman, R.E., & Harlow, H.F. (1975). Behavioral and hormonal effects of attachment object separation in surrogate-peer-reared and mother-reared infant rhesus monkeys. *Developmental Psychobiology, 8(5)*, 425-435.

Michael, R.P., Bonsall, R.W., & Warner, P. (1974). Human vaginal secretions: Volatile fatty acid content. *Science, 186*, 1217-1219.

Michelson, L. (Ed.). (1985). Meta-analysis and clinical psychology. [Special issue]. *Clinical Psychology Review, 5(1)*.

Michener, H.A., DeLamater, J.D., & Schwartz, S.H. (1986). *Social psychology*. New York: Harcourt Brace Jovanovich.

Mika, S. (1981). Some determinants of source credibility. *Polish Psychological Bulletin, 12(2)*, 79-86.

Mikulas, W.L. (1986). Self-control: Essence and development. *Psychological Record, 36*, 297-308.

Milgram, S. (1974). *Obedience to authority*. New York: Harper & Row.

Millar, S. (1968). *The psychology of play*. Baltimore: Penguin Books.

Miller, A.G. (Ed.). (1982). *In the eye of the beholder: Contemporary issues in stereotyping*. New York: Praeger.

Miller, A.R. (1986). The physical attractiveness of physiques in determining certainty of guilt, recommended punishment, and rehabilitative potential of defendants. *Dissertation Abstracts International, 47(5-B)*.

Miller, J.A. (1986). X chromosomes: Too few and too many. *Science News, 129*, 358.

Miller, J.G. (1978). *Living Systems*. New York: McGraw-Hill.

Miller, W.R., & Hester, R.K. (1980). Treating the problem drinker: Modern approaches. In W.R. Miller (Ed.), *The addictive behaviors: Treatment of alcoholism, drug abuse, smoking and obesity*. Oxford, England: Pergamon Press.

Miller, W.R., & Hester, R.K. (1986). The effectiveness of treatment techniques: What the research reveals. In W.R. Miller & N. Heather (Eds.), *Treating addictive behaviors: Processes of change*. New York: Plenum Press.

Mills, C., & Walter, T. (1979). Reducing juvenile delinquency: A behavioral employment intervention program. In J.S. Stumphauzer (Ed.), *Progress in behavior therapy with delinquents*. Springfield, IL: Charles C Thomas.

Mirsky, A.F. (1986). The Israeli high-risk study. *Schizophrenia Bulletin, 12*, 158-161.

Mirsky, A.F., & Duncan, C.C. (1986). Etiology and expression of schizophrenia: Neurobiological and psychosocial factors. *Annual Review of Psychology, 37*, 291-319.

Mischel, W. (1968). *Personality and assessment*. New York: Wiley.

Mischel, W. (1973). *Introduction to personality*, 2nd ed. New York: Holt, Rinehart and Winston.

Misle, B. (1988). Charting changing patterns of drug abuse. *Ann Arbor News*, January 13, B1-B2.

Monte, C.F. (1987). *Beneath the mask: An introduction to theories of personality*, 3rd ed. New York: Holt, Rinehart and Winston.

Montplaisir, J., & Poirier, G. (1987). Narcolepsy in monozygotic twins. *Neurology, 37*, 1089.

Mooney, D.K., Fromme, K., Kivlahan, D.R., & Marlatt, G.A. (1987). Correlates of alcohol consumption: Sex, age, and expectancies relate differentially to quantity and frequency. *Addictive Behavior, 12*, 234-240.

Moore, B.C.J. (1982). *An introduction to the psychology of hearing*, 2nd ed. London: Academic Press.

Moore-Ede, M.C. (1982). What hath night to do with sleep? *Natural History, 91(9)*, 22-24.

Moore-Ede, M.C., Sulzman, F.M., & Fuller, C.A. (1982). *The clocks that time us: Physiology of the circadian timing system*. Cambridge, MA: Harvard University Press.

Moray, N. (1959). Attention in dichotic listening: Affective cues and the influence of instructions. *Quarterly Journal of Experimental Psychology, 11*, 56-60.

Moreno, J.L. (1946). *Psychodrama*. New York: Beacon House.

Moreno, J.L. (1947). *The theater of spontaneity: An introduction to psychodrama*. New York: Beacon House.

Morris, A.J. (1979). *The ape's reflexion*. New York: Dial Press/James Wade.

Morris, N.M., & Udry, J.R. (1978). Pheromonal inferences on human sexual behavior: An experimental search. *Journal of Biosocial Science, 10*, 147-157.

Morrison, A. (1983). A window on the sleeping brain. *Scientific American, 248(4)*, 94-102.

Morrison, F.J., Lord, C., & Keating, D.P. (Eds.). (1985). *Applied developmental psychology*, Vol. 2. Orlando, FL: Academic Press.

Morrow-Bradley, C., & Elliott, R. (1986). Utilization of psychotherapy research by practicing psychotherapists. *American Psychologist, 41*, 188-205.

Mortimer, J.A., & Schuman, L.M. (Eds.). (1981). *The epidemiology of dementia: Monographs in epidemiology and biostatistics*. New York: Oxford University Press.

Mosak, H.H., & Kopp, R.R. (1973). The early recollections of Adler, Freud, and Jung. *Journal of Individual Psychology, 29*, 157-166.

Moscovici, S., Mugny, G., & Papastamou, S. (1981). Sleeper effect and/or minority effect? *Cahiers de Psychologice Cognitive, 1(2)*, 199-221.

Mosher, F.A., & Hornsby, J.R. (1966). On asking questions. In J.S. Bruner, R.R. Oliver, & P.M. Greenfield (Eds.), *Studies in cognitive growth*. New York: Wiley.

Murdock, B.B., Jr. (1961). The retention of individual items. *Journal of Experimental Psychology, 62*, 618-625.

Murray, J., & Abramson, P.R. (Eds.). (1983). *Bias in psychotherapy*. New York: Praeger.

Mussen, P.H. (Ed.). (1983). *Handbook of child psychology*, Vols. 1-4. New York: Wiley.

Mussen, P.H., Conger, J.J., & Kagan, J. (Eds.). (1980). *Readings in child and adolescent psychology: Contemporary perspectives*. New York: Harper & Row.

Mussen, P.H., & Kagan, J. (1958). Group conformity and perceptions of parents. *Child Development, 29*, 57-60.

Myers, R.D., & McCaleb, M.L. (1980). Feeding: Satiety signal from intestine triggers brain's noradrenergic mechanism. *Science, 209*, 1035-1037.

Myers, R.E., & Sperry, R.W. (1958). Interhemispheric communication through the corpus callosum. *Archives of Neurological Psychiatry, 80*, 298-303.

Myrtek, M. (1984). *Constitutional psychophysiology: Research in review*. Orlando, FL: Academic Press.

Naftolin, F. (1981). Understanding the bases of sex differences. *Science, 211*, 1263-1264.

Nagler, S., & Mirsky, A.F. (1985). Introduction: The Israeli high-risk study. *Schizophrenia Bulletin, 11(1)*, 19-29.

Nassi, A.J. (1981). Survivors of the sixties: Comparative psychosocial and political development of former Berkeley student activists. *American Psychologist, 36*, 753-761.

Nathans, J., Piantanida, T.P., Eddy, R.L., Shows, T.B., & Hogness, D.S. (1986). Molecular genetics of inherited variation in human color vision. *Science, 232*, 203-210.

Nathans, J., Thomas, D., & Hogness, D.S. (1986). Molecular genetics of human color vision: The genes encoding blue, green, and red pigments. *Science, 232*, 193-202.

Neisser, U. (1967). *Cognitive psychology*. New York: Appleton-Century-Crofts.

Neisser, U., & Becklen, R. (1975). Selective looking: Attending to visually significant events. *Cognitive Psychology, 7*, 480-494.

Nelson, K., *et al.* (1986). *Event knowledge: Structure and function in development*. Hillsdale, NJ: Erlbaum.

Newcomb, T.M. (1943). *Personality and social change: Attitude formation in a student community*. New York: Dryden Press.

Newcomb, T.M. (1961). *The acquaintance process*. New York: Holt, Rinehart and Winston.

Newcomb, T.M. (1967). *Persistence and change: Bennington College and its students after 25 years*. New York: Wiley.

Newcomb, T.M. (1981). Heiderian balance as a group phenomenon. *Journal of Personality and Social Psychology, 40*, 862-867.

Newcomb, T.M., Turner, R.H., & Converse, P.E. (1964). *Social psychology*. New York: Holt, Rinehart and Winston.

Niemark, J. (1986). Her nose knows best. *American Health, 5(5)*, 36-40.

Ninio, A., & Bruner, J. (1978). The achievement and antecedents of labelling. *Journal of Child Language, 5*, 1-15.

Nisan, M., & Kohlberg, L. (1982). Universality and variation in moral judgment: A longitudinal and cross-sectional study in Turkey. *Child Development, 53*, 865-876.

Norman, D.A., & Bobrow, D.G. (1975). On data-limited and resource-limited processes. *Cognitive Psychology, 7*, 44-64.

Norman, W.T. (1961). Development of self-report tests to

measure personality factors identified from peer nominations. *USAF ASK Technical Note*, No. 61-44.

Norman, W.T. (1963). Toward an adequate taxonomy of personality attributes: Replicated factor structure in peer nomination personality ratings. *Journal of Abnormal and Social Psychology, 66*, 574-583.

Nykodym, N., Ruud, W.N., & Liverpool, P.R. (1986). Quality circles: Will transctional analysis improve their effectiveness? *Transactional Analysis Journal, 16(3)*, 182-187.

O'Connor, W.A., & Lubin, B. (Eds.). (1984). *Ecological approaches to clinical and community psychology*. New York: Wiley.

Olds, J., & Milner, P. (1954). Positive reinforcement produced by electrical stimulation of septal area and other regions of rat brain. *Journal of Comparative and Physiological Psychology, 47*, 419-427.

Oller, D.K., Eilers, R.E., Bull, D.H., & Carney, A.E. (1985). Prespeech vocalizations of a deaf infant: A comparison with normal metaphonological development. *Journal of Speech and Hearing Research, 28(1)*, 47-63.

Olney, R.L., & Scholnick, E.K. (1976). Adult judgments of age and linguistic differences in infant vocalization. *Journal of Child Language, 3(2)*, 145-155.

Olson, J.M. (1984). Psychological versus sociological social psychology. *Contemporary Psychology, 29*, 314-316.

Olton, D.S., & Noonberg, A.R. (1980). *Biofeedback: Clinical applications in behavioral medicine*. Englewood Cliffs, NJ: Prentice-Hall.

O'Neill, P., & Trickett, E.J. (1982). *Community consultation*. San Francisco: Jossey-Bass.

Overmier, J.B. (1986). Reassessing learned helplessness. *Social Science, 71(1)*, 27-31.

Page, J. (1984). Rural stress. *Science 84, 5(2)*, 104-105.

Paris, S.G., Saarnio, D.A., & Cross, D.R. (1986). A metacognitive curriculum to promote children's reading and learning. *Australian Journal of Psychology, 38(2)*, 107-123.

Parisi, T. (1987). Why Freud failed: Some implications for neurophysiology and sociobiology. *American Psychologist, 42*, 235-245.

Parker, T., Hill, J.W., & Miller, G. (1987). Multiple family therapy: Evaluating a group experience for mentally retarded adolescents and their families. *Family Therapy, 14*, 43-51.

Parsons, H.McI. (1982). More on the Hawthorne effect. *American Psychologist, 37*, 856-857.

Patterson, M.L. (1983). *Nonverbal behavior: A functional perspective*. New York: Springer-Verlag.

Patterson, M.L., *et al.* (1984). A content-classified bibliography of research on the immediacy behaviors: 1965-1982. *Journal of Nonverbal Behavior, 8*, 360-393.

Patterson, R.E. (1986). Perceptual interaction of global stereoscopic and physical contours. *Dissertation Abstracts International, 46(8-B)*, 2847.

Pauk, J., Kuhn, C., Field, T.M., & Schanberg, S.M. (1986). Positive effects of tactile versus kinesthetic or vestibular stimulation on neuroendocrine and ODC activity in maternally-deprived rat pups. *Life Sciences, 39*, 2081-2087.

Paul, G.L., & Lentz, R.J. (1978). *Psychosocial treatment of chronic mental patients: Milieu versus social-learning programs*. Cambridge, MA: Harvard University Press.

Pavlov, I. (1927). *Conditioned reflexes*. Oxford, England: Clarendon Press.

Pellegrini, A.D. (1987). Rough-and-tumble play: Developmental and educational significance. *Educational Psychologist, 22(1)*, 22-43.

Pendery, M., Maltzman, I., & West, L.J. (1982). Controlled drinking by alcoholics? New findings and a reevaluation of a major affirmative study. *Science, 217*, 169-174.

Perlmutter, R.A., & Jones, J.E. (1985). Problem solving with families in psychiatric emergencies. *Psychiatric Quarterly, 57(1)*, 23-32.

Perls, F., Hefferline, R., & Goodman, P. (1951). *Gestalt Therapy*. New York: Julian Press.

Peterson, L.R. (1966). Short-term memory. *Scientific American, 215*, 90-95.

Petri, H.L. (1986). *Motivation: Theory and Research*, 2nd ed. Belmont, CA: Wadsworth.

Petty, R.E., & Cacioppo, J.T. (1986). *Communication and persuasion: Central and peripheral routes to attitude change*. New York: Springer-Verlag.

Petty, R.E., Ostrom, T.M., & Brock, T.C. (Eds.). (1981). *Cognitive responses in persuasion*. Hillsdale, NJ: Erlbaum.

Pfaff, D.W. (Ed.). (1982). *The physiological mechanisms of motivation*. New York: Springer-Verlag.

Pfeiffer, J. (1987). Six months and half a million dollars, all for 15 seconds. *Smithsonian, 18(7)*, 134-145.

Piaget, J. (1965). *The moral judgment of the child*. New York: Free Press.

Piaget, J. (1976). *The child and reality*. Baltimore: Penguin.

Piaget, J. (1977a). *Epistemology and psychology of functions*. Boston, MA: D. Reidel.

Piaget, J. (1977b). *The development of thought: Equilibration of cognitive structures*. New York: Viking.

Piaget, J. (1978). *Success and understanding*. Cambridge, MA: Harvard University Press.

Piaget, J. (1980a). My position. In M. Piattelli-Palmarini (Ed.), *Language and learning: The debate between Jean Piaget and Noam Chomsky*. Cambridge, MA: Harvard University Press.

Piaget, J. (1980b). *Adaptation and intelligence: Organic selection and phenocopy*. Chicago: University of Chicago Press.

Piaget, J. (1981). Intelligence and affectivity: Their relationships during child development. *Annual Reviews, 14*.

Piaget, J. (1986). Essay on necessity. *Human Development, 29*, 301-314.

Pickles, J.O. (1982). *An introduction to the physiology of hearing*. London: Academic Press.

Pilon, A.F. (1986). Education, man and his horizons. *Man Environment Systems, 16(1)*, 17-24.

Pines, M. (1982). Infant-stim. *Psychology Today, 16(6)*, 48-53.

Pinker, S. (1984). *Language learnability and language development*. Cambridge, MA: MIT Press.

Pinker, S., & Prince, A. (1987). On language and connectionism: Analysis of a parallel distributed processing model of language acquisition. *Occasional paper #33*. Cambridge, MA: MIT Press.

Piotrowski, C. (1984). The status of projective techniques: Or, "Wishing won't make it go away." *Journal of Clinical Psychology, 40*, 1495-1502.

Piotrowski, C., & Keller, J.W. (1984a). Psychological testing: Trends in masters-level counseling psychology programs. *Teaching of Psychology, 11(4)*, 244-245.

Piotrowski, C., & Keller, J.W. (1984b). Attitudes toward clinical assessment by members of the AABT. *Psychological Reports, 55*, 831-838.

Piotrowski, C., Sherry, D., & Keller, J.W. (1985). Psychodiagnostic test usage: A survey of the Society for Personality Assessment. *Journal of Personality Assessment, 49*, 115-119.

Platt, J.J. (1986). *Heroin addiction: Theory, research, and treatment*, 2nd ed. Malabar, FL: Krieger.

Pleck, J.H., Lamb, M.E., & Levine, J.A. (1985-1986). Epilog: Facilitating future change in men's family roles. *Marriage and Family Review, 9(3-4)*, 11-16.

Plomin, R., Defires, J.C., & McClearn, G.E. (1980). *Behavioral genetics*. New York: W.H. Freeman.

Plutchik, R. (1980). *Emotion: A psychoevolutionary synthesis*. New York: Harper & Row.

Plutchik, R., & Kellerman, H. (Eds.). (1980). *Emotion: Theory, research, and experience. Theories of Emotion, Vol. 1*. New York: Academic Press.

Polivy, J., & Herman, C.P. (1985). Dieting and binging: A causal analysis. *American Psychologist, 40*, 193-201.

Pomeroy, W.B., Flax, C.C., & Wheeler, C.C. (1982). *Taking a sex history: Interviewing and recording*. New York: Free Press.

Poon, L.W., Fozard, J.L., Cermak, L.S., Arenberg, D., & Thompson, L.W. (Eds.). (1980). *New directions in* memory and aging: Proceedings of the George A. Talland Memorial Conference. Hillsdale, NJ: Erlbaum.

Pope, H.G., Jr., & Hudson, J.I. (1984). *New hope for binge eaters: Advances in the understanding and treatment of bulimia*. New York: Harper & Row.

Pope, H.G., Jr., *et al.* (1986). Frequency and presentation of neuroleptic malignant syndrome in a large psychiatric hospital. *American Journal of Psychiatry, 143*, 1227-1233.

Porter, R.H., *et al.* (1985). Odor signatures and kin recognition. *Physiology and Behavior, 34*, 445-448.

Postman, L., Bruner, J.S., & McGinnies, E. (1948). Personal values as selective factors in perception. *Journal of Abnormal and Social Psychology, 43*, 142-154.

Power, T.G., & Chapieski, M.L. (1986). Childrearing and impulse control in toddlers: A naturalistic investigation. *Developmental Psychology, 22*, 271-275.

Premack, D. (1986). *Gavagai! Or the future history of the animal language controversy*. Cambridge, MA: MIT Press.

Presti, D.E. (1987). What goes around comes around . . . *Contemporary Psychology, 32*, 556-557.

Pruitt, D.G., & Rubin, J.Z. (1986). *Social conflict: Escalation, stalemate, and settlement*. New York: Random House.

Ragland, D.R., & Brand, R.J. (1988). Type A behavior and mortality from coronary heart disease. *New England Journal of Medicine, 318(2)*, 65-69.

Rak, D.S., & McMullen, L.M. (1987). Sex-role stereotyping in television commercials: A verbal response mode and content analysis. *Canadian Journal of Behavioural Science, 19(1)*, 25-39.

Raloff, J. (1983). Ear implant conveys robot-like speech. *Science News, 123*, 151.

Ramachandran, V.S., & Anstis, S.M. (1986). The perception of apparent motion. *Scientific American, 254(6)*, 102-109.

Rand Corporation. (1980). *The course of alcoholism: Four years after treatment*. Santa Monica, CA: Rand Corporation.

Raou, Y.Y. (1984). Dynamics of some characteristics of stutterer's personality in the process of psychotherapy. *Voprosy Psikhologii, 3*, 67-72.

Ratner, H.H., *et al.* (1987). Changes in adults' prose recall: Aging or cognitive demands? *Developmental Psychology, 23*, 521-525.

Ratner, N., & Bruner, J. (1978). Games, social exchange and the acquisition of language. *Journal of Child Language, 5*, 391-401.

Raven, B.H. (1987). The chronic complexity of compliance in health care. *Contemporary Psychology, 32*, 938-939.

Raven, B.H., & Rubin, J.Z. (1983). *Social psychology*, 2nd ed. New York: Wiley.

Ray, O. (1983). *Drugs, society, and human behavior*. St. Louis, MO: Mosby.

Ray, W.A., *et al.* (1987a). Psychotropic drug use and the risk of hip fracture. *New England Journal of Medicine, 316*, 363-369.

Ray, W.A., *et al.* (1987b). Reducing antipsychotic drug prescribing for nursing home patients: A controlled trial of the effect of an educational visit. *American Journal of Public Health, 77*, 1448-1450.

Ray, W.J., & Cole, H.W. (1985). EEG alpha activity reflects attentional demands, and beta activity reflects emotional and cognitive processes. *Science, 228*, 750-752.

Razel, M. (1985). In I.E. Sigel (Ed.), *Advances in applied developmental psychology*, Vol. 1. Norwood, NJ: Ablex.

Redman, J., Armstrong, S., & Ng, K.T. (1983). Free-running activity rhythms in the rat: Entrainment by melatonin. *Science, 219*, 1089-1091.

Reich, J. (1987). Sex distribution of DSM-III personality disorders in psychiatric outpatients. *American Journal of Psychiatry, 144*, 485-488.

Reigle, T.G. (1985). Increased brain norepinephrine metabolism correlated with analgesia produced by the periaqueductal gray injection of opiates. *Brain Research, 338*, 155-159.

Relman, A.S., *et al..* (1982). *Marijuana and Health*. Washington, DC: National Academy Press.

Remer, R. (1986). Use of psychodramatic intervention with families: Change on multiple levels. *Journal of Group Psychotherapy, Psychodrama and Sociometry, 3(1)*, 13-29.

Reppert, S.M. (1985). Maternal entrainment of the developing circadian system. *Annals of the New York Academy of Sciences, 453*, 162-169.

Rescorla, R.A. (1984). Associations between Pavlovian CSs and context. *Journal of Experimental Psychology: Animal Behavior Processes, 10*, 195-204.

Rescorla, R.A. (1987). A Pavlovian analysis of goal-directed behavior. *American Psychologist, 42*, 119-129.

Retterstol, N. (1986). Classification of functional psychoses with special reference to follow-up studies. *Psychopathology, 19(1-2)*, 5-15.

Reynolds, D.K., & Farberow, N.L. (1981). *The family shadow: Sources of suicide and schizophrenia*. Berkeley, CA: University of California Press.

Richards, M., & Light, P. (Eds.). (1986). *Development in a social context*. Cambridge, MA: Harvard University Press.

Richardson, A.G. (1986). Two factors of creativity. *Perceptual and Motor Skills, 63*, 379-384.

Riecken, H.W. (1952). *The volunteer work camp: A psychological evaluation*. Cambridge, MA: Addison-Wesley.

Roberts, A.H. (1985). Biofeedback: Research, training, and clinical roles. *American Psychologist, 40*, 938-941.

Robinson, B.E., & Barret, R.L. (1986). *The developing father: Emerging roles in contemporary society*. New York: Guilford Press.

Robinson, D.N. (1986, Fall). The tradition of William James. *APA Division 1 Newsletter, 47*, 5-15.

Rock, I. (1975). *An introduction to perception*. New York: Macmillan.

Rodgers, J.E. (1982). The malleable memory of eyewitnesses. *Science 82, 3(5)*, 32-35.

Rodgers, W.L., & Herzog, A.R. (1987). Interviewing older adults: The accuracy of factural information. *Journal of Gerontology, 42*, 387-394.

Rodin, J. (1984). Taming the hunger hormone. *American Health, 3(1)*, 43-47.

Rodin, J. (1986). Aging and health: Effects of the sense of control. *Science, 233*, 1271-1275.

Rogers, C.R. (1942). *Counseling and psychotherapy*. Boston: Houghton Mifflin.

Rogers, C.R. (1951). *Client-centered therapy*. Boston: Houghton Mifflin.

Rogers, C.R. (1959). A theory of therapy, personality and interpersonal relationships as developed in the client-centered framework. In S. Hoch (Ed.), *Psychology: A study of a science*, vol. 3. New York: McGraw-Hill.

Rogers, C.R. (1961). *On becoming a person*. Boston: Houghton Mifflin.

Rogers, C.R. (1962). A tentative scale for the measurement of process in psychotherapy. In E.A. Rubenstein & M.B. Parloff (Eds.), *Research in psychotherapy*, vol. 1. Washington, DC: American Psychological Association.

Rogers, C.R. (1964). The concept of the fully functioning person. *Psychotherapy: Theory, research and practice, 1(1)*, 17-26.

Rogers, C.R. (1967). Autobiography. In E.G. Boring & G. Lindzey (Eds.), *A history of psychology in autobiography*, vol. 5. New York: Appleton.

Rogers, C.R. (1983). *Freedom to learn for the 80's*. Columbus, OH: Merrill.

Rogozea, R., Florea-Ciocoiu, V., & Constantinovici, A. (1983). Retention of orienting reaction habituation in patients with epileptogenic cerebral tumors. *Neurologie et Psychiatrie, 21(1)*, 21-31.

Root, M.P.P., Fallon, P., & Friedrich, W.N. (1986). *Bulimia: A systems approach to treatment*. New York: W.W. Norton.

Rosch, E.H. (1973). Natural categories. *Cognitive Psychology, 4*, 328-350.

Rosch, E.H. (1977). Human categorization. In N. Warren (Ed.), *Advances in cross-cultural psychology*, Vol. 1. London: Academic Press.

Rosch, E.H. (1978). Principles of categorization. In E. Rosch & B. Lloyd (Eds.), *Cognition and categorization*. Hillsdale, NJ: Erlbaum.

Rosch, E.H., Mervis, C.B., Gray, W.D., Johnson, D.M., & Boyes-Braem, P. (1976). Basic objects in natural categories. *Cognitive Psychology, 7*, 573-605.

Rose, S.P. (1984). Disordered molecules and diseased minds: Biological markers in mental disorders. *Journal of Psychiatric Research, 18*, 351-360.

Rosen, C.M. (1987). The eerie world of reunited twins. *Discover, 8(9)*, 36-46.

Rosenblatt, J.S. (1983). Olfaction mediates developmental transition in the altricial newborn of selected species of mammals. *Developmental Psychobiology, 16(5)*, 347-374.

Rosenblatt, P.C., & Budd, L.G. (1975). Territoriality and privacy in married and unmarried cohabiting couples. *Journal of Social Psychology, 97(1)*, 67-76.

Rosenfeld, A.H. (1987). Fat, schmat, so long as you feel OK. *Psychology Today, 21(7)*, 18.

Rosenhan, D.L. (1973). On being sane in insane places. *Science, 179*, 250-258.

Rosenhan, D.L. (1975). The contextual nature of psychiatric diagnosis. *Journal of Abnormal Psychology, 84*, 462-474.

Rosenheimer, J.L. (1985). Effects of chronic stress and exercise on age-related changes in end-plate architecture. *Journal of Neurophysiology, 53*, 1582-1589.

Rosenthal, J., Massie, H., & Wulff, K. (1980). A comparison of cognitive development in normal and psychotic children in the first two years of life from home movies. *Journal of Autism and Developmental Disorders, 10(4)*, 433-444.

Rosenthal, R.R. (1965). *Clever Hans*. New York: Holt, Rinehart and Winston.

Rosenzweig, M.R. (1984). Experience, memory, and the brain. *American Psychologist, 39*, 365-376.

Ross, A.O. (1987). *Personality: The scientific study of complex human behavior*. New York: Holt, Rinehart and Winston.

Ross, E.D., & Mesulam, M-M. (1979). Dominant language functions of the right hemisphere? *Archives of Neurology, 36*, 144-148.

Ross, H.S., & Lollis, S.P. (1987). Communication within infant social games. *Developmental Psychology, 23*, 241-248.

Ross, R.T. (1985). *Lives of the mentally retarded: A fourty year follow-up study*. Stanford, CA: Stanford University Press.

Ross, S., & Buckalew, L.W. (1985). Placebo agentry: Assessment of drug and placebo effects. In L. White, B. Tursky, & G.E. Schwartz (Eds.), *Placebo: Theory, research, and mechanisms*. New York: Guilford Press.

Rossi, A.S. (Ed.). (1985). *Gender and the life course*. New York: Aldine.

Roth, S., & Cohen, L.J. (1986). Approach, avoidance, and coping with stress. *American Psychologist, 41*, 813-819.

Rothbart, M., & John, O.P. (1985). Social categorization and behavioral episodes: A cognitive analysis of the effects of intergroup contact. *Journal of Social Issues, 41(3)*, 81-104.

Rothbart, M., & Park, B. (1986). On the confirmability and disconfirmability of trait concepts. *Journal of Personality and Social Psychology, 50*, 131-142.

Rothman, D.J. (1971). *The discovery of asylums: Social order and disorder in the new republic*. Boston: Little, Brown.

Rotter, J. (1971). External control and internal control. *Psychology Today, 5(1)*, 37-42.

Rouan, G., & Thaon, M. (1985). Rites of consensus in cultural life. *Connexions, No. 45*, 233-242.

Rounsaville, B.J., Spitzer, R.L., & Williams, N.B. (1986). Proposed changes in DSM-III substance use disorders: Description and rationale. *American Journal of Psychiatry, 143*, 463-468.

Rowand, A. (1984). Hormone peaks level off with age. *Science News, 125*, 410.

Rowe, J.W., & Kahn, R.L. (1987). Human aging: Usual and successful. *Science, 237*, 143-149.

Roy, A. (Ed.). (1986). *Suicide*. Baltimore: Williams and Wilkins.

Rubin, J.Z. (1981). Psychological traps. *Psychology Today, 15(3)*, 52-63.

Rubin, J.Z., Provenzano, F.J., & Luria, Z. (1974). The eye of the beholder: Parents' views on sex of newborns. *American Journal of Orthopsychiatry, 43*, 720-731.

Rubin, R.T., Reinisch, J.M., & Haskett, R.F. (1981). Postnatal gonadal steroid effects on human behavior. *Science, 211*, 1318-1324.

Ruesch, J., & Bateson, G. (1987). *Communication: The social matrix of psychiatry*. New York: W.W. Norton.

Rumelhart, D.E., & McClelland, J.L. (1986). *Parallel distributed processing: Explorations in the microstructure of cognition*. Cambridge, MA: MIT Press.

Rumelhart, D.E., & McClelland, J.L. (1987). Learning the past tenses of English verbs: Implicit rules or parallel distributed processing? In B. MacWhinney (Ed.), *Mechanisms of language acquisition*. Hillsdale, NJ: Erlbaum.

Runco, M.A. (1986). Predicting children's creative performance. *Psychological Reports, 59*, 1247-1254.

Rusbult, C.E., Zembrodt, I.M., & Iwaniszek, J. (1986). The impact of gender and sex-role orientation on responses to dissatisfaction in close relationships. *Sex Roles, 15(1-2)*, 1-20.

Rushton, W.A.H. (1975). Visual pigments and color blindness. *Scientific American, 232(3)*, 64-74.

Russell, A.T., *et al.* (1979). A comparison of DSM-II and DSM-III in the diagnosis of childhood psychiatric disorders: III. Multiaxial features. *Archives of General Psychiatry, 36*, 1223-1226.

Safer, M.A. (1980). Attributing evil to the subject, not the situation: Student reaction to Milgram's film on obedience. *Personality and Social Psychology Bulletin, 6(2)*, 205-209.

St. George-Hyslop, P.H., *et al.* (1987). Absence of duplication of chromosome 21 genes in familial and sporadic Alzheimer's disease. *Science, 238*, 664-671.

Saito, K., *et al.* (1981). The development of communicative behaviour in the first two years of life: Analysis of child vocalization as related to child-mother interaction. *Japanese Journal of Educational Psychology, 29(1)*, 20-29.

Salkind, N.J., & Ambron, S.R. (1987). *Child development*, 5th ed. New York: Holt, Rinehart and Winston.

Samelson, Franz. (1980). J.B. Watson's Little Albert, Cyril Burt's twins, and the need for a critical science. *American Psychologist, 35*, 619-625.

Sandford, D.A., *et al.* (1987). Evaluation of a residential behavioral program for behaviorally disturbed, mentally retarded young adults. *American Journal of Mental Deficiency, 91*, 431-434.

Sarason, S.B. (1981). An asocial psychology and a misdirected clinical psychology. *American Psychologist, 36*, 827-836.

Savage-Rumbaugh, E.S., Rumbaugh, D.M., & Boysen, S. (1980). Do apes use language? *American Scientist, 68(1)*, 49-61.

Scarr, S. (1981). *Race, social class, and individual differences in I.Q.*. Hillsdale, NJ: Erlbaum.

Scarr, S. (1985). Constructing psychology: Making facts and fables for our times. *American Psychologist, 40*, 499-512.

Scarr, S., & Weinberg, R.A. (1983). The Minnesota adoption studies: Genetic differences and malleability. *Child Development, 54*, 260-267.

Scarr, S., & Weinberg, R.A. (1986). The early childhood enterprise: Care and education of the young. *American Psychologist, 41*, 1140-1146.

Schachter, S. (1971). *Emotion, obesity and crime*. New York: Academic Press.

Schachter, S. (1982). Don't sell habit-breakers short. *Psychology Today, 16(8)*, 18.

Schachter, S., & Hall, R. (1952). Group-derived restraints and audience persuasion. *Human Relations, 5*, 397-406.

Schachter, S., & Singer, J.S. (1962). Cognitive, social, and physiological determinants of emotional state. *Psychological Review, 69*, 379-399.

Schacter, D.L. (1983). Amnesia observed: Remembering and forgetting in a natural environment. *Journal of Abnormal Psychology, 92*, 236-242.

Schacter, D.L., & Graf, P. (1986). Preserved learning in amnesic patients: Perspectives from research on direct priming. *Journal of Clinical and Experimental Neuropsychology, 8*, 727-743.

Schacter, D.L., & Worling, J.R. (1985). Attribute information and the feeling-of-knowing. *Canadian Journal of Psychology, 39*, 467-475.

Schaeffer, J., Andrysiak, T., & Ungerleider, J.T. (1981). Cognition and long-term use of ganja (cannabis). *Science, 213*, 465-466.

Schafer, R. (1978). *Language and insight: The Sigmund Freud Memorial Lectures 1975-1976, University College London*. New Haven, CT: Yale University Press.

Schaie, K.W. (Ed.). (1983). *Longitudinal studies of adult psychological development*. New York: Guilford.

Schechter, M.D., *et al.* (1969). Sensory isolation therapy of autistic children: A preliminary report. *Journal of Pediatrics, 74*, 564-569.

Scheidlinger, S. (1982). *Focus on group psychotherapy: Clinical essays*. New York: International Universities Press.

Scherer, K.R., Feldstein, St., Bond, R.N., & Rosenthal, R.R. (1985). Vocal cues to deception: A comparative channel approach. *Journal of Psycholinguistic Research, 14*, 409-425.

Schiff, W. (1980). *Perception: An applied approach*. New York: Houghton Mifflin.

Schlenker, B.R. (Ed.). *The self and social life*. New York: McGraw-Hill.

Schmidt, H. (1981). PK tests with pre-recorded and pre-inspected seed numbers. *Journal of Parapsychology, 45*, 87-98.

Schmidt, H. (1985). Addition effect for PK on prerecorded targets. *Journal of Parapsychology, 49*, 229-244.

Schnarch, D.M. (1984). Save us from our sexual saviors. *Contemporary Psychology, 29*, 416-417.

Schneider, D.J., Hastorf, A.H., & Ellsworth, P.C. (1979). *Person perception*, 2nd ed. Reading, MA: Addison-Wesley.

Scholnick, E.K. (1985). Unlimited development. *Contemporary Psychology, 30*, 314-315.

Schuler, H. (1982). *Ethical problems in psychological research*. New York: Academic Press.

Schwager, M. (1986). Training for television. Special issue: Communications. *Training and Development Journal, 40(10)*, 62-65.

Scroggs, J.R. (1985). *Key ideas in personality theory*. St. Paul, MN: West.

Segalowitz, S.J. (Ed.). (1983). *Language functions and brain organization*. New York: Academic Press.

Segraves, R.T. (1982). *Marital therapy: A combined psychodynamic-behavioral approach*. New York: Plenum Medical.

Sekuler, R., & Blake, R. (1985). *Perception*. New York: Knopf.

Sekuler, R., and Mulvanny, P. (1982). 20/20 is not enough. *American Health, 1(5)*, 50-56.

Seligman, M.E.P. (1975). *Helplessness*. San Francisco: W.H. Freeman.

Seligman, M.E.P. (1976). *Learned helplessness and depression in animals and humans*. Morristown, NJ: General Learning Press.

Selye, H. (1976). *The stress of life*, rev. ed. New York: McGraw-Hill.

Selye, H. (1978). On the real benefits of eustress. *Psychology Today, 12(3)*, 60-70.

Selye, H. (Ed.). (1981-1983). *Selye's guide to stress research* [Series]. New York: Van Nostrand Reinhold.

Serban, G., Conte, H.R., & Plutchik, R. (1987). Borderline and schizotypal personality disorders: Mutually exclusive or overlapping? *Journal of Personality Assessment, 51*, 15-22.

Sergios, P., & Cody, J. (1985-1986). Importance of physical attractiveness and social assertiveness skills in male homosexual dating behavior and partner selection. *Journal of Homosexuality, 12(2)*, 71-84.

Shafii, M., *et al.* (1985). Psychological autopsy of completed suicide in children and adolescents. *American Journal of Psychiatry, 142*, 1061-1064.

Shah, N.S., & Donald, A.G. (Eds.). (1986). *Movement disorders*. New York: Plenum Medical.

Shell, E.R. (1986). Chemists whip up a tasty mess of artificial flavors. *Smithsonian, 17(2)*, 79-88.

Shepard, R.N., & Metzler, J. (1971). Mental rotation of three-dimensional objects. *Science, 171*, 701-703.

Shepherd-Look, D.L. (1982). Sex differentiation and the development of sex roles. In B.B. Wolman (Ed.), *Handbook of developmental psychology*. Englewood Cliffs, NJ: Prentice-Hall.

Sherif, M. (1935). A study of some social factors in perception. *Archives of Psychology, 27, (187)*, 1-60.

Sherif, M. (1936). *The psychology of social norms*. New York: Harper.

Sherif, M., *et al.* (1961). *Intergroup conflict and cooperation: The Robber's Cave experiment*. Norman: University of Oklahoma Book Exchange.

Shevrin, H., & Dickman, S. (1980). The psychological unconscious: A necessary assumption for all psychological theory? *American Psychologist, 35*, 421-434.

Shneidman, E.S. (1981). *Endeavors in psychology: Selections from the personology of Henry A. Murray*. New York: Harper & Row.

Shoben, E.J., Jr. (1957). Toward a concept of the normal personality. *American Psychologist, 12*, 183-189.

Shotland, R.L. (1985). When bystanders just stand by. *Psychology Today, 19(6)*, 50-55.

Sibicky, M., & Dovidio, J.F. (1986). Stigma of psychological therapy: Stereotypes, interpersonal reactions, and the self-fulfilling prophecy. *Journal of Counseling Psychology, 33(2)*, 148-154.

Sieber, J.E. (Ed.). (1982). *The ethics of social research: Surveys and experiments*. New York: Springer-Verlag.

Siegler, R.S. (1983). Five generalizations about cognitive development. *American Psychologist, 38*, 263-276.

Siegler, R.S. (1984). How knowledge influences learning. *American Scientist, 71*, 631-638.

Simek, T.C., & O'Brien, R.M. (1981). *Total golf: A behavioral approach to lowering your score and getting more out of your game*. Garden City, NY: Doubleday.

Simon, H.A. (1981). Studying human intelligence by creating artificial intelligence. *American Scientist, 69*, 300-308.

Simons, D.J. (1985). The relationship of sequential-simultaneous processing to emotionally disturbed children's behavior problems and to their improvement in milieu therapy. *Dissertation Abstracts International, 46(3-B)*, 971.

Simpson, P.G., *et al.* (1986). Infusion of a monoamine oxidase inhibitor into the locus coeruleus can prevent stress-induced behavioral depression. *Biological Psychiatry, 21(8-9)*, 724-734.

Sinclair, J.D. (1983). The hardware of the brain. *Psychology Today, 17(12)*, 8-12.

Singer, B., & Benassi, V.A. (1981). Occult beliefs. *American Scientist, 69(1)*, 49-55.

Sinyagin, Y.V. (1985). A method of establishing valuation statements of group members. *Voprosy Psikhologii, 6*, 139-145.

Skeels, H.M., *et al.* (1938). A study of environmental stimulation: An orphanage pre-school project. *University of Iowa Studies in Child Welfare*, no. 4.

Skinner, B.F. (1938). *The behavior of organisms: An experimental approach*. New York: Appleton-Century.

Skinner, B.F. (1950). Are learning theories necessary? *Psychological Review, 57*, 193-216.

Skinner, B.F. (1954). The science of learning and the art of teaching. *Harvard Educational Review, 24*, 86-97.

Skinner, B.F. (1960). *Walden two*. New York: Macmillan.

Skinner, B.F. (1978). *Reflections on behaviorism and society*. Englewood Cliffs, NJ: Prentice-Hall.

Skinner, B.F. (1983a). Intellectual self-management in old age. *American Psychologist, 38*, 239-244.

Skinner, B.F. (1983b). Origins of a behaviorist. *Psychology Today, 17(9)*, 22-33.

Skinner, B.F. (1987). *Upon further reflection*. Englewood Cliffs, NJ: Prentice-Hall.

Skodol, A.E., & Spitzer, R.L. (1982). DSM-III: Rationale, basic concepts, and some differences from ICD-9. *Acta Psychiatrica Scandinavica, 66*, 271-281.

Sloane, R.B., *et al.* (1975). *Psychotherapy versus behavior therapy*. Cambridge, MA: Harvard University Press.

Sluckin, A. (1981). *Growing up in the playground: The social development of children*. London: Routledge & Kegan Paul.

Smilansky, J., & Halberstadt, N. (1986). Inventors versus problem solvers: An empirical investigation. *Journal of Creative Behavior, 20(3)*, 183-201.

Smith, B.L., & Oller, D.K. (1981). A comparative study of pre-meaningful vocalizations produced by normally developing and Down's syndrome infants *Journal of Speech and Hearing Disorders, 46(1)*, 46-51.

Smith, D., & Kraft, W.A. (1983). DSM-III: Do psychologists really want an alternative? *American Psychologist, 38*, 777-785.

Smith, D.E.P., Walter, T.L., Miller, S.D., & McConnell, J.V. (1985). Effect of using an auditory trainer on the attentional, language, and social behaviors of autistic children. *Journal of Autism and Developmental Disorders, 15*, 285-302.

Smith, I.D., *et al.* (1982). Touching textured surfaces: Cells in somatosensory cortex respond both to finger movement and to surface features. *Science, 218*, 906-909.

Smith, J.L., Glass, G.V., & Miller, T.I. (1980). *The benefits of psychotherapy*. Baltimore: Johns Hopkins Press.

Smith, M.B., Bruner, J.S., & White, R.B. (1956). *Opinions and personality*. New York: Wiley.

Smith, M.L., & Glass, G.V. (1977). Meta-analysis of psychotherapy outcome studies. *American Psychologist, 32*, 752-760.

Smith, M.L., Glass, G.V., & Millter, T.I. (1980). *The benefits of psychotherapy*. Baltimore: Johns Hopkins Press.

Smith, P.B. (1980). *Small groups and personal change*. London: Methuen.

Smith, P.K. (Ed.). (1984). *Play in animals and humans*. Oxford, England: Basil Blackwell.

Smith, W.L., Merskey, H., & Gross, S.C. (1980). *Pain: Meaning and management*. New York: SP Medical & Scientific Books.

Smotherman, W.P. (1982). Odor aversion learning by the rat fetus. *Physiology and Behavior, 29(5)*, 769-771.

Smotherman, W.P., & Robinson, S.R. (1985). The rat fetus in its environment: Behavioral adjustments to novel, familiar, aversive, and conditioned stimuli presented in utero. *Behavioral Neuroscience, 99(3)*, 521-530.

Snarey, J.R., Reimer, J., & Kohlberg, L. (1985a). The kibbutz as a model for moral education: A longitudinal cross-cultural study. *Journal of Applied Developmental Psychology, 6(2-3)*, 151-172.

Snarey, J.R., Reimer, J., & Kohlberg, L. (1985b). Development of social-moral reasoning among Kibbutz adolescents: A longitudinal cross-cultural study. *Developmental Psychology, 21(1)*, 3-17.

Snyder, M. (1983). The influence of individuals on situations: Understanding the links between personality and social behavior. *Journal of Personality, 51*, 497-516.

Snyder, M. (1987). *Public appearances/private realities: The psychology of self-monitoring*. New York: W.H. Freeman.

Snyder, M.L. (1982). A helpful theory. *Contemporary Psychology, 27*, 11-12.

Snyder, S.H. (1972). *Uses of marijuana*. New York: Oxford University Press.

Snyder, S.H. (1984a). Drug and neurotransmitter receptors in the brain. *Science, 224*, 22-30.

Snyder, S.H. (1984b). Neurosciences: An integrative discipline. *Science, 225*, 1255-1257.

Snyder, S.H. (1987). *Drugs and the brain*. New York: W.H. Freeman.

Solomon, E.P., & Davis, P.W. (1983). *Human anatomy and physiology*. Philadelphia: Saunders.

Solomon, L.J., & Rothblum, E.D. (1986). Stress, coping, and social support in women. *Behavior Therapist, 9*, 199-204.

Solomon, P. *et al.*, (Eds.). (1961). *Sensory deprivation*. Cambridge, MA: Harvard University Press.

Solomon, R.L., & Wynne, L.C. (1953). Traumatic avoidance learning: Acquisition in normal dogs. *Psychological Monographs, 67(4)*, Whole No. 354.

Sommer, R. (1969). *Personal space: The behavioral basis of design*. Englewood Cliffs, NJ: Prentice-Hall.

Sonderegger, T.B. (Ed.). (1984). *Psychology and gender*. *Nebraska symposium on motivation*, Vol. 32. Lincoln: University of Nebraska Press.

Soules, M.R., & Bremner, W.J. (1982). The menopause and climacteric: Endocrinologic basis and associated symptomatology. *Journal of the American Geriatrics Society, 30*, 547-561.

Spearman, C. (1904). General intelligence objectively determined and measured. *American Journal of Psychology, 15*, 201-293.

Sperling, G. (1963). A model for visual memory tasks. *Human Factors, 5*, 19-30.

Sperry, R.W. (1968). Hemisphere deconnection and unity in conscious awareness. *American Psychologist, 23*, 723-733.

Sperry, R.W. (1982). Some effects of disconnecting the cerebral hemispheres. *Science, 217*, 1223-1226.

Spiegel, D., Bloom, J.R., & Yalom, I. (1981). Group support for patients with metastatic cancer: A randomized prospective outcome study. *Archives of General Psychiatry, 38*, 527-533.

Spiegel, D., & Yalom, I. (1978). A support group for dying patients. *International Journal of Group Psychotherapy, 28*, 233-245.

Spitz, R.A. (1945). Hospitalization: An inquiry into the genesis of psychiatric conditions of early childhood. In A. Freud *et al.* (Eds.), *The psychoanalytic study of the child*. New York: International Universities Press.

Spitzer, R.L. (1984a). A debate on DSM-III: First rebuttal. *American Journal of Psychiatry, 141*, 546-547.

Spitzer, R.L. (1984b). A debate on DSM-III: Second rebuttal. *American Journal of Psychiatry, 141*, 551-553.

Spitzer, R.L., Williams, J.B.W., & Skodal, A.E. (Eds.). (1983). *International perspectives on DSM-III*. Washington, DC: American Psychiatric Press.

Springer, S.P., & Deutsch, G. (1981). *Left brain, right brain*. San Francisco: W.H. Freeman.

Squire, L. (1982). Neuropsychological effects of ECT. In R. Abrams & W.B. Essman (Eds.), *Electroconvulsive therapy: Biological foundations and clinical applications*. New York: SP Medical & Scientific Books.

Squire, L.R. (1986). Mechanisms of memory. *Science, 232*, 1612-1619.

Squire, S. (1983). *The slender balance*. New York: G.P. Putnam's Sons.

Stabenau, J.R., Dolinsky, Z., & Fischer, B. (1986). Alcohol consumption: Effect of gender and psychopathology. *Alcoholism: Clinical and Experimental Research, 10*, 355-356.

Stack, C.B. (1986). The culture of gender: Women and men of color. *Signs, 11(2)*, 321-324.

Stanton, M.E., & Sevine, S. (1985). Brief separation elevates cortisol in mother and infant squirrel monkeys. *Physiology and Behavior, 34*, 1007-1008.

Stanton, T.L., Craft, C.M., & Reiter, R.J. (1984). Decreases in pineal melatonin content during the hibernation bout in the golden-mantled ground squirrel, Spermophilis lateralis. *Life Sciences, 35*, 1461-1467.

Star, S.A., & Hughes, H.McG. (1950). Report on an educational campaign: The Cincinnati plan for the United Nations. *American Journal of Sociology, 55*, 389-400.

Stark, E. (1985). Video playbacks: Athletes do better . . . *Psychology Today, 19(7)*, 71.

Stebbins, W.C. (1983). *The acoustic sense of animals*. Cambridge, MA: Harvard University Press.

Steele, R.S. (1982). *Freud and Jung: Conflicts of interpretation*. London: Routledge & Kegan Paul.

Steer, R.A., Beck, A.T., Riskind, J.H., & Brown, G. (1986). Differentiation of depressive disorders from generalized anxiety by the Beck Depression Inventory. *Journal of Clinical Psychology, 43*, 475-478.

Steif, B.L., *et al*. (1986). Effects of depression and ECT on anterograde memory. *Biological Psychiatry, 21*, 921-930.

Steinberg, S. (1983). Endorphins: New types and sweet links. *Science News, 1124*, 136.

Stellar, J.R., & Stellar, E. (1985). *The neurobiology of motivation and reward*. New York: Springer-Verlag.

Stephan, C.W., & Stephan, W.G. (1985). *Two social psychologies: An integrative approach*. Homewood, IL: Dorsey Press.

Stephenson, B.D., & Wicklund, R.A. (1983). Self-directed attention and taking the other's perspective. *Journal of Experimental Social Psychology, 19*, 58-77.

Stern, D.N. (1983). Le but et la structure du jeu mere-nourrison. (The goal and structure of mother-infant play.) *Psychiatrie de l'Enfant, 26(1)*, 193-216.

Sternberg, R.J. (Ed.). (1982). *Handbook of human intelligence*. New York: Cambridge University Press.

Sternberg, R.J. (Ed.). (1984). *Human abilities: An information-processing approach*. New York: W.H. Freeman.

Sternberg, R.J. (1985). *Beyond IQ: A triarchic theory of human intelligence*. New York: Cambridge University Press.

Sternberg, R.J. (1986). *Intelligence applied*. New York: Harcourt Brace Jovanovich.

Stevenson, H., Azuma, H., & Hakuta, K. (1986). *Child development and education in Japan*. New York: Freeman.

Steward, M.S., *et al*. (1986). Group therapy: A treatment of choice for young victims of child abuse. *International Journal of Group Psychotherapy, 36*, 261-277.

Storms, M.D. (1980). Theories of sexual orientation. *Journal of Personality and Social Psychology, 38*, 783-792.

Storms, M.D. (1981). A theory of erotic orientation development. *Psychological Review, 88(4)*, 340-353.

Stratton, P. (Ed.). (1982). *Psychobiology of the human newborn*. Chichester, England: Wiley.

Strauss, J.S., & Carpenter, W.T (1981). *Schizophrenia*. New York: Plenum Press.

Striegel-Moore, R.H., Silberstein, L.R., and Rodin, J. (1986). Toward an understanding of risk factors for bulimia. *American Psychologist, 41*, 246-263.

Stroebe, W., Kruglanski, A., & Bar-Ral, D. (Eds.). (1987). *The social psychology of intergroup conflict*. New York: Springer Verlag.

Strom, J.C., & Buck, R.W. (1970). Staring and participants' sex: Physiological and subjective reactions. *Personality and Social Psychology Bulletin, 5(1)*, 114-117

Stroop, J.R. (1935). Studies of interference in serial verbal reactions. *Journal of Experimental Psychology, 18*, 643-662.

Stryer, L. (1987). The molecules of visual excitation. *Scientific American, 257(1)*, 42-50.

Stuart, R.B., & Jacobson, B. (1987). *Weight, sex, and marriage: A delicate balance*. New York: W.W. Norton.

Stumphauzer, J.S. (Ed.). (1979). *Progress in behavior therapy with delinquents*. Springfield, IL: Charles C. Thomas.

Stunkard, A.J., *et al*. (1985). An adoption study of human obesity. Unpublished manuscript, University of Pennsylvania, Philadelphia.

Suedfeld, P. (1980). *Restricted environmental stimulation: Research and clinical applications*. New York: Wiley.

Suomi, S., Delizio, R., & Harlow, H.F. (1976). Social rehabilitation of separation-induced depressive disorders in monkeys. *American Journal of Psychiatry, 133*, 1279-1285.

Suomi, S., & Harlow, H.F. (1972). Social rehabilitation in isolate-reared monkeys. *Developmental Psychology, 6*, 487-496.

Suomi, S., Harlow, H.F., & McKinney, W.T. (1972). Monkey psychiatrist. *American Journal of Psychiatry, 128*, 927-932.

Sussman, N.M., & Rosenfeld, H.M. (1982). Influence of culture, language, and sex on conversational distance. *Journal of Personality and Social Psychology, 42*, 66-74.

Szabo, C. (1985). Effect of role-play on attitude change. *Magyar Pszichologiai Szemle, 42*, 495-507.

Tajfel, H. (1979). Individuals and groups in social psychology. *British Journal of Social and Clinical Psychology, 18(2)*, 183-190.

Tajfel, H. (1982a). Social psychology of intergroup relations. *Annual Review of Psychology, 33*, 1-39.

Tajfel, H. (Ed.). (1982b). *Social identity and intergroup relations*. Cambridge, England: Cambridge University Press.

Takooshian, H., & O'Connor, P.J. (1984). When apathy leads to tragedy: Two Fordham professors examine "Bad Samaritanism." *Social Action and the Law, 10(1)*, 26-27.

Tanzi, R.E., Bird, E.D., Latt, S.A., & Neve, R.L. (1987). The amyloid beta protein gene is not duplicated in brains from patients with Alzheimer's disease. *Science, 238*, 666-669.

Tavris, C. (1982). *Anger: The misunderstood emotion*. New York: Simon & Schuster.

Taylor, C.W., *et al*. (1985). Attributes of excellence in various professions: Their relevance to selection of gifted/talented persons. *Gifted Child Quarterly, 29(1)*, 29-34.

Taylor, S.E. (1986). *Health psychology*. New York: Random House.

Terman, G.W., Shavit, Y., Lewis, J.W., Cannon, J.T., & Liebeskind, J.C. (1984). Intrinsic mechanisms of pain inhibition: Activation by stress. *Science, 226*, 1270-1276.

Thatcher, R.W., Walker, R.A., & Guidice, S. (1987). Human cerebral hemispheres develop at different rates and ages. *Science, 236*, 1110-1113.

Thigpen, C.H., & Cleckley, H. (1954). *The three faces of Eve*. Kingsport, TN: Kingsport Press.

Thompson, R., & McConnell, J.V. (1955). Classical conditioning in the planarian *Dugesia dorotocephala*. *Journal of Comparative and Physiological Psychology, 48*, 65-68.

Thompson, R.F. (1986). The neurobiology of learning and memory. *Science, 233*, 941-947.

Thorndike, E.L. (1898). *Animal intelligence: An experimental study of the associative processes in animals*. New York: Columbia University Press.

Thorndike, E.L. (1935). *The psychology of wants, interests and attitudes*. New York: Appleton-Century-Crofts.

Thorne, A. (1987). The press of personality: A study of conversations between introverts and extraverts. *Journal of Personality and Social Psychology, 53*, 718-726.

Toates, F. (1985). Psychobiology. *Contemporary Psychology, 229*, 962-963.

Toller, C. van, Dodd, G.H., & Billing, A. (1985). *Ageing and the sense of smell*. Springfield, IL: Charles C Thomas.

Tolman, E.C. (1938). The determiners of behavior at a choice point. *Psychological Review, 45*, 1-41.

Torsvall, L., Akerstedt, T., & Froberg, J. (1985). On-call duty, sleep and wakefulness: An EEG study of engineers on ships in the Swedish merchant marine. *Stressforskningsrapporter, no. 184,* 22.

Toseland, R.W., & Siporin, M. (1986). When to recommend group treatment: A review of the clinical and the research literature. *International Journal of Group Psychotherapy, 36,* 171-201.

Toth, N. (1985). Archeological evidence for preferential right-handedness in the lower and middle Pleistocene, and its possible implications. *Journal of Human Evolution, 14,* 607.

Triandis, H.C. (1984). Toward a psychological theory of economic growth. *International Journal of Psychology, 19(1-2),* 79-95.

Triandis, H.C., & Brislin, R.W. (1984). Cross-cultural psychology. *American Psychologist, 39,* 1006-1016.

Triandis, H.C., & Lambert, W.W. (Eds.). (1980). *Handbook of cross-cultural psychology,* vol. 1. Boston: Allyn & Bacon.

Trotter, R.J. (1985a). A life of conflict and goals. *Psychology Today, 19(9),* 54-59.

Trotter, R.J. (1985b). The sign of music read in the face. *Psychology Today, 19(3),* 18.

Trotter, R.J. (1986a). Profile: Robert J. Sternberg. *Psychology Today, 20(8),* 56-62.

Trotter, R.J. (1986b). The mystery of mastery. *Psychology Today, 20(1),* 32-38.

Trotter, R.J. (1987). You've come a long way, baby. *Psychology Today, 21(5),* 35-45.

Truax, C.B. (1968). Therapist interpersonal reinforcement of client self-exploration and therapeutic outcome in group psychotherapy. *Journal of Counseling Psychology, 15,* 225-231.

Tschuschke, V. (1986). Relationships between psychological and psychophysiological variables in the group therapeutic setting. *International Journal of Group Psychotherapy, 36,* 305-312.

Turk, D.C., Meichenbaum, D., & Genest, M. (1983). *Pain and behavioral medicine: A cognitive-behavioral perspective.* New York: Guilford Press.

Turkington, C. (1982). Hypnotic memory is not always accurate. *APA Monitor, 13(3),* 46-47.

Turner, C.J., & Miles, H.B. (1983). *The biology of human intelligence: Proceedings of the twentieth annual symposium of the Eugenics Society.* Longon: Eugenics Society.

Turner, S.M., *et al.* (1986). Panic disorder and agoraphobia with panic attacks: Covariation along the dimensions of panic and agoraphobic fear. *Journal of Abnormal Psychology, 95,* 384-388.

Twitmyer, E.B. (1905). Knee-jerks without stimulation of the patellar tendon. *Psychological Bulletin, 2,* 43-44.

Tyler, L.E. (1973). A significant change in direction: Implications for measurement. *Proceedings of the Invitational Conference on Testing Problems, 1973,* 70-78.

Tyler, L.E. (1984). What tests don't measure. *Journal of Counseling & Development, 63(1),* 48-50.

Tyler, L.E., & Walsh, W.B. (1979). *Tests and Measurements,* 3rd ed. Englewood Cliffs, NJ: Prentice-Hall.

Tyndall, K. (1986a). Robot sense of touch. *Insight, 2(29),* 57.

Tyndall, K. (1986b). Down's syndrome. *Insight, 2(8),* 60.

Tyson, G.M., & Range, L.M. (1987). Gestalt dialogues as a treatment for mild depression: Time works just as well. *Journal of Clinical Psychology, 43,* 227-231.

Ullmann, L.P., & Krasner, L. (1975). *A psychological approach to abnormal behavior,* 2nd ed. Englewood Cliffs, NJ: Prentice-Hall.

Uttal, W.R. (1973). *The psychobiology of sensory coding.* New York: Harper & Row.

Uttal, W.R. (1978). *The psychobiology of mind.* Hillsdale, NJ: Earlbaum.

Uttal, W.R. (1981). *A taxonomy of visual processes.* New York: LEA.

Valenstein, E.S. (Ed.). (1980). *The psychosurgery debate: Scientific, legal, and clinical perspectives.* San Francisco: W.H. Freeman.

Valenstein, E.S. (1986). *Great and desperate cures: The rise and decline of psychosurgery and other radical treatments for mental illness.* New York: Basic Books.

Van Bilsen, H.P., & Van Emst, A.J. (1986). Heroin addiction and motivational milieu therapy. *International Journal of the Addictions, 21,* 707-713.

Van den Brink, G., & Bilsen, F.A. (Eds.). (1980). *Psychophysical, physiological and behavioural studies in hearing.* Delft, The Netherlands: Delft University Press.

Vaughan, G.M., Tajfel, H., & Williams, J. (1981). Bias in reward allocation in an intergroup and an interpersonal context. *Social Psychology Quarterly, 44(1),* 37-42.

Vernon, J.A. (1963). *Inside the black room.* New York: Clarkson N. Potter.

Veroff, J., & Veroff, J.B. (1980). *Social incentives: A life-span developmental approach.* New York: Academic Press.

Vinokur, A., & Ajzen, I. (1982). Relative importance of prior and immediate events: A causal primary effect. *Journal of Personality and Social Psychology, 42,* 820-829.

Voelkl, J.E. (1986). Therapeutic activities with the impaired elderly. *Activities, Adaptation and Aging, 8(3-4),* 37-45.

von Brock, M.B., & Elliott, S.N. (1987). Influence of treatment effectiveness information on the acceptability of classroom interventions. *Journal of School Psychology, 25,* 131-144.

Wachs, T.D., & Gruen, G.E. (1982). *Early experience and human development.* New York: Plenum Press.

Wagstaff, G.F. (1974). The effects of repression-sensitization on a brightness scaling measure of perceptual defense. *British Journal of Psychology, 65(3),* 395-401.

Waid, W.M., & Orne, M.T. (1982). The physiological detection of deception. *American Scientist, 70(4),* 402-409.

Wall, P.D. (1979). On the relation of injury to pain. *Pain, 6,* 253-264.

Walster, E., Aronson, V., Abrahams, D., & Rottman, L. (1966). Importance of physical attractiveness in dating behavior. *Journal of Personality and Social Psychology, 4,* 508-516.

Ward, M.S., Carlsmith, J.M., & Leiderman, P.H. (1988). *Protecting abused and neglected children.* Stanford, CA: Stanford University Press.

Warren, J.M., Zerweck, C., & Anthony, A. (1982). Effects of environmental enrichment on old mice. *Developmental Psychobiology, 15(1),* 13-18.

Wasserman, G.S. (1978). *Color vision: An historical introduction.* New York: Wiley-Interscience.

Watanabe, I. (1982). Selective attention and memory. *Japanese Psychological Review, 23,* 335-354.

Waters, E.R. (1984). Building on what you know: Techniques for individual and group counseling with older people. *Counseling Psychologist, 12(2),* 63-74.

Waters, H.S. (1987). Art though egocentric? Let me count the ways. *Contemporary Psychology, 32,* 573-574.

Watkins, C.E., Jr., Lopez, F.G., Campbell, V.L. & Himmell, C.D. (1986). Counseling psychology and clinical psychology: Some preliminary comparative data. *American Psychologist, 41,* 581-582.

Watkins, L.R., & Mayer, D.J. (1982). Organization of endogenous opiate and nonopiate pain control systems. *Science, 216,* 1185-1192.

Watson, J.B. (1929). Introduction. In G.B. Hamilton, *A research in marriage.* New York: A & C Boni.

Watson, J.B., & Rayner, R. (1920). Conditioned emotional reactions. *Journal of Experimental Psychology, 3,* 1-14.

Waxman, D., Misra, P.C., Gibson, M., & Basker, M.A. (Eds.). (1985). *Modern trends in hypnosis.* New York: Plenum Press.

Weale, R.A. (1982). *Focus on vision.* Cambridge, MA: Harvard University Press.

Webb, W.B. (1975). *Sleep: The gentle tyrant.* Englewood Cliffs, NJ: Prentice-Hall.

Webb, W.B. (1983). Theories in modern sleep research. In A. Mayes (Ed.), *Sleep mechanisms and functions in humans and animals: An evolutionary perspective.* London: Van Nostrand Reinhold.

Wegrocki, H.J. (1939). A critique of cultural and statistical concepts of abnormality. *Journal of Abnormal and Social Psychology, 34,* 166-178.

Weiman, L.A. (1986). Eye contact and perceived status in communication patterns between able-bodied and physically disabled dyads. *Dissertation Abstracts International, 47(4-A).*

Weinrich, J.D. (1987). Bisexuality: How bi? How sexual? *Contemporary Psychology, 32,* 350-352.

Weisburd, S. (1988). Computer scents. *Science News, 133,* 27-29.

Weiss, A.S., & Comrey, A.L. (1987). Personality factor structure among Hare Krishnas. *Educational and Psychological Measurement, 47(2),* 317-328.

Wells, G.L., & Lindsay, R.C.L. (1983). In S.M.A. Lloyd-Bostock & B.R. Clifford (Eds.), *Evaluating witness evidence: Recent psychological research and new perspectives.* Chichester, England: Wiley.

Wenar, C. (1982). *Psychopathology from infancy through adolescence: A developmental approach.* New York: Random House.

Wertheimer, M. (1987). *A brief history of psychology,* 3rd ed. New York: Holt, Rinehart and Winston.

West, S.G., & Wicklund, R.A. (1980). *A primer of social psychological theories.* Monterey, CA: Brooks/Cole.

White, C.J.M. (1982). *Consistency in cognitive social behaviour: An introduction to social psychology.* London: Routledge & Kegan Paul.

White, L., Tursky, B., & Schwartz, G.E. (Eds.). (1985). *Placebo: Theory, research, and mechanisms.* New York: Guilford Press.

Whitehouse, W.G., *et al.* (1983). Opiate antagonists overcome the learned helplessness effect but impair competent escape performance. *Physiology and Behavior, 30,* 731-734.

Wicklund, R.A., & Braun, O.L. (1987). Incompetence and the concern with human categories. *Journal of Personality and Social Psychology, 5,* 373-382.

Will, J.A., Self, P.A., & Datan, N. (1976). Maternal behavior and perceived sex of infant. *American Journal of Orthopsychiatry, 46,* 135-139.

Williams, J.B., & Spitzer, R.L. (1983). The issue of sex bias in DSM-III: A critique of "A woman's view of DSM-III" by Marcie Kaplan. *American Psychologist, 38,* 793-798.

Williams, J.B., Spitzer, R.L., & Skodol, A.E. (1985). DSM-III in residency training: Results of a national survey. *American Journal of Psychiatry, 142,* 755-758.

Wilson, C. (1972). *New pathways in psychology.* New York: Taplinger Publishing Co.

Wilson, E.O. (1975). *Sociobiology: The new synthesis.* Cambridge, MA: Harvard University Press.

Wilson, I.C., *et al.* (1983). Is there a tardive dysmentia? *Schizophrenia Bulletin, 9,* 187-192.

Wilson, J.D., George, F.W., & Griffin, J.E. (1981). The hormonal control of sexual development. *Science, 211,* 1278-1284.

Wilson, S.C., & Barber, T.X. (1982). The fantasy-prone personality: Implications for understanding imagery, hypnosis, and parapsychological phenomena. *PSI Research, 1(3),* 94-116.

Windholz, G. (1986). A comparative analysis of the conditional reflex discoveries of Pavlov and Twitmyer, and the birth of a paradigm. *Pavlovian Journal of Biological Science, 21,* 141-147.

Winfree, A.T. (1986). Benzodiazepines set the clock. *Nature, 321,* 114-115.

Wingard, J.A., & Maltzman, I. (1980). Interest as a predeterminer of the GSR index of the orienting reflex. *Acta Psychologica, 46(2),* 153-160.

Winick, M., Meyer, K.K., & Harris, R.C. (1975). Malnutrition and environmental enrichment by early adoption. *Science, 190,* 1173-1175.

Witelson, S.F. (1985). The brain connection: The corpus callosum is larger in left-handers. *Science, 229,* 665-667.

Wolman, B.B. (Ed.). (1983). *International encyclopedia of psychiatry, psychology, psychoanalysis, and neurology.* New York: Aesculapius Publishers.

Wolpe, J. (1981a). Behavior therapy versus psychoanalysis: Therapeutic and social implications. *American Psychologist, 36,* 159-164.

Wolpe, J. (1981b). *Our useless fears.* Boston: Houghton Mifflin.

Wood, C. (1986). The hostile heart. *Psychology Today, 20(9),* 10-11.

Wood, G. (1983). *Cognitive psychology: A skills approach.* Monterey, CA: Brooks/Cole.

Wright, A.A. *et al.* (1985). Memory processing of serial lists by pigeons, monkeys, and people. *Science, 229,* 287-289.

Wuthnow, R. (1978). *Experimentation in American religion.* Berkeley: University of California Press.

Yalom, I.D. (1970). *The theory and practice of group psychotherapy.* New York: Basic Books.

Yalom, I.D. (1983). *Inpatient group therapy.* New York: Basic Books.

Yalom, I.D. (1985). *Theory and practice of group psychotherapy,* 2nd ed. New York: Basic Books.

Yalom, I.D., Licherman, M.A., & Miles, M.B. (1973). *Encounter groups: First facts.* New York: Basic Books.

Yando, R., Seitz, V., & Zigler, E. (1979). *Intellectual and personality characteristics of children: Social-class and ethnic-group differences.* Hillsdale, NJ: Erlbaum.

Yarbrough, C. (1986). Language and communication. *Comparative Psychology Newsletter, 3(August),* 23-27.

Yarrow, L.J. (1981). The many faces of continuity. *Contemporary Psychology, 26,* 746-748.

Yarrow, L.J., & Klein, R.P. (1980). Environmental discontinuity associated with transition from foster to adoptive homes. *International Journal of Behavioral Development, 3(3),* 311-322.

Yates, A., Leehey, K., & Shisslak, C.M. (1983). Running—an analogue of anorexia? *New England Journal of Medicine, 308,* 251-255.

Yonas, A. (1979). Studies of spatial perception in infants. In A.D. Pick (Ed.), *Perception and its development: A tribute to Eleanor J. Gibson.* Hillsdale, NJ: Erlbaum.

Yulsman, T. (1985). Down's syndrome: Postponing pregnancy. *American Health, 5(5),* 8-9.

Yussen, S.R. (1977). Characteristics of moral dilemmas written by adolescents. *Developmental Psychology, 13,* 162-163.

Zajonc, R.B. (1984). On the primacy of affect. *American Psychologist, 39,* 117-123.

Zanna, M.P., Higgins, E.T., & Herman, C.P. (1982). *Consistency in social behavior: The Ontario Symposium,* Vol. 2. Hillsdale, NJ: Erlbaum.

Zarbatany, L., & Lamb, M.E. (1985). Social referencing as a function of information source: Mothers versus strangers. *Infant Behavior and Development, 8(1),* 25-33.

Zax, M., & Cowen, E.L. (1976). *Abnormal psychology: Changing concepts,* 2nd ed. New York: Holt, Rinehart and Winston.

Zax, M., & Stricker, G. (1963). *Patterns of psychopathology.* New York: Macmillan.

Zilbergeld, B., Edelstein, M.G., & Araoz, D.L. (Eds.). (1986). *Hypnosis: Questions and answers.* New York: W.W. Norton.

Zimbardo, P.G. (1975). On transforming experimental research into advocacy for social change. In M. Deutsch & H. Hornstein (Eds.), *Applying social psychology.* Hillsdale, NJ: Erlbaum.

Zimbardo, P.G., Andersen, S.M., & Kabat, L.G. (1981). Induced hearing deficit generates experimental paranoia. *Science, 212,* 1529-1531.

Zimbardo, P.G., *et al.* (1973). Pirandellian prison: The mind is a formidable jailer. *New York Times Magazine,* April 8, pp. 38-60.

Zimmerman, M., Coryell, W., Pfohl, B., & Stangl, D. (1987). Validation of definitions of endogenous depression: Reply. *Archives of General Psychiatry, 44*, 390-391.

Zinberg, N.E. (1984). *Drug, set, and setting: The basis for controlled intoxicant use.* New Haven, CT: Yale University Press.

Zinker, J. (1977). *Creative process in gestalt therapy.* New York: Brunner-Mazel.

Zuckerman, M., Spiegel, N.H., DePaulo, B.M., & Rosenthal, R.R. (1982). Nonverbal strategies for decoding deception. *Journal of Nonverbal Behavior, 6(3)*, 171-187.

Copyright Acknowledgments

The author is indebted to the following for permission to reproduce copyrighted materials:

Chapter openers 1 and 3–22 are copyright Innervisions. Chapter opener 2 is copyright R. Michael Stuckey/Comstock, Inc. All cartoons are copyright Sidney Harris, reprinted by permission. Unless otherwise credited, portraits of psychologists are provided courtesy of the individual pictured. Copyrights for all photographs belong to the photographer or agency credited, unless specified otherwise.

Chapter 1: p. 4, (top) Michael Weisbrot and Family, (bottom) Pfungst, Oskar. *Clever Hans (The Horse of Mr. von Osten),* ed. Robert Rosenthal. A Henry Holt Edition in Psychology, Holt, Rinehart and Winston, Inc.; p. 5, Ellis Herwig/The Picture Cube; p. 10, Media Vision/Peter Arnold, Inc.; p. 11, Erika Stone; p. 15, (top left) Richard Wood/Taurus, (bottom) Joan Menschenfreund/Taurus; p. 16, courtesy World Book.

Chapter 2: p. 21, Dan McCoy/Rainbow; p. 22, American Museum of Natural History; p. 24, (top) Arthur Jacques/Rhode Island Hospital; p. 28, (bottom) Erika Stone/Peter Arnold, Inc.; p. 31, (bottom) Mark Godfrey/Archive; p. 33, Martin Bell/Archive; p. 34, (top) courtesy of Norman Geschwind/Beth Israel Hospital, Boston; p. 35, (bottom left) Scala/Art Resource; p. 36, Arthur Jacques/Rhode Island Hospital; p. 37, Will and Deni McIntyre/Photo Researchers; p. 42, Gazzaniga, M.S., and LeDoux, J.E. (1978). *The Integrated Mind.* Plenum Press. Reproduced by permission of Dr. Michael S. Gazzaniga.

Chapter 3: p. 49, Comstock; p. 52, Franz Kraus/The Picture Cube; p. 54, Stuart Cohen; p. 56, adapted from Crooks, R.L., and Stein, J. (1988). *Psychology: Science, Behavior and Life.* Copyright © 1988 by Holt, Rinehart and Winston, Inc. Reprinted by permission; p. 57, (top) courtesy Wilse B. Webb, University of Florida Sleep Laboratories, (bottom) adapted from Webb, Wilse B., and Agnew, Harman, W., Jr. (1969). "Measurement and Characteristics of Nocturnal Sleep," in L.E. Abt and B.P. Riess (eds.). *Progress in Clinical Psychology, VIII.* Reproduced by permission of Grune and Stratton, Inc., and the author; p. 62, Griffith, R.M., Miyago, O., and Tago, A. (1958). "The Universality of Typical Dreams: Japanese vs. Americans," *American Anthropologist, 60:* 1172–1179. Reprinted by permission of American Anthropological Association; p. 63, Detroit Institute of Arts; p. 64, Kevin Horan/Stock Boston; p. 67, Jeff Rotman/Peter Arnold, Inc.; p. 69, Innervisions; p. 71, Addictive Behaviors Research, University of Washington.

Chapter 4: p. 78, (bottom right) Ethan Hoffman/Archive; p. 80, Innervisions; p. 82, Hank Morgan/Photo Researchers; p. 84, (bottom left) Museum of Modern Art/Film Stills Archive; p. 86, (top left) Topham/The Image Works, (top right) Manfred Kage/Peter Arnold, Inc.; p. 88 (top right) courtesy Zwiren and Wagner; p. 92, (top) Jeff Jacobson/Archive, (bottom) Innervisions; p. 94, (bottom) Manfred Kage/Peter Arnold, Inc.; p. 97, Alec Duncan/Taurus; p. 99, Alfred Pasieka/Taurus; p. 102 (top) Gregory, R.L. (1966). *Eye and Brain.* Reprinted by permission of McGraw-Hill Book Company, (bottom) © 1973 by Albert Bonniers Förlag, Stockholm, published by Little, Brown and Company, Boston, 1974; p. 104, (top right) Manfred Kage/Peter Arnold, Inc.; p. 105, Michael Weisbrot and Family; p. 106, (top right) Eric A. Roth/The Picture Cube; p. 107, Cornsweet, T. N. (1970). *Visual Perception.* Copyright © 1970 by Harcourt Brace Jovanovich, Inc. Reprinted by permission of the publisher; p. 110, (bottom) Bill Gallery/Stock Boston; p. 112, (top left) Jeffry W. Myers/Stock Boston.

Chapter 5: p. 117, p. 118, (top right) Russell Dian/Holt, Rinehart and Winston; p. 126, (bottom) Mikki Ansin/The Picture Cube; p. 128, (top) Harvey Lloyd/Peter Arnold, Inc.; p. 129, (bottom left) Innervisions, (bottom right) The Minneapolis Institute of Arts; The William Hood Dunwoody Fund; p. 130, (top right) Alec Duncan/Taurus; p. 131, (top right) © 1980 Gary Braasch; p. 132, (top right) Russell Dian/Holt, Rinehart and Winston, (bottom left) Baron Wolman/Woodfin Camp; p. 134, (bottom left) Free Library of Philadelphia/Scala/Art Resource, (bottom right) Jock Pottle/Design Conceptions; p. 135, (bottom) The Bettmann Archive; p. 136, (top left and right) Innervisions; p. 139, Enrico Ferorelli/DOT; p. 141, Innervisions; p. 142, UPI/Bettmann Newsphotos; p. 143, Mark Antman/The Image Works.

Chapter 6: p. 152, (top left) Joel Gordon, (top right) The Bettmann Archive, (bottom) Alen MacWeeny/Archive; p. 156, (bottom) Alexandra Edwards/Peter Arnold, Inc.; p. 157, Innervisions; p. 159, courtesy of Dr. Neal E. Miller, Rockefeller University; p. 161, University of Pennsylvania News Bureau; p. 162, (top) Culver Pictures, Inc.; p. 164, (top) Columbia University Office of Public Information, (bottom) The Bettmann Archive; p. 166, (top) UPI/Bettmann Newsphotos, (bottom) University of Pennsylvania News Bureau; p. 168, Comstock; p. 169, Alan Carey/The Image Works; p. 171, Innervisions.

Chapter 8: p. 197, Michael Weisbrot and Family; p. 201, (top) Jim Amos/Photo Researchers; p. 202, (top) Alan Carey/The Image Works, (bottom) Innervisions; p. 204, David H. Wells/The Image Works; p. 206, (top and middle) Michael Weisbrot and Family; p. 207, Joel Gordon; p. 208, (top) Ethan Hoffman/Archive; p. 209, Innervisions; p. 212, (top left) John Coletti/The Picture Cube, (top right) © Brownie Harris, courtesy Simon and Schuster, (bottom) CBS/Phototeque; p. 213, (bottom) The Bettmann Archive; p. 214, Bob Daemmrich/Stock Boston; p. 216, (top right) Jacques Charlas/Stock Boston, (bottom) Manny Millan © Time Inc.

Chapter 7: p. 177, Erika Stone; p. 178, (top) Dellenback/Kinsey Institute for Sex Research; p. 179, Bob Levin/Black Star; p. 180, (bottom) © Petit Format/Nestle/Science Source; p. 182, (bottom) Fred Bavendam/Peter Arnold, Inc. p. 183, Joel Gordon; p. 184, Gregg Mancuso/Stock Boston; p. 186, Innervisions; p. 187, The Museum of Modern Art/Film Stills Archive. Copyright © 1979 by United Artists Corporation. All rights reserved. By permission of Woody Allen; p. 188, Innervisions; p. 190, (top) courtesy of Peter Milner; p. 192, Peter D'Angelo/Comstock.

Chapter 10: p. 222, Blair Seitz/Photo Researchers; p. 223, The Granger Collection; p. 228, Dr. Ben Harris, University of Wisconsin-Parkside; p. 229, Jay Dorin/Omni-Photo Communications, Inc.; p. 230, (top) Erika Stone, (bottom) G. Paul Bishop; p. 232, (top) Innervisions; p. 233, Innervisions; p. 241, Susan Lapides/Design Conceptions, p. 242, courtesy Teachers College, Columbia University; p. 243, Köhler, W. (1976). *The Mortality of Apes,* copyright © 1976 by Routledge & Kegan Paul PLC; p. 249, Mary Ellen Mark/Archive; p. 246, The Bettmann Archive; p. 253, Joel Gordon; p. 255, G. Cloyd/Taurus; p. 257, Barbara Pfeffer/Peter Arnold, Inc.

Chapter 11: p. 266, Bob Hahn/Taurus; p. 271, Joel Gordon; p. 277, (bottom) courtesy of Elizabeth Loftus; p. 278, Alan Duncan/Taurus; p. 284, (top) Hazel Hankin; p. 284 (bottom), p. 285, p. 286, courtesy James V. McConnell.

Chapter 12: p. 293, Charles Harbutt/Archive; p. 295, (bottom) Hazel Hankin; p. 296, courtesy the University of California, Los Angeles; p. 301, (top) courtesy Peter Suedfeld, (bottom) Christopher Brown/Stock Boston; p. 305, (top) Designers: De Pas, D'Urbino and Lomazzi. Manufacturer: Poltronova. Distributor: Stendig International. © Stendig International; p. 306, (top) Klein, Adrian Bernard, M.B.E., A.R.P.S. (1931). *Coloured Light: An Art Medium, Being the Third Edition Enlarged of "Colour-Music."* London: The Technical Press Ltd.; p. 309, Matlin, Margaret. (1983) *Cognition.* Copyright © 1983 by CBS College Publishing. Reprinted by permission of Holt, Rinehart and Winston; p. 313, (bottom left) Mark Godfrey/Archive, (bottom right) John Lei/Stock Boston.

Chapter 13: p. 321, Innervisions; p. 323, The Granger Collection; p. 324, The Bettmann Archive; p. 325, Richard Kalvar/Magnum; p. 327, Charles Harbutt/Archive; p. 331, Kathryn Dudek.

Chapter 14: p. 346, L.L.T. Rhodes/Taurus; p. 347, (top) Charles Harbutt/Archive; p. 350, Thomas McAvoy/*Life.* © 1955 Time Inc.; p. 352, Meltzoff, A.N., and Moore, M.K. (1977). *Science 198,* 75–78. University of Washington; p. 356, Sharon L. Fox/The Picture Cube; p. 357, (bottom left and right) Harlow Primate Laboratory, University of Wisconsin; p. 358, Ken Heyman/Archive; p. 361, (bottom) Hazel Hankin; p. 361, (top) Lenore Weber/Taurus; p. 363, Bob Daemmrich/Stock Boston.

Chapter 15: p. 372, (top) Media Vision/Peter Arnold, Inc.; p. 376, (top) Erika Stone/Peter Arnold; p. 376 (bottom) courtesy of The New School; p. 384, James H. Simon/The Picture Cube; p. 385, Jackie Curtis; p. 390, Richard Choy/Peter Arnold, Inc.; p. 391, Kohlberg, Lawrence. (1976). "Moral Stages and Moralization: The Cognitive-Developmental Approach," *Moral Development and Behavior; Theory, Research, and Social Issues,* Thomas Lickona, ed. Copyright 1976 Holt, Rinehart and Winston. Reprinted by permission; p. 393, Joel Gordon; p. 394, Erika Stone/Peter Arnold, Inc. p. 395, Hazel Hankin; p. 397 (bottom) MacDonald/The Picture Cube; p. 398, Hazel Hankin.

Chapter 16: p. 406, The Granger Collection; p. 410, Bayerische Staatsgemäldesammlungen; p. 412, (bottom) Pam Hasegawa/Taurus; p. 413, James H. Karales/Peter Arnold, Inc.; p. 414, (top left) Erika Stone/Peter Arnold, Inc.; p. 414, (top right) Alec Duncan/Taurus, (middle right) The Bettmann Archive; p. 415, (top) MacDonald/The Picture Cube; p. 416, (bottom right) The Bettmann Archive; p. 417, (bottom) Scala/Art Resource; p. 420, (top) National Gallery, Oslo, Norway, photo Jaques Lathion, (bottom) The Granger Collection; p. 421, UPI/Bettmann Newsphotos; p. 422, (top) Nancy Sheehan/The Picture Cube, (bottom) Joel Gordon; p. 423, Hazel Hankin; p. 424, Charles Harbutt/Archive; p. 426, condensed from Maslow, Abraham H. (1954). "Self-Actualizing People: A Study of Psychological Health," *Motivation and Personality,* 2nd ed. Copyright 1954 by Harper & Row, Publishers, Inc., Copyright © 1970 by Abraham H. Maslow. Reprinted by permission of the publishers; p. 462, (bottom) courtesy of the Center for the Studies of the Person, La Jolla, California.

Chapter 17: p. 435, The Bettmann Archive; p. 436, courtesy WQED/Pittsburgh; p. 437, Mark Gerson FBIPP; p. 439, The Bettmann Archive; p. 440, Harvard University News Office; p. 442, (top) Maddi, S.R. (1973). *Personality Theories: A Comparative Analysis.* Copyright © 1973 by Dorsey Press. Reprinted by permission, (bottom) courtesy University of Illinois; p. 443, adapted from Norman, W. (1963). "Toward an Adequate Taxonomy of Personality Attributes: Replicated Factor Structure in Peer Nomination Personality Ratings," *Journal of Abnormal Social Psychology 66:* 574–583; p. 444, (top) The Bettmann Archive, (bottom) David Felt; p. 445, Stanford University News and Publications Service; p. 446, Marilyn Sanders/Peter Arnold; p. 448, Donald Dietz/Stock Boston; p. 449, copyright 1968 by Newsweek Inc.; p. 451, Ethan Hoffman/Archive.

Chapter 18: p. 462, (top) Ragu Rhai/Magnum; p. 467, p. 468, adapted from the *Diagnostic and Statistical Manual of Mental Disorders (Third Edition, Revised).* Copyright 1987, American Psychiatric Association. Reprinted by permission; p. 469, Michael O'Brien/Archive; p. 474, Karl Shumacher/Time; p. 476, (bottom) Danuta Otfinowski/Archive; p. 477, Twentieth Century Fox.

Chapter 19: p. 489, (bottom left) Martin Rogers/Stock Boston, (bottom right) Allan Seiden/Image Bank; p. 490, (bottom) The Granger Collection; p. 491, Paul Fusco/Magnum; p. 493, Michael Weisbrot/Stock Boston; p. 501, Michael Culloty/courtesy American Psychiatric Association; p. 502, (top) Jon Goell/The Picture Cube, (bottom) Innervisions; p. 504, Innervisions; courtesy Center for Creating Responses, Princeton; p. 506, Alex Webb/Magnum; p. 507, Michael L. Abramson/Woodfin Camp.

Chapter 20: p. 517, Richard Pasley/Stock Boston; p. 519, Bettmann Archive; p. 520, Larry Lawfer/The Picture Cube; p. 521, courtesy the University of California, Los Angeles; p. 522, (bottom) C.T. Seymour/The Picture Cube; p. 524, Barbara Pfeffer/Peter Arnold, Inc.; p. 527, John Coletti/Stock Boston; p. 528, Richard Pasley/Stock Boston; p. 530, Kevin Horan/Stock Boston; p. 532, Harvard University News Office; p. 533, Jeffry W. Myers/Stock Boston; p. 535, courtesy Philip Zimbardo; p. 536, Jeff Jacobson/Archive.

Chapter 21: p. 542, Innervisions; p. 550, copyright 1965 by Stanley Milgram. From the film *Obedience* distributed by the New York University Film and Video Library and the Pennsylvania State University, PCR; p. 553, (bottom left) AP/Wide World; p. 558, Janet Bennett/Taurus; p. 560, UPI/Bettmann Newsphotos; p. 565, courtesy Golden West Television from *Scared Straight;* p. 568, Bryce Flynn/Stock Boston.

Chapter 22: p. 577, (top) Edward L. Miller/Stock Boston, (bottom) Stanford University, Stanford, California; p. 578, Billy E. Barnes/Stock Boston; p. 579, The University of Michigan News and Information Services, photo Bob Kalmbach; p. 581, Nubar Alexanian/Stock Boston; p. 582, courtesy Dr. E. Roy John and Dr. Leslie Prichep, New York University Medical Center, copyright 1988 by the American Association for the Advancement of Science; p. 583, Carol Lee/The Picture Cube; p. 584, (top) Bob Daemmrich/Stock Boston; p. 585, Susan Van Etten/The Picture Cube; p. 587, Billy E. Barnes/Stock Boston.

Indexes

Name Index

Vinokur, A., 523
Virkkunen, M., 478, 490
Voelkl, J.E., 211

Wachs, T.D., 350
Wagner, M., 140
Walk, R., 139
Walker, A.S., 139
Walker, R.A., 37
Wall, P.D., 329, 330, 331, 332
Wallace, C.S., 283
Wallace, P.M., 203, 204
Wallerstein, R., 499
Walsh, W.B., 447, 453
Walster, E., 524
Walter, T., 565, 566
Ward, L.M., 121, 123, 130
Ward, M.S., 577
Warren, M., 284
Watanabe, I., 296
Waters, E.R., 506
Watkins, C.E., Jr., 15
Watkins, L.R., 331, 332
Watson, J.B., 177–178, 179, 228, 230, 259, 292
Weale, R.A., 103
Webb, W.B., 50, 51, 53, 54, 55, 57, 58, 59, 60, 62
Wegrocki, H.J., 462
Weiman, L.A., 528, 529
Weinberg, M.W., 464
Weinberg, R.A., 446
Weinberg, R.B., 215
Weinrich, J.D., 185
Weisburd, S., 90

Weiss, A.S., 549
Weiss, W., 561, 562, 563
Weitzman, E.D., 60, 61
Weitzman, N., 188, 189
Wells, G.L., 327
Wenegrat, B., 504
Wertheimer, M., 223, 292
West, L.J., 257
Wheeler, C.C., 178
White, C.J.M., 519
White, D.K., 63
White, L., 322
White, R.W., 568, 569
Whitehouse, W.G., 322
Wicklund, R.A., 519
Wilkins, C., 568
Will, J.A., 188
Willerman, L., 37–38
Williams, J., 557
Williams, J.B., 479, 480–481
Willows, A.O., 286
Wilson, C., 424, 425
Wilson, E.O., 187, 188, 189, 518, 519
Wilson, I.C., 495
Wilson, J.D., 180, 181
Wilson, S.C., 325
Windholz, G., 223
Winfree, A.T., 52
Winick, M., 348
Witelson, S.F., 36
Wolf, T.J., 185
Wolfe, E.L., 205
Wolpe, J., 231, 232, 256, 259, 507

Wood, C., 207
Wood, F.B., 306
Worling, J.R., 281
Wright, A.A., 275, 523, 524
Wundt, W., 292, 293
Wuthnow, R., 141
Wynne, L.C., 209, 210
Wysocki, C.J., 89

Yalom, I.D., 502, 504, 505, 508
Yando, R., 450
Yarbrough, C., 377
Yarrow, L.J., 341–342, 371
Yarrow, P.R., 568
Yates, A., 167, 168
Yerkes, R.M., 377
Yogman, M.W., 354
Yonas, A., 137
Yulsman, T., 363

Zajonc, R.B., 197, 198, 208–209, 217
Zanna, M.P., 519
Zarbatany, L., 358
Zax, M., 462, 470
Zigler, E., 450
Zilbergeld, B., 326
Zimbardo, P.G., 97, 535, 536, 552
Zimmerman, M., 480
Zinberg, N.E., 72
Zinker, J., 504
Zubin, J.Z., 556
Zuckerman, M., 528

Subject Index

Terms in the running glossary are indicated by page numbers in boldface type.